Dreamweaver CC

Second Edition

the missing manual®

The book that should have been in the box®

David Sawyer McFarland and Chris Grover

O'REILLY®

Beijing | Cambridge | Farnham | Köln | Sebastopol | Tokyo

Dreamweaver CC: The Missing Manual, Second Edition

by David Sawyer McFarland and Chris Grover

Copyright © 2015 David Sawyer McFarland and Chris Grover. All rights reserved.
Printed in the United States of America.

Published by O'Reilly Media, Inc.,
1005 Gravenstein Highway North, Sebastopol, CA 95472.

O'Reilly books may be purchased for educational, business, or sales promotional use.
Online editions are also available for most titles (*https://www.safaribooksonline.com*).
For more information, contact our corporate/institutional sales department:
(800) 998-9938 or *corporate@oreilly.com*.

November 2014:   First Edition.

Revision History for the First Edition:

  2014-11-07   First release

See *http://www.oreilly.com/catalog/errata.csp?isbn=0636920032779* for release details.

ISBN-13: 978-1-4919-4720-3

[QG]

Contents

Part Two: **Building a Better Web Page**

Part Three: **Building Websites for Mobile Devices**

Part Four: **Bringing Your Pages to Life**

Part Seven: **Appendixes**

The Missing Credits

ABOUT THE AUTHORS

David Sawyer McFarland is a teacher at Treehouse (*www.teamtreehouse. com*), an online school that teaches web design and programming. He's been building websites since 1995, when he designed his first site, an online magazine for communication professionals. He's served as the webmaster at the University of California at Berkeley and the Berkeley Multimedia Research Center, and he has helped build, design, and program numerous websites for clients including Macworld.com, among others.

In addition to building websites, David is a writer, trainer, and instructor. He's taught web design at the UC Berkeley Graduate School of Journalism, the Center for Electronic Art, the Academy of Art College, and the Art Institute of Portland. He currently teaches in the Multimedia Program at Portland State University. He's written articles about web design for Practical Web Design, Macworld, and *CreativePro.com*.

David is also the author of *CSS: The Missing Manual* and *JavaScript & jQuery: The Missing Manual*.

Chris Grover is a veteran of the San Francisco Bay Area advertising and design community. Chris is the owner of Bolinas Road Creative (*www.bolinasroad.com*), an agency that helps businesses promote their products and services. Chris has written several books in the Missing Manual series and has produced training videos for video2brain, *Educator.com*, and *Lynda.com*.

Chris welcomes feedback about this book by email at *dreameaver@bolinasroad. com*. (If you need technical help, however, please refer to the sources listed in Appendix A: Getting Help.)

ABOUT THE CREATIVE TEAM

Peter McKie (editor) has a master's degree from Boston University's School of Journalism and lives in New York City. In his spare time, he digitizes archival photos of his summer community. Email: *pmckie@oreilly.com*.

Kara Ebrahim (production editor) lives, works, and plays in Cambridge, MA. She loves graphic design and all things outdoors. Email: *kebrahim@oreilly.com*.

Murray R. Summers (tech reviewer) is an Adobe Certified Dreamweaver Developer and Community Professional. He has co-authored and contributed chapters to several books on Dreamweaver, been the technical editor for the last nine editions of the Dreamweaver Missing Manual, and presented at multiple national conferences. His company, Great Web Sights, has been active in web development since 1998. Murray lives in southern Delaware with his wife, Suzanne. One daughter works at Clemson University and lives in Greenville, SC, and the other is a skilled web developer (*carolinawebcreations.biz*). His two sons live and work in Virginia Beach.

Danilo Celic, Jr. (tech reviewer) has been using Dreamweaver since version 1.2. In the years since, he has contributed to the Dreamweaver community in a variety of capacities. He has been a co-author, technical editor, and technical reviewer for a shelf full of Dreamweaver- and web-related books. He loves sharing what he has learned over the years of the inner workings of Dreamweaver and various web technologies. Danilo lives in the suburbs of Chicago with his wife, Melissa, who patiently forgives the late hours he puts in in front of a glowing screen. Email: *danilocelic@gmail.com*.

Julie Van Keuren (proofreader) quit her newspaper job in 2006 to move to Montana and live the freelancing dream. She and her husband, M.H. (who is living the novel-writing dream), have two sons, Dexter and Michael. Email: *little_media@yahoo.com*.

Ron Strauss (indexer) specializes in the indexing of information technology publications of all kinds. Ron is also an accomplished classical violist and lives in Northern California with his wife and fellow indexer, Annie, and his miniature pinscher, Kanga. Email: *rstrauss@mchsi.com*.

ACKNOWLEDGEMENTS

Thanks to all those who have helped with this book (and all of my books over the years): my students, colleagues, and the wonderful people at O'Reilly. Thanks to Murray Summers and Danilo Celic for their careful scrutiny and erudite corrections to my writing; thanks also to Peter McKie for making my writing more energetic and clearer.

—Dave McFarland

I'm always amazed at the number of pros it takes to create a book like *Dreamweaver CC: The Missing Manual*. My thanks go out to everyone who worked on this book, including the technical reviewers. I also want to thank my wife, Joyce, for her love and support.

—Chris Grover

THE MISSING MANUAL SERIES

Missing Manuals are witty, superbly written guides to computer products that don't come with printed manuals (which is just about all of them). Each book features a handcrafted index and cross-references to specific pages (not just chapters). Recent and upcoming titles include:

iPad: The Missing Manual, Seventh Edition by David Pogue

Fire Phone: The Missing Manual by Preston Gralla

iPhone: the Missing Manual, Eight Edition by David Pogue

QuickBooks 2015: The Missing Manual by Bonnie Biafore

Photoshop Elements 13: The Missing Manual by Barbara Brundage

JavaScript & jQuery: The Missing Manual by David Sawyer McFarland

Photoshop CC: The Missing Manual, Second Edition by Lesa Snyder

Galaxy S5: The Missing Manual by Preston Gralla

WordPress: The Missing Manual, Second Edition by Matthew MacDonald

iPhoto: The Missing Manual by David Pogue and Lesa Snider

iWork: The Missing Manual by Jessica Thornsby and Josh Clark

Switching to the Mac: The Missing Manual, Mavericks Edition by David Pogue

OS X Mavericks: The Missing Manual by David Pogue

HTML5: The Missing Manual, Second Edition by Matthew MacDonald

Dreamweaver CC: The Missing Manual by David Sawyer McFarland and Chris Grover

Windows 8.1: The Missing Manual by David Pogue

Office 2013: The Missing Manual by Nancy Connor and Matthew MacDonald

Excel 2013: The Missing Manual by Matthew MacDonald

Microsoft Project 2013: The Missing Manual by Bonnie Biafore

Access 2013: The Missing Manual by Matthew MacDonald

For a full list of all Missing Manuals in print, go to *www.missingmanuals.com/library. html*.

Preface

Websites evolve every year, growing in scope, capability, and complexity, making them look and work ever better over time. Even people with personal sites use a collection of computer languages and server technologies to dish up their content.

Throughout its history, Dreamweaver has kept pace with the changing web-development landscape, and Adobe's latest offering, Dreamweaver CC (Creative Cloud) 2014, is no exception—it does more than any previous version of the program. Whether you want to use Cascading Style Sheets (CSS) for cutting-edge site design, include audio and video, create JavaScript-powered dynamic pages, incorporate HTML5, build websites for mobile devices, use content management systems like WordPress or Drupal, or simply stick to straightforward HTML, Dreamweaver has just about all the tools you need.

Any enterprising designer can create web pages, Cascading Style Sheets, and even JavaScript programs using just a simple text editor. However, typing HTML, CSS, and JavaScript code is not only a recipe for carpal tunnel syndrome; it's also a slow and typo-prone way to build web pages. Dreamweaver provides buttons, dialog boxes, and panels that let you build web pages quickly, with fewer keystrokes. For example, in a matter of seconds, a simple button lets you insert the complex HTML required to insert a video into your web page. And Dreamweaver is flexible enough to let you hand-code pages and use time-saving HTML shortcuts in tandem—the choice is yours.

NOTE To emphasize that its Creative Suite applications (Dreamweaver, Photoshop, InDesign, and so on) reside exclusively in the cloud, Adobe added "CC" to the Creative Suite product names. It's necessary to distinguish one version from another, so Adobe added the year to product names. So, for this new version of Dreamweaver, what used to be Dreamweaver CS6, then Dreamweaver CC, has become Dreamweaver CC 2014. Throughout this book, and out there in the site design/developer world, the program is usually referred to simply as Dreamweaver.

■ What Dreamweaver Is All About

Dreamweaver is a complete website development and site-management program. It works with web technologies like HTML, XHTML, CSS, JavaScript, and PHP.

It lets you use CSS to create fast-loading, easily modified pages, and it lets you tap the jQuery JavaScript framework to create complex, interactive page elements, like tabbed or collapsible content panels, with a single key click.

Dreamweaver also includes plenty of tools to help you manage your sites once you build them. You can check for broken links, use templates to implement site-wide page changes, and reorganize your site in a flash with the program's site-management features.

NOTE If you're unfamiliar with the acronym CSS, it stands for Cascading Style Sheets—a set of rules you write that dictate the look of your pages. Dreamweaver includes advanced tools to create, test, and edit CSS in your pages.

If you've built one or more sites without Dreamweaver, you don't have to start over again. The program happily opens web pages and websites created in other programs without destroying any of your carefully crafted code.

■ Why Dreamweaver?

You can find other web design programs on the market, but Dreamweaver is one of the leaders, thanks to key benefits like these:

- **Visual page-building**. If you've ever spent time using a text editor to punch out HTML for your web pages, you know the tedium involved in adding even a simple photograph. When your boss asks you to add her photo to the company home page, you launch your trusty text editor and type in something like *<img src="images/staff/bigcheese.jpg" width="100" height="150" alt="The Boss" title="Bow Down">*. Not only is this approach prone to typos, but it also separates you from what you want the page to *look* like.

  Dreamweaver, on the other hand, gives you several ways to stay in touch with your page's visual design. If your interest is in design and not HTML, you can work in the program's Design view. Drag an image to your budding web page, and Dreamweaver displays the picture on the page. Just as a word processor displays documents as they'll look when you print them out, so Dreamweaver gives you a close look at what your page will look like in a web browser.

But Dreamweaver's Design view is only an approximation of what a page will look like in a browser. Because of that, the program offers Live view, too—a real-time look at your page in a browser built right into Dreamweaver. It lets you see what a page looks like and how it behaves without leaving Dreamweaver! Not only is this a time-saver, but it's also a more accurate way to build your web page.

Another approach web designers commonly use is monitoring a page's code and appearance side by side. Dreamweaver's Split view handles that, giving you direct access to the HTML of a page in one half of the screen and to its visual look in the other half. For the visual half, you can use either Design view, or, for greatest accuracy, Live view. Using this technique, you can hammer out your HTML in the Code view half of your screen and quickly see the effect in a web browser in the Live view half.

- **Complex interactivity, simply**. You've probably seen web pages where an image (on a navigation bar, for example) lights up or changes appearance when you point to it. Dynamic effects like these, along with alert boxes and pop-up dialog boxes, usually require JavaScript programming, a language browsers understand. While JavaScript can do amazing things, it requires time and practice to learn.

  Dreamweaver embraces the wildly popular jQuery JavaScript framework and its sister project, jQuery UI, which provides easy-to-use "widgets" that make adding interactive page elements like tabbed panels, pop-up date selectors, and dialog boxes a breeze.

- **Solid code**. Every now and then, even in Dreamweaver, you may want to put aside the visual view and look at a page's underlying HTML. You may want to tweak the code that Dreamweaver produces, for example, or see how Dreamweaver writes instructions.

  Adobe realizes that many professional web developers do a lot of work "in the trenches," typing HTML, CSS, and JavaScript code by hand. In Dreamweaver, you can edit a page's raw HTML to your heart's content. Switching back and forth between Design view and Code view is seamless and, best of all, nondestructive. Unlike many visual web page programs, where making a change in the visual mode stomps all over the underlying HTML, Dreamweaver respects hand-typed code and doesn't try to rewrite it (unless you ask it to). You can even use Dreamweaver's Split view to see your HTML side by side with your final page.

  In addition, Dreamweaver can open many other types of files commonly used on websites, such as external JavaScript (.js) files, so you don't have to switch to another program to work on them. Dreamweaver's Related Files toolbar lists all CSS, JavaScript, and server-side files the current document uses. For hand-coders, this feature means that editing a page's CSS or JavaScript is just a click away (instead of a time-draining File→Open hunt for that danged file). Chapter 7 has the scoop on how Dreamweaver handles writing and editing code.

- **Site-management tools**. Rarely will you build just a single web page. More often, you'll create and edit pages that work together to form part of a website. Or you may build an entire website from scratch.

  Either way, Dreamweaver's site-management tools make your job easier. They automate many of the routine tasks every webmaster faces, from managing links, images, pages, and other media, to working with a team of people and moving your site to a web server. Part 5 of this book shows you how Dreamweaver helps you build and maintain websites.

UP TO SPEED

Hand-Coding vs. Visual Editors

At one time, creating web pages in a text editor was considered the best way to build websites. The precise control that hand-written code gave you over HTML was (and often still is) seen as the only way to ensure quality web pages.

Professional site developers championed hand-coding because many early visual page-building programs added unnecessary code—code that affected how a page appeared and how long it took to download. But hand-coding is time-consuming and error-prone. One typo can render a web page useless.

Fortunately, Dreamweaver creates solid code even in a visual environment. Since its earliest incarnation, Dreamweaver has prided itself on its ability to produce clean HTML and its tolerance for code created by other programs—including text editors. In fact, Dreamweaver includes a powerful built-in text-editing mode that lets you freely manipulate the HTML of a page—or any other code, including JavaScript, Visual Basic, XML, PHP, and ColdFusion Markup Language.

But the real story behind the code Dreamweaver produces in Design mode is that it's as solid and well-written as hand-hewn code. Knowing this, feel free to take advantage of the increased productivity that Dreamweaver's visual-editing mode brings to your day-to-day work with its one-click objects, instant JavaScript, and simplified layout tools. Doing so won't compromise your code and will certainly let you finish your website in record time.

Honestly, no web design program is really WYSIWYG ("What you see is what you get"). Because every browser renders the HTML language slightly differently, web design is more like WYSIRWYGOAGD: "What you see is roughly what you get, on a good day." That's why Dreamweaver's Live view can help make sure your pages look the way you *really* want them to. Dreamweaver is also clever enough to automatically add code "fixes" so that browsers with known issues behave better when displaying your pages.

Finally, if you have experience hand-coding HTML and CSS, you'll be pleasantly surprised by Dreamweaver's powerful text-editing capabilities. In fact, even though Dreamweaver has a reputation as a *visual* web page editor, it's also one of the best text-editing programs on the market.

- **Have it your way**. As if Dreamweaver didn't have enough going for it, the program's engineers have created a completely customizable product. If you're not thrilled about pressing Ctrl-F11 (⌘-F11 on the Mac) to open CSS Designer, no problem. You can create your own keyboard shortcut. If you have favorite tools you use to insert page elements, you can store all those tools in the Insert panel's Favorites section.

There's a large community of developers creating Adobe Add-ons, mini-programs that enhance Dreamweaver's capabilities. Anyone can add to or change Dreamweaver's menus, commands, objects, and windows. Once installed, Add-ons are literally a part of Dreamweaver, giving you new menu commands and tools to handle common (and in some cases not-so-common) web-building chores. Best of all, the Adobe Add-ons website includes hundreds of free and commercial extensions for Dreamweaver. See Chapter 23 for details.

What's New in Dreamweaver CC 2014

If you haven't used Dreamweaver before, see Chapter 1 for the grand tour. If you're upgrading from Dreamweaver CS6, Dreamweaver CC, or some other version of the program, you'll find that Dreamweaver CC 2014 offers a host of new features:

- **Editable Live View** is brand-new to Dreamweaver CC 2014. In the past, Live view was a preview mode, where you could check your work to see how it looked in a real browser. Now, you can *edit* in Live view, adding paragraphs, headings, and images. You can even add audio and video clips without ever leaving Live view.

- **Element Quick View** is one of those tools that's so handy you wonder why it wasn't part of Dreamweaver years ago. It's a simple panel that quickly shows you the structure of your HTML code in outline form and lets you isolate elements on a page with one click. This is important because web pages are made up of dozens (and maybe hundreds or thousands) of elements nested inside other elements. The order and hierarchy of nested elements affects the way your page appears and performs. Want to quickly identify which paragraphs are inside a footer and which aren't? Element Quick View is the tool to use.

- **HTML5** is touted by everyone from AT&T to Google as the next big thing (described in more detail on page 456). It's the first major change to HTML in years, and it promises to make building powerful websites easier than ever. Dreamweaver CC 2014 brings HTML5 to Design view, providing simple menu options that let you insert new HTML5 elements like <header>, <article>, and <nav>. It also lets you insert the many useful HTML5 form elements, such as web addresses, dates, email addresses, and search fields. Finally, Dreamweaver makes adding the HTML5 <video> and <audio> tags easy, so you can insert video and audio that works on smartphones as well as web browsers.

- **Mobile web design**. Web pages that you build today may be viewed on a tiny smartphone screen or in a web browser built into a big-screen TV. With each version of Dreamweaver, Adobe makes it easy to develop pages that respond to the size and orientation of screens big and small. Dreamweaver CC 2014 improves on the fluid grid design system that has been a part of the program for a few years, and its new starter templates let you quickly develop responsive pages for blog posts, email newsletters, e-commerce sites, and image portfolios. Dreamweaver also includes jQuery Mobile tools for building pages designed exclusively for phones and tablets.

- **Photoshop PSD Extract.** It's not unusual for designers to develop web page prototypes (sometimes called "comps" for "compositions") in Photoshop. Photoshop is a tool designers know, and they can quickly whip up a page design for a client. But what happens when the client says, "Yes. I'll buy it!"? Someone has to build a page that looks like the prototype. That's where Dreamweaver's new Extract tools come in. Using Extract, you can move assets like text and images from a PSD file to Dreamweaver. Equally important, you can quickly create code for your web page that defines type styles, colors, and other important formatting features.

- **CSS** is the heart of web design. While HTML provides the structure for content, CSS gives it color, layout, and graphical flair. Because CSS is so fundamental to web design, Adobe took a long look at how designers use CSS and completely revamped CSS creation and editing in CC. As a result, you use the CSS Designer panel to visually manage complex sets of styles, and you use the CSS Transitions panel to develop engaging and useful visual effects. Dreamweaver CC 2014 has refined the tools in CSS Designer, making them easier and more intuitive. You'll find these new tools covered on page 425.

- **Web Fonts.** Dreamweaver's typography options build off of the web fonts feature added in Dreamweaver CS6. In addition to being able to use your own set of fonts, CC 2014 lets you take advantage of free, hosted fonts from Adobe using its Edge Web Fonts. This free service gives you access to dozens and dozens of fonts. You'll learn more about this on page 141.

- **jQuery UI.** Adobe's outdated Spry framework (last appearing in Dreamweaver CS6) had been replaced with the wildly popular jQuery library and its user-interface toolkit known as jQuery UI. Unfortunately, jQuery UI doesn't replace all the Spry widgets available in earlier versions of Dreamweaver (see page xix for more on Spry and what's missing).

■ Life in the Cloud

Adobe programs like Dreamweaver no longer come as a disc in a box—they come from the cloud. That change may have a greater effect on your wallet than it does on your computer. Like many other companies, Adobe decided it is better to get a little money from you each month than it is to get big whopping sums every couple of years. In essence, you lease Creative Cloud software. You can pay $19.99 a month to use Dreamweaver, or $49.99 a month to use Dreamweaver and a whole suite of creative apps such as Photoshop, Illustrator, InDesign, Flash, and Premiere Pro. Those are just the major tools; the complete list is really pretty impressive. See *http://www.adobe.com/products/creativecloud.html*.

The first time you install an app like Dreamweaver from the Creative Cloud, you use the Download Center—a web page you log into after you pay the licensing fee. Click the Download button next to the Dreamweaver icon and follow the instructions to download and install the program on your computer. Yes, that's right, Dreamweaver CC gets saved on your computer's hard drive, just like the previous versions. The difference is that, periodically, Dreamweaver checks back with the mother ship to make sure you still have a license to use the program. Depending on your agreement with Adobe, that period is either 30 days or 99 days. If you don't have a valid license, you can't use the app. Web pages you created in Dreamweaver won't disappear; you just can't use Dreamweaver to work on the project until you're paid up.

When you first install Dreamweaver (or any other Creative Cloud app) on your computer, you also install the Creative Cloud desktop app, which keeps track of the CC 2014 programs on your computer and notifies you when there are updates. Once you install the CC app, you can install and update Dreamweaver or any of the other apps you're licensed to use. All it takes is the click of a button.

> **NOTE** The Creative Cloud app is compatible with Windows 7 or later and Mac OS X 10.7 or later. If you have an earlier operating system, you use the older Adobe Application Manager to download and install CC applications.

■ What's Gone in Dreamweaver CC 2014

With Dreamweaver CC, Adobe took a long, hard look at a fairly old program. It decided that it was time for some serious housecleaning:

- **Server behaviors.** Dreamweaver's innovative server behaviors were a boon to those afraid of server-side programming. They let non-programmers build websites that could tap into a database, making it easy to add forms to collect (and then store) visitor information. For several versions of the program, however, Adobe largely ignored Dreamweaver server behaviors, and the code behind their magic wasn't up to current programming standards. In CC, Adobe finally pulled the plug on these database tools. If you want to use a database with your site, you either need to learn how to program the website-database interaction yourself or use an add-on that provides the tools necessary to create database-driven web pages. For that, you can turn to a third-party solution, such as WebAssist (*www.webassist.com*) or DMXZone (*www.dmxzone.com*).

- **Spry**. Adobe's Spry JavaScript Framework for AJAX was once a cutting-edge set of tools that made building forms, drop-down menus, and other interactive page features simple. However, the programming behind these elements is out of date, and a hugely popular replacement, jQuery, has arisen out of the world of open-source software. jQuery is a free JavaScript framework that more than 40 percent of the world's websites use. Adobe wisely realized that it could never keep its Spry framework up to the level of jQuery and, in Dreamweaver CC, dropped Spry and replaced it with jQuery and the jQuery user-interface library.

However, while Adobe replaced many Spry widgets with jQuery counterparts, there are a few exceptions. For example, there's no longer a tool that lets you build drop-down navigation menus, nor are there any tools that let you validate forms. See the Note on page 609 for more.

- **BrowserLab.** Earlier versions of Dreamweaver integrated directly with BrowserLab, Adobe's online service that displayed your web pages in a variety of browsers. BrowserLab let you see, for example, if your page looked the same in Internet Explorer 7 as it did in Google Chrome. However, the company closed BrowserLab in March 2013 and removed it from Dreamweaver CC. Adobe now refers developers to BrowserStack (*www.browserstack.com/*) and Sauce Labs (*https://saucelabs.com/*) for that service, and it recommends using its Edge Inspect tool (*https://creative.adobe.com/products/inspect*) for mobile web projects.

- **Assorted changes.** Dreamweaver CC boasts a number of smaller changes, too. Among them are the removal of the panel that let you manage absolutely positioned elements (see page 483 for more on absolute positioning), the link to Adobe's Bridge program so you could browse for files outside of Dreamweaver, and the File→Convert tool that translated the HTML of one type (say, XHTML) to the HTML of another type (HTML5, for example).

■ HTML Basics

Under the hood of any web page—whether it's your uncle's "Check out this summer's fishin'" picture album or the front door of a billion-dollar online retailer—is nothing more than line after line of ordinary text. You embed simple commands, called tags, within this text. Web browsers know how to interpret these tags to properly display your pages. When you create a page with tags in it, the document becomes known as an HTML page (for Hypertext Markup Language). HTML is at the heart of most of the Web.

The HTML code that creates a web page can be as simple as this:

```
<!doctype html>
<html>
    <head>
        <meta charset="UTF-8">
        <title>Hey, I am the title of this page.</title>
    </head>
    <body>
        <p>Hey, I am some body text on this page</p>
    </body>
</html>
```

While it may not be exciting, this short bit of HTML is all you need to create an actual web page.

■ Document Types

The first line of the code above:

```
<!doctype html>
```

is called a "doctype," and it identifies the flavor of HTML you used to create the page. Developers have used different doctypes over the years—for example HTML 4.01 and XHTML 1.0. Dreamweaver can create any type of HTML—you simply tell it which you want when you create a new web page (see page 29). However, today's standard is HTML5, so that's the one Dreamweaver uses unless you direct it to use an older version.

HTML5 is much easier to use than plain old HTML in many ways, and Dreamweaver CC embraces this new version of the web's *lingua franca*. This book uses the HTML5 doctype—it's short, simple, and supported by every major browser (even back to Internet Explorer 6). And because HTML5 is the future of the Web, there's no reason to use older doctypes.

But no matter which doctype you use, it's important that you always use one, because without it, different browsers display CSS differently, and your pages will look different depending on your visitor's browser.

Different doctypes do require that you write your HTML in a particular way. For example, the line break tag looks like this in HTML 4.01:

```
<br>
```

But in XHTML, you write it this way:

```
<br />
```

HTML5 lets you write it either way. Fortunately, you won't have to worry about these subtle differences when you use Dreamweaver to insert your HTML—it automatically adjusts to the doctype you chose, inserting the appropriate HTML.

■ Of Tags and Properties

In the preceding example—and, indeed, in the HTML of any web page—you'll notice that most commands appear in *pairs* that enclose a block of text or other commands.

These bracketed commands, like the <p> command that denotes the beginning of a paragraph, constitute the "markup" part of HTML (Hypertext *Markup* Language), and they're called *tags*. Sandwiched between greater-than and less-than signs, tags are simply instructions that tell a web browser how to display a page.

The starting tag of each pair tells a browser where the instruction begins, and the closing tag tells it where the instruction ends. A closing tag always includes a forward slash (/) after the first bracket symbol (<), so the closing tag for the paragraph command above is </p>.

Fortunately, Dreamweaver can generate all these tags *automatically*. You don't have to memorize or even type them in (although many programmers still enjoy doing so for greater control). Behind the scenes, Dreamweaver's all-consuming mission is to convert your visual design into underlying code, like this:

- The <html> tag appears once at the beginning of a web page and again (with an added closing slash) at the end. This tells a browser that the information between these two tags is written in HTML, as opposed to some other language. All the contents of the page, including any other tags, appear between these opening and closing <html> tags.

  If you were to think of a web page as a tree, the <html> tag would be its trunk. Springing from the trunk are two branches that represent the two main parts of any web page: the head and the body of the page.

  The *head* of a web page contains the page's title ("Izzie's Mail-Order Pencils"). It may also include other, invisible information, such as a page description, that browsers and search engines use. You surround the head section with opening and closing <head> tags.

  The head section can also include information that browsers use to format a page's HTML and add interactivity. You can store CSS styles and JavaScript code in the head, for example, or you can embed links to external CSS and JavaScript files there. In fact, the interactivity you'll see in Dreamweaver's jQuery UI widgets (Chapter 15) work with the help of JavaScript code stored in separate files on a server; the link to these files resides in the page's head section.

  The *body* of a web page, identified by its beginning and ending <body> tags, contains all the content that appears in a browser window—headlines, text, pictures, and so on. When you work in Dreamweaver's Design view, the blank white portion of the document window represents the body area. It resembles the blank page of a word-processing program.

Most of your work with Dreamweaver will involve inserting and formatting text, pictures, and other objects in the body portion of a document. Many tags commonly used in web pages appear within the <body> tag. Here are a few:

- You can tell a web browser where a paragraph of text begins with a <p> (opening paragraph) tag, and where it ends with a </p> (closing paragraph) tag.

- The <strong> tag emphasizes text. The text between an opening and closing <strong> tag shows up as boldfaced. The HTML snippet <strong>Warning!</strong> tells a web browser to display the word "Warning!" in bold type.

- The <a> tag, or anchor tag, creates a link (hyperlink) on a web page. A link, of course, can lead anywhere on the Web. How do you tell a browser where the link should point? Simply give address instructions inside the <a> tags. For instance, you might type *<a href="http://www.missingmanuals.com">Click here!</a>*.

The browser knows that when your visitor clicks the words "Click here!" it should go to the Missing Manual website. The *href* part of the tag is called, in Dreamweaver, a *property* (you may also hear it called an *attribute*), and the URL (the Uniform Resource Locator, or web address) is the *value* of that property. In this example, *http://www.missingmanuals.com* is the value of the *href* property.

Fortunately, Dreamweaver exempts you from having to type any of this code, letting you add properties to tags (and other page elements) through an easy-to-use window called the *Properties panel*. To create links the Dreamweaver way (read: the easy way), turn to Chapter 4.

> **NOTE**   For a full-fledged introduction to HTML, check out *Creating a Website: The Missing Manual, 3rd Edition* (O'Reilly). For a primer geared to readers who want to master CSS, pick up a copy of *CSS3: The Missing Manual* (O'Reilly). And if you want to add interactivity to your web pages (beyond the cool, ready-to-use features that Dreamweaver offers), you might be interested in *JavaScript & jQuery: The Missing Manual* (O'Reilly). End of advertisements; now back to your regularly scheduled book.

■ XHTML in Dreamweaver

Like any technology, HTML has evolved over time. Although standard HTML has served its purpose well, it's always been a somewhat sloppy language. Among other things, it allows uppercase, lowercase, and mixed-case letters in tags (<body>, <BODY>, and <bODy> are all correct, for example) and permits unclosed tags (so you can use an opening <p> tag without a closing </p> tag to create a paragraph, for instance). While this flexibility may make page-writing easier, it also makes life more difficult for web browsers, smartphones, and other technologies that must interact with these pages. Additionally, HTML doesn't work with one still-useful Internet language, XML (Extensible Markup Language).

To keep pace with the times, an improved version of HTML, called XHTML, was introduced back in 2000, and you'll find it used frequently on many sites (in fact, XHTML is just an "XML-ified" version of HTML). Dreamweaver CC can create and work with XHTML files as well as plain old HTML pages.

> **NOTE**   XHTML was seen as the future back in 2000, but HTML5 has since supplanted it. While web browsers still understand XHTML (and probably will for a long time), you won't be using it in this book.

■ HTML5, the New Markup Standard

HTML5 isn't some radically new technology. In fact, unlike XHTML, which was intended to foster a new way to build web pages, HTML5 is about making sure the Web continues to work as it always has. Most of the basics of HTML are still in place. HTML5 adds a few new elements that support the way designers build websites today.

In HTML5, for example, the <header> tag contains the content you'd usually find at the top of a page, such as a logo and site-wide navigation links; the new <nav> tag encloses the set of links used to navigate a site; and the <footer> tag houses the stuff you usually put at the bottom of a page, like legal notices, email contacts, and so on.

In addition, HTML5 adds new tags that let you insert video and audio into a page, add sophisticated form elements like drop-down date-pickers, and validate forms to make sure visitors fill them out correctly. Unfortunately, browser support for these new features isn't consistent, and it's therefore difficult to use the new tags without some pretty elaborate workarounds to ensure cross-browser support.

Dreamweaver CC includes new tools that work with HTML5. Click-to-insert buttons make it easy to insert HTML5 tags like <header>, <footer>, <article>, and <section>. And CC supports the HTML5 <video> and <audio> tags that make your pages come to life with video and sound.

But new tags are just one small part of the HTML5 story. HTML5 started life as a product of the Web Hypertext Application Technology Group (WHATG), which wanted to create a version of HTML that provided the tools needed to build powerful, browser-based applications, like Google's Gmail program. So much of HTML5 is devoted to powerful (and complicated) technologies like Canvas (for drawing pictures and diagrams on a web page), data storage (for storing information like game scores, preferences, and notes on a visitor's computer), drag and drop design, "web workers" for making JavaScript programs run faster and more efficiently, and "web sockets" for streaming data from a web server. All these technologies are promising, but browser support for them varies. In addition, Dreamweaver doesn't provide any easy-to-use tools to tap into these complicated technologies, so you're a few years off from being able to easily include most HTML5 capabilities on your site.

■ Add Style with Cascading Style Sheets

In the beginning, HTML was the only language you needed to create web pages. You could build them with colorful text and graphics, and make words jump out using a limited selection of fonts, font sizes, and font colors. Today, however, you can add much more visual stimulation using Cascading Style Sheets. CSS is a formatting language that lets you design pages with sophisticated layouts and precise typographic control. For example, it gives you site-wide design consistency for headings and subheads, lets you create unique-looking sidebars, and lets you add special graphics treatment for quotations.

From now on, think of HTML as merely the scaffolding you use to organize a page. It helps identify and structure page elements. Tags like <h1> and <h2> denote headlines and reflect their relative importance. A *Heading 1* is more important than a *Heading 2*, for example (and can affect how a search engine like Google adds a page to its search listings). The <p> tag indicates a basic paragraph of information. Other tags provide further structural clues: For example, a <ul> tag identifies a bulleted list (to, say, make a list of recipe ingredients more intelligible).

Cascading Style Sheets, on the other hand, add *design flair* to that highly structured content, making it more beautiful and easier to read. Take a look at the CSS Zen Garden site (*www.csszengarden.com*). Each of the striking, very different websites profiled there uses the same underlying HTML. The only difference among them—and the sole reason they look different—is that each uses a different style sheet. Essentially, a CSS style is just a rule that tells a browser how to display a particular page element—to make an <h1> heading appear orange, 36 pixels tall, and in the Verdana font, for example.

But CSS is more powerful than that. You use it to add borders, change margins, and even control the exact placement of an element on a page.

To be a successful web designer, you need to get to know Cascading Style Sheets. You'll learn more about this exciting technology throughout this book.

■ Add Interactivity with JavaScript

A normal web page—just regular HTML and CSS—isn't very interactive. About the only way visitors communicate with a page like that is to click a link to load a new page. JavaScript is a programming language that lets you supercharge your HTML with animation, interactivity, and dynamic visual effects. It can also make a web page more responsive to visitors by supplying immediate feedback. For example, a JavaScript-powered shopping cart can instantly display the total cost of your purchase, tax and shipping included, the moment a visitor selects a product to buy. Or JavaScript can produce an error message immediately after someone attempts to submit a web form that's missing information.

JavaScript's main selling point is immediacy. It lets web pages respond instantly to visitor actions: clicking a link, filling out a form, or merely moving the mouse around the screen, for instance. JavaScript doesn't suffer from the frustrating delay associated with "server-side" interactive programming languages like PHP, which require that a web browser communicate with a remote web server before the browser does anything.

If you've visited Google Maps (*http://maps.google.com*), you've seen JavaScript in action. Google Maps lets you zoom in to get a detailed view of streets and zoom out to get a birds-eye view of how to get across town, the state, or the nation, all from the same web page, thanks to JavaScript. Earlier map sites always loaded a new page every time you changed a view (usually a slow process).

The JavaScript programs you create can do something as simple as popping up a new browser window with a web page in it, or they can be part of a full-blown "web application," such as Google Docs (*http://docs.google.com*), which lets you edit documents, build spreadsheets, and create presentations using your web browser—all as though the program were running on your computer.

JavaScript programming can be difficult, but Dreamweaver has plenty of tools that let you add sophisticated interactivity to your sites—from animations to pop-up dialog boxes—with just a few clicks of your mouse.

Mobile Web Design

There's no doubt that mobile phones have changed how we live. They're also changing how we build websites. The small screens of iPhones and Android phones don't treat wide, three-column web pages kindly. Many sites shrink down to postage-stamp size when you look at them on a phone, requiring you to pinch, zoom, swipe, and scroll to find what you're looking for. Fortunately, Dreamweaver CC 2014 includes several solutions: the new fluid grid layout tool (page 25) lets you design three layouts (for phones, tablets, and desktop screens) using the same HTML. In other words, you have only a single web page, but using CSS, you can dynamically alter the page's layout depending on the width of the viewing screen. You can also craft your own "media queries" (a CSS feature discussed on page 23) to create styles that apply only to screens at particular widths or within a particular range of widths.

Dreamweaver CC 2014 lets you create mobile-only websites, too, using jQuery Mobile (page 581), a JavaScript tool that makes traditional websites look and function more like mobile applications (and less like web pages).

How This Book Is Organized

Dreamweaver CC: The Missing Manual is divided into five parts, each with several chapters:

- **Part 1** explores Dreamweaver's main screens and takes you through the basic steps of page building. It explains how to add and format text, link from one page to another, and spice up your design with graphics. It also introduces you to Cascading Style Sheets.

- **Part 2** takes you deeper into Dreamweaver and provides in-depth CSS coverage, including that for Dreamweaver's new CSS Designer and CSS Transitions tools. In addition, you'll get step-by-step instructions for creating advanced page layouts, as well as advice on how to view and work with the underlying HTML of a page.

- **Part 3** focuses on building pages for smartphones and tablets. You'll learn to build pages that determine the dimensions of the viewing screen and then transform themselves to accommodate that size. That's called responsive Web design.

- **Part 4** helps you add interactivity to your site. From the new jQuery UI widgets that let you add tabbed content panels to forms that collect information from visitors, this section guides you through adding animation, multimedia, and other interactive effects with ease. The last chapter in this section explains how

to add HTML5 video and audio, Flash animation, and Edge Animate compositions to your web pages.

Part 4 also covers site management: working with the pages and files on your
site, testing links and pages, and moving your site to a web server connected
to the Internet. And since you're not always working solo, this section covers
features that let you work with a team of web developers, too.

- **Part 5** shows you how to take advantage of timesaving Dreamweaver features
like libraries, templates, and history-panel automation. It also covers Dreamweaver's Extension Manager, a program that can add hundreds of free and
commercial features to the site-builder.

■ About This Book

Despite the many improvements in software over the years, one feature has grown
consistently worse: documentation. Until version 4, Dreamweaver came with a
printed manual. In MX 2004, all you got was a *Getting Started* booklet. Now, most
likely, you're getting the entire application from the cloud. If you do get a physical
disc, it arrives in an otherwise empty cardboard box. To get any real information,
you need to delve into the program's online help.

But even if you have no problem reading a help screen in one window as you work
in another, something is still missing. At times, the terse electronic help assumes
you already understand the discussion at hand and hurriedly skips over important topics that require in-depth explanation. In addition, you don't always get an
objective evaluation of the program's features. Engineers often add technically
sophisticated capabilities to a program because they *can*, not because you need
them. You shouldn't have to waste your time learning tools that don't help you get
your work done.

The purpose of this book, then, is to serve as the Dreamweaver manual that should
have been in the box. You'll find step-by-step instructions for every Dreamweaver
feature, including those you may not otherwise have understood, let alone mastered,
such as libraries, Design view, behaviors, and Dreamweaver's JavaScript tools. In
addition, you'll find honest evaluations of each tool to help you determine which
are useful to you, as well as how and when to use them.

> **NOTE** This book periodically recommends *other* books, covering topics that are too specialized or tangential
> for a manual on Dreamweaver. Careful readers may notice that not every one of these titles is published by Missing
> Manual parent O'Reilly Media. While we're happy to mention other Missing Manuals and books in the O'Reilly
> family, if there's another great book out there, we'll let you know about it.

Dreamweaver CC 2014: The Missing Manual is designed to accommodate readers
at every technical level. The primary discussions are written for advanced-beginner
or intermediate computer users. But if you're new to building web pages, special

sidebars called "Up to Speed" provide the introductory information you need to understand the topic at hand. If you're a web veteran, on the other hand, keep your eye out for similar boxes called "Power Users' Clinic." They offer more technical tips, tricks, and shortcuts for more experienced readers.

■ Windows and Macintosh Commands

Dreamweaver CC works almost precisely the same way on the Macintosh as it does in Windows. Nearly every button in every dialog box is exactly the same, and the response to every command is identical. The images in this book alternate among the various operating systems where Dreamweaver feels at home (Windows 8, Windows 7, Windows Vista, and Mac OS X).

One of the biggest differences between Windows and Mac software is the keystrokes, because the Ctrl key in Windows is equivalent to the Macintosh's Command key, ⌘. And the key labeled Alt on a Windows PC (and on non-U.S. Macs) is equivalent to the Option key on American Macs. On some Mac keyboards, you need to press the "fn" key when you use the F1 through F12 keys, because the Mac's operating system uses the "F" keys for other functions, like adjusting the audio volume. Those special cases are pointed out throughout this book.

Whenever this book refers to a key combination, therefore, you'll see the Windows keystrokes listed first (using the + symbol for compound commands, as is customary in Windows documentation); the Macintosh keystrokes follow in parentheses (with - symbols, in time-honored Mac fashion). In other words, you might read, "The keyboard shortcut for saving a file is Ctrl+S (⌘-S)."

■ The Very Basics of Reading This Book

You'll find very little jargon or technical terminology in this book. You will, however, encounter a few terms and concepts you'll come across frequently in your computing life:

- **Clicking.** This book gives you three kinds of instructions that require you to use your computer's mouse or trackpad. To *click* means to point the arrow cursor at something on the screen and then—without moving the cursor—press and release the clicker button on the mouse (or laptop trackpad). To *double-click*, of course, means to click twice in rapid succession, again without moving your cursor. And to *drag* means to move the cursor while holding down the mouse button.

- **Point to.** Sometimes you need to move the cursor on the screen over another object. Just positioning the cursor in a location may make text appear, or a color change, or a tool perform some important function. Instead of saying "Move your mouse over the widget and pause," we simply say "Point to the widget."

- **Keyboard shortcuts.** Every time you take your hand off the keyboard to move the mouse, you lose time and potentially disrupt your creative flow. That's why many experienced computer fans use keystroke combinations instead of menu commands wherever possible. Ctrl+B (⌘-B for Mac folks), for example, gives you boldface type in Dreamweaver documents (and most other programs).

  When you see a shortcut like Ctrl+S (⌘-S), it's telling you to hold down the Ctrl or ⌘ key and type the letter S, and then release both keys. (This command, by the way, saves changes to the current document.)

- **Choice is good.** Dreamweaver frequently gives you several ways to trigger a particular command—by selecting a menu command *or* by clicking a toolbar button *or* by pressing a key combination, for example. Some people prefer the speed of keyboard shortcuts, while others like the satisfaction of a visual command available in menus or toolbars. This book lists all the alternatives; use whichever you find most convenient.

▪ About→These→Arrows

Throughout this book, and throughout the Missing Manual series, you'll find sentences like this one: "Open the System→Library→Fonts folder." That's shorthand for a much longer instruction that directs you to open three nested folders in sequence, like this: "On your hard drive, you'll find a folder called System. Double-click it to open it. Inside the System folder is a folder called Library; double-click it to open it. Inside *that* folder is yet another folder called Fonts. Double-click to open that folder, too."

Similarly, this kind of arrow shorthand helps to simplify the business of choosing commands in menus, as shown in Figure P-1.

▪ Online Resources

This book is designed to get your work onto the Web fast and professionally; it's only natural, then, that part of the value of this book also lies on the Web.

The Missing CD

This book doesn't have a CD pasted inside the back cover, but you're not missing out on anything.

As you read the book, you'll find a number of tutorials that show you how to build web pages using raw materials, like graphics and half-completed web pages. You can download these practice files from this book's Missing CD page (*http://www.oreilly.com/pub/missingmanuals/dreamweaverccmm2014*). If you take the time to work through the tutorials, you'll discover that they give you unprecedented insight into the way professional designers build web pages.

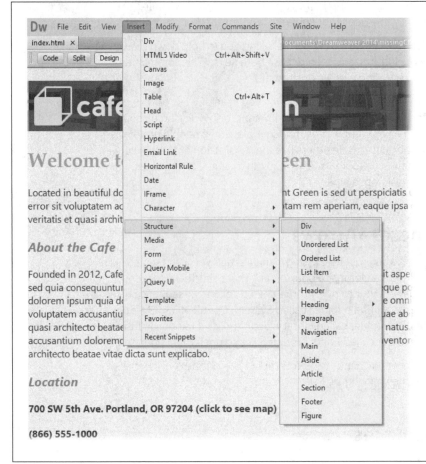

FIGURE P-1

When you read "Choose Insert→Structure→Div" in this Missing Manual, that means, "From Dreamweaver's menu bar, click the Insert command. From the drop-down menu that appears, select Structure. That opens a list of HTML tags you can add to the currently open document; select Div from that list."

The download also includes the completed tutorial pages, so you can compare your Dreamweaver work with the final result. In other words, you won't just see pictures of Dreamweaver's output in the pages of the book, you'll find the actual, working pages in this download.

Finally, the Missing CD site gives you one-click access to the reference websites mentioned in this book—that'll save your fingers some typing.

Registering Your Book

If you register this book at oreilly.com (*http://oreilly.com/register*), you'll be eligible for special offers—like discounts on future editions. If you buy the ebook from *http://oreilly.com* and register your purchase, you get free lifetime updates for that edition of the ebook; we'll notify you by email when updates become available. Registering takes only a few mouse clicks.

Reporting Errata

To keep this book as up to date and accurate as possible, each time we print more copies, we'll make any confirmed corrections you suggest. We also note such changes on the book's errata page, so you can mark important corrections in your own copy of the book if you like. Go to *http://tinyurl.com/erratadreamweavercc2014mm* to report an error and view existing corrections.

■ Using Code Examples

This book is here to help you get your job done. In general, you may use the code in this book in your programs and documentation. You don't need to contact us for permission unless you're reproducing a significant portion of the code. For example, writing a program that uses several chunks of code from this book does not require permission. Selling or distributing a CD of examples from O'Reilly books does require permission. Answering a question by citing this book and quoting example code does not require permission. Incorporating a significant amount of example code from this book into your product's documentation does require permission.

We appreciate, but do not require, attribution. An attribution usually includes the source book's title, author, publisher, and ISBN. For example: "*Dreamweaver CC 2014: The Missing Manual* by David Sawyer McFarland and Chris Grover (O'Reilly). Copyright 2015 David McFarland and O'Reilly Media, Inc., 978-1-4919-4720-3."

If you feel your use of code examples falls outside fair use or the permission given above, feel free to contact us at *permissions@oreilly.com*.

■ Safari® Books Online

Safari® Books Online is an on-demand digital library that lets you search over 7,500 technology books and videos.

With a subscription, you can read any page and watch any video from our library. Access new titles before they're available in print. Copy and paste code samples, organize your favorites, download chapters, bookmark key sections, create notes, print out pages, and benefit from tons of other time-saving features.

O'Reilly Media has uploaded this book to the Safari Books Online service. To have full digital access to this book and others on similar topics from O'Reilly and other publishers, sign up for free at *http://safaribooksonline.com*.

Building a Web Page

Dreamweaver CC Guided Tour

Dreamweaver CC is a powerful program for designing and building websites. If you're brand new to Dreamweaver, turn to page xiv for a quick look at what the program can do; if you're a longtime Dreamweaver fan, page xvii tells you what's new in this latest incarnation of the program.

This chapter gives you an overview of Dreamweaver—a guide to the windows, toolbars, and menus you'll use every time you build a web page. It also shows you how to set up the program so you can begin building pages. And, because *doing* is often a better way to learn than just *reading*, you'll get a step-by-step tour of web page design—the Dreamweaver way—in the tutorial at the end of this chapter.

■ Setting Up Creative Cloud

Back in 2013, Adobe changed the way it offered its programs. Instead of a boxed, standalone copy of say, Dreamweaver, that you bought and installed on your desktop computer, you now license Adobe programs, which reside on Adobe's site, in what the company dubs the "Creative Cloud." To sign into your Adobe account and tap into your programs, Adobe built a program called the Creative Cloud app. It acts as a hub for everything Adobe, overseeing various housekeeping chores for your programs—through it, you download Adobe programs, updates, add-ons, and individual files.

◼ Downloading Dreamweaver CC

To install Dreamweaver, go to Adobe's Download Center (*www.adobe.com/down-loads.html*). To download and install Dreamweaver, click the Dreamweaver icon, sign up for a subscription to the Creative Cloud, and then follow the links. Adobe downloads both Dreamweaver and the Creative Cloud desktop app,

Once installed, the Creative Cloud app resides in the taskbar on Windows computers (in the lower-right corner of the screen) or in the menu bar of a Mac (upper-right corner). To start working, click the cloud icon, 🌥️. If you aren't signed in, Creative Cloud displays the window in Figure 1-1, left, and won't let you go further until you type in your credentials. If you are signed in, you'll see the window in Figure 1-1, right. The Creative Cloud app has four major sections:

- **Home** reports on recent changes, such as programs Adobe updated.

- **Apps** lists all the Adobe programs you can license. Any you've already installed appear at the top of the list. To see other Adobe programs, scroll down. If you have an all-access Adobe license and you're signed into your Creative Cloud account, you can install the new program (you can also update a program you already installed). If not, you can lease the program.

- **Assets** keeps track of files you store in the cloud. They can be photos, web pages, or fonts you use in your projects.

- **Community** gives you a place to share your work or check out the work of others.

If you do a lot of work in Dreamweaver and other Creative Cloud programs, it's easiest to stay logged in to Creative Cloud. Under the standard license agreement, you can sign in from two computers at a time, say your office desktop and your laptop at home. If you need to use Dreamweaver on a third computer, you have to sign out from one of the others. To do that, click ⚙️ in the upper-right corner of the Creative Cloud app and then choose Preferences. In the dialog box, click Account, and then click "Sign Out from Creative Cloud."

◼ Getting Around the Dreamweaver Window

When you launch Dreamweaver, the program's Welcome screen greets you (Figure 1-2). This simple starting point lets you reopen the last eight most recently opened files, create a new web page, view instructional videos, and get online help.

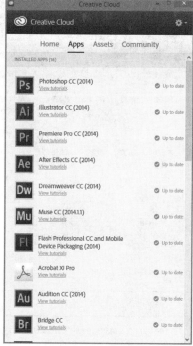

FIGURE 1-1

*Left: To work in Dream-
weaver and other Adobe
Creative Cloud programs,
you have to sign into your
account. Fill in the blanks
and then click Sign In to
see the window on the
right. If you don't have
an account, click "Get an
Adobe ID."*

*Right: The Creative Cloud
app keeps track of the
programs you've installed
and makes it easy to install
and update new ones.*

Dreamweaver CC's interface shares its look and feel with the other programs in Adobe's Creative Cloud suite, including Photoshop, Illustrator, and Flash. The various panels that make up Dreamweaver's main screen appear as a unified whole. That is, the edges of all the windows touch one another, and resizing one window affects the others around it. This type of layout is common on Windows computers, but Mac fans accustomed to independent floating panels might find it strange. Give it a chance. As you'll soon see, it has its benefits. (If you just can't stand this locked-in-place style, you can detach most panels. Drag the panel's tab (it includes the panel's name) and let it float anywhere on your screen. See page 17 for more on arranging Dreamweaver panels and windows.

Many of Dreamweaver's individual windows help you handle specific tasks, like building CSS styles. You'll read about each panel in relevant chapters of this book, but you'll frequently interact with three main groups of windows: the document window, the Properties panel (below the document window), and a set of panels on the right side of the workspace.

FIGURE 1-2

Dreamweaver's Welcome screen lets you open existing Dreamweaver files, create new ones, and learn more about the program. It disappears as soon as you open a web page. If you don't have any use for this window, go to Edit→Preferences→General (Dreamweaver→Preferences→General) and turn off Show Welcome Screen (second item from the top).

NOTE The look of Dreamweaver's windows depends on whether you use a Windows or Mac PC, and what changes you make in the program's Preferences settings. Even so, the features and functions generally work the same way on both computers. In this book, where the program's operation differs dramatically in one operating system or the other, special boxes and illustrations (labeled "For Windows Only" or "For Macs Only") will let you know.

Choosing a Dreamweaver Workspace

If you're new to Dreamweaver, setting up your workspace can be daunting. That's because Dreamweaver is impressively easy to customize—you can open a bunch of panels, windows, and toolbars. You can rearrange the Code and Design windows. You can dock the Properties panel below the document window or have it float anywhere on the screen. If you're just learning Dreamweaver, it's probably best to set up your workspace so that it matches the pictures in these pages (see below for that). Then, once you're a seasoned Dreamweaver jockey, you can set up your workspace so the tools you use the most are at hand.

Fortunately, there's an easy way to rearrange your workspace. Adobe, in its wisdom, created the Workspace Switcher—a tool that lets you change your entire workspace with the click of a menu item. Its thinking is that an ideal workspace for a JavaScript coder is different from that of a Web designer. And those two individuals probably use different workspace layouts for different tasks.

You find the Workspace Switcher in the upper-right corner of the Dreamweaver window (Figure 1-3). The button is actually a drop-down menu that displays the name of the currently selected workspace. When you open a newly installed version of Dreamweaver, that button says "Extract." That view is a good one when you work on Photoshop files (page 64), but most of the exercises in this book use the Design layout, which puts the document window on the left and the Properties panel underneath it (see Figure 1-4). It also positions other panels and tools you often need to the right of the document window. If your Dreamweaver workspace doesn't look like the one in Figure 1-4, go to the Workspace Switcher, choose Design, and then go back into the menu and select "Reset 'Design.'" When you choose Design from the workspace switcher, Dreamweaver displays the Design workspace with panels and windows positioned as they were when you last used it. When you choose "Reset 'Design,'" Dreamweaver displays the original out-of-the-box Design workspace.

FIGURE 1-3

The Workspace Switcher lives in the upper-right corner of the Dreamweaver window. Most of the exercises in this book use the Design layout, so if your screen doesn't look anything like the ones in the book, head up to the Workspace Switcher and choose Design.

You can customize your workspace, too. Once you have the panels and windows positioned and sized the way you want, go to the Workspace Switcher and choose New Workspace. When Dreamweaver opens the Save Workspace window, type in a name for the layout and then click OK. Your new workspace appears listed with the others. If you ever want to delete a workspace you created, use the Workspace Switcher's Manage Workspaces option.

Page 17 has more details on how to organize your workspace by rearranging the panels and windows. Page 21 provides additional instructions for creating and saving workspaces.

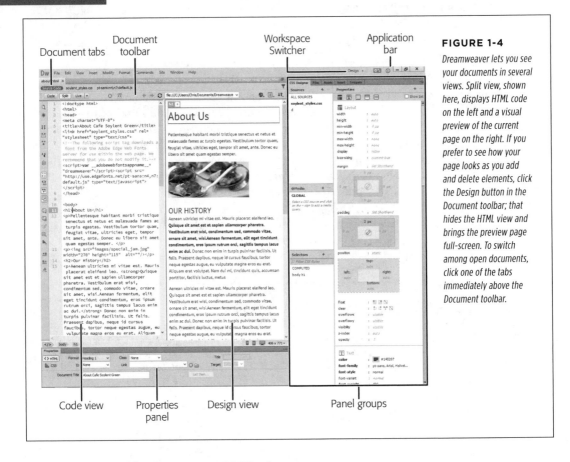

Document tabs | Document toolbar | Workspace Switcher | Application bar

Code view | Properties panel | Design view | Panel groups

FIGURE 1-4

Dreamweaver lets you see your documents in several views. Split view, shown here, displays HTML code on the left and a visual preview of the current page on the right. If you prefer to see how your page looks as you add and delete elements, click the Design button in the Document toolbar; that hides the HTML view and brings the preview page full-screen. To switch among open documents, click one of the tabs immediately above the Document toolbar.

The Document Window

What you see on a web page is the end result of the interaction between your browser and the page's underlying code: its HTML, CSS, and (sometimes) JavaScript. Because of this interrelationship, Dreamweaver's *document window* lets you view pages-in-progress four ways: as straight code (in Code view); in an editable, visual view (called Design view, pictured in Figure 1-5); with both views side by side (known as Split view, pictured in Figure 1-4); and as the page will appear in a web browser (in Live view, which turns the document window into a real web browser). One of the new features in Dreamweaver CC 2014 is the ability to edit your pages in Live view. You can make changes to your page and see the results right away. (But editing in Live view is different from editing in Design view, as you'll learn on page 348.)

Document tabs   Related files   Document toolbar   Application bar

FIGURE 1-5

A document window like this represents a web page in progress; here's where you add text, graphics, and other objects as you build the page. Useful widgets and information surround the window. For example, you can instruct Dreamweaver to display the current document at different widths and heights so you can simulate what the page will look like in different-size browsers, like those on mobile phones, tablets, and desktop computers.

Tag selector   Web page in progress   Mobile/tablet/ desktop screen sizes   Window size

If your monitor is wide enough, Split view is a great way to work: Click into the Design view half of the document window to add HTML visually, and then, when it's easier just to type HTML, click into the Code view part of the document window and type away. Split view even lets you see the code in one half, and turn on Live view in the other half so you can work on the HTML code while you see the page as it will appear in a real web browser. In addition, if you're new to HTML, Split view is a great way to learn the language. You can add elements like paragraphs, headlines, and tables in Design view and see the relevant HTML in Code view. (You work in the document window's Design view much as you do in a word processor: to add text to a page, for example, you simply click inside the window and start typing.)

> **TIP** A couple of commands in the View menu help you arrange the two windows in Split view exactly as you want them. First go to View→"Code and Design." Then, on the View menu, click View→Split Vertically (this command works like a toggle, positioning the two windows side by side or one over the other). The next command down changes depending on the current view. If you split the window vertically, click "Design View on Left" to arrange the windows. If you split the windows horizontally, the menu option changes to "Design View on Top."

When you build a page, you work in the document window, and, as you add pages to your site or edit existing ones, you open new document windows. Several screen cues provide useful information about your document. They may appear in different locations on Windows and Mac computers (Figures 1-4 and 1-5, respectively), but they work the same way.

For example:

- **Document tabs**. Small tabs appear at the top of the document window—one for each open file. The name of the file appears in the tab; to switch to a different document, just click its tab.

> **TIP** If you point to a document tab and pause, Dreamweaver displays the location of the file in a small pop-up window called a *tooltip*. Dreamweaver offers tooltips for just about every feature, so if you're ever in doubt about a button, widget, or item, just point to it.

- **Related Files bar**. The Related Files bar lists all CSS (Cascading Style Sheets), JavaScript, and server-side programming pages (like PHP pages) the current web page uses. You'll learn more about these external files later in this book, but as a quick summary, it's common in current web design to have other files supply design and interactivity to a page of HTML. Web designers frequently work on these files in addition to the basic HTML file, so the Related Files bar lets you quickly jump to and work on these "helper" files. You choose which files to display using the Filter Related Files button on the right side of the bar.

- **Document toolbar**. The Document toolbar (View→Toolbars→Document) lets you switch between Code, Design, and Live views. On the right side, click ⊕ to preview your page in the web browsers installed on your computer. Use the menu under ⬆ to manage the files on both your computer and on the web server that hosts your site. You'll read about the toolbar's various buttons and menus in the relevant chapters of this book, but you'll want to be aware of the Code view and Split view buttons and the Design/Live menu (circled in Figure 1-5). They let you see the page you're working on in the four views described earlier.

> **NOTE** You may also find Dreamweaver's Standard toolbar useful. The Standard toolbar is common on many Windows programs and includes buttons for frequent file and editing tasks, like creating a new page; opening a page; saving one or all open documents; canceling and repeating commands; and cutting, copying, and pasting page elements. Dreamweaver hides this toolbar until you summon it by choosing View→Toolbars→Standard.

- **Tag Selector**. The Tag Selector is extremely useful. It provides a sneak peek at the HTML that composes your web page, behind the scenes. It indicates how Dreamweaver nests HTML tags in your document to create what you see on the page. In addition, it lets you select, with a single mouse click, an HTML tag and all the content inside it. That means you can cleanly remove a page element or set its properties (see page 14), and precisely control the application of styles to it (Chapter 3).

You'll make good use of the Tag Selector in nearly all the tutorials to come. For experienced Dreamweaver fans, it's one of the program's most useful tools.

NOTE In Design view, clicking the <body> tag in the Tag Selector is usually the same as pressing Ctrl+A (⌘-A) or choosing Edit→Select All. It selects everything in the document window. However, if you click inside a table (Chapter 6) or a <div> tag (see page 454), choosing Edit→Select All selects only the contents of the table cell or the <div> tag. In such a case, you need to press Ctrl+A (⌘-A) several times to select everything on the page. After you do, you can press the Delete key to instantly get rid of everything in your document.

Careful, though: Pressing Ctrl+A (⌘-A) or choosing Edit→Select All in Code view selects *all* the code, including the information in the head section of the page. Deleting all the code gives you an empty file—and an invalid web page.

The Insert Panel

Dreamweaver provides many windows (also referred to as panels) for working with the various technologies required to build and maintain a website. You open and close all these windows using Dreamweaver's Window menu. For the most part, the windows appear in tidy groups on the right edge of your screen. You'll hear about the windows and their uses in relevant sections of this book, and you'll learn how to organize the panels on page 17. But two are worth mentioning up front: the Insert panel and the Files panel.

If the document window is your canvas, the Insert panel holds your brushes and paints, as you can see in Figure 1-6. You can create a page simply by typing HTML in Code view, but it's often easier to work in Design view, where the Insert panel can simplify the process of adding page elements like images, video, horizontal rules, and forms. Want to put a picture on your web page? Just click the Images icon in the Insert panel.

NOTE Adding elements to your web page using the Insert panel may feel like magic, but it's really just a quick way to add HTML to a page. Clicking the Images icon, for instance, simply inserts the <img> tag into the underlying HTML of your page. Of course, Dreamweaver's visual approach hides that code and cheerfully displays a picture on the page.

If you ever close the Insert panel by mistake or simply can't find it, you can reopen it by choosing Window→Insert or by pressing Ctrl+F2 (⌘-F2). On the other hand, if screen space is at a premium, you can close the Insert panel and use the Insert *menu* instead. The menu offers all the objects in the panel, but they're not grouped by sets, as the panel and toolbar are. (You can turn the Insert panel into a toolbar that sits above the document window as described in Figure 1-6.)

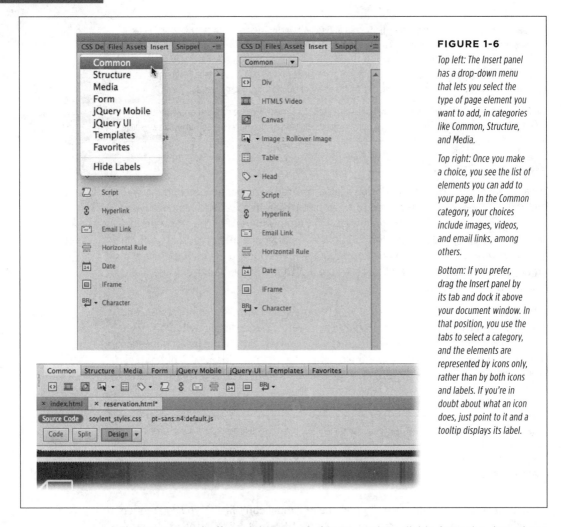

FIGURE 1-6

Top left: The Insert panel has a drop-down menu that lets you select the type of page element you want to add, in categories like Common, Structure, and Media.

Top right: Once you make a choice, you see the list of elements you can add to your page. In the Common category, your choices include images, videos, and email links, among others.

Bottom: If you prefer, drag the Insert panel by its tab and dock it above your document window. In that position, you use the tabs to select a category, and the elements are represented by icons only, rather than by both icons and labels. If you're in doubt about what an icon does, just point to it and a tooltip displays its label.

The Insert panel offers eight sets of objects, each available from the drop-down menu at the top of the window (see Figure 1-6, top) or by clicking one of the tabs on the Insert toolbar (Figure 1-6, bottom):

- **Common**. Common objects are those you'll most likely add to web pages: images, videos, hyperlinks, email links, tables, horizontal lines, heading tags, canvas tags, and the most versatile all-around utility player, the <div> tag.

- **Structure**. There's some overlap between Common and Structure objects. You'll find the <div> and heading tags here, along with paragraph, list, navigation, article, and aside tags. You use structure tags to identify elements on your web page, and you format those elements using CSS.

- **Media**. Media objects include Edge Animate compositions, HTML5 video, HTML5 audio, Flash SWF, Flash video, and a less well-defined catchall, Plugin. For details on inserting media into web pages, see Chapter 17.

- **Form**. Want to hear back from your visitors? Forms let them make comments, order products, and ask questions. You can add form elements like radio buttons, pull-down menus, and text boxes (see Chapter 16). And because Dreamweaver includes sophisticated form validation, you can make sure visitors type in the correct information *before* they submit the form.

NOTE In Web parlance, a *form* is a web page that lets visitors type in information that your web server processes. For example, you might ask a guest to type in his email address when he signs up for a newsletter.

- **jQuery Mobile**. jQuery Mobile is a JavaScript-powered toolset for building websites for mobile devices, like iPhones and Android phones. The objects listed here include page elements like lists, form text boxes, and text areas. You'll learn about these tools in Chapter 14.

- **jQuery UI**. Another part of the jQuery family, this toolset provides familiar menu and content objects like buttons, checkboxes, sliders, accordion sections, and progress bars. You don't need to reinvent the wheel every time you want to add a widget to your web page.

- **Templates**. Templates let you build basic web page designs you can use over and over again, speeding up page development and facilitating easy updates. See Chapter 22 for details.

- **Favorites**. Perhaps the most useful category, Favorites can be anything you want it to be. After you discover which objects you use the most (like the Image command, if you work with a lot of graphics), you can add those objects to this set of personal tools. You may find that once you populate this category, you'll never again need the other categories in the Insert panel. For instructions on adding objects to the Favorites category, see the box on page 14.

The Files Panel

The Files panel, another Dreamweaver element you'll turn to frequently (see Figure 1-7), lists all the files—web pages, graphics, CSS, and JavaScript—that make up your website. It gives you a quick way to open the files you want to work on (just double-click the filename), lets you switch among different sites you're building or maintaining, and provides some valuable tools for organizing your files. If the Files panel isn't open, summon it by choosing Window→Files or by pressing F8 (fn-F8 on Macs).

Adding Favorite Objects to the Insert Panel

Help! I'm tired of wading through so many pull-down menus to find all my favorite Dreamweaver objects. How can I see my most-used objects in one place?

Dreamweaver includes a marvelous productivity tool: the Favorites category of the Insert panel. It lets you collect your most-used objects in a single place, without having to wade through buttons for HTML tags and objects you never use. Maybe you use the Common category's Email Link object all the time but never touch the IFrame object, for example. This is the timesaving feature for you.

To add objects to the Favorites category, right-click (Control-click) anywhere in the Insert panel (or the Insert toolbar, if you made the changes described on page 11). From the pop-up menu, choose Customize Favorites to open the Customize Favorite Objects window. All the objects available in all the Insert categories appear in the left-hand list. Select an object and then click the >> button to add that object to your Favorites list. (You can view the objects for just one category by selecting the category from the "Available objects" menu.) Repeat with other objects if you like.

To rearrange the order of the toolbar buttons, click one and then click the up or down arrow. Depending on whether you display the panel buttons with or without labels, buttons you put higher in the list appear either toward the top of the panel or toward the beginning of the rows of buttons. You can even use the Add Separator button to insert a thin gray line between buttons—to separate one group of similar elements (graphics-related objects, say) from another (such as form objects). Unfortunately, you can't group Favorite objects into submenus; each item you add becomes a single button on the Insert bar.

To delete a button or separator from the list, select it and then click the Trash icon. Click OK to close the window and create your new list of Favorite objects, which are now available under the Favorites category of the Insert panel.

After you create your Favorites tab, you can always add more objects (or delete ones you no longer need) by right-clicking (Control-clicking) the Insert bar and then, from the shortcut menu, choosing Customize Favorites.

To use the Files panel effectively, you need to create a local site for each website you work on—setting up a site is a specific Dreamweaver task and one of the most important steps in using Dreamweaver correctly. You'll learn how to do that starting on page 23.

The Properties Panel

After dropping an image, table, or anything else from the Insert panel into your web page, you can use Dreamweaver's Properties panel to fine-tune the element's appearance and attributes (see Figure 1-8). Suppose, for example, that your boss has decided she wants her picture to link to her personal blog. After highlighting her picture in the document window, you can use the Properties panel to add the link.

FIGURE 1-7

The Files panel gives you a bird's-eye view of your site's files. But it's more than just a list—you can quickly open files, rename and rearrange them in your site, and switch among sites. Later in this chapter, you'll learn how to organize site files using this panel.

FIGURE 1-8

If you don't see the Properties panel, open it by choosing Window→Properties or by pressing Ctrl+F3. (On Macs, the keyboard shortcut is ⌘-F3, but for most Macs this conflicts with an operating system command. If you run into that problem, just use the menu command.)

The Properties panel, sometimes referred to as the Properties Inspector, is a chameleon. It's aware of what you're working on in the document window—a table, an image, some text—and displays the appropriate set of properties (that is, options). It works whether you're in Design view or Code view.

You'll use the Properties panel extensively in Dreamweaver. For now, though, here are two essential tips to get you started:

- In the Properties panel, double-click any blank light-gray area to hide or show the bottom half of the panel, where Dreamweaver displays a set of advanced options. (It's a good idea to leave the panel fully expanded, since you may otherwise miss some useful options.)

- At its heart, the Properties panel simply displays the attributes of HTML tags. The *src* (source) attribute of the image tag (<img>), for instance, tells a web browser where to find an image file.

  You can most easily make sure you're setting the properties of the correct object by selecting its tag in the Tag Selector (see page 7).

NOTE When you work with text, the Properties panel has two buttons—labeled "HTML" and "CSS"—that let you either work with the page's HTML properties related to text or create CSS styles. You'll read more about these two buttons in Chapter 3, but here's a quick pointer: When you want to create paragraphs, headlines, bulleted lists, and bold or italic text, click the HTML button. When you want to change the appearance of text (its font, color, and size), use the CSS button—or, better yet, use the CSS Designer panel, described on page 116, to choose from a much wider range of formatting options.

The Application Bar

As in most programs, the Application bar offers menus and the usual controls for expanding, shrinking, hiding, and closing the workspace window. As you can see, these controls are in their usual positions on Windows PCs (Figure 1-9, top) and Macs (Figure 1-9, bottom). The application bar gives you two other toolsets, on the right side:

- The **Workspace Switcher** lets you reorganize Dreamweaver's layout. As discussed back on page 6, you can choose one of Dreamweaver's stock workspaces, or you can design a custom layout to create the ultimate workspace. (You can find these same options from the Window→Workspace Layout menu.)

- The **Creative Cloud** tools let you sync CC files on your computer with those stored in the cloud. They also give you quick entry to Adobe's Creative Cloud site pages and let you log into your personal cloud using your Adobe ID.

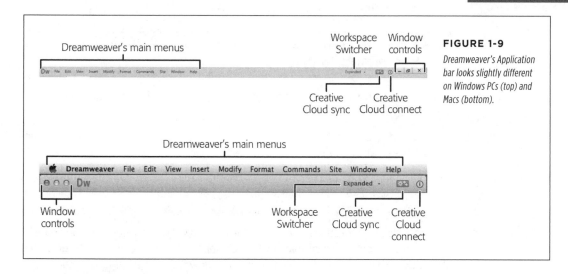

FIGURE 1-9

Dreamweaver's Application bar looks slightly different on Windows PCs (top) and Macs (bottom).

Hiding the Application Bar

On Windows PCs, the Application bar is unobtrusive—it sits just to the right of Dreamweaver's main menu items. However, if you have a particularly small monitor, the Application bar will poke up above the menu, taking up a good chunk of vertical space on the screen. In previous versions of Dreamweaver, you could hide the Application bar, but that's no longer the case.

On Macs, the Application bar always sits on its own. With just a few menu items and widgets, it's mostly a waste of space. You can hide it on Macs as well, but at a cost: You'll lose the Application Frame, which binds all the panels, toolbars, and windows into a cohesive whole. With the Application Frame turned on, changing the width of the panel groups on the right side of the screen resizes the document window and Properties panel, too. If you turn off the Application bar, however, the document window, Properties panel, and panel group act as separate windows you can resize independently of one another.

So if you're a Mac user willing to give up the unified workspace of the Application Frame, here's how to hide the Application bar: Select Window→Application Frame, and then choose Window→Application Bar to hide the bar. You can always turn the Application Frame back on, but doing so automatically brings the Application bar back.

Organizing Your Workspace

Dreamweaver's basic user interface includes the document window, Application bar, Properties panel, and panel groups. All these windows act as though they were a whole; that is, if you resize one window, the other windows readjust themselves to fit the available space. For example, you can drag the left edge of the panel groups to the left to make the panels wider or to the right to make them thinner. The windows that touch the panels (the document window and the Properties panel) change their widths accordingly. This kind of joined-at-the-hip layout is common in

Windows programs but may feel a bit weird for Mac enthusiasts. (If you prefer the "floating palette" look and feel common to a lot of Mac programs, you can set up Dreamweaver that way—see the next section.)

> **NOTE** On Macs, if you turn off the Application Frame, Dreamweaver's windows act independently of one another. See the box on page 17 for more.

You can customize your workspace in many ways when you control the panel group (Figure 1-10):

- You can open a particular panel from the Window menu. For example, to open the Files panel, choose Window→Files.

- If the panel is hidden but its tab is visible (for example, the CSS Transitions tab in Figure 1-13), click the tab once to open the panel. Double-click the tab again, and the panel (and any other panels grouped with it) collapse down to a single bar.

- If panels are stacked vertically, drag the horizontal line between two open panels to resize them. For example, if CSS Designer is below the Files panel, grab the thick border between them and then drag down. The Files panel gets taller and CSS Designer gets shorter.

- To completely close a panel so that even its tab no longer appears, right-click (Control-click) the tab and then choose Close. (Choose Close Tab Group to hide all the tabs in a group.) To get the panel back, use the Window menu or the panel's keyboard shortcut—for example, F8 (fn-F8) opens and closes the Files panel.

- To hide all windows *except* the document window, choose Window→Hide Panels or press F4 (fn-F4)—a useful trick when you want to maximize the amount of screen space for the web page you're working on. To bring back all the panels, press F4 (fn-F4) again or choose Window→Show Panels.

■ FLOATING PANELS

As mentioned earlier, you can drag a panel by its tab to another part of the screen. Releasing the panel at the edge of the screen docks it to that edge. However, if you drag a panel and drop it when it's not near a screen's edge, it becomes a floating panel (see Figure 1-11). Floating panels are often nuisances, since they hide whatever is beneath them, so you often end up having to move them out of the way just to see what you're doing. However, they come in handy when you have two monitors. If that's the case, you can dedicate your main monitor to the document window and Properties panel (and maybe your most important panels), and then drag a bunch of floating panels onto your second screen.

FIGURE 1-10

You don't have to keep all of Dreamweaver's panels on the right side of the screen—you can move individual panels to more comfortable positions. If a panel is docked, just drag the panel's tab and it becomes a floating panel.

Top: The Insert panel is being dragged toward the top of the document window. Dreamweaver provides two visual clues when a dragged panel approaches the edges of the document window where it can be docked (see below).

Bottom: Here the Insert panel is close to the top edge of the document window, so Dreamweaver does two things: it ghosts out the panel, and it displays a thin blue line. Releasing the mouse button docks the panel in its new position.

To "unfloat" a floating panel, drag it to the edge of your screen (if you have more than one monitor, drag the panel to one of the edges of your *main* monitor). If you already have panels at that edge, drag the panel to either the bottom of the panels (to dock it at the bottom of the column of panels), between the bottom edge of one panel group and the top edge of another (to insert the panel in its own group between the other panels), or next to another panel's tab to group the panels together side by side.

FIGURE 1-11

Here, the Files, Insert, and CSS Designer panels float. Each one has its own context menu (circled in the Files panel). Clicking the menu icon reveals a shortcut menu that lets you work with commands specific to that panel. The menu also offers generic panel actions, such as closing the panel. If you find you've made a mess of your workspace and want to return Dreamweaver to the way it normally lays out panels, use the Workspace Switcher. Choose Design, and then choose "Reset 'Design.'" Choosing Design switches to the Design workspace as it last appeared. That means some panels could be out of position. Choosing "Reset 'Design'" returns the workspace to the factory settings for Design.

■ ICONIC PANES

As if you didn't already have enough ways to organize your panels, Dreamweaver includes yet another one. By clicking the "Collapse to Icons" button at the top right of a column of panels, you can shrink the panels to a group of much smaller icons. To reopen the controls for a panel you shrunk, click the panel name. For example, in Figure 1-12, clicking CSS Designer opens the CSS Designer panel to the left. Once you finish working with the panel, click the panel name again or click elsewhere on the screen, and the pop-up panel disappears. This so-called iconic view is particularly good if you have a small monitor and need to preserve as much screen real estate as possible.

Expand Panels button

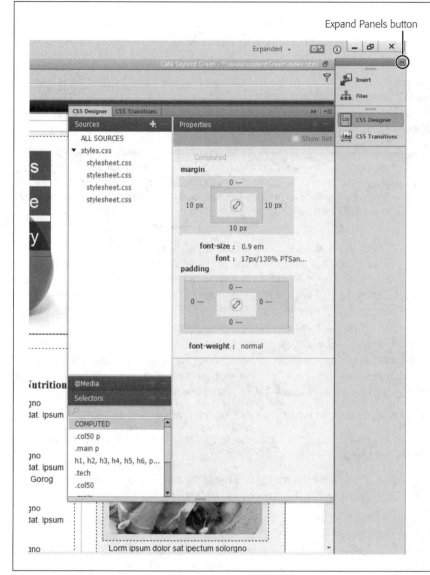

FIGURE 1-12

Iconic panes, like those for Insert and Files in the top right here, let you preserve screen real estate. To return the panels to their normal widths, click the Expand Panels button.

■ WORKSPACE LAYOUTS

Sometimes too much choice is a bad thing, and even though Dreamweaver lets you pretty much organize windows and panels any way you like, it also means you can easily accidentally click or drag the wrong thing and suddenly find panels strewn across the screen or completely gone.

Fortunately, Dreamweaver includes a wonderful, timesaving productivity enhancer that ensures you always have your windows organized the way you want, and you can return to that setup if you accidentally move anything. The Workspace Layouts feature lets you save the position and size of Dreamweaver's panels and windows as a custom "layout" you can invoke by selecting the layout's name from the Workspace Switcher menu in the Application bar or by choosing Window→Workspace Layout.

For example, when you work on a mobile website, you may like to have the jQuery swatches panel and the Snippets panel open, and the CSS Designer panel tucked away. But when you work on design-heavy sites, you probably want the CSS Designer panel open, though you couldn't care less about the Code Inspector. You can create a different layout for each situation and then switch among them.

NOTE If you have a small screen or an older, squarish screen, drag the vertical bar between the document window and the panels to the right. They squash down quite well. On the other hand, if you have a larger, or cinema-style, display, you may want to drag the vertical bar in toward the document window, making more room for important, but cluttered, tools like CSS Designer and the Files panels.

After you tweak a workspace to perfection by closing, opening, and rearranging panels, you can save the result as a custom layout. Go to Window→Workspace Layout→New Workspace; when the New Workspace dialog box appears, provide a meaningful name like "Dual Monitors" and then click OK. (You'll find the same New Workspace command on the Workspace Switcher menu in the Application bar.) If you type in a name that matches a workspace you already use, Dreamweaver gives you the option to replace the old layout with the new one. That's the only way to update a workspace layout you previously created. Once you save a custom workspace, you can call it up in the Workspace Switcher with a couple of mouse clicks. If you prefer menus, you can choose Window→Workspace Layout→[*Name of Your Layout*].

Here are a few other tips when you're ready to create a custom layout:

- Open the panels you work with most frequently. For example, choose Window→ Files to open the Files panel.

- Increase or decrease the height of a panel by dragging the empty space to the right of a panel or panel-group name up or down (see Figure 1-13).

- You can move a panel to another area of your screen by dragging its tabs as described on page 17. This trick is especially useful if you have a large monitor, since you can place one group of panels on the right edge of the monitor and another group either next to the first one or on the left side of the monitor. As described on page 18, you can also create untethered panels—if you've got two monitors, you can spread the panels across both screens.

TIP The Workspace Layout feature is also handy if you share your computer with other people. You can create your own workspace layout ("Bob's Workspace," for example) with the panels and windows exactly where you like them. Then, when you go to use the computer and the bozo before you has rearranged the entire workspace, just select your layout from the Application bar or the Window→Workspace Layouts menu.

FIGURE 1-13

Resizing a panel vertically is as easy as dragging its bottom border (circled at the bottom of the Insert panel) up or down. If you're lucky enough to have a large monitor, it's often helpful to put the Files panel by itself on either the left or right side of the screen.

■ Setting Up a Site

Whenever you build a new website or want to edit a site you created outside of Dreamweaver, you have to introduce the program to the site—a process Dreamweaver calls *setting up a site*. This is *the* most important first step when you start using Dreamweaver, whether you plan to whip up a five-page site, build a 1,000-page online store, or edit the site your sister built for you. At its most basic, defining a site lets Dreamweaver know where you store your web pages on your computer. It also helps Dreamweaver correctly insert images and add links from one page to another. In addition, if you want to take advantage of Dreamweaver's many timesaving site-management tools, such as the link checker (page 781), Library items (Chapter 21), templates (Chapter 22), and FTP feature for moving your files to a web server (Chapter 20), you *have* to set up a site.

There are a lot of ways to configure a site, depending on your needs. For example, if you're ready to move pages to the Web, you need to tell Dreamweaver how to connect to your web server. But to get started with a new site, you need only a couple pieces of information:

1. **Choose Site→New Site to open the Site Setup window (Figure 1-14).**

   You'll supply basic site info here.

2. **In the "Site name" box, name your site.**

   The name you type here is for your own reference, to help you identify the site when it appears in the Files panel; the name won't show up on the Web.

   NOTE In Web argot, a *box* is simply a box where you type in information.

3. **Click ▤ (the browse-for-file button) to the right of the "Local site folder" box.**

   The Choose Root Folder window opens, letting you select a folder on your hard drive to serve as your *local site* or, more specifically, your local site's *main*, or *root*, folder. You'll store all your site's files—HTML documents and graphics, CSS files, and so on—in this local root folder (or in a subfolder that you create in the root folder, like an Images subfolder).

   NOTE Another way to think of the local site folder is as the folder on your computer in which you'll put your site's home page.

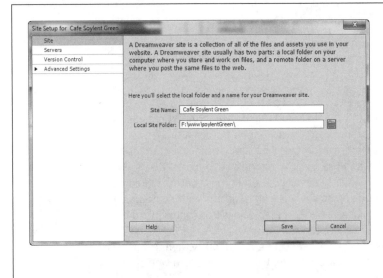

FIGURE 1-14

The Site Setup window tells Dream-weaver about your site—where you store your files, how to connect to your web server so you can upload pages to the Internet, and so on. But to get started, you only need to fill in these two boxes and designate an Images folder (step 5). You'll find the other Site Setup categories, listed on the left, discussed later: The Servers category lets you point Dreamweaver to your online web server so you can upload files to your site (Chapter 20) and to a "testing server" so you can put complex, database-driven websites through their paces before going live (Chapter 24); the Version Control category is for those using the (very complex) Subversion system (most people—the authors of this book included—never use this option, but if you're curious, see the box on page 824 for more).

4. Browse to and select a folder for your site's files.

Figure 1-15 demonstrates the process. If you're editing a site created outside of Dreamweaver, select the folder that contains the site's files. If you're creating a new site, create a folder for that site using the New Folder button in this window.

FIGURE 1-15

The dialog box for selecting a folder in Windows (top) is pretty much the same as that for Macs (bottom). You can verify which folder you're about to select by looking in the Folder box on Windows PCs (circled, top) or in the path menu on Macs (circled, bottom).

5. **For a few additional options, select Advanced Settings from the left-hand list of setup categories (see Figure 1-16).**

This step is optional and you can happily skip much of the settings listed. You'll find most of them discussed elsewhere in the book. But you should visit the Local Info category to at least set up an Images folder for your site. Here are the options you'll see in that category, including the one to set up an Images folder:

- You should always set up an Images folder whenever you set up a site. The "Default Images folder" box lets you select (or create) one inside your local site folder. It will hold the images you'll use on your web pages. Choosing a default images folder is important when you add images to your pages-in-progress from outside your local site folder—you might, for example, add images that are sitting on your desktop or in another folder on your hard drive. In that case, Dreamweaver automatically copies those files to the Images folder on your local site; that way, when you upload your local site to your web server, all your images go along for the ride. (Dreamweaver copies "outside" image files to your local site without setting this option, but each time you add an outside image, you have to tell Dreamweaver where to save the file.)

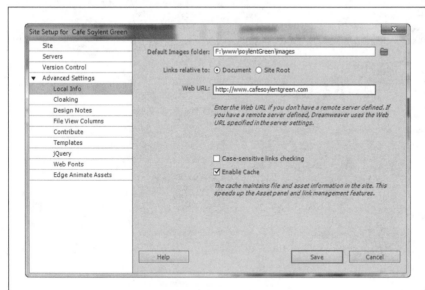

FIGURE 1-16

You can happily use Dreamweaver without ever visiting many of the advanced settings in the Site Setup window. The Local Info options are discussed earlier, and the other options are discussed elsewhere in this book: cloaking on page 818, Design Notes on page 831, File View columns on page 761, templates in Chapter 22, jQuery on page 607, Web fonts on page 141, and Edge Animate on page 718.

- The "Links relative to" setting determines how Dreamweaver writes links to other pages in your site, links to images in your site, and links to external files, like Cascading Style Sheets, Flash movies, and so on. Unless you're an experienced web designer, stick with the normal "Document" setting here—you can read about the difference between (and uses for) document- and site root-relative links on page 179.

- Type the web address for your site in the Web URL box, something like *http://www.cafesoylentgreen.com/,* for example. If you don't yet have a web address, you can leave this blank. In some cases, you may need to add information after the domain name. For example, if you're a teacher and you have a site on your college's web server, its address might look something like this: *www.somecollege.edu/~bob.* Or you might be responsible for maintaining just part of a larger site—sometimes called a "sub-site"—so you might need to append, for example, */marketing* to the end of the URL. Regardless, just type the address you normally type into a web browser to visit your site; for example, *www.mybigcompany.com/marketing.*

- Leave the checkbox next to "Case-sensitive links checking" turned off. This is useful only when you have web pages and files on a UNIX server that allows files with the same name but different letter cases: for example, *HOME.html, home.html,* and *HoMe.html.* Since Windows PCs and Macs don't let you do this, you'll probably never have a site with filenames like these.

- Keep the Enable Cache checkbox turned on. Dreamweaver creates a cache for each site you set up. That's a small database that tracks pages, links, images, and other site components. The cache helps Dreamweaver's site-management tools avoid breaking links, lets Dreamweaver warn you when you're about to delete important files, and lets you reorganize your site quickly. The only reason to turn off this checkbox is if you have a really large website (tens of thousands of pages and images) and you notice that Dreamweaver is really slow whenever you begin to work on the site, move a file, change a file's name, delete a file, or perform one of Dreamweaver's other site-management tasks. In that case, you may see a box saying "Updating the site cache" or "Checking links" that stays open and prevents you from using Dreamweaver for a minute or more—basically your site is so big that Dreamweaver has to spend a lot of time keeping track of your files and links.

6. **Click Save to finish the site setup.**

   Your site's files (if there are any yet) appear in the Files panel. Now you're ready to create and edit web pages and take advantage of Dreamweaver's powerful site-building tools.

NOTE Dreamweaver lets you set up *multiple* websites, a handy feature if you're a web designer with several clients, or if your company builds and manages more than one site. To define an additional site, choose Site→New Site and then repeat the steps above. You can then switch from one site to another using the Sites menu at the top left of the Files panel.

Creating a Web Page

After you define a site, you'll want to start building pages. Just choose File→New or press Ctrl+N (⌘-N on Macs) to open Dreamweaver's New Document window (see Figure 1-17). The window's a little overwhelming at first—there are so many options, it's hard to know where to start. Fortunately, when you just want to create a new HTML file, you can skip most of these options.

FIGURE 1-17

The New Document window lets you create nearly every type of web document under the sun. Dreamweaver includes a small set of prepackaged HTML layouts that you'll learn more about in Chapter 10. You'll find details about starter templates on page 557.

To create a basic HTML file for a web page:

1. From the left-hand list of document categories, choose Blank Page.

The Blank Page category lets you create a new empty document—maybe a web page or something a bit more esoteric, like an XML file, an external JavaScript file, or one of the several types of server-driven pages (such as a PHP file, discussed in Chapter 24).

The Fluid Grid Layout option is relatively new in Dreamweaver. It lets you create a web page that adapts to three browser widths: for a phone, a tablet, and a desktop browser. You'll learn how to use this feature on page 549.

The Starter Templates and Site Templates categories relate to Dreamweaver's Template feature discussed in Chapter 22. Within Starter Templates you'll find starter pages for common projects like blog posts or image portfolios (page 557). The Site Templates category holds templates for sites you've created, so initially it will be empty.

2. **From the Page Type list, choose HTML.**

   You can create other types of documents, too, some of which you'll learn about later in this book, such as templates (Chapter 22), Library items (Chapter 21), and CSS files (Chapter 3).

3. **From the Layout list, choose <none>.**

   This creates a blank document. The other choices ("2 column fixed, right sidebar, header and footer," "3 column fixed, header and footer," and so on) are pre-designed page layouts (you'll learn more about using these layouts in Chapter 10). They use CSS, which you'll learn about in Chapter 3.

UP TO SPEED

Terms Worth Knowing

During the tutorials in these pages—and, indeed, everywhere in Dreamweaver—you'll encounter a few terms frequently heard at web designer luncheons:

- **Root folder.** The first rule of managing a website is that every piece of the site you're working on—web pages (HTML files), images, sound files, and so on—must sit in a single master folder on your hard drive. This is the *root* folder for your website, and because it's on your computer, it's called the *local* root folder, though Dreamweaver calls it your local site folder. The *root* (a.k.a. site) folder is the master, outer, main folder. Think of it as the edge of the known universe for that site; nothing exists outside the root. Of course, to help organize your site's files, you can include any number of subfolders *within* that main folder.

  When you finish creating a site on your computer, you'll move the files in your local root folder onto a web server for the world to see. You call the folder where you place your site files on the server the *remote root folder*.

- **Local site.** The usual routine for creating web pages goes like this: Create the page on your own computer—using a program like Dreamweaver—and then upload it to a

computer on the Internet called a web server, where your handiwork becomes available to the masses. So it's very common for a website to exist in two places at once, one copy on your computer and the other on the server.

The copy on your computer is called the *local site*, or the development site. Think of the local site as a sort of staging ground, where you build your site, test it, and modify it. Because the local site isn't on a web server, the public can't see it and you can freely edit and add to it without affecting the pages your visitors see (they're on the remote site, after all).

- **Remote site.** When you add or update a file, you move it from your local site to the remote site. The *remote*, or live, site is a mirror image of your local site. Because you create the remote site by uploading your local site, the folder on your web server has the same structure as the folder on your local site, and it contains the same files. Only polished, fully functional pages go online to the remote site; save the half-finished, typo-ridden drafts for your local site. Chapter 20 explains how to use Dreamweaver's FTP features to define and work with a remote site.

---

4. **Select a document type from the DocType menu.**

   Selecting a *doctype*, or document type, identifies the type of HTML you'll use to create your page. It affects how Dreamweaver writes HTML code and how a web browser understands it. Fortunately, since Dreamweaver writes all the code for you, you don't need to worry about the subtle differences between the different doctypes.

HTML5 is the latest version of HTML, and the normal setting in Dreamweaver—it's what all the cool kids on the block are using, and you should, too. However, XHTML 1.0 Transitional, as well as HTML 4.01 Transitional, HTML 4.01 Strict, and XHTML 1.0 Strict also work just fine; so if you're working on a site whose pages use one of these older doctypes, you might want to stick with it.

If you don't really understand or care about doctypes, just select HTML5, making sure to avoid the None option (which can force browsers to display pages in what's called "quirks mode" and makes perfecting designs difficult), XHTML Mobile, and XHTML 1.1 (which is not only obsolete but also requires a special setting on your web server to work properly).

TIP If you don't want to deal with the New Document window every time you create a page using Dreamweaver's New Document keyboard shortcut (Ctrl+N in Windows, ⌘-N on Macs), choose Edit→Preferences in Windows (Dreamweaver→Preferences on Macs). In the Preferences dialog box, click the New Document category and then turn off the "Show New Document Dialog on Ctrl+N (⌘-N)" checkbox.

While you're at it, you can specify the type of file Dreamweaver creates whenever you press Ctrl+N (⌘-N). For example, if you usually create plain HTML files, choose HTML. But if you usually create dynamic pages, choose a different type of file—PHP, for example. You can also select the default doctype—choose HTML5—for all new pages.

Once you set these options, pressing Ctrl+N (⌘-N) instantly creates a new blank document using the doctype you chose. (Choosing File→New, however, still opens the New Document window.)

---

5. **Click Create.**

   Dreamweaver opens a new, blank page ready for you to save and title (see Figure 1-18).

6. **Choose Modify→Page Properties. In the panel on the left of the Page Properties window, choose Title/Encoding, and then, in the Title box, type a name for your page.**

   Every new document Dreamweaver creates has the unflattering name Untitled Document. If you do a search on Google for "Untitled Document," you'll find about 40 million pages. Dreamweaver probably created most of them. Change the Dreamweaver-given name to a descriptive one that indicates the page's main topic, like "Directions to Cafe Soylent Green," "About Cafe Soylent Green," or "Technical Specifications for the Anodyne 3000 Indoor Lawn Mower." Not only is a true page title more professional, but providing one can also improve a web page's ranking among search engines.

7. **Choose File→Save.**

   The Save As dialog box appears. You need to save the file somewhere inside your local site folder (or in any subfolder of the site folder).

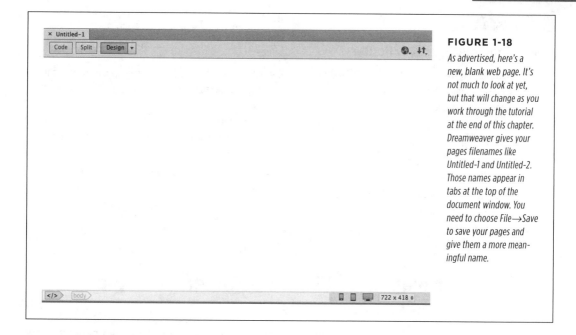

FIGURE 1-18

As advertised, here's a new, blank web page. It's not much to look at yet, but that will change as you work through the tutorial at the end of this chapter. Dreamweaver gives your pages filenames like Untitled-1 and Untitled-2. Those names appear in tabs at the top of the document window. You need to choose File→Save to save your pages and give them a more mean-ingful name.

TIP If you've set up a site, Dreamweaver provides a quick shortcut to the local root folder. When you save a web page, click the Site Root button in the Save As dialog box—this jumps directly to the local root folder. The Site Root button appears at the bottom right of the Save As dialog box in Windows, and at the bottom left of that window on Macs.

8. **Type a name for the file and then click Save.**

   Make sure the name doesn't contain spaces or any characters except letters, numbers, hyphens, and underscores, and that it ends in either .html or .htm.

   Although most operating systems let you save files with long names, spaces, and characters like #, $, and & in them, some browsers and servers have trouble interpreting anything other than letters and numbers. Furthermore, web servers rely on file extensions like .htm, .html, .gif, and .jpg to know whether a file is a web page, graphic, or some other type of file. Dreamweaver for Windows automatically adds the extension to your saved documents. But on Macs—which let you save files without extensions—you have to add the extension yourself.

Naming Your Files and Folders

The rules for naming files and folders in Windows and on Macs are fairly flexible. You can use letters, numbers, spaces, and even symbols like $, #, and !.

Web servers, on the other hand, are far less accommodating. Because many symbols—such as &, ⌘, and ?—have special significance on the Web, using them in filenames can confuse web servers and cause errors.

The precise list of no-no's varies from web server to web server, but you'll be safe if you stick to letters, numbers, hyphens

(-), and underscore characters (_) when you name files and folders. Stay away from spaces. Filenames like *company logo. gif* or *This company's president.html* may or may not work on a web server. Replace spaces with underscores or inner caps—*company_logo.gif* or *companyLogo.gif*—and remove all punctuation marks.

Sure, some operating systems and web servers permit strange naming conventions, but why take the chance? Someday you may need to move your site to another, less forgiving server.

■ Managing Files and Folders with the Files Panel

Dreamweaver's Files panel provides a fast way to add blank web pages to your site. With one click, you can create a new page in any folder, saving you several steps compared with using the File menu. In addition, you can use the Files panel to add folders, rename files and folders, and move files into and out of the folders on your site.

Adding Files

To create a new, blank web page, open the Files panel using one of the methods described on page 13 (for example, choose Window→Files), and then right-click (Control-click) a file or folder in the Files panel. In the shortcut menu that appears, choose New File. Dreamweaver creates a new, empty page in the same folder as the selected page or, if you selected a folder, it creates the page there.

The type of file Dreamweaver creates depends on the type of site you're creating. For a plain HTML site, Dreamweaver produces a blank HTML page. If you're building a dynamic, database-driven site, however (like those described in Chapter 24), Dreamweaver creates a blank page based on the type of server model you select. For example, if you build a site using PHP and MySQL, Dreamweaver creates a blank PHP page (named *untitled.php*).

NOTE The doctype (page xxi) of a new web page created with the Files panel depends on your Dreamweaver Preferences settings: Choose Edit→Preferences (Dreamweaver→Preferences on Macs), select the New Document category, and choose HTML5 (or whichever doctype you prefer) from the Default Document Type menu. You can set other options for new documents in this window as well, such as the file extension you prefer (.htm or .html, for instance).

The new file appears in the Files panel with a highlighted naming rectangle next to it; type a name for the page here. Don't forget to add the appropriate HTML extension (.htm or .html)—if you do forget, Dreamweaver creates a completely empty file, no starter HTML included (and changing the name by adding the .html extension won't fix the problem). If this happens, delete the file and create a new one. (If you're creating a PHP file, make sure the filename ends in .php.)

NOTE If, immediately after creating a new file in the Files panel, you rename that file and add a new extension, Dreamweaver updates the file to reflect the new file type. For example, changing *untitled.html* to *global. css* erases all the HTML code in the file and turns it into an empty CSS file.

Adding Folders

You can add folders to your site using the Files panel, too. Right-click (Control-click) any file or folder. From the shortcut menu, choose New Folder. If you click a filename, Dreamweaver creates the new folder in the same folder the file is in; if you click a folder, you get a new folder inside the existing one.

If you crave variety, you can add a folder another way. Select a file or folder in the Files panel, click the drop-down menu button at the very top right of the Files panel, and then select File→New Folder. Finally, in the naming rectangle that appears in the Files panel, type a name for the new folder.

Moving Files and Folders

Because the Dreamweaver Files panel looks and acts so much like Windows Explorer and the Mac Finder, you may think it does nothing more than let you move and rename files and folders. You may even be tempted to work with your site files directly on your Windows or Mac desktop, thinking that you're saving time. Think again. When it comes to moving site files and folders, Dreamweaver does more than your computer's desktop ever could.

In your Web travels, you've probably encountered the dreaded "404: File Not Found" error. This "broken link" message doesn't necessarily mean that the page doesn't exist; it just means that your web browser didn't find the page at the location (URL) the link specified. Someone working on the website probably moved or renamed the file without updating the link. Because website files are interrelated in such complex ways—pages link to other pages, which include paths to graphics, which in turn appear on other pages—an action as simple as moving one file can wreak havoc on an entire site. That's why you should always use the Files panel, rather than Windows Explorer or the Macintosh Finder, to rearrange your files.

Moving and reorganizing website files is so headache-ridden and error-prone that some web designers avoid it altogether, leaving their sites straining under the weight of thousands of poorly organized files. But Dreamweaver's Files panel makes organizing a site easy and error free. When you use the panel to move files, Dreamweaver looks for actions that could break your site's links and automatically rewrites the paths of links, images, and other media (see the cautionary Note below).

TIP Note to JavaScript coders: If your custom JavaScript programs include paths to web pages, images, or other files on your site, Dreamweaver can't help you. When you reorganize your site with the Files panel, the program updates *links* it created, but not any *paths* in your JavaScript programs.

Just be sure to do your file and folder moving from within Dreamweaver, like this: In the Files panel, drag the file or folder into its new folder (see Figure 1-19). To move multiple files, Ctrl-click (⌘-click) each and then drag them as a group; to deselect a file, Ctrl-click or ⌘-click it again. You can also select a file or folder and then Shift-click another file or folder to select all the content between the two.

NOTE Close *all* your web documents *before* you reorganize your files. Dreamweaver has been known to skip updating links in open files. But if you do end up with malfunctioning links, you can always use Dreamweaver's Find Broken Links tool (page 781) to ferret out and fix them.

When you release the mouse button, the Update Files dialog box appears (Figure 1-19); click Update and Dreamweaver rewrites the links.

NOTE If you accidentally drag a file or folder to the wrong location, click Don't Update. Then drag the file or folder back to its original location and, if Dreamweaver asks, click Don't Update once again.

Renaming Files and Folders

Renaming files and folders poses the same problems as moving them. Because links include file and folder names, altering a name can break a link just as easily as moving or deleting a file or folder.

Say you create a new site that has a page named *about.html*. You cheerfully continue building the other pages of your site, linking them to *about.html* as you go along. But that cranky boss of yours insists that you change the name of the page to *aboutus.html*. If you were to rename the file using Windows Explorer or the Macintosh Finder, every link to *about.html* would result in a "File not found" error!

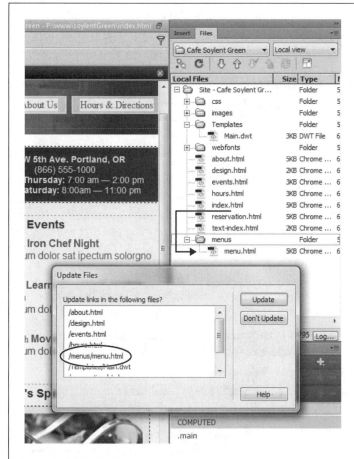

FIGURE 1-19

You can move files and folders within the Files panel just as you would in Windows Explorer or the Macintosh Finder. Simply drag the file into (or out of) a folder. Here you're moving the menu.html file from the root folder to the Menus folder. Unlike your computer's file system, Dreamweaver monitors the links between web pages, graphics, and other files. If you move a file using Windows Explorer or the Finder, you'll most likely end up breaking those links. By contrast, Dreamweaver is smart enough to know when moving files will cause problems. It displays an Update Files dialog box you can use to trigger Dreamweaver to update the links to and from the moved files so your site keeps working properly.

Dreamweaver handles this potential disaster effortlessly, as long as you rename the file in the Files panel. To do so, click the file or folder name in the panel, pause a moment, and then click it again. (The pause ensures that Dreamweaver won't think you just double-clicked the name to open the file.) Dreamweaver highlights the name, ready for you to type in a new name. Be sure to include the proper extension. For example, image GIFs end with .gif and Cascading Style Sheets end with .css. Although Dreamweaver lets you name files without using an extension, extension-less files won't work when you move them to a web server, and Dreamweaver may not open the file correctly without an extension.

Finally, in the Update Files dialog box, click Update. Dreamweaver updates all the links to the newly named file or folder.

NOTE It bears repeating: Never rename or move files or folders *outside* of Dreamweaver. If you use Windows Explorer or the Macintosh Finder to reorganize your site's files, links will break, images will disappear, and the earth will open underneath your feet. (Well, that last thing won't happen, but it can *feel* that way when your boss comes in and says, "What happened to our website? Nothing works!")

If you move files outside of Dreamweaver by accident and break links, see page 781 to learn how to fix them.

Deleting Files and Folders

It's a good idea to clean up your site from time to time by deleting old and unused files. Just as with moving and renaming files, you delete them from the Files panel.

To delete a file or folder, select it in the Files panel and then press Backspace or Delete. (To select multiple files or folders, Ctrl-click [⌘-click] them.) If no other page references the doomed file or folder, a simple "Are you sure you want to delete this file?" warning appears; click Yes.

If other files link to the file or to files within the folder you want to delete, Dream-weaver displays a warning message (Figure 1-20) informing you that you're about to break links on one or more pages.

The message even lists the first few pages that use the file.

If you're sure you want to delete the file or folder, click Yes. If you made a mistake, click No to leave your site untouched.

Clicking Yes breaks the links in all the pages. Repairing those links, which usually means linking to a new web address, requires a separate command: Site→Change Links Sitewide (see page 783).

FIGURE 1-20

When you delete files in the Files panel, Dreamweaver tells you if other site pages link to that file. If they do, you need to repair the links. Dreamweaver makes that easy via the Change Links Sitewide command (see page 783)—and it reminds you of the feature in this dialog box.

NOTE   If you move files to your site folder using Windows Explorer or the Mac Finder, Dreamweaver might not be aware of those files or links between those files and others in your site. If that's the case, when you move or delete files, Dreamweaver may not correctly update links or warn you of broken links caused by deleting a necessary file. To make Dreamweaver aware of any new files you add, choose Site→Advanced→Recreate Site Cache. Dreamweaver scans the files in the local site folder and updates the cache (its database of files and links on the site).

■ Tutorial: The Dreamweaver Test Drive

Although reading a book is a good way to learn the ins and outs of a program, nothing beats sitting in front of a computer and putting that program through its paces. Many of this book's chapters include hands-on training: step-by-step tutorials that show you how to create a real, working, professionally designed website for a fictional restaurant, Cafe Soylent Green.

The rest of this chapter introduces Dreamweaver by taking you step by step through the process of building a web page. It shouldn't take more than an hour. When it's over, you'll have learned the basics of building any web page: creating and saving a new document, adding and formatting text, inserting graphics, adding links, and using the program's site-management features.

If you already use Dreamweaver and want to jump right into the details of the program, feel free to skip this tutorial. (And if you're the type who likes to read first and try second, read Chapters 2 through 5 and then return here to practice what you learned.)

NOTE   The tutorial in this chapter requires the example files from this book's website at *http://oreilly. com/missingmanuals/cds/dreamweaverccmm13/*. Click the Download Tutorials link to save the files to your local drive. The tutorial files are in ZIP format, a technology that compresses a lot of files into one, smaller archive file. Windows folks should download the ZIP file and then double-click it to open the archive. Click Extract All Files and then follow the instructions to store the files on your computer. Mac users can just double-click the file to decompress it. After you download and decompress the files, you should have an MM_DWCC folder on your computer, containing all the tutorial files for this book.

Once you download the tutorial files and open Dreamweaver, set up a new site as described on page 23. In a nutshell, choose Site→New Site. In the Site Setup window, type *Test Drive* in the Site Name box. Click ▦ next to the Local Site Folder box, navigate to and select the Chapter01 folder inside the MM_DWCC folder, and then click Choose (Select). Finally, click OK.

FREQUENTLY ASKED QUESTION

Beware "Site-Less" Web Design

Why doesn't Dreamweaver update links when I move a file or warn me when I delete a file that other pages link to?

Dreamweaver's site-management tools always have your back—unless you're not working within a site. That can happen if you make the wrong choice in the Files panel.

The Files panel lets you browse all the files on your local drive, just like Windows Explorer or the Mac Finder does. If you click the Sites menu in the Files panel (where you'd normally switch between sites) and scroll to the top of the list, you'll see a list of all the hard drives and other storage devices on your home or office network.

Sometimes people accidentally select their hard drive (C: or Macintosh HD, for example) instead of the site they want to work on, and *then* they navigate to the folder holding their site's files. They begin working, blissfully unaware that they're doing so without Dreamweaver's safety net. When you work on your files this way, Dreamweaver doesn't monitor the changes you make to your files—like moving, deleting, or renaming them. In other words, Dreamweaver normally rewrites page links when you move a file that other pages link to, and it warns you when you delete a file that other pages use. But when you're working in "site-less" mode, with your hard drive selected in the Sites menu, Dreamweaver can't help you. Similarly, all of Dreamweaver's other site-management features, like libraries (Chapter 21), templates (Chapter 22), and file transfers (Chapter 20), don't work when you're off in Unmonitored-Site Land. In other words, it's best to always set up a local site, and always make sure you select the site's name in the Files panel to work on that site.

Phase 1: Getting Dreamweaver in Shape

Before you start working in Dreamweaver, make sure the program is set up to work for you. In the following steps, you'll double-check some key Dreamweaver settings and organize your workspace using Dreamweaver's Workspace Layout feature.

First, make sure your preferences are all set:

1. **If it isn't already open, start Dreamweaver.**

   Hey, you've got to start with the basics, right?

2. **Choose Edit→Preferences (Windows) or Dreamweaver→Preferences (Macs).**

   The Preferences dialog box opens, listing a dizzying array of categories and options (see Figure 1-21).

3. **Select the Invisible Elements category and then turn on the fourth checkbox from the top, Line Breaks (circled in Figure 1-21).**

   Sometimes, when you paste text from other programs, like Microsoft Word or an email program, Dreamweaver displays what were once separate paragraphs as one long, single paragraph broken up with invisible characters called *line breaks* (for you HTML-savvy readers, that's the <br> tag). Normally, you can't see the line break character in Dreamweaver's Design view. This setting makes sure you can—it uses a little shield to represent breaks in the document. The shield gives you an easy way to select a line break and remove it to create a single paragraph by combing the text before and after the line break, or to create two paragraphs from one long one.

FIGURE 1-21

Dreamweaver's Preferences dialog box is a smorgasbord of choices that let you customize the program to look and work the way you want. This panel lets you choose whether to keep Dreamweaver's invisible elements hidden or exposed. For example, if you turn on the checkbox next to "Line breaks" (circled), you can easily see where the breaks fall as you work on a page.

4. **Click Apply, and then click Close.**

   The Preferences dialog box closes. You're ready to get your workspace in order. As noted at the beginning of this chapter, Dreamweaver offers many windows to help you build web pages. For this tutorial, though, you need only four: the Insert panel, the document window, the Properties panel, and CSS Designer. But for good measure (and to give you a bit of practice), you'll open another panel and rearrange the workspace a little. To get started, have Dreamweaver display the Design workspace.

5. **From the Workspace Switcher on the Application bar, select Design (see Figure 1-22), or go to Window→Workspace Layout from the main menu and select Design from the drop-down list.**

If you see Design already selected, choose "Reset 'Design,'" which moves any panels you resized, closed, or repositioned back to their original locations. The Design workspace puts the Properties panel below the document window and groups several panels together on the right side of the window. You choose one or the other of these panels by clicking the appropriate tab. The panels are CSS Designer, Files, Assets, Insert, and Snippets.

In the next step, you'll turn the handy Insert panel into a toolbar, so you have easy access to its commands.

FIGURE 1-22

The Dreamweaver Welcome screen lists recently opened files in the left-hand column. Clicking a filename opens that file for editing. The middle column provides a quick way to create a new web page or define a new site. In addition, you can go to introductory videos and other getting-started material from the screen's right-hand column. Dreamweaver displays the Welcome screen when you have no documents open in the document window.

6. **Grab the Insert tab and then drag the Insert panel to just below the Application bar. When you see a blue line as shown in Figure 1-23, release the mouse button.**

When you drag the Insert panel away from the panel group, it looks like a floating palette, and that's what it would be if you let go of the mouse button. When it's near workspace edges where it can dock, you see a blue line. When you let go of the mouse to dock the panel, Dreamweaver transforms it into a toolbar with no text labels, just icons. Tabs across the top let you choose from different Insert sets like Common, Media, and Favorites. If you don't know what a button does, point to it and Dreamweaver displays a descriptive tooltip. That won't work now because the buttons are disabled since you don't have a document open.

Now the workspace looks great. It displays most of the tools you need for this tutorial (and for much of your web page building). Since this arrangement is so useful, you'll want to save it as a custom layout (OK, maybe you don't, but play along).

FIGURE 1-23

Customize your workspace to match the way you want to work. A key to this is positioning Dreamweaver's windows and palettes where you need them. Here you're positioning the Insert panel under the Application bar. When you see a thick blue line, the panel is ready to dock in that new location. When you move the Insert panel to this position, it changes into a toolbar.

7. **From the Application bar's Workspace Switcher, choose New Workspace.**

   The Save Workspace window appears, waiting for you to name your new layout.

8. **Type *Missing Manual* (or any name you like), and then click OK.**

   You just created a new workspace layout. To see if it works, switch to another one of Dreamweaver's layouts, see how the screen changes, and then switch back to your new setup.

9. **From the Workspace Switcher, choose Code.**

   This moves the panels around a bit. The Files and Snippets panels move to the left side of the window, leaving a big empty area to the right, where you can open documents and write code—but not right now. This is just a demonstration/detour, so now you'll switch back.

10. **From the Workspace Switcher, choose Design.**

Voilà! Dreamweaver resets everything to the Design workspace used for much of this book. Just keep in mind that you can create multiple workspaces for different websites or different types of sites.

Phase 2: Creating a Website

As discussed on page 24, whenever you use Dreamweaver to create or edit a website, your first step should always be to show Dreamweaver the location of your *local site folder* (also called the local root folder)—the master folder for all your website's files. You do this by *setting up a site*, like so:

1. **Choose Site→New Site.**

The Site Setup window appears. You need to provide only two pieces of information to get started.

2. **Type *Test Drive* in the Site Name box.**

The name you type here is for your own reference; it lets you identify the site in Dreamweaver's Site menu. Dreamweaver also asks where you want to store the website's files. In this example, you'll use one of the folders you downloaded from this book's website (at other times, you'll choose or create a folder of your own).

3. **Click 📁 next to the label "Local site folder."**

The Choose Root Folder window opens so you can navigate to a folder on your hard drive to serve as your local folder. (This is where you'll store the HTML documents and graphics, CSS, and other web files that make up your site.)

4. **Browse to and select the Chapter01 folder located inside the MM_DWCC folder you downloaded earlier. Click Select Folder (Choose) to set this folder as the local root folder.**

At this point, you've given Dreamweaver all the information it needs to successfully work with the tutorial files.

NOTE You'll find finished versions of all the tutorials in this book in the MM_DWCC folder; the completed files have "_complete" appended to the chapter name. The finished version of *this* tutorial is in the Chapter01_complete folder.

---

5. **Choose Advanced Settings and then click 📁 next to the "Default Images folder" box. Click the folder named *images*, and then click Select Folder (Choose).**

When you first create a website, you should identify the folder where you will store images. There are several subcategories under Advanced Settings. The first is Local, which Dreamweaver displays when you first click Advanced Settings.

6. **Click Save to close the Site Setup window.**

After you set up a site, Dreamweaver creates a *site cache* for it (see page 27). Since there are hardly any files in the Chapter01 folder, you may not even notice this happening—it goes by in the blink of an eye.

Phase 3: Creating and Saving a Web Page

"Enough already! I want to build a web page," you're probably saying. You'll do just that now:

1. **Choose File→New.**

   The New Document window opens. Creating a blank web page involves a few clicks.

2. **From the left-hand list of document categories, select Blank Page; in the Page Type list, highlight HTML; and from the Layout list, choose <none>. From the DocType menu in the bottom right, select HTML5.**

   As discussed on page xxi, HTML comes in a variety of flavors, called doctypes. HTML5 is the latest and greatest version, so use it.

3. **Click Create.**

   Dreamweaver opens a new, blank HTML page. Even though the underlying code for an HTML page differs in slight ways depending on which document type you chose (HTML 4.01 Transitional, XHTML 1.0 Strict, HTML5, and so on), you have nothing to worry about: When you add HTML in Design view, Dreamweaver writes the correct code for your doctype.

   If you see a bunch of strange text in the document window, you're looking at the underlying HTML, and you're in either Code or Split view. If your monitor is wide enough to view both the Code and Design views side by side, select the Split button at the top of the document window; if your monitor is on the small side, choose Design from the Design/Live menu (the button with the triangle opens this menu). If you don't see the Code, Split, Design, or Live buttons, choose View→Toolbars→Document. You'll work mainly in the visual Design view for this tutorial.

4. **Choose File→Save.**

   The Save As dialog box opens.

   Always save a newly created page right away. This good habit prevents serious headaches if the power goes out as you finish that beautiful—but unsaved— creation.

5. **Save the page in the Chapter01 folder as *index.html*.**

   You could also save the page as *index.htm*; both .html and .htm are valid extensions for HTML files. On most web servers, you'll name the home page *index. html* (see the box on page 751 for an explanation).

Make sure you save this page in the correct folder. In Phase 2 earlier, you told Dreamweaver to use Chapter01 as the site's root folder—the folder that holds all the pages and files for the site. If you save the page in a folder outside of Chapter01, Dreamweaver gets confused and its site-management features won't work correctly.

> **TIP** When you save a file, you can quickly jump to the current site's root folder. In the Save As dialog box, click the Site Root button—that takes you right to the root folder. This little trick also works when you link to or open a file.

6. **If the document window toolbar isn't already open, choose View→Toolbars →Document to display it.**

   The toolbar at the top of the document window provides easy access to a variety of tasks you'll do frequently, like previewing your page in a browser, and looking at the HTML.

7. **In the Properties panel, click the Page Properties button, or choose Modify→ Page Properties.**

   Dreamweaver opens the Page Properties dialog box (see Figure 1-24) where you can give your page a title and define the basic look of each page you create. Six categories of settings control page attributes like text color, background color, link colors, and page margins.

8. **Click Title/Encoding, and then, in the Title box, select the text "Untitled Document" and type _Welcome to Cafe Soylent Green_. Then click Apply.**

   The Title box holds the page's title—the information that appears in the title bar of a web browser. The title also shows up as the name of your page when someone searches the web. In addition, a clear and descriptive title that identifies the main point of a page can also help increase a page's rank among the major search engines.

   If you have Split view turned on, you'll notice that in Code view, Dreamweaver updated the <title> tag in the HTML to read "<title>Welcome to Cafe Soylent Green</title>."

9. **Click Appearance (CSS) in the Category list. From the "Page font" menu, select "Segoe, Segoe UI, DejaVu sans, Trebuchet MS, Verdana, sans-serif."**

   This sets a basic font (and backup fonts, in case your visitor's machine lacks Segoe) that Dreamweaver automatically uses for all the text on the page. But as you'll see later in this tutorial, you can always specify a different font for selected text.

   Next you'll set a basic text color for the page.

10. **Click the small gray box next to "Text color." From the palette that pops up, choose a color (a dark green color works well with this site).**

   Unless you intervene, all web page text starts out black; the text on this page reflects the color you select here. In the next step, you'll add an image as a background to liven up the page.

   NOTE Alternatively, you could type a color value, like *#333333*, into the color box. That's *hexadecimal* nota-tion, which is familiar to HTML coding gurus. Both the pop-up color palette and the hexadecimal color-specifying box appear fairly often in Dreamweaver. Dreamweaver even lets you specify a color using other values, such as RGB (red, green, blue) and HSL (hue, saturation, lightness) values. See page 151 for more on setting colors in Dreamweaver.

11. **To the right of "Background image," click the Browse button.**

   The Select Image Source window appears (see Figure 1-25) and it automatically displays the files in the Images folder. Dreamweaver knows this is where you store images, because you identified the folder when you created your site.

12. **Select the file *bg_page.png*, and then click OK (Open).**

   In Dreamweaver, you can select a file *and* close the selection window just by double-clicking the filename.

FIGURE 1-25

Use the Select Image Source window to insert graphics on a web page. The image for the background is in the Images folder, which is in your site's main, or root, folder. The Site Root button (circled) is a shortcut to that folder—a nifty way to quickly select it when you're searching for a file.

> **NOTE** Note for Windows users: Windows normally doesn't display a file's extension, so when you navigate to the Images folder in step 12, you might see *bg_page* instead of *bg_page.png*. Since file extensions are an important way people (and web servers) identify the types of files a website uses, you probably want Windows to display extensions. Here's how you do that: In Windows Explorer, navigate to and select the MM_DWCC folder. In the Windows 8 ribbon, choose View and then, in the Show/Hide group, turn on "File name extensions." If you use Windows 7 or Vista, choose Organize→"Folder and search options." If you use Windows XP, choose Tools→Folder Options. In the Folder Options window, select the View tab, and then turn off the "Hide extensions for known file types" checkbox. To apply this setting to the tutorial files, click OK; to apply it to all the files on your computer, click the "Apply to Folders" button, and then click OK.

13. **In the Left margin box, type *0*; in the Top margin box, type *20*.**

    The 0 setting for the left margin removes the little bit of space web browsers insert between the contents of your web page and the left side of the browser window. The 20 adds 20 pixels between the top of the browser window and the page contents.

If you like, you can change this setting to make the browser add more space to the top and left side of the page, or set both values to 0 to remove any space between the page's content and the browser window edges. In fact, you can even add a little extra empty space on the *right* side of a page. (The right margin control is especially useful for languages that read from right to left, like Hebrew or Arabic.)

14. **Back in the Category menu (far left of the Page Properties window), click Links (CSS).**

    Add the following properties: In the "Link color" box, type *#336633*; in the "Visited links" box, type *#999999*; in the "Rollover links" box, type *#CC9900*; and in the "Active links" box, type *#FF0000* (see Figure 1-26).

    These hexadecimal codes specify the colors for links on your web page (see page 151 for more on choosing colors in Dreamweaver).

FIGURE 1-26

You can set several hyperlink properties using the Links (CSS) category of the Page Properties dialog box. For example, you can choose a different font and size for the links, as well as specify colors for the four link states (unvisited, hovered over, clicked, and visited). Finally, you can choose whether (or when) a browser underlines links. Most browsers automatically do, but you can override that behavior with the help of this dialog box.

Links come in four varieties: regular, visited, active, and rollover. A *regular* link is a plain old link, unvisited, untouched. A *visited* link is one you've already clicked, as noted in your browser's History list. An *active* link is one you're currently clicking, so you see its color for the split second that you're pressing the mouse button. And finally, a *rollover* link changes color as you point to it without clicking. You can choose different colors for each of these states.

While it may seem like overkill to have four link colors, the regular and visited links provide useful feedback to visitors by telling them which links they already followed and which remain to be checked out. For its part, the rollover link gives you instant feedback, changing color as soon as you move your cursor over it.

The active link color isn't that useful for navigating a site since its color changes so briefly you probably won't even notice it.

NOTE Although Dreamweaver uses the term *rollover* link, in the world of Cascading Style Sheets, this is called a *hover* link.

15. **Click OK to close the window and apply your changes.**

    If you look at the top of the document window, you'll see an asterisk next to the filename—that's Dreamweaver's way of telling you that you haven't saved a page you edited, a nice reminder to save your files frequently to prevent heartache if the program suddenly shuts down (see circled image in Figure 1-27).

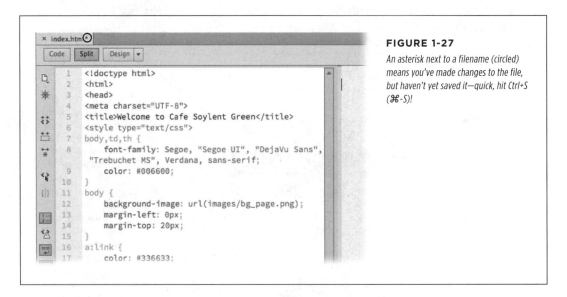

FIGURE 1-27

An asterisk next to a filename (circled) means you've made changes to the file, but haven't yet saved it—quick, hit Ctrl+S (⌘-S)!

If you've been working in Split view, you'll notice that Dreamweaver added the HTML <style> tag along with some other code—this is called a CSS style sheet, and the code dictates how a browser displays your pages (you'll learn all about this in Chapter 3).

16. **Choose File→Save (or press Ctrl+S [⌘-S]).**

    Save your work frequently. (This isn't a web technique so much as a computer-always-crashes-when-you-least-expect-it technique.)

Phase 4: Adding Images and Text

Now you'll add the real meat of your web page, words and pictures. Before you get started, make sure you have the Workspace Switcher (upper-right corner) set to Design. Also, above the document window, choose Design from the Design/Live menu.

1. **In the panels to the right of the document window, click the Insert tab. Then, in the drop-down menu at the top (Figure 1-28), choose Common. Click the triangle next to Image and then choose Image from the submenu.**

   Dreamweaver opens the Select Image Source window, showing the contents of your Images folder.

2. **Double-click the *logo.png* graphics file.**

   The Cafe Soylent Green logo appears in the upper-left corner of your web page. After you insert an image, it remains selected, as shown in Figure 1-29. Its properties appear in the Properties panel below the document window. If you click elsewhere on the page, that deselects the image and you no longer see its properties.

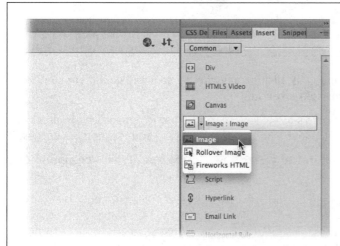

FIGURE 1-28

Dreamweaver splits the Insert commands into several categories. Use the drop-down menu at the top of the panel to select one, like the Common category shown here. Some commands, like Image, have a submenu; click the triangle button to open it. These clever menus remember the last selection you made, so if you make the same choice several times in a row, all you have to do is click the main button, without having to go into the submenu.

3. **In the Properties panel's Alt text box (circled in Figure 1-29), type *Cafe Soylent Green*.**

   "Alt" stands for Alternative, but the text you type here is really all about accessibility. It makes your pages more accessible to people who visit websites using alternative devices—for example, people with viewing disabilities who require screen readers to read the contents of a web page out loud. That's where the *alt* property comes in. This text description is useful not only for screen-reading software, but for people who deliberately *turn off* pictures in their web browser so pages load faster. (Search engines also look at *alt* properties when they index a page, so an accurate description can help your site's search-engine rankings.)

FIGURE 1-29

When you select an image in the document window, the Properties panel reveals the image's dimensions. A thumbnail of the image appears in the top left of the panel, as does the word "Image" (to identify the type of element you selected), along with the image's file size (in this case, 16 KB). You'll learn about other image properties in Chapter 5.

4. **Deselect the image by clicking anywhere else in the document window or by pressing the right arrow key.**

   Keep your keyboard's arrow keys in mind—they're a great way to deselect a page element *and* move your cursor into place to add text or more images.

5. **Press Enter (Return) to create a new paragraph. Type *Welcome to Cafe Soylent Green.***

   Make sure you're in Design view here—pressing Enter (Return) in Code view simply inserts a carriage return and no paragraph tags. Notice that the text is a dark color and uses the Segoe (or, if you don't have Segoe installed, a substitute sans-serif) font; you set these options earlier, in the Page Properties dialog box. The Properties panel now displays text-formatting options.

NOTE The key called Enter on Windows keyboards is named Return on most Macintosh keyboards (and Enter on others). So on Macs, you press either Return or Enter.

---

6. **In the Properties panel, click the HTML button and then, from the Format menu, choose Heading 1 (see Figure 1-30).**

   The text you just typed becomes big and bold—the default style for Heading 1. Right now, the text doesn't stand out enough, so you'll change its color.

7. **Select the text you just typed.**

   Do so by either dragging carefully across the entire line or by triple-clicking anywhere inside the line. (Unlike the Format menu, which affects an entire *paragraph* at a time, many options in the Properties panel—like the one you'll use next—apply only to text you *select.*)

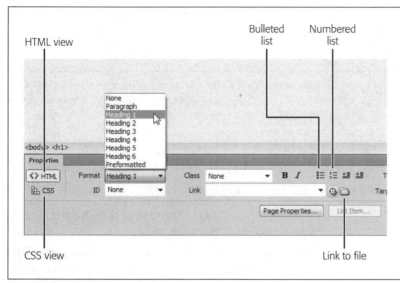

HTML view

Bulleted list

Numbered list

CSS view

Link to file

FIGURE 1-30

The Properties panel includes two views: HTML and CSS. The HTML view, shown here, lets you control the HTML tags Dreamweaver uses to create standard text elements like bulleted lists, paragraphs, and links. The CSS view provides a simple way to create fancy CSS styles that format your text to look great.

8. **In the Properties panel, click the CSS button so you can style the text. Look for New Rule under the Targeted rule drop-down menu, and then choose <New Inline Style> from the submenu. In the Color box to the right, replace the current value with #CC9900 (or select a color using the color box). Click in the document window to deselect the text so you can see its new color.**

   Congratulations! You created a new CSS style in the middle of your content using what's known as an *inline style*. With your cursor somewhere inside this headline, the Properties panel's Targeted Rule box shows it as <inline style>.

9. **In the panels group on the right, click the tab for CSS Designer. Under that is a section called Selectors. Section headers like Selectors and Properties work like an accordion—when you click a headline, the section expands to display the contents inside. If necessary, click the Selectors bar to view the contents, where you'll see a few selectors, including "<inline style>: h1."**

   This is another way of explaining that the cursor is inside an h1 heading, but the heading isn't displaying the usual style because you added an inline style for it.

10. **To see the style Dreamweaver applies to a selector, look in the Properties section of CSS Designer (just below the Selectors section). Use the scroll bar to see all the properties.**

    The items Dreamweaver displays in the Properties section change depending on what you highlight in the Selectors section. For example, if you click "<inline style>:h1" in Selectors, you see all the properties you can use to format your <h1> headings. Grayed-out properties are undefined—you haven't assigned any values to them. At the top of the list you'll see text attributes including the *color* property, along with a swatch and the hex code that defines the hue. If you click Computed in the Selectors section, Dreamweaver displays the properties in use for the currently selected element. In this example, if you position your cursor in the heading and highlight Computed in the Selectors section, the Properties section displays the color and font family you chose earlier.

> **NOTE** It's easy to get confused between the Properties panel below the document window and the Properties *section* of CSS Designer, which lives in the panel group. The Properties section of CSS Designer displays the properties of CSS styles. Chapters 3 and 9 give you more details.

11. **With your cursor still in the document window, right-click (Control-click) any text. Choose CSS Styles→Convert Inline CSS to Rule.**

    The Convert Inline CSS dialog box opens.

12. **Set the "Convert to" menu to "All h1 tags," turn on the radio button labeled "The head of this document," and then click OK.**

    You've successfully redefined the <h1> style in your document. Now all <h1> tags will sport the new color. Dreamweaver writes the CSS definition in the "head" section of your document. Want to take a peek? Change your document view to Split or Code view, and then look for <h1> in the code window.

    You're not done yet. Next, you'll make more changes to <h1> using CSS Designer.

13. **In CSS Designer's Sources section, click <style>.**

    The <style> entry represents the internal style sheet in the <head> part of your web page. When you choose <style>, CSS Designer's Selectors section displays the selectors defined in the internal style sheet.

    In CSS Designer's Selectors section, you'll see "h1" listed, but it no longer displays <inline style> because you're no longer using an inline style. Dreamweaver formats the text using the new <h1> style. What's more, when you create new <h1> paragraphs, they'll look the same as this one.

14. **In the Selectors section of CSS Designer, click h1. In the Properties section, scroll down until you see the Text group and the *font-family* property within it. Click the grayed-out words "default font" and then choose "Baskerville, Palatino Linotype, Palatino, Century Schoolbook L, Times New Roman, serif" from the drop-down menu.**

    Once again, you're changing the definition of the <h1> heading (also called the <h1> tag). No extra steps are necessary when you change the definition in the CSS Designer panel. You can confirm the change by inspecting the code in the document window as you did in the previous step.

    Time to add more text.

15. **Back in Design view, click to the right of the heading, and then press Enter (Return) to create a new paragraph.**

    Although you may type a headline now and again, you'll probably get most of your text from word processing documents or emails from your clients, boss, or coworkers. To get that text into Dreamweaver, you simply copy it from the other document and paste it into your web page.

16. **Click the tab for the Files panel. In the Files panel, double-click the file *home-page.txt* to open it.**

    This file is just plain text—no formatting, just words. To get it into your document, you'll copy and paste it.

17. **Click anywhere inside the text, and then choose Edit→Select All, followed by Edit→Copy. Click the *index.html* tab to return to your web page and, finally, choose Edit→Paste.**

    You should see a few shields sprinkled among the text (circled in Figure 1-31). If you don't, make sure you completed step 3 in Phase 1. These shields represent line breaks—spots where text drops to the next line without creating a new paragraph. You'll often see these shields in pasted text. If you find them, you need to remove them and then create separate paragraphs.

18. **Click one of the shields and then press Enter (Return). Repeat this on all the other gold shields in the document window.**

    This deletes the line break in the document (it actually deletes the HTML tag <br>) and creates two paragraphs out of one.

    At this point, the pasted text is just a series of paragraphs. To give it some structure, you'll add headings and a bulleted list.

19. **Click in the paragraph that has the text "About the Cafe." In the Properties panel, click the HTML button, and then choose Heading 2 from the Format menu.**

    That changes the paragraph to a headline, making it bigger and bolder.

20. **Using the same technique as in step 19, assign the Heading 2 tag to the labels "Location," "Hours," and "Specialties."**

    You now have one Heading 1 and four Heading 2 headlines. The Heading 2 headlines could use a little style.

21. **Triple-click the headline "About the Cafe" to select it. In the Properties panel, click the CSS button. Make sure Targeted Rule is set to <New Inline Style>. Then, in the Size box, delete "none" and type *20.***

    Once again, you've created an inline style. This time it's within this <h2> heading ("About the Cafe"). Notice that it is the only <h2> heading affected by the size change to 20 pixels (px). Next you'll update all the <h2> headings to match.

Welcome to Cafe Soylent Green

Located in beautiful downtown Portland, Oregon, Cafe Soylent Green
accusantium doloremque laudantium, totam rem aperiam, eaque ipsa
sunt explicabo.

About the Cafe
Founded in 2012, Cafe Soylent Green Nemo enim ipsam voluptatem
magni dolores eos qui ratione voluptatem sequi nesciunt. Neque porro
adipisci velit. sed ut perspiciatis unde omnis iste natus error sit volupt
ipsa quae ab illo inventore veritatis et quasi architecto beatae vitae dic
voluptatem accusantium doloremque laudantium, totam rem aperian
vitae dicta sunt explicabo.

Location
700 SW 5th Ave. Portland, OR 97204 (click to see map)
(866) 555-1000

Hours
Monday-Friday: 7:00 am — 2:00 pm
Saturday-Sunday: 8:00am — 11:00 pm

Specialities
Plankton burger*
Tomato Bisque
Melon with vegan prosciutto
Daily Surprise

FIGURE 1-31

*Line breaks (circled) often crop up when you copy and
paste text from other programs into Dreamweaver. Follow the steps on page 38 to make sure you can see the
line breaks in Design view.*

22. **With your cursor in the "About the Cafe" heading, right-click (Control-
click) and then choose CSS Styles→Convert Inline CSS to Rule from the
drop-down menu.**

    The Convert Inline CSS dialog box appears.

23. **Using the "Convert to" menu, choose "All h2 tags." In the "Create rule in"
group, turn on the radio button labeled "The head of this document," and
then click OK.**

    Notice that all the <h2> headings now look the same. The text gets a little
    smaller—the style you just created applies to all <h2> tags, and they now share
    the same font size, 20 pixels.

    Next you'll change the text's color.

24. **In CSS Designer's Sources section, choose <style>. Then, in the Selectors section, choose "h2." Below that, in the Properties section, scroll down until you see the Text group and the *color* property. Replace the color currently there with *#339966*.**

    You changed the color to a lighter and brighter shade of green.

25. **Under *font-style*, choose Italic.**

    This italicizes the text and updates the <h2> style you created earlier—that's why the other Heading 2 headlines are now italicized, too.

26. **Select the four paragraphs under the headline Specialties; drag from the start of the first paragraph to the end of the fourth paragraph.**

    You can also drag up, starting from the end of the last paragraph.

27. **In the Properties panel, click the HTML button, and then click the Unordered (bulleted) List button (see Figure 1-30).**

    The paragraphs turn into a bulleted list of items, called an "unordered list" in HTML-speak. Finally, you'll highlight the cafe's location and hours.

28. **Select the two paragraphs below the Location headline (beginning with "700 SW 5th" and ending with the phone number).**

    You'll make the address bold.

29. **Make sure you have the HTML button pressed in the Properties panel, and then click the B button.**

    Dreamweaver boldfaces the text, but you won't see any change in CSS Designer. Even though you find the Bold options in two places—the HTML Properties panel and the CSS Font Weight setting (Font→Font Weight→Bold)—they do different things. When you select bold in HTML mode, Dreamweaver inserts the HTML <strong> tag—used to "strongly" emphasize text. But when you choose Font→Font Weight→Bold in CSS mode, Dreamweaver adds CSS code to the page to make the text look bold. It's a subtle but important difference—in HTML mode, you change the formatting of just the selected text, but in CSS mode, you'd create a style, and that style could change the formatting of all the text that shares the same tag (the paragraph tag [<p>] in this example). (You'll read more about this on page 116.) In this case, you want to use the HTML <strong> tag to emphasize the selected text.

30. **Repeat the previous step for the two paragraphs below the Hours headline, and then save the page.**

    You'll add a few more design touches to the page, but first you should see how the page looks in a real web browser.

FREQUENTLY ASKED QUESTION

The Mysterious Haunted Steering Wheel

When I select a paragraph, an image…heck, anything at all, in Design view, a weird icon appears. It looks like a ship's steering wheel. What is it and how do I get rid of it?

You click this steering-wheel icon to open the Code Navigator window. That window (described on page 418) lists the CSS styles related to whatever page element you select. It's useful for people who like to skip Dreamweaver's user-friendly CSS

Designer panel and create and edit CSS by hand. If you're new to CSS, this isn't a useful tool, and that goofy icon, which looks like something Ahab's ghost misplaced, gets in the way. To hide it, click the icon to open the Code Navigator and then turn on the "Disable indicator" checkbox in the bottom right. If you ever want to turn the Navigator back on, choose View→Code Navigator to open the Code Navigator window, and then turn off the Disable checkbox.

Phase 5: Preview Your Work

Dreamweaver's Design view gives you a visual way to add and edit HTML, but its page presentation is frequently a long way off from that of a real web browser. Dreamweaver may display *more* information than you'd see on the Web, for example, including "invisible" objects, like table borders and those line breaks you removed earlier, or it may display *less* information (it sometimes has trouble rendering complex designs).

Furthermore, much to the eternal woe of web designers, different browsers display pages differently. Pages you view in Internet Explorer don't always look the same in other browsers, like Safari, Firefox, or Chrome. In some cases, the differences may be subtle (text may be slightly larger or smaller, for instance). In other cases, the changes are dramatic: Earlier versions of Internet Explorer, for example, can't display the text or drop shadows discussed on page 438.

If you're designing web pages for a company intranet and only have to worry about the one web browser your IT department puts on everyone's computer, you're lucky. Most people have to deal with the fact that their sites must withstand scrutiny from a wide range of browsers, so it's a good idea to preview your pages using whatever browsers you expect your visitors to use. Fortunately, Dreamweaver lets you do that using any browser you have on your computer.

NOTE With the increasing popularity of tablets and mobile phones, you can no longer just worry about how your web pages look in desktop browsers; you also have to think about how they look on the small screens of an iPhone, Android phone, or Windows phone. Chapter 12 has information on how Dreamweaver CC can help you make your websites mobile-ready.

One quick way to check a page in a web browser is to use Dreamweaver's built-in Live view, which lets you preview a page using a browser that's built into Dreamweaver.

1. **In the Document toolbar, switch the Design/Live menu to Live (Figure 1-32).**

   The Design/Live menu displays "Live" in the document toolbar. The page doesn't look that different—for a simple page like this it won't, but Live view is great for previewing more complex CSS and for testing JavaScript page elements (see page 607).

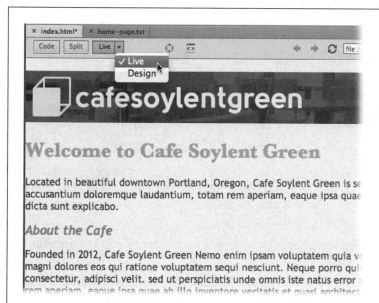

FIGURE 1-32

Dreamweaver's Live view lets you preview a page in a real web browser, one built into Dreamweaver.

There is one problem with Live view: It uses the page display engine that's behind Google's Chrome browser. Chrome isn't the only browser out there, of course, so you want to test your page designs in other browsers, too. Fortunately, Dreamweaver makes it easy to jump straight to any browser on your computer.

2. **Click the logo at the top of the page.**

   Dreamweaver displays a turquoise border around it. A blue tab at the top says "img." This is Live view's way of telling you that you selected a page element that has the <img> tag applied to it. In other words, you clicked an image. You can select page elements and make edits in Live view, which is different from editing in Design view, as you'll learn on page 348.

3. **Click some of the headings and paragraphs in your document.**

   The headings display "h1" or "h2" on their tabs, while the paragraphs display "p." If you click one of the cafe's specialties with the bullets, you see "li." In HTML code, that's the list item tag, <li>.

4. **In the document toolbar, switch the Design/Live menu back to Design.**

This is an important and easily overlooked step. When you're in Live view, you can't edit a page in the same manner as Design view. Since a page in Live view can look very much like it does in Design view, it's easy to try to work on the page while you're in Live view and say, "Hey, what's going on? Dreamweaver isn't working anymore!" When that happens, check the Design/Live menu to see which view you have selected.

To preview your page in a web browser, you need to make sure Dreamweaver knows which browsers you have installed and where they are.

5. **Choose File→Preview in Browser→Edit Browser List.**

The Dreamweaver Preferences window opens with the Preview in Browser category selected (see Figure 1-33). When you install Dreamweaver, it detects the browsers on your computer; a list of them appears in this window. If you installed a browser *after* you installed Dreamweaver, it doesn't appear here, and you need to follow steps 4 and 5 again; otherwise, skip to step 6.

6. **Click +.**

The Add Browser window opens. There are two boxes. In the Name box, type any name you want to describe one of the browsers installed on you computer. In the Application box, provide the path to the browser. The easy way to do that is by clicking the Browse button.

7. **Click the Browse button. Search your hard drive to find the browser you want to add to the list.**

Dreamweaver inserts the browser's out-of-the-box name in the Name box. To change it, select it, and then type a new name. (But don't do this *before* you select the browser, since Dreamweaver erases anything you typed as soon as you select a browser.)

8. **In the window's Browser list, select the browser you most commonly use. Turn on the Primary Browser checkbox, and then click OK.**

You just designated this browser as your *primary* one. You can now preview your pages in this browser with a simple keyboard shortcut: F12 (Option-F12 on Macs—unfortunately, Apple assigned the F12 key to the Mac's Dashboard program, so it takes two keys to preview a web page—Option and F12 together; you can change this by creating your own keyboard shortcut, as described on page 904). If you use a Macintosh laptop, you may have to press Option-F12 *and* the function [fn] key in the lower-left corner of the keyboard.

If you like, you can choose a secondary browser, which you open by pressing Ctrl+F12 (⌘-F12).

Now you're ready to preview your document in your favorite browser.

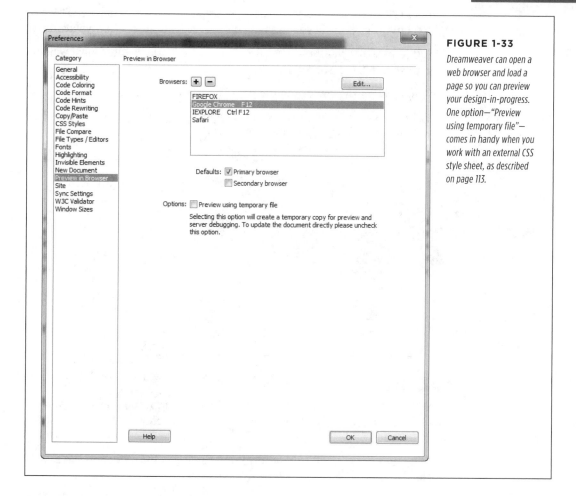

FIGURE 1-33

Dreamweaver can open a web browser and load a page so you can preview your design-in-progress. One option—"Preview using temporary file"— comes in handy when you work with an external CSS style sheet, as described on page 113.

NOTE Some Windows PCs don't list Google Chrome in the Program Files directory, as they do for most other programs. Depending on your version of Windows, you'll find Chrome in one of these locations:

- Windows 8: *C:\Program Files (x86)\Google\Chrome\Application*

- Windows 7: *C:\Users\[Username]\AppData\Local\Google*

- Vista: *C:\Users\[Username]\AppDataLocal\Google\Chrome*

- XP: *C:\Documents and Settings\[Username]\Local Settings\Application Data\Google\Chrome*

9. **Press F12 (Option-F12) or choose File→Preview in Browser and then, from the menu, select a browser.**

   The F12 key (Option-F12) is the most important keyboard shortcut you'll learn; it opens a web page in your primary browser so you can preview your work.

   You can also use the "Preview in Browser" menu, ⚙., in the document window to preview a page (see Figure 1-34).

10. **When you finish previewing the page, go back to Dreamweaver.**

    Do so using your favorite way to switch programs on your computer—the taskbar in Windows or the Dock in Mac OS X.

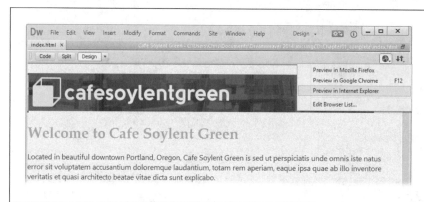

FIGURE 1-34

The document window's "Preview in Browser" option is another way to preview a page. Its menu lets you select from any browser installed on your computer, not just the ones to which you assigned keyboard shortcuts.

Phase 6: Finishing the Page

You've covered most of the steps you need to finish this web page. Now you just need to add a graphic, format the copyright notice, and provide a little more structure to the page.

1. **In Design view, scroll to the bottom of the page and select all the text in the copyright notice.**

   You can either triple-click inside the paragraph or drag from beginning to end.

2. **Click the CSS button in the Properties panel and make sure the Targeted Rule menu displays <New Inline Style>. Then, from the Size menu, choose "12."**

   You've created a new CSS style within a paragraph <p> tag. You can see the result in the CSS Designer's Selectors section. This time you want to create a reusable style that applies only to specific paragraphs of text—not every paragraph. So you need to use what's called a *class style*.

3. **With your cursor still in the copyright text, right-click (Control-click) and then choose CSS Styles→Convert Inline CSS to Rule.**

   The Convert Inline CSS dialog box makes its appearance.

4. **Leave the "Convert to" menu set to "A new CSS class." In the text box to the right, type the word *copyright*. Click the "The head of this document" button and then click OK.**

While you won't see a change in the document's design, you've successfully created a new CSS class that you can apply to any paragraph you want. Notice in the Properties panel's CSS view that the Targeted rule now displays *.copyright*. Don't overlook the period (.) that precedes the word, as that's how browsers identify the CSS style as a class. Look in CSS Designer's Selectors section (Figure 1-35) and you see *.copyright* listed there, too. Scroll through the Properties for the *.copyright* selector, and you see that it has the *font-size* property set to 12 px (pixels).

Another way to separate the copyright notice from the page's main content is to add a simple line above it. CSS lets you do that in CSS Designer with a property called Border.

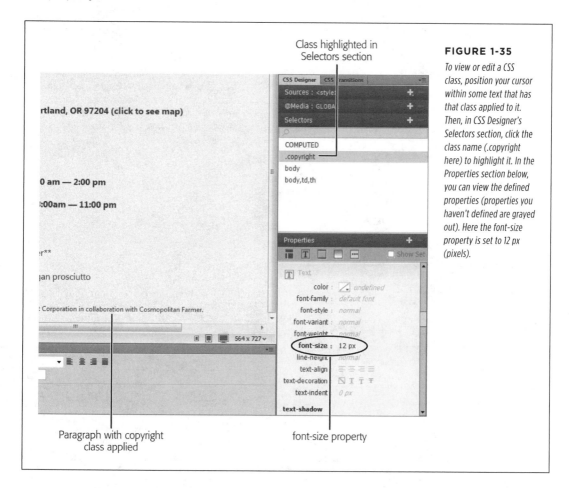

Class highlighted in
Selectors section

Paragraph with copyright
class applied

font-size property

FIGURE 1-35

To view or edit a CSS class, position your cursor within some text that has that class applied to it. Then, in CSS Designer's Selectors section, click the class name (.copyright here) to highlight it. In the Properties section below, you can view the defined properties (properties you haven't defined are grayed out). Here the font-size property is set to 12 px (pixels).

5. **In CSS Designer's Sources section, click <style>.**

   Dreamweaver displays all the CSS selectors defined in the document's head in the Selectors section.

6. **In Selectors, click the *.copyright* class.**

   You may need to scroll through the list to find it.

7. **In the Properties section of the CSS Designer, click ▢ to scroll down to the Border group (Figure 1-36). Under the word "border," click the second tab from the left ("top border"). Then, next to "style," click the grayed-out word "none" and choose "solid" from the drop-down menu.**

   The CSS Designer panel is the command center for working with style sheets (see Figure 1-36). It lists all the styles available to the current web page and lets you edit them. You can even use CSS Designer to add new styles, as you'll learn on page 116.

CSS Designer

Sources section

Selectors section

Properties section

Border button

Top border tab

FIGURE 1-36

You'll often work in the CSS Designer panel from the top down, selecting from the sections Sources, Selectors, and Properties. Here you've selected <style> in the Sources section, the .copyright class in the Selectors section, and the three top border attributes (width, style, and color) in the Properties section.

NOTE It takes three properties to define a border: *border-style*, *border-width*, and *border-color*. To add to this smorgasbord, you can place your border left, right, top, bottom, or on all sides of the selected text (see page 250).

8. **Set *width* to *1px* and *border-top-color* to *#CC9900*.**

    With all three properties defined (*border-top-style*, *border-top-width*, and *border-top-color*), your copyright notice has a handsome line separating it from the rest of the page. Borderlines touch the content of the element they surround—in other words, this top line sits very close to the copyright text. It'll look better if there's a bit of space between it and the copyright notice.

9. **In the CSS Designer's Properties section, click the Layout icon, ⊞, to scroll to Layout properties (Figure 1-37). Then find the Padding properties.**

    Padding is the space that appears between an element's content (like the text in the copyright notice, or an image) and its border. In the Padding properties section, Dreamweaver uses a rectangle to represent content. As you make changes to the properties, you see the results in the document window.

Layout button

Padding properties

padding-top property

Click to change
all properties

FIGURE 1-37

Click the Layout button in CSS Designer's Properties section to see padding and margin properties. Here the padding-top property is set to 5 px. If you want to set the padding for all four sides at once, then click the link icon in the center.

10. **Click the 0 at the top of the Padding box and then type *5px*, as shown in Figure 1-37.**

    Initially, the border setting is grayed out because you haven't defined the property. After you enter a number, you see the Padding setting reflected in the document window—there's more distance between the copyright text and the border. Next you'll link to a map that shows the location of the cafe.

11. **In the middle of the page, select the parenthetical text "click to see map."**

    To create a link, you need to tell Dreamweaver which page you want to link to. You can do this several ways, but using the Properties panel is the easiest.

12. **In the Properties panel, click the HTML button, and then click 🖿 to the right of the Link box.**

The Select File dialog box appears.

13. **Click the Site Root button and double-click the file *map.html*.**

The Site Root button takes you right to the folder containing your site. It's a quick way to select the root folder if you aren't already there, or if you want to be certain you are. Double-clicking the filename tells Dreamweaver to insert the HTML needed to create a link to the file, along with the link's address.

If you save the page and then preview it in a web browser, click the link you just added. The browser jumps to another page (one already created for you). You'll notice that there's text near the bottom of the map that reads "back to home page." Since you just learned the powerful link-adding skill, open *map. html* and add a link to that page. Select the text "back to home page" and link to the *index.html* file by following steps 11 and 12, and then save the *map.html* file. We'll wait for you.

You may have noticed that the map page's content is contained in a box that's nicely centered in the middle of the screen. That would look great on your home page. To make that happen, first create a new selector in the Selectors section of CSS Designer. Then, in the Properties section, specify the properties you want for the border and the way you want to position the page elements. Finally, apply your new selector to the page elements you want to style. You'll do all that next.

14. **In the document window, click the Index tab. In CSS Designer's Sources section, click <style>.**

The <style> source means that Dreamweaver stores selectors and their styles inline, that is, in the code for your page. In this case, <style> also stores the formatting for the headings and the *.copyright* class of the page you're working on.

15. **In the gray bar at the top of Designer's Selectors section, click + .**

A new selector appears. Dreamweaver prompts you with a name in the text box, but you're going to change it.

16. **Type *.container* in the box and then press Enter (Return).**

Make sure you begin the new name with a period (.), because that's the way you identify a class.

17. **With new *.container* class still selected, go to the Properties section of CSS Designer and click 🔲. Then choose the first border tab ("All sides"), and set the *width* property to *1px*, *style* to *solid*, and *color* to *#336633*.**

These are the same three properties you used for the border of the *.copyright* class. The difference this time is that the border will be on all four sides of the element.

18. **At the top of CSS Designer's Properties section, click the Layout button, ▥.**

    Dreamweaver scrolls to the layout properties. At the top of the list, you see "width" with the word "auto" grayed out next to it. When you see a property grayed out, you haven't set a value for it.

19. **Click "auto" next to "width," choose "px" from the list, and then type *760* in the number box.**

    The abbreviation "px" stands for pixels, a standard unit of measure for computer screens. CSS Designer often gives you several choices for units of measure. Pixels (px) is the one you'll use most frequently.

20. **Below the Width property, find the Margin box, which is a silhouette that represents a page element. In the number box for the left margin setting, click the grayed-out "px" and then choose "auto" from the list. Do the same for the right margin setting.**

    As you'll see in a moment, setting left and right margins to "auto" centers elements on the page.

21. **Scroll down to the Padding box, another element silhouette. Click the link in the middle of the box, and then type *10px* in any number box around the edge.**

    The link is a timesaver—it lets you set the padding for all sides of an element by typing in just one number. The 10 pixels you specified here puts distance between the border and the contents inside the border. When you're done, the Layout properties should look like those in Figure 1-38.

FIGURE 1-38

CSS Designer's layout properties include width, weight, margins, padding, and position. The .container class uses width, padding, and margin properties from the layout category. The class also makes use of border properties, but they're not shown here.

22. **Return to the *index.html* file; click anywhere inside the page, and then choose Edit→Select All or press Ctrl+A (⌘-A).**

    You selected all the contents on the page. You'll wrap all the text and images in a <div> tag to create a kind of container for the page contents.

23. **Choose Insert→Div.**

    The Insert Div window opens (see Figure 1-39). A <div> tag simply provides a way to organize content on a page by grouping HTML—think of it as a box containing other HTML tags and web page content. For example, to create a sidebar that includes navigation links, news headlines, and Google ads, you'd wrap them all in a <div> tag. It's a very important tag for CSS-based layouts. You'll read more about it on page 454.

FIGURE 1-39

The Insert Div window gives you an easy way to divide sections of a web page into groups of related HTML—like the elements that make up a page banner, for example (logo, navigation bar, and so on). You'll learn all the functions of this window on page 456.

24. **In the Insert Div window, leave the Insert menu set to "Wrap around selection." Then, in the Class menu, choose *container* and click OK.**

    Dreamweaver wraps the contents of your page inside a <div> that has the *.container* class applied to it. As a result, you can see the effects of the settings for the Border, Width, Margin, and Padding properties.

25. **Choose File→Save All, and then press F12 (Option-F12) to preview your work in your browser (Figure 1-40).**

    The Save All command saves the changes you made to both *index.html* and *map.html*. Test the link to make sure it works. Resize your browser and watch how the content centers itself in the middle of the window.

TIP To get a full description of every Dreamweaver menu, see Appendix B, "Dreamweaver CC 2014, Menu by Menu."

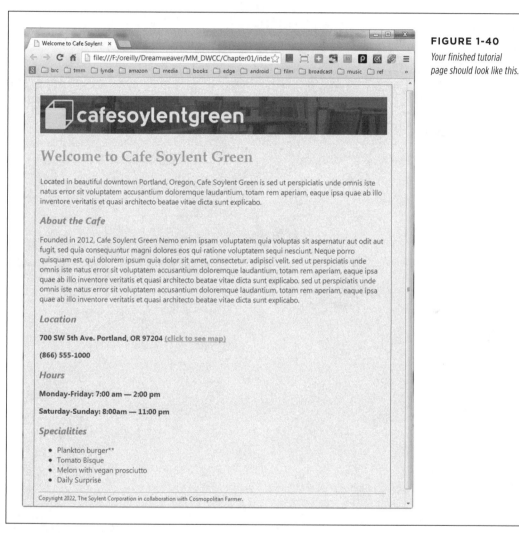

FIGURE 1-40

Your finished tutorial page should look like this.

Working with Text

The basic building block for most websites is, was, and always will be text. Oh, sure, you can stream feature films and TV shows from Netflix, but it's text, in the form of paragraphs, headings, and captions, that helps you find the film you want. Want to stream some music from Pandora or iTunes Radio? Same story. Text describes the songs, albums, and artists. You may love video, audio, and quality graphics, but you rely on the written word when you surf the Web.

As you build web pages and sites, you'll spend a lot of time adding and formatting text. To get your message across effectively, you need to understand how Dreamweaver works with it. That's what this chapter is all about—it covers the not-always-simple act of getting text *into* your Dreamweaver documents. First you'll learn how to add text to pages in *Design view*—the standard "view" you'll use to build new pages. You'll learn how to apply HTML tags that mark chunks of text as paragraphs, headings, sidebars, and so on.

Near the end of the chapter, you'll see how to add text to pages using Dreamweaver's revamped *Live view*. In the past, you could only preview pages in Live view, you couldn't edit them. But with the current version of Dreamweaver, you can now edit there, too.

In Chapter 3, you'll learn how to format the text you add here so that it looks professionally designed.

■ Adding Text to Pages in Design View

In Design view, Dreamweaver works much like a word-processing program. When you create a new document, a blinking cursor appears at the top of the blank page, ready for you to begin typing. When you finish typing a paragraph, you press Enter (Return) to start a new one. Text, as well as anything else you add to a web page, starts at the top of the page and works its way to the bottom.

If you build websites for clients or as part of a team, your writers likely send their text to you as a word-processing document. You can copy text from that document (or from another source, like an email message) and paste it into Dreamweaver's Design view in a couple of ways.

TIP If the text you want to paste comes from a Microsoft Word or Excel file, you're lucky. Dreamweaver includes special commands for pasting text from these two programs (see page 71). If you use Windows, you can *import* Word and Excel files directly into a web page. For example, to import a Word document, choose File→Import→Word Document (see page 75).

Simple Copy and Paste

For non-Microsoft-spawned documents, you can, of course, simply copy and paste text, like generations of web designers before you.

Open the document in whatever program created it—WordPad, TextEdit, your email program, whatever. Select the text you want (by dragging through it, for example), or choose Edit→Select All (Ctrl+A [⌘-A]) to highlight all the text. Then choose Edit→Copy or press Ctrl+C (⌘-C) to copy it to your virtual Clipboard. Switch to Dreamweaver and, in Design view of the document window, click where you want the text to go, and then choose Edit→Paste (Ctrl+V [⌘-V]). This drops the text into place. Unfortunately, you lose any formatting the text had (font type, size, color, boldfacing, italics, and so on), as shown in Figure 2-1.

Furthermore, you may find the pasted paragraphs separated by line-break characters instead of true paragraph tags, <p>. In HTML, the line-break tag—
—adds a "soft" carriage return, simply dropping the text that follows onto the next line. That means that when you paste in a series of paragraphs, Dreamweaver treats them as though they were one gargantuan paragraph, which can pose problems when you try to format what you *think* is a single paragraph. To get true paragraphs, you first have to make the line breaks visible. Choose Edit→Preferences (Dreamweaver→Preferences) or press Ctrl+U (⌘-U). Click the Invisible Elements category and then make sure you have the Line Breaks checkbox turned on. Now you see each line break as a small gold shield. (If you still don't see the line-break character, choose View→Visual Aids, and make sure you have the Invisible Elements checkbox turned on.) Select the shield and then hit Enter (Return) to eliminate the break *and* create a true paragraph.

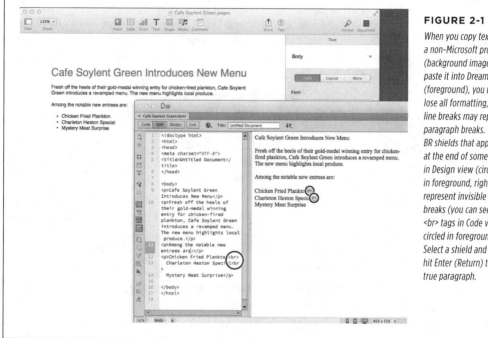

FIGURE 2-1

When you copy text from a non-Microsoft program (background image) and paste it into Dreamweaver (foreground), you usually lose all formatting, and line breaks may replace paragraph breaks. The BR shields that appear at the end of some lines in Design view (circled in foreground, right) represent invisible line breaks (you can see the <br> tags in Code view, circled in foreground, left). Select a shield and then hit Enter (Return) to get a true paragraph.

TIP If you *have* to copy and paste text from non-Microsoft programs, you do have one way to get true paragraphs (and not just lines separated by line breaks) when you paste text into Dreamweaver. Just make sure whoever's typing up the original document inserts an empty paragraph between each paragraph of text by pressing Enter (Return) twice at the end of the paragraphs. When you copy and paste, Dreamweaver removes the empty paragraphs *and* pastes the text as regular paragraphs.

Paste Special

Dreamweaver's Paste Special command supports four document formats, ranging from plain text to highly designed HTML. But in reality, Dreamweaver supports only two formats for *all* pasting operations—text only and text with structure (see page 72). The other two formats—text with basic formatting and text with full formatting—work only with Microsoft Word or Excel documents.

Note that these operations work only when you paste text in Design view—if you paste a document in Code view, Dreamweaver just dumps in the plain text, without paragraphs, line breaks, or any other formatting. For details about adding text to pages in Live view, jump ahead to page 102.

Choose Paste Special and you see the dialog box shown in Figure 2-2. It offers these choices:

- **Text only**. This is the most basic option of all. It pastes text without any formatting whatsoever, ignoring even paragraph and line breaks (this is also how text appears when you paste it in Code view). You end up with one long, uninterrupted series of sentences. Though you won't want this effect often, it can come in handy when you copy a long paragraph of text from an email program that adds unnecessary line breaks at the end of each line of text.

- **Text with structure (paragraphs, lists, tables, etc.)**. Here Dreamweaver tries to preserve the *structure* of the text, including paragraphs, headers, bulleted lists, and so on. This option doesn't retain any formatting applied to the text, however, such as boldface or italics. You use this option with most text that's not copied from a Microsoft Office program. In most cases, however, Dreamweaver ends up preserving only paragraphs, missing any bulleted lists and headers.

- **Text with structure plus basic formatting (bold, italic)**. When you paste text using this option, Dreamweaver formats elements the same way that "Text with structure" does, but it also preserves text formatting, such as boldface, italics, and underlines. This is the option Dreamweaver uses when you paste Microsoft Word or Excel text and numbers, as described next.

- **Text with structure plus full formatting (bold, italic, styles)**. This option includes everything you get with basic formatting and converts Word-formatted text into CSS styles, placing them in an internal style sheet in the <head> section of the web page.

For text you copy from most programs, "Text with structure" is the best paste option. Keep the "Retain line breaks" checkbox turned on. You still have to manually replace line breaks with paragraph markers, as described in the Note on page 71, but without "Retain line breaks" turned on, Dreamweaver removes single hard returns, resulting in one long paragraph of text.

In addition, when you paste text that includes traditional quotation marks (also called "curly" quotes), you can tell Dreamweaver to insert "straight" quotes by turning on the "Convert smart quotes to straight quotes" checkbox. This option forces Dreamweaver to replace opening and closing curly double quotes (" and ") with the " character, and curly single quotes (' and ') with straight single quotes ('). Turn on this option only if you really like the "Hey, I wrote this on a dumb computer that has no understanding of real typography" look. For Word or Excel files, there are a few better options, described next.

NOTE In most browsers, you can copy an entire page of HTML and paste it into Dreamweaver. Click inside a web page, press Ctrl+A (⌘-A) to select the entire page, and then press Ctrl+C (⌘-C) to copy the HTML. Next, switch to Dreamweaver, click inside an empty page, and then press Ctrl+V (⌘-V) to paste. Results vary depending on your operating system and the browser you use. With Google Chrome, Firefox, and Internet Explorer, for instance, Dreamweaver copies the HTML (including links to graphics) from the body of the page. The text shows up with HTML tags for paragraphs and headings, but you lose CSS styles, because Dreamweaver stores internal style sheets and links to external style sheets in the head of HTML documents. See page 113 for more on style sheets and page xx for the structure of HTML documents.

FIGURE 2-2

The Paste Special command lets you paste text copied from other programs into a budding web page. If you want Dreamweaver to use the same option each time you use Paste Special, click Paste Preferences to open the Preferences window. Select whatever settings—basic formatting, for example—you want Dreamweaver to apply when you click Paste.

Changing the Paste Command's Standard Behavior

If you use the same Paste Special option each time you copy text, you're in luck, because the Paste Special dialog box remembers the last option you used. But what if you'd like Dreamweaver to use one of the Paste Special options each time you click the Paste command (Ctrl+V [⌘-V]), and skip the Paste Special window altogether? Perhaps you'd always like to copy text "with structure" and retain some basic formatting, like bold and italic type. You can do that, too. Choose Edit→Paste Special→Paste Preferences. You see the four options described above at the top of the dialog box. Choose "Text with structure plus basic formatting (bold, italic)." Now when you press Ctrl+V (⌘-V), you'll retain the bold and italic formatting.

Pasting Text from Microsoft Word: The Basic Method

While text you paste from non-Word applications doesn't retain much formatting beyond paragraphs, Dreamweaver includes both basic and advanced ways to copy and paste Word text.

Frequently, you'll just want to preserve basic formatting, like bold or italic text, headlines, and bulleted lists. You won't need (and in most cases, won't want) more extravagant formatting, like different fonts, colors, or margin settings. After all, you're the web designer, and you'll use your own design sense and CSS formatting rules to add beauty to basic text.

You paste Word text just as you would any other: Select the desired text in Word, copy it, switch to Dreamweaver, and then choose Edit→Paste (Ctrl-V [⌘-V]) to drop the text into a web page. You don't have to spend a lot of time reformatting the text since Dreamweaver preserves much of it:

- Paragraphs formatted with Word's built-in heading styles (Heading 1, Heading 2, and so on) get HTML heading tags: <h1> for Heading 1, <h2> for Heading 2, and so on.

- Paragraphs remain paragraphs...most of the time. Actually, the way Dreamweaver pastes paragraphs depends on how Word formatted the paragraphs to begin with, and whether you turned on the Paste Special window's "Clean up Word paragraph spacing" setting (see Figure 2-2). If you did, paragraphs you paste from Word sometimes appear in Dreamweaver as one large paragraph, with line break characters at the end of the original paragraphs. To get Dreamweaver to paste each paragraph *as* a paragraph, choose Edit→Paste Special, turn off the "Clean up Word paragraph spacing" checkbox, and then click OK.

NOTE If the source Word document has an empty line between each paragraph (in other words, an empty paragraph generated by pressing the Enter [Return] key twice after each real paragraph), make sure you *do* have the "Clean up Word paragraph spacing" checkbox turned on. That eliminates the empty paragraphs.

- Bold and italic text maintain their look (Dreamweaver uses the HTML <strong> tag for bold text and the <em> tag for italicized text, as described on page 101).

- Basic text-alignment options (left, right, and center) remain intact. Justified text, on the other hand, gets pasted as left-aligned. (You can compensate for this using the Justify option in the Properties panel, as described on page 153.)

- Numbered lists come through as numbered lists in Dreamweaver (see page 91) *if* you initially created the list using Word's automatic numbered list feature.

NOTE Suppose you copy some HTML, maybe out of the Source view of an actual web page or from a "How to Write HTML" website. You'll notice that when you paste it in Dreamweaver's Design view, all the HTML tags appear in that view, complete with brackets (< >) and other assorted messiness. To get HTML into a page (and make it work like HTML), you have to go into Code view and paste the code directly into the page's HTML. (To see the HTML for a page, click the Code view or Split view buttons at the top of the document window.)

- If you paste text created using Word's built-in list-bulleting feature, you end up with a proper HTML bulleted list (see page 91). If you create your own bulleted list style in Word, make sure you select the "list" type when you create the style; otherwise, copying and pasting the custom list might just paste plain paragraphs of text.

- Graphics from Word documents get pasted as graphics. In fact, even if the original graphics aren't in a web-ready format (if they're BMP, TIFF, or PICT files, for example), Dreamweaver converts them to either the GIF or JPEG format, which web browsers understand. Dreamweaver even copies the files to your local site folder *and* links them correctly to the page. (Chapter 5 covers images in depth.)

> **NOTE** Keep a couple of things in mind when you paste material from Word: First, you can't copy and paste more than a couple hundred kilobytes' worth of text at a time, so you have to transfer really long documents in pieces (or better yet, spread them out among multiple web pages). Second, the ability to keep basic HTML formatting in place when you paste works only with versions of Word later than Office 97 (for Windows) or Office 98 (for Macs).

Pasting Text with Word Formatting

If you simply *must* keep that three-inch-tall, crazy orange font you used in a Word document, you can turn to the Paste Special "Text with structure plus full format-ting" option. After copying text from Word and returning to Dreamweaver, choose Edit→Paste Special or press Shift+Ctrl+V (Shift-⌘-V). When the Paste Special window appears, choose the full formatting option, and then click OK.

Dreamweaver pastes the text with as much formatting as possible, including mar-gins and text fonts, colors, and sizes. Behind the scenes, Dreamweaver pastes the text *and* adds CSS formatting that attempts to replicate the look of the text as it appeared in Word.

> **NOTE** Sometimes when you paste from Word (even using the standard Paste command), you end up with empty hyperlink tags (<a>) in your HTML. They appear as gold shields in Dreamweaver's Design view, like the line break marks shown in Figure 2-1. The links might look something like this: *<a name="OLE_LINK1" id="OLE_LINK1">* *</a>*. Feel free to delete them—they're unnecessary crud that Word adds.

Unfortunately, all this extra code increases the document's file size and download time and can interfere with future formatting changes. What's worse, most of your visitors won't even be able to *see* some of this formatting—if you use an uncommon font, for example, that font may not be available on your visitors' computers. For these reasons, it's best to skip this feature, paste Word text using the regular Paste command, and then create your own styles to make the text look great (you'll learn how to do that in the next chapter).

Pasting Excel Spreadsheet Information

Most companies have tons of valuable information stored in Excel spreadsheets, such as financial data, schedules, product specifications, and price lists. When it's time to transfer that information to web pages, you'll be pleased to know that Dreamweaver pastes Excel text and numbers with fidelity. In Excel, click and drag to select the cells you need. Choose Edit→Copy or use the keyboard shortcut Ctrl+C (⌘-C) to temporarily store the data in your computer's Clipboard. Move over to Dreamweaver and then, in Design view, click the spot on the page where you want to paste the data. Choose Edit→Paste or the shortcut Ctrl+V (⌘-V) to paste your Excel data. This simple paste method copies the text to your web page as a table, but without any formatting—you lose font styles, colors, and alignment. This is usually just fine when you plan on creating distinctive table styles using CSS (Cascading Style Sheets), as described on page 305.

NOTE Dreamweaver's tables don't do arithmetic. Suppose your spreadsheet has a cell that adds the values in two cells and displays the result as 4. After you copy and paste the Excel data into a web page, you see the number 4, but it's not based on an underlying formula in the table, it's based on the arithmetic Excel did before you copied and pasted the table. So even if you change the numbers in the relevant cells, the pasted table still displays a result of 4.

But if you want to retain the formatting from Excel, you need to use the Edit→Paste Special command (or press Shift+Ctrl+V [(Shift-⌘-V]). You also need to use Paste Special for the rare occasions when you want the text from a spreadsheet, but you don't want Dreamweaver to place it inside an HTML table. After you choose Edit→Paste Special, a dialog box appears with four "Paste as" options, but only the first and last are truly useful:

- **Text only.** Use this option to paste text from a spreadsheet without any tabular formatting. The words and numbers appear in a jumble because there is no table structure; everything is scrunched together. You need to spend time cleaning up the text to make it useful. You're not likely to use this option frequently, but there are occasions when it comes in handy. Suppose you want to extract the names, descriptions, and prices from a restaurant menu that's stored in a spreadsheet. In your web page, you plan to show each menu item as a paragraph. Using this option, you can copy the spreadsheet data into your web page without the table structure.

- **Text with structure (paragraphs, lists, tables, etc.).** This option produces the same results as the simple Edit→Paste command. Excel data appears in a table with no formatting.

- **Text with structure plus basic formatting (bold, italic).** When you use this option with Excel data, it doesn't quite work as advertised. For example, you won't see the bold and italic formatting that your Excel worksheet has. To get that, you need to use the next option.

- **Text with structure plus full formatting (bold, italic, styles).** Use this option when you want to retain the font size, style, and color you used in Excel. It also retains any background colors in cells and the alignment options you set. This "full formatting" option creates CSS style definitions in the <head> section of your web page. (To learn more about these so-called *internal style sheets*, see page 113.)

TIP There's a whole chapter on HTML tables beginning on page 279.

Importing Word and Excel Documents from Windows

Windows fans can import documents directly from a Word or Excel file into Dreamweaver. In Design view, position your cursor where you want to insert the text or spreadsheet, and then choose File→Import→Word Document (or Excel Document). An Open File dialog box appears; find and double-click the Word or Excel file you want.

Dreamweaver captures the document just as if you'd used Edit→Paste. That is, for Word documents, it carries over basic formatting like bold, italics, headlines, and paragraphs, and imports and converts images. The importing process doesn't create style sheets or apply advanced formatting. For Excel documents, you get just an organized table of data, without any formatting.

■ Adding Special Characters to Pages

Many useful special characters—such as copyright and trademark symbols—don't appear on your keyboard, making them difficult or impossible to type. But you can add a special character to your pages simply by clicking an icon. To do that, follow these steps:

1. **On the Insert panel, choose the Common category.**

   If you can't see the Insert panel (Figure 2-3), choose Window→Insert to open it, or use the keyboard shortcut Ctrl+F2 (⌘-F2). As explained on page 12, the Insert panel can appear as a toolbar, a floating palette, or a panel.

TIP Shortcut keys may not behave as expected on some computers. For example, some laptops use a command like Ctrl+F2 to adjust the volume of the computer's speaker. In that case, Ctrl+F2 may not be available to Dreamweaver. As a workaround, use the relevant menu command, such as Window→Insert. If you desperately want to use a shortcut key, create your own. Select Edit→Keyboard Shortcuts (Dreamweaver→Keyboard Shortcuts) to open the panel that does the job. See page 904 for instructions.

   As advertised, the Insert→Common category gives you one-click access to elements you frequently pop into web pages, such as images, videos, tables, and links.

TIP There are more characters in the Western alphabet than the Insert Other Character dialog box lists (Figure 2-3). You can find a table of these characters and the HTML code that produces them at *http://tinyurl.com/ffl5g*.

FIGURE 2-3

Left: The Character menu at the bottom of the Insert→Common panel (circled) displays some of the most common special characters, like the copyright mark.

Right: To choose from a wider range of characters, click Other Characters at the bottom of the Character menu. That opens the Insert Other Character dialog box, which offers characters that are difficult or impossible to type on a keyboard.

2. **Choose the last option on the Insert→Common menu, Character.**

   Character offers a range of symbols and international characters (Figure 2-3, left). Unlike regular Western characters, such as *a* or *z*, Dreamweaver represents special characters using an HTML code or value. For instance, the code *™* adds the trademark symbol (™); another way to write this symbol in HTML is *™*.

3. **Open the menu of characters by selecting Character, or, if you've been here before, by clicking the small arrow next to the word "Character."**

   The Insert→Common→Character menu can be a little tricky to use. For one thing, if you previously selected an option from the menu, it remembers the character you inserted, and the button reads something like "Character: Line Break" or "Character: Em Dash," accompanied by the appropriate icon. To insert that character again, click the icon or label.

TIP If you like card games or just want to add a heart to a web page without using a graphic, choose the Other Characters option from the Insert panel and type *♥*. Type *♦* for a diamond, *♠* for a spade, or *♣* for a club. (Don't forget the semicolon at the end of each—that's part of the code.)

4. **To select a different character, click the name of the character you want to insert.**

5. **Dreamweaver inserts the appropriate HTML into your web page.**

6. **If you don't see the special character you need, select Other Characters from the Character menu.**

   That opens the Insert Other Character dialog box (Figure 2-3, bottom), which has a wider range of characters you can choose from.

NOTE If you set the encoding of your page to anything other than Western European or Unicode (UTF-8) in the Page Properties window (by choosing Modify→Page Properties, and then clicking the Title/Encoding category), you can reliably insert only line breaks and nonbreaking spaces. The other special characters available from the Character menu may not work (see the box on page 80 for more on encoding).

Line Breaks

Pressing Enter (Return) in Dreamweaver's Design view creates a new paragraph, just as it does in a word processor. Unfortunately, web browsers add extra space above and below paragraphs—which is a real nuisance if you want to create several single-spaced lines of text, like this:

> 702 A Street
> Boring, OR
> 97009 USA

Here, each part of the address is on its own line, but the entire address still represents just a single paragraph (and each of the lines share that paragraph's formatting, as you'll learn in the next chapter).

NOTE If you want to dispense with the space that browsers insert between paragraphs *entirely*, don't use line breaks each time. Instead, use CSS Designer to eliminate the top and bottom margins associated with the <p> tag. See page 116 for details on creating styles with CSS Designer.

To create this single-spaced effect in HTML, you need to insert *line breaks*. For example, click after the word "Street," and then insert a line break using one of these techniques:

- Press Shift+Enter.

- Go to Insert→Common→Character and then select Line Break.

- Choose Insert→Character→Line Break from the menu bar.

Keyboard Shortcuts for Special Characters

Dreamweaver uses UTF-8 (also called Unicode) encoding when you create a new page (unless you specify otherwise). Without getting into the messy details, UTF-8 lets you include almost any type of character available to the languages of the world—it lets a Chinese speaker embed actual Chinese characters in a page, for example. When you use the Other Characters window, Dreamweaver inserts what's called an HTML *entity*—a code that replaces the real character. For example, the HTML entity for the © symbol is *©*. When a browser encounters that code, it inserts the copyright character. But UTF-8 lets you add the actual symbol to a page—the trick is knowing how to do that through your keyboard.

On the Mac, a handful of keyboard shortcuts let you type special characters, like curly quotes, directly into your budding web page. Here are the keystrokes for a few of the most common characters:

- Ellipsis (three periods in a row): Option-;
- Em dash (—): Shift+Option+-
- Opening single quote ('): Option-]
- Closing single quote ('): Shift+Option+]
- Opening double quote ("): Option-[

- Closing double quote ("): Shift+Option+[
- Copyright symbol (©): Option-G

You can also use the Mac Character Palette to insert unusual symbols. To open it, select Edit→Special Characters from the Finder.

In Windows, you have to press the Alt key, type the Unicode value using your keyboard's numeric keypad, and then release the Alt key. Note that you can't use the regular number keys for this—you must use the numeric keypad. For example, to add an ellipsis, hold down the Alt key, type *0133*, and then release the Alt key. Here are a few other codes for Windows PCs:

- Open single quote: Alt+0145
- Closing single quote: Alt+0146
- Opening double quote: Alt+0147
- Closing double quote: Alt+0148

In Windows, it's easier to use the character map to insert special symbols and characters. To open Windows' Character Map tool, press the Windows key and then type Character Map in the "Search program and files" box.

NOTE When you insert a line break in Design view, Dreamweaver may give you no visual hint that the break is even there; after all, a regular paragraph break and a line break both create a new line of text. This is especially likely if you copy text from programs other than Microsoft Word or Excel. You might find text from those programs—especially email programs—loaded with an infuriating number of line breaks. To add to the confusion, a line break may go unnoticed if it occurs at the end of a line of text that goes off-screen.

Your only workaround is to make the line breaks visible. To do that, choose Edit→Preferences (Dreamweaver→Preferences), or press Ctrl+U (⌘-U). Click the Invisible Elements category, and then make sure you have the Line Breaks checkbox turned on. Now you see each line break as a small gold shield. (If, after doing this, you still don't see the line break character, choose View→Visual Aids, and make sure you have the Invisible Elements checkbox turned on.)

You can select a line break by clicking the shield, and then delete it by pressing Delete. Better yet, select the shield and then hit Enter (Return) to eliminate the line break *and* create a new paragraph.

Nonbreaking Spaces

Sometimes, the way a sentence breaks over two lines can distort what you're trying to say, as shown in Figure 2-4. If you run into that problem, a *nonbreaking space* can save the day. It looks just like a regular space, but acts like a glue that prevents the words on either side from being split apart at the end of a line. For example, adding a nonbreaking space between the words "farmer" and "says" in Figure 2-4 ensures that those words won't get split across a line break and helps clarify the headline's meaning.

> **Hybrid potato is edible farmer says.**
>
> **Hybrid potato is edible farmer says.**

FIGURE 2-4

Headlines sometimes break between lines, leaving a single word alone on a line (top). In typography, this is known as a widow. Adding a nonbreaking space (bottom) can prevent widows and clarify a headline's meaning.

To insert a nonbreaking space between two words, delete the space already there (for example, by positioning your mouse after the space and pressing the Backspace key), and then do one of the following:

- Press Shift+Ctrl+space bar (Shift-⌘-space bar).

- From the Character menu in the Insert panel's Common category, select Non-Breaking Space.

- Choose Insert→Character→Line Break.

Multiple Spaces

You may have noticed that if you type more than one space in a row, Dreamweaver ignores all but the first one. This isn't a glitch in the program, it's standard HTML. Web browsers ignore any spaces following the first one.

Therefore, a line like "Beware   of   llama," with several spaces between each word, appears on a web page like this: "Beware of llama." Not only do web browsers ignore multiple spaces, they ignore any spaces that aren't *between* words. So if you hit the space bar a couple of times to indent the first line of a paragraph, you're wasting your time. A browser won't display any of those spaces (and Dreamweaver doesn't display them, either).

This feature makes good sense, because it prevents web pages from being littered with extraneous spaces that many people insert when writing HTML (because extra spaces in a page of HTML often make the code easier to read).

There may be times, however, when you *want* to add more space between words. For example, consider the text navigation bar at the bottom of a web page, a common element that lists the sections of a website. Visitors can click one of the section titles to jump directly to that area of the site. For clarity, many designers like to add multiple spaces between the links, like this:

News   Classifieds   Jobs

One simple way to add this space is to insert multiple nonbreaking spaces, as described in the previous section. A browser *does* display every nonbreaking space it encounters, so you can add multiple nonbreaking spaces between words, letters, or even at the beginning of paragraphs. This technique has a few downsides, though: You have to type in the code for a bunch of nonbreaking spaces, which takes work, and it adds code to your web page, making it download a bit more slowly.

Alternatively, you can enlist Cascading Style Sheets (CSS). While you won't get in-depth detail on CSS until the next chapter, here are a few CSS *properties* (formatting rules) to tuck in the back of your mind when you need to add space to your text:

- To indent the first line of a paragraph, use the CSS *text indent* property (page 157).

- To add space between words in a paragraph, use the *word spacing* property (page 157).

- To increase or decrease the space between letters, use *letter spacing* (page 157).

- And, if you want to increase the space between links, as in the links example above, you can add either left and right *margins* or *padding* to each link (page 465).

NOTE If you often add multiple spaces to a line of text, Dreamweaver offers a shortcut. Choose Edit→ Preferences (Dreamweaver→Preferences) to open Dreamweaver's Preferences window. Click the General category and then turn on "Allow multiple consecutive spaces." Now, whenever you press the space bar more than once, Dreamweaver inserts *nonbreaking* spaces.

In fact, Dreamweaver is even smarter than that. It inserts a regular space if you press the space bar just once, a nonbreaking space followed by a regular space if you hit the space bar twice, and multiple nonbreaking spaces followed by a regular space if you hit the space bar repeatedly. Why does Dreamweaver automatically add the regular spaces? Since nonbreaking spaces act like glue that keeps words stuck together, the regular spaces let the lines break normally, if necessary.

Adding a Date to Your Page

The Insert panel's Common category offers an option called Date (its icon looks like the page of a calendar) that inserts just about any combination of the current day, date, and time. Click the calendar icon or choose Insert→Date to open the Insert Date dialog box (Figure 2-5) and set your preferences.

Select the format you want from the Date Format list. You can choose from 13 configurations, such as March 7, 1974, or 3/7/74.

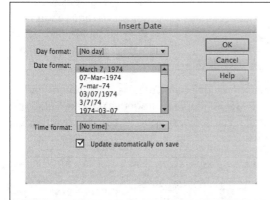

You may wonder why Dreamweaver includes a date function anyway. After all, how hard is it to type *Thursday, July 12*? But the feature's real value lies in the "Update automatically on save" checkbox. Turning on this option forces Dreamweaver to *update* the date each time you save the document. And that, in turn, tells you when you last updated the page. For example, you might type *This page was revised on:* and then choose Insert→Date, simultaneously turning on the "Update automatically on save" checkbox. Now, each time you change a page, Dreamweaver rewrites the date when you save the document. You never have to worry about dating pages again.

■ Selecting Text

After you get text into your Dreamweaver document, you'll undoubtedly need to edit it. You'll delete words and paragraphs, move sentences around, add words, and fix typos.

The first step in any of these procedures is learning how to select text, which works much as it does in a word processor. You drag your cursor across the text to highlight it, or click at the beginning of the selection and then hold down the Shift key as you click the end of the selection—that automatically selects all the text in between. You can also use shortcuts like these:

- To select a word, double-click it.

- To select a paragraph, triple-click anywhere inside it.

- To select a line of text, move your cursor to the left of the line until it changes from an I-beam to an arrow, signaling that you've reached the left-margin selection strip. Click once to highlight one line of text; click once and then drag vertically to select multiple lines.

- While pressing Shift, use the left and right arrow keys to select one letter at a time. Use Shift+Ctrl (Shift-⌘) to select one *word* at a time.

- Ctrl+A (⌘-A) selects everything in the body of a page—text, graphics, and all. (Well, this isn't 100 percent true: If you use tables or <div> tags [page 454] to organize a page, Ctrl+A may select just the text within a table cell or <div> tag; clicking the <body> tag in the Tag Selector at the bottom of the document window [page 7] is the sure-fire way to select everything on a page.)

Once you select text, you can cut, copy, or delete it. To move it to another part of the web page, or to another Dreamweaver document altogether, use the Cut, Copy, and Paste commands in the Edit menu. You can also move text around by dragging and dropping it, as shown in Figure 2-6.

FIGURE 2-6

You can move a blob of text simply by dragging it to another location. First select the text, and then point to a spot inside the selection. The cursor changes from an I-beam to an arrow, indicating that you can drag the selection. As you drag, a horizontal bar indicates the selection's landing site, circled here. Let go of the mouse button to drop the selection in that spot. This technique works with graphics and other objects, too. You can even move a copy of the selection by pressing Ctrl (Option on a Mac) as you drag and drop.

Once copied, the text remains in your Clipboard and you can place it again and again (until you copy something else to the Clipboard, of course). When you cut (or copy) and paste *within* Dreamweaver, all the text attributes come along for the ride. So if you copy a paragraph that includes bold text, you also copy the HTML tags for both creating the paragraph and for producing the bold text.

To delete any selection, press Delete or choose Edit→Clear.

> **NOTE**   Not *all* text formatting necessarily comes along for the ride. For example, if you format text using an external style sheet (page 113) and cut and paste that text into a web page that's not linked to the CSS file, then the formatting does *not* show up in the new page. So on some occasions, you may copy text from one document, paste it into another, and then find that the formatting disappears.

■ Applying HTML Tags to Text

Getting text into a web page is a good start, but effective communication requires effective design. Large, bold headlines help readers scan a page's important topics. Colorful text focuses attention. Bulleted lists crystallize and summarize ideas. Just as a monotonous, low-key voice puts a crowd to sleep, a vast desert of plain text is sure to turn visitors away from the important message of your site. In fact, text formatting could be the key to making your *Widgets Online 2015 Sale-a-Thon* a resounding success instead of an unnoticed disaster.

Styling text is a two-step process. First you apply the appropriate HTML tag to a chunk of text, and then you use CSS to create styles that make that text look great. You add HTML tags not so much to format text (though they *can* do that, with the undesired side effect that different browsers can interpret the tags differently); rather, you use them to *structure* the text into logical blocks. Once you set up those blocks, you can use CSS to format them to your liking—and not just in the current page, but across your site. That's one of the big benefits of CSS.

For example, you'd use the <h1> (Heading 1) tag to indicate the most important content on a page, and the <ol> (ordered list) tag to list a series of numbered steps. Structuring your text like this not only adds some rudimentary formatting (the resulting page has a large, boldfaced headline and a numbered list), but it also structures your text so that search engines and alternative browsing devices, like screen readers for the vision impaired, can weight the relative importance of each block of text. However, HTML's limited formatting options aren't very appealing. That's where CSS comes in. You use CSS to fine-tune the visual appeal of text by changing fonts, applying color, adjusting font size, and a lot more.

The fundamental differences between HTML and CSS styling are so significant that Dreamweaver treats the two technologies separately by splitting the Properties panel into two tabbed areas, one for HTML and the other for CSS. That way, you always know when you're applying which type of formatting code (see Figure 2-7). In this chapter, you'll learn to use HTML tags to structure text on a page; in the next chapter, you'll create beautiful typography with CSS.

Decoding Encoding

In some cases, when you copy a symbol like © from Microsoft Word and then paste it into Dreamweaver, you see © in the HTML. Other times, you see the actual symbol (©). Which you get depends on the type of *encoding* Dreamweaver uses on your web page. Unless you work with languages other than English, you can work happily without ever worrying about how Dreamweaver encodes your HTML. But if you commonly need to type characters that don't appear on the standard English keyboard, such as Chinese or Kanji letters, or simply the accented letters of French or Spanish, Dreamweaver's encoding method is helpful.

Computers don't think in terms of letters or any of the other symbols we use to communicate with one another. Computers think in terms of bits and bytes. They represent every letter or symbol on a web page by a numeric code. The process of converting those letters and symbols to computer-friendly code is called *encoding*. But since the world is filled with symbols from many languages—Latin, Chinese, Arabic, Cyrillic, Hebrew, and so on—there are many *encoding schemes* used to accommodate the alphabets of the world. Versions of Dreamweaver prior to CS3 used Western Latin encoding, which handles most of the characters in English and Western European languages. But it doesn't handle all the symbols. That's why, when you copy a © symbol from Word and paste it into a web page with Western Latin encoding, you end up with © in your HTML instead of the copyright symbol. © is called an *entity*, and browsers know that when they see that particular entity, they should display the copyright symbol.

The current version of Dreamweaver uses a newer type of encoding when it creates a web page—Unicode. Unicode, which Dreamweaver refers to as *Unicode (UTF-8)*, handles many of the alphabets of the world, so you can mix Kanji with Cyrillic with English on a single page, and all the characters display as they should. A page encoded with Unicode also produces slightly different HTML when you paste symbols from other programs. Instead of using entities in the page, like ” for a curly right quotation mark, you see the actual character (") in the HTML. This quality generally makes HTML much easier to read. However, if you previously built a site using a different encoding scheme, like *Japanese (Shift JIS)*—yes, that's the actual format name—you may want to stick to that method.

You probably won't ever need to change Dreamweaver's encoding scheme, but if you update a site and want to upgrade to the new Unicode encoding (maybe so you can type © instead of © in your HTML), choose Modify→Page Properties, click the Title/Encoding category, and then select a method from the encoding menu. To change the default encoding for all new documents (for example, if you absolutely must stick with the *Shift JIS* to match the encoding method of other pages on your site), choose Edit→Preferences (Dreamweaver→Preferences), click the New Document category, and then select an option from the Default Encoding menu.

Note that if, later on, you switch back to Unicode (UTF-8), make sure you select "C (Canonical Decomposition)" from the Normalization drop-down menu, and leave the Include Unicode Signature checkbox *turned off*. Otherwise, the page may not display correctly.

Finally, if you use the Insert Special Character menu (page 77), Dreamweaver always inserts an HTML entity (®, for example) instead of the actual symbol (™), even in a UTF-8 page. You can, however, type many of these symbols on your keyboard, as described on page 80.

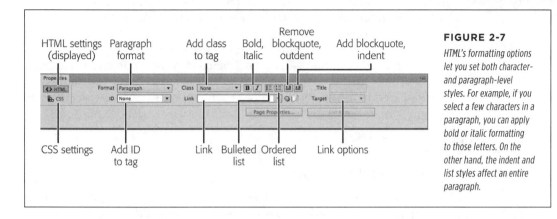

FIGURE 2-7

HTML's formatting options let you set both character- and paragraph-level styles. For example, if you select a few characters in a paragraph, you can apply bold or italic formatting to those letters. On the other hand, the indent and list styles affect an entire paragraph.

▇ Structuring Paragraphs with HTML

Just as you use paragraphs to help organize your thoughts into clear, well-structured units, so you organize content into blocks of information using HTML tags (see page xx for more about tags). The most basic block of information is the simple paragraph, which you identify in HTML with a paragraph tag, like this:

```
<p>Hello. This is a paragraph on a web page.</p>
```

A web browser considers everything between the opening <p> tag and the closing </p> tag as part of the same paragraph. You can apply many Dreamweaver formatting options—headlines, lists, indentations, and alignment, for example—only to full paragraphs of text rather than to individual words. In a word processor, you call this kind of styling *paragraph* formatting; in web design, it's called *block-level* formatting. Either way, the idea is the same: The styling you apply affects the entire paragraph (that is, it affects the *block* of text, whether that block consists of just a single sentence or of several sentences). On the other hand, you can apply *character-level* formatting to individual characters or words. Character-level formatting includes bold and italic letters or words. In the world of HTML, you get character-level formatting using *inline elements*, like the <strong> and the <em> tags (see page 101).

Paragraphs

If you create a new document in Dreamweaver and start typing right away, the text you type has no formatting at all, as indicated by the word "None" in the Format menu at the left side of the Properties panel (see Figure 2-7). (*None* isn't an HTML tag; it just means that you aren't using *any* of the text tags this menu offers—<p>, <h1>, and so on.)

However, when you press Enter (Return), Dreamweaver transforms that text into a new paragraph, complete with opening and closing <p> tags. Still, your newly born paragraph has no *design* applied to it. When a visitor looks at the paragraph in a browser, he doesn't see text in a font and size of your choosing; he sees it formatted according to his browser's Preferences settings. For example, if a visitor sets his browser to display unformatted text as Vladimir Script, your page will look as though John Hancock wrote it. Since most people don't bother to set a default font, browsers usually use some version of the widely supported Times New Roman font for paragraphs (you'll be able to specify your own fonts using CSS, as described on page 140).

UP TO SPEED

Separating Structure from Presentation

HTML isn't about good looks or fancy design, it's about architecture. HTML tags apply *structure* to your page, providing search engines with valuable insight into how you organize your content. In fact, most visitors to your site won't ever see, and probably don't care, which HTML tags you use. But Google, Bing, and other search engines do. They use your tags to determine which text is the most important and to understand what your page is really about.

Google, for example, puts a lot of stock in <h1> tags, seeing the text inside as defining the page's subject. That's why search engine experts recommend using only one <h1> tag per page, and suggest that you make the text descriptive: <h1>My page </h1> isn't good, but <h1>The Ultimate Chia Pet Resource </h1> is.

In general, use HTML to structure your page the same way you'd structure a report or term paper. For example, the Heading 1 tag (<h1>) indicates a headline of the highest level and, therefore, of greatest importance. The Heading 2 tag (<h2>) represents a smaller headline—a subhead—that flags content as slightly less important. You see this kind of structure in this book—each chapter begins with a headline and includes subheads that further divide the content into logical blocks of information.

Structure is more about organizing content than it is about making a page look pretty. Even if this book used different colors and fonts for every headline, its fundamental organization—chapter title, main headlines, subheads, bulleted lists, numbered instructions, and so on—remains the same.

HTML is also important for devices that don't read or can't display CSS. For example, people with vision impairment often rely on screen readers (programs that literally read the text on a page out loud) to surf the Web. For screen readers, good HTML structure is the only way they can understand a page—clear use of headline, paragraph, and other tags helps screen readers convey the structure of a page.

You can add the paragraph tag to any block of text. Since that tag affects all the text within the block, you don't need to select any text as a first step. Simply click anywhere inside the block of text, and then do one of the following:

- In the Properties panel, choose Paragraph from the Format drop-down menu.

- Choose Format→Paragraph Format→Paragraph.

- Press Shift+Ctrl+P (Shift-⌘-P).

NOTE Much to the chagrin of web designers, web browsers display a line's worth of blank space before and after many block-level elements, like headings and paragraphs. If you find this gap distracting, you can't, unfortunately, get rid of it with regular HTML. However, many of the formatting limitations of HTML, including this one, go away when you use CSS. Using CSS Designer (page 116), you can create a style that sets the top and bottom margin for paragraphs to 0.

Headlines

Headlines announce information ("The Vote Is In!") and help organize content. HTML headings come in a variety of sizes to reflect the content's importance, from Heading 1 (most important) to Heading 6 (least important), as shown in Figure 2-8.

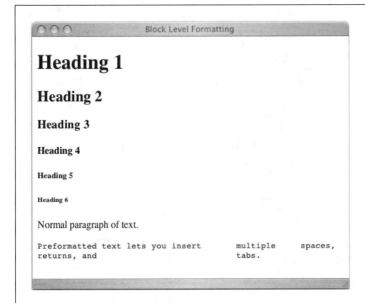

FIGURE 2-8

You can apply any of eight basic formats to a block of plain old text: Headings 1 through 6, and Paragraph and Preformatted styles. Normally, browsers vary the size, font, and weight (boldness) of the content associated with these tags (unless you add some CSS magic, discussed in the next chapter).

To turn a paragraph into a headline, click anywhere inside the line, or block, of text and then do one of the following:

- From the Format menu in the Properties panel, select one of the heading levels (Heading 1 through Heading 6) from the drop-down menu.

- Choose Format→Paragraph Format→Heading 1 (or Heading 2, Heading 3, and so on).

- Press Ctrl+1 (⌘-1) for the Heading 1 style, Ctrl+2 (⌘-2) for Heading 2, and so on.

Preformatted Text

Web browsers normally ignore extra spaces, tabs, and other blank-space characters in HTML. However, the Preformatted paragraph style overrides this behavior. Pre-formatted paragraphs display *every* text character in a paragraph, including tabs, multiple spaces, and line breaks, so you don't have to resort to multiple nonbreaking characters (page 81) to insert more than one space at a time.

Originally, the idea behind the Preformatted format was to display tabular data—like that in a spreadsheet—without the use of tables. That's why preformatted paragraphs use a *monospaced* font like Courier, where each letter of the alphabet, including *i* and *w*, have the same width, making it easy to align letters in columns. That's also why, when you use the Preformatted style, you can use tabs to align text in columns. (When you use any other paragraph format, web browsers ignore tabs.) However, an HTML table is a much better way to display data in columns; see Chapter 6.

Nonetheless, you can still find uses for the Preformatted format—when you want to display sample HTML or programming code, for example. You add the format to any block of text by clicking inside the block and taking one of these two steps:

- In the Properties panel, choose Format→Preformatted.

- Choose Format→Paragraph Format→Preformatted Text.

Keep in mind that preformatted text appears exactly as you type it. Unlike normal paragraph text, lines of preformatted text don't automatically wrap if they're wider than your visitor's display. That means that if you present your visitor with a really long line of preformatted text, she has to scroll horizontally to see all of it. To end a line of preformatted text and create another, you must press the Enter (Return) key, thus creating a manual line break.

Indented Paragraphs

Dreamweaver's Properties panel includes a button (⊞) that looks like the indent button in word processors. However, the button doesn't really create an indent; it actually inserts the HTML blockquote tag (though the Indent button has a different function when you apply it to lists, as described on page 96).

The blockquote tag was designed to set apart quoted material, such as an excerpt from a book or part of a famous speech. However, since browsers display blockquotes indented from the left edge of the page, some novice web designers use it to indent text. That's not a good idea for a couple of reasons. First, the tag indents text from *both* sides of a page, so it doesn't make sense as a way to indent a paragraph. In addition, you don't have any control over how *much* space a visitor's browser adds to the margins of a blockquote. (Most insert about 40 pixels on the left and right sides.)

As you'll see on page 465, CSS gives you precise control over indented elements using the *margin* or *padding* properties. However, if you *do* want to quote passages of text, you should use the blockquote tag. To do so, click inside a paragraph or any other block-level element, and do one of the following:

- In the Properties panel, click the blockquote button, ⊞ .

- Choose Format→Indent.

- Press Alt+Ctrl+] (Option-⌘-]).

If you ever want to remove the blockquote, you can use Dreamweaver to *outdent* it (yes, "outdent" is a real word—ever since Microsoft made it up).

To remove a <blockquote> tag, click inside the paragraph, and then do one of the following:

- In the Properties panel, click the Remove Blockquote button, ▣.
- Choose Format→Outdent.
- Press Alt+Ctrl+[(Option-⌘-[).

NOTE When you work with lists (as you will next), the Blockquote and Remove Blockquote buttons change their names and their behavior. They become Indent and Outdent buttons.

■ Formatting Lists

Lists organize the everyday information of our lives: to-do lists, grocery lists, least-favorite celebrities lists, and so on. On web pages, lists are indispensable for presenting groups of items, such as links, company services, or sets of instructions.

HTML offers formatting options for three basic types of list (see Figure 2-9). The two most common are *bulleted* lists (called *unordered* lists in HTML) and *numbered* lists (called *ordered* lists in HTML). The third and lesser-known list type, the *definition* list, comes in handy when you want to create glossaries or dictionary entries.

Bulleted and Numbered Lists

Bulleted and numbered lists share similar formatting. Dreamweaver automatically indents list items in both cases, and precedes each item with a character—a bullet, number, or letter, for example:

- Unordered, or bulleted, lists, like the one you're reading, are good for groups of items that don't necessarily follow a sequence. Browsers precede each list item with a bullet.

- Ordered lists are useful when you want to present items that follow a sequence, such as the numbered instructions in the next section. In an ordered list, Dreamweaver precedes each item with a number or letter instead of a bullet. It initially suggests ordinal numbers (1, 2, 3, and so on), but you can substitute Roman numerals, letters, and other variations.

You can create a list from scratch or apply list formatting to text already on a page.

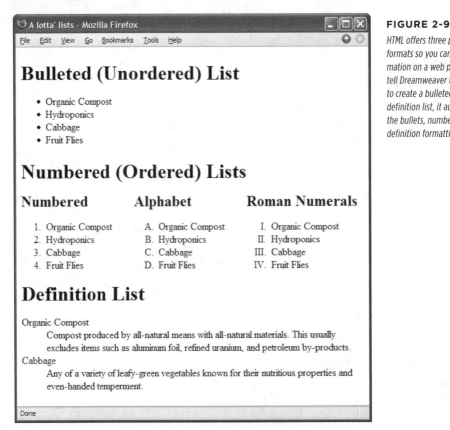

FIGURE 2-9

HTML offers three predefined list formats so you can organize information on a web page. Once you tell Dreamweaver that you intend to create a bulleted, numbered, or definition list, it automatically adds the bullets, numbers, or word/ definition formatting.

■ CREATING A BULLETED OR NUMBERED LIST

To create a list in Dreamweaver, first choose a list format, and then type in the list items:

1. **In the document window's Design view, select the point on the page where you want to start the list.**

2. **In the Properties panel, click Ordered List or Unordered List to apply the list format (see Figure 2-7). (The Unordered option is also known as a bulleted list.)**

   Alternatively, you can choose Format→List→Unordered List or Format→ List→Ordered List. Either way, the first bullet or number automatically appears in your document.

3. **Type in the first list item, and then press Enter (Return). Repeat this step until you add all the items to the list.**

The text you type appears after the bullet or number (*Organic Compost*, for example, in the list in Figure 2-9). When you press Enter (Return), a new bullet or number appears, ready for your next entry. (To move to the next line *without* creating a new bullet, insert a line break by pressing Shift+Enter [Shift-Return].)

> **NOTE** You can use the Properties panel to create a numbered or bulleted list in Code view, but Dreamweaver won't automatically add a new list item each time you hit Enter (Return). To insert a new list item, you must click outside the current item (either before an opening <li> tag or after a closing </li> tag) and choose either Insert→HTML→Text Object→List Item, or just type the HTML yourself (for example: *<li>New item</li>*). As you can see, using Design view for lists is a lot easier. The only benefit to Code view is that you can insert paragraphs, headlines, and other elements inside the <li> tags, which is perfectly valid HTML, but which Dreamweaver doesn't let you do in Design view.

4. **When you finish the list, press Enter (Return) twice.**

The double hard return ends the list and creates a new empty paragraph.

■ FORMATTING EXISTING TEXT AS A LIST

You may have several paragraphs of text you already typed up or pasted in from another program. You can easily change any such group of paragraphs into a list:

1. **Select the text you want to turn into a list.**

The easiest way to do that is to drag from the first list item straight down to the last one. Lists are block-level elements; each paragraph, whether it's a headline or a regular block of text, becomes one bulleted or numbered item in the list.

> **NOTE** You can use the Properties panel to change existing text into a list in Code view as well.

2. **Apply the list format.**

Just as you created a list from scratch as described previously, click either the Unordered List button (⊞) or the Ordered List button (⊞) in the Properties panel, or choose from the Format→List submenu. The selected paragraphs instantly take on the list formatting, complete with bullets or numbers.

> **NOTE** You may sometimes select what looks like a handful of paragraphs and apply the list format, only to end up with just a single bullet (or number). This happens when you use the line break <br> tag to move text down one line in a paragraph. While it's true that the <br> tag visually separates lines in a paragraph, the text is still part of a single paragraph, so Dreamweaver styles only *one* item with a bullet or number. The presence of multiple <br> tags can be a real problem when you paste text from other programs. See page 38 for more on the <br> tag and how to get rid of these pesky critters.

Whichever way you create your list—either by typing it in from scratch or formatting existing text—you're not stuck with the results. You can add more items, add extra spaces, and even renumber items, as described in the following section.

Reformatting Bulleted and Numbered Lists

HTML tags define lists, just as they do other web page elements. Making changes to an existing list is a matter of changing those tags, using Dreamweaver's menu commands and Properties panel.

> **TIP** Web browsers generally display list items stacked directly one on top of the other. To add a little breathing room between each item, use the CSS *margin* property to add space above or below the <li> tags, as described on page 465.

■ ADDING NEW ITEMS TO A LIST

Once you create a list, you can easily add items. To add an item at the beginning of a list, click in front of the first character of the first entry (not the first bullet point or number), type the item you want to add, and then press Enter (Return). Your added item now sits beside the first bullet or number, and pressing Enter (Return) automatically created the next bullet or number (and renumbered the other list items, if necessary).

> **NOTE** Adding items this way works only in Design view, not in Code view.

To add an item to the middle or end of a list, click at the end of the *previous* list item, and then press Enter (Return). The insertion point appears after Dreamweaver adds a new bullet or number; type your list item on this line.

■ FORMATTING BULLETS AND NUMBERS

Bulleted and numbered lists aren't limited to just the standard round black bullets or the numbers 1, 2, and 3. You can choose from two bullet types and a handful of numbering schemes. Here's how to change these settings:

1. **Click once inside any list item.**

   Strangely enough, you can't change the properties of a list if you first select the entire list, a single list item, or several list items.

> **NOTE** Most of the settings in the List Properties dialog box produce invalid HTML for HTML5, as well as for the strict versions of HTML 4.01 and XHTML 1.0. If you use this dialog box, stick to XHTML transitional or HTML transitional document types (see page xxi for more on picking a document type).

2. **Open the List Properties window (Figure 2-10).**

   Either click the List Item button in the bottom half of the HTML Properties panel or choose Format→List→Properties. (If the list is inside a table cell, your only choice is to use the Format menu, because the List Item button doesn't appear when you select text inside a table cell.)

TIP If you don't see List Item in the Properties panel, click HTML in the upper-left corner of the panel. Then, in the lower-right corner, click the expand button. It looks like a triangle.

FIGURE 2-10

The List Properties dialog box lets you select the type and style of a list. For example, if you select a numbered list, you can choose from five number styles: Number (1, 2, 3); Roman Small (i, ii, iii); Roman Large (I, II, III); Alphabet Small (a, b, c); and Alphabet Large (A, B, C). While the options in the top half of this window apply to an entire list (every item within the <ol> or <ul> tag), the options in the box labeled "List item" apply to just the single list item you clicked before opening the List Properties dialog box.

3. **Skip the "List type" drop-down menu.**

   It lets you turn a numbered list into a bulleted one, and vice versa. But why bother? You can achieve the same thing by simply selecting a bulleted list and clicking ▤ in the Properties panel and vice versa. In addition, this menu has two other options—Directory List and Menu List—which insert obsolete HTML, so avoid them.

4. **Choose a bullet or number style.**

   Bulleted lists can have one of three styles: *default*, *bullet*, or *square*. In most browsers, the default style is the same as the bullet style (a simple, solid black circle). As you might guess, the square style uses a solid black square for the bullet character.

   Numbered lists, on the other hand, offer a greater variety of options. Dreamweaver starts you off with a simple numbering scheme (1, 2, 3, and so on), but you can choose from any of five styles for ordered lists, as explained in Figure 2-10.

TIP You can achieve the same effect as step 4 above using CSS. Not only does CSS give you more options—you can use a graphic you created as a bullet, for example—but you avoid inserting obsolete HTML. See page 158 for CSS list options.

5. **Set the starting number for the list.**

   You don't have to begin a numbered list at 1, A, or the Roman numeral I. You can start it with any number you wish—a trick that can come in handy if, for example, you create a web page that explains how to rebuild a car's engine. As part of each step, say you want to include a photograph. You create a numbered list, type in the directions for step 1, hit Return, and then insert an image (as described in Chapter 5). You hit Return again, and then type in the text for step 2. Unfortunately, the photo, because it's technically an item in an ordered list, now has the number 2 next to it, and your real step 2 is listed as step 3!

If you remove the list formatting from the photo to get rid of the 2, you create one list above it and another below it. The real step 2, *below* the photo, now thinks it's the beginning of a new list—and starts over with the number 1! The solution is to make the list below the photo think it's a *new* list that begins with the number 2.

To start a list at something other than 1, type the starting number in the "Start count" field (Figure 2-10). You must enter a number, even if you want the list to use letters. So, to begin a list at D instead of A, type *4* in the "Start count" field.

You can even change the style of a *single* list item. For instance, you could change the third item in a numeric list from a 3 to the letter C. (Of course, just because you *can* doesn't mean you should. Dreamweaver is very thorough in supporting the almost overwhelming combination of options available in HTML, but, unless you're building a Dadaist revival site, how often do you want a list that's numbered 1, 2, C, iv, 1?)

6. **Click OK to apply the changes.**

■ NESTED LISTS

Some complex outlines require multiple *levels* of lists. Legal documents, for instance, may list major clauses with capital letters (A, B, C, and so on) and use Roman numerals (i, ii, iii, and so on) for subclauses.

You can easily create nested lists in Dreamweaver using the Properties panel's Indent button; Figure 2-11 shows you the steps.

You can change the style of a nested list—for example, change the nested list in Figure 2-11, bottom, into a bulleted list—by clicking the appropriate list type in the Properties panel. Changing the nested list's type doesn't affect the parent list type (that is, the outer list); for example, changing the nested list in Figure 2-11 from a numbered list to a bulleted list doesn't change the outer list to a bulleted list.

> **TIP** You can also create a nested list by hitting the Tab key to indent a list item to another level. Shift-Tab outdents the item.

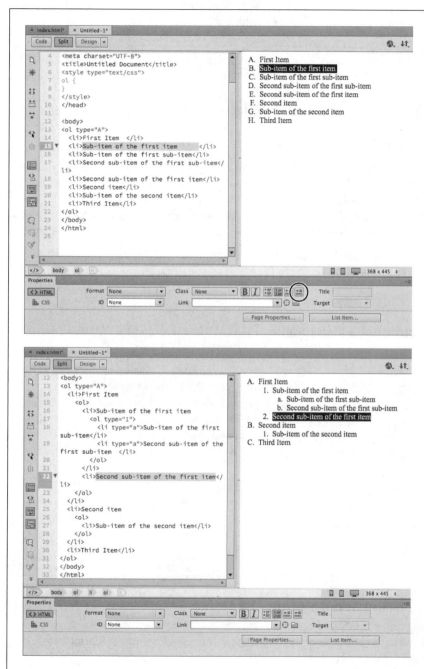

FIGURE 2-11

Top: To create a nested list, start with a single list—in this case, an ordered list using capital letters instead of numbers. Select an item in the list that you want to turn into a sub-topic, and then click the Indent button (circled), or choose Format→Indent.

Bottom: The entry becomes nested, indented from the main list and with its own numbering scheme. Here you've nested several subtopics. Notice that Dreamweaver has renumbered the major items to reflect the list's new order—item F from the top figure is item B in the bottom figure.

Definition Lists

You use *definition lists* whenever you need to present a term and its definition, such as when you create a dictionary or a glossary. Each item in a definition list comprises two parts: a word or term and its definition.

NOTE Behind the scenes, Dreamweaver creates an entire definition list using the <dl> tag. It applies two tags to each item in the list: <dt> for the word or term you want to define, and <dd> for the definition itself.

As you can see in Figure 2-9, definition lists aren't as fancy as they sound. They present the first item in the list—the word or term—on its own line with no indent, and display the second item—the definition—underneath, indented.

You can't create a definition list using the Properties panel. Instead, you start by creating a list of definitions and terms: Each term and definition should be its own paragraph, and the definition should immediately follow the term. Next, highlight the paragraphs that contain the terms and definitions, and then choose Format→List→Definition List.

To turn a definition list *back* into regular paragraphs, select the list and then choose Format→List→None, or, in the Properties panel, click ▦.

FREQUENTLY ASKED QUESTION

When Not to Approach the Insert Panel

I like the convenience of the Insert panel. Should I use its Structure category to format text?

In a word, no. At least, not when you're working in Design view. Unlike the way web designers use most of the other categories in the Insert panel, they use Structure mainly when working in Code view. It contains many of the same formatting options as the Properties panel; for instance, the Insert panel's h1, h2, and h3 headings are the same as Headings 1, 2, and 3 in the Properties panel.

However, using some of the panel's text options, such as <li>, can generate invalid HTML if you don't use them correctly. Furthermore, despite its usual tidiness, Dreamweaver doesn't clean up the code produced this way.

In fact, some of these options, when used in Design view, actually split the document window in two, showing the HTML code on one side and Design view on the other. This arrangement is confusing if you're not accustomed to seeing—or if you're not interested in seeing—the raw HTML. All major text-formatting options are available from the Properties panel and the Format menu. If you stick to these two tools, you can safely avoid the Structure category.

An exception to this rule is when you edit in Live view, a new feature in Dreamweaver CC 2014. With Live view editing, you *will* use the Structure category to insert headings and paragraphs. To learn that process, see page 365.

Removing and Deleting List Items

Dreamweaver lets you take items out of a list two ways: either by removing the list *formatting* from items (and changing them back to normal paragraphs) or by deleting their text outright.

■ REMOVING LIST FORMATTING

To remove list formatting from one or more list items (or an entire list), highlight the lines in question, and then choose Format→List→None (or, in the Properties panel, click ▦. You just removed all list formatting. The text remains onscreen, now formatted as standard paragraphs. For nested lists, you need to click ▦ once for each level of indent.

If you reformat an item in the middle of a list using this technique, it becomes a regular paragraph, and Dreamweaver turns the items above and below it into separate lists.

■ DELETING LIST ITEMS

You can easily delete a list or list item using the Tag Selector in the document window's status bar (see Figure 2-12). To delete an entire list, click anywhere inside it, click its tag in the Tag Selector—<ul> for a bulleted list, <ol> for a numbered list—and then press Delete. You can also, of course, drag through all the text in the list and then press Delete.

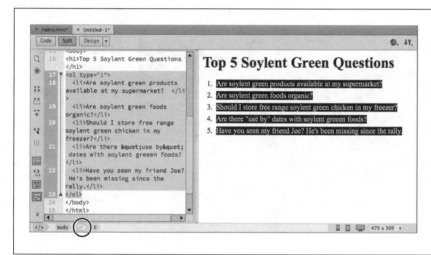

FIGURE 2-12

The Tag Selector (bottom left of the document window) is a great way to quickly and accurately select an HTML tag and its contents. Clicking the <ol> (ordered list) tag, for instance, selects the entire numbered list, as shown here. Clicking the <li> tag selects just one list item.

To delete a single list item, click that item in the document window, click the <li> tag in the Tag Selector, and then press Delete.

> **TIP** You can rearrange a list item in Design view by dragging it to another position within the list. If it's an ordered list (1, 2, 3, and so on), Dreamweaver automatically renumbers it.
>
> However, selecting a list item can be tricky. If you simply drag to select the text, you don't actually select the list item itself, with all its formatting and numbering. To be sure that you select a list item *and* its formatting, click the <li> tag in the Tag Selector (see Figure 2-12). Now, when you drag the selection to a new position in the list, the number (or bullet) goes along for the ride. You can also copy or cut the selected list item and then paste it into another position in the list.

Using HTML Text Styles

The formatting you can apply through HTML tags isn't much to write home about, much less to advertise on a resume. It's pretty basic; browsers generally display a Heading 1, for instance, as black and bold and in a large Times New Roman font. As mentioned on page 88, HTML paragraph formatting is really about *structure*, not looks. To create standout web pages, you need Cascading Style Sheets, which let you apply different fonts, colors, and sizes to your text.

And while CSS, which you'll learn about in the next chapter, is the mother lode of styles, HTML itself offers a handful of tags you can use to format text. Dreamweaver refers to these tags as *styles*, but they really just format text for specific, often obscure, purposes (see Figure 2-13). For example, the Code and Variable styles format programming code, while the Sample style represents the output from a computer program—not exactly styles you need often in promoting, say, your *Cheeses of the World* mail-order company.

FIGURE 2-13

Top: While the Properties panel lets you apply bold and italic formatting to text, the Format→HTML Style menu offers a larger selection of styles. Don't be confused by the term "styles" here, which merely refers to different HTML tags. HTML styles are unrelated to CSS styles, and are intended to customize very specific types of text, like citations from a book or magazine, or programming code.

Bottom: As you can see, the style options usually include bold and italic fonts, your browser's monospaced font (usually Courier), or some combination of the three. But don't worry about how they look "out of the box"—you can make any of these tags appear any way you want by applying CSS, as you'll learn in the next chapter.

To use an HTML style, select the text, and then select a format from the Format→HTML Style menu. (You can also use the Properties panel to apply the <strong> or <em> tags to emphasize text by making it bold or italic.)

TIP   Use italics with care. While printed material uses it frequently to add *emphasis* or to reference a book title, it can be difficult to read on a computer screen, especially at small type sizes.

Unless you intend to use HTML tags that properly format your content, like using the Code style to display computer code, you're better off avoiding HTML styles.

TIP   The Teletype (<tt>) tag is truly, genuinely, absolutely, obsolete. When was the last time you used a Teletype machine? The tag has been removed from HTML5, so avoid it.

UP TO SPEED

When Bold and Italics Are Neither

You may be confused by the HTML Dreamweaver produces when you tell it to make text bold or italic. Instead of using the <b> tag—the original HTML code for bold—Dreamweaver uses the <strong> tag. And instead of using <i> for italic, clicking the Properties panel's I button gets you the <em> tag, the one for emphasis. That's because Adobe decided to follow industry practices rather than stick to an old tradition.

For most purposes, <strong> and <em> behave identically to <b> and <i>. The results look the same—bolded or italicized text—in most browsers. However, when screen readers (programs or equipment that read web pages aloud for the visually impaired) encounter these tags, the <strong> tag triggers a loud, strong voice. The <em> tag also brings an emphasis to the voice of screen readers, though with less timbre than the <strong> tag.

Since most browsers simply treat the <strong> tag like the <b> tag and the <em> tag like the <i> tag, you'll probably never notice the difference. However, if you prefer using the simple <b> and <i> tags, choose Edit→Preferences. Select the General category, and then turn off the checkbox labeled "Use <strong> and <em> in place of <b> and <i>."

HTML5 slightly redefines these tags. It rewrote the <i> tag for text in an "alternate voice," such as a foreign word, a technical term, or typographically italicized text such as a book title. You use the <b> tag just to make text look bold so that it stands out visually. Basically, imagine you're reading text out loud. If you encounter a word that you would emphasize with your voice ("For crying out loud," for example), use the <em> tag; if you'd shout the word ("Help!!!"), use the <strong> tag. If you simply want text to look a certain way, you can use the <i> or <b> tags, or, better yet, the CSS *font-weight* and *font-style* properties described on page 154.

You can read more about HTML5 and the <b>, <strong>, <i>, and <em> tags at *http://tinyurl.com/yau4mze*.

◼ Editing in Live View

Dreamweaver CC 2014 brings major changes to Live view, where you see your page just as it looks in a web browser. Live view lets you preview the page you're building right in the document window. And unlike Design view, Live view lets you see and run fancy features like animations, video, or interactive elements.

Live view eliminates a lot of jumping back and forth between Dreamweaver and a web browser. In earlier versions of Dreamweaver, Live view simply provided a preview. To actually edit your page, you had to go back to Design view or Code view. Now you can add new elements to a page in Live view, including text, graphics, and media. It's worth noting, though, that editing in Live view is still in the "gem in the rough" stage. It can be helpful for certain chores, like minor text edits and reordering major blocks of HTML on a page, but it's less helpful for detailed text editing and working with complex pages that have multiple columns and sections. Some processes, like moving a sentence from one place to another within a paragraph, take additional steps in Live view.

Element Quick View is a new tool that works hand in hand with Live view editing. It displays the HTML elements in your page in outline form. Using Element Quick View, you can drag elements to different positions in the outline, repositioning them on your web page. For more on Element Quick View, see page 353.

Old Dreamweaver pros are likely to continue their page building in Design view, because it's faster and provides more control. You may come to the same conclusion, but it's still worth checking out Live view editing. It's likely that Adobe will continue to refine this feature over time, and it's great to see your page just as your web visitors will.

Adding Text in Live View

As mentioned at the beginning of this chapter, working in Design view is similar to working with a word processor. You see a blank page and you start typing. Later on, you apply HTML tags to the text to provide structure to the page. Working in Live view reverses that process. First, you figure out what type of element you want to add to the page—a paragraph, for example. Then, using the Insert panel's Structure category, you add a paragraph to the page. Dreamweaver provides placeholder text. At that point, you start typing (or pasting) to change the text.

To get a feel for adding text in Live view, start with a blank page in Dreamweaver, and then follow these steps:

1. **In the upper-left corner of the document window, set the Design/Live drop-down menu (circled in Figure 2-15) to Live view.**

   The Document window changes from Design view to Live view, but because you still have just a blank page, you may not notice.

NOTE   If you're in Code view when you click the Live view button, the view automatically changes to Split view, with code showing in half the window and Live view appearing in the other half.

---

2. **Go to the Insert panel and then, using the drop-down menu, change the category to Structure (circled in Figure 2-14).**

The Structure category makes it easy to add elements to your document. As explained on page 11, Dreamweaver identifies the elements (paragraphs, headings, and lists) using words and icons.

FIGURE 2-14

To add content to your web page in Live view, use the Insert panel. Standard text elements like headings, paragraphs, and lists appear in the Structure category. Here, you're about to click the Paragraph option. Some options (like Heading) offer drop-down menus that provide variations on the element. To open those menus, click the triangle button.

3. **Click the Paragraph option in the middle of the list.**

Dreamweaver inserts a paragraph in your document, indicated by a blue rectangle with the placeholder text, "This is the content for Layout P Tag." Translation: Change these words to the words you actually want in the paragraph. Below the rectangle is a blue tab with the letter P in it. That tells you that this page element is a paragraph. To the right of the tab is a button with a plus (+) sign. You don't need to worry about it now, but you'll use that button later to apply CSS formatting to your paragraph (see page 352 for details).

4. **Double-click inside the blue rectangle and then select all the text by pressing Ctrl+A (⌘-A).**

Double-clicking opens the paragraph for editing and changes the blue rectangle to gold. When you press Ctrl+A (⌘-A), you select all the placeholder text. Once you start typing, your words replace the placeholder text.

5. **Type** *The food is tasty at Cafe Soylent Green. It reminds me of Mom's cooking.*

   Your new text replaces the placeholder text.

6. **Click outside the paragraph's gold rectangle.**

   The rectangle changes back to blue. You're no longer in editing mode. You have a page with a single paragraph in it. In the next step, you'll add a heading.

7. **On the Insert panel, in the Structure category, click the small triangular arrow in the Heading option. Then, from the resulting drop-down menu, choose H1.**

   The Heading option remembers the last heading style you used: H1, H2, H3, and so forth. To choose a different option, you need to open the menu by clicking the arrow. Then you can choose the style you want.

   After you choose H1, a panel like the one in Figure 2-15 pops up in the document window. Dreamweaver is asking where you want to place the heading—before or after the paragraph? (The other two options, Wrap and Next, don't apply here; they position elements that are inside other elements.)

FIGURE 2-15

In Live view (circled), when you insert a second structural element, Dreamweaver asks where you want to place it in relation to the currently selected element. The options are Before, After, Wrap, and Nest. The gray and white tags in the simple diagrams show the relationship between the currently selected element (dark gray) and the one you're adding (white with a + sign). The Wrap option makes the new element act as a container for the currently selected element. The Nest option places the new element inside the currently selected element.

8. **Click Before.**

   A new header appears above your paragraph with placeholder text that reads, "This is the content for Layout H1 Tag." You'll want to edit the text, just like you did for the paragraph.

9. **Double-click the heading placeholder text, press Ctrl+A (⌘-A), and then type** *Comments from Cafe Customers.*

   Your new header appears big and bold above the paragraph.

The easiest way to add a second paragraph in Live view is to double-click in the first paragraph. Place your cursor at the end of the text and then press Enter (Return). Your cursor moves to a new line, and the editing box expands. This makes it easy to type in several paragraphs without returning to the Insert panel. After you finish typing and click elsewhere on the page, you see two separate, blue paragraph boxes.

You can apply simple bold and italic formatting to individual characters in Live view. For example, suppose you want to italicize the word "tasty" from the previous example. Double-click the paragraph's text to open it for editing. When the rectangle changes from blue to gold, double-click the word "tasty" to select it. (In Live view, you can use the standard selection methods, described on page 83.) A menu pops up (Figure 2-16). Click the I button to italicize the text. If you want to make the text bold, click the B button. As explained on page 101, Dreamweaver places italicized text inside <em> tags and bold text inside <strong> tags.

After you italicize the word "tasty," the HTML code for your paragraph should look like this:

```
<p>The food is <em>tasty</em> at Cafe Soylent Green. It reminds me of Mom's
cooking.</p>
```

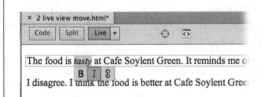

FIGURE 2-16

When you select text in Live view, this pop-up menu appears. Use it to apply bold (B) or italic (I) formatting to the selected characters. The Link button creates a hyperlink, which you'll learn about on page 177.

Moving and Removing Text in Live view

Suppose you want to move a heading below a certain paragraph when you're working in Live view. Click anywhere in the heading's text, and Dreamweaver displays a blue tab and a blue border around the heading. Double-check to make sure the tab displays "h1," for Heading 1, and then drag the headline to its new location on the page. You can drag the heading by the tab or by clicking inside the blue border and dragging. Using the same technique, you can reposition paragraphs, images, and other HTML elements on the page.

Deleting an element is just as easy. Click to select the element, and then press Delete. When you move or delete elements in Live view, you're working with the tags and the content inside those tags. So, when you delete a paragraph, you delete the words displayed on the page *and* the <p> tags that surround the paragraph.

If you want to move or delete specific words inside a paragraph or heading, you need to open it for editing. Double-click a paragraph, and the blue border changes to gold. Now you can select specific words within the paragraph. Press Delete to delete words or right-click (Control-click) to see a context menu with Cut, Copy, Paste, and Select All commands. Here's how you move text from one place to another inside a paragraph:

1. **Double-click the paragraph to open it for editing.**

2. **Select the text you want to move.**

3. **Right-click (Control-click) to display a context menu of commands, and then choose Cut to remove the text.**

4. **Position your cursor where you want to move the cut text.**

5. **Right-click (Control-click) to show the context menu, and then choose Paste to insert the text.**

That's a lot of clicking compared with the same operation in Design view, where you can just select and drag text to a new location.

Editing Pages with Element Quick View

As your pages become filled with lots of HTML elements, it becomes difficult to keep track of everything. Is this paragraph in the main body of the page or in a sidebar? How many paragraphs of text are in the footer? The Element Quick View, seen in Figure 2-17, shows you all the HTML elements of a page in outline view, making it easy to understand the relationship between page parts. To open the tool, choose View→Element Quick View or click </> in the Tag Selector (in the lower-left corner of the document window).

You can expand and collapse sections of the Element Quick View outline just as you would an outline in a word processor. Consider the paragraph you typed earlier:

```
<p> The food is <em>tasty</em> at Cafe Soylent Green. It reminds me of Mom's
cooking.</p>
```

The <em> tags that italicize the word "tasty" are nested inside the <p> tags for the paragraph. Element Quick View depicts that paragraph as a set of stacked tags, with the <p> tag on top. Click the tag stack, and it expands to show the nested <em> tags. Click again to collapse the section.

Using Element Quick View, you can reorder HTML elements and their content. Just drag the element from one place to another, as shown in Figure 2-17. For other editing chores, right-click (Control-click) a selected element to display a context menu with Delete, Duplicate, Copy, and Paste commands.

When you select an element in Element Quick View, you see the same element selected in Live view. These two tools work well together because they give you two ways to visualize your page. Live view is the literal view, showing you how your page looks to your visitors. Element Quick View is an abstract view of your page's HTML building blocks, uncluttered with all that pesky content. It's worth noting that you can use Element Quick View when you work in Design view, too, but you'll probably find it most helpful when you're in Live view.

Show/hide Element Quick View   Element Quick View

FIGURE 2-17

Top: Using the Element Quick View tool, you selected the <h2> tag (for Heading 2) and you're dragging it down below the two paragraphs on the page. A green line shows where in the page's set of elements the heading will appear when you release the mouse button.

Bottom: Here's the result of the move. The <h2> heading now appears below the two paragraphs in both the document window and Element Quick View.

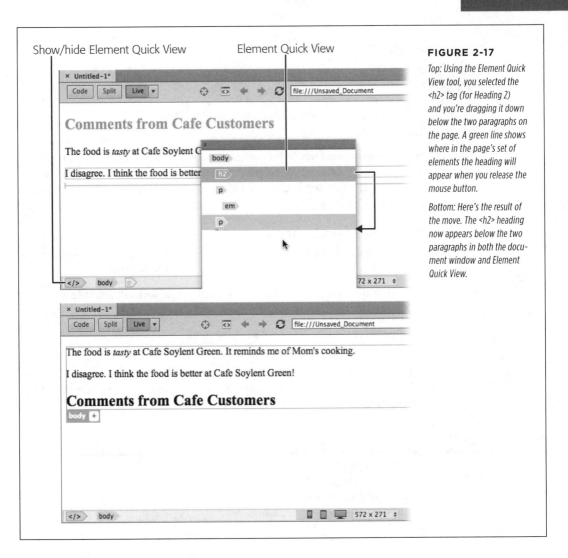

Checking Spelling

You spend a lot of time perfecting your web pages, making sure that the images look great, the text is properly formatted, and everything aligns for a beautiful visual presentation. But webmasters often forget one step, especially given the hyper-development of web content—making sure the text is free of typos.

Spelling mistakes look unprofessional and imply a lack of attention to detail. Who wants to hire an "illustraightor" or "web dezyner?" Dreamweaver's spell-checking feature can help.

About Dictionaries

Before you start spell checking, make sure you have the right *dictionary* selected. Dreamweaver comes with 47 of them, ranging from Bulgarian to Turkish (including four variants of English and four of German). When it checks your spelling, the program compares the text in your document against the list of words in one of these dictionaries.

To specify a dictionary, choose Edit→Preferences (Dreamweaver→Preferences) or press Ctrl+U (⌘-U) to open the Preferences dialog box. Select the General category and then, from the Spelling Dictionary drop-down menu at the bottom of the window, choose a language.

Performing a Spell Check

Once you select a dictionary, open the web page whose spelling you want to check. You can check as much or as little of the text as you like, as follows:

1. **Highlight the text you want to check (which can be even a single word).**

   To check the *entire* document, make sure you have nothing selected in the document window (one good way to do this is to click in the middle of a paragraph of text).

> **NOTE** Unfortunately, Dreamweaver doesn't offer a site-wide spell-checking feature. You must check each web page individually.

GEM IN THE ROUGH

Clean Up Word

In Microsoft Word, you can save any document as a web page, essentially turning it into an HTML page—except that Word produces hideous HTML. One look at it, and you'd think that your cat fell asleep on the keyboard.

Here's what happens: To let you reopen the document as a Word file when the time comes, Word injects reams of information that add to the file size of the page. This is a particular problem with the latest versions of Word, which adds loads of XML (page xxiii) and Cascading Style Sheet information.

Fortunately, Dreamweaver's Clean Up Word HTML command strips out most of that unnecessary code and produces leaner web pages. To use it, open the Word HTML file just as you would

any other web page, by choosing File→Open. Then choose Commands→Clean Up Word HTML.

The Clean Up Word HTML dialog box opens. Dreamweaver automatically detects which version of Word produced the HTML and then applies the appropriate rules.

Unfortunately, Dreamweaver doesn't always catch all the junk that Word throws in, so if you have the original Word document, you're better off just opening it, copying the contents, and pasting it into Dreamweaver. Then you can use Dreamweaver's tools for formatting the text so that it looks just the way you want it to, without any unnecessary code.

2. **Choose Commands→Check Spelling (Shift+F7).**

   The Check Spelling window opens (see Figure 2-18). If a word isn't in Dreamweaver's dictionary, it appears in the top box, along with a list of suggested spellings.

   The first suggestion is listed in the "Change to" field.

FIGURE 2-18

Dreamweaver's spell-checking feature checks only words in the document window. It can't check the spelling of comments, <alt> tags, or any text that appears in the head of a document, with the exception of the page's title. Nor can you spell check an entire website's worth of pages with a single command; you need to check each page individually.

3. **If the word in the "Change to" field is correct, click Change.**

   If Dreamweaver correctly flags a word as misspelled but the correct spelling isn't in the "Change to" box, double-click the correct spelling in the Suggestions list below it. If the correct spelling isn't *there*, type it into the "Change to" box yourself. Then click the Change button to correct this one instance, or click Change All to replace this misspelled word everywhere it appears in your document.

   Dreamweaver makes the change and moves on to the next questionable spelling.

4. **If the word is actually correctly spelled but not in Dreamweaver's dictionary, click Ignore, Ignore All, or Add to Personal.**

   If you want Dreamweaver to ignore this word *every* time it appears in the document, rather than in just this instance, click Ignore All.

   On the other hand, you'll probably use some words that Dreamweaver doesn't have in its dictionaries. You may, for instance, use a client's name throughout your pages. If that name isn't in Dreamweaver's dictionary, it consistently flags the name as a spelling error.

   To teach Dreamweaver the client's name, click Add to Personal. Dreamweaver adds the word to your personal dictionary, which Dreamweaver consults when it checks your spelling.

After you click Change, Ignore, or Add to Personal, Dreamweaver moves on to the next word it doesn't recognize. Begin again from step 3. If you didn't start the spell checker from the beginning of the document, then once Dreamweaver reaches the end, it asks if you want to continue spell checking from the beginning. Click Yes if you do.

5. **To finish the spell check, click Close.**

Introducing Cascading Style Sheets

I f you use garden-variety HTML tags like <h1>, <p>, and <ul> to style web pages, what you see onscreen pales in comparison to the styling on display in, say, a print magazine. If web designers had only HTML to make their sites look great, the Web would forever be the ugly duckling of the media world.

Fortunately for web designers, you can change the ho-hum appearance of HTML using the options you get with a formatting standard called Cascading Style Sheets (CSS). CSS gives you the tools you need to make HTML look beautiful. If you think of HTML as the basic structure of a house (the foundation, walls, and rooms), then CSS is the house's interior design (the paint; carpeting; and color, style, and placement of furniture).

CSS gives you much greater control over the layout and design of your pages than HTML does. Using CSS, you can improve the look of common web page elements like links, images, and tables. For example, you can add margins to paragraphs (just as in a word processor), colorful and stylish borders to images, and even dynamic rollover effects to text links. Dreamweaver's CSS Designer tool makes it fast and easy to create styles and then store them in a central style sheet that controls the look of all the pages in your site.

CSS is a big topic. It's also the heart of today's cutting-edge web design. So instead of dedicating just a single chapter to it, this book provides instructions in nearly every chapter. In this chapter, you'll learn the basics of CSS and how to use Dreamweaver's powerful CSS tools—with an emphasis on the program's new CSS Designer feature. You'll also learn to expand your font library using new web fonts.

Once you're comfortable with the basics, you'll find in-depth information on CSS in Chapter 9. In Chapter 10, you'll learn how to harness the power of CSS to fully control the layout (not just the style) of a web page. And in Chapter 11, you'll learn how to troubleshoot CSS problems.

◼ Cascading Style Sheet Basics

If you've formatted text in programs like Microsoft Word or Adobe InDesign, styling pages with CSS will feel familiar. A *style* is simply a rule describing how a browser should display a particular element on a web page, like a heading or an image. A *style sheet* is a collection of these rules.

For example, you might create a style that formats text in the Arial font with red letters and a left margin of 50 pixels. Or a style that aligns images along the right edge of a web page, adds a colorful border, and includes a 50-pixel margin between the image and the surrounding text.

Once you create a style, you can apply it to text, images, or other elements on a page. For example, you could select a paragraph and instantly change the text's size, color, and font just by applying a style.

Why Use CSS?

When designers styled web pages in the past, HTML alone provided the formatting options for text, images, tables, and other page elements. Today, professional web designers use CSS to style their pages.

NOTE The World Wide Web Consortium, the organization that defines Web standards, has phased out older HTML tags used to format text and other page elements in favor of CSS. Following industry practice, Dreamweaver CC has made it impossible to add these obsolete tags, such as the <font> tag (unless you write the code yourself).

CSS has many benefits over HTML. With it, you can format paragraphs to look as fancy as those that appear in a book or newspaper (with the first line indented and no space between paragraphs, for example), and control the leading (the space between lines of text in a paragraph). When you use CSS to add a background image to a page, you get to decide whether and how it tiles (repeats). HTML can't even begin to do any of these things.

Style sheets also make it easy to update your site. You can collect all your styles into a single style sheet and link it to every page on your site. When it's time to change every Heading 2 tag (<h2>) to lime green, you edit the style in the style sheet, and that change ripples throughout your site, *wherever* you used that style. You can completely change the appearance of a site simply by editing a single style sheet.

Getting to Know (and Love) CSS

Cascading Style Sheets are an exciting—and complex—addition to your web-building toolkit, worthy of entire books and websites by themselves. Here are some resources:

- For an excellent tutorial on CSS, visit W3 Schools' CSS tutorials at *http://www.w3schools.com/css/*.

- Sitepoint (*www.sitepoint.com*) provides articles on many topics, with an entire section devoted to CSS. You'll find stories on best practices for creating navigation menus, for positioning photos, and many other topics.

- If you want to get help *and* learn more about CSS, the Sitepoint CSS Forums (*http://tinyurl.com/cmeaubn*) are always busy with advice from a great community of CSS enthusiasts.

- Sitepoint also provides a great CSS reference at *http://reference.sitepoint.com/css*. It's a dictionary-like resource

of all CSS properties, and includes information on which browsers support which properties.

- For the ultimate authority on CSS, turn to the World Wide Web Consortium's website at *www.w3.org/Style/CSS*. The W3C is the body responsible for many of the standards that drive the Web—including HTML and CSS. (Beware: This site reads like a college physics textbook.)

- For a great list of CSS-related sites, visit the Information and Technology Systems and Services website at the University of Minnesota, Duluth (*http://tinyurl.com/jg2fe*).

- If you just love to curl up by the fireplace with a good tech book, try *CSS3: The Missing Manual* by David Sawyer McFarland (hey, that name rings a bell!). It's written in the same style as this book, with in-depth coverage of CSS and step-by-step tutorials on every facet of this complicated technology.

Internal vs. External Style Sheets

As you create new styles, you'll add them to a style sheet you store either in the web page itself (in which case it's called an *internal style sheet*) or in a separate file called an *external style sheet*.

NOTE There's actually a third place where CSS styles can appear: within the HTML code itself. These are called *inline styles*, but don't confuse them with internal style sheets. Inline styles are out of fashion because they mix page formatting (CSS) with page content (HTML). For details, see the box on page 115.

In Dreamweaver, the most common use of inline styles is as a temporary style that you quickly convert to an internal or external style sheet, as described on page 51.

Internal style sheets appear in the <head> portion of a web page and contain styles that apply to that page only. You use internal style sheets when you want a very specific format for a single web page. For example, the marketing department might ask you to create a one-page flyer with a unique format and its own distinctive look, the perfect use of an internal style sheet.

TIP As you design a new web page, it's often easier to add styles to an internal style sheet. Then, once you're satisfied with the design, you can export the styles to an external style sheet—for use by all your site's pages. See page 409 for details.

An external style sheet, on the other hand, contains only styles—no HTML—and you can link numerous pages to it. In fact, you can link every page on your site to it, giving your site a uniform look site-wide. For instance, you can put a headline style in an external style sheet and link every page on the site to that sheet. Every headline on every page then shares the same look—instant design consistency! Even better, when the boss (or the interior decorator in you) calls up and asks you to change the color of the headlines, you need to edit only a single file—the external style sheet—to update hundreds or even thousands of web pages.

You can easily create both types of style sheet in Dreamweaver, and you aren't limited to choosing one or the other. A single web page can have both an external style sheet (for styles that apply to the whole site) and an internal style sheet (for styles that apply to just that page). You can even attach multiple external style sheets to a single page.

Types of Styles

CSS styles come in several flavors, the three most common being *class*, *ID*, and *tag* styles. Dreamweaver's CSS Designer tool, which helps you create CSS rules, calls all these style types "selectors" because you use them to select and format specific elements on a page.

A class style is one you create, name, and attach to an HTML tag or to selected text (in other words, text you select with your cursor). Class styles work much like styles in word processing and page layout programs. To display the name of your company in bold and red wherever it appears on a web page, for example, you can create a class style named *.company* that formats text in boldface with red letters. You'd then highlight your company's name on the page and apply this style to it.

An ID style lets you format a *unique* item on a page. You use ID styles to identify an object (or an area of a page) that appears only once—like a website's logo, copyright notice, or main navigation bar. An ID style is similar to a class style in that you name the style and then apply it to a page element. But while you can apply a class to many different elements on a page, you can apply an ID to only a *single* element per page. (It's OK to use multiple IDs on a single page, as long as each ID is different.) ID styles aren't as popular as they once were—partly because you can only use the ID (and thus the style) once per page, but mostly because ID styles pose problems when your site's styles grow more complex and your style sheets longer. You'll learn the details on page 413, but for now, keep in mind that class styles can do anything ID styles can, and you'll use class and tag styles (discussed next) more frequently than ID styles in this book.

The other major type of CSS style is called a tag style, and it formats a specific HTML tag globally, as opposed to styling individual paragraphs or text selections. Suppose you want to display every level-1 heading on your site in the Arial font. Instead of creating a class style and applying it to every <h1> tag on a page, you could create a style for the <h1> tag, in effect redefining it so that browsers display all level-1 headlines in Arial.

Inline Styles vs. Internal Style Sheets

What's the difference between an inline style and an internal style sheet?

An *inline style* is attached directly to an HTML tag, and it formats the page element associated with that tag. Inline styles have no "style sheets"—you place them right within the HTML of a page—and include the HTML tag you're styling. For example, if you format a paragraph with an inline style that turns the text red, this is what the HTML would look like:

```
<p style="color: #FF0000">This paragraph
is really, really red!</p>
```

This inline style affects this particular paragraph only. You don't need to specify a "selector" (that is, a target for the style) because you just tacked the formatting command onto the paragraph tag. With no selector (in other words, without a target for the style), you can't attach this "style" to any other paragraph.

Internal style sheets, on the other hand, are legitimate style sheets. You store them in the <head> section of a web page. They use selectors to identify elements on a web page, so you can apply a single style to multiple elements using the same selector. When a web page uses an internal style sheet, you're likely to find more than one CSS rule stored there. Here's an example of an internal style sheet that has two rules:

```
<style type="text/css">
h1 {
```

```
    color: #CC9900;
    font-family: Baskerville, "Palatino
Linotype", Palatino, "Century Schoolbook
L", "Times New Roman", serif;
}
.copyright {
    font-size: 12px;
    border-top: 1px solid #CC9900;
    padding-top: 5px;
}
</style>
```

This internal style sheet has rules for the <h1> heading, and it creates a style for text tagged with the class selector "copyright" (see page 117 for more on class selectors). These rules appear inside opening and closing <style> tags, and the entire sheet gets stored in the <head> section of the web page.

The best practice these days is to separate formatting from content, so most designers don't use inline styles. If you perform all your CSS chores in CSS Designer, it's unlikely that you'll ever create an inline style. Designer doesn't create or edit inline styles. If you use the Properties panel's CSS mode, you can create inline styles, and you may occasionally create an inline style and then convert it to a class that you store in an internal or external style sheet. That process is described on page 51.

The main benefit to redefining a tag this way is convenience—you don't have to go into your site's pages, find every <h1> tag, and then apply the style by hand. The Heading 1 style you create says that *all* <h1> tags must use the Arial font, so a browser displays all <h1> tags in Arial. Styling tags globally like this is the easiest way to format a page.

Nevertheless, sometimes only a class style will do, such as when you want to format just a few words in a paragraph. Simply redefining the <p> tag won't do the trick, since that would affect the entire paragraph (and every other paragraph on your site). Instead, you have to create a class style and apply it to just the words you wish to style. In addition, class styles are handy when you want to format just one instance of a tag differently from others. For example, if you want to format the introductory paragraph on a page one way and all the other paragraphs a different way, for example, you create a class style and apply it to that first paragraph. (Another solution is a slightly more complicated, but more flexible, type of style called a *descendent selector*—you'll read about those on page 398.)

NOTE In addition to class, ID, and tag styles, other types of styles provide added control for particular situations. You'll read about these more advanced styles on page 395.

Creating Styles

Dreamweaver has a special tool to help you create and manage styles: CSS Designer, shown in Figure 3-1. Replacing an earlier patchwork of panels, palettes, and menus, CSS Designer puts everything you need to build and manage styles in one convenient, well-organized location. Learn how to use the Designer's system of *sources*, *selectors*, and *properties*, and you'll master all your CSS chores. (Dreamweaver still provides some of the old tools for specific tasks and for pros reluctant to learn new ways.)

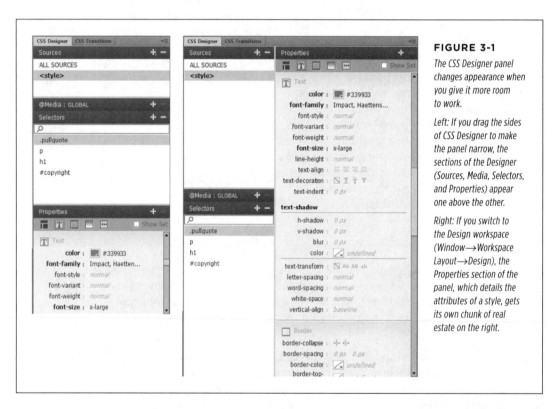

FIGURE 3-1

The CSS Designer panel changes appearance when you give it more room to work.

Left: If you drag the sides of CSS Designer to make the panel narrow, the sections of the Designer (Sources, Media, Selectors, and Properties) appear one above the other.

Right: If you switch to the Design workspace (Window→Workspace Layout→Design), the Properties section of the panel, which details the attributes of a style, gets its own chunk of real estate on the right.

In this section, you'll tour CSS Designer and learn how to create new styles. In a later section, on page 124, you'll look at the Properties panel's CSS mode, another place you can create and modify styles.

TIP If you've used earlier versions of Dreamweaver, you may groan when you hear there's a new way to create CSS rules. Why learn yet another way to work through the maze of CSS styles? The answer is that you'll probably find the new system faster and more logical. Adobe added earlier CSS tools to Dreamweaver piecemeal over the years. It designed this new system from the ground up, reflecting the way designers use CSS today. If you already have experience with CSS, it won't take long to get a handle on CSS Designer.

Creating New Styles with CSS Designer

Dreamweaver divides the CSS Designer panel into four sections: Sources, Media, Selectors, and Properties. (If you don't see the panel, press Shift+F11 [Windows only] or go to Window→CSS Designer.) In Dreamweaver's stock Design workspace, the panel appears on the right, sharing space with the Files, Assets, Insert, and Snippets panels. You can also display CSS Designer by clicking the CSS Designer tab. Its appearance changes slightly depending on the workspace you choose (Figure 3-1).

In most cases, creating a new style is a three-step process, all of which you accomplish in the Designer panel, moving from one section to another. Here's a rough outline of the procedure:

1. **Choose a source for your style rule. (The "source" here refers to the file your pages will consult for style rules.)** You add styles to an internal or an external style sheet, or you create a new style sheet.

2. **Choose a selector.** A selector is the target of a style rule. It can be a class, an ID, or an HTML tag. You can modify existing selectors using CSS Designer, or you can create new ones.

3. **Set the selector's properties.** After you choose a selector in step 2, you can set or change its properties—also known as creating a rule or editing one, respectively. For example, you can set text properties by choosing a *font-family* (Arial), *font-color* (green), and *font-size* (large).

NOTE There are four sections in CSS Designer: Sources, Media, Selectors, and Properties. This part of the book doesn't cover the Media options, which you use to create media queries. Media queries determine what type of device (computer, phone, or tablet) your guest uses to view your web pages. Knowing that, you can use CSS to format your content so that it looks great no matter what the device. Media queries are covered on page 523.

There are dozens of CSS properties. Using class, ID, and tag selectors, you can apply these properties to text, images, videos, or some arbitrary group of elements you define using HTML's versatile <div> tag (page 454). Naturally, certain properties don't apply to all elements. For example, images have no use for a *font-weight* property. Still, CSS Designer gives you access to all the styles and a consistent way to apply them. You don't have to memorize the style names or exactly the right way to define their properties. You point, click, and type in the Designer, and then Dreamweaver writes the code in your web page (for internal style sheets) or in a separate CSS document (for external style sheets).

Anatomy of a Style

When you style a page, Dreamweaver automatically writes the proper code. But if you want to impress your neighbors, here's the behind-the-scenes scoop on how that works.

When you create an internal style sheet, Dreamweaver adds a pair of <style> tags to the head of the page. The opening <style> tag tells a browser that the following information isn't HTML—it's CSS code. When the browser encounters the closing </style> tag, it knows that it's at the end of the style definition.

Within that <style> tag, you see one or more styles (reminder: in CSS-speak, styles are also called rules). An HTML tag style for the Heading 1 tag (<h1>), for example, might look like this:

```
h1 {
    font-size: 24px;
    color: #003399;
}
```

The first part—<h1>—is called a *selector*, and it identifies the style's target, a level-1 heading. Browsers apply the Heading 1 style specified above wherever they find an <h1> tag in a web page's code.

The information between the braces—{}—defines the formatting that browsers should apply. The preceding code contains two formatting instructions for the <h1> tag. Each is called a *declaration* and is composed of a *property* and a *value*. For instance, *font-size: 24px* is one declaration, which has a property of *font-size* and a value of *24px*. In other words, this rule

tells a browser that it should make the text inside an <h1> tag 24 pixels tall. The second declaration makes a browser display the text of all <h1> tags in royal blue (whose hex color code is #003399; see page 151 for more on hex codes).

A class style looks just like a tag style, except that instead of the selector being a tag, it's a name *you* supply, preceded by a dot, like this:

```
.company {
    font-size: 24px;
    color: #003399;
}
```

Styles in an external style sheet look exactly the same; the only difference is that external style sheets are separate files whose names end in .css, don't include the <style> tags, and must not include any HTML. You link an external style sheet to a web page using the <link> tag. For example, to link a style sheet named *styles.css* to a web page, you could add this HTML to the <head> section of the page:

```
<link href="styles.css" rel="stylesheet"
type="text/css">
```

In Dreamweaver, you can easily get a look at the style definitions in an external style sheet: Near the top of the document window, in the list of related files, click the CSS file's name (Figure 1-5).

TIP In CSS Designer, to enlarge or reduce the size of a section, position your cursor along the top border of the section (just above the section's name) until the arrow cursor turns into a resize cursor (two parallel lines with arrows at either end), and then drag up or down.

Here's a closer look at each of the steps you take to create a new CSS style.

Choose a Style Source

When you create a style in CSS Designer (Window→CSS Designer), you have to decide where that style will reside—as part of your web page or as an external style sheet. Go to the Sources section of CSS Designer and click ＋ on the right (Figure 3-2, top). The Add CSS Source menu opens, offering three options:

- **Create A New CSS File**. This opens a window where you can create a new, external style sheet. Style sheets contain only CSS formatting rules; they don't include any page content. You're likely to use this option when you build a website and want consistent formatting across many pages. Here's the scenario: You build pages with the usual HTML tags, like <p>, <h1>, and <h2>. Perhaps you create some classes, like *.copyright* or *.pullquote*, to handle special formatting. Then you define the style for those tags and classes in your external style sheet. A single line of code at the top of your web page identifies the relevant style sheet.

- **Attach Existing CSS File**. If you created a style sheet earlier (say in step 1 above) and you want to apply the styles it defines to the current page, select this option. You can also create a new CSS rule and store it in an attached style sheet—just keep in mind that styles you add to an existing sheet may affect other pages in your site.

  You can attach more than one external style sheet to a web page. For example, suppose your site includes several "glossary" pages with definitions. You might create an additional style sheet to format just those pages.

- **Define in Page**. This option stores a CSS style internally, in the same page where you specify the style. This method has both limitations and advantages. On one hand, if you store styles within a page, you won't be able to apply them to other pages. On the other hand, styles defined in a page can override styles applied through an external style sheet, which can come in handy. Suppose you have a website of several pages, and it uses an external style sheet called *soylent_styles.css*. You want to change the Heading 1 style for just one of your pages, so you apply the *soylent_styles.css* to that page and then use an internal style sheet to create a new definition for the <h1> heading. Web browsers will see both <h1> definitions, but they'll use the one in the internal style sheet because internal styles take precedence over external styles.

After telling CSS Designer where to find your style, the style sheet's name appears in the Sources panel (Figure 3-2, bottom). For some projects, you may see an extensive list of sources, because a single page can use several style sheets (including internal style sheets, listed as <style> in the Sources section).

The next step in creating a style is to choose the style's target, known as a Selector in CSS-speak. That's up next.

TIP　If you don't see any white space below the dark-gray Sources bar, the section is collapsed. You collapse and expand sections by clicking the dark-gray bars.

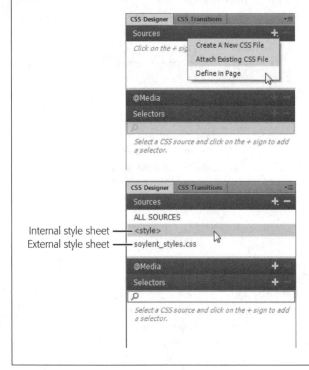

FIGURE 3-2

Top: In the Sources section of CSS Designer, click the + button to add a new style sheet.

Bottom: After you add a style sheet, Dreamweaver lists it in the Sources section. Here, <style> designates an internal style sheet, while soylent_styles.css is an external style sheet.

Choose a Selector

Selectors target specific elements in web pages. They include HTML tags like the paragraph (<p>) and Heading 1 (<h1>) tags, or you can selectively style page elements by creating class selectors. For example, you may want to create a *.copyright* class to format the copyright notice at the bottom of a page, or you may create a *.caption* class to set photo captions off from body text. Web designers use another selector, ID, less frequently because it's less flexible; you can apply an ID selector to only a single element on a page.

To see the selectors you identified in a set of CSS rules, click the source of those rules in (where else?) the Sources section of CSS Designer. To see all the selectors applied to a page, choose All Sources in the Sources section.

To create a brand-spanking-new selector, follow these steps:

1. **In the Sources section of CSS Designer, tell Dreamweaver where you want to put the new selector and its related styles.**

   To add a selector to an existing style sheet, whether internal or external, click the name of the style sheet in the Sources list (Dreamweaver lists internal style sheets as "<style>"). If the source doesn't exist, create it by following the steps on page 118.

2. **In the Selectors section, click the Add Selector button, + .**

   Dreamweaver positions your cursor in a text box at the bottom of the list of selectors. Type in a name for the selector. (If the + sign is grayed out, you probably haven't selected a valid source.)

   If you selected All Sources in step 1, the + sign isn't active because you need to identify a single, specific destination for your new style. Otherwise, CSS Designer won't know where to store the rule.

3. **Type in a name for your selector.**

   HTML tags are predefined, so you don't need to rename a selector to style tags. If you create a class selector, remember to add a period to the beginning of the class name; .caption and .pullquote are both valid class names, for example. In naming ID selectors, always precede the name with a pound sign (#); #copyright is a valid ID name, for instance.

   For both class and ID selectors, the character immediately following the period or pound sign must be a letter. After that, you can use any combination of letters, numbers, underscore characters, and hyphens you want. If you don't start typing a period or a pound sign when you name your selector, Dreamweaver displays a list of valid HTML tags as you type. You can continue typing or choose one of the tags.

■ TAG HINTS

Dreamweaver is ready to help when it comes to naming tags. In Design view, put your cursor in a block of text before you click + , and Dreamweaver displays the HTML tag applied to that block. It's a little confusing, though, because CSS Designer always suggests a *compound selector* as the tag. A compound selector is a selector within another selector. In this case, the compound selector targets a paragraph (<p>) within the body (<body>) of your HTML document. In other words, the <p> tag resides within the <body> tag. That's why Dreamweaver suggests *body p* as the selector, though you don't have to accept that. You can use *p* (the paragraph tag) only as your selector—just delete *body* from the suggestion. Compound selectors are key to the "cascading" behavior of Cascading Style Sheets. You'll find more details on page 412.

Set Properties for the Selector

Once you choose a selector, you need to specify the rules that format the content associated with that selector. You do that by setting values for the selector's properties. In CSS Designer, when you highlight a selector in the Selectors section, Dreamweaver displays its properties in the Properties section. Scroll down the list of properties to see just how extensive they are. You can easily read the property names, but most of their values are grayed out, which means you haven't set a value for the property yet. In other words, there's no rule defining the style for that property. To create a rule, you simply provide a value for the property. Dreamweaver does its best to make it easy—just highlight one of the grayed-out property values, and Dreamweaver displays a pop-up menu, a color picker, or some other widget that helps you set the value.

Say you want to set the color for the text in a paragraph. Before you create a rule to do that, you need to choose a source (the place where you'll store the rule) and a selector—the class, ID, or HTML tag you want to apply the style to. In this example, you'll style a paragraph and store its rule in an external style sheet called *soylent_styles.css*:

1. **In the Sources section of CSS Designer, click + . Then, from the drop-down menu, select "Create a New CSS Style."**

    The "Create a New CSS Style" dialog box opens.

2. **Type *soylent_styles.css* in the File/URL box, leave the Link radio button selected, and then click OK. (For details on the Conditional Usage field, also known as media queries, see page 523.)**

3. **In the Selectors section, click + to add a new selector, and then, in the selector text box that appears, type *p*.**

    When you press *p*, Dreamweaver displays a list of matching HTML tags in case you can't remember the tag name or you want to save a few keystrokes by choosing a name from the list. After you specify the tag, Dreamweaver displays a list of properties relevant to that tag in the Properties section.

4. **At the top of the Properties section, click the T (for "text") button.**

    Dreamweaver automatically scrolls to the list of text properties. It displays style rules in two parts:

    `name : value`

    The colon separating the name from the value is part of the rule, as you'll see when you inspect a CSS style sheet (page 123). The box on page 118 gives you more detail on CSS's two-part naming system.

    The first property Dreamweaver lists is *color*. It displays a color swatch next to the property, with a red line drawn through it and the word "undefined" beside it. Both the property and its value are grayed out because you haven't set a value for either yet.

TIP There are so many CSS properties that Dreamweaver organizes them in categories and provides relevant buttons at the top of the Properties section (see Figure 3-3). From left to right, the categories are Layout, Text, Border, Background, and Custom.

---

5. Click the color swatch and then choose a color from the color picker.

When the color picker opens, you dial in a color using the three sliders on the right (see Figure 3-3). They control the hue, lightness/darkness, and transparency of a color. Your chosen color appears inside the ring in the large square. You adjust the color by dragging the ring to a different spot. There are two smaller squares in the upper-left corner of the color picker. The square on the left shows the new color you're specifying; the one on the right shows the original color. If you see the exact color you want already on the web page or anywhere else on your computer screen, click the eyedropper in the lower-right corner. Then click on the color you want. That loads the color value into the color picker.

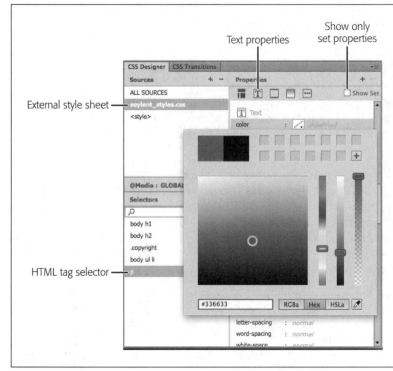

FIGURE 3-3

You're about to define a CSS style that will apply to all <p> (paragraph) tags. Dreamweaver will store the rule for the <p> tag in the external style sheet soylent_styles. css. As you define a style, you give different properties, like the text Color property illustrated here, different values. Dreamweaver helps you out with relevant tools. For example, when you want to set a color value, as above, Dreamweaver opens the color picker for you. If you want to see only properties that have their values already set (a fast way to review the styles you're using), turn on the Show Set checkbox in the upper-right corner.

When you're happy with your color, press Enter. Dreamweaver closes the color picker and writes the CSS rule for your style. So, if you inspect the innards of *soylent_styles.css*, you see this as the style for paragraphs:

```
p {
    color: #336633;
}
```

You can create multiple rules for a single selector. So, in the case of the paragraph tag, you may want to continue to define the style by choosing values for *font-family*, *font-size*, and *font-weight*. Each time you set a value, Dreamweaver writes the CSS for it in the style sheet.

The real trick to defining styles is mastering all the properties available to each style, such as borders, margins, and background colors, and *then* applying them so they work reliably in different browsers. Keep in mind that it's not necessary to define every property for a selector—just focus on the ones that are important to your page.

> **TIP** To move your CSS rules from an internal style sheet to an external style sheet, switch to Code view in the document window. Then in the <head> of your page, click inside a single rule you want to move or drag to select multiple rules. (A rule includes the selector and the properties in the curly brackets.) Choose Format→CSS Styles→Move CSS Rules. In the Move To External Style Sheet dialog box, browse to an existing style sheet. (If you haven't created an external style sheet, click the "A new style sheet" button.) Dreamweaver includes many tools for managing your style sheets; you'll learn about them on page 135.

Creating Styles Using the Properties Panel

Most of the time, you'll create new styles using CSS Designer. But you can do some of the same chores from the CSS mode of the Properties panel. (If you've used Dreamweaver in the past, the Properties panel's CSS mode and dialog boxes will be familiar, but some of the procedures, especially for creating new styles, have changed.)

Creating a new style in the Properties panel is more complex than doing so in CSS Designer because you need to wade through more dialog boxes to get the same results. But the idea is the same: First, you highlight the page element you want to style. Then you select (or create) an internal or external style sheet (the Source), choose a selector (a class, ID, or tag), and write the rule. That creates an inline style you can convert into an external CSS rule by selecting the text of the inline rule and then choosing Format→CSS Styles→"Convert Inline CSS to Rule."

> **NOTE** Keep in mind that the Properties *panel*, which resides under the document window, is a different beast from the Properties *section* of the CSS Designer panel. You can use both to work with CSS styles, but the techniques are entirely different.

For example, here's how you style an <h1> heading from the Properties panel:

1. **If the Properties panel isn't visible, go to Window→Properties.**

   The Properties panel is an indispensable tool, so you want to keep it visible almost all the time. If you're highlighting text (as opposed to an image or table), you see two buttons on the far left of the panel: HTML and CSS. (If you *are* working with an image or table, Dreamweaver doesn't display the CSS button, so you need to turn to CSS Designer for formatting chores; see page 116 for the details.)

2. **Click the CSS button.**

   The Properties panel changes to CSS mode.

3. **Triple-click within an <h1> heading.**

Triple-clicking within a paragraph selects the entire paragraph; in this case, that paragraph is a heading.

4. **In the Properties panel, click the color box and then choose a dark green.**

You could format several other properties from this panel, including the font, size, or alignment of the text you selected. And you can change more than one property at a time.

Once you choose a color, the Targeted Rule field displays <inline style>. As explained on page 115, Dreamweaver doesn't store inline styles in a style sheet (internal or external), and they don't have a selector. They're formatting instructions attached to HTML tags in the body of the page.

5. **From Dreamweaver's menu bar, choose Format→CSS Styles→"Convert Inline CSS to Rule."**

Dreamweaver displays the Convert Inline CSS window (Figure 3-4) so you can choose a selector and a source for your new rule. It also removes the inline style from the body of your document.

6. **Choose "All h1 tags" from the "Convert to" menu.**

Since you highlighted an <h1> page element, Dreamweaver assumes you want to style <h1> tags, so it automatically suggests <h1> as the selector (Figure 3-4). If you wanted to create a *class* selector, you'd choose the first option, "A new CSS class," and then name the class.

7. **In the "Create rule in" section, choose "The head of this document."**

This option creates an internal style sheet within the <head> section of the current document. Choose "Style sheet" to store your style in an external style sheet, and then click the Browse button to select or create the sheet.

8. **Click OK.**

When you click OK, Dreamweaver creates a style rule and writes the code that defines the style for <h1> tags.

FIGURE 3-4

To convert inline CSS formatting to a CSS rule, use this dialog box to identify the selector and source.

■ CREATING STYLES FOR NON-TEXT ELEMENTS

To style non-text elements using the Properties panel, the process is a little different. When you select an object like an image or table, Dreamweaver doesn't display the CSS button in the Properties panel. To create the style, right-click (Control-click) the selected element and then choose CSS Styles→New. The New CSS Rule dialog box opens, which you use to choose a selector and identify a source. You'll see four options under the Selector Type menu, but they really are just the usual selector suspects, described back on page 120:

- Class (can apply to any HTML element)

- ID (applies to only one HTML element)

- Tag (redefines an HTML element)

- Compound (based on your selection)

A compound selector, like the *body p* selector you learned about on page 121, targets a page element that sits inside another page element. (Find out more about compound selectors on page 395.)

Under Selector Name, type in a name. Precede class names with a period (.) and ID names with a pound sign (#). Tags don't have a preceding character.

By their nature, compound selectors comprise more than one selector. For example, a compound selector for an image might be *body p img*. In other words, you're targeting an image inside a paragraph, which is inside the body of the document.

At the bottom of the New CSS Rule box, use the Rule Definition menu to choose a source. These are your options:

- **This document only.** Choose this to create an internal style sheet.

- **New Style Sheet File.** Choose this to create a new external style sheet.

If you previously attached a style sheet to the page, Dreamweaver displays its name in the menu, too. Choose it to store your new style in that sheet.

After you click OK, a second window opens, where you specify the CSS rules for the style. This "CSS Rule definition for…" dialog box (Figure 3-5) is familiar to Dreamweaver veterans. Before CSS Designer, this was the tool you used to create CSS rules. The box identifies your selector at the top of the window. It says "CSS Rule definition for *selector*," where *selector* is the name of your class, ID, or tag. Dreamweaver groups the dozens of CSS properties into categories like Type, Background, and Border. To set the properties for one of the categories, click the category name on the left side of the dialog box.

The last step for creating a CSS rule in the Properties panel is similar to creating rules in CSS Designer. Use the menus, text boxes, number boxes, and color pickers to set values for properties. You can set several properties at once, and you can switch from one category's properties to another's. When you're done, click OK, and Dreamweaver writes the code and stores it in the source you identified earlier.

FIGURE 3-5

*The CSS Rule Definition
dialog box displays the same
CSS property names and values
as CSS Designer. Click a category
name to see its properties. As
you change properties, click the
Apply button to see their effect
on the page. When you're done,
click OK to apply all the property
changes and close the window.*

NOTE The CSS Rule Definition dialog box displays most of the same properties as CSS Designer, but it groups those properties into different categories, with different category names. This alone may force you to choose a single tool (CSS Designer or the Properties panel) for creating styles.

Applying Styles

If you're formatting a tag, once you create the tag style, your work is done. Browsers automatically apply that style to the appropriate tag on the page. If you create a <p> style, for example, anything in your document with the <p> tag applied to it has the style you just created.

When you create styles for class or ID selectors, however, you need to take an extra step: You must assign the class or ID to the tag you want to format.

You can apply class styles to any selection in the document window, whether it's a word, an image, or an entire paragraph. In fact, you can apply a class style to *any* individual HTML tag, such as a <p>, <td> (table cell), or <body>. You can even select just a single word within a paragraph and apply a style to *it*.

Applying a Class Style to Text

After you create a class and its style rules using the steps on page 124, you can assign that class (and its formatting) to elements in your document. For example, to style text using a class selector, start by selecting the words you want to format in the document window. Then, from the Properties panel, select the class you previously created—you can do this either in HTML mode, in which case you select the name from the Class drop-down menu (Figure 3-6, top), or in CSS mode, where you use the Targeted Rule menu (Figure 3-6, bottom).

FIGURE 3-6

The easiest way to apply a class style is through the Properties panel. When you select a non-text element, like an image or a table, a Class menu appears in the top right of the panel. For text, you apply class styles using the Class menu if the Properties panel is in HTML mode (top) or the Targeted Rule menu when it's in CSS mode (bottom). Dreamweaver uses only the bottom section of the Targeted Rule menu (the stuff below "Apply Class") to add or remove a class style from a selection of text. The other options let you create new styles or view the styles that apply to the selection.

To style an entire paragraph or heading, click within the paragraph or heading, and then use the Properties panel to select the class. When you use this method, don't inadvertently highlight a piece of text, or Dreamweaver applies the style to just that selected text, not the entire paragraph. When you style a paragraph, you're actually telling Dreamweaver to apply the style to an individual <p> tag. To accomplish that, Dreamweaver adds a special *class* property to the paragraph. Suppose you defined a class named *.company*. After you apply the class to the paragraph, its tag looks like this:

```
<p class="company">
```

■ APPLYING A CLASS STYLE IN LIVE VIEW

New in Dreamweaver CC 2014 is the ability to add class and ID styling to headlines, paragraphs, and other elements in Live view. Click an element, and Dreamweaver displays a border around it, along with a tab that identifies the HTML tag applied to it—for example "p" for a paragraph tag or "h1" for a heading. As part of that tag, you see a + button. Click it to open a text box where you type in the class or ID name you want to apply to the element. Don't forget to precede class names with a period (.) and IDs with a pound sign (#).

If the element you selected in Live view already has a class assigned to it, you see its name as part of the tab. That doesn't mean you can't apply another class. Just click the + button and then type in the name. When you're done, you'll see both classes listed in the element's tab.

■ APPLYING A CLASS STYLE TO OBJECTS

To apply a class style to an object (like an image or a table), start by selecting the object. As always, the Tag Selector at the bottom of the document window is a great way to select a tag. Then, at the top of the Properties panel, use the Class drop-down menu to select the style name.

> **NOTE**   You can apply any class style to any element, although doing so doesn't always make sense. For example, if you format a graphic with a style that specifies bold, red, Courier type, the image doesn't look any different.

■ OTHER CLASS STYLING OPTIONS

You can also apply a class style by selecting whatever element you want to style, choosing Format→CSS Styles, and then, from the drop-down menu, selecting the style. Or you can right-click (Control-click) an element in the document window and choose CSS Styles from the shortcut menu. From there, you can assign an existing class; create a new class, ID, or tag style; or apply multiple classes (covered in the next section) to a page element. Choose the option you want from the submenu.

Finally, you can apply a class from the document window's Tag Selector, as shown in Figure 3-7.

Applying Multiple Classes

The rules of HTML and CSS let you apply more than one class to a single tag, which is handy when you have page elements that share *some* formatting but have their own style requirements as well. For example, say you want to add a border and colorful background to a set of images in a portfolio (you'll learn how to do that on pages 167 and 172). You could create a class style with the properties you want (for example, *.portfolioImage*), but you might want some photos to appear on the right side of the page and others on the left (you'll learn how to do this on page 248). In other words, you'll format the images similarly but position them differently. To make that happen, you'd create two new class styles (say, *.imageLeft* and *.imageRight*).

You apply both the *.portfolioImage* and the *.imageLeft* classes to pictures you want to have a border and align to the left, and add the *.portfolioImage* and *.imageRight* classes to flush-right images.

FIGURE 3-7

You can apply a class style directly to a tag using the Tag Selector at the bottom of the document window. Right-click (Control-click) the tag you want to format (the <p> tag here is circled, but partially hidden by the pop-up menu), and then, from the Set Class submenu, select a class style. The Tag Selector also lets you know if a tag has a class style or ID style already applied to it. If so, Dreamweaver adds the style's name to the end of the tag. For example, in this figure, the body tag has a class named .container applied to it (<body.container>) and the paragraph has the class named .copyright applied to it (<p.copyright>).

Using multiple classes is increasingly common in web design, but until Dreamweaver CS6, the only way to use them was to type the multiple classes in Code view. Fortunately, Dreamweaver CC provides a simple way to use the Properties panel to add more than one class to a tag:

1. **Select an element you want to style with more than one class.**

    This could be a headline, a paragraph, an image, a <div> tag (page 454), and so on.

2. **If you're in the Properties panel's HTML mode, click the Class drop-down menu and select Apply Multiple Classes. If you're in CSS mode, choose Apply Multiple Classes from the Targeted Rule drop-down menu.**

    In either case, the Multiclass Selection window appears (see Figure 3-8).

NOTE You can also apply multiple classes to a tag using the Tag Selector at the bottom of the document window. Right-click (Option-click) the tag and choose Set Class→Apply Multiple Classes (see Figure 3-7).

FIGURE 3-8

Dreamweaver's Multiclass Selection window lets you apply more than one class to a page element. You can choose from a list of classes that already exist or type the class names (separated by spaces) in the text box at the bottom.

3. **In the Multiclass Selection window, select the classes you want to apply to the selected tag.**

   Only CSS classes you already added to a page's internal or external style sheet appear in this window, so it's best to create the styles before applying class names to HTML tags. However, you can apply the names of classes even if they don't appear in a page's style sheet. Type each class name into the text box at the bottom of the window, adding a space between each one (and leaving out the period that precedes a class name in a style sheet). For example, *portfolio-Image imageLeft* is correct, but *.portfolio.imageLeft* is not.

4. **Click OK to close the Multiclass Selection window and apply the classes to the tag.**

   Under the hood, Dreamweaver simply adds the names of the classes you chose to the HTML tag, like *<img class="portfolioImage imageLeft" src="photo.jpg">*.

You can always remove or add classes by selecting a tag and choosing Apply Multiple Classes from the Properties panel's Class menu. If you deselect all the class names, Dreamweaver removes the class attribute from the tag. Alternatively, you can use the technique described next to remove all the classes from a tag.

TIP If you're a master of the mouse, you'll be happy to know you can reach the Multiclass Selection window by right-clicking (Control-clicking) selected text and then choosing CSS Styles→Apply Multiple Classes.

Removing a Class Style

You remove a class style from a page element in one of four ways:

- To remove a class style from text, select the text and then, in the Properties panel, choose None from the Class menu (in HTML mode) or <Remove Class> from the Targeted Rule menu (in CSS mode).

- To remove a class style from any other object (like an image), select the object and then, from the Properties panel's Class menu, choose None.

- To remove a style from any selection (even non-text elements, like images and tables), choose Format→CSS Styles→None.

- To remove a class style from a particular tag, first use Dreamweaver's Tag Selector to locate the tag. Suppose you want to remove the .*copyright* class from a paragraph. In the Tag Selector, right-click (Control-click) the <p.copyright> tag. Then, from the drop-down menu, choose Set Class→None. One advantage to this method is that the Tag Selector makes it very clear what HTML tag the class is applied to.

TIP   If you applied a class style to a selection of text, you don't have to select *all* the text to remove the style. Just click anywhere inside it, and then select None from the Properties panel's Class menu or <Remove Class> from the Targeted Rule menu. Dreamweaver is smart enough to realize that you want to remove the style applied to all the text. (If you applied the style to a tag, Dreamweaver removes the *class* property from the tag. If you applied the style using the <span> tag, which groups random elements, Dreamweaver removes the <span> tag.)

You can't, however, remove *tag* styles from HTML tags. For example, suppose you redefined the <h2> tag using the steps on page 117. If your page has three Heading 2 (<h2>) paragraphs, and you want the third heading to have a different style from the other two, you can't simply "remove" the <h2> style from the third heading. You need to create a new class style with all the formatting options you want for that heading, and then apply it directly to this particular <h2> tag. (By the magic of CSS, class formatting options override any existing tag style options—see page 412 for more on this sleight of hand.)

Applying IDs to a Tag

If you're working on a site that uses ID selectors, you first need to associate the IDs with a tag. To apply an ID to text, select the text and use the ID menu in the Properties panel's HTML mode (see Figure 3-6, top). Since you can apply each ID name only once per page, the menu lists only unassigned IDs—IDs that exist in your style sheet but that you haven't applied to an element in the current page.

For non-text elements, select the element, and then, in the Properties panel, type the ID name into the ID box. (For some elements, the ID box is unlabeled, but you can always find it on the far left of the Properties panel.)

You can also apply an ID using the Tag Selector, as outlined in Figure 3-7. Right-click (Control-click) the tag, select Set ID from the drop-down menu, and then select the ID from the submenu.

TIP The Tag Selector tells you whether you applied an ID to a tag by including the # symbol with the ID name. For example, *body#catalog* indicates that the <body> tag has an ID named *catalog* applied to it. All tags in the Tag Selector, including the <body> tag discussed here, have pointed ends, making it easy to distinguish the tag from any associated class and the ID names.

Whenever you apply an ID to a tag, Dreamweaver adds a bit of HTML to your page. For instance, an ID style named *#copyright* applied to a paragraph looks like this in HTML:

```
<p id="copyright">
```

This is just like the *class* property Dreamweaver adds when you use class styles, as described on page 128.

To remove an ID from a text element, select the text, and then, from the Properties panel's ID drop-down menu, select None. For non-text elements, select the element, and then, in the Properties panel's ID field, delete the ID name.

Linking to an External Style Sheet

When you create an external style sheet while working on a page, Dreamweaver automatically links the sheet to the current document. To use that document's styles on a different page, you must *attach* the style to the page.

To do so, open the page and then, in the Sources section of CSS Designer, click + to add a source, and then choose Attach Existing CSS File (see Figure 3-2, top). (If CSS Designer isn't open, choose Window→CSS Designer or press Shift-F11.)

TIP You can also use the Properties panel to attach a style sheet; select Attach Style Sheet from the Class menu in HTML mode (see Figure 3-9, top).

The "Attach Existing CSS File" window opens (see Figure 3-9, bottom). Click Browse. In the Select Style Sheet File dialog box, navigate to and double-click the CSS (.css) file you want to attach to the document. If the style sheet you select is outside the current site—if, for example, it's in another of your websites—Dreamweaver offers to copy it to your site's root folder; click Yes.

The "Attach Existing CSS File" window provides other options. You can attach a style sheet by linking to it from the current document, or by importing it into the current web page. The choices are nearly identical—they're simply two ways of applying styles from an external style sheet to a web page. The method preferred by the pros, and Dreamweaver's suggested choice, is linking to the sheet, so go with the Link option.

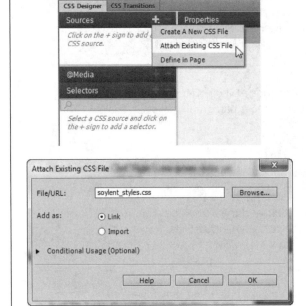

FIGURE 3-9

Top: To attach an existing style sheet, use CSS Designer's Add Source button (+) and choose Attach Existing CSS File.

Bottom: The Attach Existing CSS File window opens, where choosing an external style sheet is as simple as browsing for the file and then clicking OK. The Conditional Usage settings for media queries are optional.

You can also specify the conditions under which a page uses one style sheet over another. For example, you might use one style sheet for a page displayed on a monitor, and a second sheet for a page that visitors can print out, like a receipt. Browsers figure out which style sheet to use by performing a *media query*, that is, by figuring out the destination device. You'll find in-depth information on media queries and how to use them on page 523. In the meantime, if you simply want to attach a style sheet to a page so that the styles always apply (when viewed on a screen *or* printed out), you can ignore the Conditional Usage options in the "Attach Existing CSS File" dialog box.

After choosing your options, click OK. Dreamweaver adds the necessary HTML to the head of the web page and automatically formats any tags according to the style sheet's rules. In Design view, the formatting changes take place immediately.

If the style sheet contains *class* styles, on the other hand, you don't see their formatting effects until you apply the class to an element on the page, as described on page 128.

■ Working with Styles

As with anything in Dreamweaver, styles are easy enough to edit, delete, or duplicate; all you need is a map of the terrain.

Editing Styles

As you build a website, you continually refine your design. That chartreuse background may have looked great at 2 a.m., but it loses something in the light of day.

Fortunately, one of CSS's greatest selling points is how easy it is to update a website's styles. Dreamweaver provides many ways to edit style rules:

- In CSS Designer, select a source and a selector and then, in the Properties section, change the values for properties. Dreamweaver writes the changes to the style sheet and reformats the page to reflect your changes.

- In the Properties panel (Window→Properties), click the CSS button. Use the Targeted Rule drop-down menu to choose a selector (class, ID, or tag), and then use text formatting attributes like font, size, and alignment. This method is good for tweaking text styles. Each change takes effect as soon as you make it.

- In the Properties panel, click the CSS button. Use the Targeted Rule drop-down menu to identify a style, and then click Edit Rule. The "CSS Rule definition for..." dialog box opens (Figure 3-5), where you can change multiple properties. Use the Category list on the left to display the types of properties, and then make your changes using the menus, checkboxes, and other widgets in the main window. When you click OK, Dreamweaver records all the changes to the style sheet and updates your page to reflect those changes.

Deleting a Style

At some point, you may find that you created a style that you don't need anymore. Maybe you redefined the HTML <code> tag and realized that you never use it. You don't need to keep it around, taking up precious space in the style sheet.

To delete a style rule for a specific selector, such as an <h1> tag or a *.copyright* class, go to CSS Designer. In the Sources section, choose the source for the style rule. It can be a single specific source, like a style sheet, or you can click the All Sources option to see all the available sources. Then, in the Selectors section, choose the selector you want to delete. In the dark-gray bar at the top of the Selectors section, click the Remove Selector button, also known as the minus sign (–) button.

You can remove all the styles in a sheet by removing the source. In the Sources section of CSS Designer, click the style sheet you want to remove, and then click the Remove CSS Source button (the – sign again). In the case of an external style sheet, that removes the link between your web page (HTML document) and the CSS file. It doesn't delete the actual style sheet, however. In the case of an internal style sheet, the process removes the rules from the head of your web page.

When Formatting Disappears

Sometimes when I copy text from one web page and paste it into another, all the formatting disappears. What's going on?

If you copy an HTML tag, say an <h1> tag, from one web page to another, and both pages use the same external style sheet, you get the styling you expect in the second page because the external sheet formats the <h1> tag in both pages.

If, however, you use an *internal* style sheet and copy a headline from one page to another, you lose any styling that was applied to the <h1> tag in the first page. That's because Dreamweaver doesn't copy the internal style sheet from one page to another.

But, of course, there's an exception: If you use an internal style sheet *and* the HTML tag you copy has a class or ID applied to it, then Dreamweaver *does* copy the internal styles you defined for the tag's class or ID to the new document.

Here are a couple of examples that illustrate the point. In both cases, assume you stored the styles in an internal style sheet—that is, in the <head> section of a web page.

First, say you define a style for your <h1> tag that specifies a red font. Then you copy the <h1> heading from one page to a new page. Dreamweaver pastes the new text and its <h1> tag in the new page, but it doesn't copy the tag's style definition. As a result, the heading in your new page won't be red.

Now say you create a class called *.redhead* that specifies a red font, and you apply it to an <h1> heading in your first document. When you copy that heading to a new document, you'll see a red headline. That's because Dreamweaver copied not only the <h1> heading, but the *.redhead* class and its styles into the <head> section of the new document, too.

The best way to avoid a situation like the one you had is to use an external style sheet and attach it to all the pages in your site. That way, when you copy and paste HTML, all the pages share the same styles and formatting. So, in the preceding example, if you copy a paragraph that includes a class style—*class="company"*—into another page that shares the same style sheet, the paragraphs look the same on both pages. Page 118 has more on creating an uber, site-wide external style sheet.

Unfortunately, deleting a class style *doesn't* delete any references to the style in your site's pages. For example, suppose you create a style called *.copyright*, apply it throughout your site to a paragraph at the bottom of every page, and then delete the style from the style sheet. In the web page, Dreamweaver doesn't remove the <p> tags or class properties that refer to the style, so your pages will be littered with code like this, even though your text looks unstyled:

```
<p class="copyright">Cafe Soylent Green</p>
```

You solve this problem using Dreamweaver's powerful "Find and Replace" tool to ferret out the orphaned tags and class properties, as discussed in Chapter 8.

Renaming a Class Style

You can rename any style by selecting it in CSS Designer, pausing a second, and then clicking the name again. Dreamweaver highlights the name for editing, at which point you can type a new name in its place. Of course, if you change a style named *p* to a style named *h1*, you've essentially removed the style for the <p> tag and added an <h1> style to your style sheet—in other words, all the paragraphs in your pages would lose their formatting, and all the <h1> tags would suddenly change appearance.

Another way to edit a style name is to open the style sheet in Code view, find the style name, and then edit it.

No matter which method you choose, when it comes to class styles, just changing the name doesn't do much good if you already applied the style throughout your site. The *old* class name still appears in the HTML everywhere you used it.

FREQUENTLY ASKED QUESTION

When Undo Won't Do

Sometimes when I edit a style—say, change a font color—I can undo that change. But other times, I can't undo changes I make to a style. What gives?

You can undo changes only in a currently open document. If you're working on an HTML file in either Design, Code, Split, or Live view, you can undo any changes you make to that file. For example, say you add an internal style sheet to a document. If you edit one of those styles, Dreamweaver lets you undo those changes. Because the styles in an internal style sheet are part of the web page you're working on, choosing Edit→Undo reverses the last change you made.

However, if you're working on a web page with an *external* style sheet, you're actually working on *two* files at the same time—the web page you're building and the style sheet you're editing. So if you're designing a web page and edit a style in the external style sheet, you're actually making a change to the style sheet file. In this case, choosing Edit→Undo affects only the last change you made to the *web page*. If you want to undo the change to the external style sheet, you need to use Dreamweaver's Related Files feature. The name of the external style sheet appears in the Related Files toolbar, which appears below the title of the web page; click the filename to move to its code, and then choose Edit→Undo. Click the Source Code button to return to your web page. (You'll learn more about the Related Files toolbar on page 343.)

If you're in Split view with the HTML code displayed on the left and the Design view on the right, you can click the CSS file in the Related Files toolbar and see the code for that file on the left. At this point, the Undo command works on the active document—in other words, click in the CSS code on the left and Edit→Undo undoes the last change to the CSS; click in Design view on the right and Edit→Undo reverses the last change to the HTML of the page.

What you really need to do is rename the class style, and *then* perform a find-and-replace operation to change the name wherever it appears in your site. Dreamweaver includes a handy tool to simplify this process.

To rename a class style:

1. **In the Properties panel, choose Rename from the Class menu (on the HTML tab of the Properties panel).**

   The Rename Style window opens (Figure 3-10).

FIGURE 3-10

Dreamweaver's Rename Style tool is a fast and easy way to change the name of a class style even if you've used the style hundreds of times on your site.

2. **From the "Rename style" drop-down menu, choose the name of the style you want to rename.**

   This menu lists all the class styles in the page's style sheets, both internal and external.

3. **In the "New name" box, type the new style name, and then click OK.**

   Follow the usual rules for naming class styles (described on page 121), but don't precede the name with a period; Dreamweaver already knows that you're working with classes.

   If you're changing an internal style, Dreamweaver makes the change and your job is done.

   If the style belongs to an external style sheet, Dreamweaver warns you that other pages in your site may also use this style and suggests that you use Dreamweaver's "Find and Replace" tool to search your site and update all the old style names to the new name. You have three choices: Cancel, No, and Yes.

4. **If you get cold feet, click Cancel or No to call off the name change. Otherwise, click Yes to open the "Find and Replace" window, and then click Replace All.**

   One last warning appears, reminding you that you can't undo the find-and-replace.

NOTE If you click No in the warning box that appears after step 4, Dreamweaver still renames the style in the external style sheet, but it doesn't update your pages. That means the elements that used the old style name lose the formatting the old style applied.

5. **Click Yes.**

   Dreamweaver goes through each page of your site, dutifully updating the name of the style everywhere it appears. When you finish with "Find and Replace," it's likely that you'll still see the Search panel in your workspace. To close it, use the menu in the upper-right corner and choose Close Tab Group.

NOTE Dreamweaver doesn't supply a Rename Style tool for rechristening ID styles. While you can change the name of an ID style in the CSS styles panel—select the style, pause, and then click its name to edit it—Dreamweaver doesn't automatically update the HTML that references that style. You can use Dreamweaver's "Find and Replace" feature (Chapter 8) for that.

Duplicating a Style

Dreamweaver makes it easy to duplicate a style, which is handy when you want to use the formatting from one style as the starting point for a new style. In the Sources section of CSS Designer, choose All Sources, or choose a specific source from the list. In the Selectors section, right-click (Control-click) the name of the style you want to duplicate, and then, from the shortcut menu, choose Duplicate (Figure

3-11, left). Dreamweaver copies the file and displays both the original and duplicate filenames in the Selectors section, with the doppelganger filename highlighted and ready for editing, as shown in Figure 3-11, right. (Sometimes the name box closes before you get a chance to rename the file. If that happens, select the filename, pause for a second, and then click the name again to edit it.) As long as you have two styles with the same name, Dreamweaver won't attempt to rename the references in your web pages.

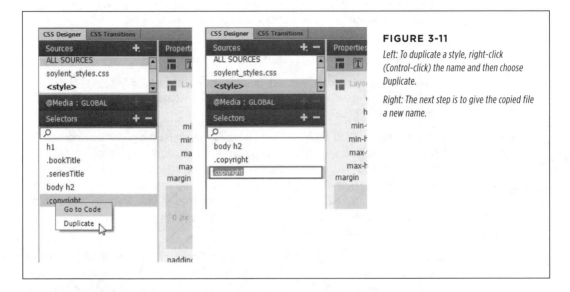

FIGURE 3-11

Left: To duplicate a style, right-click (Control-click) the name and then choose Duplicate.

Right: The next step is to give the copied file a new name.

Formatting Text with CSS

The early World Wide Web was not a pretty place. It was a sea of plain text, with a few changes in type size and a bit of bold and italic thrown in here and there. Of course, all that's changed. Today's websites dazzle the eye with stunning design that rivals the best printed pages. But artists have always faced a dilemma designing for the Web. When you create a design for a book, magazine, newspaper, or roadside sign, your audience sees exactly what you do. When you design a web page, you don't have that kind of control. Why? One major issue is fonts. (If you're a print designer, you might call them typefaces.) In the comfort of your design cubicle, you can build your web page with any font stored on your computer. But your audience won't see that font unless they, too, have that font on their systems, or unless they seamlessly get it from the Web. This section shows you how to make sure your audience sees all the fonts and formatting you want them to see.

One of the best uses of Cascading Style Sheets is converting the drab appearance of HTML text into lavishly designed prose. Alternatively, if you like a somber, corporate style, CSS can help with that, too. Whatever your design inclination, you can improve the look of your text using CSS.

The most commonly used properties for styling text appear in CSS Designer's Properties section, under Layout and Text. As the names imply, you use layout properties to form blocks of text and apportion the space around them, while the text properties focus on the font, size, style, color, and more of the type.

> **NOTE** You can apply nearly every CSS property to text. For example, you can use the *border* property to underline text and the *margin* property to remove the space between paragraphs. You'll find these properties, and others not listed in the Designer's Layout or Text categories, introduced later in this book (you don't want to blow your circuits too quickly). For now, you'll learn the most type-centric properties.

Choosing a Font

You can include fonts with your web page in two ways. The traditional method uses fonts installed on your visitor's computer, while a newer technique uses specially prepared typefaces called *web fonts*.

The traditional method relies on fonts already installed on a guest's computer. For example, as you craft a web page, you can select any font on your computer, even that fancy font you just bought from a small company in Nome, Alaska. Unfortunately, when you publish that document on the Web, not all visitors will see the page you created because not all visitors own the same fonts as you. Your guests can still read your pages—their computers will substitute a font they do have, usually some version of Times, Arial, or Courier.

You can deal with this problem in several ways. Designers coming to the Web from print might consider converting text into graphics—type your copy into an image-editing program like Photoshop, and then save that text-laden document as an image file. Unfortunately that process takes time and forces your visitors to download byte-hogging images just to read your web page. An even bigger problem is that search engines can't read the text inside the image, so they won't index your words.

A better solution is to specify the font you'd *like* to use; if your visitor's computer has that font, that's what he'll see. You can specify secondary or tertiary fonts, too, in case your preferred font isn't available. In fact, Dreamweaver offers prepackaged lists of such "first choice, second choice, third choice" fonts, as you'll see in the following section.

■ SPECIFYING FONTS

The quickest way to specify primary and backup fonts is to use the CSS mode of the Properties panel. After you click the CSS button, choose a set of fonts (which includes primary and backup fonts) from the Font menu.

You can also select font sets from CSS Designer. In the Designer's Properties section, click the big T (the Text button) or scroll down until you see the *font-family* property, and choose a font set. Either way, you're creating a new style (as described on page 116) or updating an existing one.

You'll soon discover that Dreamweaver's font menus aren't quite what you're used to. When you apply a font to text, you choose from one of the prepackaged lists just described; a typical choice is something like "Arial, Helvetica, sans-serif." In other words, you don't choose just a single font, such as Helvetica, you choose a matched set of fonts.

If the first font isn't installed on your visitor's computer, the browser looks down the list until it finds a font that is. Different operating systems use different fonts, so these lists include at least one font common on Windows PCs and another, similar-looking font that's common on Macs. Arial, for instance, is found on all Windows machines, while Macs offer the similar Helvetica.

That's it. You just selected a set of predefined fonts, and any styles you apply to text on your web page will use the font you selected (provided that it's also on your guest's computer, of course). For more control over the fonts your page displays, read on.

NOTE Technically, you can specify any number of fallback fonts in one of these lists, not just first, second, and third choices. These days, it's common to see five or more fonts listed.

Using Adobe Edge Web Fonts

While primary and fallback fonts serve their purpose, a newer way to distribute type ensures better compatibility with your guests' computers. You no longer have to rely on serendipity to make sure your guests see the page you designed; your visitors can download the fonts you used on your pages from the Web itself. These so-called *web fonts* free you from restrictive font choices.

Visitors get the web fonts either from your own site or from a site that hosts fonts (Adobe and Google are examples). When a guest loads a page that specifies a web font, his browser automatically downloads the font file. The experience isn't much different from the way browsers download images, which are also kept in files separate from the web page itself. Your visitor doesn't have to do a thing—he simply benefits from better-looking typography.

Prior to Dreamweaver CC, using web fonts was a cumbersome and confusing process. You had to hunt down the fonts you wanted at sites like Google Fonts (*www.google. com/fonts/*) and FontSquirrel (*www.fontsquirrel.com/fontface*). Then you needed to make sure you could legally use the font—some companies don't want their fonts used on the Web because an unscrupulous person could download them and use them for free. Even the process of getting and using fonts varied depending on the source. And different web browsers and devices, such as iPhones and iPads, require web fonts in different file formats. Some font providers automatically provide all the formats, while others expect you to convert the fonts. Despite all these problems, it was worth the hassle to be able to use a font other than Arial and Times Roman in your web page.

Knowing Your Font Types

You can express your every written thought by choosing from among tens of thousands of fonts, from bookish, staid, classic typefaces to rounded, cartoonish squiggles.

Most fonts are divided into two categories: serif and sans serif. Graphic designers often use serif fonts, where the letters include small decorative strokes at the extremities (the "hands" and "feet" of r's, for example)—for long passages of text, as it's widely believed that serifs gently lead the eye from letter to letter, making the text easier to read. Examples of serif fonts include Times, Times New Roman, Georgia, and Minion.

Designers often use sans-serif ("without serifs") fonts for headlines, thanks to their clean, simple appearance. Arial, Helvetica, Verdana, and Formata are all sans-serif fonts (you're reading Gotham sans-serif right now). Some people believe that you should use only sans-serif fonts on web pages because the delicate, decorative strokes of serif fonts get muddy on the coarse resolution of computer screens. But that's an aesthetic judgment, and you should feel free to use whatever font you think looks (and reads) the best.

You can find other classes of fonts as well, like monospace and script. Monospace fonts—Courier is perhaps the best known—resemble the characters a typewriter (remember those mechanical beasts?) produces—all the letters have the same width (useful for aligning text into columns). Script fonts resemble handwriting, and they're usually bold, fun, and difficult to read at small sizes. However, the different operating systems have few of these types of fonts in common, so if you do want to use a fancy-looking font, you'll have to use a web font.

Enter Dreamweaver CC and Adobe Edge web fonts, which simplify font acquisition and give you access to hundreds of free fonts you can legally use. Adobe acquired web fonts from all kinds of sources, so if you've used web fonts in the past, you'll likely find some old friends here. Best of all, you can set up web fonts without leaving Dreamweaver, by using the Modify→Manage Fonts command.

NOTE The "Edge" in Adobe Edge web fonts is a brand name for a family of tools and services that Adobe provides web developers. The other products include Animate (web animation and effects [page 718]), Reflow (responsive design prototyping), Code (text/code editor), PhoneGap Build (mobile app development [page 604]), and Inspect (preview websites on mobile devices during the design process [page 528]).

■ MANAGING ADOBE EDGE WEB FONTS

Before you can use web fonts in Dreamweaver, you have to add them to the program using the Manage Fonts window. This step simply registers the fonts with Dreamweaver so you can use them on any site you create:

1. **In Dreamweaver, choose Modify→Manage Fonts.**

    The Manage Fonts window appears (see Figure 3-12). It has three tabs across the top, labeled Adobe Edge Web Fonts, Local Web Fonts, and Custom Font Stacks. Use the first tab, Adobe Edge Web Fonts, to preview and choose a font. The second tab, Local Web Fonts, helps you manage fonts you downloaded to your computer from other sources. If you stick with the easier Adobe Edge web fonts, you may never use this tab. Use the third tab, Custom Font Stacks, to create font sets—lists of fonts and their fallback options, as described at the bottom of this page.

Dreamweaver displays all these font choices in the font menus of the Properties panel and CSS Designer.

2. **On the Adobe Edge Web Fonts tab, find one or more fonts you want to use.**

    Use the buttons along the left side of the window to narrow your choices (Figure 3-12). For example, using the top two buttons, you can limit the list of fonts to those suitable for headings and fonts better suited for paragraphs. (Naturally, you can use the fonts however you want.) Another group of buttons filters the list by font style: serif, sans serif, typewriter, cursive, and so on. If you know the name of the font you want, type it in the "Filter by font name" box. You can select more than one font. For example, fonts often come in families, so you might want to add PT Sans, PT Sans Caption, and PT Serif at the same time.

3. **Click a font name to add it to your list of available fonts.**

    A checkmark appears in the upper-right corner. If you change your mind, click again to remove the checkmark. Dreamweaver adds only fonts that have checkmarks.

4. **Click Done.**

    When you click Done, the font becomes part of your Dreamweaver fonts lists. To find it, go to the Properties panel, make sure you're in CSS mode, and then use the Font drop-down menu. You'll also find your new font in CSS Designer. Go to the Properties section and find the *font-family* property. Fonts you added with the Manage Fonts window appear near the bottom of the list in the Properties panel and in CSS Designer.

If you ever decide to remove a font, open the Manage Fonts window (Modify→Manage Fonts), go to the Adobe Edge Web Fonts tab, and then turn on the checkmark in the bottom-left corner. You'll see all the Adobe Edge web fonts you added to Dreamweaver. Click to remove the checkmarks from fonts you no longer want, and then click Done.

■ CREATING A CUSTOM FONT STACK

When you use web fonts in your pages, Dreamweaver adds a code to the page so your visitors can get those fonts from the Web. In most cases, they'll be able to get the font you specify, but it's good practice to give your visitors some fallback options. These next steps explain how to create a custom font stack:

1. **Choose Modify→Manage Fonts.**

    The Manage Fonts window opens.

Filter by name

Recommended
for headings

Recommended
for paragraphs

Styles

Show previously
added fonts

FIGURE 3-12

*The Manage Fonts window
lets you select web fonts for
your site. Initially, it displays
the Adobe Edge Web Fonts
tab, where you can choose
from more than 500 free-
to-use fonts. Buttons along
the left side of the window
help you zero in on fonts you
want to preview.*

2. **Click the Custom Font Stacks tab.**

   Dreamweaver divides the Custom Font Stacks window into three panes (Figure
   3-13). The first one, "Font list," sits at the top of the screen and displays all the
   fonts currently available in Dreamweaver. (These are the font choices you see
   in the Properties panel and in CSS Designer.) You use the two panes below that
   to build new font stacks and add them to Dreamweaver's fonts list.

3. **Click + at the top left of the Font list.**

   A message at the bottom of the fonts list says "Add fonts in list below."

4. **Scroll through the "Available fonts" list to find a font you like. If you know
   its name, type it in the text box below "Available fonts," and Dreamweaver
   scrolls through the list to display it.**

   The Adobe Edge web fonts you added appear at the bottom of the list of available fonts.

5. **Double-click a font you want to use in a new custom font stack.**

When you double-click a font, or click the << button, Dreamweaver adds it to the "Chosen fonts" list on the left. To create a stack, add several fonts to the list. Often, you start off with a web font you like and then add a fallback font popular on Windows PCs and another popular on Macs. Finally, choose a generic option, like a serif or sans-serif font, for visitors who have none of your preferred fonts on their machine.

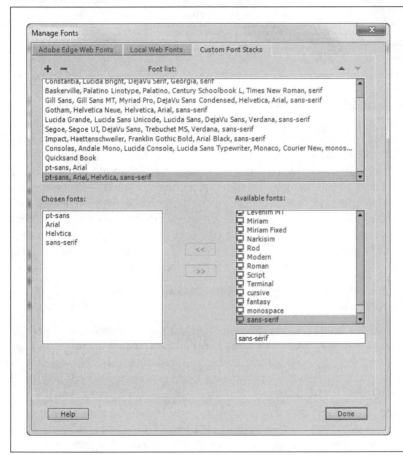

FIGURE 3-13

Use the Custom Font Stacks tab to create new lists of fonts—first choice and fallback options—to use in your styles. Click the + button (upper left) to start a new list. Then select a font in the "Available fonts" box and click the << arrow to move the font to the "Chosen fonts" box. When you finish your list, click Done. You'll find your new font stack listed in the Properties panel's drop-down Fonts menu and in the font-family menu in CSS Designer.

TIP If you're not sure how popular a font is, consult a website like *http://cssfontstack.com/*. Point to the info button to see the percentage of Windows or Mac PCs that have the font installed.

6. **Click Done.**

This closes the Manage Fonts window. Your new font stack will be available in the Properties panel's CSS mode and in CSS Designer under Properties→font-family (Figure 3-14).

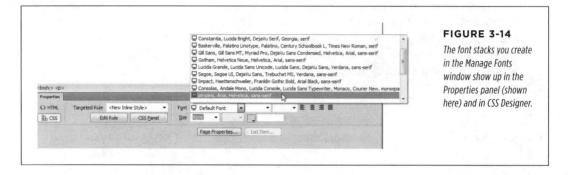

FIGURE 3-14

The font stacks you create in the Manage Fonts window show up in the Properties panel (shown here) and in CSS Designer.

USING ADOBE EDGE WEB FONTS

After using Dreamweaver's Manage Fonts tools to add fonts to your list of available fonts, you use them just like any other font. For example, you'll find the new fonts and custom font stacks in CSS Designer's Properties section. The *font-family* menu lists the newcomers along with all the usual suspects. You're not required to do anything special to use the new fonts—just pick them off the list. However, when you specify an Edge web font, Dreamweaver performs a few extra bits of web font magic. When visitors view your page, their browsers need to know where to find its fonts. Dreamweaver adds a line of code to the page that points to a JavaScript file that handles all your web font chores. For example, if your font specification includes the PT Sans font, this bit of code appears in the head of your page:

```
<script src="http://use.edgefonts.net/pt-sans:n4:default.js"
type="text/javascript"></script>
```

In most cases, the entire process takes place so fast that your visitors won't notice the difference between using web fonts and the fonts already installed on their computers.

Changing the Font Size

Varying the size of fonts on a web page is one way to direct a viewer's attention. Large type screams "Read Me!"—excellent for attention-grabbing headlines—while small type fades into the background, perfect for necessary but unexciting legal mumbo-jumbo like copyright notices.

Unless you set a type size for web page text, it appears on a visitor's monitor at the default size specified by her browser, usually 16 pixels. However, not only can people change that default size (much to the eternal frustration of web designers), but different operating systems display text at different sizes. Bottom line: You can't assume that the way text appears on your monitor is the way it'll appear on your guests' monitors.

Using Non-Adobe Edge Web Fonts

If you use web fonts other than those provided by Adobe on the Adobe Edge Web Fonts tab (Figure 3-12), you're in for some extra work and you'll need to take legal precautions. Here's a quick rundown of the issues.

First, the way you get and use web fonts depends on the source of the font. Different providers use different methods. In the case of Google Fonts, for example, you choose your fonts, copy a bit of code that Google provides, and paste it into the head of your web pages. This code tells your visitor's browsers where to find the files needed to display the fonts. In the case of Font Squirrel (*www.fontsquirrel.com*), you download font files to your computer. Initially, Font Squirrel provides OTF (Open Type Format) fonts. You use its Webfont Generator to convert OTF fonts to web font files that different browsers can use. Then you use Dreamweaver's Font Manager (Modify→Manage Fonts) to add them to the list of available fonts in the Properties panel and CSS Designer (Figure 3-15). The bottom line is that differ-

ent font providers use different methods for procuring their fonts, and you'll need to do a little digging with each provider to understand their process.

The other issue you need to consider when using third-party fonts is whether you can legally use them on the Web. The Google Fonts site says "All the fonts are Open Source" and that you are "free to use them in every way you want, privately or commercially—in print, on your computer, or in your websites."

Other font providers aren't that generous. That's why Dreamweaver passes the legal responsibility for using third-party fonts to you. To use a font you downloaded to your computer, go to Modify→Manage Fonts and then click the Local Web Fonts tab. Before you register downloaded fonts (what Dreamweaver calls local fonts) for use in Dreamweaver, you have to turn on a checkbox that says "I have properly licensed the above font(s) for website use." Translation: It's your fault, not Adobe's, if a font designer wants to sue.

To set a font size, use either the Size menu in the Properties panel's CSS mode (Figure 3-16) or the Properties section of CSS Designer (Figure 3-17); in the latter, look for the *font-size* property. Whichever method you choose, you're either creating a new style as described on page 116 or updating an existing style (page 167).

The choices available from the Size menu break down into four groups:

- The *None* option removes any size information applied to the text. The text returns to its default size.

- The numeric choices—9 through 36—indicate how tall you wish to make the text, measured in pixels. Nine-pixel-tall text is nearly unreadable, while 36-pixel copy makes a bold statement. One benefit to specifying a pixel size is that the resulting text appears nearly the same across different browsers and operating systems, obviating the problems mentioned above.

- The options *xx-small* through *xx-large* indicate fixed font sizes, replacing the sizes 1 through 7 used with the old HTML <font> tag. The *medium* size is usually the same as the standard browser font size of 16 pixels.

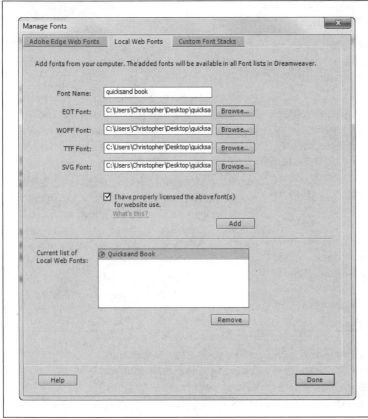

FIGURE 3-15

Use the Local Web Fonts panel to manage web fonts you downloaded from the Web. You need to include each of the font formats (EOT, WOFF, TTF, and SVG) to cover all the font variations different browsers need. If you downloaded a complete "web font kit," all the formats should be in the same folder.

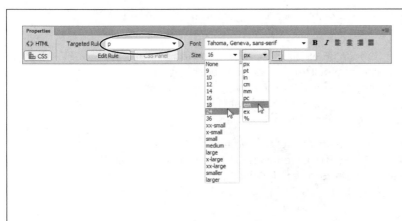

FIGURE 3-16

You can set a dizzying array of font sizes using CSS. When you use the Properties panel's CSS mode to set the size of text, you either create a new style—in which case the Targeted Rule field (circled) displays <New CSS Rule>—or you edit an existing style, as shown here. In this case, you have the tag style <p> listed, so picking a font size edits the size of text for all the paragraphs on the page.

FIGURE 3-17

While you can set some text formats from the Properties panel, CSS Designer's Properties section offers additional options. For example, you get the ability to control the space between lines of text (line-height), and an option to add drop shadows (h-shadow and v-shadow).

- The last two choices—*smaller* and *larger*—are relative sizes, meaning that they shrink or enlarge the selected text based on your page's text size. These choices come in handy when you define a base font size for an entire page using the Page Properties window (see Figure 1-26 on page 47).

   Suppose you set the text size for a page at 12 pixels. If you apply *larger* to a selection of text, the text gets bigger (the exact amount varies by web browser). If, later, you change the base size to 14 pixels in the Page Properties window, all that "larger" text will increase proportionally.

To change the size of text, select it, and then, from the Properties panel, choose a new font size or edit the appropriate CSS, as described on page 153. If you applied a pixel value, you have an additional option: You can type in any number you wish if you don't like any of the sizes listed. In fact, web browsers can handle humongous text—hundreds of pixels tall, if that's what you're into.

You don't have to specify the text size in pixels. You can use points, picas, ems, percentages, and exes (an *ex* is the width of the letter "x" in the current font). Select the unit of measure you want from the drop-down menu to the far right of the Size field. Most of these units were developed for print publishing and may have little relevance to computer, phone, or tablet screens. Of them, these are the most useful:

- *Pixels* ensure that text is the same size across browsers and operating systems.

- *Ems* are a relative measure, meaning that the actual font size varies. They're based on the size of the capital letter M in the current font.

One em is equal to the default font size. Suppose a web browser's default size is 16 pixels. In that case, 1 em means characters are 16 pixels tall, 2 ems would be twice that (32 pixels tall), and 1.5 ems would be 24 pixels tall.

The advantage of ems is that they let visitors control their browser's base font size to fit their needs. For example, if someone finds standard text too small, she can increase her browser's base font size. Any text measured in ems then changes according to the browser's new setting. (For a good set of instructions on how to change the starting font size in all major browsers, visit *http://tinyurl. com/7b9ndbg*.)

> **NOTE** You don't need to use ems to let browsers resize text. All current browsers have a Zoom command that enlarges not only text, but all other page elements (pictures, navigation links, and so on), too.

You can use pixels and ems together. You could, for instance, set the base font size of your page to 16 pixels and then use ems for other parts of the page. For example, you could set headlines to 2 ems, making them 32 pixels tall. If you later thought the overall text was too small or too large, you could change the base font size for the page, and the headlines and other text would resize proportionally.

> **NOTE** As you get more familiar with CSS, you'll probably run into some weird problems with text sizes specified in ems or percentages due to an advanced concept known as the *cascade*. The gruesome details begin on page 412.

- *Rems* are another relative measure, similar to ems. When Dreamweaver calculates the size of text in rems, it bases that size on the size of the root element—in other words, on the default font size. The advantage of rems over ems is that rems avoid the cascading issues mentioned in the Note above.

- *Percentages* (%) are another relative size measurement. When you apply a percentage to text, it's functionally equivalent to ems—100% is the same as 1 em, 200% is 2 ems, and 75% is .75 ems. If you're more comfortable with the notion of percentages than the typography-inspired ems, use percentages.

CSS Designer offers other units of measure in the *font-size* property, but not many designers use them because they don't offer advantages over pixels, ems, rems, or percentages. They include old-fashioned type measures like points (pt) and picas (pc). They also include measurements based on letter or glyph size. Ex is based on a lowercase x, for example, and "ch" is based on the number 0.

The upshot is that you're safe using pixel values—they're easier to understand, more consistent across browsers, and compatible with the Zoom feature of all currently shipping browsers.

Picking a Font Color

To set the hue of your text, use the CSS *color* property. You can do so in the Properties panel's CSS mode or in CSS Designer.

Whether for text or the background of a web page, most color formatting in Dreamweaver uses the *color picker*. When the color picker opens (Figure 3-18), you dial in a color using the three sliders on the right. They control the hue, lightness/darkness, and transparency of a color. Your selection is shown inside the ring in the large square. You adjust the color by dragging that ring to a different spot. There are two smaller squares in the upper-left corner of the color picker. The square on the left shows the new color you're specifying; the one on the right shows the original color. When you're happy with your color, press Enter.

New specified color
Previous color
Swatches
Add new swatch
Transparency
Hue
Eyedropper
#195207
RGBa | Hex | HSLa
Color specification number
Color model

FIGURE 3-18

Whenever you need to specify a color, Dreamweaver displays this color picker. To specify a color, drag the three sliders on the right or the ring inside the big square. The picker displays your chosen color as a number at the bottom of the window. The format for the color spec changes to match the color model button that's selected. The Hex color model is selected here.

In addition, you can use the eyedropper tool in the lower-right corner of the picker to choose a color. It starts out "empty," but when you click any spot on your screen, the cursor takes on that color and passes it to the color picker. That trick comes in handy when you want to use a color that appears in an image somewhere elsewhere in your document (to have headline text match the image, for example). This sample spot doesn't have to be from within Dreamweaver, either—you can switch to another program and click a color there, and Dreamweaver's color picker reflects that color.

Normally, Dreamweaver records the colors you select in hexadecimal (a.k.a. hex) notation, but it supports a much broader range of notations, including RGB, HSL, RGBa, and HSLa (see the box on page 155). To use one, click the appropriate button in the color picker (Figure 3-18).

NOTE Internet Explorer 8 and earlier support only three color formats: RGB and two hex formats (page 155). Until Internet Explorer users upgrade to IE 9 or switch to Firefox, Chrome, Safari, or Opera, you're better off sticking with RGB or hex color values for your pages.

If you decide you don't want to add a color, or you want to remove a color you already applied, click the trash can next to the color swatch in CSS Designer's Properties section. Without a color specified, web browsers use default colors for the element in question. For instance, unless you specify otherwise, text on a page is usually black.

If you know your colors—and more important, your color values—you can bypass the sliders and set a color by hand. Look for the text box in the lower-left corner of the color picker (Figure 3-18). Type the color value into this box, and the color picker displays your chosen hue. This method is sometimes faster and more precise than eyeballing it with the ring/slider combo.

Adding Bold and Italic Formatting

You can make text bold or italic using HTML tags or CSS styles. In most cases, the text looks the same, but there's a geeky, subtle difference. When you use the Properties panel in HTML mode and click the B button, Dreamweaver wraps the selected text in HTML <strong> tags, like this:

```
<strong>I'm feeling bold</strong>
```

Most browsers boldface text when they come upon this expression, but that doesn't have to be the case. Someone could build a browser that uses red text or a different font. It just doesn't happen very often. On the other hand, when screen-reading software for the impaired sees the <strong> tags, it might increase the volume of the spoken words. In the Properties panel's HTML mode, the I button works in a similar way, but it adds <em> tags (think "em" for emphasis).

The CSS rules for bolding and italicizing text work differently from the HTML tags. As always, CSS uses rules to style your text, and these rules are less ambiguous than those for HTML. For example, in the Properties panel, if you click the CSS button to switch to CSS mode, you see two menus to the right of the Font menu. The first one (*font-style*) gives you a choice of normal, italic, or oblique text. (For details on the difference between italic and oblique, see the box on page 153.) The next menu (*font-weight*) lets you set the thickness of letters. Various fonts offer different settings for font weight, so you may need to choose from numbers (like 400 or 700) or words (like normal, bold, bolder). When using the number system, 400 is a normal font weight, while 700 is bold.

FREQUENTLY ASKED QUESTION

Italic and Oblique Text

What's the difference between italic and oblique text? Which option should I use?

Choose italic over oblique text. Here's the typographic reason: Italic and oblique are both slanted typefaces, but there's a visible difference. When a type designer creates a typeface like Goudy Old Style, he often laboriously creates a set of italic typefaces that match it. He'll craft each glyph so that it looks stylish in its slanted position. Some letters, like the lowercase "f," take on a script-like appearance. On the other hand,

oblique text is created by forcing normal text to slant a bit. Oblique text doesn't have the same artistic details. Wikipedia provides a good comparison at *http://en.wikipedia.org/wiki/Oblique_type*.

Sadly, when it comes to web typography, there's often no difference between italic and oblique. Why? Because web browsers often substitute one for the other. If you specify italic and it's not available, browsers will use or create oblique text in its place. Still, it never hurts to specify the best option: italic.

So how do you decide whether an HTML tag or a CSS rule should format your text? If you just want to change the appearance of text, use CSS. But if you want to emphasize text because it's important to the sentence's meaning (and therefore to the way search engines and screen readers perceive the sentence), use HTML mode. For example, if you want the word "Monday" to stand out on a page, use CSS. But for a sentence like "He *never* makes mistakes," the emphasis on "never" is important to understanding the sentence; in that case, use HTML mode. The people viewing your site might not notice the difference, but Google, other search engines, and screen readers will.

NOTE Browsers automatically display headlines in boldface, so highlighting a headline and then clicking the B button in CSS mode has no effect. But what if you want to *remove* the bolding from a headline? Clicking the B button works for normal text, but not for headlines. To remove the bold formatting from them, you have to use the CSS Style Definition window (page 124), and then, from the *font-weight* menu, select *normal* or *400*.

Aligning Text

The alignment buttons in the Properties panel's CSS mode set the CSS *text-align* property to either *left*, *right*, *center*, or *justify*. These same options are available in the Properties section of CSS Designer.

Text Properties in CSS Designer

In CSS Designer's Properties section, click the T (Text) button to see the properties that format text.

NOTE It's a little confusing, but CSS Designer and the Properties panel in CSS mode use different names for the same properties. CSS Designer uses the same property names as those in a CSS style sheet, so you see lowercase words and hyphens between two words in Designer. For example, you use *font-family* to specify a font. But the Properties panel uses more generic terms, so you specify a font there using a Font menu. Either way, once you choose an option, Dreamweaver writes the same, correct code in a style sheet.

- **color**. Set the text color using Dreamweaver's color picker, as described on page 151.

- **font-family**. Choose a font or a font stack from the font menu for the new CSS rule. The menu offers both Dreamweaver's stock fonts and any web fonts you added to Dreamweaver, as discussed on page 141.

- **font-style**. Choose either normal, italic, or oblique from the menu.

- **font-variant**. This drop-down menu lets you specify small-caps type, if you like—a slightly formal, fancy-looking style much favored by attorneys' offices.

- **font-weight**. Weight refers to the thickness of a font. CSS Designer's *font-weight* property offers 13 thicknesses. Normal and Bold are the most common, and they work in all browsers that understand CSS. See Figure 3-19 for details.

FIGURE 3-19

According to the standards set for CSS, each of the nine numeric weight values between 100 and 900 mimic the thickness of characters in fonts that have many different weights (ultrathin, thin, light, extra bold, and so on). Four hundred is normal; 700 is the same as bold. However, given the limitations of today's browsers, you'll notice no difference between the values 100 and 500 (the top text group in the right column). Similarly, choosing any of the values from 600 to 900 just gets you bold text (bottom text group). Reflecting these limitations, CSS Designer usually offers two options: 400 (normal) and 700 (bold).

- **font-size**. As described on page 149, you can choose from many standards to size text, but the most common are pixels, ems, rems, and percentages.

- **line-height**. Line height, otherwise known as *leading* (pronounced "led-ing"), refers to the space between lines of text in a paragraph (see Figure 3-20). To set the line height, choose a unit of measure (like pixels or ems), and then type in a number. For example, to increase the amount of space between lines in a paragraph, type a number greater than the font size into the *line-height* property field.

Normal, the standard setting (third paragraph in Figure 3-20), uses a line height that's slightly larger than the height of the text. You don't see the drop-down menu of measurement units (pixels, points, percentage, and so on) unless you type a number in this box.

UP TO SPEED

Web Colors

CSS supports several color notations: hexadecimal, RGB, HSL, RGBa, and HSLa. These formats are just different ways to specify a color, and you can get the same color using any of them.

Traditionally, you specify colors in CSS using hexadecimal notation. "Hex" represents colors using a six-digit code, like this: #fe3400. (Hexadecimal notation is a system computers use for counting. In this system, you count like this: 0, 1, 2, 3, 4, 5, 6, 7, 8, 9, a, b, c, d, e, f. The # symbol tells a computer that the following sequence is a series of hexadecimal numbers.) The best way to find a color's hex value is to choose the color you want by clicking on it in the picker and then looking at the code that Dreamweaver writes in the text box below.

Hex colors comprise three pairs of numbers. For example, the number above, #fe3400, is really fe, 34, and 00. Each pair represents a number for red, green, and blue color values, which, when combined, make up a color. You sometimes see only three numbers, like this: #f00—that's shorthand used when both numbers in a pair are the same. For example, you can shorten #ff0011 to just #f01. In the color box's "Color format" menu (see Figure 3-18), Dreamweaver refers to these formats as "six-digit hex" and "three-digit hex."

However, CSS supports other color formats. RGB stands for "red, green, blue" and is the format most commonly associated with computer graphics. Most graphics programs let you pick colors using RGB, and, in fact, hex colors are really just RGB values specified using hex numbers. For example, the hex color #ff0033 looks like this as an RGB value in CSS: rgb(255,0,51). Each value represents a color and uses a number from 0 to 255, so rgb(255,0,51) means 255 red, 0 green, and 51 blue. RGB color values work in all web browsers (even Internet Explorer 6), so if you're more comfortable with RGB, feel free to use it.

HSL stands for "hue, saturation, lightness" and is yet another way to specify a color based on its color (hue), intensity (saturation), and lightness (how close a color is to white or black). You specify the hue using a number from 0 to 360 (representing the degrees around a color wheel with red being both 0 and 360, green 120, and blue 240); the saturation is a percentage from 0 (gray) to 100 (full intensity); and lightness is a percentage from 0 (black) to 100 (white). That hex color above, #ff0033, is written like this in HSL: hsl(348,100%,50%). Some people find HSL colors easier to understand than RGB or hex, but all three let you specify the same colors. However, for Internet Explorer, HSL colors work only in version 9 and later. Since IE 8 and 7 are still popular, you're better off skipping HSL for now.

Finally, RGBa and HSLa colors add the dimension of transparency to color: The "a" stands for alpha transparency and refers to how transparent the color is. In other words, you can create "see-through" colors. For example, you could make the color of a headline partially transparent so that a background image on the page shows through the headline. There are many fun and creative effects possible with alpha transparency (for example, the article at *http://tinyurl.com/ydj8658* uses RGBa color). Unfortunately, Internet Explorer 8 and earlier don't understand RGBa or HSLa, so use these formats with caution. If you do want to explore them, they work just like their non-transparent counterparts, with the addition of one extra value from 0 (completely invisible) to 1 (completely opaque). So if you wanted a vivid red color that was 50 percent transparent, you'd specify an RGBa value using this notation: rgba(255,0,0,0.50). In HSLa notation, that color is hsla(0,100%,50%,0.50). If you use Dreamweaver's Color Format menu to select an RGBa or HSLa color, Dreamweaver always sets the transparency to 1; you can change it in the color field to anything from 0 to 1 (such as .25 to get 25 percent transparency).

FIGURE 3-20

You control the space between lines using the line-height property in the CSS Rule Definition dialog box. In this example, each paragraph is set in a 16-pixel Trebuchet MS font. With CSS, you can make lines bump into one another by setting a low line-height value (top paragraph), or spread them far apart by using a larger value (bottom paragraph).

TIP A good strategy for setting line height is to use a percentage measurement, such as *120%*, which is relative to the size of the text. So if your text were 10 pixels tall, the space from the base of one line of text to the next would be 12 pixels (120% of 10). Now, if you change the size of the text, the *relative* space between lines remains the same.

- **text-align**. This property controls the alignment of a block-level element, like a paragraph or table. You choose from among the usual suspects—left, center, right, or justify. (Like the text in this paragraph, justified text aligns copy on both the left and right edges.)

  Use the "justify" option with care, however. Because web browsers don't have the advanced controls that page-layout software does, they usually do an awful job of justifying text on computer screens. The results can be difficult to read—and ugly.

- **text-decoration**. These three buttons let you dress up your text, mostly in unattractive ways. Underline, overline, and line-through add horizontal lines below, above, or directly through the selected text, respectively. An option called blink, which made text flash on and off, was so universally hated and poorly supported by web browsers that it's no longer available.

- **text-indent**. This useful option lets you indent the first line of a paragraph. If you specify 15 pixels for this property, Dreamweaver gives each paragraph an attractive first-line indent, exactly as a real word processor would.

  You can also use a *negative* number, which makes the first line extend past the *left* margin of a paragraph, creating a hanging indent (or *outdent*)—a nice effect for a sentence that introduces a bulleted list or for glossary pages. If you use a negative number, it's a good idea to set the left margin for the paragraph equal to the value of the negative text indent (see page 465). That moves everything, including the outdented line, away from the edge of the browser window. Otherwise, the first line might extend too far to the left, off the screen!

- **text-shadow**. This group of properties creates a drop shadow that sets off text from a page, but only fairly new browsers know how to interpret the settings. To create an effective drop shadow, you need to set all the *text-shadow* properties. The h-shadow and v-shadow values offset the shadow from the original line of text so that the text appears to pop off the page. The blur setting softens the shadow. Use the color setting to choose the shadow's hue. Want to experiment? Start off with these settings:

  — h-shadow : 7 px

  — v-shadow : 5 px

  — blur : 6 px

  — color : #666666

  View the results using Dreamweaver's Live view.

- **text-transform**. This menu lets you set the case for text. To capitalize the first letter of each word, choose Capitalize. The Uppercase option gives you all capital letters, while Lowercase makes all the letters lowercase. The factory setting is None, and it has no effect on the text.

- **letter-spacing**. This property governs the space between *letters*. To add space l i k e t h i s, type a value of about 5 pixels. The result can make long passages hard to read, but a little space between letters can add a dramatic flair to short headlines and movie titles.

- **word-spacing**. This property helps you clean up text by adding or removing space between *words*. The factory setting, Normal, leaves a normal, single space between words. If you want words in a sentence to be spaced   apart like   this, use a value of about 10 pixels (choose Value from the first drop-down menu, and the units of measure from the second). The bigger the number, the larger the gap between words. You can also *remove* space between words by using a negative number—a great choice when you want to make your pages difficult to read.

- **white-space**. This property controls how a browser displays extra white space (spaces, tabs, returns, and so on). Browsers normally ignore extra spaces in the HTML of a page, reducing them to a single-space character between words and other elements, as described on page 81. The *pre* option functions just like the HTML <pre> tag: Extra white space (like tabs, multiple spaces, and hard returns) that you put *in the HTML code* appears in the document itself. Setting the *nowrap* option prevents lines from breaking (and wrapping to the next line) when they reach the end of the browser window.

- **vertical-align**. With this property, you can change the vertical placement of an object—such as text or an image—relative to the items around it. For example, you can add a trademark character, chemical symbol, or footnote by offsetting the characters from the surrounding text using the options *super* and *sub*. If you wanted to add the trademark symbol to, say, *Chia Pet*™, you'd select the letters TM and set the vertical alignment to *super*. For more accurate placement, you can type a positive value, like 10 percent, to raise an object above its normal baseline, or a negative value (like –10% or –5 pixels) to move an object down.

    You can also align images vertically, and designers often use the options Top, Bottom, and Middle to position content within a cell.

> **NOTE** The *super* and *sub* alignment options don't change the size of the selected text. To create true subscript or superscript characters (for chemical symbols, trademark or copyright symbols, and so on), you should specify a font size for the super or sub text that's smaller than the font size you set for the body of the page; 75% works well.

List Properties

At the bottom of the text property category, you find properties that help you exercise greater control over bulleted and numbered lists (see Figure 3-21):

- **list-style-position**. This property controls where a bullet or number appears relative to the list item's text. The "outside" option places the bullet/number outside the margin of the text, exactly the way these lists normally look. "Inside," on the other hand, displays the bullet/number within the text margin, so that the left edge of the *bullet/number* aligns with the left margin of the text; Figure 3-21 makes the effect clear.

- **list-style-image**. For the ultimate control of your bullet icon, skip the boring options preprogrammed into a web browser (like disc, circle, square, or decimal) and supply your own bullets. Click the Browse button and then, from your site folder, select a graphics file. Make sure it's appropriate bullet material—in other words, small.

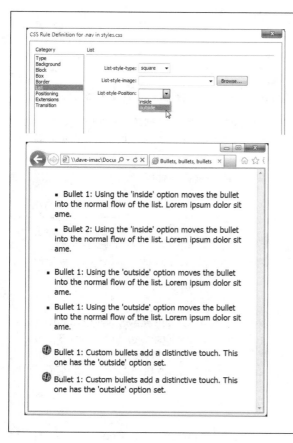

FIGURE 3-21

Top: Take control of your bulleted and numbered lists using the CSS Rule Definition window's List category. With Cascading Style Sheets, you can even supply your own graphic bullets.

Bottom: A bullet-crazed web page, for illustration purposes. Parading down the screen, you can see "inside" bullets, "outside" bullets, and bullets made from graphics.

TIP The *background-image* property, which you'll learn about on page 252, is a more versatile solution to adding customized bullets to a list. The *list-style-image* property lets you specify a graphic to use as a bullet, but CSS doesn't offer any controls to position that image. On the other hand, you can accurately position a background image, so it's much easier to tweak the placement of a bullet using the *background-image* property. Here's how: Create a style for the <li> tag (or a class style that you apply to each <li> tag). Set the *list-style-type* property type to *none* (this hides the bullet), set the background image to your graphical bullet, and play with the background position values (page 255). Playing with the padding values (page 465) helps position the text relative to the image.

- **list-style-type**. Select the type of bullet or number you want in front of a list item. Your options include disc, circle, square, decimal (1, 2, 3), lower-roman (i, ii, iii), upper-roman (I, II, III), lower-alpha (a, b, c), upper-alpha (A, B, C), and none (no bullet at all).

NOTE To adjust how much space web browsers use to indent lists, set the left *padding* property (page 465) to *0*, and then set the left margin (see page 465) to the amount of indent you'd like. Sometimes you want no indent at all—for example, when you create a list of links that you want to look like buttons, not bulleted items. In that case, set both the left padding and left margin to *0* (and while you're at it, set the bullet type to *none*, as described previously).

■ Tutorial: Creating Cascading Style Sheets

In this tutorial, you'll practice creating and editing styles. Make sure you grasp the fundamentals covered in the following pages—you'll be building lots of style sheets in the other tutorials in this book.

In this tutorial, you'll create an external style sheet that formats pages on the Cafe Soylent Green website.

NOTE To complete this tutorial, you need to download sample files from this book's Missing CD page at *http://oreilly.com/pub/missingmanuals/dreamweaverccmm2014*. (See the Note on page 37 for details.) The files you'll work on are in the Chapter03 folder, and the finished project, for comparison, is in the Chapter03_complete folder.

Setting Up a Site

Once you download the tutorial files and open Dreamweaver, set up a new site as described on page 23. In a nutshell, choose Site→New Site. In the Site Setup window, type *Cascading Style Sheets Tutorial* into the Site Name box. Click 🗀 next to the Local Site Folder box, navigate to and select the Chapter03 folder inside the MM_DWCC folder, and then click Choose (Select). Finally, click OK.

Adding Web Fonts

In the first part of this tutorial, you'll use Dreamweaver CC's web fonts feature. The first thing you want to do is add fonts to Dreamweaver's fonts manager.

1. **Choose Modify→Manage Fonts.**

   Dreamweaver opens the Manage Fonts window (Figure 3-22). You'll add your first font.

2. **From the vertical set of buttons on the left, click the second from the top, the one whose tooltip says, "List of fonts recommended for paragraphs" when you hover over it (circled in Figure 3-22).**

   The window displays fonts suitable for body text. Use the button above the paragraph button for headings. The other buttons filter the fonts so you can see different typeface styles, such as sans serif, decorative, and cursive.

3. **In the search box at the top, type a couple of the letters of *PT Sans*.**

   As you type, Dreamweaver displays fonts that match. Eventually, the only font you'll see is PT Sans.

FIGURE 3-22

Dreamweaver CC's Manage Fonts window displays free-to-use fonts on the Adobe Edge Web Fonts tab. This window makes it easy to choose attractive fonts that work well with all browsers.

4. **Click the PT Sans tile.**

   Dreamweaver puts a checkmark in the upper-right corner, indicating that it added the font to its library.

5. **Click the X at the end of the search box, and then click "List fonts recommended for paragraphs" once more (second from top).**

   Once you clear the font filter by pressing X, Dreamweaver displays all the fonts.

6. **Click the checkmark button at the bottom of the left-hand column.**

   With this button ("List of fonts previously added to font list") turned on, Dreamweaver displays only the Edge web fonts you added to its font library (which now includes PT Sans).

7. **At the top of the Manage Fonts window, click the Custom Font Stacks tab.**

   You see three boxes in the resulting window. The top one, "Font list," lists your font stacks. The list includes stacks that come with Dreamweaver, plus any custom font stacks you created. The box on the bottom right lists your available fonts, and the one on the bottom left lists your "Chosen fonts" as you build a new font stack.

8. **In the font list, select the bottom item, "(Add fonts in list below)."**

   If you don't see "(Add fonts in list below)" in the Font list box, click + in the upper-left corner to add it, and then select it. Once you do, you're ready to build a new font stack by moving fonts from the "Available fonts" box to the "Chosen fonts" box.

9. **In the text box below the list of available fonts, triple-click the current font listed to select it, and then type *pt-sans*. When Dreamweaver highlights "pt-sans" in the "Available fonts" box, click the << button.**

   As you type in a font name, Dreamweaver automatically scrolls the "Available fonts" list to any matches. When you click <<, Dreamweaver adds the font to the "Chosen fonts" list. Its position at the top of the list makes it the preferred font. Dreamweaver uses the fonts listed below that as fallbacks.

10. **Repeat the previous step to add Arial, Helvetica, and sans-serif fonts to the "Chosen fonts" list.**

    As you add the fonts, Dreamweaver replaces the "Add fonts in list below" entry in the "Font list" pane with your newly selected stack (Figure 3-23). Browsers use the fonts in the order listed. In this case, browsers will use PT Sans because your site provides it. (If Dreamweaver doesn't show Arial or Helvetica in the "Available fonts" box, then use another sans-serif font, like Gill Sans or Verdana.)

11. **Click Done.**

    The Manage Fonts window closes. As you'll see below, your new font stack, including PT Sans, will be available from the *font* and *font-family* menus.

Creating an External Style Sheet

Now that you've got Dreamweaver ready to use web fonts, you'll create a new external style sheet and start adding styles.

1. **In the Files panel, double-click *about.html*. Make sure you have the Design/ Live view menu at the top of the document window set to Design.**

   The cafe's About Us web page opens in the document window. (If you don't see the Files panel, choose Window→Files to open it.)

2. **In CSS Designer's Sources section, click the + (Add CSS Source) button.**

   Dreamweaver displays a menu with three options: "Create a New CSS File," "Attach Existing CSS File," and "Define in Page."

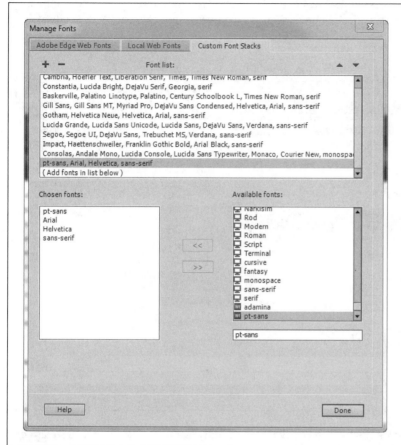

FIGURE 3-23

You use the Custom Font Stacks tab to build lists of fonts starting with a preferred font, followed by fallback options. The goal is to provide fonts with a similar, suitable appearance where at least one of the options will be available to your visitors or already installed on their systems.

3. **Choose "Create a New CSS File."**

   Dreamweaver opens the "Create a New CSS File" window, where you can name the file and choose other options.

4. **In the File/URL box, type *soylent_styles* and leave the "Add as" radio button set to Link.**

   The name of your external style sheet will be *soylent_styles.css*, but you don't need to add the .css extension—Dreamweaver takes care of that. The Link option adds a line of code to your web page that links *soylent_styles.css* to your web page.

5. **Click OK.**

The "Create a New CSS File" window closes, and Dreamweaver lists *soylent_ styles.css* in the Files panel (Figure 3-24). The same filename now appears in CSS Designer's Sources section. The next step is to create a CSS style.

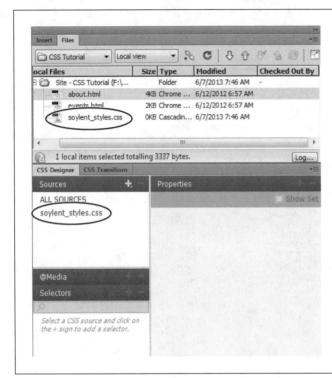

FIGURE 3-24

When you create a style sheet, Dreamweaver lists it in the Local Files panel. In this case, the style sheet (circled) sits in the site's root folder, but you can put it in any folder on your site. For example, some web developers like to reduce the clutter in the root folder by placing all their CSS files in a folder named css. *No matter where you put the style sheet, Dreamweaver lists it in the Sources panel when it's linked to the current page.*

6. **Click anywhere in the first line of text, About Us. Then, in CSS Designer's Sources section, click *soylent_styles.css*. Finally, in the Selectors section, click the Add Selector button (+).**

Dreamweaver adds a new selector called "body h1." This is a compound selector, combining the <body> and <h1> tags, and the style you create will apply to all the <h1> headings in the body portion of your document. Just to review, the term *h1 headings* indicates the text that appears between HTML tags, like this:

```
<h1>About Us</h1>
```

Dreamweaver gives you the option to keep this tag or rename it. In this case, you'll keep it, so click an empty spot in the Selectors section to deselect the editing field.

7. **In the Selectors section, choose *body h1*, and then, in the Properties section, click the Text button (T).**

Dreamweaver scrolls down the list of properties to those related to text, like *color, font-family,* and *font-style.*

8. **To the right of *font-family*, click the grayed-out words "default font." Then, near the bottom of the font stack, choose "pt sans, Arial, Helvetica, sans-serif."**

   You format CSS properties by pairing a property name and value, separated by a colon. In this case, *font-family* is the property name, and "pt sans, Arial, Helvetica, sans-serif" is the value.

9. **In Properties, set *font-weight* to 700.**

   The *font-weight* drop-down menu offers about a dozen choices to control the thickness of the characters, but in practice, there are only two variants of the font, normal and bolded. The value 400 is the same as normal-weight text, while 700 is bolded text.

   You created a style that Dreamweaver applies to all the <h1> headings in your document. Now it's time to see the results.

10. **In Design view, find the About Us heading, and then change the Design/ Live view menu to Live.**

    You have to switch to Live view to see web fonts.

    The new <h1> heading uses a sans-serif font, as did the old one, but there are differences. Note the shape of the letter "b" in "About." The Live view displays the PT Sans font.

    Now switch back to Design view, since there's more work to do.

NOTE   Because Live view often looks just like Design view, it's easy to get caught in the frustrating situation where Dreamweaver seemingly won't let you select text or edit a web page. If that happens, take a breath, look to see if you're in Live view, which limits the way you can edit your page, and then toggle the menu to Design view. Keep in mind that if you're in Split view, you can edit the HTML code and leave Live view turned on. HTML pros often work this way, typing HTML tags into the code half of Split view and then clicking in the Live view window to update the page and check the edits.

---

11. **Click the Code view button.**

    Dreamweaver displays the underlying code for your web page (Figure 3-25). Notice the line:

    ```
    <link href="soylent_styles.css" rel="stylesheet" type="text/css">
    ```

    This links your style sheet to your web page. After the <body> tag, you see the code for the <h1> heading:

    ```
    <h1>About Us</h1>
    ```

Don't put any formatting rules in the <h1> link because the CSS rules for that tag (*font-family*, *font-weight*) are already in the style sheet, and Dreamweaver will apply them to all the <h1> headings in the page. The next step is to add a bit of color to your style. You can do this in CSS Designer, but for variety and practice, you'll use the Properties panel.

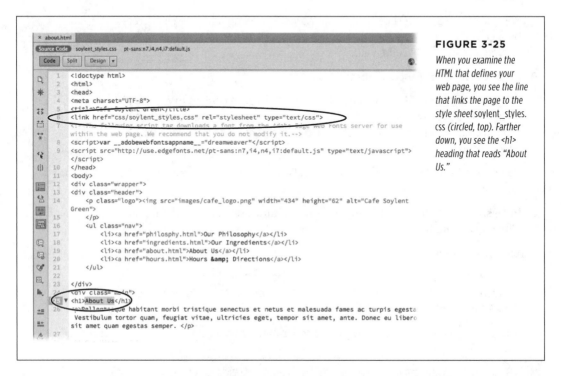

FIGURE 3-25

When you examine the HTML that defines your web page, you see the line that links the page to the style sheet soylent_styles. css *(circled, top). Farther down, you see the <h1> heading that reads "About Us."*

12. **Click the Design button to switch from Code view back to Design view. Then, in the Properties panel below the document window, click the CSS button.**

    The Properties panel displays CSS properties.

13. **Click to place your cursor in the About Us heading.**

    The Targeted Rule in the Properties panel shows "body h1." Any changes made in the Properties panel's CSS mode change the styles applied to the "body h1" selector. Notice that the *font-family* and *font-weight* styles already reflect the changes you made in CSS Designer.

14. **Next to the *color* label in the text properties section, type #145207 and then press Enter (Return).**

    The color of the <h1> heading changes. Use the color picker to select another color if you prefer.

15. **Change *font-size* to 36.**

    This sets the size of your headline to 36 pixels, as shown in Figure 3-26.

FIGURE 3-26

Choosing properties for an element that already has a style applied to it—like the "body h1" selector shown here—updates that style.

Editing a Style

You won't always create the perfect style on your first try—you may make a mistake or just want to change the font, font size, or color of text. Fortunately, Dreamweaver makes it as easy to edit a style as it does to create one.

1. **Open CSS Designer (Window→CSS Designer) and, in the Sources section, select All Sources.**

    In CSS Designer, when you click a source in the Sources section, the list in the Selectors section changes to show all the selectors (classes, IDs, and tags) defined in that source. When you choose All Sources, you see all the selectors the style sheet uses to format the page. In this case, there's only one source (*soylent_styles.css*) and, so far, you've defined only one selector (<body h1>).

2. **If the Selectors section isn't open, click the dark-gray bar at the top of the section, and then click "body h1."**

    The Properties section now displays the CSS rules for the body h1 selector. You need to click the Text button (T) or scroll down to see <body h1>'s properties: *color, font-family, font-weight,* and *font-size.* Properties with grayed-out values represent properties you haven't set yet.

3. **In the gray bar at the top of the Properties section, click the Border button (third from the left).**

    Dreamweaver displays more than a dozen styles related to borders. Why so many? You can set options for border spacing, color, thickness, and corner radius. You can set different values for many of the border properties. For example, you can set different values for the left, right, top, and bottom borders. To see more options, expand CSS Designer by dragging the top of the panel up, as shown in Figure 3-27.

4. **In the border properties area, click the Top tab (the second from left) and then set values for the following properties: width, style and color.**

    Click to the right of the *width* property (where you see the grayed-out word "medium"), choose px from the pop-up menu, and then type *2.* Next, for *style,* click the grayed-out word "none" and choose *solid*. In the color text box, type *#145207*. Click the Bottom tab and use the same values for width, style, and color.

FIGURE 3-27

Drag the top edge of CSS Designer (circled) to see more properties. You can set individual left, right, top, and bottom properties for many border options.

Here you're setting the values for the top and bottom borders independently. If you want to set the values for top, bottom, left, and right all at once, use the "All sides" tab, the first one under the "Border" area.

5. **At the top of the Properties section, click the Layout button (the first one).**

   The Properties section scrolls to display layout properties. Dreamweaver represents the *margin*, *padding*, and *position* properties using rectangles where you can set top, bottom, left, and right values independently, or as a single value.

6. **For the *padding* property, set the top value to *2px*.**

   Padding is the space between the edge of an element (where the border appears) and the stuff inside (like text). In this case, you add 2 pixels of breathing room between the top border and the headline. You'll learn more about padding on page 465.

7. **Examine your handiwork in Design view, and then switch to Live view to see your <h1> heading in all its glory.**

Now you have a distinctive-looking headline. But you've just started building styles for this page.

8. **Choose File→Save All Related Files.**

   The Save All Related Files command can be a lifesaver when you work with external style sheets. Even though you're looking at and working on a web page (*about.html* here), each time you add a style, Dreamweaver updates the external style sheet file (*soylent_styles.css*). So most of the work you've done so far has gone into updating the *soylent_styles.css* file. Unfortunately, the regular keyboard shortcut to save a file, Ctrl+S (⌘-S), only saves changes to the file you can see—in this case, the web page only, and not the style sheet that goes along with it. Use the Save All Related Files command frequently, or you could lose all the changes you make to an external style sheet if Dreamweaver or your computer crashes. (To make things easier, you can create your own keyboard shortcut for the Save All Related Files command by choosing Edit→Keyboard Shortcuts (Dreamweaver→Keyboard Shortcuts. See page 904 for details.)

> **NOTE** The File→Save All command also protects your hard work. It saves every file that has unsaved changes. Feel free to use this command frequently even if you might want to undo some of those changes—Dreamweaver is smart enough to let you undo changes you make to a file even after you save those changes (but only if you don't close the file in the meantime).

Adding Another Style

Dreamweaver lists files related to the current web page above the document window. Below the "about.html" tab, a button says *soylent_styles.css*. Click it to see the CSS code you created to format <h1> headings.

Next on the agenda—a new look for those <h2> headings, so make sure you're back in Design view and get to work.

1. **In Design view, click anywhere in the line that says "Our History." In CSS Designer's Sources section, click *soylent_styles.css*, and then, in the Selectors section, click + .**

   A new selector appears with the name "body h2."

2. **In CSS Designer's Properties section, click the Text button (T).**

   Dreamweaver scrolls to the text properties.

3. **Set *font-family* to "pt sans, Arial, Helvetica, sans-serif."**

   You'll use the same font as in Heading 1, but you'll change its size and color.

4. **Click the *font-size* value, choose px, and then type *24*. For the *color* property, click the grayed-out word "undefined," and then type *#033E00*.**

   This creates medium-sized, dark-green text. To make the headline stand out a bit, you'll make all the text uppercase. Fortunately, you don't have to hold down the Caps Lock key and retype each headline—a CSS property can handle that for you.

5. **Find the *text-transform* properties and click the AB button.**

One problem with this page is the gap between the subheads and the paragraphs that follow. Removing the gap visually ties the two together better. To make this change, you must first remove the margin below each headline.

6. **At the top of the Properties section, click the Layout button.**

Dreamweaver scrolls down the long list of properties until it gets to those related to layout, such as padding and margins.

7. **Click the grayed-out 0 at the bottom of the margin box and type *0 px*.**

It may seem like you're replacing one 0 with another, but the *margin-bottom* property was initially grayed out, meaning that it was undefined and therefore using a default value.

These settings remove any margin space that appears below the Heading 2 tags, but the space between the headlines and the paragraphs hasn't changed a bit! What gives? Paragraphs and headlines have space both above *and* below. The space you're seeing is actually the *top* margin of the paragraph tag.

Top and bottom margins have a peculiar feature: They don't add up, like 1+1=2. In other words, a web browser doesn't add the bottom margin of Heading 2 to the top margin of the paragraph to calculate the total space between the two blocks of text. Instead, a web browser uses the margin with the *largest* value to determine the space between paragraphs (a lot of text layout programs, including word processors, share this behavior).

For example, say the <h2> tag has a bottom margin of 12 pixels, while the paragraph following it has a top margin of 10 pixels. The total space between the two isn't 22 pixels (10+12)—it's 12 pixels (the value of the larger margin). And, if you remove the bottom margin of the headline, the gap between the two blocks of text isn't gone—it's now 10 pixels, the value for the paragraph's top margin. That's the situation here: You need to modify the paragraph's top margin as well. You do that by creating another style.

8. **Click somewhere in the paragraph below Our History.**

Make sure you don't actually select text; you just want your cursor placed within the paragraph.

9. **In CSS Designer's Sources section, click *soylent_styles.css*, and then, in Selectors, click + .**

A new selector appears: <body p>.

10. **In the Properties section, click the Layout button. Then, in the margin box, click the 0 at the top and type *0 px*.**

    Take a look at your page and you see the desired result (Figure 3-28).

    While you're defining <p> properties, you might as well make the text look spiffy.

11. **In the Properties section, click the Text button (T), and then change *font-family* to "pt sans, Arial, Helvetica, sans-serif."**

    This is one of the web fonts you added earlier.

12. **Click the value next to *font-size*, choose px, and then type *14*.**

    CSS provides a lot of control over type, including the ability to adjust the leading, or the space between lines in a paragraph.

13. **Click the grayed-out value next to *line-height*, choose %, and then type *150*.**

    The *line-height* property controls the space between lines of text. In this case, you set that space to 150 percent, which means that each line will be 150 percent (or 1.5 times) the height of the font. A setting of 150 adds more space than usual between each line of text in a paragraph—the result is more white space and a more luxurious feel.

FIGURE 3-28

Headings like Our History look better when they sit snug atop a paragraph. To create this look, you need to change both the heading's margin-bottom *value and the paragraph's* margin-top *value. In this example, both are set to 0px.*

Creating a Class Style

Now you'll create a style to format the copyright notice at the bottom of the page. It's inside a regular paragraph tag (<p>), so it gets all its formatting from the <p> tag style. Here's an instance where you'd like to style a single paragraph without affecting the other paragraphs on the page. A class style is the perfect solution.

1. **In CSS Designer's Sources section, click *soylent_styles.css*. In the Selectors section, click + , and then type *.copyright*. Press Enter (Return).**

   Don't forget the period at the beginning of "copyright." That identifies your selector as a class rather than as an HTML tag.

   NOTE Some beginners think that whenever you create a new style, you also need to create a new external style sheet. On the contrary, you can—and should—store more than one style in a single external style sheet. In fact, if you're creating a set of styles for an entire site, put them all in the same external style sheet.

2. **In the Selectors section, click *.copyright*, and then, in the Properties section, click the Text button (T).**

   CSS Designer scrolls to the text properties. By now, you probably know the drill.

3. **Click *font-family* and choose "pt sans, Arial, Helvetica, sans-serif." For the *font-size* property, choose px, and then type *12*. Set the *font-weight* property to 700. At the top, click the color box and choose white.**

   Because the text is now white (the same color as the page), you'll change the background color to make the copyright notice stand out.

4. **In the Properties section, click the Border button and then scroll down until you see *background-color*.**

   You'll add a background color now (background images are discussed on page 252).

5. **In the background-color box, type *#145207*.**

   To allow a little breathing room around the copyright text, you'll add some padding.

6. **In the Properties section, click the Layout button (the first one). Then, in the padding box, click the link in the center and type *5px* in any of the number boxes.**

   The link lets you set the top, bottom, left, and right padding to the same values. While margins control the space between elements (like the gap between paragraphs), *padding* controls the space between the content and the content's border, which includes the background of the page. In other words, adding padding enlarges the background around the text (or other content) you're styling.

   You'll change the copyright notice's margin settings as well.

7. **For the *margin-top*, type *25px*. For *margin-left*, type *0px*.**

   The window should look like the one in Figure 3-29. The 25 pixels of the top margin push the copyright notice away from the bottom of the paragraph above it. In addition, since Dreamweaver indents all the paragraphs 75 pixels from the left edge, you need to set the left margin here, in the copyright notice, to *0px*.

This overrides the 75-pixel margin from the <p> tag style and lets the copyright notice hug the left edge of the page.

You may have noticed that none of your *.copyright* styles have taken effect. That's because the line at the bottom of your page doesn't know it's a copyright notice. Unlike HTML tag styles, class styles don't show up anywhere until you apply them by hand.

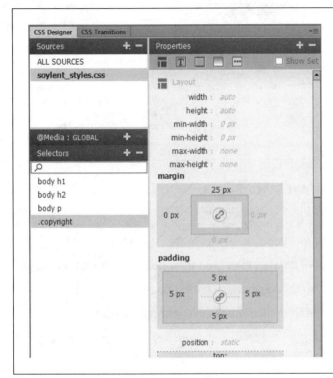

FIGURE 3-29

The difference between padding and margin settings is subtle but important. Both properties add space around content you're styling. And if you don't have a background color, image, or border, both properties pretty much act the same way. However, when you do have a background color, image, or border, padding adds space between the content and the backgrounds and borders. Margins add space outside the border and background.

8. **Scroll to the bottom of the page and select the last paragraph, the copyright notice.**

   This action sets you up for applying the style. You can also just click anywhere inside the paragraph (without selecting any text) to apply a class style.

9. **In the Properties panel, click the HTML button, and then, from the Class menu, choose copyright (see Figure 3-30).**

   Boom—the copyright notice suddenly changes size and color. Magic.

FIGURE 3-30

The Class menu in the HTML mode of the Properties panel lists all class styles. It also displays the style name using the style's formatting—in this case, bold, white text with a dark-green background. Notice that the menu lists only class styles; tag styles don't appear here, since you don't apply them manually. You can also apply a class using the Properties panel's CSS mode, as described on page 124.

Attaching an External Style Sheet

Now that you've created these styles, you may wonder how you can use them on other pages—after all, that's the beauty of external style sheets. Once created, it's a simple process to link other pages in the site to that style sheet.

1. **Choose File→Save All Related Files, and then close the *about.html* page.**

   You'll open a new web page and attach the external style sheet to it.

2. **In the Files panel, double-click the file *events.html* to open it.**

   This file is another page for the cafe's website. It has no formatting yet, so you'll attach the external style sheet you just created.

3. **In CSS Designer, click the Add Source button (+) and choose Attach Existing CSS File.**

   Dreamweaver opens the Attach Existing CSS File window.

4. **Click Browse.**

   Dreamweaver opens the Select Style Sheet dialog box.

5. **Navigate to the Chapter03 folder (or click the Site Root button), and then double-click the *soylent_styles.css* file.**

   Don't forget the Site Root button. It appears on every window in which you need to save, open, or select a file. It's a great shortcut to make sure you're working in the correct folder for your site.

   You can ignore the other settings in the Attach External Style Sheet window for now (they're described on page 523).

6. **Click OK to attach the style sheet to the page.**

   Dreamweaver instantly formats the headlines and main text of the story. Pretty cool—and very efficient. You need to apply the *.copyright* class style to only the last paragraph on the page.

7. **Scroll to the bottom of the page, and then click anywhere inside the paragraph with the copyright notice.**

   Next you'll style the paragraph.

8. **From the Class menu in the Properties panel, select "copyright."**

   This page is almost done. Preview it in a web browser to see what you need to do next.

9. **Press F12 (Option-F12) to preview the page in your browser.**

   Dreamweaver probably prompts you to save your files; go ahead and do that. The page opens in a browser; notice that the bulleted list doesn't use the same font as the paragraph text. You'll change that now.

10. **Return to Dreamweaver and add a style for the <ul> tag.**

    In other words, place your cursor in the list. In CSS Designer's Sources section, select *soylent_styles.css*. In the Selectors section, click +. The selector name "body ul li" appears in the Selectors section. Click an empty spot in Dreamweaver to accept that name. To review, the compound name identifies a list item (<li>), within an unordered list (<ul>) within the body of the page (<body>).

11. **In the Properties section, click the T button. Set *font-family* to "pt sans, Arial, Helvetica, sans-serif," choose px from the font-size drop-down menu, and then type *14*.**

    This matches the settings for the paragraph text. Lastly, change the bullet to a square shape.

12. **In the Properties section, click the Layout button, and then, beside *margin-left*, type *50px*.**

    This sets the list off from the left edge of the page.

13. **Scroll down through the text properties until you see *list-style-type*. Click the grayed-out word "undefined" and choose "square."**

    You finished the style for the bulleted list items. To see the square bullets and some of the other formatting changes, you may need to go into Live view.

14. **In the upper-right corner of the Properties section, click Show Set.**

    The Properties section displays only the properties to which you've assigned values. The Show Set feature is helpful when you want to quickly review and update the styles for a selector.

15. Press F12 (Option-F12) to preview the page in your web browser.

Dreamweaver prompts you to save your files; go ahead and do that. The finished page should look something like Figure 3-31. If you'd like to compare your finished product to the completed version, you'll find those pages in the tutorial's Chapter03_complete folder.

> **NOTE** When you view pages in your web browser, you may need to hit your browser's Refresh button to see the most recent changes you made to a style sheet. This is a problem you'll encounter when you design pages with external style sheets—web browsers often *cache* them. Normally that's a good thing—it means repeat visitors have to wait only once for the CSS file to download—the first time they visit your site. But when you're in the midst of a design, frantically switching back and forth between Dreamweaver and a web browser preview, the browser might retrieve the obsolete version of the external style sheet saved in its cache rather than the newly updated file on your computer. (The Safari browser is particularly aggressive at holding onto cached files, so if you preview in that browser, make sure to reload the page when you do.)
>
> You can work around this problem. Open the Preferences window (Edit→Preferences [Dreamweaver→Preferences]), select "Preview in Browser," and then turn on the "Preview using temporary file" checkbox. Now when you preview the page, Dreamweaver makes a temporary file on your computer that incorporates both the CSS and HTML of the page. This circumvents a browser's cache so that now you're seeing the very latest changes. It has the added benefit of stopping Dreamweaver's annoying "You must save your file before previewing" dialog box each time you preview an unsaved page.

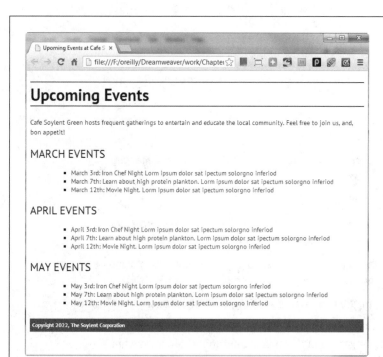

FIGURE 3-31

CSS offers a lot of design tools to produce beautiful typography for your web pages. In addition, an external style sheet lets you quickly, easily, and consistently style hundreds of pages with little extra work.

Links

The humble hyperlink may not raise eyebrows anymore, but the notion that you can navigate a whole sea of information, jumping from one island of content to another with a simple mouse click, is a powerful phenomenon. Interested in a particular band? Go to Google, type in the band's name, *click* to go to its website, *click* to see its upcoming gigs, *click* to go to the venue's website, and then *click* to buy tickets.

Although embedding links is a basic task in building web pages, and even though Dreamweaver—for the most part—shields you from the complexities of doing so, links can be tricky to understand. The first section of this chapter gives you an overview of links and explains the technical distinctions between different types of links. The rest of the chapter, with sections on formatting the appearance of your links and creating navigation menus, will help turn you into a link-crafting maestro.

NOTE If you already understand links, or if you're eager to start using them, jump to the tutorial on page 216.

■ Understanding Links

Links are snippets of HTML that give web browsers directions to get from one web page to another. What makes links powerful is that the distance covered by those directions doesn't matter. A link can lead to another page on the same site just as easily as it can lead to a page on a web server halfway around the globe. Behind the scenes, a simple HTML tag called the anchor tag (<a>) makes each and every link work. Links come in three flavors: *absolute*, *document-relative*, and *root-relative*. See page 182 for examples of each.

Absolute Links

When people want to mail you a letter, they ask for your address. Suppose it's 123 Main St., Smithville, NY 12001, USA. No matter where in the country your friends are, if they write *123 Main St., Smithville, NY 12001, USA* on an envelope and mail it, their letters will get to you. That's because your address is unique.

Similarly, every web page has a unique address, called a *URL* (most people pronounce it "you-are-el"), or Uniform Resource Locator. If you open a web browser and type *http://www.cafesoylentgreen.com/events/iron_chef.html* into the address bar, the browser opens the iron chef event page for Cafe Soylent Green.

This URL is an *absolute link*—it's the complete, unique address for a single web page. Absolute links always begin with *http://*, and they always lead to the same destination page, no matter what page you put that link on—an absolute link in a web page can call up another page within the same site or a page on an entirely different site. You'll use absolute links any time you link to a web page *outside of your own site*— they're the *only* way to link to a page on a different site. But when you want to call up a page *within* your site, there's another way to write a link, described next.

The bottom line: Use absolute links when you want to link to a page on another website.

Document-Relative Links

Suppose you, the resident of 123 Main Street, drop in on a couple who just moved into a house directly across the street. After letting them know about all the great restaurants nearby, you tell them about a party you're having at your place.

When they ask you where you live, you could say, "I live at 123 Main St., Smithville, NY 12001, USA," but your neighbors would probably think you needed psychiatric help. Instead, you'd say something like, "Just walk across the street, and there you are." Of course, you can't use these instructions as your mailing address, nor would they make sense for a neighbor who lived seven houses down. Those directions only help the neighbors directly across the street get from their house to yours.

To link from one web page to another in the same website, you use a similar shorthand, called a *document-relative link*. In essence, a document-relative link—like the directions you gave your neighbors—tells a browser where to find a page *relative* to your current location, in this case, relative to the current web page. If two pages are in the same folder, for instance, the path is as simple as the code version of "Go to that page over there"—in its entirety, the link is no more than the target filename—*index. html*, for example. You can leave off all that *http://www.your_site.com/* business, because you're already on that site and within that folder.

Document-relative links can be finicky, however, because they're completely dependent on the location of the page containing the link. If you move that page to another part of your site—putting it in a different folder, for example—the link won't work. It's as though your neighbors moved across town—they can't walk across the street to get to your house any longer. This vulnerability makes web designers reluctant to use document-relative links, even though they're ideal for linking from one page to another in the same site.

Fortunately, Dreamweaver makes working with document-relative links so easy you may forget what all the fuss is about. In Dreamweaver, whenever you save a page that has a document-relative link to a folder different from the page's original folder—a maneuver that would normally shatter all the links on a page—Dreamweaver quietly *rewrites* the links before it saves the file so that the links still work. Even better, using the program's site-management tools, you can reorganize your site with impunity, moving files and folders without harming the delicate connections between your site's files. (You'll learn about Dreamweaver's site-management features in Part 5 of this book.)

Root-Relative Links

Root-relative links, also called *site root-relative links*, tell browsers how to get from one page to another within the same site, just as document-relative links do. But in this case, the link describes the path *relative to the site's root folder*—the folder that contains your site's home page and all your other pages, folders, and files. (For a detailed description of the root folder and the structure of a website, see page 745.)

Here's how a root-relative link works: Imagine you work in a big office building. You need to get to a coworker's office in the same building, so you call her for directions. She may not know the precise directions from your office to hers, but she *can* tell you how to get from the building's entrance to her office. Since you both know where the building's front door is, these directions work well. In fact, she can give everyone in the building the same directions and they'll be able to find her office, too (they all know where the entrance is). Think of the office building as your site, and its front door as the *root* of your site. Root-relative links always begin with a slash (/). This slash is a stand-in character for the root folder—the front door—of your site. A root-relative link always leads to the same page, no matter where the link is on your website.

If you use Dreamweaver for all your web page development, you probably won't need root-relative links. Using document-relative links, Dreamweaver does a great job of mapping (and, if necessary, remapping) the connections to all the pages and files on your site, with very little effort on your end. Still, on rare occasions, you may find it necessary to create root-relative links. For example, suppose your client asks you to create a new page for an existing site. She gives you text, some graphics, and a list of the other pages on the site that this page needs to link to. The problem is, your client doesn't know where on the site the new page needs to go, and her webmaster won't return your calls.

Fortunately, you can use root-relative links to solve this dilemma. Since root-relative links work no matter where the page is on your site, you could create the page and then let the client put it anywhere in her site, and the links will still work.

There's one major drawback to root-relative links: They don't work when you test them on your own computer. If you click a root-relative link in a web page that's sitting on your computer's hard drive, the link either doesn't work or it produces only a "File not found" error. That's because you haven't defined a root directory on your local machine, so the link doesn't have a route to follow. Root-relative links work only when a website resides on a web server, because you defined a root folder when you set up the site.

> **NOTE** There's one exception to the "root-relative links don't preview correctly" problem. Dreamweaver lets you preview a web page two ways: *with* a temporary file or *without* one. The temporary-file option has a couple of advantages: You can preview a page without having to save it first, and you can preview *on your local computer* any root-relative links on the page.
>
> To turn this feature on, go to Edit→Preferences (Dreamweaver→Preferences), click the "Preview in Browser" category, and then turn on the Preview Using Temporary File checkbox. Behind the scenes, Dreamweaver rewrites root-relative links as *document-relative* links whenever it creates a temporary file. If you see files in your site with weird names like *TMP2zlc3mvs10.htm*, those are the temporary files Dreamweaver creates. Feel free to delete them.

One solution to the root-relative links problem is to install a web server on your computer and put your site files inside it (see page 921). That's the approach you'll take when you build dynamic sites, discussed in Chapter 24.

Parts of a URL

Each chunk of a URL helps a browser find the proper web page. Take the following URL, for instance: *http://www.cafesoylent-green.com/events/iron_chef.html*. Many websites these days even leave off the www, and you can find them simply by their domain name, like *http://cafesoylentgreen.com*.

- **http://.** This portion of the address specifies the *protocol*, the communications technology a browser uses to interact with a web server. *HTTP* stands for *hypertext transfer protocol*; you use it to open a web page. You use other protocols for other web tasks, such as *ftp* when you want to transfer files to and from a server, and *mailto* when you want to send email messages to mail servers. *HTTPS* stands for hypertext transfer protocol secure, and you write it as *https://* in the address bar of a browser. HTTPS requires a special server setup, and it encrypts the communications between a browser and a web server so snoops can't see the information you send and receive.

Bank websites, e-commerce sites, and other sites that deal with sensitive information use HTTPS web servers.

- **www.cafesoylentgreen.com.** This is the web address of the computer dishing out the pages for Cafe Soylent Green's website—that is, it's the address of the web *server* where all the cafe's pages reside. The *www* part identifies a website within the *domain* cafesoylentgreen. com (*http://cafesoylentgreen.com*). You can have multiple websites in a single domain, such as *http://news. cafesoylentgreen.com*, *http://secret.cafesoylentgreen. com*, and so on.
- **/events/.** This is the name of a folder (also called a directory) on the web server.
- **iron_chef.html.** This is the name of the file the web browser will open—it's the filename of the web page itself, the HTML document you created in Dreamweaver.

Unless you have a specific reason to use root-relative links (like your IT department tells you to), avoid their pitfalls by sticking to document-relative links. But keep this discussion in mind—later in the book, you'll see that, behind the scenes, Dreamweaver's site-management features use root-relative paths to track your site's files.

NOTE You can run into trouble with root-relative links if the site you're working on is located in a folder inside a web server's root folder. For example, say your buddy gives you space on his web server at *www.my_buddy. com*. He says you can put your site in a folder called *my_friend*, so your URL is *http://www.my_buddy.com/ my_friend/*. In this case, your web pages don't sit at the root of the site—they're in a folder *inside* the root. So a root-relative link to your home page would be */my_friend/index.html*. Dreamweaver can handle a situation like this, but only if you provide the correct URL for your site—*http://www.my_buddy.com/my_friend/*—when you set it up (see Figure 4-1).

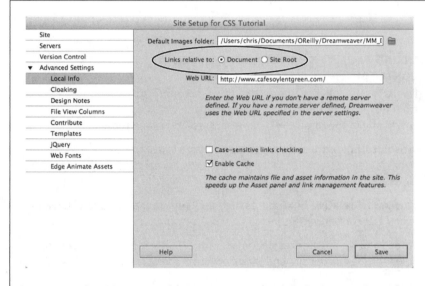

FIGURE 4-1

When you set up a new site, Dreamweaver asks you for the site's URL. Even if that address leads to a subfolder within your root folder, it's easy to figure out—it's the site's actual address, the one you need to type in to locate the site on the Internet. Expand the list of Advanced Settings options on the left of the Site Setup window, click the Local Info category, and then type the full web address of your site in the Web URL box. You can also tell Dreamweaver which type of link—document-relative or root-relative—it should use when it creates a link to another page on your site (circled). You can always return to this window to change this option; choose Site→Manage Sites, select your site, and then click Edit.

Link Types in Action

Figure 4-2 shows you the structure of a fictitious website, NationalExasperator.com, on a hard drive: folders filled with HTML documents and graphics. Here's a closer look at some links you might find on the site's pages and how they might work.

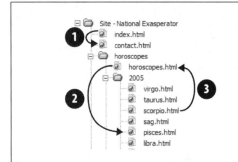

FIGURE 4-2

Here are a few examples of links for a fictitious website located at http://www.nationalexasperator.com. The three arrows show the original page (that's where each arrow starts) and the page it links to (that's where each arrow ends).

■ LINKING FROM THE HOME PAGE TO THE CONTACT US PAGE (CONTACT.HTML)

Most websites use the filename *index.html* or *index.htm* for the home page. You can link from this page to the *contact.html* page—identified by the number 1 in Figure 4-2—using any of the three link types discussed above and these addresses:

- **Absolute link address**: *http://www.nationalexasperator.com/contact.html*. What it means: Go to the website at *http://www.nationalexasperator.com* and download the page *contact.html*.

- **Document-relative link address:** *contact.html*. What it means: Look in the folder the current page is in and download *contact.html*.

- **Root-relative link address:** */contact.html*. What it means: Go to the top-level folder of the current site and then download *contact.html*.

> **TIP** If you can write an absolute URL, you can easily write a root-relative URL. Simply strip off the *http://* and the web server name. In the example above, erasing the *http://www.nationalexasperator.com* in the absolute address leaves */contact.html*—the root-relative path.

■ LINKING FROM THE HOROSCOPES PAGE TO THE PISCES PAGE

Imagine you build a web page that you want to link to a page in a *subfolder* of your site. Here's how you'd use each of the three link types to do that, as identified by the number 2 in Figure 4-2. (In this example, the subfolder is called 2005.)

- **Absolute link address**: *http://www.nationalexasperator.com/horoscopes/ 2005/pisces.html*. What it means: Go to the website *http://www.nationalexasperator.com*, look in the Horoscopes folder, look in the folder 2005, and then download the page *pisces.html*.

- **Document-relative link address:** *2005/pisces.html*. What it means: From the current page, look in the folder 2005 and then download the page *pisces.html*.

- **Root-relative link address:** */horoscopes/2005/pisces.html*. What it means: Go to the top-level folder of this site, go to the Horoscopes folder, look in the folder 2005, and then download the page *pisces.html*.

■ **LINKING FROM THE SCORPIO PAGE TO THE HOROSCOPES PAGE**

Now suppose you build a web page and store it in a deeply nested folder. You want to link that page to a document outside that folder, like link 3 in Figure 4-2:

- **Absolute link address**: *http://www.nationalexasperator.com/horoscopes/ horoscopes.html*. What it means: Go to the website at *http://www.national- exasperator.com*, look in the Horoscopes folder, and then download the page *horoscopes.html*.

- **Document-relative link address:** *../horoscopes.html*. What it means: Go up one level—outside the current folder—and then download the page *horoscopes. html*. In website addresses, a forward slash (/) represents a folder or directory. The two dots (..) mean "Go up one level" into the parent folder of the current folder. If you needed to link to a page that's up two levels—for example, to link from *scorpio.html* to the About Us page (*about.html*)—you'd use *../* twice, like this: *../../about.html*.

- **Root-relative link address:** */horoscopes/horoscopes.html*. What it means: Go to the top-level folder of this site, look in the *Horoscopes* folder, and then download the page *horoscopes.html*.

In short, use absolute URLs to link to pages *outside* your site folder, use document- relative links to link to pages *within your site*, and, unless you know what you're doing (or your IT department tells you to), avoid using root-relative links altogether.

■ Adding Links to a Page

If all this talk of links gets you confused, don't worry. Links *are* confusing, making them one of the best reasons to use Dreamweaver. If you can navigate to a docu- ment on your own computer or anywhere on the Web, you can create a link to it in Dreamweaver.

Browsing for a File

To create a link from one page to another on your local website, use the Proper- ties panel's "Browse for File" button (■; see Figure 4-3) or its keyboard shortcut, Ctrl+L (⌘-L).

Point to file   Link title

Class None ▼ **B** *I* ≣ ≣ ≣ ≣   Title
Link [   ] ▼ ⊕ 📁   Target [▼]

Link field   Browse for file   Link target

FIGURE 4-3

The Properties panel gives you three ways to add links to a web page: by typing its URL in the Link box, or by finding and selecting the file using either the "Point to File" tool (the radar icon, ⊕) or the "Browse for File" button (the folder icon, 📁).

You browse for a file in Dreamweaver using the same type of dialog box you use to open or save a file, making "Browse for File" the easiest way to add a link. (To link to a page on another website, you need to type the web address into the Link box in the Properties panel. Turn to page 188 for instructions.)

Here's how to add a link to a page:

1. **In the document window, select the text or image you want to make into a link.**

   For text links, you can select a single word, a sentence, or an entire paragraph. When you add a link to text, the selected words appear blue and underlined (depending on your visitors' web browser settings), like billions of links before them.

   You can turn a picture into a link, too—a great way to add attractive graphics-based navigation buttons. Your visitors will see the "pointing finger" icon when they point to a linked picture.

NOTE When you add a link to an image, Internet Explorer 8 and earlier versions draw a blue border around the image, just as linked text has a blue underline. Fortunately, with some simple CSS, you can create a style for the <img> tag that gets rid of the blue outline (see page 116 if you're unsure about creating styles). Under the Border category of the CSS Rule Definition window, set the border style to "none" (see page 250 for more on CSS borders).

---

2. **In the Properties panel, click 📁 (a.k.a. the "Browse for File" button), or choose Modify→Make Link, or press Ctrl+L (⌘-L).**

   Whichever command you use, the Select File dialog box opens (see Figure 4-4 for Windows, Figure 4-5 for Macs).

TIP You can also use the "Browse for File" method in Code view: Select the text and then press Ctrl+L (⌘-L).

---

3. **Navigate to and select the target file, that is, the file you want the link to open.**

   When you use the "Browse for File" technique, you can only specify a page that's part of your website—you can't "browse" to an external web page, in other words—the file needs to reside in your local root folder (see the box on page 29) or in a folder therein. Why? Remember that, to a website, the root folder is like the edges of the known universe—nothing exists outside it. If you try to link to a file *outside* the root folder—like to a file on your desktop—Dreamweaver tells you it's a problem and offers to copy the file to your root folder for you. Accept the offer.

> **NOTE**   If you double-click the name of a file in the Select File dialog box, Dreamweaver both selects the file *and* closes the Select File dialog box.

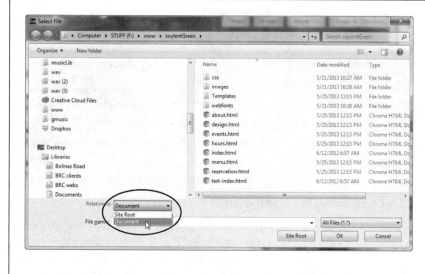

FIGURE 4-4

In Windows, use the Select File dialog box to identify a link's target page. When you set up a site, you can tell Dreamweaver whether to use document- or root-relative links (page 179). Later, if you need to temporarily switch to a different type of link (to a root-relative link if you set up your site for document-relative links, for example), use the "Relative to" drop-down menu (circled).

4. **Make sure you select the correct type of link—document- or root-relative— from the "Relative to" drop-down menu.**

   As noted earlier, document-relative links are usually your best choice. Root-relative links don't work when you preview your site on your own computer. (They do, however, work once you move the pages to your web server.)

> **NOTE**   You can skip step 4 by universally setting the type of link your sites should use in the Site Setup window (see Figure 4-1 for details).

FIGURE 4-5

Every file in a website has to be somewhere inside a local root folder (see the box on page 29). This master folder holds all your site's files, including sub-folders that hold yet other files. Because the root is so central to site management, Dreamweaver includes a Site Root button (circled) in every window that requires selecting or saving a file. (This example shows a Mac window; on Windows PCs, the button is near the lower-right corner, as shown in Figure 4-4.) Click this button to jump straight to your site's root folder so you know exactly where you are on your hard drive, making it easy to navigate to the file you need.

5. Click OK (Choose) to apply the link.

The text or image you made into a link in step 3 now opens another web page. If you haven't yet saved the target web page in your site, Dreamweaver doesn't know how to write the document-relative link to it, so it uses an interim solution: it assigns the link a temporary path until you save the page—see the box on page 187 for details.

After you apply a link, the link text appears underlined and colored in Design view (using the color defined by the Page Properties window, shown in Figure 1-24). Press F12 (Option-F12 on Macs) to preview the page in your browser, where you can click the link to test it.

Using the "Point to File" Tool

You can also create links by dragging an icon from the Properties panel to the Files panel (see Figure 4-6) to a file in the Files panel. If your site involves a lot of links, learning to use the "Point to File" tool will save you time and energy.

The Mysterious Triple Slashes

Why do my links start with file:///?

Links that begin with *file:///* (*file:///C:/missingmanual/ book_site/cafe/events.html*, for example) aren't valid on the Web. Rather, they're temporary addresses that Dreamweaver creates as placeholders for links it will rewrite later. (A *file:///* path tells Dreamweaver to look for the file on your computer.) You'll spot these addresses when you add document-relative links to a page you haven't saved, or when you work with files outside of your site's local root folder.

Suppose you're working on a web page that contains your company's legal mumbo-jumbo, but you haven't yet saved it. After adding a document-relative link to your home page, you notice that the Properties panel's Link box begins with *file:///*. Since you haven't saved your legal page, Dreamweaver doesn't know its folder location and can't create a relative link telling a browser where to go to get the page. So it creates a temporary link, which helps it keep track of which page to link to. Once you save the page somewhere on your site, Dreamweaver rewrites the link in proper document-relative format, replacing the temporary *file:///* link.

Likewise, Dreamweaver can't write a "legitimate" link (a link that really *will* work in a web browser) to a file outside the local root folder. Since it considers anything beyond the root folder outside the bounds of the site, Dreamweaver can't write a link to "nowhere." So, if you save the page you're working on *outside* the local root folder, Dreamweaver writes all document-relative links on that page as file paths beginning with *file:///*. (This problem can also crop up if you use Dreamweaver without first setting up a site—that's why that simple site setup process, described on page 23, is so important.) To avoid this invalid link problem, always save your web pages inside the local root folder or in a folder *inside* the local root folder. (To learn more about root folders and websites, see page 745.)

If you set up a site and link to a page—or you add an image to the page (Chapter 5)—that's stored outside your local root folder, Dreamweaver has the same problem. However, in this instance, Dreamweaver gives you the option of copying the out-of-bounds file to a location of your choosing within the root folder. Then Dreamweaver rewrites the link so that it opens the copy of the page (or displays the image) that's now part of your website.

To use the "Point to File" tool effectively, position your document window and Files panel side by side. Keep in mind, you must always select the text or image in the document window before you create a link.

1. **In the document window, select the text or image you want to turn into a link.**

   Make sure you open both the Properties panel (Window→Properties) and the Files panel (Window→Files). (Before using the Files window, you need to create a local site, as described on page 23.)

NOTE The "Point to File" tool works in Code view as well.

2. **Drag the "Point to File" icon (⊚) from the Properties panel to a web page in the Files window.**

   Or Shift-drag the selected text or image in the document window to any web page in the Files panel, bypassing the Properties panel altogether (this method works only in Design view, however).

FIGURE 4-6

In the document window, select the text you want to turn into a link (circled). To link to another page, drag the "Point to File" icon (the radar image in the Properties panel) to a web page in the Files panel (right). In this example, Dreamweaver creates a link to the web page iron_chef.html. You could create the same link by Shift-dragging the selected text to the iron_chef.html page in the Files panel. The text doesn't actually move, Dreamweaver just creates a link to the target page.

TIP You can also link to a file in the Files panel by dragging the file into the Link box in the Properties panel. If you haven't selected any text when you drag the file, Dreamweaver automatically adds the filename as text. For example, if you drag *mysong.mp3* from the Files panel, that filename appears on the page.

3. **Once you're pointing to the target web page in the Files panel, release the mouse button.**

   The selected text or image in your web page now links to the file you just pointed to.

NOTE Bizarre Bug Alert: If you use two monitors as you build web pages, with your main monitor (the one with the Start menu for Windows, or the one where a program's menu bar appears on Macs) on the right, and the second monitor on the left, the "Point to File" icon may not work. Then again, it might! Strange, but truly infuriating.

Typing or Pasting a Web Address

If you need to link to a page on another website, or if you feel comfortable working with document-relative links, you can simply type the target page's URL into the

Link box in the Properties panel. Note that this technique—and the hyperlink object tool discussed next—are the *only* ways to add links to pages *outside* your website.

1. **In the document window, select the text or image you want to make into a link.**

2. **In the Properties panel's Link box (Figure 4-3), type the URL (the path) to the file.**

   If the link leads to another website, type an absolute URL—that is, a complete web address, starting with *http://*.

> **TIP** An easier approach is to go to the destination web page using your browser and then copy the complete URL—including the *http://* part—from the browser's address bar and then paste it into the Link box.

To link to a page on your own site, type a document-relative link (see page 178 for some examples). Letting Dreamweaver write the correct path using the point-to-file or browsing technique described above is a good way to avoid typos. But typing the path name can come in handy when, say, you want to create a link to a page you haven't yet created, but whose eventual URL you know.

3. **Press Enter (Return) to apply the link.**

   While you don't necessarily have to hit Enter (Return)—sometimes you can just click elsewhere on the page and keep working—Dreamweaver has been known to forget the link and not apply it. This is true for most text boxes in the Properties panel. So if you type information directly into a box in the Properties panel (to create a link, add a title, and so on), get into the habit of hitting the Enter (Return) key to make sure your change sticks.

> **NOTE** If you add an absolute link to a website without specifying a web page, add a final forward slash (/) to the end of the address. For example, to link to Yahoo, type *http://www.yahoo.com/*. The final slash tells the web server that you're requesting the default page (the home page) at Yahoo.com.
>
> Although leaving out the slash works, too (*http://www.yahoo.com*), the server has to do a little extra work to figure out which page to send back, resulting in a slight and unnecessary delay.
>
> Also include the final slash when you link to the default page inside a folder on a site, like this: *http://www.oreilly.com/missingmanuals/*. That saves the browser from first requesting a file named *missingmanuals* and then requesting the default page inside the folder *missingmanuals*.

Using the Hyperlink Object

Dreamweaver gives you yet another way to add links. The Hyperlink object in the Common category of the Insert panel (Figure 4-7) lets you insert a link and set several options. Its only real benefit over the methods described above is that it lets you add text and a link in one step, instead of adding text to a page, selecting it, and then specifying a link address. Unfortunately, this tool works only with text (not graphics), and some of the optional properties don't work in all browsers.

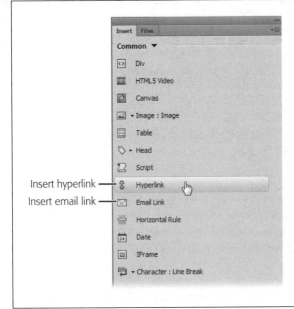

FIGURE 4-7

The Insert panel's Common category offers one-button convenience for creating hyperlinks and email links (to link to an email address).

Insert hyperlink

Insert email link

Here's how you add a hyperlink.

1. **Click the spot on a web page where you want to insert the hyperlink, or select the text or image you want to turn into a hyperlink.**

2. **Choose Insert→Hyperlink, or click the chain icon on the Insert→Common toolbar.**

   The Hyperlink dialog box opens (see Figure 4-8).

FIGURE 4-8

As an alternative to this dialog box, you can apply all the settings you see here, except the "Access key" and "Tab index" properties (see steps 7 and 8 below), to text or images using the Properties panel. Also, keep in mind one somewhat special case: If you want to add an access key and tab index to an existing link without using Insert→Hyperlink, go into Code view (as described in Chapter 7) and hand-edit the HTML.

3. **In the Text box, type the label for your link (that is, the text of the link).**

Whatever you type here is what your guests will see on the page, and what they'll click to follow the link. If you select existing text, Dreamweaver automatically displays that text in the Text box.

4. **Click ▦ and navigate to the page you want to link to.**

Alternatively, type a URL in the Link box.

5. **Set the target window for the link.**

If you want the linked page to open in the current window—as most linked pages do—don't select anything. To make the page open in a new window, select _blank (see the box below for more on targeting links).

The last three options—Title, Access key, and Tab index—are more interesting.

6. **Type a title for the destination page.**

This is optional. Most browsers display page titles in a tooltip when a visitor points to the associated link, as described in the box below.

FREQUENTLY ASKED QUESTION

Targeting and Titling Links

What purpose do the Title box and Target menu in the Properties panel serve?

A link's *title* property supplies additional information about a link, usually to clearly indicate where the link leads. For example, if you linked the words "Click here for more" to an article describing different types of termites, the link text doesn't explain where the link leads—"Click for more *of what?*" you might ask. In this case, you could, in the Properties panel, add the title "A complete list of termite species" to the page (see Figure 4-3). The *title* property is optional, and if your link text already tells you where the link leads, don't bother setting it. In fact, you can avoid thinking about the *title* property altogether if you write text that explains where the link leads: "Click here for a complete list of termite species," for example.

However, in the case of linked images (such as a logo that also acts as a link back to a site's home page), adding a title is a very good idea. Search engines like the *title* property, because it lets them know the purpose of the link; people who use screen readers (programs that help those with vision problems surf the Web) also benefit, since the *title* property can be read out loud and the visitor will know where the link goes. The *title* property has one other unique feature: Web browsers display a pop-up tooltip with the title's text in it when a guest points to the link.

The Target menu has nothing to do with the accuracy of your links. It deals with how a browser displays the destination page when you click a link. You can have the new page replace the current page in the browser window (the way most links work), open in a new browser window (choose the _blank option), or appear in a different *frame* on the same page (an obsolete HTML feature).

_blank is pretty much the only option used these days, but be careful if your pages use the Strict forms of HTML 4.01 and XHTML 1.0 (page xxi); the Target attribute isn't valid code for these doctypes. However, HTML5, recognizing the usefulness of being able to open links in a new tab or window, allows the _blank target...and so does every browser on the planet.

7. **Type a key in the "Access key" box.**

An *access key* lets you follow a link by tapping a key on your keyboard. For example, if you type *h* in the link's "Access key" box, a visitor using Google Chrome for Windows can press Alt+H to open the link. Of course, unless your visitors are psychic, you should include the access key with the link label, as in "Home Page (Alt+H)."

Actually using an access key requires a little computer savvy on the part of your visitors. In addition to knowing they can use the key, they need to know *how* to use it with their browser. The key combinations differ depending on the browser and the operating system, and in the past, browsers' key combinations were all over the place. It's a little more uniform with the latest batch of browsers. Here's the rundown on current Windows browsers:

— Alt+ the access key works in Google Chrome, Safari, and Opera.

— Alt+ the access key + Enter works in Internet Explorer.

— Alt+Shift+ the access key works in Firefox.

Recently, Mac browsers have achieved a little consistency:

— Control+Option+ the access key works in Safari (from version 4 on), Chrome, Firefox, and Opera.

8. **In the "Tab index" box, type a number for the tab order.**

In most browsers, you can press the Tab key to step through the links on a page (and boxes on a form). This feature not only gives you a handy way to go from link to link using your keyboard, but it also lets people who can't use a mouse due to disabilities cycle through the links.

Normally when you press Tab, web browsers highlight the links in the order they appear in the page's HTML. The Tab index, by contrast, lets *you* control the order in which links light up. For example, you can give your navigation buttons priority when someone presses Tab, even if those buttons aren't the first links on the page.

For the link that you want first in the Tab order, type *1* in the "Tab index" box. Number the other links in the order you want the Tab key to trigger them. If you aren't concerned about the order of a particular link, leave this option blank or type *0*. Web browsers highlight that link after your visitor tabs through all the links that *do* have a Tab index.

■ Adding Email Links

If you want to invite visitors to contact you, an *email link* is the perfect solution. When someone clicks the link, his email program automatically launches, and a new, empty message opens with your email address already in the To box. Your guest can then just type his message and click Send.

Consider the email link *mailto:chef@cafesoylentgreen.com*. The first part of any email link, *mailto*, indicates the type of link (an email link in this case), while the second part (*chef@cafesoylentgreen.com*) specifies the email address.

NOTE Email links work only if the person who clicks the link has an email program set up and running on his computer. If someone visits your site from a computer at the public library, for example, he might not be able to send mail. Likewise, if he's using a web-based email client, like Gmail, clicking an email link won't open his Gmail account in a web browser.

You create an email link the same way you create any other Dreamweaver link: by selecting text or an image and typing the *mailto* address in the Properties panel's Link box, as shown above. Dreamweaver offers a shortcut, too:

1. **Type in or select the text you want to turn into a link.** *Email me!* or *Email the webmaster* **are good options.**

    You have to have something to link from, right?

2. **Under the Insert panel's Common category, click the "Email link" icon, ⊞ (see Figure 4-7).**

    Alternatively, choose Insert→Email Link. The Email Link dialog box opens (see Figure 4-9).

FIGURE 4-9

The Email Link dialog box lets you specify a label for an email link, along with the email address itself. You can also select text in your document and click the "Email link" icon in the Objects panel. The text you select will appear in the Text box in this window.

3. **Check the Text box. The word or phrase you highlighted in step 1 should appear here.**

    You can edit the link label if you like.

4. **Type an email address in the Email box.**

    This is the address that appears in your visitors' email programs when they click the link. (You don't have to type *mailto*—Dreamweaver adds it automatically.)

5. **Click OK.**

    Dreamweaver makes the *mailto* link active.

NOTE Some people don't add email links to their websites because they're afraid of spammers' automated programs that search the Web and collect email addresses. There are some tricks to fool these "spambots," but spammers have figured most of them out. The fact is, spammers can attack even Contact Us web forms.

If you're absolutely obsessed with never being spammed, leave your email address off your site. However, many businesses rely on people contacting them for more information, and the harder you make it for a legitimate visitor to contact you, the fewer legitimate contacts you'll receive—after all, you wouldn't have much of a freelance design business if you never provided a way for someone to contact you. Your best bet is to let the spam come, but add a filter to your email program to separate the wheat from the chaff.

◼ Linking Within a Web Page

Clicking a link usually loads a web page in a browser window, but what if you want to link to a specific spot on the *same* page? Webmasters frequently use this technique on long web pages, like FAQs, where links at the top of the page let visitors jump to content lower down on the page; see Figure 4-10.

You create this type of link by adding an HTML tag to the target section of the destination page, giving it a unique ID, and then linking to that ID. Although this method is newer, it works with all current web browsers.

NOTE If you've been building web pages for a while, you're probably familiar with the "named anchor" technique for creating in-page links. That method uses an <a> anchor tag with a name attribute. Because HTML5 doesn't recognize the named anchor, Dreamweaver no longer offers the Insert→Named Anchor command. So instead of trying to use named anchors, use the ID method described here.

Adding an ID to a Target Page

To link to a specific spot in a page, assign an ID to that spot. For example, to link to a subhead way down on a page (a Heading 2, or <h2> tag, for example), you assign an ID to that heading. For text, you add an ID by clicking anywhere inside a paragraph and then, in the Properties panel's ID box, typing the ID name you want to use. (Keep in mind that you can't use spaces or punctuation marks.)

For non-text elements, like images or tables, select the tag (using Dreamweaver's Tag Selector, discussed on page 7), and then type a name in the ID box on the left side of the Properties panel.

You might use IDs in another context, too: to identify and style discrete sections of your page by adding an ID to a tag and then styling the page using CSS (see page 132 for more). The good news is you can use that same ID to both identify the destination point in a target page *and* to style the tag in a style sheet.

FIGURE 4-10

To make it easy for visitors to navigate long web pages, you might list the contents for that page first and add links for each entry so that, when a visitor clicks a link (left), she jumps to the appropriate section of the page (right).

Linking to an ID

Once you add an ID to a tag, creating a link to that ID—either from within the same web page or from a different page—isn't all that different from linking to a standard web page.

To link to an ID on the same page:

1. **In the document window, select the text or image you want to turn into a link.**

   For example, drag across some text, or highlight a graphic.

2. **In the Properties panel's Link box, type #, followed by an ID name you choose.**

   The # sign tells browsers that the link points to an ID. So, to link to an ID named *directions*, you'd type *#directions*.

You can also link from one web page to a particular location on *another* web page. First, you need to add an ID to the destination page. Then, follow the same process you followed to link to a same-page ID, except that you have to specify not only the ID, but the path to the web page as well.

1. **In the document window, select the text or image you want to turn into a link. Then, in the Link box of the Properties panel, type or choose the URL of the destination page.**

   You can use any of the methods described above to identify the target page: browsing, point-to-file, or typing in the path name. Unfortunately, if you browse to select the destination page, Dreamweaver doesn't display any of the IDs on that page, so you need to type in the ID's name as explained in the next step.

2. **Click at the end of the URL or path. Type # followed by the ID's name.**

   In the end, the Link box should look something like this: *contact.html#directions*.

FREQUENTLY ASKED QUESTION

Where Bookmarks Fall Short

When I click a link to a bookmark, my browser is supposed to go to the page and display the bookmarked content at the top of the window. But sometimes the linked-to spot appears in the middle of my browser. What's that about?

Web browsers can't scroll beyond the bottom of a web page, so if you have a bookmark ID near the bottom of a page, the browser can't pull that particular part of the page all the way to the top of the window.

If one of your own web pages exhibits this problem and it really bothers you, the fix is simple: Create a style for the <body> tag and add *bottom padding* (page 465). This adds space after the last bit of content on the page, so browsers can scroll the page all the way to the bookmark.

▪ Modifying Links

At some point, you may need to edit a link. Perhaps the URL you were linking to has changed, or you simply no longer need that link.

Changing a Link's Destination

As you'll read in Part 5 of this book, Dreamweaver provides some amazing tools that automatically update the links on your pages so your site keeps working even if you move files around. But even Dreamweaver isn't smart enough to know when a page on someone *else's* website has been moved or deleted. And you may decide you simply need to change a link so that it points to a different page on your own site. In both cases, you need to edit the links by hand:

1. **Select the text or picture link.**

   The link path appears in the Properties panel's Link box.

2. **Use any of the techniques described on page 183 to specify the link's new target.**

   For example, click ☐ in the Properties panel to target a different page on your own site, or type a complete URL that points to a page outside your site.

Removing a Link

Sometimes you want to stop a link from linking—when the web page you were pointing to no longer exists, for example. You want to keep the originating text or image, but remove the outdated link. In that case, select the link text or image and then use one of these tactics:

- Choose Modify→Remove Link, or press Shift+Ctrl+L (Shift-⌘-L).

- Delete the text in the Link box of the Properties panel and then press Enter (Return).

The text or image remains on your web page, but it no longer links to anything. If you delete a text link, the text changes from your site's link color to the normal text color for the page.

Of course, if you're feeling particularly destructive, you can delete the link's text or image itself, which simultaneously deletes the link.

■ Styling Links

You can control the basic look of links from the Links category of the Page Properties window (Figure 4-11). To open it, choose Modify→Page Properties→Links (CSS), press Ctrl+J→Links (CSS) [⌘-J→Links (CSS)], or click the Page Properties button in the Properties panel (the button appears only when you have either nothing on the page selected or text selected; it doesn't appear if you have an image selected). In the Category list, click "Links (CSS)."

The top set of options—font, size, bold, italic—sets the basic format for every link on the page. The next group of options sets the color of the links under specific conditions. Web browsers keep track of how a visitor interacts with the links on a page, such as when she points to a link. Each link has four modes (called *states*): a plain, unvisited link is simply called a *link*; a link that a visitor has already clicked (determined by your guest's browser history) is called a *visited* link; a link that a guest's mouse is currently pointing to is technically in what's called a *hover* state, though Dreamweaver refers to it as a *rollover* state; and a link in the process of being clicked (where a visitor has pressed but not released his mouse button) is known as an *active* link.

FIGURE 4-11

The Page Properties' Links (CSS) window lets you set basic properties for the links on a page, including their font, color, and size. This window is mainly a shortcut for creating CSS styles.

You can style each link state individually. In most browsers, a plain link appears blue until you visit the linked page—then the link turns purple. This helpful color-coding lets a visitor know whether to follow a link: "Hey, there's a page I haven't seen," or "Been there, done that."

The rollover (or hover) link is useful in telling visitors that they can click the link because it provides visual feedback, and it lends itself to a lot of creative potential. For example, when a visitor points to the link, you can change the link's color, add a background image, or change the background color. (To get neat effects like these, you need to go beyond the Page Properties window and set the styles using CSS, as described next.) But there's a drawback to rollovers these days: Visitors using phones and tablets can't see the rollover effect because they're using a finger instead of a mouse, and fingers don't hover.

Finally, an *active* link is for that fleeting moment when a visitor clicks a link but has yet to release the mouse button. It happens so fast that it's usually not worth spending too much time formatting the state.

NOTE Internet Explorer applies the active link style to any link a visitor *tabs* to (some web surfers can't, or don't want to, use a mouse, so they rely on the keyboard to navigate websites). Firefox, Safari, Opera, and Chrome use yet another link state, called *focus*, to style links that someone reaches via the Tab key. See the note on page 200 for more on a link's focus state.

The Page Properties window lets you change the color of each link state. In addition, the "Underline style" menu lets you control whether a browser underlines a link (the norm), displays nothing beneath the link, displays an underline when a guest points to the link, or underlines the link by default but removes it once a visitor points to it. Since web surfers are accustomed to thinking of underlined text as a big "Click Me" sign, think twice before removing underlines from links. Without some clear indication that the text is a link, visitors may never see (or click) the links on your page.

One problem with using the Page Properties window to style links is that the settings apply only to the current page. That's because the Page Properties window saves the CSS styles to an internal style sheet in the page. Fortunately, you don't need to set the Page Properties on every page of your site; you can export those styles or even drag them to an external style sheet. (To learn how, see page 405.) Alternatively, you can bypass the Page Properties window altogether and create CSS link styles from scratch—which you'll learn about next.

CSS and Links

Using CSS Designer to style links lets you tap many more formatting options than the Page Properties window offers. In fact, CSS Designer lets you apply nearly every CSS property to links. For example, you can set all the text options discussed on page 153—font size, weight, variant, letter spacing, and so on. In addition, you can add a border (page 250) and a background color to a link to make it look like a button.

To format the look of all your links, create a style for the <a> tag (the tag that creates links) using the instructions on page 116. To create a different look for a particular link (if you want that "Buy Now!" link to be bigger and bolder than other links on a page, for example), create a class style (page 114) and apply it to that link.

To control how a link looks for different states (link, visited, hover, and active), you need to dip a little deeper into the CSS pool and use what's called a *pseudo-class*. Pseudo-classes give you a way to apply special effects to CSS selectors depending on your visitor's actions. For example, you can change the way an <a> tag's link looks based on whether your visitor points to the link, has already clicked the link, and so on.

As you may remember, a selector tells a browser where it should apply a style—*h1* is the selector for formatting every Heading 1, for example. When you style links, the formatting is all about the <a> tag so you want to find and choose the *a* selector in CSS Designer's Selector section. In CSS, you distinguish pseudo-classes from selectors by using a colon between the two. So in a style sheet, the four pseudo-classes for the *a* link look like this: *a:link*, *a:visited*, *a:hover*, and *a:active*. It's easy to create a selector and pseudo-classes in CSS Designer because a pop-up menu prompts you with valid classes as soon as you type in the colon (see Figure 4-12).

You don't have to set all four pseudo-classes; if you're not interested in how your link looks during the nanosecond when a visitor clicks it, skip the *a:active* option. If you want to set more than one pseudo-class, you must create them in the order that they appear in the pop-up Class menu, or the styles may not display as you intend them. In CSS Designer's Selectors section, that means your pseudo-classes should be in this order, from the top: *a:link*, *a:visited*, *a:hover*, and, if you're using it, *a:active*. (A helpful mnemonic for remembering this rule is LoVe HAte—that is, *:link* comes before *:visited*, which comes before *:hover*, which comes before *:active*.) If your links are in the wrong order in the Selectors section, move them. Click the source in CSS Designer's Sources section, and then, in Selectors, click and drag your selectors and their pseudo-classes to the proper position. This actually rearranges the code in the style sheet.

FIGURE 4-12

Create a selector for <a> tags by clicking the Add Selector button (+) and then typing "a." To add a pseudo-class to the selector, type a colon (:). As soon as you do, Dreamweaver opens a pop-up menu that has the names of valid pseudo-classes. All you need to do is click. The first three are the most common pseudo-classes used with links: link, visited, and hover.

NOTE Safari, Firefox, and Chrome browsers understand an additional pseudo-class related to links: *a:focus*. This selector applies when a visitor uses the Tab key to move from one link to another on a page. Each time she jumps to a new link, the browser highlights it and gives the link "focus." All versions of IE treat *a:active* as if it were *a:focus*.

The focus pseudo-class has a special role in making sites accessible to people who navigate websites using a keyboard rather than a mouse. To create a style that formats a link when a visitor tabs to it (instead of pointing to it), create what's called a group style. Here's how: When you create the highlighted link style, choose Compound for the selector type. For the selector name, type in *a:focus, a:active*. This highlights the "tabbed to" link in all current browsers.

Using these styles, you can make your link text appear red and underscored before a visitor clicks the link, twice as large when he points to it, purple and boldfaced when he clicks it, and pale pink after he visits the linked site. (Granted, if you try this, Martha Stewart may never hire you to design her site, but you get the point.)

NOTE For privacy reasons, some browsers limit the styling you can apply to a visited link. In other words, say you create the pseudo-class style *a:visited* and change the font, font size, background color, underline, and set its text color to red; the only visual change the browser will make to a visited link is to change its text color to red—browsers simply ignore the font, background-color, and other settings.

Link pseudo-classes have one drawback: Setting them affects *all* the links on a page. In that respect, adding pseudo-classes to the <a> tag is like creating tag styles.

To apply a style to only certain links on a page, you need to create a class and then create CSS rules to style the class and its pseudo-classes, like link and hover. For example, to create a special look for the text link "Buy Now!", create a selector called *.buynow:link* in CSS Designer. The class, *.buynow*, has the pseudo-class *:link* tacked onto it. To make that link look different when someone points to it, create a *.buynow:hover* selector. Naturally, you need to create the style rules that go along with the *.buynow* class and its pseudo-classes. You can change the color, size, style, and other properties of the text to make the link stand out. To do that, follow the steps for creating a style on page 117. Once you define the style, all you need to do is apply the *.buynow* class to the text on your page. You can do that easily in the Properties panel's Class menu. Check your work in Live view, and you'll see the link with the *.buynow* class applied.

NOTE Descendent selectors provide a more efficient—but more complex—way to format specific links differently from all the other links on a page. You'll find this CSS concept discussed in page 398.

◼ Creating a Navigation Menu

Every website should have navigation links that let visitors jump quickly to different sections of a site. On a shopping site, for example, those links might point to the categories of products for sale—books, DVDs, CDs, electronics, and so on. For a corporate intranet, links to human resources, office policies, company events, and each department might be important. Whatever the site, you should strive to get visitors where they want to go via the shortest route possible. Navigation menus are a good solution, because everyone using a computer is familiar with them.

Dreamweaver CC doesn't have a built-in system for creating navigation menus, but with the help of some third-party tools, known as Adobe Add-ons, you can easily do so. Think of add-ons as helper programs for Dreamweaver; once you download and install them, they give the program capabilities it didn't have before. Best of all, add-ons are fairly easy to get up and running (as you'll see below), and they're integrated into Dreamweaver—their commands and tools appear in Dreamweaver's menus and panels.

Some menus rely on JavaScript and its jQuery plug-in, while others use only CSS to work their magic. Most, however, create a hierarchy of menus, submenus, and menu items using HTML unordered lists (page 91). That makes it easy to add and remove menu items over time, and keeps the structure of the menu separate from its formatting.

Getting a CSS Menu System from Adobe Add-Ons

The tutorial in this chapter uses a menu builder called Advanced CSS Menu Light from Ajatix (Menu Light for short). There are a number of menu creators out there, but this one is available from Adobe Add-ons, which means it's easy to get and install. Ajatix offers a few menu builders, but this one costs everyone's favorite price—nothing.

To automatically download and install add-ons, you need Adobe's Creative Cloud app. For details on downloading and using the app, see the steps below. On Windows computers, it runs in the taskbar in the lower-right corner of the screen. On Macs, it appears on the right side of the menu bar, along with Spotlight and the volume control.

Creative Cloud's file-synching feature handles downloading and installing add-ons. You can turn file synching on and off (though it needs to be on to manage add-ons), and you can pause and restart a download.

To see if you have file synching turned on, go to Creative Cloud→Assets→Files. When file synching is running smoothly, you see the message, "All files up to date" and you can go ahead and follow the steps below to install the CSS menu add-on. If synching is paused, a message near the bottom of the panel says "Synching Paused." Click Resume Sync to start it again. If you have synching turned off, you see a big blue button that says "Start Synching." Click that to turn synching on so you can grab the CSS menu add-on.

> **TIP** If you don't want to leave Creative Cloud's File Sync feature turned on, you can turn it on while you install add-ons and then turn it off when you're done. The master control for file synching is in the Creative Cloud Preferences area. Open Creative Cloud, click the gear-shaped button in the upper-right corner, and then choose Preferences. Click Files and then, under Sync On/Off, click Off.

Follow these steps to download and install Advanced CSS Menu Light from Adobe Add-ons:

1. **In Dreamweaver, choose Window→Browse Add-ons.**

   Your web browser opens and displays the Adobe Add-ons page (*https://creative. adobe.com/addons*). There are tons of extensions, but the buttons along the left side of the page help you find the extension you want.

2. **Click the Dreamweaver icon.**

   The page shows add-ons that work with Dreamweaver.

3. **Below the Featured Add-ons section, click Free.**

   The panel displays no-cost extensions.

4. **Set the "Sort by" menu to Most Popular.**

At this point, you may see Advanced CSS Menu Light near the top of the group of add-ons. If not, take the next step.

5. **In the search box (upper-right) type *CSS Menu*, as shown in Figure 4-13.**

Extensions related to CSS and menus appear in the list.

6. **Click Advanced CSS Menu Light.**

Details about Menu Light fill the panel. If you want more information, explore the Product Info, Rating & Reviews, Notes, and Previews sections.

7. **Click the blue Free button.**

The first time you get an add-on, you see an End-User License Agreement, displaying the usual legalese that explains that the extension is copyrighted. Have your lawyer read it thoroughly before you click "Accept and Continue." If you don't see the agreement, the download starts immediately. Some blue squares dance on the screen while you "acquire" (download) your new add-on. When the process is complete, you see the "Where to find it" section for Advanced CSS Menu Light.

The text explains that you need to restart Dreamweaver. When you do, you'll find an Ajatix category with the menu add-on in your Insert menu (Insert→Ajatix). In the Insert panel, there's an Ajatix category in the drop-down menu.

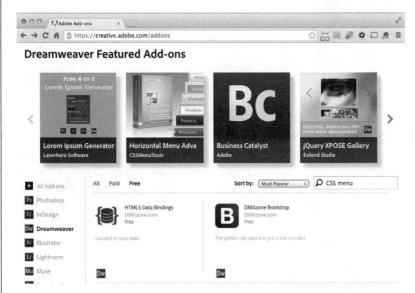

FIGURE 4-13

Adobe Add-ons is your source for finding and installing Dreamweaver tools, like Advanced CSS Menu Light, that extend the power and features of Dreamweaver and other Adobe applications. To browse add-ons, use the All, Paid, and Free buttons. To search for a specific extension, type a couple of keywords in the search box. Once you find an interesting candidate in the grid of add-ons, click it to see more details.

8. **Restart Dreamweaver, go to the Insert panel, and then select Ajatix from the drop-down menu, as shown in Figure 4-14.**

The Ajatix entry appears at the bottom of the menu. When you select it, you see Advanced CSS Drop Down Menu Light. The command to launch Menu Light also appears in the Insert menu (Insert→Ajatix→Advanced CSS Drop Down Menu Light), but you need to restart Dreamweaver before you can see it.

NOTE If you have more than one version of Dreamweaver installed on your computer (for example, Dreamweaver CC and Dreamweaver CC Release 2014), add-ons are installed for only one of the programs. Typically, it's the one you installed first.

In Adobe Exchange, the name for this extension is "Advanced CSS Menu Light," but once it is installed on your computer, the name in the Insert panel is the wordier "Advanced CSS Drop Down Menu Light." They are actually the same thing.

FIGURE 4-14

After you download and install Menu Light, you see Ajatix listed as one of the Insert panel's categories. Click it and you'll see Advanced CSS Drop Down Menu Light, ready for your projects.

Adding a Menu with Submenus

The first step in inserting a menu in a web page is deciding where on the page to put it. A horizontal menu bar, with buttons sitting side by side, works well either at the very top of a page or below the area dedicated to a logo (often called a *banner*; see Figure 4-15). A vertical menu bar, whose buttons are stacked one on top of the other, usually sits at the left edge of a page, below the banner area.

In the next steps, you'll create a menu with submenus for the imaginary Chia Vet website. You can follow along, or change the item names for your own nefarious purposes. These steps assume you've already downloaded and installed the menu builder described in the previous section.

FIGURE 4-15

Menu-builders like Advanced CSS Menu Light usually let you choose between a horizontal (top) or vertical (bottom) navigation bar. Drop-down submenus let you cram loads of links into a small space, but be merciful to your visitors: Navigating a rat's maze to reach a link in a sub-submenu is sometimes a tiring test of patience and hand-mouse coordination.

1. **Start with a web page you've already named and saved. In the document window, click the spot where you want to insert the menu.**

   You can add a menu bar in either Design view or Code view, but it's easier to position it in Design view.

2. **In the Insert panel (Window→Insert), click the drop-down menu, and then click Ajatix.**

   If you installed Menu Light as described on page 202, you see it listed here as Advanced CSS Drop Down Menu Light. If you downloaded other products from the company, they appear here, too.

3. **Click Advanced CSS Drop Down Menu Light.**

   Menu Light opens its Start Wizard, offering two choices, "Create a new menu" and "Insert an existing menu."

4. **Choose "Create a new menu," and then click OK.**

   Menu Light replaces the Start Wizard with a Select Theme panel. The box on the left shows a number of themes of different styles. Horizontal menus top the list, while vertical menus appear near the bottom.

5. **In the left-hand box, click Horizontal – Leaf Green, and then click Apply (in the lower-right corner).**

   As you click theme names on the left, Menu Light previews them on the right. Once you choose a theme that has the color, font, and styles you want, click Apply. Menu Light closes the Select Theme window and opens another window, the New Menu window (Figure 4-16). This window is worth getting to know because you use it to build your menu link by link. And later, when you need to make changes to an existing menu, you use a very similar control panel.

> **TIP** If you want to insert an incomplete menu in a page to serve as a placeholder, you can do that now. Click OK, give your menu a name, and then click Save. A menu bar appears in your document with a single item in it, "Unnamed." With your placeholder menu on the page, you can come back later and build your menu by adding items, submenus, and all the trimmings, as explained on page 209.

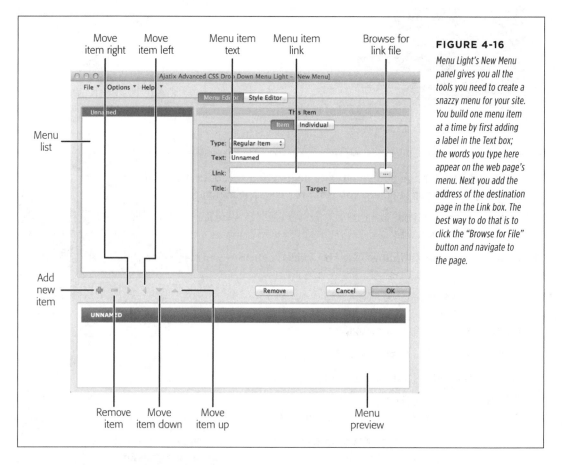

FIGURE 4-16

Menu Light's New Menu panel gives you all the tools you need to create a snazzy menu for your site. You build one menu item at a time by first adding a label in the Text box; the words you type here appear on the web page's menu. Next you add the address of the destination page in the Link box. The best way to do that is to click the "Browse for File" button and navigate to the page.

6. **In the box labeled Text, type *Home*.**

   The words you type in the Text box will appear in the menu. For this first menu item, change the word "Unnamed" to "Home." As you type, Menu Light adds your new item to the list on the left and changes the preview at the bottom to read "Home."

7. **In the Link box, type *index.html*.**

   You can type in any valid link. For this example, it makes sense to type *index. html* because that's the standard name for a website's home or default page. However, the best way to add most links is to click the Browse button ("...") next to the Link box and navigate your way to the destination page. That creates a link with the proper path and no typos!

   At a minimum, you should provide a label and URL for your menu items. As explained in the box on page 191, you don't have to add a title or target. In fact, ignore the target option unless you want the linked page to open in a new browser window. Fill in a title for the link if you feel the need to provide a better description than the one in the Text box. Titles benefit people with screen readers and they can give you a boost with search engines. In this example, you'll add a title.

8. **In the Title box, type *Welcome to Chia Vet*.**

   For most browsers, this message appears as a tooltip that pops up when someone points to a menu item. Screen readers read these words aloud to visitors, and some search engines read and evaluate the words when ranking a page.

9. **Click + on the left side of the panel.**

   That adds a new menu item. The function of the other buttons in this row are pretty easy to figure out. The − button removes an item from the list, while the arrow buttons move items up and down in the list, and in- and outdent them. The details are on page 205.

10. **For the new menu item, change "Unnamed" to *About Us* in the Text box. Then type *about.html* in the Link box. In the Title box, type *More Info about Chia Vet*.**

    It's just that easy to create a second menu item, complete with a link and title. In the next step, you'll add a submenu to About Us.

11. **Click + on the left side of the panel. Below the menu list, click the right arrow button (the Move Item Right button).**

    When you click +, Menu Light adds a new "Unnamed item" below About Us. When you click the Move Item Right button, the Unnamed item shifts to the right in the list. In the menu preview at the bottom of the page, a down arrow (triangle) appears next to About Us, telling you that this menu item includes a submenu. If you point to About Us, you see the submenu with one "Unnamed item" listed.

    Using the arrows below the menu list (Figure 4-16), move items up and down in the list. You see the results immediately in the menu preview. To create a submenu or to add an item to a submenu, click the right arrow button. The left arrow button removes an item from a submenu, bumping it up a level. If it's the last item in the submenu, it removes the submenu entirely.

12. **With "Unnamed item" selected in the list, type *History* in the Text box and then type *history.html* as the link.**

The submenu item now has both a title and a link. Continue adding items and submenus as needed.

13. **When you're done, click OK.**

The Save Menu As box appears, where you name the menu.

14. **Type *NavChiaVet* and then click Save.**

You use the CSS filename *NavChiaVet.css* to add this same menu to other pages on your site. When you click Save, Menu Light creates two new files in your site's root folder. The file *NavChiaVet.css* formats the menu and its items. The file *NavChiaVet.ajm* is an Ajatix proprietary file (.ajm) that stores information about the menu you just created. Dreamweaver uses this information when you add the menu to other web pages.

You won't need to edit these files, so don't worry about them too much, but don't move or delete them, either. If you do, your menus won't work as expected.

Once you finish a menu, you'll see something like the menu shown in Figure 4-17. It may include several submenus, like the About Us and Facilities menus do here. Naturally, you'll adapt the actual menu to match your project. Page 228 explains how to add an existing CSS menu to another page. The next section explains how to make changes to your menu after you create it.

FREQUENTLY ASKED QUESTION

Who's on First: Pages or Menus?

Should I create my navigation system before I create my pages?

This is a typical chicken-and-egg question that comes up when you develop a navigation system for a website that's still under construction. Do you build the menu before or after you create your web pages? Here's a recommended workflow:

- **Create a list of web pages for your site**. You can jot this down on the back of a napkin or work in Notepad, TextEdit, or any other app that helps you make a list. The main thing is to consider the needs of your site and to work up a list complete with the order of the pages. If your site is large, you might create sections that include groups of pages. For example, the Chia Vet site may have an About Us section. Within that section there could be a History page, a Facilities page, and a Directions page.

- **Create, name, and save empty pages**. Use File→New to create the pages, and then you can immediately use

File→Close to name and save the pages. At this point, you aren't worrying about the actual content on the page. The goal is simply to create placeholder files that you can point to when you build your navigation menu. If your plan calls for some files to be stored within folders, go ahead and create the folders and store those files there before you create your menu. Keep in mind that you need to save the folders within the root folder of your site.

- **Create your menu and link to the site's pages**. Now that you've got pages (albeit empty ones) on your site, you can build your navigation menu (see page 204 for instructions). The advantage of having actual files in your site folder is that you can use the Browse button to find those files, and Dreamweaver automatically fills in the Link box. The menu builder creates the proper path, ensuring that your links are typo-free.

Adding, Editing, and Removing Menu Links

At some point, you're going to want to edit one of your menus—your site structure may change, forcing you to relink pages, or you may add a section to your site that you want to appear in the menu.

To edit a menu, open a page that uses it. Go to the Insert panel (Window→Insert), click Ajatix from the drop-down menu, and then double-click Advanced CSS Drop Down Menu Light. Dreamweaver opens the panel shown in Figure 4-17. Here you can create a new menu, insert an existing one, or edit a menu on the page. Choose the last item, "Edit menu on page." A box at the bottom of the panel lists all the menus you've created for the site so far. Select the one you want to edit and then click OK. Dreamweaver opens the menu in a window like the one in Figure 4-16.

FIGURE 4-17

After you create a menu, you can reopen it to edit it or add new entries. To do that, use the Insert panel or go to Insert→Ajatix→Advanced CSS Drop Down Menu Light. If you already created and saved a menu, you can add it to the current page. If the current page already has a menu, you can edit it.

At this point, editing your menu is like creating a new one (described on page 204). Your menu panel should look like the one in Figure 4-18. Use the + and – buttons to add and remove menu items. Use the arrow buttons to position items in the list, or to move them back and forth between submenus. To edit a link, select the link's label from the list on the left and then use the Browse button next to the Link box to select a new destination page.

NOTE   As you work with the Light version of Advanced CSS Drop Down Menu, you're likely to encounter features that have an asterisk and a note that says "Not available in the Light version." These features let you create and edit animated effects, highlight current items, add rounded corners to drop-down menus, and manually position submenus. Bottom line: If you need to support touch devices, assign individual colors to specific buttons, or want the most recent update to the CSS menus, you're better off ponying up the cash for the full-featured version of the program at *http://www.ajatix.com/*.

Changing the Look of the Navigation Menu

When you first create a menu with Menu Light, you choose from 18 themes. They include horizontal and vertical menus, and a choice of color schemes and fonts. Some themes have a rounded, three-dimensional look, while others appear flat. Chances are, you'll find something suitable for your site.

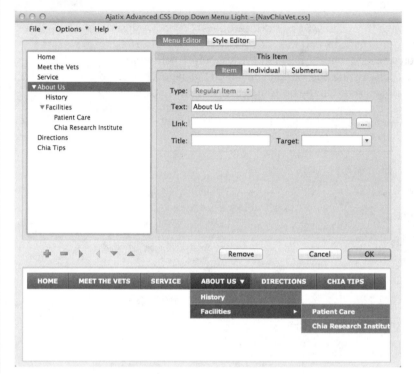

FIGURE 4-18

You'll find everything you need to change the structure of your menu under this panel's Menu Editor tab. As you make changes, Dreamweaver previews the results at the bottom of the panel. The menu actually works, so you can click submenus to open them. The structure of your menu is displayed in the list on the left. Use the buttons below to add, move, and rearrange items. You can edit the text, links, or label for any item you select in the list. Want to remove a menu from a web page? Click the Remove button.

But when it comes to making your menu "perfect," you probably have your own ideas about colors, fonts, and other styles. Menu Light formats its menus using CSS style sheets, so you could head over to CSS Designer, find the source for your menu styles, and start editing them. However, Menu Light uses some pretty cryptic names for selectors, so you'd spend way too much time just identifying the selectors that control the styles you want to change. The easier way to edit your menu is with Menu Light's Style Editor, found under the same-named button at the top of the edit window. (As you learned in the previous section, you use the Menu Editor to create the structure of your navigation menu. Here you'll use the Style Editor to modify its appearance. These two editing tools share the same window, so you fire them up in the same manner.)

The Style Editor (see Figure 4-19) makes it easy to identify page elements and apply changes. Suppose you want to change the font the Chia Vet menu uses. You first open a page that has the menu in it. Then, from the Insert panel, open the Ajatix category and double-click Advanced CSS Drop Down Menu Light. In the Start Wizard that opens (Figure 4-17), choose "Edit menu on page," select the *NavChiaVet.css* menu, and then click OK.

FIGURE 4-19

To change the appearance of your menus, click the Style Editor button and then, in the lower row of buttons, choose the type of change you want to make: Size & Position, Colors, Images, or Text (selected). You make changes using the editor's buttons, boxes, and drop-down menus. Behind the scenes, Menu Light writes the CSS that creates the styles you specify.

When Dreamweaver opens the editor, click the Style Editor button, shown in Figure 4-19. The style editor's layout is similar to the menu editor's, and you work with the two in the same way. Use the pane on the left to select a section of your menu, the main part of the window to edit button styles, and the bottom pane to preview your changes. For example, to edit the font for your menu items, select that element from the list on the left.

The entries on the left—Global, Top Menu, and Submenu—identify the major sections of any menu. To see the properties for a menu item, click Regular Items under Top Menu. Dreamweaver displays the properties for top menu items in the main part of the window. An additional row of tabs (Size & Position, Colors, Images, and Text) lets you refine their styles. Click Text, for example, and you see several text-related widgets, including one that lets you change fonts.

The key to styling menus is identifying the menu item you want to format in the Style Editor and then hunting down the property you want to tweak. The good news is that the menus all use CSS styles, and the tabbed panels are fairly well organized. So if you're familiar with CSS color, text, border, background, and positioning properties, you have a head start with the Style Editor. The next few sections explain how to style different parts of your menu.

> **TIP** The preview at the bottom of the Style Editor shows you the effect of your new style. When you click OK and close the Style Editor, you should see those changes reflected in Design view, but that doesn't always happen. Sometimes, the display gets "stuck" on the previous styles. You can take a few steps to fix this. First, choose File→Save All Related Files. If you find Save All Related Files grayed out, choose Save All. This saves your website and any changes you made to it, and saves the CSS style sheets the menu-builder uses. Switch to Live view and you should see the effect of your edits. If the page still looks odd, click the Refresh button (the one with two arrows going in a circle). One of those steps should update the menu to your new styles.

POWER USERS' CLINIC

CSS Menus Behind the Scenes

A CSS menu might look like a fancy navigation bar made up of colorful buttons and interactive menus, but under the hood it's just a simple list of links. Some pretty clever CSS creates the cool-looking menus complete with rollover effects, and shows or hides submenus.

The structure of the menu itself is an unordered list. In other words, the items in your menu and the tiered menus and submenus are the result of HTML code alone. You can find that HTML in the source code of your web page (right-click the page and then choose View Source from the pop-up menu)—just run a search for words that appear in the menu. For example, the first few lines for a menu that has Home and About Us buttons might look like this in your source code:

```
<ul>
  <li><a href="index.html">Home</a></li>
  <li class="tsub"><a class="ajxsub"
  href="about.html">About Us</a>
```

The <ul> tag begins the unordered list. List items comprise the next two lines, as you can tell by the <li> tags. In the second

line, you see a link to *index.html* and a label for the Home page link. Similarly, the third line includes a link and a label, About Us. (These CSS menus use nonbreaking spaces between words so that a browser can't break up multiword labels. HTML represents nonbreaking spaces with the code * *, so if you look at the source code for a CSS menu, you'll see plenty of * * codes where you'd normally see a space.)

The other unique thing about the third line is that it applies a class to the list tag and another class to the anchor <a> tag. These classes define the style for the navigation menus, a formatting function that's pure CSS.

If you're comfortable editing HTML code and CSS style sheets, you may want to jump in and edit your menu code by hand. You can do that, but there are consequences. If you edit the HTML by hand, Menu Light won't recognize your changes when you try to structure or style the menu. In fact, if you manually make changes and then use the Menu Editor, it overwrites your manual changes. For this reason alone, it's best to stick with Ajatix's editing tools.

■ FORMATTING TOP MENU ITEMS

Menu Light always displays the menu buttons you created for the main menu bar, whether you use a vertical or horizontal menu. You can style the background of the menu bar and of the menu buttons themselves. To change the background bar, select it in the Top Menu list. Menu Light displays the main menu properties under two buttons in the main window, Layout and Style.

Use the Layout button's settings to change the menu's orientation, set the width of the background bar, and align the menu on your web page (Figure 4-20).

- **Orientation**. This drop-down menu gives you two options, Horizontal and Vertical. Even if you initially chose a theme with a horizontal orientation, you can use this menu to change it to a vertical menu.

- **Width**. Choose *none* if you don't want to specify a width. In that case, the length of the button labels determines the width of the menu bar. Choose *Fixed* to set a specific width using pixels as the unit of measure. Choose *100%* if you want the menu bar to fill the available space. Choose *Min* to set the minimum space, in pixels, for the menu background. That way, Menu Light will always make the width of your menu bar equal to or greater than the minimum value. Choose *auto* to have the background menu bar change size depending on the size of menu items, their spacing, and their padding.

- **Menu align**. You can choose Left, Center, or Right to position your menu on the page. Most people choose Left.

- **Sublevel offset**. Use these settings to position submenus when they pop up. Left to the factory setting of *0*, the submenus will touch the menu item that triggered them. To move the menu down from a triggering item, set a positive value (in pixels) in the *y* property. To move a submenu to the right, set a positive value in the *x* property. Negative values position submenus up or to the left of their triggering items.

FIGURE 4-20

The Style Editor gives you the tools you need to change the appearance of your menus. With Top Menu selected on the left and the Layout button selected in the main part of the window, you see options that let you orient, size, and position the top menu; that is, the part of the menu that's always visible.

Using the Style Editor's Style button, you can change the color and images behind the menu. Make sure you select Top Menu in the list on the left, and then set values for these properties:

- **Background color**. Click the swatch and choose a color. Use the Transparent option to make the background invisible, so that Dreamweaver displays only the menu items (buttons), not the backgrounds. (Menu Light uses your operating system's color picker, so the Windows tools look different from the Mac tools.)

- **Border**. To add a border, turn on the checkbox and then click the swatch to choose a color.

- **Background image**. You can use an image for your menu's background. Use the alignment tools to position the image horizontally and vertically. If your image is smaller than the background bar, set the Repeat menu to Repeat. This replicates the image both horizontally and vertically. Choose repeat-x if you want to repeat the image horizontally only, or repeat-y to repeat it vertically. The repeat options are standard CSS settings, which you can learn more about on page 254.

To change the background color of a menu item (as opposed to the entire menu bar), go to the list on the left and, beneath Top Menu, choose Regular Items. The main part of the window displays the properties related to the buttons in the menu. Menu Light groups the properties under four tabs: Size & Position, Colors, Images, and Text.

■ SIZE & POSITION
- **Width**. Turn on the Width checkbox to use a fixed width, measured in pixels. Otherwise, Menu Light automatically adjusts the width to fit the text.

- **Height**. This works the same way as the width. Turn on the Height checkbox and type in a value in pixels.

- **Padding**. As usual with CSS, padding is the amount of space between the text and the edge of an element, in this case the menu button.

- **Spacing**. To add space between menu items, set a value in pixels here. When you have space between menu items, the background shows through (if the bar is transparent, you see elements on the web page peek through).

- **Overlap child dropdown**. Turn on this checkbox when you want drop-down menus to overlap the triggering menu item.

■ COLORS
Use the color settings to change the appearance of buttons in their Normal and Over states (the latter when a guest points to a button). Clicking the color swatches next to Items (the button's background), Text, and "Border standard" opens your operating system's color picker, which looks different on Windows and Mac computers. In either case, you specify colors by clicking them or typing in values.

■ IMAGES
Click this tab to choose background images for buttons. You can choose different images for buttons that lead to submenus and for those that don't. For even snazzier effects, choose different images for the normal and hover states.

■ TEXT

The Text tab lets you format the "usual suspects": the font (called Face in the Font group), size (specified in pixels), style (bold, italic, or underlined), and capitalization (none, Capitalize, Uppercase, and Lowercase), known as Transform in Menu Light. Use the Align menu to position the button text to the left, right, or center. You can add left and right padding and specify different values for items that lead to submenus.

■ FORMATTING ROLLOVER MENU BUTTONS

Visitors get instant feedback when they interact with menus. Pointing to a menu button, for example, changes the color of the button and its text, letting visitors know, "Hey, I'm a link; click me!" You set the colors when you style your menus, as described in the previous section. With the Style Editor button selected, select Top Menu→Regular Items from the list on the left to display the properties that style your Top Menu buttons. Click the Colors button. To set the colors Dreamweaver displays when a guest points to a button (what Menu Light calls a link's *mouseover* state), change the Mouseover values.

To create rollover buttons for submenus, choose Submenu→Regular Items, and then click the Colors tab. To set the background color for a submenu item, click the Normal swatch under the Item heading, and then choose a color from your color picker. Repeat the process with the Mouseover swatch under Item, but, of course, choose a different color. In this case, you choose the background color that appears when your guest points to a submenu item. If your color scheme calls for it, you can repeat the process to create different Normal and Mouseover colors for the submenu button's text and border.

■ FORMATTING SUBMENU BUTTONS

Submenu buttons appear in Menu Light's drop-down menus. In fact, with Menu Light, your submenus can have submenus. But don't get carried away nesting menus, or you'll try the patience of your visitors.

Using the Style Editor, format your submenus the same way you format the top menu. In fact, you use the same properties and have the same options as in the top menu. If you prefer an understated appearance, style your submenus with the same colors and rollover properties as your top menu. If you want your submenus to stand apart from the top menu, use different but complementary colors.

To format a submenu's background box, click Submenu in the list. To format the submenu's buttons, click Regular Items beneath Submenu.

NOTE   Menu Light displays an Animation tab when you choose Submenu from the left-hand list. This feature is listed, but not available, in the Light version of the menu-builder. Its properties control the speed, direction, and other effects used to display the submenu. If you're interested in controlling a submenu's animation, you can get the full version of Advanced CSS Drop Down Menus from Ajatix at *http://www.ajatix.com/*.

■ Tutorial: Adding Links to Pages

In this tutorial, you'll link to other pages on your own site, link to another site on the Web, and create a great-looking CSS-powered navigation bar, complete with fancy drop-down menus. (To see the completed page, skip ahead to Figure 4-28.)

> **NOTE** To complete this tutorial, you need to download sample files from this book's Missing CD page at *http://oreilly.com/pub/missingmanuals/dreamweaverccmm2014*. (See the Note on page 37 for details.) The files you'll work on are in the Chapter04 folder, and the finished project, for comparison, is in the Chapter04_complete folder.

Linking to Other Pages and Websites

Once you download the tutorial files and open Dreamweaver, set up a new site as described on page 23. In a nutshell, choose Site→New Site. In the Site Setup window, type *Links* into the Site Name box. Click 🖿 next to the Local Site Folder box, navigate to and select the Chapter04 folder inside the MM_DWCC folder, and then click Choose (Select on Macs). Finally, click OK.

Once again, you'll be working on a page from Cafe Soylent Green.

1. **In the files panel, double-click the file *index.html*.**

   You can also choose File→Open, select the filename, and then click OK (Select on Macs). You're looking at a basic web page, with a banner, some text, and a footer. It's all contained inside a <div> tag that's 800 pixels wide and centered on the screen (you learned how to do this in the tutorial in Chapter 1, on page 37).

   If your screen is wide enough to show both Code and Design views side by side, click the Split button in the top-left corner of the document window. If you can't fit both comfortably, click the Design button.

   At the end of the last paragraph on the page, in the section with the headline "All Natural Ingredients," you'll see the text "Read more about our natural ingredients." This sentence should link to another page.

2. **Select the text "Read more about our natural ingredients." In the Properties panel, to the right of the Link box, click 🖿, the "Browse for File" button.**

   Dreamweaver opens the Select File window. (If you don't see the Link box, you may be in the Properties panel's CSS mode. In that case, click the panel's HTML button.)

3. **Click Site Root (at the bottom right) to go to your site's main folder. Double-click *ingredients.html*.**

   Dreamweaver closes the Select File window. That's it? Yup. You just created a link. Now you'll learn an even faster way to do the same thing.

4. **In the last paragraph before the page's footer, select the text "Read more about our nutritional principles."**

Make sure you have the Files panel open (Window→Files).

5. **In the Properties panel, drag the "Point to File" icon (⊙) beside the Link box into the Files panel, point to the file *nutrition.html*, and then release the mouse button.**

Dreamweaver adds the link to your page. (If you have the double-monitor configuration discussed in the Note on page 188, this point-to-file technique won't work. Use the method described in steps 2 and 3 above.)

Note that if you wanted to link the text in the examples above to a page on another website, you couldn't use either of the methods outlined here. Instead, you'd need to type an absolute URL into the Link box, as you'll see in the next two steps.

6. **Scroll to the bottom of the page. In the footer, find the phrase "in collaboration with Cosmopolitan Farmer" and then select the text "Cosmopolitan Farmer."**

You want this text to link to the parent company's site.

7. **In the Properties panel's Link box, type *http://www.cosmofarmer.com/*, and then press Enter (Return).**

Now the text "Cosmopolitan Farmer" links to the CosmoFarmer.com website. Unfortunately, the blue links don't fit in with the cafe's color palette. You'll remedy that next.

Formatting Links

You can change the look of links using a little CSS.

1. **Make sure you have CSS Designer open (Window→CSS Designer). In the Sources section, choose *soylent_styles.css*.**

In the Selectors section, you see the selectors you created in *soylent_styles.css*. You haven't added a selector for links (the <a> tag) yet. (That's why the text for your link uses the standard link color, blue.)

2. **In Selectors, click + to add a selector. In the text box, type *a*, and then press Enter (Return) twice.**

When you type *a*, the new selector replaces the selector CSS Designer suggested. The first time you press Enter (Return), you select the <a> tag from the pop-up menu. The second time you press Enter (Return), you create a new selector for anchor tags.

3. **In the Properties section of CSS Designer, click the T (text) button. Make sure you have the Show Set checkbox unchecked.**

Dreamweaver scrolls the list of properties until it gets to Text.

4. **Click the swatch next to the *color* property box, type *#417F2C*, and then press Enter (Return).**

This color makes your text green. After you press Enter (Return), the links on the page change to green. You'll change one more property to remove the underline from your links.

5. **With the *a* selector still highlighted in the Selectors section of CSS Designer, find the *text-decoration* property in the Properties section. Click the first box—the one with the diagonal line through it (circled in Figure 4-21).**

Setting *text-decoration* to "none" overrides the standard value, underlined links. As a result, browsers won't underscore your links and pseudo-classes like *hover* will inherit the *text-decoration* style. In fact, *hover* is up next for some styling. (For more on pseudo-classes, see page 199.)

FIGURE 4-21

To remove an underline from a link, set the CSS text-decoration property to "none." You can create a look similar to an underline (but with a lot more design choices) by turning underlining off here, and then using the CSS border property to create a dotted, dashed, or different-color underline.

6. **In CSS Designer's Selectors section, click + to add a selector, type *a:hover* in the text box, and then click Enter (Return) twice.**

A new selector appears in the list. This time, the selector includes the pseudo-class *hover*.

7. **With *a:hover* highlighted in Selectors, click the T (for text) in the Properties section. Find the *color* property, click the swatch next to it, and then type *#0A2F02*.**

To see how this rollover style works, use Dreamweaver's Live view.

8. **In the Selectors section of CSS Designer, choose the _a_ selector.**

9. **At the top of the document window, choose Live from the Design/Live view menu (or choose View→Live View).**

Dreamweaver includes an embedded version of the Google Chrome browser, and Live view uses it to preview the look and functionality of a web page. With Live view, you can interact with JavaScript and see CSS hover effects. Point your mouse to the various links on the page, and you see the link change to dark green and the underline disappear. (Of course, to check your work thoroughly, you should also preview your pages in Safari, Internet Explorer, and Firefox. You can do that using the File→"Preview in Browser" command if you have those browsers installed.)

10. **Choose Design from the Design/Live view menu.**

It's generally easier to edit your page in Design view, so leave Live view when you're ready to work on your page again.

Adding an Email Link

You'll find the cafe's email address—_info@cafesoylentgreen.com_—at the bottom of the _index.html_ page. Clicking it, however, does nothing. Here's how you turn that address into a link that opens your visitor's email program and addresses a note to you:

1. **Select the text _info@cafesoylentgreen.com_, or place your cursor where you'd like to add the email link.**

The text you select doesn't have to be an email address—it could say "Email us" or something similar. Likewise, if you haven't selected any text, click where you'd like to insert the email link and move on to step 2.

2. **Choose Insert→Email Link (or click the Email link button under the Common category of the Insert panel, shown in Figure 4-7).**

Dreamweaver opens the Email Link window (Figure 4-22) with the link text and email address already filled in (it copies the link from the text you selected in step 1). If you didn't select any text, the Text box is blank. The Email box displays the address for the last Email link you created. You'll find this helpful if you link to the same email address all the time, or annoying if you don't.

FIGURE 4-22

When you insert an email link, Dreamweaver copies any text you selected on the page into the Text box. If the text on the page is in the form of an email address, the program helpfully copies that into the Email box as well.

3. **Click OK.**

Dreamweaver adds the email link (pretty easy, huh?).

Adding a Navigation Bar

A navigation bar with rollover effects and smooth drop-down menus gives your website a professional look and feel, and it makes navigating your site easy for visitors.

If you haven't downloaded and installed the Dreamweaver extension Advanced CSS Drop Down Menu Light, do that now by following the steps on page 202. Then:

1. **Return to Dreamweaver and make sure you have the file *index.html* open; in the banner at the top of the page, click just to the right of the word "Green."**

    You'll insert a horizontal menu bar that spans most of the page's width. Placing it near the top of the page, as part of the banner, lets site visitors easily find it.

2. **Choose Insert→Ajatix→Advanced Drop Down Menu Light.**

    The Start Wizard window opens, giving you two choices: "Create a new menu" and "Insert an existing menu."

3. **Choose "Create a new menu," and then click OK.**

    Menu Light closes the Start Wizard and opens the Select Theme window. Choose from any of the themes listed in the box on the left. Click a theme to preview it in the box on the right.

4. **Choose the Horizontal-Dark Olive theme and then click Apply.**

    Menu Light closes the Select Theme window and opens the New Menu window (see Figure 4-23).

5. **In the Text box, replace "Unnamed" with *Home*.**

    The words you type here will show up as a button in your menu. As you type, you're replacing the "Unnamed" label that Menu Light automatically gave the button with your own name for the link, "Home" in this case. You see the change in the page list on the left and in the preview window.

6. **Click inside the empty box next to Link, and then click the Browse button (the three dots) at the end of the box.**

    Menu Light opens a window displaying your website's files.

7. **Click *index.html*, and then click Open (Select on Macs).**

    A link to *index.html* appears in the Link box.

8. **In the Title box, type *Welcome to Cafe Soylent Green*.**

    You won't include a title for every link in the menu, but the label "Home" is so generic that a description will help visitors who use screen readers.

Menu item properties

List

Add
new
item

Preview

FIGURE 4-23

*With Menu Light, you build
your navigation menu one
item at a time. You use the
Menu Editor list (shown
on the left in this figure)
to add and organize menu
items. Select an item in
the list, and Menu Light
displays its properties on
the right, the most important of which are Text and
Link. As you can see from
the preview at the bottom
of the window, the words
you type in the Text box
appear in the navigation
menu. The Link box stores
the link to a specific page
or to a bookmark on a
page.*

9. **Below the list, click + (the Add New Item button).**

    Menu Light adds a new, "Unnamed" menu item to the list. Next, you'll create a
    drop-down menu that has a submenu.

10. **In the Text box, type *Menu*. Click the Browse button next to the Link box,
    select the file *menu.html*, and then click Open (Select on Macs).**

    The Menu button is at the same hierarchical level as the Home button. The next
    three items you add—buttons for Cafe Soylent Green's breakfast, lunch, and
    dinner menus—will go in a submenu of the Menu button.

11. **Click + again, and then click the right-pointing triangle, a.k.a. the Move
    Item Right button.**

    After you add a new, top-level menu item, you turn it into a submenu using the
    right arrow key to nest the item under an existing menu item.

12. **In the Text box, change "Unnamed" to *Breakfast*. In the Link box, click the
    Browse button, and then select *breakfast.html*.**

    You labeled your first button and created the first link for this submenu.

13. **Click + again. Type *Lunch* in the text box. Set the link to *lunch.html*. Repeat the process to add a Dinner menu item and link it to *dinner.html*.**

No mysteries here. The process is similar to steps 11 and 12. If you have a submenu selected when you add a new item, Menu Light creates another submenu item. You can always use the arrow buttons to move an item left, right, up, or down. When you finish, the New Menu window should look like the one in Figure 4-24. Time to move on to the About Us page.

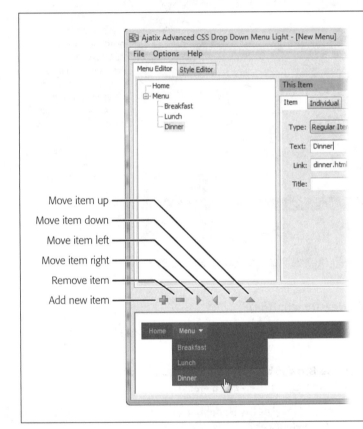

Move item up

Move item down

Move item left

Move item right

Remove item

Add new item

FIGURE 4-24

Menu Light displays the structure of your menu in standard outline form in the Menu Editor pane. You can expand and collapse the submenus by clicking the + or – buttons in Windows (shown here) or the flippy triangle on Macs. The preview pane at the bottom of the window not only shows you what your menu looks like, but it also lets you try out the drop-down menus. Menu Light automatically adds triangle icons to menu items that have submenus so visitors know they have more options.

14. **Click + to add a new, unnamed menu item to the list, and then click the left arrow to move the item left and make it a top-level button. Type *About Us* in the Text box, and then, in the Link box, browse to and select *about.html*.**

The left arrow button repositions the new Unnamed item so that it's at the same level as the Home and Menu buttons. Next you'll add two submenu items under About Us: Directions and Hours.

15. **Click + twice to create two new items. Type *Directions* and *Hours* in their respective Text boxes. Set the links to *directions.html* and *hours.html*. Use**

the right arrow to position Directions and Hours as submenu items under About Us.

As you add each button, Menu Light previews it as a submenu item under About Us.

16. **Click OK. In the "File name" box of the Save Menu As window, type *soylent_menu*. Click Save to save your menu with this descriptive name. Now is a good time to save all your work, so choose File→Save All.**

The New Menu window closes, and you see your menu in Design view in all its glory. If you're eager to give it a test drive, switch to Live view. On the document toolbar's Live View Options menu, turn on the Follow Links Continuously checkbox. You haven't added your menu to the other pages in your site, so you'll need to use the back arrow on the document toolbar to return to the Home page. Remember to switch back to Design view when you move on to the next section, where you'll style your menu.

Styling the Menu Bar

The basic look of your menu isn't bad, but it could benefit from some style changes. For example, the text is a little small, and the menu bar has only three items, so it doesn't need to extend across the banner. Fortunately, styling your menu is almost as easy as creating it.

1. **With *index.html* open in Design view, choose Insert→Ajatix→Advanced Drop Down Menu Light.**

The Start Wizard window opens, with the radio button "Edit menu on page" selected and the menu you just created listed in the filename box. If your cursor is inside your menu when you choose the Insert→Ajatix→Advanced Drop Down Menu Light command, the Start Wizard window doesn't open—the menu editor opens with your menu loaded and ready for editing. In that case, you can skip the next step.

2. **Click *soylent_menu.css*, and then click OK.**

Menu Light's Menu Editor/Style Editor window opens, with the name of the menu in the title bar. You used the Menu Editor in the previous exercise to build your menu. Now you'll use the Style Editor to make it look nice.

3. **Click the Style Editor button.**

The list on the left changes from listing the individual menu buttons you previously created, like Home and About Us, to listing the generic terms Global, Top Menu, and Submenu. In the following steps, you'll see that the Global styles apply to the entire menu, Top Menu styles affect all Top Menu items, and Submenu styles apply to all submenu items.

Initially, the Global item is selected so you see the Z-index property on the right. You see other Global properties grayed out because they're not available in the Light version of Advanced CSS Drop Down Menu.

4. **Leave the Z-index set to *100* and then, in the list, click Top Menu.**

   The Z-index determines whether your menu appears in front of or behind other elements on a web page. It's a standard CSS property covered on page 487. Here's how it works: The Z-index controls the order of stacked elements on a page. An element with a larger Z-index (a higher number) appears in front of other elements. Menu Light automatically gives your menu a very high Z-index number: 100. In most cases, you won't need to change it. However, if your menu is hidden underneath another page element, say the banner at the top of the page, you can enter a higher number here to fix the problem. If you want your menu *underneath* another element, change this to a lower number. It may take some experimenting to get the order just right.

   When you click Top Menu, the window changes. Two buttons divvy up the styling chores, Layout and Style.

5. **Click Layout, leave Orientation set to Horizontal, change the Width value to None, and leave "Menu align" set to Left.**

   When you finish, the settings should look like those in Figure 4-25. The *width* property affects the width of the bar that holds your Top Menu buttons. Set to None, Menu Light applies no specific width to the menu bar. This removes the green band (background) that extends beyond the three menu items. The "Menu align" setting—Left, Center, or Right—positions the top menu bar. The Left option works best for Cafe Soylent Green because it places the menu directly below the name of the cafe.

FIGURE 4-25

To change a menu from horizontal orientation to vertical or vice versa, use Menu Light's Orientation drop-down menu. In this example, you set the width to None, so the menu bar can stretch and shrink to fit menu items. The "Menu align" option lets you position the menu bar to the right, left, or center of the page.

6. **Click the Top Menu's Style button and then click the Background color swatch. In the Select Color window, choose Transparent. Turn off the Border option.**

   The Top Menu *color* and *border* settings apply to the background bar behind menu items. With these settings, you hide that background bar. In the following steps, you'll space out the menu buttons so you can see part of the banner behind them.

7. **In the menu list, click Regular Items under Top Menu.**

The properties here format the top-level menu buttons. Initially, the Size & Position tab is selected.

NOTE Under Top Menu and Submenu, there are options for Headings, but you can't specify these settings in the Light version of the Advanced Drop Down Menu.

8. **Set the width to *100px*, the height to *30px*, and the spacing to *20px*.**

With the Width and Height boxes checked, the dimension item (the rectangle) is set to fixed dimensions. So an item with the text "lunch" will have the same size background rectangle as an item with more text, like "early breakfast." There's one case that overrides this setting. If the text overflows the width of the box, the width remains fixed, but Menu Light automatically adjusts the height, adding more lines to accommodate the text. For this project, with a width of 100px and a height of 30px, the text in the top menu buttons has some breathing room. The Spacing setting puts some distance between each of the menu items. With the background bar hidden (step 6), you see the site's banner behind the top menu items. You can't quite see the effect at this point because the top menu items don't have any background color. You'll fix that next.

9. **Click the Colors tab and then turn on the checkboxes next to Normal and Mouseover.**

You'll pick the colors for a menu item's normal state (when the link just sits on the page) and for the state when a guest points to the button. For each state, you can choose colors for the button's background, text, and border.

10. **Click the color swatch for Normal/Item.**

The process for choosing a color in Menu Light is different for Windows PCs (Figure 4-26, left) and Macs (Figure 4-26, right). For the menu portion of this tutorial, you'll specify colors as RGB (red, green, blue) values.

On Windows PCs, you see the operating system's familiar color picker, with swatches on the left and a spectrum square on the right. Below that, boxes let you specify a color as a hex value, an HSL value, or an RGB value. For this tutorial, use the RGB system.

When you click a color swatch on Macs, you see familiar color picker options. Choose your color using the color bar sliders (second button from the left in the Colors window). Then, from the drop-down menu, choose RGB Sliders.

11. **For the Normal menu link, set the RGB values as follows:**

   — For items, use *70, 133, 49*.

   — For text, specify *242, 229*, and *194*.

12. **As a finishing touch, turn on the border checkbox and set the border color to match the text (*242, 229*, and *194*).**

With these settings, buttons in their normal state have a green background and a dark-gray border. The text is the same light color you used at the bottom of the page for the copyright background. For the menu's state when a visitor points to a link (what Menu Light calls a *mouseover* state), you'll swap the text and background colors.

FIGURE 4-26

Menu Light uses your operating system's color picker, which looks different on Windows PCs and Macs, even though you enter the same red, green, and blue (RGB) values.

Left: For Windows PCs, type the color values in the circled boxes.

Right: For Macs, choose the color bars (circled), select RGB Sliders from the drop-down menu, and then set the color by either using the sliders or by typing color values in the Red, Green, and Blue boxes.

13. **Move to the Mouseover color swatches. Set the Item color to *242, 229, 194* and the text color to *70, 133, 49*.**

Reversing colors is a good way to provide feedback for rollover items. In the next step, you'll increase the size of the button text.

14. **Click the Text tab and then, in the Face (think typeface) drop-down menu, choose "Verdana, Geneva, sans-serif." Turn on the B (Bold) button next to both Normal and Over, set the size of the text to *14px*, set the Transform menu to Uppercase, and then set "Align menu" to Center.**

CSS menus don't currently recognize web fonts, so choosing "Verdana, Geneva, sans-serif" is a reasonable substitute for PT Sans. The Bold and Size settings make the button text easier to read, and the Uppercase setting makes the text for all the items uniform in appearance. The Top Menu Text settings should now match Figure 4-27.

You style submenu items separately from top menu items. That's next on the agenda.

15. **In the list, click Submenu and then click the Style button. Set the background to Transparent and turn the Border checkbox off.**

You can use dramatically different colors for submenus, but that can be distracting. In this case, you're styling the submenu to match the top menu.

FIGURE 4-27

Use the Style Editor's Text tab to style your menu buttons. You style the top menu and submenu text separately, but the Property panel and widgets for the menu and submenu are the same.

16. **In the list under Submenu, click Regular Items. In the Size & Position tab, set the width to *100px*, the height to *27px*, and the spacing to *3px*.**

This width—100px—matches that of the top menu, while the height makes the submenus a tad shorter than the top menu. The spacing lets the submenu background show through. In effect, this creates a matching border around each of the submenu buttons.

17. **In the Colors tab, set the Normal colors to match the Normal colors in the top menu.**

— For items, use *70, 133, 49.*

— For text, specify *242, 229, 194.*

— For the border, use *242, 229, 194.*

Next pick the colors for the Mouseover state.

18. **For the Mouseover state, set the Item color to *242, 229, 194* and the text and border colors to *70, 133, 49.***

The button's background and text switch colors when a guest points to them.

19. **Click the Text tab. In the group of fonts at the top of the window, set Face to "Verdana, Geneva, sans-serif," and the font size to *12*. Turn on the bold setting (click the B button) for the Normal and Over states, set the Transform menu to Uppercase, and then set the Align menu to Center.**

The text for the submenu will be a little smaller than the text for the top menu, but the other characteristics will match.

20. **Click OK.**

Menu Light rewrites the *soylent_menu.css* file to match your specifications.

> **NOTE** If you don't see the changes in your document immediately, Dreamweaver may not have loaded the changes from the CSS file. If that's the case, choose File→Save All Related Files. If that command isn't available (it won't be if you used it recently), choose File→Save All. Then switch to Live view and, in the document toolbar, click Refresh to reload the HTML and CSS files.

21. **Choose File→Save All.**

You save any changes made to *index.html* and to your CSS files. The next step is to add your menu to the other pages in your website.

Adding the CSS Menu to Other Pages

You've built a menu that links the pages in your site. The problem is that those pages don't have the same navigation bar. Fortunately, it's easy to add an existing menu to a web page. After all, the CSS file *soylent_menu.css* has all the formatting your menu needs, and Menu Light's definition file, *soylent_menu.ajm*, stores the menu description.

1. **Choose File→Open and then select *about.html*.**

You need to have a web page open in the document window to add an existing menu.

2. **In the banner, click after the word "Green."**

This positions the cursor where you want to insert the menu.

3. **Choose Insert→Ajatix→Advanced CSS Drop Down Menu Light.**

Menu Light's Start Wizard offers two options, "Create a new menu" and "Insert an Existing menu."

4. **Click "Insert an existing menu" and then click OK.**

The dialog box closes and the Open Menu window appears, where you can select a file.

5. **Choose *soylent_menu.css* and then click Open (Select).**

The menu editor appears, where you see the Menu Editor and Style Editor buttons. You don't need to make any changes at this point.

6. **Click OK.**

The menu editing window closes, and Menu Light adds your menu to the page.

7. **Choose File→Close. When prompted to save your page, click Yes.**

   Menu Light saves and closes your web page, complete with its shiny new menu.

8. **Repeat steps 1–7 for each page in your site.**

   Once all the pages have the same menu, visitors will find it a snap to jump from one to the other.

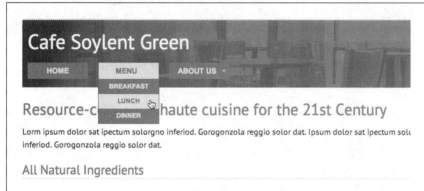

FIGURE 4-28

Adding a CSS drop-down menu may take quite a few steps, but it delivers a high-quality, dynamic navigation bar. By using a Dreamweaver extension to create the menu instead of building your own from scratch, you save yourself countless hours of CSS and JavaScript programing and testing.

Working with Images

Nobody believes that a picture is worth a thousand words more than today's web designers, as evidenced by the highly visual nature of the Internet. In fact, it's not difficult to stumble onto a home page composed almost entirely of graphics, as you can see in Figure 5-1.

Even if you don't want to go that far, understanding how to effectively use graphics on a web page is invaluable. Whether you want to plop a simple photo onto your page, cover it with clickable "hotspots," or design an interactive set of buttons that light up when a cursor passes over them, Dreamweaver makes the job easy.

■ Adding Images

If you were writing out the HTML instructions for your web page by hand, you'd insert an image using the image tag: <img>. For example, this HTML snippet:

```
<img src="images/george.jpg">
```

tells a browser to display a graphic file named *george.jpg*, which it can find in the Images folder. An image tag's primary property is the *source* of the picture, written in HTML as *src*. In the example above, the portion inside the quotes is the path to the source, which web browsers use to find the image.

FIGURE 5-1

Some websites rely almost exclusively on graphics for both looks and function. The home page of the Sesame Street website (http://pbskids.org/ sesame/), for instance, uses graphics not just for pictures of the main characters, but for the page's background and navigation buttons, too.

Dreamweaver does all the necessary coding for you when you insert a picture into your fledgling page. Here are the steps you follow:

1. **Save the web page that will include the image.**

   You don't have to save your page before you add an image, but web designers consider it a good practice. One advantage is that after you add the image, you see the path from the saved page to the image in the "src" field of the Properties panel.

2. **In the document window, position your cursor where you want the image to appear.**

   You can choose anywhere within a paragraph or in any HTML element that acts as a container. For example, <header>, <footer>, <article>, <aside>, and <div> tags are all candidates for hosting images. (You'll learn more about these elements in Chapter 7.) You can set your graphic apart from the text on a page by creating a paragraph for it. Do that now—with your cursor in the page, press Enter (Return) to create a blank line before the next step.

3. **Choose Insert→Image→Image.**

Alternatively, go to the Insert panel (Window→Insert), choose the Common category, and then click "Image : Image" (Figure 5-2). Or, if you're a keyboard shortcut fan, press Alt+Ctrl+I (Option-⌘-I).

Dreamweaver opens the Select Image Source dialog box. It's nearly identical to the Select File window you see when you add a link to a page (Figure 4-4).

4. **Browse to and select the graphics file you want to add to the page.**

The file must be in one of the formats that work on the Web: GIF, JPEG, or PNG.

Store the file somewhere in your local site folder (see page 4) or in one of its subfolders. If you don't, Dreamweaver can't add the correct path to your page.

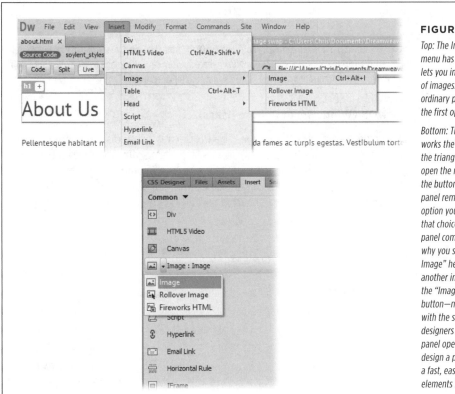

FIGURE 5-2

Top: The Insert→Image menu has a submenu that lets you insert three types of images. To insert an ordinary picture, choose the first option, Image.

Bottom: The Insert panel works the same way. Click the triangle button to open the menu. Because the buttons on the Insert panel remember the last option you chose, you see that choice listed in the panel commands. That's why you see "Image : Image" here. To insert another image, just click the "Image : Image" button—no need to futz with the submenu. Many designers keep the Insert panel open while they design a page because it's a fast, easy way to pop elements into a page.

NOTE The primary file format for Fireworks, Adobe's Web-friendly image-editing program, is PNG (just as Photoshop's format is PSD). However, native Fireworks files contain additional data the program uses to keep track of fonts, layers, and other information. That extra data significantly increases the file size and isn't needed to display a picture on your web page. So always make sure you use Fireworks' Export command to properly compress the image into a GIF, JPEG, or PNG file without all the extra info. Fireworks CS6 changed the way it names its native files (the big ones) so that you don't confuse them with compressed images. It now adds .fw to the native filename—*logo.fw.png*, for example. If you see *.fw.png* at the end of the filename, don't use the pic on your web page. Instead, open the file in Fireworks and use the File→Export command to create a smaller file.

That's why, if you try to insert a graphic that's not in your site folder, Dreamweaver offers to add a *copy* of the image to that folder. If you choose Yes, Dreamweaver opens a Copy File As dialog box so you can save the file to your local root folder, renaming it if you wish. If you choose No, Dreamweaver uses a file-relative path (beginning with *file:///*) for the image's location. But clicking No is a bad idea; while you can see the graphic as you work in Dreamweaver on your computer, the graphic doesn't appear once you move the document to the Web (see the box on page 187).

NOTE Dreamweaver lets you choose a Photoshop (PSD) file from the Select Image dialog box, but it doesn't actually insert the PSD file. It opens a second window where you can save the image as a GIF, JPEG, or PNG file with Web-appropriate optimization settings. Page 236 has the full story.

5. **Click OK (Windows) or Choose (Macs).**

   Dreamweaver inserts the image. The Properties panel displays the properties related to the image (Figure 5-3), like its size. It also offers an Alt text box where you can add a brief description of the pic. You should do that for any image that adds meaning to your page. For example, if you insert a graphic of your company's logo, the alternative text should be your company's name.

FIGURE 5-3

After you insert an image in your page, the image remains selected, and you see the properties for it in the Properties panel. Some of these properties are unique to images, such as the Edit options (circled), which you can use to crop, sharpen, and adjust the brightness and contrast of a pic.

TIP Dreamweaver offers several drag-and-drop techniques so you can quickly add images to your pages.

First, set up a site as described on page 23. Then open the Files window (press F8). You can drag any graphics file from that window right into an open Dreamweaver document. You can also drag graphics from the Assets panel, as described on page 766.

Dreamweaver even lets you drag a graphic from your desktop (including Photoshop images) onto a web page. If you do this, Dreamweaver dutifully informs you that you must copy the file into your site folder (and provides a dialog box that lets you specify *which* folder), so that the image shows up when you transfer your site files to the Web.

It is highly recommended to define a default Images folder for your site, so that when you drag an image onto a page or insert images that are outside your site, Dreamweaver automatically copies the image to the correct folder. To set up a default images folder when you create a new site (Site→New Site), click Advanced Settings in the Site Setup window. Dreamweaver displays a text box with the label "Default Images folder." Click ▦ to the right of that to choose a folder for your images. All the details for setting up a new site are on page 23.

Adding a Placeholder Image

Past versions of Dreamweaver let you add a placeholder image to your documents. Just as its name implies, the placeholder reserves real estate on the page so you can continue working while you wait for the real image. For example, you may start building a page even before your client gives you all the photos, banners, and navigation buttons a page requires. You need a properly sized, empty object to hold the spot—what graphic artists call an FPO (for placement only) object.

In earlier versions of Dreamweaver, the Insert menu provided the tools you needed to insert a placeholder. Now, however, you're on your own. Fortunately, the process is not hard.

1. **Choose any image and insert it as described on page 31.**

    Seriously, any image will do. The actual image won't stay around long.

2. **In the Properties panel, delete the text in the *src* box.**

    This breaks the reference to the image you added in step 1. As a result, in Design view, your page displays a battleship-gray box where the image used to be. Dreamweaver displays the dimensions of the box, as shown in Figure 5-4. You may not need to change them if you don't know the size of the real image, but if you do, you can change the dimensions as described in the next step.

3. **In the Properties panel, change the width (W) and height (H) properties.**

    Type in any dimension you want, and the size of the gray box changes. If the proportions are different from the image you inserted in step 1, make sure you turn off the Toggle Size Constraint padlock.

You don't need to place the actual image before you style it. You can, for example, place a margin around the image or add Alt text.

FIGURE 5-4

If an image isn't ready for prime time when you build a page, you can create a placeholder to reserve the necessary space. That gives you a way to lay out the structure of your page without waiting for all the graphics.

When the real image (that prima donna) is ready to take the stage, store it with the other images on your site. Often, that's a folder named "images," but you can also put it in the root folder or some other folder, so long as it sits inside your site.

At this point, all you need to do is identify the source for the new image. There are a couple of ways to do that. You can double-click the image and then, when Dreamweaver displays the Select Image Source window, choose the source file (described in steps 4 and 5 on pages 233 and 234). Another option is to drag the ⊡ button on the Properties panel to the image in your Files panel.

■ Inserting Images from Photoshop

Since Adobe makes the world's most popular image-editing program, Photoshop, it only makes sense that Dreamweaver's engineers provided a streamlined process for moving images back and forth between Photoshop and Dreamweaver. You can add a Photoshop document to a web page two ways: Insert a PSD file (Photoshop's native format), or copy an image from Photoshop, and then paste it into Dreamweaver.

The first method—inserting a PSD file—supports what Adobe calls *smart objects*, which lets Dreamweaver keep track of whether you update the original Photoshop file, and, if so, gives you the option to update the compressed, web-ready version of the image, too. That's great news if you're the type who constantly tweaks your artwork in Photoshop. The second method—copying and pasting from Photoshop—doesn't keep track of any changes to the original file.

Adding Photoshop Images

You can insert a regular Photoshop file using the same steps you use for inserting GIF, JPEG, or PNG files, described on page 231. For example, use the Image button on the Insert panel, or choose Insert→Image. You can then choose a Photoshop document (a .psd file).

NOTE You can also insert a PSD file by dragging it directly from the desktop (or any folder) and dropping it into a Dreamweaver document. If you stored the PSD file somewhere inside your local root folder, you can drag it from the Files panel and drop it onto the page.

UP TO SPEED

GIFs, JPEGs, and PNGs: The Graphics of the Web

Computer graphics come in hundreds of file formats. The assorted acronyms can be mind-numbing: GIF, JPEG, PNG, TIFF, PICT, BMP, EPS, SVG, and so on.

Fortunately, the limited graphics formats of the Web make things simpler. All of today's web browsers support three common graphics formats, each of which provides good *compression*, which reduces a graphic's file size so it can travel more rapidly across the Internet. The graphics format you choose depends on the image you want to add to your page.

GIF (Graphics Interchange Format) files provide good compression for images with big areas of solid color: logos, text, simple banners, and so on. GIFs also offer single-color transparency, meaning that you can make one color in the graphic disappear, permitting the background of a web page to show through that part of the image. In addition, you can create limited animations with GIF files (like a flashing "Buy Me" button).

GIF images support a maximum of only 256 shades of color, generally making photos look choppy (in other words, not completely realistic). That radiant sunset photo you took with your digital camera won't look so good as a GIF file.

JPEG (Joint Photographic Experts Group) graphics, on the other hand, pick up where GIFs leave off. JPEGs support millions of colors, making them ideal for photos. Not only that, they com-press multicolored images much better than GIFs do, because the JPEG compression formula considers how the human eye perceives adjacent color values; when your graphics software saves a JPEG file, it runs a complex color analysis to lower the amount of data required to accurately represent the image. On the downside, JPEG compression makes any text you have in an image and large areas of solid color look blotchy, so it's not a good choice for logos or simple drawings.

Finally, the PNG (Portable Network Graphics) format includes the best features of GIFs and JPEGs, but you need to know which version of PNG to use for which situation. PNG8 is basically a replacement for GIFs. Like a GIF, it supports 256 colors and basic one-color transparency. And while PNG8 usually compresses images to a slightly smaller file size than GIFs, Dreamweaver's image-optimization tool does the opposite, making PNG8 files slightly larger than GIF versions of the same graphic.

PNG24 and PNG32 offer the expanded color palette of JPEG images, without any loss of quality. This means that photos saved as PNG24 or PNG32 tend to be of higher quality than JPEGs. But before you jump on the PNG bandwagon, JPEG images offer very good quality and a much smaller file size than either PNG24 or PNG32. In general, JPEG is a better choice for photos and other images that include lots of colors.

---

4. **Choose Insert→Image.**

   To insert a Photoshop file, use the same steps you use to insert a GIF, JPEG, or PNG file, described on page 231. Alternatively, you can use the Image button on the Insert panel. Either way, Dreamweaver displays the Select Image Source window, just as it does when you insert a standard Web-ready file.

5. **Choose a Photoshop document (a .psd file), and then click OK (Open).**

   Dreamweaver places the image on the page and opens the Image Optimization window (see Figure 5-5). In the next step, you tell Dreamweaver how to convert the file from the Photoshop format to one of the standard file formats for a web page. Like the name of the dialog box, the process is called "image optimization."

6. **Use the Preset drop-down menu to choose one of six file formats.**

   The six choices are related to the file formats GIF, JPEG, and PNG. Dreamweaver provides good hints for choosing one over the other. As always, the goal is to achieve the right balance between image size and quality. Image size affects how fast your web page and photos appear in a visitor's browser. Quality affects how good your images look. Here are the choices:

   - **PNG24 for Photos (Sharp Details).** As advertised, this choice is good for photos. The file is compressed (making it smaller), but none of the image detail is lost. This compression technique is called "lossless."

   - **JPEG for Photos (Continuous Tones).** JPEG is the most common file format for photos. Unlike PNG24, the JPEG format uses a "lossy" compression technique. When you choose this preset, the image quality is set to 100. That's the highest quality setting, which means you lose a minimal amount of detail.

   - **PNG8 for Logos and Text.** This preset doesn't work well for photos, but it's good for images like logos or other graphics that have large swaths of solid color.

   - **JPEG High for Maximum Compatibility.** This JPEG preset is a good choice for many photos. It creates smaller files than the "JPEG for Photos" option above by using a quality setting of 80. You lose a little more detail than you do with "JPEG for Photos," but in many cases it may be a good size/quality tradeoff.

   - **GIF for Background Images (Patterns).** GIFs are also great for images with solid colors or any graphic that displays a repeating pattern. The GIF format can compress these types of images into very small files. But don't use the GIF format for photos or graphics with gradients (one color blending into another)—the results leave a lot to be desired.

   - **PNG for Background Images (Gradients).** This is the option to use if you have a logo or other colorful graphic that uses gradients.

   When you select a preset from this menu, Dreamweaver updates the image on the page so you can preview the optimization setting. You also see the properties for the preset displayed at the bottom of the Image Optimization dialog box. These properties vary depending on the file format. You can make adjustments, as you'll see in the next step.

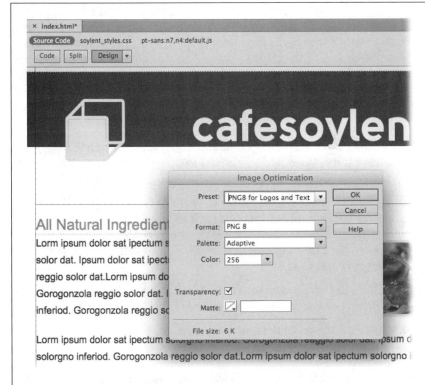

FIGURE 5-5
Dreamweaver lets you insert a Photoshop (.psd) file directly into Dreamweaver, and in the process choose a format for the file when Dreamweaver converts it into a web-ready GIF, JPG, or PNG. You can choose a file type such as PNG8 and set various options that help compress the image to a smaller file size.

7. **Optional: Tweak the image settings provided by the preset in step 3.**

   In most cases, the preset file formats provide the results you need. But if you're not happy with the look and you understand the ins and outs of different file formats, you can tweak the properties. At the top of the list, regardless of the preset you choose in step 3, you see a Format menu. Using it, you can, for example, change from a PNG to a JPEG or a GIF file format. Doing so negates any benefit you get from choosing a preset, however.

   Here's a description of the other preset settings you can tweak:

   - **PNG24 for Photos (Sharp Details).** There are really no options when you choose the PNG24 preset. The only thing you can do is change the format as described above.

   - **JPEG for Photos (Continuous Tones).** Initially, the Quality setting for JPEG for Photos is at its maximum: 100. To make the file smaller, drag the Quality slider to the left. As you lower the quality value, the file becomes smaller and the image fidelity poorer. Check the image in the document window to judge its acceptability. It's unlikely that you'll be happy with values below 50.

- **PNG8 for Logos and Text.** Set the palette to Adaptive for color images. For black and white images, you can create smaller files by choosing GrayScale. The Color menu lets you choose the number of colors in the image. Options range from 2 to 256. Fewer colors create a coarser image. If your picture has transparent areas, turn on the Transparency checkbox. The Matte option helps you minimize the jaggies that sometimes appear at the edge of images that have some transparency in them. In that case, you might want to choose a color that's closer to the background color. (The background for an image with transparency isn't part of the image, it's either the page's background itself, or the background of a section of the page, such as a sidebar.)

- **JPEG High for Maximum Compatibility.** The single option here is the Quality slider. Move it to the left for smaller file sizes and poorer image quality. If you move the slider up to 100, you get the same quality as the "JPEG for Photos" preset.

- **GIF for Background Images (Patterns).** The settings for a GIF are identical to those for PNG8 (above) with one exception, the Loss slider. That governs the quality of the image, but in this case, moving the slider *right* decreases the quality.

- **PNG for Background Images (Gradients).** These settings let you turn on transparency and choose a matte color. See PNG8 above for a description.

8. **Click OK in the Image Optimization window.**

   Dreamweaver opens the Save Web Image window.

9. **Navigate to a location in your site where you want to save the Web-ready image (for example, an Images folder in the site's root folder).**

   Click Save.

   Dreamweaver optimizes the image (converting it to GIF, JPEG, or PNG format) and saves it to the site.

NOTE You can't import animated GIFs using the Image Preview window; instead, you need to first export the animated GIF from the program in which you created it (like Fireworks or Photoshop), and then import it into Dreamweaver.

When you insert a Photoshop image this way, Dreamweaver, unfortunately, ignores images you made using Photoshop's "slice" tool. This handy tool lets web designers export just bits and pieces of a complete web page design in Photoshop—for example, you could design the look of a site's home page in Photoshop and then show it to your client for feedback. Then you can export just parts of the design as separate image files, like a logo in the upper-left corner of the document, individual navigation icons along the top, or a photo in the middle of the document. So if you want to use an exported slice as a graphic on your web page, the import-from-

Photoshop technique isn't the best; Dreamweaver tries to insert the entire image, not just slices of it. To get around this, you need to stick with Photoshop and its "Save for Web" command for pages. An even better way to convert a page designed in Photoshop into a Dreamweaver page is to use the Window→Extract tool. The box on page 264 has the details.

■ JPEG OPTIMIZATION OPTIONS

Dreamweaver doesn't give you many choices for optimizing JPEG images that it creates from Photoshop files. It offers just two presets: "JPEG for Photos (Continuous Tones)" and "JPEG High for Maximum Compatibility." These presets don't really do anything besides choose JPEG as the file format and set the image quality level to 100 or 80. You're better off selecting JPEG from the Format menu and then choosing a quality setting of from 1 to 100 (see Figure 5-6).

FIGURE 5-6

To optimize an image, move the quality slider to the left (for smaller files, but worse-looking images) or right (for larger files and better-looking images). Keep an eye on the file size listed at the bottom of the window. It tells you the size of the Web-ready JPEG file Dreamweaver will create.

The quality level you set affects both how good the image looks and its file size. The higher the quality, the larger the file; the worse the quality, the smaller the file. Dreamweaver's Quality setting runs from 1 (low quality/small file) to 100 (high quality/large file). Eighty is a good choice for very good quality and manageable file size; 60 works when you want to keep file size on the slim side. The best setting depends on the image, so move the Quality slider back and forth until the image preview (in Design view) looks good.

■ GIF AND PNG8 OPTIMIZATION OPTIONS

GIF and PNG8 files have nearly identical optimization settings. The number of colors an image has—the size of its *palette*, in other words—contributes most to its file size. Fewer colors mean a smaller file size. Most of the settings available for GIF and PNG8 images control the number and type of colors you can use (see Figure 5-7).

FIGURE 5-7

Dreamweaver offers nearly identical GIF and PNG optimization settings when you convert a Photoshop image. The only difference is the Loss option—you can use it only for GIFs, and it trades image quality for smaller file size.

For optimal compression settings with a GIF or PNG8 image, follow these steps:

1. **From the Palette menu, select Adaptive.**

   Since both image types are limited to just 256 colors, this menu determines which colors your image will use. You have two options here, but the best choice for most images is Adaptive, which means that Dreamweaver picks the best 256 colors from the image itself. The other option, Grayscale, converts the graphic to a black-and-white image.

2. **In the Color menu, select a value for the number of colors Dreamweaver should use when it optimizes the photo.**

   You can tell Dreamweaver to use two to the maximum of 256 colors. If the original Photoshop image started out with only 64 colors, then choosing 256 doesn't add colors or quality to the image. However, you can often choose a *lower* number, eliminating colors from the graphic and reducing the file size significantly without overly harming the image's quality. Again, each image is different, so trial and error is the best way to balance the minimum number of colors you need with the quality you want.

3. **Choose a value for Loss (available only for GIF images).**

   The Loss option decreases file size at the cost of image quality. In general, increasing the Loss setting makes an image look spotted and windswept, so unless you're going for a special effect, use a low setting or none at all.

4. **If the Photoshop image includes transparent areas, turn on the Transparency checkbox.**

   Transparency lets some of the content behind an image show through. Images that include transparent areas sometimes show jagged edges where the image stops and the transparent part of the background begins. You can minimize these ugly jaggies by applying a matte color, which helps blend the colors at the edge of the image with the colors of the background. When you choose a matte color, pick a hue that matches (or is at least close to) your background. You can do this by clicking the color picker and using the eyedropper to sample the color. This blends the semi-transparent areas of the image (like a see-through drop shadow or the edges around the visible part of a graphic) with the background color, creating a more natural-looking gradient.

TIP If the graphic doesn't have any transparency and you choose the GIF format, the matte setting performs a different function: It removes a selected color from the image, making that part of the image transparent. Click the Matte color picker and use the eyedropper to pick the soon-to-be-transparent color in the image. But generally the results don't look very good, so you're better off creating the transparent effect in Photoshop.

In the case of PNG8 images, you don't need to select a matte color as long as the Photoshop image has a completely transparent background. In that case, Dreamweaver is smart enough to apply an "alpha transparency" to the image, which doesn't have the same "jaggies" issues.

TIP If you're inserting an image that has a transparent background and is a good candidate for the GIF or PNG8 format (that is, large areas of solid color, as described in the box on page 237), choose PNG8 and turn on the Transparency checkbox. Dreamweaver saves PNG8 images with full alpha transparency, which looks a lot better than the color transparency GIF images offer.

■ PNG OPTIMIZATION OPTIONS

If you save a file in the PNG8 format, you have the same options you do with GIFs (see the previous section). If you choose PNG24, your choice is simple...because Dreamweaver doesn't offer any options. So, if you choose the PNG24 format, just click OK in the Image Preview window, and then save the file. As mentioned in the box on page 237, PNG24 images aren't a good choice for web pages. While they provide better quality than JPEG images, they often produce significantly larger files.

If you choose the PNG32 format, you can turn on the Transparency checkbox just as you can with PNG8 images (see Figure 5-8). In fact, you'd want to use PNG32 only if an image contains an alpha transparency channel (256 levels of transparency) and it has lots of colors, like an image with a gradient that transitions from a solid color to a transparent background, or a photograph whose edges fade to a transparent background. In other words, use PNG8 with transparency if the image has 256 colors or less (like a logo), and choose PNG32 with transparency if the image has more than 256 colors and has transparent areas. (See the box on page 237 for more on choosing a graphic file format.)

FIGURE 5-8

Saving a Photoshop file as a PNG32 image doesn't provide a lot of choices. In fact, the only advantage to using PNG32 is its transparency option. Skip selecting a matte color for PNG32 images—you only need to turn on the Transparency checkbox to use the alpha transparency that PNG32 already provides.

Modifying an Image

After you insert a graphic, you can manipulate it in several ways. You can attach a link to it, apply a CSS class style to it, and even create an "image map" so that different areas on the image link to different web pages. You can also use some of Dreamweaver's basic editing tools to crop, resize, optimize, sharpen, and adjust the image's contrast and brightness.

As with most objects on a web page, you set image properties using the Properties panel (see Figure 5-9).

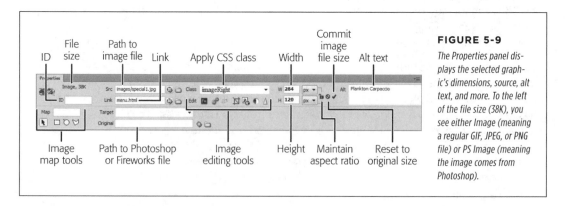

FIGURE 5-9

The Properties panel displays the selected graphic's dimensions, source, alt text, and more. To the left of the file size (38K), you see either Image (meaning a regular GIF, JPEG, or PNG file) or PS Image (meaning the image comes from Photoshop).

Adding an ID to an Image

In the Properties panel, just to the right of an image's thumbnail, you'll see a small box where you can type in an ID. The ID is JavaScript's standard way of identifying an individual object on a page. Cascading Style Sheets also use IDs, as described on page 132. For example, in CSS Designer, you use IDs as selectors so you can apply unique formatting to just a single element. For example, you might use the ID to add a border to an image.

Most of the time, you'll leave this field blank. But if you plan to add interactive effects to an image, like the rollover effect discussed on page 268 or your own JavaScript programming (see Chapter 15), you need to add an ID. Here are the rules for ID names: The first character must be a letter (upper- or lowercase). Following that, you can use numbers, hyphens, underscores, colons, and periods. Spaces and other punctuation are not allowed. The purpose of an ID is to identify a single element on the page, so IDs must be unique. If you give an image on the page the ID "logo," you can't use that ID for another element on the same page.

When you add an ID to an image in the Properties panel, Dreamweaver writes the resulting code like this:

```
<img src="images/logo.jpg" alt="" width="120" height="150" id="logo"/>
```

Adding a Text Description to an Image

Not everyone who visits your website gets to see those stunning photos of your summer vacation. Some (but not many) people deliberately turn off graphics when they surf, enjoying the web without the wait, since graphics-free pages appear almost instantly. Other people have vision impairments that prevent them from seeing the Web's visual aspects. They rely on special software that reads web page text aloud, including any labels you give your graphics.

To assist web surfers in both situations, make a habit of setting an image's *Alt* property. Short for *alternative text*, the Alt property is text that describes an image. To add a description to an image, type it in the Properties panel's Alt box (see Figure 5-9). If you're naming navigation buttons, for example, you could use the text that appears on the button, such as *Home* or *Products*. For images that carry greater meaning—such as a photo of the product itself—you might use a more detailed description: "Photo of Sasquatch relaxing at his lodge in the Adirondacks."

NOTE In some cases, a description is more of a distraction than a help. For example, you might insert an image of an intricate swirling line to act as a visual divider between two paragraphs. The image doesn't actually convey any meaningful information—it's just for decoration—so the Alt description is less useful in this case.

Changing an Image's Size

A graphic's width and height properties do more than determine its size onscreen; they also help web browsers load the graphic quickly and efficiently. Since the HTML of a web page downloads before any graphics do, browsers display the text on a page first and add images as they arrive. If you don't include width and height attributes with an image, the browser doesn't know how much space on the page to reserve, so it has to redraw the page after it downloads each image. As a result, the pages appear to "stutter" with each redraw. This disconcerting behavior does little for your reputation as a cool, competent web designer.

Fortunately, you don't have to worry about specifying a picture's dimensions yourself. Whenever Dreamweaver inserts an image into a page, it automatically calculates its width and height and enters those values into the Properties panel's W and H boxes (see Figure 5-9).

You can, if you like, *shrink* a graphic by typing smaller values into those boxes, but doing so doesn't do anything to speed up the page's download time. You make the picture *appear* smaller, but a browser still downloads the entire file. To make your graphic smaller in both appearance and file size, you have to shrink it in an image-editing program like Fireworks or Photoshop, or use Dreamweaver's Resample Image tool, described on page 257. Not only do you get an image that's exactly the size you want, but it usually looks better and you trim a few bytes off its file size (and maybe even save a second or two of download time).

On the other hand, setting width and height values that are *larger* than the dimensions of a graphic merely distorts the image by stretching it, creating an undesirable pixelated effect. If you want a larger image without distortion or pixelation, start with a larger original image. To do so, return to your digital camera or stock photo file, or recreate the graphic at a larger size in Photoshop or Fireworks.

Dreamweaver provides some helpful tools when you resize an image. For example, use the lock icon to the right of the Properties panel's Width and Height boxes to maintain an image's aspect ratio. Say you insert an image that's 200 pixels wide by 100 pixels tall. You click in the panel's W (width) box and type *100* because you want the image to be smaller. If the lock icon is closed, the H box will change to 50 pixels. Dreamweaver maintains the proportions of the image when you type a value in either the W or H box so long as the lock icon is closed. On the other hand, if you click the icon to unlock it, you can type values in the W and H boxes that stretch the image beyond its normal proportions. (You'll probably also stretch your client's patience when he sees what a mess you made of his company's logo.)

In addition, if you're not happy with the new dimension you typed (or you accidentally resized the image by typing in the W field instead of the H field, or you grabbed the image-resize handles discussed in the box on page 247), click the "Reset to original size" button (see Figure 5-9). That returns the image to its initial dimensions. Finally, if you do change the image's size and you're happy with the new look, click the "Commit image size" button, which permanently alters the file (basically, it does the same thing as the Resample Image tool described on page 257).

■ Controlling Images with CSS

Cascading Style Sheets aren't just for styling text. You can use their design power to add borders to an image, force text to wrap around an image, and even add images to the background of other elements. For example, the CSS *background-*

image property lets you place an image in the background of a web page, or add a graphical background to a link, headline, or any other HTML tag.

Making Accessible Websites

Some people using the Web have disabilities that make reading, seeing, hearing, or using a mouse difficult. Visually impaired people, for example, may not benefit from images on the screen, even if they have software that reads a web page's text aloud.

Dreamweaver includes a number of features that make your website more accessible. That's good news if you're building a site for the federal government or one of the many states that supports Section 508 of the Workforce Investment Act, which requires websites built for or funded by the government to offer equal or equivalent access to everyone. Throughout this book, you'll find tips for using Dreamweaver's accessibility features.

The Alt property described on page 245 is an important first step in assisting visually impaired web surfers. For complex images,

such as a graph that plots changes in utility rates over time, you can supply a more detailed description on a separate web page. The *Longdesc* (long description) property of an image lets you specify a link to a page containing a text description of the image. Some web browsers understand this property, letting visually impaired visitors jump to that description page.

Longdesc was officially part of HTML4 but was initially left out of HTML5. As you might imagine, this led to a debate about whether *Longdesc* was the best way to provide accessibility. When this book went to press, Dreamweaver didn't include tools for *Longdesc*, but that may change in the future. For the most current details on the subject, go to *www.w3.org* and search on the term *longdesc*. For an overview of web accessibility and helpful tips on making accessible sites, visit *www. w3.org/WAI/gettingstarted/*.

Watch Those Resize Handles!

After you insert an image in the document window in Design view, a thin black border appears around it, indicating that you selected it. Three small black squares—resize handles—appear on the right edge, bottom edge, and lower-right corner of the pic.

Dragging these handles changes the graphic's width and height—or, rather, it changes the Width and Height properties in the Properties panel. Pressing Shift while dragging the corner handle maintains the proportions of the image. The graphics file itself remains unchanged.

Dragging one of these handles to make the picture appear bigger is almost always a bad idea, resulting in distortion and ugly pixelation. And you can far too easily accidentally grab and drag the pesky handles. In fact, sometimes you may resize a graphic and not even know it. Perhaps you accidentally dragged the left resize handle a few pixels, making the graphic a bit wider, but not enough to notice.

Fortunately, the Properties panel lets you know when a graphic differs from its original size: If you see the "Reset to original size" button (the little circle with a slash icon pictured in Figure 5-9), you know you've resized the image. Click this button to roll the pic back to its original dimensions.

In general, you probably don't want to create a tag style (see page 116) for the <img> tag. That type of style affects *every* image on a page (or on an entire site if you use a site-wide external style sheet). And while you may want a bright-red, 10-pixel border around each thumbnail in a photo gallery, you probably don't want that border around the site's logo or the navigation buttons on the same page. You're more likely to create class styles you can manually apply to certain graphics. In the thumbnail example, you'd create a class style with the proper border setting, and then apply that class to each gallery image (you can be even more efficient and use a *descendent selector*, as described on page 398).

Wrapping Text Around an Image

After you add an image to a page, you might initially find yourself staring at a bunch of empty white space around the image (see Figure 5-10, top). Not only does this waste precious screen real estate, but it's also usually unattractive. Fortunately, you can wrap text around images using the CSS *float* property (see Figure 5-10, bottom).

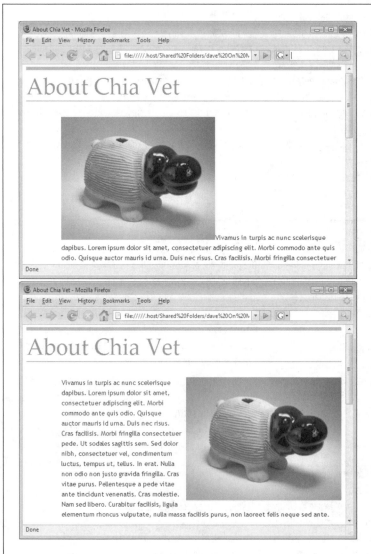

FIGURE 5-10

Placing an image on the same line as text (top) creates unsightly open space, which you can put to better use. By floating an image to the right (bottom) or left, you force content that would otherwise sit beneath the image to wrap around it.

To do so, in CSS Designer's Layout category, set the *float* property (see Figure 5-11). You can float an element to the left or right side of the page. If you want an image to appear on the right side of a page and have text flow around its left and bottom edges, choose "right" from the Float menu. The *float* property behaves just like the right and left alignment options for images (see the Note below).

FIGURE 5-11

In CSS Designer's Properties section, the Layout category contains some of the most-used CSS properties. Use the float property to align images and other page elements to the left or right. Use the margin property to add or remove space between elements (like the edge of a right-floated image and the text that wraps around it). Use the padding property to add space between the content inside an element and the edges of that element.

NOTE The *float* property has many uses, from positioning images on the right or left side of a page to creating thumbnail photo galleries to laying out entire web pages. You'll learn about using it for layout in Chapter 10. For an excellent introduction and set of tutorials on the Float property in general, visit *http://css.maxdesign.com.au/floattutorial*. Book lovers should pick up *CSS3: The Missing Manual* (O'Reilly) for an in-depth discussion, tutorials, and practical tips on using floats.

One thing to keep in mind with floats: The floated element must appear *before* anything you want to wrap around it. Say you have a paragraph of text you'd like to wrap around a right-floated image. You need to insert the image before the text (a good spot is before the first letter of the paragraph you want to wrap around the image). If you float an image to the right but place the image after the text, the image moves to the right, but the paragraph remains above the image.

You'll frequently use the *margin* property with floats. A margin is the outermost space surrounding an element. It lets you add space between one element and another. So, for a right-floated image, it's usually a good idea to add a little left, bottom, and top margin. This creates a bit of breathing room between the image and anything that wraps around it; omitting a left margin on a right-floated image can cause text to butt right up against the image.

You can specify a margin using any unit of measure—pixels, percentages, and so on—that CSS supports.

Adding Borders

As you saw in the tutorial for Chapter 3, you can add a border to any element on a page—a paragraph or even a single word. But borders can really add impact to a photo on a page, because they give the image a polished "frame-like" appearance. In addition, borders can help unify a page full of thumbnail images.

You control a border, logically enough, from the Border category of CSS Designer's Properties section (see Figure 5-12). (If CSS Designer isn't visible, choose Window→CSS Designer.)

You can set the properties of each *side* of a border independently, so that each has its own color, width, and style. Tabs at the top of the Border category determine which part of a border you format. Click the first tab to style all the sides at once. The other options (from left to right) are top, right, bottom, and left. Here are the border properties you can set:

- **border-width**. For border widths, choose one of the preset widths—thin, medium, or thick—or choose a unit of measure from the pop-up menu and then type in a value. Again, you can choose from a range of units: pixels (the most common), percentage, inches, and so on (see page 149 for more on CSS units of measure). If you want to eliminate the border, type *0* into the appropriate box, or click the Remove CSS property button (a.k.a. the Trash can).

- **border-style**. This menu lets you specify the type of line web browsers draw for the border. It gives you more options than a frame shop: none (the standard), dotted, dashed, solid, double, groove, ridge, inset, and outset (see Figure 5-13).

- **border-color**. Use the ubiquitous color picker to set the *border-color* property. If you don't assign border colors but do assign border *widths*, the border color matches that of the surrounding text.

FIGURE 5-12

Click the Border button (circled) to see the options for framing a page element. Add colorful and stylish borders to paragraphs, images, tables, and links. Turning on only the bottom border for a paragraph is a great way to add a horizontal rule between paragraphs. While HTML's Horizontal Rule object does the same thing, only CSS lets you control the rule's color.

- **border-radius.** Round off the corners of your border using this property. Choose a unit of measure, like px for pixels, and then type in a number. Click the link in the middle of the border-radius box to round all the corners, or type a value in one of the corners. Set the Design/Live menu at the top of the document window to Live to see the effect.

NOTE If you don't choose a border style, or if you set it to "none," you don't see the borders even if you set their width and color properties. The same is true if you don't set a width property or have it set to 0.

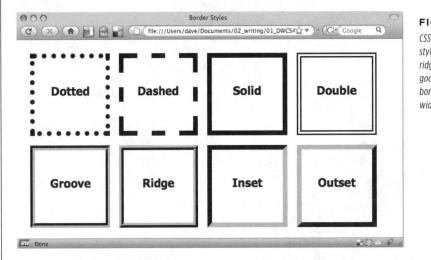

FIGURE 5-13

CSS offers eight border styles. Some, like double, ridge, and groove, look good only with a thick border (more than 1 pixel wide).

If you use borders to "frame" an image, you can use the *padding* property to add space between the image and the border—this simulates the appearance of the cardboard mat used in professionally framed photographs. Padding is the gap that separates content—such as a paragraph of text or an image—and its border.

You set the padding from CSS Designer's Layout category. To put a 1-pixel border around an image and add 10 pixels of space between the image and the border, go to CSS Designer→Properties, and then click the Layout button. In the Padding box, click the link icon ("Click To Change All Properties"). Click one of the number boxes around the edge of the box, and then type *10*.

Background Images

Adding an image to a page is one way to enhance your site, but CSS also lets you add an image to the *background* of any tag. That way, you can use a graphic as the background of a page, enhance a headline with an icon, or add your own custom graphics to links.

You control background images by setting the following properties in CSS Designer's *background-image* property (see Figure 5-14).

■ BACKGROUND-IMAGE

Add a background image to a tag in CSS Designer by choosing a source (an internal or external style sheet), a selector (a tag, such as <body>, <h1>, <header>, or <div>), and then, in the Properties section, by clicking the Background button. Dreamweaver scrolls down to the background properties. Under *background-image*, you see "URL," prompting you to locate the background image file. After clicking in the text box, click the folder icon and then browse your way to the image. If you choose an image outside your site, Dreamweaver automatically adds it to the Images folder you designated when you set up your site. You can also type in an absolute URL, starting with *http://*, to use an image from the Web.

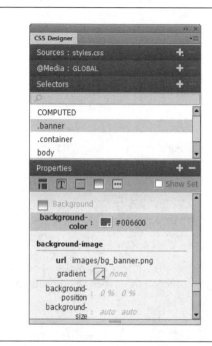

FIGURE 5-14

CSS's Background properties let you specify both a background color and a background image for a given element, such as a <div> that makes up a sidebar. While you won't frequently apply a color and image (after all, the image would usually cover up anything behind it), it can come in handy when you use it with the Padding property (see page 465) to create a customized "mat" to surround the image.

To fill the background of your entire web page with a repeating graphic, you could either redefine the <body> tag using the *background-image* property, or create a class or ID style with a *background-image* property, and then apply the class or ID to the <body> tag as described on page 127 (the tutorial from Chapter 1 uses this technique to add a background pattern to the page).

You can even control how an image tiles (repeats) and where Dreamweaver puts it on a page (see below). Furthermore, you can add background images to any *individual* element on your page: paragraphs, tables, <div>s, and so on.

Background images appear above any background color, so you can (and often will) combine the two. For example, you may want to position an interesting graphic on top of a colorful background image.

NOTE One common byte-saving technique when you use navigation buttons on a site is to create an image that has all the characteristics of a button—burnished edges and so on—except for a label. You use this generic button as the background image for navigation links on a page. The link labels themselves use regular text—"Home," "About Us," and so on—but the background behind each label makes the links look like a graphical button. The main benefit to this technique is that you don't need to create separate graphics for each button.

■ BACKGROUND-REPEAT

When a browser displays the background for a web page, it usually *tiles* the background image. That is, it repeats the image over and over again, across and down the screen. A small image of a carrot added to the background of a page appears as a field of carrots—one next to another, row after row. (Not all web designers use a background image for their pages; some leave the background white or set a color property, such as black, for sites that use white text.)

But with CSS, you can control *how* the background image repeats. In CSS Designer, you select from the following properties for background images:

- **repeat** tiles the image horizontally and vertically. This is how browsers normally display a background image.

- **repeat-x** and **repeat-y** display a horizontal and vertical band of images, respectively. If you want a single row of images at the top of a page, use the repeat-x option; it's a good way to add a graphical background to a banner. Repeat-y, on the other hand, is great for a graphical sidebar that appears down the edge of a page.

- **no-repeat** displays the image only once (see the examples in Figure 5-15).

■ BACKGROUND-ATTACHMENT

By default, the background image on a page scrolls with the rest of the page—as you scroll down to read a long page, the image scrolls "off the screen" along with the text.

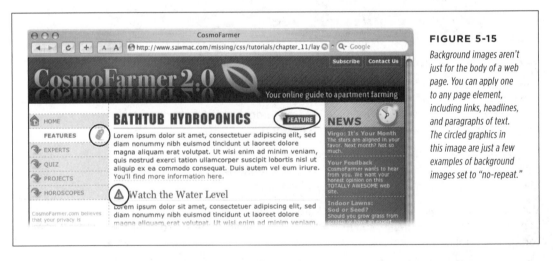

FIGURE 5-15

Background images aren't just for the body of a web page. You can apply one to any page element, including links, headlines, and paragraphs of text. The circled graphics in this image are just a few examples of background images set to "no-repeat."

But using CSS, you can lock the image in place by choosing "fixed" from the *background-attachment* menu. Say you add your company's logo to the background of a page and set the Repeat property (described above) to "no-repeat." The logo now appears only once in the upper-left corner of the page. If you use the "fixed" option for this property, when a visitor scrolls the page, the logo remains fixed in the upper-left corner. (Choosing "scroll" from the Attachment menu means, of course, that the background image scrolls with the page—this is its standard behavior, so you don't need to choose this option.) Note that "fixed" works best when you apply it to the <body> or <html> tags of a page—the image stays fixed when the rest of the content scrolls.

■ POSITIONING A BACKGROUND IMAGE

Using the horizontal and vertical settings for *background-image*, you specify a position for the image within a container, such as a <div> tag or the <body> tag of the page. There are two ways to apply the *background-position* properties. You can use select terms to define the position, like "left," "right," "top," "bottom," and "center." Or you can apply numeric values, such as 40 px (pixels) or 10%. For example, if you choose "center" for both the horizontal and vertical background position, your image is centered inside the container. Choosing "left" positions the left edge of the image at the left edge of the container.

When you choose a value and unit of measure, the top-left corner of the image is positioned relative to the top-left corner of the container. So if you set the horizontal property to *10px* and the vertical property to *45px*, the top-left corner of your image is 10 pixels to the right of the left edge of the container and 45 pixels down from the top. There's a long list of units of measure you can use when you apply values, but the most useful are pixels, percentages, and ems.

Keep in mind that these positioning options refer to the position of the background image *within the container*. Suppose you create a class style that includes a background image with both the horizontal and vertical positions set to "center." Then say you apply that class style to a paragraph. The background image would appear in the center of that *paragraph*, not in the center of the web page.

And if you wanted to place an image in the exact center of a page, you'd choose the <body> tag as the selector in CSS Designer. In other words, it's the container for the image. Then, after setting the URL for the background image, you'd set the *background-position* properties to "center" for both the horizontal and vertical. You should set the *background-repeat* property to "no-repeat."

■ Editing Images

Nothing is ever perfect, especially when you're building a website. Corrections are par for the course—not just to a web page, but to the pictures on it as well. Perhaps a picture is a tad too dark, or you'd like to crop out the rowdy coworker being escorted from your company's holiday party.

In the hands of less capable software, you'd face a tedious set of steps each time you wanted to edit a graphic. You'd have to open Photoshop, Fireworks, or whatever graphics program you prefer, choose File→Open, navigate to your website folder, find the graphic that needs touching up (if you can even remember its name), and then open it to make your changes.

But Dreamweaver simplifies all that with tools that handle many basic graphics-editing tasks. For more complex work, like changing the text on a button from "Now Firing" to "Now Hiring," you do need to switch to a different program. But even here, Dreamweaver is considerate of your time; it lets you open your favorite graphics program with just a couple of clicks.

Dreamweaver's Built-In Editing Tools

When you select an image in Design view, the Properties panel includes four tools that let you crop, resample, sharpen, and adjust the brightness and contrast of an image (see Figure 5-16). Suppose your boss emails you his portrait with instructions to put it on his "Meet the Boss" page. Unfortunately, the picture is too big and too dark. Rather than launch a separate image-editing program, you can add the photo to the page and then make the corrections within Dreamweaver.

But first, a warning: All of Dreamweaver's tools change the *original* GIF, JPEG, or PNG image in your site folder. If you shrink a graphic and later change your mind, you may be out of luck. It's a good idea, therefore, to back up your images before you use these tools. In addition, if you add a Photoshop document and create a Smart Object (page 236), the tools discussed next break the link with the Photoshop file. That means that, for Smart Objects, you're better off editing the original Photoshop document as discussed on page 261. The reason? Doing so retains the relationship between the image on your web page and Photoshop; if you edit the graphic in Photoshop at some point and then launch Dreamweaver, Dreamweaver tells you the image has changed and lets you update it on your site.

FIGURE 5-16

The Properties panel includes tools for editing images from within Dreamweaver. You won't see these tools in Live view, but you do see them when you select an image in Design view, or if you click the <img> tag in Code view.

Furthermore, remember that if you use that same file on other pages, your Dreamweaver image edits appear on those pages, too. For instance, if you shrink your company logo on one page, you may find the smaller logo on *every* page on your site! What's worse, the image's width and height settings don't change on those other pages, so the logo looks unnaturally pixelated there. If you want to change a graphic on only one page, make a copy of it first, insert the *copy* in the page you wish to change, and then modify just that image file. That way, the rest of your site keeps the original graphic.

Of course, if you discover right away that you made a change you don't want, you can choose Edit→Undo or press Ctrl+Z (⌘-Z). Until you close the page, you can undo multiple changes.

■ CROPPING AN IMAGE

Dreamweaver's Crop tool can remove extraneous or distracting parts of an image. You can use it to focus on a single person, or to get rid of those teenagers making faces in the corner.

To do so, select the graphic you want to crop and then, in the Properties panel, click the Crop tool (see Figure 5-16). Alternatively, choose Modify→Image→Crop.

A rectangular box with eight resize handles appears inside the image; anything outside the box will be cropped out. Move this box (by dragging it) and resize it (by dragging the handles) until you've got just what you want inside the box.

When you're done, double-click inside the box, or click the Properties panel's Crop tool again. Dreamweaver crops the image, discarding the unwanted areas.

To undo a crop, press Ctrl+Z (⌘-Z). In fact, you can back out before you've used the Crop tool at all; click anywhere on the page outside the image to make the cropping box go away.

■ RESAMPLING AN IMAGE

If a photo is just too big to fit on a web page, you could select the image and use one of the resize handles to alter its dimensions. Unfortunately, graphics you shrink this way give you the worst of both worlds: They look muddier than they were before, and they download slowly because you're still grabbing the larger image.

You can, however, use this resizing technique with Dreamweaver's Image Resample tool to resize the actual graphic. You'll end up with a trimmed-down file with its appearance intact.

To use the Resample tool, select an image and then resize it using the resize handles. (Shift-drag to keep the image's proportions.) When you're done, click Resample in the Properties panel (Figure 5-16), and Dreamweaver resizes the original image, altering its width and height. If you change your mind about resampling the image, your only option is the old Undo command, Ctrl+Z (⌘-Z).

You can even make an image larger than the original using this technique. The end result isn't perfect—even Dreamweaver can't create image information that was never there—but the program does its best to prevent the image from looking pixelated. You don't want to enlarge images this way often, but in a pinch, it's a quick way to make a photo just a little bit larger.

> **TIP** When working with a Photoshop Smart Object, you can make the image on the page in Dreamweaver smaller, and then click the "Update from Original" button to create a smaller version without resizing the Photoshop file (see page 261).

■ BRIGHTNESS AND CONTRAST

If an image on a page is too light, dark, or washed out, use Dreamweaver's Brightness/Contrast dialog box to fix it.

First, select the picture, and then click the Brightness/Contrast icon in the Properties panel. In the Brightness/Contrast dialog box (Figure 5-17), move the Brightness slider to the right to lighten the image (great for underexposed interior shots), or to the left to darken the image. The Contrast control works the same way: right to increase contrast (making dark colors darker and light colors lighter), left to decrease contrast (moving all colors toward gray).

FIGURE 5-17

If you've ever used an image-editing program like Fireworks or Photoshop, this dialog box should look familiar. Make sure you have the Preview checkbox turned on so you can preview your changes in the document window before you click OK.

You'll often use the Brightness and Contrast sliders together. Brightening (lightening) an image also has a fading effect. By increasing the contrast at the same time, you restore some punch to a brightened image.

As with the other image-editing controls, if you're unhappy with the changes you make, choose Edit→Undo or press Ctrl+Z (⌘-Z) to return the image to its previous glory.

■ SHARPENING IMAGES

Sometimes graphics, even those from scanners and digital cameras, can look a little fuzzy, especially if you resample the image (see page 257). Dreamweaver's Sharpen tool helps restore clarity and make such images "pop." It works like similar tools in graphics-editing programs: It increases the contrast between an image's pixels to create the illusion of a sharper, more focused picture.

To use the tool, select a graphic and then, in the Properties panel, click the Sharpen icon (Figure 5-16). Dreamweaver opens the Sharpen window, which has a single slider. Move the slider to the right to increase the amount of sharpening, or type a number in the box (*10* is maximum sharpening; *0* is no change). You probably won't use the maximum setting unless you're going for a special effect, since it tends to highlight "noise" in the image, creating an unappealing halo effect around the pixels. Once you select a level of sharpening you like, click OK.

If you're unhappy with the results, just press Ctrl+Z (⌘-Z), or choose Edit→Undo.

Setting Up an External Editor

When you double-click an image file in Dreamweaver's Files panel, the program opens the file in your favorite image-editing program, ready for you to edit. When you first install Dreamweaver, it tries to figure out which program to use by looking through the software on your computer. If you want to use a program other than the one Dreamweaver assigns, you need to tell Dreamweaver.

1. **Choose Edit→Preferences (Dreamweaver→Preferences).**

   Dreamweaver opens the Preferences dialog box, as shown in Figure 5-18.

FIGURE 5-18

You can tell Dreamweaver to use a specific program to edit different types of files, such as GIF, JPEG, or PNG files. If you have .fla (Flash files), .mp3 (music files), or other types of non-HTML files on your site, you can assign programs to those file types as well. Double-clicking the filename in the Files panel launches the associated editing program.

2. **In the left pane, click File Types/Editors.**

   The Preferences box displays your preferred editing programs for different types of files. It displays two columns, Extensions and Editors.

3. **From the Extensions list, select a graphics file extension.**

   The box lists several graphics file types, including GIFs, JPEGs, and PNGs. You can choose a different editing program for each type if you like. Add filename extensions for file types not shown by clicking + above the Extensions list.

4. **Click + above the Editors list.**

   Dreamweaver opens the Select External Editor dialog box.

5. **On your hard drive, find the program you want to use to edit the selected type of graphics file.**

   It can be Photoshop, Photoshop Elements, Fireworks, or whatever.

6. **To make this program your primary image-editing tool, click Make Primary.**

   This *primary* editor is the one Dreamweaver opens when you choose to edit a graphic. (You can define other, less frequently used editors as well. See the Tip below.)

7. **Repeat steps 3–6 for each type of graphics file you work with.**

   Dreamweaver treats GIFs, JPEGs, and PNGs as separate file types, so you need to assign an editor to each. Of course, most people choose the same program for all three types.

8. **Click OK to close the Preferences dialog box.**

   From now on, whenever you need to touch up a graphic on your web page, select it and then click Edit in the Properties panel. Alternatively, in the Files panel, you can simply double-click the file, or Ctrl-double-click (⌘-double-click) the image on the page. Either way, your graphic now opens in the program you set as your primary editor.

> **NOTE** When you insert a Photoshop image into a web page in Dreamweaver, the program always converts it to a web-friendly format like JPG or PNG. Later, clicking the Properties panel's Edit button launches Photoshop and opens the original PSD file—no matter what Dreamweaver changed the image's file type to.

Now you can edit the graphic and save changes to it. When you return to Dreamweaver, the modified image appears on the page. (If you're a Photoshop fan, you're in even better shape; read about Smart Objects below.)

> **TIP** You aren't limited to just one external editor for each file type. For instance, if there's a Fireworks feature you need, even though Photoshop is your primary editor, you can still jump to Fireworks directly from Dreamweaver.
>
> The trick is to right-click (Control-click) the image you want to edit, whether it's in the document window or the Files panel. Choose the Open With menu. If you added the image editor to your preferences (Figure 5-18), the submenu lists that editor. Otherwise, from the contextual menu, select Browse, and then, in the resulting dialog box, choose the editing program you want to use. Dreamweaver opens that program with the graphic you clicked, open and ready for your edits.

Editing Smart Objects

Since Adobe makes the ubiquitous Photoshop as well as Dreamweaver, it makes sense that the two programs work together. As you read on page 236, you can add a Photoshop image to a page by simply inserting the PSD file, just as you would insert a regular web-ready graphic. Doing this creates a *smart object*.

Smart Objects really are a, well, smart idea. They let you preserve a high-resolution Photoshop file as the original source of your now web-ready graphic (thanks to Dreamweaver automatically converting PSD files you place on a page to a featherweight format). Since producing web graphics often entails reducing a file's size, any edits you make to the image are best made to the highest-quality version you have. For example, if you want to change the font in your company's logo, don't edit the GIF or PNG file you used on the page. Instead, edit the higher-quality PSD version in Photoshop. Smart Objects make that easy.

You can launch Photoshop by itself and then open the PSD file to work on it, or, better yet, you can open the program directly from Dreamweaver—on your web page, select the Smart Object, and then click the Properties panel's "Edit in Photoshop" button (see Figure 5-19). This opens the PSD file in Photoshop, where you can make the desired edits—modify the company logo, crop the image, use creative filters, and so on. When you're done, save and close the file.

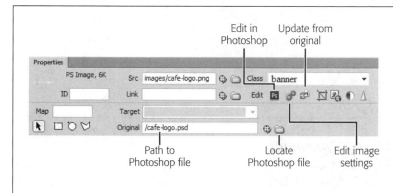

FIGURE 5-19

When you use Smart Objects on a page, the Properties panel makes the "Update from Original" button active, which lets you update the image on a page when you change the original image in Photoshop. You can also revisit the original image settings—if you decide, for example, that you want a PNG8 image instead of a GIF or if you want to change the compression settings—by clicking the Edit Image Settings button.

Edit in Photoshop / Update from original

Path to Photoshop file / Locate Photoshop file / Edit image settings

TIP You can also launch Photoshop from the Files panel to edit a Smart Object. Right-click (Control-click) the Smart Object in the Files panel and then, from the contextual menu that appears, choose "Edit Original with Photoshop."

Smart objects are "smart" because they keep track of changes you make to the original PSD file. You can recognize a Smart Object by the "recycle" logo that appears in the upper-left corner of the image in Dreamweaver's Design view (see Figure 5-20).

When you insert a Photoshop image, Dreamweaver displays an icon in the upper-left corner that looks like a recycling logo (Figure 5-20, top). If you point to the icon, Dreamweaver displays a tooltip with the current status of the smart image. If the original Photoshop image has changed, you see the message "Original asset modified." To replace the old image with the new, improved version, select the image and then, in the Properties panel, click "Update from Original" (Figure 5-19). When you update an image this way, Dreamweaver retains all its previous attributes—including the file format (GIF, JPEG, or PNG), cropping, resizing, and filename.

FIGURE 5-20

A Smart Object is a GIF, JPEG, or PNG file you import from Photoshop. The easiest way to determine the status of a Smart Object is to point to it.

Top: The "Images Synced" message means there have been no changes to the original Photoshop file.

Bottom: If the tooltip message reads "Original asset modified," then it's time to click the "Update from Original" button in the Properties panel.

■ SMART OBJECT WARNINGS

Sometimes you see a warning symbol (a yellow triangle with an exclamation mark in it) as part of the Smart Object icon (see Figure 5-20, bottom). That means one of two things: Either Dreamweaver can't locate the original PSD file, or you resized the inserted image in Dreamweaver—probably by dragging the resize handles, as discussed on page 245.

If Dreamweaver loses track of a PSD file, simply select the Smart Object (you need to be in Design view), and then click 🖿 in the Properties panel (to the right of the Original box). This opens the Select Original File window—just a basic "pick a file on your computer" dialog box. Navigate to the PSD file, and then select it. Unfortunately, once Dreamweaver loses track of a PSD file, it also loses all the file's attributes, such as its file format and the name of the web-ready file. You have to set all these options again, as described on page 236.

The second instance in which you can see the yellow warning symbol is when you resize an image in Dreamweaver. If you make the image *smaller* than the original PSD file (for example, by dragging the resize handles or entering smaller width and height values in the Properties panel), click the Properties panel's "Update from Original" button (see Figure 5-19). That re-exports the original image from your image editor, retaining all the file's attributes, so that it matches the new size you set on the page. (Note that this doesn't replace the original image in your image editor—that remains as it was.)

However, if you resize the image on the page so that it's *larger* than the original PSD file, the yellow warning icon remains, no matter what. In this case, it indicates that the PSD file doesn't have enough pixels to make the image the size you want it without affecting the image's quality. In other words, you can't make the images on your page larger than the Photoshop file they come from without getting a worse-quality image.

NOTE If you resize a Smart Object on a page, you can return it to its original size (that is, the size of the image in the original Photoshop file). In Design view, right-click (Control-click) the Smart Object, and then, from the menu that appears, choose "Reset size to original."

Optimizing an Image

You can optimize an image—compress it so it downloads faster—by clicking the "Edit image settings" button (the one with the two gears) in the Properties panel (see Figure 5-19). After you click the button, Dreamweaver opens the Image Optimization window. This is the same one that appears when you import a Photoshop file.

Although the Optimize feature does leave you with a smaller image file, you should use it only if you're applying it to a Photoshop Smart Object. If you try to optimize a regular GIF, JPEG, or PNG, you're compressing an already-compressed file. Applying additional optimization often degrades the image's quality. However, clicking the "Optimize image" button after selecting a Photoshop file lets you create a new web-ready file—GIF, JPEG, or PNG—from the original Photoshop file without any loss of quality.

If you have a JPEG file that you think should be a GIF (see the box on page 237 for guidelines), or you simply want to see if you can shave a few more bytes from a file by optimizing it again, it's best to return to the original file (Fireworks, Illustrator, or whatever program you used to create the graphic), if available, and use that program's export or "Save for Web" feature to generate a new GIF, JPEG, or PNG.

If you decide to ignore this warning (or you don't have the original image and really need to optimize the image further), follow the directions on page 241. Once you make your changes, click OK in the Preview Image window. Dreamweaver optimizes the image again. You can choose Edit→Undo to back out of the change.

Extracting Photoshop Web Page Prototypes

The ties between Photoshop and Dreamweaver are stronger than ever with Dreamweaver CC 2014. Thanks to a new feature called Extract, you or someone on your team can design a prototype for a web page in Photoshop and then, when it's time to build your page, you can extract the assets and specifications from the Photoshop file and pop them into Dreamweaver.

It's not unusual when bidding for a web job for a graphic artist to design prototype pages in Photoshop. It's a tool artists know well, and they can quickly mock up a design that includes text, color, and image specifications. They often design buttons for a navigation bar, add a company logo, and insert photos. The end result is a great-looking page to show to the potential client. When the client buys into the project, there's only one problem: The page doesn't work. After all, it's just an image, it's not a real web page. That's the point where you take advantage of Dreamweaver's shiny new Extract feature.

Here's how it works. You start by switching over to the Extract workspace (Window→Workspace Layout→Extract). In that view, the Extract panel appears on the left side of the page. Click the Upload PSD button on that panel to upload the Photoshop prototype. You only need to do this once. After Dreamweaver uploads the file to your Creative Cloud account, you see a thumbnail in this panel. When you click the thumbnail, you see the prototype full size, in all its glory. As you point to elements, like the banner at the top of the page, a panel displays the specifications for that element. Point to an image and you see its dimensions. Point to a block of text and you see the font family, font size, and font color. You also see the dimensions of the box that holds the text.

This is exactly the type of information you need to plug into Dreamweaver and CSS Designer to build a real, working web page. Extract even helps with that process. At the top of the pop-up panel (Figure 5-21) you see buttons that make it a snap to copy the text in headings and paragraphs. If you want the type specs, you can click Copy CSS and then you can paste the rule that defines the *font-family*, *font-size*, and *font-color* properties into your CSS style sheet. (Hint: After you create a Selector in CSS Designer, right-click its name and then choose Paste Styles.)

If there are photos or other images on the page that you need in Dreamweaver, you can download them by clicking Extract Asset button on the right end of the pop-up panel. You have your choice of selecting elements by clicking them or selecting them by Photoshop layer (click the Layer button in the upper-right corner of the Extract window).

Think how easy life will be when you add a dozen or so designs to your Extract panel and you can go out and grab the CSS specs and other assets from them!

Using Image Maps

As Chapter 4 makes clear, you can easily turn a graphic into a clickable link. You can also add *multiple* links to a single image.

Suppose your company has offices all over the country and you want to provide an easy way for visitors to locate the nearest one. One approach is to list all the state names and link them to separate pages for each state, but that's boring! Instead, you could use a map of the United States—a single image—and turn each state's outline into a hotspot linked to the appropriate page, listing all the offices in that state.

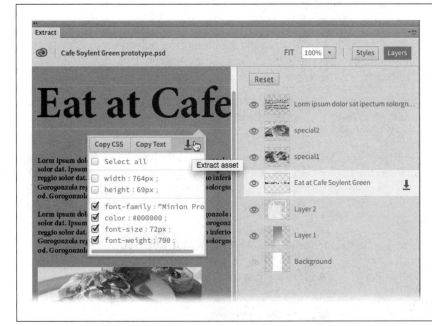

FIGURE 5-21

Point to an element in the Extract panel and you see a pop-up panel like this one. Here the panel displays the specifications for the headline. Click the buttons at the top of the panel to mine the Photoshop file for valuable details that you can use to build your web page. Click Copy CSS to get the code you need for your CSS style sheet. Click Copy Text to save yourself the chore of typing the text as it appears on the page. Click the extract asset icon to download that big headline as an image.

The array of invisible links (called *hotspots*) responsible for this magic is called an *image map*. Image maps contain one or more hotspots, each leading somewhere else.

Here's how to create an image map:

1. **Select the graphic you want to make into an image map.**

   The Properties panel displays the image's properties and, in the lower-left corner, the image map tools (see Figure 5-22). (You see these tools only with the Properties panel fully expanded—double-click the empty gray area to show the full Properties panel.)

2. **In the Properties panel's Map box, type a name for the map.**

   The name should contain only letters and numbers, and can't begin with a number. If you don't give the map a name, Dreamweaver automatically assigns it the ingenious name *Map*. You don't really need to change the name; your visitors never see it, and a browser uses it just to find the file. If you create additional image maps, Dreamweaver calls them *Map2*, *Map3*, and so on.

3. **Select one of the image map tools.**

   Choose the rectangle, circle, or polygon tool, depending on the shape you have in mind for your hotspot. For instance, in the image in Figure 5-22, the polygon tool was used to map the state of Oregon.

4. **Draw the hotspot.**

To use the rectangle and circle tools, click directly on your picture, and then drag diagonally to form a rectangle or circle. To make a perfect square, press Shift while you drag the rectangle tool. (The circle tool always creates a perfect circle.)

To draw an irregularly shaped hotspot using the polygon tool, click once to define one corner of the hotspot. Continue clicking until you define each corner of the hotspot. Dreamweaver automatically joins the corners to close the shape.

Dreamweaver fills the inside of the hotspot with a light blue tint to make it easy to see. Your visitors won't see the blue highlighting, so you don't need to draw a perfect hotspot.

If you need to adjust the hotspot you just drew, click the arrow ("Pointer Hotspot Tool") in the bottom left of the Properties panel. You can drag the light-blue square handles to reshape or resize the hotspot, or drag inside it to move the hotspot as a whole. If you change your mind about the hotspot, press Delete to get rid of it.

When you begin to draw, Dreamweaver reminds you to add an Alt property to the hotspot you're about to create. Each hotspot can have its own Alt description, which assists visitors using screen readers.

NOTE After you draw a hotspot, the drawing tool remains active so you can draw additional hotspots. To disengage it, click the arrow in the bottom left of the Properties panel again.

5. **Add a link to the hotspot.**

When you draw a hotspot, it's automatically selected and Dreamweaver displays its properties in the Properties panel. Use any of the techniques discussed on page 183 to link this hotspot to another web page or location (like an ID on a page; see page 194).

6. **If necessary, set the Target property.**

Most of the options in the Target drop-down menu are useful only when you work with frames, as discussed on page 191. The "_blank" option, however, is useful anytime: It forces your visitor's browser to load the linked page in a *new* browser window or tab. The original page remains open.

7. **Set the hotspot's Alt property.**

By typing a label into the Properties panel's Alt box, you provide a written name for this portion of the graphic. As noted on page 245, *alt* attributes are extremely important to people who surf the Web with graphics turned off or who use text-to-speech reading software.

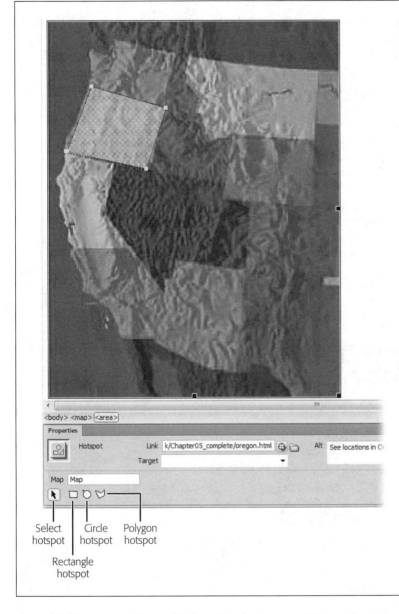

FIGURE 5-22

Each link on an image map is called a hotspot. Here you've created a hotspot for the state of Oregon. You'll create other hotspots and links for the other states. When you select a hotspot, the Properties panel displays its Link, Target, and Alt properties. The lower half of the panel displays the name of the map, as well as tools for selecting and drawing additional hotspots.

Select
hotspot

Circle
hotspot

Polygon
hotspot

Rectangle
hotspot

8. **Repeat steps 2–7 for each hotspot you want to add to an image.**

As you work, you can see the light-blue hotspots filling in your image map.

Editing a Hotspot's Properties

As noted in step 4, you can change a hotspot's shape by dragging its tiny square handles. But you can also change its other properties—like which web page it links to.

To do so, click to select the image map. Click the black arrow button—the hotspot selection tool—in the Properties panel (see Figure 5-22), and then click the hotspot you want to edit. Use the Properties panel's controls to edit the Link, Target, and Alt properties.

If you're having a fit of frustration, you can also press Delete or Backspace to delete the hotspot altogether.

■ Creating Rollover Images

Rollover images are common interactive elements on the Web. Webmasters frequently use them as navigation buttons (see Figure 5-23), but you can use them anytime you want to dramatically swap one image for another. Say you put a photo of a product you're selling on a web page. The photo links to a page that describes the product and lets your visitor buy it. To add emphasis to the image, you could add a rollover image so that when a visitor points to the photo, *another* image—for example, the same image but with a "Buy Now!" or "Learn more" banner across it—appears.

FIGURE 5-23

Rollover graphics appear frequently in navigation bars. Here, all the top and bottom buttons have a similar appearance. When you point to a button, as with "web development" here, your browser swaps in a new image, giving the button a pushed-in look.

This simple change in appearance is a powerful way to inform visitors that the graphic is more than just a pretty picture—it's a button that actually does something. Rollovers usually announce that the image is a link, though you can use them for other creative effects, as described above.

Behind the scenes, you create a rollover by preparing *two different* graphics—a "before" version and an "after" version. One graphic appears when the web page first loads, and the other appears when your visitor points to it. If your guest moves her cursor away without clicking, the original image pops back into place.

You achieve this dynamic effect using *JavaScript*, a programming language that lets you add interactivity to web pages. Dreamweaver includes many prewritten JavaScript programs, called *behaviors*, that let you add rollover images and other interactivity to your pages. (You'll find more about behaviors in Chapter 15.)

To insert a rollover image, start by using a graphics program to prepare the "before" and "after" images. Unless you're going for a bizarre distortion effect, both images should be exactly the same size. Store them somewhere in your website folder.

> **TIP** In cases where normal and "mouseover" versions of a rollover are similar, it often makes sense to create both buttons in the same Photoshop or Fireworks document. Using different layers, you can export similar but slightly different images, as in the case of Figure 5-23. When you export related rollover images, it helps to give them similar names, such as *button.gif* and *button_ro.gif*.

Then, in the document window, click the spot where you want to insert the image. If you're building a navigation bar, you might place several images (the buttons) side by side.

Choose Insert→Image→Rollover Image (or, on the Insert panel's Common category, click the triangle on the Image menu, and then choose the Rollover Image). Either way, Dreamweaver displays the Insert Rollover Image dialog box (see Figure 5-24).

FIGURE 5-24

This box lets you specify the name, link, and image files browsers use to create a rollover effect. The "Preload rollover image" option forces browsers to download the rollover image along with the rest of the page to avoid a delay when a guest points to the image the first time.

Fill in the blanks like this:

- **Image name**. Type a name for your graphic. JavaScript requires *some* name to complete the rollover effect. If you leave this field blank, Dreamweaver gives the image an unimaginative name—like *Image2*. If you plan to add additional interactive effects (Chapter 15) later, you may want to change this generic name to something more descriptive, so you can easily find the graphic.

- **Original image**. When you click the top Browse button, Dreamweaver displays a dialog box, prompting you to choose the graphic you want to use as the "before" button—the one that appears when the web page first loads.

- **Rollover image**. When you click the second Browse button, Dreamweaver prompts you to choose the "after" graphic—the image that appears when your visitor points to the original button.

- **Alternate text**. You can add a text description for a rollover button just as you can for any other graphic, as described on page 245.

- **When clicked, go to URL**. Most web pages use rollover images as navigation elements that, when clicked, take a web surfer to another page. In this box, you specify the destination page. Click ▣ to select a page from your site, or, if you wish to link to another site, type an absolute URL (see page 178), one beginning with *http://*.

When you click OK, you return to your document window, where only the "before" button appears. You can select and modify it just as you would any other image. In fact, it *is* just a regular image, with a link and a Dreamweaver behavior attached.

You can see the rollover effect in action right from Dreamweaver. Choose Live from the Design/Live menu near the top of the document window. In Live view, you see the JavaScript work just as it will in a "live" browser.

You can achieve the same rollover effect with a little more effort using Dreamweaver's Swap Image behavior, discussed on page 645. In fact, this versatile behavior lets you create multiple, simultaneous image swaps where several images change at the same time.

■ Tutorial: Inserting and Formatting Graphics

In this tutorial, you'll learn how to insert a photo, add a rollover image, and apply CSS to improve the look of a web page. You'll also learn how to use background images to enhance the look of headlines.

NOTE To complete this tutorial, you need to download sample files from this book's Missing CD page at *http://oreilly.com/pub/missingmanuals/dreamweaverccmm2014*. (See the Note on page 37 for details.) The files you'll work on are in the Chapter05 folder, and the finished project, for comparison, is in the Chapter05_complete folder.

Setting Up

Once you download the tutorial files and open Dreamweaver, set up a new site as described on page 23. In a nutshell, choose Site→New Site. In the Site Setup window, type *Images* into the Site Name box. Click ▣ next to the Local Site Folder box, navigate to and select the Chapter05 folder inside the MM_DWCC folder, and then click Choose (Select). Finally, click OK.

Adding an Image

Once again, you'll work on a page from the Cafe Soylent Green site. Before you start, set the Design/Live menu at the top of the document window to Design.

1. **In the Files panel, double-click the file *index.html*.**

   If you need a refresher on the Files panel, see page 13 and Figure 1-7.

2. **Click at the beginning of the paragraph, immediately following the headline "All Natural Ingredients" (before the "L" in "Lorum ipsum").**

   You'll add an image here.

3. **Choose Insert→Image→Image or, on the Common tab of the Insert panel, choose "Image : Image." Navigate to the Images folder, and then double-click the file *special1.jpg*.**

   A photo of one of the cafe's dishes appears. A black outline around the image and three resize handles indicate that you've selected the image—if you don't see the handles, click the image to select it. Dreamweaver inserts the image where your cursor is, pushing the text down the page to accommodate the graphic.

4. **Before you forget, type a description for the image, like *Plankton Carpaccio*, in the Alt text box of the Properties panel.**

   The Alt text provides a verbal description of the image, as explained on page 245.

   Next, you'll link this image to another page.

5. **In the Properties panel, to the right of the Link box, click the folder icon. Click the Site Root button to make sure you have the Chapter05 folder (the local site folder) selected, and then double-click the filename *menu.html*.**

   If you need a recap on linking, check out page 183.

   The image is a bit too close to the headline, and the large empty white space to the right of the graphic is distracting. Fortunately, CSS can help with both problems.

6. **Make sure you have CSS Designer open (Window→CSS Designer). In the Sources section, choose *soylent_styles.css*. Then, in Selectors, click + .**

   A new selector appears with the name box open for editing.

7. **Type *.imageRight* and then press Enter (Return).**

   The newly named selector appears in your list of Selectors. Dreamweaver displays its attributes in the Properties section. The Layout properties appear first on the long, scrolling list.

8. **In the *margin-top* property box, type *10px*; in *margin-bottom*, type *10px*; and then, for *margin-left*, type *15px*.**

   You're setting each of the margins separately. If you don't provide a value for a margin, Dreamweaver automatically sets it to zero. That's what you want for the right side, so you don't need to change a thing over there.

9. **Scroll down until you see the *float* properties (see Figure 5-25). Click the "right" icon, the middle of the three options.**

   Floating this image right forces the image to the right side of the page.

   Next you'll add a decorative border.

FIGURE 5-25

float *is one of the most commonly used CSS properties. It lets you align an element, like an image, to the left or right of a page. Content adjacent to the floated element wraps around it; when you use the* float *property on <div> tags, it helps you create multicolumn page designs (which you'll learn about in Chapter 10).*

10. **At the top of CSS Designer, click Border and then click the first tab ("All sides"). Click the box to the right of "width" and choose px (pixels), then type *4*. Click the box next to "style" and choose "solid." Click the box to the right of the color swatch, and then type *#F2E5C2*.**

    Once you make all these changes...nothing happens. You have to apply the class style.

11. **Click the image to select it. In the Properties panel's Class menu, choose "imageRight."**

    Dreamweaver adds a tan border to the image, moves the pic to the right of the content, and scoots it down from the headline 10 pixels.

12. **Click at the beginning of the paragraph immediately following the second headline. Repeat steps 3–5 to insert the image *special2.jpg*. Select the**

image, type *Grilled Mozzarella* for the Alt text, and then link the pic to *menu.html.*

You've inserted a second graphic and link; now you'll apply the class you created earlier.

13. **Click the *special2.jpg* image to select it. In the Class menu of the Properties panel, choose "imageRight."**

The cafe name at the top of the page looks a bit drab; let's replace it with the cafe's logo.

Inserting a Photoshop File

Dreamweaver makes it easy to insert and optimize files from Photoshop.

1. **Select the text "Cafe Soylent Green" at the top of the page and press Delete to remove it. Choose Insert Image→Image.**

   Dreamweaver opens the Select Image Source window so you can specify the Photoshop (.psd) file. You can also drag the PSD file from the Files panel and drop it into the empty space where the text used to be.

2. **Click the Site Root button, and then double-click *cafe-logo.psd*.**

   Dreamweaver opens the Image Optimization window.

3. **Choose "PNG8" from the Format menu and turn on the transparency checkbox.**

   The Photoshop file has a transparent background—that's not so important right now since the logo is sitting on a white page, but if you add an image behind the logo (which you soon will) it's important to make sure that the transparent areas of the graphic are truly see-through.

4. **Click OK, and then, in the "Save Web Image" box, save the file as *cafe-logo.png*. Then click OK once more.**

   A big image appears on the page (see Figure 5-26). You'll notice the Smart Object logo in the top-left corner (circled in Figure 5-26), and three resize handles. The logo is a bit large, but you can resize it in Dreamweaver.

5. **In the Properties panel's Alt box, type *Cafe Soylent Green*.**

   This is a verbal description of the cafe's logo. Even though the graphic looks like type in the logo, a screen reader just sees it as another image.

6. **Hold down the Shift key and drag the image's bottom-right resize handle up and to the left until the image is about 110 pixels tall (look in the Properties panel's H box to see the image's height).**

   If you don't see the resize handles, click the image to select it. The Shift key makes sure the image scales proportionally, which, in turn, ensures that you don't accidentally distort the image.

FIGURE 5-26

Photoshop Smart Objects look just like regular images except for the small icons in the top-left corner (circled).

Now you see a warning sign in the image's upper-left corner (see Figure 5-27). That means that the dimensions of the image no longer match the width and height specified in the HTML—by resizing the image, you changed the HTML for it, but not the actual image file. As mentioned in the box on page 247, this isn't a good idea—the image doesn't look as good, and the file is larger than it needs to be (meaning it will download more slowly). Fortunately, because this is a Smart Object, you can easily create a PNG file that matches the smaller dimensions you specified while maintaining the image's original quality.

7. **In the Properties panel, click "Update from Original" (the button with the recycle icon in it, circled in Figure 5-27).**

Dreamweaver re-optimizes the image based on the Photoshop file. This means that, behind the scenes, Dreamweaver creates a new PNG file—complete with all your original optimization settings (PNG8 with transparency in this case). Modifying an image using Smart Objects, aside from being very fast, is the best way to ensure a high-quality web image. When the image on your page is "in sync" with the original Photoshop file, Dreamweaver grays out the "Update from Original" button.

FIGURE 5-27

When you see a warning icon (the triangle) on a Smart Object, it usually means you resized the image on the page. The "Update from Original" button lets you recreate the image from the original to match the dimensions you're after.

If you own Photoshop, launch it now (if you don't have Photoshop, skip to the next section). Then, in the Chapter05 folder, open the *cafe-log.psd* file and edit it—apply a filter, add some text, whatever. Save the file, and then return to Dreamweaver. Select the image in the banner. You see that the "Update from Original" button is now active because the image is no longer in sync with the original Photoshop file. Click "Update from Original" again, and Dreamweaver creates a new image from the edited PSD file, resizes and optimizes it, and puts it on your page. You'll now see the new, filter-enhanced version of the image without having to make a stop at the Image Preview window. Very cool.

Using Background Images and Custom Bullets for Lists

You can use CSS Designer to add background images to an entire page by using the <html> or <body> tags as selectors. You can also apply background images to a portion of the page. For example, you can apply a background image to an <aside> or <footer> tag. In this example, you apply a background image to the page and choose custom bullets for your unordered list.

1. **Make sure CSS Designer is open (Window→CSS Designer). In the Sources section, choose *soylent_styles.css*. Then, in Selectors, click + .**

   Dreamweaver adds a new selector to the list, ready for you to give it a name.

2. **Type *html*.**

   As you type, Dreamweaver displays matching selectors. When you see *html*, stop typing and hit Enter (Return) twice.

   CSS Designer's Properties section displays the properties you can set for your selector.

3. **Click the Background button. Under *background-image*, next to URL, click the box, and then click ▣. Navigate to and select the file *bg_page.png*.**

   The background image is a simple, textured, sand color. But you can't see it! What gives? Again, Dreamweaver's Design view fails us—many common CSS tricks, like adding a background image to the <html> tag, just won't appear in Design view. You'll see the effect only when you view the page in a browser or in Dreamweaver's Live view.

4. **Set the Design/Live menu at the top of the page to Live.**

   The background texture looks great! Unfortunately, the color matches the word "Soylent" in the logo. To see the entire logo, you can add another background image. There's no need to go back to Design view, because you can do the next few steps in Live view.

5. **With *soylent_styles.css* selected in the Sources section of CSS Designer, locate and select the <body> tag in the Selectors section.**

   The properties for the body selector appear in CSS Designer's Properties panel. Most of the properties are grayed out, which means you haven't set them yet.

6. **In the Properties section of CSS Designer, click the Background button. Then, under *background-image*, click next to "URL," and then click ▣. Browse to and select *bg_banner.png*.**

   The image is a dark-green bar that will run along the top of the page. Normally, background images tile from left to right and top to bottom. As you can see, the image now fills the body of the page. Not pretty. Fortunately, you can control how a background image tiles.

7. **Scroll down until you see the *background-repeat* properties. Choose the "repeat-x" icon (second button from the left).**

   The CSS Designer window should now look something like the one in Figure 5-28. "Repeat-x" repeats the image horizontally, along the x-axis. Time to create a style for the list items.

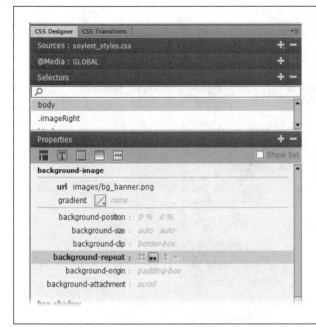

8. **In the Sources section of CSS Designer, select *soylent_styles.css* and then, in Selectors, click + .**

   You'll create a style for the list element (<li>) this time.

9. **In the "Selector name" box, type *li*, and then press Enter (Return) twice.**

   The Properties panel displays properties you can set for the <li> tag.

10. **Click the Text button at the top of CSS Designer's Properties section. Scroll down to the *list-style-image* property. Click the grayed-out word "none" and then choose "url" from the drop-down menu. Click ▤ next to the text box.**

    Dreamweaver opens the Select Image Source window.

11. **Choose *list_dingbat.png* and then click OK (Open).**

    The bullet changes from the standard circle to your custom image, as shown in Figure 5-29.

To see the finished page, choose *index.html* from the Chapter05_complete folder.

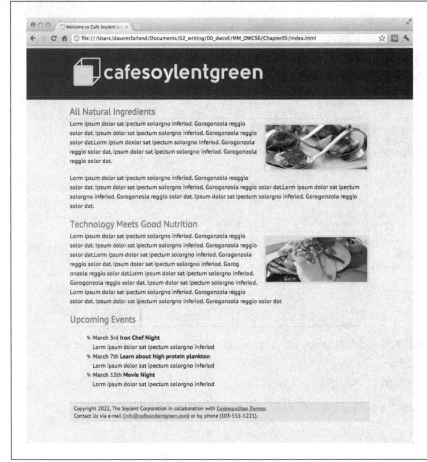

Working with Tables

The HTML <table> tag has had a somewhat infamous existence in the world of web design. It was originally intended to present scientific data in spreadsheet-like format. But as the Web grew, graphic designers got into the web design game. They wanted to recreate the types of layouts they saw in magazines, books, and newspapers (in other words, they wanted to make good-looking websites!). The most reliable tool at the time was the <table> tag, which designers used as a back-door way to create columns, sidebars, and, in general, to precisely position elements on a page.

Today, with nearly everyone on the planet using advanced browsers like Internet Explorer, Firefox, Safari, Chrome, and Opera, web designers use a more facile page-styling technique—CSS-based layout. Table-based layout is an aging dinosaur that produces pages that are heavy with code (so they download slower); harder to update; and hostile to alternative browsers, like screen readers, mobile phones, and text-only browsers.

This chapter shows you how to use tables for their intended purpose: displaying data and other information best presented in rows and columns (Figure 6-1). If you're a longtime web designer who still uses tables for page layout, you can use Dreamweaver and the instructions in this chapter to continue that technique. However, you're better off making the switch to CSS. Dreamweaver's advanced CSS tools make building well-designed pages much simpler than table-based layout does. You'll learn all about CSS layout in Chapter 10.

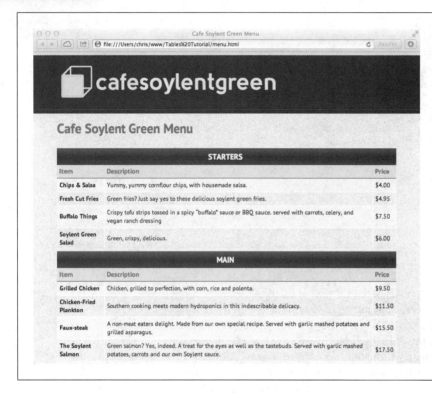

FIGURE 6-1
You can do all your page layout and design with CSS, and use tables for their intended purpose—displaying rows and columns of information. The list of tasty delights on this page is nestled inside a basic <table> tag, while the rest of the page—the logo, headline, and so on—is laid out using CSS.

■ Table Basics

A table is a grid of rows and columns that intersect to form *cells*, as shown in Figure 6-2. If you've used a spreadsheet before, an HTML table will feel familiar.

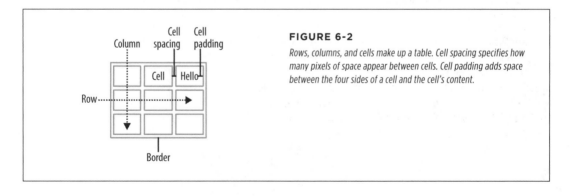

FIGURE 6-2

Rows, columns, and cells make up a table. Cell spacing specifies how many pixels of space appear between cells. Cell padding adds space between the four sides of a cell and the cell's content.

A table row usually represents a collection of data for a single item. In Figure 6-1, for example, each row holds data for one dish. A table *column* represents data of a particular type. The first column in Figure 6-1 contains the name of each dish, for example, while the second column provides a tantalizing description, and the third displays the price. A table cell, then, holds one piece of data for a particular row, like the cell that displays the $6.00 price of the Soylent Green Salad.

At a minimum, you use three HTML tags to create a table (there are actually quite a few tags related to table design, as you'll read about soon, but these three are the core table tags). You set the boundaries of the table with the <table> tag. Then, within this structure, you add rows using the *table row* <tr> tag. Finally, you divide a table row into individual cells with the <td> or *table data* tag. Each cell holds one piece of data, like the $6.00 price for the salad. Browsers align the text inside a cell to the left edge.

A fourth tag, the <th>, or *table header,* tag also creates cells within a row, but instead of holding data, table headers tell you the *kind* of information you'll find in a row or column (like Price). Text inside a <th> tag appears centered and in boldface.

Figure 6-1, for example, contains one table (it uses one <table> tag), and 12 rows (12 <tr> tags). The top row contains one table header (<th>) that identifies the type of data in the cells below. In this example, that header is Starters. The next row contains three table headers, labeled Item, Description, and Price. And the following four rows contain data in cells, which you create with simple <td> tags.

■ Inserting a Table

One of the main problems with HTML tables is that they require a lot of code. Not only is this one reason why CSS is a better page layout method than HTML, but it's also a good reason to use Dreamweaver to create tables. If you've ever hand-coded an HTML table, you know what a tangled mess of instructions it requires; one typo can sink your whole page. Fortunately, Dreamweaver makes the process simple:

1. **Choose Design from the Design/Live view menu at the top of the document window. Then, position your cursor where you want to insert the table.**

   You can add a table anywhere you can add a paragraph of text. You can even add a table inside *another* table (a common technique in the bad old days of table-based layout), by clicking inside a table cell.

2. **Choose Insert→Table.**

   You can also click the Table button in the Common category of the Insert panel. Finally, you can press Alt+Ctrl+T (Option-⌘-T). Either way, the Table dialog box opens (see Figure 6-3).

FIGURE 6-3

The Table dialog box lets you control a table's appearance. Leaving the "Cell padding" and "Cell spacing" fields empty isn't the same as setting them to 0. If you leave the values blank, most browsers insert 1 pixel of cell padding and 2 pixels of cell spacing. If you notice unwanted gaps between cells in a table, or between content in a cell and the cell's edges, blank settings are the likely culprit. To truly leave zero space, set "Cell padding" and "Cell spacing" to 0. (Dreamweaver remembers the settings you use. When you open the Table dialog box again, it starts with the settings you entered previously.)

3. **Using the Rows and Columns fields, specify how many rows and columns you want in your table.**

   Don't fret too much over your estimate, because you can always add or remove rows and columns later.

4. **Type the amount of cell padding, in pixels, you want for the table.**

   Cell padding is the buffer around the content in a cell—the space from the edge of the cell to the contents inside it (see Figure 6-2). Unfortunately, this property applies to *every* cell in a table (it also applies equally to all four sides of the cell). You can't specify cell padding for individual cells, nor can you specify different padding for each edge of the content (you can't, for example, specify 10 pixels of padding on the left side of a cell and only 5 pixels at the top) unless you use the CSS *padding* property, as described on page 465. Designers often type either *0* or leave this box empty, and then use CSS to control the spacing in individual cells (by styling the <td> and <th> tags).

5. **Type the amount of cell spacing, in pixels, you want for the table.**

   Cell spacing specifies how many pixels of empty space separate one cell from another. Like *cell padding*, this property applies to every cell in a table. CSS provides an equivalent property, *border-spacing*, and you add it to a table using CSS Designer (see page 116). But there's a catch: Internet Explorer 7 and earlier ignore the *border-spacing* property. So if you want space between each table cell, it's easiest to add a cell spacing value here (you can change it later). Type *0* to remove any space between cells. (Note that leaving these fields empty isn't the same as setting them to 0; see Figure 6-3.)

6. **In the "Table width" box, specify how wide you want the table to be (in units you specify using the drop-down menu beside the box).**

   You can create a table that has either a specified, fixed minimum width, or one whose width is a percentage of the space available on the page. To set a fixed width, choose pixels as the unit of measure, and then, in the "Table width" box, type an amount. Fixed-width tables remain the same size regardless of the browser window's size.

   Percentage-width tables grow or shrink relative to the space available. If you place a 100% wide table on a blank web page, the table stretches all the way across your visitor's browser window, no matter how wide or narrow he has it set. But the percentage isn't always based on the overall browser window width. If you place a table *inside* another object—for example, within a <div> tag—and that <div> has a set width, Dreamweaver calculates the percentage based on that <div>'s set width. Say you have a sidebar on a page, and the sidebar is 300 pixels wide; if you insert an 80% wide table inside the sidebar, the table takes up 80 percent of 300 pixels, or 240 pixels.

7. **In the "Border thickness" box, type a number, in pixels, for the border.**

   If you don't want a border, type *0*. Dreamweaver uses dotted lines in Design view to help you identify rows, columns, and cells whose border is 0. (The dotted lines won't appear on your finished page.) Again, CSS offers a much better way to add borders, so it's best to set this to *0* and use CSS for your borders (see page 259).

8. **Using the buttons in the middle of the Table dialog box, select a Header option.**

   The Table Header property creates the specialized cells in the top row or left-hand column of a table that identify the content in the associated cells. When you select one of the Header options here, Dreamweaver inserts the <th> tag to indicate that these cells are *headlines*. For instance, a table that displays a company's yearly sales figures broken down by region might have a top row of headers for each year (2012, 2013, 2014), while the left column would have table headers identifying each region (Northwest, West, South, and so on).

   The only visible change you see with a <th> tag is that web browsers display the text inside center-aligned and in bold type. However, this option also makes the table more accessible by telling screen readers (used by the visually impaired) that the cell serves as a header for the information in the related column or row. (You can always change the look of these cells using CSS; just create a style for the <th> tag.)

9. **In the bottom section of the Table dialog box, add any Accessibility notations you want.**

In the Caption box, type in a description for the table; it appears, centered, above the table. Use the Summary box when you want to explain a particularly complex table. This information doesn't show up in a browser window; it's intended to clarify the contents of a table to search engines and screen readers. Basic data tables (simple rows and columns) don't need a summary; search engines and screen readers can understand them just fine. It's only when you create a complex table with merged cells (see page 299) and multiple levels of headers that you might want to fill out the Summary box.

For more information on these options, and to get a complete rundown on table accessibility, visit *http://tinyurl.com/5vgvv2e*.

10. **Click OK to insert the table.**

Once you add a table to a page, you can begin filling its cells. A cell works like a small document window; you can click inside it and add text, images, and links using the techniques you've learned so far. You can even insert a table inside a cell.

To move your cursor from one cell to the next, press Tab. When you reach the last cell in a row, the Tab key moves the insertion point to the first cell in the row below. And if you're in the last *cell* of the last row, pressing Tab creates a new row at the bottom of the table.

Shift+Tab moves the cursor in the *opposite* direction—from the current cell to the previous one.

■ Editing a Table

Tables and their cells have independent properties. For example, a table and a cell can have different alignment properties. But before you can change any of these properties, you must first *select* the table, rows, columns, and cells you want to affect.

Selecting a Table

In Design view, you select a table in the document window a number of ways:

- Click the upper-left corner of the table, or anywhere on the bottom or right edges. (Be careful using the latter technique; it's easy to accidentally *drag* the border, adding a *height* or *width* property to cells in the table.)

- Click anywhere inside the table, and then select the <table> tag in the document window's Tag Selector.

- Click anywhere inside the table, and then choose Modify→Table→Select Table.

- Right-click (Control-click) inside a table, and then, from the shortcut menu, choose Table→Select Table.

- If the cursor is in a cell inside the table, pressing Ctrl+A (⌘-A) twice selects the table.

Once selected, the table grows a thick black border and three tiny square resize handles at the right edge, bottom edge, and lower-right corner.

Selecting Rows or Columns

You can select an entire row or column of cells by doing one of the following:

- Move your cursor to the left edge of a row or the top edge of a column. When it changes to a right- or down-pointing arrow, click, as explained in Figure 6-4.

- Click a cell at either end of a row, or the first or last cell of a column, and then drag across the cells in the row or column to select them.

- Click any cell in the row you want to select, and then click the table row tag, <tr>, in the Tag Selector. This method doesn't work for columns, however.

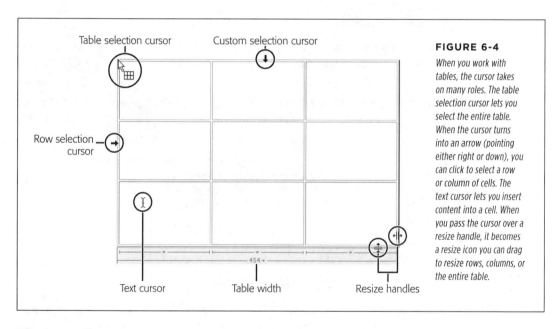

FIGURE 6-4

When you work with tables, the cursor takes on many roles. The table selection cursor lets you select the entire table. When the cursor turns into an arrow (pointing either right or down), you can click to select a row or column of cells. The text cursor lets you insert content into a cell. When you pass the cursor over a resize handle, it becomes a resize icon you can drag to resize rows, columns, or the entire table.

When you select a cell, its border turns dark. When you select multiple cells, each has a dark border.

Selecting Cells

To select one or more cells:

- Drag across adjoining cells. A solid black border appears around your selection.

- To select several cells that aren't necessarily adjacent, Ctrl-click (⌘-click) them one at a time. (You can also Ctrl-click [⌘-click] an already selected cell to deselect it.)

- Click a cell, and then Shift-click another cell. Your two clicks form diagonally opposite corners of an imaginary rectangle; Dreamweaver highlights all cells within it.

- Use the Tag Selector (page 7) to select a cell. Click inside the cell you wish to select, and then click the <td> (or <th>, for table headers) tag in the Selector.

- If the insertion point is inside the cell you want to select, press Ctrl+A (⌘-A).

Expanded Tables Mode

If you remove all the padding, cell spacing, and borders from a table, you may find it hard to select tables and individual cells. This is especially true if you nest tables within table cells (a common table-layout technique). To help you out, Dreamweaver offers Expanded Tables mode. Right-click (Control-click) inside a cell, and then choose Table→Expanded Tables Mode. That adds visible borders to every table and cell, and increases onscreen cell padding. Expanded Tables mode never changes the actual HTML of your page, it merely affects how the page looks in Design view. The guideline borders and extra spacing won't appear in browsers.

If you simply use tables to display data, you'll probably never need Expanded Tables mode, but if you have to edit old web pages built with complicated table layouts, Expanded mode is a big help.

To return the table to its normal look, click the Exit link that appears in the black toolbar above the document window (this toolbar appears only in Expanded Tables mode).

TIP Go to View→Visual Aids to see your options for displaying or hiding table widths and borders, as well as for other features, like the ability to have your <div>s outlined or to see normally invisible elements, like paragraph markers. In general, the Visual Aids options are design-time tools that help you understand why your page looks like it does.

■ Modifying Table Properties

When you first insert a table, you set its number of rows and columns, as well as its cell padding, cell spacing, width, and borders. You're not stuck with the properties you first give a table, however; you can change any or all of these settings—and set a few additional options—using the Properties panel.

When you select a table, the Properties panel changes to reflect that table's settings (see Figure 6-5). You can adjust the table by entering different values for width, rows, columns, and so on in the appropriate boxes.

FIGURE 6-5

When you select a table, you can do all kinds of editing in the Properties panel, everything from adjusting the table's basic structure to fine-tuning its appearance. Dreamweaver includes two drop-down menus—Table on the far left and Class on the far right—that let you apply an ID or assign a class (page 117) to a table.

In addition, the Properties panel lets you set alignment options and add colors or a background image to a table, as described next.

Aligning Tables

In the normal flow of a web page, a table acts like a paragraph, header, or any other HTML block-level element. Browsers align it to the left of the page. Initially, other page elements are either above or below the table. But, as explained in the first bullet point below, you can change that, making text and other elements wrap around the table.

You can make several useful changes to the way a table interacts with text and other page elements. After selecting the table, use one of the three alignment options in the drop-down menu on the right of the Properties panel:

- The Left and Right options align the table with the left or right page margins. Anything you then add to the page—including paragraphs, images, or other tables—wraps around the right or left side of the table. You can apply the CSS *float* property to a table (just as with images) to achieve the same effect (see page 248).

- The Center option makes the table sit in the center of a page, interrupting the flow of the elements around it. Nothing wraps around the table.

NOTE Some of the properties Dreamweaver lets you adjust to make tables look better aren't technically valid for some of the different HTML doctypes (see page xxi for details on doctypes). Dreamweaver can create HTML 4.01 Transitional, XHTML 1.0 Transitional, and several other types of HTML documents. In general, HTML 4.01 Transitional and XHTML 1.0 Transitional are commonly used document types—HTML5 is the factory setting in Dreamweaver. However, the more "strict" doctypes, like HTML 4.01 Strict and XHTML 1.0 Strict, don't support some HTML table properties, and the *align* property, discussed above, is one of them.

HTML5 is even more restrictive. Not only is the *align* property considered obsolete, but so are the *table width*, *cell padding*, and *cell spacing* options.

This discrepancy is more a technicality than a design nuisance; most web browsers still display the alignment you select, even when you create HTML5, HTML Strict, and XHTML Strict documents. The newer and recommended method of alignment is to use CSS properties to accomplish the same display goals; for example, using CSS to set the left and right margins of a table to *auto* to automatically center the table on the page, while applying a CSS *left float* or *right float* property does the same as the Left and Right alignment options. The CSS *width* (page 464) and *padding* (page 465) properties for tables are fine replacements for their HTML equivalents.

Clearing Width and Height Values

When you create complex tables, it's easy to get into a situation where width and height measurements conflict and produce unreliable results. For example, it's possible to set one cell to 300 pixels wide, and later set another cell *in the same column* to 400 pixels wide. Since a browser can't do both (how can one column be both 300 *and* 400 pixels wide?), you might not get the results you want.

In tables with many cells, these kinds of problems are tough to ferret out. That's when you'll find the following timesaving tools—located behind the obscure-looking buttons in the Properties panel's bottom half when you have a table selected (see Figure 6-5)—handy. They let you delete the width and height measurements and start from scratch (see page 289).

- Clicking the Clear Height Values button removes the height properties from the table and each cell. Doing so doesn't set the heights to 0, it simply deletes the property altogether.

- Clicking the Clear Width Values button does the same thing with the width properties of a table and its cells.

Two additional buttons let you convert pixel-based table widths to percentage measurements and vice versa. In other words, if a table is 600 pixels wide and you click Convert Widths to Percentages, Dreamweaver assigns percentages to the table and each cell whose width you specified using pixels.

These percentages depend on how much of the document window your table takes up when you click the button. If the document window is 1200 pixels wide, that 600-pixel-wide table changes to a 50% wide table. Because you'll rarely do this, don't waste your brain cells memorizing such tools.

NOTE Dreamweaver doesn't let you set outdated HTML table properties like *border color, background color*, and *background image* from the Properties panel. Instead, use the CSS equivalents: *border* (page 292), *background-color* (page 291), and *background-image* (page 91). You'll find examples of how to use CSS to add table borders, background colors, and background images in the tutorial at the end of this chapter. In addition, you'll learn how to use the very valuable *border-collapse* property on page 292.

Resizing a Table

While you define the width of a table when you first insert it, you can always change it. To do so, select the table, and then take either of these steps:

- Type a value in the W (width) box in the Properties panel, and then choose a unit of measure, either pixels or percentages, from the drop-down menu.

- Drag one of the resize handles on the right edge of the table. Avoid the handle in the lower-right corner—this adds a *height* property to the first cell in the bottom row. If you do add a *height* property this way, you can easily remove it using the Clear Height Values button in the Properties panel.

In theory, you can also convert a table from a fixed unit of measure, such as pixels, to the stretchy, percentage-style width setting—or vice versa—using the two Convert Table Width buttons at the bottom of the Properties panel (see Figure 6-5). What these buttons do depends on the size of the document window in Dreamweaver. Suppose the window is 700 pixels wide, and you insert a table that's 100 percent wide. Clicking "Convert Table Widths to Pixels" sets the table's width to around 700 pixels (the exact value depends on the margins of the page). However, if your document window was 500 pixels wide, clicking the same button would produce a fixed-width table of around 500 pixels.

NOTE The HTML <table> tag doesn't officially have a *height* property. Dreamweaver, however, adds height properties to table cells when you drag their top or bottom borders, but it won't add a *height* property to the table tag, which is a good thing, since it's invalid HTML. You could add it manually—<table height="500">—since most browsers understand the *height* property and would obey your wishes. But since it's not standard HTML, there's no guarantee that newer browsers will support it.

You have a couple of alternatives: First, you could decide not to worry about height. After all, it's difficult to control the height of a table precisely, especially if there's text in it. Since text sizes appear differently on different operating systems and browsers, the table may grow taller if your guest's text is larger than yours, no matter what height you set.

Your second option is to use the CSS *height* property (page 64) to set the table's stature, but this is a bad idea because the table text may overflow the allotted space, making your page look haphazard.

The "Convert Table Widths to Percent" button takes the opposite tack. It sets the width of a table and its cells to a percentage based on the amount of the document window's width and height the table occupies. The bigger the current document window, the smaller the percentage.

Because the effects of this button depend on the document window's size, you'll find yourself rarely, if ever, using it.

Modifying Cell and Row Properties

Cells and rows have their own properties, separate from the properties of the table itself. Table columns, however, don't have separate properties (see the box on page 293).

When you click inside a cell, the top half of the Properties panel displays the cell's text formatting settings, while the bottom half shows the properties of the cell itself (see Figure 6-6).

Split cells

Merge cells

FIGURE 6-6

The Properties panel displays the settings of a cell. If you select an entire row of cells, or select <tr> from the Tag Selector, the background-color property (listed as "Bg" in the Properties panel) applies to the <tr> tag—to the whole row, in other words. But the W, H, "No wrap," and Header options affect individual cells in the row only.

Alignment Properties

At the outset, a cell's contents hug the left wall and float halfway between the top and bottom of the cell. After selecting a row, a cell, or several cells, you can change these alignments in the Properties panel. For example, the Horz (horizontal) menu offers Left, Center, Right, and Default alignment. (Default gives you the same effect as Left without adding any extra HTML code.)

Note that these options are distinct from the *paragraph* alignment options discussed in Chapter 3. In fact, you can mix and match the two. Suppose you have a cell containing four paragraphs, and you want to center-align all but the last one, which you want right-aligned. To do that, you could set the alignment of the *cell* to Center, and then select just the last paragraph and set *its* alignment to Right. The paragraph's alignment overrides the alignment applied by the cell.

You set the *vertical alignment* property the same way. Select the relevant cells, and then use one of the five options available in the Properties panel's Vert (vertical) menu: Default (the same as Middle), Top, Middle, Bottom, or Baseline. The Baseline option aligns the bottom of the first line of text in the cell to the baseline of text in all the other cells in the row—really only useful if you have different size type in different cells and you're an extremely picky designer (which you might be, and that's OK).

> **NOTE** The CSS *text-align* property (in the Text category of CSS Designer) provides the same effect as horizontal cell alignment; the *vertical-align* property (also in the Text category of CSS Designer) is the CSS replacement for a cell's vertical alignment.

Header

The Header option lets you convert a <td> tag to a <th> tag, which is useful when you want to turn, say, the row at the top of a table into a header. It works just like the column or row header options available in the Table dialog box, described on page 282.

> **NOTE** You can also turn off the Table Header checkbox to turn a table header into a regular table cell. This is handy when you insert a table that shouldn't have headers, but you forgot to unselect the header option in the Table dialog box.

You usually use the Header option for tables that include tabular data (like a spreadsheet) to identify the type of data in the cells in a row or column. For example, you may have a table containing data from different years; each cell in the top row could identify the year the data in the cells below it was compiled.

While Dreamweaver lets you change a single cell into a header, you'll most likely apply this to the top row or left column of cells.

A Property to Forget

The No Wrap property prevents a web browser from wrapping a line of text within a cell onto multiple lines. The browser widens the cell instead, so that it accommodates the line without breaks. The result is almost never useful or attractive, and it's of such little value that you'll probably go your entire web career without using it. Furthermore, in some browsers, if you specify a width for the cell, the browsers ignore the No Wrap option!

Cell Backgrounds

Table cells needn't be drab. As with tables themselves, you can give individual cells background colors or even background graphics. But also just as with tables, you should avoid decorating cells through the options available in the Properties panel. Using those options fills your page's HTML with formatting instructions that may be difficult to edit later. In other words, it breaks the rule for separating content from formatting. Instead, use CSS's *background-color* property to add color to a cell and the *background-image* property (see page 291) to add a graphic to the background of a cell. Use the border properties covered next to dress up cell perimeters.

Cell Borders

Each cell in your table has four borders: top, bottom, left, and right. When you first add a table to a page, Dreamweaver adds extra space between the cells so you can easily identify individual units (see Figure 6-4). Dreamweaver's CSS rule-writing tool, CSS Designer, lets you set border attributes like width and color, and even change the border style from solid lines to dotted or dashed lines.

To style a single cell in a table, first select the cell: click inside it and then, using the Tag Selector at the bottom of the document window, click <td>, the HTML tag for an individual table cell (think "table data," because cells are the containers for a table's data). In Design view, Dreamweaver highlights the selected cell with a bold rectangle to make it easy to see, but the rectangle doesn't show up in your finished page.

To change the borders for *all* the cells in all your tables, go to CSS Designer and choose a source. Then, in the Selectors section, click + (Add Selector) and type *td* in the box. Then go to the Properties section of CSS Designer and click ▢, the Border button. Generally, you want to set values for cell width, color, and border style (solid, dashed, and so forth). At a minimum, you want to set the *border-style* property, because if you don't, guests won't see any cell borders at all, and all the data in the cells will run together.

To add rounded corners to any or all of a cell's corners, set the *border-radius* property. Below that, you can set the *border-collapse* and *border-spacing* properties. (Note that there are two boxes for the *border-spacing* property—the first sets the space between columns, and the second sets the space between rows.)

The *border-collapse* property provides a solution to a problem that might not be apparent when you first work with tables. Because each cell has four borders, you get a double border wherever two cells meet. The problem is most apparent when you have thick borders with space between them, as in Figure 6-7. The resulting table can look pretty ugly. To turn those double borders into a single border and remove the space between them, set the *border-collapse* property to "collapse." You won't see the result in Design view, so switch to Live view to preview your table.

If you want some of the borders in your table to look different from others, you need to create a class selector in CSS Designer's Selectors section. Something like *.orangeBorder* will do the trick. Then apply that class to the specific <td> elements whose borders you want to tint. Use the Tag Selector to isolate the cell, and then set the class using the Properties panel, or go to Format→CSS Styles→orangeBorder. (For a refresher on applying classes to HTML tags, see page 128.)

TIP Tables have yet another border, one that goes around the outside edges of the table itself. To style that border, select the <table> tag in the Tag Selector and then use the techniques described here to apply width, color, and a border style and border radius to it.

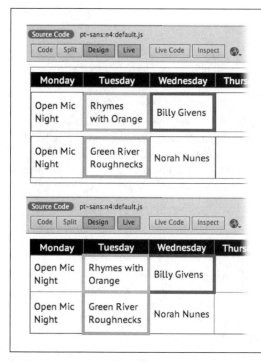

FIGURE 6-7

Top: In this somewhat exaggerated example, you can clearly see that each cell has its own border, creating double borders where the cells intersect. In addition, the setting for the border-spacing property adds 7px of space between the table rows.

Bottom: If that's not the look you want, remove the double borders and the space between rows by setting the table's border-collapse property to "collapse."

The Dawn of Columns

As far as the standard HTML language is concerned, there really isn't any such entity as a column. You create tables with the <table> tag, rows with the <tr> tag, and cells with the <td> tag—but there's no column tag. Dreamweaver calculates the number of columns in a table based on the number of cells in a row. If you have seven rows in a table, each with four cells, the table has four columns. In other words, the number of cells you add to a row determines the number of columns in a table.

Two tags introduced in HTML 4—<colgroup> and <col>—let you control various attributes of columns in a table. Unfortunately, Dreamweaver provides no easy way to add the tags. You can find out more about them, however, from *http://tinyurl. com/3whpctc*.

Suddenly Jumbo Cells

When I add text to a cell, it suddenly gets much wider than the other cells in the row. What gives?

It isn't Dreamweaver's fault; it's how HTML works.

Web browsers (and Dreamweaver) display cells to match the content inside. For example, say you add a three-column table to a page. In the first cell of the first row, you type in two words, leave the second cell empty, and add a 125-pixel-wide image in

the third cell of that row. Since the image is the biggest item, its cell is wider than the other two. The middle cell, with nothing in it, is given the least amount of space.

Usually, you don't want a web browser making these kinds of decisions for you. By specifying a width for a cell, as explained below, you can force a browser to display a cell with the dimensions you want. But keep in mind that there are exceptions to this rule; see "Tips for Surviving Table-Making" below.

Setting Cell Dimensions

Specifying the width or height of a particular cell is simple: Select one or more cells, and then type a value in the Properties panel's W (width) or H (height) box. You can specify the value in either pixels or percentages. For instance, if you want a 50-pixel-wide cell, type in *50*. For a cell that you want to take up 50 percent of the total table width, type in *50%*. Read the next section for details on the tricky business of controlling cell and table dimensions.

You can also resize a column or row of cells by dragging a cell border. As your cursor approaches the cell's edge, it changes into two parallel lines with arrows beside each to indicate that you can begin dragging. As you do, Dreamweaver dynamically lists the cell's width (circled in Figure 6-8). This helpful feature lets you know the exact width of your cells at all times, so you can drag a cell to a precise measure. When you resize table cells this way, Dreamweaver shows the width of the cell using the same unit of measure you specified for the table itself, pixels or percentages. So if you set a table's width to 100%, Dreamweaver shows you cell widths using a percentage value, too (30%, for example). And if you initially set the table to 500 pixels wide, Dreamweaver displays the cell widths as pixel values when you resize them.

Tips for Surviving Table-Making

Nothing is more confounding than trying to get your tables laid out exactly as you want them. Many beginning web designers throw their hands up in despair when working with tables, which often seem to have minds of their own. Here are a few problems that often confuse designers—and some ways to make working with them more straightforward.

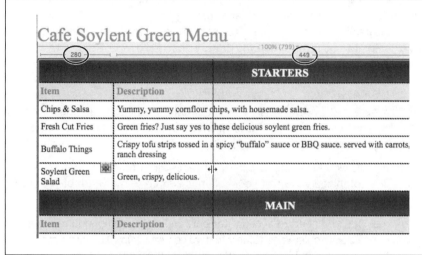

FIGURE 6-8

As you drag the border between cells, Dreamweaver displays the changing widths of the cells in real time.

■ THE CONTENTS TAKE PRIORITY

Say you create a 300-pixel-wide table and set each cell in the first row to 100 pixels wide. You insert a large graphic into the first cell, and suddenly—kablooie! Even though you set each cell to 100 pixels wide, as shown in Figure 6-9, the column with the graphic is much wider than the other two.

FIGURE 6-9

Because a web browser can't shrink an image or hide part of it, the top-left cell in this table has to grow to fit it. That first column of cells now measures 161 pixels wide; the other two columns must shrink in order to keep the table 300 pixels wide. The numbers at the top of each cell indicate its width as set in the HTML—100—and, in parentheses, the actual width as displayed in Dreamweaver (161, 58, and 59).

That's because an individual table cell can't be smaller than the largest piece of content inside it. In this case, although you set the cell to 100 pixels wide, the image is 161 pixels wide, which forces the first column to grow—and the other columns to shrink—accordingly.

■ SETTING COLUMN WIDTHS

To set the width of a column of cells, you set the width of only *one* cell in that column. Say you have a table with three rows and three columns. You need to set only the width for the top row of cells; you can (and should) leave the cell widths for the remaining cells in the two bottom rows empty. In fact, that's what Dreamweaver does automatically—when you drag a vertical border between cells, Dreamweaver modifies the *width* property of only the top cells.

This principle can save a lot of time and, because it reduces the amount of code on a web page, make your pages load (and therefore appear) faster. The same holds true for the height of a row. You need to set the height of only a single cell to define the height for its entire row. When you drag a horizontal border, Dreamweaver adds a *height* property to the first cell in the row above the border.

■ DO THE MATH

Calculators are really useful when you build tables. Although you *could* create a 400-pixel-wide table with three 700-pixel-wide columns, the results you'd get on the screen could be unpredictable (after all, 700 plus 700 plus 700 does not equal 400).

As it turns out, web browsers' loyalty is to *table* width first, and then to column width. If the combined widths of your columns add up to the width of your table, you'll save yourself a lot of headaches.

Don't forget that you need to account for borders, cell padding, and cell spacing. Say you create a 500-pixel-wide table with two columns and 10 pixels of padding. If you want the first column 100 pixels wide, you'd set the width to 80 pixels: 10 pixels of left padding plus 80 pixels of cell space plus 10 pixels of right padding equals 100 pixels total width.

The same is true when you use percentage values for tables and cell widths. Just make sure the value of the widths of the cells in a row totals 100 percent. That is, if you have three columns and you want the first to be twice as wide as the other two, you could set its width to 50% and the other two cells' widths to 25% each. This is true even if you set the initial width of the entire table to something smaller than 100%, say, 80%. That 80% table width simply means that the table will be 80% of the width of its container—the page, for example, or a <div> tag. Even though the table takes up only 80% of the browser window, all the cells together still make up 100% of the table width.

UP TO SPEED

Beware the Resize Handles

Dreamweaver provides several ways to resizing tables and cells in Design view. Unfortunately, the easiest way to resize a table—dragging a cell or table border—is also the easiest way to make a mistake. Because pointing to any border turns the cursor into the Resize tool, almost every Dreamweaver practitioner drags a border accidentally at least once, overwriting carefully calculated table and cell widths and heights.

In addition, if you grab either of the two bottom resize handles (they look like black squares) when you have a table selected,

you'll set the table's *height* property. As mentioned in the note on page 289, it's actually invalid HTML to add a Height attribute to the <table> tag.

On occasions like these, don't forget Dreamweaver's Undo feature, Ctrl+Z (⌘-Z). And if all is lost, you can always clear the widths and heights of every cell in a table (using the Properties panel's buttons) and start over by typing in new cell dimensions (see Figure 6-5).

■ Adding and Removing Cells

Even after you insert a table into a web page, you can add and subtract rows and columns. The text or images in the columns move right or down to accommodate their new next-door neighbors.

Adding One Row or Column

To add a single row to a table, use any of these approaches:

- Click inside a cell, and then choose Modify→Table→Insert Row (Figure 6-10).

- Select Ctrl+M (⌘-M) to insert a new row of cells above the current row.

- Right-click (Control-click) a cell, and then, from the shortcut menu, choose Table→Insert Row.

- To add a new row at the end of a table, click inside the last cell in the table, and then press Tab.

The new row inherits the properties of the row you originally clicked.

Here's how to add a single *column* of cells:

- Click inside a cell, and then choose Modify→Table→Insert Column.

- Click inside a cell, and then press Shift+Ctrl+A (Shift-⌘-A).

- Right-click (Control-click) a cell, and then, from the shortcut menu, choose Table→Insert Column.

In each case, a new column appears to the left of the current one.

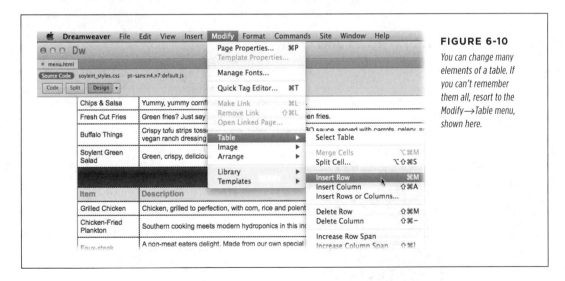

FIGURE 6-10

You can change many elements of a table. If you can't remember them all, resort to the Modify→Table menu, shown here.

Adding Multiple Rows or Columns

To add a *lot* of rows or columns to a table, you use a special dialog box.

1. **Click inside a cell. Choose Modify→Table→"Insert Rows or Columns."**

   The "Insert Rows or Columns" dialog box appears (see Figure 6-11).

FIGURE 6-11

The "Insert Rows or Columns" dialog box lets you add multiple rows or columns to a table at once. The wording of the options changes depending on which you want to do.

2. **Turn on either the Rows or Columns radio button. Type the number of rows or columns you want to add.**

   Windows users can also click the tiny up and down arrow buttons next to "Number of rows" (or "Number of columns").

3. **Tell Dreamweaver where you want the new rows or columns to appear relative to the cell you selected by clicking Above or Below (for rows), or Before or After (for columns). Click OK to insert them.**

Using this dialog box gives you an advantage over the single row/single column expansion described above. There, new rows always go above the current cell, and new columns always go to the left. Here, you can choose whether the new row or column comes *before* or *after* the selected cell.

Deleting Rows and Columns

To delete a row from your table, use one of the following techniques:

NOTE When you remove a row or column, Dreamweaver eliminates everything inside the cells. So before you start hacking away, it's a good idea to save a copy of the page.

- Select the row (see page 285) and then press Delete to remove all the row's cells—and all the content in them.

- Click a cell and then choose Modify→Table→Delete Row, or use the keyboard shortcut, Shift+Ctrl+M (Shift-⌘-M).

- Right-click (Control-click) inside a cell, and then, from the shortcut menu, choose Table→Delete Row.

Deleting a column is equally straightforward:

- Select the column, and then press Delete. You just eliminated all the selected cells and everything in them.

- Click a cell, and then choose Modify→Table→Delete Column, or use the keyboard shortcut Shift+Ctrl+hyphen (Shift-⌘-hyphen).

- Right-click (Control-click) inside a cell, and then choose Table→Delete Column from the shortcut menu.

NOTE Dreamweaver doesn't let you delete a row if you *merged* one of its cells with a cell in another row. Nor can you delete a column if it contains a cell merged with an adjacent cell. (You'll learn about merged cells next.)

Merging and Splitting Cells

When you first create a table, cells are very basic creatures. All the cells in a row are the same height and all the cells in a column are the same width. That's not always the best way to express the underlying information. Sometimes you want to merge cells, as shown in Figure 6-12. This table shows you the number of subscribers to *CosmoFarmer* magazine for the years 2006 and 2007. Since the data for each year is further broken down into Men and Women, each year generates two columns' worth of information. To accurately label these columns, the cells that contain the year labels would have to span the two columns below them. The trick to making that happen is to *merge* cells—combine the area of one or more—to create a larger cell that spans multiple rows or columns.

CosmoFarmer Subscriber Information by Year

Year	2006		2007	
Gender	Men	Women	Men	Women
Number	10,000	15,000	25,000	27,000
Average Age	39	34	33	30
Avg Yearly Income	$65K	$66K	$100K	$100K

FIGURE 6-12

You can create cells that span multiple rows or columns by merging adjacent cells. When you do, you can represent multiple related rows or columns of information using a single table header.

To merge cells, select the cells you want to combine using any of the usual methods, like clicking and dragging through them or Ctrl-clicking (⌘-clicking) individual cells. You can only merge cells that form a rectangle or square. You can't, for instance, select three cells in a column, and only one in the adjacent row, to create an L shape. Nor can you merge cells that aren't adjacent; in other words, you can't merge a cell in one corner of a table with a cell in the opposite corner.

Then do one of the following:

- Click the M key. This undocumented keyboard shortcut is much easier to use than the "official" shortcut, Alt+Ctrl+M (Option-⌘-M).

- From inside a selected cell, right-click to open the shortcut menu and then choose Table→Merge Cells.

- In the Properties panel, click the Merge Cells button (Figure 6-13).

- Choose Modify→Table→Merge Cells. Dreamweaver joins the selected cells, forming a single new super cell.

FIGURE 6-13

Dreamweaver makes the Merge Cells button active only when you select multiple cells. The Split Cells button becomes active only when you select a single cell or when you click inside a cell.

You may also find yourself in the opposite situation: You have one cell that you want to *divide* into multiple cells. To split a cell (including a cell you previously merged), click or select the cell. In the Properties panel, click Split Cells. You can also right-click (Control-click) the selected cell, and then, from the shortcut menu, choose Table→Split Cell); or choose Modify→Table→Split Cell; or press Alt+Ctrl+S [Option-⌘-S].

When the Split Cell dialog box opens (Figure 6-14), click one of the buttons to indicate whether you want to split the cell into rows or columns. Type the number of rows or columns you want, and then click OK.

FIGURE 6-14

The Split Cell dialog box lets you divide a single cell into multiple cells. You can divide the cell into rows, with multiple cells on top of one another, or columns, with multiple cells side by side.

If you split a cell into columns, everything in the original cell winds up in the left column, with the new, empty column or columns to the right. When you split a cell into rows, the current contents end up in the top row, and the new rows appear underneath.

■ Working with Tabular Data

Since tables are meant to display information, Dreamweaver provides useful tools that let you import and work with data.

Importing Data into a Table

Say your boss emails you your company's yearly sales information, which includes data on sales, profits, and expenses organized by quarter. She asks you to get this up on the Web for a board meeting she's having in half an hour.

This assignment could require a fair amount of work: building a table and then copying and pasting the information into each cell of the table, one piece at a time. Dreamweaver makes your task much easier, because you can create a table and then import data into its rows and columns in one pass.

For this to work, the data you want to import must be in *delimited* format. Most spreadsheet programs (including Excel) and database programs (such as Access or FileMaker Pro) export delimited data easily. In most programs, you select File→Export or File→Save As and then choose a tab-delimited or comma-separated text file.

NOTE If you use Dreamweaver for Windows, you don't need to create a delimited-format file for Microsoft Excel data. Dreamweaver directly imports the data and converts it into a well-organized table. See page 75 for details.

In a delimited file, each line of text represents one table row. You separate the individual pieces of information in that line using a special character called a delimiter—most often a tab, but possibly a comma or colon. Each discrete piece of data will go into a single cell in the row. In a colon-delimited file, for example, Dreamweaver would convert the line *Sales:$1,000,000:$2,000,000:$567,000:$12,500* into a row of five cells, with the first cell containing the word *Sales*.

Once you save your boss's spreadsheet as a delimited file, you're ready to import it into Dreamweaver as a table:

1. **Choose File→Import→Tabular Data.**

   The Import Tabular Data dialog box appears (see Figure 6-15).

2. **Click Browse. Navigate to and select the delimited text file you want to import.**

   The delimited file isn't a spreadsheet; it's a plain text file. Find the filename and double-click it to insert it into the "Data file" box.

3. **From the Delimiter drop-down menu, select the delimiter you used to separate the data in the file.**

   You can select a tab, comma, colon, or semicolon as the delimiter, or specify your own by selecting Other. When you do the latter, an additional box appears where you type in your delimiter character.

FIGURE 6-15

You import a data file and set formatting options for the resulting table using the Import Tabular Data dialog box.

4. **Select a table width.**

   Choose "Fit to data" if you want the table to fit itself to the information you're importing—an excellent idea when you aren't completely sure how much information the file contains. (You can always modify the table later.)

   On the other hand, if your web page needs a table of a certain size, you can specify its dimensions by selecting the "Set to" button and then typing a value in the box next to it. Finally, select Pixels or Percent from the drop-down menu (see page 283).

5. **Set values for cell padding, cell spacing, and a border, if you like.**

   See page 282 for details.

6. **Select a formatting option for the top row of data.**

   If the first line in the text file has column headings—1st Quarter Sales, 2nd Quarter Sales, and so on—Dreamweaver lets you choose Bold, Italic, or Bold Italic to set this row apart from the rest of the table. Unfortunately, this option doesn't turn the cells in the first row into table header (<th>) tags, which is what they should be. It's best to choose no formatting, manually select the cells, and then turn them into table header tags as described on page 291.

7. **Click OK to import the data and create the table.**

   Dreamweaver adds the table to your web page. It's a regular HTML table at this point, and you can edit the contents as you normally would, or modify the table itself (add rows and columns, for example) using any of the techniques discussed in this chapter.

Sorting Data in a Table

If you have a table that lists employee names, you probably want to present that list in alphabetical order—or alphabetically *and* by department. Dreamweaver's Sort command takes a lot of the drudgery out of that task. Keep in mind that the Sort command is a tool you use as you build your page; it's not something your site visitors can use.

NOTE You can't sort tables that have merged cells in them using Command→Sort Table. The easiest workaround is to sort your table *before* you merge any cells. For more on merged cells see page 299.

1. **Select the table you want to sort.**

   See page 285 for some table-selection techniques.

2. **Choose Commands→Sort Table.**

   The Sort Table dialog box appears (Figure 6-16).

FIGURE 6-16

The Sort Table command is an excellent complement to Dreamweaver's Import Tabular Data feature. Once you import data into a table, Sort Table lets you organize that information. Imagine you get a text file listing all your company's employees, import the data into a table, and then realize that the names aren't in any particular order. This dialog box lets you granularly dictate the sorting scheme.

3. **Using the "Sort by" drop-down menu, choose the column by which you want to sort.**

   You can choose any column in the table. Suppose you have a table listing a bunch of products. Each row has the product name, number, and price. To see the products listed from least to most expensive, sort by the Price column.

4. **Use the next two drop-down menus to tell Dreamweaver how to sort the data.**

   You can sort it alphabetically or numerically. To order the products in the example above by price, choose Numerically from the Order drop-down menu. To sort the products by name, choose Alphabetically.

   Use the second drop-down menu to specify whether you want an Ascending (A–Z, 1–100) or Descending (Z–A, 100–1) sort.

5. **If you like, choose an additional column to sort by, using the "Then by" drop-down menu.**

   This secondary sort can come in handy when several cells in the *first* sorting column have the same value. If several items in your product list cost $100, a sort by price would place them consecutively in the table; you could then specify a secondary sort that would place the products in alphabetical order within each price group. Doing so lists all the products from least to most expensive *and* lists all same-priced products alphabetically within their group.

6. **If the first row of the table contains data you want to sort, turn on the "Sort includes the first row" checkbox.**

   If, however, the first row contains *headings* for the columns, leave this checkbox turned off. If you have multiple rows that you don't want to include in the sort, make sure you use the table heading tag <th> in those cells, discussed on page 291. Then leave the "Sort header row" checkbox turned off in the Sort Table dialog box.

7. **Choose whether you want to sort header and footer rows.**

   The "Sort header rows" option isn't referring to cells that have the Table Header property set (see page 291). This option and the next one, "Sort footer rows," refer to the <thead> (table header) and <tfoot> (table footer) tags, which let you turn one or more rows into repeating headers and footers for long tables. Since Dreamweaver doesn't insert these tags for you, you'll most likely never use these options.

8. **Choose whether to keep row colors with the sorted row.**

   One way to visually organize a table is to add color to alternate rows. This every-other-row pattern helps readers focus on one row of information at a time. However, if you sort a table formatted with tinted rows, you could wind up with a crazy pattern of colored and uncolored cells. The bottom line: If you applied colors to your rows and want to keep those colors in the same order, leave this checkbox turned off.

   Dreamweaver is even in step with current web design practices, which don't assign a background color to table rows using the outmoded *bgcolor* HTML property, but instead use CSS. A common approach to coloring table rows is to apply a CSS class style to every *other* row in a table. That class style might have the *background-color* property set so that alternating rows are colored. When you use the Sort Table command, Dreamweaver keeps the class names in the proper order. That is, it keeps the classes applied to every other row, even when you reorganize the data in those rows. This works only if you *don't* turn on the "Keep all row colors the same" checkbox—so don't turn it on!

9. **Click Apply to see the effect of the sort without closing the dialog box.**

   If the table meets with your satisfaction, click OK to sort the table and return to the document window. (Clicking Cancel, however, doesn't undo the sort if you already clicked Apply. To return the table to its previous sort order, choose Edit→Undo after closing the sort window.)

Exporting Table Data

Getting data *out* of a table in Dreamweaver is simple, too. Just select the table and then choose File→Export→Table. In the Export Table dialog box, select the type of delimiter (tab, comma, space, colon, semicolon, or Other) and the destination computer's operating system (Windows, Mac, or Unix), and then click OK. Give the file a name and save it on your computer. You can then import this delimited file into your spreadsheet or database program.

■ Tutorial: Creating Tables

In this tutorial, you'll create a menu for the cafe site you've been working on. In addition, you'll use some Cascading Style Sheet magic to make the table look great (skip ahead to Figure 6-27 if you want to see the finished page).

> **NOTE** To complete this tutorial, you need to download sample files from this book's Missing CD page at *http://oreilly.com/pub/missingmanuals/dreamweaverccmm2014*. (See the Note on page 37 for details.) The files you'll work on are in the Chapter06 folder, and the finished project, for comparison, is in the Chapter06_complete folder.

Once you download the tutorial files and open Dreamweaver, set up a new site as described on page 23. In a nutshell, choose Site→New Site. In the Site Setup window, type *Tables* into the Site Name box. Click ■ next to the Local Site Folder box, navigate to and select the Chapter06 folder inside the MM_DWCC folder, and then click Choose (Select). Finally, click OK.

Adding a Table

Once again, you'll be working on a page for the good people who run Cafe Soylent Green.

1. **Choose File→Open.**

   You'll work on a page similar to the ones you've built so far.

2. **Navigate to the Chapter06 folder and double-click the file named *menu. html*. Click in the empty space beneath the headline "Cafe Soylent Green Menu."**

   You'll insert a table into this space.

3. **Choose Insert→Table.**

   You can also click the Table button in the Insert panel's Common category. Either way, the Table window appears (see Figure 6-17). You need to define the table's basic characteristics.

FIGURE 6-17

Inserting a table into a web page is a matter of making a few choices in the Table dialog box. Any text you type into the Summary box doesn't appear in a browser window, so you probably won't use this field much. It's intended to explain a particularly complicated table to non-visual web browsers (like search engines such as Google and Bing, or screen readers used by the visually impaired).

4. **Type *10* in the Rows box and *4* in the Columns box.**

   Time to set the table's width, spacing, and padding properties.

5. **Set "Table width" to *100 percent*. Type *0* in the "Border thickness," "Cell padding," and "Cell spacing" boxes.**

   Setting a table's width to 100 percent makes it fit the space available to it—in this case, you're about to insert this table into a <div> tag that has a set width of 800 pixels. The browser will make this table fill that space and, in effect, display an 800-pixel-wide table. Using a percentage value is a good idea, because if you decide to change the width of the main content area of the page (make it 1,000 pixels wide instead of 800 pixels, for example), the table grows to fit the new dimensions. If you use pixels for the width, you'd have to go back to the table and change its width every time you decided to change the width of the page. Setting the other three properties here to *0* is common—you get greater control over border and cell attributes using CSS.

6. **In the window's Header section, select Top.**

   The header setting indicates which cells Dreamweaver will mark as "table headers"—the cells that contain labels describing the information in the cells below (when you select Top), or in the cells of a row (when you select Left). Now that you've picked Top, the top row of cells will hold labels like Product, Cost, and Manufacturer.

   You can skip the caption. It's not a requirement, and the page's title makes clear what the table is all about. The window should now look like Figure 6-17.

7. **Click OK.**

A new table appears on the page, filling the space provided by the main content <div> tag. At this point, you could begin adding content by typing in a cell. However, this book isn't about improving your typing skills, so forget about typing in the menu items and use Dreamweaver's very useful Import Tabular Data command instead.

Importing Tabular Data

While it's not difficult to type data into a table, it does take time. And if you already have the data in spreadsheet format, there's a better way to add it to the table. In this section of the tutorial, you'll use the Insert Tabular Data command to create and fill a table in several easy steps—but first you need to remove the table you just added.

1. **Select the table you created in the steps above and then press Delete (or select Edit→Cut).**

You can select a table in several ways (see page 284). One is to click the top-left corner of the table to get the Table selection cursor (Figure 6-4). But when a table has no borders, padding, or cell spacing, that can be tricky. For a surefire method, right-click (Control-click) and then choose Table→Select Table.

Another easy way is to just click inside any cell in the table and then, in the Tag Selector (page 7) in the bottom left of the document window, click the <table> tag to select the table and all its contents. Then press Delete to remove the table.

Now you'll import a text file.

2. **Make sure your cursor is in the empty space below the cafe's headline and then choose File→Import→Tabular Data.**

Dreamweaver opens the Import Tabular Data window (Figure 6-18).

FIGURE 6-18

Dreamweaver makes it easy to import a text file's worth of data into a brand-new HTML table. Leave the "Format top row" setting on No Formatting. You're better off controlling the formatting—including the border, padding, and spacing attributes you earlier set to 0—with CSS.

3. **Click Browse to open a file selection window, and then double-click the file** ***menu.txt*** **in the Chapter06 folder.**

This file contains tab-delimited data. That is, each line in the file represents one row in a table, and within that line, you separate the content for each cell using the Tab key. This is a common way to export information from a spreadsheet program like Microsoft Excel or Apple Numbers, or even from database programs.

4. **Make sure you have Tab selected in the Delimiter menu.**

The option you select from the Delimiter drop-down menu depends on the delimiter used in the file you're importing. The file you just selected separates each piece of information by a tab character. Dreamweaver can use that tab to identify the data for individual cells and figure out how many columns the table will need. When you export a spreadsheet, you can use other delimiting characters, including commas, semicolons, and colons, to demarcate each cell.

5. **In the "Table width" section, select "Set to," type** ***100,*** **and then choose Percent from the drop-down menu. Set the "Cell padding," "Cell spacing," and Border boxes to** ***0,*** **and make sure the "Format top row" drop-down menu is set to No Formatting.**

The window should now look like the one in Figure 6-18.

6. **Click OK to import the data and create a new table.**

Dreamweaver creates the new table, three columns wide by 16 rows high, and inserts all the information for the cafe's menu (see Figure 6-19).

The menu includes three categories: Starters, Main, and Dessert. In the first row, you'll see the word "Starters" in a single cell on the left. This really should span the entire table, since it introduces this section of the menu. Fortunately, that's an easy task to accomplish.

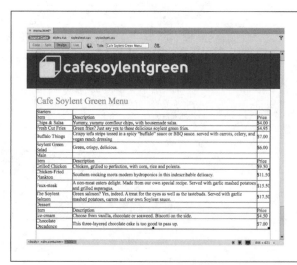

FIGURE 6-19

Dreamweaver's Import Tabular Data feature makes it easy to convert a comma- or tab-delimited file into a complex HTML table. It's certainly a lot easier than adding data to each cell individually. When you need to create an HTML table filled with data, try to get your data into a CSV (comma-separated value) file first.

7. **Ctrl-click (⌘-click) the three cells in the top row. Press the M key to merge them.**

The three cells turn into one big cell that spans the width of the table. You could also have selected the row using any of the methods described on page 285—for example, in Expanded Table Mode (right-click [Control-click]→Table→Expanded Tables Mode), you could click the left edge of the first cell to select the row, or you could click in the left cell and then drag to the right until you select all the cells.

You can also merge those cells by clicking the Merge Selected Cells icon in the Properties panel (labeled in Figure 6-20).

Because this row introduces the content that follows, it's a good candidate for the table header (<th>) tag described on page 291.

8. **In the Properties panel, turn on the Header checkbox.**

This converts a regular table cell (a <td> tag) into a table header (a <th> tag).

Merge   Split
cells   cells

Header
check box

FIGURE 6-20

The Header checkbox (lower right) turns the selected table cell into a table header by applying the <th> tag to the cell. You see the Header box only if you click inside a table and you have the Properties panel completely expanded, as described on page 14. The "Merge selected cells using spans" button (lower left) combines table cells.

9. **Repeat steps 7–8 for the two rows that have the text "Main" and "Dessert" in them.**

Below these three rows is another set of cells that make good candidates for table headers: the Item, Description, and Price cells all indicate what type of information will appear in each of those columns.

10. **Click inside each of the three Item, Description, and Price cells (that's nine cells altogether), and then turn on the Header checkbox in the Properties panel.**

A quick way to do this is to Ctrl-click (⌘-click) all nine cells, and then turn on the Header checkbox. Just as in step 8, this turns each <td> tag into a <th> tag.

You've discovered that a couple of items are missing from the menu, so it's time to add them.

11. **Click in the very last cell of the table, the one with the $7.00 price, and then press the Tab key.**

Dreamweaver adds a new row to the bottom of the table.

12. **Type** *Hot Fudge Sundae,* **and then press Tab to jump to the next cell. Type** *The ultimate dessert experience.* **Press Tab again, type** *$5.00,* **and then press Tab one last time.**

You added a row's worth of information and then added another blank row to the end of the table. Unfortunately, that was a mistake. You don't need that last row. What an excellent time to learn how to delete a row.

13. **Click inside the last cell in the bottom-right corner of the table. Drag to the left until you select all three empty cells, and then press Delete.**

Dreamweaver removes the row easily. Now you need to add another row in the middle of the table. The Tab-to-add-a-row technique works only if you're in the last table cell. To add a row in the middle of a table, you need to try something else.

14. **Click in the cell with the text "The Soylent Salmon." Select Modify→Table→ Insert Row.**

Dreamweaver inserts a new, blank row above the one with the selected cell in it. The last step is to add another entrée to the menu.

15. **Click in the first cell of the newly inserted row. Type** *Shiitake Burger,* **and then press Tab to jump to the next cell. Type** *The best hamburger mushrooms money can buy.* **Press Tab one last time and then type** *$12.00.*

The menu is complete. Now it's time to make it look good.

Formatting the Table

Tables, like everything HTML, are drab by themselves. To make data really stand out, you need to turn to the power of Cascading Style Sheets. In this section, you'll format the table's basic font attributes, make the headers stand out, and add lines around the cells.

1. **Make sure CSS Designer is open (Window→CSS Designer). In the Sources section, click** *soylent_styles.css* **and then, in Selectors, click** + .

A new selector appears in the list, ready for you to give it a name. You'll create a class style for the table tag headers and store the CSS information in an already attached external style sheet—*soylent_styles.css.* (For a recap on creating a style sheet, called a Source in CSS Designer, turn to page 118.)

2. **Type** *.menu* **in the Selector Name box and then hit Enter (Return).**

CSS Designer's Properties section shows the properties you can set for the *.menu* class.

Instead of creating a style for the <table> tag here, you're creating a class style. That's because, if you created a *tag* style, it would apply to every instance of that HTML tag. So if this site had other tables in it, that single <table> tag style would format *all* the site's tables, and that might not be what you want. By using a class style, you have the flexibility to create different designs for different tables.

3. **In the Properties section, click the Text button. From the *font-family* menu, select "pt-sans, Arial, Helvetica, sans-serif." In the *font-size* box, choose "px," and then type *14*.**

You'll see PT Sans only if you completed the tutorial in Chapter 3, which added the PT Sans web fonts to Dreamweaver (see page 160).

The table is a bit close to the bottom of the headline above it; adding a little margin to the top of the table will help.

4. **In Properties, click Layout, and then, in the top position of the Margin box, type *20*.**

This class style doesn't take effect until you apply it.

5. **Click the bottom border of the table to select it (or use any of the techniques described on page 284). From the Properties panel's Class menu, choose "menu."**

The menu scoots down the page a bit, and the font gets smaller. You won't see the effect of the PT Sans font, since Dreamweaver can't display web fonts in Design view; however, if you preview the page in a browser or view the page in Live view, you'll see the new font in action.

The table headers don't really command enough attention. You'll make them stand out by using a background graphic and increasing the space inside each cell.

6. **With *soylent_styles.css* still selected in Sources, click + in the Selectors section. For the selector name, type *.menu th*, as shown in Figure 6-21.**

Selectors with two names are called *compound selectors*, or what CSS veterans know as *descendent selectors*—a style name composed of two or more CSS selectors. You'll learn more about compound selectors in the next chapter, but for now, keep in mind that you want to create a style that affects only the table headers that appear inside the table on the page—<th> tags that appear inside a table that's styled with the *.menu* class, in other words.

7. **In the Properties section, click the Text button. For *font-family*, choose "pt-sans, Arial, Helvetica, sans-serif." For *font-size* choose *16 px*. Set *font-weight* to "700" and color to *#468531*.**

This makes the text bold, green, and 16 pixels tall. Now you'll add a background color.

8. **In the Properties section, scroll down past the Background box and then, beside *background-color*, type *#F2E5C2* (a tan).**

Dreamweaver centers the column headers in their cells. To have them match the appearance of the other cells, you'll align them to the left.

9. **Click the Text button, and then, from the *text-align* options, choose *left*.**

You could also use the Properties panel to set the horizontal alignment of each table header to Left, but not only is that more work, it also adds extra HTML to your page. The CSS method is easier and makes for faster-loading web pages.

Review your page using Live view. The text is a bit cramped inside the cells. To add some breathing room between the edges of each cell and the text inside it, you'll use the CSS *padding* property.

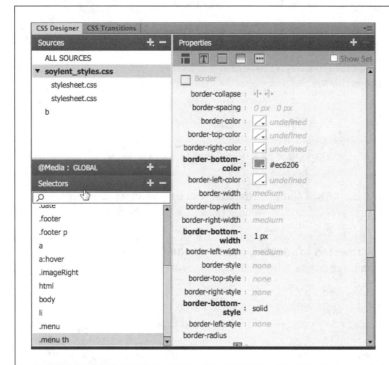

FIGURE 6-21

Dreamweaver uses the catchall term "compound style" for selectors that have two names. The names can be a combination of class, ID, and tag styles. For example, Dreamweaver uses compound styles to create one of the most important types of CSS style, descendent selectors, like the .menu selector pictured here. This selector homes in on a very specific group of tags: <th> tags inside any other tag that has the class .menu applied to it.

NOTE In CSS Designer, if you accidentally drift away from the *.menu th* properties, choose *soylent_styles. css* in Sources, and then choose *.menu th* in Selectors.

10. **Click the Layout button. In the *padding* properties box, click the link icon (whose tooltip says "Click to change all the properties"), and then set any of the sides to *5 px*.**

Dreamweaver applies the 5-pixel setting to all four sides of the table header. One last touch: a border separating the table headers from the rows below it.

11. **Click the Border button, and then click the tab for the bottom border (fourth from the left, as shown in Figure 6-22). Set *border-bottom-color***

to *#EC6206*. Set *border-bottom-width* to *1 px*. Set *border-bottom-style* to "solid," as shown in Figure 6-22.

This adds a border below each table header. In this particular table, you have two rows of different types of headers: the category headers (Starters, for example) and the headers that announce the dish, its description, and its price. Sharing the same style, the stacked header rows look a bit...well, boring. You'll create a class style for each category of dish.

12. **Make sure you have *soylent_styles.css* chosen in CSS Designer's Sources section. Then, in Selectors, click + . To name the new selector, type *.menu .course*.**

This is another descendent selector. This one is composed of two class names and can be translated to mean "Use this style on any element that has the class *.course* applied to it, but only when it's inside another element with a class of *.menu*." In other words, you're about to create another style that includes a new class name, *.course*, which you'll apply to the first table header in each section of the menu.

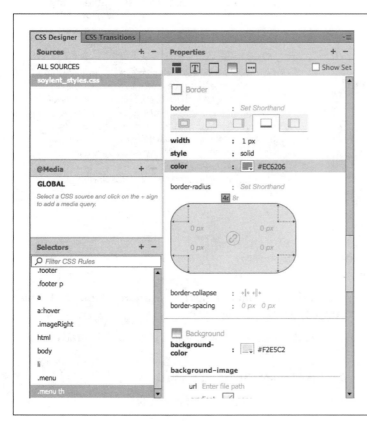

FIGURE 6-22

You can apply borders to any or all sides of an element. For example, when you set border-style *to "solid," you're putting a solid line around the outside of the entire table. On the other hand, you can set* border-bottom-style *to "solid," which makes only the bottom border solid.*

13. **In Properties, click the Text button. Then set *color* to white (*#FFFFFF*), *font-size* to *18 px*, and *text-transform* to "uppercase."**

You may need to scroll down a little to find the *text-transform* property.

14. **In Properties, click the Background button. In *background-color*, type #0A2F02. Click in the "url" box of the *background-image* property, click , and then, in the site's Images folder, select the file *bg-th.png*. For *background-position*, click the % sign for the value on the left (X), and then choose "center." Set the value on the right (Y) to "top."**

The Properties panel should look like the one in Figure 6-23. Just a few last touches and you'll be done.

15. **Click the Text button and then choose "center" from the *text-align* options.**

This centers the text in the row. To scoot these table headers down a little, you'll add a bit of padding.

16. **Click the Layout button. In the padding box, type *13 px* in the top position.**

Nothing happens...you need to apply the class style to the table header.

FIGURE 6-23

Why add a background color when you're already using a background image? Remember that, in step 13, you made the text white. To make sure visitors can read your text, you need a dark background. If, for some reason, the background graphic doesn't appear (your visitor may have turned off her graphics, for example, or the image might not have downloaded properly), the table headers would appear as white text on a white background. By setting a dark background color in addition to a background image, you're covered—if the image doesn't download, the text is still readable—white text on a dark-green background.

17. **Click inside the table header that has the text "Starters." From the Properties panel's Class menu, select "course."**

Dreamweaver centers the text, turns it white, and adds a green gradient background.

18. **Repeat step 17 for the table headers Main and Dessert.**

Now it's time to tackle the look of the main table cells.

19. **With *soylent_styles.css* still selected in CSS Designer's Sources section, click + in Selectors. Give the new style the name *.menu td*.**

You should be getting the hang of these descendent selectors by now. This style will apply to every <td> tag (that's an individual table cell) within another tag that has the class named *.menu* applied to it. You'll add padding and border lines to clearly differentiate each cell.

20. **Click the Layout button. In the *padding* box, click the link ("Click to change all the properties"), and then type *5 px* in any one of the fields.**

Each cell will have 5 pixels of padding around all four sides. Time to add some borders.

21. **Click the Border button, and then click the "All sides" tab. Set *border-color* to white—*#FFFFFF*. Set *border-width* to *1px*, and then set *border-style* to "solid."**

If you preview the page in a browser (press F12 [Option-F12]) or switch to Live view using the menu at the top of the document window, you'll notice that, where two cells touch, the borders are a bit thick (see Figure 6-24). Because you added a border around all four sides of each cell, the border is twice as thick and looks a little chunky where two cells meet You could edit the style and then add a border to only some sides of the cell (like the left and bottom sides) so that the borders don't double up, but CSS gives you an easier way.

STARTERS		
Item	**Description**	**Price**
Chips & Salsa	Yummy, yummy cornflour chips, with housemade salsa.	$4.00
Fresh Cut Fries	Green fries? Just say yes to these delicious soylent green fries.	$4.95
Buffalo Things	Crispy tofu strips tossed in a spicy "buffalo" sauce or BBQ sauce. served with carrots, celery, and vegan ranch dressing	$7.50
Soylent Green Salad	Green, crispy, delicious.	$6.00

FIGURE 6-24

Adding a border to table cells creates slightly chunky double borders where cells touch. Here the interior borders are 2px wide, while the outside border is only 1px. Fortunately, with a little-known CSS property, you can overcome this aesthetic nuisance.

> **NOTE** Make sure to exit Live view when you finish viewing your page—set the Design/Live view drop-down menu to Design. If you don't leave Live view, it's harder to edit your page.

Final Improvements

To finish this tutorial, you'll get rid of the double-border problem and make the table rows easier to read by coloring every other row.

1. **Make sure CSS Designer is open (Window→CSS Designer) and that you have *soylent_styles.css* chosen in the Sources section.**

   When you choose *soylent_styles.css* in Sources, the Selectors section shows the tags, classes, and IDs for the styles from that source.

2. **In Selectors, locate the style named *.menu*, click it, and then, in the Properties section, click the Border button.**

   The Properties pane scrolls so that *border-collapse* is the first property listed (see Figure 6-25).

3. **In the *border-collapse* property, choose "collapse."**

   border-collapse is a special CSS property that forces adjoining cell borders to "collapse" into each other. Essentially, it reduces the space between cells, thus preventing the double border. You don't see the effect of this in Dreamweaver's Design view, but if you switch to Live view or preview the page in a browser, you will.

   Now you'll highlight alternating table rows. This technique makes tables easier to scan. To accomplish this, you'll create an advanced CSS style.

FIGURE 6-25

The border-collapse property (circled) offers you two options, represented by icons: collapse and separate. The collapse option (on the left above) resolves the double-border issue.

4. **In Selectors, with *soylent_styles.css* still chosen, click + . When the new selector appears, name it *.menu tr:nth-child(odd)*.**

As you type a name, CSS Designer may prompt you with suggestions. This style is an advanced CSS selector. In a nutshell, it selects every odd table row inside a table that has the class *.menu* applied to it. There's a similar style for every even table row: *tr:nth-of-type(even)*. All you need to do now is define a background color for the shaded rows.

5. **In CSS Designer's Properties section, click the Background button. Then, for the *background-color* property, click the swatch to open the color picker. Click the RGBa button (Figure 6-26), and then drag the middle slider (lightness/darkness) all the way to the top.**

As mentioned on page 151, CSS supports several color formats; RGBa stands for "red, green, blue, alpha," and it lets you pick a color that is partially transparent. This gives your table a neat effect since it lets colors or images below the element show through.

You'll see *rgba(255,255,255,1.00)* in the *background-color* box. If the box can't fit all that in, either use your keyboard's arrow keys to move right until you see the 1 at the end of the value, or drag the left edge of the CSS Styles panel to make it wider. The *255,255,255* specifies the color white, while the *1* means 100% opaque—in other words, you can't see through it. Time to change that.

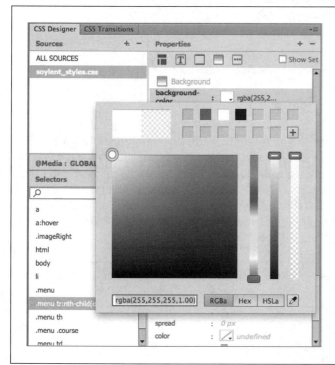

FIGURE 6-26

Dreamweaver's color picker lets you choose different color formats. Here the RGBa model is selected, so the color specification is displayed as rgba(255,255,255,1.00). Translation to humanese: white. Changing that last number (1.00) to a fraction makes the color semi-transparent.

6. **Change the 1 to .5 so that the color value now reads rgba(255,255,255,.5).**

You won't see any effect in Design view, but if you preview the page in Live view or a web browser, you'll see that every other table row has a slightly lighter background. One last design change and you're done. The menu items don't really stand out. Simply making them bold will help guide visitors' eyes to the tasty food the cafe offers.

> **NOTE** Neither the nth-of-type selector nor RGBa colors work in Internet Explorer 8 or earlier. While all other browsers, including IE 9 and above, display this style correctly, if you want to add striped rows to your tables and you want it to work in Internet Explorer 8, you need to create a class style—*.odd*, for example—with a background color of your choosing (but using only hexadecimal [#FFFFFF] or RGB [for example, *rgb(255,255,255)*] colors). Then you need to manually apply the style to every other table row by selecting the row and using the Properties panel to apply the class to that row (which is a lot of work!).

7. **With *soylent_style.css* chosen as the Source, click + in Selectors. When the new selector appears, name it *.menu td:first-child*.**

CSS Designer may prompt you with the *:first-child* option as you type. If you see those words highlighted, press Enter (Return) to complete the name. The *:first-child* style is a new type of style called a *pseudo-element*, and it selects an element that's the first child nested inside another tag. In this case, *td:first-child* means "Select the first table cell (the first <td> tag) that's nested inside its parent." To understand how it works, it helps to examine the HTML for one row from the table:

```
<tr>
    <td>Chips & Salsa</td>
    <td>Yummy, yummy cornflour chips, with housemade salsa.</td>
    <td>$4.00</td>
</tr>
```

Here, the <tr> tag wraps around all the <td> tags. In CSS-speak, the <tr> tag is called a parent, while the <td> tags that appear immediately inside it are called children. In this example, there are three <td> tags, and thus three children. The first child is the <td> tag with the menu item Chips & Salsa in it. So the selector *.menu td:first-child* will select that <td> tag and every other first table cell inside a row that's also inside a table with the class *.menu* applied to it. Wow, that seems like a pretty complex selector, but you'll see in a moment how it will make formatting this table easy.

> **NOTE** Unlike the *:nth-of-type* selector, the *:first-child* selector works in Internet Explorer 7 and later. Only the nearly extinct IE 6 doesn't understand it, so you should feel free to use it.

8. **In the Properties section of CSS Designer, click the Text button, set *font-family* to "pt-sans, Arial, Helvetica, sans-serif," and then set *font-weight* to "700."**

Press F12 (Option-F12) to preview your hard work in a browser. The complete page should look like the one in Figure 6-27. Notice that the name of each food item is bold, but none of the other cells in each row are. Without that *:first-child* selector, the only way to achieve this effect would be to apply a class style to the Name cells, or to manually select each food item and make it bold.

You'll find a completed version of this tutorial in the Chapter06_complete folder that accompanies the downloaded tutorial files.

FIGURE 6-27

With Dreamweaver and a little CSS, you can make elegant HTML tables.

Working with HTML

Dreamweaver started life primarily as a visual web page editor, but over the years, its code-editing tools have evolved to rival those of the best text editors, including those that hard-core hand-coders use. Some people bypass Dreamweaver's Design view entirely and use only its Code view, where they edit their HTML, CSS, and JavaScript files directly. In fact, you can use Dreamweaver to edit any text-based file, including XML, Java, ActionScript, and just plain text itself.

Dreamweaver's code editor includes professional features like customizable syntax highlighting, auto indenting, line numbering, and code hints; code collapse, so you can concentrate on just the code you want; and the Code view toolbar, which provides one-click access to frequently used hand-coding commands. Many of Dreamweaver's recent improvements were aimed at those who use Code view to edit pages built with HTML, CSS, JavaScript, and the server-side programming language PHP.

In Dreamweaver CC Release 2014, Adobe added HTML tools for designers. In this chapter, you'll see how to create web pages in Live view, and then, in the tutorial at the end, you'll build a page from scratch in that view.

■ Controlling How Dreamweaver Handles HTML

Unlike many other visual HTML editors, Dreamweaver has always graciously accepted HTML written by hand (and even by other programs). This openness lets you write code the way you want, without worrying that Dreamweaver will change it. For example, suppose you format your handwritten code a particular way. Maybe you insert an extra hard return after every <td> (table cell) tag, or you use multiple tabs to indent nested tags. In cases like these, Dreamweaver doesn't rewrite your code to fit its own style—unless you ask it to.

Auto-Fixing Your Code

That's not to say that Dreamweaver doesn't *ever* change your code. In fact, when you open a page created in another program, Dreamweaver can automatically fix errors, including these:

- **Overlapping tags**. Take a look at this example:

```
<p><strong>Fix your tags!</p></strong>
```

This HTML is invalid because both the opening and closing <strong> tags should appear *inside* the <p> tag. Dreamweaver rewrites this snippet correctly:

```
<p><strong>Fix your tags!</strong></p>
```

- **Unclosed tags**. Tags usually come in pairs, like this:

```
<em>This text is in italic</em>.
```

But if a page is missing the ending tag (<em>This text is in italic), Dreamweaver adds it.

- **Extra closing tags**. If a page has an *extra* closing tag (<strong>bold text</strong></strong>), Dreamweaver helpfully removes it.

> **NOTE** If you use Dreamweaver's Design view to create the HTML for your web pages, you don't have to worry about Dreamweaver rewriting code; it automatically writes the correct HTML.

This auto-fix feature comes turned *off* in Dreamweaver. If you work on a site that was hand-coded or created by a less capable web-editing program, it's wise to turn this feature on, since the errors Dreamweaver fixes are improper HTML that can cause problems for browsers. (Once upon a time, for example, some web developers deliberately omitted closing tags to save a few kilobytes in file size. Although most browsers can still interpret this kind of sloppy code, it's poor practice.)

You activate auto-fixing in the Code Rewriting category of Dreamweaver's Preferences window (see Figure 7-1). There, turn on the checkboxes next to "Fix invalidly nested and unclosed tags" and "Remove extra closing tags." If you leave these options turned off, Dreamweaver doesn't fix the HTML, and there's no command you can run to correct the tags. Dreamweaver does, however, highlight the mistakes in Design and Code views (skip ahead to Figure 7-5 to get a glimpse of that).

> **NOTE** The "Warn when fixing or removing tags" option doesn't really warn you so much as report code that Dreamweaver went ahead and fixed on its own. You can't undo these auto-changes, but you can close the file without saving it to retain the old (improperly written) HTML.

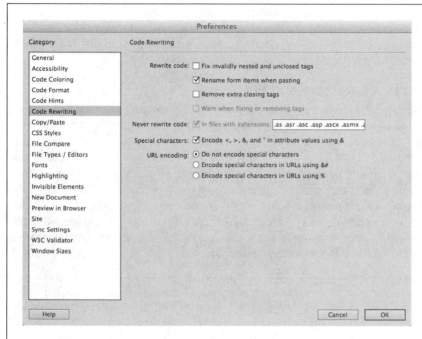

FIGURE 7-1

You don't want Dream-weaver trying to "fix" some types of code. For example, many server-side programming languages mix HTML and server-side code in a way that confuses Dreamweaver's code-rewriting tool. For that reason, turn on the checkbox next to "Never rewrite code." The text box to the right of that lists the most common server-side file extensions, such as .php and .asp. If you write pages that end in an extension not listed—for example, Ruby on Rails files end in .rb—add the extension in this box.

Dreamweaver can also change the capitalization (case) of HTML tags and properties if you want. For example, you might prefer lowercase letters for tags and proper-ties, like this:

```
<a href="nextpage.html">Click here</a>
```

Dreamweaver can convert uppercase tags (<A HREF="next.html">) to lowercase (and vice versa) when it finds them in pages created by other programs. You turn on this feature in the Code Format section of the Preferences menu (Edit→Preferences [Dreamweaver→Preferences]), as described in "Line breaks" on page 38.

Server-Side Web Pages

Dreamweaver can leave pages that have certain file extensions untouched—pages created with a server-side programming language like PHP, Cold Fusion, C#, or Ruby, for example. (Server-side programming lets web pages talk to databases, process HTML forms, and send email.) Server-side programming relies on code within the HTML of a page—code that Dreamweaver might otherwise "fix," mistakenly inter-preting it as error-prone HTML.

Unless you change its settings, Dreamweaver doesn't rewrite the code in files whose names end in .asp (active server pages that run on Microsoft's IIS Web Server), .aspx (Microsoft's .NET technology), .cfm and .cfml (pages written in ColdFusion markup language that run on Adobe's ColdFusion server), .jsp (JavaServer pages that run on any Java Server), or PHP files (PHP pages), among others. Nor does it rewrite code inside an external JavaScript file (a .js file), since many websites use JavaScript to create HTML on the fly, and JavaScript coders often add HTML fragments (incomplete tags and code) to their files. If you edit other types of files with Dreamweaver and don't want it interfering with them, add their extensions to the "Never rewrite code" list in the Preferences window, as shown in Figure 7-1.

Special Characters and Encoding

Some characters have special meaning in HTML. For example, the "less than" symbol (<) indicates the beginning of an HTML tag, so you shouldn't use that character in a filename. A link that tries to open the file *bob<zero.html*, for example, won't work because a browser reads the filename as the start of a new HTML tag called *zero*. The solution is to have Dreamweaver *encode* special characters, like <, >, &, and ", whenever you type them into a dialog box or set an option in the Properties panel. Dreamweaver represents these characters using a code. For example, it produces a space on a web page using the code *%20*, and the < symbol using the code *<* (think "less than"). Thus, Dreamweaver rewrites the infamous *bob<zero.html* filename as *bob<zero.html*, and your link will work just fine.

> **TIP** Whenever possible, avoid strange characters when you name pages, graphics, CSS styles, or any other object in your site. Stick to letters, numbers, hyphens, and underscores (_) because they're the only characters that web servers can universally read.

To set up encoding, choose Edit→Preferences (Dreamweaver→Preferences on Macs) and select Code Rewriting from the category list. Your options are as follows:

- **Special characters**. Turn on this checkbox to have Dreamweaver convert the <, >, &, and * characters to the specially encoded formats mentioned above. (This doesn't apply to code you type in Code view, nor to text you type into the document window in Design view.)

- **Do not encode special characters**. Select this option, the first of three under "URL encoding," to tell Dreamweaver not to touch any web addresses you enter (in the Properties panel's Link box, say). (Again, selecting this option has no effect on links you add in Code view.)

- **Encode special characters in URLs using &#.** This is the best of the three "URL encoding" options. Unlike the option above, this one gives you encoding help when you need it. It's especially helpful if you use a language that has a non-Latin alphabet. If you name your files using Japanese characters, for example, choosing this option translates them into code that successfully transmits over the Internet.

- **Encode special characters in URLs using %** is intended for use with older browsers (and we're talking *old*, as in pre-Internet Explorer 4), so unless you've got a time machine and plan on going back to 1998 to build websites, skip this option.

■ Viewing HTML Markup in Code View

Dreamweaver provides several ways to view a page's HTML:

- **Code view (View→Code)**. In Code view, Dreamweaver displays your page's raw code, just as any text editor would.

- **Split view with Design (View→Code and Design)**. This view displays both the HTML and the visual design of a web page (Design view) side by side: code on the left, design on the right (Figure 7-2). You can reverse this order (View→Design View on Left) or stack one view on top of the other by turning off the checkmark next to View→Split Vertically. In addition, if the page has an external style sheet, you can use Dreamweaver's Related Files feature (page 343) to display the CSS code in one half of the document window and the Design view in the other half.

- **Split view with Live (ViewCode and Live).** This view works almost exactly like Split view with Design discussed previously. The major difference is that the page is displayed in Live view rather than Design view. To switch from Design to Live view, choose View→Live View or press Alt+F11 (Option-F11). An even easier option is to use the Design/Live menu at the top of the document window.

- **Split Code view (View→Split Code)**. This option is for serious coding junkies. It lets you view the code *twice*, so you can work on two sections of a page at once. That's useful for pages with lots of HTML and can come in handy when you want to edit the CSS in the <head> region of a page while you write HTML in the <body> section. It also works with Dreamweaver's Related Files feature (page 343); in Split Code view, you can check the HTML for a web page in one half of the document window and the CSS for an external style sheet in the other half (or the JavaScript from an external JavaScript file, for that matter).

- **Code Inspector (Window→Code Inspector)**. The Code Inspector displays your HTML in a floating window so you see your working pages in their full glory in the document window, rather than have them cut in half in Split view. To open the Code Inspector, choose Window→Code Inspector, or press F10 (Option-F10). If you have multiple monitors, the Code Inspector is especially handy, because you can display your HTML code on one monitor and the document window on the other. Multitasking code warriors can also use the Code Inspector to look at one area of code while using the main document window to work on another area of code (though the Split Code view works well for this, too).

The rest of this section assumes that you're using Code view to edit your HTML.

Keep in mind that, in addition to using the menu commands mentioned above, you can use the document window toolbar with its buttons and the Design/Live menu to select Code, Split, Design, or Live view.

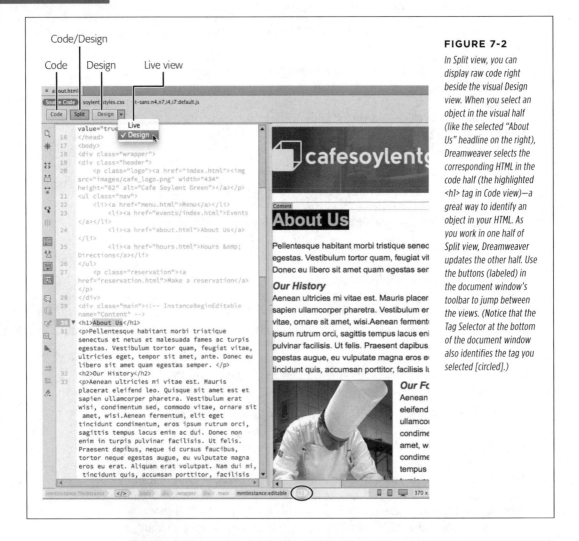

Code/Design

Code   Design   Live view

FIGURE 7-2

In Split view, you can display raw code right beside the visual Design view. When you select an object in the visual half (like the selected "About Us" headline on the right), Dreamweaver selects the corresponding HTML in the code half (the highlighted <h1> tag in Code view)—a great way to identify an object in your HTML. As you work in one half of Split view, Dreamweaver updates the other half. Use the buttons (labeled) in the document window's toolbar to jump between the views. (Notice that the Tag Selector at the bottom of the document window also identifies the tag you selected [circled].)

> **TIP**   You can quickly jump between Code and Design views by pressing Control+` (on both Windows and Macs). In Split view, this shortcut jumps between the two views, so you can insert an image in the design half of Split view, and then press Control+` to jump right into the HTML for that image in the code half of the window. (If you have the Code Inspector open, this keyboard shortcut jumps between the Code Inspector and the document window.)

Code view functions much like a text editor (only better, as you'll soon see). You can click anywhere inside the window and start typing in HTML, JavaScript, CSS, or any other programming code you want (such as PHP or ColdFusion).

You don't have to type out *everything* by hand; the Insert panel, Insert menu, and Properties panel also function in Code view. Use these sources of canned HTML to combine hands-on coding with convenient, easy-to-use Dreamweaver objects. This trick can be a real timesaver when you need to add a table, which would otherwise be a multiline exercise in typing accuracy.

You can also select a tag (like a photo's <img> tag) in Code view and use the Properties panel to modify it.

NOTE When you add HTML in Code view, Dreamweaver doesn't automatically update Design view, which can be disconcerting when you work in Split view (after all, how would Dreamweaver display a half-finished tag like this: *<img src="*?). In the Properties panel, click the Refresh button (see Figure 7-3) or press F5 to update the visual display.

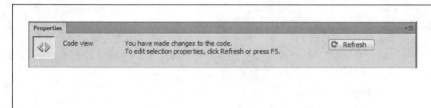

FIGURE 7-3

After you change the HTML on the code side of Split view, click the Refresh button in the Properties panel to update the Design view.

To help navigate your code, Code view provides several visual cues. They include:

- **Syntax coloring**. Dreamweaver displays different page elements in different colors, making it easy to distinguish comments from code and tags from text. The actual colors Dreamweaver uses depends on settings in Edit→Preferences→Code Coloring (Dreamweaver→Preferences→Color Coding). In Preferences (Figure 7-4), you can choose one of the pre-designed themes, such as Raven (black background) or Blanche (white background). Most of the pictures and examples in this chapter use the Classic theme. The background is white, comments are gray, and text is black.

  To really make a tag stand out, you can underline, boldface, or italicize it, and even give it a background color. Dreamweaver offers separate color schemes for 25 types of documents, such as CSS, ASP, and XML files. (But do you really need different colors for HTML forms in JavaScript files, HTML pages, and PHP pages? You be the judge.)

- **Bad code highlighting**. When you type incorrect code (say an opening tag without a closing tag, or improperly nested tags), Dreamweaver highlights the error (circled in Figure 7-5), but only if you turn on the Highlight Invalid Code option (View→Code View Options→Highlight Invalid Code) or click the Highlight Invalid Code button in the Coding toolbar (see Figure 7-6).

FIGURE 7-4

From Dreamweaver's Preferences window (Edit→Preferences in Windows, Dreamweaver→Preferences on Macs), you can control the hue Dreamweaver uses to color-code your web page's HTML, CSS, and script in Code view. Select the Code Coloring category, choose the type of document you're working on—HTML, CSS, PHP, or whatever—and then apply one of the themes. For even more fine-tuning, click the Edit Coloring Scheme button. That displays another dialog box (not shown here) with even more options, where you can customize colors for nearly every syntactical element in Code view.

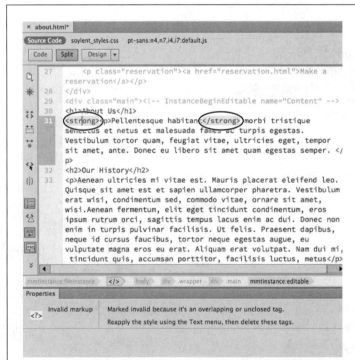

FIGURE 7-5

Dreamweaver highlights incorrect HTML in Code view (like the <strong> tags circled here). Here the highlights are light gray. If you click the gray area, the Properties panel reveals your mistake. In this case, you improperly nested a tag—part of it lies outside the surrounding <p> tag. (In Design view, on the other hand, Dreamweaver indicates mistakes by showing the HTML tag—</strong>, for example—in front of a bright yellow background.)

FIGURE 7-6

In Code view, the Coding toolbar (left edge) gives you easy access to common code-writing commands. Using the toolbar, it's easy to wrap a selection of HTML in an HTML comment, hide code you don't want to see or edit, and turn on or off Code view options like line numbering and highlighting invalid code.

- **Non-editable highlighting in templates**. You'll learn about templates in detail in Chapter 22, but for now, templates include both editable and non-editable regions. Dreamweaver displays non-editable regions in light gray. This is a little confusing because Dreamweaver displays HTML comments in gray, too, and you *can* edit those. You can change either color, however, as shown in Figure 7-4.

- **Browser compatibility highlighting**. Much to the anguish of web designers, different browsers can interpret CSS formatting rules differently. What looks great in Firefox may crumble in Internet Explorer 6. Dreamweaver's Browser Compatibility Checker alerts you to possible cross-browser CSS problems. When you see a squiggly line underneath code, Dreamweaver is telling you there's a potential issue.

- **Library item highlighting**. Code from Library items (Chapter 21) has a light-yellow background.

You can also control the following Code view display options from the View→Code View Options submenu:

- **Word Wrap**. This option makes long lines of code wrap (at the window's edge) to the next line, so you don't have to scroll horizontally to see the entire line. It affects only how Dreamweaver *displays* the line; it doesn't actually change your code by introducing line breaks. Dreamweaver turns this option on by default; if it got turned off, go to View→Code View Options→Word Wrap.

- **Line Numbers**. Automatic line numbering can come in handy when you encounter an error in a page containing JavaScript or server-side code (such as PHP, described in Chapter 24). In Code view, you can click a line number to select the entire line, which is a great way to delete a line of code. Normally, Dreamweaver displays line numbers, but if you don't see them in Code view, click the Show Line Numbers button in the Coding toolbar (Figure 7-6) or choose View→Code View Options→Line Numbers to turn them on.

- **Hidden Characters**. Some characters you type on a keyboard don't show up onscreen: the end of a line, created by hitting the Enter (Return) key, for example. Occasionally, these hidden characters can cause big trouble. When you work with dynamic, server-side web pages, for example, you might find some cool code on the Web and copy it to your own page. Sometimes copying and pasting code from a web page introduces hidden characters that prevent the code from working. Turning on the Hidden Characters option (View→Code View Options→Hidden Characters) helps ferret out problem characters so you can eliminate them. Spaces appear as dots, paragraph breaks as paragraph symbols, and tabs as a set of double arrows (see the code in Figure 7-6).

- **Highlight Invalid Code**. This option is the on/off switch for highlighting bad HTML in Code view (see Figure 7-5). Dreamweaver normally turns this option off, but it's a good idea to turn it on: Go to View→Code View Options→Highlight Invalid Code.

- **Syntax Coloring**. This option turns tags, comments, and text into colorful (and informative) text (see Figure 7-4). Dreamweaver comes with this option turned on.

- **Auto Indent**. When you work with nested HTML tags, it's often helpful to press Tab to indent each level of nested tag, making it easier to identify large blocks of HTML (such as a table and all its contents). The Auto Indent option left-aligns the indent for multiple lines of content each time you hit Enter (Return).

  Suppose you hit the Tab key twice, type a line of code, and then hit Enter (Return). Dreamweaver puts the insertion point on the next line, indenting it two tabs. To outdent, press the Backspace key. Dreamweaver normally turns this option on.

- **Syntax Error Alerts in Info Bar**. This feature benefits JavaScript and PHP programmers. When you turn it on (View→Code View Options→Syntax Error Alerts in Info Bar), Dreamweaver highlights potential syntax errors in both languages (meaning it signals typos and improper code) and displays a yellow info bar at the top of the document window. You can also turn this feature off and on from the Coding toolbar (Figure 7-6).

The Coding Toolbar

Dreamweaver includes a handy toolbar on the left edge of the document window in Code view that makes many basic hand-coding tasks go much more quickly. If you don't see it, turn it on by choosing View→Toolbars→Coding or by right-clicking (Control-clicking) another toolbar, such as the Standard or Document toolbar, and then, in the drop-down menu, selecting the Coding option. Use the same technique to close the toolbar if you don't use it.

The toolbar's buttons duplicate tasks and preference settings from other parts of Dreamweaver. If you can't figure out the purpose of a button, point to it. In a second or two, a tooltip appears identifying the button's function. Here's a quick rundown of what the buttons in the toolbar do and, when applicable, a cross-reference to a more detailed description of the tool or action:

- **Open Documents**. This pull-down menu displays all your open documents so you can switch among them. Since it's actually easier to click a document's tab at the top of the document window, you probably won't use this button much.

- **Show Code Navigator**. Dreamweaver's Code Navigator lets you see which CSS styles affect the currently selected HTML. If you have no HTML selected, the Navigator displays the HTML tag in effect at the cursor location. It also lets you jump quickly to the code in a style sheet so you can edit it. Read more about this feature on page 418.

- **Collapse Full Tag/Collapse Selection/Expand All**. These three buttons work with Dreamweaver's Code Collapse feature described on page 338. They let you collapse (and expand) multiple lines of code, essentially hiding those lines onscreen so you can concentrate on another section of code.

- **Select Parent Tag**. This handy feature lets you quickly select the tag that surrounds your current selection. Say you select the text inside a link tag (<a>), or just click inside that tag, and your cursor is blinking happily. Click this button, and Dreamweaver selects the entire <a> tag and all its contents. Click it again, and you select that link's *parent* tag. If you really want to be productive, the keyboard shortcut Ctrl+[(⌘-[) is quicker.

- **Balance Braces**. If you do a lot of programming in JavaScript or a server language like PHP, .NET, ColdFusion, or Java Server Pages, this button helps you find the matching brace ({ or }) in a chunk of code—actually this tool selects *all* the code between an opening and closing brace, but doing so lets you identify where the braces begin and end. Just click to the right of an opening brace ({), and then click this button to find the closing brace. To find a *closing* brace's mate, click to the left of the brace, and then click this button. You can also find matching parentheses this way. The keyboard shortcut Ctrl+' (⌘-') is even faster.

- **Apply/Remove Comments**. Comments let you include helpful notes in your code, which don't appear when a browser displays the page. For example, you may want to leave explanatory notes to help future generations of web developers. Or you might put a comment before a <div> tag that explains what should go inside it—"Put corporate logo and navigation bar here." People frequently use comments to mark the end of a page section—"End of navigation bar," for example. These buttons let you add or remove comments in HTML, CSS, JavaScript, PHP, and VBScript code, as demonstrated in Figure 7-7.

FIGURE 7-7

Dreamweaver's Coding toolbar lets you wrap HTML, CSS, JavaScript, and other code within comment characters. Select the code you want to turn into a comment, click the Apply Comment button (circled), and then select the type of comment you want to add. Use an HTML comment to "comment out" (hide) HTML code; the /* */ option to hide multiple lines of CSS, JavaScript, or PHP; the // option to hide each line of JavaScript or PHP code; and the ' option to hide VBScript code. The last option, Apply Server Comment, hides server-side code; use it to comment out both HTML and server-side programming code in one step. To remove a comment, select all the code (including the comment markers), and then click the Remove Comment button (hidden in this figure; it's just below the Apply Comment button).

> **TIP** You can easily turn style properties on and off in Cascading Style Sheets by taking advantage of "comment" behavior. Open a CSS file, select a property inside a style, and stick a pair of comment tags around it (/* at the beginning and */ at the end). When you preview a page that uses the style, you see the style minus the property you "commented out," as programmers call it. This maneuver lets you add a new style and preview it, temporarily hiding the effect of one or more other styles without permanently deleting them. It's also a great help in debugging problematic styles. In fact, it's so useful that CSS Designer's Properties section provides a button that makes it easy to turn style properties on and off (see Figure 9-5).

- **Wrap Tag**. When you select some text or a page element and then click this button, Dreamweaver opens a window listing HTML tags. Choose one and Dreamweaver wraps the selected text or element in that tag. (The Quick Tag editor, described on page 356, works the same way.)

- **Recent Snippets**. This drop-down menu lists all the snippets (pieces of reusable code; see page 841) you've recently used. Select an item and Dreamweaver inserts it into your page.

- **Move or Convert CSS**. This drop-down menu lets you move an inline CSS style to either an internal or external style sheet, or lets you move a rule from an internal to an external style sheet. You'll find more details on page 405.

- **Indent/Outdent**. These buttons indent or outdent lines of selected code, using the settings you defined in the Indent box of the Code Format preferences window (see page 340).

- **Format Source Code**. This button lets you enforce a consistent style for your code by applying specific formatting to an entire web page or to just a section of code. It uses the code-formatting options you set in the Code Format preferences window (see page 341) and the rules defined in the Type-A-ubergeek-what-a-lot-of-work Tag Library described in the box on page 345. In other words, if you want to make your HTML easier to read (by making Dreamweaver write every opening <tr> tag and closing </tr> tag on their own lines, for example), you can.

Code Hints

Typing code can be a chore, which is why even longtime hand-coders take advantage of anything that speeds up the process. A perfect example is Dreamweaver's Code Hints feature (shown in Figure 7-8). It lets you select tags, attributes, and even Cascading Style Sheet styles from a drop-down menu as you type.

FIGURE 7-8

Dreamweaver's Code Hints feature saves your tired fingers from typing tags and tag properties. As soon as you type <, the program launches a list of tags. Select the one you want, and Dreamweaver types it in for you. Dreamweaver is even thoughtful enough to show you all the available CSS styles when you add a class attribute to a tag.

> **NOTE** Code hints work with other tags, too, as well as scripting languages like JavaScript, PHP, ASP.NET, and ColdFusion. In addition, Dreamweaver includes CSS code hints, so if you write your style sheets by hand, you can take advantage of Code Hints' auto-complete feature to quickly write CSS styles.

Here's how it works: When you begin a new tag by typing an opening bracket (<), Dreamweaver displays a menu listing all the available HTML tags. Use your mouse or arrow keys to select a tag, or type in the first few letters of it, and Dreamweaver finds the closest match. When you press Enter (Return), Dreamweaver automatically adds the tag to your code. Even better, a second menu pops up, listing all the properties that tag can have.

TIP You can also open the Code Hints menu by pressing Ctrl+space bar when your cursor is in a tag. This shortcut is really useful when you're editing code and want to add a property or when you edit the property of a tag you already created. For example, you could click inside the name of a class style applied to a tag—inside the word "copyright" in the code *class="copyright"*, for instance—and then press Ctrl+space bar. This action not only selects the name so you can change it, but it also opens a menu listing all the classes available to the page. Then you can use the up and down arrow keys (or even your mouse) to select a different style.

If code hints annoy you, you can turn them off completely, rein them in by setting a delay (so that lists don't appear immediately), or turn them off for selected types of elements (such as tag properties). To make any of these adjustments, open Dreamweaver's Preferences window (Ctrl+U [⌘-U]), and then select Code Hints. Make your desired changes, and then click OK.

Dreamweaver also simplifies writing closing tags: As soon as you type </ (the first two characters for any closing tag), Dreamweaver automatically finishes your thought by closing the tag for you. For example, after you type an opening <p> tag and add the paragraph's content, Dreamweaver finishes the closing tag—</p>—the moment you type </. For a longer tag, like </address>, this feature saves your fingers a lot of work. You can change this behavior to make Dreamweaver automatically insert the closing tag immediately after you finish typing the opening tag, or, if you just can't stand the feature, turn off "Enable code hints" in the Code Hints preferences window.

NOTE If you like Code Hints, you'll love the Snippets panel, which makes reusing code a snap. See Chapter 21 for details.

■ JAVASCRIPT CODE HINTS

JavaScript programmers also have access to a wide array of code-hint features. In general, JavaScript hints work just like HTML hints—as you type JavaScript code, Dreamweaver pops up a box of suggestions that match what you're typing. But JavaScript code hints go much further than simple lists of JavaScript keywords. Dreamweaver provides hints for basic JavaScript objects like arrays, dates, numbers, and strings. For example, say you create an array (gentle reader, if you have no idea what a JavaScript array is, feel free to skip this section). If you then write the array's name in your code, a hint box pops up listing all the methods and properties of JavaScript array objects.

In addition, Dreamweaver keeps track of JavaScript functions *you* create and provides code hints using your own function names, as well as custom-created classes. Even better, Dreamweaver is aware of document object model (DOM) properties and provides hints for all the properties and methods of DOM objects.

■ JQUERY CODE HINTS

jQuery is a popular JavaScript library used on millions of websites, from one-person blogs to ESPN, NBC, and even Microsoft. jQuery lets web designers jump into JavaScript programming by simplifying many common JavaScript programming tasks. It's so popular that Dreamweaver CC adds detailed code hints for jQuery. If you've no idea what jQuery is, skip this section, or better yet, pick up a copy of *JavaScript & jQuery: The Missing Manual* (O'Reilly Media), which covers the programming language in detail.

Dreamweaver's jQuery code hint feature is very sophisticated. Not only does it provide hints for all of jQuery's built-in functions, but it also offers hints for all class and ID selectors on a page, along with tooltips for functions that have multiple properties (see Figure 7-9.)

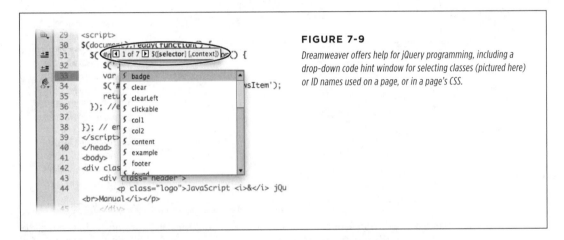

FIGURE 7-9

Dreamweaver offers help for jQuery programming, including a drop-down code hint window for selecting classes (pictured here) or ID names used on a page, or in a page's CSS.

Dreamweaver CC adds a kind of built-in jQuery cheat sheet as well. When you type in a jQuery function, a yellow box appears above the code (circled in Figure 7-9). It displays the function's name as well as which *arguments* it accepts (in programming, an argument is a piece of information that you can hand off to a command, and it affects how that command works). In some cases, a built-in jQuery function might work in several ways, each requiring a different kind of argument. In the example in Figure 7-9, you've begun typing jQuery's $() function. The yellow pop-up box indicates that you can use that function seven ways. Clicking the left or right arrow keys steps you through examples of the methods, indicating the number and type of arguments you need to provide in each case.

■ PHP CODE HINTS

Dreamweaver includes advanced code-hinting for the server-side programming language PHP, too (but not for other server-side technologies, like .NET, ColdFusion, Ruby on Rails, or Java Server Pages). Not only does Dreamweaver support code-hinting for built-in PHP functions, it also makes note of variables, functions, and classes you create (see Figure 7-10).

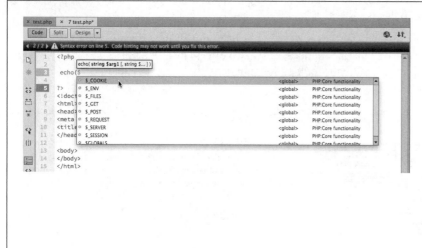

FIGURE 7-10

Dreamweaver is pretty unforgiving of syntax errors (typos or missing punctuation) in PHP code. Most of the time, you start typing PHP code and Dreamweaver displays a "Syntax error" message at the top of the document window, along with a red mark at the point it thinks you made an error. Don't worry, this happens a lot as you program. The important thing is that, once you finish, you have no remaining syntax errors. If there are, you probably left off a closing), }, ', or ".

Since it's common for programmers to create multiple PHP files and add them all to (or include them all in) a master file, Dreamweaver CC searches through all the files the current page references and analyzes (or *parses*) them. Then, as you type more PHP code, Dreamweaver displays code hints based on the names of the variables, functions, and classes you defined in those files. In other words, Dreamweaver personalizes its code hints for your site and for the PHP programming you add to it.

In addition, since many PHP frameworks, like CakePHP and Zend, and many PHP-based content management systems (CMSes), like Drupal, Joomla, and WordPress, rely on many separate PHP files, Dreamweaver includes something called site-specific code hints. This is available only for PHP-based websites (you'll learn how to set one up in Part Six of this book), and it lets you identify which folders Dreamweaver scans to create code hints for your site.

Dreamweaver's site-specific hints have a few benefits. First, if you often include PHP files outside your root folder (for example, the Zend framework keeps its Include files outside the web-accessible root folder), you can tell Dreamweaver to scan the folder above the current local root folder. Second, many CMSes and PHP frameworks use tons of files with tons of variables, functions, and class names. Sites like these use the files internally, in the programming that drives the systems. You, as a programmer, don't ever need to see most of them, and you certainly don't want their elements cluttering up your code hint window.

With your PHP page open, you can turn site-specific code hints on by choosing Site→Site-Specific Code Hints. This opens a new window (see Figure 7-11). If you're using Drupal, Joomla, or WordPress, you can select your environment from the top Structure menu, and Dreamweaver automatically identifies the proper folders, files, and paths. Click OK and you're done.

FIGURE 7-11

To add the function names, class names, and variable names you use in your site's PHP code to Dreamweaver's Code Hints feature, choose Site→Site-Specific Code Hints and tell Dreamweaver which files and folders to scan.

If, however, you're using a PHP framework or some other PHP CMS, you need to tell Dreamweaver which folders to analyze by following these steps:

1. **Click ▤ and navigate to the folder containing your site and all the PHP files you want Dreamweaver to scan.**

   If you don't have any PHP files outside your local root folder, you can skip this step because Dreamweaver automatically scans the local root folder. However, you may have PHP files one level up from the root folder. In that case, click ▤ and select the folder one level up that contains both the PHP files and your local site root.

2. **Click +.**

   The Add File/Folder window opens. You can click another icon to select either one particular PHP file or a folder's worth of PHP files. If you pick a folder, turn on the checkbox labeled "Recursive" if you want Dreamweaver to scan the files in subfolders within this folder. You can ensure that Dreamweaver searches only .php files by clicking + to the right of the Extensions label and then typing in *.php*. Dreamweaver won't look through any other files and, as a result, it displays code hints faster. But if you do use other extensions for your PHP files, such as .inc, make sure to add them as well.

You can prevent Dreamweaver from scanning a folder you added from the main Site-Specific Code Hints window, too. Select the folder from the Files list, and then turn off the "Scan this folder" checkbox. You can also turn off recursive scanning and change the file extensions from this window.

3. **Click OK to finish.**

Dreamweaver scans the selected files and creates a list of code hints for your site.

> **NOTE** You may find that Dreamweaver doesn't always automatically pop up a box of site-specific code hints as it does when you use regular PHP functions. You may need to coax Dreamweaver into displaying them by using the keyboard shortcut Ctrl-space bar.

Code Collapse

One problem with raw HTML, CSS, JavaScript, and PHP is that, well, it's raw—a bunch of letters, numbers, and symbols that tend to blend together in a mind-numbing sea of code. This can make locating a particular bit of code needle-in-a-haystack tough. On pages with lots of code, you can easily get lost as you scroll up and down to make a change. In many cases, you don't need to see all the code, because you're not likely to change it—like the doctype and HTML declarations at the top of a page—or because you *can't* change it—like the HTML embedded in template-based pages (Chapter 22), or pages that have Dreamweaver Library items (Chapter 21).

Fortunately, Dreamweaver lets you get that code out of your face. Its Code Collapse feature condenses multiple lines of code into a single highlighted box of 10 characters. Collapsing the code is a simple process: Select the code you want to collapse—like all the code above the <body> tag—and then click one of the icons that appears just to the left of both the first and last line of code you want to collapse. In Windows, this icon is a small box with a minus sign (–) in it (Figure 7-12 top, circled); on Macs, it's a down-pointing arrow at the beginning of the selection and an up-pointing arrow at the end. The code collapses into a gray box. To expand it, select the condensed code and then click the "expand" icon (a + sign in Windows, a flippy triangle on Macs).

> **TIP** To quickly select multiple lines of HTML (or any code, for that matter), click in the line-number area to the left of the code at the beginning of your selection, and then drag to the end of your selection. (If you don't see any line numbers, turn them on using the Coding toolbar or by clicking View→Code View Options→Line Numbers.)

Dreamweaver includes a few more nuanced ways to collapse code:

- **Collapse an individual tag**. Say you want to hide a long paragraph of text. Instead of selecting it, click anywhere inside the paragraph tag (<p>), and then either click the Coding toolbar's Collapse Tag button, choose Edit→Code Collapse→Collapse Full Tag, or press Shift+Ctrl+J (Shift-⌘-J).

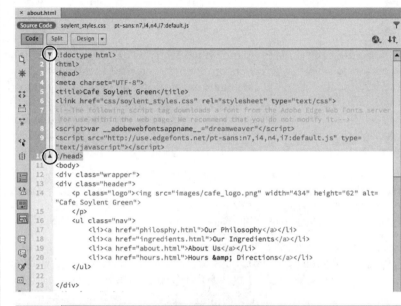

FIGURE 7-12

Now you see it, now you don't. You can collapse multiple lines of code (top) into a compact little gray box (bottom, circled) by clicking one of the Code Collapse icons (top, circled). The collapsed code is still there in your page—you haven't deleted it—but now it's conveniently tucked out of sight. If you need a reminder of what it is, point to the gray box, and a tooltip displays the hidden code.

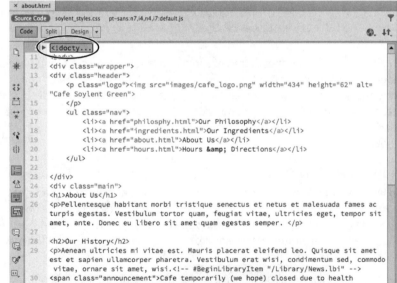

This feature works on the tag nearest the cursor. Say you have a paragraph of text and, inside it, a link. If you click inside the <a> tag and use this feature, the <a> tag collapses. But if you click anywhere else inside the paragraph (but not inside any other tag), the paragraph itself collapses. This behavior is a little confusing, but it can be really useful. Say you want to hide everything inside a page's <head> tags. Instead of having to select all the lines inside the tag, click anywhere between the beginning and ending <head> tags (but make sure you're not inside *another* tag, like the <title> tag), and use any of the commands mentioned in the previous paragraph.

- **Collapse the code outside an individual tag**. This lets you hide everything *except* the code you want to work on. Suppose you want to see only the code inside the <body> tag. Click immediately after the opening <body> tag (in other words, inside the <body> tag, but not inside any other tag), press Alt (Option) and then, in the Coding toolbar, click Collapse Tag. Choosing Edit→Code Collapse→Collapse Outside Full Tag or pressing Alt+Ctrl+J (Option-⌘-J) does the same thing.

- **Collapse the code outside the current selection**. This is another way to view only the code you want to work on. Select the code and then press Alt (Option) and click the Coding toolbar's Collapse Selection button, or choose Edit→Code Collapse→Collapse Outside Selection, or press Alt+Ctrl+C (Option-⌘-C).

- **Expand All**. If you miss all that hidden code, you can quickly restore it to its full glory by clicking the Coding toolbar's Expand All button, choosing Edit→Code Collapse→Expand All, or pressing Alt+Ctrl+E (Option-⌘-E).

> **NOTE** You can use the Collapse Full Tag and Collapse Outside Full Tag commands only when you work with HTML. They have no effect on CSS, JavaScript, or PHP pages.

You can hide any number of code regions in a page—for example, the top portion of a page, a navigation sidebar that never gets edited, or the copyright notice at the bottom of a page—so you can easily identify the code you really want to work on. Dreamweaver even remembers the state of these sections, so if you collapse a code section and then close the document, the collapsed section remains hidden when you reopen the file.

Setting Code Formats

As you work away building your web page in the document window, Dreamweaver writes the relevant HTML behind the scenes. Web browsers read that code and display your page. As long as you write the code properly, web browsers don't care how the code looks in writing. For example, here's a chunk of code from the menu of the Cafe Soylent Green site:

```
<table width="100%" border="0" cellpadding="0" cellspacing="0"
class="menu"><tr><th colspan="3" class="course">Starters</th></tr>
<tr><th>Item</th><th>Description</th><th>Price</th>
</tr>
```

Browsers don't care if there's any white space in the lines of code; they just read what's there and display the elements defined by the code.

You, on the other hand, may care a lot if you're trying to troubleshoot your HTML. White space like line breaks and indents can detangle your code. Here's the same chunk of code as above, but with a little white space added:

```
<tr>
    <th colspan="3" class="course">Starters</th>
</tr>
<tr>
    <th>Item</th>
    <th>Description</th>
    <th>Price</th>
</tr>
```

Here, it's easier to see that there are two table rows, the first of which spans three columns. It's also easier to identify the text that appears inside the table header (<th>) tags: Starters in the first row, then Item, Description, and Price in the second row.

Out of the box, Dreamweaver adds white space, like line breaks and indents, to your code automatically. And while these standard settings work fine, you can tweak them in the Preferences window (Edit→Preferences [Dreamweaver→Preferences]). For example, you might want to change the size of the indent, or automatically have Dreamweaver write all tags in lowercase. Click the Code Format category in the Preference window's left-hand column to see your options (Figure 7-13).

FIGURE 7-13

To control the way Dreamweaver writes HTML, go to the Code Format category of the Preferences window. For most people, this degree of control is overkill, but if the way HTML appears on a page matters to you, go wild. (These settings don't affect how the page looks in a web browser, only how the code appears when you view it in Dreamweaver's Code view, another text editor, or when you look at the page's source code in a browser.)

■ INDENTS

To make your code easier to read, it helps to indent nested tags and other block-level elements. But if you prefer that Dreamweaver stop auto-indenting such elements, turn off the Indent checkbox. This is also your opportunity to tell Dreamweaver whether you want to indent code using the space or tab character, and to set the amount of indentation:

- If you select Spaces in the Indent menu, in the Indent box, type in the number of spaces you want Dreamweaver to move the code over. The default setting is 2, meaning that Dreamweaver will indent the code for block-level elements two spaces in from the edge of the preceding code.

- If you select Tabs in the Indent menu, the number in the "Tab size" box indicates the size of each tab, measured in spaces. (The size you specify here affects only the display in Code view. In the code itself, Dreamweaver simply inserts a plain tab character.)

NOTE If you choose to indent using tabs, you can save yourself a few bits of file size. Since Dreamweaver indents tabbed code two spaces, switching to tabs saves you one character—your document will use just one tab instead of two spaces for each indent.

■ LINE BREAKS

The Windows, Mac, and Unix operating systems each look for a different invisible character at the end of each line of code. This can cause problems if you create a page under one operating system and your remote server uses another. Fortunately, Dreamweaver fixes the problem when it transfers files to your server.

However, if you later plan to edit Dreamweaver-built pages you copy from a server using another text editor, select that server's operating system from the "Line break type" drop-down menu. Doing so ensures that the program on the receiving end will properly read the line breaks in your Dreamweaver-produced pages.

■ CHARACTER CASE FOR TAGS AND ATTRIBUTES

In standard HTML, you can write tag and property names using either uppercase letters (<B>bold</B>) or lowercase letters (bold); browsers don't care. However, *you* may care how they appear in Code view. Choose your preference from the two "case" drop-down menus, "Default tag case" and "Default attribute case." Most web developers write tags in lowercase, so if you share your pages with colleagues, you're best off selecting lowercase (see the Note below).

NOTE HTML may treat upper- and lowercase tags identically, but XML does not. Both it and the hybrid language *XHTML* require all-lowercase tag and property names. That's why many web developers now strictly use lowercase characters, even in their HTML. And that's why, if you select the XHTML option when you create a new page, Dreamweaver ignores any uppercase preferences you set—even if you turn on the "Override case of" checkboxes.

If you turn on the "Override case of" checkboxes, Dreamweaver scans tags and properties when it opens a page someone else (or some other program) created. If the case doesn't match your preference, Dreamweaver rewrites the code so that it does.

■ THE <TD> TAG

Adding a line break after an opening <td> (table cell) tag may look good in Code view, but in some browsers it adds an unwanted extra space in the table cell. The extra space can wreak havoc on your design, so make sure you always turn this checkbox on.

■ ADVANCED FORMATTING OPTIONS

For real format sticklers, two Advanced Formatting buttons, CSS and Tag Libraries (Figure 7-13), let you control the way every aspect of your CSS and HTML code looks. The CSS button opens the CSS Source Format Options window, which lets you dictate how Dreamweaver writes your CSS—whether it indents properties, whether it uses separate lines for each property, where it puts the opening brace in CSS rules, and whether it inserts a blank line between rules to make your CSS more readable. All these options are matters of personal preference and don't affect the performance of your web page or CSS. The Tag Libraries button opens the same-named dialog window, discussed in the box on page 345.

If you find yourself wading through lots of CSS and HTML, you might want to experiment with these settings to make the code Dreamweaver produces more readable. Both the CSS and Tag Libraries windows have panes that preview your customized CSS and HTML.

Keep in mind that these settings don't affect how *you* write code. But if you find that your own CSS or HTML hand-coding doesn't look as elegant as Dreamweaver's, you can turn to the Apply Source Formatting command (Commands→Apply Source Formatting) to make Dreamweaver clean up your code. That command changes a page's code—adds indents, line breaks, and so on—based on the instructions defined in the CSS and Tag Libraries options.

> **NOTE** Another set of options affects how Dreamweaver creates CSS code. The Preferences window's CSS Styles category tells Dreamweaver whether or not to use CSS shorthand properties (see page 405).

Related Files

With external style sheets, JavaScript libraries, and server-side programming becoming more and more a part of the average web designer's toolbox, Dreamweaver includes a feature that makes it easier for code jockeys to jump around the vast collection of files required to make a single web page work. The Related Files toolbar lists all the files a current web page uses (see Figure 7-14). (Can't find the toolbar? See the Note on page 344.) This includes external style sheets, external JavaScript files (like the ones jQueryUI uses), and server-side files, such as *server-side includes*. Web developers use server-side includes like building blocks for web pages. For example, if you use the same header on every page of your site, you can store the HTML header code in a single file on your web server. Then, using a server-side include, you can automatically attach the header to every page on your site as the server dishes it out.

Web page   Related files

FIGURE 7-14

The Related Files toolbar is a big help for JavaScript programmers, server-side programmers, and those who like to code their CSS by hand. It gives you instant access to any CSS or programming file the current web page uses, so you can quickly summon and edit its CSS, JavaScript, or server-side programming. That saves you a trip to the Open File dialog box and the need to hunt and peck through your files to find the right one.

Currently selected related file

The first item in the Related Files toolbar—Source Code—refers to the web page you're currently editing. The other items represent linked files. For example, the web page you're building in Figure 7-14 has 10 related files—eight external style sheets (including web fonts) and two JavaScript files (related to jQueryUI).

NOTE If you don't see the Related Files toolbar, it may have gotten turned off. To turn it on, choose Edit→Preferences (Dreamweaver→Preferences), click the General category, and then turn on the Enable Related Files checkbox. A dialog box explains that you need to restart Dreamweaver to see the change.

When you click the name of a related file in the toolbar, Dreamweaver displays that file's code. If you're in Design view, Dreamweaver switches to Split view and displays the web page in the Design window and the code for the related file in the other pane. If you're in Code view, Dreamweaver simply switches from the HTML of the web page to the CSS, JavaScript, or server-side code of the related file.

When you work on a related file, all the normal file operations apply only to that file. For example, if you select a CSS file from the Related Files toolbar and edit and save it, Dreamweaver saves only the CSS file when you choose File→Save; it doesn't record any changes you made to the web page's code or to any other related files (see the Tip below). Likewise, if you choose Site→Put to move a file to your web server (see page 812), that CSS file gets whisked off to the server, but the web page itself stays put. This sequence gets a little confusing when you work on related files in Split view, because the web page appears on one half of the screen while the code for a different file appears in the other half.

TIP When you work with the Related Files feature, you may be editing multiple files (for instance, the web page, the CSS, and the JavaScript code) at the same time. To make sure you save the changes to *all* the files, use the File→Save All Related Files command, which saves the current web page and all its helper files. Better yet, create a keyboard shortcut for this useful command by going to Tools→Customize Keyboard. See page 904 for more details.

POWER USERS' CLINIC

Take Control of Code Formatting

For ultimate control over tag formatting, Dreamweaver includes the Tag Library Editor. Not only does it let you control *exactly* how Dreamweaver formats every HTML tag it inserts into a page, but it also lets you dictate the formatting for nine other tag libraries, such as those for PHP, ASP, JSP, ColdFusion, and SVG graphics.

Even if you use some new bleeding-edge tag language unfamiliar to Dreamweaver, you're not out of luck. You can create additional tag libraries and even import custom ASP, .NET, and JSP tags, as well as DTD schemas for XML. You can also add tags to (and remove them from) any library; so if the HTML standard suddenly changes, you can add new or remove obsolete tags.

To control the way Dreamweaver formats tags in a library, choose Edit→Tag Libraries, which opens the Tag Library Editor. Dreamweaver displays a list of all the tag libraries. Click the + sign (flippy triangle on Macs) to the left of a library name to see a list of tags for that library. Select a tag, and then, from the Tag Format area in the bottom half of the window, set your formatting options.

Here's a shortcut for quickly reformatting a particular tag already present on a page: Select the tag in the Tag Selector and then choose Edit→Tag Libraries; Dreamweaver preselects that tag. You can control where a line breaks in relation to the tag through four settings:

- **No line breaks at all**. If you apply this option to the <a> tag example above, for instance, you'd end up with code like this:

```
<p>Here is a <a href="home.html">link</a></p>
```

- **Line breaks before and after the tag**:

```
<p>Here is a
<a href="home.html">link</a>
</p>
```

- **Line breaks before, inside, and after the tag**:

```
<p>Here is a
<a href="home.html">
link
</a>
</p>
```

- **Line break after the tag only**:

```
<p>Here is a <a href="home.html">link</a>
</p>
```

In addition, you can choose whether Dreamweaver applies formatting rules to the contents of a tag, and choose the case—upper, lower, or mixed—that Dreamweaver uses when it adds the tag to your code.

The Related Files feature works hand in hand with the Code Navigator. As described on page 418, the Code Navigator (the small ship steering wheel floating above page elements) displays a drop-down list of all the CSS styles applied to the page element under your cursor. If you click one of the styles and it happens to be in an external style sheet, Dreamweaver switches to Split view, opens the CSS file, and positions your cursor on the appropriate style so you can edit it. (That said, you might find the other methods of editing CSS, described on pages 135 and 402, easier and more error-free.)

■ **FINDING NESTED PHP FILES**

When programmers write pages in the server-side language PHP, they commonly use server-side includes to have that page load and run several helper PHP files to complete the page. For example, the popular blogging system WordPress uses a single file, *index.php*, to control an entire blog—this one file manages every one of the blog's pages, from the home page to a category page to a single blog post.

To do this, the *index.php* file includes tons (really, a *lot*) of other PHP files. If you wanted to edit your WordPress site using a text editor other than Dreamweaver, the only way to do that would be to open each file manually. But with Dreamweaver, you simply open the *index.html* file and let Dreamweaver "discover" all the related PHP files. To see how that works, follow these steps:

1. **Set up a testing server.**

   A testing server (also called a staging server) is a computer you set up (frequently on your own computer or a networked computer in your office) so you can test PHP files before moving them to the Internet for all the world to see.

   It's not hard to set up a testing server on your own computer (page 921). Windows users can learn how at *http://uptospeedguides.com/wamp* and Mac fans can go to *http://uptospeedguides.com/mamp*.

   After you set up the testing server, you need to edit the Site Definition settings (Site→Manage Sites) to let Dreamweaver know about it. Follow the instructions on page 23.

2. **Open a PHP file.**

   When you open a PHP file, you won't see the familiar HTML tags; you'll see PHP code (see Figure 7-15), which often uses multiple server-side includes to build a page. There are a couple of ways to "include" a PHP file in another PHP file. Dreamweaver has a command that lets you add basic includes: Insert→Server-Side Include (see page 928). When you insert an Include using this command, Dreamweaver automatically recognizes the PHP files and displays them in the Related Files toolbar with no further effort on your part. But you might also use PHP files within *other* Include files. In cases like these, you need to tell Dreamweaver to "discover" them.

3. **Click the "Discover" link in the Document toolbar above the document window (see Figure 7-15, top).**

   Dreamweaver displays a warning box saying that it will execute the scripts on this page. That's not a problem, so turn on the "Don't warn me again" checkbox to skip this window in the future. Dreamweaver finds all the PHP files the currently open dynamic page uses. This may be just a few files, or, in the case of a complex PHP application like WordPress, quite a few. For example, in the bottom image of Figure 7-15, you can see that the Related Files toolbar is chock-full of filenames.

4. **Select a related file to work on.**

   Once Dreamweaver discovers all the related PHP files, you can use the Related Files toolbar as you normally would to open a file. If there are a lot of files, as in the case of a WordPress site, navigate through the list by clicking the left and right arrow buttons, or click Show More to see a drop-down menu of all the related files. Select a name from that list to open the file in Code view.

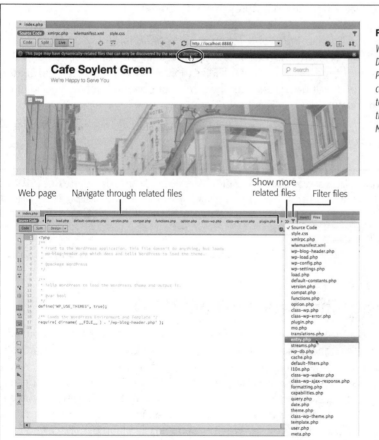

FIGURE 7-15

With PHP pages, you need to click the Discover link (top) to find all related PHP files. You work on a related file by clicking its name in the Related Files toolbar, or, if there are more filenames than can fit there, by clicking the Show More button (bottom).

Web page   Navigate through related files   Show more related files   Filter files

5. **Filter the list if necessary.**

You may not want to see or work on some of the files in the Related Files toolbar. For example, in the case of WordPress, you'll see many PHP files listed, most of which you never want to touch since they're part of the core WordPress program and editing them might break your blog.

Fortunately, you can filter the list of related files so you see just the ones you want. The Filter button in the top-right corner of the Related Files toolbar lets you do two things. First, clicking it pops up a menu that lets you filter by file type—meaning you can show or hide CSS, PHP, or JavaScript files, or any other file type that your web page references. Out of the box, Dreamweaver displays all file types. To hide one, click the Filter button and then click the extension (.css, .php, .js, and so on) for the file type you want to hide. To show those file types later, select them again from the same menu.

You can create a custom filter, too. Click the Filter button, and then choose Custom Filter to bring up a dialog box. Type in the filenames and/or file types you want to see. For example, with WordPress, you may want to edit the PHP theme files—the ones WordPress uses to create your blog's look. To have Dreamweaver display the relevant files, enter their filenames separated by a semicolon, like this: *index.php; footer.php; header.php*, and so on. You can also filter by file type. To show all JavaScript files plus *index.php, footer.php*, and *header.php*, type this in the Related Files toolbar: *index.php;footer.php;header. php;.js*. Don't include spaces after the semicolons or you'll get an "invalid filter" error message.

When you're done, click OK. Dreamweaver displays only the files you specified in the Related Files toolbar.

NOTE Custom filters are useful but, unfortunately, Dreamweaver doesn't save them, so once you close a file, that filter is lost and you have to recreate it the next time you open the file. In addition, you can't filter by folder—all PHP files within a particular folder only, for example—although that would be helpful when you work with certain CMS systems, like WordPress, which keep files related to the design of the site in a dedicated folder. Maybe next time.

■ Designing Pages in Live View

Time to take a break from hardcore coding by hand. The next sections deal with HTML from a designer's perspective. The focus is on Live view, but that doesn't mean you shouldn't keep an eye on the code Dreamweaver writes as you build a page using visual tools. Before Dreamweaver CC Release 2014, the sole purpose of Live view was to preview your page as it appears in a web browser. Now you can build and edit pages in Live view. In addition to the instant gratification of seeing your page in its true glory, you save the time and hassle of jumping back and forth between your browser and Dreamweaver.

To enter Live view, choose Live from the Design/Live menu at the top of document window. If, initially, you're in Code or Split view, you see Live view in one pane of the document window and the code in the other. This is a great way to work, because you can watch Dreamweaver write the underlying code as you add elements to the page. It's like an interactive HTML tutorial. If you want to fine-tune the positioning of the two panes, use the View menu options. Want to see the two panes side by side? Click View→Split Vertically. Want the page on the left and code on the right? Choose View→Live View on Left.

There are three stages to building a page in Live view:

- **Insert HTML structural elements**. In Live view, you can't just click somewhere in your nascent web page and start typing. You first need to structure the page by adding HTML elements like headings and paragraphs using the Insert panel (Figure 7-16) or the Insert menu. These elements use placeholder text ("This is the content for Layout H1 Tag") that identifies the content. You can insert elements from the Insert panel's Common, Structure, Media, and Form groups. When you first start building a page, the Structure group has the elements you need the most.

- **Add text and graphics**. After you structure your page using HTML elements like headings and paragraphs, you'll want to change the placeholder text to something more useful. Double-click the text to open it for editing. Highlight the placeholder copy and type in new text. (You can also copy and paste text from other sources.) You add photos and other graphics to the page through the Insert panel (Insert→Common→Image) or the Insert menu (Insert→Image→Image).

- **Apply CSS formatting**. As usual, you make that stark-looking HTML look great by applying CSS styles. Using CSS Designer, you can create styles for headings and paragraphs. Live view also provides tools that let you apply classes and IDs to elements.

TIP As a new feature, editing in Live view has a few quirks. Dreamweaver old-timers may prefer to continue doing most of their page building and editing in Design view, which in some cases is faster. However, it's worth investing some time learning to work in Live view, since it's likely that it will become a more powerful feature in future versions of Dreamweaver. Also, you're not limited to working in just one view. The Design/Live menu at the top of document window lets you toggle between Design and Live view, so you can use whichever works best for the job at hand.

Inserting HTML Structural Elements in Live View

Adding elements to your page in Live view is a point-and-click procedure. Naturally, the first step is to choose Live from the Design/Live menu at the top of the document window. Then head over to the Insert panel. (You can use the Insert menu, too, but the panel is easier and quicker.) So, for example, to add a paragraph to your page, choose Structure from the Insert panel's menu and then click the Paragraph button. The new paragraph appears in Live view with placeholder text inside a turquoise box, as shown in Figure 7-16.

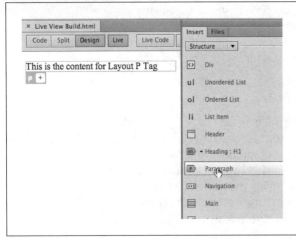

FIGURE 7-16

The Insert panel, shown on the right, is the best tool for adding HTML elements in Live view. Once you place elements in your document, the easiest way to select them is to click on the placeholder text. Once you select an element, you see a turquoise box marking its place on the page. A tab attached to the box shows the HTML tag for the element. The tab with the p, shown here, identifies this element as a paragraph.

When you build a web page element by element, the order of those elements is critical to the look and logic of the page. You want your header at the top and footer at the bottom, and you may want to insert a banner or company logo inside the header tags. Live view provides a positioning dialog box to help you place new elements right where you want them (see Figure 7-17). It makes its first appearance when you add a second element to the page. For example, to place an <h1> heading before a paragraph, click inside the paragraph's blue box, and then select Insert→Structure→Heading: H1. The positioning dialog box opens, giving you four options for placing the <h1> header in relation to the paragraph: Before, After, Wrap, and Nest. Choose Before to place the heading before the paragraph on your page. The After option is equally straightforward.

FIGURE 7-17

The positionng dialog box gives you four options for adding a new element in relationship to the currently selected element. The first two (Before and After) are pretty clear and work as advertised, placing your new element before or after the selected <div> tag. Use the Wrap option to place the tag for the element you're inserting around the selected element. The Nest option places the new tag inside an existing element.

The last two options let you position elements inside each other. Suppose you want to insert a logo inside an existing header. Select the header on the page, and then choose Insert→Common→Image→Image to insert the logo. When you see the positioning dialog, choose Nest. Dreamweaver puts the image between the opening and closing header tags.

To do the reverse of that, that is, to add a header to a logo that's already on the page, select the image and then insert the header using the Wrap option. The end result is the same: Dreamweaver writes the header opening tag in front of the image URL, and the closing tag after the image location. In HTML-speak, this makes the image a "child" element of the header.

When you insert some elements, you see different dialog boxes and windows. For example, when you insert an image, a Select Image Source window opens where you identify the source file for the image. When you insert a Table, you see a Table dialog box where you specify the number of rows and columns and other table formatting details (see page 281). These are the same dialog boxes you see when working in Design view.

■ Editing Pages in Live View

Dreamweaver includes placeholder text with the HTML elements you insert in Live view, so one of the first things you want to do is replace those words with something more meaningful. In Live view, double-click an element to open it for editing. At that point, use the usual editing techniques to replace the placeholder text. If you're replacing everything in an element, triple-click inside it to select all its contents. Then all you need to do is start typing. Just make sure there aren't any nested elements you want to keep. If you do make a mistake, Ctrl+Z (⌘-Z) undoes your error.

If the text you want to add resides in another program, copy it from its source and paste it into the element in Live view. If you copy multiple paragraphs and paste them into a paragraph element, you get a single paragraph with no breaks—Dreamweaver doesn't recognize the original text's paragraph breaks. You need to manually break the now-single paragraph into multiple paragraphs by placing the cursor where you want a break and pressing Enter (Return). Initially, it may not seem as though Dreamweaver creates a new paragraph, but when you click another element on the page to leave editing mode, you'll see the multiple paragraphs.

Sooner or later you'll want to delete or move an element. Perhaps you added a photo but then decide not to use it. Right-click (Control-click) the element and then choose Delete from the shortcut menu. This menu puts the usual editing suspects at your disposal: Cut, Copy, and Paste. So if you want to move an element from one position to another, you can cut it from one spot and paste it in another. (If you're a menu-driven person, the Edit menu also provides the standard editing commands.) Paste always positions the copied element after the currently selected element—you don't get the benefit of the positioning dialog box. So, for example, there's no way to paste a copied paragraph inside a header.

TIP In Live view, one element is always selected (unless your page is empty). That means there's always a turquoise box with a tab wrapped around something on the page. This can be distracting if you want to get a feel for the look of your page *exactly* the way it will look for visitors. The solution is tucked away in the Live View Options menu at the top-right of the document window. Open the menu and select Hide Live View Displays to make the turquoise box disappear. Toggle it back on when you're done admiring your page. The shortcut key for Hide Live View Displays is Alt+Ctrl+H (Control-⌘-H). You can also find Live View Options in the View menu, at View→Live View Options.

Changing Tag Attributes, Classes, and IDs in Live View

Some HTML tags have attributes that provide additional information. For example, <img> tags always use an attribute to identify the source file for the image. You can inspect and edit these attributes in Live view. Elements with editable attributes include a menu button—a stack of three horizontal lines—on the tag (Figure 7-18, circled). Click the button to open the attributes menu.

You add a class or ID to an element in a similar way. Every tag has a + sign button on the tab. Click it and a text box appears where you can type in a class or ID name. Remember to start class names with a period (.) and IDs with a pound symbol (#). If you already defined the class or ID rule, Dreamweaver prompts you with its name. For example, as soon as you type the period to begin a class name, a list of available classes appears. If you haven't already defined a class, no problem; just type the name here. Later, in CSS Designer, you can create the style rules for it (see page 118 for details on creating CSS styles). You can add multiple classes and IDs to an element in Live view. To remove a class or ID, point to its name in the Element tab, and then click the X to the right of the name.

NOTE Want to test drive Live view editing? Jump to the end of this chapter (page 365), where there's a tutorial on building and editing pages in Live view.

FIGURE 7-18

Click the menu button (circled) to see the attributes for this image. To make changes, type in new values. Want to change the source file? Click the folder button to browse your way to a new image.

■ Examining Page Elements

The busier your page gets, the tougher it is to get a complete picture of the way HTML tags interact with one another. After all, you have paragraph tags inside <header> tags inside <div> tags inside <body> tags. Fortunately, two good tools help you keep the hierarchy straight: the Tag Selector (introduced on page 7) and Element Quick View.

You find the Tag Selector at the bottom of the document window. When you select an element in any view (Code, Split, Design, or Live), the Tag Selector displays that element's tag along with any parent tags. So, if your cursor is in a paragraph in Design view, you see the <p> tag in the Tag Selector. If that paragraph is inside a <div> tag, you see a <div> tag as well. Dreamweaver lists parent elements to the left of child elements, so you'll always see the <body> tag on the left and your selected element on the right.

Dreamweaver displays tags in gray tag icons (see Figure 7-19). If any of the tags have classes or IDs assigned to them, you see those names as well. For example, if you apply the *.wrapper* class to a <div> tag, you see the gray <div> tag followed by *.wrapper*. The Tag Selector makes isolating page elements easy—you can click any tag displayed to select the associated element and all its content. Want to select everything on your page? Click the <body> tag.

The Tag Selector is extremely helpful when you try to figure out the relationship between an element and its parent, but it only shows you part of the HTML picture. It doesn't list every HTML element on the page, for example, only the elements that are parents of the selected element. To see every element, you need to turn to Element Quick View. Click the </> button to the left of the Tag Selector to open the Element Quick View window, circled in Figure 7-19, left.

Unlike the Tag Selector, Element Quick View shows you all the elements in the body of your page. You can collapse the outline of elements—clicking a tag hides its child elements. (It works like a toggle, so click again to show the child elements.) You can use Element Quick View to select elements in your web page. It works the same way as the Tag Selector—click a tag to select the element (and its children) in the document window.

Element Quick View has one other trick that you don't find in the Tag Selector. You can use it to edit the basic structure of your web page. Right-click an element to open a shortcut menu that has the commands Delete, Duplicate, Copy, and Paste. You change the order of elements on the page by dragging and dropping them in Element Quick View. Perhaps you want to move a headline and a couple of paragraphs to a different position on the page. As you drag an element, a green line in the Element Quick View panel shows you where Dreamweaver will position the element when you release the mouse button.

As your pages become more complex, you'll be grateful that you have two tools that let you select HTML elements on a page.

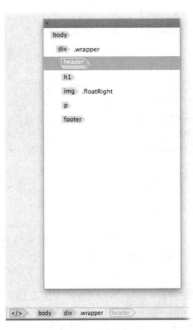

FIGURE 7-19

Left: Element Quick View shows every HTML tag in the body of your web page in outline fashion. Here you see that the <header>, <h1>, <img>, <p>, and <footer> elements are all at the same level (they're all indented two levels). The <div> that has the .wrapper class applied to it is parent to all of them. You can also see that the <header> element has a child image and a child paragraph. Right: Collapsed tags appear as a stack of tags, like the <header> tag shown here. This collapsed tag hides the child elements <img> and <p>. Click tags to collapse or expand the display.

Troubleshooting Interactive Pages

When you see animated effects on a page, like photo slideshows or drop-down navigation menus, there's usually a *script* (a chunk of programming code, like Java-Script) behind the scenes, rewriting the HTML and CSS of your page to make those effects happen. The same thing is true with interactive pages that display additional text or images when you click a button or check a box in a form. Scripting tools like JavaScript and PHP literally rewrite the HTML or CSS of a page before a browser displays it. So, as a web developer, how do you troubleshoot pages like these, written on the fly? The answer is Live Code.

Back on page 348, you learned that Dreamweaver's Live view lets you see what an in-progress web page looks like in a real browser, right from within Dreamweaver. You may have noticed that, when you click the Live view button, another button shows up in the document toolbar: Live Code (Figure 7-20 middle). Live Code works in conjunction with Live view to give you an option you don't get with Live view alone: the ability to see the HTML code as it gets rewritten in response to programming.

That means you can see how the page's components—its HTML, CSS, JavaScript, and so on—work together in real time to create a web page (or not, if you've got programming problems).

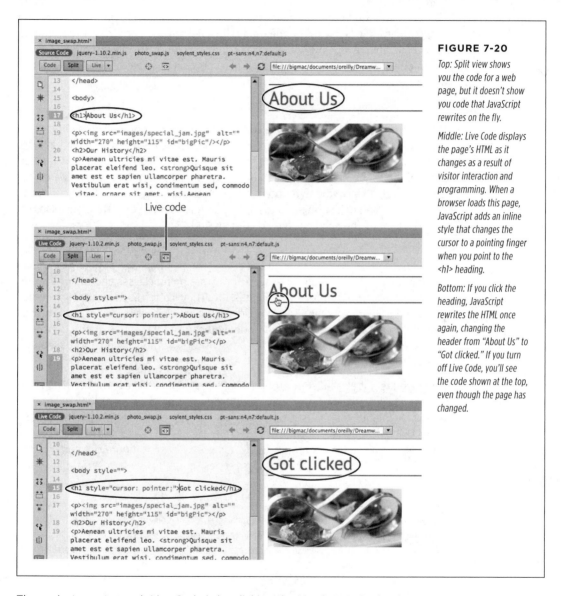

FIGURE 7-20

Top: Split view shows you the code for a web page, but it doesn't show you code that JavaScript rewrites on the fly.

Middle: Live Code displays the page's HTML as it changes as a result of visitor interaction and programming. When a browser loads this page, JavaScript adds an inline style that changes the cursor to a pointing finger when you point to the <h1> heading.

Bottom: If you click the heading, JavaScript rewrites the HTML once again, changing the header from "About Us" to "Got clicked." If you turn off Live Code, you'll see the code shown at the top, even though the page has changed.

The easiest way to reach Live Code is by clicking the Live button in the document window and then clicking the Live Code button that appears. If you're a fan of menus, choose View→Live Code. Either way, Dreamweaver displays the page's Live view in one half of the document window and the underlying HTML in the other half (against a yellow background, a not-so-subtle reminder that you can't edit code in this view). Click an interactive element in Live view, and Dreamweaver highlights the relevant HTML in pink to help you zero in on the code responsible for dynamically created pages.

Here's an example: Figure 7-20 shows three views of the same page. At the top, you see the page in Dreamweaver's Split view with the HTML on the left and the page displayed in Live view on the right. The <h1> heading (circled) is programmed to change when a visitor interacts with it, but you can't tell that from this view. In the middle view, you have Live Code turned on, and you see that the <h1> tag has an inline style:

```
style="cursor: pointer; "
```

When a browser loads this page, it also runs a JavaScript program that rewrites parts of the page's HTML. In this case, it adds the inline style above to the <h1> heading, and changes the cursor to a pointing finger whenever you point to the heading. You can see the rewritten code in Live Code (Figure 7-20, middle), and see the cursor change in Live view when you point to the heading. When you actually *click* the heading (instead of just pointing to it), JavaScript rewrites your HTML again. In this case, it changes the heading to read "Got clicked."

This is a simple example, but the ability to rewrite HTML and CSS on the fly is extremely powerful. You can change the color, size, position, and appearance of any element on a page through inline styles or by assigning classes and IDs to the element on the fly. PHP scripts rewrite pages, too. They'll often use server-side includes (page 928), where your web server builds just-in-time pages by adding code blocks stored in separate files. Using Live Code, you can see the actual instructions web browsers follow to display the page to your visitors. Without being able to see that final HTML, it's difficult to troubleshoot a problem.

And if you're not a JavaScript programmer? You might still have an interest in Live Code if you use someone else's JavaScript code or a program you found online, like one of the many marvelous jQuery plug-ins for web pages (*http://plugins.jquery. com*). Using Live Code, you can see the HTML and any class and ID names it creates. Looking at JavaScript-generated HTML, it's pretty easy to figure out some of the CSS that formats the page, such as class styles (page 114), ID styles (page 114), and descendent selectors (page 398).

TIP Pressing the F6 key freezes any currently running JavaScript program, so you can make a drop-down menu "stick" in place when you point to it. It's like freezing the entire page, and it's great for working with Live Code, since you can freeze a dynamic rollover effect and see how the JavaScript programming affects the HTML of the page.

■ Adding Tags with the Quick Tag Editor

Code view is great when you really need (or want) to jump into the trenches and fine-tune your HTML. But if you're aesthetically oriented, you probably spend most of your time in Design view, enjoying the pleasures of its visual authoring environment.

Occasionally, however, you want to dip into the HTML pond, especially when you need to use some HTML that's unavailable from the Insert panel. You might wish you could type out a quick HTML tag on the spot, right there in Design view, for example, without having to make the mental and visual shift to Code view.

That's what Dreamweaver's Quick Tag Editor (Figure 7-21) is all about—it lets you tweak the underlying HTML while remaining in Design view. To see the Quick Tag Editor, press Ctrl+T (⌘-T) in Design view—or, if you're feeling especially menu-driven, choose Modify→Quick Tag Editor.

FIGURE 7-21

The Quick Tag Editor lets you insert new tags (top), edit old ones (middle), or wrap a new tag around a selection (bottom). If the Quick Tag Editor window blocks part of the page you're editing, drag it out of the way.

Depending on what you select in the document window, the Quick Tag Editor opens one of three windows:

- **Insert HTML**. If you haven't selected anything in the document window, you see this window. It inserts a new tag on the page.

- **Edit tag**. Lets you edit the tag of whatever element you select in the document window (a graphic, for example). You can also edit all of that element's properties.

- **Wrap tag**. If you select a swath of text or other objects (like two images), the editor opens this window, which lets you easily wrap a tag around your selection.

> **TIP** You can cycle through Quick Tag windows by repeatedly pressing Ctrl+T (⌘-T).

Using the Quick Tag Editor

You can type tag names, properties, and property values directly into the Quick Tag Editor. If you're editing a selected tag, you can change any of the properties listed, and even add new ones. When you're done, press Enter (Return). The Quick Tag Editor closes, and the changes take effect.

To make all this even easier, the Quick Tag Editor sports a helpful list—called *tag hints*—of HTML tags and properties for your selection pleasure. It's much like Code view's Code Hints (in fact, in the Preferences window, the Code Hints category also controls tag hints). The Insert HTML window displays a list of available tags, for example (Figure 7-21, top). Use the up and down arrow keys or the scroll bar to move through the list, or type in the first few letters of a tag or property, and Dreamweaver jumps to the nearest match. To choose the highlighted tag, press Enter (Return). Dreamweaver adds that tag or property name to the Quick Tag Editor. If you select a tag property, Dreamweaver inserts the tag into your document.

> **TIP** When you edit an existing tag in the Quick Tag Editor, press Tab to select the next property or property value. Shift+Tab selects the *previous* property or value.

■ Comparing Versions of a Web Page

Sometimes you make a change to a page, save it, preview it, close it, and move along to the next assignment for the day. Only later, when you take a second look at your day's changes before moving pages to your web server, do you see that one of them has a problem you didn't notice before. Perhaps the left sidebar is suddenly wider than it used to be. Since you already closed the file, you can't use the Undo command to reverse whatever pesky mistake you made. You could, of course, retrieve the current version of the page from the server, thus overwriting your changes. But what if you did a lot of good work on the page—added text, graphics, and links—that you don't want to lose? Ideally, you'd like to see all the changes you made to the page, and selectively undo the mistake you accidentally introduced.

Enter the Compare File command. With it, you can compare two files and identify lines of code that differ between them. This tool is a perfect solution for problems like the sidebar mentioned above. Compare the local file (the one with the messed-up sidebar) with the remote file (the live version of the page that works, but lacks your most recent edits). You can then identify any changes you made and smoke out your mistake. Before you can tackle that, you need to download and install a file-comparison program and then tell Dreamweaver where to find it. Fortunately, you have to do the installation and setup only once.

Downloading and Setting Up Diff Tools

Dreamweaver doesn't actually have a built-in file-comparison program. Instead, it passes the files to a separate file-comparison utility (often called a *diff tool*, since it identifies *differences* between files). Before you can use Dreamweaver to compare files, you need to download one of these programs, and you have a lot to choose from. Fortunately, several are free for both Windows and Mac PCs (see the following boxes for suggestions).

After you download and install the file-comparison utility, you need to tell Dreamweaver where to find it:

1. **Open Dreamweaver's Preferences panel by choosing Edit→Preferences (Dreamweaver→Preferences) or pressing Ctrl+U (⌘-U), and then click the File Compare category.**

   There's not much to this Preferences category, just a single box and a Browse button.

2. **Click Browse, and then navigate to and select the file-comparison program.**

   For example, on Windows PCs you might find your utility at *C:\Program Files (x86)\WinMerge\WinMergeU.exe*.

WINDOWS ONLY

Getting Your Hands on the Goodies

You can find lots of file-comparison tools for Windows. One commercial product, Beyond Compare from Scooter Software (*www.scootersoftware.com*), costs $30 and offers a range of comparison options.

But for a free alternative that provides all the basics you need, check out WinMerge. Go to *http://winmerge.org* and click Download Now. At this point you may be asked to save the file to your computer. Of course, if you're using Internet Explorer, one of those orange "Warning, warning, enemy attack" banners appears—you need to click Save (to download the file) or Run (to download the program and then run its installer).

Once you download WinMerge, the process of installing it is like that for most other Windows programs: Double-click the filename to launch an installer, and then follow the step-by-step instructions. You have several options along the way, but accept the suggested settings and you'll be fine.

Once you install WinMerge, you're ready to proceed as described below.

On Macs, the process is slightly different. Instead of selecting the text-editing program TextWrangler or BBEdit in Dreamweaver, you need to specify the proper diff tool, which is stored in a special location on your computer. Navigate to the */usr/local/bin* folder—*Macintosh HD→usr→local→bin* for most Macs—and select the correct file. For TextWrangler, it's *twdiff*; for BBEdit, it's *bbdiff*; and for FileMerge, it's *opendiff*.

3. **Click Apply and then click Close to close the Preferences window.**

   Dreamweaver has been notified of the utility's location, so you're ready to compare files.

Comparing Files from the Files Panel

The most common use of a diff tool is to see how a local file (one stored on your computer) differs from a file on your web server. You can start the process from Dreamweaver's Files panel. For example, to compare a local file called *about.html* with a file of the same name on the remote server, follow these steps:

What Difference Does It Make?

The Mac version of Dreamweaver supports only three file-comparison tools: File Merge (which is a Mac developer program that comes with the XCode tools on your Mac OS X installation disc), BBEdit (the powerful, $125 commercial text editor), and TextWrangler (the free little brother of BBEdit). Bare Bones Software (*www.barebones.com*) produces both BBEdit and TextWrangler, but since TextWrangler is free, it's the best place to begin.

Point your Web browser to *http://www.barebones.com/support/textwrangler/cmd-line-tools.html* and click any of the download links to save the program to your computer. As with many Mac applications, this download opens a disk image—which is just like a folder—with the program inside it. Just drag it to your Applications folder to install it.

1. **In the Files panel, choose "Local view."**

   The panel displays files stored on your computer.

2. **Right-click (Control-click) *about.html* and then, from the pop-up menu, select "Compare with Remote Server," as shown in Figure 7-22.**

   Dreamweaver does a little behind-the-scenes trickery before passing your files off to the file-comparison program. First, it creates a folder (if it doesn't already exist) named *_compareTemp* in the local root folder. Then it creates a temporary copy of the remote file and stores that in the new folder. As you can see, you're not actually comparing the live web page on your server with the local web page on your computer, you're comparing a *copy* of the remote file with a *copy* of the local file.

   Then your selected file-comparison program—for example, WinMerge or Text-Wrangler—starts up and compares the two files. If it finds no differences—if they're *exactly* the same—you'll most likely get a message saying something like "The selected files are identical." Your work is done. If there *is* a difference, the file-comparison program displays the two files and identifies the differences (see Figure 7-23 and Figure 7-24).

3. **Evaluate the differences, and incorporate any changes into your local file.**

   All file-comparison programs work the same way. As they compare two files, you see the code for each side by side. In addition, they highlight the differences in the code in some way. You can then review the differences and merge the changes into one of the files. For example, say you accidentally delete a table from your local file; a comparison of this file with the remote file shows the table intact in the remote file but missing from the local file. You can copy the table code from the remote file into the local file. If, however, you deleted the table from the local page purposefully, move on to evaluate the next difference.

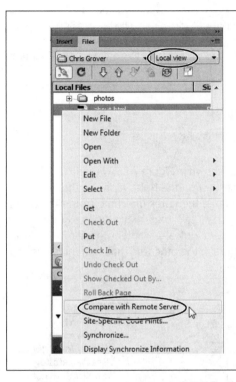

FIGURE 7-22

You start the file-comparison process by choosing a location from the Files panel, such as "Local view"(top circle), and then right-clicking (Control-clicking) a filename. From the menu that pops up, choose "Compare with Remote Server" (bottom circle). The steps for the rest of the comparison process vary depending on the diff tool you use.

You want to move changes in only one direction—from the temporary server file to your local file. That's because any changes you make to the temporary file have no effect on the live file on your web server. So how do you update the remote file? Make changes to your local file, save it, return to Dreamweaver, and then upload the local file to your web server. Then pour yourself a cup of tea and be thankful you don't have to do *that* very often.

4. **Save any changes to the local file, return to Dreamweaver, and then move your newly updated local file to your web server.**

    The exact process varies from program to program, but see the next sections for details on WinMerge and TextWrangler.

It's easy to get confused as you compare files, make changes, and then move the files between your computer and your web server. To introduce as little worry as possible, it helps to compare the files the same way each time. The steps above explain how to compare a local file to one on a server, save changes to the local file, and then upload those changes to the server. This is a good work path that helps prevent mistakes from going live on your website. But you aren't required to follow this path. You can, instead, start with a file on the remote server (by choosing

"Remote server" in step 1 on page 360). Then you can save changes to the file on your server. It works, but it's a bit riskier.

> **TIP** You can compare two files on your local hard drive (the home page of the site you're working on with a backup of the page you made last week, for example) if the two files are in the same site (perhaps you have a backup folder in your local root folder). Ctrl-click (⌘-click) to select the two files in the Files panel. Then, right-click and choose Compare Local Files from the pop-up menu.

Comparing Files with WinMerge

WinMerge is a popular diff tool for Windows PCs, in large part because it's free. Here's how it works.

WinMerge compares files side by side, as shown in Figure 7-23, with the first file you select (in this case, a file on the local server) on the right. It shows the file you're comparing it to on the left. In this example, the latter file came from the remote server. The Location Pane (far left) displays two bars that graphically represent the two files. A gold band in one of the bars indicates content that's missing from the other file. A gray band indicates where in the other file that content is missing.

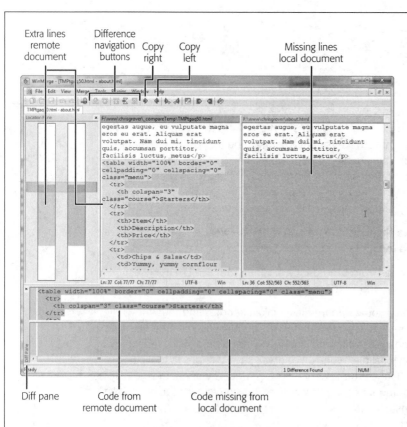

Extra lines remote document | Difference navigation buttons | Copy right | Copy left | Missing lines local document

Diff pane | Code from remote document | Code missing from local document

FIGURE 7-23

WinMerge includes a kind of bird's-eye view of code differences in the far-left Location Pane. Here, the gold band marks a table that's present in the remote file, while the gray band marks the location in the local file where that table is missing. One click of the Copy Right button and you'll copy the missing table over to the locally stored file.

If you want to check every difference between the two files, start at the top of the diff report and choose Merge→Next Difference to work your way down through all the differences. Even better, use the "next diff," "previous diff," "first diff," and "last diff" buttons on the toolbar to navigate between the differences. As you review the differences, the two versions of your document scroll to the spot where those differences occur. WinMerge highlights the currently displayed difference in red and shows the nature of the difference in the Diff Pane below the files. You can now figure out which code you want to keep.

Once you zero in on a spot where the two versions differ, you can copy changes from the local file to the remote file or vice versa. For example, Figure 7-23 shows a table in the remote version of a file (left) that isn't in the local version (right). Choose Merge→Copy to Right, or just click the toolbar button as shown in the figure, to copy the table to the local file.

The next step is to save the changes you made using the File→Save command. You leave WinMerge and go back to Dreamweaver, which displays the warning "This file has been modified outside of Dreamweaver. Do you want to reload it?" Click Yes to accept the changes you just made.

Now you have a single file with all the elements you want in it. You just need to upload it to your web server. You do that in the Files panel by selecting the file and then clicking the "Put file to remote server" button. (See page 812 for the details on moving files to your web server.)

> **NOTE** WinMerge is a standalone program, so you can fire it up and run it like any other program on your Windows computer. That means you can use it to compare *any* two files on your computer. You can even use it to compare the contents of two folders.

Comparing Files with TextWrangler

TextWrangler is a standalone text editor for Macs. You download and install it as described in the box on page 360. Included in that package is a program called "twdiff" that is installed in a special location for tools. That means you won't find "twdiff" in your application folder, you'll find it in *Macintosh HD→usr→local→bin*.

> **NOTE** The popular program BBEdit is a more powerful version of TextWrangler, so this description works for that commercial program as well.

You start comparing files as usual, in Dreamweaver's Files panel. Choose a location, right-click (or Control-click) the file you want to check, and then choose the "Compare..." command from the pop-up menu. For example, you might set the location menu to "Local view," right-click *about.html*, and then choose "Compare with Remote Server." At this point, TextWrangler's diff tool starts up. It displays the first file you selected (in this example, the local file) on the right and the temporary file copied from the remote server on the left. It displays the differences between the two files and breaks out the problematic code in the Differences panel below the two pages (see Figure 7-24).

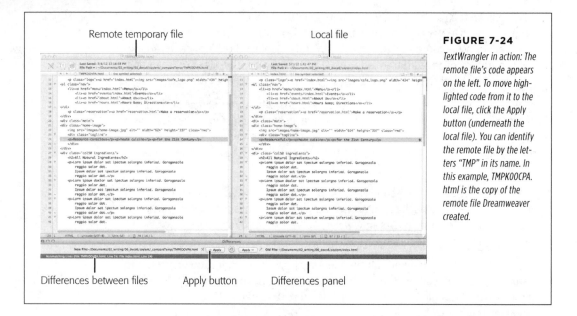

Remote temporary file   Local file

FIGURE 7-24

TextWrangler in action: The remote file's code appears on the left. To move high-lighted code from it to the local file, click the Apply button (underneath the local file). You can identify the remote file by the letters "TMP" in its name. In this example, TMPK00CPA.html is the copy of the remote file Dreamweaver created.

Differences between files   Apply button   Differences panel

TextWrangler tells you how the lines differ. For example, "Nonmatching lines" means the lines are similar (some of the code is the same) but not identical, while "Extra lines before line 678" means that one file uses a line of code that's completely different from the line of code in the other file.

In the Differences panel, double-click the anomaly you want to inspect. TextWrangler scrolls to the point of difference in both files. To make sure you catch all the differences, start at the top of the report and work your way down. If the code from the server file looks correct, click the Apply button to transfer the code from the remote file to your local file.

After you make changes to the local version of your file, choose File→Save, and then, choose File→Quit to leave TextWrangler and return to Dreamweaver. Once back in the comfortable environs of Dreamweaver, you see a message that says, "This file has been modified outside of Dreamweaver. Do you want to reload it?" Click Yes to accept your changes.

At this point, the "perfect" copy is your local file. It has all the correct code from the remote file, and all the correct code originally in the local file. If you don't have any other changes to make, you can upload the local file to your web server. You do that in the Files panel by selecting the file and clicking the "Put file to remote server" button. See page 812 for the details.

■ Finding References on Site-Building

When it comes to building websites, there's a lot to know. After all, HTML, Cascading Style Sheets, and JavaScript are filled with cryptic terms and subtle nuances. Dreamweaver used to provide a Reference panel to make your search for knowledge a little bit easier. Unfortunately, the references became outdated, and Adobe removed the Reference option from Dreamweaver CC.

But you can still find great references on the Web. Here are a few resources to get you started:

- For CSS help, SitePoint.com's free, online reference to CSS is great: *http:// reference.sitepoint.com/css*.

- For JavaScript, W3Schools.com provides an in-depth reference: *www.w3schools. com/jsref/default.asp*. For in-depth coverage in book format, check out *JavaScript & jQuery: The Missing Manual* (O'Reilly Media).

- For PHP, you can't beat the Source. The official PHP site has excellent documentation on every aspect of PHP: *www.php.net/manual/en*.

■ Tutorial: Building Pages in Live View

This tutorial focuses on building pages and editing HTML in Live view. That's something that previous versions of Dreamweaver couldn't do. To review how Live view editing works, flip back to page 351. To learn by doing, roll up your sleeves and follow the steps below.

This exercise shows you how to build a page from scratch, but you'll find some support material (images and a CSS file) in the Chapter07 folder of the Missing CD (see the Tip below).

TIP To complete this tutorial, you need to download sample files from this book's Missing CD page at *http:// oreilly.com/pub/missingmanuals/dreamweaverccmm2014*. (See the Note on page 37 for details.) The files you'll work on are in the Chapter07 folder, and the finished project for comparison is in the Chapter07_complete folder.

Once you download the tutorial files and open Dreamweaver, set up a new site as described on page 23. In a nutshell, choose Site→New Site. In the Site Setup window, type Working with HTML into the Site Name box. Click ▣ next to the Local Site Folder box, navigate to and select the Chapter07 folder inside the MM_DWCC folder, and then click Choose (Select). Finally, click OK.

Then, to build a page in Live view:

1. **Go to File→New. In the New Document window, click Blank Page, choose HTML, and then press Create. Save your page by choosing File→Save. Give it the name *ingredients.html*.**

   Dreamweaver opens a new page that appears to be empty. However, if you click the Code button, you see that the page includes several HTML tags, including <html>, <head>, and <body>. These are the basic building blocks of any web page.

2. **Position your cursor in the blank page in Design view, and then choose Live from the Design/Live view menu at the top of the document window.**

   You're now officially in Live view, but you're still gazing at a blank page. Next, you'll begin adding structural elements in the form of HTML tags with place-holder text. Later, you'll tweak the content.

3. **Go to the Insert panel and choose Structure from the drop-down menu at the top. Click the Div button.**

   A new HTML element shows up in Live view. A turquoise box appears on the screen with a tab that says "div." The placeholder text says "Content for New div Tag Goes Here." This first HTML block serves as a wrapper for all the other page elements you'll add—headings, paragraphs, and graphics. Later, you'll see how this wrapper makes it easy to format and position the contents of the page.

4. **With the <div> element selected, go to Insert→Structure→Header.**

   A positioning dialog box appears, asking you where you want to place the header in relation to the selected div tag. There are four options: Before, After, Wrap, and Nest.

5. **In the Positioning dialog box, click Nest.**

   The Nest option inserts the new tag inside the selected element (the <div>), which is exactly what you want. The new element appears at the top of the page. In fact, it looks like the header was placed above the <div>, because the <header> placeholder text appears above the placeholder text for the <div>. Actually, the <header> is nested inside the <div>. It's just placed at the top, with the <div> placeholder text below. The turquoise box has a tab that says "header" and the placeholder text reads, "Content for New header Tag Goes Here." The <header> tag is an HTML5 tag dedicated to (you guessed it) page headers. Later, you'll insert its partner, Footer.

TIP The <header> tag is a different beast from head*ing* tags like <h1>, <h2>, and so forth. You usually insert a header at the top of a web page to identify the page and its website. In addition, you'll often tuck a logo, company name, and maybe navigation tools in the header. You use *headings* (<h1>, <h2>, and so on) to place headlines above paragraph text.

Click the second line of text to select the <div> element again, and you see that its box surrounds the header, indicating that the header is indeed nested inside the opening and closing <div> tags. A quick look at Code view or Split view confirms this:

```
<div>
  <header>Content for New header Tag Goes Here</header>
Content for New div Tag Goes Here
</div>
```

6. **Now you'll add a headline for a paragraph that you'll insert in step 8. Back in Live view, click the first line of text to select the header, and then choose Insert→Structure→Heading: H1.**

   The positioning dialog box opens, giving you the choices Before, After, Wrap, and Nest.

7. **Choose After.**

   Dreamweaver inserts the placeholder headline's tag, <h1>, immediately after the <header> tag. Both are nested inside the <div> element. The <h1> element is selected after the insertion. You see the turquoise box wrapped around text that reads, "This is the content for Layout H1 Tag." It also shows a turquoise <h1> tab. You now have three elements on the page in Live view. You can click to choose any of them. For now, you'll keep adding elements.

8. **With <h1> selected, go to Insert→Structure→Paragraph, and then choose After from the positioning dialog box.**

   A paragraph and its placeholder text appear below the <h1> heading. Next, you'll add the bottom building block for the page, the footer.

9. **With the <p> (paragraph) element selected, choose Insert→Structure→Footer, and then choose After from the positioning dialog box.**

   Your page now has a footer, as shown in Figure 7-25. At this point, the content for the page consists entirely of placeholder text, and the formatting isn't likely to win a Webby award. But this is just the start. It's probably a good time to save the page (File→Save).

Each time you add an element to a page in Live view, Dreamweaver inserts tags and placeholder text. Usually, the tags come in pairs. For example, the paragraph element is made up of an opening <p> tag, followed by the placeholder text, "This is the content for Layout P Tag," followed by the closing </p> tag.

Next up, you'll change the placeholder content to something more useful.

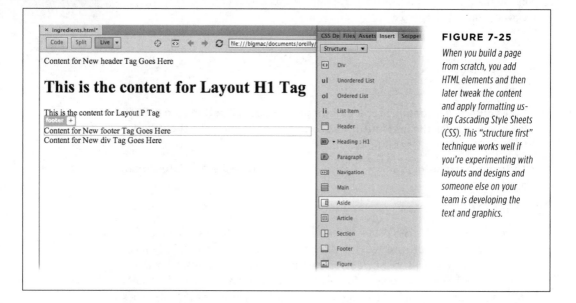

FIGURE 7-25

When you build a page from scratch, you add HTML elements and then later tweak the content and apply formatting using Cascading Style Sheets (CSS). This "structure first" technique works well if you're experimenting with layouts and designs and someone else on your team is developing the text and graphics.

Editing Pages in Live View

It's time to add some meaningful content to the page. You want to replace the placeholder text with something more substantial, starting with the header.

1. **Click the header, and then double-click the text.**

   Clicking the header produces the familiar turquoise box and the tab that reads "header." Double-clicking the text opens the element for editing. Often, you'll merely want to replace the text with your own words.

2. **Triple click the text, and then type *a place for people to eat*.**

   If you're not a fan of triple-clicking, you can press Ctrl+A (⌘-A) to select all the placeholder text.

3. **Click outside the header.**

   You leave edit mode. If you click a blank spot on the page, the header remains selected. If you click another element on the page, that other element is selected.

4. **Repeat the process to change the <h1> text to *Our Ingredients*.**

   The new heading appears on the page and, as with any respectable <h1> tag, the text is large.

5. **Edit the paragraph text.**

   By now you know the drill. Open the <p> element to edit it and then type the text you want. If you want, you can use the text in the *paragraph.txt* file in the Chapter07 folder. Open it in a text editor like Notepad or TextEdit, and then copy and paste it into the paragraph element.

6. **Edit the footer, changing the text to *Copyright 2015, The Soylent Corporation*.**

   Your last task is to remove the placeholder text from the <div> element.

7. **Click the text that reads, "Content for New div Tag Goes Here." Double-click the text to open the <div> element for editing. Then, carefully, delete the words.**

   The <div>'s placeholder text is helpful when there's no other content in the <div>, but now that the <div> contains a header, footer, <h1> heading, and a paragraph, the placeholder isn't necessary. If you need to select the <div> for editing purposes later, use the Tag Selector at the bottom of the document window or Element Quick View (View→Element Quick View).

Now your page has real text as opposed to placeholder text. The next step is to place a couple of images on the page.

Inserting Images in Live View

When you work in Live view, the steps for adding graphics are almost identical to those for adding other page elements. Here you'll insert one image in the header section of the page and another between the <h1> heading and the paragraph.

1. **Click the header text, which now reads "a place for people to eat." In the Insert panel's category menu, choose Common, and then click Image: Image.**

   Dreamweaver displays the positioning dialog box, asking where you want to place the image relative to the header. You want the image inside the header, appearing before the text, which will serve as a tagline.

2. **In the positioning dialog box, click Nest.**

   The Select Image Source window appears. This is the standard window you see when you need to identify a file. The banner graphic you need is in the Images folder.

3. **If necessary, click the Site Root button, select *cafe_logo.png* from the Images folder, and then click Open.**

   The logo for Cafe Soylent Green appears in the header. It looks a little faint and awkwardly placed at the moment, but you'll fix that next.

4. **Double-click the text "a place for people to eat." Position your cursor between the logo and the letter "a" and then press Enter (Return).**

This puts the logo and the text on separate lines by creating two paragraphs. Now the <img> tag is in one paragraph and the text is in a separate paragraph. It looks a little better. You'll fine-tune the look later, using CSS.

5. **Click the paragraph following the <h1> heading and then select Insert→ Common→"Image : Image."**

The positioning dialog box appears, as shown in Figure 7-26. The Before option will place the image between the heading (<h1>) and the paragraph.

FIGURE 7-26

Use the positioning dialog box to place your images before, after, or nested inside of another element. Here you selected a paragraph; if you select Before from the dialog box, Dreamweaver positions the image above the paragraph.

6. **Click Before.**

The Select Image Source window opens.

7. **Select *special1.jpg* in the Images folder, and then click Open.**

An image of a scrumptious Soylent Green delicacy appears in your web page. You placed this image between the heading and the paragraph text, and like those elements, as well as the header and footer, it sits inside the <div>.

8. **Go to File→Save.**

You saved all the work you did in the single file *ingredients.html*. In the next part of the tutorial, you'll attach an external Cascading Style Sheet.

At this point, the text and graphics for the page are complete, but it still looks pretty homely. You'll remedy that now.

Applying CSS to Your Web Page

As explained in Chapter 3, web experts consider it a best practice to keep content separate from formatting. That's done very efficiently when you build pages in Live view, as shown in this tutorial. As you can see from your page at this point, the content is there, but it desperately needs some formatting. You'll take care of that rather quickly by attaching a previously developed style sheet.

1. **With your page open in Live view, go to CSS Designer (Window→CSS Designer).**

   CSS Designer has four sections: Sources, Media, Selectors, and Properties. For this task, you'll work in the Sources section.

2. **In the Sources section, click + in the top right.**

   A pop-up menu appears showing three options: Create A New CSS File, Attach Existing CSS File, and Define in Page.

3. **Choose Attach Existing CSS File.**

   This opens the Attach Existing CSS File window, where you identify the file you want to attach and choose the manner for using it on your page (Figure 7-27).

4. **Click Browse.**

   The Select Style Sheet File window opens. It looks similar to all the other "file finder" windows in Dreamweaver.

FIGURE 7-27

You can use the Link option to attach an external CSS style sheet to your web page. When you use the Import option, Dream-weaver copies the CSS rules in the style sheet and stores them in the head section of your HTML document.

5. **Navigate to the tutorial's Chapter07 folder and then choose *live_build. css*. Leave the "Relative to" menu set to Document, and then click Open.**

   The Select Style Sheet File window closes, and you're back in the Attach CSS File window.

6. **Leave the "Add as" option set to Link and then click OK.**

   The Link option links your web page (the HTML file) to the CSS file using a single line of code that appears in the <head> of the document:

   ```
   <link href="live_build.css" rel="stylesheet" type="text/css">
   ```

Using this link, your web page can find the styles that format the header, footer, paragraphs, and images. The results are dramatic, as the style sheet applies backgrounds and formats the text on the page. In the next steps, you'll apply classes to elements in Live view.

Applying Classes to Page Elements in Live View

In the Sources section of CSS Designer, click *live_build.css*. You'll see a list of selectors in the Selectors section. The three selectors preceded by periods (.) are classes. The other selectors are HTML elements like <h1> and <p>. Once you link *live_build. css* to your web page, the HTML elements there adopt that file's style rules. That's not the case with classes, however. Before the CSS file can style classes, you need to add them to specific elements on the page. In the next steps, you'll add the *.wrapper* class to the page's <div> element. That will position all the elements in the <div>, applying a fixed width and centering the contents in the browser window. Then, you apply the *.tagline* class to, you guessed it, the tagline. That positions the tagline in relation to the cafe logo. As a final touch, you'll apply the *.floatright* class to the image between the heading and the paragraph. That pushes the image to the right edge of the <div> and lets the text wrap around it.

1. **Click any element on the page and then, in the Tag Selector at the bottom of the document window, click <div>.**

   Once you remove the placeholder text for a <div>, as you did earlier (page 368), the Tag Selector is the easiest way to select a <div>. Once you do that here, you see the turquoise box wrapped around the header, footer, and everything in between. You also see "div" on the turquoise tab.

2. **Click the Add Class/ID (the + sign) button on the <div> tab.**

   A text box opens in the tab where you identify a class or an ID.

3. **Type a period (.) and pause for a second.**

   After you type the period, Dreamweaver displays a list of classes available to this web page, as shown in Figure 7-28. These are three classes defined in *live_build.css*: *.wrapper*, *.floatright*, and *.tagline*.

FIGURE 7-28

As you begin to type in a class or ID name, Dreamweaver prompts you with a list of previously defined styles. Just click a name to save yourself a bit of typing.

4. **Click .wrapper.**

The contents of your page takes a major shift to the right as the style sheet sets the page width and margins.

5. **Click the text "a place for people to eat," and then click the Add Class/ID button (+) on the <p> tab. Type a period, and then choose .tagline from the list of classes.**

The .tagline class positions the tagline text so that it lines up with the text in the logo. The tagline CSS style uses margin properties, including a negative top margin, to put the line in just the right spot.

6. **Click the image between <h1> and the paragraph. Then click the Add Class/ID button (+) for <img>. Type a period and then choose .floatright.**

The styles for the .floatright class position the image and apply a border, and the paragraph text wraps around the image.

TIP You can apply more than one class to an element on a page. To do so, add the first class, click the Add Class/ID button again, and then identify the additional class (Figure 7-29). To remove a class or ID from an element, click inside the text box with the class or ID name. Then click the small *x* at the end of the name.

This chapter is about HTML rather than CSS, so you'll find the details for creating CSS styles in other parts of the book, especially Chapter 3, Introducing Cascading Style Sheets, and Chapter 9, Learning Advanced CSS Techniques. To get you pointed in the right direction for specific CSS topics, here's a roadmap:

- To apply background colors and images to elements, see page 252.

- To specify text properties using CSS, go to page 153.

- To apply margins so you can position elements, see page 465.

- To apply the CSS *float* property to images, go to page 248.

FIGURE 7-29

When your web page is complete, you can see that it uses a number of CSS rules to specify text properties, apply background colors and images, center the page contents, and position everything.

Finding and Replacing Text, Tags, and Code

At some point, you've probably encountered a find-and-replace tool in a word processing program. As its name implies, the feature *finds* a piece of text ("webmaster," for example) and *replaces* it with another piece of text ("webmistress"). Like Microsoft Word, Dreamweaver can search and replace text in the body of your web pages, but it offers a richer set of options, too, geared to the world of web-page creation. For example, you can search and replace HTML tags.

Dreamweaver also lets you find and replace text on *every* page of your site simultaneously, not just in the current, open document. In addition, you can *remove* every appearance of a particular HTML tag, or search and replace text that matches very specific criteria. For example, you can find every instance of the word "Aardvark" that appears within a paragraph styled with the class name *.animal*. These advanced maneuvers are some of the most powerful—and underappreciated—tools in Dreamweaver. If you learn how to use them, you can make changes to your pages in a fraction of the time it would take otherwise.

> **TIP** You can use Dreamweaver's "Find and Replace" feature to search an entire site's worth of files. This is powerful, but it can also be slow, especially if some folders hold files you don't want to search—like old archive files. Fortunately, you can hide files from the "Find and Replace" tool using Dreamweaver's Cloaking feature (see page 818 for details).

■ "Find and Replace" Basics

To start a search, you need to be in Design view, so make sure you have the Design/ Live drop-down menu (above the document window) set to Design. Then, press

Ctrl+F (⌘-F), or choose Edit→"Find and Replace." The "Find and Replace" window opens (see Figure 8-1). Now all you have to do is fill in the blanks and set your options.

NOTE You can use any of the pages you created from the tutorials in this book to hone your find-and-replace skills. If you skipped the tutorials (take a time out!), you can download a sample file from this book's Missing CD page at *http://oreilly.com/pub/missingmanuals/dreamweaverccmm2014*. (See the Note on page 37 for details.) For a page perfect for find-and-replace practice, open *about.html* in the Chapter04_complete folder, and then search the placeholder text.

FIGURE 8-1

Dreamweaver's "Find and Replace" tool lets you replace text and HTML code quickly and accurately. By using the Save Query and Load Query buttons, you can even save complex searches and reuse them later.

Whether you perform a simple text search or a complex, tag-based search-and-replace, you use the "Find and Replace" feature the same way. First, you need to tell Dreamweaver *where* to search (within highlighted text on a page, for example, or in a file, a folder, or across your website). Next, tell it *what* to search for (text, HTML, or a particular tag with a specific attribute). Finally, specify the replacement item. (This last step is optional; you can use "Find and Replace" simply as a way to locate an item on a page or on your site, without changing the item to anything.)

TIP After you enter the "Find and Replace" criteria, click the Save Query button (see Figure 8-1). A Save dialog box appears where you type in a name for your query. Dreamweaver saves it as a .dwr ("Dreamweaver replace" query) file. (If it's a query you'll use for a particular site, you might want to save it with that site's files.) To reuse a query, click the Load Query button in the "Find and Replace" window and locate the .dwr file. Then click any of the four action buttons—Find Next, Find All, Replace, or Replace All.

■ Searching Text and HTML Markup

Dreamweaver can search all the source code in a page or focus on just the text in the document window. Here's the difference:

- Source code searches let you find and replace any code on a page, including words, letters, and symbols. This means *anything* you see in Code view, such as HTML, CSS, or the server-side programming used to create the dynamic websites described in Part Six of this book. Code searches are the only type of search Dreamweaver allows on non–web page files, such as external JavaScript files or external CSS files.

- Text searches are more refined. They only look for text that appears within the <body> element of a page. That is, Dreamweaver ignores HTML tags, properties, and comments when it executes a text search—in short, it ignores anything that doesn't appear as actual words in the document window. By using a text search when you want to change the word "table" to "elegant wood table," for example, you won't accidentally change the useful HTML <table> tag into a browser-choking <elegant wood table> tag.

If you've used the "Find and Replace" feature in other programs, the process will seem familiar. The degree to which you can refine a search is unique to Dreamweaver, however.

Phase 1: Set the Scope of Your Search

In Dreamweaver, select Edit→"Find and Replace" to open the "Find and Replace" window. Using the "Find in" drop-down menu (see Figure 8-2), choose any of these search options:

- **Selected Text**. Searches only the highlighted section of the page you're working on. You might find this useful if you're working in Code view and you want to search the code in just a certain part of the page, like the head section of a document. But it also comes in handy if you have a large HTML table full of data, and you want to search and replace just the content inside that table—you'd select the table (for example, click <table> in the Tag Selector [see page 7] or use any of the techniques described on page 284), and then choose the Selected Text option from the drop-down menu.

- **Current Document**. Searches the web page you're working on.

- **Open Documents**. Searches all currently open Dreamweaver documents, handy if you're working on a bunch of pages at once and you realize you made the same typo on each.

- **Folder**. Searches all the web pages in a particular folder. Dreamweaver also searches web pages in all the folders *within* the selected folder. You can use this option to search pages that aren't part of the current site.

- **Selected Files in Site**. To use this option, open the Files panel and then select the files you want to search in the Local Files list (see page 24 for details).

- **Entire Current Local Site**. Searches every web page in the current site folder, including pages in folders *inside* the site folder. This option is invaluable when you need to change a basic piece of information throughout your site. If your company hires a new boss, for instance, you can replace every instance of "Mark Jones" with "Joe Smith."

NOTE Using the "Find and Replace" command is one of the best ways to quickly make changes to an entire site, but it's also one of the easiest ways to wreck a site's worth of web pages. Dreamweaver *can't undo* "Find and Replace" changes to files that aren't open when you execute the command. So be careful. If you plan to make extensive changes, back up your files first!

FIGURE 8-2

The search that the "Find and Replace" command executes isn't limited to the current document. You can also search multiple web pages, or even an entire site.

Phase 2: Specify What to Search For

For your next trick, you'll tell Dreamweaver what you want to search for. Use the "Find and Replace" window's Search pop-up menu to choose one of these two options:

- **Text**. This makes Dreamweaver search for a certain word or phrase that appears in the <body> section of the documents you specify. Type the text you want to find in the Search field. To search for text using wildcard characters, enter a *regular expression* here and turn on the "Use regular expression" checkbox. (See the box on page 386 to learn about regular expressions.)

- **Source Code**. Basic text searches are useful, but they're limited to text that appears in the body of a page (what you see in the document window). To search and replace *code*, you need the Source Code option.

  Source code searches work identically to text searches, except that Dreamweaver searches *everything* within a file—text, HTML, JavaScript, CSS, and so on—and replaces any part of the file. Using this option, you could search for any instance of the tag <img src="mark_jones_photo.jpg">, for example, and replace it with <img src="joe_smith_photo.jpg">. (If you're in Code view when you initiate a search, Dreamweaver automatically selects the Source Code option.)

  As you fill in the Find box, be aware that some plain-English words are also special words in HTML, JavaScript, or CSS. If you replace *table* with *desk* using a source-code "Find and Replace" command, for instance, you'll destroy any <table> tags on the page.

  Just as you can search for patterns within text (page 375), so you can search for patterns in your source code (see the box on page 382).

Phase 3: Provide Replacement Text

To change the text that Dreamweaver finds, type the replacement text into the Replace box. It may be the word or words you want to swap in (for a text search), or actual HTML code (for a source-code search).

TIP Dreamweaver won't let you create a new line in the Search or Replace boxes—you can't, for example, replace one line of HTML with two lines of HTML, at least not in the normal way. That's because, when you hit the Enter key to add the second line, Dreamweaver executes the search instead. To add another line, use Shift-Enter (Shift-Return).

If you just want to find text without replacing it, skip this step and use Find Next or Find All, described in Phase 5 next.

Phase 4: Choose the Search Settings

Dreamweaver gives you three options to govern its search and replace, some quite complex:

- The **Match Case** option limits the Find command to text that exactly matches the case (upper- and lowercase) of the text in the Search field. If you search for the text *The End* with the Match Case checkbox turned on, Dreamweaver finds a match in "The End is near," but not in "You're almost at the end." Use this trick to find every instance of *Web* and replace it with *web*, for example.

- **Match Whole Word** searches for an entire word—not a portion of a larger word. With this option turned on, a search for *Rob*, for example, matches only "Rob," and not any parts of "Robert," "robbery," or "problem." If you don't select this option, Dreamweaver stops on all four instances of "rob." This could cause serious problems if you also *replace* "Rob" with something like "Bob" (unless, of course, you've come up with a new word for thefts committed by people named Bob: Bobbery). Note that if you selected the Match Case option here, Dreamweaver matches *Rob* in "Rob" and "Robert," but *not* in "robbery" and "problem," since they don't include a capital R.

- The **Ignore Whitespace** option treats multiple spaces, tabs, nonbreaking spaces, and carriage returns as single spaces during a search. For instance, if you search for *the dog* with this option turned on, Dreamweaver matches "the dog" as well as "the   dog"—even if the multiple spaces are actually the HTML nonbreaking space character, * * (see page 81).

NOTE Note to Mac users: Unfortunately, in the Mac version of Dreamweaver, the "Find and Replace" function doesn't treat nonbreaking space characters as spaces, so if you have *the dog* in your HTML and search for *the dog* with the Ignore Whitespace box checked, Dreamweaver will report no matches.

Unless you have a good reason, always leave this option turned on. The HTML of a page can contain lots of extra spaces, line breaks, and tabs that don't appear in a web browser or in Dreamweaver's document window. For example, in the HTML of a document, it's possible to have two lines of code that look like this:

```
<p>This sentence will appear on one
line in a Web browser.</p>
```

Even though this text would appear on a single line in the document window, a search for "one line" *without* the Ignore Whitespace box turned on would find no match—the carriage return after "one" is not an exact match for the space character in "one line."

NOTE You can't turn on the Ignore Whitespace option when you have the "Use regular expression" checkbox turned on.

- The **Use regular expression** option lets you use wildcard characters in a search. For a discussion of this advanced technique, see the box on page 386.

Phase 5: Take Action

Finally, you're ready to set the search in motion by clicking one of four buttons in the "Find and Replace" window (see Figure 8-1):

- **Find Next** locates the next instance of your search term. If you're searching the current document, Dreamweaver highlights the matching text. If you're searching an entire website or a folder of pages, Dreamweaver opens the file *and* highlights the match. You can cycle through each instance of the search term by clicking this button repeatedly.

TIP As in other programs (notably Microsoft Word), you can press Enter to repeat the Find Next function. If you click in the document window—or even close the Find window—you can press F3 (⌘-G) to repeat the command.

- **Find All** locates every instance of the search term and lists them under the Search tab of the Results panel (Figure 8-3). The name and location of each file (if you searched multiple files) appear to the left, and the matched text appears to the right. Dreamweaver displays part of the sentence in which the matched word or words appear, and it underlines the exact match with a squiggly red line, so you can see the search term in context.

  Unlike the Find Next action, Find All doesn't automatically open any of the web pages containing matches. To open a matched page and highlight the matches, double-click its filename in the results list.

- **Replace** locates the next instance of the search term and replaces it with the text in the Replace field, leaving the replaced text highlighted for your inspection.

  You can use this button in combination with Find Next to selectively replace text. First, click Find Next. Dreamweaver locates and highlights the next match.

To replace the text, click Replace. Otherwise, click Find Next to search for the next match, and repeat the cycle. This cautious approach lets you supervise the replacement process and avoid making changes you didn't intend.

- **Replace All** is the ultimate power tool. It finds every instance of the search term and replaces it with the text in the Replace box. Coupled with the "Find in Entire Local Site" option, you can quickly make site-wide changes (and mistakes—so back up all your files before you click Replace All!).

  When you click this button, Dreamweaver warns you that it can't undo this operation on any closed files. You can erase mistakes you make with "Find and Replace" in *open* documents by choosing Edit→Undo in each document, but Dreamweaver *permanently* alters closed files that you search and replace. So be careful!

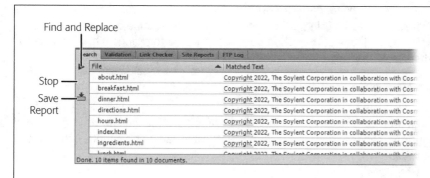

FIGURE 8-3

In the panel that displays the results of a search, click the arrow button to reopen the "Find and Replace" window. The Stop button becomes active when you run a search. Click it to abort the current search (when you inadvertently search for "the" in a 10,000-page website, for example). You can also save a rather useless XML file that reports the results of the search (but remember the old adage: Just because you can, doesn't mean you should).

TIP Before you take the plunge and click Replace All, it's a good precautionary step to click Find All first and then preview the results in the Results panel (Figure 8-3). That way, you can be sure that you're going to change exactly what you *want* to change.

If you use the Find All or Replace All commands, the "Find and Replace" window closes, and the results of your search appear in the Search tab (see Figure 8-3). You can reopen the window—with all your previous search criteria still in place—by clicking the green arrow (called the "Find and Replace" button), but only if you haven't selected anything else first—like text on a page.

■ Creating Advanced Text Searches

For greater control over a text search, use the "Find and Replace" command's *advanced* text search option, which lets you hunt down text either inside or outside a specific tag.

For example, when Dreamweaver creates a new blank document, it sets the page's *title* property to *Untitled Document*. Unfortunately, if you forget to change the name, your site will quickly fill up with untitled web pages. A basic text search doesn't identify this problem, because it searches only the <body> portion of a page, and titles appear in the <head> section. And a source-code search for *Untitled Document* would turn up the words "untitled document" *wherever* they appeared in the page, not just inside the <title> tag.

In cases like this, an advanced text search is your best choice. You set the "Find and Replace" command to search for *Untitled Document* whenever it appears within the <title> tag. To search using this technique, follow the routine described above, but before you click one of the action buttons, you need to change a few more things in the dialog box.

Limiting a Search by Tag

To see "Find and Replace's" expanded controls, choose Text (Advanced) from the Search drop-down menu (see Figure 8-4). Now, from the menu next to the + and – buttons, choose either Inside Tag or Not Inside Tag. For example, consider this line of code:

```
Stupid is as <strong>stupid</strong> does.
```

The first instance of "stupid" sits outside the <strong> tag, but the second instance is inside it. Depending on your choice on the Inside Tag/Not Inside Tag menu, Dreamweaver will highlight one of these words when you search for "stupid."

FIGURE 8-4

Use an advanced text search to limit your pursuit to words that appear within a particular HTML tag. Conversely, you can search for text that doesn't appear within a tag.

NOTE A more descriptive name for Inside Tag option is *Enclosed by* Tag. Dreamweaver executes tag searches by examining the text between opening and closing tags. In fact, a text search using the Inside Tag option doesn't literally identify text inside the brackets of a single tag, it searches the text between opening and closing tags. For example, searching for "Aliens" inside an <img> tag—<img src="ufo.jpg" alt="Aliens live among us.">—won't work. The <img> tag has no closing tag, and Dreamweaver doesn't search inside the angle brackets of a single tag, so it won't find the *alt* text. But a search for "Aliens" between opening and closing <strong> tags—<strong>Aliens live among us.</strong>—would work. In the first example, *Aliens* appears as part of the <img> tag, while in the second, *Aliens* is enclosed by the opening and closing <strong> tags.

Once you specify whether you're looking for text inside or outside a tag, you can choose that tag from the Inside Tag/Not Inside Tag drop-down menu (Figure 8-4). The menu lists all HTML tags, not just those with both an opening and a closing tag. So the image tag (<img>) appears here, even though Dreamweaver won't search for text inside it.

TIP A great way to search for text in both the title and the body of a web page is to choose the Inside Tag option and then select "html" from the Tag drop-down menu. That way, you can search for any text between the opening and closing <html> tags of the page—which, since those tags start and end any web document, is *all* the text on the page. This trick is handy when you want to change text that might appear in the body *and* in the title section of a page (to change a company name, for example).

Limiting a Search by Attribute

To limit your search further, click + to launch the Tag Modifier menu (Figure 8-5). It offers six more options for your search:

- **With Attribute/Without Attribute**. To limit your search, you can specify that a tag either must have a specific property (*With Attribute*) or must not have that property (*Without Attribute*).

  For example, say the following lines of code appear throughout a site:

  ```
  <p>For assistance, please email<a href="mailto:mail@chia-vet.com">

  Chia Vet.</a></p>
  ```

  For the sake of argument, assume you need to change that line to read "For assistance, please email Customer Service." A basic find-and-replace search would incorrectly change the words "Chia Vet" to "Customer Service" *everywhere* on the site.

  However, an advanced text search using the With Attribute option lets you find the text "Chia Vet" wherever it appears inside an <a> tag whose *href* attribute is set to *mailto:mail@chia-vet.com*. That way, you tell Dreamweaver to replace "Chia Vet" with "Customer Service" in this case only, leaving all other instances of "Chia Vet" alone. (For tips on where to find more HTML references, see page 365.)

After you choose With Attribute, use the menu on the right to select *which* of the tag's properties you want to find. Dreamweaver automatically lists properties appropriate for the tag you specify. For example, if you search inside a <table> tag, Dreamweaver lists properties such as *align*, *background*, and *bgcolor*.

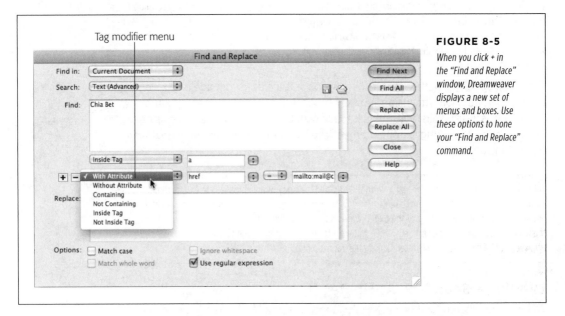

FIGURE 8-5

When you click + in the "Find and Replace" window, Dreamweaver displays a new set of menus and boxes. Use these options to hone your "Find and Replace" command.

Advance to the next drop-down menu to tell Dreamweaver how to compare your search term with what it finds on the page. Choose equal to (=), not equal to (!=), greater than (>), or less than (<). You'll only use the less than or greater than options when a property's value is a number, such as the *width* property of a table cell. For example, you could locate all the table cells wider than 100 pixels using the width > 100 parameter. And while you can compare values expressed as numbers, you can't compare values expressed as words—how do you evaluate one word against another? So the "Find and Replace" command has no effect on *center* in this code example:

```
<td align="center">
```

Finally, type the value of the property in the last box. If you were searching for a black-colored background, for example, you'd type *#000000* (the hex value for black).

You can also click the menu and choose "[any value]"—a useful option when you want to find tags that have a certain property, but you're not concerned with the property's value. For example, to find all <table> tags with a background color (no matter whether the color's #336699, #000000, or #FFFFFF), choose the *bgcolor* attribute and "[any value]."

- **Containing/Not Containing**. These options let you specify whether a tag contains or doesn't contain specific text or a particular secondary tag.

  When you choose this option, Dreamweaver displays a new set of boxes and menus. Choose either Text or Specific Tag from the drop-down menu to the right, and then, in the last box in the row, enter either type in some text or select a tag. For example, another (less error-proof) solution to the find-and-replace problem above would be to search for the text "Chia Vet" wherever it appears inside a <p> (paragraph) tag that *also contains* the text "please email."

- **Inside Tag/Not Inside Tag**. These last two choices let you specify whether a search term is inside—or not inside—a specific tag. For example, you can use these options to limit a search to text that appears within a <span> tag that itself is *inside* an <h1> tag. As the Note on page 383 explains, inside a tag actually means within the opening and closing tags. To search within the *brackets* of a tag, you need to search the "source code" not the "text." For details, see Phase 2 on page 378. For even more searching power within tags, use the advanced tag search features described in the next section.

If you like, you can add even more restrictions to your search by clicking + and specifying a second set of attributes. If you're really on a roll, you can add so many modifiers that the "Find and Replace" window grows past the bottom of your monitor. To remove a modifier, click –.

Creating Advanced Tag Searches

If you find the number of options an advanced text search offers overwhelming, you haven't seen anything yet. Dreamweaver's tag search adds even more choices to help you quickly search for, and modify, HTML tags. You can use a tag search to strip out unwanted HTML tags (for example, if you're migrating a very old site to CSS, you could remove the obsolete <font> tag), transform one tag into another (you could turn the old-style *bold* [<b>] tag into the more widely accepted *strong* [<strong>] tag), and perform a host of other powerful actions.

In its basic outline, a tag search is much like the text search described on page 376. But this time, you choose the Specific Tag option from the Search menu. Now, a Tag menu appears next to the Search menu, and the dialog box expands to display a new set of boxes and drop-down menus (see Figure 8-6). Some of them are the same as the controls you see with an advanced text search (page 382), such as the Tag Modifier menu and the + button that lets you refine the search.

Turbocharge Your Searches

If you want to find the phone number 555-123-5473 on your site, no problem: Just type *555-123-5473* into "Find and Replace's" Search field. But what if you want to find *every* phone number—555-987-0938, 555-102-8870, and so on—on a web page or across your site?

In such a case, you need to use a *regular expression*, the geeky name for a delightfully flexible search language that lets you use wildcard characters to search for *patterns* of text instead of actual letters or numbers. Each phone number above follows a simple pattern: three numbers, a dash, three more numbers, another dash, and four more numbers.

To search for a pattern, you use a variety of symbols combined with regular text characters to tell Dreamweaver what to find. For example, in the world of regular expressions, "\d" stands for "any number." To find three numbers in a row, you could search for \d\d\d, which would find 555, 747, 007, and so on. There's even shorthand for this: \d{3}. The number between the braces ({}) indicates how many times in a row the preceding character must appear to match. To search for phone numbers, then, you could use a regular expression like this:

\d{3}-\d{3}-\d{4}

The two \d{3}s finds three numbers, while the hyphen (-) following it is just the hyphen in the phone number, and \d{4} finds four numbers.

Here are some of the other symbols you'll encounter when using regular expressions:

- . (period) stands for any character, letter, number, space, and so on.

- \w stands for any letter or number (but not spaces, tabs, nonbreaking spaces, or line breaks).

- * (asterisk) represents the preceding character zero or more times (and is always used after another character). For example, the regular expression colou*r matches both "colour" and "color"—the * following the u indicates that the u is optional (it can appear zero times). This search term would also match "colouuuuur" (handy for those times when you've fallen asleep on the keyboard).

To see a complete list of regular-expression characters Dreamweaver understands, as well as a brief tutorial on regular expressions, visit *http://tinyurl.com/3zw4oj6*. For a quick reference, there's a great cheat sheet for regular expressions at *http://www.visibone.com/regular-expressions/*. A full-length discussion of regular expressions could—and does—fill a book of its own. Check out *Mastering Regular Expressions*, Third Edition (O'Reilly Media) (*http://oreilly.com/catalog/9780596528126*) or, for made-to-order regular expressions, visit the Regular Expression Library at *http://regexlib.com*. For an example of using regular expressions in Dreamweaver, see the box on page 386.

But a key difference here is the Action drop-down menu (Figure 8-7), which lets you specify the action Dreamweaver takes on tags that match the search criteria when you click Replace or Replace All. If you intend to search, but not replace, these options don't apply:

- **Replace Tag & Contents**. Replaces the tag and anything enclosed by the tag (including other tags) with whatever you put in the With box to the right of this menu. You can type or paste either text or HTML here.

- **Replace Contents Only**. Replaces everything enclosed by the tag with the text or HTML you specify. The tag itself remains untouched.

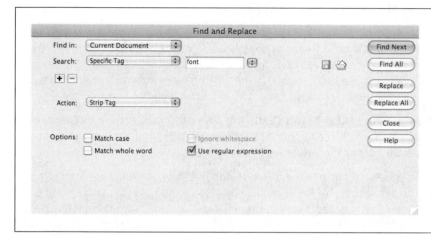

FIGURE 8-6

It's a snap to remove tags using the Specific Tag option with Dreamweaver's "Find and Replace" command—just select the Strip Tag action. This option is handy if you want to replace old-style text formatting with Cascading Style Sheets. Use it to strip out unwanted <font> tags from old sites, for example.

FIGURE 8-7

Once Dreamweaver finds a specific tag, it can perform any of 11 actions on the tag or its contents.

NOTE Dreamweaver doesn't offer "Find and Replace" options for all HTML tags. For example, the <img> tag has just an opening tag (<img>), not the opening and closing tags of, say, a paragraph (<p> and </p>). In cases like this, Dreamweaver doesn't offer the option to let you change the content between opening and closing tags because there are no tag pairs.

- **Remove Tag & Contents**. Deletes the opening and closing tags and *everything* inside them.

- **Strip Tag**. Deletes the tag from the page, but leaves anything enclosed by it untouched. The outmoded <font> tag is a perfect candidate for this action.

- **Change Tag**. Let's you swap one tag for another. This is the option to use if you want to change antiquated <b> tags to state-of-the-art <strong> tags.

- **Set Attribute**. Adds an attribute to the tag. For example, you could use this command to set the *alt* property of an image (see the tutorial on page 388).

- **Remove Attribute**. Removes an attribute from a tag. You could remove the not-at-all-useful *lowsrc* attribute from all image tags on your pages, for example. (Since you're dying to know, in the olden days of slow web connections, the *lowsrc* attribute provided faster-loading, low-resolution versions of images.)

- **Add Before (After) Start (End) Tag**. The last four actions in the menu offer variations on the same theme. Each lets you place content in a web page just before or after the tag for which you're searching.

To understand how this works, remember that most HTML tags come in pairs. The paragraph tag, for example, has an opening tag (<p>) and a closing tag (</p>). Say you search for a paragraph tag; you could add text or HTML *before* or *after* the start tag (<p>), or *before* or *after* the end tag (</p>). To see when you might use this feature, see the box on page 391.

■ Tutorial: Adding Alt Text Fast

You've just put the finishing touches on the last page of your brand-new, 1,000-page site. You sit back and smile—and then snap bolt upright when you notice you forgot to add an *alt* description for the site's banner graphic (see page 245). This graphic, called *site_banner.gif*, appears on every single one of those 1,000 pages. With rising dread, you realize you have to open each page, select the graphic, and add the *alt* attribute by hand. And then you remember Dreamweaver's advanced tag-based "Find and Replace" feature. So you press Ctrl+F (⌘-F) to open the "Find and Replace" window, and then you go to work.

NOTE For this tutorial, you can use any of the pages you created from the earlier tutorials in this book. If you skipped those tutorials, download a sample file from this book's Missing CD page at *http://oreilly.com/pub/missingmanuals/dreamweaverccmm2014*. (See the Note on page 37 for details.) For a page perfect for find-and-replace practice, open *about.html* in the Chapter04_complete folder, and then search the placeholder text.

Once you download the tutorial files and open Dreamweaver, set up a new site as described on page 23. In a nutshell, choose Site→New Site. In the Site Setup window, type Tables into the Site Name box. Click ▦ next to the Local Site Folder box, navigate to and select the Chapter06 folder inside the MM_DWCC folder, and then click Choose (Select). Finally, click OK.

1. **From the "Find in" menu, choose Entire Current Local Site.**

   You want to fix *every* page on your site (remember to make a backup first!).

2. **Choose Specific Tag from the Search drop-down menu, and then, from the drop-down menu to its right, choose "img."**

You start by identifying every image on your site (via the <img> tag).

3. **In the next row, use the three drop-down menus to choose With Attribute, "src," and the equal-to sign (=).**

This tells Dreamweaver to look for specific images—in this case, images with a *src* attribute (the path that tells a browser where to find the image) that has a specific value.

4. **Type .*site_banner\.gif in the box next to the = sign.**

For this exercise, assume you stored the graphics file in a folder called *images* located in the root folder of your site. The filename of the image is *site_banner. gif.* The .* is the magic "wildcard" that matches any text, and you'll see how it works in a moment (ditto the backslash hanging out before the second period).

5. **Click + .**

Dreamweaver displays another row of Tag Modifier menus.

6. **From this new row of menus, choose Without Attribute and "alt."**

You've further limited Dreamweaver's search to only those images that don't already have an *alt* attribute. (After all, why bother setting the *alt* property on an image that already has it?)

7. **From the Action menu, choose Set Attribute, and then, from the drop-down menu, choose "alt."**

You just told Dreamweaver to add an *alt* attribute if it finds an *alt*-less <img> tag that matches your search criteria.

In this example, you might type *Chia Vet* in the To box to specify the *alt* text you want Dreamweaver to add to the image.

8. **Turn on the "Use regular expressions" checkbox.**

Regular expressions, described on page 386, let you search for patterns of characters and, in this case, help you accurately identify the banner graphic everywhere it appears.

You know you're looking for the file *site_banner.gif* wherever it appears on your site. Unfortunately, if you type just *site_banner.gif* as the value of the *src* property in step 3, Dreamweaver can't find the file. That's because the *src* attribute—the part of the <img> tag that includes the location of the file—varies from page to page. Depending on where a page is relative to the graphic, the src path might be *site_banner.gif, images/site_banner.gif,* or even *../../../images/site_banner.gif.* What you need is a way to find every *src* attribute that ends in *site_banner.gif.*

A simple regular expression, .*site_banner\.gif, does the trick. The period stands for *any* character (6, g, or even %, for example), while the asterisk means "zero or more times." When you prepend these codes to the image filename, you instruct Dreamweaver to find every *src* value that ends in *site_banner.gif*.

In other words, .* matches *images/, ../../images/,* and so on. It even matches nothing at all, such as when the page actually sits inside the *images* folder; in that case, the *src* property is just *site_banner.gif.*

Note the backslash before the last period: \.*gif.* In the world of regular expressions, a period means "any character," so if you specified just *site_banner.gif* as the search term, Dreamweaver would not only match *site_banner.gif*, but also *site_banner1gif, site_bannerZgif,* and so on—in other words, any character that sits between *site_banner* and *gif.* The backslash tells Dreamweaver to treat the next character literally; it's just a period with no special regular-expression power.

The "Find and Replace" dialog box should now look like the one in Figure 8-8.

9. **Click Replace All and sit back.**

In a matter of moments, Dreamweaver updates all 1,000 pages of your site.

To test this out, you might try a more cautious approach first: Click the Find Next button to locate the first instance of the missing *alt* attribute, verify that it's correct by looking in the Search box (see Figure 8-8), and then click Replace to add the proper *alt* value. Double-check the newly updated page to make sure everything worked as planned. You can continue updating pages one at a time this way, or, once you're sure the search works correctly, press Replace All.

FIGURE 8-8

The numbers shown here correspond to the steps in this example, in which you want to add an alt attribute to every occurrence of the banner logo for the benefit of people who can't, or don't want to, see graphics in their browsers.

Convenient Copyright Notices

I want to add a copyright notice to the bottom of each page in my website. Is there a way to automate this process so I don't have to edit every page by hand?

You bet. Use Dreamweaver's "Find and Replace" command to add text or HTML to the bottom of any web page. The trick is knowing how to use the command's Specific Tag option.

First, choose Edit→"Find and Replace" to open the "Find and Replace" window. Next, choose Entire Current Local Site from the "Find in" menu, and then choose Specific Tag from the Search menu. Choose "body" from the Tag menu. Remember, the <body> tag in HTML encloses everything that appears inside a browser window—it's equivalent to what you see in the document window.

From the Action menu, choose Add Before End Tag. The end tag in this case is </body>. Since </body> marks the end of any content in a web page, whatever appears directly before this closing tag will appear at the bottom of the page (you can probably see where this is going).

In the text field next to the Action menu, type (or paste) the copyright notice you want on each page. (You may want to first design the copyright message using Dreamweaver, and then copy and paste the HTML into this field.)

Now, click Replace All. Dreamweaver handles the rest.

You may not want to put the copyright notice at the *very end* of a page's HTML, as in this example. You might want it to go inside a particular <div> tag that's already on the page. Say that that <div> has an ID of *footer*. You'd search for a <div> tag from the Tag menu and then click +. Then, in the next four drop-down menus, select "With attribute," "id," the equal-to sign, and, finally, "footer." Then you use either the Add Before End Tag or Add After Start Tag options to place the copyright notice either at the end or the beginning of that <div>.

TIP   To get a full description of every Dreamweaver menu, see Appendix B, "Dreamweaver CC 2014, Menu by Menu."

Building a Better Web Page

Learning Advanced CSS Techniques

C hapter 3 introduced you to the basics of Cascading Style Sheets. In other chapters, you learned how to use CSS to style links, navigation bars, text, and tables. You can go a long way in web design with those skills alone (and many people do), but to really become a web design expert, you should learn a handful of advanced CSS concepts. Fortunately, Dreamweaver includes tools to help you master these concepts so you can work more efficiently and avoid those head-scratching "Why the heck does my design look like that?!" moments. In addition, Dreamweaver CC includes a few approaches for adding shiny new CSS3 properties and a fun tool for adding basic CSS animations. (Even if you're not ready for some of the advanced CSS concepts discussed in this chapter, don't skip the section on CSS Transitions [page 425], because they're fun and easy to create.)

NOTE This chapter will help you on your journey from CSS novice to master. But keep in mind that it's the rare mortal who understands everything about CSS from reading a single chapter. If you really want to know the ins and outs of CSS, check out *CSS3: The Missing Manual* (O'Reilly Media).

■ Fine-Tuning Page Design with Advanced Selectors

It's pretty easy to learn how to use class, ID, and tag styles. Technically, however, these aren't really styles at all. In CSS lingo, they're *selectors*, instructions that tell a browser *what* page element to look for so it can apply CSS formatting. For example, a tag selector (not to be mistaken with Dreamweaver's time-saving selection tool, *the* Tag Selector) tells a browser to apply formatting to *any* instance of a particular tag on a page. Thus, browsers apply Heading 1 tag styles to *all* <h1> tags on a page. They apply class selector styles, on the other hand, only when they encounter an element in your HTML that has the right class name attached to it. Similarly, browsers apply ID selector styles to a tag with a matching ID, like *<body id="home">*. (Flip back to page 114 for a review of key differences between class and ID selectors.)

> **NOTE** For a detailed discussion of selectors, visit *http://tinyurl.com/29dnb4*.

But class, ID, and tag selectors are just the tip of the selector iceberg. CSS offers many other types of selectors, and they let you format even the smallest page element. In the past, Dreamweaver lumped these laser-focused selectors under the term *compound selectors* (a Dreamweaver term, not an official CSS term, so don't go using it at your weekly web designer get-togethers). Dreamweaver used the term to describe advanced selectors, such as the "pseudo-class" styles you use to format different link states (*a:link*, *a:visited*, *a:hover*, and *a:active*), as described on page 199, or the *descendent selectors* used with some JavaScript widgets, like JavaScript/jQuery menu bars (page 607). With its new CSS Designer (Window→CSS Designer), Dreamweaver is moving away from the term "compound selector"; these days you're more likely to see the program use the more common term "descendant selector."

The CSS arsenal includes a variety of advanced selectors—you'll find a few of the most common and useful ones mentioned below—but in Dreamweaver, you write all of them using the same three-step process:

1. **Choose or create a source for the CSS rule.**

   The source is the style sheet where your CSS rules live. If you were adding a style to your web pages, you could either start a new style sheet or use an existing one.

   Web browsers look up formatting rules in the source document. You can use an internal style sheet as the source document, which goes in the <head> section of a web page, or use an external style sheet, which is a separate .css file. If you're styling a page-in-progress, you may already have defined one or more sources. To add a new one, click + in CSS Designer's Sources section and select one of three options: create a new style sheet, attach an existing one, or define the style in your web page (in the <head> section, to create an internal style sheet). For a complete explanation of these choices, turn to page 118.

2. **Choose or create a selector.**

   You can use a class, ID, or tag as a selector. When you combine two or more selectors, you create a "descendant" selector. For example, Figure 9-1 shows a descendant selector that defines an anchor tag, listed as "a" in the selector. But the style rules apply only when that anchor tag is inside a list tag (<li>) that's inside an unordered list tag (<ul>) that's inside the body (<body>) of the page.

You create a selector like this by clicking the add selector button (+) and then typing the tags in the Selector text box. If you don't remember the exact name for each tag, in Design view, put your cursor inside the text you want to style or, to style an image or other media, select that media. Then, after you choose a source, click + . Dreamweaver suggests a descendant selector that targets the text or media file. You can edit Dreamweaver's suggestion however you want.

3. **Set values for the CSS properties.**

Highlight your selector in the Selectors section of CSS Designer, and Dreamweaver displays the selector's properties in the Properties section. When you turn on the Show Only Set Properties checkbox, you see only properties that have already been defined for that selector. To see *all* the properties available to a selector, leave this box unchecked. The result is a very long, scrolling list. Use the buttons at the top of the Properties section to jump to the properties for a page's layout, text, borders, and background. After styling a page or two, you'll become familiar with the location of the properties you use most often and you'll zip right to them.

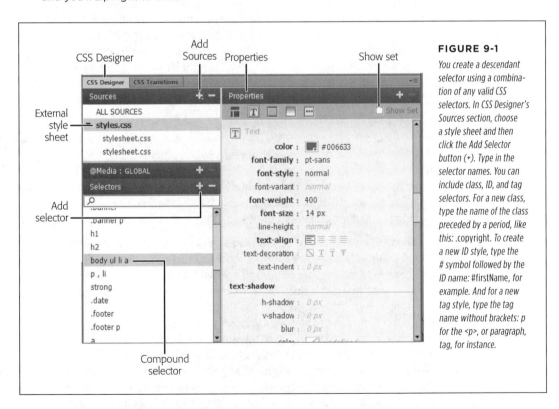

FIGURE 9-1

You create a descendant selector using a combination of any valid CSS selectors. In CSS Designer's Sources section, choose a style sheet and then click the Add Selector button (+). Type in the selector names. You can include class, ID, and tag selectors. For a new class, type the name of the class preceded by a period, like this: .copyright. To create a new ID style, type the # symbol followed by the ID name: #firstName, for example. And for a new tag style, type the tag name without brackets: p for the <p>, or paragraph, tag, for instance.

As described in the following sections, you use a different naming convention for each type of selector. The rest of the process for creating advanced styles works just like creating regular class or tag styles, and you edit and delete advanced styles the same way, too.

Descendent Selectors

Tag styles have their drawbacks. A tag style for the <p> tag, for example, makes simple work of formatting every paragraph on a page, but it's also indiscriminate. You may not *want* every paragraph to look the same.

Suppose you want to divide your web page into sections—a sidebar and a main content area, say—and use smaller text in the sidebar. You *could* create two class styles—such as *.sidebarText* and *.mainText*—and apply them to the appropriate paragraphs (*<p class="sidebarText">* for sidebar paragraphs, and *<p class="mainText">* for body text), but who has that kind of time?

What you really need is a "smart" tag style, one that understands its surroundings and formats an element based on where the element is on the page. Enter *descendent selectors*.

You use descendent selectors to format every instance of a particular tag (the same way tag selectors do), but only when those tags appear in a particular *part* of a web page. In effect, it's like saying, "Hey, you <a> tags in the navigation bar, listen up. I've got some formatting for you. All you other <a> tags, move along, there's nothing to see here." In other words, a descendent selector lets you format a tag based on its *relationship* to other tags. To understand how descendent selectors work, you need to delve a little more deeply into HTML.

Think of the HTML that forms any web page as a kind of family tree, like the one shown in Figure 9-2. The first HTML tag you use on a page—the <html> tag—is the grandpappy of all the other tags. In essence, when a tag is *inside* another tag, it's a *descendent* of that tag. In Figure 9-2, the text "wide range of topics" is bolded in the long paragraph. You get that format by applying a <strong> tag to that phrase. Because that bolded text sits inside a paragraph (inside a <p> tag, in other words), the <strong> tag is a descendent of the <p> tag—a descendent of that paragraph.

Descendent selectors let you take advantage of the HTML family tree by formatting tags differently when they appear inside certain other tags. For example, say you have an <h1> tag on your page, and you want to emphasize a word within that heading. One option is to select the word and press the B button on the Properties panel—that applies the <strong> tag to that word. The trouble is, most browsers boldface the words in headings anyway, so your visitors won't see any difference between the emphasized word and the other words in the headline. Creating a tag selector to change the <strong> tag's color and make it stand out from the headline isn't much of a solution—you end up changing the color of *every* <strong> tag on the page, even those inside paragraphs or lists. A descendent selector lets you do what you really want: Change the color of the <strong> tag *only when* it appears inside an <h1> tag.

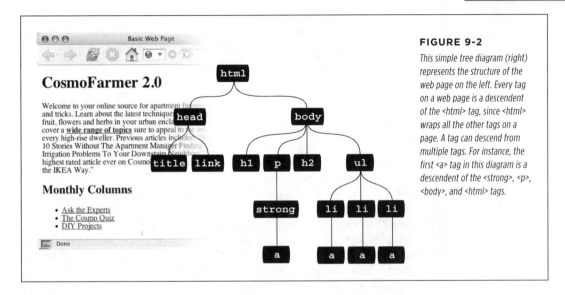

FIGURE 9-2

This simple tree diagram (right) represents the structure of the web page on the left. Every tag on a web page is a descendent of the <html> tag, since <html> wraps all the other tags on a page. A tag can descend from multiple tags. For instance, the first <a> tag in this diagram is a descendent of the <strong>, <p>, <body>, and <html> tags.

Creating descendent selectors isn't much more difficult than creating any other type of style. You follow the same three-step process described on page 120. After you choose a source for your styles, click ＋, and then type in a name for your selector. Figuring out how to name the selector is the tricky part, but Dreamweaver can help with that, too. In Design view, put your cursor inside the text or image you want to target. Say you click inside a <strong> tag that's inside an <h1> tag. In this case, when you click ＋, Dreamweaver suggests the name "h1 strong."

NOTE After you click ＋ and start typing, Dreamweaver prompts you with HTML tags. So, after you press *b* you see *base, basefont, bgo, bgsound*. If you continue to type, adding *o*, you see *body* and *tbody*. If you select <body>, add a space, and then start typing another tag name, you'll see more prompts related to the letters you type. Want to see a list of the classes already defined for your page? Press period (.) and then begin typing. For a list of IDs, enter the pound character (#) first.

You name a descendent selector by tacking together the series of parent selectors (separated by spaces) that identify the location in the family tree of the element you want to style. The most distant ancestor is on the far left and the element you wish to style is on the far right. Consider the example of the bolded word inside the headline discussed above. To style that bolded text (but leave any other bold text as is), the descendent selector is *h1 strong*. You read this from right to left, so <strong> is the actual tag you're formatting, but only when it's inside an <h1> tag.

Figure 9-2 shows another example of descendent selectors. There are four links (<a> tags) on the page. Three of them appear inside bulleted list items (that's the <li> tag). To create a style that applies only to those three links, leaving the fourth untouched, you'd create a *li a* descendent selector. Again, the actual tag you want to format—the <a> link here—appears on the far right, while the tag that wraps around the link—the <li> tag—appears to the left.

You can have descendent selectors with more than just two elements. The following are all valid selectors for the <a> tags inside the bulleted list in Figure 9-2:

- li a

- ul li a

- body li a

- html li a

- html body ul li a

These five selectors, all of which do the same thing, demonstrate that you don't have to describe the entire lineage of the tag you want to format. For instance, in the third example—*body li a*—you don't need the ul found in the previous selector so long as there's an <a> tag that's a descendent (somewhere along the lineage) of an <li> tag (which itself is a descendent of the <body> tag). This selector can just as easily apply to an <a> tag inside an <em> tag inside a <strong> tag that's inside an <li> tag, and so on.

> **NOTE** One reason you might make a descendent selector longer by tacking on additional selectors is if you've written several rules that simultaneously format a tag. The more selectors that appear in a style name, the more powerful that style is and the more likely it is to override any conflicts with other styles. (More on this concept on page 412.) However, it's best to keep your selectors as short as possible to get the job done—that way, you keep your pages as lean as possible. In the above example, all five selectors work, but *li a* is the shortest, and therefore the best one to use.

When you click + in CSS Designer's Selectors section, Dreamweaver suggests a descendent selector based on the position of the cursor in your page, or what you currently have selected on the page. For example, say you had the page in Figure 9-2 open in Dreamweaver. If you select the link with the label "Ask the Experts," choose a source, and then click +, you'd see a screen like the one in Figure 9-1. Having Dreamweaver compose the selector for you is, as you can imagine, a brain-cell saver. In this case, Dreamweaver suggests *body ul li a*—a descendent selector that formats every link (every <a> tag) inside a list item (<li>) that's part of an unordered list (<ul>) that is itself inside the body of the page (<body>).

That's a pretty long-winded style name and, as mentioned above, you don't have to use the whole thing to accurately target an element on a page. For example, a simpler name, *li a*, would get the job done. Dreamweaver generally suggests the most complete descendent selector, meaning the tag you want to format and every ancestor tag (every tag that wraps around the selected element). In most cases, you won't need such complicated descendent selector names. Often, you can dispense with the tags on the left side, because those are the most general. For example, everything in your page is likely to be within the <body> tag, so you don't need to include it in your selector. Or you can replace Dreamweaver's suggested selector with a simpler one; just delete what Dreamweaver provides and type in another selector.

■ DESCENDENT SELECTORS WITH CLASS AND ID STYLES

Descendent selectors aren't limited to tags. You can build complex versions by combining different types of selectors. Suppose you want links to appear in yellow in introductory paragraphs to which you assign the class style *.intro*. The following selector does the trick: *.intro a*. This descendent selector formats any link (<a> tag) inside any other tag that has the *.intro* class applied to it.

Web designers frequently format the same tag differently, depending on where the tag appears in a layout. For instance, you'll often want paragraphs in the main area of your page to look different from paragraphs in sidebars (you might use a different font and a smaller font size in the sidebar, for example). You'll usually wrap each section of a page inside a <div> tag and apply a class to it. For example, you might wrap the main content area in a <div> and apply the class name *.content* to it. To format just the paragraphs inside the <div>, you'd use the descendent selector *.content p* (don't leave out the period). You'll use this technique frequently when you work with CSS layouts like those discussed in the next chapter.

You can apply either class or ID names to <div> tags so you can target—and then style—specific sections of a web page. Designers used to apply IDs to <div>s to identify unique page sections like banners (for example, *<div id="banner">*), but classes work just as well (*<div class="banner">*). Either way, the process of naming the selector is the same. If you want to define the look of bulleted lists wherever they appear inside a tag that has an ID named *#banner*, for example, you'd type *#banner ul* in the Selector Name box; if the tag had the class *.banner*, you'd name the selector *.banner ul*.

TIP When you work with descendent selectors, it helps to read the selector name *backward*, from right to left. Take, for example, the selector *#content .nav li*. The *li* means "This style applies to the <li> tag." The *.nav* means "but only when it's inside a tag with a class of *.nav* applied to it." And *#content* means "and only when that tag is inside another tag that has the ID *#content* applied to it."

To review, after you choose (or create) a style sheet to use as the source of a style and use + to name a descendent selector, you're ready to start adding the CSS properties that define the style for the selector. That's simply a matter of finding properties in the Properties section of CSS Designer and setting their values (see page 121 for a refresher).

Styling Groups of Elements

Sometimes you want several page elements to share the same formatting. Say you'd like all the headers on a page to share a certain color and font. Creating a separate style for each type of header—h1, h2, h3, h4, h5, and h6—is way too much work. In addition, if you later want to change the color of all the headers, you have to update all six styles. A more streamlined approach is a *group* selector, which lets you apply a style to multiple selectors at the same time.

As always in CSS Designer, you choose your source first. Then, in the Selectors section, click + . In the Selector Name box, type a list of selectors separated by commas. To style all heading tags with the same style, for example, you'd create the following selector: *h1, h2, h3, h4, h5, h6*. For a similar example, see Figure 9-3.

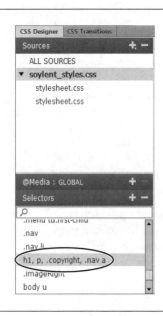

FIGURE 9-3

To style more than a single tag at a time, use a group selector. You can use any valid selector (or combination of selectors) as the group selector. For example, the selector circled here applies styles to the <h1> tag, the <p> tag, any tag that has the .copyright class applied to it, and any links inside a tag that has the .nav class applied to it.

> **TIP** At times, you may want a bunch of page elements to share *some*—but not all—formatting properties. Suppose you want to use the same font for several tags but a different font color for each tag. You can create a single rule for the shared styles using a group selector and then create separate styles with unique formatting for the individual tags. That's a perfectly valid (and common) approach. Web browsers just "tally up" all the different CSS properties applied to a tag to create a kind of uber-style, as described on page 418.

■ Editing Styles with the Properties Pane

The CSS Rule Definition window can be a rather tedious way to edit CSS properties. Just getting to the window takes several steps: In Design view, click the text you want to format or select an image or other piece of content. Then, in the Properties panel just below the document window, make sure you have CSS selected, and then click Edit Rule.

Opening this Rule Definition window and jumping around the categories and menus may slow you down if you're an experienced CSS jockey. Fortunately for you, CSS

Designer (Window→CSS Designer) streamlines the process so you can edit styles in a jiffy (Figure 9-4). After you select the page element you want to format, CSS Designer displays the selectors that trigger the style for that element. Click a selector, and Designer displays the properties for that element in the Properties section. If you're adjusting an already-defined property, turn on the Show Set checkbox so you see only properties whose value you've already set—in other words, you see the style's old rules. This makes it easier to find the exact property you want to tweak.

FIGURE 9-4

Click an element somewhere in your web page and then check out the Selectors section of CSS Designer. It shows you all the selectors that govern the formatting for that element. Here you can see the selectors that apply CSS rules to the word "price," which happens to be in a table header, which is itself in a table that has the .menu class applied to it. Clicking ".menu th" highlights the selector and displays the rules for it in the Properties section. With the Show Set checkbox turned on, you see only properties that already have values defined. To see other properties, turn off the Show Set checkbox.

Show set

Selected element on page | Related selectors | Highlighted selector | Properties for highlighted selector

When you make changes, Dreamweaver rewrites the rule for that selector in the style sheet. Keep in mind that the changes you make may affect other elements on your page. If the rule is in an external style sheet shared by multiple pages, you may be changing more than one page. How do you know which style sheet holds the rule definition? That's easy. When you choose a selector, CSS Designer highlights the style source in the Sources section.

Using Designer's Show Set option, it's easy to edit property values. To increase the size of a page's text, for example, find *font-size* in CSS Designer's Properties section, and then bump it up to a larger size.

For many properties, CSS designer displays the name of the property on the left and a value box on the right. You can type in a value or click the value box and drag to scrub in a value. You see the number change as you drag. Drag left to decrease the value and right to increase it. Menus help you provide values in the proper format, using the correct units of measure. Some properties, such as *color, border-radius, margin*, and *padding*, give you more visual tools for setting the value. If you don't see the property you want to change, make sure you have the Show Set checkbox turned off.

Sometimes you'll want to remove a property from a rule. For example, you may have set your <h1> headings to have 5px of padding all the way around and decided that wasn't the right choice after all. To remove the padding from the <h1> selector, go to the Selectors section of Designer and select "h1." In the Properties section, turn on the Show Set checkbox. Point to the *padding* property and then, on the right side, click the trash can icon to delete the style from the <h1> rule (Figure 9-5). To preview the effect before you make the change, click the disable button, (⊘).

FIGURE 9-5

Click the trash can icon to remove a property and its rule from a selector. Use the Disable button to the left of the trash can (⊘) to see the effect the rule has on your layout. It works like a toggle, so you can disable and then enable specific rules. Remember to do all this in Live view, so Dreamweaver displays the style in a real browser. Otherwise, you may not get the complete picture.

You can learn a lot about CSS styles by watching Dreamweaver edit the style sheet as you work with CSS Designer. For example, after you click inside your web page to identify an element and then choose a selector in CSS Designer, you'll notice that Dreamweaver highlights the source for the style in the Sources section. If you used an external style sheet, you'll see a filename ending in .css. You'll see that same filename in the group of related files above your web page. Click the name, and Dreamweaver automatically switches to Split view, showing the style sheet on the left. It displays a blinking cursor in the rule for the selector you chose in Designer. As you make changes, you can watch Dreamweaver edit the style sheet.

If your styles are in an internal style sheet, the process is slightly different. When you choose a selector in CSS Designer, the highlighted style sheet is "<style>." In that case, click the Source Code button to the left of the related files tabs. Scroll through the <head> of your document until you see the CSS rules. The code for your styles appears between two tags. The first will read:

```
<style type="text/css">
```

And the closing tag is:

```
</style>
```

After you zero in on the CSS rules in the head of your document, you can watch Dreamweaver edit the code as you work in CSS Designer.

TIP Another quick way to find the code for a selector is to right-click the selector in CSS Designer, and then choose "Go to Code" from the pop-up menu. Dreamweaver launches Split view, displays the CSS code in the left pane, and places your cursor in the rule for the selector so you can edit it.

FREQUENTLY ASKED QUESTION

CSS Shorthand

In CSS Designer's Properties section, I'll sometimes see all the font properties grouped into a single property named font; other times, font properties are listed individually, like font-family, font-size, and so on. Why is that?

Some CSS properties seem to go together: font properties, background properties (like *background-color*, *background-image*, *background-repeat*, and so on), margin, border, padding, and *list-style* properties. CSS supports a shorthand that combines related properties into a single property name. For example, it can combine the properties *font-family*, *font-size*, *font-weight*, *font-style*, and *line-height* into a single property it calls *font*. This shorthand makes writing CSS by hand faster. Instead of typing all the above font properties—one line of CSS code per property—you can combine them into a single line like this:

```
font: italic  bold 16px/150% Tahoma,
Verdana, Arial, Helvetica, sans-serif;
```

Dreamweaver uses either the shorthand or longhand method depending on your Preferences settings. Choose Edit→Preferences (Dreamweaver→Preferences) or use the keyboard shortcut Ctrl+U (⌘-U). Then click the CSS Styles category to view the settings Dreamweaver uses when it writes CSS code. The top group of checkboxes lets you turn on and off shorthand mode for specific categories. The second group of buttons and boxes controls how and when you can use the shorthand. Initially, Dreamweaver uses shorthand for borders and transitions. That's a good setting when you're still getting used to all the mysteries of CSS.

If you hand-edit your CSS, you might want to turn on other shorthand checkboxes. If Dreamweaver writes all your CSS, it's best to turn off these boxes. Unless you know your CSS well, shorthand versions of CSS properties can be harder to edit—it's very easy to mistype something.

■ Moving and Managing Styles

In the old days, when CSS support in web browsers was new, site designers would create just a handful of styles to format headlines and text. Keeping track of a site's styles back then wasn't too hard. Today, with great support for CSS and CSS-based layouts the norm, you can easily create a style sheet with hundreds of styles.

You might want to take a really long, complicated style sheet and split it into several smaller, easier-to-read external style sheets, however. One common design practice is to store styles that serve related functions in separate style sheets—for example, all the styles related to web forms would be in one style sheet, styles for text in another, and styles for page layout in yet another. You can then link each of the style sheets to your site's pages as described on page 162.

Or you might find yourself in the opposite situation: You have too many style sheets and want to combine them into a single one to cut down on the number of files a browser needs to download from your web server.

NOTE For really busy websites, the conventional wisdom is to use only a single external style sheet. That's because each request for a new file takes time and server power, so the more requests a browser makes for files, the slower the server performs. But unless your site is as busy as Yahoo, Google, or Amazon, your visitors won't notice if you use one or five external style sheets.

Even if you're not worried about creating new external style sheets (or cutting down on the number you already have), it's still useful to organize the styles *within* a style sheet. Web designers frequently use this strategy. For example, they keep all the styles for basic layout in one section of a style sheet, basic tag selectors in another section, and styles for text, images, and other content grouped according to where on the site they use them (sidebars, banners, and so on). By grouping related styles, it's a lot easier to find a particular style when it comes time to edit it.

Fortunately, you don't need to venture into Code view to move styles around in your sheets. Dreamweaver provides a simple and logical way to do so (and to move styles from one sheet to another, too).

- To move a style from one place to another in the same style sheet, drag the style's selector in CSS Designer (see Figure 9-6, top). Dreamweaver lists styles in the order in which they appear in the actual style sheet, so when you drag one style below another, for example, Dreamweaver repositions the CSS code in the style sheet. Order can be important in CSS for reasons you'll learn on page 412, but in a nutshell, CSS gives styles listed lower in a style sheet (closer to the bottom) greater priority if that style conflicts with styles higher up. You can select and move more than one style at a time by Ctrl-clicking (⌘-clicking) each style and then dragging the highlighted group (Ctrl-click [⌘-click] a selected style to deselect it). Select a range of styles by clicking one style and then Shift-clicking another style: That highlights every style between the two mouse clicks.

- To move one or more styles *between* two style sheets, drag the selectors from the Selectors section of CSS Designer onto the name of the destination style sheet in the Sources section. Dreamweaver removes the selector and its related CSS rules from one style sheet and adds them to the other. Using this method, you can move CSS rules from internal style sheets to external sheets and vice versa. (Internal style sheets are represented in CSS Designer as "<style>," while external style sheets have filenames that end in .css.)

FIGURE 9-6

In CSS Designer, you can drag selectors to different locations within a style sheet (top). In this case, dragging the .banner class below the .container class groups all the banner selectors together (bottom).

- To copy one or more CSS rules to another style sheet without deleting the originals, hold the Alt (Option) key down as you drag.

You need to give Dreamweaver a little help if you drag a style onto a style sheet that has a style with the same name. Say you define a style for the <body> tag in an internal style sheet, and you have an external style sheet attached to the same page that also has a <body> tag style (perhaps with different properties). If you drag the <body> tag style from one style sheet onto the other, Dreamweaver thinks you're trying to add the same-named style a second time and informs you of the potential problem (see Figure 9-7).

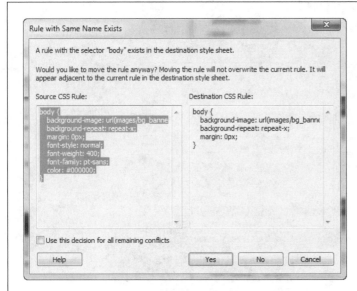

FIGURE 9-7

When you drag a style from one style sheet to another and a style by the same name exists in the destination sheet, Dreamweaver opens this dialog box, letting you either cancel the move or move the style anyway. To help you figure out what to do, Dreamweaver lists the properties in both the style you're trying to move (left) and the one already present (right). Use this information to determine which of the two styles you want to keep, or to figure out which properties from each style are most important.

> **NOTE** Unfortunately, Dreamweaver doesn't give you a way to reorder the sequence of internal and external style sheets on a page. They're attached to the page in the order in which you added them. For example, if you attach an external style sheet to a web page and then create an internal style sheet, the internal style sheet's code appears *after* the link to the external style sheet. The order of style sheets dictates the order in which a browser downloads those style sheets and can affect how a browser applies styles that have conflicting properties (thanks to the cascade in Cascading Style Sheets, described on page 412). To change the order of the style sheets in the HTML, you have to go into Code view (View→Code) and reorder the <link> tags in the <head> section of the HTML document.

You have two choices at this point. You can decide not to move the style and click No (Cancel has the same effect), and Dreamweaver closes the window without moving the style. Or you can click Yes and Dreamweaver moves the style, but it doesn't replace the old style, nor does it merge the properties of the two styles. It simply adds the new style to the destination style sheet—in other words, you end up with a style sheet that has two separate styles, each with the same name. Even though this is perfectly valid CSS, it's confusing. Delete one of the styles, and, if necessary, edit the remaining one to add any properties you wanted from the deleted style.

NOTE Dreamweaver says that it places a duplicate rule "adjacent" to the rule with the same name when it moves like-named rules, but it doesn't. It positions the rule at the end of the list.

- You can also move one or more styles from an internal style sheet to an external style sheet that's not attached to the current page. As discussed on page 113, external style sheets are the most efficient way to style a website's collection of pages. But it's often easier to use an internal style sheet when you first start a design. That's because, as you tweak your CSS, you only have to edit one file (the web page with the internal style sheet in it) instead of two (the web page *and* the external CSS file). But once you finish your design, it's best to move your styles from an internal sheet to an external one. You can do that from Code view.

TIP If you're most comfortable working within CSS Designer, you can add a source to the Sources section. Use Shift-click or Ctrl-click (⌘-click) to highlight selectors and then Alt-drag to move styles to the new source.

To find your styles in the page's code, start in CSS Designer. Right-click (⌘-click) a selector that has <style> as the source. From the pop-up menu, choose "Go to Code." Dreamweaver changes to Split view if you aren't already there and displays the CSS code that's in the <head> section of your page. To move all your code, select everything between *<style type="text/css">* and *</style>*, but don't select the tags themselves. Right-click (Control-click) the selection and choose CSS Styles→Move CSS Rules (see Figure 9-8, top). The Move To External Style Sheet window opens (Figure 9-8, bottom). You can then either add the rules to an existing external style sheet by clicking the Browse button and navigating to the CSS file, or turn on the "A new style sheet" radio button to create a new CSS file and move the styles there. When you click OK, Dreamweaver either moves the styles to an existing style sheet or it displays a dialog box letting you name and save the new style sheet. Either way, Dreamweaver removes the styles from the internal style sheet and places them in the external sheet. Even better, if the external CSS file isn't already attached to the current page, Dreamweaver attaches it for you, which saves you from doing so manually.

NOTE If you move all the styles from an internal style sheet to an external one, Dreamweaver still leaves some useless <style> tags in your web page. To remove them, select "<style>" from CSS Designer's Sources section and then click the Remove CSS Source button (–). You can also edit the source code for your page by clicking the Source Code button in the document window. To remove the style tags, delete the starting tag <style type="text/css"> and the closing tag </style>. If you moved all the CSS Rules to an external style sheet, there shouldn't be anything between the two tags.

FIGURE 9-8

Moving internal styles to an external style sheet is a two-step process. First, select the styles you want to move and then right-click to select Move CSS Rules from the pop-up menu (top). Second, tell Dreamweaver where you want the style to go (bottom).

Resolving CSS Conflicts

As you begin to pile more and more styles into your pages, you may notice that a page might not look exactly as you expect. A paragraph of text might be green even though you didn't create a style for a green paragraph. Or you may have styled a paragraph to appear with green text, but it refuses to change color. Most of the time, peculiar behaviors like these occur when styles collide. The rules governing these interactions can be complex, but they boil down to two main concepts: *inheritance* and *the cascade*.

Inheritance

Imagine you create a new style by redefining the paragraph tag (<p>). The style specifies red text displayed in the Arial font at a height of 24 pixels. Then you select a single word in a paragraph and apply bold formatting to it. When you use the Properties panel's Bold button to do this, Dreamweaver wraps that word in a pair of <strong> tags.

When a browser loads the page, it formats all the paragraphs in red Arial text with a font size of 24 pixels, because that's how you defined the <p> tag. But what happens when the browser encounters the paragraph with the <strong> tag in it? Since you didn't redefine the <strong> tag in red, Arial, 24 pixels, the browser scratches its little silicon head and asks, "Should I resort to my *default* font, text size, and color when I get to the <strong> tag, ignoring your style rules?"

And you can answer, "Of course not!" The bolded word should look just like the rest of the paragraph: red, Arial, 24 pixels high—and now boldfaced to boot. And indeed, that's how CSS works: The <strong> tag *inherits* the formatting of the surrounding <p> tag.

Just as human babies inherit traits like eye color from their parents, nested HTML tags inherit the properties of tags that surround them. In fact, a tag nested inside another tag—such as that <strong> tag inside the <p> tag—is called a *child*, while the enclosing tag is called the *parent*.

> **NOTE** As you read on page 398, a tag inside another tag is also called a *descendent* tag, while a tag that surrounds another tag is called its *ancestor*.

Inheritance passes from parent to child and ancestor to descendent. So in this example, the <p> tag (the parent) passes on the red text, Arial font, and 24-pixel size to the <strong> tag (the child). But just as children have their own unique qualities, the <strong> tag adds its own quality—boldness—to the properties it inherits from its parent.

> **NOTE** Inheritance applies to all styles, not just tag styles. For example, if you apply a class style to the <body> tag, then all the tags inside the <body> tag—paragraphs, images, and so on—inherit the properties of the class style.

Inheritance comes in quite handy at times. Say you want to display *all* the text on a page (paragraphs, headings, unordered lists, and links) in the Verdana font. You could dedicate yourself to a lengthy tagging extravaganza and redefine *every* HTML tag used to format text—<h1>, <h2>, <p>, <a>, <ul>, and so on—or create a class style and then manually apply it to all the text on the page.

But there's a better and faster technique, and it takes advantage of inheritance. Every web page contains a <body> tag, which contains *all* the elements of your page. The <body> tag, therefore, is an ancestor to *all* the HTML you see on a page—images, paragraphs, headings, and so on. To quickly format all the page's text, you can create a style for the <body> tag and set the font to Verdana, or create a class style using that font and apply it to the tag. Every bit of text inside the <body> tag—all the children—will inherit the Verdana *font* property.

> **NOTE** Actually, tags don't inherit *all* CSS properties. For the most part, the exclusions are logical. For example, say you create a border around an unordered list to visually set it off in its own box. If the *border* property were inherited, all the elements *inside* the unordered list—like list items, links, or bolded words—would each have their own boxes around them as well. Padding and margin are two other common properties that tags don't inherit.

The Cascade

At times, styles can conflict. Say you redefine the <h1> tag in an external style sheet, so that all <h1> headings show up in red in the Arial font. Then you attach this external style sheet to a web page that has an *internal* style sheet where you set the <h1> tag style to the Times font at 24 pixels high.

Now, when a browser tries to display an <h1> heading, it runs into a little dilemma. The page specifies two styles—two sets of formatting rules—for the *same tag*. To make matters even more confusing, suppose one <h1> tag has a class named *.highlight* applied to it. The *.highlight* class style sets the font to Trebuchet MS and makes all the text uppercase. So which style does the browser choose: the style from the internal style sheet, the style from the external style sheet, or the class style?

The answer is "All of them." The browser adopts elements of the three styles according to these hierarchical rules (hence the term "cascading" in "Cascading Style Sheets"):

- Properties that don't conflict are applied as usual. In the previous example, the red *color* property exists only in the external style sheet, while the internal style sheet is the only one to specify a font *size*. And the class is the only style to specify uppercase text. So far, the browser knows that, for this page, text inside <h1> tags should be red, 24 pixels tall, and uppercase.

- When properties *do* conflict, the browser uses the style with the greatest specificity. *Specificity* is just CSS jargon that means "the style with the most authority." The type of selector you use on a page is one way to affect specificity: ID styles are considered more specific than class styles, which are more specific than tag styles. In general, this means that properties from an ID style override properties from a class style, and properties from a class style override conflicts with a tag style.

> **NOTE** For an amusing—but accurate—description of specificity, read the article *CSS: Specificity Wars* (*http://tinyurl.com/7ogaq*). Make sure you print out the accompanying *Star Wars*-themed chart (*http://tinyurl.com/dz9cf*), which visually explains specificity by equating class selectors with Darth Vader and IDs with the Emperor himself. May the force be with you. (If you're more an aquatic type, there's also a CSS "SpeciFISHity" chart at *http://tinyurl.com/89bafl2.*)

- If two styles with the same specificity conflict—like the *h1* style in the external style sheet and the *h1* style in the internal style sheet in this example—the browser chooses the properties from the styles that were added to the page last. Say you first create an internal style sheet (at which point Dreamweaver inserts the appropriate HTML and CSS into the web page) and *then* attach an external style sheet. That means the link to the external style sheet appears *after* the internal style sheet in the web page. In this case, a style from the external style sheet with the same name as a style from the internal style sheet wins out. Similarly, if you attach the external style sheet first and then create the internal style sheet, the internal style sheet wins.

To summarize, then: Once the browser sorts things out, it determines that the text inside the <h1> tag on this web page should be Trebuchet MS and uppercase (from the *.highlight* class style), red (from the *h1* style in the external style sheet), and 24 pixels high (from the *h1* style in the internal style sheet).

NOTE Descendent selectors, which include combinations of class, ID, and tag names, such as *.main p*, *#banner h1*, or *h1 strong*, have even more authority than a tag or class style by itself, since Dreamweaver calculates specificity by combining all the selectors listed. Say you create a <p> tag style that produces bright-red text, and a descendent selector, *.sidebar p*, with purple text. Any paragraphs inside another element (like a <div> tag) that use the *.sidebar* style are purple—*not* red. Fortunately, Dreamweaver provides several ways to decipher this confusing jumble of conflicting styles (described in the next section).

Inherited properties, however, have no specificity, so when child elements inherit properties from parent elements (as described on page 411), any style applied directly to the child element overrules properties inherited from the parent element—no matter the specificity of the parent tag's style. Suppose you create an ID style named *#homepage* with the following properties: purple text and the Arial font. If you apply the *#homepage* ID to the <body> tag, the child elements (anything within the <body> tag) inherit those properties. If you then redefine the paragraph tag so that it displays text as green, the paragraph text inherits the Arial font from the <body> tag but ignores the purple color in favor of the green. Even though an ID style like *#homepage* has greater authority than a simple <p> tag selector, the properties applied to the paragraph through the <p> tag style overrule the properties inherited from the ID selector.

TIP Because ID selectors are so powerful (they have greater specificity than either class or tag selectors), many web designers steer clear of them. For example, when you create a descendent selector like *#main p*, you can't override that style unless you create an even more powerful selector like *#main .special*. This can lead to some really long descendent selectors. If you stick with class and tag selectors, you won't need to work so hard to overcome conflicts the cascade causes.

To learn more than you probably ever wanted to know about the cascade, visit *www. w3.org/TR/css3-cascade/*.

NOTE In *CSS3: The Missing Manual* (O'Reilly Media), you'll find chapters dedicated to both inheritance and the cascade.

CSS Sleuthing with Computed Properties

If you haven't yet put this book down in hopes that the swelling in your brain will subside, you've probably absorbed the notion that using multiple styles can get complex. With all this inheritance and cascading going on, it's easy for styles to collide in hard-to-predict ways. To help you discern how styles interact and to ferret out possible conflicts, Dreamweaver has some useful tools, starting with the Computed feature in CSS Designer, which tells you how a web browser formats a selected item—such as an image, paragraph, table, or <div> tag—*once it takes into account inheritance and the cascade*. That's pretty cool.

The Computed feature, found in the Selectors section of CSS Designer, is an invaluable tool for diagnosing weird CSS behavior associated with inheritance and the cascade. But like any incredible tool, it requires a good user's manual to learn how it works. First of all, even though the word "Computed" appears in the Selectors section, it's not really a selector—it's better to think of it as a tool.

As usual, your first step is to click some text, select a picture, or highlight some other media on your web page. CSS Designer displays the selectors that govern that element's formatting. It includes the computed "selector" at the top of that list (in all caps). Click Computed, and Designer highlights the label in blue to indicate that you selected it. Now a different set of properties appears in the Properties section: the *computed properties*. The Computed tool automatically displays the post-inheritance and post-cascade properties and values that format the element you selected in the document window. The different properties CSS Designer displays may be associated with different selectors. For example, the *font-family* property may be defined by a style attached to a <div> tag, while the color of the text may be defined by a style attached to a heading. In other words, different selectors produce the end result, but by clicking Computed, you see all the properties associated with a style at one time. You can go ahead and make changes to the values for the properties while viewing the effect those changes have on your page (remember to review the page in Live view). When you click the name or value for a property in CSS Designer's Properties section, the related selector appears in bold in the Selectors section. That way, you know which CSS rule you're editing. That's important because your changes will affect other elements on the page, or even other elements on other web pages that use the same CSS rule.

So how does the computed value help you in the real world? Suppose you have a headline that's orange but you never created an <h1> tag that specified orange text. You can find out which selector passed the hideous orange on to the heading by clicking inside the headline. Then, in CSS Designer's Selectors section, click Computed. At that point, the Properties section displays the headline's computed properties (see Figure 9-9), one of which is *color*. You'll see an orange swatch next to it. Click either the *color* property name or value, and Dreamweaver boldfaces the selector that has the CSS rule that sets the color for the headline. Perhaps your <h1> is inside a <div> tag that has the *.uglyOrange* class applied to it. In your page's HTML, that would look like this:

```
<div class="uglyOrange">
```

When you select the *color* property in the Properties section of CSS Designer, the program displays ".uglyOrange" in bold type in the Selectors section. Now you know which selector defines that ugly orange color. You can change the color value for the selector, but that also affects any other element that has the *.uglyOrange* class applied to it. To fix the problem, you could create a color rule specifically for your <h1> tag. That rule would override the *.uglyOrange* class, but it will affect other <h1> elements. A third option is to create a new class, say *.notOrange*, where you set a color value and then apply the *.notOrange* class to your <h1> heading. You need to specifically set a color value for this new class, or the style sheet will have no color rule, and so it won't override *.uglyOrange*.

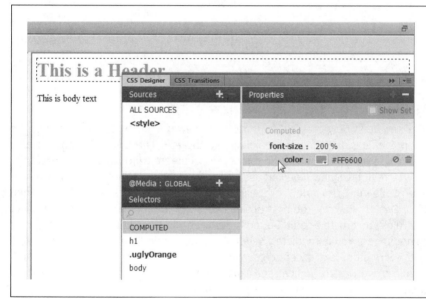

FIGURE 9-9

Here, the computed selector displays all the rules that affect the <h1> header in the sample document. Clicking the color property highlights the .uglyOrange class in Selectors, telling you which selector defined the color.

When you finish, click inside your <h1> heading again to check out the computed properties and values. Notice that the *color* property displays your new shade. Select *color* or its assigned value and you'll see the selector that now governs the <h1> tag is something other than that *.uglyOrange* class.

You may be surprised to notice that you can still find the *.uglyOrange* class listed in the Selectors section. That's because you're still applying the class to a "parent" of your <h1> header. The *.uglyOrange* class may even have other rules that still affect your heading. Now, if you click *.uglyOrange* in Selectors and find the text *color* property (Figure 9-10), you see the property name with a strikethrough line. Pause with your cursor over the property and a message appears that says "color does

not apply to your selection because it has been overridden by the rule *.notOrange.*"
If you changed the color for <h1> tags, Dreamweaver would cite that rule instead
of *.notOrange*.

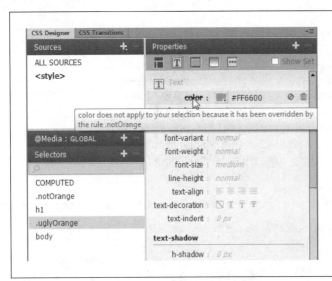

FIGURE 9-10

When you see a property name with a strikethrough, Dreamweaver hasn't applied the rule to the current selection. The color property shown here isn't in effect because the .notOrange class has overridden the original setting. Note that even though Dreamweaver displays both classes in the Selectors section of Designer, only one of the rules is in effect.

CSS Sleuthing with Inspect View

One of the most powerful features of Dreamweaver CC is that you can tweak the
rules in CSS Designer and immediately see the effect in Live view (choose Live
from the Design/Live menu at the top of the document window). Don't forget that,
while you're in Live view, you can use any of the other view options Dreamweaver
offers—Code view, Split view, or Design view. When you work with CSS Designer,
Split or Design view are the best options because you immediately see the effect
of the rules you create or edit. Suppose, for example, you change the text color for
the <body> tag. You immediately see that change ripple through your web page. It
affects every bit of text, except those where another rule overrides the color. And if
your rule is overridden, you can see exactly where that occurs in the context of the
entire page using Inspect view.

When you're in Live view, you see two additional buttons to the right of the Live op-
tion. Point to the first one and a tooltip explains that it will "Turn on Inspect mode."
The second one "Shows the Live view source in Code view," an option also known as
Live Code (View→Live Code). When you click Inspect or press Shift+Alt+F11 (Shift-
Option-F11), the behavior of your cursor changes. Now if you point to a page element,
CSS Designer shows you that element's computed properties. You also see colorful
highlights around the element; blocks of text appear in blue, margins in orange, and
padding in green. This visual representation of CSS properties is extremely helpful
as you make design decisions. You can use CSS Designer to change or disable values
momentarily to understand their effect on your page.

If you're not sure exactly which page element is under the Inspect microscope, check the Tag Selector at the bottom of the document window, where Dreamweaver displays the current selection's class, ID, and tag names. In Figure 9-11, for example, you can see an inspected element and its entire hierarchy of tags and classes. You can see that the <img> tag is highlighted, indicating that it's currently under inspection.

As you check out page elements in Inspect view, CSS Designer displays the elements' computed properties and their values. You can position your cursor on a value and edit it as you normally would.

All Natural Ingredients

img 292px × 137px

Lorm

solor dat ipsam color sat ipectum solorgno infe
solorgno inferiod. Gorogonzola reggio solor dat.
solor dat.

</> body div .container p a img

FIGURE 9-11

With the Inspect view turned on, Dreamweaver highlights elements on the page as you point to them. Here, you're inspecting an image, and you can see the padding around it (the green border). At the bottom of the document window, you see the entire family of tags and classes. The highlighted <img> tag tells you that it's the focus of the inspection. To move the focus to a different tag, click it in the Tag Selector. Throughout the process, CSS Designer displays the associated selectors and properties.

TIP Sometimes, when you're sleuthing through your CSS rules, you may need more room for CSS Designer. To provide more breathing room for Source, Selectors, and Properties, click and drag any of the gray bars (vertical or horizontal) between the sections to adjust the spacing. In some cases, it may help to drag the CSS Designer tab away from the dock to create a floating palette. For more workspace details, see page 21.

Analyzing the Cascade

When CSS Designer displays computed selectors and properties, it's showing you the cascade of CSS rules. In the Selectors section of CSS Designer, the rules that have the most precedence are at the top of the list. You can click each selector to see how it contributes to the style of the currently selected element. If you see a property name with a strikethrough, the rule doesn't apply to the current selection. To learn which selector governs that property, point to the property name and a tooltip pops up with its name.

You can also see the cascade of rules listed in the Properties panel. Select the text you want to analyze, click the CSS button in the Properties panel, and then select the Targeted Rule menu—the top group of items in the menu lists the cascade. In this case, the cascade is shown in reverse order. The rules with the least precedence are at the top, while the most powerful selectors are at the bottom.

TIP One way to make a style more "powerful"—so that its properties override properties from conflicting styles—is to use a descendent selector. For example, a *body p* descendent selector has more authority than just a plain <p> tag style, even though both styles target the exact same tags. Likewise, a *.content p* style is more powerful than a *body p* style since it applies a class selector (which is more powerful than a tag selector) and one tag selector. You can quickly rename a style or create a more long-winded and powerful descendent selector using CSS Designer. Just select a target element on the page, choose a source for the CSS code in the Sources section, and then click Add Selector, +. CSS Designer then suggests a verbose selector, which you're free to edit.

◼ Using the Code Navigator to Identify Styles

Dreamweaver includes yet another valuable tool, this one aimed at CSS pros who like to use Code view when they write and edit CSS. The Code Navigator gives you a quick way to see all the CSS styles applied to any element you select. It's kind of like CSS Designer's Computed feature, but the CSS styles appear in a pop-up window instead of in CSS Designer (see Figure 9-12).

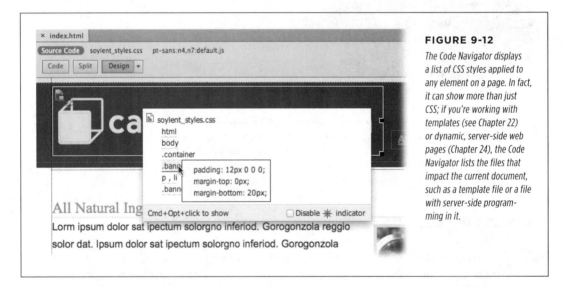

FIGURE 9-12

The Code Navigator displays a list of CSS styles applied to any element on a page. In fact, it can show more than just CSS; if you're working with templates (see Chapter 22) or dynamic, server-side web pages (Chapter 24), the Code Navigator lists the files that impact the current document, such as a template file or a file with server-side programming in it.

To launch the Code Navigator, hold down the Alt key and click an element on the page (Mac owners need to press Option-⌘ and click). You can click any element whose CSS you wish to examine: an image, a heading, a paragraph, a table, and so on. For example, in Figure 9-12, Alt-clicking (Option-⌘-clicking) the cafe's logo opens the Code Navigator, which lists the styles that apply to that headline.

Code Navigator won't appear in Live view, but as long as you're in Design view, you can launch it several ways:

- Click the Code Navigator icon (the ship steering wheel, circled in Figure 9-13). It appears next to an element you select on a page (or above an element when you point to it). It usually takes a second or so to appear, so you may want to stick with the keyboard shortcut (Alt-click or Option-⌘-click).

- Right-click any item on the page and then choose Code Navigator from the pop-up menu.

- Select an item on the page and choose View→Code Navigator, or press Alt+Ctrl+N (Windows) or Option-⌘-N (Macs).

FIGURE 9-13

If the Code Navigator's ever-present steering wheel icon bothers you, get rid of it by turning on the Disable checkbox in the Code Navigator window (see Figure 9-12). From that point on, you open the Code Navigator using the keyboard shortcut (Alt+Ctrl+N for Windows, Option-⌘-N for Macs) or one of the other methods discussed above.

Once the Code Navigator window opens, you see all the styles that affect the current item. In Figure 9-12, for example, the Navigator lists seven styles that format the logo. If you point to a style, you'll see a list of that style's CSS properties. In Figure 9-12, pointing to the *.banner* style lists that style's properties: *padding* of 12px; *margin-top* of 0px; and a *margin-bottom* of 20px. Although this is a quick way to view styles and their properties, it isn't as useful as CSS Designer's Computed feature, which shows you exactly which *properties* (not just which styles) apply to the current selection. In addition, the Code Navigator doesn't always accurately display the CSS cascade (page 412)—it does list the styles in order of specificity, but it splits up the list by style sheet, so if a page has more than one style sheet, you may not get a clear picture of the cascade. CSS Designer's Computed feature (page 414), on the other hand, shows a complete list of styles from least to most specific, regardless of how many style sheets you use.

If you're a code jockey who prefers to type CSS code instead of relying on Dreamweaver's windows and panels, the Code Navigator lets you jump immediately to a style sheet. Open it and click any style listed. Dreamweaver jumps into Split view and displays the CSS for the selected style. Of course, you need to know how to write CSS for this to be useful. If you're not comfortable with that, you should stick with CSS Designer and the methods for editing styles discussed on page 135.

■ Styling Pages for Print

You may be surprised to see a section on print design in a book dedicated to creating beautiful onscreen presentations. However, it's common for people to print web pages—directions to a concert, a list of product names and ratings, or a long-winded treatise that's easier to read on paper while reclining in a favorite chair.

Unfortunately, some web pages just don't print well. Sometimes the banner is too big to fit on one sheet of paper, so it spans two printed pages, or the heavy use of ads wastes ink. And some CSS-based layouts simply print as jumbled messes. Fortunately, CSS has an answer: *printer style sheets.* The creators of CSS realized that people might use web pages in different ways. In fact, they went so far as to define a large group of potential "media types" so web designers could customize pages for different output devices, including Teletype machines, Braille readers, and so on.

Basically, by specifying a media type, you attach an external style sheet that Dreamweaver applies *only* when someone sends the page to a particular device. For instance, you could have a style sheet that comes into play only when someone looks at a web page on a monitor, and another that applies only when he prints the page. Using this technique, you can tweak the way a page looks when guests print it out without affecting the way it looks onscreen. Figure 9-14 shows the concept in action.

FIGURE 9-14

When you print a web page (left), you really don't need its navigation links or information unrelated to the topic at hand. Create a printer style sheet to eliminate unnecessary content and format the page so it looks nice on paper (right).

The basic process involves creating an external style sheet that contains styles suited to a particular media type (like a printer or monitor), and then attaching that style sheet to a web page and identifying the destination device. The Sources section of CSS Designer automates the process for you. Simply click + and choose either "Create a New CSS File" or "Attach Existing CSS File."

That opens a window like the one in Figure 9-15, where you name the CSS file. Next to "Add as," choose Link. To specify a style sheet for print, expand the Conditional

Usage panel by clicking the right-pointing arrow (lower left). Set the first menu to "media" and the second to "print," and then click OK.

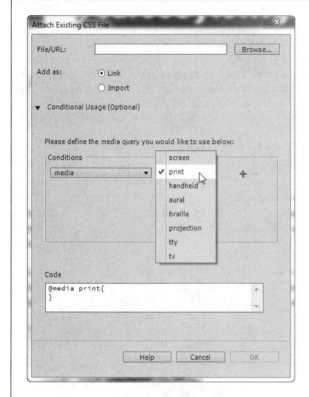

FIGURE 9-15

When you attach an external style sheet to a web page, you can assign it to a specific output device, such as a printer ("print") or monitor ("screen"). If you don't specify one or the other, the browser uses the style sheet for all output devices. By clicking +, you can continue to add conditions like max-width or min-color. You use them to specify styles when a browser encounters certain conditions (like a screen that's no wider than 480 pixels). Most of the options aren't that useful, but some are great for creating specific page designs for phones and tablets. You'll learn about "media queries" on page 523.

Say you name your style sheet *print.css*. When you follow the steps above, you add a line to the <head> section of your web page that looks like this:

```
<link href="print.css" rel="stylesheet" type="text/css" media="print">
```

The key feature of this line is the last bit, *media="print"*, which tells Dreamweaver you'll be sending this page to a printer.

NOTE If you attach an external style sheet and select a media type, Dreamweaver displays the media type in CSS Designer. For example, if you attach an external style sheet named *print.css* and specify the "print" media type, Dreamweaver displays "print.css [print]" in Designer's Sources section.

Although Dreamweaver lists many media types, there are only three related to crafting printer style sheets: *print*, *screen*, and *all*. "Print" specifies that the styles apply only when someone prints the page; "screen" indicates a style sheet that takes effect only when the page appears on a display; and "all" is the same as not selecting anything—the style sheet applies when you print the page, view it on a monitor, feel it on a Braille reader, and so on. The "all" option comes in handy when you want to create a style sheet that defines the basic look of your website—such as its font, line height, and text alignment—no matter whether someone prints pages or views them onscreen. You can create two additional style sheets from this basic one, one designed for print, the other for monitors.

> **NOTE** When you use CSS Designer to add a style sheet to the Sources section and to set a media type, Dreamweaver doesn't give you "all" as an option, because it's the same as not specifying a media type. However, if you write the code by hand in Code view, you'll see a code hint listing "all," as well as a ream of other media options.

Previewing Media Styles in Dreamweaver

Web designers use Dreamweaver mainly to create pages that people view onscreen. Because of that, the program displays formatted pages only when you either haven't selected a media type at all or when you specify the "all" or "screen" type. So how can you see what a printed version of the page will look like when you design a printer style sheet? Use the View→Style Rendering→Design Time options shown in Figure 9-16.

FIGURE 9-16

The Design-Time Style Sheets dialog box lets you pick and choose which styles Dreamweaver applies as you work. That gives you a way to view your "print" media styles and turn off the "screen" styles that format your page for a computer monitor.

> **NOTE** If you're in Live view, the Style Rendering toolbar has no effect. In Live view, Dreamweaver displays only what the page will look like in a web browser.

To see the effect your printer style sheet has on your document, you want to use its styles. At the same time, you want to turn off the styles used to display the document onscreen. That's exactly what you can do in the Design-Time Style Sheets box (Figure 9-16). Click + above "Show only at design time," and then navigate to your printer style sheet. To temporarily hide the screen styles, add the name of that style sheet to the "Hide at design time" list. After you click OK, you'll see the formatting as advertised. Keep in mind that you can add as many style sheets as necessary to the show and hide lists. For example, if your web page uses more than one style sheet for the screen, you'll want to hide them all to see the printed view. For more details on the uses of Design-Time style sheets, see the box on page 425.

NOTE If your CSS styles don't seem to have any effect on a page, you might have turned them off. Make sure that you turn on the View→Style Rendering→Display Styles checkbox or you won't see any CSS styling.

Tips for Printer Style Sheets

A printer style sheet can redefine the look of any element on a page when you print that page. You can change fonts, adjust type size, increase the leading (space) between lines of text, and so on. You can use any CSS property you want, and modify any style to your liking, but most printer style sheets handle a few common tasks.

- **Override properties from another style sheet**. If you attach an external style sheet after selecting the "all" media type, or if you didn't specify any media type at all, the printed page uses styles from the external style sheet. When you create the printer style sheet, you may need to override some of the settings in the web page's style sheet. The best way to do this is to simply create styles with names that match the names of the styles you want to override. For example, if a style sheet attached to a page has a <p> tag style that specifies a font size of 12 pixels, you can create a <p> tag style in the printer style sheet that changes the font size to 12 points. (Due to the rules of the cascade [page 412], the printer style sheet needs to be attached to the web page *last* for its styles to overrule similarly named styles in another sheet.)

  Another solution is to simply create two style sheets—one for print and one for monitors—and attach each with its respective media type. This way, there won't be any overlap between styles in the two sheets. The web browser uses the print style sheet when it sends a page to a printer, but it uses the monitor style sheet when it displays the page onscreen.

- **Text size and color**. You size text that appears onscreen using pixels, ems, or percentages (see page 149). Unfortunately, these units of measure don't make a lot of sense to an inkjet printer. If you've ever used Microsoft Word, you know the measurement of choice for printed text is points. If you don't like the size of the type when you print a page, use a printer-friendly font size in the printer style sheet. In addition, while bright yellow type on a black background may look cool onscreen, black type on white paper is the easiest to read. If you colored your text, it may print out as a shade of gray on a black-and-white printer. Setting text to black in a printer style sheet can help your visitors' weary eyes.

- **Hide unnecessary page elements**. Guests don't really need to (and often don't want to) print some parts of a web page (a navigation menu or a sidebar of links, for example). After all, you can't click them on paper! Fortunately, CSS provides a property that lets you hide unwanted elements when you print a web page. Just create a style that applies to the part of the page you want to hide—for instance, with CSS-based layouts, you typically divide a page into sections using <div> tags, each with its own unique ID. Say you have the site's navigation bar inside a tag that has an ID named *#navbar* attached to it. To hide the nav bar when someone prints the page, create another ID named *#navbar* in your printer style sheet. In the CSS Rule Definition window, click the Block category and then choose None from the Display property menu. (In Figure 9-14, right, for example, the banner and both sidebars don't appear in the printed version of the page.)

- **Adjust margins and widths**. To make a website look more elegant, you might increase the margins around the edges of a page, but this extra space only wastes paper when printed. In the printer style sheet, remove any margins you applied to the <body> tag. In addition, if you hide parts of a page when you print it, the remaining page elements may not fill the printed page. In that case, add a style to the style sheet that changes the widths of the printed elements. For example, if you have a two-column design—a sidebar with links and other site-specific info, and a main column filled with all the useful info that should appear on a printed page—and you hide one column (the sidebar), you'd then set the width of the remaining column to 100% and remove any margins on its left and right sides. That way, the information fills the width of the printed page.

- **Take advantage of *!important*.** Sometimes the printer style sheet needs to override certain CSS properties from another style sheet. Thanks to the cascade (page 412), a style must have greater "specificity" to overrule another style. If you're trying to override, say, the font color used for a descendent selector named *body #wrapper #maincontent p*, you have to add the same long-winded style name to your printer style sheet. Fortunately, CSS provides a less labor-intensive method: the *!important* directive. Adding *!important* to a property in a CSS style lets that property overrule any conflicting property values from other styles, even if those other styles are more specific.

Unfortunately, Dreamweaver doesn't give you a way to easily add this option. You have to manually edit the style sheet in Code view. Say you want the text of all paragraphs to print black. Create a <p> tag style in the printer style sheet and set the *color* property to black. Then open the printer style sheet in Code view and add *!important* after the color value and before the semicolon. Here's what that would look like:

```
p {
    color: #000000 !important;
}
```

When you print the page, this style overrides any color settings for any paragraph tags in a competing style sheet—even a much more specific style.

A Time to Design

A Dreamweaver feature called *Design-Time style sheets* lets you quickly try different CSS style sheets as you develop web pages. With it, you can hide external style sheets you've attached to a page and substitute new ones.

Design-Time style sheets come in handy when you work on HTML that, later on, you intend to make part of a complete web page. Dreamweaver Library items are a good example; this feature (discussed in Chapter 21) lets you create a chunk of HTML that any number of pages on your site can use. When you update a Library item, Dreamweaver updates every page that uses it. A timesaving feature, for sure, but since a Library item is only *part* of a page, it doesn't include the <head> portion needed to either store styles or link to an external style sheet. So when you design a Library item, you're working in the dark (or at least without any style). By using Design-Time style sheets, you can use all the styles in an external style sheet and even preview the effects directly in Design view.

You apply a Design-Time style sheet by clicking the Design-Time style sheet button in the Style Rendering toolbar (see Figure 9-16) or by choosing Format→CSS Styles→Design-Time.

The Design Time Style Sheets window appears. Click the top + button to select an external style sheet. Note that clicking this button doesn't attach the style sheet to the page, it merely lets you tap the properties of the .css file as you work on a page.

To properly view your page with this new style sheet, you may need to get an attached external style sheet out of the way. To do that, use the bottom + button to add the old style sheet to the Hide list.

You can only use Design-Time style sheets when you work in Dreamweaver. They have no effect on how a page looks in a web browser. That's both the good news and the bad news. Although Dreamweaver lets you apply class styles from a Design-Time style sheet to your web page, it doesn't actually attach the sheet to the page. For example, if you use a Design-Time style sheet to design a Library item, Dreamweaver doesn't guarantee that that style sheet is attached to the web page that uses the item. You have to attach the sheet yourself, or your visitors will never see your intended result.

Animating Style Transitions

In Chapter 4 you learned about the *:hover* pseudo-class, which lets you change the style of a link when a visitor points to it. For example, the background color of a link in a navigation bar might be deep blue, but when a guest points to it, it changes to bright orange. That change occurs instantaneously, but it might feel a bit abrupt to some. What if you could animate the change so that the link starts out blue and then moves through a range of colors as it morphs to solid orange? Then, when a guest move his mouse somewhere else, the color would go from orange back to blue. Now *that* would be cool...and, thanks to CSS3's Transitions and Dreamweaver, it's easy to achieve.

In a nutshell, a CSS transition is a change over time from one CSS property value to another. But wait! There's more! A single CSS transition can change more than one property. So, in addition to changing the background color, you could change the link's font color at the same time and have a border grow or fade in. Web browsers handle the animation; that is, they create all the in-between steps from one property value to another. You need to focus on only a few aspects of the process. What do you want to animate? You identify HTML elements with your old friend the CSS selector—that could be a tag, a class, or an ID. Then you specify which CSS properties you want to change in the transition: Background color? What starting color do you want to use? What does that change to? There are timing considerations, too: How long should the transition last? Fortunately, Dreamweaver supplies all the tools you need to answer those questions and create the transition. Choose Window→CSS Transitions to open the Transitions panel. You provide the details in the panel and its dialog boxes, and Dreamweaver writes the code in your CSS style sheet.

NOTE CSS transitions are fun and look great, but they're relatively new, so not all browsers support them. While Safari, Firefox, and Chrome understand CSS transitions, only version 10 (and higher) of Internet Explorer does. That means that about half of the web-surfing world won't be able to enjoy your finely crafted CSS transitions...yet. But since CSS transitions are really just eye candy anyway, visitors coming to your site with IE 7, 8, or 9 won't miss anything crucial.

Here's a list of the steps you take to create a transition. (To actually build one, see the tutorial on page 442.)

1. **Choose or create a selector to identify the page element you want to change with a transition.**

   You can use transitions with a class, ID, tag, or any other CSS selector. For example, if you want to create a transition for an <h2> heading, you have three options:

   — Use the <h2> tag if you want to apply the transition to all <h2> headings.

   — Create a class if you want to apply the transition to a few, but not all, of your <h2> headings.

   — Create an ID if you want to be certain that you animate only one <h2> heading on each page.

   If you create a class or ID, you can do that in CSS Designer as you normally would. Choose a source (an internal or external style sheet) and then, in Selectors, click + to create a new selector. (See page 116 for a refresher on using CSS Designer.)

2. **Decide which CSS properties you want to change in the transition. Then, if necessary, set initial values for those properties.**

   You can create transitions using a bewildering number of CSS properties, like *color*, *border-width*, *margin-left*, or *border-right-color*. You can find a complete list at *http://tinyurl.com/dxjbdhd*, but you don't have to memorize the properties—Dreamweaver's CSS Transitions tool prompts you with a list when it's time to set values for the transition. That's the good news. The bad news is that not all browsers support all those properties.

Even though Dreamweaver provides a list of properties you can use in a transition, it pays to plan ahead. You'll usually want to set the starting value for a property because, if you don't, browsers use a default property and the result may not be what you expect. So, if you're changing the background color of an <h2> heading from blue to orange, for example, you want to create an <h2> selector in CSS Designer and set the *background-color* property to blue. Now you're ready to use the CSS Transitions panel to create your transition.

3. **Choose Window→CSS Transitions to open the CSS Transitions panel (see Figure 9-17).**

   It lists any existing CSS transitions you created, organized by selector—for example, if you already have a transition that works with <h2> headings, you see h2 in the list. If you have a transition that works with the *orangebg* class, you see that listed.

Create new transition

FIGURE 9-17

The CSS Transitions panel lets you add, edit, and delete animations between CSS properties. It lists all the selectors in the current page that have CSS transitions.

4. **Click + to add a new transition.**

   Dreamweaver opens the New Transition window (Figure 9-18).

5. **From the Target Rule menu, choose the selector from step 1.**

   This menu lists all the selectors in the page's style sheet, including class, ID, and tag styles. It also lists any IDs applied to page elements, even if you never created style definitions for them by setting properties and values.

> **TIP** You're not limited to the list of selectors shown in the Target Rule menu. If you don't see the selector you want, you can type in a new selector name. When might you do this? Suppose you skipped steps 1 and 2 and you want to change the background color of your page's <footer> using a transition. So far, no CSS properties are defined for <footer>, but you're perfectly happy to start with the default background color (white). In that case, you just type "footer" in the text box for Target Rule, and then go ahead and follow the steps to build the transition.

FIGURE 9-18

The New Transition window looks a bit overwhelming at first, but it's really an easy way to create CSS transitions: Choose a selector from the Target Rule drop-down menu, specify a trigger for the animation (the "Transition on" option), choose a CSS property you want to animate, and then set some timing options.

6. **From the Transition On menu, select the event that triggers the transition.**

Unfortunately, you can't just animate an element whenever you like—some action needs to trigger the transition, and you're limited to a handful of events related to CSS selectors. The *:hover* pseudo-class is the most well known, but there are others you can tap into:

— *active* refers to the moment you click a link. It's the same as the *:active* pseudo-class discussed on page 199. Browsers also apply an active state anytime you click an element and hold the mouse button down. In other words, you could create a CSS animation so that when a visitor clicks a particular <div> element and holds his mouse button down, that <div>'s background color changes and its width increases.

— *checked* applies to checkboxes (page 671) and radio buttons. However, there aren't a lot of CSS properties for checkboxes and radio buttons that are worth animating.

— *disabled* and *enabled* apply to form elements visitors can't select or change. Since you can't disable or enable a form element without JavaScript, you probably won't ever need to use either of these settings.

— *focus* refers to page elements guests can select, like text boxes in web forms. When a visitor either clicks into or tabs to a box, that box receives what's called "focus" from the browser. You can apply a separate set of styles to a box when it receives focus, and animate the change between the look of the box as it normally appears and as it appears when a guest clicks inside it to type a response. For example, you could set the height of a multiline text box (also called a *textarea*, as described on page 662) to 100 pixels, and then create a CSS transition that changes the box's height to 500 pixels. When a visitor clicks into the box, it grows to 500 pixels high, and when she tabs or clicks out of the box, it shrinks back to 100 pixels. Likewise, you could set the background color of a text box to white but have it change to bright yellow when a visitor clicks in it.

— *hover* is the most commonly used option. It applies when a visitor points to a page element. While you'll commonly use the hover transition with links, you can apply it to any page element: paragraphs, <div> tags, headlines, and so on. Keep in mind that the hover effect works well with desktop computers, but not so much with phones and tablets—a mouse hovers, but a finger doesn't.

— You probably won't ever use the *indeterminate* setting. It applies only to checkboxes and radio buttons, and refers to a checkbox or radio button that is neither turned on nor turned off. Sounds very Zen, but it's also very useless. You can specify the *indeterminate* setting only using JavaScript, and since you probably won't ever need to use the state, there's no need to create an animation for it.

— *target* applies to locations in a page that are bookmarked using IDs. Visitors click a link to jump to a different part of the page. The technique is described on page 194, and this event applies when a visitor clicks a link that jumps to that bookmark. For example, say you add a link at the top of a page that jumps down the page to a bookmark. You could add a background color and a CSS transition to that bookmark so that when a visitor clicks the link and jumps to that spot on the page, the section's background color fades into view.

NOTE For some ideas on what you can do with the CSS *:target* pseudo-class, check out *http://tinyurl.com/6mxqbz7* and *http://css-tricks.com/on-target/*.

7. **Choose either "Use the same transition for all properties" or "Use a different transition for each property."**

As you'll see in steps 8–10, you can set a duration for the animation (how long it takes), a delay (how long before it begins), and a "timing function" (the rate of change during the animation). You can apply the same settings to all CSS properties or set different timings for each property. For example, if, when a visitor points to a navigation button, you want that button to change from blue to orange, have its text grow from 16 to 25 pixels, and enlarge its border from 1 pixel to 10 pixels in width, you have a choice. You can have all three animations occur at the same rate, or set different rates for each. You could, for instance, have the background color change quickly, make the border change more slowly, and wait a second before the text increases in size. To create these transitions, choose "Use a different transition for each property."

Depending on which selection you make, the next steps will vary. If you selected the "Use the same transition" option, then continue to the next step. If you selected "Use a different transition," then skip to steps 11 and 12 to add a CSS property that you can animate, and then jump back to steps 8–10 to set the duration, delay, and timing function for that property.

8. **Type a number in the Duration box and select either "s" (for seconds) or "ms" (for milliseconds) from the menu to the right.**

The duration specifies how long an animation takes. While it may seem cool to slowly change the background color over the course of 10 seconds, most web surfers are impatient and don't want to wait to savor your carefully choreographed animation. A good value is .25 seconds (250 milliseconds)—that speed is fast enough for anxious visitors, but slow enough so they can see the transition. However, you may want to try .5 seconds (500 milliseconds) or longer to see how the effect looks.

As mentioned in step 7, you can set different timings for each property, so you might want one animation, like a change in the text weight, to happen really quickly, but another, like a change in background color, to happen more slowly.

> **NOTE** Don't leave the Duration box blank. Otherwise, the transition takes place immediately, with no animation.

9. **Type a number in the Delay box and select either "s" (for seconds) or "ms" (for milliseconds) from the menu to the right.**

The delay value indicates how long the browser should wait before starting the animation. In general, it's best to type *0*, since waiting for any significant amount of time before starting the animation might confuse visitors. In addition, an animated transition reverses itself the moment the "trigger" stops: In other words, if a visitor points to a link, the animation begins, but when he moves the mouse off the link, the animation stops (even if the animation hasn't ended) and goes back to the original CSS property. If you add a long delay, your visitors may never see the animation.

10. **Choose an animation speed from the Timing Function drop-down menu.**

While the duration setting indicates how long the animation takes from start to finish, the timing function (also known as an "easing" function) controls the rate of change in an animation. Normally, a CSS transition doesn't progress at the same speed for the entire animation. That is, if you change the background of a link from blue to orange, the background color will start moving toward orange slowly at first; more quickly in the middle, reaching a more orange-ish color rapidly; and then slowly turning solid orange at the end. Different timing functions specify different rates of change. You can get some interesting and more "natural"-looking animations with different options:

— The cubic Bezier setting is the most complex. It requires four numbers that plot four "control points" along a line. Each point is a number from 0 to 1. In reality, all the timing functions follow what's called a Bezier curve that plots the amount of visual change over time (if you've worked with a drawing program like Photoshop Elements, you've probably used Bezier "handles" to add curves to lines). The math isn't worth explaining (that's just our way of saying it's too confusing even for us), so you're better off using an online tool to create and test different settings. The "CSS cubic-bezier Builder" tool at *http://tinyurl.com/bljzsxl* is particularly good. It lets you drag the control handles around and test how the animation changes over time. Once you find a curve you like, note the four numbers listed beside "cubic-bezier" (for example, "cubic-bezier(.17, 1, .78, .42)") and then type them into the Timing Function box.

— The Ease option is the normal way a transition animates: slowly at first, rapidly in the middle, and then slowly at the end.

— The Ease-In setting begins the animation slowly at first, and then picks up speed to finish the animation rapidly.

— The Ease-In-Out option's animation begins very slowly, proceeds very rapidly in the middle, and ends very slowly.

— The Ease-Out option's animation begins very quickly, and then ends slowly.

— The Linear option's animation is smooth, where every step in the show represents the same amount of progress. There's a reason this setting isn't the standard for animations...it's boring.

TIP The best way to pick a timing function is to simply experiment. Try different settings and see which you like best. You can always go back and edit the setting, as described in Figure 9-19.

11. **From the Property menu (Figure 9-18), pick the CSS property you want to animate.**

While the list of properties is long, a few work particularly well. Any property that uses color, like *background-color*, *border-color*, and *color*, is a good candidate; positioning properties like *left*, *right*, *top*, and *bottom* (used with absolutely positioned elements, described in Chapter 10) also look great when animated, as do the *width* and *height* properties. If you want to change the size of text, the ems or % unit of measure works well. For example, to make text twice as big, go with 2em or 200%. To make text appear bold, set the *font-weight* property to "700."

Remove selected transition

Edit selected transition

FIGURE 9-19

To edit a transition, select the triggering event (hover, active, and so on) in the CSS Transitions panel, and then click the ✎ button. Deleting a transition is a bit more complicated, as explained below.

As mentioned in step 2, if you haven't already specified a value for the property you're using in the transition, you may get unexpected results.

12. **Set the end value for the property in the End Value box.**

What you add to this box depends on the property you selected in the previous step. If you picked *background-color*, for example, Dreamweaver displays a color picker; either select a color from it or type a color value into the box (see page 151 for more on CSS colors). If you picked a property that requires a numeric value, like *width*, *height*, *margin-left*, and so on, Dreamweaver displays two options: a box to enter a value and a menu for selecting a measurement unit, like pixels (px), ems, or percentages (see page 149 for more on CSS measurement units).

If, in step 7, you chose to set a different transition for each property, go back to steps 8–10 to set the timing options for this particular property.

13. **Repeat steps 11 and 12 to continue adding properties.**

You don't need to animate every CSS property applied to an element. Adding too many not only slows down the browser, but it probably distracts your audience, too. One or two animated changes is often enough to capture people's attention.

14. **From the "Choose Where to Create the Transition" menu, select the style sheet to which you want to add the transition.**

CSS transitions are really just CSS styles, so you store them in either an internal or external style sheet. This is the same choice you make when you create any CSS style, as described on page 118. In general, it's best to store the style in the same external style sheet you use for all the other styles in your site.

15. **Click Create Transition.**

Dreamweaver closes the New Transition window, adds the required CSS to the page's style sheet, and lists the animation in the CSS Transitions panel (see Figure 9-19).

NOTE If you choose to create a CSS transition using a class style as the target (step 5 on page 427), Dreamweaver adds the class name to the HTML element currently selected (or where your cursor is currently positioned). This can be a bit disorienting since, if you aren't paying attention and simply create a CSS transition, Dreamweaver will apply that class to the current element, possibly significantly altering the look of that element. The solution is to remove the unwanted class from the tag (see page 132). That doesn't remove the CSS transition, so it will still work for the elements you intended.

Understanding the CSS Transitions Panel

Dreamweaver's CSS Transitions panel isn't really intuitive. You have to specify three components for each transition you want to create: the target selector, the triggering event, and a list of matched elements. On the far left are the CSS selectors—they represent the selectors that the transition targets, and they're the same as the targets you selected in step 5 on page 427, when you created the transition. For example, in Figure 9-19 you can see *.imageRight*, *.nav a*, and *.footer*. Those represent three selectors: two class selectors and a descendent selector (*.nav a*), which targets links inside an element that has the class *.nav* applied to it.

Next, Dreamweaver lists (and indents) the action that triggers the transition underneath each selector. For example, the *.imageRight* class has a hover transition, as do all the links inside a page element that has the class *.nav* applied to it.

You can have more than one trigger for a target. For example, you could create one transition that comes into play when a visitor points to an element, like a link, and a different transition that takes place when the guest clicks the link (or makes it active). That's the case for the *.footer* element in Figure 9-19.

Dreamweaver lists (and indents once again) the elements that match the target selector below the trigger event. While the target selectors and triggers are defined in the style sheet the page uses, the elements list is specific to each page. For example, in Figure 9-19, Dreamweaver lists the hover transition for the *.imageRight* class selector as "[Not Applied]." That means that Dreamweaver won't apply the transition to any element on the page because no HTML tag has the *.imageRight* class applied to it; there may be a tag with that class on another page that uses the same style sheet, but not on this page.

The same transition may also apply to more than one element on a page. This is common when you apply a transition to each button in a navigation bar. In Figure 9-19, for example, the panel states that there are "[3 Instances]" of the button transition on the page, meaning three links on this page use the same transition. Likewise, you see *td.footer* and *div.footer* listed under both the active and hover triggers of the *.footer* selector. That means there's one <td> tag and one <div> tag that has the *.footer* class applied to it, and both of these elements have a CSS transition for the hover and active states. If you apply the *.footer* class to any other element on the page, Dreamweaver lists that here as well.

Deleting a Transition

Deleting a CSS transition is more complicated than you might think. As discussed in the box on page 436, Dreamweaver acts on two style rules each time you add a transition: the style before the animation begins and the style at the end of the transition (a pseudo-class like *:hover* or *:active* [see page 199]). So when you go to delete a CSS transition, Dreamweaver knows immediately which styles you wish to edit.

To remove a CSS transition:

1. **Select the target selector (for example, *.imageRight*, *.nav a*, or *.footer*) and then click – (a.k.a. the Remove Transition button).**

   Dreamweaver opens the Remove Transition window (Figure 9-20).

   If you have more than one trigger event (like hover and active triggers) on the same element, you can select just one trigger to remove that transition from the selector. For example, if a link (the <a> tag) has two trigger events, hover and focus, you could remove hover, and focus would still trigger the transition.

FIGURE 9-20

The trick to removing a transition is figuring out exactly what you want to remove.

2. **In the Remove Transition window, turn on the checkboxes that tell Dreamweaver what you'd like to remove.**

   Here's the confusing part about deleting a transition. Dreamweaver gives you several options, which have different effects.

— "Remove Target rule" relates to the style rule that defines the initial appearance of the target element, the way the element looks before the transition begins. As mentioned in the box on page 436, that initial style includes the CSS *transition* property, which tells a browser that you want to animate a change in the CSS.

— Choose the "Transition properties" radio button if you simply want to remove the *transition* property but leave the rest of the style untouched. You'll usually select this option, since the style will also contain properties you'd like to preserve, like the *font, font-size, background-color, margin*, and *padding* properties. But if you *really* want to remove a style, formatting and all, turn on the "Entire rule" radio button. Just keep in mind that this removes all the formatting applied by that style to the target element.

— Turn on the "Remove Transition On rule(s)" checkbox to delete the pseudo-class style (*:hover, :active*, and so on) that Dreamweaver added to your style sheet. This removes the end result of the animation—the style that formats the element when a visitor interacts with it (by pointing to the element, for example). Leave this checkbox turned off if you simply want to remove the animation. For example, you may find that you like the abrupt change in background when a visitor points to a link and you prefer to not have that change animated. If that's the case, turn on the "Remove Target rule" checkbox, and select the "Transition properties" button, but leave the "Remove Transition On rule(s)" and the "Remove class from element(s)" checkboxes turned off.

— The "Remove class from element(s)" checkbox appears only if you apply a transition to a class selector (*.imageRight*, for example). Turning on this checkbox simply removes the class from any HTML tag on the page, so use this checkbox when you want to completely remove all traces of a transition, including the styles and classes used in it. However, if you're keeping the initial class style and its formatting (but not its transition properties), don't turn on this checkbox—that way, you'll leave the class on the HTML tag, and the remaining styling information will still apply to that element.

So, in a nutshell, if all you want to do is remove an animation, turn on the "Remove Target rule" checkbox, turn on the "Transition properties" radio button, and leave all the other checkboxes turned off. If you want to erase everything Dreamweaver added, turn on the "Remove Target rule" checkbox, select the "Transition properties" button, and then turn on the "Remove Transition On rule(s)" checkbox.

3. **Click Remove.**

The Remove Transition window closes and Dreamweaver makes the requested changes, altering styles and the HTML where needed.

Behind the Scenes of CSS Transitions

Dreamweaver's CSS Transitions panel makes it easy to create complex animated transitions. Behind the scenes, however, Dreamweaver generates quite a bit of CSS. As you've read, a CSS transition changes the value of one or more CSS properties over time. A CSS selector (a tag, class, or ID) identifies the page element that changes. So, at a minimum, you have a selector with a CSS property with two values—it has two CSS rules, in other words. The first defines the beginning of the animation—what the element looks like initially—and the second specifies the final set of properties at the end of the animation. For example, a style rule for the <a> tag sets the style for links on a page, while the style for *a:hover* defines the appearance of those links when a visitor points to them.

When you create a CSS transition and set the *transition* property to "hover" (see step 6 on page 428), Dreamweaver creates a new style with the *:hover* pseudo-class for whatever selector you chose in step 5 on page 427. For example, say you had an image on the page with the class *.imgBorder* applied to it. You want to add a cool animation that changes the image's border color when a visitor points to the pic. By following the steps on page 426, you add a new CSS transition. Dreamweaver creates a new style named *.imgBorder:hover* with the new border color you specified. The CSS for that would look something like this:

```
.imgBorder:hover {
    border-color: #457348;
}
```

By itself, this new rule doesn't have any special CSS transition magic. It simply changes the border color when someone points to the image. To animate the border, Dreamweaver has to add another CSS property, the *transition* property, to the original style—in this example, to the *.imgBorder* class style. The *transition* property includes details about the timing of the transition.

That's how CSS transitions work. You add the *transition* property to the starting point for the animation, that is, to the style rule that formats the element when the page first loads. That way, a web browser knows that it needs to animate the changes from this style to the *:hover* style.

Unfortunately, because the *transition* property hasn't yet been finalized by the W3C (the group that determines how CSS works), each browser requires its own special version of it, which Dreamweaver precedes with a special prefix: *-ms* for Internet Explorer, *-webkit* for Safari and Chrome, *-moz* for Firefox, and *-o* for Opera. That means that, to add a CSS transition, Dreamweaver actually has to write several lines of code, not just one. For example, the CSS code for the transition that changes a border might look like this:

```
.imgBorder {border: 10px solid #758837;
    -webkit-transition: border-color .5s
ease-out;
    -moz-transition: border-color .5s ease-
out;
    -ms-transition: border-color .5s ease-
out;
    -o-transition: border-color .5s ease-
out;
    transition: border-color .5s ease-out;
}
```

Thankfully, Dreamweaver takes care of all this coding for you.

■ Using CSS3

The Web continually evolves—not only do new websites appear, but the fundamental technologies used to build websites change and grow. Web designers who used HTML tables to lay out pages in the past, for instance, now use CSS. The web design world today is abuzz with the next incarnation of the CSS standard: CSS3. CSS3 offers amazing new design effects for websites, such as drop shadows for text or page elements, animated effects, rounded corners on images, gradient backgrounds, and more (see a list of the most popular CSS3 properties on page 438).

But there are drawbacks to CSS3. First, it's a work in progress; the W3C is still hammering out the list of CSS3 properties and how they work. As a result, browser support for CSS3 varies significantly. The still-popular Internet Explorer 6, for example, was created long before CSS3, and even Internet Explorer 9 doesn't understand many aspects of the standard. Some browsers don't support *any* of the properties proposed in CSS3. In addition, to get some CSS3 properties to work in the browsers that *do* support them, you have to use special "browser vendor prefixes." For example, here's the HTML to add a drop shadow to page elements like a sidebar, <div>, or headline:

```
box-shadow: 2px 3px 4px #000;
```

But to get that box shadow in Safari and Chrome browsers, you have to write that same code like this:

```
-webkit-box-shadow: 2px 3px 4px #000;
```

And for Firefox, you'd write it like this:

```
-moz-box-shadow: 2px 3px 4px #000;
```

In other words, to add a drop shadow to an element, you have to write three lines of code, and even then the style won't work in Internet Explorer 8 or earlier!

Because the CSS3 standard isn't complete and doesn't work universally across browsers, Dreamweaver doesn't support it in the same way that it supports the W3C-sanctioned CSS 2.1 standard. CSS 2.1 has wide support among browsers—even Internet Explorer 6 understands most of its properties—and Dreamweaver's CSS Rule Definition window reflects this. You can find most of the CSS 2.1 properties in that window, but you won't find many of the new CSS3 properties there. On the other hand, you'll find a slew of CSS3 properties in the new CSS Designer and, of course, in the CSS Transitions window. Web fonts, covered back on page 141, are also part of CSS3.

TIP If you want to know which browsers support which CSS properties, visit the "When can I use…" website at *http://caniuse.com/*. It's an invaluable resource for web designers.

Code-Hinting

Dreamweaver also includes CSS3 code hints. You read about code-hinting in Chapter 7, but in a nutshell, it's a helpful aid for designers who like to type their HTML, CSS, and JavaScript by hand. As you type away to add CSS properties to a style sheet, Dreamweaver lists properties that match. For example, type *co* and Dreamweaver lists *color*, *column-count*, and other CSS properties that begin with *co*. In Figure

9-21, for instance, after typing -webkit-, Dreamweaver lists all WebKit-specific CSS3 properties. You can hit Enter (Return) to accept Dreamweaver's suggestion, select a different property with your mouse, or use the up and down arrows on your keyboard to select a property. Unfortunately, code-hinting is really a power user's tool: You need to know how the CSS3 property works to correctly fill out the required value.

FIGURE 9-21

Dreamweaver's code-hinting feature is a time-and finger-saver. As you type a few letters of a CSS property, Dreamweaver opens a window that lists matching properties. You can select a property from the list and let Dreamweaver type the rest. This feature works with HTML tags and JavaScript programming as well.

Common CSS3 Properties

Although parts of CSS3 are still in development, a range of browsers support a limited set of its properties. Many web designers have begun testing the CSS3 waters and include judicious amounts of CSS3 in their pages. Here are some of the most exciting (and supported) properties:

- **Text-shadow**. Adds a drop shadow to headlines or any other text. Unfortunately, Internet Explorer 9 and earlier versions don't support this property, but it works in Safari, Firefox, Chrome, and Opera without a special vendor-specific prefix (like -webkit or -moz). You can use CSS Designer to add the text-shadow property to a style (see page 157). For more on the property and a useful tool for previewing its effect, visit http://tinyurl.com/cxxhavg.

- **Box-shadow**. Adds a drop shadow to any HTML element, like a sidebar, banner, or any box on a page. You can even add a rectangular shadow around headlines and paragraphs of text. All major browsers (except IE 8 and earlier) support this property. Unfortunately, like many CSS3 properties, you need to use special prefixes to make this work in some browsers (for example, you need to specify -webkit-box-shadow instead of box-shadow for version 5 of Safari and early versions of Safari for iOS). Visit *http://tinyurl.com/c2h2rrv* to get a useful tool for previewing box-shadows.

- **Border-radius**. If you've ever struggled trying to create rounded corners on an HTML element using multiple background images, this CSS3 property is for you. The *border-radius* property lets you round the corners of any element—you can even round just one, two, or three corners, or provide different radii for each. Again, IE 8 and earlier can't take advantage of this fun property.

- **Gradient**. CSS3 lets you add a gradient to the background of any element, so you could, for example, create a background that fades from white to dark gray without using graphics. You can create either linear (top to bottom or left to right) or radial (circular from the center outward) gradients. Internet Explorer doesn't support this property, and the other major browsers require different property names for it. For a great tool to help you preview and write the required CSS, visit *http://www.colorzilla.com/gradient-editor/*.

- **Transforms**. Have you ever wanted to rotate an element on a page—perhaps make a <div> tag look like a piece of paper that's been set down askew on a table top? Well, even if you haven't, you can! Thanks to CSS3 you can rotate, skew, and scale an element with the *transform* property. You need vendor-specific prefixes for Internet Explorer 9 (*-ms-transform*), Safari and Chrome (*-webkit-transform*), Firefox (*-moz-transform*), and Opera (*-o-transform*). Of course, IE 8 and earlier are left out of the party. To learn how to use this property and test it out, visit *http://tinyurl.com/d8dle98*.

■ Tutorial: Using Advanced Styles

In this tutorial, you'll create a descendent selector, and use Dreamweaver's CSS Designer and CSS Transitions.

NOTE To complete this tutorial, you need to download sample files from this book's Missing CD page at *http://oreilly.com/pub/missingmanuals/dreamweaverccmm2014*. (See the Note on page 37 for details.) The files you'll work on are in the Chapter09 folder, and the finished project, for comparison, is in the Chapter09_complete folder.

Once you download the tutorial files and open Dreamweaver, set up a new site as described on page 23. In a nutshell, choose Site→New Site. In the Site Setup window, type *Adv CSS Tutorial* into the Site Name box. Click 📁 next to the Local Site Folder box, navigate to and select the Chapter09 folder inside the MM_DWCC folder, and then click Choose (Select). Finally, click OK.

Creating a Descendent Selector

Once again, you'll be working on a page for the good people who run Cafe Soylent Green.

1. **Choose File→Open.**

   You'll work on a page similar to the ones you built in Chapter 5.

2. **Navigate to the Chapter09 folder and double-click the file *index.html* to open it, or double-click *index.html* in the Files panel.**

   You'll notice a simple navigation bar in the upper-right corner of the page. These links would look a lot better as buttons, so you'll add a style to make that happen.

3. **Make sure you have CSS Designer open (Window→CSS Designer). In the Sources section, click *soylent_styles.css* and then, in the Selectors section, click +.**

   Dreamweaver creates a new selector and suggests a name for it, one that reflects your cursor's position on the web page (see Figure 9-22). It also positions your cursor in the selector's text box so you can edit the proposed name.

   You follow the same process you do to create any style (see page 116 if you need a recap). You want to style the navigation links, but if you create an <a> tag style to do that, it would affect every link on the page (the links at the bottom of the page and those associated with the two images). A better option is a descendent selector that targets just the navigation links (About Us, Menu, and Home). In this case, the links are actually bulleted list items that already have a bit of styling. The outer <ul> tag has a class applied to it: *<ul class="nav">*. This class name is all you need to create a style that affects just the links inside the bulleted list.

4. **In the box for the new selector name, type *.nav a*. CSS Designer's Properties panel should look like the one in Figure 9-22.**

   The selector you just typed—*.nav a*—is a descendent selector. The element on the far right of the selector, "a," is the target. The selector to the left, *.nav*, is a class applied to the list element that wraps around the <a> tag. Time to create the style.

5. **In CSS Designer's Properties section, make sure you have the Show Set box unchecked.**

   If you have the Show Set box checked, Dreamweaver displays only the properties whose values you've already set. If there are no rules for a property, as is the case with *.nav a*, you won't see any properties set.

6. **With *soylent_styles.css* selected in the Sources section and *.nav a* selected in Selectors, click the T button in the Properties section to jump to the text properties. Then, in the box for *font-family*, choose "pt-sans, Arial, Helvetica, sans-serif," and then set *font-weight* to 700.**

   If you don't see PT Sans, you may not have installed it yet. This is a web font introduced in the Chapter 3 tutorial. You can either go back to page 160 and follow the instructions to install PT Sans, or select another font from the font-family list.

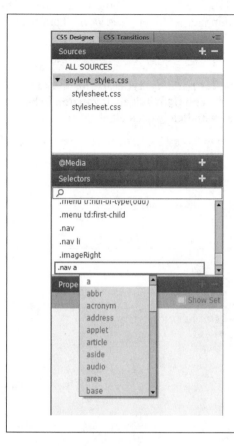

FIGURE 9-22

You can create any type of CSS selector, like the descendent selector .nav a pictured here, by clicking + in the Selectors section of CSS Designer and then typing a selector name. You use the same technique to create basic tag, class, and ID styles.

7. **Stay in the Properties section of CSS Designer and click the Background button. Beside *background-color*, click the value box to the right of the color swatch (it should be labeled "undefined"). Type in the hex color value *#0A2F02*.**

   The pound sign (#) tells Dreamweaver that the value is in hexadecimal format.

8. **Click the Layout button and then scroll down to the *display* property. Using the drop-down menu, set the value to "inline-block."**

   The inline-block setting is useful if you want to add margins and padding to an inline element.

9. **Click the Border category button. Click the All Sides icon, the first one under the word "border." In *width*, choose "px" as the unit of measure and then type *1* in the value box. Set *style* to solid. For *color*, type in *#1C6300*.**

When you choose the All Sides tab, CSS uses the *border-style* value for all the edges. This is true for the color and width, too. When you finish, you have a green border around all four sides of each link, creating a button-like box effect. Preview the page in Live view, but don't forget to turn Live view off afterward.

Because the border lines come very close to the link text, you'll add some padding to push the border away from the text.

10. **Click the Layout button, and then, for** *padding*, **type** *3px* **for the top and bottom values. Type** *10px* **for the left and right values. If you don't choose a unit of measure, CSS Designer automatically uses pixels (px).**

The window should look like the one in Figure 9-23. You're all done with this style. Now it's time to add a CSS transition.

11. **Choose File→Save All Related Files.**

Dreamweaver saves your web page (*index.html*) and the CSS source file (*soylent_styles.css*).

FIGURE 9-23

Whenever you add a border around an element that has text in it, it's a good idea to add some padding as well. Padding pushes the border away from the text so the text doesn't look cramped.

Adding a CSS Transition

CSS transitions are simple animations between two sets of CSS rules. Dreamweaver CC makes it easy to add these fun CSS3 effects.

1. **Choose Window→CSS Transitions.**

Dreamweaver displays the CSS Transitions panel. If you want, you can drag the panel by its tab to move it or dock it someplace in your workspace.

2. **Click + (the Create New Transition button).**

The New Transition window opens. You'll specify the element you want to animate.

3. **From the Target Rule drop-down menu, select ".nav a."**

   The menu lists all the CSS styles available to the page, as well as any IDs the page's HTML uses. In this case, you choose the descendent selector you just created since you want to add a transition to the navigation links.

4. **From the Transition On menu, select "hover."**

   While Dreamweaver gives you other options, many aren't useful. "Hover" is by far the most common option, as it animates an element's appearance when a visitor points to it.

5. **Make sure you have "Use the same transition for all properties" selected from the drop-down menu. Type *.25* in the Duration box, *0* in the Delay box, and choose "ease-in-out" from the Timing Function drop-down menu.**

   This creates an animation that takes .25 seconds from start to finish, begins without delay, and starts slowly, then changes rapidly, and then slows down as the .25 seconds comes to an end.

6. **Click + below the Property box, and choose "background-color" from the pop-up menu. Type *#E1EBEB* in the End Value box.**

   The window should now look like the one in Figure 9-24. You're done.

FIGURE 9-24

It's possible to animate each CSS property for a style differently (choose "Use a different transition for each property"). However, animating each property at a different rate, with a different delay and a different timing function, can result in a confusing set of transitions.

7. **Click Create Transition to create the transition and close the window.**

Behind the scenes, Dreamweaver adds a new style, *.nav a:hover*, and the proper CSS transition code to the *.nav a* style. Time to check your work.

8. **To preview the transition, choose Live from the Design/Live menu at the top of the Document window. Point to various links.**

The background color gently fades into view when you point to a link, and fades out when you move your mouse away. If you don't see this effect, you may have accidentally selected a different transition trigger (like "active" or "focus" instead of "hover"). If that's the case, select the transition in the CSS Transitions panel and then click – to delete it.

9. **Set the Design/Live menu back to Design for the next part of the tutorial.**

Now you'll add a CSS3 property to the links.

Adding CSS3 Properties

You won't find many CSS3 properties in the Rule Definition window you open from the Properties panel's CSS mode, but you can add CSS3 properties using CSS Designer.

1. **Open CSS Designer (Window→CSS Designer). In the Sources section, click *soylent_styles.css*, and then, in Selectors, click ".nav a."**

The Properties section of CSS Designer shows all the properties you can set for the selector *.nav a*. If you see only a few properties, make sure you have the Show Set checkbox turned off.

2. **In the Properties section of CSS Designer, click the Border button, and then find the *border-radius* properties.**

The border-radius widget looks, appropriately enough, like a rounded rectangle, as shown in Figure 9-25.

3. **Click the link icon in the center of the border radius settings to make all the border radii the same, and then, type *3* in any of the corner boxes.**

You won't see the rounded corners in Dreamweaver's Design view, but if you preview the page in a browser or switch to Live view, you'll see the effect (make sure you exit Live view before continuing to step 4). Next, you'll add some CSS3 magic to the two photos on the page.

4. **In Design view, select the first photo (the one below "All Natural Ingredients") and then, from the Properties panel, choose "imageRight" from the class menu.**

This is the same style you created in Chapter 5's tutorial. It floats the image to the right and adds a border around it.

5. **Repeat the previous step for the next photo (the one below the headline "Technology Meets Good Nutrition").**

   Now you'll add another CSS3 property.

6. **In the Sources section of CSS Designer, click either *soylent_styles.css* or All Sources. Then, in the Selectors section, click ".imageRight" (it's near the bottom of the list). In Properties, scroll down until you see *opacity*, and then type *.75* in the box to the right.**

   The *opacity* property controls the transparency of an element. You can use a value of between 0 and 1. Zero makes the element completely invisible, while 1 makes it completely opaque. A value in between, like the .75 here, lets a little bit of the background show through while still displaying the element. Why would you want to do this? So you could animate it with a CSS transition, of course!

FIGURE 9-25

The CSS border-radius *property adds rounded corners to elements. You can give all four corners the same radius (as in this case) by clicking the center link button before you set a value. To create a completely rounded "box," use 50% for all four corners.*

> **NOTE** As with the *border-radius* property, you can't see the effect of the *opacity* property in Dreamweaver's Design view.

Adding One Last Transition

1. **Click to select one of the two images.**

   When you create a CSS transition from a class selector (here, the *.imageRight* style you applied in the previous step), Dreamweaver has the unfortunate habit of adding that class to whatever element is currently selected on the page. If you don't select one of the images, Dreamweaver ends up adding the *.image Right* class to another element on the page, causing unwanted animation when someone points to that element.

2. **Open the CSS Transitions window (Window→CSS Transitions), and then click the New Transition button (+).**

You'll specify the element you want to animate.

3. **From the Target Rule drop-down menu, select ".imageRight."**

This is the class style where you just added the *opacity* property.

4. **From the Transition On menu, select "hover."**

This time, you'll set different timings for two different CSS properties.

5. **Choose "Use a different transition for each property" from the drop-down menu.**

The window changes.

6. **Click + below the Property box, and then choose "border-color" from the pop-up menu. Type *1* in the Duration box and *0* in the Delay box. Choose "ease-in-out" from the Timing function menu, and then type *#0A2F02* in the End Value box.**

This creates an animation that lasts 1 second (pretty long), gradually changing the border color around the image to dark green.

Now you'll add the *opacity* property.

7. **Click + below the Property box and then choose "opacity" from the pop-up menu. Type *.5* in the Duration box and *0* in the Delay box. Choose "ease-out" from the Timing function menu, and then type *1* in the End Value box.**

The window should look like the one in Figure 9-26. This animation makes the images appear vibrant and colorful when a visitor points to them. Since it only takes half a second to complete, it will happen more quickly than the border-color change.

8. **Click Create Transition to close the window and complete the transition.**

Behind the scenes, Dreamweaver adds a new style, *.imageRight:hover*, and the proper CSS transition to the *.imageRight* style. Time to check out your work.

9. **Choose Live from the Design/Live menu at the top of the document window. Point to the two photos.**

They should pop vibrantly from the page, while the border will more slowly change to dark green (see Figure 9-27).

You can find a completed version of this tutorial in the Chapter09_complete folder that accompanies the downloaded tutorial files.

FIGURE 9-26

You can animate different CSS properties at different rates when you create CSS transitions.

FIGURE 9-27

You can enliven any web page by adding CSS transitions to links, navigation bars, and even images. In this example, a "soft" image becomes vibrant and its border slowly turns dark green when a visitor points to the picture. There's no need for JavaScript—just a little CSS3 magic. (Unfortunately, you'll find that these effects won't work in Internet Explorer 9 or earlier.)

Choosing a Page Layout

W eb design isn't, unfortunately, like most other forms of graphic composition. For magazine and book projects, programs like Adobe InDesign let you place text and images anywhere you want, and even rotate and overlap them. But web designers are stuck with the basic technology of HTML, which wants to flow content from the top of a browser window to the bottom, in one long column. To place elements around the page and create multiple columns of content, you need to resort to some fancy footwork, and that's where this chapter comes in.

For much of the Web's short life, designers have used the HTML <table> tag to control the position of elements on a page—to create columns, sidebars, banners, and so on. But the tag was intended to display information in spreadsheet-like format, and bending it to a web designer's vision often resulted in complex HTML that downloaded slowly, displayed sluggishly, and challenged coders.

Now that CSS-friendly web browsers like Internet Explorer, Safari, Firefox, Chrome, and Opera rule the Web, designers can safely rely on a much better (though sometimes frustrating) method of page layout: Cascading Style Sheets. That's right, not only is CSS great for formatting text, navigation bars, images, and other bits of a web page, but it also has all the tools you need to create sophisticated designs, like the ones in Figure 10-1.

CSS provides a couple of ways to control the placement of elements on a page. The most common is to create multiple-column layouts using the CSS *float* property (the same property you used in Chapter 5 to position an image to the left or right of a page).

FIGURE 10-1

*CSS Zen Garden (www.csszengarden.com) is the original
showcase for CSS layout. Over the years, it has caused many
a web designer to bow down and proclaim, "I'm not worthy,
I'm not worthy." The site not only demonstrates great design,
but it also shows you the power of CSS-based layout. Each
page includes the same content and the same HTML; the only
difference is their external style sheets and graphics. CSS lets
you redesign sites without rewriting any HTML.*

Dreamweaver includes a starter set of layouts that use this float-based approach. These stock pages cover the most commonly used layouts—designs with two or three columns of content, a header for a logo and banner, and a footer for copyright notices, for example. The files aren't really complete page designs; they're basic web page building blocks you can modify to match your sensibility.

CSS also includes a *position* property, which lets you place elements "absolutely"— that is, at a pixel-specific position on the page. While this might sound like the answer to page layout, absolute positioning has its own problems, and web designers don't usually use it to lay out entire pages. Instead, they use it to accurately place small elements in precise positions on a page. They also use absolutely positioned elements, in conjunction with JavaScript, to make elements pop onto the page over other components—a menu bar (page 201), for example, may use absolute positioning to display drop-down menus over the page's content.

NOTE CSS layout is one of those complex topics that is sometimes better learned by doing instead of reading. To get a taste of how CSS layout works, try the tutorial on page 496, and then flip back to the beginning of this chapter for all the messy details.

This chapter introduces the basic concepts behind float-based layouts—what they are, how they work, and how to create one. It also shows you how to modify Dreamweaver's CSS designs and how to absolutely position elements so you can place them where you want them.

■ Types of Web Page Layouts

Being a web designer means dealing with the unknown—what kind of browsers your visitors use, whether your design work in all of them, and so on. Perhaps the biggest challenge designers face is creating attractive designs that work across different-size screens. Monitors vary in size and resolution, from petite 15-inch 640 x 480 pixel models to 30-inch monstrosities displaying, oh, about 5 million x 4.3 million pixels. In addition, designers have to cope with the small displays found on millions of smartphones and tablets. (Chapters 12–14 show you how to use CSS to create sites for mobile devices.)

NOTE A new approach to web layout, called responsive Web design, uses a "liquid" layout and some fancy CSS to completely change a page's design depending on the destination screen size. That is, you can create one design for a phone, a different design for a tablet, and a third layout for desktop browsers, and have the appropriate page appear on each type of device, thanks to a technique called media queries. You'll learn about this technique, as well as the tools in Dreamweaver that let you build these kinds of layouts, starting in Chapter 12.

Float-based layouts come in two flavors, *fixed-width* and *liquid* (the latter also called *fluid layouts*). A fixed-width layout gives you the most control over your design but can inconvenience some of your visitors—folks with really small monitors have to scroll to the right to see everything, and those with large monitors see wasted space that could display more of your excellent content. Liquid layouts make designing pages more challenging, but they also make the most of your guests' screen sizes.

- **Fixed-width layout**. Many designers prefer the consistency of a set width. Regardless of how wide a browser window is, the page's width remains the same (see the top two images in Figure 10-2). In some cases, the design clings to the left edge of the browser window. More often, the content is centered. With the fixed-width approach, you don't have to worry about what happens to your design on a very wide (or very small) monitor.

  Fixed-width designs can range anywhere from 760 pixels wide to 1000 pixels or more wide. These days, however, the screens on even tiny 10-inch netbooks or Apple iPads are at least 1024 pixels wide, and all desktop computers support at least 1024 x 768 pixels, so most new sites use much bigger dimensions—960 pixels wide is now a common baseline for fixed-width designs, but you'll also see 1000 pixels and even a bit more on some sites.

- **Liquid layout**. Sometimes, it's easier to roll with the tide instead of fighting it. A liquid design adjusts a page's dimensions to fit a browser's width—whatever that may be. Your page gets wider or narrower as your visitor resizes his browser window (Figure 10-2, bottom two images). While liquid design makes the best use of browser real estate, you have to do more work to make sure your design looks good at different window sizes. On very large monitors, these types of designs can look ridiculously wide.

Fixed-width designs are probably the most common type of layout on the Web, since they provide a consistent display that makes it much easier for designers to work with.

■ Float Layout Basics

Float-based layouts take advantage of the CSS *float* property to position elements side by side and create columns on a page. As you read on page 248, you can float an image to make text wrap around it. But the *float* property is also a powerful layout tool that lets you move a bunch of related page elements (like a list of links you want to appear in a left-hand column) to one side of the page or the other. In essence, the *float* property moves a page element to the left or right. When that happens, any HTML that appears *after* the floated element moves up on the page and hugs the side of the floated element.

Float is a CSS property, available when you create a CSS style (see page 116 for instructions on creating styles). You'll find it in CSS Designer's Layout category (see Figure 10-3). Choose the "Left" option, and the styled element floats to the left; choose "Right," and the element moves to the right.

FIGURE 10-2

CSS gives you several ways to deal with the uncertain widths of browser windows and browser font sizes. You could simply ignore the fact that your site's visitors have different-resolution monitors and force a single, unchanging width on them, as the Target.com website does. As you can see in the top two images, resizing the browser window doesn't change the page—it remains the same width (but centered in the browser window) when you make the browser window wider. Many websites take this approach. Alternatively, you could create a liquid design whose content flows to fill whatever width window your visitor uses. That's how Amazon's site works (bottom two images).

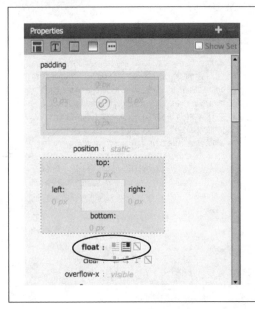

FIGURE 10-3

You have just three options when you float an element: left, right, and none. You might never need "none"—it simply positions the element as though it were a normal, unfloated element. Since this is standard behavior for any element, you need this option only if you want to turn off a float applied by another style (see page 412 for more on how multiple styles can affect the same element).

The Mighty <div> Tag

Whatever layout method you use, web page design involves putting chunks of content into different regions of a page. With CSS, the most common way to organize content is with the <div> tag. The <div> tag is an HTML element that has no inherent formatting properties (besides the fact that browsers treat it as a block element, with a line break before and after it); you use it to define a logical grouping of elements (a *division*) on a page, a chunk of HTML that belongs together, like an article and accompanying images. For example, the elements comprising the logo and navigation bar in Figure 10-4 occupy the top of the page, so it makes sense to wrap a <div> tag around them (labeled "Banner div" in the figure).

At the very least, you would include <div> tags for all the major regions of your page, such as the banner, main content area, sidebar, footer, and so on. But it's also possible to wrap a <div> tag around one or more *other* <div>s. Web designers often wrap all the HTML inside the <body> tag in a <div> tag. This tag, therefore, wraps around all the other <div>s on the page, and you can set some basic page properties by applying CSS to this *wrapper* <div>. For example, you can style the <div> to set the overall width for the page, set left and right margins, or center all the page's content. A wrapper like this is also a good place to define a basic global style for your fonts. For example, if you define the *font-family* here, you don't need to define it for your paragraphs and headings.

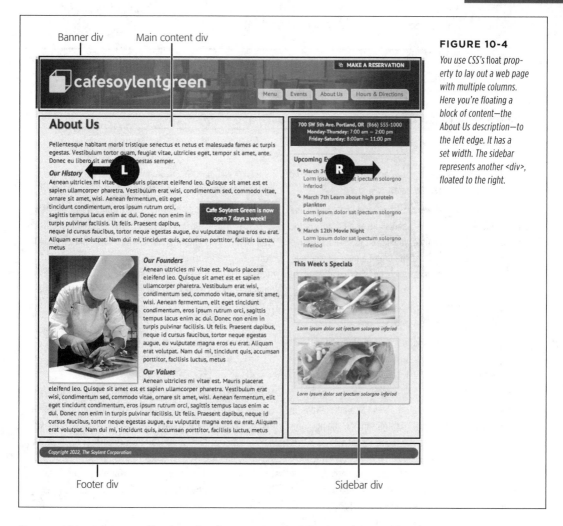

FIGURE 10-4

You use CSS's float property to lay out a web page with multiple columns. Here you're floating a block of content—the About Us description—to the left edge. It has a set width. The sidebar represents another <div>, floated to the right.

Once you've got your <div> tags in place, you assign them a class or ID selector (page 128). This makes it easy to identify the basic building blocks of a page. For example, the <div> tag for a page's banner area might be *<div id="banner">* or *<div class="banner">*.

There are only a few differences between using a class selector and an ID selector to identify a region of a page. Recall that you can use an ID only once per page, so if you have an element that appears multiple times, use a class selector. For example, if you have several <div>s that position photos and their captions, you'd add a class to each <div> rather than an ID, like this: *<div class="photoBox">*. Another difference is that, in the case of a style conflict, ID selectors in CSS take precedence over class selectors. For example, if you apply both an ID and a class selector to the same <div> tag and then you create class and ID styles, any properties in the ID style that conflict with those in the class style would win out. This is one of the basic rules of the CSS cascade, described on page 412.

NOTE If you select a <div> tag in the Tag Selector, the Properties panel provides two menus, one to apply a class style to the <div> and the other to apply an ID style to it.

HTML5 Elements

I hear that HTML5 has lots of new elements that replace the <div> tag. Is the <div> tag still relevant?

HTML5 introduces many new tags to help organize web page content. These "sectioning elements" let you group specific types of content. For example, you'd use the <header> tag to group content that appears at the top of a page (like a banner), the <article> tag to for corral all the tags that make up an individual article, and the <aside> tag to wrap content related to other content on the page, like an article-and-sidebar pair. HTML5 offers many other tags as well.

Basically, you use these tags to group related elements on a page, and they're meant to take the place of the humble <div> tag for all the content types listed above (headers, articles, and so on).

However, the <div> tag works just as well as all those tags. In fact, there's nothing inherently different in how the new tags act in a web browser, and from a site visitor's perspective, there's no difference whatsoever. You can style <div>s the same way you'd style the new HTML5 tags, by using Cascading Style Sheets. Then why the new tags? The HTML5 sectioning elements are intended to help *computers* understand a page's structure

better. For example, Google might look for an <article> tag in a page to better identify key content.

Internet Explorer 8 and earlier don't understand the new HTML5 tags, so Dreamweaver uses a standard solution called "html5shiv." This chunk of JavaScript code makes Internet Explorer 8 and earlier play well with the new <header>, <footer>, <article>, <section>, and <aside> tags. Dreamweaver's templates automatically add a line in the header of web pages to get the code necessary for IE to play well with HTML5:

```
<!--[if lt IE 9]>
<script src="http://html5shiv.googlecode.
com/svn/trunk/html5.js"></script>
<![endif]-->
```

The <script src> line tells older browsers to get the JavaScript code from the googlecode archive, an online library that delivers code when a page requests it. It works as long as guests have JavaScript turned on (the factory setting for Internet Explorer) and the browser has access to the Internet. To add the same capability to web pages you didn't create from Dreamweaver templates, just copy that code into the <head> portion of the page.

The Insert→Div Command

Because grouping parts of a page using <div> tags is such an important part of CSS layout, Dreamweaver includes a tool to simplify the process. The Insert→Div command lets you wrap a <div> tag around selected content, or simply drop an empty <div> into a page that you can fill with images, links, paragraphs of text, or whatever. In other words, the Insert→Div command creates both the opening and closing tags for a <div> element. They look like this:

```
<div> </div>
```

To use this tool, either select the content you want to wrap (for example, click at the beginning of the selection and drag to the end of it) or click in the page where you want to insert an empty <div> tag. Then choose Insert→Div, or better yet, use the Insert panel—the Div button appears at the top of both the Common and Structure categories (see Figure 10-5).

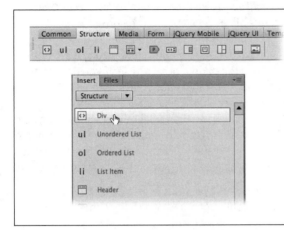

FIGURE 10-5

The Common and Structure categories of the Insert panel include a button that adds both opening and closing <div> tags. In this figure, the top image shows the Insert bar displayed as a toolbar (learn how to do this on page 12), and the bottom image shows the Insert panel as Dreamweaver displays it out of the box.

Either way, Dreamweaver opens the Insert Div window (Figure 10-6).

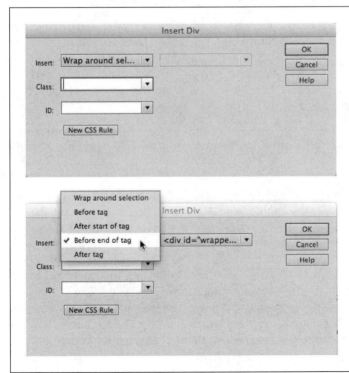

FIGURE 10-6

The Insert Div window's left-hand Insert drop-down menu (top) lets you tell Dreamweaver where to put a <div> tag in relation to other tags on the page (bottom). The Insert menu to the right of that lists tags that have an ID applied to them, or, if you chose "After start of tag" or "Before end of tag," it lists the <body> tag. Suppose, for example, you want to insert a <div> tag to display a footer at the bottom of the page. Because you know the footer will go last on the page, you click the Insert Div button, select "Before end of tag" from the left Insert menu, and then <body> from the right menu. Dreamweaver puts the <div> at the very end of the page's content, just before the closing </body> tag.

If you click OK, Dreamweaver wraps the content you selected in a <div> tag, or, if you didn't select anything on the page, it drops a new <div> tag into the page with the text "Content for New Div Tag Goes Here." (Of course, you'll replace that with your own content.) But usually, you'll take an additional step, applying either a class or ID selector to the <div>. You do this in a couple of ways:

- **Choose a class from the Class drop-down menu or an ID from the ID menu**. The Class menu lists all the class styles available to the current page. A class selector is the way to go if you want to format several <div>s the same way. For example, you might use a <div> tag to position an image and a caption on a page, or to create a pull-quote in the middle of an article. If you had multiple instances of photos with captions, you could create a class style (like *.figure*) to format each photo-caption pair. You could then select a photo and caption on the page, use the Insert→Div command, and then select the class name (*.figure* in this example) from the Class menu. You could repeat this process multiple times on a single page. But you can also apply a class to a <div> even if you use that <div> for a unique set of elements—such as the banner at the top of a page.

  The ID drop-down menu on the Insert Div window lists any ID selectors you created. Since you can use an ID only once per page, the ID menu lists only those IDs you haven't applied to a page element. For example, after you apply the *#banner* ID to the logo and navigation bar at the top of your page, *banner* no longer appears in the ID menu. And while you're limited to using an ID once per page, you can apply the same ID to more than one page.

- **Create a new class or ID**. If you haven't yet created a style to apply to the new <div> tag, click the New CSS Rule button. It opens the familiar New Style Rule window. The process is the same as that for any style, described on page 116. Once you define the style, it appears in the appropriate menu on the Insert Div window (in other words, if you create a class style, that style name appears in the Class drop-down menu).

TIP If you're more comfortable using CSS Designer, by all means, go ahead and create class or ID selectors there. Once you do, their names will show up in the Insert Div window's menus.

After you apply a class or ID selector and click OK, Dreamweaver inserts the new <div> tag, complete with the appropriate HTML needed to apply the style. For example, that tag might look like *<div class="photo">*. (Note that when you create a class style, you add a period—for example, *.photo*—but when Dreamweaver inserts the HTML for the class name, it omits the period. The same applies to ID names: *<div id="banner">* is correct; *<div id="#banner">* is not.) In addition, Dreamweaver applies any styling you create for the class or ID to the <div>. In the case of a CSS layout, that could mean sizing the <div> and positioning it on the page, as well as adding a background color, changing the size of the text, or any other CSS formatting. You can add new content inside the <div>, edit what's there, or delete the <div> completely.

NOTE CSS-based layout is a big topic, worthy of a book or two by itself. For more in-depth coverage, including solutions to common float problems, pick up a copy of *CSS3: The Missing Manual* (O'Reilly Media).

A Simple Example

To get a better idea of how <div>s help with page layout, look at the designs in Figure 10-7. These layouts include a banner (a logo and navigation bar), sidebar, and main story. The left images show the order in which the HTML appears on the page: the banner elements come first, the sidebar second, and the main story (headlines, paragraphs, photo, and so on) last. (Remember, what you're seeing demonstrates the power and beauty of the HTML/CSS tango. Your HTML file contains your structured chunks of content, while your CSS controls how a browser displays that content.) Viewed in a web browser, without any CSS styling, these different HTML sections would all appear stacked one on top of the other.

NOTE You don't have to create and name <div>s to get started laying out your pages with CSS. Dreamweaver ships with a couple of premade CSS-based layouts. To find templates for two-column and three-column layouts, go to File→New. Click the Blank Page category and then, under Page Type, choose HTML. In the Layout pane you'll see *2 column fixed, right sidebar, header and footer* and *3-column fixed, header and footer*.

To create a two-column design using CSS, follow these steps in Design view:

1. **Select the page's banner.**

   For example, click before the logo image and drag until you select it and the navigation bar. With this HTML selected, you can wrap it in a <div> tag.

2. **In the Structure category of the Insert panel, click Div.**

   Dreamweaver opens the Insert Div window. In the Class box, type a class name (or type an ID name in the ID box, if you prefer).

   You can name the style several ways, depending on whether you want to create the style immediately, whether you've already created the style, or whether you want to create the style later on.

   — To create a class or ID style right away, click the New CSS Rule button. The process at this point is the same as that for creating any new style, described on page 116. In this case, you might name the class style *.banner* (or the ID style *#banner*). You can set any CSS properties you want for the banner: Add a border around all four sides, color the background, specify a width, and so on.

   — Select a class name from the Class menu or an ID name from the ID menu. The web page may already have an external style sheet that contains all the necessary styles for the layout attached. Just select the class name for the <div> you're inserting (for example, *.banner*).

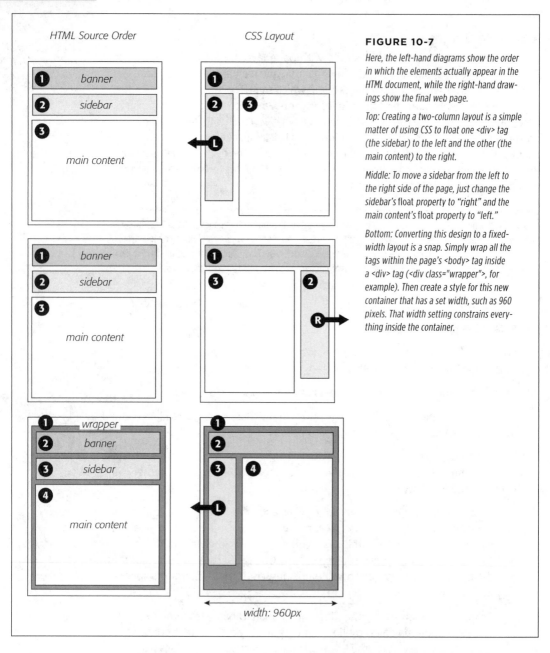

HTML Source Order

CSS Layout

FIGURE 10-7

Here, the left-hand diagrams show the order in which the elements actually appear in the HTML document, while the right-hand drawings show the final web page.

Top: Creating a two-column layout is a simple matter of using CSS to float one <div> tag (the sidebar) to the left and the other (the main content) to the right.

Middle: To move a sidebar from the left to the right side of the page, just change the sidebar's float property to "right" and the main content's float property to "left."

Bottom: Converting this design to a fixed-width layout is a snap. Simply wrap all the tags within the page's <body> tag inside a <div> tag (<div class="wrapper">, for example). Then create a style for this new container that has a set width, such as 960 pixels. That width setting constrains everything inside the container.

— Type a name in the Class (or ID) box. If you don't want to create a style right away, you can just type *banner* in the Class or ID box and create the rules later.

NOTE When you create a class style using the New CSS Rule box, you have to start the class name with a period, like this: *.banner*. However, when you type the class name in the Insert Div window, you omit the period; you just type *banner* (or select "banner" from the Class menu). The same applies to ID styles—use a # when you create a style in the New CSS Rule box (*#banner*, for example), but omit it in the Insert Div window.

3. **Click OK to close the Insert Div window.**

   Dreamweaver wraps the selected HTML in a <div> tag and, if you created a new style, formats the banner.

4. **Select the contents of the sidebar, and then, from the Insert toolbar, click Div. Click the New CSS Rule button and create another class (or ID) style. Name it whatever you like, such as *.sidebar* or *.section-Nav*, and then click OK.**

   This style formats and positions the left sidebar. You're finally getting to the "float" part of this design.

5. **In the New CSS Rule window, click the Box category, and then, from the Float menu, select "left" (see Figure 10-8).**

   When you work with floats, the order in which page elements appear in the HTML code is important. The HTML that positions the floated element must appear *before* the HTML for the element that wraps around the floated content.

FIGURE 10-8

Whenever you float an element (other than an image), always set a width. It constrains the floated element so that a browser can wrap other content around it.

Figure 10-7 shows three two-column layouts. The diagrams on the left show the page's HTML source order: a <div> for the banner, followed by a <div> for the sidebar and, lastly, a <div> for the main content. On the right, you see the actual page layout. The sidebar comes *before* the main content in the HTML, so it can float either left (Figure 10-7, top and bottom) or right (Figure 10-7, middle). The main text area then moves up the page and wraps around the floated element.

6. **Type a value in the Width box (circled in Figure 10-8).**

Unless you're floating an image with a predefined width, you should always give your floats a width. That way, you create a set size for the floated element, allowing the browser to wrap other content around it.

You can use a fixed width, say *250px*, or you can specify a percentage for a flexible design based on the width of the browser window (see page 451 for more on set versus variable dimensions). For example, if you set the sidebar to 20% of the width of the browser window and the window is 700 pixels wide, then the sidebar will be 140 pixels wide. If a visitor stretches her window to 1000 pixels wide, the sidebar grows to 200 pixels. Fixed-width sidebars make page design easier, since you don't have to fret over differently sized browser windows.

> **NOTE** If you set a fixed width for your overall design (by wrapping all the page contents in a <div> tag and setting its *width* property), percentage width values for the sidebar are based on the containing element, not on the window size, and that percentage doesn't change when someone changes the size of her browser window. This is true of any element whose width you specify using a percentage value. That percentage is based on the width of the "parent" element.

7. **Add any other styles you like, and then insert the <div>.**

At this point you can continue to style the sidebar. You could add a background color, set a font family that, thanks to inheritance (see page 411), will apply to all the text inside the <div>, and so on.

When you're done with the Style Definition window, click OK. Dreamweaver returns you to the Insert Div window, which has the Class box filled in with your freshly created style's name. Click OK to insert the <div>, and then watch the sidebar float.

Now it's time to style the main column.

8. **Follow steps 4–7 for the main content <div>, too. Select the page elements that form the main content of the page, click Insert→Div, and then create a new class (or ID) style.**

In this instance, you don't need to float anything. You merely have to add a left margin to the main content <div> so that the content won't wrap *below* the end of the sidebar. If the sidebar is shorter than the main content area, the text from the main column wraps both beside and underneath the sidebar, much as the main text interacts with the left-floated photo in Figure 10-4. But if the main content wrapped underneath the sidebar, you wouldn't get two side-by-side columns; you'd get one long column of content. Adding a left margin that's equal to or greater than the width of the left-floated sidebar indents the main content of the page so that it sits beside the sidebar, creating the illusion of a second column.

By the way, it's usually a good idea to make the left margin a little bigger than the width of the sidebar. That creates some empty space—a gutter—between the two elements. So if the sidebar is 170 pixels wide, setting a left margin of 185 pixels for the main content <div> adds an extra 15 pixels of space for the gutter. If you use percentages to set the width of the sidebar, use a slightly larger percentage value for the main content's left margin.

In addition, avoid setting a width for the main content <div>. It's not necessary, since browsers simply expand the width of the content to fit the available space. Even if you want a fixed-width design, you don't need to set a width for the main content <div>, as explained in Figure 10-7.

Expanding the two-column design to a three-column layout isn't difficult, either (see Figure 10-9). First, add another <div> *between* the two columns and float it to the right. Then add a right margin to the middle column, so that if the text in the middle column runs longer than the text for the right sidebar, the main content's text won't end up underneath the sidebar.

FIGURE 10-9

A three-column design uses the same concepts as a two-column design. In this case, you float both the left and right sidebars and add both left and right margins to the center column. The left-hand diagram shows the order of the HTML; the right side shows the final web page.

TIP If you're concerned about displaying your HTML in a specific order—for example, you'd like the main content region to appear before a sidebar—you can do that by simply floating both the main content and the sidebar. You'll see an example of this in the tutorial at the end of this chapter.

■ Understanding the Box Model

It's no coincidence that you find the *float* property in the Box category of the CSS Rule Definition window (Figure 10-10) and in the Layout category of CSS Designer. Float is fundamental to the "box model" that website developers use for page layout. That model states that all page elements (text, pictures, and so on) are boxes, and you build your page by arranging the boxes.

Starting on the inside and moving out, those boxes are made up of content, padding, a border, and a margin. A page element may not always have all those features. For example, a picture may not have a border, and you might set the margin and padding properties to *0*. In any case, the size of a page element is the sum of those features: content, padding, border, and margin.

FIGURE 10-10

Use the CSS Rule Definition window's Box category to define the dimensions of a style, to position an object on the page, and to add space between the styled object and the objects around it. If you're working in CSS Designer (not shown here), use the Layout category.

To fully understand CSS layouts and make the most of floats, you need to understand the other CSS properties in the Rule Definition window: *width*, *height*, *clear*, *padding*, and *margin*.

- **Width and height**. You can specify the dimensions of any styled object using these properties. If you want a paragraph that's 100 pixels wide, create a class style with the *width* property set to 100 pixels, and then apply it to the paragraph. You'll often use the *width* property in conjunction with the *float* property to do things like create a box with a set width that floats to either the left or right side of a page—a common format for pull-quotes, message boxes, and sidebars (see the bullet point below).

  Be careful with the *height* property. Many designers use it for precise control over page elements. Unfortunately, height is tricky to control. If you set a height for a sidebar that contains text and you later add more text, you can end up with text spilling outside the sidebar—the same thing can happen if a visitor increases the text size in his browser. In other words, set the height of an object only if you're *sure* the content inside will never get taller—for example, if the content is an image.

- **Float**. To force an object to the left or right side of a page and have other content wrap around it, use the *float* property. Of course, that's been most of the point of this chapter, so you probably understand this by now. However, there's one important thing to keep in mind: floating an object doesn't necessarily move it to the side of a page or browser window. A floated object merely goes to the left or right edge of what's called its "containing block." If you float a <div> to the left of a page to create a sidebar, and then insert an image into the sidebar and float that image to the right, the image goes to the right edge of the sidebar, *not* to the right edge of the page. In addition, if you float multiple elements, they can often end up sitting beside each other—you use this technique to create four-column layouts, where each column floats next to the other.

- **Clear**. Clear *prevents* an element from wrapping around any object with a right or left *float* property. It comes in handy when you want to force an element to appear *below* a floated object instead of wrapping around it. The classic example is a page's footer (the area at the bottom of a page that usually contains contact information and a copyright notice). If a page has a left-floated sidebar that's longer than the main content, the footer could move up the page and wrap around the sidebar, which is not what you want. In this case, the bottom of the sidebar is at the bottom of the page, and the footer is now somewhere in the middle of the page. To fix this problem, set the footer's *clear* property to "both." That forces the footer to drop below both left- and right-floated elements. (If you merely want something to drop below a left-floated element but still wrap around anything floated right, choose the "left" option; to clear a right-floated element, choose "right.") In other words, if you ever see page content next to a floated element instead of underneath it, use the *clear* property to properly position that content.

- **Padding**. Padding is the gap that separates the content of a page element—like a paragraph of text or an image—from its border. If you put a 1-pixel border around an image and want to add 10 pixels of space between the image and that border, make sure you have the "Same for all" checkbox turned on, type *10* into the Top padding box, and then choose "pixels" from the drop-down menu. To set the padding around each edge separately, turn off the "Same for all" checkbox and then type values into each of the four boxes.

- **Margin**. Margin is the amount of space *surrounding* an element. It surrounds the border and padding properties of the style and lets you add space between elements. Use any of the values—pixels, percentages, and so on—that CSS allows.

Padding, margins, borders, and the content inside a styled tag make up what web designers call the CSS Box Model, seen in Figure 10-11. Margins and padding are invisible. They also have similar effects: 5 pixels of left padding adds 5 pixels of space to the left edge of a style; the same happens when you add a 5-pixel left margin. Most people use margins to put space between elements (for example, between the right edge of one column and left edge of an adjacent column) and padding to add space between an element's border and its content (like a column of text and its surrounding borderline). Because you can't see padding or margins (just the empty space they occupy), it's often difficult to know if the gap between, say, the banner at the top of your page and the main content area results from the banner's style or the main area's style.

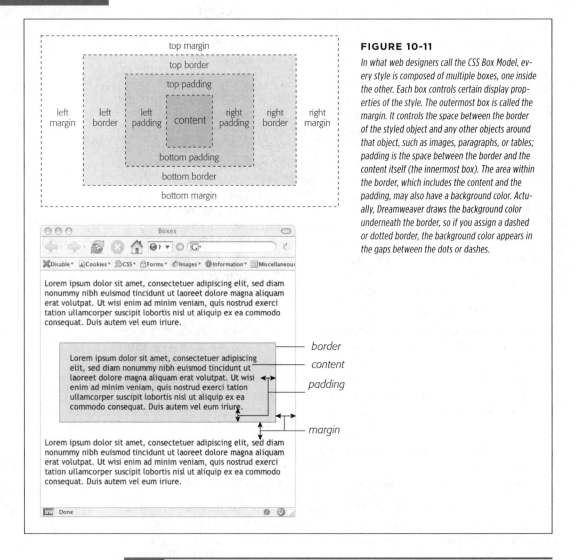

FIGURE 10-11

In what web designers call the CSS Box Model, every style is composed of multiple boxes, one inside the other. Each box controls certain display properties of the style. The outermost box is called the margin. It controls the space between the border of the styled object and any other objects around that object, such as images, paragraphs, or tables; padding is the space between the border and the content itself (the innermost box). The area within the border, which includes the content and the padding, may also have a background color. Actually, Dreamweaver draws the background color underneath the border, so if you assign a dashed or dotted border, the background color appears in the gaps between the dots or dashes.

> **NOTE** Dreamweaver includes a tool called Inspect Mode that helps you visualize margins and padding. It works in Live view and displays margins and padding in different colors. To learn how to use it, see page 513.

You also can't always tell if the extra space comes from the padding or the margin setting. Dreamweaver includes a helpful diagnostic tool (View→Visual Aids→CSS Layout Box Model) that lets you see these invisible properties (see Figure 10-12).

When you select a <div> tag that has its margin or padding properties set, Dream-weaver draws a box around the <div> and adds slanting lines to indicate the space the margins and padding occupy.

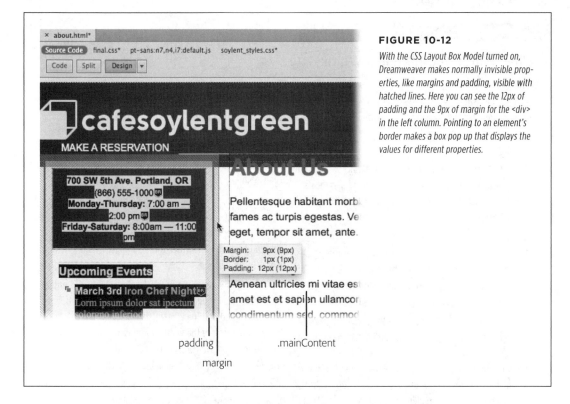

FIGURE 10-12

With the CSS Layout Box Model turned on, Dreamweaver makes normally invisible prop-erties, like margins and padding, visible with hatched lines. Here you can see the 12px of padding and the 9px of margin for the <div> in the left column. Pointing to an element's border makes a box pop up that displays the values for different properties.

Margins, the space between a piece of content and its border, appear outside of padding, and Dreamweaver represents margins with lines that slant *downward*, from left to right. Padding appears inside margins, and Dreamweaver indicates it with lines that go *upward*, from left to right. When you select a <div> tag (the Tag Selector, discussed on page 7, is a great way to do so), Dreamweaver highlights the margins and padding values defined by the selector (class or ID) you applied to the <div>.

If you find these visual aids confusing, turn them off by choosing View→Visual Aids→CSS Layout Box Model. These same steps turn the margin and padding visual aids back on.

Dreamweaver's HTML Templates

You'll contend with many details as you build CSS-based layouts. For example, you need to understand the intricacies of the CSS Box Model, as well as the sometimes-bizarre behavior of floats. In addition, different browsers handle some CSS properties differently, which means that a design that looks great in Firefox can completely fall apart in Internet Explorer 6. (Remember, even though much of the Windows-loving world has upgraded to IE 8 and 9, there are still some folks cruising around the Web in IE 6 jalopies.) Fortunately, Dreamweaver is ready to give you a helping hand with predesigned HTML Layouts.

When Width Doesn't Equal Width

In my style sheet, the CSS width property of one of my styles is 150 pixels. But when I preview the page in a web browser, the <div> tag I applied the style to is much wider than 150 pixels. Is there a bug in my browser?

No, your browser is fine. The problem lies with the difference between the CSS *width* property and the final calculated width of an element onscreen. The width you see onscreen is the sum of several CSS properties, not just the *width* property. The *width* property merely defines the width of the content area, where the text, images, or other nested tags sit.

The actual width—that is, the amount of screen real estate given to the page by a browser—is the *total* of the widths of the left and right margins, left and right padding, left and right borders, *and* the *width* property.

Say you create a style with a width of 100 pixels, 10 pixels of padding on all four sides, a 2-pixel border, and 20 pixels of space in the left margin. While the space dedicated to the content inside the style is 100 pixels wide, any tag with this style will have an onscreen width of 144 pixels: 100 (width) + 10 (left padding) + 10 (right padding) + 2 (left border) + 2 (right border) + 20 (left margin).

This can cause problems if you're not careful. For example, in a fixed-width layout, you might create a <div> that wraps around all other page elements. Its width is 960 pixels, so everything inside that <div> must fit in that 960-pixel-wide space. If you wanted to create a four-column layout, you might insert four <div>s and create styles that set the width of each to 240 pixels (960 divided by 4).

However, if you added even a 1-pixel border to one of the <div>s, they'd suddenly take up more than 960 pixels, and you'd find that the last column wouldn't fit—in fact, it would drop down *below* the other three columns, creating a very weird-looking layout.

So if you find yourself floating lots of elements and one of them drops below another when it should sit beside it, odds are pretty good that the elements are just too wide to sit side by side. So decrease the width, margins, padding, or borders until the elements fit (breaking out a calculator and adding up the margins, padding, borders, and widths helps).

The CSS *height* property and the final height of a style behave the same way. The onscreen height of an element is a combination of the height, top and bottom margins, padding, and borders.

Dreamweaver's HTML templates aren't finished web page designs. They don't have graphics, fancy text, drop-down menus, or any whiz-bang features. They're intended to lay the foundation for *your* design talents. Each layout is a simple HTML file and style sheet, each works with all current browsers, and each design's handcrafted CSS irons out the many wrinkles in troublesome browsers (most notably Internet Explorer 6). In other words, instead of spending a day stretching and sizing your own canvas, a Dreamweaver HTML template is like going to the art store and buying a ready-made and primed canvas so you can get busy painting.

NOTE If you used previous versions of Dreamweaver, you may be surprised at how few templates there are in Dreamweaver CC Release 2014. Adobe has been trimming the ranks of templates for the last few versions. One reason, Adobe says, is that it found that most people used the same two- or three-column templates and were confused by the other options. Another reason is the move to mobile web surfing and the need for responsive designs to accommodate smartphones and tablets. To meet that need, Adobe developed the fluid grid layouts discussed in Chapter 13. If you're looking for a template you don't see in Dreamweaver, check out the Adobe Add-ons (Window→Browse Add-ons). Type "template" in the Search box. Use the "Sort by" menu to fine-tune your search based on cost, ratings, age, or popularity. For details on using templates, see Chapter 22.

Creating a new page from one of Dreamweaver's templates takes just a few steps:

1. **Choose File→New.**

   This is the same first step you take when you create any new web page. You can also create a new file by choosing the Ctrl+N (⌘-N) keyboard shortcut. Either way, Dreamweaver launches the New Document window (Figure 10-13).

   You can skip this clunky window when you use the keyboard shortcut. First, click Preferences at the bottom of the New Document window. Then, at the bottom of the Preferences dialog box, turn off the "Show New Document dialog box on Control+N" checkbox. (For Macs the label reads, "Show New Document dialog box on CMD+N.") After you turn off this option, you won't see the New Document window when you use the shortcut.

FIGURE 10-13

This New Document dialog box for a blank web page lists Dreamweaver's ready-made layouts. For example, "2 column fixed, right sidebar, header and footer" indicates a design with two columns: a column of main content on the left, and a thinner sidebar (for supplementary info like links) on the right. The design uses a fixed width (you can tell by the lock icon), and the HTML5 tags <header>, <footer>, <article>, <aside>, and <nav>. A preview of the selected layout appears in the top-right corner of the window; a brief description below the preview provides more detail on how the layout works.

2. **Choose Blank Page from the left column, and then select the type of page you want to create—HTML, PHP, and so on—in the Page Type column.**

Usually, you'll select HTML from the Page Type category, since most of the time you'll create regular web pages. However, if you're creating a page that uses a server-side language like PHP, you'd select PHP from the list.

TIP You can choose from four layout categories on the left side of the New Document window (Figure 10-13). Blank Page includes empty templates, Fluid Grid holds templates for smartphones and tablets (page 549), Starter Templates get you going with jQuery Mobile pages (page 581), and the last category, Site Templates, holds templates you create (see page 861).

---

3. **From the Layout column, select a page layout.**

This is where the fun begins. As you read before, choose "<none>" to create an empty web page. The other options let you choose one of Dreamweaver's prefab templates. For example, you can select either a two- or three-column fixed-width layout.

A fixed-width design maintains a constant page width no matter the width of a visitor's browser. The fluid grid layouts let the overall width of the page change with the size of the browser window and device. (See page 549 for more on fluid grid layouts.)

Dreamweaver previews each design in the top-right corner of the New Document window. See Figure 10-14 to decipher the visual codes that help you understand how the layouts behave.

FIGURE 10-14

The design Dreamweaver previews in the Blank Page New Document window visually identifies the type of layout you select. A small lock icon indicates a fixed-width design (top); the layout sets the width of each column using pixel values, and the widths don't change when a guest resizes her browser window. The % symbol indicates a liquid design (bottom). It defines column widths using percentage values that change based on the width of the browser window; a wider browser window means wider columns.

4. **Choose a doctype from the DocType menu.**

Here's where you decide which type of HTML/XHTML you want to use for the page. It's the same option you face when you create a new, blank web page, as described on page xxi. You're safe going with the default option of HTML5.

5. **From the Layout CSS menu, select where you want to store your page's CSS code.**

Each Dreamweaver HTML Layout requires its own style sheet, which includes all the styles that make the design work. When you create a new page from a template, you specify where Dreamweaver stores the associated style sheet. The "Add to Head" option creates an internal style sheet in the HTML file Dreamweaver creates. Most of the time, you don't want this option, since external style sheets are more efficient (see page 118 for an explanation).

You can also store the layout styles in a new, external style sheet (select Create New File). Choose this option when you use one of Dreamweaver's layouts to build a new page. It creates a separate file with all the CSS necessary to control the page's layout. To add another page to your site using a layout you've already used (for example, a two-column fixed-width design with a header and footer), read on.

The "Link to Existing File" option sidesteps the entire process of creating new CSS styles. It assumes you have the appropriate styles defined in another external style sheet. If you previously created a web page using the same type of layout, choose this option.

Say you create a two-column fixed layout using a Dreamweaver template. You saved the necessary styles for that layout in an external style sheet and saved the sheet to your site. Now you can create a *new* two-column fixed-layout page using the same style sheet. Choose "Link to Existing File," and then proceed to step 6 to link the external style sheet to the new page.

Keep in mind, however, that each template has its *own* style sheet. So if you create a two-column fixed-layout page and then want to create a page with three columns and a liquid layout, you can't link to the style sheet Dreamweaver created for the two-column layout. In other words, whenever you create a new *type* of layout (two-column fixed, three-column liquid, and so on), choose the Create New File option so Dreamweaver creates the appropriate CSS file in a new, external style sheet.

TIP You don't need to go through these steps each time you create a page using a layout you've used before. Suppose you want to build a 40-page site with a two-column, fixed-layout design. Instead of going through the New Document dialog box (and the steps listed here) 40 times, use the New Document dialog box to create the initial page, and then choose File→Save As to save a copy of that design for the next two-column page you want to create. Better yet, use Dreamweaver's Template tool described in Chapter 22 to manage pages that have the same layout.

---

6. **Click Attach Style Sheet to link an external style sheet to the page (see Figure 10-15).**

This is an optional step. Dreamweaver's HTML Layouts come with lots of pre-defined CSS styles, but you probably need to define some of your own for your unique content. For that reason, you likely want to use your own external style sheet to format your site. If you already created one, now's the time to link to it. In addition, if you chose "Link to Existing File" in the previous step, you have to link to an external style sheet to create a particular layout type. The process of linking to external style sheets is the same as with any other web page, described on page 162.

> **NOTE** If, when you create a new web page, you link to an external style sheet as described in step 6, Dreamweaver may pop up a warning message that says something about needing to save your web page in order to correctly attach the style sheet. You can safely ignore this message. In fact, turn on the "Don't show me this message again" checkbox to stop this annoying message in the future.

FIGURE 10-15

You can attach more than one external style sheet when you create a CSS-based layout. For example, one sheet might define the basic look of headlines, text, images, and other elements, while another controls column layout, and a third handles "printer" styles that dictate how the page will look when printed (see page 420).

7. **Click Create to bring your new web page to life.**

If you selected the Create New File option in step 5, Dreamweaver asks you to name the new style sheet and select where you want to save it (just like when you create any new external style sheet, as described on page 118). Dreamweaver suggests names for the CSS files for each of its layouts—such as *HTML5_twoColFixRtHdr.css* for an HTML5, two-column, fixed-width design with a right sidebar and a header and footer. You can change the name if you like, but the name Dreamweaver suggests is descriptive.

After all that, you end up with a page that has a basic structure and some tutorial text telling you how CSS formats the different areas of the page (see Figure 10-16). Don't forget to save and title the page.

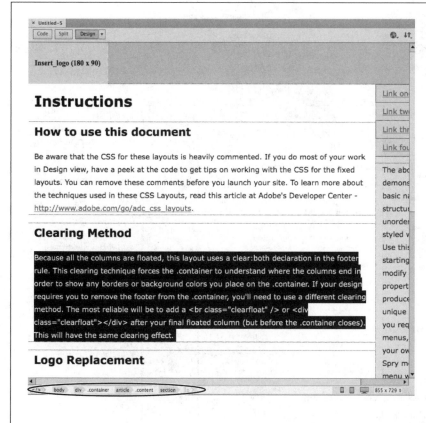

FIGURE 10-16

It doesn't look like much, but this Dreamweaver pre-designed layout has the basic scaffolding of a bona fide web page in place: HTML tags to organize the page and CSS styles to position and format them. Click inside any area of the page, and the Tag Selector (circled) shows you the structure of the HTML at that point. In this case, if you click inside a paragraph in the main column, the Tag Selector shows you which tags wrap around that paragraph. You read this info from right (the selected <p> tag) to left (the <body> tag that contains everything you see inside the document window). For this two-column design, the <p> tag is inside an HTML5 <section> tag, which is inside an <article> tag with the class .content applied to it (that's what "<article> .content" means), which is itself inside a <div> that has a class of .container. Finally, the <body> tag encloses all the other tags.

The Structure of Dreamweaver's HTML Layouts

Dreamweaver's HTML Layouts include a handful of page elements that suggest their intended use. As explained in the box on page 456, Dreamweaver templates use HTML5's descriptive tags, like <header>, <article>, and <section>, to architect a new page. It also adds some JavaScript to the page so that these newfangled tags work with older browsers. When you examine the structure of Dreamweaver's templates, you'll see the descriptive HTML tags used in the same way that <div> tags have been used in the past. They stake out territory on a page for the header, footer, sidebars, and main article of the page, as shown in Figure 10-17. In some cases, these descriptive tags will have classes assigned to them. For example, click in the main article on the page, and in the Tag Selector at the bottom of the document window, you'll see something like this:

```
<body><div.container><article.content><section><p>
```

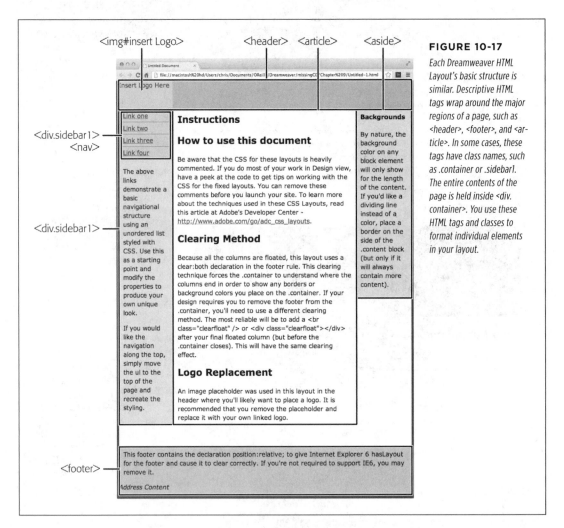

FIGURE 10-17

Each Dreamweaver HTML Layout's basic structure is similar. Descriptive HTML tags wrap around the major regions of a page, such as <header>, <footer>, and <article>. In some cases, these tags have class names, such as .container or .sidebar1. The entire contents of the page is held inside <div.container>. You use these HTML tags and classes to format individual elements in your layout.

Remembering to analyze this line from right to left, you know that your cursor is inside a paragraph's <p> tags, which happen to be inside <section> tags. That section, in turn, appears inside the <article> tag, which has the *.content* class applied to it. Then, there's a <div> tag with the *.container* class applied to it (*<div.container>*). As explained previously, this tag usually represents the page's outer container, and you use that container to position all the content on the page. For example, you can center the page by centering the <div>. Just outside of *<div.container>* is the <body> tag for the page.

The good news is that once you get a handle on one of Dreamweaver's pre-designed layouts, you can apply that knowledge to the other layouts. Whether you structure page elements with descriptive HTML tags or <div> tags and classes, you format and position them the same way, through CSS.

You may wonder how, if all of Dreamweaver's HTML Layouts share the same name for their <div>s, do you end up with different types of designs? Easy: each page has its own style sheet. When you create a new HTML Layout page and save those styles in an external style sheet (as described in step 5 on page 471), Dreamweaver suggests a name such as *HTML5_thrColFixHdr.css* (for a three-column, fixed design with a header and footer), or *HTML5_twoColFixRtHdr.css* (for a two-column, fixed design with a right sidebar). Each style sheet has different rules for the layout's container, content, sidebar, header, and footer styles. This means that if you plan to use more than one HTML Layout page, you need separate style sheets for each—in other words, if you attach *twoColLiqRt.css* to a three-column, fixed design, you end up with some weird results.

So what do you do if you want to, say, have the same design for all the paragraphs inside the main content <div> (*<div class="content">*) when you use two different HTML Layouts? Create a third style sheet, named something like *global.css* or *site. css*, attach it to both types of pages, and then create a descendent selector (page 398) like *.content p*. This formats just the paragraphs that live inside a tag that has the class *.content* applied to it, and since it's in a style sheet shared by both pages, it works in both designs.

◼ Modifying Dreamweaver's HTML Layouts

The basic look of a freshly minted Dreamweaver HTML Layout page doesn't have much to recommend it. The fixed-width layouts, for example, have a green and tan color scheme. One of the first things you want to do with an HTML Layout is remove any Dreamweaver formatting that doesn't fit with your design ideas. In addition, you might want to tweak some of the basic layout properties, like the width of a fixed-width design or the width of sidebars and main columns.

Editing HTML Layouts

Unless you really like Dreamweaver's green and tan color scheme (and if you do, your job is a lot easier), one of your first tasks is to remove (or change) the background colors for the sidebar and other page elements of an HTML Layout. This generally means editing the CSS in the Dreamweaver-supplied style sheet. You already know the basics for creating a CSS rule: choose the source of the style, choose the selector that triggers the style, and then set the values for the style's properties. (These steps are covered in detail on page 116.) Editing an existing style rule is similar, but you may be able to take some shortcuts when it comes to zeroing in on the property you want to tweak.

Suppose you want to edit the styles for the main part of your web page—change the font, say, or adjust the size of the margins. Here's how to find the relevant CSS rule:

1. **Click inside a paragraph in the main part of your web page.**

   Clicking inside a paragraph selects the <p> element. If you're working with a photo or video clip, click it to select it. In either case, you can examine the tags that define the element in the Tag Selector at the bottom of the document window (Figure 10-18, top).

2. **In CSS Designer's Sources section, examine the Computed properties.**

   When you highlight "Computed" in the Selectors section of CSS Designer, the Properties section displays the rules that style the selected tag (Figure 10-18, bottom). Dreamweaver may store these rules (property/value pairs) in different sources. For example, one source may be the template's external style sheet *HTML5_twoColFixRtHdr.css*, and another could be a style sheet like *soylent_styles.css*, where you create styles to format specific page elements.

3. **If you don't see the property you want to edit in the list of Computed properties, go to the Tag Selector (Figure 10-18 top, circled) and click another tag.**

   In a case like this, a page element a little higher up on the food chain probably governs the property. For example, a rule that positions a sidebar isn't going to be in the paragraph selector (<p>). It's more likely to be in the <div> that includes the sidebar. So, if you assigned the sidebar the class *.sidebar1*, look in the Tag Selector for the <div> with a *.sidebar1* class. As you click different tags, Dreamweaver displays different properties in CSS Designer's Properties section. Usually, it takes only a couple of clicks to find the property and CSS rule you need.

4. **When you see the property you want to edit, click the property/value pair to identify the selector and source.**

   Dreamweaver highlights the source and selector that define the CSS rule in their respective sections. The source appears in bold type, while the selector has a blue background.

   In many cases, you can tweak a value—that is, edit a CSS rule—just by changing the value in Designer's Properties section. However, it's always best to understand exactly which *selector* you're changing and which *source* style sheet holds the rule. After all, you may use that same CSS rule elsewhere on the current page, or on some other page in your website. Often, instead of changing the rule, you want to create a new rule for an element on the page that overrides the existing style.

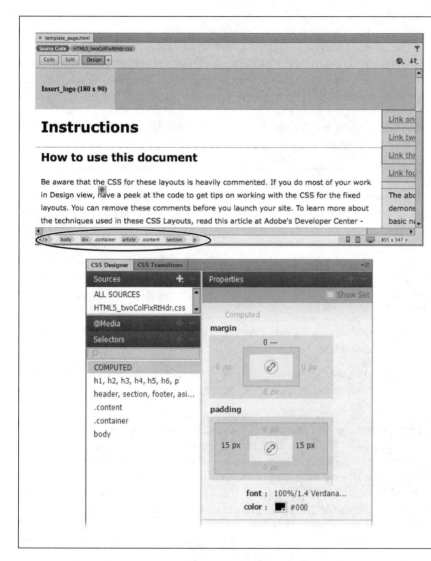

FIGURE 10-18

Finding the style that formats a particular tag can be tricky—unless you use Dreamweaver's Tag Selector (top) and CSS Designer's Computed view (bottom). That way, you can quickly identify and edit a style applied to any tag on a page.

5. **Set values for the properties you want to change.**

   At this point, you can change the property values in CSS Designer's Properties section. Suppose you want to change the background color of a sidebar that has the selector *.sidebar1*. You'd go to the Tag Selector and click *<div.sidebar1>*. Dreamweaver highlights the source file *HTML5_twoColFixRtHdr.css* in bold and the selector *.sidebar1* in blue. The Properties section displays the *background-color* property for the sidebar with the current color highlighted. Click the color swatch and choose a new shade, or enter a number for it. You can also remove the rule entirely by clicking the trash bin icon.

Sometimes you want to override an existing rule rather than change it. You may use the *.aside* class on multiple pages, but you want to use red text on one page to flag an important passage, and you don't want to change *.aside* for all those other pages. To override an existing rule in *HTML5_twoColFixRtHdr.css* (rather than change it), you do the CSS Designer three-step: Choose a source, add and then name a new selector, and then tweak the properties. Place your new rule in a new external style sheet. Then make sure that the link to the external style sheet comes *after* the link to *HTML5_twoColFixRtHdr.css* in the <head> section of your page. (If the link comes before, it won't override the rule.)

NOTE The styles for Dreamweaver HTML Layouts use what's called CSS "shorthand properties." For example, you can combine the values for *background-color* and *background-image* into a single property named *background*, while you can specify all four margins of an element (top, right, bottom, and left) with just one property: *margin*. This makes for more compact styles, but it also means that, to edit a shorthand property in the Properties section, you need to know how to write the values yourself.

Dreamweaver doesn't provide a color box, link button, or any other of the helpful tools it gives you when you set the values of a "longhand" property like *background-color*. In other words, unless you know CSS well, use CSS Designer to select a source and selector, and to set property values for a layout's styles.

Once you select a layout region on the page (header, sidebar, and so on), you probably want to make a few common changes:

- **Background color**. To completely remove a <div>'s background color, delete the value next to the *background-color* property in the Properties section of CSS Designer.

- **Text formatting**. You can modify the text and other content of a page to your heart's content. This book's earlier chapters show you how to format headlines, paragraphs, images, and links. However, when you create styles for these elements, use an external style sheet other than the one Dreamweaver supplies for the layout. You can store these types of styles in a generic style sheet like *styles.css* instead of the layout-specific style sheet, such as *twoColFixLtHdr.css*. By using two external style sheets, you keep your custom-built styles separate from the generic template styles. To give your whole site a unified look, attach both style sheets to multiple pages.

FREQUENTLY ASKED QUESTION

Paying Attention to Conditionals

When I create a page using Dreamweaver's fluid grid layout, the page has some weird-looking code just above the ending </head> tag. What's that about?

If you go into the Code view of any fluid grid layout, you'll notice some grayed-out HTML that begins with *<!—[if lt IE 7]>* and ends with *<![endif]—>*. It's grayed out because Dreamweaver treats this code as an HTML comment. People who hand-code their pages use HTML comments to annotate their code—to explain why they added a particular chunk of HTML, for example, or to identify which <div> a particular closing </div> tag belongs to. Dreamweaver and browsers ignore HTML comments.

However, this particular HTML comment, while ignored by every other browser, has special significance for Internet Explorer. HTML comments that begin with *<!—[if IE]>* are actually secret messages, called *conditional comments*, intended just for Internet Explorer. Conditional comments let you send HTML, CSS, and JavaScript to Internet Explorer only; you can even send special HTML to particular versions of Internet Explorer. For example, *<!—[if lt IE 7]>* sends HTML to versions 6 and earlier

of Internet Explorer (the "lt" part stands for "less than," so it addresses versions of Internet Explorer before version 7).

You'll encounter comments in Dreamweaver's fluid grid layouts that link to the JavaScript code for HTML5 (*html5shiv.google-code.com/svn/trunk/html5.js*), too, as described on page 456. It makes older versions of Internet Explorer play well with new HTML5 features. You'll also find conditional comments that identify different versions of Internet Explorer and then apply a class (like *ie6 oldie* or *ie7 oldie*) to the page's <html> tag. The template code uses these classes to handle special problems with each version of Internet Explorer.

Fortunately for web developers everywhere, IE 6 is nearly gone (see the box on page 521), and IE 7 is following close behind it. Odds are that soon you won't need to worry about either of these browsers and, depending on how tech-savvy your audience is, you might be able to stop supporting IE 7 now.

For a brief tutorial on conditional comments, visit *http://tinyurl.com/commentsforexplorer*.

Modifying Fixed Layouts

Dreamweaver's fixed HTML Layouts are 960 pixels wide, a common page width that works well on 1024-pixel-wide screens (that is, most netbooks, laptops, tablets, and desktop computers). However, that width may be too wide or too narrow for your tastes. If you're designing for the cinema-screen audience, you might want a page that takes advantage of a wider screen, so you might bump the width to 1100 pixels or more. In addition, you may want to change the widths of columns on a page. Here's how you make a few key layout changes to HTML Layouts like these:

- **Page width**. Dreamweaver fixes the area of the page that includes the header, sidebars, and main content at 960 pixels. It defines this width in the *container* <div>. Select the <div> and then change 960 to whatever width you want.

NOTE Of course, 960 pixels is way too wide for smartphones held vertically. Fortunately, Dreamweaver CC includes support for a CSS technique called "media queries," which lets you adjust a page's layout based on the screen dimensions and orientation of the destination device. In other words, you can design both a 960-pixel-wide layout for desktop computers and a 640-pixel-wide layout for phones. See Chapter 12 to learn how to use media queries.

- **Column width**. In its two-column layouts, Dreamweaver makes the sidebar column 180 pixels wide and the main content region 780 pixels wide. For three-column designs, it makes the main content area 600 pixels wide and adds a second 180-pixel-wide column. Select the column you wish to make wider or narrower, and then adjust its *width* property.

Unfortunately, you often have to do a little math if you want the three columns to sit side by side. Since the container has a set width (Dreamweaver uses 960 pixels), the width of all three columns should add up to 960 pixels. If their total is bigger, the content area's width actually becomes smaller than the width of the two sidebars. So if you increase the size of one sidebar, you need to decrease the width of the main content area (the *.content* style) by the same amount. For example, in a two-column fixed design, if you increase the sidebar to 200 pixels wide (20 pixels more than it starts out with), you need to subtract 20 pixels from the width of the *<article>.content* selector. In other words, in the Tag Selector, click *<article>.content*, and then, in CSS Designer's Selectors section, click *.content*. Finally, in the Properties section, change the column width to 760 px.

Things get even trickier if you add margins, padding, or a border to the left or right of any column. As discussed in the box on page 468, the actual horizontal space of any element is the sum of its width, left and right margins, left and right padding, and left and right border. If you add a 1-pixel right border to a sidebar, you increase the total width of all the columns to 961 pixels (1 pixel more than the container's 960-pixel width). The result? The main content area drops below the sidebar. Ay caramba! In other words, if you make a change to a sidebar or the main content area, and the *<article>.content* <div> suddenly drops down on the page, check your math!

TIP If you use Dreamweaver HTML Layouts often, you may make the same adjustments over and over again. For example, you might always remove the padding and background color and adjust the column widths. Instead of repeatedly doing that, edit the default HTML and CSS files Dreamweaver uses when it creates a new blank HTML Layout page. In Windows, you find them in *C:\Program Files\Adobe\Adobe Dreamweaver CC2014.1\Configuration\ BuiltIn\Layouts.* (If you're running the 32-bit version of Dreamweaver on a 64-bit Windows computer, your layouts are in *C:\Program Files (x86)\Adobe\Adobe Dreamweaver CC 2014.1\Configuration\BuiltIn\Layouts.*) On the Mac, they're in the *Applications→Adobe Dreamweaver CC 2014.1→Configuration→BuiltIn→Layouts* folder.

You can clean up the Layout folder by deleting designs you don't use. Just make sure you back up the folder beforehand. And then back up your new designs, too, so that if you ever have to reinstall Dreamweaver, you have a backup of your modified templates.

Creating and Modifying Liquid Layouts

Liquid layouts adjust to the width of a browser window. Columns grow wider on bigger screens or as visitors widen their browser windows, and shrink when they narrow it. For example, you can create a layout where Dreamweaver displays all the content in 80% of the space allowed by the browser window. Then you can divvy up that space between one or more sidebars and a main article. You designate these regions using <div> tags with classes, or by using HTML5's new descriptive tags, like <article> and <aside>.

For example, to quickly whip up a liquid layout, you might create a class called *.container* that you apply to a <div> tag. You plan to place all the elements of your web page inside this <div>, and then apply formatting. So you create CSS rules for *.container*, setting the *width* to 80% and *margin-left* and *margin-right* to "auto." Dreamweaver sizes the resulting page to 80% of the browser width and centers the content. That leaves 10% empty space on the left and right sides of the main content area. You can add borders, color, or an image to the background, or any other formatting that's appropriate for your container. To create a sidebar, use the HTML5 <aside> tag. You can then create styles for the major regions of the page, such as the header, footer, sidebar, and article.

Here are some of the properties you can use to format your page:

- **Page width**. In a liquid layout, the content on a page adjusts to fit the available width. So, if the width is set to 80%, you have empty space on one or both sides of the page. If you center the content, Dreamweaver leaves 10% of free space on either side. To remove this space to make the page fill the entire width of the browser window, edit the *.container* style. You should delete the width entirely—don't set it to 100% of the browser window because that'll make the page appear a little *wider* than the window, forcing visitors to scroll right to see all of a page's content. See the box on page 468 for an explanation.

> **NOTE** You can provide built-in limits for the width of a container <div> using Dreamweaver's *max-width* and *min-width* properties. *Max-width* defines the maximum width of the <div> and keeps it from becoming unreadably wide on extremely large screens. So, for example, a value of 1260 px would be appropriate for many web pages. The *min-width* property, by contrast, keeps the <div> from shrinking past the point of readability. A value of 780 pixels is common. To change or delete these values, go to the Layout category of CSS Designer's Properties section (see the Tip on page 122).

- **Column width**. As with fixed-width layouts, you can set the sidebar and main content widths using CSS's *width* property. The only difference for liquid layouts is that you use percentages, with the combined width of the sidebars and the content <div> totaling 100%. Just as with fixed layouts, if you change the width of one <div>, you need to adjust the width of another. So in a three-column liquid design, to make the left sidebar, say, 25% instead of the usual 20%, you need to remove 5% from the *.content* <div>, the right sidebar, or split that between the two: For example, change the *.content* style to a width of 57% (from its normal 60%) and the *.sidebar2* style to 18%.

Other Styles to Change

You might want to modify or delete a few other styles:

- **Text spacing**. It's common for web designers to add some empty space between the edge of a column and the content inside it. This "white space" makes the text feel less cramped and more readable. You can add padding to the <div> that creates the column—for example, to the *<div class="content">* element that HTML Layouts use to create the main content region. However, as mentioned above, adding padding to that <div> increases its overall width, potentially making the column too wide to fit next to other columns. So, instead of adding padding to the sidebars or main content styles, Dreamweaver uses a group style ("h1, h2, h3, h4, h5, h6, p") that includes left and right padding. Because it applies the padding to tags *inside* the column and not the column itself, the overall width of each column remains the same. You get the same visual result—added white space on either side of each column—without having to futz with width settings.

The only downside to this approach is that it will apply to *every* header and paragraph on the page. What if you want a little less white space inside the left sidebar and a little more inside the main content area? The answer is descendent selectors (see page 398). For example, to create a style that affects the padding of just the headings and paragraphs in the first sidebar, you'd create this (long-winded) group style:

.sidebar1 h1, .sidebar1 h2, .sidebar1 h3, .sidebar1 h4, .sidebar1 h5, .sidebar1 h6, .sidebar1 p

Then, any left and right padding you add to the *.sidebar* style applies only to the headings and paragraphs *inside* the sidebar (see page 401 for instructions on creating a group style).

You'll also find styles named *.content ui* and *.content ol*, which Dreamweaver uses to add white space around bulleted and numbered lists inside the main content area. You may want to adjust or delete these styles as well.

Links. Dreamweaver's HTML Layouts also include styles for the link states discussed on page 199 (*a:link, a:visited,* and so on). You may not like these styles, so feel free to change or delete them. And if the pages in your site use more than one HTML Layout (two-column fixed and three-column fixed pages, for example), you're better off creating a shared, external style sheet (*site.css* or *styles.css,* for instance), putting your link styles there, and then linking the external style sheet to all your pages (see page 162 to learn how to do that, and page 405 to learn how to move styles between style sheets). That way all your pages, even the ones with different layouts, will have consistent link styles.

- **Navigation bar**. Some of Dreamweaver's layouts include a simple navigation bar in a sidebar. If you like the basic design but want to change a few details, you can edit the various styles that begin with *ul.nav* in the layout's style sheet. They control the appearance of the list and the links inside. If you don't plan to use the navigation bars, feel free to delete the styles entirely by clicking the <nav> tag in the Tag Selector and then pressing Delete.

NOTE The style sheets Dreamweaver supplies with HTML Layouts are chock-full of CSS comments. This is a good thing when you're getting started, because they're like a mini-lesson in CSS layout. Read through the comments in at least one of the style sheets, and you're sure to learn a few things. However, when it's time to put your site on the Web, all those comments are unnecessary bloat that slow page downloads. You can delete them by hand (CSS comments are gray in Code view and begin with /* and end with */) or you can use Dreamweaver's "Find and Replace" tool to quickly remove them all.

For a little help, download Dreamweaver expert David Powers' Stored Query to Remove CSS Comments (basically, a saved find-and-replace command) from *http://tinyurl.com/4ywjk42*. You can read about Dreamweaver's powerful "Find and Replace" tool in Chapter 8.

■ Using Absolute Positioning

Beyond float-based layouts, CSS's other main technique for placing elements on a page, *absolute positioning*, lets you specify the exact position of any element. But before you start thinking you've found page-layout heaven, keep in mind that the Web is a fluid environment that's difficult to control with pixel-level precision. If a visitor increases the font size in her browser, the enlarged text may spill out of your carefully crafted layout. In addition, it's nearly impossible to force a footer to the bottom of a page laid out using absolute positioning (a trivial task with float-based layouts). That's why most of Dreamweaver's HTML Layouts use floats and the techniques discussed at the beginning of this chapter.

That's not to say you shouldn't use absolute positioning. It's great for moving small elements, like a logo, image, or short set of links, to a specific position on a page. And it's the only way to have one element overlap another (see Figure 10-19). As long as you don't try to dictate the exact width, height, and position of every page element, you'll find absolute positioning powerful and helpful.

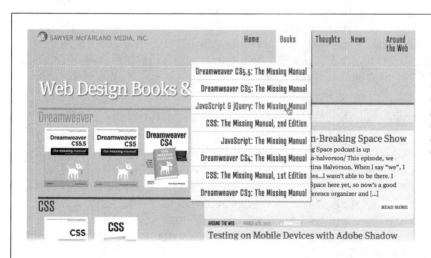

FIGURE 10-19

One unique aspect of absolute positioning is its ability to position an element on top of other page content. That lets the drop-down menu pictured here overlap the page content below it.

The CSS Positioning Properties

Several CSS properties position elements onscreen. You'll find them under the Layout category of the CSS Designer window (Figure 10-20).

FIGURE 10-20

Dreamweaver gives you easy access to its many CSS positioning properties in the Layout category of CSS Designer. After you click the button for the Layout category, scroll down past the padding and margin boxes to find the position box shown here.

■ POSITIONING TYPE

Normally, browsers position elements on the screen in the order they appear in the HTML. The first element tagged in the HTML appears at the top of the browser window, while elements at the end of web page files appear at the bottom of the browser window. In Figure 10-21, the top-left image shows a headline, followed by a paragraph of text, followed by a headline, an image, and another paragraph. This is the order in which the elements appear in the HTML, top to bottom.

The CSS *position* property, however, lets you alter this order by assigning one of four available position types: *absolute, relative, static,* and *fixed*.

- **Absolute** is the most common option. It lets you place a tag anywhere on a page, regardless of the tag's position in the page's HTML. The top-right image in Figure 10-21 displays a graphic of a sticky note. Even though the image falls after the headline Malorum Gipsum in the page's HTML, it appears at the top of the page (and even a little bit above the top) because it's absolutely positioned. The space the graphic used to occupy (top-left image) is now filled by the paragraph of text beneath the second headline.

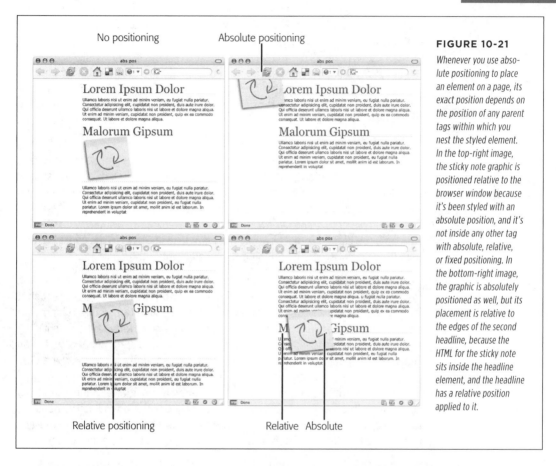

No positioning   Absolute positioning

Relative positioning   Relative   Absolute

FIGURE 10-21

Whenever you use absolute positioning to place an element on a page, its exact position depends on the position of any parent tags within which you nest the styled element. In the top-right image, the sticky note graphic is positioned relative to the browser window because it's been styled with an absolute position, and it's not inside any other tag with absolute, relative, or fixed positioning. In the bottom-right image, the graphic is absolutely positioned as well, but its placement is relative to the edges of the second headline, because the HTML for the sticky note sits inside the headline element, and the headline has a relative position applied to it.

In other words, with absolute positioning, HTML code can go *anywhere* inside a <body> tag and still appear *anywhere* on a page—its location in the code has nothing to do with its location onscreen. In addition, absolutely positioned (AP) elements are removed from the normal flow of a page—other tags on the page aren't even "aware" that the AP element exists.

After you select the Absolute option, use the Position properties to place the element with precision (see page 489 for details).

Browsers, however, don't always put absolutely positioned elements in relation to the page itself. If you create a style to position an element inside another element that's either positioned relatively (see the next bullet point) or absolutely, the browser positions the first element *in relation to the latter element*, not in relation to the page itself. The next bullet point clarifies this confusing concept.

- The **Relative** option lets you position a tag relative to its position in the HTML. When you choose this option, the positioned element appears relative to where it appears in the HTML. The bottom-left image in Figure 10-21 shows the same sticky note positioned using the Relative property. Although it has the same top and left position values (page 489) as the top-right image, the browser now positions the sticky note relative to where its tag sits in the HTML—just below the Malorum Gipsum line. Even so, the note sits in the top-left position of that line, reflecting the values in the Relative property. Another side effect of relative positioning is that the space formerly taken up by the image (top-left in Figure 10-21) remains. Notice that the last paragraph doesn't try to fill up the space where the graphic was—there's still a big empty area.

  At first glance, the Relative option might seem less than useful. After all, what's the point of positioning something on a page, just to leave a big empty space? In many cases, you don't actually apply relative positioning to an *element* you want to position, you apply it to a *tag* that wraps *around* the element you want to position in order to create a new set of coordinates for an absolutely positioned element. You can think of it as applying relative positioning to the container and then applying absolute positioning to the element in the container.

  Say you put an image inside a headline, and you want the image to appear on the left edge of that headline. If you simply position the image in an exact spot in the browser window on the left edge of the headline tag, you're taking your chances. If the headline moves (say you add some new body text above it), the absolutely positioned image stays glued to its assigned spot. Instead, what you want to do is position the image *relative* to the headline tag, so that when the headline moves, so does the image. Look at the bottom-right image in Figure 10-21. The headline Malorum Gipsum is relatively positioned, and the sticky note is absolutely positioned, but it's absolutely positioned *inside the headline tag*. Even when, later on, you add a little more text above the header (thereby forcing the headline to move down), the sticky note travels along for the ride.

- **Static** positioning is the normal behavior of HTML. Static simply means the content follows the normal top-down flow of HTML. Why would you want to assign an element static positioning? The short answer: You probably never will.

- **Fixed** positioning is similar to the "fixed" value of the CSS Attachment property that locks background images in place (see page 486). This option "fixes" an element in place in a browser window. When you scroll down the page, the fixed element doesn't move—it remains in a precise spot in the browser window. It's a cool option with exciting possibilities, though sites frequently use it for annoying ads. For a non-evil example, you could create a navigation bar that sticks to the top of the browser window. When visitors scroll down the page, the navigation bar stays at the top of the window. Internet Explorer 6 ignores the "fixed" option, but since that browser is nearly extinct, it's worth experimenting with this property.

■ WIDTH AND HEIGHT

These properties, logically enough, set the width and height of an element. You can use any of the available CSS units of measure, like pixels, ems, or percentages. In most cases, when you want precise control over the dimensions of your tags—that is, if you want a page element that's *exactly* 200 pixels wide and won't change even if a visitor changes the size of his browser window—use pixels. If, however, you want the element to resize as the visitor resizes his browser, use percentages. That way, you can specify a style that's 50% the width of the browser window, no matter the size of the window. Width and height are at the top of the Properties list in CSS Designer's Layout category.

NOTE The Width and Height properties available under the Positioning category of the CSS Rule Definition window are identical to the same-named options under the Box category (see Figure 10-10) in the same window. Also note that CSS calculates the total width of a style as the width value *plus* any borders, margins, or padding (see the box on page 468 for more). The same is true for the height of an element.

■ VISIBILITY

Left to its own devices, a web browser makes the contents of all tags visible on a page, so you'll usually leave this property blank. After all, if you put something on your page, it's usually because you want people to see it. But there are situations in which you may want to make a certain tag (and its contents) invisible to your visitors.

For example, you might want a page element to appear when a visitor clicks a button or points to another element (that's how tooltips work). However, most web designers use the Display property (page 423) for this, not the Visibility property. Why? Because when you hide an element using the Visibility property, the element is still there taking up space. When you hide it by setting Display to "none," poof! It's as if it isn't there at all. To make an element visible, set the Display property to *block* (for block-level elements like headlines, paragraphs, and <div>s) or *inline* (for inline elements like images, links, and <span> tags).

In other words, skip the Visibility property.

■ Z-INDEX

Welcome to the third dimension. Absolutely positioned tags are unique in the world of web elements because they "float" above (or even behind) a web page and can overlap each other, completely or partially.

If you were awake in high school geometry, you may remember the graphing system in which the x-axis specified where a point was in space from left to right and the y-axis specified where the point was from top to bottom. And if you were awake *and* paying attention, you may remember that the z-axis denotes a point's position in *front-to-back* space. When you draw a three-dimensional object on this type of graph, you need to use all three axes: x, y, and z.

The Z-Index of an absolutely positioned element doesn't make your web page appear three-dimensional, it simply specifies the "front-to-backness" of overlapping AP elements. In other words, the Z-Index, represented by a number in the Z-Index box, controls the stacking order of AP elements on a page.

The page itself lies behind all AP elements, and the AP elements stack up from there. In other words, the higher the Z-Index number, the higher above the page the AP element sits, so an AP element with a Z-Index of 4 appears *behind* an overlapping AP element with a Z-Index of, say, 7.

Z-Index numbers have no relation to the actual number of absolutely positioned items on a page. You can have three AP elements with Z-Indexes of, say, 2, 499, and 2000 if you choose. You'd still have just three AP elements, one on top of the other in ascending order. Spacing your Z-Index numbers in this somewhat arbitrary manner is helpful, since it lets you insert new <div>s between already positioned <div>s as you develop your page, without having to renumber the Z-Indexes of all your AP elements.

■ OVERFLOW

Suppose you create a square <div> that's 100 x 100 pixels and then fill it with a graphic that's 150 x 162 pixels—that is, an image that's larger than the <div> itself.

You've already seen how a table cell reacts to this situation: it simply grows to fit the content inside. But <div>s (and other elements) are different; their reaction depends on your choice of Overflow settings in the Properties panel. The following options let you decide how browsers handle the excess part of an image:

- **Visible** displays any content that doesn't fit inside the element. The element doesn't expand to fit the content (something you'll notice if you apply a background or borders to the element); it lets the graphic "pop out" of the box.

- **Hidden** chops off the excess content. In the example above, you'd see only the top-left 100 x 100 pixels of the image.

- **Scroll** adds scroll bars to the element, so that visitors can scroll to see all the element's contents. It's like having a miniature browser window embedded in the page. This feature offers an interesting way to add a small, scrollable window within a web page. Imagine a small "Latest Company News" box that visitors can scroll through to read the text inside without disturbing anything else on the page.

- **Auto** adds scroll bars to an element *only* if necessary to accommodate oversize contents.

In Design view, you see the complete element, overflow and all. Switch to the Live view and the overflow reflects the *hidden, scroll*, or *auto* properties. If you select any option besides Visible, you see the <div>'s set dimensions—for example, 100 pixels by 100 pixels. Dreamweaver doesn't display any content outside that area.

> **NOTE** You can use the Overflow property on any element, not just absolutely positioned <div>s. For example, to create a 100-pixel-tall <div> with scrollbars and lots of content inside that visitors can scroll through, just create a style with a 100-pixel height and the Overflow property set to "scroll," and apply that style to the <div>, no positioning required.

■ POSITION

Dreamweaver's Position properties let you specify where you place an absolutely positioned element, which is, after all, the whole point of AP elements. The four Position properties control where each of the four edges of the element begin. Setting the Top box to 200 pixels positions the top of the element 200 pixels down the screen, whereas the Bottom option identifies where the bottom of the element starts. Similarly, the Left and Right properties set the beginning of the left and right edges of the element.

> **NOTE** Dreamweaver is inconsistent when it comes to the terminology for Position properties. If you're in the CSS Rule Definition window, you position elements using the Positioning category's *Placement* properties: Top, Right, Bottom, and Left. In CSS Designer, the terminology matches the official CSS terms you see in style sheets. Go to Designer's Layout category where you find the *position* properties.

You'll frequently use a combination of the Width property (page 464) and the Top and Left or Right properties to position AP elements. To place a 150-pixel-wide sidebar 200 pixels from the top of a page and 15 pixels in from the left, you'd set the Width property to 150 pixels, the Top property to 200, and the Left property to 15 pixels.

You'll also find the Right property handy in some situations. Say you want to put a 200-pixel-wide sidebar on the right side of a page. Since you don't know the exact width of a visitor's browser—580 pixels, 1200 pixels?—you can't know ahead of time how far the AP element needs to be from the left edge of the window. The solution is to set the Right property. Specify *0* if you want the sidebar to touch the right edge of the page. If you want to indent the AP element, say 20 pixels from the right edge of the window, type *20*.

In addition, you can skip setting a width by assigning both Left and Right positioning simultaneously—say, by placing an AP element 50 pixels from the left edge and 20 from the right. You can do the same with Top and Bottom settings as well—don't set the height of an element, just set its Top and Bottom values.

> **TIP** Here's a cool trick: Absolutely position a <div> and set its top, left, bottom, and right positions to *0*. You'll have a <div> that fills the browser window—even when someone resizes the window.

Positioning isn't quite as straightforward as it may seem. The exact location of a positioned <div> is a combination of not only these position values, but also of the type of position you choose for the positioned element—absolute or relative. As noted earlier, with relative positioning, the numbers you type for Top or Left, for instance, are calculated based on where the AP element already appears in the HTML and on the screen. So setting the Top property to 100 pixels doesn't place the AP element 100 pixels from the top of the browser window; it places it 100 pixels from where it would appear on the screen based on the HTML.

Absolute positioning, however, lets you place an AP element at an exact spot on a page. So setting the Top and Left properties for an absolutely positioned element to 100 and 150 pixels *will* place that AP element 100 pixels from the top of the browser window and 150 pixels from the left edge.

NOTE There's one additional wrinkle to absolute positioning: For a <div> nested inside another <div> that has either a Relative or an Absolute position setting, the browser calculates position values based on the position of the *parent* <div>. If you have one AP element 300 pixels from the top of a page, and an absolutely positioned element nested inside *that* AP element with a Top position of 20, it doesn't appear 20 pixels from the top of the page. It appears 20 pixels from the top of the parent AP element, in this case, 320 pixels from the top of the page.

■ CLIP

The Clip property can hide all but a rectangular piece of an AP element. In most cases, you should avoid this property, since it's rarely useful except for animated special effects.

Suppose you put a large graphic into an AP element but you want to display only one small area. You *could* use the Clip property, but a browser still has to download the *entire* graphic, not just the clipped area. You're much better off preparing the smaller graphic at the right size to begin with. The kilobytes you save may be your visitor's.

You can use JavaScript to *move* the clipping area, creating an effect like a spotlight traveling across the AP element. Although that may be a more useful purpose for the Clip property, Dreamweaver doesn't support it, unfortunately. Those effects are frequently created using a program such as Edge Animate.

The four Clip settings—top, right, bottom, and left—specify the positions of the clipping box's four edges. In other words, these indicate the borders of the visible area of the AP element.

■ Adding an AP Element to Your Page

In most cases, the <div> tags you position will contain a variety of HTML elements—images, paragraphs, headlines, and so on. For example, to place a series of links at the top of a page, you could use the Insert→Div command (page 454) to wrap the links in a <div> tag. Then you'd position the <div> so that it sits atop the page.

Start out by selecting existing content, or click in the spot where you want to add a new absolutely positioned <div>. Next, create a class or ID style (with the positioning properties discussed above), and then select that style from the Class or ID menu of the Insert Div window. Alternatively, you can create the class or ID style by clicking the New CSS Rule button in the Insert Div window (see Figure 10-6). If you're working in Live view, as discussed on page 352, you can assign classes and IDs by clicking the element and then clicking + in CSS Designer's Selectors section.

But absolute positioning isn't just for <div> tags; you can absolutely position any HTML element—forms, paragraphs, headlines, and images. You just need to create a style and set the *position* property to Absolute (page 484), and—voilà!—you have an absolutely positioned element.

Unless you add a background color or border to your AP element, it's difficult to identify its boundaries. To make working with AP elements easier, Dreamweaver provides visual cues in Design view, as shown in Figure 10-22, and explained below:

- **AP element marker**. The shield with the letter C on it (huh?) represents where in the underlying HTML the code for the AP element actually appears. (Actually, the shield appears for any tag with either absolute or relative positioning.)

  Dreamweaver doesn't normally display these markers. To see them, you have to turn them on in the Preferences window: Press Ctrl+U ($\mathcal{H}$-U) to open the window, click the Invisible Elements category, and then turn on the "Anchor points for AP elements" checkbox.

  While HTML objects generally appear in the document window in a top-to-bottom sequence that mirrors their order in the page's HTML, the position of AP elements *doesn't* depend on where the AP code appears in the markup. In other words, you can have an AP element in the first line of the page's HTML, while the element itself actually appears near the bottom of the final line on the page.

  To move the HTML of an AP element, drag the shield icon. You can also reposition elements in the HTML by dragging them to a new location in Element Quick View (View→Element Quick View). You can place the icon (and therefore the code) at the beginning, end, or anywhere else in your HTML, but you need to be careful. As discussed on page 484, when you position an element absolutely, its exact location depends on whether its parent element has a relative or absolute position. If the parent element is itself absolutely positioned and you drag the element outside its parent, then its top, left, bottom, and right coordinates will change—a browser may now position that element in relation to the browser window. Likewise, if you drag an AP element inside another absolutely positioned element, the browser displays that element in relation to the new parent element. In other words, it can get pretty confusing when you start dragging the AP elements around, so be careful and remember to use the Undo command, Ctrl+Z ($\mathcal{H}$-Z), if your design breaks as you do so.

  Conversely, if you drag the selection handle of an element (described next), it moves the element but leaves the HTML in the same location.

  That distinction often confuses web designers. For instance, if you want to reposition an AP element, don't drag the AP element's marker—the shield that represents the HTML code—that simply moves the HTML to another spot inside the code, it doesn't reposition the element onscreen.

FIGURE 10-22

Unlike other page components, absolutely positioned elements don't appear in the same place on the page as their HTML code. Here, a block of text hovers over an image several hundred pixels below the top of the page. The image and text are both inside a <div> tag that has its position set to "relative." The block of text ("Resource conscious...") is absolutely positioned 34 pixels from the top of the <div> and 55 pixels from its right edge. Dreamweaver represents the text's position in the HTML using an AP element marker—it's in the lower-left corner of the <div> tag.

HTML position for AP div   Selection handle   Positioning information for AP div   Resizing handle

NOTE   The AP element marker (the shield) takes up room onscreen in Design view and can push text, graphics, and other items out of the way. In fact, even the thin borders that Dreamweaver adds to indicate <div>s take up space in the document window, and the space they occupy may make it difficult to place AP elements precisely. The keyboard shortcut Shift+Ctrl+I (Shift-⌘-I) hides or shows invisible items like AP element markers. The Visual Aids→Hide All menu command does the same thing (see Figure 10-23).

- **Selection handle**. The selection handle provides a convenient way to grab and move an AP element around a page. The handle appears when you select the element, or when you click inside the element to add material to it. The handle lets you move the position of the AP element without changing the position of its code. Behind the scenes, Dreamweaver updates the CSS by updating the element's positioning values. For example, if you originally placed an image by setting the left and top values, Dreamweaver changes those numbers to match the new location. The same thing happens if you used right and bottom settings...pretty nifty.

- **AP element outline**. Unselected absolutely positioned elements have a thin, gray, 3-D border. Like the AP element marker and selection handle, it's only there to help you see the boundaries of the element and doesn't show up in web browsers.

- **AP element positioning summary**. If you select an AP element in Design view's document window and then point to it on the page, Dreamweaver pops up a box with information about the element (see Figure 10-22), including the name of the class or ID assigned, what type of positioning you used, the AP element's dimensions, and so on. This gives you a bird's-eye view of the CSS properties defining the AP element's position on the page.

FIGURE 10-23

The options in the Visual Aids menu help you visualize HTML Layouts in Design view. For example, the CSS Layout Backgrounds option lights up each <div> tag on a page with a hideous, randomly selected background color. It also highlights any element whose display property you set to "block" (page 487), or that uses either absolute or relative positioning.

NOTE If one AP element overlaps another, the top AP element—the one with the higher Z-Index, as described on page 487—has a solid outline; the lower element's outline appears dashed where the top AP element overlaps it.

■ Modifying AP Elements

Once you add an AP element, you don't need to go back to CSS Designer to edit many of its positioning properties. Using the Properties panel, you can rename, resize, move, and align the <div> with other AP elements, and set many other properties.

But, first, you have to select the AP element in Design view using one of these methods:

- Click the AP element's selection handle (see Figure 10-22).

- Click the AP element's border. Square handles appear on the blue border.

- Click the AP element marker (the shield) that indicates where the HTML for the absolutely positioned item resides. Out of the box, Dreamweaver hides these markers, since they can get in the way of your design work. To see them, select Ctrl+U (⌘-U) to open Dreamweaver's Preferences window, click the Invisible Elements category, and then turn on the "Anchor points for AP elements" checkbox.

And if those aren't enough ways to select an AP element—Adobe's programmers never sleep—you can also Shift-click them to select multiple AP elements simultaneously, and then set the properties of (or align) all the AP elements at once. If you're working with an AP element or have one selected, Shift-clicking another AP element selects them both. (Shift-click a selected element a second time to deselect it.) You can continue to Shift-click to select additional AP elements.

NOTE The techniques for modifying AP elements discussed here work only in Design view; you can't select multiple items in Live view, and you won't see the positioning and resizing handles described next.

Resizing Absolutely Positioned Elements

When you select an AP element, eight resize handles appear around its edges (see Figure 10-22). You can drag any of them to change the element's dimensions. The corner handles resize both the width and height simultaneously and proportionately.

You can also resize an absolutely positioned element via the keyboard. First, select the AP element, and then do one of the following:

- Press the Ctrl (⌘) key, and then press the arrow keys to change the AP element's size. The up and down arrow keys adjust the element's height one pixel at a time, while the left and right arrows affect its width.

- To change the size *10* pixels at a time, press Ctrl+Shift (⌘-Shift), and then press the arrow keys.

For better precision, use the Properties panel (or CSS Designer) and the W and H boxes to set an exact width and height for the element (see Figure 10-24). You can specify any unit of measure that CSS understands: px (pixels), pc (picas), pt (points), in (inches), mm (millimeters), cm (centimeters), em (height of the current font), ex (height of the current font's x character), or % (percentage)—see page 149. To pick your measurement unit, type its abbreviation *immediately* after you type in the size value. For example, type *100px* into the W box to make the AP element 100 pixels wide. Don't include a space, and don't leave out the measurement unit—px, em, or %, for example—or browsers won't display the AP element at its correct dimensions.

FIGURE 10-24

The Properties panel controls many AP element properties (although some require you to edit CSS styles).

Moving AP Elements

Moving an absolutely positioned element is just as simple as resizing it—drag any border of the element, or the element's selection handle. Avoid the eight resize handles, however, because they'll change the size of the element when you drag them.

For less speed but greater precision, you can use the keyboard. Select the element and then do one of the following:

- To move an AP element one pixel at a time, press the corresponding keyboard arrow key.

- Press Shift while using an arrow key to move the element 10 pixels at a time.

Placing AP Elements

As you'd guess, you can also control an AP element's placement using the Properties panel or CSS Designer. Dreamweaver measures an AP element's position relative to the left and top edges of a page (or, for nested AP elements, from the left and top edges of the parent <div> when you set the Position property to either absolute or relative). The Properties panel provides two boxes for these values: L specifies the distance from the left edge of the page to the left edge of the selected AP element, and T specifies the distance from the top of the page to the top of the selected AP element. In CSS Designer's Properties section, go to the Layout category's Position box and then set the top, bottom, left, and right values.

NOTE You can't edit an AP element's Right or Bottom positioning properties from the Properties panel. To change them, use CSS Designer.

To position an AP element using the Properties panel, select the <div> (for example, by clicking the <div>'s border), and then type distances in the L and T boxes. You can use any of the units of measure mentioned previously. You can even use negative values to move part or all of an AP element off the page entirely (offstage, you might say), which you might want to do if you intended a subsequent animation to bring it *onstage*, that is, into the document window using JavaScript.

If you draw a 100-pixel-tall by 50-pixel-wide AP element, you can move it to the very top-left corner of the page by selecting it, and then typing *0* in both the L and T boxes. To position that same element so that it's just off the left edge of the page, type *-50px* in the L box.

Aligning AP Elements

At times, you may want to align several AP elements so that their left, top, bottom, or right edges line up with one another. Dreamweaver's Align command does just that. It can even make the width and height of selected AP elements the same.

To use this feature, select two or more AP elements (by Shift-clicking them), choose Modify→Arrange, and then select one of the following options from the submenu:

- Align Left aligns the left edges of the selected AP elements. In other words, it gives each AP element the same L property.

- Align Right aligns the right edges.

- Align Top aligns the top edges, so that all the T properties are the same.

- Align Bottom aligns the bottom edges of the AP elements.

- Make Same Width sets the same width for all the selected AP elements (in the W box in the Properties panel). Make Same Height does the same for the height of the AP elements.

The AP element you select *last* dictates how Dreamweaver aligns the AP elements. Say you have three AP elements—A, B, and C—and you select them in order from A to C. You then set their Align property to Left. Dreamweaver uses the left edge of AP element C (the last one you selected) as the value for the other AP elements.

Background Image and Color

To add a background image to an AP element, click ▣ next to the "Bg image" box, and then select an image from your site folder. As usual, Dreamweaver tiles the image, if necessary, to fill the entire element's area with repeating copies of the graphic. (To adjust how or whether the image tiles, you need to edit the AP element's style using the standard CSS style-editing techniques, described on page 167.)

Setting a background color is even easier. Just use the "Bg color" box to select a color or to sample one from your screen.

◼ Tutorial: Building a CSS-Based Layout

In this tutorial, you'll create a two-column web page using CSS floats. You'll also use absolute positioning to control the placement of navigation elements (skip ahead to Figure 10-33 to see the final page). You can achieve a design like this in many ways.

You could, for example, use Dreamweaver's HTML Layouts (page 473), add <div>s, position them using CSS, and then add content. In this exercise, though, you'll start with an already created web page: It contains basic HTML but no <div>s to organize the content or style sheets to format the page.

NOTE To complete this tutorial, you need to download sample files from this book's Missing CD page at *http://oreilly.com/pub/missingmanuals/dreamweaverccmm2014*. (See the Note on page 37 for details.) The files you'll work on are in the Chapter10 folder, and the finished project, for comparison, is in the Chapter10_complete folder.

Once you download the tutorial files and open Dreamweaver, set up a new site as described on page 23. In a nutshell, choose Site→New Site. In the Site Setup window, type *Page Layout* into the Site Name box. Click ▣ next to the Local Site Folder box, navigate to and select the Chapter10 folder inside the MM_DWCC folder, and then click Choose (Select). Finally, click OK.

1. **In the Files panel, double-click the file *about.html*.**

   Alternatively, choose File→Open and double-click *about.html*. Dreamweaver opens a web page with a little content and basic HTML formatting. You'll start by grouping the banner content—the logo, nav bar, and "Make a reservation" link.

2. **In Design view, click to the right of "Make a reservation" and drag up until you select the link, navigation bar, and logo at the top of the page.**

   You'll wrap all this in a <div> tag.

3. **Choose Insert→Div or click the Div button under the Common or Structure tabs of the Insert panel.**

   Either way, Dreamweaver opens the Insert Div window. You want to create a CSS style to format this <div>.

4. **Click the New CSS Rule button, and in the New CSS Rule Window, choose Class from the Selector Type menu, type *.header* in the Selector Name box, and then choose New Style Sheet File in the Rule Definition menu.**

   The window should look like the one in Figure 10-25.

5. **Click OK and save this style sheet file as *soylent_styles.css* in the CSS folder of the site.**

   Dreamweaver opens the CSS Rule Definition window. You're creating a style for the page's banner, and, as you can see in Figure 10-4, it's just a box that stretches across the page. You don't need to float or absolutely position it, but you'll add a background image and a few other properties.

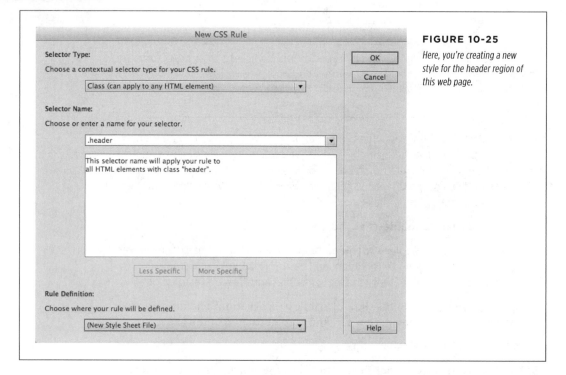

FIGURE 10-25

Here, you're creating a new style for the header region of this web page.

6. **Select the Background category from the Rule Definition window. Click Browse to the right of the *background-image* property, select the file *bg_banner.jpg* from the Images folder, and then click Open.**

   This box holds only a bit of content—the logo and navigation elements—so you'll set a height for it to match the final design.

7. **Select the Box category and then type *140* in the Height box.**

8. **Turn off the margin setting's "Same for all" checkbox, type *20* in the Bottom margin box, and then click OK.**

   You return to the Insert Div window. Notice that "header" (the style you just created) appears in the Class box (see Figure 10-26).

9. **Click OK.**

   Dreamweaver adds the <div> tag to the page. There's something a bit wrong with it—the navigation bar and the link to the "Make a reservation" page don't fit. That's OK for now. Later in this tutorial, you'll use absolute positioning to relocate these elements to the upper-right corner of the banner.

FIGURE 10-26

The Insert Div window not only inserts a <div> tag, but it also lets you create a new CSS style and apply a class or ID (or both) to the tag.

10. **Click to the left of the About Us headline and drag down until you select the headlines, paragraphs, and images—everything up to the cafe's address and phone number—don't select those.**

This area is the main content of the page and should be in its own <div>.

11. **Choose Insert→Div.**

Dreamweaver opens the Insert Div window. You want to create a CSS style to format this <div>, too.

12. **Click the New CSS Rule button, and in the New CSS Rule window, choose Class from the Selector Type menu, type *.main* in the Selector Name field, select *soylent_styles.css* from the Rule Definition menu, and then click OK.**

These are the same steps you followed for the previous <div>.

13. **Select the Box category, type *64* in the Width box, and then select "%" from the drop-down menu to the right. Choose "left" from the Float menu, turn off the margin setting's "Same for all" checkbox, and then type *25* in the Bottom margin box.**

The CSS Rule Definition window should look like the one in Figure 10-27. Here, you're using a percentage width, so the main column will change its width as a guest changes the width of his browser window. The "left" float places this column on the left side of the browser window.

14. **Click OK to return to the Insert Div window, and click OK again to close the window and insert the new <div> tag.**

The main content's text floats to the left of the page, and the content that was previously below it wraps around the right side, creating two columns (see Figure 10-28).

You'll also float the sidebar column.

15. **Click to the left of the address (700 SW 5th Ave), and then drag down to select everything up to the copyright notice (the black-highlighted area in Figure 10-28).**

This area is the sidebar, and you'll add a <div> to it as well.

16. **Choose Insert→Div to open the Insert Div window. Click the New CSS Rule button, and in the New CSS Rule window, choose Class from the Selector Type menu, type *.sidebar* in the Selector Name field, and then click OK.**

These are the same steps you followed for the previous <div>.

17. **Select the Background category and, in the "Background-color" box, type *#E7EBE0.***

This adds a greenish background to the sidebar. You'll add a border next.

FIGURE 10-27

Percentage-width values make a nested element change size based on the width of its parent element. For example, a 64% wide box placed inside the body of a web page makes that box 64% of the browser window's width. As a visitor resizes the window, the box changes width. However, if you place that box inside another <div> with a fixed pixel-value width—say 1000 pixels—that box will now be a fixed width (64% of its 1000-pixel-wide container, or 640 pixels).

18. **Select the Border category.**

Select "solid" from the Style menu, type *1* in the Width box, and then type *#E5E5E5* in the color box.

You added a gray border to the box. Time to position it.

19. **Select the Box category, type *33%* in the Width box, choose "right" from the Float menu, turn off the margin setting's "Same for all" checkbox, and then type *25* in the Bottom margin box.**

You'll float this <div> to the right of the browser window. Notice that the width of this column (33%) and the main column (64%) don't add up to an even 100%.

There are a couple of reasons for that. First, since you floated the two columns in opposite directions, the remaining space (3%) will appear as a bit of white space (a "gutter") between the two columns, giving the content some breathing room. Second, when using percentage widths, you need to be careful when you add padding, margins, or borders. As you read in the box on page 468, the actual width of an element is a combination of the border, padding, and width values.

Because you added a border to the sidebar, its screen width will be slightly wider than the 33% you specified. If you set the two columns' width values to equal 100%, they wouldn't fit side by side, since 100% width plus 2 pixels of left and right borders would total greater than 100%. The sidebar would end up dropping below the main column of content.

20. **Click OK to return to the Insert Div window, and then click OK again to close the window and insert the new <div> tag.**

Dreamweaver adds the tag to the page. The sidebar column appears with a light-green background. You'll add a couple of CSS3 properties next.

FIGURE 10-28

A simple left float and a set width is the easiest way to get multiple columns to sit side by side.

Adding CSS3 Properties

CSS Designer makes it easy to add CSS3 properties—it's your best bet when you work with the latest, greatest CSS features.

1. **In CSS Designer's Sources section, click *soylent_styles.css*, and then, in Selectors, click ".sidebar."**

   Properties for the *.sidebar* class appear in the Properties section of CSS Designer. Turn on the Show Set checkbox if you want to examine the properties that are already part of the CSS rule for *.sidebar*, but make sure you turn off the checkbox before moving on to the next step.

2. **In the Properties section, click the Border button and then scroll down until you see the *border-radius* box.**

   The *border-radius* box looks like a rounded rectangle and has value boxes at each corner. There's a link in the middle whose tooltip says "Click to change all the properties."

3. **Click the link to change all the properties to the same value. Then, click Value for any of the corners and type *5*, as shown in Figure 10-29.**

   This adds rounded corners to the sidebar. The *border-radius* property works only in modern browsers (that excludes IE 8 and earlier). Next, you'll add a drop shadow.

FIGURE 10-29

The CSS3 border-radius property lets you add rounded corners to one, two, three, or all four corners of an element. Make sure you add either a background color or border to the element—otherwise, you won't be able to see the rounded corners!

4. **Scroll down in the Properties section until you see the *box-shadow* properties.**

   You style a box shadow by setting six properties: *h-shadow, v-shadow, blur, spread, color,* and *inset.*

5. **Type *2px* in the "h-shadow," "v-shadow," and "blur" boxes. Type *#999999* in the color box (see Figure 10-30).**

This adds a drop shadow to the sidebar, but you won't see anything in Dreamweaver's Design view. You need to use Live view or preview the page in a browser. (Be sure to return to Design view to tackle the next steps.)

You're almost done with the layout. If you look at the page, you'll notice that the copyright notice appears below the sidebar and to the right of the main column of content. It should drop below both columns.

6. **Select the paragraph with the copyright notice ("Copyright 2022, The Soylent Corporation").**

You're going to wrap this in a new <div>. You should have a sense of déjà vu at this point.

FIGURE 10-30

The CSS3 box-shadow property lets you add drop shadows to any element. You can learn more about this property at http://css-tricks.com/ snippets/css/css-box-shadow/.

7. **Choose Insert→Div to open the Insert Div window.**

Click the New CSS Rule button, and in the New CSS Rule window, choose Class from the Selector Type menu; type *.footer* in the Selector Name field, and then click OK.

These are the same steps you followed for the previous <div>.

8. **Select the Box category and then, from the Clear menu, select "both."**

The Clear property prevents an element from wrapping around a floated element. The "both" setting prevents the footer from wrapping around either the left- or right-floated element.

9. **Click OK to return to the Insert Div window, and then click OK again to close the window and insert the new <div> tag.**

The page's basic structure is in place. You have a two-column layout with a header and footer. If you preview the page in a browser, you'll see that the design uses a liquid layout—that is, it grows wider or becomes narrower as the browser window's width changes. That's because you used percentage widths for the columns. However, you can easily turn this design into a fixed-width layout.

Creating a Fixed-Width Design

To turn the current liquid \layout into a fixed-width layout, you simply wrap the contents of the page in a <div> tag with a set pixel width.

1. **In the Tag Selector at the bottom left of the document window, click <body>.**

   You just selected the entire body of the web page. (The Tag Selector, discussed on page 7, is the best and quickest way to select a tag.)

2. **Choose Insert→Div to open the Insert Div window. Click New CSS Rule and, in the New CSS Rule window, choose Class from the Selector Type menu, type *.container* in the Selector Name field, and then click OK.**

   Now you'll set the width for this tag and position it in the middle of the screen.

3. **Select the Box category, type *1000* in the Width box, turn off the "Same for all" checkbox in the Margin settings, and then choose "auto" from both the Left and Right margin menus.**

   The window should look like the one in Figure 10-31.

FIGURE 10-31

To center a <div> on a page, give it a fixed width and set its left and right margins to "auto."

4. **Click OK to return to the Insert Div window, and then click OK again to close the window and insert the new <div> tag.**

   The new <div> wraps around all the other content on the page. By giving this container <div> a set width, you constrain all the contents inside to that width.

Adding Styles and Using Absolute Positioning

At this point, you could format this page by creating new styles using the techniques you read about earlier in this book—change the font and font sizes, add underlines to headlines, rejigger the look of links, and so on. For the sake of keeping this book shorter than *War and Peace* (actually, this edition is just about 50 pages shy of that), we assume you already have those skills under your belt, so you'll attach a style sheet with some ready-made styles.

1. **In the Sources section of CSS Designer, click + and then choose Attach Existing CSS File from the menu.**

   The Attach Existing CSS File window opens.

2. **Click Browse, navigate to the css folder, double-click the filename *final. css*, and then click OK.**

   Dreamweaver links the style sheet to the page and styles the page's content. The new styles really change the look of the page, but there's nothing about them that you haven't already seen. For example, the picture of the chef is simply aligned to the left using the *float* property, the text is set to different sizes and colors with CSS, and so on.

   One thing that does need some changing is the banner. The navigation bar and the reservation link are crowded together, and there's too much empty space on the right. You'll use absolute positioning to move these elements into place.

3. **In CSS Designer's Sources section, click *final.css* and then, in the Selectors section, click ".nav."**

   A list of properties appears in the Properties section.

4. **In Properties, click the Layout button, scroll down until you see the *position* properties, and then choose "absolute."**

   Type *0 px* in the "right" box and *32 px* in the "bottom" box (see Figure 10-32).

   Where did the navigation bar go? If you preview the page in a browser (or switch to Live view), you'll find it at the bottom and right edge of the document window. Normally if you absolutely position an element on a page, the coordinates you use (top, left, right, and bottom) are set in relation to the browser window. But that's not what you want here. You want to position the navigation bar in relation to the bottom and right edges of the header <div>. To do that, you just need to give the header <div> a position of "relative."

5. **In the Sources section of CSS Designer, click *soylent_styles.css* and then, in Selectors, click ".header."**

   Dreamweaver displays the properties for the *.header* class in the Properties section.

6. **In Properties, click the Layout button, and then scroll down to the *position* property, and set the value to "relative."**

   The navigation bar pops into place inside the header (you may need to click in the document window to see the change). Now you'll position the reservation link.

FIGURE 10-32

When absolutely positioning an element, you need to type a value for only one of the horizontal (left or right) and only one of the vertical (top or bottom) settings.

7. **In CSS Designer's Sources section, click *soylent_styles.css* and then, in Selectors, click + to add a selector, and then type *.reservations* as the class name for the new selector.**

A new class style named *.reservations* appears in the Selectors section.

8. **In the Properties section, go to the *position* property, set the value to absolute, set its top position to *8 px* and its right position to *0 px*.**

These absolutely positioned properties position the reservations button above the navigation bar.

9. **Press F12 (Option-F12) to preview your hard work in a browser.**

The complete page should look like Figure 10-33.

You'll find a completed version of this tutorial in the Chapter10_complete folder that accompanies the downloaded tutorial files.

> **NOTE** To get a full description of every Dreamweaver menu, see Appendix B, "Dreamweaver CC 2014, Menu by Menu."

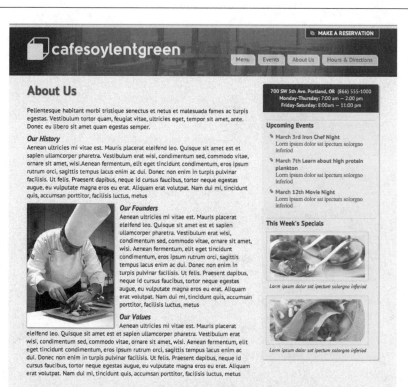

FIGURE 10-33

It doesn't take much CSS to create a multicolumn layout, or to accurately place elements, like a navigation bar.

Troubleshooting CSS

C ascading Style Sheets are the most important technology in a web designer's toolkit. Unfortunately, they're also the source of many frustrations. As you pile style upon style to transform drab HTML into beautiful web pages, you increasingly run the risk that those styles will interact in ways you don't expect. As discussed in Chapter 9, the CSS concepts of inheritance and the cascade dictate how styles interact on a page, and those concepts have their own complicated rules. Adding to the confusion, different browsers can display CSS differently—which is especially true with older versions of Internet Explorer. Even newer browsers exhibit some frustrating inconsistencies in how they display CSS.

In this chapter, you'll look at Dreamweaver's tools for diagnosing CSS problems, as well as solutions to common problems you'll encounter as you build the kinds of CSS layouts discussed in Chapter 10.

■ Analyzing CSS with Dreamweaver

Dreamweaver's CSS tools are as good as they come—you can use them to build complex designs without ever dipping your toe into code, manage style sheets easily, and quickly add external sheets to your pages. But building and managing styles is only one part of the CSS puzzle. You also need to analyze what the CSS is doing to the tags on your page—to see why text, for example, is purple instead of the green you specified.

As described on page 116, CSS Designer gives you different ways to explore the rules that format your pages. As you're building a web page, CSS Designer's Properties section can display just about every CSS property known to mankind. When you're troubleshooting, you can use the section's Show Set checkbox to limit the CSS properties Designer displays to those that have set values in your style sheet. In other words, you see only the CSS rules you already established.

In addition, if you're not sure which class, ID, or tag selector a page uses for formatting, or you're not sure where you stored a style rule, you'll be grateful for CSS Designer's Computed feature (see Figure 11-1). It displays the CSS properties for a selected element—such as an image, paragraph, table, or <div> tag—and helps you zero in on the element's source and selector, which tells you how a web browser formats the item *once it takes into account inheritance and the cascade.*

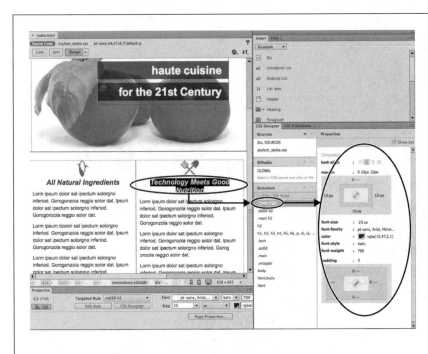

FIGURE 11-1

CSS Designer's Computed feature is a great tool for learning why a section of your web page looks the way it does. After you click an element on the page (like the headline selected here), CSS Designer highlights the Computed entry in Designer's Selectors section with a blue background, and displays all the properties that format your selection in the Properties section. Even though you may have applied CSS rules to different selectors and stored the rules in different style sheets, Computed performs the handy task of gathering all the relevant style rules in one spot.

Using the Computed View to Identify Styles

The Computed view is the place to start analyzing styles and their effect on your page. As you read on page 411, tags can inherit properties (like color and font) from tags that wrap around them. If, for example, you create a style for the <body> tag that has a color property of *#F00*, a browser displays that text, as well as the text inside tags within the <body> tag, such as <p>, <h1>, and <li>, as red. In other words, the styling of any one tag may result from a combination of properties from multiple styles and how they interact when you take into account the rules of CSS inheritance (page 411) and the cascade (page 412). The Computed view untangles all this for you.

You can view this combined, "computed" style by clicking an element in Design view. When you do, CSS Designer highlights "Computed" in the Selectors section.

That's its way of saying, "I'm displaying the results of multiple selectors." Then, in the Properties section, Designer displays the properties and values that give the element its final style. In Figure 11-1, for example, the Properties section shows rules for *text-align*, *margins*, *padding*, *font family*, *size*, *color*, and *weight*. If you point to one of the property names or values, a tooltip appears that may or may not help you. Often they simply repeat the property name, but sometimes they explain why that particular property doesn't apply to the page element you selected.

Editing CSS Properties

There are lots of ways to change CSS styles in Dreamweaver. To quickly format an element, use the CSS settings in the Properties panel below the document window. For more complete control, turn to CSS Designer. In its Properties section, with the Show Set box unchecked, you see a complete list of CSS properties. That's great for creating new rules. Using the Category buttons at the top of the section, you can zero in on Layout, Text, Border, Background, and List properties. To fine-tune an already created style, turn on the Show Set checkbox (in the upper-right corner of the Properties section) to see the properties whose values you've already set. Want to bump up the size of the type or adjust a color? Go ahead: click the value assigned to that property and change it.

These techniques are all well and good if you know which style you need to edit, but if you have a really long list of styles or you're working on a site for the first time in a while, you may not know which style you're after or where you stored the style rule. Is it in an internal style sheet? External? Which class, ID, or tag is the selector? In a case like this, use the Computed view to home in on just the properties you want to change. Here's a step-by-step guide to that process:

1. **In the document window, select the element whose style you want to change.**

   For example, if a paragraph has green text and you want to make it blue, select that paragraph using one of the many techniques Dreamweaver offers: Triple-click to select the paragraph, click once in the paragraph and then click the tag's name in the Tag Selector at the bottom of the document window, or just drag to highlight the whole paragraph. When you select a page element in Design view, CSS Designer displays the sources, selectors, and properties for that element. It highlights the relevant style sheet in bold and the selector in blue.

   NOTE These same selection techniques work in Code view.

2. **In CSS Designer's Selectors section, click Computed.**

   Designer highlights "Computed" with a blue background and, in the Properties section, displays a seemingly random bunch of properties. They may be a mix of styles from different categories in the Properties section, like Layout, Text, Border, or Background. No matter their origin, these are all properties that format the element you selected.

3. **Click one of the property names.**

When you click either a property name or its value, CSS Designer highlights both the source (the style sheet) and selector (the tag that triggers a style) for that CSS rule. This is important because you need to know if the changes you are about to make to a rule will affect other elements on the page, or elements on another page in your site that uses the same selector.

If CSS Designer lists more than one source, it's worth noting the order. For example, if you see an internal style sheet (<styles>) listed before an external style sheet (*styles.css*), the external style sheet link appears after the internal styles in your page's HTML. Style sheets listed later in your HTML have precedence over any competing styles listed earlier.

The order of selectors is also worth noting. Those at the top of the list are the most specific to the selected element, making them "more powerful" should two or more style rules conflict. In such a case, the tags and classes at the top of the list win out when a browser formats the selection.

Occasionally, in CSS Designer's Properties section, you'll see a property name with a line through it. This strikethrough means there's a rule for that property, but it's not in effect because another rule overrides it. To learn more about the conflict, point to the property name. Dreamweaver displays a tooltip explaining why it isn't applying the style, and names the selector that won the formatting battle.

4. **To edit a property's value, click the value and make the change.**

CSS Designer offers a variety of widgets that help you set values for properties. If there's a choice for the unit of measure, you'll see a drop-down menu. For example, *font-size* gives you a choice of 17 units of measure, from pixels to ems to percentages!

Sometimes you won't find the property you expect to see in the list of Computed properties. If that's the case, head to the Tag Selector at the bottom of the document window. Start from the right and click the next tag to the left. If you still don't see the property, click the *next* tag to the left. You're moving from the most specific tags to those that are less specific, but one of them should have that *font-color* property you need.

As you can see, you can go a long way in tweaking a site's styles simply by selecting elements in the document window and using CSS Designer to quickly locate and edit the properties you want to change.

TIP Even if you're not as interested in editing an existing property as you are in *adding* properties, CSS Designer is a big help. Select the element you want to embellish with a new property—the font for the copyright notice, for example. You can examine all the CSS rules that apply to that paragraph. If you see a selector that specifically targets the paragraph (like a class selector named *.copyright* or a descendent selector like *.footer p*), you can click it and set a value for the *font-family* property. Or, if you find there isn't a selector that formats the copyright notice's font, you can create one.

Analyzing CSS in JavaScript and Server-Side Pages

CSS Designer is great at locating and editing styles that affect the elements on a page, but what about the HTML you don't normally see in the document window? These days, lots of sites use fancy JavaScript effects to display content; tooltips, form validation notices, and menu bars display certain page elements only when someone interacts with the page, for example. Likewise, when you create server-side-driven pages, like PHP pages that retrieve information from a database, you see the completed page and all its elements only *after* a web server processes the server-side programming and sends the page back to you.

So how do you make sure pages that require real-time interaction with a web browser look and act the way you want? Easy: Dreamweaver includes a Live view feature called Inspect mode. Once in Live view, click the Inspect button (circled in Figure 11-2) to mouse around a page and analyze its CSS. You can even interact with JavaScript-driven effects like drop-down menus, and analyze the CSS of page elements that aren't normally visible in Design view.

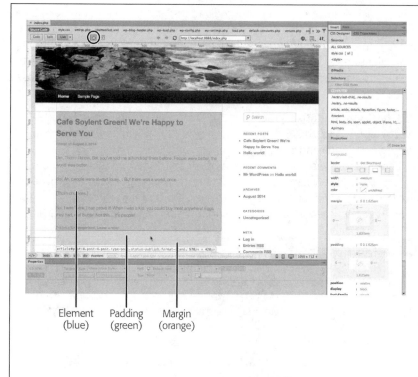

Element   Padding   Margin
(blue)   (green)   (orange)

FIGURE 11-2

Dreamweaver's Inspect mode is a great way to see which CSS styles affect which elements on a page. It's especially useful for pages with a lot of JavaScript-created elements (like drop-down menus and tooltips), or pages that include server-side programming, like PHP files. This figure shows a post from the popular WordPress blogging system. In WordPress and other "content management systems" like Joomla and Drupal, web "pages" aren't individual files like the ones you've been building in this book, they're dynamically created screens that pull information from a database and construct the HTML for the page on the fly. Live view lets you see what a page created with server-side programming looks like in a browser; Inspect mode lets you analyze the CSS that formats the different parts of the page, as shown here.

A few things happen in Inspect mode:

- **Dreamweaver highlights a tag's box, padding, and margins.** As you mouse around a page, Dreamweaver highlights the box model of each tag you point to. As you may remember from page 463, every block-level tag (like a headline, <div>, or paragraph) is basically a box with a width, height, margins, padding, and borders. When you point to a tag in Inspect mode, the underlying "box" turns blue to reveal its dimensions; padding appears in green, and margins show up in orange. Not every element has all these properties, so you may see some but not others. In fact, since you can set padding and margin values individually for each side of a tag, you might see padding or a margin on only one side of an element. As an added bonus, Inspect view also displays a tooltip that identifies the element's selector and its properties. For example, a tooltip might read *div#main 410px x 1100px*. That means you're pointing to a <div> that has the ID *#main* applied to it, and the style for that selector sets the box's width and height to 410 x 1100 pixels.

- **The Tag Selector displays the HTML structure.** When you point to page elements, such as images, paragraphs, <div> tags, and so on, the Tag Selector at the bottom of the document window identifies the tag you point to, as well as the tags that wrap around that tag. For example, in Figure 11-2, the Tag Selector is highlighting *<article>*, meaning you're pointing to an element whose selector is the <article> tag (<article> is a new HTML5 tag). The page's HTML encloses that tag in several other tags—in this case, a bunch of <div>s.

- **CSS Designer updates.** When you use Live view and its Inspect mode, CSS Designer displays the Computed properties for a selected element in the Properties section and updates the Sources and Selectors lists. In other words, Inspect mode gives you an element-by-element view of the page's CSS. In Figure 11-2, you can see this level of detail. The mouse points to an article, and in the Selectors section, you see the classes, IDs, and tags that format it. In the Properties section, you see the styles that Dreamweaver applies to the article.

NOTE You can't change any text that JavaScript or server-side code creates for your page in Live view—that is, you can't, for example, click inside a paragraph and add new text to that created by JavaScript or server-side code. However, you *can* edit the HTML, CSS, and JavaScript in Split view (page 325), and Live view will reflect those changes. You can also edit the CSS of a page in Live view using CSS Designer. To exit Live view, click the Live button in the Document toolbar or choose View→Live View. You can also use the keyboard shortcut Alt-F11 (Option-F11) to turn Live view off and on.

If you decide to edit the styles for a particular element in Inspect mode, click the element. This turns off Inspect mode, but you remain in Live view. CSS Designer highlights the selector(s) for the element, and you can edit the styles in the Properties section, as described on page 121. To re-enter Inspect mode, press the Inspect button again (or use the keyboard shortcut Shift+Alt+F11 [Shift-Option-F11]).

TIP In Inspect mode, it's sometimes hard to select the exact tag you want to analyze in CSS Designer. For example, when you point to a <div> nested inside another <div>, Dreamweaver highlights the innermost <div>, and selecting the outer, parent <div> may not be easy. The solution? While you point to an element in Inspect mode, press the left arrow key to highlight the next-nearest parent element (the tag that wraps around the currently highlighted tag). You can keep pressing the left arrow key to move up the nested HTML tags. (Pressing the right arrow key incrementally moves you back down to the original element.) Finally, when Dreamweaver highlights the tag you're interested in, click to select it. Dreamweaver displays all the tag's CSS rules in CSS Designer's Properties section.

■ FOLLOWING LINKS IN SERVER-SIDE PAGES

Dreamweaver includes a Browse function in Live view that lets you click links to jump to different pages within your site. The linked page appears in the document window. This is kind of cool, but not that useful for links that call up web pages outside your site, because you can't edit those live pages. It's not even that useful for pages within your site—after all, you can just as easily open those pages from the Files panel to edit them.

NOTE The information in this section applies to server-side-driven pages, such as pages written in the PHP programming language. To interact with these types of pages, you need to host them on a web server, which can process the commands in the code. So, to really understand what's going on with your server-side pages, you need to set up a web server on your computer, as described on page 921. Chapter 24 discusses server-side programming.

To follow the links on a page, here's what you need to do:

1. **Enter Live view.**

   Choose Live from the Design/Live menu above the document window.

   In Live view, Dreamweaver displays the Navigation toolbar seen in Figure 11-3. It's made up of buttons, text boxes, and menus that give you the same features as a web browser—you can refresh the current page, go to the next or previous link you visited, and type a web address in the URL box.

2. **Ctrl-click (⌘-click) a link.**

   Dreamweaver replaces the current page with the linked page. In the case of some dynamic pages, like WordPress, Dreamweaver doesn't actually load a page; it sends a request to the relevant web server and the *index.php* file, which does a bunch of behind-the-scenes magic to generate a new chunk of HTML and display a newly minted page on the fly.

   In Live view, you Ctrl-click (⌘-click) links to follow them. But you can make the links respond as usual, that is, with just a click of your mouse, by going to the Live view options menu and selecting Follow Links Continuously.

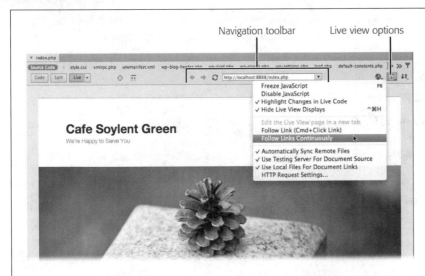

Navigation toolbar   Live view options

Overcoming Common CSS Problems

As you get more adventurous with CSS, you'll probably encounter—as many web designers before you have—some of the weird intricacies of working with floated elements ("floats"). This section describes a few common problems and their solutions. (And if you ever stumble on a problem not listed here, you can always take it to one of the online forums listed in Appendix A, "Getting Help.")

Clearing and Containing Floats

As you learned in the last chapter, the CSS *float* property is a powerful design tool. It's the only way to get content to wrap around other content. Floating a photo lets text below it move up and wrap around the image. When you create float-based column designs, though, sometimes you *don't* want content to move up and next to a floated element. For example, you probably want to keep copyright notices, contact information, and other housekeeping details at the bottom of your web page, below all the other content. The last thing you want is for any of these elements to move up the page and wrap around core page content.

> **TIP** Don't forget to give "floated" elements a width. If you float an image but don't specify its width, text or other page elements won't wrap around it.

In the CSS layouts discussed in the last chapter, you saw that if the main column of content is shorter than either of the floated sidebar columns, the footer moves up and around the left-floated column (Figure 11-4, left, circled). To make the footer stay below the sidebars, add the *clear* property (page 465) to the style, which prevents elements from wrapping around floats (Figure 11-4, right, circled). You find the property in the Layout category of CSS Designer and in the Box category of the CSS Rule Definition window.

FIGURE 11-4

You don't always want an item to wrap around a floated element (left, circled). Copyright notices and other housekeeping info that belong at the bottom of a page usually need to clear any floats they encounter. Turn to the clear *property for that—it forces the copyright notice to the bottom of the page, below any floated elements (right).*

You can make an element drop below a left-floated object by selecting "left" from the Clear drop-down menu, or below a right-floated object by selecting "right." For footers and other items that need to appear at the bottom of a page, select "both" so the item drops below both left- and right-floated elements.

Another problem occurs when you float one or more elements inside a non-floated containing tag, like a <div>. When the floated element is taller than the content inside the <div>, it sticks out the bottom of the <div>. This snafu is especially noticeable if that tag has a background or a border. The top image in Figure 11-5 shows a <div> tag that has an <h1> tag and two columns of text created by floating two <div>s. The enclosing <div>'s style applies background and border properties to the entire box, but they appear only around the <h1> tag. That's because the floated columns are bigger than their container. So, instead of expanding the borders of the box, the columns pop out the bottom of it. What you really want is something like the bottom image in Figure 11-5, where the columns of text and the headline all appear over the same background.

You see a similar problem with the three boxes that contain photos in Figure 11-5, top. In this case, the style floats each image to the left inside a containing <div> that has a border. Because the images are taller than their boxes, they pop out of the bottom. Unfortunately, this problem is even worse than the previous one, because each image causes the image below it to wrap to the right, creating an ugly staggered effect.

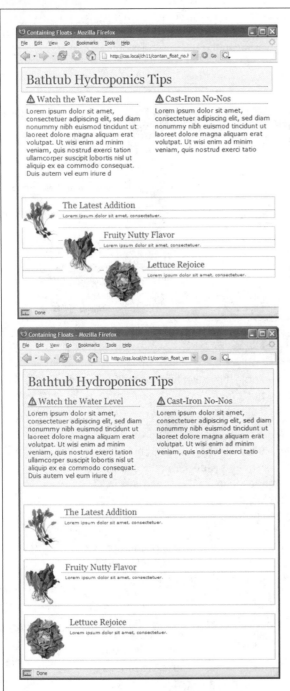

FIGURE 11-5

A floated element can escape its containing <div> if it's taller than the container. If the containing tag includes a background or border, the escaping elements can look like they're not even part of the container, as you can see in the top image—the bathtub tips should have the same tinted background as the headline does (bottom image), but they're popping out of their container (the tinted box with the headline in it). In addition, a floated element can bump into other elements—including other floats, thereby creating a "stair-step" effect, like the one you see in the three boxed elements in the top image. You really want the nicely stacked boxes you see in the bottom image.

You can tackle the problem of renegade floats in many ways. You'll learn several of the most common techniques in the bullet points below. They use Figure 11-5 as an example, but the solutions apply to all dropped floats.

- **Add a clearing element at the bottom of the containing <div>.** This solution is the most straightforward. Simply add a tag—like a line break or horizontal rule—as the last item in the <div> containing the floated element (that is, right before the closing </div> tag). Then use the *clear* property to force that extra tag below the float. This trick makes the enclosing <div> expand, revealing its background and border. For example, you could add a line break (<br>) *before* the closing </div> tag and then add a class to it: *<br class="clearfloat">*. (The quickest way to do this is to manually type the code in Code view.) Then, in CSS Designer's Selectors section, create a CSS class (say, *.clearfloat*) and, in the Properties section, set the class's *clear* property to "both" (see below).

- **Float the containing element.** An easier solution is to float the <div> that contains the floated elements. A floated container <div> expands to fully include the floated elements inside it. In Figure 11-5, bottom, for example, the *float* property has been added to the <div> containing the heading and the two floated columns. In the process, the <div>'s entire box—right down to its background and borders—expands to fit everything inside it, including the floated elements. Strange but true.

   If you go this route, make sure you add a *clear* property to whatever element follows the floated container so that the following element drops below the container.

- **Use overflow:hidden.** Another common technique is to add the *overflow* property (page 488) to the tag that wraps around the floated elements. In CSS Designer's Properties section, set the *overflow* property to "hidden."

   The *overflow:hidden* property is just another one of those weird CSS things: It forces the containing block to expand and contain the floated elements.

   In general, this technique works very well. However, if you have any absolutely positioned elements (see page 483) inside the container, they may not show up. Because the CSS hides the "overflow," it hides the stuff beyond the width and height dimensions of the container. You'll experience this if you have a drop-down menu inside a container, and the drop-downs extend beyond the container element. If that's the case, use one of the float-taming methods described above.

Avoiding Float Drops

Say you call up your website-in-progress and find that one of your page's columns simply drops down below the others (see Figure 11-6). You've got the dreaded "float drop," a symptom of there being too little room to fit the float. "But," you say, "it looks like there's plenty of room for all the columns to exist side by side." It may look that way, but there's a problem with your math.

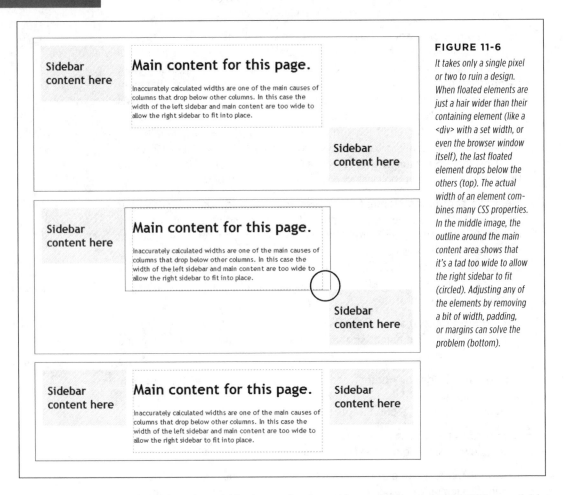

FIGURE 11-6

It takes only a single pixel or two to ruin a design. When floated elements are just a hair wider than their containing element (like a <div> with a set width, or even the browser window itself), the last floated element drops below the others (top). The actual width of an element combines many CSS properties. In the middle image, the outline around the main content area shows that it's a tad too wide to allow the right sidebar to fit (circled). Adjusting any of the elements by removing a bit of width, padding, or margins can solve the problem (bottom).

Be careful setting widths for *each* column in a multicolumn layout. If the available space in a browser window (or in a <div> containing the columns in a fixed-width design) is less than the *total* widths of the columns, you're asking for a float drop. For example, if you're using one of Dreamweaver's fixed-width layouts, a <div> tag with the ID *.container* wraps around the other tags on the page. Dreamweaver's stock style sheet sets the <div> to a width of 960 pixels. In a two-column design, you'll find two other <div>s, one for the main content and the other for a sidebar. If the combined widths of these two <div>s is greater than 960 pixels, the main content <div> drops below the sidebar.

Also, keep the CSS box model in mind. As discussed in the box on page 468, the width of an element displayed in a browser window isn't the same as its *width property*. The displayed width of any element combines the element's width, left and right borders, left and right padding, and left and right margins. For columns to fit side by side, the browser window (or containing <div>) must be wide enough to fit the total of all these widths.

While miscalculated column widths are the most common cause of dropped floats, they can also result from rounding errors if you use percentage widths. Browsers sometimes make mistakes when calculating the actual number of pixels needed to display something onscreen. That is, they can round numbers up, making elements slightly too large for the available space. So be careful when you set widths in percentages—err on the side of caution and make your percentages total slightly less than 100.

Bottom line: The only reason you'll see a float drop is because there's not enough room to hold all of a page's columns side by side. Rather than strive to use every last pixel of screen space, give your elements a little wiggle room. Get in the habit of making the overall column widths a bit smaller than the max, and you'll spend less time troubleshooting float drops.

FREQUENTLY ASKED QUESTION

Should I Care About IE 6?

I keep hearing that Internet Explorer 6 is dead and we don't need to worry about it anymore. Is this true?

If you're a web designer, you've probably got the latest version of Internet Explorer, Safari, Firefox, Chrome, or Opera on your computer. Previous versions of this book talked quite a bit about Internet Explorer 6 and even provided a section on how to deal with IE 6 bugs. You won't find that section in this edition because IE 6 is rapidly disappearing.

For example, in the U.S., fewer than 0.2 percent of web surfers use that outdated browser; in the UK, it's 0.5 percent. The exact figure varies depending on whom you ask and your geographic location. For example, when this book went to press, the website Internet Explorer 6 Countdown (*http://www. IE6countdown.com*) says that worldwide IE 6 usage is just 3.8 percent, but in China, IE 6 is still widely used.

Even when you know the geographic region of your site's audience, you can't assume which browser your visitors use. For example, if you build a site aimed at tech-savvy web designers, odds are that IE 6 hasn't tapped your site in a long time. But if your site is aimed at people in China, you may need to contend with IE 6.

The best way to find out how much of your traffic comes via IE 6 is to look at your web server's log files or sign up for Google Analytics (*http://www.google.com/analytics*) so you can track your visitors' browsers (among many other things).

For the great majority of web design projects, IE 6 is effectively gone. Hooray!

Building Websites for Mobile Devices

Designing Websites
for Mobile Devices

W̲eb designers used to build web pages for the 800 x 600 pixel resolution
of 15-inch monitors. Then, as large LCD screens became popular, most web
wizards designed pages for monitors that measured 1024 pixels wide and
larger. Today, the explosive growth of smartphones makes it clear that designers
need to craft sites for much smaller screens, too. A majestic, panoramic web page
that looks beautiful on a 27-inch monitor may turn into a tiny, unreadable postage
stamp on an iPhone.

You design for the multitude of mobile browsing devices in several ways. Some
designers build separate, mobile versions of their sites (see Figure 12-1). Using
server-side programming, these sites detect the type of device you have and deliver a web page customized for it. An Android phone web surfer, for example, will
see the mobile version of a site, which provides a greatly simplified experience: a
single-column design with most of the navigation elements removed, but with a
prominent search box added.

Of course, not all of us have the time to create two versions of a website, or the
technical skills to program a server to detect a visitor's browser. Fortunately, Dreamweaver includes several tools that tackle the problem of mobile site design. The most
straightforward of them uses CSS; CSS3 allows *media queries* that let you check
the resolution of a device (how many pixels wide a screen is) and supply styles for
just that resolution. For example, if a screen is 320 pixels wide (typical for phones
held vertically, in "portrait" mode), you can apply styles that format the page for
that dimension. In other words, instead of sending out different versions of the site
to different-size devices, you distribute the same site, but use different style sheets
to format the HTML.

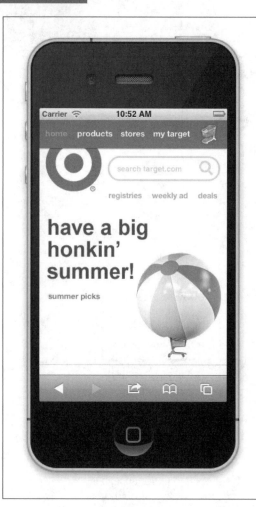

FIGURE 12-1

Many big companies, like Amazon.com and Target.com (pictured), create mobile versions of their sites, optimized for display on handheld devices like the iPhone.

This chapter begins by showing you how to preview your website at different screen sizes. You'll be pleased to learn you don't need to own every mobile device on the planet to see how your page looks on different screens. Next, you'll learn all about media queries, which ask a device, "What size screen do you have?" Then, media queries apply styles and formatting to the page so that it looks great on that device.

NOTE Two other chapters in this book address aspects of mobile site design. Chapter 13 covers fluid grid websites, which resize themselves for desktops, tablets, and phones, and which you build using special templates. Sometimes, though, you want to build a site specifically for phones and mobile devices. In Chapter 14, you'll learn about the jQuery Mobile library that provides building blocks to do just that.

■ Previewing Pages at Different Resolutions

Testing web pages in different browsers has always been a chore for webmasters, and that's especially true for mobile designs. As smartphone and tablet makers battle for market share, they change screen sizes and pixel density (the number of pixels per inch). That means web designers are left to cope with new challenges. In the past, to preview a web page on a phone, you had to store the page on your server and then use your mobile phone to connect to the website to see how it looked. Now, Dreamweaver jockeys can see their layouts on a variety of screens in a couple of ways. You can use Dreamweaver's built-in Window Size feature in Design or Live view, or, if you have an Apple or Android phone or tablet, you can use Adobe Edge Inspect to examine your Dreamweaver pages on that device. In addition, there are a few resources on the Web that can help you. This section explores all these options.

Previewing Different Screen Sizes in Dreamweaver

Dreamweaver simulates different mobile devices' screen sizes right within Design view. You find these so-called Window Size controls in the lower-right corner of the document window. Three icons of different sizes look suspiciously like smartphone, tablet, and desktop displays (Figure 12-2). Beside them, a drop-down menu displays the dimensions of the Design window's current view.

FIGURE 12-2

Dreamweaver has three preset window sizes for phones, tablets, and desktop computers. These views are key when it comes to working with fluid grid layouts (page 549), but they're also useful when you want to see how your page will look on different devices. To target sizes other than the three presets, or to change from portrait to layout orientation, use the Window Size drop-down menu by clicking the screen dimension numbers in the lower-right corner of the document window.

Click one of the icons for a quick look at your page in phone, tablet, or desktop lay-out. For all but the shortest of web pages, you'll see a scroll bar on the right to help you see all your content. As you click the device icons, you'll see the dimensions in the Window Size menu change. The phone, tablet, and desktop buttons use preset dimensions, but you're not limited to those.

Click the Window Size numbers to open the drop-down menu. It lists close to a dozen screen dimensions. Each indicates a screen size and a type of device, like "768 x 1024 Tablet," which are the dimensions of the original iPad. Want to see that tablet screen in landscape mode? Choose Orientation Landscape from the bottom of the menu.

If you don't see the size you need (perhaps you want to know what your design looks like on an 800 x 600 screen), you can create a new option. Click Edit Sizes from the Window Sizes menu, and Dreamweaver's Preferences window opens with the Window Sizes category already selected (Figure 12-3).

FIGURE 12-3

You can add options to Dreamweaver's Window Sizes list by going to Preferences→Windows Sizes. Click + to add a new size, and then enter a width, height, and name for the new size. For example, you can create an 800 × 600 window and dub it "Old Monitor."

Previewing Your Layout with Edge Inspect

Simulating screen sizes is all well and good, but there's nothing like viewing a page you're designing on an actual device. You get to see how your page looks in the real world and discover any quirks that pop up on mobile touchscreens. If you own an iPhone, iPad, or Android phone or tablet, Adobe has a tool that can help. Adobe Edge Inspect works through your wireless network and uses the Google Chrome browser with a special Inspect plug-in. Your mobile device uses a free app you download from the app store (Apple or Android). Once you set everything up, your desktop computer can literally beam a web page you're looking at in Chrome on your desktop straight to your phone or tablet. In fact, you can send a page to all your iOS or Android devices simultaneously. So, after you make changes to a page in Dreamweaver, you can use File→"Preview in Browser" to view the page in Chrome.

To use Inspect, you need a Creative Cloud account, and you have to download and install the desktop application through the Creative Cloud panel. On your mobile device, download the free Edge Inspect app from your app store. If you don't have Google Chrome, you should have a copy for cross-browser testing even if you don't want to use Inspect. You can download it for free at *http://www.google.com/chrome*.

NOTE One significant drawback to Inspect view is that you need to set up a local server to view the pages you're designing in Dreamweaver. See page 721 to learn how to install a testing server for Windows or the Mac.

After you install the desktop and mobile apps, you need to fire them up on your computer, phones, and tablets. The first time you run Inspect on your desktop, you'll be asked to install the Edge Inspect plug-in for Google Chrome. This is a one-time chore.

Once you have Inspect running on your desktop and mobile devices, you need to establish a connection between the two. Your mobile app will request the name of your local network or the IP (Internet Protocol) address of your desktop computer (see the Tip below to find it). After you type in the info, you get a six-number code to type into the Google Chrome plug-in. Fortunately, you only have to do this once.

TIP To find the IP address for a Windows computer, press the Windows key and then type *cmd* in the search box. This opens a primitive DOS-like window where you can type in commands. Type *ipconfig* and then press Enter. Several details about your network connection appear. The line "IPv4 address" displays the number you need. It'll be in a form like this: 192.168.1.104.

To find the local IP address for a Mac, click the Apple icon and then choose About This Mac. In the window that opens, click More Info. In the next window, click System Report. In the report that appears, click Network in the left-hand column of categories. At the top of the page you'll see a line that says AirPort. To the far right of that is the IP address—four numbers separated by periods.

The process is simpler the next time you use Inspect. Start the apps on your desktop and mobile devices, turn on Inspect in Chrome (as shown in Figure 12-4), and then, in your mobile app, click the name of the desktop device you want to connect to (Figure 12-4, bottom).

When your page shows up on the mobile device, you can take screenshots of the display. That way, you can show a client how a page looks on a phone or a tablet. You get a screen grab two ways: through controls within the mobile app or by requesting one through the desktop program. As icing on the cake, the desktop program includes a button to easily open the folder where it stores the snapshots.

Refresh all devices   Full screen   Request snapshots

Plug-in menu

On button

Snapshot folder

FIGURE 12-4

Top: To use Edge Inspect, open Google Chrome on your desktop, launch the Inspect plug-in from the plug-in menu, and then click the On button. Once you make a connection with a mobile device, using Inspect is pretty easy. Generally, when you click links and go from one page to another in your desktop browser, the page shows up on the connected mobile device so you can check its fit and finish. If necessary, you can force a refresh with the button shown here. Click the camera icon to request snapshots from each of the connected devices. Click the folder icon to retrieve those shots.

Bottom: Inspect's mobile apps remember connections they've made, so after your first session, reconnecting is a matter of clicking a name like Studio or Gravenstein shown here.

Third-Party Help for Window Size Dilemmas

You're not alone in trying to figure out how your web pages will look on the variety of devices out there, so you may as well learn from those who have gone before you. In fact, some of those folks have created tools that can give you a hand.

For example, if you go to *www.websitedimensions.com*, you find helpful information about devices and their pixel count, and the actual space available to web pages (Dreamweaver calculates this usable space by subtracting the area taken up by toolbars and scrollbars). The two most interesting features on the site are the "Live pixel checker" and the "Does your site fit?" tools. The "Live pixel checker" displays the resolution of your browser window. So if you connect to the site with your smartphone, you'll see a grid that measures the height and width of the screen in pixels, as shown in Figure 12-5.

FIGURE 12-5

Here's the display from the live pixel-checker at www.websitedimensions.com. The grid shows you the screen resolution of your browser window. Here, it measures the window of an iPhone 4s (320 pixels high by 415 pixels wide) using Google's Chrome browser. The grid doesn't include the area occupied by Chrome's navigation bar, so the space you see is the space that's available to a web page.

The "Does your site fit?" tool simulates what a site would look like on iPhones, iPads, and desktop computers. Feed the tool a web page address, and you see how the page squeezes into the browser windows of the devices in both portrait and landscape orientations. The site displays all the screen simulations on a single web page, so the view is similar to the Multiscreen Preview tool in Dreamweaver CS6, but removed from Dreamweaver CC. The downside to the tool is that the page you're checking needs to be live on the Internet.

Another site, Screenfly (*http://quirktools.com/screenfly/*), provides a similar tool for viewing live web pages. After you type in a web address, Screenfly displays your page below a toolbar (Figure 12-6) that has silhouettes of several mobile device screens. By clicking a screen icon, you can see what your site looks like on different devices, in landscape or portrait orientation, and with or without scroll bars. Many tools like this focus only on iPhones and iPads; Screenfly is noteworthy because it includes mock-ups for many other devices, like the Kindle Fire.

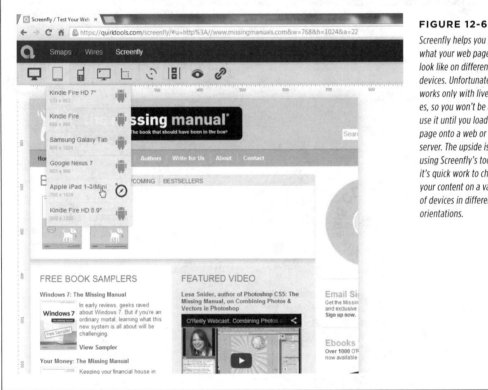

FIGURE 12-6

Screenfly helps you see what your web page will look like on different devices. Unfortunately, it works only with live pages, so you won't be able to use it until you load your page onto a web or testing server. The upside is that, using Screenfly's toolbar, it's quick work to check your content on a variety of devices in different orientations.

If you're feeling particularly geeky, you may want to head over to CSS-Tricks (*http://css-tricks.com*). Check out some of the lively forums, where you'll find questions and answers on all sorts of CSS, JavaScript, and PHP topics ("Why doesn't this slider work?" "Can I use JavaScript to delete a row in a table on the fly?"). CSS-Tricks'

CSS-Combat forum is a good place to learn more about CSS and strategies for different window sizes. The Snippets section provides examples of working code. So, for example, this page (*http://css-tricks.com/snippets/css/retina-display-media-query/*) shows you how to fashion a media-query that specifically targets Apple devices equipped with high-resolution Retina displays. Not sure what a media query is? Read on.

■ Media Queries

As mentioned at the beginning of this chapter, CSS3 includes a concept called *media queries*, which let you assign styles to a page based on the width and height of the destination browser. So you can create styles for mobile phones, tablets, and desktop PCs to customize your site's formatting so that it looks its best on each type of device. Because media queries are part of the yet-to-be-finished CSS3 standard, not all browsers support them. Fortunately, the browsers you're most interested in—those for mobile phones and tablets—do, so even though Internet Explorer 8 doesn't know what a media query is, your good old iPhone or Android device does.

TIP You can make IE 8 and earlier understand your media queries by adding a bit of JavaScript to the <head> section of your page. First, you need to download a zipped (compressed) file from *http://tinyurl.com/7w49a6z*. Unzip the file, and then, in the "dest" folder, copy the JavaScript file *respond.min.js*. Put that file in your site's root folder (or wherever you want to store your JavaScript files) and then link to it from your page using the <script> tag. For example:

```
<script src="respond.min.js"></script>
```

This little maneuver forces IE 6, 7, and 8 to understand media queries. In fact, Dreamweaver's fluid grid layouts automatically add this JavaScript to your pages (see page 562).

A "query" is just a question asked of a web browser: "Is your screen 320 pixels wide?" If the answer is Yes, the browser launches a style sheet for just that size device (a style sheet that you supply, as explained on page 116). The code that makes this happen looks pretty much the same as that for any external style sheet:

```
<link href="css/phone.css" rel="stylesheet" type="text/css" media="only
screen and (width:320px)">
```

The one addition to this standard style sheet link is the *media* attribute, which sets up the conditions under which Dreamweaver uses a particular sheet. You encountered the media attribute in Chapter 9, where you told a browser to apply different styles depending on whether you wanted to print out a web page or view it onscreen (see page 420). Media queries are just an addition to the media attribute. In the example above, a browser loads the *phone.css* external style sheet when someone views your site with a browser whose width measures 320 pixels.

Because 320 pixels is very precise—what if there's a phone with a slightly smaller screen, say one that's just 300 pixels wide?—it's best to use a range of values in your media query. For example, you might want to link a style sheet for screens that are less than or equal to 480 pixels wide:

```
<link href="css/phone.css" rel="stylesheet" type="text/css" media="only
screen and (max-width:480px)">
```

The notation "max-width:480px" is the same as saying "for screens that are at most 480 pixels wide." So the <body> tag style would apply to screens that are 480px wide, 320 pixels wide, and 200 pixels wide, for example.

Likewise, there's a min-width option that determines whether a browser is at least a certain width. This is useful when you target devices that are bigger than mobile phones or tablets. For example, you could write this link to apply styles to screens wider than the 768 pixels of many tablets:

```
<link href="css/desktop.css" rel="stylesheet" type="text/css" media="only
screen and (min-width:769px)">
```

To use this style sheet, a browser window must be at least 769 pixels wide—that's 1 pixel wider than most tablets in portrait orientation.

And, finally, you can set both maximum widths and minimum widths to target devices that fall between phones and desktop browsers. For example, you could use this code to create styles for a tablet that's 768 pixels wide:

```
<link href="css/tablet.css" rel="stylesheet" type="text/css" media="only
screen and (min-width:481px) and (max-width:768px)
```

In other words, the browser's screen must be at least 481 pixels wide, but not more than 768 pixels wide. This style sheet wouldn't apply to a 320-pixel-wide smartphone, nor would it apply to a desktop browser with a screen width of 1024 pixels.

In the discussion about media queries, you may notice a lot of emphasis on browser window width. There's a reason for that. The biggest problem with viewing most websites on a phone is that their pages are just too wide, forcing you to either zoom in and scroll left and right to read the page, or to squint and try to make out the tiny-tiny type of a three-column web page displayed at 320 pixels. Most web pages are already too tall to fit inside a browser window without scrolling anyway, so worrying about a browser's height doesn't make much sense.

Fortunately, Dreamweaver doesn't require you to know how to write media queries. CSS Designer gives you the tools you need to create them for desktop, phone, and tablet browsers. When you click +, the Add Sources button, in CSS Designer's Sources section, you define your media query using Conditional Usage options. Below the Sources section, you'll see the Media section, which you use to insert media queries into existing files. The media query retrieves the dimensions of the web browser window and then tells the browser which CSS rules to use.

With CSS Designer, you can create a media query, and Dreamweaver will write the necessary code. Used in conjunction with the window size previews discussed above, you can build media queries and preview their effects directly in Dreamweaver. Read on to learn how.

NOTE   CSS3 media queries can do more than just check the width of a browser window. The current media queries standard states that you can check for height, orientation (whether a phone is held upright in portrait mode, or sideways in landscape mode), and even whether a device uses a color or monochrome screen. There are a few other browser characteristics you can check with media queries, but not all browsers support them. You can learn more from the W3C website at *www.w3.org/TR/css3-mediaqueries.*

Two Approaches to Media Queries

Dreamweaver provides the tools you need to attach separate external style sheets for each screen size you target: a phone style sheet, a tablet style sheet, a desktop style sheet, and so on. You can have as many style sheets as you want, each for a different screen resolution.

You can either attach those style sheets directly to a web page (see Figure 12-7, top) or to an intermediary style sheet—called a site-wide media queries file—that is, in turn, attached to the web page (Figure 12-7, bottom). The benefit of the site-wide file is that you need only one line of code to attach a style sheet to the page, instead of one line of code for each style sheet you create (for example, three lines of code that load phone, tablet, and desktop style sheets).

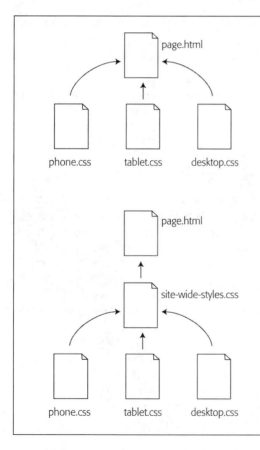

FIGURE 12-7

CSS Designer lets you attach multiple style sheets to a web page, each for a custom screen width (top). You need to write a line of code for each style sheet you want to link to—for example, if you have three style sheets attached to a web page, you need three links on the page. Alternatively, you can attach a site-wide media queries file to each page on the site. That file contains links to device-specific style sheets (bottom). To target another device with another style sheet, you simply add one more line of code to the site-wide file.

In addition, by using the site-wide media queries file, it's easier to add or remove style sheets for different devices. Say you start off with three style sheets, one for smartphones, one for tablets, and a third for desktop browsers, and you attached those sheets to each page on your site. If you later decide you only need style sheets for phones and desktop browsers, you need to edit every page on your site to remove the link to the tablet style sheet. If, however, you use a site-wide media queries file, you need to edit only the site-wide file to remove the tablet style sheet. Since each page on your site links to the site-wide file, Dreamweaver automatically applies any changes you make to that file to every page.

> **NOTE** If you use a site-wide file, you need to create a link to that file using the regular \<link\> tag—the same way you'd attach any external style sheet (see page 162). However, the site-wide media queries file itself won't have the CSS styles; instead, it uses a rule called *@import* in conjunction with a media query to attach device-specific style sheets:
>
> ```
> @import url("phone.css") only screen and (max-width:320px);
> ```

Creating Media Queries with CSS Designer

In CSS Designer, sources are locations where Dreamweaver stores CSS rules. When you identify a source, Dreamweaver lets you create a media query at the same time. Here, for example, are the steps to create an external style sheet named *phone.css* and a media query that links that style sheet to a web page if the destination screen is less than 480 pixels wide.

1. **In CSS Designer, with your web page open in the document window, go to the Sources section, click + to add a CSS source, and then choose "Create a New CSS File."**

   Dreamweaver opens the "Create a New CSS File" window.

2. **In the File/URL box, type *phone.css* and leave "Add as" set to Link.**

   Dreamweaver names your external style sheet *phone.css* and links it to this web page using code in the \<head\> portion of the HTML. Naturally, you can give your external style sheets any name you want, as long as they end in .css. Usually, something short and descriptive works best, so *phone.css*, *tablet.css*, and *desktop.css* are good choices.

3. **Click the flippy triangle next to Conditional Usage.**

   The window expands and displays two sections, one titled "Conditions" and the other labeled "Code." As you add conditions using the two drop-down menus in the first section, you can see Dreamweaver write the code for your media query in the Code section. Initially, the Conditions menu on the left displays the word "media" and the one on the right shows "screen." This is exactly what you want when you create a media query for screen properties. In effect, you're saying that the first condition for this media query is that the *media* must be a *screen*. That's just the beginning of your query, as you'll go on to add more conditions.

4. **Point to either the "media" or "screen," menu and Dreamweaver displays a + sign to the right. Click it to add another condition.**

Two more drop-down menus appear beneath the others. You'll notice the word AND replaces the + sign after the first condition. This logical AND operator is Dreamweaver's way of telling you that you must meet *both* conditions before Dreamweaver will link the style sheet.

5. **Click the left menu and choose "max-width."**

When you open the menu, you see all the conditions Dreamweaver supports (Figure 12-8)—screen orientation, screen size, resolution, aspect ratio, and device size. After you choose "max-width," the value portion of the condition changes so you can specify the value in the proper format. Use the text box to enter a value and the drop-down menu beside it to choose a unit of measure (like px (pixels), pt (points), or % (percentage).

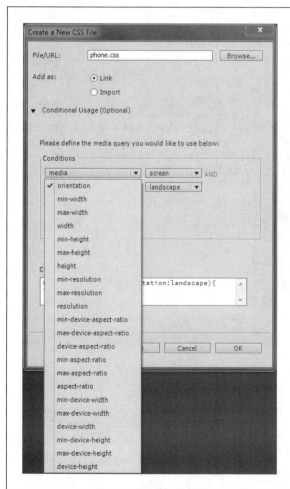

FIGURE 12-8

Using the Conditional Usage option in the "Create a New CSS File" window, you can develop media queries while you link an external style sheet to your page. You build your query by adding conditions. Here, the first condition queries the destination device about a media setting ("media"), specifically, the device's screen size ("screen"). The menu for the next condition is open, showing the variety of media queries Dreamweaver supports.

6. **Type *480* in the text box and then select "px" from the drop-down menu beside it.**

The *max-width* property accepts a value and a unit of measure. When you're done, the "Create a New CSS File" window should look like the one in Figure 12-9.

7. **Click OK.**

Dreamweaver closes the "Create a New CSS File" window. The external style sheet *phone.css* appears in Designer's Sources section, with a description of the media query in brackets, like this: [screen and (max-width:480px)]. Behind the scenes, CSS Designer has added the code for the media query to the <head> section of your web page. Check the Code view and you see a line that looks like this:

```
<link href="phone.css" rel="stylesheet" type="text/css" media="screen and
(max-width:480px)">
```

The first part is a normal link to an external style sheet. The part following the word "media" is the condition you set. In effect it says, "Use the *phone.css* style sheet for screens that are 480 pixels wide or less."

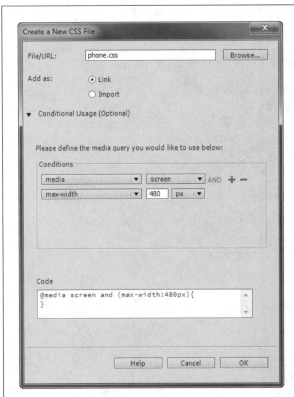

FIGURE 12-9

This window sets the conditions for a media query that checks a device for a screen width of 480 pixels or less. That's a good size for identifying smartphone screens. The Code box shows the instructions for the query. Keep an eye on the box as you add queries, and before you know it, you'll be able to hand-code media queries.

The media query described above has a single condition, but it could have more. For example, you could add "Orientation Portrait" as another condition. In that case, when both conditions are met (the screen is 480 pixels wide *and* it's positioned in portrait mode), the query will link the *phone.css* style sheet to your web page.

■ MEDIA QUERIES FOR DESKTOP AND TABLET BROWSERS

After you create a media query for phone-sized screens, you'll want to create CSS style sheets (sources) and media queries for the other screen sizes you want to target. For example, you might create style sheets named *desktop.css* and *tablet. css* and then link those to your pages via media queries. In general, you follow the same steps described on page 536 to build your queries, but you identify different screen sizes.

To create a media query for desktop browsers, use "min-width" instead of "max-width" in your conditional statement ("max-width" targets phone screens). By using "min-width," you're saying, "The browser window must be at least this wide." For example, if you set "min-width" to *769px*, only browsers at least 769 pixels wide will load the style sheet. It also applies to wider browser windows (1024 pixels wide, 2000 pixels wide, and so on), but not to narrower ones—768 pixels, 480 pixels, and so on.

To create a media query for the desktop, follow the steps on page 536, but create or attach the file *desktop.css* in step 2, choose "min-width" as a condition in step 5, and then set the value to 769 pixels in step 6.

Creating media queries for tablets requires some strategic thinking. Tablets come in a variety of dimensions. The Kindle Fire measures 600 x 1024 pixels, for example, as does the Samsung Galaxy Tab 2. The iPad is 768 x 1024 pixels. Of course, if you hold any of these tablets in landscape mode, they'll measure 1024 pixels wide. Since 1024 pixels is wide enough to fit most web pages, there's really no reason to create a separate style sheet for tablets held in landscape mode, but you might want to tighten up the design for tablets held in portrait mode—for example, you might take a three-column design for the desktop and convert it to a two-column design for tablets. To do this, you create a media query that handles screens larger than your phone's (480 pixels), but smaller than your desktop's browser window (769 pixels). So you write a media query for tablets the same way you build one for phones and desktop browsers—you create or attach a tablet style sheet, include a min-width condition of 481 pixels, and then add a condition (see step 4 on page 537) that sets *max-width* to 768 pixels. These conditions target screen sizes between those for phones and those for desktops.

At this point, your style sheets have no CSS rules. You need to add selectors and set property values for the formatting you want to apply through your style sheets.

Using a Site-Wide Media Queries File

A site-wide media query is a single, external style sheet that points to other style sheets, depending on the target device. Each page in your site links to the site-wide file, which in turn loads the appropriate style sheet once the destination device is identified. As mentioned on page 535, this approach means you add just one line of

HTML to your page (for the site-wide file), and makes it easy to add or remove a media query from your site because you have to edit only one file. In addition, as you'll see next, it's faster to add the site-wide file to a web page using Dreamweaver. Because of these advantages, it's generally a good idea to use a side-wide media query.

> **NOTE** The one downside to site-wide media queries is that they require one additional request of the web server—the receiving browser has to download the site-wide file *and* the style sheet for your visitor's device. Downloading that additional file results in a slight performance hit, but unless you get huge amounts of traffic, no one will notice.

The steps for setting one up include these:

- Creating an external style sheet to hold the media queries—this is your site-wide media query file.

- Adding links to web pages that point to the site-wide file.

- Creating media-query import rules in the site-wide file for the separate style sheets that handle phones, tablets, and desktop browsers.

- Developing CSS rules for different screens and storing them in the separate style sheet for phones, tablets, and desktop browsers.

In CSS Designer, it's easy to create a new external CSS file and link it to a web page at the same time, so you can tackle the first two tasks in one step. Here's the process:

1. **With a web page open in the document window, in CSS Designer's Sources section, click + and then choose "Create a New CSS File."**

   Dreamweaver opens the "Create a New CSS File" window.

2. **In the File/URL box, type *sitewide.css* and leave "Add as" set to Link.**

   You can use any name that seems appropriate for the external CSS file. As always, something short and descriptive works best.

3. **Click OK.**

   Dreamweaver creates the file *sitewide.css* and adds a link to the currently open page. There's nothing special about the link that attaches the CSS file to your page; it looks like any other link:

   ```
   <link href="sitewide.css" rel="stylesheet" type="text/css">
   ```

   You want to add this line of code to the other pages in your site that use the media queries in *sitewide.css*.

After you create the *sitewide.css* file, you can add the link to your pages in a couple of ways. In CSS Designer's Sources section, click + . Then follow the instructions in step 1 above, but instead of choosing "Create a New CSS File," choose "Attach Existing CSS File." When the Attach Existing CSS File window opens, use the Browse button to identify your style sheet (*sitewide.css*). If you're comfortable in Code view, an even quicker method is to simply copy and paste the line of code in step 3 above from one web page to another. Just make sure to paste the code into the <head> section of the new pages.

At this point, your site-wide queries file is empty, so the next step is to add queries to *sitewide.css*. If you plan on having separate CSS files for phone, tablet, and desktop browsers, create three media queries. It doesn't require much code, so the easiest method is to just open the *sitewide.css* file in Dreamweaver's Code view and type in the rules (see Figure 12-10). For example, a media query to import *phone.css* might look like this:

```
@import url("phone.css") only screen and (max-width:480px);
```

The instruction to import the file is "@import." The "url()" portion defines which file you want to import. In this case, that's *phone.css*, so type that between the parentheses, putting the filename in quotation marks.

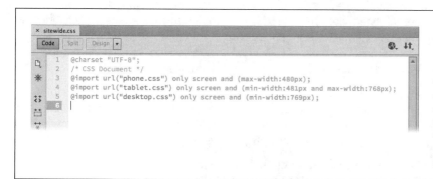

FIGURE 12-10

Here, a site-wide media queries file, sitewide.css, is open in Code view so you can edit it. Three lines of code identify the external CSS files that apply different formatting depending on the width of the destination screen.

The word "only" in the code sample above is meant for older browsers, those that don't handle media queries. When those browsers see the word "only," they ignore the query.

The last portion of the media query file ("max-width:480px") should look familiar. It's the conditional statement used to target phones with screens that are 480 pixels wide or less. When Dreamweaver imports the file, it's as if it copied the CSS rules from *phone.css* to the *sitewide.css* file at the point of the import instruction. The position is important because the usual CSS rules of inheritance (page 411) and the cascade (page 412) apply. That can become an issue if you combine media queries with global CSS styles, as described on page 544.

To query tablets and desktop browsers, you can edit the line of code above so that it calls up the relevant external style sheets and uses different conditions:

```
@import url("desktop.css") only screen and (min-width:769px);
@import url("tablet.css") only screen and (min-width:481px) and (max-width:768px);
```

The last step in developing a site-wide queries file is to add CSS rules to your *phone.css*, *tablet.css*, and *desktop.css* files. You do that from within CSS Designer, as described on page 116. What *is* a little different from the normal site-wide query file are the strategies behind the rules you create when you develop styles for phones, tablets, and desktop browsers. For those details, see page 545.

NOTE There's an issue you need to be aware of when you develop media queries that target desktop browsers. Internet Explorer 8 usage is shrinking but still stands at about 2 percent of your worldwide audience. The problem is that IE 8 doesn't understand media queries. Without some help, it fails to load the CSS styles used in the query. The best solution is to add a bit of JavaScript code to the <head> of your document, as described in the box on page 456.

Using @media to Add Queries to Internal Style Sheets

As usual with Dreamweaver and CSS, there's more than one way to get the job done. On page 536, you saw how to use a media query to apply styles you saved in an external style sheet. On page 539, you saw how to create a site-wide queries file that imports external style sheets. But you can also use media queries in an internal style sheet. That style sheet may include other styles, too, styles that Dreamweaver applies globally, for example, as explained on page 544.

Suppose you want to create a single rule that sets the font size for <h1> headings to "large." You want to apply this rule to devices with screen widths of 480 pixels or less. You can create a media query for that rule and place it in the <head> section of your web page, along with any other styles you want to store internally.

1. **With your web page open in Design view, in the Sources section of CSS Designer, click + and then choose "Define in Page."**

   If you already have an internal style sheet for the page, you can simply select <style> from the Sources section.

2. **With <style> selected in the Sources section of CSS Designer, go to the Media section and then click the Add Media Query button, +.**

   Dreamweaver opens the Define Media Query window opens. It looks like the Conditional Usage section of the "Create a New CSS File" window (Figure 12-9). The only difference is that the media query doesn't include tools to identify a file because you're going to put the query in the currently open page.

3. **For the first condition, set the left menu to "media" and the right one to "screen." Then click + to add another condition.**

   A new row appears where you define the second condition.

4. **For the second condition, set the left menu to "max-width" and then type *480* in the box next to px.**

The instructions in the Code box should look like this:

```
@media screen and (max-width:480px){
}
```

That is your media query. As you'll see next, Dreamweaver applies any CSS rules that appear between the curly braces ({}) when the media query's conditions are met.

5. **Click OK.**

   A new media query appears in the Media section of CSS Designer. As you can see in Figure 12-11, its name actually describes the query.

6. **With the media query "screen and (max-width:480px)" selected in Media, click + in the Selectors section.**

   A text box opens where you name your selector. If you don't see the media query in Media, you probably don't have <style> selected in Sources. The media query will appear only when you select <style> or All Sources.

7. **In the selector name box, type *h1*.**

   The selector targets <h1> headings.

8. **In the Properties section of CSS Designer, click + to see Text properties. Click to the right of the *font-size* property, and then choose "large" from the menu.**

   This style rule sets the *font-size* property for <h1> headings to "large." CSS Designer puts the rule inside the media query's curly brackets ({}) in the page's internal style sheet. In the document window, click Source Code to see the code Dreamweaver uses. It should look like this:

```
@media screen and (max-width:480px){
h1 {
    font-size: large;
}
}
```

   The CSS rule for the heading appears in the second, third, and fourth lines.

At this point, you can continue to add CSS rules to your media query. Make sure you select <style> in Sources and "screen and (max-width: 480px) in Media (Figure 12-11). Then add selectors and set property values. With your media query selected in Media, Dreamweaver puts all the rules you create inside the curly braces of your media query.

You can create additional queries for other screen sizes and store them in your internal sheet. Just follow the steps above and provide different conditions for the query. You can also create CSS rules in the internal style sheet that don't use media queries. For details, see the next section.

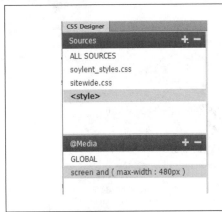

FIGURE 12-11

With the internal style sheet <style> selected in the Sources section of CSS Designer, you see the media queries that Designer uses in the Media section. In this example, you have a media query called "screen and (max-width:480px)." If there were other queries in <style>, Dreamweaver would list them here, too. If you select a source and don't see any queries in the Media section, that style sheet has no media queries.

Using Media Queries and Global CSS Styles

As the previous sections explain, you can include media queries in external or internal style sheets, just as you can any old CSS rule. No matter where Dreamweaver stores media queries, it's not unusual for web pages to use styles that result from a combination of rules—those from your media query and those that you apply globally, to all the pages on your site (in other words, rules that aren't governed by media queries). For example, you might have a set of styles that apply to all devices: *background-color*, *font-family*, and *font-color*. In addition, you may have styles specific to phone, tablet, or desktop browser windows. These device-specific styles might change the page's font size, image size, layout widths, and float arrangement of columns.

So, after you create a combination of styles that use media queries and styles that don't, how can you tell the difference within CSS Designer? If Dreamweaver stores your media query and its rules in an internal style sheet, that media query's name appears in CSS Designer's Media panel. For example, you might see "screen and (max-width : 480px)," as shown in Figure 12-11. If your media query links to an external style sheet, its filename appears in the Sources section, with a description of the query in brackets. If you created a site-wide media query file, with multiple media queries inside it, you'll see the name of the site-wide query file listed in the Sources section with a flippy triangle next to it. Click the triangle to display all the media queries in the file (see Figure 12-12). When you select a specific query in CSS Designer, the Selectors section shows you the selectors the query governs, while the Properties section displays related properties. Turn on the Show Set checkbox to see only properties with established rules. To see styles ungoverned by media queries, click a source or select All Sources in the Sources section. Then click Global in the Media section. When you do, Dreamweaver displays only those selectors independent of media queries. In other words, you see only styles that Dreamweaver applies globally. With Show Set turned on, the Properties section of CSS Designer shows only the properties that have values set.

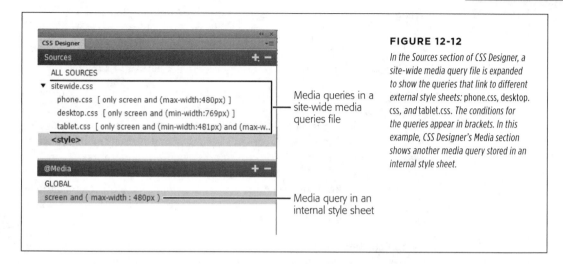

FIGURE 12-12

In the Sources section of CSS Designer, a site-wide media query file is expanded to show the queries that link to different external style sheets: phone.css, desktop.css, and tablet.css. The conditions for the queries appear in brackets. In this example, CSS Designer's Media section shows another media query stored in an internal style sheet.

Sometimes you'll want to approach the issue of style ancestry from the style end. Say you have a green <h2> heading. Is the rule that triggers green text global or governed by a media query? Here's how you find out. In Design view, click the heading text, and then, in CSS Designer's Selectors section, click Computed. As explained on page 414, Computed shows all the styles applied to a selection, even if different selectors from different style sheets trigger them. In the Properties section, turn on the Show Set checkbox to see only those properties that have values, and then click the *color* property—that's the one making your text green. Now look in the Sources and Media sections of Designer. Dreamweaver displays the source for the *color* property in bold. You may see that it's an external style sheet loaded with a media query. In that case, you see the query's filename with the query in brackets.

If you see a source displayed in bold without brackets or a media query, that means your style isn't controlled by a media query.

On the other hand, you may see a query in Designer's Media section that's bold. In that case, a media query stored in an internal style sheet governs your CSS rule. If Dreamweaver highlights <style> in the Sources section and Global in the Media section, that means the program stores your style in an internal style sheet, but one that's independent of any media queries.

Strategies for Using Media Queries

Now that you know how to add media queries to a page, what's the best way to use them to make your site mobile-friendly? Most site pages are just too wide to look good on a mobile phone. Phone browsers typically zoom out to give you a bird's-eye view of the page. If the page has multiple columns and was designed at a width of 960 pixels, it's impossible to read the page without zooming in and dragging it around.

Web designers use a few techniques when they design for mobile devices:

- **Remove columns**. Multiple side-by-side columns look great on a big monitor (and even on a tablet in landscape mode), but not so much on a phone. Remove the floats (see page 452) to stack a page's content <div>s one on top of the other.

- **Remove widths**. If you use a fixed-width design, your pages won't look good on a phone. A 960-pixel-wide page is just too much for cellphones, even the newer ones with bigger screens. A better approach is setting the widths of your content <div>s to "auto" or *100%*. This converts your page from a fixed-width design to a liquid, or flexible, design. In other words, no matter how narrow or wide a phone's screen, the <div>s will fit 100 percent of it. If a person holding an iPhone in portrait mode (so that the screen width is 320 pixels) suddenly turns the phone horizontally (changing the screen width to 480 pixels), <div>s set to "auto" or *100%* simply resize to fit the new space.

- **Tighten up white space**. Ample space between headlines, graphics, and other page elements adds breathing room to a design on a 23-inch monitor but creates a scattered layout and wastes space on a phone's small screen. Shrinking *margin* (page 465) and *padding* (page 465) values lets you fit more content on those small screens.

- **Shrink fonts**. Large fonts look good on large screens but take up too much room on handheld devices. Change the fonts on your page so they're smaller but still readable.

- **Hide content**. Many designers strip away content from mobile versions of sites. While it's easy to scan several columns and hundreds of lines of text on a desktop monitor, too much information on a phone can be overwhelming. You can use CSS to simply hide content that you think is superfluous for mobile users by setting the CSS *display* property to "none" (page 423).

- **Use background images**. If you put a 960-pixel banner on a page, no phone will display it without zooming out. One approach is to make sure your images are small enough to fit inside a phone's screen; another is to use CSS background images instead (see page 252). For example, you could create a <div> and add a class to it, say *<div class="logo">*. Then, in the style sheet for the desktop browser, set the <div>'s width and height to match the size of the large logo, using the *background-image* property to insert the image into the background. For example:

```
.logo {
    width: 960px;
    height: 120px;
    background-image: url(images/large_logo.png)
}
```

You could then put another style inside the style sheet used for mobile phones that resizes the logo <div>, using a smaller background image:

```
.logo {
    width: 320px;
    height: 60px;
    background-image: url(images/small_logo.png)
}
```

TIP Web designer Ethan Marcotte suggests another way to deal with images in mobile design. His "fluid images" technique is described at *http://tinyurl.com/ch9e43*. It's a lengthy but amusing explanation that shows you how to use an image's *max-width* property to resize images on the fly. It includes a workaround to accommodate Internet Explorer. Fluid images are part of what make up responsive Web design, used in Dreamweaver's new Fluid Grid Layouts tool and described in the next chapter. If you follow the link above, be forewarned: geeky waters ahead.

Organizing Your Style Sheets for Media Queries

So how do you actually resize your site based on screen resolution? You can take several approaches:

- **Create separate style sheets for each device**. In other words, create a phone style sheet, a tablet style sheet (if you're concerned about those), and a desktop style sheet, and then use Dreamweaver's media queries tool to attach each sheet to its respective page. However, since Internet Explorer 8 and earlier don't understand media queries, attaching a desktop style sheet using a media query in IE 8 and earlier won't work. One way around this is to use JavaScript to make IE 8 understand media queries (see the Tip on page 533). Another approach is to use an IE conditional comment (see the box on page 456) to attach the desktop style sheet. To do this, add the following code after the media queries on your page:

```
<!--[if lt IE 9]>
<link href="desktop.css" media="screen" rel="stylesheet">
<![endif]-->
```

You need to change the *href* value above to specify the path to your desktop CSS file. Dreamweaver can't insert this code for you, and its link management tools don't know how to locate and track it, so if you move the CSS file, you need to manually change the *href* value to point to the new location.

The other downside to this approach is that you need to specify all the styles in *each* style sheet. If you want to use the same font for an <h1> tag, for instance, and you use three style sheets (one each for phones, tablets, and desktop browsers), you need to add the <h1> style to each sheet.

- **Use a master style sheet and then individual style sheets for each device**. This method is similar to the one described for print style sheets on page 420. Basically, you start by creating a style sheet for the desktop version of the site, just as you'd normally do. Then you use CSS Designer and media queries to attach style sheets for other devices, like phones. In this second style sheet, you add styles that override the styles in the master sheet.

For example, say the main style sheet (the one attached without a media query) has a style for a <div> with the class *content*. Name the style *.content*, and float it to the right, with a fixed width of 564 pixels. In the phone style sheet, add another style named *.content*, but set its *float* property to "none" and its *width* property to "auto." Because of the rules of the cascade (see page 412), and because the phone style sheet appears second in the HTML, its *.content* style overrules the style with the same name in the master style sheet. You can continue adding styles to the phone style sheet that override those in the master sheet.

The phone style sheet doesn't have to override *all* the styles from the master sheet—that's one of the benefits of this approach. So if you don't create a style with the same name as one in the master sheet, the style from the master sheet prevails. Because of this, you need to create only a single style (in the master style sheet) for any site-wide formatting you want to see in phone, tablet, and desktop browsers (like fonts, page colors, and so on). Having the desktop styles in the main style sheet also avoids the need to use the IE conditional comment mentioned above.

Adding Styles to Media Query Style Sheets

As noted earlier, after you use CSS Designer to create a style source that has a media query, you still need to define the styles within the style sheets. In other words, media queries merely control when a browser uses a specific style sheet—the actual style sheet (*phone.css, tablet.css, desktop.css*) is otherwise the same as any other external style sheet. You use the same CSS Designer tools and techniques described elsewhere in this book to add, edit, delete, and manage the styles in those sheets. For example, follow the steps on page 116 to add a style, page 167 to edit a style, and page 135 to delete a style.

Building Fluid Grid Websites

I f you want to design a single set of web pages that people can read whether they're on a smartphone, tablet, or desktop computer, you need the power of fluid grid layouts. Fluid grid layouts let you create a single HTML file whose design morphs to fit phone, tablet, and desktop browsers. They combine the results of a media query (page 533) with a fancy grid-based design to create pages customized for the destination device (a practice called "responsive Web design" in Internet argot). The page's responsive layouts are based on three basic browser widths representing mobile, tablet, and desktop devices (see Figure 13-1). The pages then use percentage widths to scale the layout for specific devices—after all, not all mobile phones have screens that are precisely 320 pixels wide, nor do all tablets have displays that are exactly 760 pixels wide. Using fluid grid layouts, you can create designs that scale to a range of widths and adapt for the myriad screen sizes on mobile, tablet, and desktop devices.

NOTE Responsive Web design (RWD) is a term coined by the web designer Ethan Marcotte. You can learn more about it from the article that kicked off the RWD movement at *www.alistapart.com/articles/responsive-web-design/*.

FIGURE 13-1

The web design site Smashing Magazine (http://smashingmagazine.com) uses responsive Web design to customize the site's layout for phones (top left), tablets (top right), and desktop browsers (bottom). Each device receives the same HTML file, but CSS media queries apply different styles to the pages, creating a layout appropriate for each device.

Understanding Fluid Grid Layouts

Dreamweaver's fluid grid layouts combine lots of concepts, and to use them correctly you need to understand a few key ideas:

- **Grid layout**. Graphic designers have used grids to design books, brochures, and other printed material for centuries. A grid is an invisible pattern that underlies the design of a page (see Figure 13-2). In web design, a grid is a pattern of columns used to define the width of major elements on a page. Those elements are often <div> tags, but Dreamweaver's fluid grid layouts also support the new HTML5 tags, like <article>, <aside>, <header>, and <nav>. You decide how many columns make up the grid. The layout then determines how wide the <div> tags will be.

For example, the layout grid in Figure 13-2 has 12 columns. Think of each as a single unit, and the width of the page as 12 units wide. A header <div> that spans the entire page, then, would measure 12 units across. To add side-by-side columns, you simply divide those 12 units among the number of columns you want. For example, if you want to place the page's main content in a wide column and include some sidebar information in a narrower column to the right, you might divide that page into two columns, specifying a main content column of 8 units, and a sidebar of 4 units. Likewise, you could create two equal-width columns of 6 units each, or three side-by-side columns of 4 units apiece.

Finally, as you'll read on page 553, when you set up a new fluid grid layout page, you get to define the underlying grid yourself. For example, you may not like 12 columns as an organizing principle; you might want more or fewer columns. Dreamweaver lets you pick a grid of anywhere from 2 to 24 columns wide. In fact, you'll specify three grids—one for mobile phones, one for tablets, and one for desktop browsers.

- **Fluid layout**. The width of each unit in a grid can vary. That is, there's no fixed width of, say, 100 pixels for a unit. Each unit represents a part of the overall grid's width, and that unit's width can vary depending on the destination device and that device's browser width. That's the "fluid" part of fluid layout. When you add columns to a fluid grid layout, Dreamweaver uses percentage values to size those columns. That means that the columns resize to fit the available space in the browser window.

- **Breakpoints**. The CSS media queries you read about in Chapter 12 make it possible to apply different styles depending on the destination device. For example, you can send one style sheet to a mobile browser whose screen is 480 pixels wide, and another to a browser that's at least 789 pixels wide. The dimension at which a browser applies a different style sheet is referred to as its "breakpoint." And while Dreamweaver's Media Query tool (page 523) lets you set any number of breakpoints in a page (and apply any number of style sheets to it), Dreamweaver's fluid grid layouts put the brakes on that idea—they offer only three breakpoints: one for mobile devices, one for tablets, and one for desktop browsers.

Dreamweaver applies styles to mobile devices when their width is 480 pixels or less. Tablet layouts kick in when pages are between 481 and 768 pixels wide, and desktop layouts take over for pages between 769 and 1232 pixels wide. These numbers are hard-wired into Dreamweaver's fluid grid system, and you can't change them without breaking the fluid grid tools.

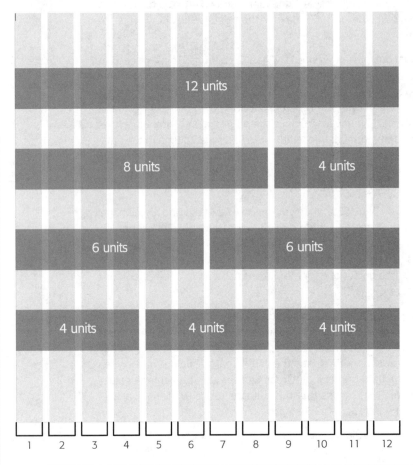

FIGURE 13-2

A layout is simply a grid of columns that gives a page structure. In this example, the layout comprises 12 columns. The page's designer distributes those columns among any number of page elements. For example, a <div> tag that houses the page's header might fill the entire page, taking up all 12 columns (or units).

- **Flexible media**. Another key feature of responsive Web design is "flexible media," or images that resize based on the width of their containers. In responsive Web design, if a column containing an image gets thinner, the image gets narrower, too. So an image that's, say, 600 pixels wide when you look at it in a desktop browser automatically scales down to fit the limited space of a mobile phone. This happens thanks to some clever CSS (in fact, you don't need to do anything to get this feature, other than insert images as you normally would, as explained on page 231).

■ Getting Started with Fluid Grid Layouts

Fluid grid layouts are different from the other pages described in this book, so it may come as no surprise that you build them differently. First of all, you must start with a special template, which you find at File→New→Fluid Grid Layout. For fluid grid layouts, the New Document Window is a form where you provide basic information about the page you plan to build (see Figure 13-3). In short, you define the grid you want to use for each of the three layouts: mobile, tablet, and desktop. For example, you might specify four columns (grid units) for a mobile device, eight columns for a tablet, and 12 columns for a desktop display. Here are some strategies and issues to consider for each of the three screen sizes:

- For mobile design, web designers often use just a single column for content (see the top-left image in Figure 13-1). Because smartphones have narrow screens (480 or fewer pixels wide), placing more than one column on a screen makes the design look squished. However, for reasons only Adobe knows, Dreamweaver won't let you type *1* in the Mobile column box, so you need to type *2* or a larger number. If you're going to simply stack content blocks one on top of the other (as many web designers do), it doesn't make a difference that you designated 2 units for the mobile screen. In most cases, you'll make your content span both the column units for the mobile layout. If you *do* plan to place columns side by side (and you should probably stick with two columns as the maximum for mobile designs), then the number you type here can help you set up the relative sizes of the columns. For example, type *2* if you want two equally sized columns sitting side by side. If you want columns of different proportions, type a larger number here. For example, if you type *3*, you can make one column 2 units wide and the second column 1 unit wide.

- For tablet design, type a number large enough to accommodate the different combinations of columns you envision for the device. If you think you might want two equally sized columns, make sure you enter an even number; if you want three equally sized columns, you need a number divisible by 3. Twelve is a good number to use since it's divisible by both 2 and 3, so you can create two columns that are each 6 units wide, or three columns that are each 4 units wide. In short, 12 units gives you lots of combinations of column number and browser width. Keep in mind that this number applies only to devices whose width is greater than 480 pixels (that is, wider than a mobile screen) and less than 768 pixels. In other words, this layout would apply to an iPad in portrait orientation (768 pixels wide), but not to an iPad you hold in landscape mode (1024 pixels wide). Nor would this apply to a Kindle Fire or Samsung Galaxy Tab 2, no matter which way you hold it, since the screens on those tablets measure 1024 x 800 pixels. In these cases, the tablet's browser would use the desktop design.

- For a desktop layout, use the same logic you apply to tablets: how many columns do you want, and what proportion do you want for them? Twelve is a good value here, too, since it gives you many unit combinations for a wide number of columns, but Dreamweaver lets you have up to 24 columns.

FIGURE 13-3

The Fluid Grid Layout category of the New Document window lets you specify the number of columns and their percentage widths for each of the three layouts this tool creates. If you make changes you regret, click "Reset to Default" to return the window to its out-of-the-box settings.

Another box in the New Document window—"% of column width"—asks how much space you want to leave between columns. Designers refer to that space as a "gutter," and you define it as a percentage of an individual column's width. A good value is between 20% and 30%, though you might want to create a couple of pages with different values and test them before you build an entire site. You can't specify different gutter values for each type of layout: the mobile, tablet, and desktop layouts all share the same setting (see Figure 13-3). However, since you can set different numbers of columns for each layout, the actual width of the gutter will vary.

Unfortunately, once you set "% of column width" and close this window, there's no way to return to this screen to change the percentage. Dreamweaver uses this value to make some complex calculations concerning the columns you insert, so even trying to change it by editing the CSS is a bad idea.

There's one last fill-in-the-blanks chore you need to do before you create your page. The content for a fluid grid page sits inside a container <div>, and you set a width for that <div> to control how much of the browser window your design will fill. Dreamweaver's out-of-the-box values are 91% for mobile, 93% for tablets, and 90% for desktop displays. Why? We don't know. It seems weird that you'd choose not to use the entire width of a mobile phone's already thin screen. In fact, it seems weird that you wouldn't use all of the horizontal space allowed. So it makes sense to set the value to 100% for each layout.

Building Fluid Grid Layout Pages

After you fill in all the blanks in the New Document window and hit Create, Dreamweaver rewards you with a brand-new fluid grid layout page in the document window. You'll notice that this isn't any old vanilla web page right away. Initially, you see the "mobile" view of the page as it looks on a phone held in portrait orientation. The background of the page shows columns—those units of measure you specified in the New Document window. Your visitors won't see the columns, they're just for your use while you design the page. Click the tablet or desktop icons in the lower-right corner of the document window to see the layouts for those devices.

After a moment or two, you'll notice that there's no Design/Live drop-down menu at the top of the document window, just a Live button. That's because you design fluid grid layouts in Live view. While you may think that Dreamweaver is tying one of your designer arms behind your back, that's not the case. Live view editing is a perfect match for fluid grid layouts because it keeps you from messing up the grid. You use the Insert panel or Insert menu to add paragraphs, headings, and images, and Dreamweaver guides you through the process. One way it does that is by asking where you want to place new page elements—before or after the current element, wrapped around other content, or nested inside another element.

In fluid grid layouts, as with many CSS designs (see Chapter 10), the fundamental element of page layout is the humble <div> tag (page 454), the box that holds your content. Creating a page layout using Dreamweaver's fluid grid tool is largely a process of inserting <div>s, sizing them to fit the grid of columns, and then filling the <div>s with content.

You use the usual tools (the Insert panel or menu) to add new <div>s, so it may seem that there's nothing unusual about them. When you insert a <div> in a fluid grid layout, Dreamweaver adds an HTML <div> tag to the page, just as it does for a regular web page. You place your content (images, headlines, paragraphs, and so on) inside the <div>. Every device—phone, tablet, and desktop browser—downloads the same HTML file with the same <div> tags and content. However, unlike a regular web page, these <div>s can look different on each device, thanks to the power of CSS media queries. That is, on a phone, the <div>s might stack one piece of content on top of another to form a single column. On a tablet, some <div>s might sit side by side to form a two-column layout, while the wide screen of a desktop browser lets you organize the same <div>s into a four-column design.

Before you start inserting <div>s, keep in mind a couple of rules:

- You must place your <div>s (or HTML5 tags like <article>, <header >, and so on) inside the container <div>, to which Dreamweaver applies the class *grid-Container*. That's not a problem if you select an element on the page and then use the Insert panel or Insert menu to add a new element.

- For major sections of your page, put new <div>s either before or after existing <div>s. For example, you don't want to nest your main article <div> inside the page's header—your design won't work.

- When you insert a <div> in one of the device views—desktop, for example—Dreamweaver adds that same <div> to the phone and tablet pages as well. Remember, the basic HTML is always the same for the three devices, though the page's appearance might differ because the browser applies different CSS styles based on the browser window width.

Laying Out Fluid Grid Pages

Once you insert <div>s into a fluid grid page, you organize them into a layout. HTML5 has several page elements that work exactly like <div>s, but have names that reflect their function on the page. For example, you can use <header>, <article>, <aside>, and <footer> tags anywhere you use a <div> tag and, like <div>s, they act as containers for page content. They simply have the advantage of a name that describes their role in the page's structure. You'll use these tags in the tutorial on page 559. For now, just keep in mind that you can use any of these elements in your fluid grid page where you'd otherwise use a <div> tag. Dreamweaver's Insert panel makes it easy to insert <div>s and page elements like <header>, <article>, and <footer> into your page. But first you need to understand that Dreamweaver creates a unique view for each device—mobile, tablet, and desktop—which you switch among by clicking the appropriate icon in the bottom-right corner of the document window. When you change the width of a <div> or turn it into a column that sits next to one or more other <div>s, Dreamweaver updates the CSS for just that one view. In other words, you create separate layouts for mobile, tablet, and desktop browsers by clicking the appropriate window-size icon and resizing the <div>s for that view.

To resize a <div>, simply click it and use the Resize Div handle on the right border of the <div>. The sole purpose of this handle is to make the <div> a certain number of grid units wide so you can place it next to one or more other <div>s in the same row. Skip the handle on the left border—it increases the margin to the left of the <div>, not the width of the <div> itself.

You can adjust your layout after you add content to the <div>s, but it's often helpful to get your layout bearings by building an initial layout before you add the clutter of content. In the tutorial at the end of this chapter, you start in the mobile view and add a <header> tag, two <article> tags, an <aside> tag, and a <footer> tag. All these elements are stacked on on top of one another in mobile view. In tablet and desktop views, there's more horizontal space. For those views, you arrange some elements side by side. For example, you poisition the <aside> tag to the right of the <article> tags so that the content in the <aside> serves as a sidebar to the main content.

Styling Fluid Grid Layout Pages

Dreamweaver's fluid grid layout tools control just the layout of <div>s and other page elements—they don't do anything to help style the look of the content you place *inside* those <div>s. For that, you turn to the regular CSS tools.

The first step in styling raw text is to add HTML tags to it. Then you create CSS rules for those tags and use IDs as selectors to target the major sections of your layout: banner, story1, sidebar, and so on.

When you first get started with fluid grid layouts, keep things simple by creating just a few global styles and storing them in a new external style sheet. Remember, you just want to set style rules here, not lay out the page—that's the work of the fluid grid's layout CSS. So avoid specifying sizes, widths, and heights for the <div>s in this style sheet.

Suppose, for example, that you want all the copyright <div>s to have a green background and white text in the PT Sans font. In your external style sheet, you create a rule for the *copyright* class selector that applies that formatting. In the web page's HTML, you link to this style sheet after you link to the fluid grid layout style sheet, so that this style sheet's rules override any competing rules in the fluid grid layout's CSS sheet.

One advantage of this technique is that it separates your global typographic and background formatting from the complex CSS that handles different-sized page elements in the fluid grid layout. In short, with this method, you're less likely to foul up the fluid grid layout. Also, when you work with global rules in a separate, external style sheet, you don't have to worry as much about where you place the rule within the media query hierarchy. (See the bullet points on page 119 for details.) Best of all, there's an easy solution if your styles don't work. Suppose you accidentally override a style you shouldn't have with a global rule. You can fix it by editing the rule or by removing a selector from your typographic style sheet. If more drastic measures are needed, you can click – (otherwise known as the Remove CSS Source button) to completely disconnect your global styles from the web page. At that point, only the fluid grid styles and their respective media queries govern the page.

■ Using Responsive Starter Templates

If you don't have the time or inclination to build your own fluid grid pages from scratch, take a look at Dreamweaver's Responsive Starter Templates (Figure 13-4). To use one, go to File→New→Starter Templates→Responsive Starters. In many ways, they work like fluid grid templates. The difference is that, here, Dreamweaver has finished the HTML page-building, and all you need to do is fill in the blanks. Naturally, each of these templates will resize gracefully for phones, tablets, and desktop screens. The layouts are modern and attractive, and there's plenty of opportunity to customize them by adding your own logo and other images.

When you create a page from the template, Dreamweaver adds a style sheet with a recognizable name to your site files. For example, the portfolio template's style sheet is *portfolioStyle.css*, and the blog post style sheet is *blogPostStyle.css*.

Using your CSS knowhow, you can tweak the fonts, text colors and styles, and background colors for headers, footers, and other sections of the page. For instance, to change the background color for the header of a page, click the header in the document window and then, in the Tag Selector, click the <header> tag. At that point, CSS Designer highlights the selector for the header in its Selectors section.

Go to the Properties section of Designer, click the Background button, and then set a new value for *background-color*.

FIGURE 13-4

The Responsive Starters templates work a lot like fluid grid layouts. After you select the template here and click Create, Dreamweaver opens your fledgling page and adds the necessary style sheets to your website. You'll find them in your Files panel (Window→Files). From that point, building a page is a matter of adding your own text and images. You can also use CSS Designer to change the formatting of the text and colors used in the page.

Here's a rundown on each of the Responsive Starters templates that come with Dreamweaver.

- **About page**. Tell the world a little about yourself with this template. There's room for a picture, some biographical information, and contact details. The bottom of the page includes room for your work experience. If you've ever filled in a LinkedIn page, you have everything you need to fill in the blanks here.

- **Blog post**. As you'd expect, the blog template provides a form where you can drop in text and images. It comes with two paragraphs as placeholders, but you can add more—open a paragraph for editing, press Enter (Return), and then let Dreamweaver add a new paragraph.

- **eCommerce**. This sales-oriented page gives you spots to drop in nine product images, prices, and descriptions. A large section at the top is just waiting for you to add your best sales pitch: 50% OFF! TODAY ONLY. Links along the left side are perfect for additional product categories. If you have hundreds of products, you can create several pages from this one template. The template's header provides room for your logo, along with links for signing into the site and for reviewing your shopping cart—but that's the catch. Before you can operate an e-commerce site, you or someone on your team needs to write the back-end programming that lets customers make purchases on a secure server.

- **Email**. Do you communicate regularly with your contacts by sending them a newsletter stored on your website? If so, this template may be for you. It has a clean, simple layout with room for one large image, a headline, a subhead, and a block of body text. The sections at the bottom give you room to point to related subjects or previous newsletters.

- **Portfolio**. In the mood to show off your past projects? The portfolio template makes it easy to drop in images and accompanying descriptions. See Figure 13-5.

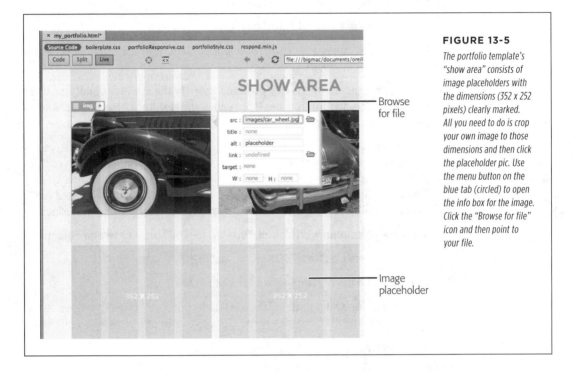

FIGURE 13-5

The portfolio template's "show area" consists of image placeholders with the dimensions (352 x 252 pixels) clearly marked. All you need to do is crop your own image to those dimensions and then click the placeholder pic. Use the menu button on the blue tab (circled) to open the info box for the image. Click the "Browse for file" icon and then point to your file.

Tutorial: Building a Fluid Grid Layout

In this tutorial, you'll use Dreamweaver's fluid grid layout tools to create a design that adapts to mobile, tablet, and desktop browsers. Dreamweaver's fluid grid layout pages use some special CSS, media queries, a bit of JavaScript, and a dedicated visual tool to get the job done. Because of this, you can't "turn" a regular web page into a fluid grid page with the push of a button. In fact, the CSS and HTML for a grid layout is so complex that the only way to create a new one is to use the fluid grid layout template.

> **NOTE** To complete this tutorial, you need to download sample files from this book's Missing CD page at *http://oreilly.com/pub/missingmanuals/dreamweaverccmm2014*. (See the Note on page 37 for details.) The files you'll work on are in the Chapter13 folder, and the finished project, for comparison, is in the Chapter13_complete folder.

Once you download the tutorial files and open Dreamweaver, set up a new site as described on page 23. In a nutshell, choose Site→New Site. In the Site Setup window, type *Fluid Grid Layouts* into the Site Name box. Click ▤ next to the Local Site Folder box, navigate to and select the Chapter13 folder inside the MM_DWCC folder, and then click Choose (Select). Finally, click OK.

The first thing you need to start this project is a new fluid grid document.

1. **Choose File→New→Fluid Grid Layout.**

   Dreamweaver opens the New Document window with the Fluid Grid Layout category selected (see Figure 13-3).

2. **In the boxes inside the device outlines, specify the number of columns you want for each destination device. Type *5* for Mobile, *12* for Tablet, and *12* for Desktop.**

   You're not saying how many columns you'll insert into the web page; you're letting Dreamweaver know how many columns to draw on the screen to form the page grid. You use these columns as units of measure when you specify how much room you want a page element to use. What you type here really depends on the design you're after. The steps below offer a few guidelines.

3. **In the "% of column width" box, type *20* for the space between columns.**

   A value between 20% and 30% works well for most designs.

4. **Type *100* as a percentage width for each layout.**

   The content for a fluid grid page sits inside a container <div>. This value specifies the width for that container. You want to use all of a browser's real estate.

5. **Click Create.**

   Dreamweaver opens the Save Style Sheet File As dialog box. You're about to save an external style sheet that contains all the styles necessary to control the layout of the page.

6. **Type a style sheet name— *layout.css*—and then click Save.**

   Dreamweaver saves the style sheet to your site and displays the page in Split view with the Live view half of the screen showing the mobile layout. You can examine the code if you want, but it's pretty cryptic at this point. You'll notice some directives embedded in the comments at the top of the page that deal with Internet Explorer.

NOTE There is no Design view option when you work with fluid grid layouts. You create pages using just the Live view and the Insert panel.

7. Click the Live button to close the Code view portion of the window.

In Live view, you see the tall, thin mobile layout (see Figure 13-6). You can switch to other views (tablet and desktop) using the buttons in the lower-right corner of the document window. However, to get started with fluid grid layouts, it makes sense to begin with the mobile layout because it's usually the simplest to build. When you first create a fluid grid page, Dreamweaver inserts a single <div> at the top of it.

Fluid grid layout div

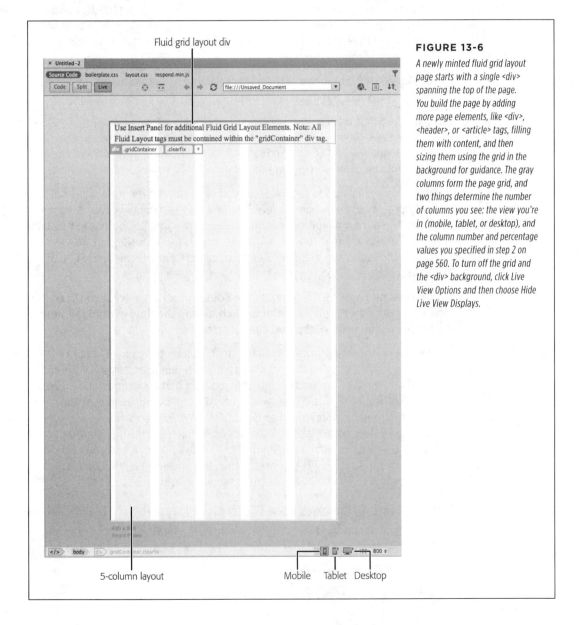

FIGURE 13-6

A newly minted fluid grid layout page starts with a single <div> spanning the top of the page. You build the page by adding more page elements, like <div>, <header>, or <article> tags, filling them with content, and then sizing them using the grid in the background for guidance. The gray columns form the page grid, and two things determine the number of columns you see: the view you're in (mobile, tablet, or desktop), and the column number and percentage values you specified in step 2 on page 560. To turn off the grid and the <div> background, click Live View Options and then choose Hide Live View Displays.

5-column layout

Mobile Tablet Desktop

8. **Choose File→Save. Type *soylent_green_fluid.html* into the Save As box and then click Save to store the HTML page on your site. When you see a follow-up dialog box that mentions dependent files, click OK.**

Dreamweaver saves the web page and opens a window informing you that it needs to save two other files to your site, *boilerplate.css* and *respond.min.js*. *Boilerplate.css* is an external style sheet based on the HTML5 boilerplate template (*http://html5boilerplate.com/*); it sets up many basic CSS properties and provides a baseline for displaying various HTML tags. The *respond.min.js* file targets just Internet Explorer 8 and earlier, and forces that browser to understand the media queries that fluid grid layouts use. You won't be altering either of these files—they just work their magic behind the scenes.

9. **Click the <div> at the top of the page. Examine its details in the Tag Selector at the bottom of the document window.**

When you first create a fluid grid page, you see a single <div> with some text in it and the ID *#div1*. The placeholder text provides important advice: "Use Insert Panel for additional Fluid Grid Layout Elements. Note: All Fluid Layout tags must be contained within the 'gridContainer' <div> tag."

When you examine the Tag Selector, you see "div1" on the right side and "div. gridContainer.clearfix" on the left. That means that Dreamweaver nested div1 inside the gridContainer <div>. You have to nest elements you add to the page inside gridContainer, too. How do you know if you positioned an element properly? Select the element and then, in the Tag Selector, you should see "gridContainer" listed to the left of the selected element.

10. **Go to Window→CSS Designer. In the Sources section, click *layout.css*. You see three "#div1" entries. Point to each, taking the time to read the tooltip that pops up, which describes the selector.**

Yes, there are actually three selectors with exactly the same ID (Figure 13-7). This works because each selector is inside a different media query. Point to the #div1 at the top of the list, and a tooltip explains that it's defined under Global. This rule styles #div1 for mobile devices. The following rules override these rules to create layouts for other devices. The middle #div1 works for tablets, that is, screens with a minimum width of 481 pixels, and the last #div is for desktops—screens with a minimum width of 769 pixels. When you add a new element to the page using the Insert panel, Dreamweaver automatically creates three selectors—one for each of the three media queries.

Adding New Elements to a Fluid Grid Layout

Once you create a fluid grid layout page, it's time to insert the basic building blocks of the design. You'll add a header, article, aside, and footer sections to your page.

1. **Click the <div> in your layout.**

Right now, it's the only element on the page.

FIGURE 13-7

Unlike the media queries you read about on page 523, fluid grid pages put media queries (and their accompanying styles) in a single external style sheet. In this example, that sheet is layout.css. As you can see in CSS Designer's Selectors section, a style sheet associated with a fluid grid layout has triplicate selector names. In fact, there are three sets of styles for each layout <div>. In this case (a page with a single layout <div>), you see the ID style #div1 listed three times. In addition, since Dreamweaver wraps all fluid grid layouts in a <div> that has the class gridContainer applied to it, the Selectors section also lists the .gridContainer class style three times. The first instance of the triplicate styles is associated with the mobile layout, the second with the tablet layout, and the third with the desktop layout.

2. **In the Insert panel, choose the Structure category, and then click Header.**

   Dreamweaver opens the Insert Header dialog box, shown in Figure 13-8. Using it, choose a position for the new element relative to the current <div>: Before, After or Nest(ed) within it. You also need to give the element a class name or an ID.

3. **Choose Before and then select the ID radio button. Click inside the ID text box, and then type *banner*. Make sure you have "Insert as Fluid Element" selected, and then click OK.**

   Dreamweaver positions your new header element before the gridContainer <div>, but still inside it. The header has an ID of *banner*, and it's a "fluid element," which means that Dreamweaver lists it three times in CSS Designer's Selectors section, just as it did with div1.

FIGURE 13-8

After you choose Insert→Header, Dreamweaver displays this special window for fluid grid layouts. It makes it easy to assign a class or ID to the new element, and it has an option (already turned on) to insert your content as a fluid element.

After you click OK, you see the new element in the document window with the text "This is the content for Layout Header Tag 'banner'."

Time to add more sections to your page. As you do, keep in mind that the HTML5 elements header, footer, article, and aside work just like <div>s. Their main advantage is that the tag names describe the elements' function.

4. **Click div1 again. In the Insert panel's Structure category, click Article. In the Insert Article dialog box, choose After. Select the ID radio button, and in the text box, type *story1*. Leave "Insert as Fluid Element" checked and then click OK.**

Your layout now has a section for a main article. The placeholder text reads, "This is the content for Layout Article Tag 'story1'." Every element you add to the page has placeholder text that identifies the element.

You'll add another article in the next step so that your page can hold two stories.

5. **Select story1. In the Insert panel, click Article. In the Insert Article dialog box, choose After. Give this article the ID *story2*.**

You have two article elements for two different stories. Next, you'll create an aside element to add additional, but less important, information. (An aside is similar to a sidebar in printed material.)

6. **Select story2. In the Insert panel, click Aside. When Dreamweaver displays the Insert Aside box, choose After. Give the aside the ID *sidebar*, and then click OK.**

Your aside appears under story2. Time to add the final element for the page, a footer.

7. **Click the aside. In the Insert panel, click Footer and then choose After. Se-lect the ID radio button, type *copyright* in the text box, and then click OK.**

   You page has a header, two articles, an aside, and a footer. It also has the original <div>, which is no longer necessary.

8. **Select div1 by clicking its placeholder text, which starts off with, "Use the Insert Panel..." Click the Trash can icon on the tab in the lower-right corner of the <div>.**

   The document window shows the elements you added to your fluid grid layout, minus the original <div>, which you just deleted. The mobile view looks like the screen in Figure 13-9, with all the page elements stacked on top of one another.

9. **Choose File→Save All Related Files.**

   This command saves your web page and the CSS files that format its elements.

You've built the basic structure for your fluid grid layout page. There are two direc-tions you could head from here. One is to replace the placeholder text with real content, the text and images you want on your final page. The second is to work on the layout for the tablet and desktop versions of your page. Up to now, you've only worked on the mobile view. You'll add real content next, which makes it easier to envision the tablet and desktop layouts for your page.

FIGURE 13-9

Here's your page as it looks on smartphones and other de-vices with narrow screens. So far, it's not so impressive. All you have are HTML5 elements and a bunch of placeholder text. That changes when you add your own content.

Adding Text to Fluid Grid Layout Pages

Adding content to a fluid grid page is no different from adding content to any other web page. You insert images and text inside the layout <div>s or, in this case, the HTML5 elements. In this example, you'll copy and paste text from a file called *website_copy.txt*. You'll make a few edits to add paragraph breaks and identify headings, and you'll also insert a few images using the Insert→Image command or the Insert Image tools in Dreamweaver's Insert panel.

1. **Make sure you're still in the mobile view. If necessary, click the mobile icon in the lower-right corner of the document window.**

   You see the mobile layout with the HTML5 elements (header, article, aside, and footer) stacked vertically.

2. **In the Files panel, double-click *website_copy.txt*.**

   This text file opens in a new tab in the document window. You'll copy and paste text from this file into the elements in your fluid grid layout.

3. **Select the headline "All Natural Ingredients" and the three paragraphs below it, and then press Ctrl+C (⌘-C).**

   Dreamweaver copies the text into the Clipboard.

4. **At the top of the document window, click the tab for *soylent_green_fluid.html*. Click inside story1 to select it, and then double-click to open the article for editing in Live view. Triple-click to select all the placeholder text, and then press Ctrl+V (⌘-V) to insert the copied text from the Clipboard.**

   Yes, that's a lot of clicking, but it's the quickest way to open a <div> for editing to replace its contents. The copied text appears as one big block of text. You'll break it into a heading and separate paragraphs later.

5. **Repeat steps 2–4 to copy the headline "Technology Meets Good Nutrition" and the three following paragraphs from *website_copy.txt* into the article story2.**

   When you copy and paste multiple paragraphs into a <div> in Live view, it appears as a single block of text. You need to manually break the text into separate paragraphs and headings.

6. **Click to select<article>#story1, and then double-click to open it for editing. Click at the end of the words "All Natural Ingredients," right before the W in the word "We," and then press Enter (Return).**

   The words "All Natural Ingredients" are now in a paragraph by themselves. The rest of the text is in a separate paragraph. Live view automatically creates paragraphs as you press Enter (Return) while editing text. Both paragraphs are inside story1. Double-check to make sure this is the case: First click outside the article, say on the footer, and then go back and click the two paragraphs in the article, examining their structure in the Tag Selector at the bottom of the document window. Reading from right to left, you see that there is a <p> tag inside an article#story1 tag that's inside the gridContainer <div>.

TIP Another great tool for analyzing the structure of your web page is Element Quick View. To use it, click </> at the bottom left of the document window, or choose View→Element Quick View.

7. **Continue to break the inserted text into paragraphs.**

   In story1, create new paragraphs at "As always" and "Not sure." In story2, do the same at "The Soylent Corporation," "We're always," and "Avoid the empty."

   Now your two stories look more like articles on a web page.

   In mobile view, the two stories appear stacked.

8. **Go back to the text file *website_copy.txt* and copy the line that reads "This Week's Specials." Paste it into #sidebar and then press Enter (Return).**

   The aside will eventually hold captions and pictures. For now, this heading is enough to identify the element. Pressing Enter (Return) puts the text inside paragraph tags (<p>), and also creates a second, empty paragraph that you don't need.

9. **Click the space below "This Week's Specials" to select the empty paragraph, and then press Delete.**

   As an alternative to pressing Delete, you can right-click an element to display a context menu with editing options that include cut, copy, paste, delete, and duplicate.

10. **Copy the last two lines in *website_copy.txt* (the copyright message) and paste them into the #copyright element.**

    There are two lines in the copyright, but you don't need extra space between them, so instead of adding a paragraph break, you'll add a line break between them.

11. **Double-click #copyright to open it for editing. Click before the letter "C" in "Contact" and then press Shift+Enter (Shift-Return).**

    A line break forces the line that begins with the word "Contact" below the first line.

The text is in place and your page is beginning to look more like a real page. It could still use some images, some color, and some styling. That will come later. Now you have enough content in place to lay out the pages for the tablet and desktop views.

Laying Out Tablet and Desktop Views

It's time to design the page layouts for devices that are wider than a smartphone. You tackle this part of the job one view at a time. First you'll switch to tablet view and rearrange the page elements there. Then you'll move on to desktop view and do the same. The process involves resizing the elements (header, articles, aside, and footer) where necessary and repositioning some of the elements so that they sit side by side on the wider screens. You'll be surprised at how simple it is.

1. **In the lower-right corner of the document window, click the tablet view icon.**

   You see the same elements as in the smartphone view, but on a wider page. All the elements are still stacked on top of one another.

2. **Click any of the text in story1 and then, in the Tag Selector, click "article."**

   When you select the <article> tag in the Tag Selector, Dreamweaver displays a turquoise border around all the paragraphs in the article. The tiny square in the middle of the right border is the element's resize handle. You'll use it next to resize the article on the grid.

3. **Drag the resize handle (Figure 13-10, circled, top) to the left, until the accompanying tooltip identifies the width as 6 columns.**

   When you're done, the text covers six columns.

> **NOTE** When you resize a <div> that you want to move up and to the right of another <div>, it's tempting to grab the handles on the left side of the <div>. Don't!!! See Figure 13-10 for an explanation.

4. **Repeat steps 2 and 3 to resize story2.**

   Both stories now occupy only half the page. There's plenty of room to arrange them side by side.

5. **Select article#story2 in the Tag Selector and then click the "Move up a row" icon (the slanting arrow) on the tab at the bottom right of the element.**

   The two stories now sit side by side. The <header> appears above, spanning all 12 columns. The <aside> and the <footer> elements are below, spanning all 12 columns. The layout needs some CSS formatting, but it'll work well for tablets. Now it's time to lay out the desktop view, where the stories and the aside will all sit side by side.

6. **Click the desktop icon in the lower-right corner of the document window.**

   You see your elements stacked as they were in the mobile view.

7. **Click any of the text in story1. In the Tag Selector, click "article," and then drag the resize handle left until the article is four columns wide.**

   For this view, you'll make both articles and the aside four columns wide.

8. **Repeat the process to resize story2 and the sidebar.**

   The three elements are now each four columns wide. It's time to move them to the same row.

9. **Click the text in story2. In the Tag Selector, click "article," and then click the "Move up a row" arrow icon.**

   The two articles sit next to each other on the same row. There's still room for the aside.

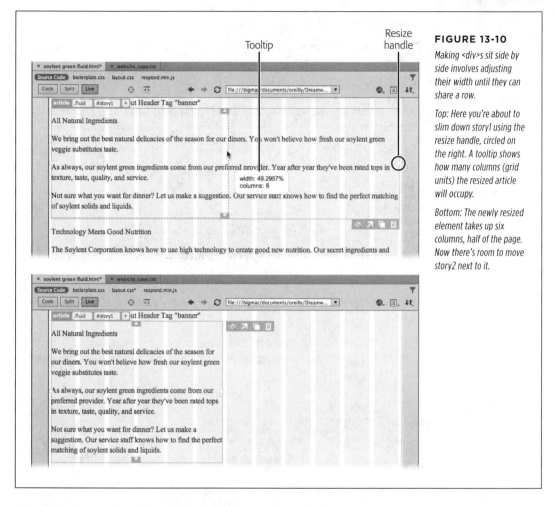

FIGURE 13-10

Making <div>s sit side by side involves adjusting their width until they can share a row.

Top: Here you're about to slim down story1 using the resize handle, circled on the right. A tooltip shows how many columns (grid units) the resized article will occupy.

Bottom: The newly resized element takes up six columns, half of the page. Now there's room to move story2 next to it.

10. **Click the text in aside#sidebar. In the Tag Selector, click "aside" and then click the "Move up a row" arrow icon.**

    Your desktop layout of the major HTML elements is complete. There's a header at the top of the page, two articles and a sidebar that share a row, and a footer for the copyright notice.

With some content in place and the basic layout for mobile, tablet, and desktop complete, you start to get a feeling for the way the page will look on different devices. There's still quite a way to go. This is a good time to start adding images.

Adding Images to Fluid Grid Layouts

You add images to your fluid grid layouts using the Insert panel or the Insert menu. In this section, you'll add an image to the header. Later in this tutorial, you'll add three images to the sidebar and a background image to the entire page.

1. **Click the mobile icon in the lower-right corner of the document window and then click the <header> section of the page.**

   The header still contains placeholder text.

2. **In the Insert panel, set the categories menu to Common and then click "Image : Image."**

   Dreamweaver displays the positioning window, which has three options: Before, After, and Nest. The Wrap option is grayed out because you can't wrap an image around the header.

3. **Click Nest.**

   Dreamweaver opens the Select Image Source window.

4. **Choose *cafe_logo.png* and then click OK (Open).**

   The image file appears in the <div>, pushing the text aside.

5. **Delete the placeholder text so that the banner image is the only element in div1.**

   If you clicked elsewhere after you added the image, you need to double-click the placeholder text to open the <div> for editing. When you're done, the header should look like the one in Figure 13-11.

FIGURE 13-11

The Cafe Soylent Green logo appears faint when you add it to your page because it includes semitransparent colors. Later in this tutorial, you'll add a background color to the <header>, which will sharpen up the logo.

Nesting HTML Elements

In these steps, you'll add three images and three captions to the aside. You want the images and captions to stay together as a single unit even as your fluid grid changes, so place each image and caption in a <div>. Here's the procedure in brief: first, nest a <div> inside the aside. Then nest one caption and one image inside that <div>. To speed things up, you'll duplicate the first <div> twice, and then modify the copies for the second and third image-and-caption set.

1. **Click the text "This Week's Specials" in aside#sidebar and then, in the Tag Selector, click <aside>.**

   When you select aside#sidebar, you see a turquoise border around the sidebar and a tab that identifies it.

2. **In the Insert panel, click Div. In the position dialog box, choose Nest, turn on the class radio button, type *special* into the ID box, turn on the "Insert as Fluid Element" checkbox, and then click OK.**

   A new <div> appears nested inside the <aside>. The Tag Selector displays <div>. fluid.special to the right of aside#sidebar.fluid.

3. **Go to the text file *website_copy.txt* and copy the line that begins "Soylent green fluid." Then select the <div> you just inserted, double-click inside it to open the <div> for editing, and then triple-click to select all the placeholder text. Finally, press Ctrl+V (⌘-V) to paste the new text.**

   The new text takes the place of the placeholder text, and the <div> remains in "edit" mode until you click something else.

4. **In the Tag Selector, click <div>, and then, in the Insert panel's Common category, click "Image : Image." When Dreamweaver displays the position dialog box, choose Nest, and then, in the Select Image Source window, select *special1.jpg*. Finally, click OK (Open).**

   The image appears in front of the text.

NOTE   When you insert an image into a fluid grid layout page, Dreamweaver doesn't assign a width or height to the image as it does for other types of web pages (see page 245). Instead, it leaves those values blank and uses some tricky CSS to make the image "fluid"—that is, to make it shrink in size as the <div> gets smaller. (To learn how this works, read the original article on this technique by Ethan Marcotte at *www.alistapart.com/articles/fluid-images/*.)

---

5. **Double-click the text to open the <div> for editing, place your cursor between the image and the "S" in "Soylent," and then press Enter (Return).**

   There are now two paragraphs in the <div>. The paragraph at the top holds the image, and the one below it has the caption. For a clear view of the hierarchy of the nested elements, open Element Quick View by clicking the button circled in Figure 13-12.

6. **In the Tag Selector, click <div>.fluid.special. In the document window, click the Duplicate DIV button in the tab on the lower-right corner of the <div>. When the duplicate appears, click *its* Duplicate DIV button.**

   There are three identical pictures and captions in the <aside>. You'll edit the last two to change their text and images.

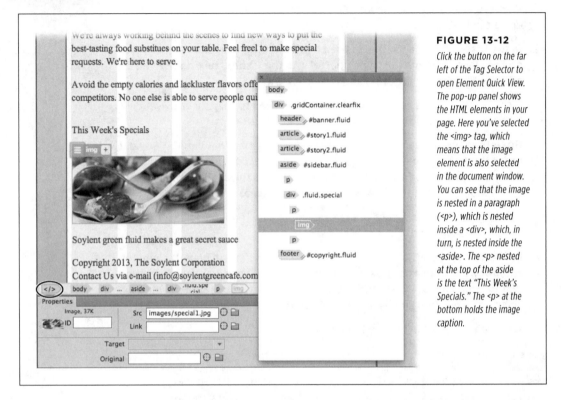

7. **In the text file *website_copy.txt*, copy the line that begins "Our special." Then, on the Soylent green fluid web page, select the caption for the second image and paste in the new text. Go back to *website_copy.txt* and copy the line that begins "Yummy grilled" and paste that into the third caption.**

   Each image has a different caption. Now it's time to change the pictures.

8. **Click the second image in the <aside>, and then click the menu button (three bars) on the tab in the top-left corner.**

   Dreamweaver displays a panel with details about the image. The "src" details on the top line identify the image file.

9. **Click the browse for file icon (a folder) and then, in the Select Image Source window, choose *special2.jpg* and click OK (Open).**

   The new image appears in the <aside>. While the panel is open, it's a good idea to provide a title and "alt" description for the image.

10. **Repeat steps 8 and 9 to set the source for the third image to *special3.jpg*.**

    Your aside has three images and three captions. The image and caption pairs are nestled safely in <div>s that will keep them together when the fluid grid changes for the different views.

Now that you have some pictures in place, this is a good time to save your work with the File→Save All Related files command. It's also a good time to take another look at the three views. The content is in place, crying out for some formatting and CSS magic. If things don't look the way they should, see the box below for some troubleshooting suggestions.

UP TO SPEED

Troubleshooting Fluid Grid Layouts

Sometimes, you'll preview your fluid grid layout and it won't look the way you think it should. Previewing your work is a task you should do early and often, because it's easier to catch and fix problems if you work incrementally. For example, after you set up a new row of <div>s, save your work and then preview it. After you add content to your <div>s, save and preview once more. And when you save the file, use the Save All Related Files command. Dreamweaver transforms your work of arranging different layouts for mobile, tablet, and desktop devices into CSS code. If you don't save that CSS file before previewing your work, you won't see any changes.

If your layout doesn't look as expected, the first thing to do is use the Save All Related Files command again, just to make sure you saved the associated CSS file. When you preview the page in your browser, press F5 to reload the page and the style sheet. Sometimes, even this doesn't solve the problem. In previous versions of Dreamweaver, fluid grid layouts were a bit fragile. The situation has improved in Dreamweaver CC 2014, but if you do run into major problems, sometimes the best (and quickest) solution is to start over. To do that for this tutorial, you'd close all the documents and then, in the Files panel, delete all the files except for *website copy.txt* and the images folder.

Styling Your Fluid Grid Web Page

Here's how you create a style sheet that specifies fonts and colors for your page. You start by applying basic HTML tags to your headlines. You can work in any of the three device views, but it's usually easier to work in the mobile view:

1. **In story1, select the paragraph "All Natural Ingredients," and then, in the Properties panel's Format menu, choose Heading 1.**

    That changes the HTML <p> tag to an <h1> tag. It doesn't change the style sheet, even though it changes the appearance of the text. In addition, since all the layouts share the same HTML and style sheet, your tag change affects *all* the fluid layouts, mobile, tablet, and desktop.

TIP If you don't see the Format menu in the Properties panel below the document window, you may be in CSS mode. In that case, click HTML (upper left).

---

2. **Using the same technique as in step 1, create an <h1> heading in story2 and an <h2> heading in the aside#sidebar.**

Both articles and the aside now have HTML headings. It's time to add some style using CSS. First, you need to create a new external style sheet.

3. **In the Sources section of CSS Designer, click + and choose Create A New CSS File from the menu. In the dialog box that pops up, type *soylent_styles.css* in the File/URL box. Leave the "Add as" option set to Link and then click OK.**

Dreamweaver lists your new external style sheet in the Sources section, below the fluid grid style sheets *boilerplate.css* and *layout.css*. You'll leave those sources alone, while you add new rules to *soylent_styles.css*.

4. **In Sources, click *soylent_styles.css* and then, in the Selectors section, click + to add a selector. Type *body* in the box for the selector name.**

Dreamweaver adds *body* to the list of selectors. You can format the tag and the style will apply to any text between the beginning and ending <body> tags. Dreamweaver applies the style rules in *soylent_styles.css* to all three fluid layouts. They're not governed by the media queries, and browsers apply the style rules after the media queries do their magic.

5. **In the Properties section of CSS Designer, make sure that you still have "body" highlighted in the Selectors section and that you have the Show Set checkbox turned off. Click the T button to see the text styles available, and then set *font-family* to "pt-sans, Arial, Helvetica, sans-serif." Dreamweaver automatically sets the value for *font-style* to "normal," and sets *font-weight* to "400." When you finish, CSS Designer's Properties section should look like the one in Figure 13-13.**

This global style sets the basic font for your layout to sans-serif. (If you haven't added the PT Sans web font as explained on page 160, use a sans-serif alternative.) All the text in your layout will use this font unless you change it for a specific selector (and you'll do that in the step 7).

FIGURE 13-13

You create a new style sheet (here called soylent_styles.css) to apply formatting to elements in all of the views. Here the <body> selector specifies font-family, font-style, and font-weight values. You see the effect in the mobile, tablet, and desktop views.

6. **With the <body> selector still highlighted, click the Background button in the Properties section. Find *background-image url* and click inside the text box. (The *background-image url* property shows the grayed-out letters "url" when you haven't set a value.) Click 🖿 on the right and then, in the Select Image Source window, choose *bg_page.png*. Then click OK (Open).**

   The background image provides a textured, colored background (as long as the browser supports background images, of course).

7. **With *soylent_styles.css* still selected in the Sources section of CSS Designer, click + in the Selectors section. In the name box for the selector, type *h1*. In the Properties section, set the text color to *#006600* (a dark green), and then set *font-family* to "pt-serif" or another typeface with serifs. Set *font-weight* to "700."**

   Your <h1> headings reflect these changes.

8. **Use the technique from step 7 to create an h2 selector, and then set the text color to *#FFFFFF* (white), the *font-family* to "pt-serif," the *font-variant* to "small-caps," and *text-align* to "center."**

   This creates a unique look for the <h2> heading in the sidebar.

9. **Click the Background button and set the background color to *#006600* (dark green).**

   Your sidebar now sports a green bar for the title.

10. **With *soylent_styles.css* still selected in Sources, click + and then, in the name box, type *header, footer*.**

   This shortcut makes it easy to apply the same style to more than one selector at a time. Just make sure you put a comma between the two selector names. In this case, you're targeting the header (with the banner) at the top of the page, and the footer (with the copyright notice) at the bottom of the page.

11. **Click the header, footer selector, and then, in Properties, click the Background button. Set the background color to *#006600*.**

   The background for the banner and copyright notice is now dark green. At last you can see your logo!

12. **In CSS Designer's Properties section, click the Layout button and then, in the padding box, click the link to change all the properties at once. Set the value of one of the padding boxes to *7px*. Next, click the Text button at the top of Properties and set the text color to *#FFFFFF* (white).**

   The padding provides a little breathing room around the contents of the <div>s. The text in the copyright inherits its sans-serif font from the <body> style rule (steps 4 and 5) and its color from the *#banner, #copyright* rule (step 11). This is probably a good time to save and preview your work.

13. **Choose File→Save All Related Files, and then press F12 to preview your page in your browser. Resize the browser window (by dragging the left edge, for example) to see the layout at different breakpoints for the mobile, tablet, and desktop designs.**

At the mobile screen width, Dreamweaver stacks everything vertically, but the way you formatted the heading and body text gives the layout an attractive appearance. At the tablet screen width, the main stories appear in side-by-side columns. The sidebar appears, a little awkwardly, in a vertical orientation below them (you'll fix this in the last part of the tutorial, on page 576). At the desktop screen width, the page has three equal columns, one for each of the two main stories, and one for the sidebar. In addition, the sidebar's green headline bar sets it off from the two stories.

In each of the views, the sidebar could use some adjustments.

You can continue to add to or tweak the global styles, being sure to follow a few straightforward rules:

- Make sure you edit the *soylent_styles.css* source, not one of the other style sheets.

- Keep in mind that you want to apply these styles *after* you apply the fluid layout styles, so in the Sources section of CSS Designer, keep *soylent_styles.css* below *boilerplate.css* and *layout.css*.

- Avoid making changes to width, height, or other size or position properties that might override the fluid grid layout's hard work.

- Be cautious about applying margins and padding. The wrong settings can look awkward in one or more of the views.

- Double-check the results after you create a rule. If you override the wrong property, it may disturb the fluid grid layout.

If you run into problems, try disabling or deleting specific rules (property/value pairs or selectors) in *soylent_styles.css*. Point to the property in CSS Designer's Properties section and then use the disable or delete buttons that appear to the right of the property. If that doesn't work, try detaching *soylent_styles.css* using the Remove CSS Source button (-) in CSS Designer's Sources section.

Next, you'll fix some of those sidebar issues.

Adjusting the Layout for Different Views

The sidebar looks pretty good in mobile and desktop views, but it would look better if the images and captions were centered. In tablet view, the sidebar looks awkward in the vast space beneath the two stories. It would look better if each of the image/caption <div>s sat on the same row side by side. Here's the fix:

1. **In CSS Designer's Sources section, click *layout.css*. Then, in the Selectors section, click the top instance of the class selector *.special*.**

   Remember, there are three instances of the *.special* selector—one for each media query. When you point to the top instance of *.special*, the tooltip says "special defined under GLOBAL." This selector sets the rules for the mobile view, and those rules will apply to the other views as well (unless you override them with new rules in the tablet or desktop views).

2. **With *.special* highlighted in Selectors, click the Text button in the Properties section and then set the *text-align* property to "center" (second button from the left).**

   You assigned the *.special* class to the <div>s you added back on page 571. The images and captions are in paragraphs inside the <div>, so their contents gets centered. This looks good in mobile and desktop views. Tablet view needs some more tweaking.

3. **Click the tablet view icon in the lower-right corner of the document window.**

   The images and captions appear stacked on top of one another.

4. **Click the top image and then, in the Tag Selector, click <div>.fluid.special. In the document window, drag the handle on the right side of the <div> to the left to make the <div> four columns wide.**

   All three of the <div>.special elements change to four columns in width.

5. **Click the second image. In the Tag Selector, click <div>. Then, in the tab at the bottom-right of the <div>, click the "Move up a row" arrow icon.**

   The image and caption for the second image pop into place next to the first. However, if you try the same thing with the third image, you won't see the "Move up a row" arrow because there isn't quite enough room. The solution is to make more room by removing the margin.

6. **Click the first image and then select <div> in the Tag Selector. Click the button at the top-left corner of the <div>. Its tooltip reads "Apply .zeroMargin_tablet" (see Figure 13-14).**

   The <div>'s turquoise tab lists .zeroMargin_tablet as one of the classes applied to the <div>. Even more important, the <div> shifts to the left, making more space for your image.

7. **Click the third image and then, in the Tag Selector, click <div>. In the lower-right tab, click the "Move up a row" arrow icon.**

   In tablet view, all three images and captions sit horizontally in a row. The <div>s in mobile and desktop view remain centered (Figure 13-15). For more details on applying CSS rules to elements in specific views, see the box on page 580.

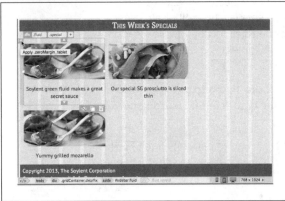

FIGURE 13-14

The zero margin button (with its tooltip displayed) adds a class to the <div> that removes the margin on the left side. That class is applied to only the <div> in the current view—in this case, tablet view. It won't affect the same element in the mobile or desktop views.

FIGURE 13-15

The sidebar "This Week's Specials" is a garland of fluid grid elements: a fluid grid element holds each of the photo-caption pairs, and they appear inside the sidebar, which is itself a fluid grid element.

Top left: In mobile view, the nested elements are centered horizontally and stacked on top of one another.

Top right: On a tablet, the photos and captions appear side by side.

Bottom: In desktop view, the images and captions are centered, and the sidebar sits to the right of the two main stories.

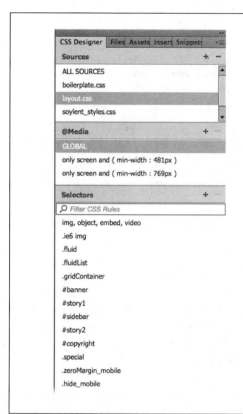

FIGURE 13-16

The source file for this fluid grid layout is layout.css. In the Media section of CSS Designer, you've selected Global, so in the Selectors section, you see the selectors for styles that Dreamweaver applies globally (unless a media query below Global overrides those styles). For example, to create a rule that applies to tablet screens, you select the media query "only screen and (min-width: 481px)." Styles you edit or create with this media query selected won't apply to smaller screens. Want to target desktops? Use the "only screen and (min-width: 769px)" media query.

Creating CSS Rules for Specific Screen Sizes

If your fluid grid layout project demands more complex formatting than you can get from a global style sheet, you may want to create individual style rules for different screen sizes. For example, you may want to add a background color or background image to a sidebar in the desktop view, but not in the other two views.

To create this kind of rule, you need to understand how Dreamweaver organizes the media queries and rules for fluid grid pages in a single, external style sheet. If you create a CSS rule specifically for desktop screens, you need to make sure that you place the rule in the right spot in the style sheet.

You can create or edit rules by writing the code yourself or by letting CSS Designer do the work. You get a good understanding of the structure of the fluid grid CSS file if you open it up and take a look, so consider the hand-coding option first.

To hand-code a new CSS style, open the fluid grid style sheet in Code view. (In the tutorial, that style sheet is *layout.css*.) Within the CSS rules, you see comments (gray text) explaining where to place your code. For example, about a quarter of the way into the code, there's this comment:

```
/* Mobile Layout: 480px and below. */
```

If you want a rule to apply to phone-size screens, place it between this comment and the next one (for tablets). The styles in this section apply to mobile screens, but they apply to the other screen sizes too, unless you override them with a different rule later in the style sheet. Move down through the code and you see another comment:

```
/* Tablet Layout: 481px to 768px. Inherits
   styles from: Mobile Layout. */
```

Thanks to the CSS cascade (page 412), these styles override the same-named selectors used for mobile devices. It's kind of like the style sheet saying, "Hey, browser, here are some styles to use...oh, wait a minute, I see that you're wider than 480 pixels, so why don't you use these styles instead?"

The last screen-size comment is for desktops:

```
/* Desktop Layout: 769px to a max of
   1232px. Inherits styles from:
   Mobile Lay-out and Tablet Layout. */
```

So, if you want to add background color to the sidebar for desktops without changing the background for mobile and tablet devices, place that rule after the comment for the desktop layout. In that case, your rule for the sidebar might look like this:

```
#sidebar {
    width: 32.2033%;
    margin-left: 1.6949%;
    clear: none;
    background-color: #FAFFCD;
}
```

You use the same principles when you add device-specific styles using CSS Designer. Instead of manually editing the code, use the media queries in CSS Designer's Media section. By choosing the correct query, CSS Designer places your rules in the proper location in the CSS file.

To add a device-specific style, first select the fluid grid style sheet—that's *layout.css* in this example. The Media section displays three media queries (Figure 13-16): Global, "only screen and (min-width: 481px)," and "only screen and (min-width: 769px)." They correspond to the screen size comments in the CSS file.

By choosing one of the media queries before you edit or add a style, you can target specific screen sizes. So, for example, to add a background color to a sidebar when it's viewed on a desktop screen, follow these steps: In CSS Designer's Sources section, click the name of the fluid grid CSS file (for example, *layout.css*). In the Media section, click "only screen and (min-width: 769px)." In the Selectors section, click "#sidebar" (the ID you applied to the sidebar <div>), and then, in the Properties section, go to the background properties and set *background-color* to a specific value.

Creating Pages for jQuery Mobile Sites

M edia queries and Dreamweaver's fluid grid layouts let you take one website and give it different designs for different devices, but what if you want to create a mobile site from the get-go? Perhaps you want to design a "mobile-only" version of your site, one optimized to look and perform like a native phone application, like the one shown in Figure 14-1? Dreamweaver lets you do just that with its support for jQuery Mobile.

jQuery Mobile is a JavaScript library that helps you build websites tailored to mobile devices. For example, instead of small text links, these mobile sites have big finger-sized buttons that your guests can easily tap on phone and tablet touchscreens. With some simple HTML, some fancy CSS, and some complex JavaScript programming, jQuery Mobile lets you quickly create the navigation elements commonly found on smartphones. You can build a mobile website that really feels like a phone application, or you can use HTML, CSS, and jQuery Mobile to actually *create* a phone application that you can install on Android devices or upload to Apple's App Store for use on iPads, iPhones, and iPod Touches. Dreamweaver CS5.5 introduced this jQuery tool, and since then, each version of Dreamweaver has added to and refined it.

■ jQuery Mobile

jQuery Mobile is a "mobile development framework," which means that it provides the tools you need to build web pages that act more like mobile applications than traditional web pages. A page built with jQuery Mobile includes screen transitions (one web page slides into view as the old one slides out), a more phone-like interface (large, round buttons and smooth color gradients), and support for non-mouse-like interactions (like screen taps and swipes).

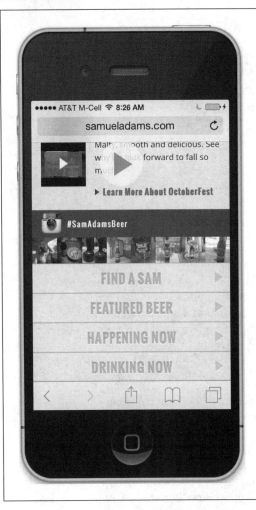

FIGURE 14-1

Unlike a regular website, a jQuery Mobile site, like this sales-oriented site for Samuel Adams Brewery (www.samueladams.com), replicates the screen elements found in phone applications.

jQuery Mobile (*http://jquerymobile.com*) is a project of the enormously popular jQuery JavaScript framework (*http://jquery.com*), which simplifies the process of writing JavaScript. jQuery solves cross-browser problems and makes normally complicated JavaScript programming a lot easier. It creates JavaScript code specific to phones, as well as the CSS that formats the HTML, so your site looks as though it was designed from the ground up as an iPhone or Android app.

So how do you use jQuery Mobile? In a nutshell, you construct a regular web page using the basic building blocks of HTML—<div>s, images, paragraphs, and headers—and have jQuery Mobile transform them, through the power of JavaScript and some fancy CSS, into something that looks and feels a lot different from a standard web page. For example, the Sam Adams Brewery website, pictured in Figure 14-1, uses basic HTML that jQuery Mobile transforms into a phone-like presentation when guests look at the site on a phone.

If you have a smartphone, now is a good time to whip it out and visit a few sites that use jQuery Mobile—it's more informative to experience it rather than read about it. Here are a few mobile sites worth trying: Sam Adams Brewery (*www.samueladams.com*), Macworld (*www.macworld.com*), and Moulin Rouge (*http://m.moulinrouge.fr*).

> **NOTE** You can build a great jQuery Mobile site using the tools you find in the jQuery Mobile category of the Insert panel. If you're a proficient JavaScript programmer you can create remarkably complex sites. In fact, with some programming chops (and some patience), you can build true, native phone applications that work on iPhones, Android devices, BlackBerry devices, and more (see the box on page 604).

Creating Mobile Pages

Fortunately, while there's a lot of complex programming behind jQuery Mobile web pages, actually adding content and building pages uses techniques you've already learned: inserting <div>s (page 454), typing in text, and adding images. When you build a jQuery Mobile site, you start off with a standard blank HTML page and then add jQuery Mobile elements to the page using the Insert menu or the Insert panel's jQuery Mobile category. Here's the process:

1. **Choose File→New. Then, in the New Document window, choose Blank Page. In the Page Type column, select HTML. In the Layout column, select <none>, and then click Create.**

   Dreamweaver displays the usual blank web page in the document window.

2. **In the lower-right corner of the document window, click the "Mobile size" button, a.k.a. the phone icon.**

   The document window changes to phone-like proportions, perfect for building your jQuery mobile project.

3. **Choose Window→Insert and then, from the categories menu at the top of the Insert panel, choose jQuery Mobile.**

   The jQuery Mobile category displays 22 elements you can insert in your page. The element at the top of the list is Page. You need to create at least one jQuery page for your site. Then, you can place other elements on that page.

4. **Click Page.**

   Dreamweaver opens the jQuery Mobile Files window (Figure 14-2). Using this window, you tell Dreamweaver about the related files you'll use for the project. It's not as hard as it sounds, because all you do is click the relevant radio buttons and Dreamweaver fills in the filename boxes for you. Here's a rundown on the decisions you need to make.

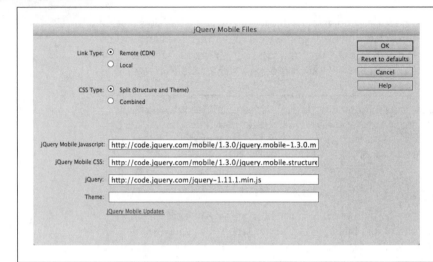

FIGURE 14-2

The first time you insert a jQuery Mobile page in your HTML file, Dreamweaver collects some details about your site with this window. Using the radio buttons, you choose where to keep the jQuery and CSS files needed to run the site. See steps 4 and 5 for all the details.

5. **For Link Type, choose Local.**

    You have two choices here, Remote (CDN) and Local. Here's how to decide which one to use: Every jQuery Mobile site uses a few standard files, including two libraries (the basic jQuery library and the jQuery Mobile library) and the CSS files that format the jQuery Mobile widgets. You can add code to your web page that automatically downloads these files from the jQuery website, or you can store the files on your own site. Either way, Dreamweaver does the heavy lifting for you.

    To have a page retrieve the files from the jQuery site, choose Remote (CDN). Then, when someone visits your site, their browser downloads the HTML page that has both your content in it, and the instructions to fetch the JavaScript, CSS, and graphics files from jQuery.com. There are two potential drawbacks to this setup, however: first, you need an Internet connection, and second, you're relying on jQuery.com's servers—if they break down, your site won't work. (In addition, since the CSS file sits on jQuery's server, you can't edit it.)

    The second option, Local, saves all the required files to your site folder, giving your site everything it needs to work with jQuery Mobile pages.

    Either way, Dreamweaver fills in the Web URL boxes that point to the necessary files at the bottom of the screen.

6. **For CSS Type, choose Split.**

You have two options here, Split (Structure and Theme) and Combined. Your decision determines whether your site uses one or two CSS files. If you choose Combined, a single CSS file governs both the stuctural layout of the elements and their visual aspects, such as the colors, text styles, and so on. If you choose Split, your site uses a separate jQuery Mobile Theme file. Split is a better option here, particularly if you think you might want to change the colors and other visible features of the page later.

7. **Click OK, and then, in the Page dialog box, click OK.**

You jQuery Mobile "pages" can include pre-designed headers and footers. If you aren't going to use a header or footer on your site, you can turn them off here. You can also give your page an ID. If you don't, Dreamweaver gives this first page the name "page."

This is a good place to explain how jQuery Mobile "pages" work. For jQuery Mobile sites, a single HTML file contains several pages. When you build the jQuery site, you work on the content for the "pages" in a single file. When visitors come to the site using their smartphones, they see the content as individual pages, even though you stored everything in that single HTML file.

When you click OK here, Dreamweaver closes the dialog box and displays a single jQuery Mobile page in the document window with placeholder text for a header, content, and footer (see Figure 14-3).

8. **Choose File→Save and give the page a name like *cafesoylentmobile.html*.**

If you store the jQuery Mobile files locally, as described in step 2, Dreamweaver displays a dialog box showing the files it will copy to your site. Dreamweaver stores these files with your site, and uploads them to your remote server when you put your site online for the public to see. It stores the JavaScript and CSS files in the *j-query-mobile* folder. It stores the graphics jQuery Mobile uses in an Images folder.

On the other hand, if you chose the Remote (CDN) option, you won't see the dialog box, and Dreamweaver saves your page in your site. The <head> section of the page includes instructions to link the needed JavaScript and CSS files to the page.

NOTE At the time of this writing, jQuery Mobile is at version 1.4.4. Dreamweaver CC 2014 October Release ships with jQuery Mobile version 1.3. To upgrade to the most recent release, go to the jQuery Mobile site (*http://jquerymobile.com*) and download the latest version of the program. Replace the files in the *jquery-mobile* folder that Dreamweaver created. You also need to remove the links to the old files from the <head> of your pages and attach the new style sheet (see page 162 for a refresher on attaching external style sheets) and the two JavaScript files (see the Tip on page 533 for an example that shows how to attach a JavaScript file to a web page).

FIGURE 14-3

Here's the humble beginning of a jQuery Mobile site. The HTML page inserts a single jQuery Mobile "page" and displays areas designated as Header, Content, and Footer. To build a more complex site, you add additional "pages" to this single HTML file, using the Insert→jQuery Mobile→Page command. For example, the Soylent Green Cafe mobile site could include a home page, a Menus page, an Hours page, and so forth. When viewed on a mobile device, its browser displays only a single page at a time.

Touring a Mobile Page

One peculiar feature of a jQuery Mobile site is that it's just a single page of HTML. When a guest visits the site, his browser downloads that single file but displays only a *portion* of the HTML at a time. For example, the left image in Figure 14-4 represents a basic jQuery Mobile site: one page of HTML that has multiple <div> tags in it. However, when you look at the page in a mobile browser, the browser converts that HTML into separate "pages" (really just bookmarked sections of the same page). The top image in Figure 14-4 represents the "home page." It lists three links: Page Two, Page Three, and Page Four. Clicking the Page Four link loads that "page's" <div> and its contents (Figure 14-4, bottom). You can find a copy of this barebones jQuery site on this book's Missing CD page at *http://oreilly.com/pub/missingmanuals/dreamweaverccmm2014.*

TIP The combination of Dreamweaver's Live view (page 348) and its Window Size menu (Figure 12-2) let you preview jQuery Mobile sites right on your screen. Choose the "320 x 480 Smart Phone" option and then click the Live button in the Document toolbar—it's like having a smartphone built right into Dreamweaver (minus the roaming charges)!

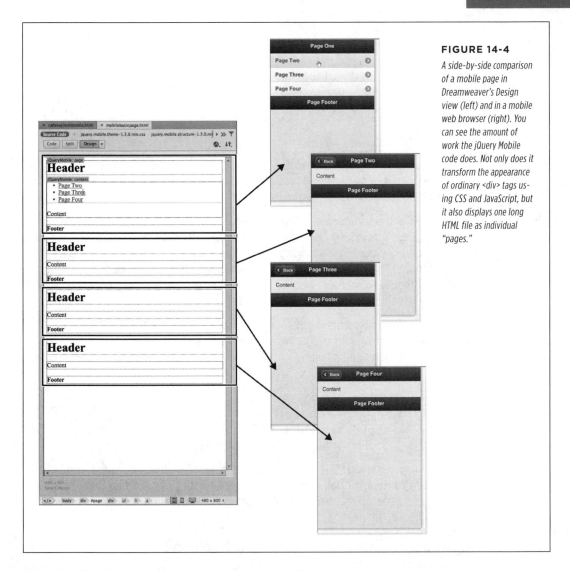

FIGURE 14-4

*A side-by-side comparison
of a mobile page in
Dreamweaver's Design
view (left) and in a mobile
web browser (right). You
can see the amount of
work the jQuery Mobile
code does. Not only does it
transform the appearance
of ordinary <div> tags using CSS and JavaScript, but
it also displays one long
HTML file as individual
"pages."*

jQuery Mobile's programming converts those <div>s into separate screens and applies the CSS that formats the page elements. But how does jQuery Mobile know
which <div> is a page, and how does it make the other elements, such as links, look
like buttons? The secret is a creative use of HTML attributes applied to HTML tags.
The jQuery Mobile programming reads the attributes you apply to a tag and then
formats that tag based on those attributes. For example, the structure of Dreamweaver's stock mobile page looks like this:

```
<div data-role="page" id="page2">
    <div data-role="header">
        <h1>Page Two</h1>
    </div>
    <div data-role="content">
        Content
    </div>
    <div data-role="footer">
        <h4>Page Footer</h4>
    </div>
</div>
```

As you can see, "page" 2 is actually a <div> tag with the value *data-role="page"* added to it. When a browser loads the "page," the jQuery Mobile programming kicks in and transforms the <div> into a "page."

You can find a sample file called *mobilebasicpage.html* on this book's Missing CD page (*http://oreilly.com/pub/missingmanuals/dreamweaverccmm2014*). It includes three other <div>s in each "page": one for a header, one for the content, and the third for a footer. Thanks to their respective "data-role" values, each <div> looks different. jQuery Mobile formats the header and footer as dark stripes with light text, while it gives the content area a light background with dark text (Figure 14-4, right images).

jQuery Mobile also applies special attributes to other HTML tags. For example, it creates the list of links (Page Two, Page Three, and so on) in the top-right image in Figure 14-4 (called a "list-view" in jQuery Mobile) using a simple unordered list:

```
<ul data-role="listview" data-inset="true">
    <li><a href="#page2">Page Two</a></li>
    <li><a href="#page3">Page Three</a>
    <li><a href="#page4">Page Four</a></li>
</ul>
```

By adding *data-role="listview"* to a <ul> tag, you can change the list from a basic bulleted set to a special, mobile-enhanced list with large buttons that are easy to use on a smartphone. jQuery Mobile provides other, similar mobile elements, as described in the next section.

Adding Content to a jQuery Mobile Page

As you can see in Figure 14-3, a jQuery Mobile page is made up of just some very basic HTML: <div>s, unordered lists, and links. To add content, select the dummy text Dreamweaver provides and change it. For example, to change the "Header" headline that appears on the first page, highlight the text and type in your own headline: *My Great Web App*, for example. Likewise, you can change the footer text—"Footer"—by selecting it inside the footer <div> and typing in something new.

> **NOTE** If you type a long sentence in either the header or footer and then preview the page in a phone, you'll notice that jQuery Mobile keeps the text to a single line and simply cuts off anything that doesn't fit. Because of that, keep your header and footer text short.

Each page has a central <div> where you add the main content. Dreamweaver places the word "Content" inside that <div>, but you can delete it and add whatever HTML you like—headlines, paragraphs, bulleted lists, and images—as you normally would. In addition, you can insert special jQuery Mobile elements—lists, layout grids, collapsible blocks, link buttons, and additional "pages"—using Dreamweaver's Insert panel (see Figure 14-5).

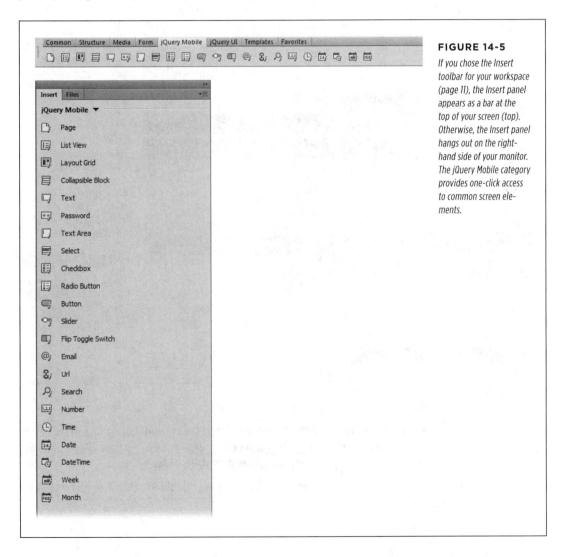

FIGURE 14-5

If you chose the Insert toolbar for your workspace (page 11), the Insert panel appears as a bar at the top of your screen (top). Otherwise, the Insert panel hangs out on the right-hand side of your monitor. The jQuery Mobile category provides one-click access to common screen elements.

■ **ADDING LISTS**

jQuery Mobile includes its own "widgets"—elements for links, layout, and content display. The page, header, and footer <div>s are widgets, for example. You can also insert a list of links that lets guests navigate from page to page on your mobile site. The sample home page, *mobilebasicpage.html*, includes a list of links to Page Two, Page Three, and Page Four, for example (Figure 14-4, top). Dreamweaver calls a list like this the "list view," and jQuery Mobile supplies several variations (see Figure 14-6).

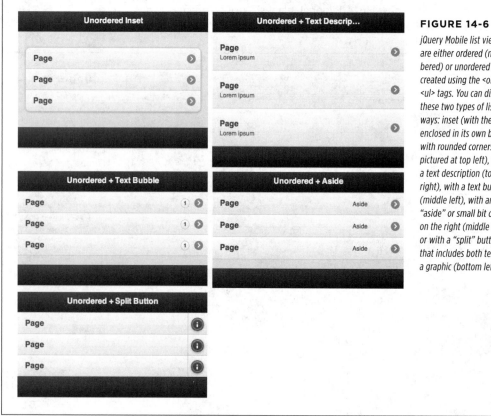

FIGURE 14-6

jQuery Mobile list views are either ordered (numbered) or unordered lists, created using the <ol> and <ul> tags. You can display these two types of list five ways: inset (with the list enclosed in its own box with rounded corners, as pictured at top left), with a text description (top right), with a text bubble (middle left), with an "aside" or small bit of text on the right (middle right), or with a "split" button that includes both text and a graphic (bottom left).

To add a list, make sure you're in Design view, and then do the following:

1. **Click inside the content <div> of a "page" <div>, and then click the List View button from the jQuery Mobile section of the Insert panel (Figure 14-5). Alternatively, choose Insert→jQuery Mobile→List View.**

    Either way, Dreamweaver opens the jQuery Mobile List View window (Figure 14-7).

FIGURE 14-7

jQuery Mobile lets you pick from a range of list types. If you select the Split Button option, which lets you include both text and a graphic in the same button, you can choose from one of 19 icons for the graphic.

2. **Choose Ordered or Unordered from the List Type drop-down menu.**

   Ordered lists include numbers to the left of each item. Use ordered lists for "Top 10" items, or to indicate the order of steps in a process, like baking a soufflé. If the order isn't important, then use an unordered list.

3. **Choose the number of list items from the Items menu.**

   You can choose from 1 to 10 items—a reasonable number for a small phone screen. However, since a list view is simply an HTML list, you can manually add more items later if necessary, by editing the HTML code.

4. **In the jQuery Mobile List View window (Figure 14-7), turn on one or more checkboxes to pick the type of list you want.**

   jQuery Mobile provides five basic list types, but you can combine them to add to your options. For example, you can create a self-contained, boxed "inset" list (Figure 14-6, top left) that also includes a "split" button, which has both a label and a button graphic (Figure 14-6, bottom left). Try different combinations of checkboxes to produce different types of lists.

5. If you select the Split Button option, choose an icon from the Split Button Icon menu.

NOTE A Split Button list type inserts both text and an icon in a button, and each provides a link that can point to separate pages. For example, the text portion might lead to a page of detailed information, but the icon might link to a short page of supplementary information.

6. Click OK to insert the new list view.

Depending on the list type you select, Dreamweaver inserts either an HTML unordered list (the <ul> tag) or a numbered (ordered) list (the <ol> tag). You can edit these list items as you would any other list item (see page 91).

TIP If you add *data-rel="dialog"* to a link (an <a> tag) on a jQuery Mobile page, the linked page pops into view like a dialog box, complete with a Close button.

7. Change the label and link for each list item.

Each list item includes the text "Page" and an empty link (# appears in the Properties panel's link box). You can select the text and type in whatever label you wish. Then link that text to another page by typing its URL in the link box. If you link to another website, just type a complete, absolute URL there, beginning with *http://*. If you link to another HTML file on your site, you can use any of the techniques described on page 183.

If you use Dreamweaver's suggested approach to mobile site development—one HTML file with multiple "page" <div>s inside it—you link to another "page" using IDs to bookmark the destination, as described on page 194. For example, if you want to link to a "page" <div> with an ID of "page8," you type *#page8* in the Properties panel's link box.

Some of the list view types include additional text you can edit. For example, the "Text Description" option (Figure 14-6, top right) includes text ("Lorem ipsum") you will want to change. This is a good list type to pick when you need a bit of explanatory text ("See a complete list of our products"). In some cases, like the Text Bubble list type, the extra text isn't visible in Design view—you have to look in the HTML code to see and change it.

Unfortunately, as with all of Dreamweaver's jQuery Mobile objects, once you insert a list view into a page, there's no way to return to the List View window and change its settings. For example, you can't change an insert list into a "split button" list. You can, however, go into Code view and edit the HTML. The jQuery Mobile website provides helpful information on creating lists, including some even fancier ones, at *http://tinyurl.com/d8sjfhz*.

■ ADDING A LAYOUT GRID

Although phone screens are small, that doesn't mean all your content has to sit inside an unbroken column. You might want to present some content in a grid of rows and columns. For example, if you have a bunch of 30- by 30-pixel thumbnail images, you can arrange them in several side-by-side columns. jQuery Mobile provides "layout grids" for just that purpose.

A layout grid is a series of <div> tags that jQuery floats to create columns, the same technique you used to create the multicolumn layouts described in Chapter 10. Here's how to insert a layout grid:

1. **Click inside the content <div> of a "page" <div> and then click Layout Grid in the Insert panel's jQuery Mobile section (Figure 14-5), or choose Insert→ jQuery Mobile→Layout Grid.**

   Either way, Dreamweaver opens the jQuery Mobile Layout Grid window (Figure 14-8, top).

2. **Choose the number of rows and columns you want.**

   There's not too much to this step, but keep in mind the limitations of a phone's screen. Choosing five columns and trying to put a lot of text into each one in a row will probably make the page wider than a phone's screen can handle.

3. **Click OK.**

   Dreamweaver inserts a number of <div> tags into the page. They don't look like much in Design view, but you can add any content you like (just make sure it isn't too big for a phone's screen).

You can't revisit the Layout Grid window, so if you want to change a three-column grid to two columns, you have to dip into the HTML. Fortunately, it's not so difficult. Here's the HTML for a one-row, two-column grid:

```
<div class="ui-grid-a">
    <div class="ui-block-a">Block 1,1</div>
    <div class="ui-block-b">Block 1,2</div>
</div>
```

jQuery Mobile uses a <div> tag to define layout grids. In the above example, that's *<div class="ui-grid-a">*. The letter in the class name determines the grid's number of columns: For example, *ui-grid-a* is a two-column grid, *ui-grid-b* gives you three columns, and so on.

FIGURE 14-8

To add a grid to a mobile page, use the jQuery Mobile Layout Grid window. The layout grid in Dreamweaver's Design view (middle image) looks decidedly less glamorous than it does in a web browser (bottom).

jQuery Mobile includes additional <div>s within this tag that define each block of content. So the above example includes two <div> tags. The class on those tags determines which column jQuery Mobile inserts the content into. For example, *ui-block-a* is the first column in a row. Say you want to turn the above two-column, one-row grid into a three-column, one-row design. You simply change the class name on the grid's <div> and then add a <div> for the new block, like this:

```
<div class="ui-grid-b">
    <div class="ui-block-a">Block 1,1</div>
    <div class="ui-block-b">Block 1,2</div>
    <div class="ui-block-c">Block 1,3</div>
</div>
```

In other words, you change *<div class="ui-grid-a">* to *<div class="ui-grid-b">* and add another block: *<div class="ui-block-c">*. You just have to be sure you keep the block's class names in order—a, b, c, and so on—and that you have the proper number of blocks for the type of grid you specify. For example, since the *ui-grid-b* class defines a three-column layout, you need three <div> tags per row. To add an additional row, duplicate the <div> tags from the previous row, like this:

```
<div class="ui-grid-b">
    <div class="ui-block-a">Block 1,1</div>
    <div class="ui-block-b">Block 1,2</div>
    <div class="ui-block-c">Block 1,3</div>
    <div class="ui-block-a">Block 2,1</div>
    <div class="ui-block-b">Block 2,2</div>
    <div class="ui-block-c">Block 2,3</div>
</div>
```

You can read more about jQuery Mobile grids at *http://tinyurl.com/cdwdlk7*.

■ ADDING A COLLAPSIBLE BLOCK

A collapsible block is a combination of a header and a hidden chunk of content. Click the header, and the content reveals itself (bottom image in Figure 14-9). It's a good way to keep your page simple and short for phone viewing—content appears only when a guest clicks a headline, and it disappears when he clicks the headline a second time.

To insert a collapsible block in Dreamweaver:

1. **Click inside the content <div> of a "page" <div> and then click the Collapsible Block button in the Insert panel's jQuery Mobile section (Figure 14-5).**

   Alternatively, choose Insert→jQuery Mobile→Collapsible Block. Unlike other jQuery Mobile objects, there's no dialog box for this: Dreamweaver just drops a series of <div> tags into the page (Figure 14-9, top).

FIGURE 14-9

Collapsible blocks are a good way to keep a page's appearance simple, because the blocks hide content until a visitor wants to read it.

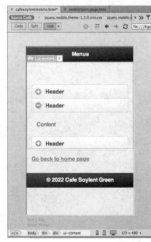

2. **Edit the headline and the content.**

   Select the dummy "Header" text and then type in your own headline. Remember to keep it short, since jQuery Mobile limits the header to a single line. You can change the dummy content Dreamweaver inserts—a simple <p> tag with the text "Content" inside it—to anything you want. You can even insert multiple paragraphs, lists, and images.

Dreamweaver inserts four <div> tags when you add a collapsible block to a page:

```
<div data-role="collapsible-set">
    <div data-role="collapsible">
        <h3>Header</h3>
        <p>Content</p>
    </div>
    <div data-role="collapsible" data-collapsed="true">
        <h3>Header</h3>
        <p>Content</p>
    </div>
    <div data-role="collapsible" data-collapsed="true">
        <h3>Header</h3>
        <p>Content</p>
    </div>
</div>
```

The outer <div>—*<div data-role="collapsible-set">*—indicates that the <div> tags inside are part of a group (a "block") of collapsible elements. Each collapsible element—a header/content pair—sits inside another <div>, *<div data-role="collapsible">*. If you want only two collapsible elements, then delete one of the <div>s Dreamweaver inserts. If you want more, then copy the <div> (including the header and content) and paste it before that last closing </div> for the set.

By default, all collapsible blocks start life closed. You can make sure that a collapsible block's content is visible by adding *data-collapsed="false"* to the <div> tag for a header/content pair. The first header/content pair in a collapsible block starts off hidden:

```
<div data-role="collapsible">
        <h3>Header</h3>
        <p>Content</p>
</div>
```

But you can show the content when the page first loads by adding an attribute to the <div> for that block:

```
<div data-role="collapsible" data-collapsed="false">
        <h3>Header</h3>
        <p>Content</p>
</div>
```

You can read more about collapsible blocks at *http://tinyurl.com/n5vfu5t*.

■ ADDING BUTTONS

The jQuery Mobile category of the Insert panel includes many form elements—text boxes, password boxes, checkboxes, radio buttons, and so on. However, these boxes and buttons don't work like traditional form elements (which you'll learn about in the next chapter). In fact, they don't work at all unless you add JavaScript programming. And, unfortunately, Dreamweaver CC doesn't provide the tools to do so. In other words, to use any of these form elements effectively, you need to learn JavaScript and jQuery programming.

However, the button element isn't restricted to forms; you can use it anywhere to insert links that *look* like buttons.

To insert button links:

1. **Click inside a <div> in one of the "pages" in the jQuery Mobile file.**

   For example, click in the "content," "header," or "footer" <div>s described on page 587.

2. **Click the Button button in the Insert panel's jQuery Mobile section (Figure 14-5), or choose Insert→jQuery Mobile→Button.**

   Either way, Dreamweaver opens the jQuery Mobile Button window (Figure 14-10).

FIGURE 14-10

Unless you know how to write JavaScript, select only "Link" from the Button Type menu. This lets you insert regular page links that look like attractive buttons. The Input Type menu is available only when you select "Input" from the Button Type menu, and it lets you select one of the HTML form buttons discussed on page 599—but, again, this is an option only if you're comfortable programming the buttons yourself to make them do something.

3. **Select the number of buttons you want on the page.**

   You can choose from 1 to 10 buttons, but remember you're designing for a small phone screen, so 10 buttons won't sit side by side.

4. **Choose Link from the Button Type menu.**

   The two other options (Button and Input) insert buttons in a form (like a "Submit" button); they require custom programming to work.

5. **Choose either Inline or Group from the Position menu.**

   The Inline option creates separate pill-shaped boxes for each button, while the Group option arranges the buttons as a unit, either stacked vertically or side by side (see the two bottom examples in Figure 14-11).

FIGURE 14-11

jQuery Mobile uses CSS3 and a few images to craft impressive-looking smartphone-like buttons.

6. **Choose a vertical or horizontal layout.**

   These options are available only when you select Group in the previous step, and they affect how the grouped buttons appear on a page, either stacked one on top of the other ("Vertical") or side by side ("Horizontal"). Keep in mind that if you place too many buttons side by side, some will drop down on the page and turn into stacked rows of buttons.

7. **Choose a button graphic from the Icon menu.**

   This step is optional, but it adds a neat touch to each button. jQuery gives you 18 shapes to choose from (Right Arrow, Gear, Star, and so on), and if you don't want any of them, choose None. (In Figure 14-11, the bottom row of buttons have a right arrow icon applied to them.) You can see all 18 icons in action at *http://tinyurl.com/c2z6hyu*.

8. **If you selected an icon in the previous step, place it using the Icon Position menu.**

   You can choose Left or Right to put the icon at either the left or right edge of the button, and Top or Bottom to place the icon either above or below the button's text. Choose No Text to display only the icon.

9. Click OK to insert the button(s).

Dreamweaver inserts as many buttons as you selected in step 3. In Design view, they don't look like much—just the word "button" repeated once for each one you added. Select that text to change it to something better. In addition, the text has a regular HTML link attached to it, just like the ones you learned about in Chapter 4. You can change the link in the Properties panel, just as you would for any other link.

If you plan to link to another "page" within the jQuery file, use the # symbol followed by the ID you applied to the <div> tag for that "page." For example, to link to "page2" in the sample jQuery Mobile file Dreamweaver supplies, type *#page2* in the Properties panel's Link box. This is the same as linking to a named anchor within a page, as described on page 194.

Unfortunately, once you insert one or more buttons, you can't revisit the jQuery Mobile Button window (Figure 14-10) to edit them—in other words, you can't change the buttons' icons, grouping, or positioning once you insert them. Well, you can, but you have to go into Code view and change the attributes applied to the buttons. For example, to change a button's icon, go into Code view, locate the <a> tag for that button, and change the *data-icon* attribute to the proper value. For instance, changing *data-icon="arrow-r"* to *data-icon="gear"* changes a button's icon from a right-pointing arrow to a gear. The web page for jQuery Mobile buttons (*http://tinyurl.com/d78s8pt*) is an invaluable aid in this process.

■ ADDING NEW "PAGES"

As you read above, you can put multiple "pages" into a single HTML file by applying an ID and a special HTML attribute (like *<div data-role="page" id="page4">*) to <div> tags in the file. jQuery Mobile then hides all but one "page" when a browser loads the file. As you click links, the browser displays different portions of the HTML page as if they were separate web pages (thanks to jQuery Mobile's JavaScript programming).

The example HTML file (*mobilebasicpage.html*) from the Missing CD page has four "pages," but you can add more. It's important to make sure, however, that you don't insert a page inside another page's <div>. The best way to ensure that you don't is to use the Tag Selector (page 7). For example, say you want to insert another page after the last page in a mobile file:

1. Click inside the <div> for the last "page."

For example, click inside the header, footer, or content <div>.

2. In the Tag Selector, click the <div> for that page (see Figure 14-12).

You'll see something like *<div#page4>* in the Tag Selector. At this point, you have the <div> for an entire page selected. In the next step, you position the cursor up a level to where you want to insert a new page.

3. **Press the right arrow key to move the cursor outside the <div> you selected in step 2.**

The right arrow key moves the cursor below the <div> so you can insert a new page after the currently selected one. (To insert a page *before* the currently selected one, press the left arrow key.)

FIGURE 14-12

The Tag Selector is the most accurate way to select and navigate among HTML tags.

4. **Click the Page button from the jQuery Mobile category of the Insert panel, or choose Insert→Query Mobile→Page.**

Either way, Dreamweaver opens the jQuery Mobile Page window (Figure 14-13).

FIGURE 14-13

jQuery Mobile "pages" are just a series of <div>s—one for the header, one for content, and one for a footer. You can choose to leave out either the header or the footer (or both).

5. **Type an ID for the page, and then select whether you want a header and footer.**

You can name the ID anything you like. For example, if the page contains information about your company, you might name it "about." You use the ID you provide to create the link that points to this new "page," as described on page

194. Normally, pages include a header and a footer; if you don't want them, turn off their checkboxes.

6. **Click OK.**

Dreamweaver inserts the <div> tags needed to add a page to the file. You can add content to this new page by following the instructions on page 588.

Formatting a jQuery Mobile Page

When viewed in Dreamweaver's Design view, a jQuery Mobile page is pretty unimpressive (Figure 14-4, left), but the browser view of the same HTML is astonishingly different (Figure 14-4, right). The formerly ho-hum HTML turns into a slick, mobile page with subtle gradients, rounded corners, shadows, and sophisticated icons. Where does this design come from? jQuery Mobile is more than JavaScript—it's also complex CSS that makes the HTML for mobile devices look like an application for a smartphone.

You can use the CSS skills you picked up in this book to change the appearance of your jQuery Mobile site, but you're in for a lot of work. The CSS is complex, and there are literally hundreds of styles required to make a jQuery Mobile site look good. If you want to give it a try, Dreamweaver's Inspect mode (described on page 513) is your best bet at deciphering the CSS.

Another way to bolster the appearance of your site is to use one of jQuery Mobile's five themes. That's right; jQuery Mobile has five built-in "page" designs you can switch among simply by adding an attribute to the page's <div> tag. The special attribute looks like this: *data-theme="a"*. You can use five different pre-designed themes by changing the letter in the attribute to anything from "a" through "e."

To change a theme, specify a *data-theme* for a jQuery Mobile-specific tag. For example, to change one page to the "b" theme, add *data-theme="b"* to that page's <div> tag, like this:

```
<div data-role="page" id="page" data-theme="b">
```

To change a jQuery list to the "e" theme, add *data-theme="e"* to the List View <div>:

```
<ul data-role="listview" data-theme="e">
```

Fortunately, you don't need to add that theme attribute by hand. Dreamweaver CC includes a handy, context-sensitive panel that lets you change themes (what jQuery calls "swatches"; see Figure 14-14). You open the panel by choosing Window→jQuery Mobile Swatches.

FIGURE 14-14

Dreamweaver CC's new jQuery Mobile Swatches panel makes it easy to apply formatting to mobile page elements. You're not stuck with just the five basic swatches that jQuery Mobile offers, either. Click the "Get more themes" link to launch a web browser and visit the jQuery Mobile ThemeRoller—an online program that lets you visually create mobile theme files.

You apply a theme by clicking into a jQuery mobile element and choosing a swatch from the panel. For example, in Figure 14-14, Dreamweaver displays the options for the selected link (circled) inside a jQuery Mobile list view (page 590). In this instance, you could apply one of five swatches (labeled "a" to "e") to the list itself, as well as other swatches for the different types of available lists. Clicking into another element, like a page header, updates the Swatches panel to list just the swatches available for page headers. Click a swatch to apply it to the selected page element.

If you want to create your own look for a jQuery Mobile site, visit the jQuery Mobile ThemeRoller website (*http://jquerymobile.com/themeroller/*). There you can try different fonts, colors, borders, and shadows, and see a live, interactive rendering of your design choices. Once you're satisfied, click the Download button. You'll end up with a CSS file containing your design, as well as an Images folder containing the icons for the design. Simply move those files into the *jquery-mobile* folder in your site (replacing the original files). Change the filename in the link from the CSS name Dreamweaver supplies (*jquery.mobile.theme-1.3.0.min.css*) to your new theme filename and you're done. In fact, Dreamweaver is smart enough to realize you're using a new theme, and displays it in the jQuery Mobile Swatches panel.

GEM IN THE ROUGH

Mobile Application Development

Using jQuery Mobile, you can build a website that looks great on mobile phones but is still a website: A visitor uses the browser in her phone to go to the site and clicks through pages just as she would on any other site.

But you can also use jQuery Mobile to build a true application for iPhones, Android phones, and other devices. Although you use HTML, CSS, and JavaScript to build the application, you can turn it into a native phone application so that, instead of viewing the jQuery Mobile site in a browser, your audience downloads it from the app store, installs it on their phones, and launches it just like any other mobile app.

The real trick lies in converting the HTML to a native application. Usually, this involves downloading an "SDK," or software development kit, for each phone you want to target—iPhones, Android phones, Windows Phones, and so on. This step is fraught with peril for all but diehard software developers.

Adobe hosts a site called the PhoneGap Build Service" (*http://build.phonegap.com/*) that can ingest your HTML, JavaScript, and CSS and, through some magic, turn out native applications you can install on a phone.

Unfortunately, Dreamweaver doesn't provide the tools for actually creating the application; you need to be a very competent JavaScript programmer to get your app to actually do anything. Mobile application development is a world unto itself, and this book can't even begin to scratch the surface of the intricacies involved. However, there are a couple of books devoted to the subject, both by Jonathan Stark: *Building iPhone Apps with HTML, CSS, and JavaScript* and *Building Android Apps with HTML, CSS, and JavaScript*.

For more information on how this works, check out the video at *http://tinyurl.com/lykqdj6*.

Launching Your jQuery Mobile Site

When you finish building your mobile website, put it on the Web just as you would any other site. Use the tools discussed in Chapter 20 to connect to your web server and transfer your files. Once on the Web, any phone with a web browser can visit the page and see its awesome mobile-enabled beauty.

If the mobile site is a supplement to a regular site, you may want to add a "See the mobile version of this site" label somewhere on your main site, with a link to the mobile version that points to the HTML file you created using jQuery Mobile elements. When the HTML file is opened in a browser, visitors see the first jQuery Mobile "page." The other "pages" remain hidden until they click buttons that link to the <div>s for those pages.

Bringing Your Pages to Life

Building Interactive Pages

JavaScript has grown from the simple language behind pop-up windows and swapped images to a full-blown programming tool that can change the content on a web page even as you look at it. It can even download new data behind the scenes and dynamically update a page (that's why you can scroll to new sections of a Google map without loading new pages—your browser has already downloaded the rest of the map). JavaScript is the key to today's interactive websites.

Dreamweaver, which always tries to provide features that meet web designers' needs, includes a set of JavaScript tools that let you add interactive elements—like content sections that expand and collapse, tabbed panels, and pop-up calendars—to a page. That's what this chapter is all about.

The first section discusses the relationship between the programming languages JavaScript, jQuery, and jQuery's library of interactive elements (like buttons and pick-a-date calendars), often called jQuery "user interface (UI) widgets." The sections that follow describe the features of jQuery UI widgets along with tips on how to use them in your pages. At the end of the chapter, you'll learn about Dreamweaver behaviors, pre-packaged JavaScript programs that add interactive elements to a page. Behaviors have been part of Dreamweaver for some time, but with Dreamweaver CC, Adobe trimmed those that were out of date. You're likely to find uses for the ones that remain.

■ The Roles of JavaScript, jQuery, and jQuery UI

JavaScript is a programming language that web browsers understand. When a browser opens a web page that has a JavaScript program (a *script*) in it, it reads the script and performs the indicated actions. JavaScript isn't part of HTML, but you use it to *manipulate* HTML elements on a page. For example, webcrafters often use JavaScript to show or hide parts of a web page—it's the magic behind the collapsible content and tabbed windows in Figure 15-1. You can also use JavaScript to rewrite your page's underlying code. Consider a photo gallery in a page that has one main picture and several thumbnail images. When you click one of the thumbnails, its image replaces the main picture. Behind the scenes, JavaScript rewrites the name of the source file for the main picture.

Accordion —

Tabs —

FIGURE 15-1

Here are two good examples of jQuery widgets: an expandable content area and a set of tabbed panes. Both let you cram a little more info on a page by showing or hiding content on demand. Interactive elements like these put your guests in charge of your page—they decide if and when they need more detail on a subject.

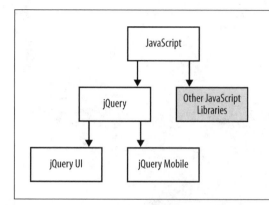

FIGURE 15-2

You can think of jQuery UI as the third generation of a programming language. First there was JavaScript, the general-purpose scripting tool, which begat jQuery. jQuery made it easier to select elements on a page and work with CSS. Then, jQuery begat jQuery UI and its sibling, jQuery Mobile (discussed on page 581). Each helps with even more specific website-development chores.

When you add a jQuery widget to a page, Dreamweaver creates a jQueryAssets folder in your site and stores the widget's files there. These files make the widget work and format the web page element it affects. In the web page itself, Dreamweaver writes links to these files so guests can trigger their actions.

NOTE Want to know more about these interactive languages? A complete review of JavaScript and jQuery can be found in *JavaScript and jQuery: The Missing Manual* by David Sawyer McFarland (O'Reilly). You can also find information at *www.w3schools.com/js* or *https://developer.mozilla.org/en/JavaScript*. (At this point, you might want to know that if you have experience with any programming language, you'll have a head start with JavaScript, because it shares many concepts with other languages.)

Versions of Dreamweaver prior to CC included the Spry framework, a library of tools and widgets similar to those in jQuery UI. Those tools fell out of date, and Adobe dropped them from Dreamweaver. If you're interested, you can still download them. Go to Adobe's blog at *http://tinyurl.com/ly4zhr8* to see why Dreamweaver no longer includes Spry, and to download the Spry framework.

■ Adding Collapsible Content

The jQuery element that adds collapsible content to a page is called an accordion, but you don't have to study music theory to use it. Even more surprising, you don't have to study JavaScript or jQuery. All you need to do is pick a spot in your web page and head over to the Insert panel (Window→Insert). Choose jQuery UI from the drop-down menu and then click Accordion. Voilà! You added a set of collapsible sections to your web page. Your accordion doesn't look very impressive in Design view, so click Live from the drop-down menu in the Document toolbar. You can see that your accordion has three sections (Figure 15-3), imaginatively named Section 1, Section 2, and Section 3. To the left of each section heading is a flippy triangle that tells guests they can expand (or collapse) that part of the page. Initially, the first panel is expanded, but if you click Section 2, the second section expands while Section 1 collapses.

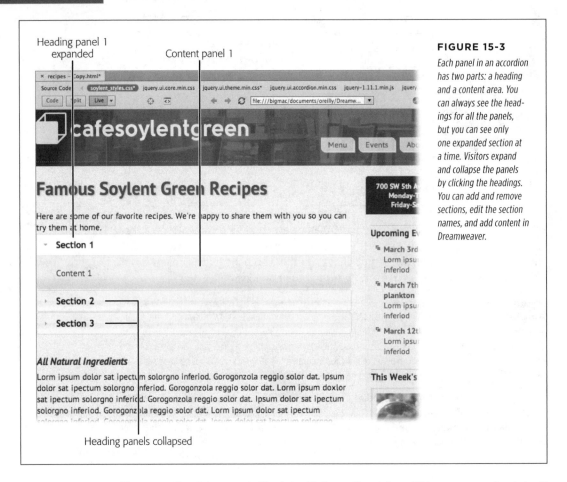

Heading panel 1 expanded

Content panel 1

Heading panels collapsed

FIGURE 15-3

Each panel in an accordion has two parts: a heading and a content area. You can always see the headings for all the panels, but you can see only one expanded section at a time. Visitors expand and collapse the panels by clicking the headings. You can add and remove sections, edit the section names, and add content in Dreamweaver.

The accordion lets you stuff a lot of information into a little screen real estate. If you're worried about overwhelming your guests with information, an accordion lets you hide content until your visitors elect to see it. Suppose your web page sells digital cameras. Along with the usual product pictures and sales pitch, you add an accordion full of details. The first panel is open when the page loads, so you fill it with an overview of the camera's features. The second panel is collapsed at first, but the heading "Specifications" lets visitors know that there are some geeky details inside. A third panel describes the items that come with the camera: a detachable lens, a battery, and a case. The fourth panel sells optional accessories like tripods, memory cards, and additional lenses. And the last panel displays the camera's glowing reviews. Using an accordion, you can put all these details on a single page. The panel headings tell visitors what info is underneath. As any good salesperson knows, once customers start interacting with the details, you're on your way to a sale.

To add a jQuery accordion:

1. **Click the location on your web page where you want to insert the accordion.**

   Here are some design issues to keep in mind when choosing a location: The shape and size of an accordion widget can vary. Initially, the accordion fills the width of the page or of the <div> that holds it. Depending on the options you set, the sections can grow to accommodate large chunks of content, or they can remain at a single, fixed size.

2. **On the Insert panel (Window→Insert), select jQuery UI from the drop-down menu (Figure 15-4).**

   The jQuery UI library offers several widgets, such as a date picker, buttons, and a slider. The accordion tops the list.

FIGURE 15-4

The Insert panel's jQuery UI category holds 11 widgets from this popular library. When you choose one, Dreamweaver adds the necessary code to your web page.

3. **Click Accordion.**

   When you do, Dreamweaver inserts a three-panel accordion in your web page and adds several lines of code to the <head> section of your document. This code links to the JavaScript and jQuery files needed to display and format the accordion. If you try to insert an accordion before you've saved your page, Dreamweaver displays a warning telling you that you need to save. Click OK to save the page or Cancel to back out.

4. **Click inside the accordion, and then click the blue tab at the top.**

   Unselected, your accordion looks a little like an HTML table (page 297). When you click anywhere inside it, though, a blue line marks its boundaries and a tab at the top identifies it as "jQuery Accordion: Accordion1" (Figure 15-5). (The portion after the colon is the widget's ID.) Clicking the tab selects the accordion, whose properties appear in the Properties panel.

FIGURE 15-5

After you insert a jQuery UI widget, click it to select the widget, and then click its blue tab. At that point, the Properties panel displays the widget's properties, and you can add or remove content panels and control how the accordion works on the page.

5. **In the Properties panel, give your accordion a new ID, such as *acc-recipes*.**

   If your page has lots of elements, it may be helpful to add a prefix like "acc" to the ID to remind you that this is an accordion. The ID works like any other in Dreamweaver—you use it in conjunction with CSS to format your content. For example, if you want to change the width of the accordion, you do that in CSS Designer by choosing a source (an internal or external style sheet), adding the accordion ID as a selector, and then setting a value for the Width property.

Of course, adding an accordion to the page is only half the battle. You'll always want to change the section headings and add content to the expandable panels. Most of the time, you also want to tweak the widget's properties.

Adding Content to an Accordion

For the most part, you edit an accordion's panel headings and content just as you would any other web-page element. To change the tab heading "Section 1," for example, select the text then type in a new label. The words "Content 1" identify the collapsible portion of Section 1. You can add images, tables, or any other element you'd use on a web page. Keep in mind, however, that accordions change shape depending on their content and the options you set in the Properties panel. The JavaScript/CSS combo gives the element the organization and formatting it needs to look good (Figure 15-6).

NOTE In Design view, if a panel is collapsed so that its content is hidden, you can expand the panel by pointing to the section heading until an eye icon appears (Figure 15-6, circled top). When it does, click the icon to see the content.

Famous Soylent Green Recipes

Here are some of our favorite recipes. We're happy to share them with you so you can
try them at home.

jQuery Accordion: Accordion1

Sumptious Soylent Sauce

Create your own special treats, simply by adding
our sumptious soylent sauce to any meal.

Section 2

Section 3

All Natural Ingredients

Famous Soylent Green Recipes

Here are some of our favorite recipes. We're happy to share them with you so you can
try them at home.

▾ Sumptious Soylent Sauce

Create your own special treats,
simply by adding our sumptious
soylent sauce to any meal.

› Section 2

› Section 3

FIGURE 15-6

*Top: When you add text
and pictures to a panel in
an accordion, things often
look like they're getting
pushed out of shape. Have
faith and select Live from
the Document toolbar's
drop-down menu.*

*Bottom: In Live view, you
see your page as it will
appear in a web browser.
You can see that the
JavaScript/CSS code have
worked their magic—the
content that was overflow-
ing in Design view is all
tucked away in Live view.*

There is one trick you need to know about adding content to an accordion. In Design view, if a panel is collapsed so that the content is hidden, you can expand it by
pointing to the section heading until an eye icon appears (Figure 15-6, circled top).
When it does, click it to see the content for that panel.

NOTE Formatting jQuery UI widgets gets pretty complex. You'll see more details on page 615, but for now,
it's worth noting that widget attributes for fonts, position, and color come from jQuery UI style sheets. You'll see
how to add your own CSS rules to change that formatting on page 620. For example, at the bottom of Figure 15-6,
you see a picture floated to the left. The CSS rule positioning that picture is in the web page's main style sheet,
not in the jQuery UI code.

Changing an Accordion's Properties

The great thing about accordions is that they're flexible. (Sorry, bad pun.) After you add an accordion to a page, chances are you'll want to add or remove sections, and, perhaps, change the way the widget opens and operates. You can do all these things in the Properties panel. First, click somewhere inside the accordion, and then click the blue tab at the top left. The Properties panel displays the accordion's attributes. Many jQuery UI widgets use these same properties. Here's what they do:

- **ID**. Dreamweaver needs to keep track of each widget on a page, so it uses IDs to uniquely identify them. As usual, to tweak the accordion's formatting, use its ID as a CSS selector and then create styles to position or size the element on the page.

- **Panels**. Use the Panels property to add, remove, and position accordion panels. Click + to add a new panel or – to remove one. Each panel you add includes a heading and a content section. To change the position of an accordion panel, select its name in the Panels box, and then use ▲ and ▼ to move the panel up and down.

- **Active**. You can specify which accordion panel a browser should expand when it opens the page, but keep in mind that computers like to number things starting with 0. So the top panel of an accordion is 0 and the panel *second* from the top is 1. Why do they always do that?

- **Event**. This menu specifies which action expands an accordion panel. Initially, it's set to "click," so a visitor has to click a heading to expand the panel beneath it. If you think that requires too much effort on the part of your guests, choose "mouseover" as the event. That way, visitors only have to point to (a.k.a., "mouse over") the heading to expose the content underneath.

- **Height Style**. Initially, a widget's Height Style menu is set to "auto." In most cases, that's the right choice, because it sets the height of *all* the panels in their open state equal to the height of the tallest panel when it's expanded. The advantage is that if the accordion sits in a block of text or other page elements, it won't constantly push those elements up and down the page as guests look at the panels. The "content" option changes the height of *each* collapsible panel to accommodate its content. In this case, the height of the entire accordion widget may change as your guest clicks different headings. This means that elements below the accordion will move up or down the page. The "fill" option is supposed to change the height according to the "parent" element, such as a <div> that includes the widget. In some cases, this creates an accordion panel with scroll bars. The "fill" option can be temperamental in other ways, too, so if you decide to use it, double-check the results in different browsers.

- **Disabled**. You can disable an accordion, but that pretty much defeats its purpose. With Disabled selected, a browser displays the accordion, but guests can't open the collapsed sections (unless you apply some JavaScript code to open it later—but, again, the whole point of a collapsible section is to be able to open and close it at will).

- **Collapsible**. Choose this option to let your visitors close all of an accordion's collapsible panels at once. With this option on, if a visitor clicks the heading of an open panel, that panel closes, leaving all the other panels closed, too. Consider this option the ultimate space-saver for accordions.

- **Animate**. Accordion panels don't pop open instantly—they slide open, using a little animation for entertainment. The widget's Animate property lets you select the type of animation (from about two dozen options), and change its timing and motion, using a property known as "easing." (See the box below for details about easing.) The box beside the Animate drop-down menu determines how long the entire action takes. You specify the time in milliseconds, so 1,000 is 1 second and 400 (the pre-set value) is four-tenths of a second.

- **Icons**. Two menus determine the look of an accordion's "expand" and "collapse" icons in panel headings. Out of the box, both display the "flippy" triangles familiar to Mac users. You can change these to ▲ and ▼ arrows or + and – buttons. Go crazy. You can even mix and match, but it will be darn confusing to visitors.

FREQUENTLY ASKED QUESTION

Easing into Animation

What's "easing" and why do I care?

Web designers often use jQuery to animate web page elements—moving headlines, sliding menus, bouncing graphics, and so on. In animation terms, "easing" smooths those motions, so they act like they would in real life. Think about how a car moves. It doesn't travel at the same speed for its entire journey. It starts off slowly, gains speed, and then slows down again before it comes to a stop. Likewise, a ball falling to the ground probably bounces once or twice before it comes to a stop. By applying easing to an animation, you give elements more realistic, or at least amusing, motion.

Give it a try with an accordion panel. Set the Animate menu to "easeOutBounce" and then set the time to *1000* (1 second). Switch to Live view or select View→"Preview in Browser" and then click some of the headings. The panels bounce into place, taking a second to complete the action.

There are a number of standard jQuery easing options with names like easeOutSine and easeInCubic. They work with many types of jQuery widgets, not just accordion panels. If you're a math whiz, these names may give you a clue as to how they work, but if you're a mere mortal who forgot everything you learned in high school trig, try different easing options and choose the one that looks best. To see examples of easing, head over to *http://easings.net/*.

Changing the Look of an Accordion

When you add an accordion (or any other widget) to your web page, it comes styled, thanks to a Cascading Style Sheet (CSS) that comes with the widget. The smart folks who wrote the code for jQuery UI followed best practices and separated the widget's content from its formatting. So you can change a widget's colors, background images, and text styles by creating a different style sheet, or by editing the one that came with the widget. jQuery UI refers to this combination of style sheets (.css) and graphic files (.png) as *themes*.

When you first insert a widget, Dreamweaver gives it a somewhat generic look, known as the Smooth theme. With its light-gray colors and standard text formatting, the greatest virtue of Smooth (Figure 15-6, bottom) is that it won't look out of place on most pages. But it won't make anyone say "Wow!" either.

Dreamweaver provides no easy way to change a widget's theme, but if you're up for a visit to the jQuery UI website (*http://jqueryui.com/*), and game for a little file-swapping, you can do it yourself. This gives your widget a dramatically different appearance. (If that sounds too risky, skip ahead to page 620, where you learn how to make minor changes using CSS Designer.)

After you add a widget and save the page, Dreamweaver creates a folder called jQueryAssets. Inside it, you'll find a file named *jquery.ui.theme.min.css* That file formats your widget. It has style rules for the widget's font family, font size, and font style. It also specifies the heading bars' background colors and images (Dreamweaver stores the latter in an *images* folder it creates inside the jQueryAssets folder). So, to change the look of a widget, replace the *jquery.ui.theme.min.css* file and add new graphics. You can think of this process as swapping themes.

■ CHOOSING A THEME

The first step in styling an accordion is finding a theme you like. Head to the website jQuery User Interface (*http://jqueryui.com/*) and then, on the navigation bar at the top of the page, click Themes. That launches a page called ThemeRoller, where you "roll your own" (as the site says) custom theme. Using the panel on the left, choose the fonts, colors, and background images you want for your accordion, and then check out the results on the sample widget in the main part of the page.

You don't have to create a theme to replace one, however. You can use one of the themes offered in the ThemeRoller gallery. Click Gallery at the top of the left-hand panel and check out the thumbnail themes. Click an example to see the sample widget take on the look.

■ DOWNLOAD JQUERY UI THEMES

Theme files are small, so if you're going to use a ThemeRoller theme, download all of them (go to *http://jqueryui.com/download/*) so you can choose from among all your options.

ThemeRoller is designed for web developers working outside of Dreamweaver, and as such it lets them download packages that combine the widget and its themes (Figure 15-7). Obviously, you need just the theme, so click the link in parentheses labeled "Themes" to download only those files (*jquery-ui-themes-1.11.1.zip*). ThemeRoller offers three versions of each theme, "Stable (Themes)" and two different versions of "Legacy (Themes)." From the Stable option, click Themes. (If you click the word "Stable" or "Legacy," you'll download both the widget and the theme.)

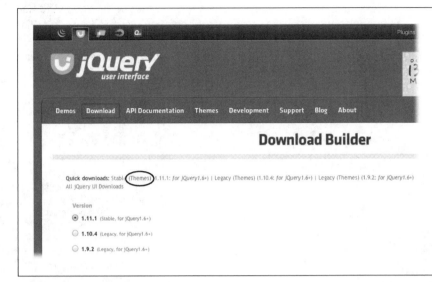

FIGURE 15-7

*To download a set of
jQuery UI themes, go to
jQuery User Interface's
ThemeRoller page
(http://jqueryui.com/
download/). Near the top
of the page, you'll see
"Stable (Themes) 1.11.1:
for jQuery 1.6+." Click the
word "Themes" (circled)
to download a .zip file that
has all the themes from
the jQuery gallery.*

NOTE When you install a jQuery UI widget, Dreamweaver adds jQuery version 1.11.1 and jQuery UI version 1.10.4 to your site. The version numbers appear in the names of the files in the jQueryAssets folder. When you choose a theme from the jQuery site, you need to make sure it's compatible with the version of jQuery you're using. You'll see a message like the one in Figure 15-7 on the download page regarding compatibility that says "Stable (Themes) (1.11.1: for jQuery 1.6+)." That's the file you want to download. Here's why. For one thing, "stable" is always a good feature in the world of programming. That means the library has been tested and vetted. Also, the version number 1.11.1 matches the jQuery version Dreamweaver uses. Even if your project uses a different version of jQuery, say 1.9 or 1.10, you'd still choose this package of themes because the version number is greater than 1.6. (Keep in mind that Dreamweaver may use a different version of jQuery by the time you read this. That's OK; just double-check to make sure the themes you download are compatible with your version of jQuery.)

■ SWAPPING THEMES

Once you download the gallery of themes, you should see a file named *jquery-ui-themes-1.11.1.zip* on your computer. It's an archive file that compresses several files into one and stores them as a single, small file. You need to expand this .zip file before you can get at the files inside (see step 1 below). Once there, you'll choose the CSS file and *images* folder you want to copy to your site so you can replace your widget's theme.

TIP To avoid theme confusion, it's best to add all the jQuery UI widgets you plan to use to your page *before* you swap themes. Otherwise, you end up with more than one CSS file applying theme styles.

1. **Double-click *jquery-ui-themes-1.11.1.zip*, and then extract the compressed files.**

   The process for extracting the contents of a zip file varies from Windows to Mac computers and depends on the version of the operating system you use. For Windows 8, double-click the filename and then, in the ribbon, click Extract→Extract All. For Macs running OS X Mavericks, double-clicking a .zip file creates a folder of the same name with the uncompressed files in it. You'll find a few text files in that folder, along with a *themes* folder like the one in Figure 15-8.

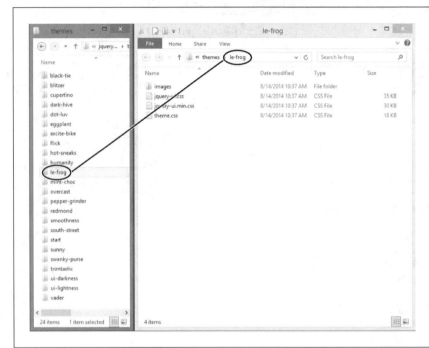

FIGURE 15-8

You'll see more than a dozen subfolders inside the jquery-ui-themes-1.11.1 folder. They have names like dark-hive, eggplant, and le-frog. Each holds one theme. If you can't guess what a theme looks like from its name, see "Choosing a theme" on page 616. To change a widget's theme, first copy the theme.css file and the images folder to your website.

2. **Double-click a theme folder.**

   If you double-click *le-frog*, for example, the folder opens to reveal a file named *theme.css* and a folder called *images*. In step 4, you'll copy this file and folder to your Dreamweaver site, but before you do that, you need to rename a file.

3. **In Dreamweaver's Folders panel, find the jQueryAssets folder and then find the file *jquery.ui.theme.min.css*. Change its name to *theme.css*. When Dreamweaver asks if you want to update your web pages, click Update.**

   The name Dreamweaver gives the CSS file it saves to your computer when you add a widget to a page differs slightly from the name of the file you downloaded from ThemeRoller. In this step, you change the theme's style sheet filename to match the one Dreamweaver gave your widget's CSS file. That way,

Dreamweaver will automatically update the links in your pages. In the next step, you'll replace the widget's original theme file with the one you downloaded.

4. **Drag *theme.css* and the *images* folder from Dreamweaver's Files panel to your jQueryAssets folder as shown in Figure 15-9.**

   A warning box asks if you want to overwrite the files on your website.

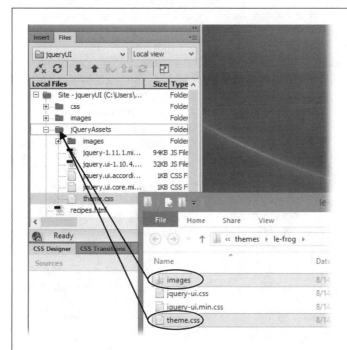

FIGURE 15-9

To change the theme of your jQuery UI widgets, open one of the downloaded theme folders and then drag the theme.css file and the images folder to the jQueryAssets folder in your website. No need to include the other files—you don't need them to change themes.

5. **Click "Yes to all."**

   Dreamweaver copies the new theme files to your site. The CSS file replaces the style sheet Dreamweaver added when you first inserted the widget. The *images* folder stores graphics in the PNG format (page 237), and most of them have different filenames from the ones Dreamweaver uses, so Dreamweaver adds the theme's images to the PNG files already in the folder.

6. **Select Live from the drop-down menu in the Document toolbar and then click Refresh.**

   If you copied the le-frog theme to your jQueryAssets folder as described in step 2, your accordion should now have a greenish hue (Figure 15-1). If you don't see the expected changes, you may need to press F5 or click Refresh at the top of the document window.

When you swap one jQuery UI theme for another, the formatting for all the jQuery UI widgets you added to your project changes. So if your page has, say, an accordion, a date picker, and some buttons, when you swap in a new theme, all those widgets look different. The same is true when you use CSS Designer to make changes to the theme, as you'll see next.

Custom-Formatting Widgets with CSS Designer

When you change the theme of a widget, you dramatically change its look in one fell swoop. But you can make minor changes, too, that have a subtle but less stark effect. You can, for example, change the text color for headings and paragraphs, or float images to the left or right. There are a couple of ways to make these kinds of changes. One is to tweak the theme—that is, to figure out which CSS selector governs the property you want to change and then set that property to a new value. The steps immediately below show you how to do that. The other method is to create a new selector for the property, and then make sure you apply a new style that over-rides the one from the theme. To use this second method, you need to understand the rules that govern the cascade, as explained back on page 412. The second set of instructions below, the ones that show you how to "float" an image in the widget, illustrate this method.

Keep in mind that developers use some advanced techniques to format jQuery UI widgets, which results in dozens upon dozens of CSS rules. Custom formatting is definitely more work than choosing a theme (described in the previous section). But by understanding the CSS cascade and with a little trial-and-error testing, you can customize your widgets.

Figure 15-1 shows two widgets: an accordion and a tabbed content window. Both have headings formatted using CSS Designer. In addition, both have an image in their content—in the accordion, the picture floats to the left, while in the tabs, it floats to the right. In the steps below, you'll change the heading text color and standardize the image positions to either the left or right of the content.

Here are the steps to change the look of the text in the accordion headings. The headings have two states: selected and not selected. You'll change the text color for both states, starting with the selected heading.

1. **In Design view, one accordion panel always displays content. Click inside the text of the heading for that panel.**

   When your cursor is in the heading text, the Tag Selector displays a long string of tags. On the right side of those tags you see *<div#Accordion1><h3><a>*. (If you've given your accordion a different ID, you'll see that ID instead of *#Accordion1*.)

2. **In CSS Designer's Selectors section, click Computed.**

   It's at the top of the list. When you click it, Designer's Properties section displays all the heading properties that have assigned values—all the properties that format the element, in other words. Multiple selectors might govern these properties. For example, a heading selector like <h3> may specify a font family, but because headings are also clickable links, a link selector (<a>) may include the rule for the text color. Among those properties, you see *color(visited)*, the property that sets the color for the heading's text once a guest clicks it.

3. **Click *color(visited)* at the top of the list in CSS Designer's Properties section.**

   When you click a property name or value in Properties, Dreamweaver highlights the source and selector for that property. So when you click *color(visited)*, Dreamweaver displays one filename in the Sources section in bold type. If you followed the steps on page 618 and changed the name of the theme, you see *theme.css* in bold. If you didn't change its name, you see *jquery.ui.theme.min. css*. Either way, the presence of the word "theme" lets you know that if you change the text *color* property, you're changing a theme color, which may affect the way other widgets look.

   If all you want to do is change the heading text color, you don't need to worry about its selector because you're editing an already defined property, and you can go on to the next step. But if you want to *add* styles to the heading text, like a drop shadow, you need to identify the text's selector. In this case, it's the rather lengthy selector *.ui-state-active a, .ui-state-active a:link, .ui-state-active a:visited*. There are actually three <a> selectors here, separated by commas, and they target very specific links—<a> tags that have the *.ui-state-active* class applied to them. The last two selectors are pseudo-classes that target an unclicked link and a visited link, respectively.

4. **Click the swatch next to *color(visited)* and choose a new color.**

   You'll see the color of the heading text change in Design view, but to see your page as your visitors will, switch to Live view. (Just remember to select Design view from the drop-down menu before you try to make additional changes.)

The accordion (and other jQuery UI widgets) use CSS to differentiate between expanded sections and collapsed sections. That way, the headings for expanded sections can have a different color, font size, and style from collapsed sections. To change the color for collapsed-section headings, follow the steps above, but in step 1, click the heading for a collapsed section. (In Design view, clicking an accordion heading doesn't expand the section.)

You can continue to make changes to the heading styles so long as your cursor is inside the heading. Sometimes it takes a little trial-and-error experimenting to zero in on the selector and property you need to tweak. To make it easier, use the Properties section's Disable Property button (⊘) to turn the property on and off so you can quickly identify the element you want to style.

As mentioned in step 3 above, when you click a property like text color, Dreamweaver highlights both the source and the selector in their respective sections of CSS Designer. Once you identify the selector that styles a particular element, like a heading or content, you can add new style rules by setting values for additional properties. For example, to create a drop shadow for the text, set *h-shadow* and *v-shadow* to a value like 3 pixels. Then set *text-shadow color* to black.

■ MORE FORMATTING INSIDE JQUERY UI WIDGETS

Formatting the text inside an accordion's collapsible panel is similar to formatting any other text in your page. You use the same HTML tags to define blocks of text: <p> for paragraphs, <a> for links, and <h1>, <h2>, and so on for headings. The accordion uses <h3> tags for the headings you click to show and hide panels, so, to avoid conflict, use <h4> or some other tag when you create a heading inside the collapsible panel. At that point, you can use CSS Designer to create a rule for the headlines inside the content (see Figure 15-10).

FIGURE 15-10

Here you've selected the style sheet soylent_styles.css in the Sources section of CSS Designer, and, in the Selectors section, created a selector named #Accordion1. You'll use that selector to format the <h4> headings' font color and text shadow in the accordion widget.

Collapsible panels can hold just about any type of HTML, including images. In Figure 15-1, you see an image inside a panel floated to the left. You create that look using a class attribute and the CSS Float property. Here are the steps involved.

1. **In CSS Designer's Sources section, choose a source (style sheet) for your "float left" rule.**

   If you already have an external style sheet, choose that sheet in the Sources section. Otherwise, click + , choose "Create a New CSS Style," and then name the new sheet.

2. **In the Selectors section, click + . In the box for the selector name, type *.float-left.***

   Don't forget the period in front. You just created a class called *.float-left.*

3. **In the Properties section, click the Layout tab and then scroll down to the Float property. Set its value to "left."**

   Your new *.float-left* class has a single rule that positions elements on the page to the left.

4. **In Design view, click an image in your accordion. Then, in the Properties panel below the document window, select "float-left" from the Class drop-down menu.**

   The image in the collapsible panel floats to the left, and the text wraps around the right side of the image.

■ Adding Tabbed Content

In many ways, jQuery tabs are similar to accordions. They both conserve space on a page by hiding content, present guests with familiar controls, and share many of the same properties. So if you edited the accordion in the previous section, you have a jump start on using tabs.

Here are the basics for inserting a set of tabs and changing the tabs' label and content.

1. **Click in the page where you want to insert tabbed content.**

2. **Go to the Insert panel (Window→Insert) and choose the jQuery UI category from the drop-down menu.**

   Tabs are second on the list of jQuery UI widgets, right under Accordion.

3. **Click Tabs.**

   Dreamweaver inserts a set of three tabs in your page, labeled "Tab 1," "Tab 2," and "Tab 3." Initially, the Tab 1 panel is open, and the content portion of it says "Content 1."

4. **In the document window, select Live from the drop-down menu to preview your tabs.**

   Tabbed panels have two parts: the labeled tab itself and the content area below it. To see them in action, switch to Live view. When you click another tab, like Tab 2, the content area displays "Content 2."

5. **Select Design from the drop-down menu to exit Live view.**

   It's easier to edit the tab text in Design view.

6. **Click Tab 1, press Ctrl+A (⌘-A) to select the entire label, and then type *Bruschetta*.**

   The label for Tab 1 now reads "Bruschetta."

7. **Repeat step 6 for the other tabs. Change Tab 2 to *Prosciutto* and Tab 3 to *Mozzarella di Bufala*.**

If you use a long name for the tab heading, it may look odd in Design view, but it will look better in Live view or a browser—the tab changes width to accommodate the longer name. Still, it's best to keep those tabs short and sweet because there's limited horizontal space after you add a few tabs.

8. **Click the Bruschetta tab. In the text area beneath it, click Content 1, press Ctrl+A (⌘-A) to select all the text, and then type *Soylent bruschetta is a delicacy that brings back memories of summer feasts al fresco*.**

This text will appear when a guest selects the Bruschetta tab.

9. **Repeat step 8 for the other two tabs, Prosciutto and Mozzarella di Bufala. Click the eyeball icon that appears, and then replace the placeholder content with your own text.**

In addition to editing the text, you can insert HTML elements in the content area. For instance, you can add pictures or tables. You can even add headings, though it's best to use <h4> headings since the tabs themselves use <h3> headings. In addition, if you use <h4> headings, you can style the two types of headings separately.

Setting Properties for Tabs

You use the Properties panel below the document window to change the way tabs look and operate. To display the tabs' properties, click inside a tab. Dreamweaver displays a blue line around the tab set and a blue tab above it that says "jQuery Tabs: Tabs1." Click the blue tab to see the widget's properties (Figure 15-11). With only a couple of exceptions, the properties for tabs are identical to those for accordions.

FIGURE 15-11

The jQuery UI accordion and tabbed panels widgets perform similar jobs, so it's not surprising to see similar properties for both. One place they differ is the Orientation property (circled), where you choose whether your tabs align horizontally or vertically on the page. Here you see the horizontal orientation, which has the tabs at the top. The vertical orientation puts the tabs on the left side of the screen.

- **ID**. jQuery UI widgets use ID selectors to give each widget a unique name. You use the ID as a selector in CSS Designer to style the widget.

- **Panels**. Use the Panels property to add, remove, and position the tab panels. Click + to add a new panel or − to remove one.

- **Active**. Choose which tab panel a browser displays when it loads the page. The tab on the left is *0*, the second from the left is *1*, and so on.

- **Event**. This drop-down menu controls which action opens the tabbed panel. Choices include "click" and "mouseover."

- **Height Style**. You have three options here: "auto," "fill," and "content." "Auto" sets all the tabbed panels to the height of the tallest one. So if the tab set sits in a block of text or other page element, it won't constantly push those elements up and down the page as it displays new panels. The "fill" option changes the panel's height according to the "parent" element—for example, a <div> on the page. "Content" changes the height of the panel to accommodate its content.

- **Disabled**. When you turn on the Disabled checkbox, the widget appears on the page, but clicking the tabs has no effect. If you're a JavaScript/jQuery programmer, you can control this property through a script. Otherwise, leave the checkbox turned off.

- **Collapsible**. When you turn on this option, clicking an open panel's tab hides its content, leaving only the tab visible.

- **Hide** and **Show**. The Hide and Show properties change the animated effect used to display the tabs. Your choices for the animation include options like "bounce" and "slide." The boxes next to Hide and Show let you specify how long the animation takes. The unit of measure is milliseconds, so *1000* equals 1 second and *400* (the standard) is four-tenths of a second.

- **Orientation**. Usually, tabs appear across a page horizontally, so that they sit at the top of the content panels. You can change that to "vertical," so that the tabs roost on the left side of the tab set.

Adding a Date Picker

The jQuery UI date picker does the same job as the HTML5 date picker (see page 668), though it has a different look from its HTML counterpart (see Figure 15-12). In short, you plop the date picker down in a form when you want visitors to choose a date from a calendar. When your visitor submits the form, it includes a complete date in a format of your choosing.

Make a Reservation

Your name

Your e-mail address

Number in party -- number of diners -- ▾

Date 01/09/2014

Time of reservation

Location Preference

Any comments or requests?

	January 2014					
Su	**Mo**	**Tu**	**We**	**Th**	**Fr**	**Sa**
				1	2	3	4
5	6	7	8	9	10	11
12	13	14	15	16	17	18
19	20	21	22	23	24	25
26	27	28	29	30	31	

FIGURE 15-12

The jQuery UI date picker feels right at home in a form, where guests specify a date. Initially, the date picker looks like an ordinary text box, but the calendar appears as soon as someone clicks in it. Turn on the date picker's Button property to display a button to the right of the text box, as shown here.

As with all jQuery UI widgets, you fine-tune your calendar in the Properties panel (Window→Properties). Other than the ID (which all widgets have), the properties you use with the date picker are unique to the job it performs. Here's a description:

- **ID**. As usual with jQuery UI widgets, name your date picker with an ID, and then use that ID as a selector to format the calendar.

- **Date Format**. This menu changes the way the widget displays the date. Initially, it appears as mm/dd/yy and, when a visitor chooses a date from the calendar, the box displays it like this: 01/09/2014. However, you can choose an alternative date format, like Thursday, 9 January 2014.

- **Locale**. Choose a country, and the date picker provides the month and days of the week in the appropriate language.

- **Button Image**. The date picker opens when someone clicks in a form's Date text box. This option lets you add a button to the right side of the box to indicate that this widget has extra talents (a pop-up calendar, in this case). The stock button has ellipses (...) as a label, but you can change that by specifying an image file—turn on the Button Image checkbox and then specify the pic's location in the box underneath.

- **Change Month, Change Year**. The date picker displays forward and back arrows at the top of the calendar so visitors can move through time. Turn on these options to display month and year drop-down menus as well.

- **In line**. This option displays the date picker as a calendar only, leaving out the text box.

- **Show Button Panel**. Turn on this option to add a panel of buttons to the bottom of the date picker's calendar. The buttons perform different functions; Today, for example, jumps to the current date in the calendar, and Done closes the date picker.

- **Min Date** and **Max Date**. If you want guests to choose a date within a certain range, supply a Min Date and Max Date.

- **Number of Months**. Normally, the date picker displays a single month at a time, but you can display multiple months by putting a number in this box.

■ Adding Pop-Up Messages

When you need to display a pop-up message, turn to the jQuery UI dialog widget. You've probably visited enough websites to know that some pop-up dialog boxes are useful. For example, you might see a dialog box warning you that you're about to send your credit card information using an unencrypted form. In other cases, however, pop-ups are just annoying—consider pop-up advertisements.

It's up to you to decide whether to use the dialog widget for good or evil. Lots of them are small, with just a few words, but they certainly aren't limited in size. You can add images, forms, and any other element you want and, as you'll see, still control the box's size.

You insert the dialog widget by clicking somewhere on the page and then selecting Insert→jQuery UI→Dialog. The truth is, it doesn't matter where on the page you click because the dialog box, by design, floats independently of it.

In the Properties panel, give your widget an ID. Fill in the Title box with a message that'll get the attention of your visitors—something like Breaking News! or Buy Now! These words appear at the top of the dialog box (see Figure 15-13). You position the box's onscreen location by choosing "center," "left," "right," "top," or "bottom" from the Position menu.

A few settings in the Properties panel deal with the dialog box's dimensions. Its stock width is 300 pixels, and its height is set to "auto." That works well for brief messages. With the height set to "auto," the box grows to accommodate the content. If your message is bigger than can comfortably fit in the standard window, increase the Width value. (There is no "auto" setting for Width.) When you set the height to a specific value instead of to "auto," there's always a chance the text won't fit in the box. In that case, the dialog box automatically adds scroll bars. You can also set Min Width, Min Height, Max Width, and Max Height properties to limit the amount of fun your visitors can have resizing the box. If you really want to restrict box-resizing, turn off the Resizable checkbox. While you're at it, you can turn off the Draggable checkbox so they can't reposition the box, either.

FIGURE 15-13

The ribbed tab in the lower-right corner of this dialog box means that a guest can resize the window. That's not really necessary for a small dialog box like this, but it's helpful for boxes that have lots of text and images.

Here are some of the other properties that govern the dialog box:

- **Auto Open**. Check this box to have the dialog box appear when a browser loads the page. If you don't use Auto Open, you need to provide some other way to trigger the dialog box. As you'll see below, you can use a stock trigger or, if you're a JavaScript/jQuery programmer, you can write some code to do the job.

- **Close on Escape**. With this option turned on, your guests can close the dialog box by pressing the Esc key.

- **Modal**. This option makes the dialog box a bit more demanding. On display, it dims the rest of the screen and prevents your visitor from selecting anything on it, except the button that dismisses the dialog box.

- **Hide** and **Show**. These options control the animation that makes the dialog box appear and disappear. You have a number of choices. You can, for example, make the dialog window appear with a shake and then disappear in a puff. Use the box to the left of Hide and Show to specify how long the animation lasts. As with the other jQuery UI time settings, the unit of measure is milliseconds, so *1000* milliseconds gets you 1 second of animation.

- **Trigger Button**. If you don't want your dialog box to appear the instant the page loads, turn off the Auto Open option. You can use a jQuery UI button to trigger the box. (To add a button, see page 631.) After you add the button, its ID appears in the Trigger Button menu. Choose it and you've got your button/dialog box action going.

- **Trigger Event**. This property works hand in hand with the trigger button. Initially, Dreamweaver sets the trigger event to "click." That's what most visitors expect to do with a button, but it's not your only option. You can choose "dblclick" or "mouseover," which work as expected. Two other options may seem curious at first. They are "keydown" and "keypress," and they're almost identical. They trigger an event when a visitor presses a key on his keyboard. The main difference is that "keydown" triggers the event when you press almost any key on the keyboard, including non-printing keys like Shift or Esc. The "keypress" option works only with letters, numbers, and other characters that display onscreen. Both keydown and keypress work when someone uses the Tab key to move from one page element to the next. When he tabs to the triggering button, giving it focus, Dreamweaver highlights the button on the page, and pressing any keyboard key opens the dialog box. Unfortunately, you can choose only one option in Dreamweaver, so you can't use both the click and keypress options.

jQuery UI Widgets for Programmers

Some of the jQuery UI widgets Dreamweaver offers are useful only if you can write JavaScript/jQuery code. For example, you can assign a value to the Progressbar and Slider widgets, but you need to write a script to do something useful with that value. Other widgets, like buttons, are natural triggers to initiate an action, but you usually need to define the action in a script. The next few sections describe what these programmable widgets do, but you need to turn to a book like *jQuery UI* by Eric Sarrion (O'Reilly) to learn how to write code to use them.

Progressbar

The purpose of a progress bar is to let your visitors know something is going on behind the scenes. They may have to wait for a moment...but just this much longer. For example, it's typical for a website to display a progress bar as guests download a particularly large file. For a progress bar to show how far along you are in the download and how much is left, it needs two pieces of information: the size of the file being downloaded and how much of that file has already been transferred. With these two values, you can display a status bar like the one in Figure 15-14.

TIP   Usually, the code behind the Progressbar widget displays an instant-by-instant report on the status of a download. But there are times when you might want to use a "static" progress bar. Suppose you develop a quiz that has 10 questions, each on its own page. You could place a progress bar at the top of each page, setting a value for the length of the bar that reflects how far a student has progressed in the quiz. None of the bars would be animated, but each would inform the student.

FIGURE 15-14

A progress bar reassures the impatient. It shows you how much of a process has been completed. Ideally, a browser updates the progress bar periodically, but that requires a bit of JavaScript/jQuery know-how.

Your file is being downloaded...

Autocomplete

The jQuery UI Autocomplete widget looks like a mild-mannered text box, but its purpose is to help visitors fill in text boxes. To work its magic, Autocomplete needs a list (also known as an *array*) of suggested answers. Then, when visitors begin to type, the list appears with answers that match. Visitors can click a suggestion on the list to save time and avoid extra typing.

You list appropriate answers in an external JavaScript file or create a script that has the list of suggestions in the <head> section of your page. Suggested answers are in the form of a JavaScript list (an array). For example, here are the instructions that appear in the <head> section of a page that lists five states in an Autocomplete widget that has the ID *weststates*. (As usual, the code for the Autocomplete widget itself appears in the <body> of the page.)

```
<script>
    $(function() {
        var availableTags = [
            "Arizona",
            "California",
            "Nevada",
            "Oregon",
            "Washington"
        ];
    $( "#weststates" ).autocomplete({
        source: availableTags
    });
});
</script>
```

Slider

The Slider widget is similar to the Progressbar element, but instead of the widget passing a value to the guest, the slider lets your guests provide a value to the widget. For example, the Progressbar widget sent a value to your visitor that said, in essence, "Your download is 35% done." The slider, on the other hand, lets your guests pass a value *back* to the widget. Visitors move the knob on the slider to select a specific value, one the widget can use in its calculations and then act upon. You've seen sliders like this before, such as when a visitor sets the volume for a media file. As with the other widgets in this section, you need some knowledge of JavaScript and jQuery to use the slider.

jQuery Buttons and More Buttons

The jQuery UI Insert panel gives you several types of buttons and checkboxes: a single button, a related set of buttons, a checkbox, and radio buttons. The Properties panel provides very few tools for you to work with the buttons, so in most cases, you need to write the code to place them in a form or otherwise use them. For example, with the help of some code, you can program the single button to trigger an event, such as opening a new browser window. The Buttonset element groups multiple push-buttons together. You can name, add, and remove the buttons in the Properties panel. The Checkbox boxes work as expected—they let visitors choose several options at once. For example, if you sell magazine subscriptions online, you could put a checkbox next to a picture of each magazine and let your visitors select the ones they want to receive. On the other hand, radio buttons give visitors several choices, but they can choose only one. The Soylent Green Cafe's reservation form (page 691) uses HTML5 radio buttons to let guests select where they want to sit (anywhere, at the bar, or at a corner table).

If you're prepared to write some scripts, you may be interested in the jQuery UI buttons. Otherwise, their usefulness is limited.

■ Working with Dreamweaver Behaviors

Dreamweaver behaviors are prepackaged JavaScript programs that let you add interactivity to your pages, even if you don't know the first thing about JavaScript. While the behaviors were once revolutionary—JavaScript programming without any programming!—Adobe hasn't updated them in years. In fact, many of the behaviors are outdated—you can get some of the same results with CSS, for example, and jQuery widgets supplant other behaviors. On top of that, some of the behaviors just didn't work as advertised. That said, a few are still worth considering.

Behavior Basics

To use a behavior, you need three elements: an HTML tag, the behavior itself, and an event that gets the ball rolling:

- First, you select an HTML tag to apply the behavior to— you have to associate the behavior with some element on the page.

- Next, pick a behavior. That's what the behavior is supposed to *do*, such as open a new browser window or hide an element on a page.

- Finally, you assign an event to the behavior. The event *triggers* the behavior, and it usually involves a visitor interacting with your site, like clicking a Submit button, pointing to a link, or loading a web page into the browser.

For instance, say that, when a visitor clicks a link, instead of just sending him to another page, you want a new browser window to open and load that linked page. In such a case, the HTML tag is the link itself—an <a> tag. The *behavior* is opening another browser window and loading a web page in it. And the *event* takes place when your visitor clicks the link—his browser opens a new window and loads the new page. Voilà—interactivity!

■ Applying Behaviors

Dreamweaver makes adding behaviors as easy as selecting a tag and choosing a behavior from a drop-down menu in the Behaviors panel.

The Behaviors Panel

The Behaviors panel is the control center for Dreamweaver behaviors (Figure 15-15). In it, you can see the behaviors applied to a tag, add more behaviors, and edit existing behaviors.

FIGURE 15-15

Dreamweaver's Behaviors panel lists all the behaviors applied to the currently selected HTML tag. Because the same event can trigger multiple actions, Dreamweaver groups the behaviors by event. In this example, the onClick event for an <a> tag (a link) triggers one action. When a visitor clicks this link, a page element appears or fades away (the Fade effect) and a new browser window opens. The order in which the behaviors occur is determined by their order in this panel. For instance, when a visitor clicks the link in this example, she sees the Fade effect first, and then a browser window opens. To change the order of these events, use ▲ and ▼. To change the type of event, click the event name and then select a different one from the drop-down menu. If a unique event triggers each action, the order in which the events appear in the panel is irrelevant.

To open the Behaviors panel, choose Window→Behaviors. Dreamweaver shows you the currently selected tag at the top of the panel; a list of the behaviors applied to that tag (if any) appears below that. The panel breaks down each behavior into two parts: events and behaviors.

You can choose from two views in the Behaviors panel, and switch between them using the buttons in the upper-left corner:

- 🔳 "Show set events" gets down to the specifics: which behaviors you applied to a tag and which events trigger them. When you work on a web page, this view moves extraneous information out of your way.

- ▤ "Show all events" lists all the events *available* to a particular tag. This view isn't that useful, since you see a complete list of events for that tag when you select the tag and add a behavior.

Applying Behaviors, Step by Step

Open the Behaviors panel (Window→Behaviors) and proceed as follows:

1. **Select the object or tag to which you want to assign a behavior.**

   You have to attach a behavior to an HTML tag, such as a link (an <a> tag) or the page itself (the <body> tag). Take care, however, because it's easy to ac-cidentally apply a behavior to the wrong tag. Form elements, like checkboxes and text boxes, are easy to target—just click one to select it. For other kinds of tags, consider using the Tag Selector described on page 7 for more precision.

2. **In the Behaviors panel, add a behavior.**

   Click ➕ in the Behaviors panel and, from its drop-down menu, select the be-havior you want to add (see Figure 15-16). (You'll find a list of these behaviors and what they do beginning on page 636.)

   The menu dims behaviors you can't use when your page doesn't include an ele-ment that the behavior can affect. If your page lacks a form, for instance, you won't be able to select the Validate Form behavior. Other behaviors are grayed out because you have to apply them to a particular page element. For example, Jump Menu is off-limits until you add a Select menu (Insert→Form→Select) to the page and highlight it.

3. **In the dialog box that opens, set options for the behavior.**

   Each behavior has properties specific to it, and you set them in this dialog box. For instance, when you choose the Go To URL behavior, Dreamweaver asks what web page you want to load.

4. **Click OK to apply the behavior.**

   At this point, Dreamweaver adds the HTML and JavaScript required for the be-havior to your page's code. The behavior and the event that triggers it appear in the Behaviors panel.

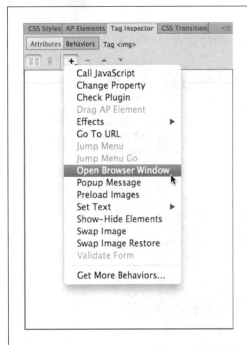

FIGURE 15-16

Dreamweaver grays out behaviors you can't apply to a currently selected tag. The reason? Your page is either missing a necessary element or you selected an element that can't exhibit that behavior. For example, you can't apply the Show-Hide Elements behavior if your page doesn't have at least one tag with an ID applied to it.

Unlike HTML objects, behaviors usually add JavaScript code in two places in a document: to the head section of the page *and* to the target HTML tag in the body of the page.

5. **Change the event, if desired.**

When your newly created behavior shows up in the Behaviors panel, Dreamweaver displays a default event (a trigger) in the Events column for the selected tag and action. For example, if you add an Open Browser Window behavior to a link, Dreamweaver suggests the *onClick* event.

However, this event may not be the only one available. Links, for instance, can handle many events. A behavior could begin when your visitor points to the link (the *onMouseOver* event), clicks the link (the *onClick* event), and so on.

To change the event for a particular behavior, click the event's name. In the Events drop-down menu that appears, select a new trigger from the events available for that tag.

When you're done, you can leave the Behaviors panel open to add more behaviors to the current tag, or to add behaviors to other tags. For the latter, select another tag using the document window or the Tag Selector, and then repeat steps 2–5.

NOTE Dreamweaver sometimes displays a warning bar above a document after you insert a behavior. It tells you that the code in a JavaScript program was written incorrectly. In fact, this warning bar occasionally appears even when there is no JavaScript error. Close and reopen the page to make the error bar go away.

Editing Behaviors

Once you apply a behavior, you can edit it anytime. Double-click the behavior in the Behaviors panel to reopen the Settings dialog box as described in step 3 of the previous instructions. Make any changes you like, and then click OK.

To remove a behavior, select it in the Behaviors panel, and then click − or press Delete. (If you *accidentally* delete a behavior, choose Edit→Undo Remove Behavior.)

A Quick Example

The brief example below shows you the behavior-creation process. In it, you'll use a behavior that makes an important message appear when a web page opens.

1. **Choose File→New to create a new, untitled HTML document.**

   You'll start with a fresh page.

2. **Choose File→Save and save the file to your computer.**

   It doesn't matter where on your computer you save the page since you won't include any graphics or links to other pages.

   You start the process of adding a behavior by selecting a tag—in this case, the page's <body> tag.

3. **In the Tag Selector, click <body>.**

   Once you select a tag, you can apply one or more behaviors to it. But, first, make sure you have the Behaviors panel open. If you don't see it, press Shift+F4 or choose Window→Behaviors.

4. **Click ⊕ in the Behaviors panel. From the "Add behavior" drop-down menu, choose Popup Message.**

   Dreamweaver opens the Popup Message dialog box.

5. **In the Message box, type *Visit our store for great gifts!* and then click OK.**

   Dreamweaver adds the required JavaScript to the page. Notice that the Behaviors panel now lists a behavior called Popup Message next to an *event* called *onLoad*. The *onLoad* event triggers the behavior *after* a page and everything on it—graphics and so on—loads.

   To see the page in action, click Live in the drop-down menu at the top of the document window or preview the page in a browser by pressing F12 (Option-F12).

NOTE Dreamweaver behaviors rely on little JavaScript programs that run inside web browsers. For security reasons, Internet Explorer doesn't always like running JavaScript programs that reside on your own computer, like those in web pages you save locally. If the JavaScript you add to a page doesn't work when you preview it in IE, look for a warning at the bottom of the browser window. (Older versions of IE display a similar warning at the top of the window.) Click "Allow blocked content" to see the pop-up message. This fussy behavior happens only when you view a page that's sitting on your computer; once you move the page to the Web, Internet Explorer eases its security precautions and runs the JavaScript without the warning.

■ Specifying Behaviors

Events are at the heart of interactive web pages. They trigger behaviors based on your visitors' actions. Events include clicking a link, pointing to an image, or simply loading a page. But you can't apply just any event to a tag—not all events work with all tags. For example, you can use the *onLoad* event with web pages and images only, not paragraphs, <div>s, or any other page element. When you specify an event, the Event menu in the Behaviors panel helps you out—once you select a tag on a page, the drop-down menu lists only those events available for that tag.

Current browsers—Internet Explorer 9 and newer, Safari, Firefox, and Chrome—support events for many HTML tags. Many events work with other tags as well, such as headline, paragraph, and <div> tags. But don't go crazy peppering your page with events and behaviors. Making an alert message appear when someone double-clicks a paragraph is more likely to win your site the Hard-To-Use Website of the Month award than a loyal group of visitors.

■ A Sampler of Behaviors, One by One

As mentioned earlier, many Dreamweaver behaviors are out of date. This section lists some of the behaviors you may still find useful. After you set up a new behavior as described on page 632, it appears in the Behaviors panel, and your web page is ready to test.

Effects

Dreamweaver gives you a bundle of visual effects to apply to the elements on your page. In the Behaviors panel, when you click ⊕, Dreamweaver displays a menu of behaviors. Point to the Effects item in the menu to see a submenu of visual effects. They do things like highlight elements on a page, make a photo fade in, or shake an entire sidebar of information as though it were in an earthquake. The effects are mostly eye candy and work well when you want to draw attention to an element or to create a dramatic introduction, but it's easy to abuse them. If every part of your page blinks, shrinks, shakes, and flashes, most visitors will quickly grow tired of the nonstop action.

In some cases, you'll highlight a page element, choose an event, and then, in the event's dialog box, select Current Element from the Target Element drop-down menu. For example, you could make a picture fade away when someone clicks it. In other cases, you'll want to target a specific element on the page. Perhaps you want that picture to fade away when someone clicks some text. To do that, you first have to apply an ID to the target element.

You usually think of IDs as a way to format a unique element on a page using Cascading Style Sheets. But IDs are also handy when you want to add interactivity to a page. In fact, you can add an ID to HTML without ever creating a CSS style for it.

Recall that the HTML ID attribute marks a tag with a unique name. Because that name targets a specific element in your page, you can control that element using JavaScript. How you apply the ID depends on the tag, but here are the most common techniques. Note that you name the ID from the Properties panel's HTML menu, not its CSS menu.

- **<div> tags**. Assign an ID to a <div> tag using the Properties panel. Select the <div> tag and then, in the panel's HTML menu, use the ID field to give the <div> a unique name. You can also apply an ID by wrapping any collection of HTML tags (or even a single element, like an image) inside a <div> tag (select Insert→Div) and then using the Insert Div window (see page 454).

- **Images**. When you select an image in the document window, you can type an ID for that image in the Properties panel's ID box.

- **Forms**. Select the form and type an ID in the ID field on the left edge of the Properties panel.

- **Form elements**. When you insert a form element, like a Submit button or text box, you can set the element's ID in the Input Tag Accessibility Options window. You can later set or change that ID by selecting it and then using the name field on the left edge of the Properties panel. Form elements have both a name and an ID, but Dreamweaver's Properties panel shows a text box just for Name, not for ID. That's because, when you type in a name, Dreamweaver assigns it to both the element's name and its ID in the HTML for the element. For example, here's the HTML for a text box named "city":

```
<input type="text" name="city" id="city">
```

- **Other elements**. To add an ID to paragraphs, headlines, bulleted lists, and other tags, select the tag in the Properties panel and then type a name in the ID field.

After you apply an ID to a target tag, specify the event that triggers the behavior. For example, say you want your site's banner image to appear on a page after the page loads. The target—the element that will change as a result of the behavior—is the banner image, The element that triggers the behavior is the page itself, because the event occurs when the page loads. So, in this case, the event is tied to the <body> tag using the *onLoad* event.

■ FADE

The Fade effect makes an element fade in or out. To add a dramatic introduction to your site, you can fade in a large photograph on your home page after the page loads. Or you can have an "Important Announcement" box disappear when a visitor clicks it.

Here's how to use this effect:

1. **Select the tag for the element that will trigger the fade in or out behavior.**

   For example, you might apply a behavior to an image inside a <div> tag, or you could target the <body> tag and choose *onLoad* as the event.

2. **Choose Window→Behaviors, click ⊹ to open the Actions drop-down menu, and then choose Effects→Fade.**

   Dreamweaver opens the Fade window (see Figure 15-17).

FIGURE 15-17

Use the Fade effect to have, say, a photograph fade into view on your site's home page, or to make an element fade out.

3. **Select a target element from the first menu in the Fade window.**

   Here's where you specify which page element should appear or fade away. The menu lists every tag on the page that has an ID applied to it. In addition, you may see Current Selection listed, which refers to an element you highlighted on the page, in this case, the tag you selected in step 1. Choose this option to apply the behavior to any <div> tag that contains some kind of message—like "We'll be closed February 2nd to celebrate Groundhog Day!" When a visitor clicks the message, it fades away.

4. **Type an amount in the "Effect duration" field.**

   This setting controls how long the fade in or out lasts. You set the duration in milliseconds, so typing *1000* gets you 1 second. If you want the target element to appear or disappear immediately, enter *0*.

5. **Set the Visibility attribute of the effect. Your choices are Show, Hide, or Toggle.**

   Choose Show to make the element fade in, or Hide to make it fade out. Use Toggle to go back and forth—if the element is visible, the toggle action hides it, and vice versa. If you want the target element to fade into view, you have to hide it to begin with. Otherwise the fade-in effect looks really weird: First you see the photo, then you don't, and *then* it fades in.

TIP To make the element invisible initially (so that it fades *in*), add (or edit) a style for the target element, and then set the CSS *display* property (page 423) to "none." Of course, if you go this route, you need to use another page element to trigger the behavior.

---

6. **Click OK to apply the behavior.**

   Once you add the effect to a tag, you can edit or delete it just as you can any other behavior; see page 632 for details.

■ BLIND

Don't worry, the Blind effect won't hurt your eyes. It's actually just a way of simulating a window blind—either being drawn closed over an element to hide it or opened to reveal it. The basic concept and behavior are the same as that for the Appear/Fade effect: It lets you hide or reveal an element on a page. Follow the steps described in the previous section to apply the effect.

Once you select Blind from the Effects menu in the Behaviors panel, you can set the effect's options from the Blind dialog box (Figure 15-18). Use the Direction pull-down menu to choose the motion you want. If you want to make an element hide and you choose "down," the top begins to disappear first. On the other hand, if you want your element to appear with a bit of flair and you choose "down," the bottom of the element appears first, and it grows upward (in this case, the Down attribute is counterintuitive). So the watchword here is, choose your settings, but test them to make sure your blind works the way you want it to.

FIGURE 15-18

The Blind effect's window is similar to the Fade window. You choose a target element, set the duration for the effect, and decide whether to show, hide, or toggle the element's visibility. The attribute specific to the Blind effect is the direction of the animation. The choices are up, down, left, right, vertical, and horizontal.

■ HIGHLIGHT

Adding a background color to a paragraph, headline, or <div> is one way to create visual contrast on a page and make an important piece of information stand out. A red box with white type will draw the eye quicker than a sea of black type on a white page. But if you really want to draw someone's attention, use the Highlight effect. Highlighting an element lets you add a flash of bright background color to it. For instance, in a form, you may have an important instruction for a particular box ("Your password must be 10 characters long and not have !, #, or $ in it"). You could add the Highlight effect to the form element so that when a visitor clicks in the box, the instruction's background color quickly flashes, ensuring that the visitor sees the important information.

As with other effects, use the Behaviors panel to apply the Highlight effect to some triggering element (like a form element you click in, or a link you point to). Then use the Highlight window (Figure 15-19) to set the target element (any tag with an ID), the duration of the effect, its visibility, and its color. To choose a color, click the swatch and select from the standard Adobe color picker. When you do, the Highlight window displays the hex color specification (page 151) beside the swatch. If you have a color specification in number form, you can enter it in the color picker. For details on coloring by number, see page 151.

FIGURE 15-19

Use the Highlight effect (sparingly) to draw attention to elements on the page for a moment. The Effect Duration property shown here determines just how long that moment lasts. Set the Visibility to "show" unless you're turning off a highlight. Click the color swatch to use Adobe's standard color picker to choose a hue for the highlight.

■ SHAKE

The Shake effect is like adding an earthquake to a web page. The target element shakes violently left to right for a second or so. And that's all there is to it. You can shake any element that has an ID—a <div> or even just a paragraph of text. When you apply this behavior, you can choose the shake's duration and direction (left, right, up, or down). To make a quake bigger, increase the number in the Distance box. You can also set the number of times your element shakes. It's kind of a fun effect...once...and maybe just for kids.

■ SLIDE

The Slide effect is just like the Blind effect, but instead of a "window blind" moving over an element to hide it (or moving off an element to reveal it), the element itself moves. Say you have a <div> tag that contains a gallery of photos. If you target that <div> with a "slide up" effect, the images all move upward and disappear at the top edge of the <div>. Think of the <div> as a kind of window looking out onto the photos. When the photos move up past the "window," you can't see them any longer.

Suppose you want to make an image slide up and out of view when your visitors click it. In the Slide dialog box (Figure 15-20), set the Target Element to Current Selection. (Always choose Current Selection when you want the trigger to serve as the target, too.) Set the duration to *2000* because you want the animation to last 2 seconds. Set the visibility to "hide." (If you leave it set to "show" and the element is already visible, you won't notice any effect at all.) Choose "up" as the direction. In the Distance box, enter the number of pixels you want the image to move before it disappears. For example, if you leave this option set to 20, the image moves up 20 pixels and then fades away. However, if the image is 320 pixels tall, that may look a little funny. To make the image appear to slide away entirely, set the distance to *320*.

FIGURE 15-20

The Slide effect works just like the Blind effect described on page 639. The only difference is that here, the element itself moves and disappears (as opposed to a "blind" being drawn over the element).

Open Browser Window

Sometimes, when a visitor's action opens a new browser window, you want to dictate the size of that window. If you have a link to a "Sign up for our newsletter" form, for example, you may want to open the sign-up page in a window that matches the exact width and height of the subscription form. Or, when a visitor clicks a thumbnail image, you may want to open a window whose dimensions match that of the full-size photo—and prevent that window from displaying all the distracting browser "chrome," like the location bar, status bar, toolbar, and so on.

Enter Dreamweaver's Open Browser Window action (Figure 15-21). Use it to tell your visitor's browser to open a new window to a height and width you set. In fact, you can even dictate what *elements* the browser window includes. Don't want the toolbar, location bar, or status bar? No problem; this action lets you include or exclude the frills.

FIGURE 15-21

Here you can define the properties of the new window, including what web page loads into it, its dimensions, and so on. If you leave the "Window width" and "Window height" properties blank, you'll get different results in different browsers. In Firefox, Chrome, and Opera, you won't get a new window—the page opens up a new tab. In Internet Explorer and Safari, you get a new window, but it's the same size as the window that spawned it.

To open a new browser window, you start, as always, by selecting the tag to which you want to attach the behavior. You can attach it to any HTML tag, but you usually want to add it to a link with an *onClick* event, or to the <body> tag using the *onLoad* event.

> **NOTE** Most browsers have pop-up blockers. This nifty feature prevents a browser from opening a new browser window unless the visitor initiates the request. In other words, you probably won't be able to open a new browser window when a page loads in the current window, but you can open a new browser window based on a visitor's action—like clicking a link.

Once you select Open Browser Window from the ⊕ drop-down menu in the Behaviors panel, you see the dialog box shown in Figure 15-21.

Specify the following options:

- **URL to display**. In this box, type the URL or path to the page you want to load, or click Browse and find the page on your computer (the latter is a near-foolproof way to ensure functional links). To load a web page on somebody else's site, don't forget to type in an *absolute* URL, one beginning with *http://.*

- **Window width, Window height**. Next, define the width and height of the new window using pixels as the unit of measure. Note that most browsers won't display a window smaller than 100 x 100 pixels. Also, if the width and height you specify are larger than the available space on your visitor's monitor, the window fills the monitor (but won't ever generate a wider or taller window).

- **Attributes**. Turn on the checkboxes for the browser elements you want the new window to include. Figure 15-22 shows the pieces of a standard browser window. Because Dreamweaver behaviors are an older feature, you won't find some of these attributes on modern browsers. For example, in most browsers, you can't really get rid of the resize handle, so even if you leave that option turned off, it still appears and a visitor will still be able to resize the window.

FIGURE 15-22

The parts of a browser window shown on an older version of Firefox. Note that the menu bar appears only on older browsers on Windows machines. On Macs, the menu bar appears at the top of the display (not at the top of the browser window), and you can't hide it. In addition, you can't hide the resize handle or the scroll bars (if they're needed) in the Safari browser.

- **Window name**. Give the new window a name (using letters and numbers only). If you include spaces or other symbols, Dreamweaver displays an error message and lets you correct the mistake. The name won't actually appear on your web page, but it's useful for targeting links or actions in the new window from the original one.

Once you set up the Open Browser Window action, you can load web pages into the new window from the original page; simply use the name of the new window as the link's target. For example, you could add the Open Browser Window behavior to a link labeled "Open photo gallery" that, when clicked, opens a small window showcasing a photo. You could include additional links on the main page that load additional photos into that small window.

If you use more than one Open Browser Window behavior on a single page, make sure you give each new window a unique name. If you use the same name, your page might retain the first new window's settings and you might not get the width, height, or other settings you want in the new window.

When you finish making selections and click OK, Dreamweaver displays your newly created behavior in the Behaviors panel's Actions list.

Image Actions

Images make web pages stand out, but using Dreamweaver behaviors with images can make them come to life.

■ PRELOAD IMAGES

It takes time for images to download from the Internet. A 64 KB image, for instance, takes about 1 second to download over a DSL modem. Add 10 images of this size to a page, and it can take a while to actually load the page. However, once a browser loads an image, it stores that image in its *cache*, a temporary storage locker, so if the page requires that same graphic again, it loads extremely quickly. The Preload Images action takes advantage of this concept by downloading images and storing them in your browser's cache *before* the page actually needs them.

Preloading is especially important when guests trigger effects by pointing to a page element. When a visitor points to a button, for example, it may light up. If the light-up graphic weren't preloaded, it would take a while to appear when your visitor points to the button; in fact, it wouldn't even begin to download until she started pointing. The resulting delay would make your button feel less like a rollover and more like a layover.

If you use the Insert Rollover Image command (see page 268), you don't need to apply the Preload Images action by hand because Dreamweaver adds it automatically. But there are exceptions. For example, when you use the CSS *background* property (page 252) to add an image to a link (see page 183), a new background image appears when a visitor points to the link. But the browser loads that image only when a visitor triggers the rollover state, not before. In a case like this, you want to add the Preload Images action to the event.

To do so, select the <body> tag. While you can apply the Preload Images behavior to any tag, it really only makes sense to attach it to the <body> tag using an *on-Load* event, so that when a web page first loads, the browser begins downloading its images.

If you add rollover images to your page, Dreamweaver may have already applied this behavior to the <body> tag. If that's the case, just select the tag (click <body> in the Tag Selector) and then double-click the Preload Images action that should be listed in the Behaviors panel. If you don't see it, choose Preload Images from the ✛ drop-down menu in the Behaviors panel. Either way, Dreamweaver displays the Preload Images dialog box.

Click Browse and navigate to the graphics file you want to preload, or type in its path. If the graphic lives on the Web, use an absolute URL. Dreamweaver adds the image to the Preload Images list. To preload another image, click ✢ and repeat the process. Continue until you've added all the images you want to preload.

To remove an image from the preload list, select it and then click −. (Be careful not to delete any images required for a rollover effect you already created—the Undo command doesn't work here.)

When you click OK, Dreamweaver returns you to your document and displays your new action in the Behaviors panel. You can edit it, if you like, by changing the event that triggers it. But unless you're trying to achieve some special effect, you usually use the *onLoad* event on the <body> tag. That's all there is to it. When your page loads in a browser, the browser quietly continues to load and store the graphics you specified in the background. They appear almost instantly when a guest triggers the action, or even when she shifts to another page that incorporates the graphics.

■ SWAP IMAGE

The Swap Image action exchanges one image on your page for another (see Figure 15-23). (See below for details on Swap Image Restore, Swap Image's sibling behavior.)

Simple as that process sounds, swapping images is one of the most visually exciting things you can do on a web page. It works something like rollover images, except that you don't have to trigger the swap by pointing to or clicking the image. You can use *any* tag-and-event combination. For instance, you can create a mini slideshow by listing the names of pictures down the left side of a web page and inserting an image in the middle of the page. Add a Swap Image action to each slide name, and the appropriate picture replaces the center image when a visitor clicks a new name.

To make this behavior work, your page has to include a *starter image*, and the images you want to swap in have to match the width and height of that starter graphic. If they don't, the browser resizes and distorts the swapped pictures to fit the "frame" dictated by the original image.

To add the Swap Image behavior, first identify the starter image (choose Insert→Image, or use any of the other techniques described in Chapter 5). Give your image an ID in the Properties panel so JavaScript knows which image to swap out. (JavaScript doesn't really care about the original graphic itself, but rather about the space that it occupies on the page.)

TIP You can swap in and out more than one image at a time with a single Swap Image behavior. Using this trick, not only can a button change to another graphic when you point to it, but any number of other graphics on the page can also change at the same time. An asterisk (*) next to the name of an image in the Swap Image dialog box (Figure 15-24) indicates that the behavior will swap in a new image for that particular graphic. In the example in Figure 15-23, you can see that two images—*horoscope* and *ad*, both marked by asterisks in Figure 15-24—swap as a result of a single action.

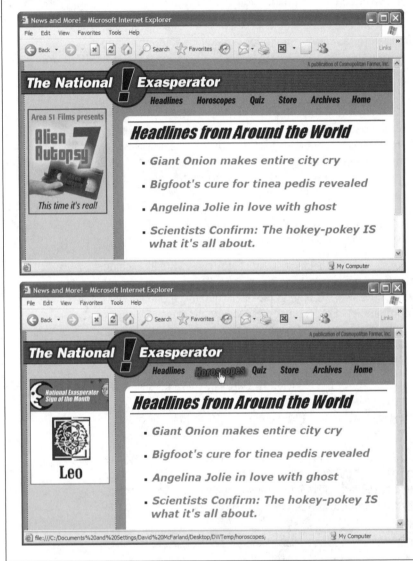

FIGURE 15-23

You can use the Swap Image behavior to simultaneously change multiple graphics when a visitor points to just one. A humble web page (top) comes to life when a visitor points to the Horoscopes button (bottom). Not only does the graphic for the button change, but so does the ad in the left sidebar; it now offers a tantalizing look at the Sign of the Month. The Swap Image action lets you easily get this type of effect, sometimes called a disjoint rollover.

Now select the tag you want to associate with the Swap Image behavior—you can choose a link, a paragraph, another image, or even the starter image itself. When you choose Swap Image from the Behaviors panel, Dreamweaver opens the Swap Image dialog box so you can set the behavior's options (Figure 15-24).

- **Images**. From the list, click the name of the starter image.

- **Set source to**. Here's where you specify the image file you want to swap in. If it's a graphics file in your site folder, click Browse to find and open it. You can also specify a path or an absolute URL to another website, as described on page 178.

- **Preload images**. Preloading ensures that image downloads don't slow down the swap-in, so check this box.

- **Restore images onMouseOut**. You get this option only when you apply the Swap Image behavior to a link. When you turn on this checkbox, the previous image reappears when a visitor moves his mouse *off* the link.

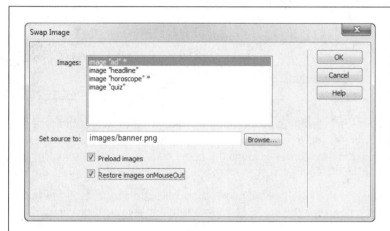

FIGURE 15-24

Some actions, like Swap Image, can automatically add behaviors to a web page. In this case, the "Preload images" and "Restore images onMouseOut" options actually add a Swap Image Restore action to the onMouseOut event of the currently selected tag and a Preload Images action to the onLoad event of the <body> tag.

■ SWAP IMAGE RESTORE

The Swap Image Restore action returns the last set of swapped images to its original state. Most designers use it in conjunction with a rollover button so that the button returns to its original appearance when the visitor moves his cursor off the button.

You'll probably never find a need to add this behavior yourself; Dreamweaver automatically adds it when you insert a rollover image and choose the "Restore images onMouseOut" option when you set up a regular Swap Image behavior. (The Swap Image Restore dialog box offers no options.)

Popup Message

Use the Popup Message behavior to send important notes to your visitors, as shown in Figure 15-25. Your visitor must click OK to dismiss the message. Because a pop-up message demands immediate attention, reserve this behavior for important announcements.

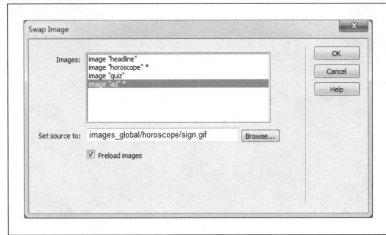

FIGURE 15-25

Here, a pop-up message indicates a sale going on at Chia-Vet.com. While the Popup Message behavior is easy to use, you can't customize the look of the dialog box. The browser controls that, and it looks different from browser to browser. In this case, Safari titled the pop-up box "JavaScript." By contrast, Chrome titles it "JavaScript Alert." This is an example of Dreamweaver behaviors being out of step with modern browsers.

To create a pop-up message, select the tag that you want to trigger the behavior. For example, adding this action to the <body> tag with an *onLoad* event makes the message appear when a browser loads the page; adding the same behavior to a link with an *onClick* event makes the message appear when a visitor clicks the link.

From the + menu in the Behaviors panel, choose Popup Message. In the Popup Message dialog box, type the message you want to appear, and then click OK.

TIP JavaScript programmers, your message can also include any valid JavaScript expression. To embed JavaScript code in a message, place it inside braces ({ }). If you want to include the current date and time in a message, for example, add {new Date()}. If you just want to display a brace in the message, add a backslash, like this: \{. That tells Dreamweaver that you really do want a { character—and not just a bunch of JavaScript—to appear in the dialog box.

Adding Forms to Pages

A website is a great way to brand your company, announce a new product, post late-breaking news, or rant about the state of the world. But all that's *one-way* communication, and you may want to interact with your audience more directly—to get feedback on your product or company, for example, or to gather vital statistics from customers.

If you want to *receive* information as well as deliver it, it's time to add *forms* to your website design repertoire (see Figure 16-1 for a simple example). For instance, if you want site visitors to sign up for your email newsletter, build a form to collect their names and email addresses. Accepting lunch reservations for Cafe Soylent Green? Create a form to get the details of date, time, and number of guests. Whatever type of information you need to collect on your site, Dreamweaver's *form objects* make the task easy.

■ Form Basics

A form begins and ends with the HTML <form> tag. The opening tag (<form>) indicates the beginning of a form and sets its properties, and the closing tag (</form>) marks the form's end.

You put form elements that your visitors interact with— radio buttons, text boxes, pull-down menus, and so on— between those two tags. It's perfectly OK to include other HTML elements inside a form, too. In fact, your visitors would be lost if you didn't add (and format) text that explains each element's purpose. And if you don't use Cascading Style Sheets to lay out your form in an organized way, it can quickly become an unreadable mess (see the box on page 677).

FIGURE 16-1

A form can be as simple as a single empty text box (or text field in geek-speak) and a button, or as complex as a survey of 100 fill-in-the-blank and multiple-choice questions.

Every form element, whether it's a text box or a checkbox, has a *name* and a *value*. You supply the name, which should reflect the information you're trying to collect. For example, if you want a visitor to type his email address into a text box, you might name that box *Email*. The value, on the other hand, is what your *visitor* types in—the text he enters into the box, for example, or the selections he makes from a pull-down menu.

After a visitor fills out a form and clicks the Submit button, his browser sends each form element as a name/value pair, like this: *email=bob@bobville.com*. You need to provide a name/value pair for each form element. After all, without a name, a value of "39" doesn't mean much (39 what? Potatoes, steps, days until Christmas?). The name/value pair (*age=39*) provides context for your visitor's input.

Processing Form Information

Creating a form is just the first step in collecting information. You also need to *transmit* that information to a program that actually *does* something with it. That program may simply email the data from the form to you. But it could also do something as complex as contacting a bank, processing a credit card payment, creating an invoice, or notifying the shipping department to deliver a poster of Taylor Swift to someone in Nova Scotia.

A form is pretty useless if you don't have a form-processing program running on your web server. These information-crunching programs come in a variety of languages—Perl, C, C#, Visual Basic, VBScript, Java, ColdFusion Markup Language, PHP, Ruby—and may be part of a dedicated application server, like Adobe's ColdFusion Server or Microsoft's .NET technology.

While writing the necessary behind-the-scenes forms software can be complex, the concepts behind the forms themselves are straightforward:

1. First, someone fills out a form on your website and clicks the Submit button (or Search, Buy, or whatever you actually label the button that transmits information).

2. Next, the browser transmits the form data over the Internet to a processing program on your web server.

3. The form-processing program collects the data and takes action, doing whatever you decide it should do. It could, for example, send data off as an email to you, search a vast database of information, or store the information in a database.

4. Finally, the server returns a page to the browser, which your visitor sees. It may be a standard web page with a message like "Thanks for the info," or a page the program generates on the fly that includes information like a detailed invoice or the results of a search.

So how do you create the processing half of the forms equation if you're not a programmer? Your web hosting company may offer free form-processing programs as part of its services. Contact it and ask; most companies provide basic instructions on how to use these programs. If you're part of a company's web development team, you may already have programmers on staff who can create the processing program. You can also find Dreamweaver extensions that can help with a variety of form-processing tasks (see the boxes on pages 679 and 682).

If you feel adventurous, many form-processing programs are available for free on the Web. For a thorough sampling, see the CGI Resource Index at *http://cgi.resourceindex.com*. Using these free programs can be tricky, however, because you need to download a program and install it on your web server—something not every web host allows.

Lastly, you can use a form-processing service like Wufoo (*http://wufoo.com*), which handles all the complicated parts of collecting and storing information from forms and provides tools for retrieving that information in a variety of formats.

■ Creating a Form

In Dreamweaver, you can build forms with one-click ease using the Insert panel's Forms category (see Figure 16-2).

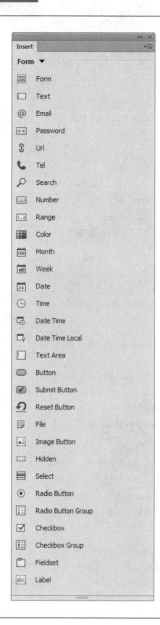

FIGURE 16-2

Dreamweaver's Insert panel has a category devoted to form elements, complete with icons that make it easy to identify each element's purpose. You may want to keep the elements handy as you build forms—just drag the Insert panel by the tab and position it within easy reach.

To begin, you need to insert a <form> tag in your web page to indicate the boundaries of the form:

1. **In Design view, click the location in the document where you want to insert the form.**

   You might decide to place it after a paragraph of introductory text, for example, or into a <div> tag that holds the page's main content.

> **NOTE** If you plan to use an HTML table to organize a form (see page 279), insert the form tags first, and then insert the table inside the tags. Better than that, use CSS to organize your form, as the tutorial at the end of this chapter shows you (page 682).

2. **On the Insert panel, select the Forms category.**

   The panel reveals 30 form-building tools.

3. **Click the Form icon (the first one in the list).**

   If you're a menu-driven person, choose Insert→Form→Form.

> **NOTE** What you see when you insert an object using the Insert panel depends on whether you're working in Design view, Live view, or Code view. These instructions assume you're inserting form elements in Design view, because it provides the most intuitive way to build forms. Live view requires extra steps to do simple things like editing labels. In Code view, Dreamweaver inserts the tag for the selected element, but the underlying code is sometimes different from what you see in either Design view or Live view. For example, in Design view, the Insert→Text command adds a text box and a label to your page, along with an ID and other helpful HTML. In Code view, the Insert→Form→Text command adds just a single, stripped-down tag, *<input type="text">*. So, unless you consider hand-coding forms a recreational activity, you're better off working in Design view.

   Either way, a rectangle with a red line appears in the document window, indicating the form's boundaries. The line is dashed on Windows PCs and solid on Macs. (If you don't see it, choose View→Visual Aids→Invisible Elements.) The top line represents the opening <form> tag; the bottom represents the closing tag. It's best to insert form objects, like buttons and menus, *inside* these lines. With HTML5, you can associate elements in any location to a specific form, but not all browsers support this feature.

   Since you can place so many other HTML elements inside a form, you'll often find it easier to insert the form first, and then add tables, graphics, text, and form objects later.

4. **If it isn't already selected, click the red line to select the form.**

   This step not only selects the form; it highlights everything inside the red lines, too. The Properties panel displays the Form ID ("reservation" here) in the upper-left corner, as shown in Figure 16-3.

FIGURE 16-3

*If you find selecting a form
by its thin red line hard,
click inside the form and
then, in the Tag Selector,
click the <form> tag
(circled). Unless you're
creating a search form,
you'll want to send data
to a processing server
using the Post method of
transmission; step 7 has
the details.*

5. **Type a name for your form into the Form ID box.**

   This step is optional. Dreamweaver supplies a generic ID, *form1*. The name doesn't
   appear anywhere on the page, so you can leave the default name if you wish.
   However, a descriptive name is useful if you need to identify the form later, and
   you might want to add one to your CSS or JavaScript code. For example, if you
   have two forms on a page, a descriptive name makes it easier to remember the
   difference between them.

   > **TIP** The "Title" attribute is another optional naming device. In most browsers, text you enter in the Title box
   > appears as a pop-up tooltip when a visitor points to the form.

6. **In the Action box, type a URL, or select a file by clicking 📁.**

   Your mission here is to specify the location of the program that processes the
   form. If someone else is responsible for the programming, ask that person what
   to enter here. It's a standard web address—either an absolute URL (one that
   begins with *http://*) or the path to the server's form-processing program (see
   page 178 for more on these different kinds of links).

   Either way, the filename you add to the Action box *doesn't* end in *.html*. The
   path might be, for example, *../scripts/mail-form.php*. In this case, the .php extension indicates a program written in the PHP programming language. Other
   common file extensions for web programs include .cfm (for ColdFusion Markup
   Language), .aspx (.NET pages), .jsp (Java Server Pages), or .cgi (CGI programs).

7. **Using the Method pop-up menu, specify how you want a browser to transmit
   the form data to the processing program (see Figure 16-3).**

   Basically, browsers can transmit form data to a web server two ways. You'll
   use the more common method, called Post, most often. It sends form data in

two steps. First, the browser contacts the form-processing program at the web address you specified in step 6, and then it sends that data to the server. This method gives your data a bit more security, and it can easily handle forms with lots of information.

The Get method, on the other hand, adds the form data to the destination URL, like this: *http://search.yahoo.com/search?p=dogs*. (Even though the Get method *sends* data, it's named Get because its purpose in life is to *receive* information—such as the results of a search.) The characters following the *?* represent the form data. This code submits a single form element named *p*, with the value *dogs*, to the server. If a form has lots of text boxes, radio buttons, and checkboxes, a Get URL can become extremely long. Some servers can't handle very long URLs, so don't use the Get method if your forms collect a lot of data.

> **NOTE** The Get method has one big benefit: You can *bookmark* it, which is great if you want to save and reuse a Google search, for example, or you want to send someone Google Maps driving directions, or a list of Dreamweaver books you searched for on Amazon. The reusability of bookmarks is the reason search engines use the Get method for form submissions.

8. **If you're using frames, select a Target option.**

   You'll most likely skip this menu. Frames are *so* 1998 web design that they pose serious problems for today's web designers and search engines. But even if you don't use frames, you can choose the "_blank" option to display the data collected by the form in a new browser window. (See page 191 for more on the Target property.)

9. **Select an encoding type, if you like.**

   You usually don't have to select anything from the Enctype menu. Leaving the encoding type set to Default is almost always correct, and it's the same as selecting the much more long-winded "application/x-www-form-urlencoded" option.

   But if you use a File box in your form (see page 677) so visitors can upload files to your site, you should select the "multipart/form-data" option, a special Internet protocol that encodes the file for transmission and then reassembles it after it reaches the web server. In fact, Dreamweaver automatically selects this setting when you add a File box to a form. See the box below for more on potential problems with File boxes in forms.

   You've laid the foundation for your form. Now you're ready to add the controls—menus, checkboxes, and so on.

■ Adding Form Elements

Unless you've never used a computer before, the elements of an HTML form should look familiar (Figure 16-4): text boxes where people type in information (names, addresses, phone numbers, and so on), checkboxes for making multiple-choice selections, and menus for picking items from a list. The Insert panel's Forms category lets you create all these elements and more.

FREQUENTLY ASKED QUESTION

Using a Form to Upload Files

I want to let visitors upload photos to my site, but when I include a File box in one of my forms, I get an error message from the server when I try to submit the form. Why?

To upload files from a web page, you need to do two things: Change the encoding method to "multipart/form-data" (see step 9 above) and set up your server to receive files. Dreamweaver automatically takes care of the first part. Whenever you insert a File box, it changes the form's encoding method to "multipart/form-data."

The second part is up to you (or your web hosting company). Many web servers have this option turned off for security reasons. Check to see if your web host lets you use forms to upload files to your server. If it doesn't, find a hosting company that does.

In addition, you have to tell the form-processing program to accept data in the "multipart/form-data" format. Since this task is challenging, you might want to enlist some help. The box on page 679 provides several resources for commercial Dreamweaver extensions.

If you decide that's too much trouble and delete the File box, you're still in trouble. Dreamweaver doesn't reset the encoding method to the original "application/x-www-form-urlencoded," so when visitors try to submit the form (even without the File box), they get a nasty error message from the server. You must remedy the situation manually, by selecting the form and using the Properties panel to change the encoding method back to "application/x-www-form-urlencoded."

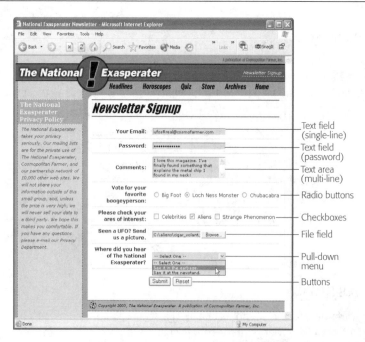

FIGURE 16-4

Forms collect information using a variety of form elements, like text boxes, password boxes, and pull-down menus. You can even add a file box so visitors can upload files to your site.

The elements you insert into a form have many things in common. The example below uses a basic text box—the second item in the Form category of the Insert panel—to walk you through the common features.

> **TIP** As an alternative to using the Insert panel, you can use the Insert→Form command and its submenus (for example, Insert→Form→Text Field). It lets you tap the same form elements as are on the Insert panel. However, the order of the elements differs between the two, so it's a good idea to choose one method and stick with it.

Setting Form Element Properties

No matter the specific type of element, adding form elements to your document always involves the same steps:

1. **In Design view, insert a form (Insert→Form→Form).**

   If the page already has a form, click inside its red border.

2. **In the Insert panel's Forms category, click Text.**

   One click adds two elements to the form on your web page: the blank box for the text and a label that displays the words "Text Field" followed by a colon. The text box remains selected after you add it to the form, so you see its properties in the Properties panel (Figure 16-5). They include Name, Value, Class, Title, Form, and Tab Index. You'll find these properties for many (but not all) of the form elements. It's worth taking a little closer look at the function of each:

   — **Name.** When you first add a form element, Dreamweaver gives it a generic name, like *textfield*. Add a second text element, and you end up with *textfield2*. That's not very helpful, so you'll want to rename elements as you create them. Be sure to follow the same naming conventions you use for CSS ID names: Begin with a letter; use only numbers, letters, hyphens, or underscores; and skip spaces, punctuation, and other characters. Depending on its purpose in life, you might want to change the *textbox* name to something like *city*, *first-name*, or *search_words*. The name you give an element serves two purposes. It's both the identifying name for the form element and the element's ID. When a web server processes a form, it works with name/value pairs. The name you type here is available later, when you process the form. For example, *numberGuests=24* is easier to understand than *textfield2=24*. As usual, the ID identifies a unique element on a page. For example, you can use the ID as a selector in CSS Designer to format the text box.

   — **Value.** The primary purpose of forms is to deliver name/value pairs to a program that processes the information and does something useful with it, like order airline tickets. Text boxes, URL boxes, password elements, radio buttons, and most other form elements have a value. It's the information your visitor provides when she types in text, clicks a button, or chooses an item from a drop-down menu. As the form designer, you can provide an initial value for an element. For example, a text box labeled "My favorite baseball team" could be set to "San Francisco Giants." Visitors would type in something else if they disagree.

— **Class.** The Properties panel also displays a class name for many elements. If your form is inside another page element, like a <div> or <body> tag that has a class applied to it, Dreamweaver displays the class name in the Class menu. As usual, you'll use the class as a selector to apply CSS formatting, but for forms, the class isn't as vital to the form's function as the ID is. That's because forms need to send unique pieces of information, like a guest's name and address, to form-processing programs, and the way to identify a unique piece of information in a web page is with an ID, which you can use only once per page.

— **Title.** In most browsers, text you enter in the Title box appears as a pop-up tooltip when a visitor points to the form element. Screen readers audibly say these words for web visitors when the focus is on the element.

— **Form.** This is a newer HTML5 property that connects a form element with a particular form. Using this property, you can put a form element outside of the form's red border but still associate it with the form. Browser support for this feature is still hit or miss, so it's best to stick with the old ways. Put your form elements into a form.

— **Tab Index.** When visitors enter data in a form, their hands are on the keyboard much of the time. Most savvy computerists know they can hit the Tab key to move from one form element to the next. As a web designer, you can control the order of that journey using Tab Index numbers. Suppose your form has street, city, state, and postal code text boxes. Assign tab index numbers like this:

Street, 3
City, 4
State, 5
Postal code, 6

Each press of the Tab key takes your web visitors to the next logical box. That said, you may not need to manually type in a value for each form element. Even if you don't provide a Tab Index value, web browsers still move the focus from one element to the next. If you arrange your form elements in a fairly logical left-to-right, top-to-bottom order, most browsers handle it well. So it makes sense to build your form and add its elements at the same time. Then test Tab key navigation with a few browsers. If you're not happy with the results, it's time to set the Tab Index property for each element.

3. **In the Name box of the Properties panel, type *first-name*.**

This name appears in the name/value pair that goes to your web server for processing. Dreamweaver simultaneously sets the element's ID to *first-name*.

FIGURE 16-5

When you select a form element, the Properties panel displays its attributes. Many elements have Name, Value, Class, Title, Form, and Tab Index properties. It's not necessary to set properties for every little box in the panel, but it's always a good idea to change their names to something descriptive. For accessibility purposes, you should always add a title in the Title box.

4. **In Design view, select the label's text (Text Field:) and change it to describe the form element. For example, type** *First Name:*.

   The label's text appears on your web page, telling visitors what type of information they should type in. Depending on the tone and style of your site, you can be long-winded and folksy, or terse and businesslike. Editing the label is no different from editing any other text on your web page. Labels differ from ordinary text in that you associate labels with a particular form element. The Text Field label is associated with the first-name text box. If you click the "First Name" text and then click <label> in the Tag Selector at the bottom of the document window, you see the For property in the Properties panel, with the menu set to "first-name." When you first inserted your text box, it was named "textfield" and the label's For property was set to textfield. When you renamed the text box, Dreamweaver cleverly updated the label's For property to "first-name."

   Click the Source Code button, and you see that the underlying code for your label and text field looks like this:

   ```
   <label for="first-name">First Name:</label>
   <input name="first-name" type="text" id="first-name">
   ```

   The label comes before the "input" (text) box in the HTML, just as it appears on the page. Both elements are independent, the only link between them being the attribute in the label tag, *for="first-name"*. Dreamweaver sets both the name and ID of the tag to "first-name." (For a closer look at the HTML underlying form elements, see the box on page 662.) So, if labels are just text on a page, what's the big fuss about associating a label with a specific form element? One good reason is that screen readers can audibly identify form elements whose labels use the For property.

NOTE Sometimes you don't need or want a label. In those cases, Dreamweaver doesn't automatically create them. HTML's buttons, like Submit or Reset, are an example—the name you gave the button also serves as its label.

5. **In the Properties panel's Title box, type an explanatory message, like "Please type in your first name."**

   The words in this box appear as a tooltip when someone points to the form element. Screen readers say these words aloud to web visitors.

6. **Optionally, in the Properties panel's Tab Index box, type a number.**

   The Tab Index lets you number each element in your form and, in the process, sets the focus order for the elements as a visitor presses the Tab key.

7. **Optionally, set the Properties panel's Form menu (Figure 16-6) to identify a specific form on the page. The drop-down menu lists the names of any forms on the page.**

   Using this feature, you can place form elements outside a form's border. However, as explained in the bullet point on page 658, this feature is still a gem in the rough because not all web browsers support it.

Each form element has different properties, suited for its specific function, as you can see in Figure 16-6. The good news is that you can always use the Properties panel as command central to set up the form elements to retrieve just the information you need from your visitors. The next sections focus on the settings for different form elements.

FIGURE 16-6

The Properties panel looks slightly different depending on the type of form element you choose. The Text Area form element (top) handles large amounts of text, like comments or (gasp!) complaints. When you place the Select form element (bottom) on a page, visitors choose from a set of predefined menu options.

Many elements have properties in common, and you can see that in the four identical checkboxes in the lower-left corner of the Properties panel. Here's how each option works:

- **Disabled**. This grays out the text box and prevents visitors from clicking into it, or even selecting any text that's already there (from the Value property discussed above). In addition, when you disable an element, a browser doesn't submit that element's data when it submits the completed form. So, you may ask, why have an unusable element that doesn't provide information when the form is processed? JavaScript turns this property on and off based on what your visitor does. For example, you might have a Spouse's Name box disabled until someone checks a Married box.

- **Required**. Turn on the Required property to make sure someone provides information in a text box. If you require a piece of info and the guest doesn't provide it, the page won't send the form data to your web server. Instead, your visitor sees a prompt asking him to complete the form. Sadly, browser support for this helpful property is mixed. It doesn't work in Safari or Internet Explorer 9 and earlier.

- **Auto Complete**. We all get tired of entering the same information over and over into forms. Auto Complete helps alleviate this annoyance. When you turn Auto Complete on for a form element, the web browser anticipates the response. For example, if you name the element "Email," the browser prompts the visitor with a list of email addresses she's entered into similar boxes.

- **Auto Focus**. Nope, this doesn't have anything to do with camera lenses. In form-speak, the term *focus* means a page element is selected and ready for input. So if your guest's cursor is blinking in the Last Name box, the Last Name box has the focus. Using the Auto Focus property, you can give a particular form element focus when a browser loads the page.

- **Read-only**. The Read-only option lets a visitor select and copy anything in the text box but doesn't let him change it. Since forms are meant to collect information from visitors, it's best not to taunt them with uneditable boxes.

The Datalist Form Element

Another property you can use with many form elements is the *datalist*. Just as its name implies, a datalist stores a set of answers to a question on a form—when a guest goes to reply to the question, the datalist pops up, displaying common responses. Your visitor can then select from the answers.

HTML already gives you several ways to elicit answers in a form—checkboxes (page 671), radio buttons (page 673), and menus (page 675). HTML5 adds the datalist option for text boxes and many of the new form elements, like Number, Range, and Color.

Suppose you ask guests to name their favorite sport. Normally, you'd just give them an empty text box to fill in, where they'd type *football*, *biking*, or *fly fishing*. But by using a datalist, you can suggest answers and save them some typing at the same time.

Forms' Chameleon: The <input> Tag

Form elements have many properties in common, as explained in this chapter. Most have another, somewhat surprising feature in common: the HTML <input> tag. Your web page creates text boxes, checkboxes, radio buttons, pull-down menus, and even the Submit button using the <input> tag. So why do they all look so different? That's the job of the "type" attribute in a form element—it lets you select different versions of the same "type" of element, such as the text box. For example, a text box's input tag might look like this:

```
<input type="text" name="first-name"
id="first-name">
```

While the input tag for a radio button looks like this:

```
<input type="radio" name="delivery"
id="delivery" value="UPS">
```

As the examples show, there are no closing input tags. Everything input elements need is between the opening and closing angle brackets. Simply changing the *type* attribute gives a form element an entirely different look and way of functioning. The first 16 form elements in the Insert panel's Form category are

text boxes at their core. By using different "types," such as *email, url, color,* or *date,* they look different in a browser. For example, when a visitor needs to select a color, the Chrome browser displays a swatch and a color-picker. Similarly, it displays a pick-a-date calendar when a visitor needs to type in a date. Less savvy web browsers simply show a text box where the guest has to manually type in a response.

Both the File form element and the Image element (type="image") use the <input> tag, but with different type attributes. All three "buttons" (a label-free button and the Submit and Reset buttons) in the Form category of the Insert panel use the input tag, but they all have different type attributes: *button, submit,* and *reset.*

While most form elements share the <input> tag, there are some exceptions. The Text Area element, used to handle large quantities of text, has its own tag, <textarea>. The Label element doesn't store data for processing, so it's not considered an input element. It has one attribute (for="formelement"), used to associate the label with a specific form element.

You follow two steps to add a datalist to a form element. First, you need to build the list, and then you need to tell the element the name of the list you want it to use. You can use the same list with more than one element in a form. For example, if you sold football caps, jerseys, and jackets with team names on them, you could create one datalist with the names and use it for each of the products.

Right now, the only way to build a list in Dreamweaver CC is by writing the code in Code view. Fortunately, it's pretty simple. You begin with an opening tag that includes an ID so you can associate a form element with an answer set, say *<datalist id="sportlist">*. You close your list with a typical closing tag, *</datalist>*. In between the tags, you provide possible answers, like this:

```
<datalist id="sportlist">
    <option value="Fly Fishing">
    <option value="Baseball">
    <option value="Biking">
    <option value="Football">
    <option value="Soccer">
</datalist>
```

The value in quotes is what actually appears in the list on your form.

Once you write the code for your datalist, you can use it with a form element. Select an element like a text box and check out its properties in the Properties panel. In the lower-right corner, click the drop-down List menu shown in Figure 16-7. (Dreamweaver calls a datalist a list in the Properties panel, but it's also known as a datalist because it uses the new HTML5 <datalist> tag.) Dreamweaver displays the names of any datalists you created in the web page. Select the name of the list you want to use, and your datalist work is done.

To test the list, choose File→Preview in Browser. Recent versions of Chrome, Firefox, Internet Explorer, and Opera support datalists. Safari and older browsers don't, so they treat form elements that use a datalist as ordinary text boxes. That means visitors who have older browsers will need to fill in the blanks themselves, without the help of a list.

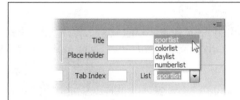

FIGURE 16-7

After you create a datalist, you can use it with form elements like text boxes. Here you've selected an element in Design view. Open the drop-down List menu in the lower-right corner, and Dreamweaver displays all the datalists you've stored on this web page.

The Text Form Element

To collect a specific piece of information, like a person's name, city, or brand of tooth-paste, use a text box (shown in Figure 16-4). Text boxes accept typed responses, and they're great for open-ended questions. They take up just a single line on a form, and they give rise to a variety of form elements that collect information, like phone numbers, web addresses, ordinal numbers, or dates (see page 668). You can also choose the Password form element, which hides your keystrokes from snooping eyes as you type in your passcode. And if you want visitors to supply a lengthy, multiline freeform response, use the Text Area element (page 665).

All these examples are just variations on the text box theme. You'll learn more about text boxes at the end of this section.

Once you insert a text box, you can adjust the following settings in the Properties panel:

- **Size**. Dreamweaver measures the width of a text box in characters, so if you type *20* for the size setting, the program creates a box that holds 20 typed letters. If someone enters more than 20 characters, they won't see them all. Be aware, however, that the *physical* width of the box (how many inches or pixels wide it is) can vary from browser to browser. (You can use Cascading Style Sheets to set an exact width using the *width* property, as described on page 464.)

- **Max Length**. This setting lets you limit the number of characters a box accepts. It's a good way to ensure that guests type in the right information in the right place. For instance, if you ask for a visitor's age, odds are you don't need to allot more than three characters; very few 1,000-year-olds surf the Web these days (and those who do don't like to reveal their ages).

- **Place Holder**. Use this option to suggest a response. The words initially appear in the text box, but they disappear when someone clicks in the box to start typing. If your visitors don't enter any new information, your server doesn't consider the placeholder text a value when it processes the form.

- **Pattern**. Use the Pattern option to ensure that guests type in a valid response. In other words, you can specify acceptable answers in the Pattern property. The challenge of this property is that it requires *regular expressions*, a geeky shorthand used to describe valid responses. For example, here's a Pattern attribute that has a regular expression inside the quotes:

```
pattern="[A-Za-z]{2}"
```

The letters in the brackets specify that your visitor must type upper- or lower-case letters only. The number in the curly brackets specifies that they can enter a maximum of two characters.

That's a simple example, but regular expressions get complicated pretty quickly. Entire books explain how to use regular expressions. If you're looking for a good reference, get hold of *Mastering Regular Expressions*, Third Edition (O'Reilly). To see a complete list of regular-expression characters that Dreamweaver understands, as well as a brief tutorial on regular expressions, visit *http://tinyurl. com/3zw4oj6*. For an online reference, check out the Regular Expression Library at *http://regexlib.com*.

The Label Form Element

As explained on page 659, the <label> tag lets you associate a label, like "First name:", with a particular form element, like a text box. Labels don't store information, so web servers don't process them. When you add a form element to a page, Dreamweaver includes a label and automatically associates the label with the element using the *for* property. For example, a label for a textfield named "diner" looks like this:

```
<label for="diner" class="label">Your name:</label>
```

The part that reads *for = "diner"* associates the label with the form element named "diner." The words "Your name:" appear in the form. Of course, you can always use plain text as a label, but an associated label helps people who use assistive technologies, like screen-reading software, understand the function and layout of your form.

> **NOTE** Labels also make forms more usable. By adding a <label> tag to a checkbox, for example, a visitor can reply by clicking either the checkbox itself or the label next to it, extending the "clickable" region. Likewise, clicking a label on a text box places your visitor's cursor inside the box so she can start typing.

In the case of text boxes, the label precedes the element. In other cases, like check-boxes and radio buttons, the label comes after the element. Either way, you can move a label to a different position without breaking the connection between the label and the element, because the label's *for* property handles that association.

In most cases, you won't need to change the *for* property because Dreamweaver automatically sets up the association between an element and its label when you add the element. If you change the name of the element, the *for* drop-down list reflects the new name. For example, if you change the Dreamweaver-supplied name for a text box, "textfield," to "first-name," the *for* property lists "first-name" for the element.

Even so, for those rare moments when you do need to change the *for* property, here's how: First, select the label by clicking its text. Then click the <label> tag in the Tag Selector and find the For property in the Properties panel. Click the *for* drop-down menu and choose the label whose name you want to change. Then, in either Split or Code view, find the label. In your source code, a label with its For property looks like this:

```
<label for="sport">What's your favorite sport?</label>
```

The attribute *for="sport"* handles the association between the label and the form element. To rename the element, select the text between the quotation marks and type away.

The Password Form Element

The Password form element is similar to the Text box element, but it conceals the text a guest types, usually displaying big dots instead of characters. The purpose is to keep the folks at your favorite cafe from learning how to log into your bank account. As a form designer, you can set the size (width) and the maximum length of the element when you create it. The password box takes up a single line, like the text box does. You set the viewable width of the box by typing a value in the Size property, so if you set Size to *20*, the box can show 20 characters. To limit the number of characters your visitors can type into a password box, type a number in the Max Length property.

The Text Area Form Element

Like text boxes, the Text Area element accepts text your guests type in. The difference is that the Text Area element is designed to accommodate large amounts of text. Use it when you ask visitors to submit a short story or to explain why they're returning an item. The text area box handles multiple lines of copy and automatically sprouts a scroll bar when necessary. In many browsers, your visitor can drag the lower-right corner of the text box to resize it on the screen, making it easier to type in his rant.

As with other form elements, use the Max Length box to limit the number of characters a guest can type in. Beyond that, the Text Area element has some unique properties:

- **Rows and Cols**. When you design your form, you set the size of the text area box using the Rows and Cols properties. You aren't creating rows and columns as you would in a spreadsheet, you're just specifying the height (Rows) and width (Cols) of the box, using characters as the unit of measure. So a modest-sized box might be 10 rows high and 50 columns wide.

- **Wrap**. This property determines whether a form stores text as a single string of characters or whether it breaks it up using line breaks (a.k.a. *newline characters*). Most of the time, you want to leave the Wrap menu on its factory setting, the Soft option, which means the form stores text as one long line of characters. When your server processes that text or opens it in a program like Word, that program decides how to display multiline text. The other option, Hard, inserts line breaks so that the text fits in the text area box. Usually, that's not how you want it on the processing end.

The Email, Number, Date, and Other Special Form Elements

It's not surprising that forms on many sites ask for the same type of information: phone numbers, email addresses, website addresses, and so on. HTML5 has a slew of text elements specifically designed to collect certain types of information. Sure, you could use a plain, old-fashioned text box, but HTML5's new input-specific form elements have advantages for guests and for you.

Your guests benefit because browsers can prompt them for the right information. For example, when Google Chrome finds the Date form element on a web page, it displays a calendar so visitors can just click a date rather than type it in. There are some great tools for the other form elements too, when it comes to choosing numbers, times, and colors. Input-specific form elements help guests using smartphones and tablets, too. When you use the *email* or *url* input type in your forms, visitors on iPhones see extra, helpful keys like @ and *.com* on their screen-based keyboards.

The advantage to you as a web developer is that you receive the data you want in usable form. Web browsers that recognize input-specific elements check your visitor's entries when he clicks the Submit button. If he hasn't provided information in the proper format, your web server won't process the form. It stays onscreen, usually with a message explaining the problem.

Unfortunately, there are still lots of browsers that don't support many input-specific elements. When a browser doesn't recognize an element, like the Time element, it displays a simple text box, ready for input. That's just the way browsers work. For example, if a browser sees this in your code:

```
<input type="mysterious" id="dunno">
```

It automatically becomes a text box. You can draw two conclusions from this. First, there's no downside to using input-specific form elements. Some of your guests will see and use the data-collecting widgets, while others will see a text box where they supply info the old-fashioned way—by typing it in. Second, you need to do everything you can to make it clear what information you want from your guests. The tools for doing that include labels, explanatory text, titles, and placeholders. For example, if you want visitors to format the date a certain way, like January 1, 2015, you should specify that in the label's text or in the Date element's Place Holder property.

Here's a rundown on the different input types available in Dreamweaver:

- **Email**. Surprise! This element is designed for email addresses, like *sol@soylent-greencafe.com*. For the convenience of your visitors, turn on the Auto Complete checkbox. Then, as they type the first few letters of the email address they always use to answer this question, they'll be prompted with the full address. As with all input-specific elements, you don't have to turn on validation. Browsers that recognize the element will check a visitor's answer when she presses Submit. They won't actually check to see if the email address exists, but they will check details. For example, email addresses should have an @ symbol and a period, and should be absent spaces or strange characters. Browsers won't send the form to your web server until the email address passes format muster. Instead, a message like the one in Figure 16-8 appears.

FIGURE 16-8

Firefox, Chrome, and Internet Explorer pop up a message like this if someone enters something other than an email address in an email form element. Web browsers that don't recognize the email element simply treat it as a text box.

- **URL**. The form element for web addresses works a lot like the one for email. It checks to make sure the URL looks like a web address, complete with *http://* at the front.

- **Tel**. The Tel element is intended to validate telephone numbers. If you've ever made a phone call outside your own country, you're probably aware that the number formats vary a lot. So it may come as no surprise that none of the major browsers support this input-specific option. Still, it doesn't hurt to use this element in your pages. Browsers will treat it as a text box until the day they begin to validate phone numbers.

- **Search**. Add a Search element to your page instead of a simple text box for your search term, and Chrome and Safari display an input box that looks like the operating system's search tool. You even get an "x" button on the right end to clear the box for a new entry. Don't get too excited, though. If you want to provide true search features, you or your programmer need to provide the form-processing functions for it. It's likely that as time goes on more browsers will recognize the Search element, so this is a form element to keep your eye on. Search is such a basic function on the web that, in the future, there will be more ways to tie this element into Google and other search engines.

- **Number**. The Number form element ensures that you get just the information you need from your guests. In the Properties panel, you can set a minimum, maximum, and step value for the number. Suppose that, for example, you sell LED lightbulbs at 5-, 10-, 15-, 20-, 25-, and 30-watt options. Set *Min* to *5*, *Max* to *30*, and *Step* to *5*. Visitors use the Number element on your site (a box with up and down arrows in it called *spinarrows*) to select a value. They can type in other values, but number-savvy browsers will display an error message when the guest submits the form. Most recent browsers, except Firefox, support the Number form element, so it's well worth using on your web pages starting today.

- **Range**. The Range element appears as a slider in browsers that support it. Sliders are great because they give people a visual way to adjust a value. You can set the same properties for the Range element as you do for the Number element: Min, Max, and Step.

  The biggest problem with the HTML5 Range element is that it doesn't automatically display a value when your visitor adjusts the slider, making it useless for most jobs unless you're willing to roll up your JavaScript/jQuery programming sleeves and head over to Code view. Before you make that journey, however, check out working examples of the range element and the necessary jQuery code at (*http://tinyurl.com/3ta7ejw*).

- **Color**. If you're selling iPhones, kitchen mixers, or Porsches, your customers need a way to choose the color they want. The Color form element can help. Sadly, as this book went to press, only recent versions of Chrome, Firefox, and Opera recognize the element. In other browsers, your visitors see a simple text box. So, until more browsers catch up with the Color element, you may be better off using radio buttons (described on page 673) to provide color options. In the browsers that support color input, visitors see a color swatch like the one at the top of Figure 16-9. You should provide a label that prompts them to select a color (something like "Click the swatch to choose a color"). You'll also want to set a color in the Value property; otherwise, the swatch is black.

  When your guest clicks the swatch, the browser opens her operating system's color-picker. One of the best things about the Color element is that it works well with the datalist option mentioned on page 661. If you're selling Porsches in a limited number of colors, you can provide color swatches by creating a datalist.

- **Date**. The Date element works well in browsers that support it. Pop it into a page, and Chrome, for example, displays a text box with a prompt that looks like this: mm/dd/yyyy (see Figure 16-10). That lets visitors know the format you expect for a date. It gets better. Chrome displays spinner arrows on the right side of the box. So, for example, when your guest wants to type in a month, he can use the spinner to choose a number between 1 and 12. The spinner shows only valid numbers, and it gracefully rolls over from the maximum value to the minimum value and vice versa. But, as the infomercial folks say, "Wait! There's more!" Click the arrow at the very end of the box to open a date-picker calendar, where it's easy to browse from month to month and choose a specific date. Current versions of Chrome, Safari, and Opera support the Date element. They also support the elements for Month and Week (see the next bullet points).

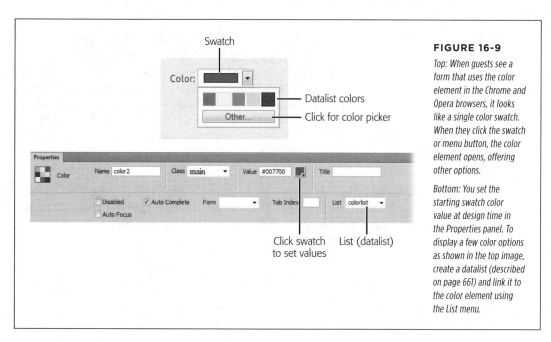

FIGURE 16-9

Top: When guests see a form that uses the color element in the Chrome and Opera browsers, it looks like a single color swatch. When they click the swatch or menu button, the color element opens, offering other options.

Bottom: You set the starting swatch color value at design time in the Properties panel. To display a few color options as shown in the top image, create a datalist (described on page 661) and link it to the color element using the List menu.

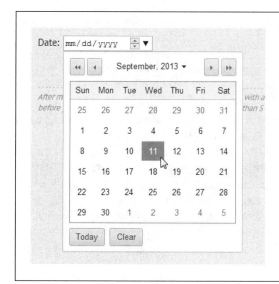

FIGURE 16-10

If your website is in the business of making appointments, your guests will love the Date element for web forms. To specify a date, they just choose from a pop-up calendar. The Date element ensures that, when your guest submits a date-containing form, the date is in a format that web servers understand.

- **Month**. The Month element works like the Date element above, except that it lets your guests select a month rather than an individual day.

- **Week**. Selecting a week is probably a lot less common than choosing a specific day or month, but when you need it, you can find this element on your trusty Insert panel.

- **Time**. Need the time? Put the Time element in your form and visitors can dial up a specific hour before they submit the form. Browsers display the time as hours, minutes, and AM or PM. In the Properties panel, Dreamweaver lets you set Min, Max, and Step values. So, for example, if you're creating a form for a dentist's office, you can choose hours between 8:00 a.m. and 6:00 p.m. in hourly increments. To give visitors a choice of times that don't fall neatly into regular intervals, the "step" option won't work. In that case, create a datalist as described on page 661. Then, in the Properties panel, set the List property to the name of the datalist.

- **Date Time**. The Date Time element simply combines the functions of the Date and Time elements into one. The Date Time element also lets your guest select a time zone, such as Pacific or Mountain. His browser sends the date/time value to your server as a single name/value element. Current versions of Safari and Opera support this element.

- **Date Time Local**. This element works like Date Time except that visitors can't specify a time zone. So Date Time Local works well if you and your guest are in the same general neighborhood. Current versions of Chrome, Safari, and Opera support this element.

FREQUENTLY ASKED QUESTION

Using the Password Box for Credit Card Numbers

Can I use the Password box for credit card numbers and other sensitive information?

Yes, but it doesn't give the information any extra security.

The Password box does one thing: It hides what people type into it. Someone looking over your shoulder can't read what you're typing—it looks like a bunch of dots—but once a browser submits that information over the Internet, it's unprotected.

To provide real security for form information, you need an encrypted connection between your web server and your visitor's computer. Most website creators use SSL (Secure Socket Layer) technology for this purpose. You can identify a site using SSL by its web address, which always begins with *https://*. The

"s" stands for "secure," and browsers usually indicate a secure connection by displaying a padlock icon at the top or bottom of the browser window.

Web browsers understand SSL, but your web server must be specially configured to work with it. Contact your web host to see if its servers support SSL (the answer is usually yes). If so, it can tell you where to put your files and how to manage them from a browser. You don't have to make any special changes to your web pages, and once the secure server is set up, you transfer your web pages to it just as you would for a non-secure website (Chapter 20 covers moving your files onto the Web).

The Checkboxes and Checkbox Group Form Elements

Checkboxes (see Figure 16-4) are simple and to the point; a guest either checks them or not. They can come solo or in groups. For example, you'll often see a single checkbox when you register with a website—"By checking this box you agree to our terms and conditions." But you can also find grouped checkboxes for questions that can have more than one answer. Suppose you offer visitors their choice of three email newsletters. In your form, you might include some text—"Check the boxes for the newsletters you want to receive"—and three corresponding checkboxes with labels that indicate the names of each newsletter.

Once you add a checkbox to a form, you can set its options in the Properties panel (see Figure 16-11):

- **Checked**. If you like, you can have a checkbox already filled in when your web page loads. You've probably seen this if you've ever signed up for something on a commercial site. There's usually a checkbox—already checked—near the bottom of the form with fine print like this: "Check here if you want to get daily, unsolicited email from our marketing department."

- **Value**. This is the information a browser sends to your form-processing program when a visitor selects a checkbox. Since visitors never actually see this information, it doesn't have to match the checkbox's label; it could transmit a coded response.

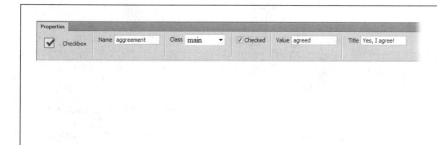

FIGURE 16-11

The Value property defines a checkbox's actual value—that is, the information it sends to your form-processing web server when a guest submits the form.

Checkboxes don't have to come in groups, but they often do. Dreamweaver includes an element to make inserting multiple checkboxes easier, as discussed next.

■ CHECKBOX GROUPS

Checkboxes can travel in groups if you ask a question with more than one possible answer, like "What activities do you like? Check all that apply." Here's how you set up a checkbox group.

1. **On the Insert panel, click the Checkbox Group button near the bottom of the list of form elements.**

   Dreamweaver opens the Checkbox Group window (see Figure 16-12).

FIGURE 16-12

The Checkbox Group dialog box lets you quickly add multiple checkboxes to a page.

2. **In the Name box, type a name.**

   This name applies to all the checkboxes in the group, saving you the trouble of typing in the same name for each checkbox. (To see how Dreamweaver differentiates checkboxes when they all have the same name, see the box on page 673.) The name you type is the name the browser submits to your web server, so follow the formatting rules for naming form elements: letters and numbers only, no spaces or funny characters except underscores and hyphens. Although each checkbox shares the same name, Dreamweaver treats them individually—if someone selects multiple checkboxes, the browser sends the data from *all* the checked boxes to the server.

3. **In the Label column, click Checkbox and then type in a label for the first box.**

   For example, if you add a set of checkboxes so visitors can sign up for one or more newsletters, you might type the name of the newsletter here—"Design Newsletter," for example. This label will appear next to the checkbox.

   NOTE If you use the Checkbox Group element, Dreamweaver places the element inside the label's beginning and ending tags. (See the code in the box on page 673.) This is valid HTML, but it's difficult for screen readers to decipher, so you may want to skip the Checkbox Group element and just insert checkboxes one at a time.

4. **Hit the Tab key to jump to the Value column for that checkbox, and then type in a value.**

   This is the value the browser passes to the web server when somebody selects the checkbox and submits the form—for example, the value for the Design Newsletter might be "design."

5. **Repeat steps 3–4 for the second checkbox in the group.**

   You can create additional checkboxes by clicking + . Follow steps 3 and 4 for each checkbox you add.

6. **Select a layout for the group.**

   Dreamweaver puts each checkbox on its own line. You can choose whether you want Dreamweaver to do that using a line break (<br>) or by creating a table with one checkbox per row. Don't care for either option? Pick the "Line breaks" option—it's easier to modify—and then read the Note below.

NOTE   If you want checkboxes in a group to appear side by side instead of stacked one on top of the other, choose the "Line breaks" option in the Checkbox Group dialog box. Then, with Dreamweaver set to display the invisible line break character (see page 38), click the line break's gold shield in Design view, and hit the Backspace or Delete key to move the checkbox on the line below onto the same line as the current checkbox.

---

7. **Click OK to add the group of checkboxes to your page.**

   The checkboxes and their labels are essentially text on the screen. You can move the checkboxes around, change their labels, and, in the Properties panel, alter each checkbox's properties.

UP TO SPEED

How Dreamweaver Uniquely IDs Checkboxes

When you insert checkboxes using the Checkbox Group tool, Dreamweaver inserts all the checkboxes using the same name but gives each a unique ID. For example, if you insert two checkboxes, you might end up with HTML that looks like this:

```
<label><input type="checkbox"
name="newsletter" value="design"
id="newsletter_0" />Design newsletter
</label>
<br />
<label><input type="checkbox"name="newslet
ter" value="programming"id="newsletter_1"
/>Programming newsletter</label>
```

Notice that the two boxes have the same name—newsletter—but, since you need to uniquely identify each newsletter, Dreamweaver creates unique IDs for the checkboxes by tacking _0, _1, and so on onto the end of each ID.

It's perfectly valid to use the same name for multiple checkboxes, but keep in mind (and tell your programmer) that your browser submits the checkbox data as an *array*—a data format common to programming languages that lets you store multiple pieces of information under a single name. So a browser sends the values of all the checked boxes as a single group using the name you supplied in step 2, but also using the unique ID that Dreamweaver added.

The Radio Buttons and Radio Group Form Elements

Radio buttons, like checkboxes, are simple page elements (see Figure 16-4); they appear either selected (represented by a solid circle) or not (an empty circle).

Unlike checkboxes, radio buttons require your visitor to make a single choice from a group, just like the radio buttons on a car or the buttons on a blender. Radio buttons are ideal for multiple-choice questions that require a single answer, like "What is your income: A. $10,000–35,000, B. $35,001–70,000, C. $70,001–100,000, D. None of your business." Of course, you'd replace the letter choices here with radio buttons.

In the Properties panel, set the following options for a radio button (Figure 16-13):

- **Name**. Dreamweaver supplies the generic name *radio* (or *radio2*, *radio3*, and so on) when you insert a radio button. Make sure you change the name to something more descriptive, and, when you insert a group of related radio buttons, give them all the *same name*. Your visitors should be able to select only one button in the group. To make sure that's the case, every button in the group needs to share the same name. On the other hand, each radio button should have a different value (see the bullet point below), because that's the information sent to the program that processed the form. So, if you're selling cars, the name of a radio button group might be "color" and the individual value buttons could be "burgundy," "slate," and "forest." (They'd never be just red, gray, and green.)

FIGURE 16-13

Radio buttons let you offer visitors a choice of answers to a single question.

If, when you test your page, you notice that you can select more than one radio button at a time, you must have given them different names. (Consider using Dreamweaver's Radio Group object, described in the next section. It acts like a wizard, simplifying the process of creating groups of radio buttons.)

- **Checked**. When you create a radio-button form, you can have one of the buttons pre-checked when the page opens. To do your visitors this timesaving courtesy, turn on the Checked checkbox for the button that holds the value they'll choose most often.

Of course, if making a choice here is optional, leave all the buttons unselected by setting their initial state to Unchecked. However, once somebody *does* select a radio button, only the Reset button (if you add one) can unselect them *all* again (see page 680 to learn how to create a Reset button).

- **Value**. This is the information a browser submits to the server if your visitor selects the related button. Once again, the info doesn't have to match the button's onscreen label. If you filled out the Accessibility window's ID box, Dreamweaver uses the ID you supplied as the checked value. If you don't like it, change it here.

Finally, you should add a text description for the entire group. For example, if you use radio buttons to let visitors choose a method of payment, then your introductory text might say, "How would you like to pay for your item(s)?" There isn't any special HTML for creating a label for an entire group of buttons, so you just type the descriptive text next to the group of radio buttons.

■ **RADIO GROUP**

Although you can easily create a group of radio buttons using the Radio Button object, Dreamweaver makes it even simpler with the Radio *Group* object, a single dialog box that creates a group of radio buttons and their labels in one fell swoop. It works the same way as the Checkbox Group element discussed on page 671, except that Dreamweaver inserts radio buttons instead of checkboxes.

The Select Menus and List Form Elements

While checkboxes and radio buttons let you ask multiple-choice questions, use them when your questions offer relatively few answers. Otherwise, your form can quickly become overcrowded with buttons and boxes. And therein lies the beauty of Select drop-down menus and List form elements—they offer many choices without taking up a lot of screen space (Figure 16-14 shows an example).

FIGURE 16-14

A Select menu (left) takes up a single compact line on a page but opens up to show a list of options. The list (right) can be as long as you choose. Use the first list item to tell visitors what to do. For example, you could say, "—please select an island—" or "—Select One—".

Once you insert a menu or list object into your document, adjust its settings in the Properties panel.

• **List Values**. This is the most important setting, because it opens a dialog box where you type in the items that make up your menu or list. You specify two pieces of information for each item: a *label* (the text that appears in the menu or in the list) and a *value* (the information the form submits to the web server, which isn't necessarily the same thing as the label). To use this dialog box, type in an item label. Press Tab (or click in the Value column), and then type a value, if you like. Values are optional; if you don't specify one, the form submits the item's label *as* the value. Still, you'll often find a separate value useful. Imagine you design a pull-down menu on an e-commerce site so your visitors can select their credit cards' expiration month. Figure 16-15 shows what the items might look like. It displays the names of the months, but the form actually transmits the *number* of the month to your form-processing program—when a visitor selects April, for example, the form submits 4.

FIGURE 16-15

Using the + button, you can add items to the end of a list. When you click inside the last item's Value column, pressing Tab creates a new list item. To delete an item, select it, and then click –. You can move an item higher or lower in the list by selecting it and then clicking the up or down arrow buttons. Like radio buttons, pop-up menu items and list items always flock together—nobody ever creates a set of options with just one entry.

Computer programs often work more easily with numbers than with names, while humans do the opposite. So when you offer visitors a pop-up menu of products, the label might use the human-friendly name of the product ("Blue Wool Cap"), while the value sent to the server reflects a model number that your form-processing program readily understands (XSD1278, say).

As with other form elements, you can, and probably should, add some explanatory text alongside the menu or list in the document window. As shown in Figure 16-14, it's common to use one line in the list to explain what you want visitors to do. In that example, the item reads, "please select an island."

- **Selected**. The Selected box displays your list items. You can pick one of them to appear selected in the list when a browser loads the page.

Two properties change the look of your select menu and turn it into a list. Enter a value in the Size box or turn on the Multiple checkbox, and your menu turns into a list like the one on the right of Figure 16-14. If there are more list items than fit in the space, Dreamweaver adds a scroll bar to the list.

- **Size**. You might not guess it from the name "size," but when you place a value in this box, it changes the height of the box. Here, type in the number of lines you want the list to take up on the page. That can vary from a single line (in which case you might as well use a drop down menu) to many lines (displaying a number of choices at once). If you specify a height that's smaller than the number of items in the list, Dreamweaver adds a vertical scroll bar.

- **Multiple**. Here's a key difference between Select menus and Lists: If you turn on the Multiple option for your list, a visitor can simultaneously select more than one item from the List by pressing the Ctrl (⌘) key while clicking items. (If you choose this option, be sure your instructions tell visitors they can select multiple items.)

Giving Order to Your Forms

If you're not careful, creating forms can quickly lead to visual chaos. The different shapes and sizes of text boxes, radio buttons, and other form objects don't naturally align well with text. One solution: Use tables to control each form's appearance.

If you simply place form labels and boxes line after line, you end up with an ungainly zigzag pattern created by the differing lengths of label text and form elements. The result is not only ugly but hard to read.

To better organize a form, you can insert the <form> tag, and then insert an HTML table made of two columns and as many rows as you have form elements; one column holds the label, the other the text box (or other form element). Align the text in the first column to the right, and you'll create a clean edge that effectively mirrors the edge created by the form elements.

To make this table-based solution work most effectively, set each text box to the same width using the Size property (page 665) or the CSS Width property (page 464).

You can also use CSS to lay out a form. You'll use this technique in the tutorial starting on page 682.

The File Form Element

Receiving responses to checkboxes, radio buttons, and pull-down menus is all well and good, but what if you want your visitors to submit something a little meatier—like an entire file? Imagine a bulletin board system that lets guests post .jpg images of themselves, or upload word processing documents to share with others. Dreamweaver's File form element (Insert→Form→File), shown in Figure 16-4, can help (but not without a little magic from your web server).

Before you get carried away with the possibilities the File box offers, you need to do a little research to see whether you can use it on your site. Although Dreamweaver lets you easily *add* an element so guests can upload images, text files, and other documents, you need to check with your web host to see if it permits anonymous file uploads (some don't for fear of receiving viruses or performance-choking large files). Then, of course, you have to ensure that the program that processes the form actually *does* something with the incoming file—stores it on your server, for instance. Dreamweaver doesn't have any built-in functions that help with this back-end work, but you can enlist some third-party solutions, as described in the box on page 679.

When you click the File button on the Insert panel's Forms category (or choose Insert→Form→File), Dreamweaver inserts a text box *and* a Browse button; together, they constitute a single File form element. When you click either one, you automatically select both.

NOTE Browsers display File form elements in different ways. For example, in Firefox and Internet Explorer, the element looks like a text box with a button next to it. In Chrome and Safari, the element is simply a button with the label "Choose File" on it and, to the right of the button, either the text "No file chosen" (when the page first loads) or the name of the file you choose from your computer.

The Browse button opens the standard Windows or Macintosh Open File dialog box, letting your visitor navigate to and select the file she wants to upload.

The Properties panel offers few settings, as shown in Figure 16-16. At the very least, you want to give your File element a name and add instructions or a label in the document window, saying something like "Click the Browse button to select a file to upload."

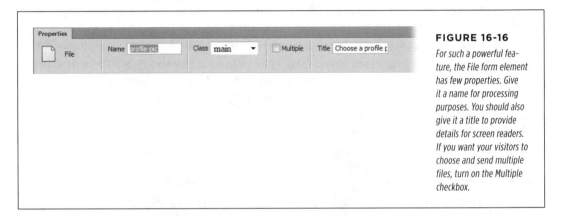

FIGURE 16-16

For such a powerful feature, the File form element has few properties. Give it a name for processing purposes. You should also give it a title to provide details for screen readers. If you want your visitors to choose and send multiple files, turn on the Multiple checkbox.

The Hidden Form Element

Most form elements are designed to accept input from your guests—the selected radio button, the text from a text box, or the choice from a menu, for example. But visitors don't even know about, and don't ever see, one kind of form element: the *hidden* element.

> **NOTE** Hidden elements aren't exactly hidden—it's true that visitors don't see them in a browser, but they (and their data) are visible if a visitor checks the page's HTML (using the browser's View→View Source or View Page Source command). In other words, despite their name, don't put anything into a hidden element that you wouldn't want someone to see.

Why, you're probably asking, would you need to submit a value you already know? Because hidden elements supply information to the programs that process forms—information that the program has no other way of knowing. Many web hosting services, for example, offer a generic form-processing program that collects information submitted with a form and emails it to the site's administrator. But how does the program know where to email the data? After all, it's a *generic* program that many other people use. The solution: A hidden element that stores the information required for the program to properly process the form—like *email=me@mydomain.com*.

To insert a hidden element, click the Insert panel's Hidden button (under the Forms category), or choose Insert→Form→Hidden. A gold shield appears on the page, Dreamweaver's symbol for HTML you can't see in web browsers. Use the Properties panel to give the box a name and a *value*—that is, the info you want the browser to submit to your form-processing program (in the example above, that would be your email address).

NOTE Gold shields indicating hidden elements appear only if, in the Preferences window's Invisible Elements category, you turn on the "Hidden form fields" checkbox (see the note on page 80), and, in the View menu, you turn on Invisible Elements (View→Visual Aids→Invisible Elements).

The Button Element

No form is complete without a Submit button so your visitors can register their choices (see Figure 16-4). Only when guests click this button do their responses set out on their way to your form-processing program. People sometimes add a Reset button, which visitors can click if they make an error; it clears all their form entries, and resets all the form elements to their original values. Dreamweaver provides a third button, a generic one that's essentially a blank canvas—it's up to you to tell it how to behave.

WORKAROUND WORKSHOP

Adding File-Upload Ability to Your Site

Imagine adding a "Job Application" page to your site, where applicants can upload their resumés for review. Or a web-based way for your clients to submit graphics files and word processing documents they want included in the pages you're building.

Dreamweaver lets you add a File element to a form, but it doesn't provide the tools you need to make this useful feature work on your site. To compensate for that glaring omission, you can turn to extensions that add this power. But before you shell out any hard-earned cash for the extensions listed next, make sure your web hosting company allows anonymous file uploads from a web form—some don't.

DMXZone (*www.dmxzone.com/index?3/1019*) offers fee-based extensions for the programming tools ASP, ASP.NET, and PHP. The Pure Upload extension offers many settings to manage the process of uploading files to a site, including the ability to rename duplicate files and to add file information to databases.

WebAssist (one of the big players in the Dreamweaver extensions market) offers a commercial product, Universal Email, for uploading *and* downloading files from a server (*http://tinyurl.com/68dj2lt*). As its name indicates, this extension also handles sending the contents of a form as an email message. This extension works for PHP pages.

You find all three buttons on the Insert panel's Forms category. Click any of them to insert it in your form. Dreamweaver doesn't include a separate label when it inserts a button, since the button itself has "Submit," "Reset," or whatever text you wish emblazoned across its face.

NOTE Like other form elements, buttons appear in your source code as <input> elements (see page 662). It's the Type attribute that dictates their function *and* their appearance. For example, the Submit button has the attribute *type="submit"*. For the Reset button, the type is "reset." The generic button's type is "button."

The Properties panel's controls (Figure 16-17) for a freshly inserted button differ depending on the button's function. The Submit button sends information to a web server, for example, so it requires properties that the Reset or generic buttons don't. All the buttons have name and value properties:

- **Name**. The button's name ("submit," "reset," and so on) provides the first half of the name/value pair that a browser sends to your server (see page 650).

- **Value**. The value is the button's label. Dreamweaver proposes *Submit*, but you're free to substitute *Buy Now, Make It So,* or *Send my data on its merry way.*

What your visitors see printed on the button—Click Me, for example—is the value a browser transmits (along with the button's name) when a guest submits the form. This characteristic opens up some interesting possibilities. You could, for example, include *several* Submit buttons, each with a different label. If you create a form that works with a database, one button might say "Delete," while another says "Edit." Depending on which button your visitor clicks, the program processing the form either deletes the record from the database or modifies it.

FIGURE 16-17

The Submit button has more properties than the Reset or even the generic button, but most of the time, the only thing you need to change is the Value. The button displays the words you put in the Value box.

The Submit button has the same properties as the Form element, but you don't need to set them for the Submit button if you already set them for the Form element, as described on page 654. Type the web address of your forms-processing program in the Form Action box. In the Form Method menu, choose between using the Get or Put methods to communicate data. And for the Form Enc Type drop-down menu, choose how you want the form info encoded when a browser sends it.

■ THE RESET BUTTON

The Reset form button resets all the form options to their original values. The text boxes, checkboxes, or menu items aren't left blank or unselected; they return to their *initial* state, which you specified when you created the control. For example, if you set the initial state of a checkbox to Checked and your visitor unchecks it and then clicks the Reset button, the box becomes checked once again.

The Reset button used to appear on nearly every form on the Web; these days it's much less frequent, mainly because it's unlikely that anyone would want to *completely* erase *everything* she's typed into a form. In addition, its presence offers the unfortunate possibility that a visitor, after painstakingly filling out a form, will mistake the Reset button for the Submit button, and click it—erasing all her work. So if you include a Reset button, it's probably best not to put it right next to the Submit button.

NOTE While Reset buttons aren't common on forms used to collect new information—"Sign up for our newsletter"—they do come in handy on a page intended to *update* information. An update form contains previously recorded information, like the shipping address for your Amazon.com account. On a form like that, the Reset button can come in handy. Say you make a mistake when you update your account information. Click the Reset button, and the form goes back to displaying the original information, like your original shipping address.

■ THE BUTTON BUTTON

The generic button you get by clicking Button in the Form category of the Insert panel doesn't trigger an action related to the form, it triggers one of Dreamweaver's built-in behaviors (see Chapter 15), like a pop-up message. It's valuable because it gives you a way to trigger many different actions, like opening a new browser window, and lets you type in a custom label that visitors see on the button. If you're a JavaScript programmer, you can also use this button to launch your own programs. For example, if you wrote a program that adds items to a website shopping cart, you can use the Button button to trigger that action.

NOTE You can use a graphic as a Submit button, too, thus freeing you to be more creative with the look of the button. That's thanks to something called an Image Button. On the Insert panel, click Image Button or choose Insert→Form→Image Button to select the graphic you want to use. When a visitor clicks the image, it submits the form and all its data. (Image buttons do only one thing: submit form data. You can't use them as a Reset button, for example.)

The Fieldset Form Element

The <fieldset> tag is a form-organization element that lets you group related form elements together. To add a fieldset, go to the Form category on the Insert panel and choose Fieldset. That creates opening and closing <fieldset> tags in your page's code. You can think of Fieldset as a box that holds other form elements. For example, if you create an online order form, you can organize all the "ship to" information—address, city, state, Zip code, and so on—as a self-contained component of the form. You'd put the form elements for these details between the opening and closing <fieldset> tags. This arrangement not only straightens out your forms, but it also helps those using assistive technology to understand the organization and intent of a form.

The <fieldset> tag also has a visual benefit: Browsers display a border around fieldsets. And, if you prefer, you can use CSS Designer to create a custom border (page 250) or background color (page 252). In addition, the <legend> tag (which Dreamweaver automatically adds whenever you insert a fieldset) lets you add a description of the fields that make up the fieldset. Dreamweaver displays the legend at the top of the set.

To use this tag, select the form elements you want to add to the fieldset in the document window. You have to position the form elements next to one another onscreen, and you can organize them within other HTML elements, like a table. Then, on the

Insert panel's Forms category, click Fieldset. In the Label window that appears, type a label (called, somewhat dramatically, a legend) for the fieldset, and then click OK.

In addition to displaying the label you type, Dreamweaver creates a simple border around the group of elements you selected. Because different browsers display this border differently, make sure you preview the page (F12 [Option-F12 on a Mac]) in a recent version of Internet Explorer, Firefox, Chrome, Safari, and Opera (page 775) to see how the label and surrounding border look.

FREQUENTLY ASKED QUESTION

Emailing Form Results

I don't want to store form submissions in a database or anything fancy like that. I just want to get an email message that includes the information a guest submits. How do I do that?

This common function—available on countless websites—may seem like an easy task, but Dreamweaver doesn't supply a tool to automate the process. Basically, you need a program to collect the data and send it off in an email message. Most web hosting companies provide just such a program. They generally work like this: You build a form, set the form's Action property (see page 683) to point to the address of the server's form-emailing program, and then add one or more hidden elements. They contain information that the program uses—your email address, for example, and the web address of the page the browser should load after it submits the form. Since this form-emailing program varies from server to server, you need to contact your hosting company for details.

Many commercial Dreamweaver extensions can help, too. Here are two that, in addition to form handling, offer much more advanced emailing features, including the ability to mass-mail newsletters to email addresses stored in a database:

- WA Universal Email ($99) from WebAssist (*http://tinyurl.com/5uhm4g4*) works for PHP pages and also supports file uploads.

- DMXZone sells both an ASP (*www.dmxzone.com/go?5578*) and a PHP (*www.dmxzone.com/go?5628*) version of its Smart Mailer extension ($46).

For all these extensions, however, your server has to support the appropriate programming language (ASP or PHP)—Part 6 of this book has more on server-side programming.

■ Tutorial: Adding Forms to Pages

In this tutorial, you'll build a simple reservation form for Cafe Soylent Green's website (skip ahead to Figure 16-29 to see the final result). To make sure the folks at the cafe get all the information they need to book a reservation, you'll use HTML5's new form elements.

> **NOTE** To complete this tutorial, you need to download the practice files from this book's Missing CD page at *http://oreilly.com/pub/missingmanuals/dreamweaverccmm2014*. (See the Note on page 37 for details.) The files you'll work on are in the Chapter16 folder (which is inside the MM_DWCC folder), and the finished project, for comparison, is in the Chapter16_complete folder.

Once you download the tutorial files and open Dreamweaver, set up a new site as described on page 23. In a nutshell, choose Site→New Site. In the Site Setup window, type *Forms* into the Site Name box. Click 📁 next to the Local Site Folder box, navigate to and select the Chapter16 folder inside the MM_DWCC folder, and then click Choose (Select). Finally, click OK.

Insert a Form

The first step in building a form is inserting the <form> tag. This tag encloses all the form's elements and indicates where the form begins and ends. As noted earlier in this chapter, you can insert other HTML elements into the form, like text blocks and <div> tags.

1. **Choose File→Open. Double-click the filename *reservation.html* in the Chapter16 folder to open it.**

   If you have the Files panel open in Dreamweaver (Window→Files), just double-click *reservation.html*. The page is partly designed. It has a banner, sidebar, and footer in it.

2. **Click the empty white space directly below the headline "Make a Reservation."**

   You're going to stake out the place on the page where you'll insert the form.

3. **On the Insert panel, select the Forms category from the drop-down menu (see Figure 16-2) and then click Form at the top of the list.**

   A red rectangle appears in the document window, indicating the boundaries of the inserted form. (The rectangle's line is dashed in Windows and solid on Macs.) In later steps, you'll insert form elements inside the form's border. First, though, you'll set the properties for the form itself.

4. **If necessary, select the form (click inside it), and then, at the bottom of the document window, use the Tag Selector to locate the <form>#form1 tag. When you do, click it.**

   When you first insert a form on your web page, Dreamweaver automatically selects it. If you click elsewhere, you deselect the form. You can select it again by clicking its red border, but that takes a bit of mouse marksmanship. The surefire way to select a form is to click inside its red border, and then choose the form using the Tag Selector. Once you select your form, Dreamweaver displays its properties in the Properties panel.

5. **In the Properties panel's ID box, type *reservation* (see Figure 16-18).**

   You just changed the form's ID from *#form1* to the more meaningful *#reservation*.

6. **In the Action box, type *http://cafesoylentgreen.com/reserve.php.***

   Leave off the period after the URL in the sentence above (we added it to make our copy editors happy).

   A form's Action property identifies the Internet address of the program that processes the form. In this case, you've been spared the effort of writing (or hiring a programmer to write) the required form-processing software. That program already exists on the website whose address you just typed in, and it's waiting to process the form you're about to design.

7. **In the Method box, make sure you see Post selected. Leave the Target and Enctype boxes set to Default.**

   The Method specifies how a form sends information to a form-processing program, and the Post option is the most common way (see page 654).

   The reservation form you're working with already includes properties that help a web server process it, but it relies on other form elements to collect information from your visitors. You'll add those elements now.

Add a Text and Email Form Element

Your guests type text in boxes, click buttons, and perform other form-filling tasks to send information to the forms-processing program. In the next steps, you'll add two form elements that get information *from* your visitors: a text box and an email box.

1. **In the document window, click inside the form—anywhere within the red lines. On the Insert panel, click the Text button or choose Insert→Form→Text.**

   Dreamweaver inserts two elements, one beside the other: a label and then, to the right of that, a text box. The label reads "Text Field," and the text box is empty.

2. **Click inside the text box.**

   There are three clues that you've selected the text box: A dotted line appears around the box, you see <input#textfield> as the last tag in the Tag Selector, and the properties for the box appear in the Properties panel.

3. **In the Name box, replace "textfield" with *diner.***

   Dreamweaver adds "diner" to both the *name* and *ID* properties of the box's HTML. The form-processing program uses the *name* property to associate the value a visitor types in (in this case, his name) with the box's ID. When a guest clicks Submit, his browser sends information to the form-processing program in what's called a name/value pair—*diner=Bob*, for instance (see page 650 for details).

The ID uniquely identifies the form element. If you want, you can create an ID style to format this particular element—for example, to assign it a width or a background color.

Next you'll tweak some form properties, and then you'll change the label text.

4. **With the diner box still selected, turn on the checkboxes in the lower-left corner for Required, Auto Complete, and Auto Focus.**

The people at the cafe aren't really picky about what their visitor types in the diner box—for example, they'll allow names like "Jenny Stadler" and "Omicron 9 from *@^$(&!(%^." However, they do require that they have at least *some* name for the day of the reservation—"Omicron 9, your table is ready!" When browsers see that a form includes a Required element, they check to see if that element has a value before they send the form to a web server. If the element has no value, the browser doesn't submit the form. Instead, your guest sees the form still in place, with a message asking him to fill in the blank box. Auto Complete helps your guest fill in form details. Chances are that if a guest has entered his name over and over in text boxes like this (and haven't we all?), the browser will prompt the visitor by name here. Auto Focus places the cursor in the diner box when the page first loads.

5. **In the Properties panel, find the Title box and then type *Please enter your name.* In the Place Holder box, type *name required.***

The Title and Place Holder properties are options, but they let your guest know the kind of information you want, so why not use them? Title text appears as a tooltip when your guest points to the text box. The Place Holder text appears inside the box but disappears once your guest enters her name, since browsers ignore placeholder text .

6. **In the document window, select the text "Text Field," and then type *Your name:.***

After you change the label's text, the document window should now look like the one in Figure 16-19. Next you'll add another text box.

FIGURE 16-19

After you insert a form into your web page (indicated by the red line here), you add form elements one at a time. Here you see a Label form element ("Your name:," which you changed from the Dreamweaver-supplied "Text Field") and the first text box (the rectangle beside the label). As explained on page 665, Dreamweaver associates the label with the text box through the box's For attribute.

7. **Click to the right of the text box and hit Enter (Return) to create a new line. In the Insert panel's Form category, click Email.**

As in step 1, Dreamweaver inserts two elements, a label and a text box. In this case, the Type attribute for the box is "email." It doesn't look much different from the text box you set up in step 1, but when a browser goes to submit the form, it checks to make sure the text your visitor types in is valid. In other words, it ensures that the address includes the @ symbol and a period, and that it doesn't have any spaces or strange characters.

8. **While you have the Email element selected, turn on the checkboxes for Required and Auto Complete in the lower-left corner of the Properties panel.**

Now you have two text boxes. Guests need to fill in both before they can submit the form to a web server and its processing program. When the page first loads in a browser, it puts the cursor in the "diner" text box, ready for your guest to enter his name. Both boxes try to help him by suggesting a name or email address he's used in the past, and the browser checks the validity of the email address when he submits the form.

9. **Choose File→Save.**

Dreamweaver saves the page and its form. You feel good, knowing that if the power goes out or some other disaster strikes, you won't have to repeat all your work.

> **NOTE** As mentioned in other parts of this chapter, not all browsers support the new HTML5 Form features. For example, a browser that doesn't recognize the *email* attribute will treat it as any old text box. In that case, it won't validate the text before submitting the form. The same holds true for other HTML5 input types and attributes. Using HTML5 features won't break your form if someone has an old browser—your forms still work—but you and your guest lose some of HTML5's benefits.

Adding (and Removing) a Number Form Element

The Number box makes it easy for your guests to tell you how many diners to expect. You could simply provide a text box and ask for the number, but if you use the Number form element, you'll minimize the hassle of receiving something that isn't a number. For the sake of learning, you'll add the number box and then learn how to remove it and other form elements.

1. **Click to the right of the email address field and press Enter (Return) to create a new, empty paragraph.**

You'll use the paragraph for your next input element. Dreamweaver placed both the previous text boxes inside paragraph (<p>) tags, and you'll place this box inside a paragraph, too.

2. **In the Insert panel's Form category, click Number.**

Dreamweaver displays the label "Number" beside a text box. Just to make sure there's a difference between this text box and the other boxes you've worked on, check out the Number box in Live view.

3. **In the document window, select Live from the drop-down menu in the Document toolbar.**

In Live view, you see your form as it appears in the Google Chrome browser. Click the spinner arrows to change the value in the number box. Say you decided to offer visitors the choices 1 through 7 in the number box, with a final option of "8+" for visitors bringing in eight or more diners. That won't work with the number box, because 8+ isn't a number. So you decide to use a Select menu instead, because it displays both numbers and text. Time to remove an element from your form, the number box.

4. **Turn off Live view by selecting Design from the drop-down menu in the Document toolbar. Then click inside the number box and look at the Tag Selector.**

The right-most tag reads <input#number>. That represents the number box. The <p> tag to the left of it means that the number box resides inside a paragraph.

5. **Click inside the label "Number" and check out the Tag Selector.**

The rightmost tag, <label>, sits next to a <p> tag, so both the label and the number box live inside the same paragraph.

6. **In the Tag Selector, click the <p> tag next to <label> and then press Delete.**

Choosing the <p> tag selects the paragraph, the label, and the number box all at once. Pressing Delete removes all three elements from the page.

You can use the same technique to delete any form element(s) inside a paragraph. To delete form elements or labels from elements other than paragraphs, select the appropriate tag in the Tag Selector and then press Delete.

Adding a Select Menu Form Element

Select menus let you predefine values for information boxes. Your guest's response is limited to the options you provide. That's perfect for the "number in party" box of the reservation form.

1. **Click to the right of the email address box, and then press Enter (Return) to create a new, empty paragraph.**

You just replaced the paragraph you removed in the previous section.

2. **Using the Insert panel's Form category, click Select (toward the bottom of the list).**

Dreamweaver adds a label and an empty Select menu to the page. The settings for the Select menu appear in the Properties panel.

3. **Type *diners* in the Name box of the Properties panel, and then type *Number of diners* in the Title box.**

You named your Select menu "diners," and Dreamweaver uses this same name as the ID for the element (to see, check the HTML in Code or Split view). When a browser submits this form, it connects the name "diners" with the number your guest selects from the menu you're about to build. In addition, the words "Number of diners" will appear in a tooltip when a guest points to the box, and screen readers will read those words aloud.

4. **In the Properties panel, click the List Values button.**

Dreamweaver opens the List Values window (Figure 16-20), where you add labels and values for the Select menu. Dreamweaver highlights the first menu option, ready for your text.

FIGURE 16-20

When you work with Select menus, you build their lists in the List Values window. Under Item Label, add the text you want to appear on the menu. In this case, the item label ("--Number of diners--") can serve as the value, too, so there's no need to add one. A browser includes this label as the value in the name/value pair it sends to a web server for processing.

5. **Type -- *Number of diners* --.**

The first label in the Select menu prompts your guests for *their* number of guests. If you don't provide a value for the label, the menu uses the label *as* the value. That shortcut works fine for this reservation form.

6. **Click + and then, under "Item Label," type the number *1* and then press Enter (Return).**

Repeat this step to add the numbers *2* through *7* as labels. Then, instead of typing the number *8* for the last label, type *8+*.

7. **Click OK.**

Your label appears in the form's drop-down menu. Dreamweaver displays the first item, "Number of diners," at the top of the list. That's great for this list, but if you wanted to display a different item from the list, you'd choose the item in the Selected box in the Properties panel.

8. **With the Select menu still highlighted on the page, click Required in the lower-left corner of the Properties panel.**

You want to make this box required so you know how many diners to expect.

9. **Click the label "Select" in the document window and then replace it with the words *Number in party*.**

   Your Select menu has everything it needs to function. This is a good time to save your work and check out Live view.

10. **Choose File→Save and then choose File→Preview in Browser.**

    At this point, the form elements should look like those in Figure 16-21. In Live view, you can try out the Select menu, but you can't edit your page.

> **TIP** Glitch alert! Select menus are a bit temperamental in Live view. If they don't work for you, go to the Live View Options (upper-right of the document toolbar) and turn on Hide Live View Displays. If they still don't work, do your previewing in a web browser as described in this step.

FIGURE 16-21

The Select menu offers several responses via a drop-down menu, but it takes up only a little space on a form. It's helpful to provide text at the top of the menu that prompts your visitors to action.

Adding Date and Time Form Elements

Next you'll add Date and Time boxes. Some of your visitors will see these boxes as date-pickers; others will see plain text boxes. That means it's important that you provide labels that describe the information you want. Web browsers that don't recognize HTML5 Date and Time elements treat them as ordinary text elements. You can save yourself some aggravation by including good descriptive text for everyone, no matter what browser they use.

1. **Click to the right of the "Number in party" element and press Enter (Return).**

   A new line appears, ready for the next element.

2. **Click Date in the Form category of the Insert panel.**

   Dreamweaver displays the Date box in the form, along with the label "Date."

3. **In the Properties panel's Title box, type *Please enter a date (mm/dd/yyyy)*.**

   Dreamweaver inserts the date box using the perfectly suitable name "date," so there's no need to change it. Adding placeholder text gives you an opportunity to describe how you want visitors to format the date. You'll change the label to reflect the format you want.

4. **With the date box selected, type *12 01* in the Min boxes of the Properties panel and *2015 12 31* in the Max boxes, and then turn on the Required checkbox.**

   You can restrict the dates the date box accepts by setting minimum and maximum values (Figure 16-22, circled). If you bought this book at a yard sale 20 years from the publication date, use more appropriate dates here.

FIGURE 16-22

In the Properties panel of the Date form element, set the earliest (Min) and latest (Max) dates you want displayed in the date-picker that web browsers like Chrome provide. You can set similar limits for the Time form element. That way, guests can reserve a table only when Cafe Soylent Green is open.

5. **In the document window, select the label "Date" and then type *Date (mm/dd/yyyy)*.**

   The label provides another opportunity to show guests how you want the date formatted.

6. **Click to the right of the Date box, and then press Enter (Return). On the Insert panel, click Time.**

   Dreamweaver displays the Time label and box on a new line in the form, with the time box selected and its properties displayed in the Properties panel. Dreamweaver places the time box with the perfectly suitable name "time," so you don't need to change it.

7. **In the Title box, type** *Please enter the time (hh:mm:pm)* **and then turn on the Required checkbox.**

Again, you use the title and its tooltip to signal the format you want for the time. The Required setting means that visitors can't submit the form without providing an answer in this box.

8. **In the Min box, type** *07 00 00*, **and then, in the Max box, type** *23 00 00*.

The Soylent Green Cafe staff put in long hours to serve the public. They'll take reservations from 7 a.m. to 11 p.m. Yes, the Min and Max properties use military time to distinguish a.m. from p.m.

9. **Change the label text from "time" to** *Time (hh:mm:pm)*.

The label shows the format you expect for the time.

10. **Choose File→Save, and then select Live to preview your form.**

In Live view, you see the date and time widgets in all their glory, just as they will look in the Chrome browser. Don't forget to go back to Design view when you finish.

Adding Radio Button Form Elements

When you want a visitor to select one option among many, as with a multiple-choice question, a group of radio buttons is the perfect solution. You'll add a set to handle seating arrangements.

1. **Click to the right of the Time box and press Enter (Return). Then click Radio Button from the Insert panel's Form category.**

A radio button and its associated label appear in a new line on the form. For this task, you'll add two more radio buttons and put them all on the same line.

> **TIP** Instead of inserting three individual radio buttons, it's tempting to use the radio button group. But, as explained on page 675, the group option wraps the radio button element inside the label for the radio button group, so screen readers can't announce the labels for the individual buttons. To accommodate all potential diners, Cafe Soylent Green opts to add radio buttons one at a time.

2. **Click to the right of the radio button's label** *without* **clicking Enter (Return) this time. Then, on the Insert panel, click Radio Button again. Finally, repeat this step to add a third radio button.**

Two more radio buttons with labels appear on the same line. If you select each button and look at the Name box of the Properties panel, you see that Dreamweaver has named the buttons *radio*, *radio2*, and *radio3*. That would be fine for most form elements, but for the radio buttons to operate as a group, they all need to have the same name. That way, your guests will be able to choose only one of the radio buttons (see page 673).

3. **Select the first radio button. Change its name from "radio" to** *location.* **Repeat the process for the other two radio buttons.**

Now the three buttons operate as a single form element named "location." When a browser processes the form, it sends a single value for "location."

It's time to start identifying the role of each button. Rewording the labels is a good start.

4. **In the document window, select the label's text for the first radio button. Change it from "Radio Button" to** *Anywhere is fine.* **Select the label text for the second button and then type** *At the bar.* **Finally, set the text for the last label to** *Corner table.*

The labels provide a good description for each option, but the entire group needs a description.

5. **Click to the left of the first button. Then, from the Insert panel's Form category, choose Label. In the Properties panel, click Refresh. Type** *Location preference.*

When you choose Label from the Insert menu, Dreamweaver adds opening and closing <label> tags to the HTML code for the page, but it doesn't include any text for the label. After you click Refresh in the Properties panel, look at the Tag Selector at the bottom of the document window and you see the <label> tag. When you type *Location preferences,* that text appears on the page. In the code, the words are placed between the opening tag <label> and the closing tag </label>.

6. **Click the first radio button, turn on the Checked checkbox in the Properties panel, type** *anywhere* **in the Value box, and then type** *Any seating location is fine* **in the Title box.**

When a browser submits the form with this option selected, it sends the name "location" and the value "anywhere" to the server that processes the information. The cafe's maître d' hopes all guests choose Anywhere, so you make it the default by turning on the Checked property (Figure 16-23).

FIGURE 16-23

Selecting the Checked option for a radio button ensures that a browser preselects that button. In other words, if you want to make one button in a group of buttons the standard answer, set its initial state to Checked. The same setting works for checkboxes.

7. **Select the second button. Change the value to** *bar*. **In the Title box, type** *Seat us at the bar*. **Select the third button, set the value to** *corner*, **and then, in the Title box, type** *Give us a corner table*.

You've now given all the radio buttons a value and a descriptive title. The first option, "Any seating location is fine," will automatically be selected when the page loads.

8. **Choose File→Save. Select Live view, and give the radio buttons a test drive.**

You can choose a menu option by clicking its button or the button's label. You can select only one button at a time. If your page doesn't work that way, make sure all the buttons have the same name, "location."

Adding Text Area and Submit Button Form Elements

To retrieve more than a single line of text—a lengthy comment, complaint, recommendation, or movie review, for example—turn to the Text Area form element.

1. **In Design view, click to the right of the "Corner table" label for the last radio button. Hit Enter (Return) to create a new paragraph, and then, from the Insert panel's Form category, click Text Area.**

A Text Area box, complete with a scroll bar, appears in the form. To the left of the box is its label, Text Area.

2. **Select the Text Area box, type** *comments* **in the Name box, and type** *Let us know of any comments or special requests* **in the Title box. Type** *300* **in the Max Length box and, for the Place Holder box, type** *Please type no more than 300 characters*.

The Max Length box limits the number of characters a visitor can type in the text area box. After all, you don't want those special requests to get out of hand. The placeholder text delivers its message in gray but disappears as soon as your guest enters a comment. On a similar note, you don't need to make this box required.

3. **In the document window, change the Text Area label to read** *Any comments or requests?*

You've got all your form elements in place; now you just need to add a Submit button.

4. **Put the cursor after the text area box and then press Enter (Return) to add a new line to the form. Then, on the Insert panel, click Submit Button.**

Dreamweaver adds a Submit button to the form. The Properties panel displays its attributes.

5. **Change the Submit button's Value property to** *Make Reservation*. **For the Title, enter** *Click to make a reservation*.

The value appears on the button as its label. The words in the title appear as a tooltip. You don't need to make any other changes to the Submit button.

6. Select File→Save and then click the Live view button for another look.

If you have different browsers installed on your computer, this is a good time to see how the form looks and functions in each. Figure 16-24 shows the form in Google Chrome. Figure 16-25 shows it in Firefox.

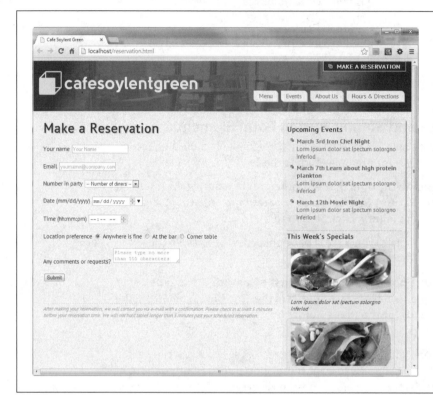

FIGURE 16-24

Your form is complete— well, sort of. All the form elements are there, but the labels and text boxes are staggered all over the page, making it hard to read and navigate from one box to the next. It's time for a CSS makeover.

Styling Labels

At this point, you have a functioning form, but it doesn't look very good (Figure 16-24). The form boxes create a jagged line that's neither easy to read nor attractive. You'll improve that by adding some style to the text and positioning the boxes so that their left edges align. To do this, you'll create and apply a style to the labels—in essence, you'll float (page 452) the labels to the left and give them a set width. That makes them behave much like the floating columns you created in Chapter 10.

1. Make sure you have the Workspace Switcher (upper-right corner of Dreamweaver) set to Design, and then choose "Reset 'Design'" from the Switcher menu.

In the Design workspace, CSS Designer's Properties section sits to the right of the other sections, giving you plenty of room to work with CSS properties.

Make a Reservation

Your name [Your Name]

Email [yo] Please fill out this field.

Number in party [-- Number of diners -- ▾]

Date (mm/dd/yyyy) [   ]

Time (hh:mm:pm) [   ]

Location preference ⦿ Anywhere is fine ◯ At the bar ◯ Corner table

Any comments or requests? [Please type no more than 300 characters]

[Make Reservation]

FIGURE 16-25

This figure shows just the form-containing part of your web page (so you don't see the banner, sidebar, and footer). In Firefox, if you click Make Reservation without filling in the blanks, the view looks like this. The browser helpfully marks required boxes left empty in red, and error messages explain what's missing.

2. **In CSS Designer, go to the Sources section and click *soylent_styles.css*.**

   Soylent_styles.css is the external style sheet for the page. When you select it in Sources, the Selectors section shows the names of the classes, IDs, and tags defined in the style sheet. (If you need a refresher on this whole CSS styles thing, turn to page 116.)

3. **Click + in the light-gray Selectors bar.**

   Clicking + adds a new selector to the list. Dreamweaver opens the selector's Name box and highlights the placeholder name ("#reservation p #comments") so you can rename the selector (Figure 16-26).

4. **Replace the suggested name with *.label*.**

   You created a new class called *label*. Next you'll style that class.

5. **With *soylent_styles.css* still selected in the Sources section of CSS Designer and your new *.label* class selected in the Selectors section, go to the Properties section and click the T (text) button.**

   Dreamweaver scrolls the list of properties to display those related to text. Your labels inherit the "pt-sans, Arial, Helvetica, sans-serif" font-family property from the *.main p* selector because the labels live inside paragraphs that live inside a <div> tag that has the *main* class applied to it. So, as long as your labels remain within paragraphs, you don't need to change the *font-family* property. You can spruce things up by changing the labels' *color* and *font-weight* properties, however.

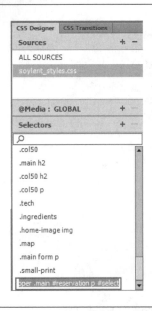

FIGURE 16-26

When you add a new selector in CSS Designer, it always suggests a name based on the location of the cursor in the document window. See the highlighted Selector name Dreamweaver suggests at the bottom of the list? Often, that's not the name you want, so type in the new one over the highlight. In this case, type ".label" to create a new class called "label."

6. **In the Properties section of CSS Designer, make sure you have the Show Set box turned off. Change the text's Color property to #205B0A (or use the color box to select a dark green). Click the value for *font-weight* and choose "700."**

   Your *.label* class now has a rule that changes the color of the text. The font-weight of 700 makes the text bold. The way CSS Designer organizes its Properties section, it makes sense to set all the text properties first and then move on to another category.

   Next you'll change the alignment of the labels so they line up next to the form boxes.

7. **Below the *font-weight* property, set *text-align* to "right."**

   That forces Dreamweaver to line up the text's right edge with the right edge of its box—in other words, you want to move the label to the right. Next, you'll use the Float property to position the label.

8. **At the top of the Properties section, click the Layout button, ▦. Set *width* to 30%. Scroll down to the *float* property and choose "left," and then, below that, choose "left" for the *clear* property. Go to the Padding settings and set the Right value (circled in Figure 16-27) to *10px*.**

   Your *label* class now styles the text and formats the layout. It's time to apply that class to the labels (but *not* to the entire paragraph, which includes both the label and the form element). You can't apply the class to labels in the Properties panel, so you need to switch to Split view, where you can see your source code.

> **NOTE** You might wonder why you didn't just create a style for the <label> tag instead of creating a class style that you had to apply manually. Good question. In some cases you can, but if you add checkboxes or radio buttons and their labels to a form, *all* the form's labels will have the same style, and that might not be what you want. Creating a class style—*.label*—lets you pick and choose which labels get the CSS formatting.

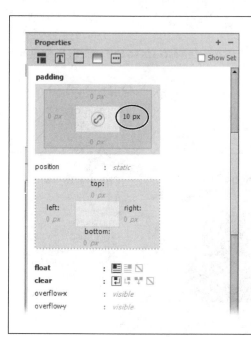

FIGURE 16-27

When you float a form label to the left, it's a good idea to set the Clear property (page 465) to "left" at the same time. That tells the label to always appear below other floated labels, preventing the label from wrapping around the right side of a cousin.

9. **In the document window, click the Split view button. In the Design half of the window, click anywhere inside the label "Your name." In the Tag Selector, click <label> to select the label tag.**

When you click <label>, Dreamweaver highlights the entire label (opening tag, closing tag, and the text in between). You'll insert the class attribute at the end of the opening tag.

10. **Click to the left of the closing bracket (>) for the opening <label> tag, click the space bar once, and then type *class="label"*.**

Code view prompts you with suggestions as you type. You can type in all the text, or choose "class" and "label" from the prompts. When you're done, the opening tag for the label should look like this:

```
<label for="diner" class="label">
```

11. **Select the text *class="label"*, including the space before the letter "c," and then press Ctrl+C (⌘-C) to copy it.**

    To save time and typing, you're going to paste this text in the other <label> tags.

12. **In Design view, click inside the label text "Email." In the Tag Selector, click <label>. In the Code window, click to the left of the closing bracket in the opening email <label> tag. Press Ctrl+V (⌘-V).**

    At the end of this operation, the email label has the *.label* class applied to it, just as the diner label does. As you apply the class to the labels, they begin to fall into line, as shown in Figure 16-28.

13. **Repeat the previous step to assign the *.label* class to the rest of the form's labels.**

    Wow! You're really getting some practice in the finer details of obsessive-compulsive web design. No time to wash hands—we need to move on to our next task, indenting the Submit button.

FIGURE 16-28

It takes some hand-coding to apply the ".label" class to the labels in your form, but the results are worth it. The labels align right, crisply up against the form elements, aligned left.

14. **In CSS Designer, with *soylent_sources.css* still selected, go to the Selectors section and click + . Name the new selector *.submit*.**

You're creating a special class that you can then apply to the paragraph containing the Submit button. By now, you're probably familiar with this drill.

15. **With *.submit* selected in the Selectors section, click ▦ in the Properties section. In the Margin box, set the left margin to *32%*.**

Nothing happens yet. Because you created a class style, you need to apply it to the paragraph containing the button.

16. **In Design view, click the line containing the Submit button (either to the left or right of the button) and then choose "submit" from the Properties panel's Class menu.**

The button indents to line up with the form elements. You're almost done styling the form. Your last task is to set a width for the form's text boxes. As you read on page 663, you can use the Size property, but if you use a class to do the job, it's easier to edit your layout in the future. For example, if you later need to resize all the text boxes, you need to change the width property for only a single class.

17. **In CSS Designer, with *soylent_sources.css* still selected, go to the Selectors section and click + . Name the new selector *.textbox*, and then, at the very top of the list in the Properties section, set *width* to *50%*.**

Next you need to assign the *textbox* class to your form element. You can do that in the Properties panel, no mucking about in the code necessary.

18. **In Design view, click the box next to "Your name." In the Properties panel, set the class to "textbox."**

The box for the "diner" text box changes size. Its actual size takes into account the way Dreamweaver nests page elements. The text box's width is half the width of the form. The form is contained inside a <div> tag with the class *main* applied to it. The width property for that class is 64%, so the form takes up 64% of the browser window, and the text box itself takes up 32%.

19. **Repeat the previous step to apply the *textbox* class to all the other form elements except the radio buttons and the Submit button.**

Your form is complete.

20. **Choose File→Save, and then choose File→Preview in Browser. Choose your favorite browser from the list and enjoy the view!**

Your form should now look like the one in Figure 16-29.

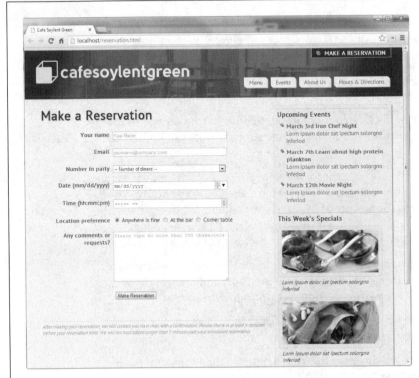

FIGURE 16-29

Thanks to CSS and the careful application of classes to labels and form elements, your reservation form looks pretty stylish. Everyone is going to want to eat at Cafe Soylent Green.

Adding Sound, Video, and Animation

As you learned in previous chapters, you can bring your website to life with interactive and animated pages using Cascading Style Sheets (Chapter 3), JavaScript widgets, Dreamweaver effects and behaviors (Chapter 15), and images (Chapter 5). But as you've probably seen by now, today's web pages go even further—they blink, sing, and dance with sound, videos, and interactive animations. Creating these sophisticated pages is the subject of this chapter.

You'll start off learning how to use the HTML5 tags to add audio and video to your pages. Along the way, you'll learn about the file formats (also known as "containers") that today's web browsers work with. There's one fly in the ointment of web audio and video, however: browser compatibility. Internet Explorer, Safari, Chrome, and Firefox expect you to deliver video and audio in specific file formats. This chapter tells you what the issues are and shows you how to convert media into formats that reach the widest audience. YouTube is a good option for storing video on the Internet and then serving it up on your own site. You'll learn how to do that in this chapter, too.

For years, Adobe's Flash program dominated the web universe in a couple of areas: animated graphics (think web ads and games) and video delivery (think YouTube and movie trailers). The reason was simple: nearly all desktop computers had the Flash player installed. The world changed once everyone started using phones and tablets to view web pages. Flash isn't the only game in town these days, but it's still used, so this chapter includes details on how to add Flash animations and Flash video to your site. The heir apparent to Flash animation is Adobe's Edge Animate, and you'll learn how to add Animate creations to your web pages, too.

Adding Sound to a Page

There are plenty of reasons to add sound to your web page. Perhaps you have a band to promote and you want to put some of your original songs online. Maybe you run a corporate website and want to include an audio message from the CEO. (He's not photogenic, so audio works best.) Or maybe you're the Cornell Lab of Ornithology (*http://macaulaylibrary.org/*) and you post bird sounds, as shown in Figure 17-1.

FIGURE 17-1

These days, you find audio used all over the Web. One great example is Cornell University's Macaulay Library of Natural Sounds (http://macaulaylibrary.org/), where visitors can pause, rewind, and play audio clips of bird calls.

In the past, webmasters had to turn to browser plug-ins like Adobe Flash to add sound clips. (See page 721 for more on Flash.) Thanks to HTML5 and its new <audio> tag, that's no longer the case. So why isn't it as easy to add a song to a web page as it is to add a photo? It's the same old culprit making things difficult—browser incompatibility.

Modern browsers are designed to understand the <audio> tag, and they can play audio files out of the box—you don't need any add-ons or plug-ins. That's the good news. The bad news is that each of the big five browsers—Internet Explorer, Chrome, Firefox, Safari, and Opera—play some, but not all, audio formats. The bottom line is that you can't choose a single audio format (like MP3) and be sure that your audience will hear your song. If you want to reach a wide audience, you need to provide the audio clip in at least two formats. As you'll see, your good friend Dreamweaver helps you do that. As a result, each web browser gets to play the sound clip that it understands.

There are two things you have to do to use audio on your website. First, you produce the audio files—some basic tips follow in the next section. Second, you add code for the audio files as part of your web page. Dreamweaver handles the second task; you handle the first.

Producing Audio Files in Browser-Friendly Formats

Before you can add an audio clip to a web page, you need to record it and then convert it to the file formats you plan to offer. Your original recording may come from a handheld audio recorder, or it may have been recorded on the same computer you're using to build your website. In any case, the process involves capturing sound with a mic, converting that sound to bits and bytes, and then storing it in a computer file. There are dozens of audio formats, just like there are different formats for storing photos. Original recordings are often saved in high-quality formats (such as WAV or AIFF) that result in very big files. You almost always want to convert your recording to a smaller file, even at the expense of some audio fidelity. The smaller file will take up less room on your server and, more importantly, it will download faster when a guest visits your page.

Web browsers can play three audio formats. The first two, MP3 and Ogg, are the most common for web pages:

- **MP3**. This is the most popular file format, and the one most people think of when it comes to music. Internet Explorer, Chrome, and Safari all support MP3 files, which can be relatively small and yet provide pretty good sound quality. They perform this feat by compressing the audio signal, losing some sound quality along the way. So why don't all browsers support the MP3 standard? It comes down to patents and money. If you can provide audio in only a single format, this is the one to choose, but you'll lose Firefox and Opera users.

- **Ogg**. This audio file format was developed as an open source, patent-free alternative to MP3. It's pretty common on Linux computers, but less so with Windows PCs and Macs. Chrome, Firefox, and Opera support Ogg (sometimes called Ogg/Vorbis).

- **WAV**. Sometimes called Audio for Windows, Microsoft and IBM developed the WAV file format back when computers could barely beep. Unlike the other two formats, WAV files usually contain "uncompressed" audio. That means the sound quality is great, but the files are huge. You most likely won't use WAV files on your website because they take a long time to travel over the Internet. However, if you need to provide uncompressed audio for the best quality sound, Chrome, Firefox, Safari, and Opera support this format. (Yes, that's every browser except Microsoft's Internet Explorer. Wasn't that the company that developed this audio format in the first place?)

If you're responsible for converting audio files to browser-friendly formats, you'll need to use a program like Adobe's Audition or the open-source program Audacity. If you have a subscription to Adobe Creative Cloud, you probably have access to Audition. You can download Audacity from *http://audacity.sourceforge.net/*. There are versions for Windows, Macs, and Linux computers, and best of all, it's free. These power-user audio programs do much more than convert files from one format to another. They can mix sound and take the audio from an entire orchestra and turn it all into a commercial-quality CD. You don't need all that power to convert files to web formats. In fact, the entire process is almost as easy as opening a word processing file and saving it in a different format.

Here are the basic steps for converting an audio file:

1. **In your audio program, choose File→Open to open your original audio clip. (The command is the same for Audition and Audacity.)**

   Use the original recording or the best quality audio file you can get your hands on. That way, you'll get the best possible sound after the conversion. Initially, audio programs display the sound as a waveform—a visual representation of sound. You'd work on this waveform if you were editing the sound file, but fortunately, you just want to convert it, so you can use the File menu.

2. **If you're using Audition, choose File→Export→File. For Audacity, choose File→Export (Figure 17-2).**

   This command opens a window where you can name the audio file you're creating and choose a file format.

FIGURE 17-2

Most audio programs, like Audacity (shown here), are complex and take a while to learn thoroughly. But if you just want to convert an audio file from one format to another, that's easy. You do most of your work in Audacity's File menu, where you open the sound file and then export it in a new format.

3. **Save the audio as an MP3 file. In Audition, set the format menu to MP3 Audio. In Audacity set "Save as type" to MP3 Files. Click OK (Audition) or Save (Audacity).**

   Your audio program creates a file with the .mp3 extension. The format menus give you an idea of the variety of audio files. The important ones for web developers are MP3, Ogg, and WAV. In most cases, you want to offer your web visitors an MP3 and an Ogg audio file. Next you'll create the Ogg file.

TIP　When you export a file from your audio program, it uses the original filename and adds an extension like *.mp3* or *.ogg*. You need to keep those extensions, but you can change the rest of the name. However, as you'll see in the next section, you save yourself some work when your audio clips use the same name to the left of the extension. For example, you could create *ceo_message.mp3* and *ceo_message.ogg*.

---

4. **Save the audio as an Ogg file. In Audition, set the format menu to Xiph Ogg Container. In Audacity, set "Save as type" to Ogg Vorbis Files. Click OK or Save.**

   Your audio program creates a file with the *.ogg* extension.

In most cases, you won't create a WAV file for your web page because the files are usually too big. It might be appropriate if you need top-notch audio quality or if the sound clips themselves are just a couple of seconds long. In any case, if you decide to produce a WAV file, choose that format (as in step 4) and then save the file.

Adding Audio to Web Pages

As explained in the previous section, when you put a sound file on your website, you should offer both an MP3 file and an Ogg file.

Using those two file formats, you can reach just about everyone with a modern browser. Once you have an audio clip, you need to store it with your other website files and create links in your web pages to it. Use the Insert panel to add the <audio> tag to your page, and use the Properties panel to manage the technical details. For example, you use the Properties panel to identify the audio source files and to choose whether or not you provide playback controls.

Here are the steps for adding an audio clip to a web page. It's best to do so in Design view and then test your pages in Live view. Your first task is to add your audio files to your website:

1. **In Dreamweaver, make sure you have the Files panel open (Window→File), and then click the Files tab.**

2. **Drag your audio clips (MP3 and Ogg) from Windows Explorer or the Mac Finder to the Files panel.**

   Dragging the audio files into the Files panel is the easiest way to add them to your website. If your root folder is cluttered, you can create a separate folder for your sound or other media files.

3. **In the Files panel, double-click the web page that will provide the audio. Then click the spot on the page where you want to insert the audio file and its playback controls.**

   The playback controls are the only visual indicator that there's an audio clip there. You might also want to identify the clip with a label or other visual element.

Say the boss asks you to post a message on the company intranet. You could create a heading like "A Message from Our CEO" and then place the audio in a paragraph under it.

4. **Open the Insert panel (Window→Insert) and then, using the menu at the top, choose the Media category.**

The Insert panel's Media category provides options for audio, video, Flash, and Edge Animate files.

5. **Click HTML5 Audio.**

Dreamweaver displays a rectangular placeholder with a speaker in the middle of it on your web page (Figure 17-3), indicating the presence of the <audio> tag in your page's HTML code. Now you need to identify the source of the audio.

NOTE Don't just drag your audio clip from the Files menu onto a web page. That creates a link to the sound file, but it doesn't insert the <audio> tag that browsers need to actually play the clip.

6. **Click in the Properties panel (next to the Source box), and then browse to the MP3 file.**

The file has the .mp3 extension. This is one of two file formats you're providing for your visitors. If your files share the same name but different extensions (such as *ceo_message.mp3* and *ceo_message.ogg*), Dreamweaver automatically fills in the Alt Source 1 box with the second audio file. If the two files have different names, you need to fill in the Alt Source box manually. (If the Properties panel doesn't show the same properties as those in Figure 17-3, you need to select the audio placeholder on your web page.)

FIGURE 17-3

When you insert an <audio> tag in Design view, a speaker icon shows where it will appear in your document. You use the Properties panel to name the source audio files, include playback controls, and display a "fallback" message for visitors whose browsers can't play audio.

7. **In the Title box, give your audio clip a short, descriptive name.**

This message appears in a tooltip whenever a visitor points to the audio controls.

8. **In the Fallback Text box, type something like *Sorry, your browser doesn't support this audio clip.***

   If your visitor's browser doesn't support any of your audio clip formats, she'll see this message.

9. **Set the Preload menu to "auto"—and then change it back to "none." (Why the odd menu two-step? See the None option below.)**

   As the name implies, the "preload" attribute determines whether your visitor's browser starts downloading the audio file while it downloads text, photos, and other parts of the web page. Audio files can be large, so you might not want automatic preloading. Here's what the different options do:

   — **None.** Tells the browser not to preload the audio. This is the option to use if your audio file is particularly large (over a minute long) or when some of your visitors are unlikely to play the audio. You may reasonably ask why you need to go through the rigmarole of changing the menu from none to something else and then back again. When you first insert an audio clip, Dreamweaver displays the word None in the Preload menu, but it doesn't actually write the *preload="none"* code in your web page. To have Dreamweaver do that, you need to change the preload option to something other than None first, and then change it back to None. Switch to Split view to double-check the code if you're in doubt.

   — **Auto.** Tells web browsers to automatically download the audio file while the page loads. Use this option if the main purpose of the page is to play the audio file and you're sure nearly everyone will want to listen. Depending on the size of the audio file, this choice may make the entire page load slowly.

   — **Metadata.** This option tells browsers to download information about the audio, such as its track list and duration. This is a good option for audio clips several minutes long.

10. **Make sure you have the Controls checkbox turned on.**

    It's almost always best to give your audience audio controls so they can start and stop playback and adjust the volume. Controls also provide information about the length of the audio clip.

11. **Leave the Autoplay, Loop, and Muted checkboxes turned off.**

    There may be cases where it's appropriate to turn these controls on, but too often they're just plain annoying. Here's what they do:

    — **Autoplay.** The audio clip starts playing as soon as it loads. But what if your web visitor is in the library or a quiet office?

    — **Loop.** As advertised, this makes your clip play over and over and over and over. Few things are more annoying than a short clip that loops. This is especially true if you haven't given your audience controls to stop it, as described in step 10.

— **Muted.** This turns off your audio clip's sound, which may be confusing to less savvy web visitors. Also, if you don't provide audio controls, guests have no way of turning the sound on.

When you finish adding audio to your page, test it on different browsers and devices (Figure 17-4). You can test-drive your audio in Live view, too—you'll see and hear how it works for visitors using the Chrome browser. If you have other browsers on your computer, you can use File→Preview in Browser to check your page.

FIGURE 17-4

The look of the playback controls differs depending on your browser—you can see Internet Explorer 10 here. But no matter the browser, the controls all do the same thing—you'll find Play/Pause and volume controls, as well as indicators for the length of the clip.

Using HTML5 Video

Video on the web isn't the novelty it used to be. Everyone is familiar with YouTube by now, and we've all seen video clips on web pages. Web video makes it possible to see your favorite band in action, to catch up on a missed episode of *Game of Thrones*, and to learn how to cast with a fly fishing rod. As a web designer, you should use video when still pictures and text can't adequately handle the job. At Cafe Soylent Green, you might produce a walk-through video that shows the dining room and a friendly welcome from the maître d'.

Videos have great instructional value, too. For example, if your website sells doors, you could create a video that shows how easy it is for a homeowner to install her own door.

With HTML5, the steps for adding video to your pages are similar to those for adding audio (described on page 702). It wasn't always that easy, though. In the past, web builders used the Adobe Flash plug-in to provide video (see page 731). Another popular option was to post video on YouTube and then add the code that embeds the clip and its controls on a web page. For details, see page 716.

Those options still work, but HTML5 gives you a shiny new <video> tag that you use to place video files in web pages. Modern desktop, tablet, and phone browsers play video files without needing plug-ins like Flash. That all sounds good, but the fly in the ointment, yet again, is browser compatibility. The five major browsers play video files, but they support different file formats. To reach a wide audience, you need to supply clips in more than one format. For video, you reach the widest audience with three file formats: MP4, WebM, and Ogg. Fortunately, Dreamweaver does the hard work of writing the HTML that offers up a source video file and two alternatives. For tips on producing video clips in the needed file formats, read the next section. If you already have your web-friendly clips in hand, jump ahead to page 712.

Converting Video Files to Browser-Friendly Formats

To attract as many visitors as possible, you need to convert your video to formats that web browsers can play: MP4, WebM, and Ogg. Video-editing programs like Premiere Pro or Final Cut Pro can open video files and then save them in a different format, but they may not export to all the formats you need, and they are complicated to use. A simpler tool for the job is Miro Video Converter (*http://www.mirovideoconverter.com*). You'll find versions for Windows, Macs, and Linux computers. The icing on the cake is that Miro is free and easy to use.

Fire up Miro Video Converter, and you see a window with five menus and one big Convert Now button, as shown in Figure 17-5. Drag the files you want to showcase from Windows Explorer or the Mac's Finder onto the top part of the window. Converting video files can take some time. For example, a 3-minute video takes 3 minutes or longer to convert. The actual processing time depends on the content and how hard the encoder has to work to compress the files. So it's a boon that Miro lets you batch-convert files. That way, you can set up a bunch of files for conversion and head off for a coffee break.

Here are the steps for converting video files to web-friendly formats with Miro Video Converter:

1. **Start up Miro Video Converter.**

   Initially, the menus and buttons are grayed out and inactive. The only thing you can do is add the video clips you want to convert. This is Miro's gentle way of guiding you through the process. Menus and buttons become active only when it's time to use them. So if you're wondering why you can't do something, you probably missed a step.

FIGURE 17-5

*Drag the video files you
want to convert to Miro
Video Converter's main
window. Once you do, use
the menus at the bottom
of the screen to choose
a format. In addition
to creating videos for
the Web, the converter
can produce videos for
Apple and Android mobile
devices. Miro keeps the big
Convert Now button faded
out until you choose a
video format.*

2. **Drag the video clip you want to convert to the top portion of the converter window, as shown in Figure 17-5.**

   As usual, you want to use an original recording or the best quality uncompressed video that's available. After you add the video, Miro activates the "Convert to" buttons at the bottom of the window. Their text turns white, and when you click them, they open to display options for the conversion. If you want to convert more than one file, drag the additional clips onto the converter now. Miro lists the videos in the conversion queue, one above the other.

3. **Click the Format menu (Figure 17-6), choose Video, and then choose one of the format options: WebM (HD or SD), MP4, or Ogg Theora.**

   Ideally, you want to provide clips in all three formats, so you'll repeat these steps for each format—see below for file format descriptions. (If you've heard the term "codec" thrown around by video or sound pros and wonder how that relates to file formats, see the box on page 712.)

   — **MP4 (.mp4).** This file format is sometimes referred to as MPEG-4. That name comes from the Motion Picture Experts Group that developed the standard. Apple has championed this format for several years, and Internet Explorer, Chrome, Safari, and Firefox version 21 on Windows 7 and 8 support it. iPhones and iPads use the same format. Bottom line: You'll reach a lot of browsers with this format.

   — **WebM HD or SD (.webm).** The WebM format was developed specifically for web video, and it's royalty free. So, naturally, all browsers support it, right?

Well, not quite. Chrome, Firefox, and Opera play WebM files. Miro offers you a choice of HD (high definition, larger file) or SD (standard definition, smaller file) with the WebM format.

— **Ogg Theora (.ogv).** Theora is similar to WebM in that it's free and open source. Ogg file sizes are often larger than the file sizes of other formats. This format works with Firefox, Chrome, and Opera.

4. **Click the Convert Now button.**

After you choose a format, the text on the big Convert Now button changes, so you might see something like "Convert to WebM SD" or "Convert to MP4." When you click the button, Miro makes a copy of the video in the file format you specified. The process takes some time. If you added more than one video to the queue, Miro processes them one at a time and automatically puts the converted file in its output folder. You're stuck with that destination (Miro doesn't let you specify a different folder), but you can easily get to that folder by clicking the Show File link under the name of the video, post-conversion. You can also get there by clicking the "gear" menu and then clicking the "Show output folder."

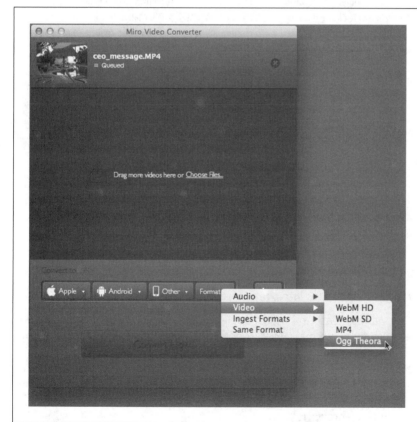

FIGURE 17-6

To create web-friendly videos, click Miro's drop-down Format menu, choose Video, and then choose a video file format. Ideally, your web page will offer video in three formats: MP4, WebM, and Ogg Theora. As a result, you need to go through the conversion process three times.

As explained in step 2, you can queue several videos and convert them all at once, but you can only choose one output file format. That means that, if you load several videos to the conversion queue and then choose WebM as the file format, Miro converts all those videos to WebM. It would be handier for web developers if you could add one original file and output to the three web-friendly formats, but sadly that's not the case. You need to repeat the process for each file format.

Video Containers and Video Codecs

Is a video file the same thing as a codec?

Video pros refer to video files, like those with the extensions .mp4 or .webm, as "containers." They store both video and audio data as well as other information. When you create a video, you "encode" that information in the resulting file. When you watch the video, that information gets decoded for playback.

The tools that perform this feat are called "codecs," short for coder/decoder. As usual in the world of computers, there are a slew of different codecs out there that provide different levels of image quality and file size. Specifying a file format such as MP4 isn't the same thing as specifying a codec, though you usually don't need to know the difference—as a web developer, you only need to worry about the file format. For example, when you use the Miro Video Converter described on page 709, you only need to choose a video *container*. The converter automatically chooses the codecs that work with web browsers. But if you want to know all the technical details, here are the video containers and the codecs that today's web browsers use:

- MP4 video containers (.mp4) use the H264 video codec and the AAC audio codec. Apple championed this combination—it produces good quality video in a relatively small file size.

- Google developed the WebM video container (.webm) as an open, royalty-free alternative to the existing video file formats. It uses the VP8 video codec and the Vorbis audio codec.

- Ogg video containers (.ogv) use the Theora video codec and Vorbis audio codec. As with the Ogg audio file format, this format is popular on Linux computers.

Adding Video to Your Page

If you followed the steps to add an audio file to your web page on page 704, the procedure for adding web video will seem familiar. The first thing to do is place your three video files on your website's server. Then you add the <video> tag to your page using the Insert panel. To finish things off, you use the Properties panel to identify the video files and provide playback controls.

Here are the steps for adding a video clip to your web page:

1. **Drag your video files into Dreamweaver's Files panel.**

   If you want to reach the widest audience, provide your video clip in all three web-friendly file formats: MP4, WebM, and Ogg Theora. That means that for every video on your web page, you'll have three video files on your web server. Each browser automatically uses the file format it supports letting, guests play your videos in all the most recent desktop browsers and on all smartphones and tablets. (See the box on page 735 for adding a Flash video fallback for older desktop browsers.)

2. **In Design view, open the page where you want to display the video, and then click where you want the playback window to appear.**

Placing a video on a page is similar to placing a photo. If the video is important (like a message from your CEO), you may want to center it at the top of the page all by itself. If your video is more of a side story, you can float it right or left and wrap text around it. In short, once your video is in place, you format it using the same CSS techniques you used to format a photo, as described on page 246.

3. **Go to the Insert panel's Media category and then click HTML5 Video, as shown in Figure 17-7.**

Dreamweaver inserts a rectangular placeholder labeled with a film icon into your web page to represent the video clip in Design view.

FIGURE 17-7

Use the commands on the Insert panel (shown here) to add video to your web pages. If you just drag a clip from the Files panel to your page, Dreamweaver creates a standard link to the file (using the anchor tag, <a>); it doesn't insert the <video> tag. But when you use the Insert panel to add video, Dreamweaver does indeed add the <video> tag that browsers require to play movies.

4. **Select the film icon on your web page to display the video's properties in the Properties panel.**

When you select the film icon, the Properties panel displays fields for additional info, like Source, Alt Source 1, and Alt Source 2.

5. **Tell Dreamweaver where to find the source video (Figure 17-8) using either the folder icon next to the Source box or by dragging the radar icon (beside the folder icon) to the MP4 video file.**

You can choose any of the file formats as your Source, but your MP4 video clip is a good choice because so many browsers and devices support it. If a browser can't play the MP4 video clip, it will try the Alt Source option, described in the next step. If all your video files have the same name but different extensions (such as *ceo_message.mp4*, *ceo_message.webm*, and *ceo_message.ogv*), you can skip the next step. Dreamweaver will automatically identify the Alt Source files in the Properties panel.

6. **Set the WebM file as Alt Source 1 and the Ogg file as Alt Source 2.**

Browsers will work their way through the options and play the first video file they can. If they can't play any of the options, the browser displays the fallback text described next.

TIP If it's important that visitors with older browsers view your video, then provide a Flash video fallback. See the details on page 735.

---

7. **In the Fallback Text box, provide a message for visitors whose browsers don't support video.**

For example, you can say, "Sorry, your web browser can't play this video."

8. **Type a brief, descriptive title for your video in the Title box.**

This appears as a tooltip when a visitor points to the video link. Screen readers read the Title property aloud, and search engines use it to improve their search results.

9. **Set Preload to Auto, and then set it back to None.**

The Preload attribute determines whether your visitor's browser downloads the video file at the same time as it downloads text, photos, and other parts of your web page. Since video files can be large, you probably don't want visitors to wait until the video downloads before they see your page. The Preload option works the same way here as it does for audio files—if you select it, a browser downloads all of a page's elements, including your video, before it displays the page. But because video files are so large, preloading may be an issue with video. Here are the options for preloading video, and the situations when you'd choose preloading over not preloading.

— **None.** Tells the browser not to preload the video. This is the option to use if your movie is particularly large (more than a minute or two long) or if your visitors are unlikely to play the video. When you first insert a clip, the preload menu in the Properties panel is set to None, but Dreamweaver hasn't actually written *preload="none"* in the code. To actually produce the code in the HTML, you need to change the Preload option to one of the other values and then change it back to None. Switch to Split view to double-check the code if you're in doubt.

— **Auto.** Tells web browsers to automatically download the video file while the page loads. Use this option if the main purpose of the page is to play the video and you're sure nearly everyone will want to. Depending on the size of the video file, this choice may make the entire page load slowly.

— **Metadata.** This option tells browsers to download information about the video, such as its dimensions, the first few frames of video, its track list, and its duration. This is a good middle-of-the-road option for video clips several minutes long. It gives browsers enough information to size the video playback window and display an image. The rest of the video will load when your guest hits the Play button.

NOTE The preload behavior varies among different browsers and on different devices. Surprising, isn't it? Given that, your preload settings serve more as suggestions than the law of the Web. For example, phones and tablets tend not to preload video even if there is an instruction to do so, and the amount of data that desktop browsers download with the Auto and Metadata options varies from browser to browser.

10. **In the lower-left corner of the Properties panel, make sure you have the Controls checkbox turned on so that your audience can play, pause, and adjust the video's volume.**

    As you can see in the next step, you can control how and when your video plays. In most cases, it's best to give the power to the people. Let them start and stop the video and control the audio volume.

11. **Leave the Autoplay, Loop, and Muted checkboxes turned off.**

    There may be cases where it's appropriate to turn these controls on, but too often they're just plain annoying. Here's what they do:

    — **Autoplay.** The video starts playing as soon as the page loads. (Most mobile devices ignore the Autoplay option.)

    — **Loop.** When your video reaches the end, it starts playing again from the beginning.

    — **Muted.** This turns off the sound for your clip. If you provided playback controls as explained in the previous step, visitors can use the volume control to turn the sound on. But how will they know that?

12. **Optional: In the Properties panel, set the width of the video playback window.**

    You can set the size of the video window using the width (W) and/or height (H) values. If you don't provide a value, browsers display your video at its original size. To make the video window smaller, set W (width) to a smaller size. If you try to make it bigger than the original clip, the image gets fuzzy. You don't need to set both the W and H values. Set one and leave the other empty. That way, your video keeps its original proportions. If you set both the width and height and they aren't in the same proportion as the original clip, you may get a distorted image.

13. **Optional: In the Properties panel, choose a file for the Poster property.**

    The Poster property displays a placeholder image when your video isn't playing. Usually, you create the image by capturing a frame of the video and saving it as a JPG, GIF, or PNG file. However, you can use any image you want as the poster. If you don't specify a poster, most browsers display the first frame of the clip.

TIP On Windows 7 and 8, you can use the snipping tool to capture an image while you play a video. Press the Windows key, and then type "snip" to start up the app. On Macs, you can capture an image by pressing ⌘-C while you play a video in the QuickTime player. After you snag the image, you need to paste it into a program that works with graphics, like Fireworks or Photoshop. Then you should save it, usually as a JPG file. If the image has lots of solid colors, like a logo, you can save it as a PNG, which will create a smaller file.

After you finish adding video to your web page, you can preview the results using Dreamweaver's Live view. You'll see how your video looks when a guest plays it using the Google Chrome browser. If you have other browsers installed on your computer, you can use the File→Preview in Browser command to play the video there.

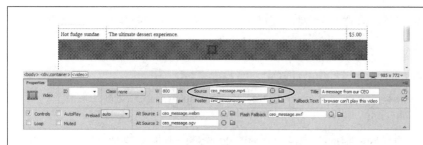

FIGURE 17-8

Use the Properties panel's Source attribute (circled) to tell Dreamweaver where to find your video file. You should provide alternative file formats in the Alt Source 1 and Alt Source 2 boxes, too.

Embedding YouTube Videos

When it first appeared on the web scene, YouTube seemed to be just a place to stash your home videos, blooper reels, and illegally copied TV shows. Now, it's more and more a place where businesses offer product demos, instructional videos, and other videos promoting their companies. In addition to showcasing the video on your site, you can make it possible for a few of the billions of eyeballs that visit YouTube each month to stumble across your video and learn about your product or business—you can't beat free marketing.

There are a few other reasons why YouTube is a good video-hosting option. Video takes a lot of bandwidth and server processing power. Putting video on your own server can easily slow down your site and cost you money once you hit your web host's monthly bandwidth allotment. In addition, YouTube does all the hard work of making your video ready for pretty much any browser or device—Internet Explorer 6, Firefox, iPad, iPhone, Android—and not just the newer video-ready browsers. So you can also use YouTube as the ultimate fallback option for browsers that don't support the <video> tag. For example, you could provide a message that says, "Can't see the video in your browser? Try the YouTube version." Then you can link the message to a page that has the YouTube video embedded in it, as explained below.

Here's how to put video on YouTube.com and include it in a web page on your site:

1. **Get a video.**

    Obviously, you'll need to create a video, have one already made, or get one from your client or boss. YouTube accepts the video formats QuickTime .mov, Windows .avi, .mpg files, Flash Video (.flv), and the new Google-owned WebM format. You can even record a video directly from a webcam. You don't have to worry too much about the video's resolution. YouTube handles every file from a tiny 426- x 240-pixel phone-sized video to the 1920- x 1080-pixel movie you see on your big-screen TV. The playback window is in the standard 16:9 aspect ratio of modern widescreen TVs. If your video has a different aspect ratio, the playback browser adds black bars at the edges to achieve the right proportion when it plays the video.

    NOTE In some cases, you can upload really long videos—up to 11 hours long—to YouTube. If you really want to upload your "My Sleeping Habits in Real Time" long-form video, visit *http://support.google.com/youtube/bin/answer.py?hl=en&answer=71673*.

2. **Get an account at *www.youtube.com*.**

    If you don't already have an account, you need to go to YouTube and sign up. It's free and easy.

3. **Upload a video.**

    Once you have an account and log into YouTube, click Upload at the top of the home page. Then click "Select files to upload," choose a video from your computer, and then click Open. The video begins to upload, and you'll see a page that lets you set its properties.

4. **Go to the YouTube page that hosts your video.**

    When your video finishes uploading, you see the message "Your video will be live at..." followed by a link to the page. Click the link to see the YouTube page with your video on it.

5. **Right-click (Control-click) the video's image, and a menu appears. Choose "Get embed code" as shown in Figure 17-9.**

    The embed code is a snippet of HTML that lets you put the video on any page of your site. You can use the same technique to find the embed code for any video on YouTube, in case you want to embed a video you didn't create.

6. **Return to Dreamweaver and add the code to your page.**

    You copied a snippet of raw HTML, and now you need to add it to your page in Code view. The easiest way to do that is to click where you want to add the video in Design view, and then click the Code view button; Dreamweaver positions the cursor in the right place, and you simply choose Edit→Paste to add the code.

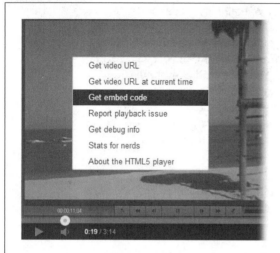

FIGURE 17-9

Right-click (Control-click) any video on YouTube and you see this menu. Choose "Get embed code" to get the code you need to add the video to your web page. If you just want to share the video with a friend, choose the first option, "Get video URL," to get the address of the YouTube page—you can then paste it into an email or instant message.

Adding Adobe Edge Animate Animations

When Apple decided not to support Flash on its extremely popular iPhones and iPads, it created ripples throughout the web world, but it created a tsunami over at Adobe. The writing was on the wall—HTML5 was poised to take over at least a portion of the interactive duties that Flash used to handle. As the earlier sections of this chapter explained, HTML5's new <audio> and <video> tags make it easy to add sound and video to your pages, no Flash plug-in or downloads needed. But what about Flash's other area of Web dominance—animation? Apple's response was that nonproprietary technologies like HTML, CSS, JavaScript, and jQuery could create moving text and graphics. That's true, but just about everyone, except Apple, agrees that the animation capabilities of JavaScript and jQuery don't quite match the snappy response you get with Flash. However, Adobe didn't simply argue the merits of Flash. It created a tool for developing animation using HTML, CSS, JavaScript, and jQuery. The result is Adobe Edge Animate.

If you're a jQuery and CSS whiz, you can animate elements on a page by writing all the code yourself. That's a lot of work, and it's not much help for most designers— they're more comfortable with the kinds of tools you find in Photoshop, Illustrator, Dreamweaver, and Flash. That's where Animate comes in. Using familiar tools for drawing, adding text, and specifying colors, designers can put their ideas in motion. Animate uses a Properties panel similar to the one in Dreamweaver and a timeline similar to the one in After Effects, Premiere, and Flash to work. In short, you arrange text, photos, and other graphics on an Edge Animate "stage." As you change the elements over the course of time, the program rewrites the necessary HTML, CSS, and JavaScript. Animate, part of Adobe's Creative Cloud, gets regular updates, adding features and making it easier to use.

So what does all this mean for web developers using Dreamweaver? First of all, if you're interested in web animation, you may want to dip your toe in the Edge Animate waters. Second, Dreamweaver streamlines the process of adding animations to your pages. An Animate animation comprises several files that Animate compresses into a single file (giving it the extension .oam) to make it easy to move them from one computer to another. When you add an Animate project file to your web page, Dreamweaver automatically opens the file and then extracts the individual files that make up the animation, and stores them in a folder on your site. Here's how to add an Animate mini-movie to your page:

1. **Click the spot on your page where you want to add the Edge Animate animation.**

   Placing an animation on a page is like placing a still image or a video. You want to consider the element's importance to the subject matter. After you add the animation, you can use CSS to add margins and padding, and to position it in relation to text and other page elements.

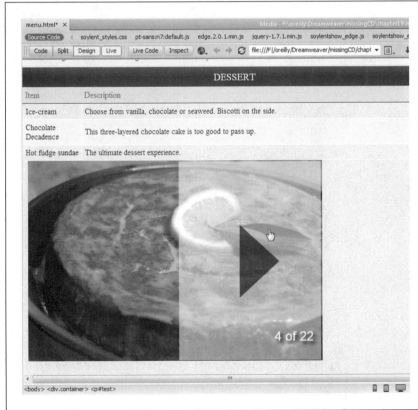

FIGURE 17-10

Edge Animate created this interactive slideshow. It uses HTML, CSS, and JavaScript/jQuery to work its magic. Animate can handle many of the interactive chores that used to be the exclusive domain of Flash. In addition to animating text, graphics, and photos, Animate projects can also include audio and video.

2. **Open the Insert panel by clicking its tab or choosing Window→Insert. At the top of the Insert panel, choose the Media category.**

   "Edge Animate Composition" is at the top of the list of elements (Animate calls its projects "compositions"—how highfalutin!).

3. **Click Edge Animate Composition, browse to find the project file you want, and then click OK (Open).**

   Animate project files have the .oam extension. You don't need to store the file in your website folder, because Dreamweaver extracts the files it needs, creates a folder in your website, and puts all the files inside. In fact, you may be surprised at the number of files that make up an Animate composition.

4. **Click the Live view button in the document window to view your animation on the page.**

   You can see Edge Animate projects in Live view because they're made up of HTML, CSS, and JavaScript code. Live view uses the same technology as Google Chrome, so it has no problem playing the animation.

FIGURE 17-11

When you use the Insert panel to add an Edge animation to your page, you identify a single, compressed "project" file (one with the .oam extension) that includes all the files the animation requires. Dreamweaver unpacks the file, putting the contents in an edge-animate_assets folder on your website. You'll find files and folders like the ones shown here inside that file. They include JavaScript, jQuery, and HTML files, as well as any other resources the project needs, such as the .jpg files used in this slideshow.

Once you embed the animation in your page, you see just a few properties in the Properties panel: ID, Class, W (width), and H (Height). All of them work as you'd expect. For example, Animate gives your project the ID "EdgeID." You can change that to something more meaningful if you want. You can also use the ID as a selector in CSS Designer to create styles and to format the animation window and position it on the page. The same is true of the project's Class property. (See page 117 for details on using CSS and classes.) The W and H properties let you change the width and height of the animation, but keep in mind that you could distort the image using these properties.

When you add an Animate project to your website, Dreamweaver creates an *edge-animate_assets* folder. You'll find other folders and files inside it. For example, if you added a project file called *soylentshow.oam* in step 3 above, Animate creates a *soylentshow* folder in the *edgeanimate_assets* folder. Within that, you'll find HTML and JavaScript files, an *images* folder, and an *edge_includes* folder. You don't need to do anything with these folders or files—but don't move or delete them, either. If you do, your animation won't work. When it comes time to move files to your web server, Dreamweaver takes care of moving the necessary files over.

> **NOTE** Interested in learning more about Edge Animate? Check out *Adobe Edge Animate: The Missing Manual* (O'Reilly).

■ Flash: An Introduction

A few years ago, if you wanted to add smooth animation, video, slideshows, or any other high-quality interactive effects to a web page, Flash was the only game in town. Thanks to the Flash plug-in (available for almost all browsers), web developers could use the Flash authoring program to make "videos" that played inside a browser and add programming logic so that those videos responded to visitor feedback—mouse movement, clicks, and keyboard input. However, the JavaScript programming language and the speedy JavaScript engines in today's browsers provide an alternative to many simple forms of animation and interactivity. Edge Animate compositions (page 718) are good examples of the interactive effects JavaScript offers.

But for really high-quality animation, games, and interactivity, Flash is still a viable option. For example, the games on the website *www.addictinggames.com* (Figure 17-12) were created in Flash and use the Flash plug-in to provide quick, responsive gameplay. JavaScript and its jQuery companion library are still playing catch-up when it comes to this kind of animation. You'll also find many entertainment company websites (especially those for video companies) and consumer-oriented product sites still turn to Flash to create an immersing, interactive experience (see *http://video.disney.com/movies*, for example).

Flash provides other benefits as well. It plays third-party audio and video files, and its advanced programming features let you add a level of sound, video, and interactivity that makes plain HTML pages look dull by comparison.

In addition, Flash animations and videos look and work exactly the same way in every browser, whether you use a Windows, Mac, or even Linux PC. That kind of cross-platform compatibility is rare. And finally, the ubiquity of Flash on the web means that nearly every desktop browser—in fact, 90 percent of them—have a Flash player installed.

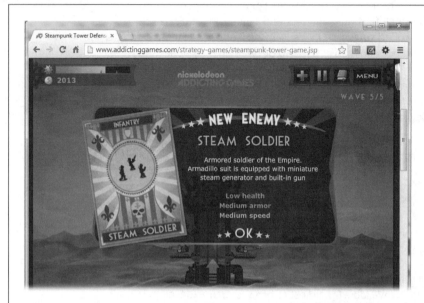

FIGURE 17-12

Some websites, like Addicting Games, use Flash because it facilitates interactivity, animation, and video playback. To add a Flash file to your site, create a page in HTML and then add your Flash file using the <object> tag. Web browsers need to have the Flash player plug-in installed for playback, but that's usu-ally not an issue, because 90 percent of desktop computer browsers do.

However, that 90 percent figure covers desktop computers only. Two of the most popular devices for surfing the Web, the iPhone and the iPad, don't support Flash at all. So if you think you'll have visitors using their iPhones or iPads to search for your business's hours, street address, and phone number, make sure you at least provide your most crucial information in HTML format. Said another way: Don't make your site's home page one big Flash video (as some sites do). Otherwise, iPhone/iPad guests will be staring at a blank page.

Of course, all this power comes at a price. You need Adobe Flash or a similar program, like Swish (*www.swishzone.com*), Toon Boom (*www.toonboom.com*), or Anime Studio (*http://anime.smithmicro.com*) to produce full-fledged animations. And although these programs aren't necessarily difficult to get started with, they represent one more expense to bear and one more technology you have to learn.

NOTE Creating external videos, animations, and applications is an art (and a book or two) unto itself. This chapter is a guide to *inserting* these goodies into your web page and assumes that a cheerful programmer near you has already *created* them. For the full scoop on creating Flash files, pick up a copy of *Flash CS6: The Missing Manual* (O'Reilly).

Is Flash Still Important?

I hear that Flash is dead. Is that true?

When Apple famously announced that it wouldn't ever support Flash on the iPhone or iPad, many people believed that was the beginning of the end for Flash. In many ways, it was. While Adobe still promotes Flash, it's developed a new tool, Adobe Edge Animate, to create animations using HTML5, CSS, and JavaScript. See page 718 for details on using Animate compositions in your web pages.

As explained at the beginning of this chapter, the latest browsers can play audio and video without the assistance of the Flash plug-in. Likewise, faster computers and browsers now make it possible to create slick animations using JavaScript only.

And while a Flash-less future may be here one day, right now Flash is still useful in some cases. HTML5's <video> and <audio>

tags are exciting, but Microsoft's still-used Internet Explorer 8 browser doesn't understand them, and thus can't play video or audio files embedded that way. In addition, different browsers support different video formats, so while you can use the high-quality H.264 video format in Safari, Chrome, and Internet Explorer 9 and above, you need to use a different format for Firefox and Opera. In other words, using the <video> tags means you need to create three versions of your video for it to work in common browsers.

In a nutshell, it may not be the best time to take on a career as a Flash programmer. In addition, if you need to build sites for mobile devices (including the popular iPhone and iPad), you probably want to stay away from Flash. However, in some cases, including video, Flash still has a role to play...for now.

Inserting a Flash Animation

To add a Flash animation to a page, position your cursor where you want the animation to appear and then choose Insert→Media→Flash SWF (.swf is the file extension for Flash animations) or, in the Media category of the Insert panel, choose Flash SWF from the Media menu (Figure 17-13). Either way, you'll see the Select File dialog box. Navigate to the Flash file you want to embed (look for the .swf extension) and double-click it. Dreamweaver automatically recognizes the width and height of the animation and writes the appropriate HTML to embed it in your page. You'll see a gray rectangular placeholder with the Flash logo in the center; you can adjust the animation's settings as described in the next section.

TIP You can also drag a Flash animation from the Files panel into the document window. Dreamweaver automatically adds the correct code.

When you insert a Flash animation, Dreamweaver opens the Object Tag Accessibility Options window. It lets you set options intended to make viewing Flash content easier, but they don't really work in most browsers. If you don't want to set these options, just click Cancel, and Dreamweaver still inserts the animation. To permanently turn off this window, open the Preferences window (Edit→Preferences [Dreamweaver→Preferences]), click the Accessibility category, and then turn off the Media checkbox.

Dreamweaver adds two helper files when you add Flash media to your page: *expressInstall.swf* and *swfobject_modified.js*. They make it possible to notify Flash-less visitors (and those with older versions of the program) that they need to download the current Flash plug-in (see page 730 for details).

FIGURE 17-13

You can use either the Insert menu (pictured) or the Insert panel to add media to your web page. When you use the Insert menu, go to Insert→Media→Flash SWF to add a Flash animation; go to Insert→Media→Flash Video to add a video and playback controls (see page 737).

POWER USERS' CLINIC

The Two Lives of the <object> Tag

If you choose View→Code after you insert a Flash animation, you may be surprised by the amount of HTML Dreamweaver deposits in your page. You may also encounter some HTML tags you've never heard of, including <object> and <param>. These tags provide browsers with the information they need to open the Flash player and play an animation.

Due to differences between Internet Explorer and all other browsers, Dreamweaver has to insert the <object> tag twice: once for IE (with all the proper settings for that browser) and once for the other browsers. To do this, Dreamweaver uses IE conditional statements—HTML comments that only Internet Explorer understands—to send special instructions to just IE (and even to specific versions of IE). You can learn more about conditional comments at *http://tinyurl.com/9osegt*.

Dreamweaver started using the <object> tag like this in Dreamweaver CS4. It replaces the old way of embedding Flash animations, which involved inserting two tags, <object> and <embed>. This new method is standards-compliant, which means that most pages where you use Dreamweaver to add an animation will pass W3C validation (the same validator that Dreamweaver's W3C Validation tool uses; see page 789). That wasn't true in versions of Dreamweaver prior to CS4, which produced invalid HTML that failed the W3C validator.

Ironically, if you insert a Flash animation into an HTML5 document (page xxi), the code Dreamweaver inserts actually produces invalid HTML5! One step forward, two steps back.

Change Animation Properties

You'll rarely have to change the default properties Dreamweaver assigns Flash animations. But if you do—say you resize an animation and want to change it back to its original size, or you want to swap in a different animation altogether—the Properties panel is the place to go.

■ PLAY YOUR ANIMATION

To view Flash media on your computer, switch to Live view, where you can watch the action and click the buttons. On Windows computers, you can play the animation right within Design view. In the Properties panel, click the Play button to start the animation (at which point the Play button becomes a Stop button). Once you have the video playing, the page's interactive features, like buttons, will work. Of course, by using the File→Preview in Browser command, you can also watch the animation in Live view. Naturally, you'll need a browser with the Flash Player plug-in installed.

■ RENAME YOUR ANIMATION

Just as JavaScript can control images and buttons, so it can control Flash animations. Dreamweaver assigns a generic name to each animation you embed—*FlashID*, *FlashID2*, *FlashID3*, and so on. This act of naming your animation is important—the auto-install option discussed on page 730 requires a name—but the exact name isn't critical. If you want, you can change it in the Name box directly below "SWF" at the top left of the Properties panel (see Figure 17-14). But there's no real need to since no one visiting the page will ever see it.

■ REPLACE YOUR ANIMATION

The Properties panel's File box specifies your animation's location on your hard drive. To swap out the current animation, type a new path into the box or click the nearby folder icon and browse to the new animation.

■ SET THE SRC PROPERTY

The Src field indicates the location of your original Flash file (the one with the .fla extension). When you first insert a Flash animation, the Src box is blank. If you think you'll want to edit the original Flash file, tell Dreamweaver where to find it.

To do that, click the Edit button in the Properties panel. Dreamweaver asks you to locate the original file. When you do, double-click it, and Dreamweaver opens the Flash program and the file you specified for editing. Make any changes you wish (or not) and then in Flash, click Done. Flash exports the updated .swf file to your site, replacing the previous version. In addition, the Src property box now points to your original .fla file. That way, if you need to work on the animation in the future, you just press the Edit button. Dreamweaver launches Flash and opens your original animation for editing.

FIGURE 17-14

Use the Properties panel to set the display and playback controls for a Flash animation. Avoid the V space, H space, and Align settings because you'll use CSS to handle those formatting chores. The "Reset size" button (circled) can get you out of a jam; see below.

■ CHANGE YOUR ANIMATION'S SIZE

Enlarging GIF or JPEG images by dragging their edges usually results in a pixelated mess, but if you use Flash's vector-based tools to create your animation, you can scale it nicely. However, if the animation contains bitmap images, such as GIFs, PNGs, JPEGs, or embedded video, leave the animation at its original size. If you resize an animation that has bitmaps, the images distort and pixelate.

To resize an animation, do one of the following:

- Select the animation in the document window and then drag one of the three resizing handles at its edges. To maintain the animation's proportions, press Shift as you drag the lower-right corner.

- Select the animation in the document window and then type new width and height values into the Properties panel's W and H boxes. You can also use percentage values, in which case your animation scales to fit the browser window.

If you make a complete mess of your page by resizing your animation beyond recognition, just click the "Reset size" button in the Properties panel (circled in Figure 17-14).

NOTE If you want to insert a Flash animation that fills 100% of a browser window, you first need to set the animation's height and width to 100%. Then you need to create a few CSS styles. First, create a tag style for the <body> tag with the *padding* (page 465) and *margin* (page 465) values set to *0*, and the *height* and *width* (page 464) values set to *100%*. Next, create a style for the <html> tag with the same settings as the <body> tag (a group selector—discussed on page xx—makes the process of creating the styles more efficient). If the Flash animation is nested within other tags, like <div> or <p> tags, you need to remove the padding and margin for those tags and set their heights and widths to 100% as well. Finally, choose an appropriate Scaling setting for the animation, as discussed on page 728.

■ SET PLAYBACK OPTIONS

The Loop and Autoplay checkboxes control animation playback. When you turn on Loop, the animation plays over and over endlessly, an approach advertisers often use in animated banner ads. The Autoplay option starts playback as soon as the page loads in a browser.

However, neither of these options overrides any programming instructions you embed in the Flash animation. So if you added a Stop command to the final frame of your animation, the animation stops at that frame regardless of the Loop setting.

■ LEAVE MARGINS UNSPECIFIED

Skip the V space and H space settings in the Properties panel. They're intended to add space to the top and bottom (V) and the left and right (H) edges of your animation, but they produce invalid code for the HTML 4.01 Strict and HTML5 document types (see page xxi for more on doctypes). In addition, you can't control each of the four margins individually.

Instead, use Cascading Style Sheets and the CSS *margin* property (discussed on page 465) to add space around your animation. You can create an ID style (page 117) using the animation's name. For example, you might create an ID style named *#FlashID*.

■ SELECT A QUALITY SETTING

If your Flash animation requires a lot of processing muscle—if it's heavy on animation and action, for example—it may overwhelm older computers, making playback slow and choppy. Not every computer has a 3-gigahertz processor and 16 gigabytes of memory (not yet, anyway). Until that day, you may need to adjust the quality settings of your Flash animation so it looks good on all computers.

Out of the box, Dreamweaver sets the animation quality to High, but you can choose any of the following four settings from the Quality menu in the Properties panel:

- **High** provides the best quality, but the animation may run slower on older computers.

- **Low** looks terrible. This setting sacrifices quality by eliminating all *antialiasing* (edge-smoothing) in an animation, leaving harsh, jaggy lines on the edges of every image. Animations set to low quality look bad on *all* computers, so pass it by.

- **Auto Low** forces the animation to start in low-quality mode, but switches automatically to high-quality playback if the visitor's computer is fast enough.

- **Auto High** makes the animation switch to low-quality mode only if the visitor's computer requires it. This mode is the best choice if you want to provide a high-quality image but still make your animation play back at reasonable speed for those with older computers.

■ ADJUST YOUR ANIMATION'S SCALE

Scaling becomes an issue only when you specify *relative* dimensions for your animation, setting its size to, say, 90% of the width of a browser window. That's because the animation grows or shrinks as your visitor's browser grows or shrinks, and you have no control over what your visitor does with her browser—one person may prefer a small horizontal browser at the bottom of the screen, while another has a tall, narrow window.

Enter Dreamweaver's Scale property. It lets you determine *how* Flash scales your animation. For example, in Figure 17-15, the top animation's original size is 334 pixels high by 113 pixels wide. If you resize the animation using the W and H attributes so that it's *350* pixels high and 113 pixels wide, one of three things will happen, depending on your Scale setting:

- **Show All**. This setting, the standard, maintains the original aspect ratio (proportions) of your animation (second from top in Figure 17-15). In other words, although the overall *size* of the animation may change as a visitor fusses with his browser, its width-to-height ratio won't. Show All keeps your animation from distorting (but it may also cause white borders on the top, bottom, or either side of your animation; to hide the borders, make the animation's background color the same color as your web page).

- **No Border**. This setting resizes an animation according to your specifications *and* maintains its aspect ratio, but it may also crop the sides of the animation. Notice how the top and bottom of the Chia Vet logo are chopped off in Figure 17-15, third image from the top.

- **Exact Fit**. Despite its name, this option may stretch your animation's picture either horizontally or vertically. In Figure 17-15, bottom, "Chia Vet" is stretched wider than normal.

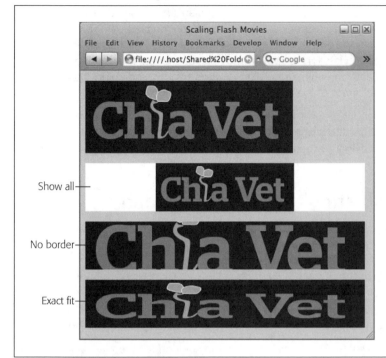

FIGURE 17-15

This browser window shows the results of choosing different settings in the Properties panel's Scale menu. A Flash animation's Scale property specifies how an animation resizes when you set its Width and Height properties to something different from the original. If you resize an animation, press F12 (Option-F12) to see how it looks in a web browser, and then, if necessary, choose a different setting from the Scale drop-down menu.

Show all

No border

Exact fit

◼ ALIGN YOUR ANIMATION

You can align Flash animations relative to the paragraphs around them just as you can align images relative to the surrounding text. In fact, the Properties panel's animation alignment options work exactly the same way as its text alignment properties. For example, when you choose Right from the Align menu, Dreamweaver positions the animation at the right edge of the screen and wraps text around its left side. (If the animation is inside a cell, Align→Right moves the animation to the right edge of the cell.) However, for Strict document types and HTML5, the Align property is invalid. As with the margin settings discussed above, you're better off using CSS properties, such as the *float* property described on page 452.

◼ BACKGROUND COLOR

To set a background color for a Flash animation, use the Bg Color box in the Properties panel. This color overrides any background color set in the animation itself and becomes the animation's placeholder color when a browser has loaded a page, but not its animation.

■ WMODE

Wmode stands for "Window mode" and it controls how your animation interacts with other HTML elements on the page. The standard setting, *opaque*, is useful when you include HTML that needs to appear on top of an animation—the classic example is a drop-down menu like the ones you learned about on page 201. The opaque setting ensures that the drop-down menu appears on top of the Flash animation. The *transparent* option lets HTML appear above an animation, too, but it also lets any HTML *underneath* the animation—like a page's background color—show through any transparent areas of the animation.

Finally, the *window* option is the exact opposite of the opaque option: It makes sure a Flash animation always appears above any HTML element on a page—even above a drop-down navigation menu that would normally appear over the animation.

■ Automating the Flash Download

Even though the Flash plug-in is nearly universal, you can't be sure that every visitor's browser has it. In addition, you may have created a Flash animation or video that runs only in the latest version of the plug-in, so a visitor might have the Flash plug-in, but not the correct *version* of it. The result? A video that either doesn't play back at all or doesn't play back as it should. Guests who fall into this category have to choose from three equally unpalatable options: Go to a different website to download the plug-in, skip the multimedia show, or skip your website entirely.

Fortunately, Dreamweaver provides a built-in solution for the playback scenarios mentioned above. When you embed Flash media in a web page, Dreamweaver includes code that detects your visitor's browser plug-ins. If she either doesn't have the Flash plug-in or doesn't have the right version of it, the page displays a message alerting her (see Figure 17-16) and offering a button (labeled "Get Adobe Flash Player") that takes her to the plug-in download. If your visitor has at least version 6 of the plug-in, she can take advantage of its "express install" feature, which lets her upgrade to the latest version with just a mouse click.

You won't see the "missing Flash file" message in Design view; Dreamweaver keeps it hidden. But you can see and edit it by clicking the eye icon (circled in Figure 17-16).

NOTE Make sure you edit the message that appears when the Adobe plug-in isn't available. It assumes that you can download and install the Flash player. Mobile devices that don't support Flash (like the iPhone and iPad) will display this same message, and telling visitors to download software that won't run on their devices is just rude. Instead, change the message to something like "Your browser either doesn't support the Flash plug-in or you need to download a newer version of it to see this content."

To make all this happen, Dreamweaver adds two files to your website, both of them inside a folder named Scripts: *expressInstall.swf* and *swfobject_modified.js*. When you move your finished web pages and Flash animation to your web server (see Chapter 20), be sure to move the Scripts folder as well.

FIGURE 17-16

Here's the message a web browser displays if a visitor doesn't have the Flash player installed, has an old version of it, or is viewing the page on a device that doesn't support Flash (like an iPhone or an iPad). You can customize the message, but it's a good idea to leave the Flash player icon in place—it includes a link to Adobe.com, where your visitor can download the player.

■ Adding Flash Videos

In addition to playing back animations and hosting games, the Flash player plays back videos, too. If you've visited a little site called YouTube, you've probably seen Flash video in action. Dreamweaver makes it a snap to embed videos. Unfortunately, Flash can't play back videos in just any old format, like MPEG or AVI, without a little help. And Dreamweaver can't transform videos in these formats to the Flash video format (which has the extension .flv). This file format (and Flash video in general) is losing in popularity compared to the .mp4, .webM, and .ogv formats mentioned in the section on HTML5 video (page 708). In the past, you needed to use the Adobe Media Encoder to produce Flash video files in the .flv and .f4v formats. These formats are no longer available in the latest version of Media Encoder—a sign of the times. Still, you'll find Flash video on the web at many sites. In fact, your company may have used Flash video for years and you may have some already-encoded Flash video files that you want to place on your web page. If that's the case, read on.

NOTE For a quick (albeit dated) intro to creating Flash videos, visit *http://tinyurl.com/63lkad9*. Adobe also devotes an entire section of its site to Flash video: *www.adobe.com/devnet/video*.

Fortunately, creating the .flv file is the hard part. Dreamweaver makes the rest easy. Follow these simple steps to insert a Flash video into your page, complete with DVD-like playback controls.

1. **Click the place on the page where you want to insert the video.**

   Like other Flash videos, you'll want an open area of your page.

2. **Choose Insert→Media→Flash Video.**

   Or, from the Common category of the Insert panel, select FLV from the Media menu, and the Insert FLV window appears (see Figure 17-17). You can also just drag the .flv file from the Files panel onto the document window.

FIGURE 17-17

The Insert FLV window makes it easy to add video to your website. To play the video, all your visitors need is the Flash player, which in many cases comes preinstalled with their browsers.

3. **Select Progressive Download Video from the "Video type" menu.**

   Dreamweaver provides two download options, the one above and Streaming Video. The latter requires you to have some expensive software (a Flash server) or a Flash video-streaming service, which can run you anywhere from $10 a month to a couple of hundred dollars a month. Streaming video is usually reserved for live events or to handle very large numbers of viewers. That's why websites for TV networks like ABC.com use streaming servers—it's an efficient way to distribute video when thousands of people watch the same video at the same time.

   If you choose Progressive Download, your video doesn't have to download completely before it begins playing back.

4. **Click 🗁 and select the Flash video file (.flv) you want to add to the page.**

   Due to differences in how operating systems work, you're best off putting your Flash video file in the same folder as your web page. If you want to put it elsewhere (in a dedicated Flash video folder, for instance, or even on a different web server), use absolute links (see page 178).

5. **Select a skin.**

   A *skin* is a set of playback controls for your video; it includes buttons that start, pause, and stop the video; a progress bar; and various volume-adjustment controls (see Figure 17-18).

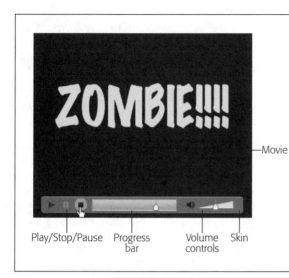

FIGURE 17-18

The Clear skin controls lie directly over your video (Clear Skin 3 is shown here). They disappear when the mouse isn't anywhere inside the video but reappear the moment you point to the video. Try each skin to see which fits your taste.

—Movie

Play/Stop/Pause Progress Volume Skin
bar controls

Dreamweaver adds the controls to your video, and offers nine styles—actually, three types of controls, each with three different graphical styles.

6. **Click the Detect Size button.**

   Flash videos contain *metadata*—information embedded inside the file that describes its features, like its dimensions, file size, and so on. The Flash video encoder adds this metadata when you create a video. Clicking the Detect Size button extracts the video's width and height measurements, adds the width and height of the playback controls, and then automatically fills in the width and height boxes in the Insert FLV window (see Figure 17-18).

   If, for whatever reason, your file doesn't include metadata, you have to enter the width and height values yourself—these settings specify how much space the video occupies on your page. Note that entering these dimensions won't actually distort your video—making it really, really thin or really, really wide, for example. No matter what size you enter, Dreamweaver preserves the original aspect ratio of your video and adds extra, empty space to fill any area not occupied by it. For example, say your video is 352 pixels wide and 288 pixels tall. If you enter a dimension of 100 x 288, the video won't stretch like you're watching it in a fun-house mirror. Instead, it appears 100 pixels wide and 82 pixels tall, with 53 pixels of blank space above and below it.

7. **If you want, turn on the Autoplay checkbox.**

   Doing so makes the video play as soon as enough video data has been downloaded from the Web. Otherwise, a visitor has to press the Play button to begin the video.

8. **If you want, turn on the "Auto rewind" checkbox.**

   After playback, your video automatically "rewinds" to the first frame if you turn on this checkbox. But you may not always want to abide by the old video-store credo "Be Kind, Rewind." If your video ends with a dramatic message—"Stay tuned for the next exciting installment of Blind Mole Rats from Mars!"—you might prefer to leave the video on its last frame when it's complete.

9. **Click OK to add the Flash video to your page.**

   This step installs the necessary code not only for the video, but for detecting the Flash plug-in as well (described on page 730). You can check out the newly inserted video by pressing F12 (Option-F12) to preview the page in a browser.

NOTE When you upload your web page and Flash video to your site (see Chapter 20), you need to upload four additional files that Dreamweaver secretly adds: the two files (and the *Scripts* folder) discussed on page 730, the file *FLVPlayer_progressive.swf* and the .swf (Flash video) file for the skin you selected. That last file is named after the skin you chose—for example, *Clear_Skin_1.swf*. Save yourself some work: When uploading your Flash-filled web page (uploading details are on page 730), choose to include "dependent files": that way, Dreamweaver grabs these three files for you.

■ Tutorial: Embedding Sound, Video, and Animation in Pages

In this tutorial you'll add audio and video clips to Cafe Soylent Green's web pages. You'll use HTML5 tags to identify the media, and provide audio and video clips in more than one format so visitors can see them, no matter which browser they use. In the last part of the tutorial, you'll add an Adobe Edge Animate project to a page. It is a slideshow, but Animate compositions vary a great deal; they can include images, video, sound, text, and graphics.

NOTE To complete this tutorial, you need to download sample files from this book's Missing CD page at *http://oreilly.com/pub/missingmanuals/dreamweaverccmm2014*. (See the Note on page 37 for details.) The files you'll work on are in the Chapter17 folder, and the finished project, for comparison, is in the Chapter17_complete folder.

Once you download the tutorial files and open Dreamweaver, set up a new site as described on page 23. In a nutshell, choose Site→New Site. In the Site Setup window, type *Audio Video Animation* into the Site Name box. Click ▣ next to the Local Site Folder box, navigate to and select the Chapter17 folder inside the MM_DWCC folder, and then click Choose (Select). Finally, click OK.

WORKAROUND WORKSHOP

Using Flash as an HTML5 Video Fallback Option

Soon everyone will be using web browsers that know how to play video without the help of a plug-in like Flash. In the meantime, web developers need to make decisions about how to support visitors who still use older web browsers. The first question to ask is, Who is my audience? If your site focuses on cutting-edge technology and gadgets, your visitors are likely to have up-to-date browsers. You may not need to worry about supporting older versions. However, if you have a site that discusses the virtues of reverse mortgages, you may be catering to an older audience, and you may need to accommodate older versions of Internet Explorer.

First here's a list of the browsers that can play HTML5 video, and therefore don't need a Flash fallback option:

- Internet Explorer 9 +
- Firefox 3.5 +
- Safari 4 +
- Opera 10.5 +
- Chrome

Your HTML5 video will also play well with most smartphones and tablets. That said, your biggest concern may be web visitors who still use Internet Explorer 8. (According to StatCounter, worldwide web traffic using Internet Explorer 8 dropped from about 10% to about 6% from October 2013 through September 2014.)

If you're concerned about reaching visitors with older computers and older browsers, you can provide a Flash video fallback. If the computers don't understand HTML5 video, and if they have Flash player installed, they'll still see your video. Copy the SWF and FLV files to your website's Files panel. Follow the steps on page 712 for adding HTML5 video. When you reach step 6, where you add Alt Source 1 and Alt Source 2 video clips, you can add one more option. In the Properties panel's Flash Fallback box, identify the SWF file for the Flash video. You can use the folder button to browse to the file, or you can use the file picker tool that looks like a radar screen (see Figure 17-19).

FIGURE 17-19

If you think your visitors may be using older browsers that don't support HTML5 video, you can use Flash video as a fallback option. In the Properties panel, after you insert the video using the Insert panel's HTML5 Video option, type in the Flash fallback file (.swf) for your clip. Older desktop browsers will play the Flash file as long as they have the Flash plug-in installed.

Adding a Sound Clip to a Page

For this tutorial's first project, you'll add a sound clip to Cafe Soylent Green's About Us page. The clips have already been produced, as described on page 703. All you need to do is insert them in the page.

1. **In the Files panel (Window→Files), double-click *about.html*.**

2. **In Design view, position your cursor after the "s" in the heading "About Us."**

   You'll place the audio clip and its controls between the heading and the first paragraph.

3. **In the Insert panel (Window→Insert), choose Media from the drop-down menu and then click HTML5 Audio (see Figure 17-20).**

   An audio speaker icon appears on the page. In the Tag Selector at the bottom of the document window, you can see the <audio> tag. The Properties panel below the document window displays the properties for the <audio> element. They're blank now, but you'll fill in the blanks.

FIGURE 17-20

Use the Media category of the Insert panel to add HTML5 audio, HTML5 video, and Edge Animate compositions to your web pages. If you prefer menus, you'll find the same commands at Insert→Media.

4. **In the Properties panel, to the right of the Source text box, click 🗀, the "Browse for file" button. In the Select Audio window, open the *media* folder, and then open the *audio* folder. Double-click the filename *ceo_message.mp3* to select the audio clip.**

   Dreamweaver closes the Select Audio window. The Properties panel displays the filename in the Source box (Figure 17-21). "Alt Source 1" shows the alternate audio file *ceo_message.ogv*. The audio folder held two *ceo_message* files with different extensions. Dreamweaver used the .mp3 file you selected as the primary source and automatically added the .ogv file as an alternate. You don't have to do anything else to have workable audio on your page, but it's a good idea to give your audio clip a title and fallback text.

5. **In the Properties panel, with the speaker icon selected, click the text box next to Title and type *Message from Our CEO*. Then, in the Fallback Text box, type: *Soylent Green Cafe's CEO discussed the importance of fresh ingredients.***

   Search engines and screen readers use the title of your audio clip to get a brief description of it. The fallback text provides information for web visitors who are unable to listen to the clip.

6. **Set the Preload property to "auto," and then set it back to "none."**

   The Preload property determines whether or not a web browser downloads the audio file when it first loads the page. Often, "none" is the best option, because you don't need to make people download the clip if they aren't going to listen to it. The odd little two-step from "none" to "auto" and then back to "none" forces Dreamweaver to add the Preload property to the file, as explained in step 9 back on page 707.

7. **Above the document window, change the Design/Live view menu to Live. Click the Play button on the audio controls to hear your clip.**

FIGURE 17-21

Your audio clip works as soon as you select a source file. You can test it in Live view or in a browser. It's a good idea to add a title and fallback text. The audio controls (Figure 17-4) seldom need additional formatting, but when they do, apply an ID or class to the clip using the Properties panel, and then develop the CSS to format the element in CSS Designer.

Adding audio clips to a web page is a fairly short and painless job. In this case, you placed the clip between a heading and a paragraph of text. You could just as easily have placed it in a sidebar or in the footer of the page. You can use CSS to apply formatting for margins, paddings, or borders.

You may want to edit the four audio properties in the lower-left corner of the Properties panel, but Dreamweaver uses the best settings for most situations. For example, it automatically includes controls with the audio clip so visitors can start, stop, and replay the clip. It automatically turns off Autoplay so it won't annoy people who don't want to hear the clip, and it turns off Loop because it's usually annoying. It also turns off Muted, because what purpose does a muted audio clip serve?

Adding Video to a Page

The steps for adding video to a page are nearly identical to those for adding audio.

1. **In the Files panel, double-click the filename *index.html*.**

   Dreamweaver opens the home page for Cafe Soylent Green in the document window. There are a couple of images floated to the right side of the page. You'll add your video to the bottom, between Upcoming Events and the page's footer.

2. **Click after the last line in Upcoming Events. In the Tag Selector, click <ul>, the unordered list tag, and then press the right arrow. Finally, press Enter (Return).**

   Dreamweaver adds a new paragraph between Upcoming Events and the footer.

3. **In the Insert panel (Window→Insert), choose the Media category from the menu at the top and then click HTML5 Video.**

   A video icon appears in the web page. Your first task is to choose a source for the clip.

4. **In the Properties panel, to the right of the Source box, click ▣. Open the *media* folder and then open the *video* folder. Double-click *our_philosophy. mp4*.**

   The Source box shows the path to and name of the video file. The box Alt Source 1 points to another video file, *our_philosophy.webm*, while Alt Source 2 points to *our_philosophy.ogv*. These two files were in the same folder as the .mp4 video and, other than the extensions, their filenames are all the same. Dreamweaver automatically added these two clips as alternates for web browsers that don't play back the .mp4 file format. (See page 712 for details on web file formats.)

5. **Switch to Live view and then, in the Properties panel's W box, type *350*.**

   The HD video file is too big for the web page, but by changing the width of the playback window to 350 pixels, it fits. However, anyone who's viewed web video knows that he can click the Full Screen button in the lower-right corner of the window to see a larger version.

6. **In the Title box, type *The Cafe Soylent Green Philosophy*, and then, in the Fallback Text box, type *Images of Cafe Soylent Green's gardens and kitchens*.**

   Screen readers and search engines use the title text to identify the inserted video. The fallback text provides a description for visitors who are unable to view the video because they have sight impairments, or because they turned off the graphics setting in their browser.

7. **Set the Preload property to "auto," and then set it back to "none."**

   The Preload property determines whether or not a web browser downloads the video clip when it first loads the page. Video clips are big, and it takes time and bandwidth to download a long clip. Often, "none" is the best option, because you don't want to make people download the clip if they aren't going to watch it. The odd little two-step from "none" to "auto" and then back to "none" forces Dreamweaver to add the Preload property to the page, as explained back on page 714. But if you think everyone who comes to your page will want to see the clip, choose "auto."

8. **Optional: If you have a still image you want to display when the video isn't playing, click ▤ next to Poster in the Properties panel and then select the image.**

   If you don't identify a poster image, Dreamweaver displays the first frame of the video. That usually works well. (See the note on page 715 for details about capturing a specific frame of your video to use as a poster.)

9. **Optional: If you have a Flash Video version of your clip, click ▤ next to Flash Fallback. Then, in the Select Video window, browse to the .swf version of your video.**

   Visitors with older browsers that can't play back HTML5 video will see the Flash video if they have the Flash player installed.

10. **Click the Play button on the clip's controls to preview the video in Live view (Figure 17-22). Then use File→Preview in Browser to watch the video in the different browsers on your computer.**

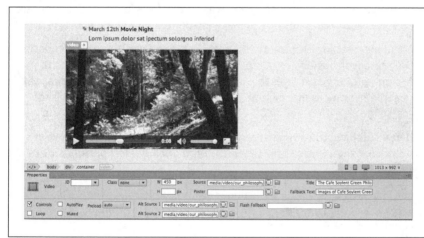

FIGURE 17-22

When you insert an HTML5 video in your web page, it arrives with video controls that just about anyone will understand. From left to right you see a Play/Pause button, a progress bar, a volume control, and a button to expand the video to full screen.

You'll see four checkboxes in the lower-left corner of the Properties panel: Controls, AutoPlay, Loop, and Muted. When you first insert a video, Dreamweaver turns on Controls and leaves the others off. This is the best setting for most web pages. It puts your visitors in control and doesn't overly annoy them with sound and video.

Adding Adobe Edge Animate Compositions to a Page

Edge Animate is part of Adobe's Creative Cloud family. Graphic artists use it to create presentations, slideshows, and other interactive animations in web pages. Animate compositions are made up of multiple files that may include HTML, JavaScript, image, audio, and video files. However, when you finish a project, Animate creates a single, compressed file that has the extension *.oam*. That's the file you work with when you add an Animate composition to a page.

1. **In the Files panel, double click *menu.html*.**

    Dreamweaver opens the menu page. The biggest element on the page is a table that includes different restaurant dishes and their prices. Makes your mouth water, doesn't it? The Animate composition is a slideshow of those pictures. You'll place it under the menu.

2. **In Design view, click inside the table. In the Tag Selector, click the <table> tag, and then press the right arrow on your keyboard.**

    This deselects the <table> tag and moves the cursor to the next position in the HTML code—outside the table.

3. **In the Insert panel, choose Edge Animate Composition. Then, in the Select Edge Animate Package window, open the *media* folder, and then the *animate* folder. Finally, double-click *soylentshow.oam*.**

    The Animate composition appears in the document window as a large gray rectangle. Behind the scenes, Dreamweaver creates a folder on your site called *edgeanimate_assets* and stores the animation's files and folders there.

    There aren't many properties associated with an Edge Animate composition. Dreamweaver has already determined its size and added W (width) and H (Height) properties. It gives the animation the ID "EdgeID." You can change this to something more meaningful, but it's not something your web visitors will see. In the next step, you add a note to tell visitors how to use the slideshow.

4. **If you still have the animation selected, press the right arrow on your keyboard and then press Enter (Return). Type *Click the left or right side of the picture*.**

    If it's not perfectly clear how an animation works, provide instructions for your visitors. Next you'll wrap both the animation and the instruction in a <div> and center them under the menu.

5. **Click in front of the animation and drag to the end of the instructions. Go to the Insert panel, choose the Common category from the menu at the top, and then click Div.**

    Dreamweaver opens the Insert Div window.

6. **Leave the Insert Div menu set to "Wrap around selection" and set the Class to *centered*.**

The *.centered* class has already been created in CSS Designer. It uses the *text-align* property to center text in a paragraph. Here it centers both the animation and the instructions. It also has the top margin set to 15px, which moves the animation down away from the cafe's menu.

7. **Switch to Live view and try out the animation (Figure 17-23).**

FIGURE 17-23

Switch to Live view to test an Edge Animate animation inside Dreamweaver. This composition works like a slideshow, but projects can vary a great deal. Some include audio and video clips, while others are like ebooks, displaying multiple pages of text and images.

Managing a Website

Introducing Site Management

As the dull-sounding term *site management* implies, organizing and tracking your website's files is one of the least glamorous, most time-consuming, error-prone aspects of being a web designer. On the Web, your site may look beautiful, run smoothly, and appear as a gloriously unified whole, but behind the scenes, it's nothing more than a collection of various files—HTML pages, images, Cascading Style Sheets, JavaScript code, Flash movies, and so on—that must all work together. The more files you have to keep track of, the more apt you are to misplace one. And a single broken link or missing graphic can interfere with the operation of your entire site, causing personal—even professional—embarrassment.

Fortunately, computers excel at tedious organizational tasks. Dreamweaver's site-management features take care of the complexities of dealing with a website's many files, freeing you to concentrate on the creative aspects of the site. In fact, even if you're a hand-coding HTML junkie and you turn your nose up at all visual web page editors, you may find Dreamweaver worth its weight in gold just for the features described in this and the next two chapters.

The first four parts of this book described how to create, lay out, and embellish your site. This part offers a bird's-eye view of the process of seeing your site through to completion and, ultimately, putting it up on the Internet.

But to get the most out of Dreamweaver's site-management features, you need to be familiar with some basic principles for organizing web files.

■ Structuring a Website

When you build a website, you probably spend hours adding carefully planned links, helpful labels, and clear, informative navigation tools. You want your *site architec-ture*—the structure of your site—to make it easy for visitors to understand where they are, where they can go, and how to return to where they just came from (see Figure 18-1). Behind the scenes, it's equally important to organize your site files with just as much clarity and care, so you can find *your* way around when you want to update or modify the site. And, just as on your computer, a website's main organizational tool is the humble *folder*.

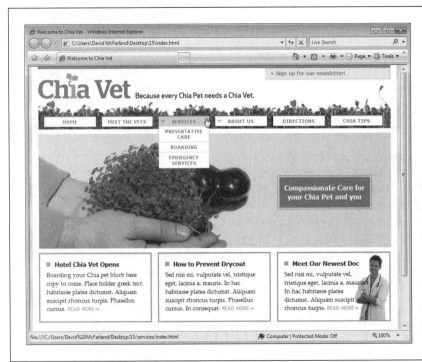

FIGURE 18-1

A good site (even a made-up one) has an easy-to-understand struc-ture. It divides content into logical sections and includes a prominent navigation bar—the row of buttons below the Chia Vet logo in this image—to give visitors quick access to that content. When you build a site, its architecture provides a useful model for creating and naming the behind-the-scenes folders that hold the site's files.

You probably organize files on your computer every day, creating, say, a folder called Personal, within which are folders called Financial Planning and Vacation Pictures. Inside the Vacation Pictures folder, you might have separate folders for memories of Maui, Yosemite, and the Mall of America.

The same principle applies to the folders that make up a website: All websites have one primary folder—the *root folder*—and that folder usually contains additional folders where you further subdivide and organize your site's files. Collectively, the root folder and its subfolders hold all of a site's web pages, graphics, and other files.

A sensible structure (see Figure 18-2) makes it easy to maintain your site because it's logically organized—it gives you quick access to whatever graphic, style sheet, or movie you're looking for. But don't fall into the trap of becoming so obsessed with bins that you put every graphic or web page in its own folder; adding structure to your site should make your job easier, not harder.

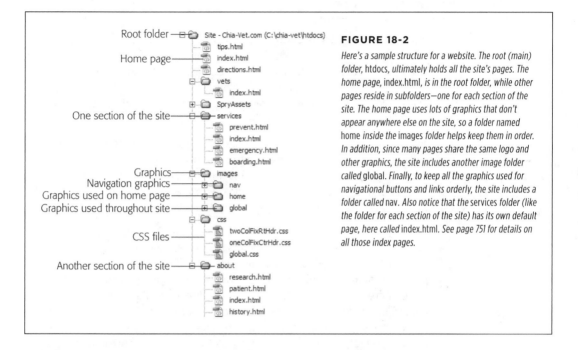

FIGURE 18-2

Here's a sample structure for a website. The root (main) folder, htdocs, ultimately holds all the site's pages. The home page, index.html, is in the root folder, while other pages reside in subfolders—one for each section of the site. The home page uses lots of graphics that don't appear anywhere else on the site, so a folder named home inside the images folder helps keep them in order. In addition, since many pages share the same logo and other graphics, the site includes another image folder called global. Finally, to keep all the graphics used for navigational buttons and links orderly, the site includes a folder called nav. Also notice that the services folder (like the folder for each section of the site) has its own default page, here called index.html. See page 751 for details on all those index pages.

NOTE   If you already have a website that suffers from lack of organization, it's not too late. Dreamweaver can help you organize your files quickly and accurately. Take the following rules to heart, and then turn to "Managing Files and Folders" on page 32.

Here, then, are some guidelines for effective site organization:

- **Plan for future growth**. Like ever-spreading grapevines, websites grow. Today you may have only enough words and pictures for 10 pages, but tomorrow you'll put the finishing touches on your new 1,000-page online catalog. It may seem like overkill to create a lot of folders for a small site, but better to start with a solid structure today than to find yourself knee-deep in files tomorrow.

  For instance, it's useful to create separate folders for graphics that appear within each section of the site. If a section is dedicated to promoting your company's products, for example, create a folder called *products* for your product web pages. Create a subfolder called *images* to store the pictures of those products. Then, when you add more products or images, you know right where to put them.

NOTE While you can start with no organizational plan and later use Dreamweaver to bring your site into shape (see page 32), you may run into unforeseen problems if your site has been up and running for a while. That's because search engines may have already indexed your site, and other websites may have linked to your pages. If you suddenly rearrange your site, people who try to visit your site from a search engine may be foiled, and those cherished links from the outside world may no longer work. If that's the case, you're better off leaving the site as it is and beginning the organization process with new files only.

- **Follow the site's architecture**. Take advantage of the work you've already done in organizing your site's content. For instance, the Chia Vet site content is divided into five sections: Meet the Vets, Services, About Us, Directions, and Chia Tips, as shown in Figure 18-1. Following this structure, it makes sense to create folders—*vets*, *services*, *about*, and so on—in the site's root folder for each section's web pages. If one section is particularly large, add subfolders.

- **Organize files by type**. After you create folders for each section of your site, you'll probably need to add folders to store other types of files, like graphics, Cascading Style Sheets, external JavaScript files, and PDF files. Most sites, for instance, make extensive use of graphics, with several images per page. If that's the case for you, file those images neatly and efficiently.

  One way to organize your graphics is to create a folder for images that appear on your home page and another for images that appear elsewhere on your site. Often, the home page is visually distinct from other site pages and contains graphics that are not only unique to it, but which might also change frequently. You can create a folder—such as *images_home*—in the root folder to hold home-page images. Create another folder—*images_global*—to store graphics that appear on all or most of the other pages, like the company logo, navigation buttons, and other frequently used icons. When you add these images to other pages on your site, you'll know to look for them in this folder. Alternatively, you could create an *images* folder in the root of your site and add subfolders such as *home*, *global*, and *nav* (see Figure 18-2). The choice of an organizational system is yours; just make sure you have one.

- **Use understandable names**. While filenames like *1a.gif*, *zDS.html*, and *f.css* are compact, they aren't very obvious. Make sure your filenames mean something. Clear, descriptive names like *site_logo.gif* or *directions.html* make it a lot easier to locate files and update pages.

  This principle is especially important if you work as part of a team. If you're constantly explaining to coworkers that *345g.gif* is the banner for the home page, changing the filename to *home_banner.gif* could save you some aggravation. There's a tradeoff here, however, as long filenames can waste precious bytes, bloating your pages and slowing down load time. For instance, a site full of filenames like *this_is_the_image_that_goes_in_the_upper_right_corner_of_the_home_page.gif* is probably not a good idea.

NOTE Dreamweaver employs the industry-standard .html extension for web pages—as in *index.html*. Another common extension is .htm (a holdover from the days when Windows could handle only three-letter extensions). It doesn't really matter which you use, and if you're used to .htm, you can easily change the extension Dreamweaver uses. Choose Edit→Preferences (Dreamweaver→Preferences) to open the Preferences window, select the New Document category, and then type *.htm* in the default extension box.

It's also helpful to add a prefix to related files. For example, use *nav_* at the beginning of a graphic filename to indicate that it's a navigation button. That way, you can quickly identify *nav_projects.png*, *nav_quiz.png*, and *nav_horo-scopes.png* as graphics used in a page's navigation bar, or *bg_body.png* and *bg_column.png* as graphics used as backgrounds. As a bonus, when you view the files on your computer or in Dreamweaver's Files panel (see Figure 18-3), they appear neatly sorted by name; in other words, all the *nav_* files cluster together in the file list. Likewise, if you have rollover versions of your navigation graphics, give them names like *nav_projects_hover.gif* or *nav_horoscopes_h.gif* to indicate that they're the highlighted (or rollover) state of the navigation button. (If you use Fireworks, its button-creation tools automatically use names like *nav_projects_f1.gif* and *nav_projects_f2.gif* to indicate two different versions of the same button.)

And, as mentioned in "Naming Your Files and Folders" on page 32, to make sure your files work on any web server, stick to letters, numbers, hyphens (-), and the underscore (_) character in file and folder names.

- **Be consistent**. Once you come up with an organization that works for you, follow it. Always. If you name one folder *images*, for instance, don't name another *graphics* and a third *pretty_pictures*. And certainly don't put web pages in a folder named *images* or JavaScript files in a folder named *style_sheets*.

In fact, if you work on more than one website, you may want to use a single naming convention and folder structure for all your sites, so that switching from one project to another goes more smoothly. If you name all your graphics folders *images*, then no matter what site you're working on, you know where to look for GIFs, PNGs, and JPEGs.

NOTE It's usually best to put files that make up your website in the root folder and its subfolders only. Keep your source files—the original Photoshop, Fireworks, Flash, or Word documents—stored elsewhere on your computer. That way, you're much less likely to accidentally transfer a 14.5 MB Photoshop file to your web server (a move that would *not* gain you friends in the IT department). That said, if you do like keeping all your files together, check out Dreamweaver's *cloaking* feature (described on page 818). Using it, you can prevent Dreamweaver from transferring certain file types to your web server when you use the program's FTP feature.

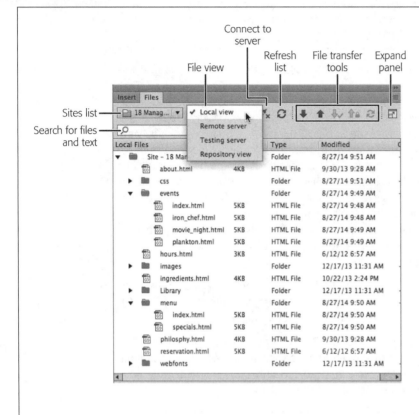

Connect to
server

File view

Refresh
list

File transfer
tools

Expand
panel

Sites list

Search for files
and text

FIGURE 18-3

*Dreamweaver's Files panel,
logically enough, lists files in
the currently active website.
A list of all the websites you
defined in Dreamweaver appears in the Sites drop-down
menu. To work on a different
site, select its name from the
list (but be aware that you
could inadvertently select files
on your local drive, potentially
tripping up Dreamweaver's
site-management tools—see
the box on page 38 for details).
You can use the Files panel
to connect to a web server
and transfer files back and
forth between your local and
remote sites, as described on
page 812. In addition, you can
tell whether you're looking
at files on your computer, the
web server, the testing server,
or a Subversion repository
(page 824) by looking at the
checkmarked name at the top
of the file view column. In this
figure, "Local view" is checked,
so you're looking at files on
your computer.*

▪ Setting Up a Site

Organizing and maintaining a website—creating new folders and web pages; moving,
renaming, and deleting files and folders; and transferring pages to a web server—can
require going back and forth between a couple of programs. With Dreamweaver's
site-management features, however, you can perform all those tasks from within the
program. But to take advantage of this simplicity, you must first make Dreamweaver
aware of your site.

Setting up a site in Dreamweaver involves showing the program which folder contains
your website files (the *root folder*) and setting a few other options. You already know
the basics of setting up a site using Dreamweaver's Site Setup window (page 23).
Here you'll get a detailed explanation of the options available.

All Those Index Pages

Why are so many web pages named index.html (or index.htm)?

If you type a URL like *www.missingmanuals.com* into a web browser, the Missing Manuals home page opens on your screen. But how did the web server know which of the site's pages to send to your browser? After all, you didn't ask for a particular page, like *www.missingmanuals.com/index.html*.

When a web server gets a request that doesn't specify a page, it looks for a default web page—often named *index.html* or *index.htm*. It does the same thing even when the URL you type specifies (with a slash) a folder inside the site root, like this: *www.missingmanuals.com/cds/*. In this case, the server looks for a file called *index.html* inside the "cds" folder, and, if it finds the file, it sends it to your browser.

If the server doesn't find an *index.html* file, two things can happen, both undesirable: The browser displays either an ugly error message or a listing of all the files inside the folder. Neither result helps your visitors.

While your site still functions if you don't give the main page inside each folder a default page name, it's good form to name that file *index.html*. This avoids the "404 File Not Found error" when someone requests just a folder name and not a specific file inside that folder.

Web servers can use different names for these default pages—*default.html*, for example—although *index.html* works on most web servers. In fact, you can specify any page as a default, so long as you set up your web server to look for that page. When you work with a server-side programming language like PHP, ASP, or .NET, the index page will end with a file extension appropriate for that language, like *index.php*, *index.asp*, or *index.aspx*. Most web servers already predefine multiple default page names, so if it doesn't find a file named *index.html*, it may automatically look for one called *index.php*.

Start by choosing Site→New Site. That opens the Site Setup window (see Figure 18-4). It includes four categories of options where you specify the details of your site—Dreamweaver labels the categories Site, Servers, Version Control, and Advanced Settings.

You've encountered the Site category several times already (page 23, for example). It's where you tell Dreamweaver where on your computer it can find your website files. The Servers and Version Control settings help Dreamweaver work with your remote server; you'll learn about them in Chapter 20 (see page 812).

You'll find the Advanced Settings options (Figure 18-4, bottom) useful for different situations, described later in this chapter. You'll learn about the Local Info options next, the Cloaking options on page 818, the Design Notes category on page 831, the Templates option in Chapter 22, and the Web Fonts option on page 141. The settings are called "Advanced" for a reason, and you may not ever feel the need to visit or change them.

The most important category in the Site Setup window is the first one listed: Site (Figure 18-4, top). Filling out the following two options is all you need to get started using Dreamweaver effectively.

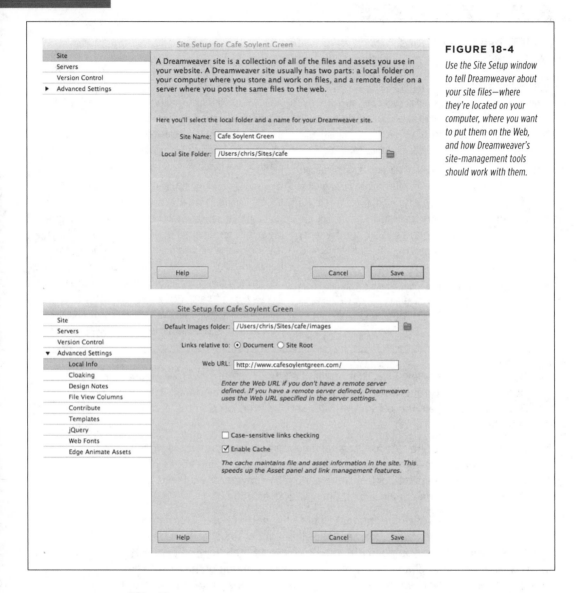

FIGURE 18-4

Use the Site Setup window to tell Dreamweaver about your site files—where they're located on your computer, where you want to put them on the Web, and how Dreamweaver's site-management tools should work with them.

Site Name

In the "Site Name" field, type a name that briefly identifies the site for you—and Dreamweaver. This is the name that appears in, among other places, the File panel's Sites drop-down menu (see Figure 18-3 for a glimpse of that), so you can choose the site you want to work on. The site name doesn't appear on your actual site pages.

Local Site Folder

Identify your site's local folder—the folder on your hard drive that contains all the site's files. (This is also known as a *local root folder*.) Click 📁 to the right of the Local Site Folder box to browse for the folder. See the box on page 758 for more on local site folders.

> **NOTE** If you're confused about which folder is your local site folder, ask yourself this: "Which folder on my computer will contain (or contains) my site's home page?" That's your local site folder. All your site's other files and folders should go inside this one.

The Dreamweaver tools that manage your sites' files rely on the local site folder. Once you set up a site, you see all its files listed in the Files panel. In the Advanced Settings area, the Local Info tab tells Dreamweaver how to work with the files on your computer.

That tab (Figure 18-4), bottom) has other useful settings that can help Dreamweaver work with your site's files, as described below.

Default Images Folder

When you want to display a graphic on a web page, you tell the page where to find the image by pointing to its file location. That location has to be inside the local root folder or one of its subfolders. In other words, if you link to a graphic that's sitting *outside* the root folder on your hard drive, a web browser will never find it when you upload your site to the web server.

Dreamweaver offers a feature that puts images in the right place even if you forget to. When you add a stray graphics file to a page on your site, Dreamweaver automatically copies that file to your default images folder. In fact, even if you drag a graphic from your desktop onto a web page in progress, Dreamweaver copies the file to the images folder without missing a beat.

You identify the default images folder the same way you select the local site folder: Click 📁 and locate the folder on your local drive. If you haven't set up the folder yet, click New Folder to create it on the spot. (For example, you might add a folder to your local root folder and name it *images*.)

Links Relative To

As discussed on page 177, you can set up links in your web pages in a variety of ways. When you link from one page to another, Dreamweaver lets you create either a *document-relative* link or a *root-relative* link. As explained on page 178, document-relative links are often the easiest way to go, but Dreamweaver gives you the flexibility to choose. Click either the Document or Site Root radio button. Then, whenever you embed a link in your pages, Dreamweaver creates the link using that setting.

> **NOTE** You can override this setting and use whichever type of link you wish when you create the link, as described in step 4 on page 185.

FREQUENTLY ASKED QUESTION

Bringing Your Own Website

I already have a website. Will Dreamweaver work with it?

Yes. In fact, Dreamweaver's site-management features are an invaluable aid in organizing the files of an existing site. You can use Dreamweaver to rearrange, rename, and reorganize files—tasks that are extremely difficult and time-consuming to do by hand (see "Managing Files and Folders" on page 32).

Furthermore, Dreamweaver lets you clean up and reorganize a site without breaking links. So it's just as useful for working with a finished site as it is for creating one from scratch.

To work on an existing site, make sure it has its own root folder—in other words, that its home page, graphics, CSS files, other web pages, and any subfolders all reside in one main site folder. Then set up a new site in Dreamweaver as described above, and choose this folder as the local site folder.

Web URL

This option serves two functions: First, if you use absolute URLs to link to pages within your site (see page 178), you must fill out the Web URL field for Dreamweaver's link-management features to work (page 183). Type in your site's full web address, beginning with *http://*. Dreamweaver uses this address to check for broken links within your site and correctly rewrite them if you move pages around. For example, say your webmaster told you to link a form to *http://www.yourdomain.com/cgi/ formscript.php* instead of using a document-relative link. In this case, you'd type *http://www.yourdomain.com/* in the Web URL box. Now, if you move or rename the *formscript.php* page from within Dreamweaver, the program is smart enough to update the absolute link in the form.

This setting is also incredibly valuable in one particular situation: if you use site root-relative links but the site you're working on isn't actually located in the site root on the web server. For example, say you run the marketing department at International ToolCo. You manage just the web pages for your department, and they're located in a folder called *marketing* on the web server. In essence, you manage a sub-site, which acts as an independent site within the larger International ToolCo site. Maybe your webmaster demands that you use site root-relative links—man, is that guy bossy.

NOTE If you set up Dreamweaver to upload and download files from your web server as described on page 812, you've already told Dreamweaver your website's URL (see step 10 on page 805). If that's the case, the Web URL option in the Local Info box will be grayed out.

This is a potentially tricky situation. Here's why: Site root-relative links always begin with a forward slash (/), indicating the root folder on the web server (for a refresher on this concept, see page 179). Normally, if you add a root-relative link to, say, the main page in a folder named *personnel* located inside the local root folder, Dreamweaver would write the link like this: */personnel/index.html*. But in this case, that wouldn't work. The *personnel* folder is actually located inside the *marketing* folder on the web server. So the link should be */marketing/personnel/index.html.* In other words, Dreamweaver normally thinks that your local root folder maps exactly to the web server's root folder.

You can solve this dilemma by adding a web address that points to the sub-site in the Site Definition window's Web URL box. In this example, you'd type *http://www. intltoolco.com/marketing/* in the box. Then, whenever you add a root–relative link, Dreamweaver begins it with */marketing/* and then adds the rest of the path. In summary, *if* you use site root-relative links *and* you're working solely on pages located inside a subdirectory on the actual server, *then* fill out the absolute URL to that subdirectory. Finally, add this whole rigmarole to the list of reasons why document-relative links are easier to manage in Dreamweaver.

NOTE   Strangely, the first use of the Web URL box mentioned above—that is, managing absolute URLs pointing to files in your site—doesn't work with the second option—sub-sites. For example, if you specify a subdirectory like *http://www.intltoolco.com/marketing/* in the Web URL box, Dreamweaver isn't able to keep track of absolute links within this site. So if you had to use the URL *www.intltoolco.com/marketing/cgi/form.php* to point to a form page within your site, and then you move that form page, Dreamweaver won't update the page that uses that absolute link.

Case-Sensitive Links

Some web servers (namely, those that use the Unix and Linux operating systems) are sensitive to the case you use in filenames. For example, both OSes consider *INDEX. html* and *index.html* different files. If your server uses either operating system, turn on the "Use case-sensitive link checking" checkbox to make sure Dreamweaver doesn't mistake one file for another when it checks links. Say you link to a file named *INDEX.html* but change the name of another file named *index.html* to *contact.html.* Without this option turned on, Dreamweaver may mistakenly update links to *INDEX. html* because it considers that file the same as *index.html.*

In real-world use, you probably won't need this option. First, it's not possible to have two files with the same name but different combinations of upper- and lowercase letters in the same folder on a Windows or Mac machine. So if your local root folder is on a Windows or Mac computer, you'll never be able to get into this situation. In addition, it's confusing (and just plain weird) to use the same name but different cases for your files.

■ CACHE

The cache is a small database of information about the files in your site. It helps Dreamweaver's site-management features work more efficiently. In almost all cases, you want to keep this checkbox turned on. However, if you have an old computer and a really large site, composed of tens of thousands of web pages, Dreamweaver might act pretty sluggishly when you perform basic tasks like moving files around within the site or checking for broken links.

Once you provide the local information for your site, click Save to close the Site Definition window and begin working.

Managing Dreamweaver Sites

When you work with Dreamweaver, keep in mind that you'll have a set of files on your computer for each site you work on as well as a "site" that you set up in Dreamweaver. Dreamweaver sites aren't websites in the true sense of the word—that is, they aren't Internet-based web pages that anyone with a browser can open. Rather, Dreamweaver sites comprise just the information Dreamweaver needs to locate and work with your local web files and to connect to your web server.

The files on your computer will always be there (until you or your mischievous cat delete them); they exist even without Dreamweaver. But when you use Dreamweaver for site development, you have a list of all the sites you set up within the program (using the process described on page 750). You can edit and delete these Dreamweaver "sites" without doing any harm to the actual site files on your computer.

Editing or Removing Sites

Sometimes you need to edit the information associated with a site. Perhaps you want to rename the site, or you reorganized your hard drive and moved the local root folder, so you want to let Dreamweaver know the new location.

To edit a site, open the Manage Sites dialog box (choose Site→Manage Sites or, in the Files panel, choose Manage Sites from the bottom of the Site drop-down menu) and then double-click the name of the site you want to edit. The Site Setup window opens (Figure 18-4, top). Now you can type a new name in the Site Name box, choose a new local root folder, or make any other changes you want. Click OK to close the window when you're done.

TIP If you want to edit the current site's information, there's a shortcut. In the Files panel (Figure 18-3), double-click the name of the site in the Sites menu.

Once you finish designing a site, you may want to remove it from Dreamweaver's list of sites. Open the Manage Sites dialog box (see Figure 18-5) as described above, click to select the site you want to delete, and then click – (that's the Delete Site button).

A warning appears telling you that you can't undo this action. Don't worry; deleting the site here doesn't actually *delete* the site's web pages, images, or other files from your computer. It merely removes the site from Dreamweaver's list of sites. (You can always go back and set up the site again by following the steps on page 750.) Click Done to close the Manage Sites window.

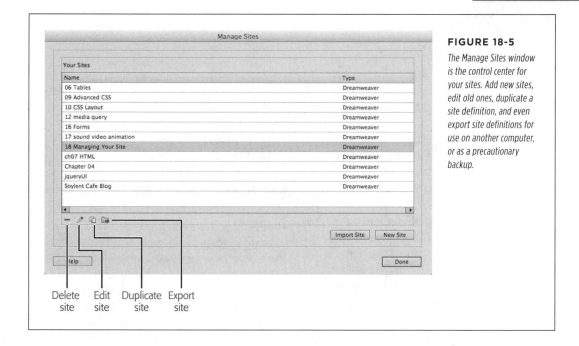

FIGURE 18-5

The Manage Sites window is the control center for your sites. Add new sites, edit old ones, duplicate a site definition, and even export site definitions for use on another computer, or as a precautionary backup.

NOTE If you do, in fact, want to delete the actual web pages, graphics, and other site components, you can either switch to your computer's file-management window (Windows Explorer or the Mac Finder, for example) and delete them manually, or delete them from within Dreamweaver's Files panel, as described on page 32.

Exporting and Importing Sites

When you set up a site, Dreamweaver stores that site's information in its own private files. If you want to work on your site using a different computer, therefore, you must set up the site again for *that* copy of Dreamweaver. In a design firm where several people work on many different sites, that's a lot of extra setup. In fact, even if there's just one of you working on two computers, duplicating your efforts takes extra work.

Dreamweaver lets you import and export site settings so you can put your time to better use. For example, you can back up your site set-up files in case you have to reinstall Dreamweaver, and you can export a site setup for others to use.

NOTE Exporting a site setup in Dreamweaver doesn't actually export your site files—all of the web pages, folders, and so on—it just exports the setup options you used when you set up the site. In other words, you just export and import the information that lets Dreamweaver work with your site's files, not the files themselves.

Local vs. Live Site Folders

A site folder (also called a *root* folder) is a site's main, hold-everything bin. It contains every component that makes up your website: all web pages, graphics, CSS style sheets, JavaScript files, and so on.

The word "site" in the name "site folder" implies that this folder holds your entire site. It's the master, outer, main folder, the folder in which you may have plenty of subfolders. Remember that, in most cases, your website exists in two locations: on your computer as you work on it and on the Internet where people can enjoy the fruits of your labor. In fact, most websites in the universe live in two places at once—one copy on the Internet and the original on some web designer's hard drive. (In some cases, you'll also have what's called a "testing server," often used so you can test dynamic, database-driven websites locally before publishing them to the Internet—you'll learn about them in Chapter 24.)

The copy on your own computer is called the *local site*. Think of it as a sort of development area, where you build your site,

test it, and modify it. (With database-driven sites, you do your testing on a testing server and use the local site to store the files as you work on them. As you'll read on page 921, it's common for the files on your local site and testing server to be one and the same.)

Because the local site isn't on a web server, the public can't see it, and you can freely edit and add to it without affecting the pages your visitors see. The folder for the version of the site you keep on your computer, therefore, is called the *local site folder*.

After you add or update a file, you move it from the local site to the *remote server*. The site on the remote server mirrors your local site. Because you create a remote site by uploading your local site to a server, it has the same folder structure as your local site and contains the same polished, fully functional web pages. The local site also includes all the half-finished, typo-ridden drafts you're working on. Chapter 20 explains how to use Dreamweaver's FTP features to upload your ready-for-prime-time local site and how to work with a remote server.

To export a site setup:

1. **Choose Site→Manage Sites.**

   The Manage Sites window appears, listing all the sites you've defined (Figure 18-5).

2. **Select a site from the list, and then click the "Export site" button (the folder with an arrow on it).**

   The Export Site panel appears.

   If you haven't told Dreamweaver about your remote server, skip to step 4.

3. **Select either "Back up my settings" or "Share settings with other users" and then click OK.**

   If the site setup includes remote server information (so Dreamweaver can connect to your web server and move files onto it, as described on page 812), you'll see a dialog box called "Exporting site" (Figure 18-6). If you simply want to make a backup of your site definition because you need to reinstall Dreamweaver, select the "Back up my settings" radio button.

The other option, "Share settings," isn't all that useful. It's intended to let you share your site settings with a person working on another copy of the same site on her own computer. When you elect to share settings, Dreamweaver doesn't include the username and password you use to connect to the remote (web) server, a good thing. But it also excludes the site-file paths you defined because, presumably, the person you're sharing the settings with has her site files in a different location on her computer. For that reason, it's just as easy for that person to simply create her own site setup following the instructions on page 750.

FIGURE 18-6

This dialog box lets you back up your site settings or share them (minus your login information) with other people.

4. **In the Export Site panel, specify where you want to save the file, and give it a name.**

   If you're making a backup, save the file outside the local root folder (for example, with the Photoshop, Fireworks, and Word source files for your site). Because the export file can potentially contain the username and password you use to move files to your remote site, you don't want to keep the file anywhere in your local root folder—you might mistakenly upload it to the web server, where someone might find it and wreak havoc with your site.

   Dreamweaver uses the extension .ste for site-definition files.

TIP You can export multiple sites in a single step. Select all the sites you want to export (Ctrl-click [⌘-click] the names of the sites), and then click Export. You won't, however, be able to name each export file in this step—just the first one. In addition, Dreamweaver saves all the site definitions you export this way in the same folder. You can, of course, move and rename the files. Just make sure to keep the .ste extension at the end of each filename.

Once you create a site setup file, you can import it into Dreamweaver as follows:

1. **Choose Site→Manage Sites.**

   The Manage Sites panel appears.

2. **Click the Import Site button (see Figure 18-5).**

   The Import Site panel appears. Navigate to the setup file—look for a file ending in .ste. Select it, and then click OK.

If you import the site setup options to a computer other than the one you used to export it, you may need to perform a few more steps. If Dreamweaver can't find the location of the local site folder in the site setup file, it asks you to select a local site folder on the new computer, as well as a new default Images folder.

Viewing Files in the Files Panel

Once you set up your local site, you can use Dreamweaver's Files panel as command central for organizing your files, creating folders, and adding new web pages. To open the Files panel, choose Window→Files, or press F8.

In its most basic incarnation, the Files panel lists the files in the current site's local root folder. This list looks and acts very much like Windows Explorer or the Mac's Finder; you see names, file sizes, and folders. You can view the files inside a folder by clicking + on Windows machines and the flippy triangle next to the folder on Macs (or simply by double-clicking the folder name). Double-click a web page to open it in Dreamweaver. You can also see the size of a file, the type of file it is, and the last time you modified it. That's a lot of information to fit in that space, so if you find this new view a little too cramped, hide any columns you don't like—see page 834.

> **NOTE** You can open certain types of files in an outside program of your choice by defining an external editor for that file type. For example, you can tell Dreamweaver to open GIF files in Fireworks, Photoshop, or another image editor. See page 258 for more.

You can view your site's files in four ways, using the View drop-down menu (shown in Figure 18-3):

- **Local view** lists the files in your local root folder. Dreamweaver displays folders in this view as green.

- **Remote server** displays the files in your remote site folder; in other words, the files on your web server (see the box on page 758). Of course, before you post your site to the Web, this list is empty. Dreamweaver adds files to this folder only after you set up a connection to the remote server and upload files to it. Dreamweaver displays folders in this view as yellow on Windows PCs and blue on Macs.

- **Testing server view** is useful when you create the dynamic, database-driven sites discussed in Chapter 22. No files appear in this view until you set up a testing server (see page 921) and connect Dreamweaver to it. When you do, Dreamweaver displays folders in this view in red.

- **Repository view** gives you a peek inside a file-versioning system called Subversion. You'll learn about this advanced file-management tool on page 824.

You can view any combination of these two views side by side—for example, you can see a list of your local files next to a list of the files on your web server—by clicking the Expand Panel button (see Figure 18-3). This undocks the Files panel from the side of the screen, turning it into a floating window (see Figure 18-7). You'll find this most useful when you want to compare files on your local computer with those on your web server or testing server.

TIP If you've got a small monitor, the Files panel (and other panel groups) might take up too much space to let you comfortably work on a web page. On a Windows computer, you can hide (and show) all panels, including the Properties panel and Insert bar, by pressing F4. On Macs, go to View→Hide Panels.

FIGURE 18-7

Click the Expand Panel button shown in Figure 18-3 to maximize the Files panel and display two views simultaneously. This way, you can see both your remote site and local site at the same time. Local files normally appear on the right, but might be on the left, depending on the preference you set under the Site category of Dreamweaver's Preferences window. (To change this arrangement, press Ctrl+U [⌘-U] to open the window, and then click the Site category.) The view that appears opposite the local files list—Remote Server, Testing, or Repository—depends on which view you selected before clicking the Expand Panel button. To change views, click a different view button.

Modifying the Files Panel View

Dreamweaver stocks the Files panel with loads of information on its inhabitants: the filename, file size, file type (web page, graphic, and so on), and the date you last modified it. That's all useful to know, but if you have a small monitor, you may not be able to display everything without having to scroll left and right. What's worse, the filenames you want front and center often get clipped by other columns of information.

There are a couple of ways to fix this. First, you can resize the width of each column by dragging one of the dividers that separates the column names (for example, the vertical line between the Local Files and Size columns in Figure 18-3). Using this technique, you can at least display the full name of each file.

If you don't like the number of columns Dreamweaver displays, you can hide any or all of them. After all, how useful is listing the type of each file? The folder icon clearly indicates when you're looking at a folder, and each filename's extension—for example, .html for a web page or .jpg for a JPEG graphic—clearly indicates the file's type. For most folks, that's enough.

Unfortunately, there's no program-wide setting to control which columns appear. You have to define the visible columns on a site-by-site basis:

1. **Choose Site→Manage Sites and then double-click the name of the site whose Files panel you want to modify.**

   Dreamweaver opens the Site Setup window.

2. **Click the Advanced Settings category to display the list of options, and then select File View Columns (see Figure 18-8, top).**

   Dreamweaver lists all the columns the Files panel can display and indicates which it currently displays ("Show") or hides ("Hide"). Under the Type heading, all the files initially say "Built In" to indicate columns that Dreamweaver displays out of the box. As you'll read on page 835, you can add your own customized columns to this list.

3. **Double-click the row that holds the column you want to change.**

   For example, double-clicking the Type row displays the options you see in Figure 18-8, bottom: Column Name, "Associate with Design Notes," and "Share with all users of this site." Most of the options are dimmed out because they apply only to custom-created columns, described on page 835.

4. **Change the alignment of the column (Left, Right, or Center) from the Align menu, and turn on or off the Show checkbox to show or hide a column.**

   For example, to hide the Size column, turn off the Show checkbox in the Size column's options window.

5. **Click Save to close that column's settings.**

   Repeat steps 3–5 for any other columns you want to edit, and when you're done, click Save in the Site Setup window.

You can change the order of the columns, too—perhaps a file's Modified date is more important to you than its size. Select a column and click the up or down arrow. The up arrow moves the column to the left in the Files panel, while the down arrow scoots it over to the right.

■ Editing Page Elements from the Assets Panel

Web pages integrate lots of page elements: PNGs, GIFs, JPEGs, links, colors, Java-Script files, and Flash movies, to name just a few. On a large site with lots of files, it's a challenge to locate a particular image or to remember an exact color.

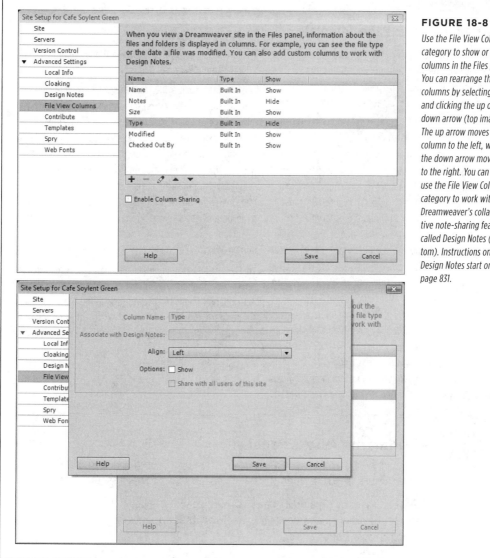

FIGURE 18-8

Use the File View Columns category to show or hide columns in the Files panel. You can rearrange the columns by selecting one and clicking the up or down arrow (top image). The up arrow moves the column to the left, while the down arrow moves it to the right. You can also use the File View Columns category to work with Dreamweaver's collaborative note-sharing feature called Design Notes (bottom). Instructions on using Design Notes start on page 831.

To simplify the process, Dreamweaver provides the Assets panel. For want of a better word, Dreamweaver defines the term *asset* to mean any element you use on a web page, such as a JPEG, a link, or even an individual color.

Changing the New-Page Template

Whenever you create a new web page—by choosing File→New or by right-clicking (Control-clicking) an existing file in the Files panel—Dreamweaver gives you a blank document. But what if you always want your pages to have special HTML comments indicating that your company created the page, or you always want to include a link to the same external style sheet?

Every new web page you create is actually an untitled copy of a Dreamweaver-supplied template document called *Default.html*. You can find this file in Dreamweaver's configuration folder. On Windows 64-bit computers, it's in *C:\Program Files\Adobe\Adobe Dreamweaver CC 2014.1\configuration\DocumentTypes\NewDocuments*. If you have a 32-bit version of Dreamweaver, it will be *C:\Program Files (86)\Adobe\Adobe Dreamweaver CC2014.1\configuration\DocumentTypes\NewDocuments*. On a Mac, you can find it in the *Applications→Adobe Dreamweaver CC 2014.1→ Configuration→DocumentTypes→New-Documents* folder. Save a copy of this folder so you can always return to the original file. In Windows XP, use the folder name *C:\Documents and Settings\[your user name]\Application Data\ Adobe\Dreamweaver CC 2014.1\en_US\Configuration*. In Windows Vista, use *C:\Users\[your user name]\AppData\Roaming\ Adobe\ Dreamweaver CC 2014.1\en_US\Configuration*. On a Mac,

try *Volume Name→Applications→Adobe Dreamweaver CC 2014.1→ Configuration→DocumentTypes→New Documents*.

You can then open a file from the NewDocument folder in your personal configuration folder and edit it however you like: change or add HTML comments, meta tags, pre-canned links to a style sheet, or whatever, so that all subsequent new pages inherit these settings. Also, make sure you don't touch an HTML fragment that may look incorrect, namely, the *charset="* snippet, which appears at the end of the <meta> tag. This fragment of HTML is indeed incomplete, but when you create a new page, Dreamweaver correctly completes the code according to the alphabet (a.k.a. character set) your page uses—Chinese, Korean, Western European, or UTF-8, for example.

You'll notice lots of other files in this folder. Since Dreamweaver can create lots of different file types—Cascading Style Sheets, Active Server Pages, and so on—you'll find a default blank file for each. You can edit any of these—but don't, unless you know what you're doing. You can easily damage some of the more complex file types, especially those that involve dynamic websites.

Viewing the Assets Panel

Dreamweaver lists your site's assets on the seven category "pages" of the Assets panel (Figure 18-9). To open the panel, choose Window→Assets.

Select an asset by clicking its name. Dreamweaver previews the asset above the Assets list. To preview a movie, click the arrow that appears in the upper-right corner of the preview pane.

Dreamweaver divides your site's assets into eight categories, represented by icons on the left side of the Assets panel. To view the assets in a particular category, click its icon:

- **The Images category lists all the GIF, JPEG, and PNG files in your site**. Dreamweaver lists the dimensions of each image next to its name so you can quickly identify whether *logo1.gif* or *logo2.gif* is your 728 x 90-pixel banner logo. You can also see the images' file sizes, types, and locations (you may need to scroll to the right to see all this).

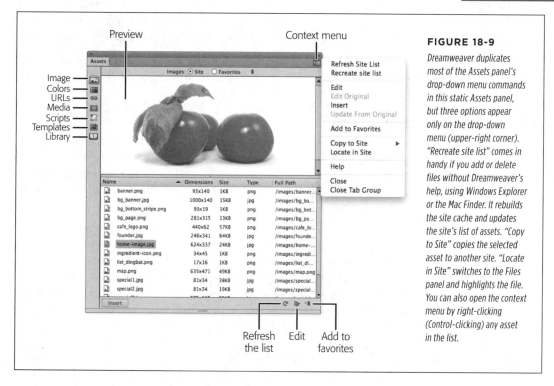

FIGURE 18-9

Dreamweaver duplicates most of the Assets panel's drop-down menu commands in this static Assets panel, but three options appear only on the drop-down menu (upper-right corner). "Recreate site list" comes in handy if you add or delete files without Dreamweaver's help, using Windows Explorer or the Mac Finder. It rebuilds the site cache and updates the site's list of assets. "Copy to Site" copies the selected asset to another site. "Locate in Site" switches to the Files panel and highlights the file. You can also open the context menu by right-clicking (Control-clicking) any asset in the list.

- **The Colors category shows you all the colors specified in your site's pages and style sheets**. These include link colors, background colors, and text colors.

- **The URLs category lists all external links.** And not just standard http:// links, but also email links, FTP addresses, and JavaScript links.

- **The Media category lists audio and video files.** It displays movie files with their corresponding extensions: .swf (Flash), .flv (Flash video), and .mov or .mpg (QuickTime and MPEG). Unfortunately, the Movies category hasn't kept up with the times: Thanks to HTML5 video (see page 708), there are other movie formats to think about, such as MPEG4 (.mp4), Ogg Vorbis (.ogv), and WebM (.webm). Unfortunately, Dreamweaver doesn't support them.

- **The Scripts category lists JavaScript files**. It includes only external program files your web pages link to. Dreamweaver doesn't include scripts embedded *in* a web page, like Dreamweaver behaviors.

- **The last two categories—Templates and Library—are advanced assets that streamline website production**. You'll find them discussed in Chapters 19 and 20.

You can switch between two views for most asset categories—Site and Favorites—by clicking the radio buttons near the top of the Assets panel. (There are no Favorites in the Templates and Library categories.) The Site option lists all the assets in your site for the chosen category. Favorites lets you create a select list of your most important and frequently used assets (see page 767), like a company logo.

If you add assets as you work on a site—for example, if you create a GIF file in Fireworks and import it into your site—you need to update the Assets panel. To do so, click the Refresh Site List button (see Figure 18-9).

Inserting Assets

The Assets panel's prime mission is to make it easy for you to add elements to your site by dragging an asset from the panel into your document window. This drag-and-drop operation works in both Design view and Live view. For example, you can add graphics, colors, and links with a simple drag-and-drop. Note that most of the categories on the panel refer to external files you commonly find on web pages: images, Flash files, movies, and scripts.

You can drop an asset anywhere on a page where you'd normally insert an object—in a table cell, a <div> tag, at the beginning or end of a page, or within a paragraph. You can also add script assets to the head of a page (see Figure 18-10). (If you're billing by the hour, you may prefer the long way: Click in the document window to plant the insertion point, click the asset's name, and then click Insert at the bottom of the Assets panel.)

■ ADDING COLOR AND LINK ASSETS

Color and link assets work a bit differently from other asset files. Instead of standing on their own, they *add* color to any text selection in the document window or *link* to text or images selected in the document window. This makes it easy to quickly add a frequently used link—the web address of Adobe Reader, for example.

To do so, start by highlighting the text whose color you want to change, or by highlighting the words or an image that you want to turn into a link. In the Assets panel, click the appropriate category button—Colors or Links. Click the color or link you want, and then click Apply. Alternatively, you can drag the color or link asset from the panel onto the selected text or image.

In the case of links, Dreamweaver simply adds <a> tags to the selection, along with the proper external link. For color, Dreamweaver pops up the New CSS Rule window and asks you to create a new CSS style—you then need to go through the whole rigmarole described on page 151. Unfortunately, Dreamweaver isn't smart enough to update the text color of any style already applied to the selected text. In other words, applying colors with the Assets panel is more trouble than it's worth.

However, there is one way to use the color assets effectively, sort of. As you'll recall (or not) from page 151, the Dreamweaver color picker lets you sample colors that appear on your monitor. So if you want to use a color from the Assets panel, make sure you have the Assets panel open and the color assets visible. Then, when you want to select a color (for example, to add a color to text in the CSS Rule Definition window), click the color box (the cursor changes to an eyedropper), and then click a color in the Assets panel.

FIGURE 18-10

Although you'll insert most assets into the body of a web page, you can (and usually should) place script files at the head of the page. To do this, view the page in Code or Split view, and then drag the script from the Assets panel into the head portion of the page—that is, after the opening <head> tag and before the closing tag (</head>), as shown here. Adding a script asset doesn't copy the JavaScript code into the web page. Instead, just as with external style sheets, Dreamweaver links to the script file so that when a browser loads the page, it looks for and then loads the associated JavaScript file from the website.

Favorite Assets

On a large site, you may have thousands of images, movies, colors, and external links. Because scrolling through long lists of assets is a chore, Dreamweaver lets you create a compact list of your favorite, frequently used assets.

For example, you might use five main colors in your site, which you'll apply much more often than the miscellaneous colors in the Assets list. Add them to your list of favorite colors. Likewise, adding graphics you use over and over—logos, for example—to a list of favorites makes it easy to locate and insert those files into your pages. (You can also use Dreamweaver's library and template features for this function. They're similar but more powerful tools that keep frequently used items at the ready. Turn to Chapters 21 and 22 for details.)

■ **IDENTIFYING FAVORITES**

If the color, graphic, or other element you want to add to your Favorites list already appears in your Assets panel, highlight it in the list and then click "Add to Favorites" (see Figure 18-9).

Even quicker, you can add favorites as you go, snagging them right from your web page. If you're working on your site's home page, for example, and you insert a company logo, that's a perfect time to make the logo a favorite. Simply right-click (Control-click) the image. From the shortcut menu, choose "Add Image to Favorites." Dreamweaver instantly adds the graphic to your list of favorites *within that asset category*—meaning that you'll see the file when you're in the Favorites view *and* you have the Image category selected. You can use the same shortcut for colors, links, program files, or media files.

When it comes to colors and links, you can turn them into favorites another way: In the Assets panel, select the Color or URLs category, click the Favorites radio button, and then click the New Asset button (see Figure 18-11).

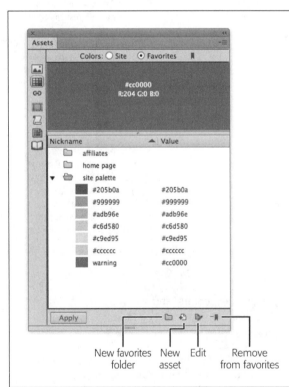

New favorites   New   Edit   Remove
folder   asset   from favorites

FIGURE 18-11

In addition to using folders to organize your favorite assets, you can give them an easily identifiable nickname. Instead of listing a favorite image using its filename—148593.gif, for instance—use an easily understood nickname, like New Product. Naming favorite colors is particularly helpful; a nickname like Page Background is more descriptive than #FF6633. To name a favorite asset, click to select it, pause a moment, and then click again to edit its name. (These nicknames apply only in the Assets panel; you don't rename or retitle your files.)

Then:

- If you're adding a favorite color, Dreamweaver opens its color box. Select a color using the eyedropper (see page 151).

- If you're adding a favorite link, Dreamweaver opens the Add URL window. Type either an absolute web address (one starting with *http://*) in the first field or an email address (for instance, *mailto:info@cafesoylentgreen.com*). Next, type a name for the link—such as *Acrobat Download* or *Info Email*—in the Nickname field and then click OK.

Your new color or link appears in your Favorites list.

■ USING FAVORITES

You insert assets from your Favorites list into web pages just as you would any other asset. For example, for an image or other media, just drag it from the Assets panel onto your page.

■ REMOVING FAVORITES

Removing an asset from your Favorites list is just as straightforward as adding one: Select it in the Favorites list and then press Delete. The "Remove from Favorites" button on the Assets panel does the same thing (see Figure 18-11). Yet another approach is to use the shortcut menu (Figure 18-10).

Don't worry; removing an asset from your Favorites list *doesn't* delete that asset from your site (or the Assets panel). You can still find it by clicking the Site radio button.

■ ORGANIZING FAVORITE ASSETS

On a large site with lots of important assets, even a Favorites list can get unwieldy. That's why you can set up folders within the asset categories of the Favorites panel. For example, if you use lots of ads on a site, create a folder in the Image category called Ads or, for even greater precision, create multiple folders for different types of ads: Banner Ads, Half Banner Ads, and so on.

You can then drag assets into the appropriate folders and expand or contract the folder to show or hide the assets inside. These folders simply help you organize your Assets panel; they don't actually appear anywhere within the structure of your site. Moving a Favorite asset into a folder doesn't change the location of files within your site, either.

To create a Favorites folder, make sure you're in Favorites view by clicking Favorites at the top of the Assets panel (Dreamweaver doesn't let you create folders in Site view), and then click the appropriate asset category button on the left edge of the Assets panel (any except the bottom two, since, alas, you can't create folders for templates and Library items). Click Favorites at the top of the Assets panel, and then click the New Favorites Folder button (see Figure 18-11) at the bottom of the Assets panel. When Dreamweaver displays the new folder with its placeholder name, type a new name and then press Enter (but don't use the same name for more than one folder).

To put an asset into a folder, just drag it there from the list. And if you're really obsessive, you can even create subfolders by dragging one folder onto another.

Nothing Could Be Kuler

Adobe's Kuler web tool (*http://kuler.adobe.com*) is an online gallery of color palettes. It lets you build your own sets of colors and offers tools based on the science of color theory to create harmonious color combinations for your site. Even better, by clicking the Explore link at the top of the page, you can see thousands of palettes created by *other* web designers, showcasing everything from cool and subtle color schemes to loud and vibrant mixes. It's a great site if you're eager for a little color inspiration.

Dreamweaver's cousin, Photoshop, has an add-on that makes it easy to browse colors from Kuler and bring them into projects. To use Kuler with Dreamweaver, you need to improvise. Open the website in one window on your computer and then open Assets→Colors in another window. At the bottom of the Assets panel, click New Color—it looks like a swatch with a plus sign. Adobe's color picker opens with the eyedropper button in the lower-right corner. Click the eyedropper and then click a color in the Kuler window that you want to add to your project. Repeat the process to add an entire set of colors to the assets panel.

Testing Your Site

As you no doubt realize by now, building a website involves quite a few steps. At any point in the process, you can easily introduce errors that affect the performance of your pages. Mistakes both small (like typos) and site-shattering (think broken links) occur frequently in the web development cycle.

Unfortunately, web designers often neglect to create a set of best practices for testing their sites. This chapter offers helpful techniques for that, and shows you how Dreamweaver's wide array of site-testing tools can help.

■ Site Launch Checklist

Don't wait until you finish your site before developing a thorough strategy for regular testing. If you do, serious design errors may have so completely infested your pages that you have to start over, or at least spend many hours fixing problems you could have prevented early on. These guidelines help you avoid such a predicament:

- **Preview early and often**. The single best way to make sure a page looks and functions the way you want it to is to preview it in as many browsers as possible. For a quick test, switch to Live view using the Design/Live drop-down menu in Dreamweaver's Document toolbar (page 57). This is a great way to quickly check JavaScript components, web fonts, and the way a browser displays pages that have complex CSS. You see pages as your web visitors will see them in the Google Chrome web browser, because Live view uses a related browser called Chromium. Your page will look similar in Safari and many mobile browsers.

  Chromium is a fast, modern browser that adheres to Web standards, so it makes sense that Adobe chose it for Live view. In short, it doesn't muck up the works inside Dreamweaver. Unfortunately, you can't stop testing once you finish with Live view, because people will visit your site using other browsers, some not so well-behaved. So you need to check your pages in other popular browsers, like Internet Explorer, Firefox, and Opera.

To see how your layouts, CSS, and JavaScript features hold up in those browsers, use Dreamweaver's Preview command (File→Preview in Browser) to test your pages in every browser you can get your hands on (Dreamweaver lists the browsers installed on your computer when you click Preview, and you select one from the list). Make sure the graphics look right, your layout remains intact, and Cascading Style Sheets and Dreamweaver behaviors work as you intend.

For a thorough evaluation, however, you should preview your pages using every combination of browser *and* operating system you think your site's visitors may use. How do you know what browser web surfers use? StatCounter (*http:// gs.statcounter.com/*) is a good place to start your research. This free-to-use website shows you which browsers are popular in different countries and regions of the world. You should also examine the stats on browser *versions*, because all Internet Explorers are *not* created equal. As you can see in Figure 19-1, the StatCounter window is pretty easy to use. Make a few choices from the drop-down menus and StatCounter provides information—on browser use, visitors' country of origin, and so on—in graph or map form.

For example, when this book went to press, browser stats indicate that for the past 12 months, Internet Explorer 10, 8, 9, and 11 (in that order) were the most popular desktop browsers in the United States. Combined, the IE versions account for 36% of Web traffic. Other versions of Internet Explorer account for less than one-half of a percent. Looking at the stats, Google Chrome usage is significant at 35%, followed by Firefox (17%) and Safari (10%). So, if you're designing a site focused on the U.S., you should test your pages in Internet Explorer 8, 9, 10, and 11; Chrome; Firefox; and Safari. That way, you know your pages will look good on 98% of the browsers out there. If you're designing pages for a site in another country or region, study the statistics for your target audience. For example, in China during the same period, Internet Explorer 8 accounted for over 25% of Web traffic, and even Internet Explorer 6 held a 3% share. So if a significant part of your audience is in China, consider testing earlier versions of Internet Explorer, too.

TIP If you already have a site up and running, you can find useful browser information in your site's *log files*. They track visits to your site, including which browsers and type of computer (desktop, tablet, and so on) your visitors use. Most web hosting companies provide access to these files and the software that analyzes the confusing code inside them. You can use this information to see, for example, whether *anyone* who visits your site still uses Internet Explorer 6. If no one does, that's one less browser you have to design for. And if you don't have access to your log files, you can use Google Analytics (*www.google.com/analytics/*), a free service that tracks guests who visit your site. You just need to sign up for a free Google Analytics account and add a little snippet of JavaScript to each page of your site.

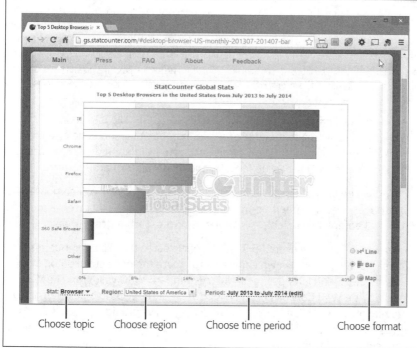

FIGURE 19-1

StatCounter (http:// gs.statcounter.com/) is a valuable research tool for web developers. Dial in a topic you want to research, such as browsers, browser versions, screen resolution (size), or operating system, and then choose a country or region and a time period. StatCounter displays the information it's collected from web logs as line charts, bar charts (shown here), or maps. This display shows overall browser stats. By choosing Browser Version as the topic, you can see which versions of a browser are popular.

Choose topic   Choose region   Choose time period   Choose format

Unfortunately, you'll discover that what works for one browser/operating system combination may not work for another. That's why you should preview your designs *early* in the process of building your site. If you design a page that doesn't work well in Internet Explorer 8, for example, it's better to catch and fix that problem immediately than to discover it after you build 100 pages based on that design. In other words, once you create a page design you like, don't plow ahead and continue building pages! Check that page in multiple browser/operating system combos, fix any problems, and then, Grasshopper, begin to build.

To test your site, enlist your friends and family so you can check your pages on as many setups as possible. You may even need to turn to websites like BrowserStack (*http://www.browserstack.com/*), where you can explore even more browser, operating system, and screen size combinations.

NOTE Internet Explorer 6 is often where most web pages fall apart. This old and crotchety browser is full of bugs that often cause hair-pulling bouts of hysteria among web designers. Most of the problems relate to the CSS that lays out your page (see Chapter 10). Fortunately, in the United States, Internet Explorer 6 is all but dead—most statistics report that less than 1% of the U.S. population uses it. Many U.S. web designers don't even test for IE 6 any longer. However, it still has a presence in China and other nations around the world, so if you're designing for a global audience, you may still need to test your designs in IE 6. Professional web designers recommend previewing your page using Dreamweaver's Live view and Firefox, Safari, or Internet Explorer 9 first. Get the page working right in those browsers, and then preview it in IE 6 to fix bugs. If you design with just IE 6 in mind, you'll find that your site might not work in Firefox, Safari, and, in many cases, the more recent versions of IE.

- **Validate your pages**. HTML and CSS errors can easily slip into your code if you edit your files with a text editor or work on pages that someone else created. These errors, called validation errors, are often the source of cross-browser display problems, messed-up layouts, and incorrect formatting.

  Previous versions of Dreamweaver included a tool that let you compare your web pages against agreed-upon standards for HTML and other web languages. It wasn't completely reliable, so Adobe removed it from Dreamweaver CS5.

  However, in Dreamweaver CS5.5, Adobe resurrected the validator! But this time, instead of relying on its own engineers to create the perfect validator, Dreamweaver CS5.5 and later use the industry-standard W3C validator. The W3C, or World Wide Web Consortium, develops most of the technologies web designers rely on, like HTML and CSS, and they've always provided a good validator. It resides online, but Dreamweaver CC makes the testing process simple by connecting to it from within the program. You'll learn how to use it on page 78.

  While you do the bulk of your checking during page development, you should do some troubleshooting at the end of the process, too, just before you move a page (or an entire site) to your web server.

- **Check your spelling**. Amazingly, people often overlook this simple step. As a result, you can easily find otherwise professional-looking pages undermined by sloppy spelling. To use Dreamweaver's built-in spell-checker, see page 107.

- **Check your links**. A website can be a complex and twisted collection of interconnected files. Web pages, graphics, videos, and other types of files all have to work together. Unfortunately, if you move or delete a file, problems can ripple through your entire site. Use Dreamweaver's Check Links command to identify and fix broken links (see page 781).

- **Run site reports**. It's always the little things. When you build a website, small errors inevitably creep into your pages. While not necessarily life-threatening, forgetting to title a page or add an Alt property to an image does diminish the quality and professionalism of a site. Use Dreamweaver's site-reporting feature to quickly identify these problems (see page 794).

■ Testing Web Pages with BrowserStack

Web browsers are free, so you can download and install several of them on your computer. But you'd soon find it unwieldy to install every version of every browser available and then test all your pages in each one. And if the browser issue weren't enough, you need to consider the different operating systems and devices (tablets, smartphones, and so on) out there. In the past, you could test pages using Adobe's BrowserLab service, which let you see your web pages in a variety of browsers and operating systems. Adobe stopped offering the service in March 2013 and now recommends third-party services like BrowserStack. As the box on page 780 explains, there are plenty of page-testing options.

> **NOTE** BrowserStack's basic service costs $19 a month, but you can sign up for a free 30 minutes of testing time. If you're organized, that's actually enough time to check out a moderately sized website. You can sign in and sign out of BrowserStack as often as you like, so you don't need to check all your pages in one session. If you sign up for BrowserStack through Microsoft's modern.IE website (*http://www.modern.ie*), you can get a 3-month trial with time restrictions on certain features. The Microsoft site also provides web testing tools, with an emphasis on the most recent versions of IE.

BrowserStack uses a "virtual machine"—a computer that loads and runs the operating system/browser combo you chose—to preview your web pages. You choose an operating system and a specific version of a browser—for example, Safari 5.1. You also specify the page you want to preview. BrowserStack runs that operating system and browser, opens the page you want to preview, and sends a "live" copy to your computer. You can click buttons, operate menus, and browse your way to other pages either on your site or on the Web. In short, you experience your website just as a visitor will when she uses that operating system/browser combo. There's a slight delay, because BrowserStack plays interference between you and the web pages you request, but you can trust the results.

Here's how you sign up with BrowserStack and then view a page on the Web.

1. **Go to *http://www.browserstack.com* and then click the Free Trial button.**

   It's in the upper-right corner. After you click it, BrowserStack displays a simple form.

2. **Fill in your email address, password, and name. Check the "Remember me" box, and then click the Sign Up button.**

   You don't need to provide a credit card for the free trial. A new page appears when you click the Sign Up button. It displays two tabs: "Test a public URL" and "Test an internal URL" (see Figure 19-2).

FIGURE 19-2

BrowserStack lets you preview individual web pages or entire sites. You can choose an operating system and a specific version of a browser simply by choosing options from a menu.

Top: Here are the browser options available when you choose the Windows 7 operating system.

Bottom: There are fewer options when you choose the mobile iOS operating system, but your choices include several models of tablets and phones.

3. **Click the "Test a public URL" tab and then fill in the address of the website you want to preview.**

   Initially, BrowserStack displays the "public" option and automatically fills in the URL text box with the website cited in your email address, but you can change that to any web address you want, so long as it's publically accessible.

4. **Below the web address, use the menu on the left to choose an operating system.**

   There are options for Windows, Macs, and mobile devices.

5. **Use the menu on the right to choose a browser.**

Your choice of operating system determines your browser options. You can choose a specific browser and version.

6. **Click "Start testing."**

BrowserStack entertains you with the play-by-play shown in Figure 19-3 while it sets up a virtual machine with the operating system and browser combination you specified. Once that's done, you see the test results on your computer.

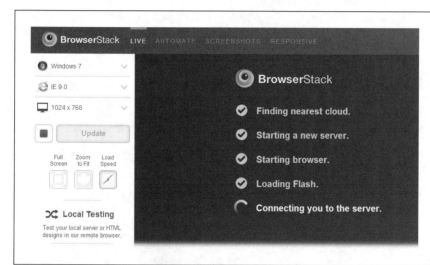

FIGURE 19-3

After you choose an operating system and browser, BrowserStack creates a virtual machine on its computers. It takes time for BrowserStack to run the necessary software, so you see this progress report in the interim. Once BrowserStack previews your page, you can use the controls on the right to test another operating system, browser, or screen size.

Previewing Pages with BrowserStack

Ideally, you want to preview your web pages before you send them off to a web server where everyone in the world can see them. BrowserStack has a pretty ingenious way of handling that, too. The process is called "tunneling." Here's how it works: You create a connection (a tunnel) between your computer and the BrowserStack computer. The BrowserStack computer runs a version of the operating system and browser you specify, and then it loads the web page from your computer. The results appear on your computer screen as if the operating system and browser were installed on your computer. It requires a few extra steps and means that you have to give BrowserStack permission to look at the files on your computer. After all, BrowserStack can't display files without reading them.

Here are the steps to set up a "tunnel."

1. **Click the "Test an internal URL" tab.**

The tab has two buttons, Web Tunnel and Command Line. Web tunnel is the easier one to use, because you don't have to type in cryptic Java commands in a terminal window.

2. **Click "Start local testing."**

   BrowserStack displays a page telling you that it takes a few seconds to set up a web tunnel. Depending on your computer's operating system and security settings, you probably need to provide permission to run the Java program that creates the tunnel between you and BrowserStack. Figure 19-4 shows the message and permission buttons for Windows 7. After you let the program run, BrowserStack displays a panel with two options: "Local server" and "Local folder." Use the "Local server" option if you have a testing server running on your computer. (See page 921 for details on setting one up.) If you want to view a web page that isn't on a testing server, use the "Local folder" option, as explained next.

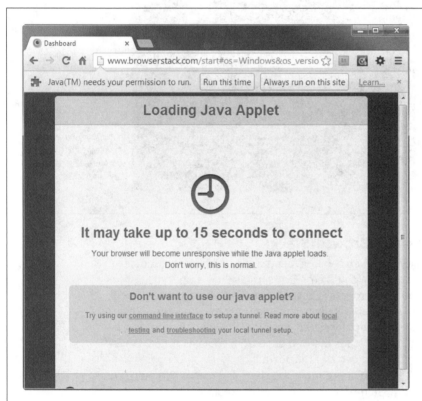

FIGURE 19-4

To view pages on your local computer but not on the web, Browser-Stack creates a "tunnel" between its computer and yours. You probably need to provide permission to complete the process. Here, Windows 7 asks permission to run the Java program that creates the tunnel. If you have a different operating system and security settings, you'll see different warnings and permission requests.

3. **Choose "Local folder." Use the Browse button to identify a folder.**

   When you click Browse, BrowserStack displays a window so you can choose a folder on your computer. Then BrowserStack returns you to the "Setup a local tunnel" page, where you see the Finish button.

4. **Click Finish to create the tunnel, and then click Finish again to view the results.**

The first time you click Finish, BrowserStack lets you know that it's creating the "local connection." Once it does, it tells you that you can access your local folder. You need to click the Finish button again to actually view the contents of the folder. Since you provided only the name of a folder, BrowserStack still needs to know what file to display.

5. **Click the HTML file that you want to preview as a web page.**

BrowserStack displays the web page, as shown in Figure 19-5.

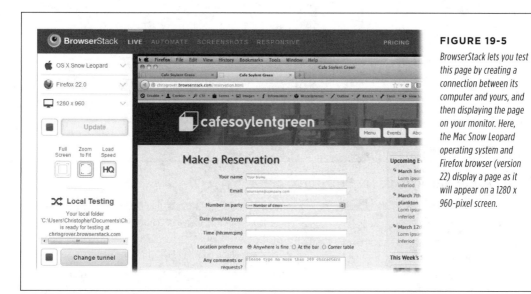

FIGURE 19-5

BrowserStack lets you test this page by creating a connection between its computer and yours, and then displaying the page on your monitor. Here, the Mac Snow Leopard operating system and Firefox browser (version 22) display a page as it will appear on a 1280 x 960-pixel screen.

Changing Settings in BrowserStack

Fortunately, you don't have to go through all those steps just to see your web page in a different browser. Once you view your first page, you can change the operating system and browser settings using the controls on the left side of the BrowserStack page (Figure 19-6). One of the great things about BrowserStack is the number of options available. Don't forget to preview your pages in the iOS and Android operating systems.

FIGURE 19-6

The controls on the left side of the BrowserStack page let you change the operating system, browser, and screen size combination on the fly. Choose your options from the top three menus. The square red button stops the virtual machine (handy if you're trying to squeeze every second out of your 30 minutes of free testing time). Click Update to display the page using the new settings.

FREQUENTLY ASKED QUESTION

Testing Your Site in Multiple Browsers

How can I test my website if I have only a couple of the most common browsers on my computer?

If you don't have every browser ever created on your Windows, Mac, and Linux machines (you *do* have all three, don't you?), you can use the BrowserStack service discussed on page 775 (at least to tackle the Windows, Mac, and mobile sides).

However, there are other options. Browsershots (*www.brows-ershots.org*), for example, is a free alternative that provides screenshots of the page you want to test for a wide range of browsers that run on Windows and Linux systems.

You can see what a page looks like in Internet Explorer 5.5 all the way through 10 for free with NetRenderer, though your pages need to be on a public website. Visit *http://ipinfo.info/netrenderer*, type in the URL of the page you want to see, and in a few moments NetRenderer displays a screenshot. Unfortunately, it doesn't take a picture of a complete web page—just the top part of it—if it's a long page, you won't see the bottom.

CrossBrowserTesting.com (*http://CrossBrowserTesting.com*), which costs $30 a month (ouch) for 150 minutes of use, offers an added benefit: interactive testing. You see your page running remotely on a PC under your control, so you can test features that a screenshot doesn't help you with, like Flash movie playback, animation, and JavaScript interactions.

Windows users can try out a program named IETester (*http://www.my-debugbar.com/wiki/IETester/HomePage*). It lets you see how your pages look in multiple versions of IE, including 6, 7, 8, 9, and 10. Microsoft also offers a browser testing program called modern.IE (*http://www.modern.ie*), which focuses on the more recent versions of Internet Explorer.

If you're a Mac person with an Intel chip at the heart of your system, you can install Windows on your machine using Apple's Bootcamp program (*www.apple.com/support/bootcamp/*) or use third-party "virtualization" software that runs Windows and Mac OS X simultaneously on the same computer (and believe it or not, the universe does *not* implode). VMWare Fusion for Macs (*www.vmware.com/products/fusion*) and Parallels Desktop (*www.parallels.com/products/desktop*) let you run multiple versions of Windows (XP, Vista, Windows 7, and Windows 8), as well as Mac OS X.

■ Finding and Fixing Broken Links

Broken links are inevitable. If you delete a file from your site, move a page or a graphic outside of Dreamweaver, or simply type an incorrect path name to a file, you may end up with broken links and missing graphics. In the B.D. era (Before Dreamweaver), you could fix such problems only by methodically examining every link on every page in your site. Fortunately, Dreamweaver's link-checking features automate the process.

> **NOTE** In this context, a link doesn't mean just a hyperlink connecting one page to another. Dreamweaver checks links to external files, such as PNGs, GIFs, and JPEGs that reside in different folders, external CSS style sheets, and JavaScript files. For example, if a graphic is missing or isn't in the place your page specifies, Dreamweaver reports a broken link.

Finding Broken Links

Dreamweaver's Check Links Sitewide command (Site→Check Links Sitewide) scans an entire site's worth of files and reports all the links and paths that don't lead to a file. (It's one of Dreamweaver's site-management features, meaning that you have to set up a local site before you can use this tool; see page 750 for instructions.) Note that Dreamweaver checks only links and paths *within* the local site folder; it doesn't check links that lead to other people's sites (see the note at the bottom of this page for a tool that helps with *that* annoying chore).

> **TIP** If your local site contains a lot of pages, you may not want to check links in one or more folders whose pages *you know* have no broken links. You can exclude files from the Check Links Sitewide operation using the Cloaking feature described on page 818. Doing so also makes the link-checking operation go faster.

■ CHECKING AN OPEN PAGE

To check links on an page you're working on, save it in your local site folder and then choose Window→Results→Link Checker. Dreamweaver scans the page and opens the Link Checker window, which lists any broken links (see Figure 19-7). If Dreamweaver doesn't find any—you HTML god, you—the window comes up empty.

> **NOTE** Although Dreamweaver can't check links to the outside world, a free tool from the W3C, called the Link Checker (*http://validator.w3.org/checklink*), can. It checks both internal links (to pages on the same site) and external links (to pages on other sites). The only possible downside: The pages you check must already be on the Web. Likewise, Webmaster Toolkit (*http://bit.ly/hcik3*) and 1-hit.com (*http://bit.ly/4v8wwi*) provide free online link-checking services.

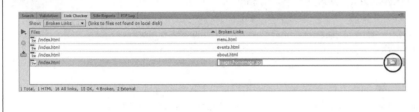

FIGURE 19-7

In addition to checking internal links, the Check Links Sitewide command generates a list of all external links and orphan files (files with no links to them). To see these details, use the Show menu. If you wish, click the Save button (the hard drive with a down arrow) to store all this information in a tab-delimited text file. You can fix a broken internal link directly inside this panel using the "Browse for File" button (circled).

■ **CHECKING SPECIFIC PAGES**

You can check links on specific pages of your site using the Link Checker panel:

1. **Choose Window→Results→Link Checker.**

   Dreamweaver opens the Link Checker panel.

2. **Use the Files panel to select the site that has the pages you want to check.**

   If you're already working on the site, skip this step.

3. **In the Files panel, select the files you want to check.**

   To learn all the ways you can select files and folders in the Files panel, see the box on page 13.

   NOTE Selecting a folder in the Files panel makes Dreamweaver scan all the files in that folder.

4. **In the Link Checker, click the gray arrow on the left. From the menu that opens, choose "Check Links for Selected Files in Site."**

   Alternatively, you can right-click (Control-click) the selected files, and then, from the shortcut menu, choose Check Links→Selected Files.

   Either way, Dreamweaver scans the pages and displays any broken links (Figure 19-7).

Selection Shortcuts for the Files Panel

You'll often want to use the link-checking tools in Dreamweaver's Results panel on more than one page in your website. Fortunately, the link checker can work on multiple pages in the Files panel.

To select several consecutively listed files at once, click the first filename, scroll if necessary, and then Shift-click the last filename. Dreamweaver highlights your first and final clicks, and all the files in between.

To select nonconsecutive files, click each one while pressing the Ctrl (⌘) key.

Once you select one or more files, you can deselect any single one by Ctrl-clicking (⌘-clicking) it once again.

Dreamweaver also includes a snazzy command that selects recently modified files in the Files panel. Suppose you want to select all the files you created or changed today (to see if the links work or to upload them to your web server). To do so, click the panel's drop-down menu button in the upper-right corner of the Files panel. From the menu that appears, select Edit→Select Recently Modified.

Dreamweaver opens the Select Recently Modified window. You can either specify a range of dates (for files you created or changed between July 1, 2014, and July 7, 2014, for example) or a number of days (to specify all the files you modified in, say, the last 30 days). (The last option—Modified By—works only with Adobe's Contribute program.) Select the options, click OK, and Dreamweaver selects the appropriate files in the Files panel.

■ CHECKING AN ENTIRE WEBSITE

You can check all the links on all the pages in your site in three ways. For all three techniques, you have to have your website selected in the Files panel (press F8 [Shift-⌘-F] to open the Files panel, and then use the panel's menu to select your site).

- Choose Site→Check Links Sitewide or use the keyboard shortcut Ctrl+F8 (⌘-F8).

- Open the Files panel and then right-click (Control-click) any file. From the shortcut menu, choose Check Links→Entire Local Site.

- Open the Link Checker panel (Window→Results→Link Checker), click the arrow on the upper-left side of the panel, and then, from its menu, choose "Check Links for Entire Current Local Site."

Once again, Dreamweaver scans your site and lists broken links in the Link Checker panel.

Fixing Broken Links

Of course, simply finding broken links is only half the battle. You also need to *fix* them. The Link Checker provides a quick and easy way to do that.

1. **In the Link Checker panel, click a filename in the Broken Links column.**

   Dreamweaver highlights the file's path and displays a tiny folder icon to the right (Figure 19-7, circled).

The Link Checker shows you which pages *contain* broken links but doesn't show you the text or images for the link itself, which can make it difficult to figure out how to fix it ("Was that a button that links to the home page?"). In cases like that, *double-click* the file name in the Link Checker panel's left column. Dreamweaver opens the relevant web page and, even better, highlights the link on the page.

Once you determine where the link should lead ("Oh yeah, that's the button to the haggis buffet menu"), you can fix it right on the page or go back to the Link Checker and make the change as described in the next step.

2. **Click the tiny folder icon on the right.**

   Dreamweaver opens the Select File dialog box. From here, you can navigate to the correct page—the one the link *should* have opened.

   If you prefer, you can type the correct path directly in the Link Checker. But that's usually not a good idea, since it's difficult to understand the path from one page to another just by looking at the Link Checker. Searching for the proper page using the Select File dialog box is a much more accurate and trouble-free method.

3. **Double-click the filename of the correct web page.**

   The Select File dialog box disappears, and Dreamweaver fixes the link.

   If your site contains other links that point to the same missing file, Dreamweaver asks if you'd like to fix those links, too—an amazing timesaver that can quickly repair broken links on dozens of pages.

NOTE Dreamweaver's behavior is a bit odd when it comes to fixing the same broken link, however. Once you fix a link, that link remains selected in the Link Checker panel. You must click another broken link, or one of the buttons in the window, before Dreamweaver asks if you'd like to fix that same broken link on other pages.

4. **Continue to fix broken links, following steps 1–3.**

   Once you repair all the broken links, you can close the Results panel by double-clicking anywhere along the top row of tabs (for example, double-click the Link Checker tab). Double-clicking any tab reopens the Results panel.

Listing External Links

Although Dreamweaver doesn't verify links that lead to external websites, it can *list* those links after you run the link-checker. To see the list, choose External Links from the Link Checker's Show menu (see Figure 19-8). The list includes absolute URLs leading to other sites (like *www.yahoo.com*) as well as email links (like *mailto:reservations@cafesoylentgreen.com*).

This window is especially useful if you include a link to a certain external website several times throughout your site and decide to change it. For example, if you discover through testing (or through the W3C Link Checker) that an external link you peppered throughout your site no longer works:

1. **Choose Site→Check Links Sitewide (or press Ctrl+F8 [⌘-F8]).**

   Dreamweaver scans your site and then opens the Link Checker panel.

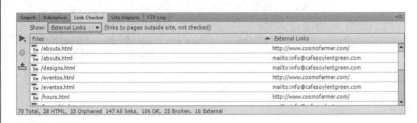

FIGURE 19-8

Although Dreamweaver can't check external links, you can use this window to change the URL of one.

2. **From the Show drop-down menu, choose External Links.**

   The window lists links you created to sites outside your own.

3. **Click the external link you want to change.**

   Dreamweaver highlights it, ready for editing.

4. **Type in the new web address, and then press Enter (Return).**

   If other pages contain the old URL, Dreamweaver asks if you want to fix them as well. If so, click Yes and the deed is done.

Orphaned Files

The Link Checker also provides a list of files that aren't used by *any* of your site's pages—*orphaned files*, as they're called. You wind up with an orphaned file when, for example, you save a GIF to your site folder but then never use it on a web page. Or you might delete the only link to a page you don't need anymore, making the destination page an orphaned file. Unless you think you may link to that file in the future, delete it to clean up unnecessary clutter.

In fact, that's the primary purpose of the Orphaned Files list: to identify old and unused files so you can delete them. Here's how it works:

1. **Choose Site→Check Links Sitewide, or press Ctrl+F8 (⌘-F8).**

   Dreamweaver opens the Link Checker panel.

2. **From the Show menu, choose Orphaned Files.**

   Dreamweaver displays the list of orphaned files (see Figure 19-9).

3. **Select the files you want to delete.**

   Ctrl-click (⌘-click) files to select them.

4. **Press Delete.**

   Dreamweaver asks if you really want to delete the files. Click OK if you do, or Cancel if you get cold feet.

FIGURE 19-9

Identify (and delete) unused files with Dreamweaver's Orphaned Files option in the Link Checker panel. This panel can also list external links and broken links; use the Show menu to choose a view.

Before you get spring-cleaning fever and delete all orphaned files in your site, however, keep a few pointers in mind:

- Just because your site doesn't *currently* use a file doesn't mean you won't need it again later. For example, say you have an employee-of-the-month page. In March, you included a photo of Robin Albert, your best salesperson. In April, someone else got the award, so you removed Robin's photo from the page. The photo still resides in your site; it's just that no web page currently uses it, making it an orphan. But next month you may need the photo again, when Robin develops a spurt of motivation. So make sure a file really is useless before deleting it.

- More important, Dreamweaver may flag files your site actually *needs* as orphaned. For example, some sites include what's called a *splash page*: an introductory page that first appears when someone comes to the site. It can be a page with a bold graphic and the text "Click here to enter the site," or it may be a fancy Flash movie intended to make a big impact on your visitors. Usually, this page is nothing more than a welcome mat that leads to the *real* home page. Since it's simply an introductory page, no other page in the site links to it. Unfortunately, that's precisely what Dreamweaver considers an orphaned file.

- If you write your own JavaScript, you may link to graphic files and web pages. Dreamweaver doesn't keep track of file references in your JavaScript code, so it identifies those files as orphans (unless you insert or link to them elsewhere in the page or on your site).

On the other hand, Dreamweaver is somewhat smarter when it comes to Dreamweaver behaviors—it tracks files in its *own* JavaScript programs—for example, graphics files you use in a rollover effect—and doesn't list them as orphaned.

The bottom line is that while this report can be useful, use it cautiously when you delete files.

Changing a Link Site-Wide

Suppose you create a page to teach your visitors the basics of HTML. You think this page would be really, really helpful, so you create links to it from every page on your site. After a while, you realize that you just don't have the time to keep the page up to date, but you still want to help your visitors get this information. Why not change the link so that it points to a more current and informative source? Using Dreamweaver's Change Link Sitewide command, you can do just that. The process differs depending on whether you want to change a link that points to the outside world or one that points to another page on your site.

1. **Choose Site→Change Link Sitewide.**

   Dreamweaver opens the Change Link Sitewide window (Figure 19-10), revealing two text fields, labeled "Change all links to" and "Into links to." Understanding what you're supposed to do at this point is easier if you imagine that the first label actually says "Change all links that *currently* point to." In other words, you first indicate where those links point to now, and then you indicate where they *should* point. To change links that point outside your site, go to step 2; to change links that lead within your site, see step 3.

FIGURE 19-10

Dreamweaver uses a root-relative link to specify the page whose web address you want to change, as indicated by the slash (/). Don't worry, this doesn't mean that Dreamweaver makes the link root relative. It's just how Dreamweaver identifies the location of the page in the site. See page 179 for more on root-relative links.

2. **For links to a page outside your site, type the old web address in the "Change all links to" field.**

   For example, if your aim is to round up every link that now points to Yahoo and redirect it to Google, type *http://www.yahoo.com* here. Then, in the "Into links to" field, type the new web address, *http://www.google.com* in this case. The links on your site that used to lead to Yahoo will now point to Google. Skip to step 4.

   TIP As a shortcut to following steps 1, 2, and 3, you can select a file in the Files panel and *then* choose Site→Change Link Sitewide. Dreamweaver automatically adds the selected file's path to the "Change all links to" field.

3. **To change links to a page *within* your site, click the folder icon to the right of the "Change all links to" field.**

   This brings up the "Select Link to Change" dialog box. Browse to the old link, the one you want to change throughout your site, and then click OK (Open).

Next, specify the file that the link should point to *now*. Click the folder icon beside "Into links to" to open the "Select Link to Change" dialog box again. Select a file in the local site folder, and then click OK (Open).

Your new link can point to graphics, Cascading Style Sheets, or any other file you can include in a web page. You'll get unpredictable results, however, if you change a link that points to a graphic file into, say, a link that points to a web page, or vice versa. Make sure the "before" and "after" links share the same file type, whether that's a web page, style sheet, or graphic.

TIP For another way to change one external link into another, see Figure 19-8.

4. **Click OK in the Change Link Sitewide box to make the change.**

   The same Update Files dialog box you encountered in the last chapter appears now, listing every page Dreamweaver will change.

5. **Click Update.**

   Dreamweaver scans your site and updates the pages.

■ Validating Web Pages

The Web is a far-flung collection of technologies, programming languages, and people, all working together. When you think about it, it's pretty amazing that an 11-year-old in Fargo, North Dakota, can create a website millions of people around the world can view, and that dozens of different browsers, from Internet Explorer to those on smartphones, can browse the same sites. This kind of global communication owes its success in large part to the World Wide Web Consortium (the W3C), the organization composed of representatives from universities, research institutions, corporations, and government agencies dedicated to creating standards for Internet-related technologies.

The W3C developed standards for HTML5, CSS, XML, and other Web languages, and continues to create new standards as technologies evolve. Thanks to these standards, companies have a guide to follow when they create new websites or new web browsers.

It sure would be great if all companies followed the W3C's standards when building web browsers, and if all web designers followed those standards when building web pages. Then anyone with any web browser could view any web page. What a wonderful world *that* would be—you'd never have to test your pages in different browsers!

Of course, this kind of utopian thinking hasn't always been applied by the major browser makers. As a result, web developers have been forced to come up with techniques to deal with the way different browsers display HTML. Dreamweaver CS4 and earlier included a built-in web page validator, but it wasn't always accurate and frequently came up with results that were different from the definitive online validator offered by the W3C (*http://validator.w3.org*). As a result, Adobe switched to that validator beginning with Dreamweaver 5.5.

NOTE Because Dreamweaver CC uses the W3C's online validator, you have to have an Internet connection to use this feature.

Steps for Validating Web Pages

Dreamweaver's validation tool works on only one page at a time, and only with a page you have open in the document window. To validate an open page:

1. **Choose File→Validate→Validate Current Document (W3C).**

   If it's not already open, the W3C Validation tab opens in the results panel at the bottom of the screen.

NOTE There's another choice under the File→Validate menu: Validate Live Document (W3C). You can select this option when you use Dreamweaver's Live view (page 348). For a plain HTML file, the Validate Live Document option isn't any different from the Validate Current Document command, but it's handy when working with some types of server-side pages, like the PHP pages discussed in Chapter 24, or a page created by a content management system like WordPress, Joomla, or Drupal.

In content management systems, what looks like a single web page from a visitor's perspective is usually many different files pieced together using information from a database to create a single HTML file. This means you can't just open a file in a WordPress site in Dreamweaver and validate it—instead, you need to view a WordPress page in Live view to see the finished HTML page and then choose File→Validate→Validate Live Document (W3C).

2. **Review the results.**

   Dreamweaver displays the results in the Validation panel (Figure 19-11) and divides each message into four columns: the first includes an icon that indicates the severity of the error; the second lists the filename; the third lists the line of code the message applies to; and the fourth describes the validation error or message.

   The icon at the beginning of the message helps you determine which errors are important. A red stop sign identifies a violation of the page's doctype (HTML 4.01 Transitional, XTHML 1.0 Transitional, HTML5, and so on).

   In some cases, this warning can indicate that a mandatory tag (like the <body> tag) is missing—a serious problem.

   Other stop-sign errors aren't necessarily fatal. For example, some JavaScript widgets may use tag attributes that are technically invalid but won't cause problems on the page. Less serious problems are flagged with little message balloons. These may inform you that the page has *no* problems or point out optional fixes.

Run validator/change validator settings

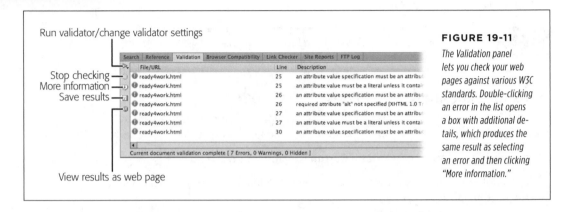

Stop checking
More information
Save results

View results as web page

FIGURE 19-11

The Validation panel
lets you check your web
pages against various W3C
standards. Double-clicking
an error in the list opens
a box with additional de-
tails, which produces the
same result as selecting
an error and then clicking
"More information."

NOTE Dreamweaver's validation feature doesn't help with CSS files. To make sure your CSS files are valid, you can use the W3C's CSS Validator (*http://jigsaw.w3.org/css-validator*), which lets you either point to a file out on the web, upload a CSS file (or an HTML file with an internal CSS style sheet), or simply paste a CSS style sheet into an online form. The CSS Validator then checks your style sheet to make sure you didn't make any mistakes in writing your CSS.

3. **Fix the errors.**

   Alas, Dreamweaver can't fix all validation errors. It does fix errors related to improperly written code, as described on page 322. But for other errors, you need to go into the code and use your knowledge of HTML to fix any problems. For help with HTML code, see Chapter 7 (page 365).

   To get started, double-click one of the errors listed in the Validation results panel. If you start in Design or Live view, Dreamweaver switches you to Split view and puts your cursor next to the invalid HTML. You can then delete or modify the offending code. Keep in mind, though, that the code Dreamweaver produces is the result of many thousands of hours of engineering and testing. Unless you're sure you know how to fix a problem, you may just want to trust the code Dreamweaver produces.

TIP You may find that you constantly get a particular validation error, like the "there is no attribute tabindex" error, with some older JavaScript widgets because the widget requires that extra attribute. To hide particular types of errors, right click (Control-click) the error message in the W3C Validation tab of the results panel and then choose Hide Error. From then on, when you validate any page that has this error (even pages on other sites), you won't see an error message in the results panel. (To make Dreamweaver display an error you previously hid, click the triangle icon in the top left of the results panel and choose "settings." The W3C Validator Preferences menu opens; click Manage to open the hidden errors window, select the error that you want to make visible, and then click Remove.)

▪ Cleaning Up HTML (and XHTML)

You've been reading about what great HTML Dreamweaver writes, and how, no matter what doctype you use (XHTML 1, HTML 4.01, or HTML5, for example), Dreamweaver adds the correct tags in the correct order. But there are exceptions to every rule. In the process of formatting text, deleting elements, and—in general—building a web page, it's quite possible to end up with less-than-optimal HTML. While Dreamweaver usually catches potentially sloppy code, you may nonetheless run across instances of empty tags, redundant tags, and nested tags in your Dreamweaver pages.

For example, in the normal course of adding, editing, and deleting content on a page (either by hand or even in Dreamweaver's Design view), you can occasionally end up with code like this:

```
<div> </div>
```

This empty tag doesn't serve any purpose, it just adds unnecessary HTML to your page. Remember, the less code your page uses, the faster it loads. Eliminating redundant tags can improve your site's performance.

Another possible source of errors is you. When you type HTML in Code view or open pages created by another (perhaps inferior) program, you may introduce errors you need to clean up later.

Aware of its own limitations (and yours), Dreamweaver provides a command designed to streamline the code in your pages: Clean Up HTML (if you're using Dreamweaver's XHTML mode, the command is called Clean Up XHTML). This command not only improves the HTML in your page, but it also strips out nonessential code like comments and special Dreamweaver markup code, and it can delete HTML tags you specify.

NOTE The Clean Up HTML command doesn't fix really bad errors, like missing closing tags or improperly nested tags. You can have Dreamweaver automatically fix mistakes like these when it opens a file by turning on the code-rewriting features in Dreamweaver's preferences. Choose Edit→Preferences and then, in the list on the left, click Code Rewriting. Turn on "Fix invalidly nested and unclosed tags" and "Remove extra closing tags."

To clean up your HTML:

1. **Open the web page you want to clean up.**

   Unfortunately, this great feature works on only one page at a time—no cleaning up a site's worth of pages in one fell swoop! Accordingly, it's best to first use the Site Reports feature (see page 794) to identify problem pages, and then open them in Dreamweaver and run this command.

2. **Choose Commands→Clean Up HTML (or Clean Up XHTML).**

   Dreamweaver opens the Clean Up HTML/XHTML window (see Figure 19-12).

FIGURE 19-12

The Clean Up HTML/XHTML command lets you strip out redundant and useless code. You can even use it to delete unnecessary tags by targeting them in the "Specific tag(s)" box (although the "Find and Replace" command provides a much more powerful way to identify and remove HTML tags; see Chapter 8).

TIP The Clean Up HTML command is extremely useful. Once you try it a few times, you'll probably want to use it on all your pages. Unfortunately, it doesn't come with a keyboard shortcut. This is a classic example of where Dreamweaver's keyboard-shortcut editor is just the white knight you need; using it, you can add a keystroke combination to trigger this command from the keyboard. See page 904 for details.

---

3. **Turn on the checkboxes for the options you want.**

   Here's a rundown:

   — **Empty container tags** deletes tags that don't actually contain anything. For example, you may have deleted text you set in boldface, leaving behind opening and closing <strong> tags without any text in between. Or you may have deleted an image within a link, leaving behind a useless pair of <a> tags. It's always a good idea to turn on this option.

   — **Redundant nested tags** deletes tags that appear within other tags of the same type, like this:

   `<strong>You can't get any <strong>bolder</strong> than bold</strong>`

   The inner set of bold tags does no good, so choosing this option produces this HTML:

   `<strong>You can't get any bolder than bold</strong>`

   This option is extremely useful, so turn it on.

   — **Non-Dreamweaver HTML comments** deletes any comments *not* inserted by Dreamweaver as part of its site-management tools. For example, the Dreamweaver template tool (Chapter 22) inserts HTML comments to help you identify different parts of a template. But web designers also place notes within their code as instructions or to explain parts of the code. (These comments are invisible in a browser, by the way. They appear only in Code view, or in Dreamweaver's document window as a gold comment icon.) If you've finished with the page and doubt you'll need the information the comments contain, you can decrease the page's file size a little bit by using this option.

NOTE Dreamweaver's Clean Up HTML command doesn't strip out CSS comments. If you use Dreamweaver's CSS Layouts, you'll find the style sheets loaded with CSS comments. To remove them, visit *http://tinyurl.com/6kcmq4g*. There you can download a "stored query" (a reusable search) to use with Dreamweaver's "Find and Replace" tool to target CSS comments.

— **Dreamweaver special markup** deletes any special code Dreamweaver inserted in your pages. Dreamweaver relies on special programming code to make some of its features, including tracing images, libraries (Chapter 21), and templates (Chapter 22), work. Choosing this option eliminates that special code, so use it with care. (Since the template feature can add a fair amount of this specialized code, Dreamweaver includes a Template Export command that lets you export an entire site with all the template code removed; see page 891.)

— **Specific tag(s)** deletes HTML tags you specify. Type the name of the tag (without brackets) in the box like this: *font*. To remove multiple tags at once, separate each tag name by a comma, like this: *font, blink*.

Be careful with this option. Since it lets you remove *any* tag from a page, you could easily delete an important and necessary tag (like the <body> tag) from your page by accident. Furthermore, Dreamweaver's "Find and Replace" command provides a much more powerful tool for doing this kind of surgery (see Chapter 8).

— **Combine nested <font> tags when possible** combines multiple *font* properties into a single tag. Hopefully, you've moved to CSS for all your text formatting needs, so you don't use the <font> tag in your HTML, nor do you need this option.

To see a report of all the changes Dreamweaver makes to a page, turn on the "Show log on completion" checkbox.

4. **Click OK to clean up the page.**

If you turned on the "Show Log on completion" checkbox, Dreamweaver displays a dialog box listing the types and number of changes it made to the page.

NOTE When running this command on an XHTML page, Dreamweaver also checks to make sure the syntax of the page matches that of an XHTML document. Among other concerns, all tags in XHTML must be lowercase, and you have to correctly terminate any empty tags—
 for the line break tag, for example. Dreamweaver fixes such problems.

As long as you keep the page open, you can undo the changes Dreamweaver makes. Suppose you asked Dreamweaver to remove comments, and then you suddenly realize you really did need them. Ctrl+Z (⌘-Z) is your savior.

TIP While Dreamweaver generally does a good job of avoiding extra, and unnecessary, HTML tags, you'll still find pages that have empty paragraphs with just a single nonbreaking space (page 81) in them, like this:

```
<p>  </p>
```

Dreamweaver inserts these paragraphs whenever you're in Design view and hit the Enter (Return) key. It fills the <p> tag with whatever you type; if you don't type anything, Dreamweaver leaves the <p> tag empty. Well, it's not quite empty since it holds a nonbreaking space, so the Clean Up HTML command's "Empty container tags" option won't help here since the container isn't empty. Instead, turn to Dreamweaver's "Find and Replace" tool (Chapter 8), and search the source code for *<p> </p>*; leave the Replace value blank, and Dreamweaver strips these almost-empty <p> tags from your page (or site).

■ Fixing Page Problems with Site Reports

The Clean Up HTML command is a great way to make sure you have lean code, but what if you forget about it until after you build all 500 pages of your site? Do you have to open each page and run the command, whether there's a problem or not?

Fortunately, no. Dreamweaver's Site Reports feature makes identifying problems throughout a site a snap. Dreamweaver not only locates problems that the Clean Up HTML command can fix, but it also checks your pages for other problems, such as missing titles, empty Alt properties for images, and other issues that can make your site less welcoming to disabled web surfers.

TIP To save time when running a report, you can exclude selected folders from the report using the Cloaking feature described on page 818.

After you run a report, Dreamweaver lists pages with problems. Unfortunately, the Site Reports feature only *finds* problems; it doesn't fix them. You have to open and fix each page individually.

To run a report on one or more web pages:

1. **Choose Site→Reports.**

   Dreamweaver opens the Reports window (Figure 19-13).

FIGURE 19-13

Dreamweaver's Site Reports feature makes quick work of finding common page errors. You won't use all these options, but at the very least, make sure you check for missing Alt text (page 245) and any untitled documents before you put a new website up on the Internet.

2. **From the "Report on" menu, select the files you want to analyze.**

   Dreamweaver can report on a single web page, on multiple pages, or on an entire site. Choose Current Document to check the web page you have open at the moment. Select Entire Current Local Site to check every page in your local site folder, including folders within the site folder. This option is great when you want to check your entire site prior to uploading it to a web server and making it "live" (more on that in the next chapter).

   Choosing "Selected Files in Site" checks only the files you choose in the Files panel. You need to open the Files panel and then select the files from the local file list for this option to work. (See the box on page 793 for ways to select files.) Choose this option when you modify pages in, or add pages to, a site and you're ready to move them to your server.

   Select the Folder option to check all web pages in a selected folder. After you choose it, Dreamweaver displays an empty box and a folder icon. Click the folder icon to locate and select the folder you want to check; Dreamweaver automatically checks folders within your selected folder. You can also use this option to check pages that aren't actually part of the current site.

3. **Select the types of report you want Dreamweaver to generate.**

   Dreamweaver displays two kinds of report in the Reports window. The first set, Workflow Reports, deals mostly with collaboration features that facilitate team work environments (see the following chapter). The last option in this group—

Recently Modified—generates a list of files that you either created or modified within a certain number of days or within a range of dates (February 1 of last year to the present, say). When you run this report, Dreamweaver lists the files in the Site Reports panel *and* opens a web page listing those files.

NOTE The Recently Modified site report looks for files created or changed in the last seven days, but you can adjust that timeframe. In the Reports window, select Recently Modified, and then click Report Settings (Figure 19-13). A window appears where you can change the range of dates.

In fact, you'll find the technique described on page 783 more useful. It not only identifies recently modified files, but it also selects them in the Files panel, giving you many more options for acting on this information. For example, with your recently modified files selected, you can upload them to your server, run find-and-replace operations on just those files, or apply many other tools.

The second type of report, HTML Reports, is useful for locating common errors, such as missing page titles or Alt properties.

Three of the HTML Reports options—Combinable Nested Font Tags, Redundant Nested Tags, and Removable Empty Tags—search for pages that have common code mistakes. These problems are the same ones the Clean Up HTML command fixes (see page 791).

Turn on the Missing Alt Text checkbox to search for images that lack a text description (see page 245).

Finally, turn on the Untitled Documents checkbox to identify pages that are either missing a title or that still have a Dreamweaver-supplied title.

NOTE The Site Report command doesn't identify XHTML syntax errors like those the Clean Up XHTML command fixes (see page 791).

4. **Click Run.**

   Dreamweaver analyzes the pages you specified and produces a report based on the options you set in step 3 (see Figure 19-14). Each line in the Results window displays the name of the file, the line number where the error occurs, and a description of the error.

5. **In the Results panel, double-click the filename.**

   Dreamweaver opens the file and highlights the offending code.

6. **Fix the problem according to its type.**

   For a page containing Combinable Nested Font Tags, Redundant Nested Tags, or Removable Empty Tags errors, use the Clean Up HTML command as described on page 791.

   For pages missing a title, add one by opening the page and typing a title in the document window's Title box, as described on page 30.

FIGURE 19-14

If you decide that Dreamweaver is taking too long to generate the error report, you can always stop the operation. In the Results panel's left-hand toolbar, click the icon that looks like a stop sign with an X through it (the icon is normally grayed out, but it's bold when Dream-weaver is busy creating a site report).

You can add missing Alt properties using the Properties panel. Select the image and type in a description, as described on page 245. If the same image is missing its Alt property on several pages, you may find it faster to use Dreamweaver's powerful "Find and Replace" command (see Chapter 8).

7. **Continue opening files from the Results window and fixing them until you correct each mistake.**

   Unfortunately, Dreamweaver doesn't provide a quick, one-step method to fix most of these problems. Except for missing Alt text, which you can universally add using the "Find and Replace" command, you must open and fix each page individually.

If you want to save the results of your report, click Save Report. Dreamweaver opens a Save As dialog box and lets you save the report as an XML file (so you can file it in the "Files I don't really need" folder on your desktop).

Moving Your Site to the Internet

B uilding web pages is a big accomplishment, but it's not the whole job. Your beautifully designed and informative site will languish in obscurity unless you move it from your hard drive to a web server.

Fortunately, once your site is ready for prime time, you can put it on a server without ever leaving the comfort of Dreamweaver. The program includes simple commands for transferring files back and forth between the server and your desktop. All you need to do is provide Dreamweaver with the information it needs to connect to your server.

NOTE Dreamweaver CC 2014 includes many enhancements to make transferring files fast and efficient. Since Dreamweaver CS6, it has allowed multiple, simultaneous connections to a server. In other words, the old Dreamweaver transferred files one at a time, but the recent versions can send multiple files at once.

■ Adding a Remote Server

As you work on your website—whether you build the site from scratch or modify existing pages—you keep your files in a *local root folder* (see page 29), often called a *local site* for short. You can think of a local site as a work in progress; you'll routinely have partially finished documents sitting on your computer.

After you perfect and test your pages using the techniques described in Chapter 19, you're ready to transfer those pages to a server that's connected to the Internet; this server stores copies of your site files so it can dispense them to visitors.

Dreamweaver calls this server the *remote server*, and you can transfer your local site files to it in several ways. You select the way you want from the "Connect using" drop-down menu:

- **FTP**. By far, the most common method is *FTP*, or File Transfer Protocol. Just as HTTP is the process by which web pages are transferred from servers to web browsers, so FTP is the traditional way to transfer files from one drive to another over the Internet. If your site resides at a web hosting company or your Internet service provider (ISP), you'll use this option or, even better, the SFTP option discussed next. One downside of FTP is that none of the information you transfer using it—including your user name and password—is encrypted. It's possible, therefore (though very unlikely), for someone monitoring the flow of data over the Internet to spot your user name and password and log into your web server and wreak havoc on your site.

- **SFTP** stands for *Secure* FTP. This transfer method encrypts *all* your data, including your user name and password, so information you transfer this way is unintelligible to Internet snoops. It's the ideal way to connect to a web server, and in many cases, it's also faster. Unfortunately, not all web hosting companies offer this advanced option, so you may be stuck with regular FTP. If you're not sure if you can use SFTP, try it—Dreamweaver will tell you if it's unable to transfer files that way. Should that be the case, switch to FTP.

- **FTP over SSL/TSL**, also called FTPS, provides security that regular FTP lacks. It encrypts your login information, and, optionally, all the data—web pages, images, and so on—that you transfer as well. Because your user name and password are secure, SFTP (discussed in the the previous bullet point) is better than FTP for file transfers, but if your server runs Windows, SFTP isn't available. You can try a couple of other options. FTP over SSL/TSL comes in two flavors, Implicit (an older and less-well-supported method) and Explicit (the newer, now-standard form of FTPS). You can choose either option from the "Connect using" drop-down menu. For example, you could choose "FTP over SSL/TSL (explicit encryption)." If your web server runs Windows, try connecting to it in this order: FTP over SSL/TSL (Explicit encryption); if that doesn't work, try Implicit encryption and, finally, if that fails, use plain old FTP.

- **Local/network**. If you work on an intranet, or if your company's web-server is connected to the company network, you may also be able to transfer files as you would any other file on your office network (using the Network Neighborhood, My Network Places, or the "Connect to Server" command, depending on your operating system).

- The last two options—**WebDAV and RDS**—are file-management systems for collaborative web development. They're not very common, so you're unlikely to ever use them, but you'll learn about them on pages 809 and 810.

Beyond Dreamweaver

Do I have to use Dreamweaver to move my files to the Web?

No. If you use another program to transfer files, like FileZilla (Windows, Mac, and Linux), Cyberduck (Windows and Mac), CuteFTP (Windows), or RBrowser (Mac), you can continue to use it and ignore Dreamweaver's Remote Site feature.

But if you've never used Dreamweaver to move files, you may want to at least try it because it simplifies the process. For example, to move a file from your computer to a web server using a regular FTP program, you must first browse for the file on your local machine and then navigate to the proper folder on your server. Dreamweaver saves you both steps; when you select the file in the Files panel and click the Put button (see page 812), Dreamweaver automatically locates the file on your computer and transfers it to the correct folder on your server.

Setting Up a Remote Server with FTP or SFTP

You can set up a remote server only if you first set up a *local* site on your computer, as described on page 750. If you built your site in Dreamweaver, you should already have a local site set up. Once you do, you need to tell Dreamweaver how to connect to the remote server so it can transfer your local site files to your server:

1. **Choose Site→Manage Sites.**

   Dreamweaver opens the Manage Sites dialog box, which lists all the sites you've defined so far. You're about to tell Dreamweaver how to connect to a web server so you can create a living, Internet-based *copy* of one of these hard drive-based local sites.

NOTE Even if all you want to do is copy a live website from the Internet to your computer, you need a local site on your computer, and you want to point Dreamweaver to a folder within that local site—even if it's simply an empty folder—so it has a place to store the files you download.

2. **Click the name of the site you want to put on the Internet, and then click ✐, the "Edit the currently selected site" button, also known as the pencil icon in the lower-left corner of the Manage Sites window.**

   Alternatively, double-click the site name in the list. Either way, Dreamweaver opens the Site Setup window, as shown in Figure 20-1.

NOTE You can set up your local site and remote server simultaneously, when you first begin building your site, as described on page 23. Even then, however, Dreamweaver requires that you first give your local site a name and choose a local site folder. At that point, you can rejoin the steps described here.

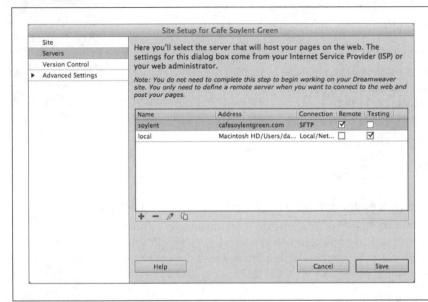

FIGURE 20-1

In addition to setting up a local site, Dreamweaver lets you set up both a "remote" server (meaning the web server on the Internet where people go to see your site) and a "testing" server (a server—frequently running on your own computer—used to test dynamic sites, like the PHP-driven pages described in Chapter 24).

3. **Click the Servers option.**

This is where Dreamweaver lists your remote and testing servers. The remote server contains the site the world can see, while the testing server acts as a test bed, usually for dynamic, database-driven sites. If you're building a site without using PHP, ASP, ColdFusion, or some other server-side programming language, you don't need to set up a testing server.

Initially, the Servers category is empty: You need to add a remote server.

> **NOTE** Dreamweaver lets you define as many remote and testing servers as you want, but you probably won't ever have a need for "infinity" servers. However, you may need to upload the same site to two different servers—perhaps you have a high-traffic website and put the site on several servers to balance the load. In that case, you can define a second, third, and even a fourth server. Even though you can create names and add details for multiple remote sites in the Site Setup window (Figure 20-1), you can only connect and transfer files to and from one remote site at a time. Choose the site you want to connect with by checking its Remote box in the Site Setup window. You can check only one Remote box at a time. So, for example, if you have a "main" server and a "backup" server and you want to transfer a file from your computer to both, you need to do so in two batches, sending the file first to the "main" server and then, after changing the Site Setup window to designate "backup" as the remote server, you'd send the files again. To see the Site Setup window, choose Sites→Manage Sites. Choose the site you want to work with (for example, Cafe Soylent Green) and then, in the lower right corner, click "Edit the currently selected site" (the pencil icon). In the Site Setup window, choose Servers and Dreamweaver opens a window like the one in Figure 20-1, where you can turn on the Remote box for the "backup" server. When you do, Dreamweaver removes the Remote checkmark from "main."

4. **Click + .**

A new pane pops up (see Figure 20-2). Here you supply the information Dreamweaver needs to connect to the server.

5. **Type a name in the Server Name box.**

Dreamweaver only uses this name internally. It's not something anyone else will see, so name it anything you like, such as "My Server" or "Hosting Company."

FIGURE 20-2

To connect to a server, you need to know its Web address (which is usually its FTP address), the FTP user name and password, and the name of the folder where the server stores your files. You get all this information when you sign up with a web hosting company. You usually don't need to change the More Options settings when you transfer files using FTP, though they can help if you're having connectivity problems (see the box on page 806). (If you use SFTP, the More Options menu doesn't appear.)

6. **From the "Connect using" drop-down menu, choose either FTP or SFTP.**

Ideally, you'll use SFTP—it's more secure and usually faster—but your web hosting company may not offer it, in which case you'll have to choose FTP.

NOTE If you're not sure whether your server supports SFTP, try it out. Follow these set-up instructions using SFTP as the "Connect using" option, and then click the Test button. If Dreamweaver can't connect, try FTPS (discussed next). If you still can't tap the server, try regular FTP. And if Dreamweaver *still* can't connect, you probably typed the wrong user name, password, or FTP address.

7. **Fill in the "FTP address" box.**

This is the address of your web server. It's usually something like *www.cafesoylentgreen.com*. It never includes directories, folders, or slashes (like *www.cafesoylentgreen.com/menu*); never includes codes for the FTP protocol (*ftp://*

ftp.cafesoylentgreen.com) or HTTP protocol (*http://www.cafesoylentgreen. com*); and it may simply be a domain name, such as cafesoylentgreen.com (*http://cafesoylentgreen.com*). It can also be an IP address, like *64.226.43.116*. In most cases, it's the address you type in a web browser's address window (minus the *http://*) to get to your site's home page.

If you don't know the address, there's only one way to find out: Call or email your web hosting company or ISP, or check its website.

8. **In the Username box, type your user name, and then, in the Password box, type your password.**

   Dreamweaver uses bullets (••••) to display your password so that office evil-doers can't see what you type. If you want Dreamweaver to remember your password so you don't have to type it each time you connect to the server, turn on the Save checkbox.

> **NOTE** For security reasons, don't turn on the Save checkbox if you access the Web using computers at, say, your local library, community college, or anywhere else where people you don't trust can use the machine. Otherwise, you might awaken one morning to find the following splattered across your home page: "Hi there! Welcome to Jack's house of illegally acquired and unlawfully distributed music, featuring One Direction's greatest hits."

9. **In the Root Directory box, type the path to your server's root directory.**

   Here you specify the path to the *folder* on the web server that contains your web page files. This folder, known as the root folder, is the counterpart to the folder on your hard drive that holds your site files as you work on them. Common names for this folder include *docs, www, htdocs, public_html, httpdocs*, and *virtual_html*.

   The path you type in the Root Directory box depends on where on the remote server Dreamweaver's FTP tool connects—and that all depends on how your web host set up the server, so the only way to know what to type into this box is to contact your web host.

   In many cases, you only have to type the name of the root folder followed by a slash, like this: *htdocs/*. You're specifying the path from the folder that Dreamweaver initially connects to via FTP—the web hosting company's administrative folder—to your site's root folder. In this example, Dreamweaver connects to a folder that contains the root folder, so you simply say, "Hey, Dreamweaver, you're in the wrong place. Go inside the *htdocs* folder to find my site."

   Sometimes, however, you need to use a much longer path, one that includes lots of folders, like this: */var/www/mysite.com/htdocs*.

   This type of address includes the entire path from the top level of the server's hard drive through several folders and, finally, to your root folder (*htdocs*) on the server. Again, there's no real way to determine the path without asking your web hosting company.

10. **Type your site's web address in the Web URL box.**

    This is simply what you'd type in a web browser's address line to get to your site: *www.cafesoylentgreen.com/,* for example. Sometimes, though, you might work on files the get stored in a subdirectory of the site's root folder. For example, if you work in corporate web design, you might oversee a self-contained site for the marketing department, which means the URL to reach the files you work on might be at *www.mycompany.com/marketing.* If that's the case, include the subdirectory's name in the web address you type in, as in *www.cafesoylent-green.com/marketing.*

> **NOTE** What you type into the Web URL box when you set up a remote server can affect how Dreamweaver checks and updates links. See page 754 for details.

11. **Click the Test button.**

    Dreamweaver attempts to connect to your server. If it succeeds, you'll see a box that says, "Dreamweaver connected to your Web server successfully." If it didn't succeed, you'll get an error message. See the box on page 806 for the most common problems and solutions.

> **NOTE** When Dreamweaver can't connect to a server, one of the first things you should try (after double-checking your user name and password) is turning on the "Use passive FTP" checkbox. See the box on page 806 for more.

12. **Click Save to store these settings.**

    Dreamweaver returns to the Servers category of the Site Setup window.

13. **Click Save once again to return to the Manage Sites window, and then click Done.**

    At this point, you're ready to connect to your web server and transfer files. If you're the only person working on the site, Dreamweaver's Get and Put commands will do the trick (page 812). If, however, you're part of a development team, you can use Dreamweaver's Check In/Check Out feature, described on page 821, to make sure a coworker doesn't accidentally erase your hard work (or his).

More Remote Server Options for FTP

The steps discussed above will probably be all you ever need to transfer your files to your server by FTP, but Dreamweaver offers a few more options, as well as some advanced settings that apply to all types of connections (see page 810).

> **NOTE** The options listed below aren't available (or necessary) when you connect using SFTP.

To see the additional options for FTP connections, click the More Options arrow from the Basic server setup window (see Figure 20-2). Most of these checkboxes should remain turned off, but here's what they do:

- **Use Passive FTP**. Select this setting if you can't make an FTP connection and you know you typed your FTP address, user name, password, and root directory name correctly (see steps 7–9 on page 803). Use this option to address firewall lockout—where hardware or software that protects your (or your company's) computer from hackers by limiting what you can send and receive to and from the outside world.

FREQUENTLY ASKED QUESTION

When Your Remote Site Is Too Remote

Help! I can't connect to my web server. What should I do?

Things don't always go smoothly when you try to connect to the outside world. That's doubly true when you try to connect to a web server, since you depend on a variety of things—your Internet connection, the networks connecting you to the server, the server itself, and the FTP software that runs the show—working together in harmony. Dreamweaver presents an error message if you can't successfully establish an FTP connection with your server. The error box frequently contains useful information that can help you diagnose the problem. Here are some of the most common messages and their meanings:

- **"Remote host cannot be found"** usually means that you typed in an incorrect FTP address (step 7 on page 803).

- **"Cannot open server folder"** usually means you mistyped the name of the remote root directory, or you've got the wrong name for it (see step 9 on page 804).

Unfortunately, there are lots of reasons why Dreamweaver may not be able to connect to a server, so sometimes the error message isn't particularly helpful—you'll often get a really large dialog box listing all those reasons. Even if you simply got your login info or password incorrect, Dreamweaver spits out a long list of possible problems.

The first thing to do is double- (and triple-) check your user name and password. Here are a few other suggestions: Make sure you're connected to the Internet (open a web browser and see if you can visit a site); return to the Site Setup window, open the Servers pane, and turn on the "Use passive FTP" option under More Options (sometimes this just makes things work). In the same window, turn off the "Use FTP performance optimization" checkbox, and if you have another FTP program, like FileZilla or Cyberduck, see if you can connect using the same settings you gave Dreamweaver. If all these steps fail, visit the Adobe website at *http://tinyurl.com/2crmqey* for more troubleshooting tips.

- **Use IPV6 Transfer Mode**. You probably won't need to turn on this checkbox, but the day has finally arrived when the IP addresses we've used for years—like 192.16.16.62—have all been used up. The new standard—called IPV6—contains many, many, many more possible addresses (340,282,366,920,938,463,463,374, 607,431,768,211,456, to be precise), so we shouldn't be running out anytime soon. If your web server uses an IPV6 address (which looks something like 1A23:120B :0000:0000:0000:7634:AD01:004D), your web hosting company will tell you.

- **Use Proxy**. If you can't connect to your remote server and your company's system administrator confirms that you have a firewall, turn on the Use Proxy checkbox (also found in Site Setup→Servers→More Options), and click the Preferences link to open the Site category of the Preferences window. Enter the name of the computer hosting the firewall, along with its port number. Your firewall configuration may also require that you transfer files using passive FTP. Check with your administrator to see if this is the case, and, if so, head back to the More Options section and turn on the checkbox next to "Use passive FTP."

- **Use FTP performance optimization**. Dreamweaver normally turns on this checkbox because it helps speed up file transfers between your computer and your web server. However, it can also be a source of connection problems. If you can't connect to your server, try turning off this checkbox.

- **Use alternative FTP move method**. If everything is OK when you connect to your server but you're getting errors when you move files there, then turn on this option. It's slower than FTP, but more reliable. It's also handy if you use Adobe's Contribute program for editing web pages and take advantage of its "rollback" feature (to learn more about Contribute, visit *www.adobe.com/contribute/*).

> **NOTE** When you set up a remote server, you'll see an Advanced button, which lets you set additional options. You can usually skip these settings, but turn to page 810 if you want to know what they do.

Setting Up a Remote Server Using FTP over SSL/TLS

As mentioned earlier, FTP isn't the safest way to transfer files: It transmits your username and password over the airwaves, and some nefarious hacker could grab that information and use it to log into your web server, wreck your site, and ruin your reputation. That's pretty unlikely, but still possible. SFTP is a much better option, but it's not available on Windows servers, so if your web host uses a server running Windows (as opposed to Linux/Unix, the more common web server operating system), try to use "FTP over SSL/TLS."

FTP over SSL/TLS (also known as FTPS or FTPSE) comes in two flavors, Implicit encryption and Explicit encryption. Use Explicit encryption since it's newer, has more features, and is an agreed-upon standard. Implicit encryption is offered only to support older servers that don't offer Explicit encryption.

Most of the settings for FTP over SSL/TLS are the same as those for regular FTP, so you can follow steps 1–10 on page 801, but instead of choosing FTP from the "Connect using" menu, choose "FTP over SSL/TLS." The main difference between regular FTP and FTP over SSL/TLS is the use of a "server certificate" to "authenticate" the web server. That simply means that the web server has a special file on it (kind of like an identification card) that "proves" it is the web server it says it is, so you know that you're really connecting to your server and not some evil server pretending to be yours (jeez, these web guys are slick).

Basically, if your server is set up for FTPS, you choose either None or Trusted Server from the Authentication menu (see Figure 20-3). You need to contact whomever is in charge of your server (your web host or your company's IT department) to determine which option you need. Once you make a selection, click Test to see if

Dreamweaver can connect to your server. If not, see the troubleshooting advice in the box on page 806.

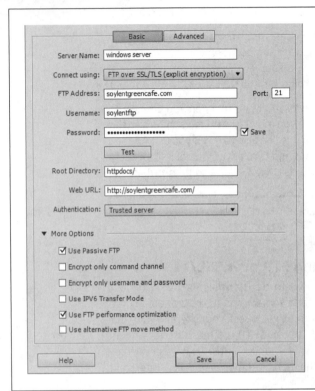

FIGURE 20-3

If you use FTP over SSL/TLS to connect to your web server, you'll find a few additional options under More Options. "Encrypt only command channel" obscures only your login information and the commands you send to the server. The actual data, like web pages and images, goes out uncloaked. This translates to faster uploads and downloads. The "Encrypt only username and password" option hides only your login information (not your commands). Still, this is a reasonably secure choice in most cases because it prevents snoopers from stealing your login information.

Setting Up a Remote Server over a Local Network

If you work on an intranet, or if your company's web server is connected to the company network, you may be able to transfer site files just as you'd move any other files from machine to machine. In this case, Dreamweaver provides the same file-transfer functions as the FTP option, but the setup is simpler.

Follow steps 1–5 from the previous instructions (page 801), but in step 6, choose Local/Network from the "Connect using" menu. That brings up options for your connection information (see Figure 20-4).

Click the folder icon next to "Remote folder," and then navigate to and select your site's remote site folder. On a local network, this folder isn't *truly* remote, because your company's web server is still within the walls of your building, but you get the idea.

Wrap up with steps 10, 12, and 13 of the previous instructions. At this point, you're ready to connect to the "remote" server and transfer files as described on page 812.

FIGURE 20-4

If your company keeps its web server in your office, the "remote site" might not be that remote. In such a case, choose a folder on your local network as the "remote" folder.

Setting Up a Remote Server with WebDAV

Dreamweaver also lets you transfer files to a remote site using *WebDAV*, short for Web-based Distributed Authoring and Versioning. Like FTP, it's a standard, or *protocol*, for transferring files. Like SFTP, it uses a secure connection (called SSL, or Secure Socket Layer) that encrypts all your data as it passes back and forth between your computer and your web server. But unlike both of those technologies, WebDAV addresses the kinds of problems you encounter when you collaborate on website development with other people.

For instance, all kinds of havoc can result if two people edit a page simultaneously; whoever uploads the page to the server *second* winds up wiping out the changes made by the first person. WebDAV supports a check-in and check-out system that works similarly to Dreamweaver's Check In and Check Out tools (see page 821) to make sure only one person works on a file at a time, and that no one tramples on anyone else's files. In fact, Dreamweaver's Check In/Check Out feature works seamlessly with WebDAV.

Both Microsoft Internet Information Server (IIS) and Apache Web Server work with WebDAV. Colleges and universities commonly use WebDAV, but that's not the case with web hosting companies, so it's pretty unlikely that you'll find commercial web hosts that offer it. To find out if your server can handle WebDAV (and to find out the necessary connection information), consult your web server's administrator (for example, call or email your web hosting company).

Setting up WebDAV access to a remote site is similar to setting up FTP access. Follow steps 1–5 on page 801, and then do the following:

1. **Choose WebDAV from the "Connect using" menu.**

   The Site Definition window displays the WebDAV settings, which require only four pieces of information.

2. **In the URL box, type in the address of the WebDAV server.**

In most cases, that's the URL of your website, so it begins with either *http://* or *https://*. The "s" in *https* means you'll connect securely to the server using SSL. The normal *http://* method doesn't use encryption, which means that, just as with regular FTP, your computer sends your user name, password, and data "in the open" as it travels across the Internet. Note that simply adding an "s" won't suddenly make your file transfers secure; the receiving server needs to be set up to accept *https* connections (a technically challenging task).

3. **In the Username and Password boxes, type in your credentials.**

Turn on the Save checkbox so you don't have to type in your password each time you move files to your server (but heed the note on page 804).

4. **Click Test to see if your connection works.**

If Dreamweaver succeeds, it proudly tells you. If it fails, you'll get an error message that, unfortunately, isn't exactly helpful. WebDAV isn't nearly as finicky as FTP, so if there's an error, you most likely just typed the URL, password, or login info incorrectly, or WebDAV isn't available on that particular server.

NOTE Due to the different possible server configurations for WebDAV, Dreamweaver may not be able to connect even if your server has WebDAV turned on. If that's the case, you'll need to use FTP or another method to connect to your server.

The rest of the process is identical to the FTP setup process, so follow steps 10, 12, and 13 starting on page 805. At that point, you're ready to connect to your server and transfer files, as described on page 812.

Setting Up a Remote Server with RDS

RDS (Remote Development Services) lets designers work on web files and databases in conjunction with Adobe's ColdFusion server. If you use a server other than ColdFusion, you don't need to worry about this option.

To create a remote site in Dreamweaver that works with RDS, follow steps 1–5 on page 812. In step 6, choose RDS from the "Connect using" drop-down menu.

The Site Definition window displays a version number, a brief description, and a Settings button. Click Settings to open the Configure RDS Server window. Fill in the dialog box as directed by your server administrator or help desk.

Advanced Remote Server Settings

No matter which connection method you use (FTP, Local/Network, and so on), each remote server has a set of advanced options that you find by clicking the Advanced tab in the server setup window (see Figure 20-5):

- **If you don't want to synchronize files, turn off the "Maintain synchronization information" checkbox**. Dreamweaver's synchronization feature ensures that all the files in your site mirror the files on your computer; when you synchronize a site, Dreamweaver moves your most recent site files to your server (you'll learn about this feature in detail on page 827).

If you don't want Dreamweaver to do this, turn off this checkbox. When it's on, Dreamweaver inserts little files named *dwsync.xml* throughout your site in folders that have *_notes* appended to their name. These files hold synchronization information about each site file. If you don't synchronize, don't clutter up your site with the files. In addition, Dreamweaver spends time determining the synch status of each file, so your file transfers go more quickly with this turned off.

- **Leave "Automatically upload files to server on Save" turned off**. Not only will this slow things down—Dreamweaver has to connect and move the saved file to the server every time you press Ctrl+S (⌘-S)—it also means you may save half-finished pages on your remote server.

- **If you work with a team of developers, you may want to use Dreamweaver's Check In/Check Out tools discussed on page 821.** To do that, turn on "Enable file check in and check out." Then fill in the corresponding options as explained in Figure 20-5. You can save yourself some clicks when you use the Check Out feature (see page 821) by turning on "Check out files when opening" and filling in your name and email address. Now you can check out a file from the remote server by simply double-clicking its name in the Site Files list. If you work on your own, *do not* turn on this setting, since it slows down the process of moving files to and from the server and adds unnecessary files (used to determine who has what file checked out) to both your server and your own computer.

FIGURE 20-5

If you use Dreamweaver's Check In/Check Out feature and you work on your site in several locations (for example, from home and from your office), use a different check-out name for each location (BobAtHome and BobAtWork, for example). That way, you know which files you checked out to your home computer and which to your computer at work.

■ Transferring Files

Once you tell Dreamweaver *how* to send off your web pages to your server, you can set about actually *doing* so. Thanks to Dreamweaver's Files panel, the whole process takes only a few steps.

Moving Files to Your Web Server

To transfer files to your server:

1. **Open the Files panel.**

   Choose Window→Files or the keyboard shortcut F8 (Shift-⌘-F).

2. **From the drop-down Site menu in the Files panel, choose the name of the site whose files you want to move (if it isn't already selected).**

   The Files panel displays files for the selected site. You can use the File View drop-down menu to see either a list of the files on your local site or a list of the files on your remote server (see Figure 20-6). You can see local and remote server files side by side if you first choose "Remote server" from the File View menu and then click the Expand button on the Files panel.

3. **From the list in the Files panel, select the files you want to upload to the server.**

   To move a folder and every file inside it, simply select the folder. (In other words, you can transfer your *entire* website to the server by simply selecting the local site folder—the folder listed at the very top of the Local Files list.) If you change only a few files on your site, you can selectively upload those files (or folders of changed files) using any of the techniques described in this section.

> **NOTE** If you don't see the files you want to upload in the Files list, you may have selected "Remote server." Select "Local view" to see only those files on your computer, and then click the Refresh button on the Files panel (Figure 20-6).

When you use do-it-yourself FTP programs like FileZilla or Cyberduck, you have to specify a folder location for every file you transfer to your web server. Here's one of the great advantages of letting Dreamweaver do your file shuffling; it already *knows* where your files should go on the remote server. The local and remote sites are, after all, mirror images, so Dreamweaver simply puts your local files in the corresponding folders on the remote server.

For example, suppose you select the file *mayo.html*, which is in a folder called Condiments, which itself is in the local root folder. When you transfer *mayo.html*, Dreamweaver automatically puts it in the Condiments folder in the root folder on the remote server. In fact, if the Condiments folder doesn't exist on the remote server, Dreamweaver creates it for you and *then* puts the file into it. Now that's service!

You're now ready to go live with your web page.

Site   Put   Check   Expand/
menu   files   out   collapse   File view

Connect/
disconnect

Refresh list

Get files

Check in

Synchronize

FIGURE 20-6

*The Files panel offers toolbar buttons for upload-
ing and downloading your web files to and from
the server that actually dishes them out to your
site's adoring public. (See Chapter 18 for much
more on this important window.)*

Local view

Remote server

Testing server

Repository view

Local Files	Size	Type	
▼ 🗁 Site – CSS La...		Folder	7/22/13 12:28 PM
🗎 about.html	5KB	HTML File	7/22/13 2:45 PM
▶ 🗁 css		Folder	7/22/13 12:30 PM
▼ 🗁 images		Folder	7/16/13 10:56 AM
🖼 bann...	1KB	PNG File	6/12/12 6:57 AM
🖼 bg_b...	15KB	JPG File	6/12/12 6:57 AM
🖼 bg_b...	1KB	PNG File	6/12/12 6:57 AM
🖼 bg_p...	13KB	PNG File	6/12/12 6:57 AM
🖼 cafe_...	57KB	PNG File	6/12/12 6:57 AM

4. **Click the "Put files" button—the up arrow icon in the Files panel.**

   Alternatively, you can use the keyboard shortcut Shift+Ctrl+U (Shift-⌘-U).

   Several things happen when you do this. First, if you're connecting via FTP,
   Dreamweaver attempts to hook into your server. As you can see from the status
   window that opens, it may take a moment or so to establish the connection;
   once that happens, the Connect button (see Figure 20-6) displays that pushed-
   in look that means you're connected.

   Next, if any of the files you're transferring are currently open and have unsaved
   changes, Dreamweaver asks if you want to save the files before it transfers them.
   Click Yes; if you have multiple unsaved files, click Yes To All. Dreamweaver then
   begins the transfer.

   In addition, as Dreamweaver transfers your pages, it asks if you want to transfer any *dependent files* (see Figure 20-7). That includes graphics, external
   CSS files, or movies that a browser needs to display your pages the way you
   designed them.

   The dependent files feature can save you considerable time and hassle because
   you don't have to hunt for and upload each graphic or external style sheet
   yourself. On the other hand, if all the dependent files are *already* on the server,
   having Dreamweaver transfer the same files again is a waste of time. Fortunately,
   Dreamweaver prevents this wasted effort, as described in the next step.

Dependent Files – will dismiss in 28 second(s)

Should dependent files be included in the transfer?

☐ Don't show me this message again

[Yes] [No] [Cancel]

FIGURE 20-7

The File Transfer command's Dependent Files feature makes sure that Dreamweaver copies to the server all the files a browser needs to display your web pages—graphics, external style sheets, videos, and so on. The feature also includes a time limit—you'll see a "will dismiss in 30 seconds" message. If you don't click a button within 30 seconds, Dreamweaver assumes you mean "No" to whether you want to upload dependent files, and it uploads only the files you selected.

NOTE If you turn on the "Don't show me this message again" checkbox in the Dependent Files dialog box and then click Yes, from that moment forward, Dreamweaver copies dependent files without asking you. On the other hand, if you turn on the "Don't show me this message again" box and then click No, Dreamweaver *never* copies dependent files.

If you turn off the Dependent Files dialog box and change your mind later, hold down the Alt (Option) key when you transfer a file (using any method except a keyboard shortcut). Or choose Edit→Preferences→Site Category (Dreamweaver→Preferences→Site Category) to turn this feature on or off.

5. **Click Yes to transfer dependent files, or No to transfer only the files you selected.**

   Dreamweaver copies the files to the server. If you copy a file that's inside a folder that doesn't exist on the remote server, Dreamweaver creates a same-named server-side folder, too. In fact, Dreamweaver creates as many subfolders as necessary to make sure it transfers every local file to a mirror folder on the remote site. (Try doing *that* with a regular FTP program.)

   If you choose to transfer dependent files, Dreamweaver streamlines the process if you left the Maintain Synchronization Information checkbox turned on when you defined your remote site (see page 827). It determines whether the dependent file already exists on the server and, if it does, whether your local copy is newer. If the dependent file doesn't exist on the server, or if your local copy is newer (meaning you made changes to it locally but haven't yet moved it to the Web), then Dreamweaver sends it when you tell it to transfer dependent files.

   However, if Dreamweaver thinks that it's the same file, or that the copy of the file on the server is newer, it won't make the transfer. This behavior is a huge time-saver, since you won't have to repeatedly upload the same 50 navigation buttons each time you say "Yes" to transferring dependent files. But best of all, Dreamweaver still transfers dependent files that really *are* new.

NOTE Dreamweaver's ability to correctly determine whether a dependent file on your computer is the same as a file on the server depends on its Site Synchronization feature, described on page 827.

Dreamweaver's accuracy with this tool is good, but it has been known to get it wrong. If Dreamweaver isn't moving a dependent file, you can select that file and upload it manually (by selecting it in the Files panel and then clicking the Put button). Dreamweaver always obeys a direct order to move a selected file.

6. **Continue using the Put button to transfer all the files in your local website to the remote site.**

   Depending on the number of files you transfer, this operation can take some time—transferring files over the Internet using FTP isn't nearly as fast as copying files from one hard drive to another (see Figure 20-8).

FIGURE 20-8

Click the File Status button (circled) and choose Put to quickly move a file to your server. You can also use this menu to retrieve a copy of a file from the server (Get), use Check In and Check Out tools (page 821), or review Design Notes (page 831) for the page. Note that Check In and Check Out are available only if you turned on the Check In/Check Out tool as described on page 821. To highlight this file in the Files panel, choose "Locate in Site."

■ **OTHER WAYS TO MOVE FILES TO YOUR SERVER**

To copy a current document to your server without using the Files panel at all, you can go directly to the Put command. Say you finish building or modifying a page and want to immediately move it to the Web. Just choose Site→Put, or press Shift+Ctrl+U (Shift-⌘-U), or use the toolbar shortcut shown in Figure 20-8; Dreamweaver automatically copies the fresh page to the proper folder online.

A Little More Background on File Transfers

Dreamweaver lets you keep working as it dutifully transfers files in the background. You can edit a web page, create a new style sheet, and so on. However, there are some things you *can't* do while Dreamweaver moves files. For example, you can't edit the site definition (since that could affect how you connect to the remote server). Dreamweaver lets you know if you try to take a forbidden action while it's working with the server.

If you find Dreamweaver's background activity window a nuisance, click the Hide button and it temporarily disappears. In addition, if you accidentally start uploading a 10,000-page website, click the Cancel button to stop the transfer.

When Dreamweaver finishes moving files around, you can see a record of its actions by clicking the Log button in the bottom-right corner of the Files panel. This log differs from the raw FTP log discussed in the box on page 818. In a plain-language report, it lets you know what Dreamweaver did—"Put successful," "Get successful," and so on. If you see a "Not transferred" message, Dreamweaver tried to Get or Put a file, but both the local and remote server copies were identical, so it didn't do anything. See the previous Note for more.

Getting Files from Your Web Server

So far, this chapter has described getting your hard drive-based pages *to* the Internet. Sometimes, however, you want to download one or more files *from* your server. Perhaps you made a horrible (and irreversible) mistake on the local copy of a file and you want to retrieve the unblemished version from the Web, effectively using the remote server as a last-ditch backup system. Maybe you took over a design job for a client, and the only files they have are on the server, so you need to copy the entire site to your desktop computer. Or perhaps someone uploaded files to the site and you want to download a copy to your own computer (although the Synchronize feature described on page 827 would also work).

To get files from your remote site to your local drive, open the Files panel (press F8 [Shift-⌘-F]) and proceed as follows:

1. **From the Site pull-down menu, choose the site whose files you wish to retrieve.**

   As with all of Dreamweaver's site-management features, downloading files from a web server depends on first defining a site.

2. **From the Files panel's View menu, choose "Remote server."**

   Dreamweaver tells you that it's attempting to connect to the server. Once it succeeds, it lists the files and folders on the server and then activates the Connect button—it looks pushed in. (Dreamweaver automatically disconnects after 30 minutes of inactivity, at which point the Connect button pops back out.)

NOTE To change the disconnect time limit, press Ctrl+U (⌘-U) to open the Preferences window. Click the Site category and change the number listed in the Minutes Idle box. Be aware, however, that some web servers have their own settings and may disconnect you sooner than you specify.

3. **From the Remote Server file list, select the files you want to download.**

   The Shift-click and Ctrl-click (⌘-click) techniques for selecting files work, as explained on page 783. To download a folder and every file inside it, click the folder. This technique also lets you get your *entire* website from the server; just select the remote server's root folder, which appears at the very top of the Remote Server file list.

TROUBLESHOOTING MOMENT

Don't Replace the Wrong File

One strange feature of the Files panel's Get and Put commands may get you in trouble. Suppose, having just added new information to your home page (*index.html*), you want to transfer that page to your server. You select it in the Local Folder list—but then you accidentally click Get instead of Put.

Not knowing your true intention, Dreamweaver dutifully prepares to retrieve the file from the server, which, of course, will replace (wipe out) the newly updated home page on your computer.

Fortunately, before causing such damage, Dreamweaver also displays a warning message asking if you really want to overwrite the local file. Click No or Cancel to save your hard work.

There may be times when you *do* want to wipe out your local copy—if, for example, your cat walks across your keyboard,

types illegible code, presses Ctrl+S to save the ruined page, and Ctrl+Q to quit Dreamweaver (keeping you from using Undo to fix the mistakes). In this common situation, you'll want to replace your local copy with the remote copy. To do so, press Yes when Dreamweaver warns you, and you'll rectify your cat's errors. Oh yeah, this is also a useful trick if *you* ever make a mistake on a page you can't fix and want to return to the working copy on your server.

Dreamweaver also includes a useful Compare button to help you sort out the differences between a local and a remote file. Click the button to compare the two files and identify the changes you made. This way, you can salvage changes you made to the local copy and discard errors you (or your cat) may have introduced to the page. You can learn more about this feature on page 358.

---

4. **Click the "Get files" button (the down arrow).**

   Alternatively, click Shift+Ctrl+D (Shift-⌘-D).

   If, as you retrieve a file from your server, you have the *local* version of that file open with unsaved changes in it, Dreamweaver warns you that you'll lose those changes. (No surprise there; copying a file from the remote server automatically replaces the same file on the local site, whether it's open or not.) Dreamweaver also warns you if you're about to replace a local file that's *newer* than the remote one. And finally, Dreamweaver offers to transfer any dependent files, as described in Figure 20-7.

5. **Click Yes to transfer dependent files, or No to transfer only the files you selected.**

Dreamweaver copies the files to your local site folder, creating any folders necessary to replicate the structure of the remote site.

Troubleshoot Using the FTP Log

If you have trouble moving files using Dreamweaver's FTP command, you may be able to find some clues to the problem in the records Dreamweaver keeps when it transfers files. If you've used other FTP programs, you may have seen little messages that the web server and FTP program send back and forth, like this:

```
< 200 PORT command successful
>LIST< 150 Opening ASCII mode data connec-
tion for file list
```

Dreamweaver sends and receives this information, too, but it keeps it hidden. To see the FTP log, choose Window→Results,

and then click the FTP Log tab. Any transfer errors that Dreamweaver encounters appear here.

For example, if you come across a "cannot put file" error, it may mean that you're out of space on your web server. Contact your ISP or your server administrator for help. WebDAV connections also produce a log of file-transfer activity, but it's not very easy to decipher.

And Secure FTP (SFTP) produces no log in Dreamweaver—hush, hush, it's a secret.

Cloaking Files

You may not want *all* your files transferred to and from your remote site. For example, as part of its library and template tools, Dreamweaver creates folders inside your local root folder. These folders don't do you any good on the web server; their sole purpose is to help you build your site locally. Likewise, you may have Photoshop (.psd), Flash (.fla), Illustrator (.ai), or Fireworks CS6 (.fw.png) files in your local site folder. Browsers can't open them, and they can take up a lot of disk space, so you shouldn't transfer them to your server when you move your site online.

> **NOTE** If you work on a website with other people, you probably *will* want to have the Library and Templates folders on the server. That way, your colleagues can get at those files as well.

To meet such challenges, Dreamweaver includes a feature called *cloaking*. It lets you hide folders and specific file types, or even a single file, from many file-transfer operations, including Get/Put, Check In/Check Out (page 821), and site synchronization (page 827). In fact, you can even hide files from many site-wide Dreamweaver actions, including site reports (see page 794), search-and-replace functions (Chapter 8), the ability to check and change links site-wide (page 787), and the Assets panel (page 764). There's one exception: Files linked to Library items (see Chapter 21) or templates (Chapter 22) can still "see" items even if you cloak them in the Library and Templates folders.

Implementing each type of cloak requires a different technique.

To hide specific types of files:

1. **Choose Site→Manage Sites.**

   The Manage Sites window opens, listing all the sites you've defined in Dream-weaver.

2. **Double-click the site of interest to open it for editing.**

   Alternatively, select the site, and then click ✏, the Edit button in the lower-right corner of the Manage Sites window. Either way, Dreamweaver opens the site's Site Setup window.

3. **Click ▶ next to Advanced Settings to expand that list of options. Click the Cloaking category.**

   You see the cloaking settings (see Figure 20-9). The factory setting is On for every site you define. (To turn cloaking off, turn off the "Enable cloaking" checkbox.)

> **TIP** You can quickly turn cloaking on and off by right-clicking (Control-clicking) any file or folder in the Files panel and then selecting Cloaking→Enable Cloaking from the shortcut menu. A checkmark next to Enable Cloaking means that cloaking is turned on.

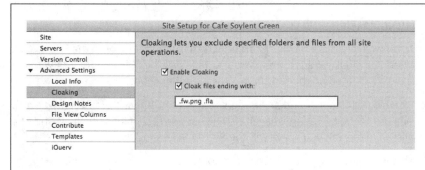

FIGURE 20-9

The Cloaking category of the Site Definition window lets you turn on or off cloaking, a feature that lets you hide folders, specific file types, and individual files from site-wide operations, like transferring files to the web server or searching and replacing text. In this window, you can specify which types of files to hide by listing their extensions (.psd for Photoshop files, for example).

4. **Turn on the "Cloak files ending with" checkbox.**

   Dreamweaver identifies file types by their extensions—.fla for Flash files, for example. If you use Fireworks, which uses the extension .png, don't add the .png extension to this box. If you're using Fireworks CS6, add .fw.png to the list (the latest version of Fireworks adds .fw to its older .png file extension so as not to confuse the byte-heavy Fireworks file with the lean, compact PNG file format).

NOTE Mac programs don't always add these filename suffixes, but without them, Dreamweaver can't cloak, so if you use a Mac, make sure you add an extension when you save a file. Some programs have a Hide File Extension checkbox that appears when you save a file—make sure you have this *turned off*.

5. **In the text box, type the extensions of the files you want to cloak.**

   Each extension should start with a period followed by three or four letters. Fireworks CS6 is an exception: for those files, type *.fw.png*. To specify multiple extensions, separate them with a space.

6. **Click Save and then Done to close this and the Manage Sites window.**

   Dreamweaver puts a red slash through files you cloak.

You can also cloak a single folder or file using the Files panel, like this:

1. **Open the Files panel by pressing F8 (Shift-⌘-F).**

   Alternatively, choose Window→Files.

2. **Right-click (Control-click) any folder or file in the Local Files view.**

   A shortcut menu appears, offering many site-related options.

3. **Select Cloaking→Cloak.**

   Dreamweaver adds a red slash through the file or folder's icon in the Files panel. When you cloak a folder, Dreamweaver hides all the files and folders *within it* as well, indicated by the red slashes through their icons.

Once you cloak a folder, it and any folders inside it disappear from Dreamweaver's file-transfer functions. Dreamweaver also hides individual files you cloak and any files with an extension you specify in the Preferences window.

As with everything in life, there are exceptions. You can override the cloaking, for example, by selecting a cloaked file or folder and then using the Get or Put buttons as described on page 812. Dreamweaver assumes that, since you specifically selected that file or folder, you want to override the cloaking feature.

Dreamweaver also ignores cloaking if you answer Yes in the Dependent Files message box when you Put or Get files. In that case, Dreamweaver transfers all dependent files, even if you cloaked them (this applies when you try to Put or Get library and template files as well).

■ Check In and Check Out

If you're the sole developer for a website, the Files panel's Put and Get buttons are fine for transferring files. But if you're on a team of developers, those simple tools can get you in trouble.

Suppose your boss emails you an important announcement that she wants posted on your site's home page immediately. You download the home page from the web server and start to edit it. At the same time, your coworker Bob notices a typo on the page. He downloads it, too.

You're a much faster worker than Bob, so you add the critical news to the home page and move it back to the server. But then Bob transfers *his* corrected home page, *overwriting* your edits and eliminating that urgent notice you just added. (An hour later, your phone rings. It's the boss.)

Without some kind of way to monitor who has what file and to prevent people from overwriting each other's work, collaborative web development is a chaotic mess. Fortunately, Dreamweaver's Check In and Check Out system provides a civilized answer to the problem, specifically designed for group web development. It works like your local public library: When you check out a file, no one else can have it. When you finish with the file, you check it back in, releasing control of it and allowing someone else on the team to check it out and work on it.

To use the Check In/Check Out feature, you first need to turn on "Enable file checkout" in the Advanced section of the Site Setup window when you set up your remote server (as described on page 811 and pictured in Figure 20-5). In addition, you must keep a few things in mind:

- **When you develop a website solo,** your local site usually contains the most recent versions of your files. You make any modifications or additions to the pages on your computer and *then* transfer the edited pages to your server.

  In a collaborative environment, where many people work on the site at once, the files on your hard drive may not be the latest ones. After all, your coworkers, like you, have been updating pages and transferring them to the server. The home page sitting in your local site folder may be several days older than the file on the remote site, which is why checking out a file from the *remote server*, rather than editing the copy on your computer, is so important. It guarantees that you'll be working on the latest version of the file. (Dreamweaver can automatically check out a file whenever you open it from the list of local files. See page 822 for details.)

- **In a collaborative environment,** nobody should post files to the server using any method except Dreamweaver's Check In/Check Out system.

  The reason is technical but worth slogging through: When Dreamweaver checks out a file, it doesn't actually *lock* the file. Instead, it places a small, invisible text file (with the three-letter suffix .lck) on both the remote server and in your local site folder. This file indicates who has checked out the website file. When

Dreamweaver connects to the remote server, it uses these text files to determine which web files are in use by others.

And that's why your site-development team needs to use Dreamweaver exclusively to transfer files: Only Dreamweaver understands the .lck files. Other FTP programs, like WS_FTP (Windows) and Fetch (Mac), gladly ignore those who-has-dibs files and can easily overwrite checked-out files. This risk also applies when you simply copy files back and forth over the office network.

NOTE Adobe's word processor-like web page editing program Contribute also takes advantage of the Check In/Check Out feature, so you can use the two programs on the same site.

* **All Dreamweaver-using team members** must configure their remote site to use Check In and Check Out. If even one person doesn't do it, you risk overwritten files.

NOTE WebDAV people are free from the constraints of Dreamweaver's Check In/Check Out system. As long as everyone working on the site uses programs that support the WebDAV protocol, they can work seamlessly with people using Dreamweaver, and vice versa.

Checking Out Files

When you work collaboratively and want to work on a file, you check it out from the web server. Doing so makes sure that *you* have the latest version of the file and that nobody else can make changes to it.

NOTE Dreamweaver's Check In/Check Out feature works only if everyone on the team uses it. Everyone needs to use Dreamweaver and everyone needs to turn on the Check In/Check Out feature, as described on page 811. If even a single person doesn't use Dreamweaver and this system, you'll probably run into problems.

If you're used to creating sites by yourself, this Check In/Check Out business may feel a little strange; after all, when it's only you working on a site, the local site (the files on your computer) contains the latest version of all your files. But when you work with a group, you need to consider the *remote server*—the drive that everyone can access, edit, and add new pages to—the master repository of your site's files.

NOTE There's nothing to check out when you create a new page. Since the only version of that file in the universe lies on your computer, have no fear that someone else may work on it at the same time as you. In this case, you only need to check the file *into* the site when you finish with it.

You check out a file using the Files panel; if it's not open, press F8 (Shift-⌘-F) or choose Window→Files. Then select the site you want to work on from the Site drop-down menu (shown at the top of Figure 20-10).

Site menu

Check out

Check in

FIGURE 20-10

The Check In/Check Out buttons transfer files between your local site and your web server. A padlock identifies files checked into the remote site—the lock means you can't edit the file until you check it out (and therefore simultaneously "unlock" the file). A checkmark appears next to checked-out files, green for those you've checked out, red for those someone else has.

Checked out — Checked in

Now you're ready to begin. From the Local Files list in the Files panel, select the files you want to check out from the server—or, to check out an entire folder and every file inside it, select the folder itself.

> **TIP** If, when you set up your remote server (see page 811), you select the "Check Out File when Opening" option, you can also check out (and open) a file by double-clicking it in the Files panel. This is a quick way to open a page you want to edit while still using Dreamweaver's Check Out feature.

In some instances, you may want to select a file from the "Remote server" list as well. For example, you might need to modify a page you didn't create and which you've never checked out before. In such a case, the file isn't *in* your local site, so you have to get it from the remote server. Select "Remote server" from the Files panel; Dreamweaver connects to and then displays the remote server files. Select the one you want to check out. Then click the Check Out button in the Files panel, or use the keyboard shortcut Shift+Alt+Ctrl+D (Shift-Option-⌘-D). (Not enough fingers? See page 904 to learn how to change Dreamweaver's shortcuts.)

Subversion in Dreamweaver

Dreamweaver includes support for a popular version control system (software that tracks the lifecycle of a document) called *Subversion*. Well, at least it's popular among coders. Subversion is a free program that developers usually use to manage files as part of a large programming project. It has powerful features to make sure that multiple users don't overwrite one anothers' changes, and to make it easy to "roll back" to previous versions of a file if something goes wrong.

To take advantage of Dreamweaver's Subversion support, you first need to set up a *Subversion server*—a separate piece of software running on either your own computer, on a server on your network, or even on a server somewhere on the Internet. Download the software at *http://subversion.apache.org/packages.html*. You can also find companies that offer free or cheap Subversion hosting (in other words, they take care of the mess of setting up a Subversion server for you). Next, you need to create what's called a Subversion *repository*—an online storage locker for a set of files that belong to a particular project. For example, you would probably set up each web project as its own repository. You can learn more about how to set up Subversion at *http://svnbook.red-bean.com*.

For Dreamweaver users, it's important to keep in mind that a Subversion repository is independent of the website running on your web server. In other words, you'll have a Subversion repository, local files on your computer, and another set of files out on the Web (that is, on your remote server).

You can set up Subversion in Dreamweaver by choosing Site→Manage Sites and then choosing a site to edit. In the Site Setup window, select the Version Control category and choose Subversion from the Access menu. Then fill out the other settings, such as the server address, repository path, your user name, and password.

Once you do, Dreamweaver connects to the repository when you choose Repository View from the File View menu (see Figure 20-6). In addition, when you use the Check In and Check Out buttons on the Files panel, you'll check files in and out from the Subversion repository. Dreamweaver CC includes the ability to copy, move, delete, and revert (go back to a previous version of) files in the repository.

Unfortunately, if you want to perform site-wide changes, like updating templates or changing a footer, you need to check out the *entire* website from the repository.

If you develop websites on your own, Subversion is definitely overkill. Even if you toil in a small workgroup, unless you have someone with the system administrator know-how to set up a Subversion server and repository, you're probably better off with something simpler, like Dreamweaver's Check In/Check Out system or even WebDAV. Probably the most important feature of Subversion is its ability to go back to a previous version of a file that has somehow been wrecked.

If you're not going to use Subversion, it's definitely worth investing in some basic backup software like Retrospect Remote or Apple's Time Machine. Even most simple backup software lets you keep hourly, daily, weekly, or monthly file backups, and lets you go back in time to retrieve older versions of files. Alternatively, take the low-tech approach: back up your site every day and store the copied files in a folder named something like *June_10_2014*. That way you'll have a daily backup you can turn to if you need to recover a lost file.

However, if your company or organization does use Subversion, you can get in-depth information on using it with Dreamweaver at *http://tinyurl.com/3kxo5wu*.

Dreamweaver asks if you want to check out dependent files, too. Click Yes if you think the page you're checking out uses files you haven't downloaded. Dreamweaver then copies the dependent files to your computer, so the page you check out displays its current images, CSS style sheets, and any other linked files. It doesn't *check out* a dependent file, however, so if you do want to *edit* the dependent file—if, for example, you need to edit the styles in a linked external style sheet—you must also check out that dependent file, by selecting it from the Files list and clicking Check Out.

> **NOTE** When you edit a web page you check out, you may run into a weird problem if the page uses an external style sheet and you didn't check out the style sheet: You won't be able to edit any styles on the page. Instead, you'll get a message saying that the styles file is locked, and Dreamweaver will ask if you want to check it out. Click the Check Out button, and Dreamweaver tries to obey. If it informs you that someone else has checked out the file, click Cancel and wait until the other person checks the style sheet back in. Then check it out and make your changes. Bottom line: Check out your site's external style sheets if you want to edit the CSS in your pages.

When you check out files, Dreamweaver copies them to your computer and marks them as checked out so others can't change them. Like uploading and downloading files, checking out files can take time, depending on the speed of your Internet connection.

After you check out a file, Dreamweaver displays a green "checked-out" checkmark in the Files panel next to its name (see Figure 20-10). You can now open and edit the file, and, when you're done, check the file back in.

If you attempt to check out a file that someone has already checked out, Dreamweaver tells you as much. It also gives you the option to override the person's check-out—but unless you're the boss, resist the temptation, for two reasons. First, your colleague may have made some important changes to the page, which you'll wipe out with your shenanigans. Second, because you so rudely stole the file, he may stop bringing you donuts in the morning.

A better way to work with someone who's checked out a file that you need is to use Dreamweaver's email feature. You can see who checked out the file by consulting Dreamweaver's Checked Out By column (see Figure 20-10, circled). Even better, if you click the name, Dreamweaver opens your email program and addresses a message to that person, so you can say, "Hey Bob, you've had the home page checked out for two days! I need to work on it, so check it back in!"

The name and email address Dreamweaver uses depends on the information your coworkers provide when they configured their computers for remote site use (you provided the same information when you configured your computer). See the Advanced options on page 810 for more.

Checking In Files

When you're ready to move a page you've been editing back to the server, check it in. (You also check in *new* files you create.)

To check in files, open the Files panel (press F8 [Shift-⌘-F]), choose the relevant site from the Site drop-down menu, and then, using the Local Folder file list in the Files panel, select the files you want to check into your server. As always, you can click a folder to check it in, too, along with every file inside it.

The files you check in should be files you checked out, or brand-new files that have never been on the server. If you attempt to check in a file that someone else has checked out, Dreamweaver warns you with a message box. Click Cancel to stop the check-in so you don't overwrite the checked-out file. Dreamweaver also warns you if you try to check in a file that's older than the copy on the server. Again, unless you're sure this is what you want to do, click Cancel.

POWER USERS' CLINIC

Overriding Checked-Out Files

Occasionally, you may want to erase the checked-out status of a file. Suppose, for example, someone who's checked out a lot of files suddenly catches the plague and can't continue working on the site. To free those files so others can work on them, you have to undo his check-out (and quarantine his cubicle).

To do the former, make sure you have the Files panel in Remote Server view (this trick won't work with the local files displayed). Then right-click (Control-click) the checked-out file and select Undo Checkout from the menu that appears.

Dreamweaver warns you that whoever checked out the file won't be able to check it back in. (This is, in fact, false. That person can still check in the file, overwriting whatever is on the web server. So you can see why you should override the checked-out file only when the person who checked it out is very unlikely to check it back in—if she's stranded on a desert island, for example.)

When the operation is complete, a padlock icon appears next to the filename.

You can use this technique on a file *you've* checked out, too, if, for example, after you check out a file, you make a horrible mistake on the page and want to revert to the copy on the server.

NOTE If you want to check in the page you're currently working on, use the toolbar in the document window (see page 815).

You can check in the selected files in any of the usual ways:

- Click the Check In button on the Files panel (see Figure 20-6).

- Use the keyboard shortcut Shift+Alt+Ctrl+U (Shift-Option-⌘-U). (See page 904 to learn how to change any Dreamweaver shortcut to something less cumbersome.)

Dreamweaver asks if you want to check in any dependent files at the same time. You should transfer dependent files only if you first checked them out, or if the dependent files are new and have never been uploaded to the server. If you attempt to check in a dependent file that someone else has checked out, Dreamweaver warns you with a message box—click the No button in this box so you don't overwrite someone's checked-out file.

After you click through all the message boxes, Dreamweaver copies the files to your remote server. Once you check in a file, Dreamweaver locks your local copy—you'll see a padlock icon next to its name in the Local Files list of the Files panel—that's so you don't accidentally change the local version of the file. If you wish to modify the file in some way, check it out from the server.

NOTE Dreamweaver's Site Report feature (page 794) lets you see which files are checked out and by whom. Skip it. On a large site, the report can take a long time to run, it isn't always accurate, and you can't do the things you're most likely to do with checked-out files (like checking them back in).

FREQUENTLY ASKED QUESTION

Get and Put, In and Out

I'm using Dreamweaver's Check In and Check Out buttons to transfer my files. What do the Get and Put buttons do if I use the Check In/Check Out feature?

If you use Check In and Check Out, the Get and Put commands function slightly differently than described on page 812. *Get*, in this case, copies the selected file or files to your local site. However, Dreamweaver adds a small lock icon next to each of the "gotten" files in your "Local files" list. The files are locked, and you shouldn't edit them. Remember, checking out a file is the only way to prevent others from working on it simultaneously. If you edit a locked file on your computer, nothing stops someone else from checking out the page, editing it, and checking it back in.

But you may still find the Get command useful in such a situation. For example, suppose someone just updated the site's external style sheet. The pages you're editing use this style sheet, so you want to get the latest version. You don't want to edit the style sheet itself, so you don't need to check it out. If you use Get instead of checking out the pages, you can keep a reference copy on your computer without locking anyone else out of the file and without having to check it back in.

Put, on the other hand, simply—and blindly—transfers the file on your local site to the remote site. If you use the Check In/Check Out feature and you haven't also checked out the file, using Put is a bad idea. The remote site should be your reference copy; several rounds of revisions may have been made to a file since you last checked it out. Your local copy will be hopelessly out of date, and moving it to the server destroys the most recent version of the file.

However, if you *do* have the file checked out, you can use Put to transfer your local copy to the server so your site's visitors see it. For example, say you're updating the home page with 20 new news items. To keep your site up-to-the-minute fresh, you can Put the home page on your server as you add each news item. Then the whole world will see each item as soon as possible. When you completely finish editing the home page, check it in. At that point, other members on your team are free to check it out and make their edits.

◼ Synchronizing Site Files

As you may suspect, when you keep two sets of files—on your local site and remote server—it's easy to lose track of which files are the most recent. For example, say you finish working on your website and move all the files to the server. The next day, you notice mistakes on a bunch of pages, so you make corrections on the copies in your local site. But in your rush to fix the pages, you didn't keep track of which ones you corrected. So, although you're ready to move the corrected pages to the server, you're not sure *which* ones you need to transfer.

When you use the Check In/Check Out feature, you avoid this problem altogether. Using this system, the version on the server is *always* considered the latest and most definitive copy—*unless* you or someone else has checked out that file. In that case, whoever checked out the file has the most recent version.

But if you're operating solo and don't use the Check In/Check Out feature, you may get good mileage from Dreamweaver's Synchronize command, which lets you compare the remote and local sites and transfer only the newer files in either direction. (In fact, since the Synchronize command uses Get and Put to transfer files, you may not get the results you expect if you synchronize your site while also using Check In and Check Out, as described in the box on page 827.)

To synchronize your sites:

1. **Make sure you turn on the "Maintain synchronization information" checkbox when you set the server options (see the Advanced options mentioned on page 810).**

   Dreamweaver automatically turns this option on when you set up a server.

2. **Choose Site→Synchronize Sitewide.**

   Alternatively, you can right-click anywhere inside the Files panel. From the shortcut menu that appears, select Synchronize. In either case, the Synchronize with Remote Server dialog box appears (see Figure 20-11).

FIGURE 20-11

Using the Synchronization command, you can copy newer files from your computer to your web server or get newer files from your remote site.

3. **Using the Synchronize drop-down menu, specify the files you want to update.**

   You can either synchronize all the files in the current site or only the files you select from the "Local site" list. This last option is useful when you have a really big site and want to limit the sync operation to just a single section of the site—one folder, for example.

4. **Using the Direction drop-down menu, choose the destination for newer files.**

   You have three choices. "Put newer files to remote" updates the web server with any newer files in your local site folder. It also copies any *newly created* files in your local site to the remote server. Use this option when you've heavily edited your local site and you want to move all the new or modified pages to your server.

   "Get newer files from remote" does the reverse: It updates your local site folder with any newer (or new) files from the remote site. Here's one instance where the Synchronize feature comes in handy in team-design situations. If you've been out of the office for a while, click this option to download copies of the latest site files. (Note that this doesn't check out any files; it merely makes sure you have copies of the latest files on your computer. This is one example where synchronization works well with Check In/Check Out, since it refreshes your local copy of the site with the latest files, including graphics and external style sheets, that any pages you do check out may depend on.)

"Get and put newer files" is a two-way synchronization. Dreamweaver transfers any new files on the local site to the remote site and vice versa. For example, if you update a page on your computer, Dreamweaver moves that file to the web server. If someone has made changes to a file on the server and the file is more recent than the copy on your computer, Dreamweaver downloads that file to your hard drive. The result is that both "sides" contain the latest files.

5. **Turn on the Delete checkbox, if desired.**

The way Dreamweaver words this option reflects the option you selected in the previous step. If you move newer files to the remote site, it says, "Delete remote files not on local drive." It's a useful option when, for example, you spend the afternoon cleaning up the local copy of your site, deleting old, orphaned graphics files and web pages, and you want Dreamweaver to update the web server to match.

If you chose to transfer newer files *from* the remote site, Dreamweaver lets you "Delete local files not on remote server." Use this feature when your local site is hopelessly out of date with the remote site. Perhaps you work on the site with a team, but you've been on vacation for two months (this is, of course, a hypothetical example). The site may have changed so significantly that you want to get your local copy in line with the website.

NOTE Of course, you should proceed with caution when using *any* command that automatically deletes files. There's no Undo for these delete operations, and you don't want to accidentally delete the only copy of a particular page, graphic, or Cascading Style Sheet.

If you chose the "Get and put newer files" option in step 4, Dreamweaver dims and makes unavailable the Delete checkbox. This option truly synchronizes the two; Dreamweaver copies newer files on the remote site (including files that exist on the server but not on your computer) to your local site, and vice versa.

6. **Click Preview to begin synchronizing.**

Dreamweaver connects to the remote site and compares the two sets of files—if your site is large, this takes a long time. When Dreamweaver finishes, it opens the Synchronize preview window (Figure 20-12), listing which files it will delete and which it'll transfer, and providing an additional set of options for working with the listed files.

NOTE Synchronization is a slow process. Dreamweaver needs to connect to the remote server and then compare the remote server files with your local files. On a site with even a dozen or so pages and lots of graphics, synchronizing files can take minutes. This is one reason why, if you only need to synchronize files in one folder, you should first select that folder in the Files panel, and then, in step 3, choose "Selected files only." Also, make sure to take advantage of the cloaking feature described on page 818 so Dreamweaver doesn't waste time synchronizing files that you don't want on your server to begin with.

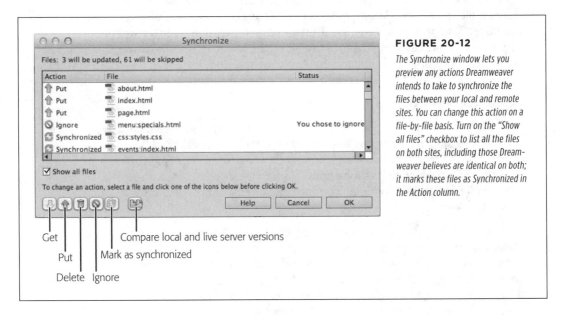

FIGURE 20-12

The Synchronize window lets you preview any actions Dreamweaver intends to take to synchronize the files between your local and remote sites. You can change this action on a file-by-file basis. Turn on the "Show all files" checkbox to list all the files on both sites, including those Dreamweaver believes are identical on both; it marks these files as Synchronized in the Action column.

Get

Put

Delete Ignore

Compare local and live server versions

Mark as synchronized

7. **Change the action Dreamweaver takes on the listed files.**

The preview box tells you what Dreamweaver plans to do with a file—Get it, Put it, or delete it. You can override these actions by selecting a file from the list and clicking one of the action buttons at the bottom of the window. For example, if you realize that Dreamweaver is going to delete a file that you *know* you need, select the file in the list and click the "Ignore file" button (the circle with a line through it).

Most of these options are useful only if you know Dreamweaver made a mistake—for example, when the program says you should Get a file, but you know your local copy is identical to the server's copy. In that case, you could select the file and then click the "Mark as synchronized" button to tell Dreamweaver that they're identical. However, if you knew exactly which files were identical and which ones needed updating, you wouldn't need to use the Synchronize feature in the first place, right?

One option can come in quite handy. The "Compare local and remote versions" button lets you compare the code in the local file to the code in the remote file so you can identify exactly what differs between the two. You can use this feature to, for example, see precisely what changes were made to the remote copy of a file. You'll learn about this feature in detail on page 358.

8. **Click OK to proceed or Cancel to stop the sync.**

   If you click OK, Dreamweaver commences copying and deleting the chosen files. If you want to stop the process, click Cancel in the Background File Activity window.

9. **Click Close.**

TIP If you only want to *identify* newer files on the local site without synchronizing them (to run a report on them, for example), click the contextual menu in the top-right corner of the Files panel and then choose Edit→Select Newer Local. Dreamweaver connects to the remote server and compares the files, and then, in the Files panel's "Local view" list, highlights files on the local site that are newer than their remote counterparts.

You can also identify newer files on the remote server: Choose Edit→"Select Newer on Remote server" from the Files panel's contextual menu.

Finally, you can identify files on your computer you either created or modified within a given date range, using the Select Recently Modified command described in the box on page 783.

■ Communicating with Design Notes

Lots of questions arise when a team works on a website: Has this page been proofread? Who authored this page? Where did that graphic come from? Usually, you must rely on a flurry of emails to ferret out the answers.

But Dreamweaver's Design Notes feature (Figure 20-13) eliminates much of that hassle by letting you attach information, such as a web page's status or author, to a file.

You can open these notes from the Files panel, from a currently open document, or automatically (by selecting the "Show when file is open" option in the Design Notes dialog box; note that Dreamweaver can't, however, automatically open files, like images, that it can't open and edit on its own). You can also edit the notes and share them with others; that makes it easy to leave your collaborators a note saying, for example, "Hey, Bob, can you make sure that this is the most recent photo of Kim and Kanye?" You can even add notes to folders and to files other than web pages, including images and external Cascading Style Sheets—to anything, in fact, that appears in the Files panel.

Setting Up Design Notes

To use Design Notes, open the Site Setup window by double-clicking the site's name in the Manage Sites window (choose Manage Sites from the Site menu or from the drop-down menu in the Files panel). In the Advanced Settings window, click Design Notes. As you can see in Figure 20-14, you can set two options:

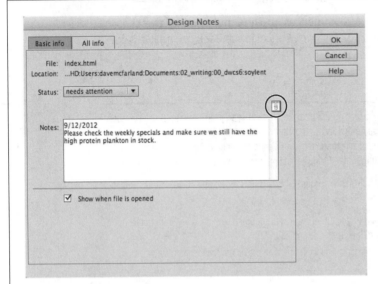

FIGURE 20-13
If you want the Design Notes window to open whenever someone opens a page, turn on the "Show when file is opened" checkbox. That ensures that no one misses important information about a page. (This option has no effect on images [GIFs, JPEGs, PNGs] or anything other than a file that Dreamweaver can open and edit, such as a web page or an external style sheet.)

- **Maintain Design Notes**. Turn on this checkbox to create and read notes using Dreamweaver's File→Design Notes command (see "Viewing Design Notes" on page 834).

- **Enable Upload Design Notes for sharing**. If you use Design Notes as part of a team, turn on this checkbox—it makes Dreamweaver upload your notes to your remote site so your fellow team members can read them.

> **NOTE** Design Notes are especially useful for keeping track of pages built and maintained by a team of web developers. But if you're a solo operator and still want to use them—maybe you're the type with 100 Post-it notes taped to the edges of your monitor—then turn off the "Enable Upload Design Notes for sharing" checkbox. You'll save time and server space by preventing Dreamweaver from transferring the notes to your server.

Click Save to close the Site Setup window. You can double-click another site in the Manage Sites dialog box to turn on its design notes, or click Done.

To add a Design Note to a document you're working on:

- Choose File→Design Notes.

- From the File Status menu in the Document toolbar (see Figure 20-8), choose Design Notes.

- Right-click (Control-click) a file in the Files panel (or an external object, such as a graphic or a movie, in the document window), and choose Design Notes from the shortcut menu.

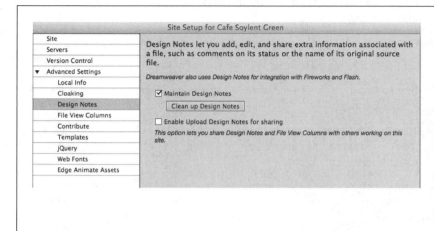

FIGURE 20-14

The "Clean up Design Notes" button deletes orphan notes—those that were attached to now-deleted files. (To avoid stray note files in the first place, always delete pages in Dreamweaver's Files panel, as opposed to Windows Explorer or the Mac's Finder.) If you turn off the Maintain Design Notes checkbox, clicking "Clean up" removes all Design Notes files from the site.

In any case, the Design Notes window opens (Figure 20-13). If you like, you can use its Status drop-down menu to let your team members know where the file stands. For example, is it ready to move to the server? Is it just a draft version? Or is there something wrong with it that requires attention? Dreamweaver provides eight options: "draft," "revision1," "revision2," "revision3," "alpha," "beta," "final," and "needs attention."

The note itself, which you type into the Note box, could be a simple question for the page's author ("Are you sure 'Kings of Leon: Defining a New Musical Language for the Modern Age' is an appropriate title for this article?") or it could offer more information about the status of the page ("Still need studio shot for high-energy plankton milkshake").

TIP Click the calendar icon (circled in Figure 20-13) to pop the current date into your note—a great way to track the dates notes were written.

When you click OK, Dreamweaver creates a file with all the note information in it. For the filename, Dreamweaver begins with the original filename and adds .mno to the end. So, for the file *index.html*, Dreamweaver uses *index.html.mno*.

Dreamweaver stores notes in a folder called *_notes* that it keeps in the same folder as the relevant page or file. For example, if you add notes to the home page, Dreamweaver stores the *_notes* folder inside the root folder.

Viewing Design Notes

You can view Design Notes in a number of ways. If the note's author turned on "Show when file is opened," of course, the Design Notes window opens automatically when you open that page.

Otherwise, to look at a note, you have any number of options:

- Choose File→Design Notes.

- Choose Design Notes from the File Status drop-down menu in the document window's toolbar.

- Double-click the small yellow balloon in the Notes column of the Files panel. (You'll see this column only if you turned on this option in the Site Definition window, as described below.)

- Right-click (Control-click) an embedded object, like a graphic or a Flash movie, in the document window, and then choose Design Notes from the shortcut menu.

- Right-click (Control-click) a file in the Files panel and choose Design Notes from the shortcut menu.

Organizing the Columns in the Files Panel

Columns in the Files panel identify a file's name, size, modification date, type, and so on.

This may be more information than you're interested in—or it may not be enough. So remember that Dreamweaver lets you show or hide columns, change their order, and even create new ones. You set your preferences when you set up a website, from the File View Columns category in the Site Definition window (Figure 20-15).

> **NOTE** You can adjust the relative width of these columns by dragging the dividing line between the column names. You can also sort all the pages listed in this window by clicking the relevant column's name. Click Modified, for example, to sort the files so the newest ones appear first. Click a second time to reverse the sort, placing oldest files first.

Once you see the screen shown in Figure 20-15, you can perform any of these stunts:

- **Reorder columns**. Click a column name in the Site Definition window to select it. Then click the up and down arrow buttons to move the column one spot to the left or right, respectively, in the Files panel.

- **Deleting columns**. You can delete only the custom columns you create. Dreamweaver doesn't let you delete the built-in columns Name, Notes, Type, Modified, and so on. To delete a custom column, click the column name, and then click –.

- **Adding Columns**. You can add columns of your own, as described next.

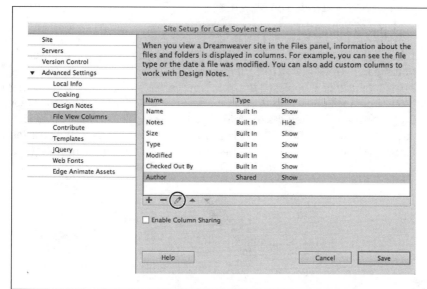

FIGURE 20-15

Dreamweaver's Files panel can display information from a handful of set columns: Name, Notes, Size, Type, Modified, and Checked Out By. You can't delete these columns, but you can hide them after you click the Edit button (circled), as described below. You can also create custom columns to display information that matches your work requirements (for example, a column listing the author of each web article).

To hide a column (or show a hidden column), select the column in the File View Options category of the Site Setup window, and then click the Edit button. In the window that opens, hide the column by turning off the Show checkbox, and display a hidden column by turning on the checkbox. You can also change how Dreamweaver aligns the text in the column (left, right, or center) using the Align menu. It's a good idea to hide columns you don't need, since they take up space in the Files panel, often hiding parts of filenames.

Creating Custom Columns

Your Files panel offers columns for all the usual information: Name, Checked Out, and so on. But you may someday wish there were a column that showed each page's status, so that your Files panel could show you which files need proofreading, who wrote each article, or which pages are being held until a certain blackout date.

You can add columns of your own design, although the process isn't streamlined by any means. It involves two broad efforts: First, using an offshoot of the Design Notes feature described earlier, you set up the new columns you want to display. Then, using the column-manipulation window shown in Figure 20-15, you make the new columns visible in the Files panel.

■ PHASE 1: DEFINING NEW COLUMNS

You create new kinds of informational flags—primarily for use in creating new columns in the Files panel—using the Design Notes dialog box. Here's the rundown:

1. **Choose File→Design Notes.**

   Dreamweaver opens the Design Notes window. (You can summon it in various other ways, as described on page 832.)

2. **Click the "All info" tab.**

   This peculiar window shows the program-ery underbelly of the Dreamweaver Notes feature (see Figure 20-16). It turns out that it stores every kind of note as a name/value pair. If you used the main Notes screen (Figure 20-13) to choose "beta" from the Status drop-down menu, for example, you'll see a notation that says "status=beta." *Status* is the info nugget's description; *beta* is its value. If you turned on the "Show when file is opened" option (page 831), you'll see "showOnOpen=true." And if you typed *Badly needs updating* as the note itself, you'll see "notes=Badly needs updating" on this screen.

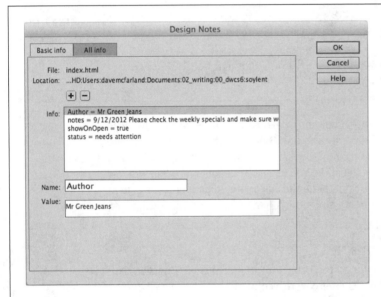

FIGURE 20-16

Dreamweaver lets you create your own types of notes in the "All info" tab of the Design Notes window. This lets you add more information to a page, such as its author or designer. Deleting a note you added is a simple matter of clicking the note in the Info box and then clicking –.

   But those are just the built-in info types; you're free to create your own.

3. **Click +.**

   You may wonder why you'd add a custom column; after all, you can type a lot of information in the Notes box itself, under the Basic Info tab. The primary benefit is that you can display the information in this new column in the Files panel.

4. **Label the new note in the Name box.**

   You may choose *Author* as a label, for example, so you can record who wrote the text of each page. Or it could be *Artist*, if you wish to add a note to each image specifying who created it. Maybe you need a column called *Hold Until* to remind you when it's OK to publish certain classified information.

5. **Press Tab to jump to the Value box, and then type the contents of the note.**

You can enter the actual name of the author or artist—Jennifer Jones, for example—or the actual "Hold Until" date.

Repeat steps 3–5 to add more notes.

NOTE Keep the value short—one or two words. Otherwise, the narrow Files panel column chops off the latter part of it. If you've got enough screen real estate, you can resize the columns by dragging the divider bars between column names.

---

6. **Click OK.**

Dreamweaver closes the dialog box.

■ PHASE 2: ADDING THE COLUMN TO THE FILES PANEL

Just creating a new note type gets you halfway home; now you have to tell Dreamweaver to display that information in the Files panel.

To add a column to the Files panel:

1. **Open the Site Setup window for the site and then select the File View Columns category under the Advanced Settings options.**

To edit a site, choose Site→Manage Sites, and then double-click the name of the site from the Manage Sites window. Expand the Advanced Settings category on the left side of the window, and the File View Columns options appear.

2. **Click +.**

Dreamweaver displays a pane where you specify details about the new column (Figure 20-17).

3. **In the Column Name box, type the column heading you want to appear in the Files panel.**

Make it short and descriptive. If possible, it should match the note type (*Author*, *Artist*, *Hold Until*, or whatever).

4. **Press Tab. Type the name of the Design Note you wish to use for this column.**

This is the "name" part of the name/value pair described in step 4 of the previous instructions. For example, if you add a note named Author to a file, you would type *Author* here. Capitalization matters, so if you named the Design Note *Author*, type it with a capital A.

There's a drop-down menu here, too, but it always lists the same four options: Status, Assigned, Due, and Priority. If you choose Status, you'll get a column that reflects your choice from the Status drop-down menu in the Design Notes window (see step 2 on page 836). The other three options do nothing *unless* you create a matching note type in step 4 of the previous instructions. (It would be nice if this drop-down menu listed *all* the notes you created, so you didn't have to remember their names.)

FIGURE 20-17

Creating your own columns is definitely for the hyper-organized. To keep special information about your pages always visible in the Files panel (such as an author name or a "hold until" date), this feature may be worth the trouble of setting up special Design Notes and columns.

Before you wrap up the column-adding procedure, you can, if you wish, choose an alignment option for the text in the column (left, right, or center). Check to make sure that the Show checkbox is turned on; otherwise, your new column won't appear, and you've just defeated the purpose of this whole exercise.

Finally, turn on the "Share with all users of this site" checkbox if you like. The Share feature works like this: The next time you connect to your remote server, Dreamweaver uploads a file containing your newly defined column and its information. The next time another member of the team connects to the remote site, *his* copy of Dreamweaver downloads this file, so that his Files panel shows the same columns yours does.

NOTE The column-sharing feature can be very handy; it lets everyone working on a site share the same information. But it works properly only if everyone on the team has the "Enable column sharing" checkbox turned on (see Figure 20-15).

5. **Click Save.**

   You should now see the new column in your Files panel. (You may need to widen the panel to see all the columns. You can also click the Expand Files Panel button [Figure 20-6] to expand the Panel.)

Dreamweaver Power

Creating Reusable Page Elements

O K, so you finished designing your company's new website. It looks great and your boss is ecstatic. But you've really only just begun— before you can launch the site, you have to build hundreds of pages. And once the site's online, you need to keep updating it so it stays fresh and inviting.

That's where Dreamweaver's snippets and library features come in, streamlining the sometimes tedious work of building and updating site pages.

As you create more and more web pages (and more and more websites), you may find yourself crafting the same page elements over and over again. Many pages may share elements that always stay the same: a copyright notice, a navigation bar, or a logo, for example. And you may find yourself frequently using complex components, such as a pull-down menu that lists all the countries where you ship products or a unique design for your site's photos and captions.

Recreating the same components time after time is tiresome and—thanks to Dreamweaver—unnecessary. The program provides two subtly different tools that let you reuse common page elements: *snippets* and *Library items*.

■ Snippets Basics

Snippets aren't fancy or complex, but they sure save time. A snippet is simply a chunk of code you store away and then plunk into your web pages as necessary. Snippets can be as simple as boilerplate legal text, or as complex as HTML instructions, CSS formatting rules, or JavaScript program code. For example, say you always use the same type of table to list product specifications in your company's online catalog.

Each time you create a similar table, you could go through all the same steps to build it—or you could turn that table into a snippet, and then, with a simple double-click, add it to page after page of your site. Or say you use the popular jQuery JavaScript library on each of your sites. When you do, you have to include the code that links your pages to the JavaScript file. Rather than type that code each time, you can just drop pre-typed instructions into the page.

You find these code chunks in Dreamweaver's Snippets panel (see Figure 21-1), and summon them in a couple of ways:

- Choose Window→Snippets.

- Windows people can press Shift-F9. (There's no Mac keyboard shortcut for the Snippets panel, but you can create one by going to Dreamweaver→Keyboard Shortcuts; see page 904 for details.)

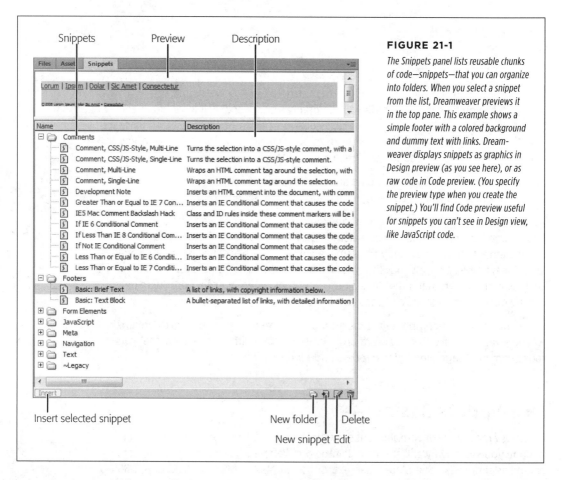

FIGURE 21-1

The Snippets panel lists reusable chunks of code—snippets—that you can organize into folders. When you select a snippet from the list, Dreamweaver previews it in the top pane. This example shows a simple footer with a colored background and dummy text with links. Dreamweaver displays snippets as graphics in Design preview (as you see here), or as raw code in Code preview. (You specify the preview type when you create the snippet.) You'll find Code preview useful for snippets you can't see in Design view, like JavaScript code.

When you first open the Snippets panel, you see a set of stock Dreamweaver snippets. But you can quickly add to that collection by building your own.

■ Using Snippets

Snippets come in two varieties: those that are simple blocks of code, and those that wrap around a selected element in a document. For example, the Snippets panel's Text folder includes a snippet called Service Mark. Add it to a page and it instantly inserts the code *^{sm}*, creating a superscript service mark (sm) symbol.

But occasionally, you'll want to wrap code around something you've already typed. You may, for example, want to add an HTML comment to your page (a message that won't appear in web browsers, but that helps you or other web designers decipher the page). The "Comment, multi-line" snippet (in the Comments folder of the Snippets panel) helps you quickly do so. It wraps whatever you select with opening and closing HTML comment markers (<!-- and -->, respectively). Adding an HTML comment is as easy as typing the comment in your page, selecting it, and then double-clicking this snippet. This may sound a lot like the Coding toolbar's Apply Comment button (described in Figure 7-7), but this snippet works in Design view, too, not just Code view.

NOTE Unfortunately, unless the snippet's description (in the Snippets panel's Description column) specifies that the snippet wraps, you can't tell whether it will or not. You either have to try out the snippet or open it in Editing mode to see. (And while you have the snippet open, you can add to its description, indicating whether it wraps or not.)

To add a snippet to a web page, click where you want the item to go, or select the object you want to wrap with a snippet. Then do one of the following:

- In the Snippets panel, double-click the snippet name.
- In the Snippets panel, select the snippet, and then click Insert.
- Drag the snippet from the panel into the document window. (If the snippet is supposed to wrap around a selection, drag the snippet *onto* the selected object.)

You can work with snippets in either Design or Code view, but some snippets make sense only in Code view. For example, you typically have to insert JavaScript snippets in the <head> section of a page, inside <script> tags. To use these snippets, you have to switch to Code view, insert the <script> tags, and then put the snippets inside.

TIP To quickly insert a snippet you recently used, select the snippet's name from Insert→Recent Snippets. Better yet, create a keyboard shortcut for your favorite snippets, and then insert them with a keystroke. Go to Edit→Keyboard Shortcuts (Dreamweaver→Keyboard Shortcuts), and then follow the instructions on page 904.

Inserting snippets simply dumps their contents into a document—essentially copying the snippet code and pasting it into your web page. Dreamweaver doesn't step in to make sure that you're adding the code correctly. Unless you're careful—and have some knowledge of HTML—you may end up adding snippets that make your page impossible to view. (To avoid such pitfalls, see the box on page 848.)

■ Creating Snippets

Dreamweaver comes with a lot of snippets, some of which may be relevant to your work. On the other hand, there may be no pre-rolled snippets that match your needs. No problem—you can easily create your own. Here's how:

1. **Select the content you want to turn into a snippet.**

   You can select either an object, like a company logo, or a block of code, like a set of JavaScript instructions. You could, for instance, select a table in Design view, or the opening and closing <table> tags (as well as all the code in between) in Code view.

   To make a snippet out of code that Dreamweaver doesn't display in Design view, like a JavaScript program or content that appears in the <head> section of a page, you need to switch to Code view.

2. **In the Snippets panel, click the New Snippet button, + .**

   The Snippet window opens (Figure 21-2).

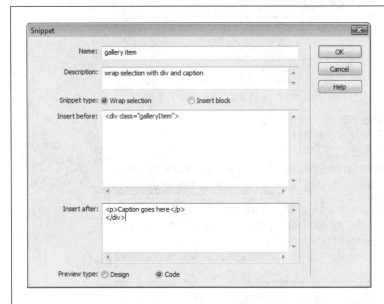

FIGURE 21-2

You create snippets in Dreamweaver's Snippet window. For snippets that you want to wrap a currently selected object—for example, a snippet that adds a link to selected text or to a graphic—you put the code in the two Insert boxes shown here. The code that comes before the selected text or object goes in the top box, and the code that goes after the selection appears in the bottom box. In this example, the snippet wraps the current selection in a <div> tag that has a predefined class applied to it.

> **NOTE** If you skip step 1 and just click the New Snippet button, you can either type the snippet code by hand or, in the Insert box, paste a previously copied selection (see step 6).

3. **Title the snippet.**

   The label you type in the Name box appears in the Snippets panel. Make sure it clearly identifies what the snippet does.

4. **In the Description field, provide details about the snippet.**

   This step is optional but useful. Use this box to describe when and how to use the snippet, and whether or not it wraps a selection.

5. **Select a snippet type.**

   The "Insert block" option simply plops down a chunk of HTML in the code of a web page. The "Wrap selection" option adds two chunks of HTML code that appear before and after a selected page element. For example, you could wrap snippet code around an image you selected.

6. **If necessary, add the code for the snippet.**

   If you're turning a block of code into a snippet, that code appears in the "Insert code" box.

   If you're creating a snippet that wraps around an element on the page, you need to add code in the "Insert before" and "Insert after" boxes. For example, say you create a lot of photo galleries, and you want to wrap each photo in its own <div> tag with some room for a caption. You can create a snippet that wraps the image with the appropriate HTML. For example, the code that goes before the image might include an opening <div> tag with a class applied to it, and the code that goes after the image might include the HTML for the caption and the closing </div> tag. In this case, you might type *<div class="galleryItem">* in the "Insert before" box, and the HTML that goes after the image in the "Insert after" box, maybe something like *<p>Caption goes here</p></div>*.

7. **Select a preview type.**

   The preview type determines how the snippet appears in the Snippets panel's Preview pane. *Design* means the snippet looks as it would in Design view—a table snippet appears as a table, for instance. *Code* means the code itself appears in the Preview pane, so a snippet for a horizontal rule would preview like this: <hr>. Use Code preview for snippets you can't see in Design view, like JavaScript instructions.

8. **Click OK.**

   Dreamweaver adds the snippet to the Snippets panel. You drop it into your web pages using any of the techniques described on page 843.

If you need to edit a snippet—change the code, snippet type, description, or name—select the snippet in the Snippets panel and then click the Edit Snippet button, ✏. You can also right-click (Control-click) the snippet name, and then, from the shortcut menu, select Edit.

Whichever method you choose, the Snippet window opens. Make your changes, and then click OK.

Organizing Snippets

To keep your snippets organized, create folders and store them by category. To add a folder to the Snippets panel, click + (see Figure 21-1). Dreamweaver creates an untitled folder; type in a name for it. If you select a folder and then click ▣, Dreamweaver creates the new folder *inside* the selected folder. You can move folders around by dragging them into and out of other folders. However, Dreamweaver always lists folders in alphabetical order, so you can't reorder them by dragging them in the Snippets panel.

TIP To drag a folder or snippet outside a folder to the top level of the Snippets list, you have to drag it all the way to the *bottom* of the Snippets panel, below any other folders. If you try to drag it to the top, Dreamweaver puts the folder or snippet inside the list's topmost folder.

To move a snippet into or out of a folder, simply drag it. If you drag a snippet over a closed folder without releasing the mouse, that folder expands to reveal the folders and snippets inside, if any.

To delete a snippet, select it in the Snippets panel and then click T or press Delete.

NOTE Storing lots of snippets slows down the Snippets panel's response time. You'll probably never use many of the stock snippets Dreamweaver includes, so it's best to remove the ones you don't want. An excellent candidate is the Legacy folder listed at the bottom of the panel. This folder, which really should be called the Old Garbage folder, is full of out-of-date, you-really-shouldn't-use-them snippets that Adobe added to much earlier versions of Dreamweaver. If you don't want to permanently delete these snippets, you can move them out of the Snippets folder found in the main Adobe Dreamweaver CC Configuration folder and store them in a separate folder on your hard drive. (For more on the Configuration folder and how to find it, see the box on page 907.)

■ Using Built-In Snippets

Most of Dreamweaver's stock snippets offer solutions to problems you may never encounter, like a page footer with two lists of links and a copyright notice in it. In addition, many Dreamweaver snippets use older design techniques (like tables to lay out content) that are best avoided. However, most web developers find at least a few of Dreamweaver's factory snippets worthwhile. Here are some highlights:

- **Close Window Button**. This snippet adds a Close button to pop-up windows (page 641) so people can dismiss the window. The Close Window Button snippet (in the Form Elements folder) creates a button with the words "Close Window" on it, complete with the JavaScript necessary to close the window when your visitor clicks the button.

- **Dropdown Menus**. If you create a lot of forms for your sites (see Chapter 16), you'll find some other useful snippets in the Form Elements folder, especially in the Dropdown Menus subfolder. For example, the "Numbers 1-12" snippet inserts a menu with the numbers 1 to 12 already coded into it—great for capturing credit card expiration dates on an e-commerce site. (To create an even more useful drop-down snippet, see the tutorial at the end of this chapter.)

- **HTML Comments**. You can use the Comment Multi-Line snippet (in the Comments folder) to "comment-out," or hide, HTML. Even better, this snippet works in Design view, so if you want to temporarily remove an element from a page-in-progress to see the result, just select the element you want to hide and apply this comment. To make the HTML visible again, switch to Code view, because the Coding toolbar has a handy tool for quickly un-commenting HTML (see Figure 7-6).

- **IE Conditional Comments**. Some older versions of Internet Explorer just don't get things right. This is frequently the case with CSS. To overcome browser differences, you sometimes need to provide IE with CSS code (or HTML or JavaScript code) that differs from the code you send to other browsers. You can insert special code (in the form of so-called conditional comments) that only IE understands. Dreamweaver provides a handful of code snippets (the last five listed in the Snippets panel's Comments folder) that create the necessary code for adding IE-oriented conditional comments. (For a good tutorial with lots of examples on how and why to use IE conditional comments, visit *http://bit.ly/H9m6UT.*)

◼ Library Basics

Imagine this: You manage a relatively large website consisting of thousands of pages. At the bottom of each one sits a simple copyright notice: "Copyright MyBigCompany. We reserve all rights—national, international, commercial, noncommercial, and mineral—to the content on these pages."

Each time you add another page to your site, you *could* retype the copyright message, but that invites both typographic errors and carpal tunnel syndrome. And if you must *format* this text, too, you're in for even more work.

Fortunately, Dreamweaver's library feature can turn anything you select in the document window (a paragraph, an image, a table) into a reusable chunk of HTML that you can drop into any Dreamweaver document. The library, in other words, is a great place to store copyright notices, navigation bars, announcements, or any other chunk of frequently used HTML.

So far, library items sound pretty much like the snippets described in the previous section. But library items have added power: When you add HTML to a web page using a Library item, that code remains linked to the original item, the one Dreamweaver created and stored in your site. Thanks to this link, whenever you update the *original* Library item, you can automatically update every page that uses that item, too.

A Snippet of Caution

Snippets aren't as smart as other Dreamweaver features. While the program usually warns you before you make a mistake, it doesn't make a peep if you incorrectly add a snippet.

For instance, if you use one of Dreamweaver's Form snippets to add, say, a text box to a page, it doesn't check to see if you're really putting the snippet into a form. Therefore, it doesn't let you know if you're missing the required <form> tag, and it certainly doesn't add the tag itself. And if you're working in Code view, Dreamweaver lets you add snippets to the <head> section of a page (or even outside the <html> tags altogether), which is useful for creating dynamic web pages that include server-side programming but creates messy and invalid HTML in normal web pages.

Furthermore, snippets don't take advantage of Dreamweaver's site-management features to keep track of links or paths to images. Suppose you create a snippet that includes an image. If you insert that snippet into another page, the image may not show up correctly. This could happen if the original page and the page where the snippet is used are in different folders on your site. The path for the image file would be incorrect. If you create a snippet that includes a document-relative link (page 178) that takes you from one page to another page on your site, that link may not work when you add the snippet to yet another page.

So it's best to create snippets that don't involve images or links—but there are workarounds. For instance, you can create snippets with fake links—you could use nothing but the # symbol for the link, for example—and update the link after you insert the snippet into the page. For images, you can use a placeholder object to simulate a graphic in a snippet, something as simple as a GIF or JPG file with the text "Placeholder" in it. After you add the snippet to the page, update the placeholder image with the details (location, size, and so on) for the real image.

To create reusable content that *does* keep track of links and images, create a Library item (see page 847).

Suppose someone buys your company, and the legal department asks you to change the copyright notice to "Copyright MyBigCompany, a subsidiary of MyMuchBigger-Company" on each of the website's *10,000 pages.* If you had cleverly inserted the original copyright notice as a Library item, you could take care of this task in the blink of an eye. Just open the item in the library, make the required changes, save it, and let Dreamweaver update all the pages for you (see Figure 21-3).

NOTE You can achieve a similar effect to Dreamweaver Library items using server-side includes. This option, discussed on page 928, is a bit more technical, but provides even faster site updates than Library items.

Compared to snippets, library items are smart. They possess the unique ability to update the same material on an entire site's worth of files in seconds, and can successfully deal with links and images. Unlike the snippets feature, however, Dreamweaver's library feature is site-specific: Each site you set up in Dreamweaver has its own library, and Dreamweaver stores the library's files along with all the site's other files. If you need to use a Library item from one site on a different site, you have to copy the item to the new site. To do that, in the original site's Assets panel, right-click the Library item, choose Copy to Site, and then choose the new site from the pop-up menu.

NOTE Keep in mind that Library items can contain only page elements that appear in the document window—in other words, only HTML from the <body> section of a web page. You can't include anything that appears in the <head> area of a page, like Cascading Style Sheets, JavaScript widgets (Chapter 15), or meta tags. This means you can't store Dreamweaver behaviors or JavaScript widgets in your library (but you *can* include them in Dreamweaver templates, discussed in the next chapter). Furthermore, Library items must include a complete set of HTML tags—both an opening and a closing tag—as well as all the tags necessary to re-create the original object. For example, Dreamweaver won't let you turn just a single table cell, row, or column into a Library item. If you try, it adds the *entire* table to the library.

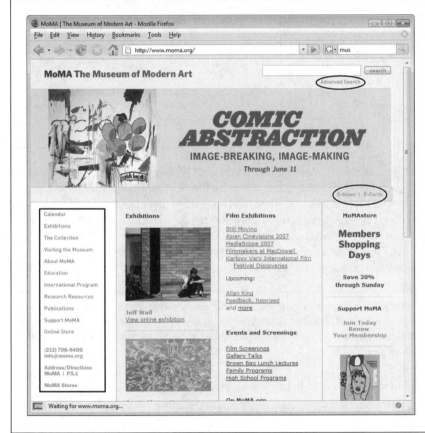

FIGURE 21-3

Library items are a great way to store small chunks of HTML you use frequently. Here, on an old version of The Museum of Modern Art's home page, many of the navigation options (circled) are Library items. If the Museum needed to add or remove a navigation link, it could simply update the Library item and change every page on the site in one step. In fact, since a Library item is a chunk of HTML, you could replace the left-hand navigation bar with plain-text links (instead of graphics), or any other valid HTML code.

■ Creating and Using Library Items

To create a Library item, start by opening the Library window. Click the Assets tab (to the right of the Files tab) or choose Window→Assets, and then click the Library button (📖), circled in Figure 21-4, to reveal the Library items.

FIGURE 21-4

The Assets panel's Library category lists the name, file size, and location of each Library item in the current site. When you select an item from the list, Dreamweaver previews it. In this example, the Library item "Copyright" is, shockingly, a copyright notice.

Now select the part of your document you want to save as a Library item: a blob of text, a graphic, whatever. You can even use the Tag Selector at the bottom of the document window to select a <div> tag (page 454) that contains other tags. Keep in mind that you should only create Library items out of elements that appear on the page—that is, within the <body> section of your page. You can't use Library items in the <head> section of a page. While Dreamweaver lets you create library items from the code there, it doesn't let you insert it into the <head> section of another page.

> **TIP** Use the Tag Selector (page 7) at the bottom-left corner of the document window to make sure you choose the precise tag you want. If you want the content *inside* a tag, however, like the content inside a table cell, click at the beginning of the content, and then drag until you select all the content in the cell, or click in the cell and then choose Edit→Select All.

Next, add the selection to the library in one of several ways:

- Drag the selection into the list of Library items.
- Click the New Item button, + .
- Choose Modify→Library→Add Object to Library.

The new item appears in the Assets panel, bearing the jaunty name "Untitled." Type in a more useful name, such as *Copyright notice* or *Logo*. Your new Library item is now ready to use.

NOTE Even though you can't turn a CSS style into a Library item, you *can* turn HTML you've styled with CSS into a Library item. For example, you can add to the library a paragraph that has a CSS class style applied to it. When you attempt to add this paragraph to the library, Dreamweaver warns you that the item may not look the same when you place it in other documents, because the style sheet information doesn't come along for the ride. To make sure the Library item appears correctly, attach the style sheet to any page where you use that item. External style sheets (page 113) make that easy.

Adding Library Items to a Page

To add a Library item to a web page, drag it out of the Assets panel's Library items list and onto your page. (The long way: Click to plant your insertion point on the page, click the Library item you want in the Assets panel, and then click Insert.)

When you insert a Library item into a page (or turn a selected item *into* a Library item), it sprouts a light-yellow background, indicating that Dreamweaver intends to treat the item as a single object, even though it may include many different HTML elements. You can select the item or drag it around, but you can't edit it. (Unfortunately, if you turn a nontransparent graphic—like a logo, for example—into a Library item, Dreamweaver doesn't give you the helpful yellow background.)

Remember, too, that the placed Library item links to the original item in the library. The copy in your document automatically reflects any changes you make to the original version in the library, using the technique described next.

TIP At some point, you may want to sever the connection between a Library item you placed on a page and the original—to modify a copyright notice on just a single page, for example. To do that, select the item on the page, and then, in the Properties panel, click "Detach from original" (Figure 21-5). Dreamweaver removes the comment tags (see the box on page 854), thus breaking the link to the library.

You can also insert the HTML of a Library item *without* maintaining a link to the library by pressing the Ctrl (Option) key as you add the item to your document. This treats the HTML more like a snippet, and Dreamweaver doesn't update the HTML if you change the original library file.

◼ Editing Library Items

You'll appreciate the real power of Library items when you need to change one. Update the original file in the library, and all the pages graced with that item update, too.

To edit a Library item, start by opening the Assets panel (Window→Assets), click 📖 in the bottom-left corner, and then do the following:

1. **Open the Library item you want to edit.**

   Double-click the Library item in the Assets panel, or highlight it in the Library item list, and then click the Edit button, ▶, or highlight the item in your web page and then, in the Properties panel, click Open (Figure 21-5). (You can also open the Library item in the Library folder of your site's root folder by double-clicking its filename—look for files that end in .lbi.)

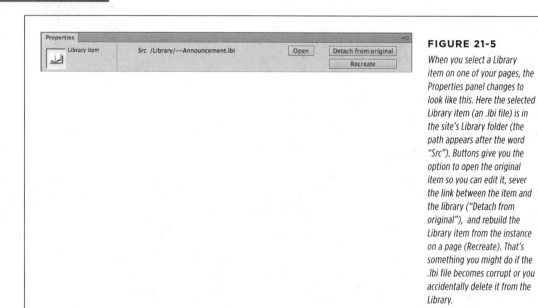

FIGURE 21-5

When you select a Library item on one of your pages, the Properties panel changes to look like this. Here the selected Library item (an .lbi file) is in the site's Library folder (the path appears after the word "Src"). Buttons give you the option to open the original item so you can edit it, sever the link between the item and the library ("Detach from original"), and rebuild the Library item from the instance on a page (Recreate). That's something you might do if the .lbi file becomes corrupt or you accidentally delete it from the Library.

Dreamweaver opens what looks like a normal web page in Design view, but it contains only the text, graphics, or other elements of the Library file.

2. **Edit away.**

A Library item is just a selection of HTML markup; it's not a complete web page. That means you shouldn't add *page* properties, like a title, background color, or one of the behaviors discussed in Chapter 15, to it. (Dreamweaver actually allows this, but it adds invalid HTML to the Library item as well as to every page that uses the item.)

Library items can't contain style sheets, either, so if the item relies on a style, you'll have trouble previewing it correctly. Dreamweaver's Design-Time Style Sheet tool comes in handy here. It lets you temporarily "add" a style sheet while you design a page, without actually adding the CSS code to the page. For more on this useful feature, turn to page 425.

3. **Choose File→Save.**

Dreamweaver checks to see if any pages use the Library item. If they do, it opens the Update Library Items window and lists those pages.

4. **Click Update.**

Dreamweaver opens the Update Pages window, updates the HTML in all the pages that use the Library item, and then lists all the files it changed.

There are times when you might not want to update embedded Library items, however. Perhaps you have a lot of changes to make to the item, and you just want to save the work you've done so far without wasting time updating pages you'll just have to update again later. If that's the case, click Don't Update. You can always update the item another time (see the box on page 875).

Once you finish making changes, save the file for the final time, and *then* update your site.

5. **Click Done.**

As you can see, the library is an incredible timesaver that greatly simplifies the process of changing common page elements.

Renaming Library Items

To rename something in your library, click its name in the Assets panel, pause briefly, and then click again. Dreamweaver highlights the name, ready for your edit. Type the new name, and then press Enter (Return).

If you already added the item to your web pages, Dreamweaver asks whether you want to update those pages. Click Update. Otherwise, the link between those pages and the library breaks.

NOTE If you accidentally click Don't Update, don't panic. Simply change the Library item back to its original name, and then *re*-rename it. And don't forget to click Update this time!

Deleting Library Items

You can delete Library items anytime, but use caution. When you delete something from the library, every copy of the item you placed on your pages—including the item's links to the now-deleted Library item—remains on those pages. You can't edit the copies until you break the links. Unfortunately, you have to do that manually by opening each page that has the item, selecting it, and then clicking "Detach from original" (see Figure 21-5). Ugh.

Now that you've been warned, here's how you get rid of a Library item. In the Assets panel, click the item, and then do one of the following:

- Click 🗑 .

- Press Delete.

- Right-click (Control-click) the item's name, and then, from the shortcut menu, choose Delete.

TIP If you ever accidentally delete an item from the library, you can re-create it if you used it on one of the web pages in your site. Open the page containing the item, and click it to select it. Then, in the Properties panel, click Recreate (Figure 21-5). A copy of the item appears in the library, using the same name as the item you selected.

■ Tutorial: Using Snippets and Library Items

In this tutorial, you'll do two things: create some useful snippets for common form elements, and turn an announcement on the Cafe Soylent Green site into a reusable Library item, finally adding it to several pages.

> **NOTE** You need to download the tutorial files from *http://www.oreilly.com/pub/missingmanuals/dream-weaverccmm2014* to complete this tutorial. See the note on page 37.

Once you download the tutorial files and open Dreamweaver, set up a new site as described on page 23. In a nutshell, choose Site→New Site. In the Site Setup window, type *Snippets and Library*. In the Site Name box, click the folder icon next to the Local Site Folder box, navigate to and select the Chapter21 folder (it's inside the MM_DWCC_2014 folder), and then click Select (Choose). Finally, click Save.

POWER USERS' CLINIC

Under the Hood of Library Items

Behind the scenes, Dreamweaver stores the HTML for Library items as basic text files. The files' names end with the extension .lbi, and Dreamweaver puts them in the Library folder inside your local site folder.

When you add a Library item to a web page, Dreamweaver inserts the item's HTML and a set of comment tags. Those tags refer to the original library file, and help Dreamweaver remember where the Library item begins and ends. For instance, if you turn the text "Copyright 2015" into a Library item called *copyright* and insert it into a web page, Dreamweaver adds the following HTML to the page:

```
<!-- #BeginLibraryItem "/Library/
copyright.lbi" -->Copyright 2015<!--
#EndLibraryItem-->
```

Avoid using hyphens in Library item names. Why? Since HTML comments use hyphens (<!-- at the beginning of the comment and --> at the end), some versions of Firefox get tripped up by additional hyphens and respond by hiding the contents of the item or displaying raw HTML code instead.

In addition, although you can't edit a Library item on a page in Design view, you can muck around with it in Code view. In the example above, you could change 2015 to 2051 in Code view. Don't do it! Dreamweaver obliterates your changes the minute you try to save the web page. If you want to make a change to a Library item, edit the *original* item, or break the link between the item and the library (as described in the Tip on page 851) and then edit the item.

Creating a Snippet

1. **With your site freshly defined, make sure you have the Files panel open.**

   If it isn't, press the F8 key (Shift-⌘-F) or choose Window→Files.

2. **In the Files panel, double-click *snippet.html*.**

   A page with three pull-down menus opens. It includes menus for the months of the year, the names of U.S. states, and the numbers 1 to 31. You can use menus like these on your web pages for a variety of jobs: to let readers specify task to-do dates, for example, or to select a destination state for a product shipment.

Dreamweaver's own snippets don't include these useful menus, but, fortunately, you can add them yourself.

3. **In Design view, click the menu at the top of the page, the one to the right of the words "Months of year."**

   You selected the menu and its underlying HTML code. To add this as a snippet, you need to open the Snippets panel.

4. **Choose Window→Snippets.**

   The Snippets panel is your control center for adding, editing, and deleting snippets.

5. **At the bottom of the panel, click +.**

   The Snippet window opens. Dreamweaver automatically copies the code for the menu into the "Insert before" window. You just need to name the snippet and add a few more details.

6. **Type *Month Menu* in the Name box, and then *A list of month names, with numeric values*, in the Description box. The Snippet window should look like the one in Figure 21-6.**

   Once you create the snippet (by clicking OK in step 9 below), Dreamweaver displays its name and description in the Snippets panel. In this case, the description you wrote identifies what appears in the menu (a list of month names) and what type of value the snippet applies when a visitor selects a month from the list—a "numeric value." In other words, your description identifies the name/value pair for this form field. (See Chapter 16 for more on how name/value pairs work in forms.)

7. **Turn on the "Insert block" radio button.**

   That identifies the snippet as a chunk of standalone HTML, and Dreamweaver changes the code's directive from "Insert before" to "Insert code." You can simply plop down standalone code like this anywhere on a page.

   If you want a snippet to wrap around a selected graphic or text, like a link or table cell, turn on the "Wrap selection" radio button and include the closing code in the "Insert after" box.

8. **At the bottom of the window, make sure you have the Design radio button turned on.**

   Selecting Design (instead of the alternative, Code) tells Dreamweaver to display the snippet itself in your pages, and not just a bunch of code.

9. **The window should now look like the one in Figure 21-6. Click OK to create your new snippet.**

   The snippet should appear in the Snippets panel, ready for you to insert it into a page.

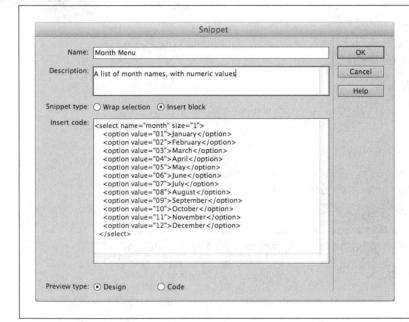

FIGURE 21-6

The HTML for the Month Menu snippet appears in the "Insert code" box. You can add or remove HTML, and you can have the snippet wrap around a selected page element by turning on the "Wrap selection" radio button.

NOTE If you select a folder (or a file inside a folder) in the Snippets panel when you create a snippet, Dreamweaver stores the new snippet in that folder. To move it out of there and up to the top-level list of the Snippets panel, drag it to the very bottom of the panel. Or, to move it to another folder in the Snippets panel, just drag the snippet to that folder—for the Month Menu here, the Form Elements folder would be appropriate.

10. **Select the Files panel by clicking the Files tab or by pressing the F8 key (Shift-⌘-F), and then double-click the file *reservation.html*.**

    Cafe Soylent Green's reservation form opens. You'll insert your new snippet here.

11. **Return to the Snippets panel once again by clicking the Snippets tab or by choosing Window→Snippets.**

    Now for the moment of truth.

12. **Drag your new snippet—Month Menu—from the Snippets panel to the right of the label "Month."**

    Ta-da! Dreamweaver adds the new menu. Now, whenever you need to add a menu that lists the months of the year, don't bother creating it from scratch, just use this snippet!

13. **At the top of the document window, click the *snippet.html* tab. Click the third menu (the one with the days of the month), and then repeat steps 5–12.**

Name this new snippet *Days of Month* and then type *Numerical days of the month* in the Description box.

14. **Click the *reservation.html* tab.**

Insert the Days of Month snippet to the right of the label "Day." You can close the *snippet.html* file when you finish.

Creating a Library Item

Now you'll see one way in which Dreamweaver's powerful site-management tools can help you create and update your site more effectively:

1. **Open the file *about.html*.**

Double-click its name in the Files panel or choose File→Open and then select *about.html* in the site's root folder.

In the column of content near the middle of the page, a green box says "Cafe Soylent Green is now open 7 days a week!" This box is a simple <span> element with some text in it. The cafe uses it for important announcements, and it appears on various pages of the site. Since you need to keep these announcements up to date, creating an easily updated Library item is an efficient tactic.

2. **Click anywhere inside the box (in the text, for example), and then, in the Tag Selector, click <span.announcement> (Figure 21-7).**

You can use this selected <span> as the basis for a new Library item.

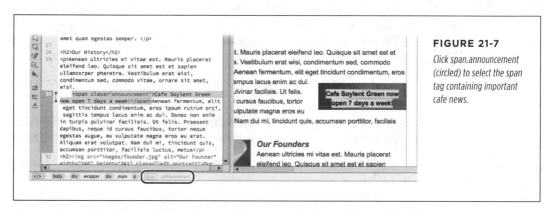

FIGURE 21-7

Click span.announcement (circled) to select the span tag containing important cafe news.

3. **Choose Window→Assets, and then click 📖.**

The Assets panel opens and displays the Library category.

4. **On the Assets panel, click + (Figure 21-4).**

A warning message appears, saying that the Library item may not look the same in other pages. Dreamweaver is telling you that Library items can contain only HTML from the body of a web page—they can't include Cascading Style Sheets. So if your item uses styles from a linked style sheet, it may look different on pages that use a different style sheet. (You can still include HTML that has a style applied to it, just as this <div> tag does, so long as you make sure that any *pages* to which you add the Library item have the appropriate style sheets attached.)

The text in this example *is* formatted using a style sheet, so, sure enough, it won't look the same in pages that don't have the same style sheet applied to them. In this exercise, however, that's not a problem, since all the pages on the site share the same linked external style sheet.

Click OK to dismiss the warning (and feel free to turn on the "Don't warn me again" checkbox while you're at it). The announcement item appears in the Library list, with a number (1, 2, and so on) for a name. The number is highlighted for editing.

5. **Type *News* to name the new item in the Assets panel, and then press Enter (Return).**

You just added this standard blob of text to your snippets library. It's ready to use anywhere else on your site. Notice the yellow highlight around the edges of the News item on the page. In Design view, Library items have a yellow hightlight, Dreamwever's way of identifying Library items. In this case, the highlight appears only in the margin because the page element has a background color applied through CSS formatting.

6. **In the Files panel, double-click the filename *hours.html*.**

You'll frequently jump between the Files panel and the Assets panel, so the keyboard shortcut to open the Files panel comes in handy: F8 (Shift-⌘-F). The Assets panel lacks a keyboard shortcut, but you can create one using Edit→Keyboard Shortcuts (Dreamweaver→Keyboard Shortcuts); see page 904 for details.

The Hours & Directions page doesn't have an announcement box, so you'll add one.

7. **Switch back to the Assets panel and drag the News Library item to the left of the letter "H" in the second headline—"Hours"—as pictured in Figure 21-8.**

If you accidentally drop the Library item somewhere else on the page, choose Ctrl-Z (⌘-Z) or Edit→Undo and try again. You can recognize the newly inserted item by its yellow highlight around the edges. Click the text in the item, and notice that you can't edit it; Dreamweaver treats the item—really a mixture of HTML, CSS, and JavaScript—as a single object. The source for this object is in the Assets panel, which is where you'd do any editing (see step 11). When you add the Library item to another page, as you'll do in the next step, it will look the same.

8. **Add the News Library item to two other pages on your site: *ingredients. html* and *philosophy.html*.**

Open each page (double-click its name in the Files window), and then repeat step 7. Insert the Library item anywhere you want on these pages.

(You can close and save the pages as you go, but for now, leave at least one open and go on to step 9.)

9. **Save the pages you added the Library item to by selecting File→Save All.**

10. **This just in!**

    New things are happening at the cafe all the time, so it's time to update this announcement. Fortunately, you used a Library item, so it's easy to make the change.

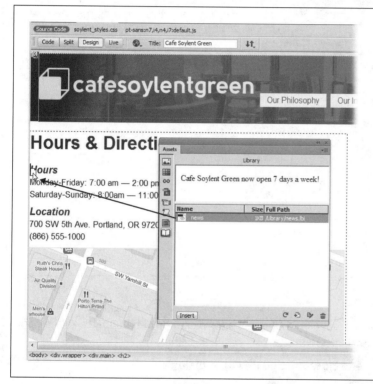

FIGURE 21-8

You can insert a Library item into a page by dragging it into the document window or by highlighting it in the Assets panel, clicking at the insertion point in the document window, and then, back in the Assets panel, clicking the Insert button.

11. **From the list of Library items in the Assets panel, double-click "News."**

    The Library item opens in the document window, ready for editing. Notice that it doesn't have any of the formatting you saw on the web page—that's because there's no CSS file attached to the item, so you see only the plain HTML version of the announcement box.

12. **Select all the text in the document window and then type *Cafe temporarily (we hope) closed due to health inspection. We are sorry for the inconvenience.* Choose File→Save.**

    The Update Library Items dialog box appears (Figure 21-9), listing the four pages in the site that use this announcement box.

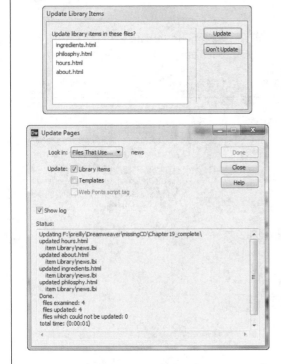

FIGURE 21-9

Top: The Update Library Items dialog box appears whenever you update a Library item.

Bottom: After you click Update, the Update Pages box appears. If you turn on the "Show log" checkbox, Dreamweaver displays all the files it changed, including the filenames of the pages it updated and the total number of pages affected. This window also appears when you update template files, as discussed in the next chapter.

13. **Click Update.**

    Dreamweaver opens the Update Pages dialog box and updates all the pages that use the News item.

14. **Click Close to close the Update Pages dialog box.**

    Now, if you open *about.html*, *hours.html*, *philosophy.html*, or *ingredients.html*, you'll see that Dreamweaver updated the announcement box.

    Now imagine that you just used this auto-update feature on a 10,000-page site. Sit back and smile.

TIP If you use a particular Library item on some, but not all, of the pages on your site, you'll want to know which pages you changed so you can move just those pages to your server—you don't want to spend time uploading your entire website when you changed just a handful of pages. Dreamweaver's Select Recently Modified command can help (see the box on page 783). You can also use Dreamweaver's Synchronization feature to make sure you get the most recent pages from your computer to your server (see page 827).

Templates

S ome web designers handcraft their sites with loving care, changing layouts, colors, fonts, and banners page by page. But that approach isn't always practical—or desirable.

Consistency from one page to another is a good thing. Web pages that look and act similarly reassure visitors; they can concentrate on each page's unique content when the navigation bar and left sidebar stay the same. But even more important, a handcrafted approach to web design is often unrealistic when you need to crank out content on a deadline.

That's where Dreamweaver *templates* come in. Frequently, the underlying design of many website pages is identical. An employee directory at a company site, for instance, may consist of individual pages dedicated to each employee. Each page has the same navigation bar, banner, footer, and layout. Only a few particulars change from page to page, like the employee's name, photograph, and contact information. This is a perfect case for templates.

This chapter shows you how templates can make quick work of building web pages where most, if not all, of the pages use repetitive elements.

■ Template Basics

Templates let you build pages that share a similar structure and graphic identity, quickly and without having to worry about accidentally deleting or changing elements. They're especially handy if you design a site where other, less Dreamweaver-savvy individuals will build pages. By using a template, you, the godlike Dreamweaver guru, can limit the areas those underlings can modify on each page.

A new page based on a template—also called a *template instance*, or a *child page*—looks just like the template, except that you can edit only designated areas of the page, called, logically enough, *editable regions*. In Figure 22-1, you can see that the question-and-answer text is an editable region; the rest of the page remains consistent (and is, in fact, locked).

FIGURE 22-1

These three web pages are part of a site dedicated to frequently asked questions. Each page provides the answer to a different question, but the pages are otherwise identical, sharing the same banner, navigation buttons, sidebar, and footer. Why re-create the design for each page? Enter one of Dreamweaver's great timesavers—templates—which help you quickly build similar-looking pages and make updating pages a snap.

A Dreamweaver template can be very basic, consisting of nothing more than one or more areas that a page author can change (the editable regions), along with other areas that he can't edit (the *locked regions*). At the same time, you can build templates that give page authors an impressive amount of flexibility. Here's an overview of the features you can tap when you create and use templates:

- **Editable regions**. These are the basic building blocks of a template. An editable region is that part of a page—a paragraph, the contents of a <div> tag, or a headline, for example—that page authors can change as they build template-based pages. Templates can include multiple editable regions—a sidebar and the main content of a page, for example.

- **Editable tag attributes**. There may be times when you want to make a particular tag *property* editable. For example, say you have a banner ad at the top of a page—the banner ad is just a basic image file, and each page should have a different ad. You want to make sure that no one can delete the image (after all, those ads are paying for your site), but you do want someone to be able to swap in a new image. In other words, people shouldn't mess with the <img> tag; they should only be able to change the <img> tag's *src* attribute. To keep someone from deleting the image placeholder but still allow her to change pictures, you'd make just the *src* property editable. (You could also make the image's *alt* property editable, and if the *width* and *height* properties vary from image to image, you can make those editable as well.)

  Or you might want a unique headline design for each section of your site. To get that, when you build the site template, assign a class to the <body> tag and make the class name editable. Then, when you create pages for different sections of the site, add a class name specific to each section. For example, for a site's About Us page, you could set the body's class to *.about*. Once you do, you can use a descendent selector (like *.about h1*) to create a custom style for all the headlines on just that page. On template-based pages showcasing your company's products, change the class name to *.products*, and then add a descendent selector style like *.products h1* to your style sheet, and you'll have a unique look for all the <h1> tags on all your product pages.

- **Repeating regions and repeating tables**. Some web pages, like those that showcase the products a company sells, include *lists* of items. For pages like these, Dreamweaver lets you define *repeatable regions* in your template. For example, your design for a page of product listings might include each product's picture, name, and price, organized in a table with multiple rows (Chapter 6). As the template builder, you may not know in advance how many products the page will eventually list, so you can't fully design the page. You can, however, use Dreamweaver to define a row—or any selection of HTML—as a repeating region, so that page authors can add new rows of product information as needed.

- **Optional regions and editable optional regions**. *Optional regions* make templates even more flexible. They let you show or hide content—from a single paragraph to an entire <div> tag full of other tags—on a page-by-page basis.

Suppose you create a template that showcases your company's products. Some products go on sale while others remain full price, so you add an *optional region* to the product descriptions that displays a big "On Sale" logo. When you create a new product page, you could *show* the optional region for products that are on sale and keep it *hidden* for the others.

Editable optional regions are similar but have the added benefit of being editable. Maybe you're creating a template for an employee directory, giving each employee his own page with contact information. Some employees want their picture displayed on the page, while others don't (you know the type). Solution: Add an editable optional region that includes space for a photo. You add a different photo for each page, except for the shyer types; for them, you simply hide the photo area.

Facilitating page creation is only one benefit of templates. They also greatly simplify the process of updating a website's design. Like Library items (Chapter 21), pages based on templates retain a reference to the original template file. Dreamweaver passes any changes you make to that template to all the pages you created from it, which can save you hours of time and trouble when it comes time to update your site's look or structure. Imagine how much time you'll save when your boss asks you to add "just one more" button to a site's navigation bar. Instead of updating thousands of pages by hand, you need to update only a single template file.

■ Creating a Template

The first step in creating a template is to build a basic web page and tell Dreamweaver that you'd like to use it as a template. You do that two ways: Build a regular, plain old web page and turn it into a template, or create a blank, empty template file and add sections for text, graphics, tables, and other content.

Turning a Web Page into a Template

The easiest way to create a template is to base it on a web page in your current site folder. Although you can create templates based on web pages that *aren't* part of your current site, you may run into problems with links and paths to images, as described in the Note on page 865.

Once you open the page, choose File→Save As Template or, on the Insert panel (Figure 22-2), choose the Templates category from the drop-down menu and then click Make Template. The Save As Template window (Figure 22-3) includes the name of the current local site in the Site drop-down menu, and all the templates for that site show up in the Existing Templates list.

FIGURE 22-2

The Insert panel's Template category gives you all the tools you need to create templates and add a variety of template components, like a table that keeps growing until it runs out of data.

NOTE At this point, you could theoretically use the Site drop-down menu to save a template in any local site folder you set up (see Chapter 18 for a discussion of local sites), but be careful with this option. If your page contains images, external style sheets, and links and you save it as a template for another local site, Dreamweaver doesn't copy the images or style sheets from the first site folder to the second one. As a result, the paths to the image files and links don't work correctly, nor will the page show any styling.

If you must use a page from one site as a template for another, copy the web page, graphics, and style sheets into the new site's root folder, open the page there, and then create the template as described here.

FIGURE 22-3

The Save As Template dialog box lets you store templates in any of the local site folders you've defined. Stick to your current local site to avoid broken links, missing images, and disappearing style sheets.

Dreamweaver includes a Description field where you can add a brief note characterizing the template. The description appears when you select a template as the basis for new pages. It's useful when *other* people build a site using your templates and they're not sure whether *templateA1*, *templateA2*, or *templateA3* is the correct choice; a simple note that says "Use this template for all FAQ pages" makes it clear. Finally, in the "Save as" box, type a name for the new template, and then click Save. Choose Yes when Dreamweaver asks if you want to update links on the page. If you choose No, all page-relative links break, styles from external style sheets won't work, and all the images on the page appear as broken-image icons.

Dreamweaver saves the page in the Templates folder of your local site root folder. It adds the extension .dwt to indicate that it's a Dreamweaver template. (For dynamic web pages, Dreamweaver adds the .dwt *before* the file's extension. For example, a PHP template may have a name like *maintemplate.dwt.php*.)

NOTE Don't get carried away building too many templates for a site. It doesn't make any sense to create 20 templates for a 20-page site. You should need only a handful of templates to cover the different types of pages you have. In fact, you might just need a single template to dictate the look of all your site's pages.

Building a Template from Scratch

It's easiest to create a web page first and then save it as a template, but you can also build a template from scratch. Open the Assets panel's Templates category by choosing Window→Assets and then clicking 🖾 (see Figure 22-4). Then click the New Template button at the bottom of the panel. Once Dreamweaver adds a new, untitled template to the list, give it a new name. Something descriptive like "Press release" or "Employee page" helps you keep track of your templates.

Preview

Template assets

Template in the
current site

Apply selected
template

Refresh
list

New

Edit

Delete

FIGURE 22-4

The Templates category of the Assets panel lists the name, file size, and location of each template in the current local site. The Apply button assigns a template to the currently open web page. The Refresh Site List button updates the list of templates—if you just created a template and don't see it listed, click this button. The New Template button creates a new, blank template in the Templates folder. Select a template from the list and then click Edit Template to open and change a template.

After you create a blank template, open it by double-clicking its name in the Assets panel (or by selecting its name and then clicking the Edit button at the bottom of the panel). It opens just like any other web page, so you can get busy designing it with the unchanging elements of your site—logo, navigation bar, and so on. You'll learn how to add editable regions next.

■ Defining Editable Regions

Your next task is to specify which parts of your template you want locked and which you want editable. Initially, Dreamweaver templates lock *all* the elements in the body of a page. After all, the main reason to use a template is to maintain a consistent, unchanging design and structure among pages. To make a template usable, you have to define the area or areas that page authors *can* change.

To add an editable region to a template, start by selecting the part of the page you want to make changeable. You can designate as editable anything in the document window (that is, any HTML between the <body> tags).

> **NOTE** You can always add Cascading Style Sheets, JavaScript, and meta tags to the <head> of a template-based page. Any <head> content in the original template files stays put in the page you create from it, however. For example, you can't remove an external style sheet applied to a template from a page based on that template.

For templates you create from scratch, place your cursor where you want to insert an editable region. For templates you build from an existing page, drag across the page to select the elements you want to make editable or, for greater precision, use the Tag Selector (see page 7) to select the exact HTML you want.

Now tell Dreamweaver that you want to make the selected elements editable. You can use any of these techniques:

- In the Templates category of the Insert panel (Figure 22-2), select Editable Region.
- Choose Insert→Template→Editable Region.
- Press Alt+Ctrl+V (Option-⌘-V).
- Right-click (Control-click) the selection and then, from the shortcut menu, choose Templates→New Editable Region.

When the New Editable Region dialog box appears, type a name for the region (you can't use the same name twice) and then click OK. You return to your template, where the name you gave the editable region appears in a small blue-green tab above the region, which is itself outlined in blue-green.

NOTE When you use CSS to lay out a page, you usually create separate <div> tags (see page 454) for the different areas of a page. For example, you might wrap the main content in one <div>, the banner in another, and the footer in yet another. For <div>s you use to *structure* a page, you want to make just the *contents* of the <div> tag editable, not the tag itself. Here's one instance where you want to *avoid* the Tag Selector (page 7), which selects the entire <div> element, tags and all. If you turned that <div> tag into an editable region, someone modifying the page could delete the tag entirely, which could wreak untold havoc on your CSS-based layout.

Fortunately, Dreamweaver has a handy shortcut for selecting just the contents of a <div> tag. Click anywhere inside the tag and then press Ctrl+A (⌘-A), or choose Edit→Select All. Then choose Insert→Template→Editable Region to turn this selection into an editable region. The <div> tags will remain *outside* that region, so no one can inadvertently delete them.

You may find that a single editable region is all you need—for example, when you put a product review in just a single place on a page (a section of a page enclosed by a <div> tag, for example). However, if you need to be able to edit *multiple* areas of a page, just add more editable regions to the template. For instance, when you create a template for an employee page, you can create editable regions for the employee's name, telephone number, and photo. If you change your mind and want to lock a region later, select the editable region and then choose Modify→Templates→Remove Template Markup. Dreamweaver removes the code that makes the region editable.

NOTE You can rename an editable region by clicking the blue-green tab on the template page and typing a new name in the Properties panel. But if you've already built pages based on the template, that's not a good idea. Because template-based pages identify regions by their names, Dreamweaver can lose track of where content should go if you rename a region.

Once you add at least one editable region to a template, you're ready to start adding pages to your site and filling them up with content. (Of course, you may need some of the more advanced template features—you'll learn how to add them starting on page 876.)

■ Building Pages Based on a Template

Building a template is the prelude to the actual work of building your site. Once you finish your template, it's time to produce pages.

To create a new document based on a template, choose File→New to open the New Document window (see Figure 22-5). Click the Site Templates button, and then, from the Site list, select the site you're working on. All the templates for that site appear in the right-hand column. Select the template you want to use, and then click Create.

FIGURE 22-5

The Site Templates category of the New Document window lets you build new pages based on a template. Be careful of the middle "Site" column—it lets you pick any site you set up in Dreamweaver and open a new page based on a template from that site. It's a bad idea to pick a site other than the one you're working on. In fact, if you do, Dreamweaver doesn't bring along any of the assets that that template uses (for example, style sheets, images, linked-to pages, and so on) so you'll end up with a broken template-based page. Why, Adobe, why?

NOTE If you don't want your new web page linked to a template (so that future changes to the template won't affect this page), turn off the "Update page when template changes" checkbox. The result is a new page that looks just like the template but has no locked regions; you can edit the entire page. This is a useful technique when you want to create a new template starting with the general design and structure of an existing one. (Be aware that Dreamweaver remembers this choice the next time you create a new template-based page, so pages you create from a template in the future will *also* be unlinked—unless you remember to turn the "Update page" checkbox back on.)

A new web page opens, based on the template, and bearing a tab in the upper-right corner labeled with the underlying template's name. In Design view, Dreamweaver outlines any editable regions in blue-green; a small blue-green tab displays each region's name (Figure 22-6). In Live view, you see the editable region outlined in orange, with the region's name in the tab at the top.

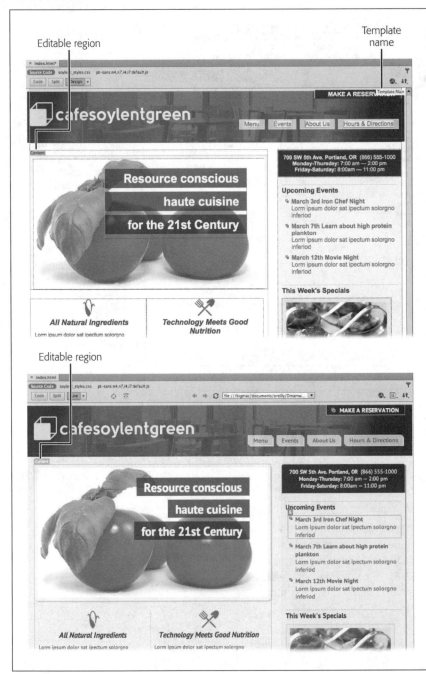

Editable region

Template name

FIGURE 22-6

Top: This page, shown in Design view, is based on a template called "Main," as you can tell from the little tab in the document window's upper-right corner. You can modify this page's editable region, which Dreamweaver identifies by name in the blue-green tab and outlines with a thin blue-green line. In this example, one editable region, called "Content," fills the main section of the page. All other parts of the page are locked. When you point to a locked portion of the page, the cursor changes to the "no" symbol.

Bottom: In Live view, you won't see the name of the applied template, but you do see the editable region marked by a thin orange line with a tab at the top showing its name: Content.

Editable region

When Save Won't Behave

I keep getting a warning message when I save my template. What's going on?

If you add an editable region *inside* certain block-level elements, like a paragraph or a heading, Dreamweaver pops up a warning message when you save the template, explaining that you can't create additional paragraphs or headings inside this region on any pages you build from this template. This just means that you selected the *contents* of a paragraph or heading, not the actual paragraph or heading tag itself, when you made the region editable. Dreamweaver considers anything outside the editable region locked, so you can't change those tags. Since it's improper HTML to have a paragraph, heading, or other block-level element inside *another* paragraph or heading, Dreamweaver won't let you add a paragraph, heading, bulleted list, or any other block-level element inside the editable contents of the locked paragraph or heading.

This characteristic may not be such a bad thing, however. Imagine you create a template for other people to use as they build a website. You have a Heading 1 with a style applied to it, and you want to make sure that it looks the same on every page. You wouldn't want anyone changing the <heading> tag and possibly erasing the style. In addition, you don't want a page editor to change the Heading 1 to a Heading 2 or a Heading 3; nor do you want her to completely erase the <h1> tag and thereby have the page display paragraph after paragraph of random thoughts. You just want the editor to type in new text for the heading. Selecting just the text inside the heading (as opposed to the <h1> tag *and* the text) and turning it into an editable region does just that. Viva micro-management!

If this is, in fact, what you want to do, you can save yourself the bother of having to constantly see the "You placed an editable region inside a block tag" warning box each time you save the template by simply turning on the "Don't show me this message again" checkbox. However, if you made a mistake and *do* want to let people change the heading or add more headings and paragraphs in this region, you need to do two things: First, unlock the editable region you created (see above), and then select the text *and* the tag (the Tag Selector [page 7] is the best way to do that), and then turn that selection into an editable region.

Dreamweaver makes it obvious which areas of a page are off limits; your cursor changes to a "forbidden" symbol (a circle with a line through it) when you venture into a locked area.

To add content to an editable region, click anywhere inside the region. You can add text to it, include graphics, or add any other object or HTML you can normally add to a document. As long as you're working in an editable region, you can insert jQuery widgets (Chapter 15) and audio and video files (Chapter 17) in the usual manner, using the Insert panel or Insert menu. Dreamweaver automatically adds the necessary code to the <head> portion of your page. You can also change the document's title by choosing Modify→Page Properties→Title/Encoding. To change the page's keywords, description, or metadata, use the Insert→Head menu.

Once you finish adding content, save the file and close it. You can create additional pages based on the same template by following the steps above (choose File→New to open the New Document window, click the Site Templates button, select the template, and so on). If you need to make a site-wide change to template-based pages (to add a navigation button, for example), you edit the template as described on page 874.

You might also find that the editable region doesn't provide all the control you want. Fortunately, Dreamweaver's advanced template regions—described on page 876—might help.

Applying Templates to Existing Pages

What happens if you create a web page, and *then* decide you want it to share the look of a template? No problem. Dreamweaver lets you apply a template to any page in your site. You can even swap one template for another.

To apply a template to a page you already created:

1. **Choose File→Open to open the page you want to alter.**

   Dreamweaver opens the page.

2. **Choose Window→Assets, and then click the Assets panel's Templates button.**

   The Assets panel lists your site's templates.

> **NOTE**   You can also apply a template to a page by choosing Modify→Templates→Apply Template to Page. Select the name of the template from the window that Dreamweaver opens, and then skip to step 5.

POWER USERS' CLINIC

Templates Under the Hood

Dreamweaver saves templates as HTML files in the Templates folder inside your current local site folder (see Chapter 18 for more on local sites). Each template bears the file extension .dwt to distinguish template pages from regular web pages.

Dreamweaver treats files in the Templates folder differently from normal web pages, so don't save anything but .dwt files there. In addition, since Dreamweaver expects to find the Templates folder in the local root folder of your site, don't move it or change its name in any way (don't even change the capital "T" in "Templates," even if you're a low-key type of person). If you do, your templates won't work.

As with Library items, Dreamweaver uses HTML comments to indicate the name of a template. If you inspect the HTML of a template-based document, you'll see that, immediately following the opening <html> tag, Dreamweaver inserts a comment

tag with the text "InstanceBegin" followed by the location and name of the template. Additional comment tags indicate areas of the page you can modify and special template features, like template settings used for optional regions. For instance, the title of a page based on a template is always editable; its comment tag might look like this:

```
<!-- InstanceBeginEditable
name="doctitle" -->
<title>My New Page</title>
<!-- InstanceEndEditable -->
```

The first comment indicates the editable region's beginning and also includes the editable region's name. When you edit pages based on this template, you can change only the HTML between these comment tags. Everything else on the page is locked, even when you work in Code view.

---

3. **Click a template in the list in the Assets panel, and then click Apply.**

   Dreamweaver opens the Inconsistent Region Names dialog box (Figure 22-7).

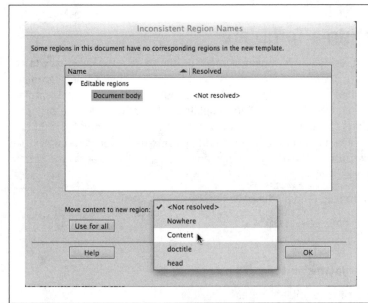

FIGURE 22-7

When you apply a template to an existing page, you must tell Dreamweaver what to do with the elements already on the page by assigning them to one of the template's editable regions from a pop-up menu. You do that in the Inconsistent Region Names window.

4. **Under "Editable regions," choose "Document body."**

   In the Resolved column to the right, you see <Not resolved>. This is Dreamweaver's way of saying that it doesn't know what to do with the elements in the current page. You need to copy those elements to one of the template's editable regions.

5. **From the "Move content to new region" menu, select an editable region.**

   If you want to keep the unassigned material, select the name of an editable region from the list—that copies the content there. Otherwise, choose Nowhere, which, in effect, creates a new blank page based on the template.

   Unfortunately, you get only a single editable region in which to stuff page elements, even if the template page has several editable regions. If the original page had several editable regions, Dreamweaver pushes them all into the single editable region in the template you're applying.

6. **If "Document head" also appears in the window, select it and choose "head" from the "Move content to new region" menu.**

   This step transfers any special information you added to the head section of your original page, like Cascading Style Sheets, meta tags, and custom JavaScript programs, to the head of the new, template-based page. Unfortunately, Dreamweaver always replaces the title of your original page with the default title of the template, so you have to re-enter the title after you apply the template.

7. **Click OK.**

Dreamweaver opens your new page.

■ Updating a Template

Templates aren't just useful for building pages quickly; they also make fast work of updating your site. Template-based pages maintain a link to their original template, and Dreamweaver automatically passes changes you make to the original template to every page built from it. If you used templates to build your site, you probably won't cry on your keyboard when the boss asks you to add an additional button and a link to the navigation bar. Instead of editing every page, you can simply open the template file, update the navigation bar, and let Dreamweaver apply the update to all your pages.

You update a template (and all the pages based on it) like this:

1. **Choose Window→Assets.**

Dreamweaver opens the Assets panel.

2. **Click the Templates button.**

A list of the site's templates appears.

3. **Double-click a template's name to open it.**

Alternatively, you can select the template in the Assets panel, and then click Edit to open the original template (.dwt) file.

> **TIP** You can also open a template by double-clicking its filename in the Templates folder of the Files panel.

4. **Edit the template as you would any web page.**

Since this is the original template file, you can edit any of the HTML in the document, including Cascading Style Sheets, meta tags, and layers. You can also add or remove editable regions.

Take care, however, to edit *only* the areas that you did *not* mark as editable regions. The reason: When you update your pages, any region marked as editable in a template file isn't passed on to pages based on that template. After all, the template dictates only the design of those pages' *non*-editable regions. In other words, if you make a change to an editable region in a template, Dreamweaver won't pass that change on to any existing template-based pages.

> **NOTE** Be careful when you remove editable regions from a template. If you already built pages based on that template, Dreamweaver warns you that your change will affect pages previously built from the template when you save the newly configured version. As described below, you can either *delete* the content that was originally in the region you removed, or you can move that content to another editable region of the page.

5. **Choose File→Save.**

   If you already created pages based on this template, Dreamweaver opens the Update Template Files window. It lists all the files that use the template.

6. **Click Update to update all the files based on the template.**

   Dreamweaver automatically applies the changes you made to the template-based pages. Then it opens the Update Pages dialog box. To see a list of all the files Dreamweaver changed, turn on the "Show log" checkbox.

   On a large site, this automatic update feature can be an incredible time-saver, but you may *not* want to click Update, at least not right now. Perhaps you're just saving some of your hard work on the template but aren't quite finished perfecting it—why waste time updating all those pages more than once? In such a scenario, click the Don't Update button. Remember, you can always update the pages later (see the box below).

7. **Click Close.**

   Dreamweaver closes the Update Pages window.

Remember that you need to update all your files, even if you make a simple change to the template, like changing its name.

POWER USERS' CLINIC

Wait to Update

Whenever you modify and save a template, Dreamweaver gives you the option of updating any child pages on the site. The same holds true for Library items; if you change a Library item, Dreamweaver asks if you want to pass that change on to all the pages that use that item. Very often, you'll say yes.

But there are times when you want to wait to update your site. If you're making a lot of changes to templates or multiple Library items, you may wish to wait until you finish all your edits before you let the changes ripple through your pages. After all, it can take some time to update a large site.

Dreamweaver lets you update pages that use templates and Library items anytime. Just choose Modify→Templates→Update Pages or Modify→Library→Update Pages.

Both menu options open the same window, the Update Pages dialog box.

At this point, you can update pages that use a specific template or Library item by going to the "Look in" menu, choosing "Files that Use," and then selecting the appropriate name from the drop-down menu. If you want to update all the pages in a site, choose Entire Site, and then, from the drop-down menu, select the name of the local site. Turn on both the Templates and "Library items" checkboxes to update all the pages.

To see the results of Dreamweaver's work, turn on the "Show log" checkbox, which lists all the files Dreamweaver updated.

Unlinking a Page from a Template

If you're confident that you won't make any further changes to a page's template and you want to edit a page's locked regions, you can break the link between the page and its template by choosing Modify→Templates→Detach from Template.

You can now edit all the HTML in the page, just as you can on a regular web page—which is, in fact, what you have now. You removed all references to the original template, so any changes to the template no longer affect this page.

> **NOTE** If you unlink a nested template from its master template, Dreamweaver removes only the code provided by the original master template. Any editable regions you added to the nested template remain.

■ Using Repeating Regions

The humble editable region is the heart of all templates—after all, the whole point of a template is to provide an easy way to create new pages. You may find that templates with editable regions are all you ever need for your site, but Dreamweaver provides several other template features that might come in handy.

Some web pages have types of content that repeat over and over. For example, a catalog page may display row after row of the same product information—picture, name, price, and description. An index of Frequently Asked Questions may list questions and the dates visitors posted them. Dreamweaver provides a couple of ways to turn content like this into an editable region in a template.

You could, of course, make the entire area where the repeating content appears editable. For example, you could use one of Dreamweaver's HTML layouts (see Chapter 10) to build a template for an FAQ page. The list of questions and answers goes inside the page's main <div> tag, and you can turn that <div> into an editable region. The downside to this approach is that you won't have any ability to enforce (or easily update) the HTML used to lay out the questions and answers, since another designer could edit or delete everything in the <div>.

Fortunately, Dreamweaver provides a pair of template tools to address the problem: *repeating regions* and *repeating tables*. Both let you create areas of a page that include editable and uneditable regions that you can repeat any number of times (see Figure 22-8).

Adding a Repeating Region

You add a repeating region the same way you add an editable region. Select the area of the template where you want to repeat information; it usually contains at least one element you've made editable. It could be a single list item (the <li> tag), a table row (the <tr> tag), or even an entire <div> tag.

> **NOTE** You can make a repeating region that *doesn't* include an editable region. For example, a template for a movie review web page could include a repeating region that's simply a graphic of a star. A page author adding a new movie review could repeat the star graphic to match the movie's rating—four stars, for example. (There's just one caveat—see the Tip on page 881.)

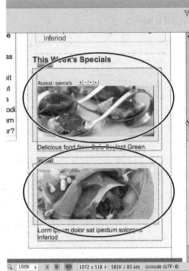

FIGURE 22-8

A repeating region lets page authors add multiple instances of information. Left: In this template, you see a repeating region labeled "specials" (circled). Right: A complete page based on this template includes two repeating editable regions (circled). If another page requires more cafe specials, you can easily add one to each list by clicking the + button at the top of the repeating region in the template-based page (right). Even though you can dictate how many repeating regions appear on a page, the master template still controls the page's editable and uneditable regions. That means page authors can't change the box that surrounds the specials, nor the headline "This Week's Specials."

Next, tell Dreamweaver that the elements you selected represent a repeating region. You can use any of these techniques:

- In the Templates category of the Insert panel, select Repeating Region.

- Choose Insert→Template→Repeating Region.

- Right-click (Control-click) the selection and choose Templates→New Repeating Region from the shortcut menu.

When the New Repeating Region window appears, type a name for the region and then click OK. You return to your template, where the name you gave the region appears in a small blue-green tab above it (see Figure 22-8).

> **NOTE** Dreamweaver lets you name a repeating region even if that name is already in use by an editable region. But don't repeat names—multiple template areas with the same name make Dreamweaver act unpredictably.

FREQUENTLY ASKED QUESTION

Hindered by Highlighting

I'm distracted by the tabs and background colors that Dream-weaver uses to indicate template regions and Library items. How do I get rid of them?

When you use templates or Library items, you see blue-green tabs and yellow backgrounds to indicate, respectively, editable regions and Library items. Although these visual cues don't appear in a web browser, they can get in your way and even alter a page's layout while you work in Dreamweaver. Fortunately, you can change the background color of these items and even turn highlighting off altogether.

Choose Edit→Preferences or press Ctrl+U (⌘-U). In the Preferences category list, click Highlighting. To change the

background color of editable regions, locked regions, and Library items, use the color swatch (see page 151) or type in a hexadecimal color value (see page 155). To remove the highlighting, turn off the Show checkbox next to the appropriate item.

On the other hand, you may prefer to have the highlighting on when you edit but off when you review your work. In that case, you can toggle the highlighting on and off by choosing View→Visual Aids→Invisible Elements or using the keyboard shortcut Shift+Ctrl+I (Shift-⌘-I). This technique has the added benefit of hiding table borders, layer borders, image maps, and other normally invisible elements.

Adding a Repeating Table

Dreamweaver's *repeating table* tool is essentially a shortcut for creating a table with repeating rows. If you had time on your hands, you could achieve the same effect by adding a table to the page, selecting one or more rows, and applying a repeating region to the selection.

To use the repeating table tool:

1. **In the template page, click where you want to insert the table.**

   You can't insert a repeating table into an editable, repeating, or optional region, as you'll see on page 876. You must add it to an empty, locked area of the template.

2. **In the Common category of the Insert panel, select Repeating Table from the Templates menu.**

   Alternatively, you can choose Insert→Template→Repeating Table. Either way, Dreamweaver opens the Insert Repeating Table window (Figure 22-9).

3. **Fill out the basic properties of the table.**

   The top part of the window lets you set up the basic structure of the table: rows, columns, cell padding, cell spacing, width, and border. Basically, it's the same information you provide when you create any table, as described on page 281. You usually start a repeating table with two rows—one for a heading, another to contain the information you want to repeat.

FIGURE 22-9

The Insert Repeating Table dialog box lets you kill three birds with one stone: It adds a table to a page, turns one or more rows into a repeating region, and adds editable regions in each table cell inside the repeating region.

4. **In the "Starting row" box, type the number of the row where the repeating region should begin.**

   Often you'll have just one repeating row: a row of product information, for example. You may want to use the top row for headings, to label the information contained in the rows below. If that's the case, enter *2* at this step, leaving the first row as an uneditable part of the template.

   It's conceivable, however, that you may want each entry to take up *two* rows. The first would list Product Name and Description; the second would contain a cell for a photo and a cell for the price. You set up this effect in this step and the next.

5. **In the "Ending row" box, type the number of the last repeating row.**

   If you want to repeat only a single row, enter the same number you provided in step 4. If you want to create a double repeating row, add 1 to the number you provided in step 4. If you need three rows for each repeating entry, add 2 to the number you entered in step 4.

6. **Type a name for this repeating region.**

   Don't use the same name as another editable template region; you'll run the risk of unpredictable results on template-based pages.

7. **Click OK.**

   Dreamweaver inserts the table into the page. A blue-green tab with the name of the repeating region appears, as do blue-green tabs in each cell of each repeated row. These tabs indicate editable regions—one per cell.

   Since these new editable regions have uninformative names like *EditRegion4*, you may want to rename them. Click the blue-green tab and type a new name in the Properties panel. (But do so *before* you create any pages based on the template—see the Note on page 876.)

To remove a repeating region, select it by clicking the blue-green Repeat tab, and then choose Modify→Templates→Remove Template Markup. A more accurate way to select a repeating region is to click anywhere inside the region and then click <mmtemplate: repeat> in the Tag Selector (see page 7). Note that removing a repeating region doesn't remove any editable regions you added inside the repeating region. To do that, select the tab for the editable region and then press Delete.

If you want to rename a repeating region, heed the Note on page 877.

Working with Repeating Regions

Repeating regions work a bit differently from editable regions. In most cases, a repeating region includes one or more editable regions (which you can edit using the instructions above). However, Dreamweaver provides special controls to let you add, remove, and rearrange repeating entries (see Figure 22-10).

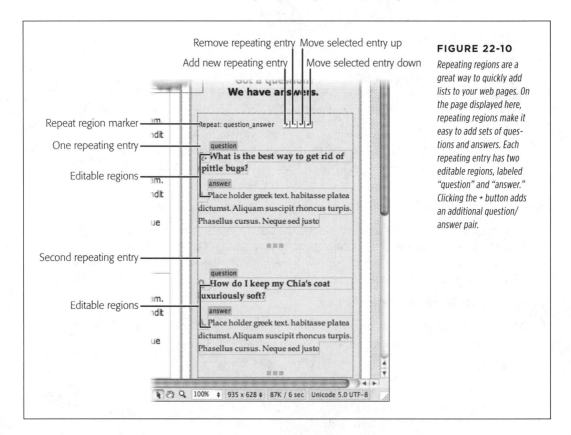

FIGURE 22-10

Repeating regions are a great way to quickly add lists to your web pages. On the page displayed here, repeating regions make it easy to add sets of questions and answers. Each repeating entry has two editable regions, labeled "question" and "answer." Clicking the + button adds an additional question/ answer pair.

These regions let page editors add repeating page elements—like rows of product information in a list of products. To add a repeating entry, click the + sign button to the right of the Repeat region's blue-green tab. You can then edit any editable region within the entry. Click inside an editable region inside a repeating entry, and then click + again to add a new entry *after* it.

Deleting a repeating entry is just as easy; click inside an editable region within the entry you want to delete, and then click the – sign button.

TIP You can create repeating regions that don't have any editable regions—for example, you can create a repeating region with a star in it, and repeat the region several times to indicate the rating for a product. Although you can use the + sign button to repeat such regions, you can't delete those regions using the – sign button. In other words, you're stuck with any extra stars you add. The only workaround is to add an editable region to the repeating region—then Dreamweaver lets you remove the repeating regions.

To rearrange entries in a repeated-region list, click inside an entry's editable region, and then click the up or down arrow to move the entry up or down in the list (to alphabetize it, for example).

■ Using Editable Tag Attributes

An editable region lets you—or, more likely, page-author jockeys—edit the underlying HTML, like a paragraph, image, or an entire table, on new pages they create from your template. But when you create a template for others to use, you may want to limit the authors' editing abilities. For example, you may want to allow budding web designers to change the source of the image used in a banner ad without letting them change the width, height, or class applied to it. Or you might want to let others assign a class to the <body> tag in a template—a move normally forbidden on template-based pages. You can use Dreamweaver's Editable Tag Attribute to specify which tag properties your successors can change.

FREQUENTLY ASKED QUESTION

Editable Regions, Repeating Regions, and Errors

When I try to insert an editable region inside a repeating region, I get the following error: "The selection is already in an editable, repeating, or optional region." What's that about?

This message essentially means you're trying to add a template region where it doesn't belong. It appears most often when you attempt to put a repeating or optional region inside an editable region. That kind of nesting is a no-no; page authors can change anything inside an editable region on template-based pages, and, as such, Dreamweaver can't touch it.

However, you may get this error message seemingly by mistake. For instance, it's perfectly OK to add an editable region inside a repeating region, and it's even OK to add a repeating region inside an optional region, and vice versa.

But say one day you select text inside a repeating region and try to turn it into an editable region—boom, you get an error message. What probably happened is, when you selected the text, Dreamweaver actually selected part of the hidden code used to define a template region (see the box on page 872) and thought you were trying to put an editable region inside it. To avoid confusion, use the Tag Selector to select the page element you want to turn into an editable region. There, click <p> to select the paragraph inside the repeating region. Alternatively, go into Code view (see page 325), and then select whatever part of the code inside the repeating region you want to make editable.

Making an Attribute Editable

To make a tag attribute editable:

1. **Select the tag whose property you want to make editable.**

   Using the Tag Selector (see page 7) is the most accurate way.

2. **Choose Modify→Templates→Make Attribute Editable.**

   Dreamweaver opens the Editable Tag Attributes window (Figure 22-11).

3. **Select an attribute from the menu or add a new attribute with the Add button.**

   The Attribute menu displays only those properties you already set for the selected tag. In other words, if you select an image, you probably see the *src*, *width*, and *height* properties listed. But unless you set the image's alternative text, the *alt* property won't appear.

   To add a property, click + . In the window that appears, type in the appropriate property name. For example, to make the *alt* (alternate text) attribute of a graphic editable, you'd type *alt* here.

FIGURE 22-11

Dreamweaver gives you detailed control over template pages. To make just a single property of a single tag editable on pages based on your template, turn on the "Make attribute editable" checkbox. In this case, you've made the ID attribute of the middle paragraph tag editable, allowing page designers the freedom to apply different CSS styles to that paragraph. Because designers can edit the CSS file, they can create entirely new styles for the paragraph.

4. **Make sure you turn on the "Make attribute editable" checkbox.**

If you decide at some point that you no longer want people to be able to edit this property, you can return to this dialog box and turn off editing, as described in a moment.

5. **Type a name in the Label field.**

What you type here should be a simple description of the editable tag and property, which helps page authors correctly identify editable properties. For example, you could use *Product Image* if you make a particular image's *src* property editable.

6. **Choose a value type from the Type menu.**

Your choices are:

— **Text.** Use this option when a property's value is a word. For example, you can change the image tag's *align* property to "top," "middle," "baseline," and so on. Or, when using Cascading Style Sheets, you could make a tag's *class* property editable to allow page authors to apply a custom style to the tag—*content*, *footer*, and *URL*. The text option lets page authors edit the path to a file, like an image's *src* property or a link's *href* property. That way, using its site-management tools, Dreamweaver keeps track of these paths and updates them whenever you move pages around your site.

— **Color.** If the property requires a color value, like a background hue, select this option. It makes Dreamweaver's color box available to people who build pages from the template.

— **True/False.** You shouldn't use this option. It's intended for Dreamweaver's Optional Regions feature (discussed below) and doesn't apply to HTML properties.

— **Number.** Use this choice for properties that require a numeric value, like an image's Height and Width properties.

7. **Type a placeholder value in the Default box.**

This step is optional. The default value defines the initial value for this property, when people first create a page based on the template. They can then modify this value for that particular page. If you already set this property in the template, its value automatically appears in this box.

8. **Click OK to close the window.**

Dreamweaver adds code to the template page that allows page authors control of the attribute. To set this attribute on pages created from the template, see the instructions on page 884.

If you later decide that you *don't* want a particular tag property to be editable, Dreamweaver can help. Open the template file, select the tag with the editable attribute, and choose Modify→Templates→Make Attribute Editable. In the window that appears, turn off the "Make attribute editable" checkbox (Figure 22-11). Unfortunately, doing so doesn't remove *all* the template code Dreamweaver adds. Even after you turn off editing for an attribute, Dreamweaver leaves behind the info used to control the tag's property. To eliminate *this* code, see the box on page 890.

Changing Properties of Editable Tag Attributes

Unlike editable or repeating regions, you can't readily see an editable tag attribute on template-based pages. Dreamweaver doesn't identify them with blue-green tabs, as it does with editable regions. In fact, nothing in Design view indicates that there are editable tag properties on the page. The only way to find out is to choose Modify→Template Properties to open the Template Properties dialog box (see Figure 22-12).

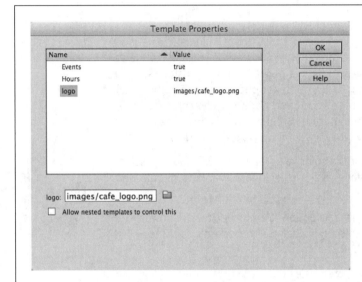

FIGURE 22-12

The Template Properties window lets you control editable tag attributes and other settings for a template's optional regions. Depending on which property you select, the options at the bottom of the window change. In this case, you made the src property of an image tag editable. To change the image tag's src property, click Dreamweaver's familiar "Browse for File" button and select a new graphic.

Dreamweaver displays all the editable tag attributes for this page in this window. In addition, it displays all the elements defined for this page, including optional regions, as discussed in the box on page 890.

To change the value of a template property—in other words, to edit the property of an editable tag—select its name from the list and set its options at the bottom of the window. For example, in the case of color properties, use the color box to pick a color. If the property is a path (like a link's web address or an image's *src* property), click ▤ to browse for the file.

When you finish, click OK.

The Broken-Link Blues

Why aren't the links in my template working?

When you created the link in the template file, you probably typed a path in the Properties panel's Link box—a recipe for heartbreak. Instead, always select the target page for a link by clicking ▣ in the Properties panel, or by pressing Ctrl+L (⌘-L). In other words, when you add links to a template, always link to pages within the site by *browsing* to the desired file.

Dreamweaver saves templates in the Templates folder inside the local root folder; all document-relative links need to be relative to this location. (Absolute links, like those to other websites, aren't a problem. Neither are root-relative links; see page 178 to learn the difference.) The reason you should browse to, rather than type in, your links is so that Dreamweaver can create a proper relative link.

Imagine this situation: You create a template for all the classified ads that appear on your site. You store all the ads for April 2013

inside a series of folders like this: *classifieds→2013→april*, as shown in the site diagram below.

A link from a page in the April folder to the home page would follow the path marked 1 here. So, when you add that link to your template, you'd type the path *../../../index.html*. That makes sense if you're thinking about the page you'll create from the template—but it won't work.

Since Dreamweaver stores templates in the Templates folder, the correct path would be path 2, or *../index.html*. When you create a new page based on the template and save it in the April folder, Dreamweaver, in its wisdom, automatically rewrites all the paths in the page so that the links work correctly.

The beauty of Dreamweaver is that you don't have to understand how all this works. Just remember to use document-relative links in your templates and create them by clicking ▣ in the Properties panel and then identifying the destination page.

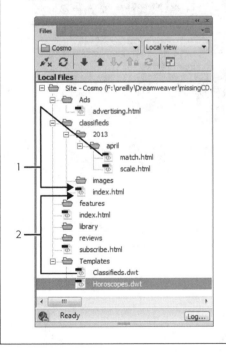

■ Using Optional Regions

Templates provide consistent design. While consistency is generally a good thing, it can also get boring. Furthermore, there may be times when you want the flexibility to include information on some template-based pages but not on others.

Dreamweaver provides a template tool that lets you vary a page's design while maintaining page-to-page consistency: *optional regions*. An optional region is simply part of a template you can hide or display on each template-based page (see Figure 22-13). When a page author creates a new page based on the template, she can turn the region on or off.

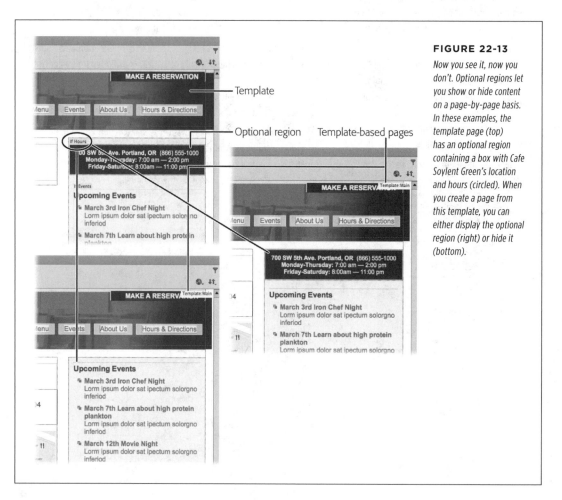

FIGURE 22-13

Now you see it, now you don't. Optional regions let you show or hide content on a page-by-page basis. In these examples, the template page (top) has an optional region containing a box with Cafe Soylent Green's location and hours (circled). When you create a page from this template, you can either display the optional region (right) or hide it (bottom).

Adding an Optional Region

Creating an optional region is a snap. Just select the HTML you want to make optional and do one of the following:

- In the Template category of the Insert panel, select Optional Region.

- Choose Insert→Template→Optional Region.

- Right-click (Control-click) the selection and choose Templates→New Optional Region from the shortcut menu.

In the New Optional Region window, type a name (see Figure 22-14). Make sure you don't use the same name as any other region on the page, and—although Dreamweaver lets you—don't use spaces or other punctuation marks. (Following the rules for naming files as described on page 32 ensures that the optional region works properly.) Click OK to close the window and create the new optional region. Dreamweaver adds a blue-green tab with the word "If," followed by the name you gave the region (Figure 22-13).

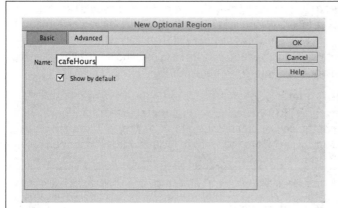

FIGURE 22-14

The Optional Regions feature lets you show or hide content on template-based pages. Turning on the "Show by default" checkbox tells Dreamweaver to display the region when you first create a template-based page. That's a good idea if you want most of your pages to display the content—you'll save yourself the effort of turning on the optional region each time you create a template-based page.

A FEATURE TO AVOID

Nested Templates

Dreamweaver includes yet another template feature called *nested templates*. Nested templates let you create a template with a very basic design so you can create new templates based on that original one, refining the design as you go along. This way, you can have a single template that dictates your core layout and then create specialized templates for particular types of pages or sections of your site.

This might sound like a great way to provide templates that both maintain your site's basic layout via a master template

and let you create pages designed for different purposes. But practically speaking, nested templates are confusing, don't always work, and aren't that necessary. With the flexibility that the optional regions discussed in this chapter give you, you can customize individual template-based pages while using only a single template file.

When it comes to nested templates, you probably want to stay away.

Locking Optional Regions

An optional region can include editable regions, repeating regions, *and* locked regions. For example, if you want to allow a page editor to turn on or off a graphic ("This item on sale!"), insert the graphic outside an editable region, and then make it an optional region as described above. Since anything not inside an editable region is locked, a page editor can't change the graphic or ruin its formatting—he can only make it visible or hidden.

Repeating Optional Regions

An optional region can also include repeating regions. For example, suppose you create a repeating region (see page 876) that lets a page editor add row after row of links to a list of related articles. You could then turn this repeating region into an optional region, as described above, so that if a particular page has no related articles, the page editor could simply hide the entire "related articles" section of the page.

Optional Editable Regions

Dreamweaver's Optional Editable Region command inserts an optional region with an editable region *inside* it. To use it, click in the template where you'd like to add the region, and then choose Insert→Template→Editable Optional Region. (Alternatively, choose this option from the Templates category of the Insert panel.) Dreamweaver displays the New Optional Region window; give it a name, and then follow the steps above for adding an optional region (see page 886).

This technique doesn't offer a lot of control; for example, it's hard to insert HTML *outside* the editable region. So if you want an image or table that's optional but *not* editable, it's usually better to just create the editable region as described on page 867 and turn it (and any other HTML you want to include) into an optional region.

> **NOTE** The Optional Editable Region command doesn't let you name the editable region; it automatically assigns a generic name like *EditRegion7*. You can select the editable region and change its name in the Properties panel, but do so *before* you build any pages based on this template (see the Note on page 868).

Advanced Optional Regions

A basic optional region is a rather simple affair—it either appears or it doesn't. But Dreamweaver's advanced optional regions give you more display options. For example, you may want several different areas of a page to be either hidden or visible at the same time—perhaps an "On Sale Now!" icon at the top of a page *and* a "Call 1-800-SHIZZLE to order" message at the bottom of the page. When one appears, so does the other.

Because these elements sit in different areas of the page, you have to create two optional regions. Fortunately, using Dreamweaver's advanced settings for optional regions, you can easily have a *single* region control the display of one or more areas of a page. Here's how:

1. **Create the first optional region by following the steps on page 887.**

   Give the region a name using the Basic tab of the New Optional Region window (Figure 22-15).

2. **Select the part of the page—an image, paragraph, or table—you want to turn into a second optional region.**

   In this case, you want to make the display of this region dependent on the optional region you added in step 1. If the first region is visible on the page, so is this region.

3. **Choose Optional Region from the Templates category of the Insert panel.**

   Dreamweaver opens the New Optional Region window.

4. **Click the Advanced tab.**

   Dreamweaver displays the optional region's advanced options (Figure 22-15). You want the first optional region to control the display of this new region, so instead of giving this region its own name, simply select the name of the first optional region in the next step.

FIGURE 22-15

The Advanced section of the New Optional Region dialog box lets you more precisely control the display of optional content. You can make the region appear only when another region is visible, or use a special code, called a "template parameter," to create a more complex behavior (see the box on page 890 for more on template parameters). In this case, the selected region appears only when another region—named "cafeHours"—isn't visible (the ! is the programming equivalent of "is not"). Writing code for templates is a complex subject. For more details about template parameters and expressions, see http://tinyurl.com/m3p7xgh.

5. **Turn on the "Use parameter" radio button and then select the name of the first optional region from the drop-down menu.**

   This is what makes the first optional region control the second. If a browser displays the first region, it also displays the second one.

6. **Click OK to close the window and create the new optional region.**

   You can continue adding optional regions this way, with the end result being that the first optional region controls the display of many other areas of the page.

Editing and Removing Optional Regions

After you insert an optional region in your template, you can always return to the New Optional Region dialog box to change the region's name or settings. To edit an optional region, select it using one of these techniques:

- Click the region's blue-green tab in the document window.

- Click anywhere inside the optional region in the document window and then click the <mmtemplate:if> tag in the Tag Selector (see page 7 for details on the Tag Selector).

When you select an optional region, Dreamweaver displays an Edit button in the Properties panel. Click it to reopen the New Optional Region window and change the region's properties.

To remove an optional region, select it and then choose Modify→Templates→Remove Template Markup. Dreamweaver removes most of the code associated with the optional region (but see the box below).

Understanding Template Parameters

When you insert an optional region, Dreamweaver adds special code to the head of the web page. Called a *template parameter*, this code is responsible for showing or hiding an optional region.

In fact, Dreamweaver uses parameters when you make a tag attribute editable, too. A typical parameter for an optional region might look like this:

```
<!-- TemplateParam name="SaleBug"
type="boolean" value="true" -->
```

The <!-- and --> are HTML comment markers that hide this code from web browsers. *TemplateParam* tells Dreamweaver that the comment is actually part of the program's template feature—specifically, a template parameter.

A parameter has three parts: name, type, and value. The name is the name you give the editable region, like SaleBug. The type—"Boolean" above—indicates that this parameter can have a value of only true or false. In this example, the value is "true," which simply means that the optional region called SaleBug is visible. (Don't worry; you don't have to actually edit this code by hand to turn optional regions on and off, as you'll see next.)

In programming jargon, a template parameter is known as a *variable*. In simpler terms, it's just a way to store information that can change. Dreamweaver reacts differently depending on the parameter's value: show the region if the parameter is true; hide it if the parameter's false.

Editable tag attributes also use parameters to store the values you enter for the attributes. For example:

```
<!-- TemplateParam name="PageColor"
type="color" value="#FFFFFF" -->
```

On template-based pages, you can change the value of an editable tag's parameter using the Modify→Template Parameters menu (see page 884).

Unfortunately, when you delete an optional region from a template, or remove the ability to edit a tag attribute, Dreamweaver leaves these parameter tags hanging around in the head of the template document. Keeping in mind that Dreamweaver adds these parameter tags directly before the closing </head> tag, you can find and remove them in Code view.

Hiding and Showing Optional Regions

When you work with template-based pages, you can hide or show optional regions. As with Editable Tag Attributes, you use the Template Properties window to control the regions. On template-based pages, you show or hide an optional region by choosing Modify→Template Properties to open the Template Properties dialog box (see Figure 22-16). Next, select the name of the optional region. To make all the page elements in the region visible, turn on the "Show" checkbox at the bottom of the window. To hide all the optional regions, turn off the checkbox.

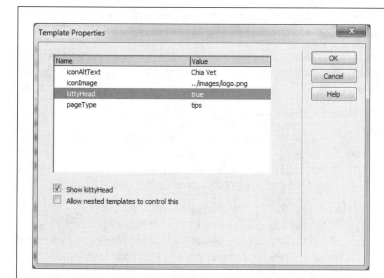

FIGURE 22-16

The Template Properties window displays a page's optional regions as well as its editable tag attributes. Template properties for optional regions—in this example, "kittyHead"—have a value of either true or false. "True" lets people see the contents of the region, while "false" hides it. (You use the "Allow nested templates to control this" option with nested templates—see the box on page 887.)

■ Exporting a Template-Based Site

The good news about Dreamweaver's sophisticated template features is that they let you build complex web pages that are easy to create and update. The not-so-good news is that you need some behind-the-scenes code to achieve this ease of use. Dreamweaver's template features rely on HTML comment tags to identify editable, optional, and repeating page regions, as well as nested templates and editable tag attributes (see the box on page 885).

Although this code is only for Dreamweaver's use and has no effect on how a web browser displays the page, it does increase, by a small amount, the size of your pages. That's probably why Dreamweaver includes a feature that lets you export an entire site into a new folder on your computer *without* any template markup code—to give you the leanest HTML possible. The following steps show you how to save this featherweight site.

NOTE While it's certainly possible to perform this file-slimming procedure, truth be told, it's not really necessary—the code Dreamweaver adds is minimal, so it won't have much effect on the download speed of your site.

1. **Choose Modify→Templates→Export Without Markup.**

   Dreamweaver uses the currently active site, so make sure you select the site you want to export in the Files panel. The Export Site Without Template Markup window appears.

2. **Click the Browse button, and then select a destination folder for the exported site.**

   Select a folder *other* than the current local site folder. You always want to keep the original files in the local folder, since they're the ones that retain the template markup, making future updates possible.

3. **Turn on the export options you want.**

   The Export window includes two options. The first, "Keep template data files," creates an XML file for each template-based page. In other words, when you export the site, there's an HTML page (without any template code) and an XML file (which includes all the template code as well as the page contents).

   Theoretically, you could then go back and choose File→Import→XML into Template to recreate the page, complete with the original template information. But in practice, you probably won't. For one thing, this process creates lots of additional files that you wouldn't want to move to a website. In addition, when you want to edit and update the site, you should use the original files in the site's local folder.

   The "Extract only changed files" option speeds up the process of exporting a large, template-based site by spitting out only those pages you changed since the last export. Unfortunately, it doesn't tell you *which* files it exports until after the fact. So, to make sure you get all those newly exported files to your server, you need to keep track of the files you change by hand.

4. **Click OK to export the site.**

   Dreamweaver goes through each page of the site, stripping out the template code and exporting it to the folder you specified.

   You can then use Dreamweaver's FTP feature to upload the files to your server (see page 812), but you need to create a new site locally and define the folder with the *exported* files as a local root folder.

   Whenever you need to add or update template-based pages, use the original site files, and then export the changed files. You can then switch to the site containing the exported files and transfer the new or updated files to your server. If that sounds like a lot of work, it is. Every change you make means exporting the site again. You're better off just leaving the template code in your pages, or use this command only if you're absolutely sure that you're done using templates for your site.

Tutorial: Building Templates

In this tutorial, you'll create a template for the Cafe Soylent Green website. Then you'll build a page based on that template and enjoy an easy, site-wide update.

> **NOTE** To complete this tutorial, you need to download sample files from this book's Missing CD page at *http://oreilly.com/pub/missingmanuals/dreamweaverccmm2014*. (See the Note on page 37 for details.) The files you'll work on are in the Chapter22 folder, and the finished project, for comparison, is in the Chapter22_complete folder.

Once you download the tutorial files and open Dreamweaver, set up a new site as described on page 23. In a nutshell, choose Site→New Site. In the Site Setup window, type *Templates* into the Site Name box, click ▣ next to the Local Site Folder box, navigate to and select the Chapter22 folder inside the MM_DWCC folder, and then click Choose (Select). Finally, click OK.

Creating a Template

1. **Open the Files panel by pressing F8 (Shift-⌘-F).**

   Of course, if it was already open, you just closed it. Press F8 (Shift-⌘-F) again.

2. **In the Files panel, find and double-click the page *design.html*.**

   It's usually easier to create a template from an existing web page rather than from scratch. For the purpose of getting to bed before midnight tonight, pretend that you just designed this beautiful page.

3. **Choose File→Save As Template.**

   Dreamweaver opens the Save As Template dialog box (see Figure 22-17).

FIGURE 22-17

The first step in creating a template from a regular web page is to choose File→Save As Template. You only need to provide a name for the new template, but a brief description can help when you have lots of templates in a site; the description appears in the New Document window when you create a new template-based page.

4. **In the Description box, type *main cafe template.***

This description appears in the New Template window when you create a page based on the template.

5. **In the "Save as" box, name the template *Main,* and then click Save. In the Update Links window, click Yes.**

Behind the scenes, Dreamweaver creates a new folder—Templates—in the site's root folder and saves the file as *Main.dwt* inside it. A new template is born. You can see it in the newly created Templates folder in the Files panel, and in the Templates page of the Assets panel (see the Note below).

The template is a model for other pages, and although those other pages will be *based* on this page, they won't be identical. The next step is to identify the areas of the design you want to change from page to page—the editable regions, in other words.

NOTE Templates don't always immediately show up in the Templates category of the Assets panel (Window→Assets). Sometimes you need to click the Refresh Site List button (the circular arrow in the bottom-right of the Assets panel) to see a newly added template.

6. **Click inside the word "Headline" and choose Edit→Select All.**

The headline and the paragraph of text below it live inside a <div> tag on this page. Choosing Select All with the cursor inside a <div> selects everything inside the <div>, but not the <div> tag itself. In this case, you want to put content inside this <div> when you create new pages based on this template, so you'll turn the current selection into an editable region.

7. **Choose Insert→Template→Editable Region.**

Alternatively, from the Insert panel's Common category, go to the Templates menu and choose Editable Region, or just press Alt+Ctrl+V (Option-⌘-V).

Dreamweaver displays the New Editable Region dialog box.

8. **Type *Content,* and then click OK.**

A small blue-green tab labeled "Content" appears above the headline (see Figure 22-18). You just added one editable region—the most basic type of template region. You'll add other types of template regions later, but build a few template-based pages first.

9. **Choose File→Save, and then File→Close.**

Congratulations! You just created your first template.

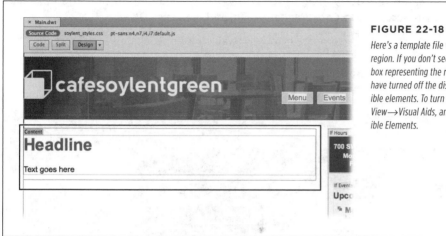

FIGURE 22-18

Here's a template file with an editable region. If you don't see the blue-green box representing the region, you may have turned off the display of invisible elements. To turn them on, choose View→Visual Aids, and then click Invisible Elements.

Creating a Page Based on a Template

Now it's time to get down to business and build some web pages, which you do in Design view:

1. **Choose File→New.**

   Dreamweaver opens the New Document window.

2. **On the window's far left side, click Site Templates.**

   A list of the sites you've defined appears in the column labeled "Sites."

3. **Make sure you have the site you set up for this tutorial (Templates) selected in the Sites column.**

   From the list of templates to the right, select Main, and then make sure you have the "Update page when template changes" checkbox (on the right of the window) turned on.

   If you don't turn on the "Update page" checkbox, the new page doesn't link to the template, and therefore won't update when you make changes to the template.

4. **Click Create.**

   Lo, a new web page appears—one that looks (almost) exactly like the template (Figure 22-19).

5. **Choose File→Save. Click the Site Root button and save the file as *index. html* in the root folder.**

   To indicate that it's your template's offspring, the document window displays a yellow tab in the upper-right corner that reads "Template:Main." Dreamweaver indicates your editable region with a blue-green tab. Now it's time to add some content.

6. **Go to Modify→Page Properties→Title/Encoding. In the Title box, type *Welcome to Cafe Soylent Green*, and then click OK.**

Several basic properties for your web page appear in the Page Properties window. "Title" is at the top of the list. The title you give your web page appears in most browsers on the page tab.

FIGURE 22-19

In template-based pages, blue-green tabs identify editable areas, and the yellow tab at the top right (circled) lists the template's name.

7. **Choose File→Open. In the Open window, click the Site Root button, and then double-click the filename *text-index.html*.**

You can also open this file by double-clicking its name in the Files panel. The *text-index.html* page contains the content for the site's home page. It's just a matter of copying and pasting the text from one page to the other.

8. **Click the <body> tag in the Tag Selector (bottom left of the document window) to select all the page contents, and then choose Edit→Copy.**

Clicking the <body> tag is the best way to select an entire page's worth of content. As you read in step 6 on page 894, just clicking into a page and choosing Edit→Select All doesn't necessarily select everything on the page; if the cursor were inside a <div> tag, for example, you'd select only the contents inside that <div>.

9. **At the top of the document window, click the *index.html* tab to switch to the template-based page. Click the blue-green tab labeled "Content" (just above the headline).**

Remember that you can add content only to an editable region. If you point to the banner, navigation buttons, or footer areas of the page, you see a black "forbidden" symbol. You can't insert the cursor anywhere but inside an editable region. Clicking the blue-green tab selects everything inside that region. Since it's just placeholder text anyway, you'll replace it with the content you just copied.

10. **Choose Edit→Paste.**

Dreamweaver replaces the dummy text with the new content. Thanks to the power of CSS, Dreamweaver instantly formats the plain-looking HTML you just pasted (if only web design were so simple!). Of course, on your own site, you'd probably copy and paste text from an email message or a Word document. Then you'd use Dreamweaver's tools to create headlines, paragraphs, links, and bulleted lists, and then add CSS to style the page.

You're done with this page!

11. **Save and close the file. (You can close *text-index.html*, too—you won't be using it again.)**

Time to create another page...well, actually, four more pages! You could repeat steps 1–9 above to create the new pages, but if you're starting off with a simple HTML page that you'd like to associate with a template, there's a better way.

12. **Open the file *about.html*. Choose Modify→Templates→Apply Template to Page.**

Dreamweaver opens the Select Template window. Since there's only a single template for this site, the choice isn't hard.

13. **Choose Main and then press Select.**

Dreamweaver opens the Inconsistent Region Names window (see Figure 22-20). Since you're starting with an HTML file, you need to tell Dreamweaver where on the template-based page to move this existing content. In general, you simply tell Dreamweaver to place the <body> tag contents of the existing page into an editable region of the template-based page, and, if necessary, the <head> content of the existing page (which includes its title, if any) into the head of the gestating page.

14. **Select "Document body" and then choose "Content" from the "Move content to new region" menu.**

This pastes the page's content into the editable "Content" region from the template.

15. **Go to Modify→Page Properties→Title/Encoding. In the Title box, type** *About Cafe Soylent Green,* **and then click OK.**

You need to do something similar for your other site pages.

16. **Repeat steps 12–14 for the** *events.html, menu.html, hours.html,* **and** *reservation.html* **files. Add appropriate titles to each page. Choose File→Save All to save all the new pages, and then choose File→Close All to close all the open files.**

Now you'll turn to an advanced template feature, optional regions.

FIGURE 22-20

The oddly named Inconsistent Region Names dialog box lets you tell Dreamweaver where, in a templates' defined regions, to put the page elements you're pasting. You do that by matching the template regions (on the left) with the existing page elements (on the right).

Creating and Using Optional Regions

You may have noticed that two of the pages you just created—*hours.html* and *events.html*—have the same content in the right sidebar. While it's useful to display the hours and location on other pages, it's a bit weird to duplicate that information on the *hours.html* page. The same is true for the *events.html* page and the events listing in the sidebar. Fortunately, using optional regions, you can hide or show that information on a page-by-page basis.

1. **Return to Dreamweaver. In the Assets panel (Window→Assets), click the Templates button, and then double-click the Main template to open it.**

Dreamweaver opens the original template, *Main.dwt.* You can also open the template by double-clicking its name inside the Templates folder in the Files panel.

You'll turn the box with the location and hours in it into an optional region.

2. **Click inside the dark-green box in the sidebar on the right. In the Tag Selector in the bottom left of the document window, click "<div>.hours" to select the entire <div> tag.**

   Alternatively, you could click inside that <div> and choose Edit→Select All twice, the first time to select the contents of the <div>, and the second to select the <div> tag itself.

3. **Choose Insert→Template→Optional Region.**

   You can also use the Template menu on the Insert panel. Either way, Dreamweaver opens the New Optional Region window.

4. **Type *Hours* in the Name box and then click OK.**

   You'll turn the events listing into an optional region as well.

5. **Click at the beginning of the "Upcoming Events" headline and then drag down until you select the headline and all three bulleted items.**

   The events listings aren't contained in their own <div> tag; they're just made up of a headline followed by a bulleted list.

6. **Choose Insert→Template→Optional Region. In the New Optional Region window, type *Events* in the Name box, and then click OK.**

   The template should look like the one in Figure 22-21.

FIGURE 22-21

Dreamweaver identifies optional regions with a blue-green tab and the word "If." In this case, there are two optional regions (circled), one named Hours, the other Events. You can show or hide either region on a page-by-page basis.

7. **Choose File→Save.**

   Dreamweaver opens the Update Template Files window. Whenever you update a template, Dreamweaver updates any pages you built using that template.

8. **Click the Update button, and when Dreamweaver completes the update, click Close.**

   Now you'll hide the hours box on the *hours.html* page.

9. **Open the file *hours.html*, and then choose Modify→Template Properties.**

   Dreamweaver opens the Template Properties window (Figure 22-22).

10. **Select Hours, turn off the Show Hours checkbox at the bottom of the window, and then click OK.**

    The Template Properties window closes and the hours/location box in the sidebar disappears. You bring the box back by opening the Template Properties window again, selecting Hours, and then turning on the Show Hours checkbox.

11. **Open the file *events.html*. Choose Modify→Template Properties. Select Events and then turn off the Show Events checkbox at the bottom of the window. Click OK.**

    The Template Properties window closes and the events listing in the sidebar disappears.

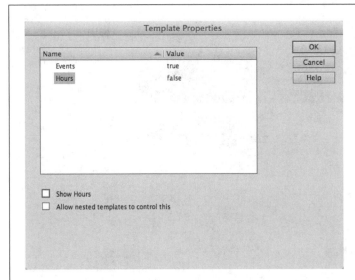

FIGURE 22-22

The Template Properties window does double duty. It lets you hide or show optional regions, and lets you set values for editable tag attributes. The "Allow nested templates to control this" option applies only to nested templates, which, as mentioned in the box on page 887, you should avoid.

12. **Choose File→Save All to save all the new pages, and then choose File→Close All to close all the open files.**

Now you'll see the real power of Dreamweaver templates.

Updating a Template

Remember, the pages you just created maintain a link to the original template. In this final phase of the tutorial, you're going to make a few changes to that template.

1. **Return to Dreamweaver. In the Assets panel, click the Templates button, and then double-click *Main.dwt*. (You can also open the file by double-clicking its name inside the Templates folder in the Files panel.)**

   Dreamweaver opens the original template, *Main.dwt*. You need to change a couple of things. First, you should update the copyright notice.

2. **In the footer, locate "Copyright 2022" and change it to the current year.**

   Change the year to 2014 or whatever the current year happens to be. You'll also add a link here.

3. **On the same line in the footer, select the text "Cosmopolitan Farmer." In the Properties panel's Link box, type *http://www.cosmofarmer.com*.**

   There's a new food special that you should add to the sidebar.

4. **In the sidebar, click at the end of the last paragraph and then press Enter (Return).**

   You want to add an image and some text.

5. **Choose Insert→Image→Image. In the Select Image Source window, navigate to the *images* folder and then double-click *special3.jpg* to insert the image.**

   The picture appears in your page.

6. **With the image still selected, type *Grilled Mozzarella* in the "Alternate text" box. Press the right arrow key to deselect the image and move the cursor to the right, and then type *Yummy grilled mozzarella*.**

   You could add more specials, update the events listing, and change the banner and navigation bar. In short, Dreamweaver will pass on any changes you make to the non-editable areas of the template to the pages you built using that template. Time to see the magic happen.

7. **Choose File→Save.**

   Dreamweaver displays the Update Template Files window. This is the moment of truth.

8. **Click Update.**

   Dreamweaver opens the Update Pages dialog box and updates the appropriate web pages, correcting the copyright year and adding the link and the new cafe special. In addition to making the changes, Dreamweaver lists them so you know which pages have changed.

NOTE If, after you update pages based on a template, you don't see the number of updated pages listed in the Update Pages window, turn on the Show Log checkbox in the lower-left corner of the Update Pages window.

9. **Click Close to close the Update Pages dialog box. Finally, open the template-based files you just created (*index.html*, *about.html*, and so on).**

   Notice that Dreamweaver updated the copyright notice and sidebar on all those pages (see Figure 22-23). That happened because you changed the template on which all those pages were genetically linked. Ah, the power!

FIGURE 22-23

Here's the finished tutorial page, complete with an editable region (content) and optional regions (hours and events).

Customizing Dreamweaver

W hether you're a hard-core HTML jockey who prefers to be knee-deep in
Code view or a visually oriented, drag-and-drop type who never strays
from Design view, Dreamweaver lets you work the way you want.

By now you're probably using the Favorites tab on the Insert panel to store your most
frequently used objects, as discussed on page 13. But don't stop there. Dreamweaver
lets you add, customize, and share keyboard shortcuts, too, giving you a simple way
to tailor the program to your needs. And if that's not a big enough efficiency boost,
you can add features that even Adobe's engineers never imagined, from productivity
add-ons like CSS Menu systems (page 202) to advanced server behaviors that help
power complete e-commerce sites. Dreamweaver lets amateur and professional
programmers alike write new features using HTML, JavaScript, and XML (Extensible
Markup Language). You can explore hundreds of these extras, called *add-ons*, right
from within Dreamweaver. And best of all, you can try many of them for free.

Keyboard Shortcuts

As you work in Dreamweaver, you'll use the same keyboard shortcuts and travel
to the same palettes and menus time and again. Perhaps you have a lot of HTML5
videos on your site, and you constantly use keyboard shortcuts to insert them. You
may find that, after the thousandth time, Shift+Alt+Ctrl+V (Shift-Option-⌘-V) hurts
your pinkie and uses too many keys to be truly efficient. On the other hand, the
things you do all the time—like adding rollover images or inserting text boxes into
forms—have no shortcuts at all, so you have no choice but to go to a menu.

To speed up your work and save your tendons, you can define or redefine shortcuts for most Dreamweaver commands using the program's keyboard shortcut editor.

Dreamweaver's Stock Shortcuts

Dreamweaver includes three sets of shortcuts. It's easy to switch among them, a useful feature when you share your computer with someone who likes a different set of shortcuts from the one you like.

If you opt for a set of shortcuts, you'll most likely never need to switch from the standard one, but here are your options:

- **Dreamweaver Standard**. When you first fire up Dreamweaver, the program turns on this set of shortcuts. It's the one available since Dreamweaver 8.

- **Dreamweaver MX 2004**. Some shortcuts have changed since Dreamweaver MX 2004—for example, Shift+F5 now opens the tag editor, whereas Ctrl+F5 did so in MX 2004. But the changes are so minor that you don't really need to use this set.

- **HomeSite**. Likewise, if you're adept at the Windows HTML text editor HomeSite, you may want to use its keyboard shortcuts. Don't remember HomeSite? That's because it hasn't been available for years, so you probably won't ever need this.

Choose a set of shortcuts by going to Edit→Keyboard Shortcuts (Dreamweaver→ Keyboard Shortcuts). Be patient; the sets can take some time to load. When you see the dialog box pictured in Figure 23-1, you can switch sets by choosing a new one from the Current Set drop-down menu.

Make Your Own Set of Shortcuts

But what if you want a set of shortcuts that *combines* Dreamweaver's timesavers with those from BBEdit? Or you're a radical individualist who wants to remap *every* command to keys of your liking? No problem; you can create your own set of shortcuts. Since Dreamweaver doesn't let you change the key assignments in any of its three standard shortcut sets, you should make a copy of one of them to use as the basis for your own set.

Choose Edit→Keyboard Shortcuts (Dreamweaver→Keyboard Shortcuts). In the Keyboard Shortcuts window, use the Current Set drop-down menu to choose the set you want to copy, and then click the Duplicate Set button, 🗐. Dreamweaver asks you to name the new set; do so, and then click OK.

You can delete or rename any set you create—once you figure out that ⓪ is the Rename Set button. The 🗑 button, of course, lets you delete a set.

> **NOTE** Dreamweaver lets you delete the three main keyboard shortcut sets. If you want one of them back, don't worry. The file isn't gone; you just need to edit a file called *mm_deleted_files.xml* in your Dreamweaver configuration folder. Remove the line that lists the shortcut set you want to get back and save the file. Then quit and restart Dreamweaver. (Note that each Dreamweaver account holder has his own configuration folder. See the box on page 907 for more.)

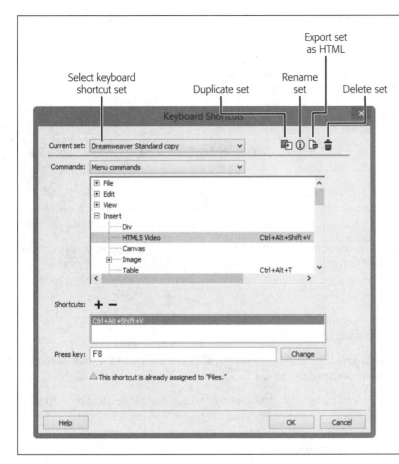

FIGURE 23-1

The Keyboard Shortcuts window lets you select or duplicate a set of Dreamweaver's stock shortcuts, as well as add or remove your own timesavers, for every menu item in the program. (You can also create keyboard shortcuts for snippets; see Chapter 21.) If you try to create a shortcut that another command already uses, Dreamweaver warns you. If you want, you can ignore the warning and reassign the keys to the new command.

Changing Keyboard Shortcuts

Once you duplicate a set of timesavers, you can select any command in the set and edit its shortcut. Start by choosing Edit→Keyboard Shortcuts (Dreamweaver→Keyboard Shortcuts) to open the Shortcuts window, and then do the following:

1. **From the Commands drop-down menu, choose the command type.**

   Dreamweaver organizes shortcuts into seven (Windows) or four (Macintosh) categories ("Menu commands," "Code editing commands," and so on), which doesn't always make sense. For example, the Copy and Paste commands appear in the "Code editing" category, even though you use them at least as frequently in Design view. In addition, quite a few commands appear in multiple categories (though you only need to change a keyboard shortcut once to change it across all categories).

Browse the types of commands to see which have (or could have) keyboard shortcuts:

— Menu commands, such as Insert→HTML5 Video, are those that appear in Dreamweaver's menus.

— You might use the code editing commands when you edit HTML. However, you could just as easily use them in Design view—they include Cut, Paste, and "Move to Top of Page," to name a few.

— Document editing commands let you select text and objects on a page, as well as preview a page in a browser.

— The Files panel options (Windows only) show up when you right-click a file in the Files panel.

— Site panel commands (Windows only) include those available from the contextual menu at the top right of the Files panel, such as Site→New Site. (On the Mac, many of these commands are in the "Menu commands" set.)

— The site window commands (Windows only) are an odd assortment of actions that let you close a window, quit Dreamweaver, or cancel an FTP session. On the Mac, you'll find these commands in the "Document editing" group.

— Snippets are pieces of reusable code you select from the Snippets panel, as discussed in Chapter 21.

2. **In the list below the Commands menu, click the command whose keyboard shortcut you want to change.**

   You'll find menu commands grouped by name. Commands you see in the File drop-down menu, like Open and Save, fall under File. Click ⊞ (Windows) or ▶ (Mac) next to a menu name to display its commands. For example, Figure 23-1 shows the Insert menu expanded.

   If the command already has a keyboard shortcut, it appears in the right-hand column. If it doesn't, you see an empty space.

3. **Click inside the "Press key" box, and then press the keys you want to use as the shortcut.**

   Unless you assign the shortcut to an F-key or the Esc key, you must begin your shortcut with the Ctrl key (⌘ key). For example, you can assign a shortcut to the F8 key, but not to the letter R; you'd have to press Ctrl+R (⌘-R) instead.

NOTE Your operating system may use some of its own keyboard shortcuts, and you can't assign any of your OS shortcuts to Dreamweaver. For example, in Windows, Ctrl+Esc opens Windows' Start menu, while on Macs, F12 increases the sound volume. If you try to reassign an operating system shortcut to Dreamweaver, your computer won't let you.

Of course, many commands already have shortcuts. If you choose an already-assigned key combination, Dreamweaver tells you which command has dibs. You can pick a different key combination, or click the Change button to reassign the existing shortcut to your command, leaving the original command without a shortcut.

4. **Click Change.**

Dreamweaver saves the new shortcut in your custom set.

Repeat the steps above to assign other keystrokes. When you finish, click OK.

FREQUENTLY ASKED QUESTION

Sharing Shortcuts

How do I share my keyboard shortcuts with other people?

If you work on two computers—for example, a desktop in your office and a laptop at home—you can synchronize your keyboard shortcuts so that they're identical. You do that through the Creative Cloud. First, set things up in your Preferences window. Choose Edit→Preferences (Dreamweaver→Preferences), and then click Sync Settings. In the "Settings to Sync" section, turn on the Keyboard Shortcuts checkbox. When you open Dreamweaver on a different computer but with the same user account, click the Sync Settings gear in the upper-right corner.

Sharing your shortcuts with someone else takes a little more work, as explained next.

Dreamweaver stores your keyboard shortcuts as XML files, but finding them can be tricky. They're in different locations depending on your operating system. Each keyboard set's filename ends with the extension .xml. For example, if you create a new set of shortcuts named "My Shortcuts," the XML filename is *My Shortcuts.xml*.

Windows stores your keyboard shortcuts in *C:\Users\[User Name]\AppData\Roaming\Adobe\Dreamweaver CC 2014.1*

en_US\Configuration\Menus\Custom Sets. Note that Windows normally hides these files from you; see the Note on page 908 to get around this little problem.

Mac OS X Mavericks [version 10.9] squirrels these files away in *[User Name]→Library→Application Support→Adobe→Dreamweaver CC 2014.1→en_US→Configuration→Menus→Custom Sets*. Since Mac OS X Lion [version 10.7] Apple has been hiding your Library folder from view, but see the Note on page 908 to flush it out.

Depending on your language choice in Dreamweaver, you might see something other than "en_US" (which stands for English) in the path name, such as "de_DE" for German, or "ja_JP" for Japanese.

You can copy these files and place them in the Custom Sets folder on other computers. Once you do, web designers on those machines can use the Keyboard Shortcuts window (Edit→Keyboard Shortcuts [Dreamweaver→Keyboard Shortcuts]) to select the new set, just as though you created it in that copy of Dreamweaver.

What if a command you use often doesn't have a shortcut at all? No problem; you can create one. As a matter of fact, Dreamweaver lets you assign *two* keyboard shortcuts to every command—say, one for you, and one for your left-handed spouse.

Here's how to give a command a first or additional shortcut:

1. **Choose the command.**

Follow the first two steps of the preceding instructions.

2. **Click + next to the word "Shortcuts."**

   Your cursor automatically pops into the "Press key" field.

3. **Press the keys for the shortcut, and then click Change.**

   Repeat these steps to assign another set of keystrokes; when you finish, click OK.

Deleting shortcuts is just as easy. Simply click the command in the list, and then click − next to Shortcuts.

> **NOTE** Windows normally hides certain files, such as important system files, from sight. This includes the configuration folder discussed on page 907. To open these folders, you need to make hidden files visible. Here are the steps for Windows 8: In Windows Explorer's ribbon, choose File→View→Show/Hide→Hidden Names. For more details see *http://tinyurl.com/win8hiddenfiles*. It's a bit more complicated to show hidden files in Windows 7. You need to change the folder options in the Control Panel's Appearance and Personalization section. You'll find the details at *http://tinyurl.com/win7hiddenfiles*.

Create a Shortcut Cheat Sheet

Unless your brain is equipped with a 2-terabyte hard drive, you'll probably find it hard to remember all of Dreamweaver's keyboard shortcuts.

Fortunately, you can print out a cheat sheet. Find the handy "Export Set as HTML" button at the top of the Shortcuts window (labeled with the odd icon 📄; see Figure 23-1). Click it to name and save a simple HTML page listing all the commands and keyboard shortcuts for the currently selected command set. Once you save the file, print it out or use it as an online reference—it's a great way to keep a record of your shortcuts for yourself or a team of designers.

> **NOTE** If you're a Mac OS X Lion owner, some versions of the operating system let you view application preferences, plug-ins, and data in your Library folder. But OS X Lion (version 10.7) and Mountain Lion (version 10.8) hide the Library folder from you. Here's how you uncover it: In the Finder, click Go to see a list of destinations (Documents, Desktop, and so on). Hold down the Option key, and the Library folder pops up in the list. Then click Library→Application Support→Adobe→Dreamweaver CC 2014.1→en_US→Configuration.

■ Dreamweaver Add-Ons

While keyboard shortcuts give you an easy way to use common commands, they're not much help if the command you want doesn't exist. Suppose, for example, you use Dreamweaver's Open Browser Window behavior (page 641) to load a new web page into a window that measures exactly 200 x 300 pixels. What if you want to center the window in the middle of your visitor's monitor? Dreamweaver's Open Browser Window behavior doesn't do that, so what's a web designer to do? You could go to the Adobe site and request the new feature (*http://tinyurl.com/jbmlm*)

in hopes that the bustling team of programmers will add it to the next version of the program. But you'd have to wait—and there's no guarantee that it'd be there.

Instead, legions of hard-core Dreamweaver fans and third-party app developers have taken this wish-list feature into their own hands. As it turns out, amateur (and pro) programmers can enhance Dreamweaver relatively easily by writing new feature modules using the basic languages of the Web: HTML, JavaScript, and XML. (In fact, HTML forms, JavaScript programs, and XML documents constitute much of the Dreamweaver program's code. The objects in the Insert panel, for example, are actually HTML pages stored within Dreamweaver's configuration folder, and Adobe wrote all of Dreamweaver's menus as an XML file.)

Because of this "open architecture," you can add new functions and commands— called *add-ons*—to Dreamweaver by downloading and installing the work of one of these programmers.

Add-ons take many forms, and they change how Dreamweaver works in a variety of ways. You can add an icon to the Insert panel, for example, a behavior to the Behaviors panel, or a command in the Commands menu. You might even add an entirely new floating window, like the Properties panel, to alter some aspect of your pages.

Best of all, while you might need some programming ability to *create* add-ons, you don't need any to *use* them. You can download and install hundreds of add-ons, many for free. In addition, you can find many sophisticated add-ons, like those for creating e-commerce sites, commercially available.

NOTE In earlier versions of Dreamweaver, Adobe called add-ons "extensions." The new name and method for distributing add-ons arrived with Dreamweaver CC 2014. If you used extensions with Adobe products in the past, the methods for using add-ons will feel familiar.

Browsing for and Installing Add-Ons

The Adobe Add-ons website hosts a large collection of free and commercial add-ons for Dreamweaver and other Creative Cloud applications. Although some come from Adobe itself, most come from an army of talented Dreamweaver fans and third-party program developers. Because add-ons are such an important part of Dreamweaver, there's a shortcut in the Window menu (Window→Browse Add-ons) that takes you right to the Adobe Add-ons site. When you find an add-on you need, a few clicks of a button let you download and install it so that it becomes a part of Dreamweaver.

1. **In Dreamweaver, choose Window→Browse Add-ons.**

   Your browser opens the Adobe Add-ons page, with the Dreamweaver category automatically selected (see Figure 23-2). Dreamweaver automatically signs you into the Add-ons store using your Adobe Creative Cloud credentials.

2. **Browse the extensions.**

   Click the All button near the top of the panel to see the entire add-on library. Likewise, click Paid or Free to narrow the list to just those types of add-ons.

There are several pages of add-ons for Dreamweaver, so you may want to use the "Sort by" menu to move the newest, most popular, or cheapest add-ons to the top of the list. If you know the name of the add-on you want, type it in the Search box in the top-right corner.

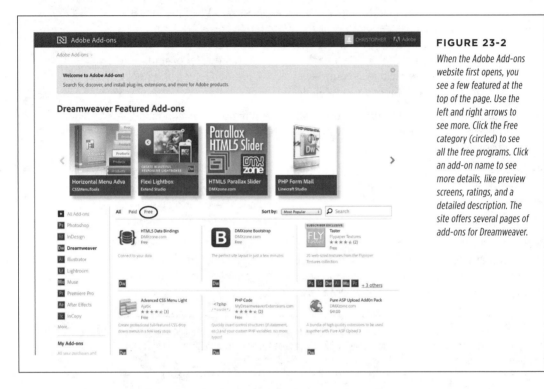

FIGURE 23-2

When the Adobe Add-ons website first opens, you see a few featured at the top of the page. Use the left and right arrows to see more. Click the Free category (circled) to see all the free programs. Click an add-on name to see more details, like preview screens, ratings, and a detailed description. The site offers several pages of add-ons for Dreamweaver.

3. **Click an add-on name to learn more about it.**

    Once you do, the site rewards you with a page devoted to that particular add-on, as shown in Figure 23-3. Under its name, you see a blue button that lists the price for the add-on. If the web gods are smiling on you, it will say Free. Under that, the site displays details like the add-on's version number, publication date, and file size. The top-right section of the page tells you about the program's compatibility. You can check to make sure it works with Windows or Mac computers, or your specific version of Dreamweaver.

    Below that, you find a list of other add-ons from the same source. Most folks call add-on creators "developers" so that's the term the rest of this chapter will use. In any case, the list of other add-ons from a developer are often helpful because you're likely to find related products. For example, a developer may focus on e-commerce, so she offers several online shopping cart add-ons designed for different needs.

4. **Click either the Free or price button, and then, when you see the End-User License Agreement, click "Accept and Continue."**

The agreement is between you and the add-on developer, so its wording is likely to vary from one extension to another. After you accept the license agreement, your path varies depending on whether the add-on is free or costs money. If it's free, Adobe's Creative Cloud tool downloads the extension and installs it. The formerly blue button with the word "Free" on it changes to a silver button with the words "View My Add-ons." You can jump to step 6.

If there's a price for your add-on, there's the little matter of forking over some money, as explained in the next step.

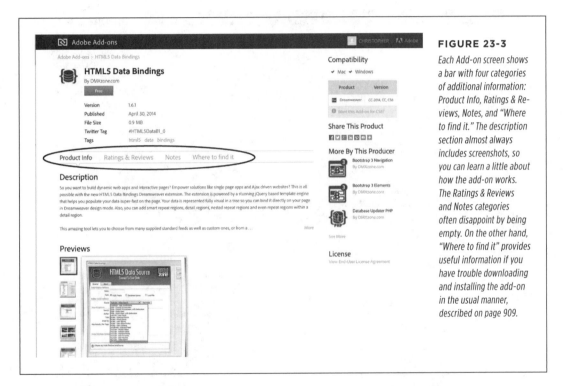

FIGURE 23-3

Each Add-on screen shows a bar with four categories of additional information: Product Info, Ratings & Reviews, Notes, and "Where to find it." The description section almost always includes screenshots, so you can learn a little about how the add-on works. The Ratings & Reviews and Notes categories often disappoint by being empty. On the other hand, "Where to find it" provides useful information if you have trouble downloading and installing the add-on in the usual manner, described on page 909.

5. **For "pay to play" add-ons, choose a payment method, provide your billing info, and then click Complete Order. When you see your receipt, click Continue.**

The Add-ons site accepts payment by PayPal or credit card. If you have an Amazon account (and who doesn't?), you can pay for add-ons through Amazon, too. In any case, you know the drill—fill in your name, number, security code, and other pertinent details. At the end of the process, the site displays your receipt. When you click Continue, you return to the page for the add-on you just purchased. The button that previously showed the price is silver and now reads View My Add-ons.

6. **Click View My Add-ons.**

   You see your own personal My Add-ons page listing all the add-ons you installed (Figure 23-4). Check the "Where to find it" section of the add-on you just installed to see instructions. For example, you may learn that you need to restart Dreamweaver to get the command for the add-on to appear in a specific Dreamweaver menu, like Commands.

7. **Quit Dreamweaver and then restart it.**

   Most add-ons won't work until you quit and then restart Dreamweaver.

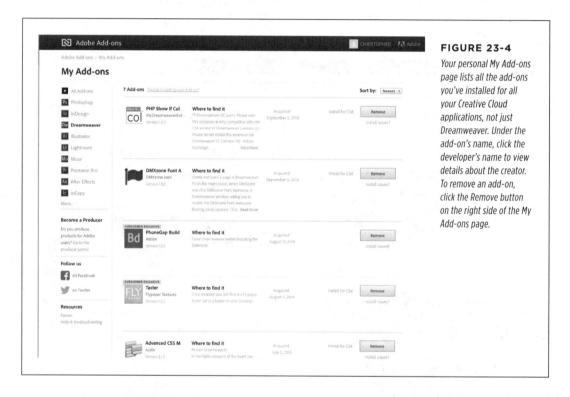

FIGURE 23-4

Your personal My Add-ons page lists all the add-ons you've installed for all your Creative Cloud applications, not just Dreamweaver. Under the add-on's name, click the developer's name to view details about the creator. To remove an add-on, click the Remove button on the right side of the My Add-ons page.

TIP If you need more details on how to work with a particular add-on, your best bet is to visit the developer's website. Unfortunately, web addresses for the developers are scarce on the add-ons site. It's almost as if Adobe doesn't want to let you go. To actually get to the developer's site, you may need to do a web search on her name.

Building and Selling Your Own Add-Ons

The Adobe Add-ons site is a great resource for helper programs, but what if you can't find an extension that suits your needs? One option is to create your own.

Writing add-ons requires in-depth knowledge of HTML and JavaScript, and it's beyond the scope of this book. But when you create a command that lets you complete a weekly task in a fraction of the time it previously took, the effort may just be worth it. For details on writing your own extensions, visit the Dreamweaver Exchange Producer Portal at *https://www.adobeexchange.com/producer*.

■ Downloading and Installing Extensions

Before there were add-ons, there were extensions. If you don't find what you need at the Adobe Add-ons website, you may find it at one of the sites listed below or someplace else on the Web in the form of an extension. Once you find a great extension, download it. You can save the file anywhere on your computer, but you may want to create a special folder for it. That way, if you ever need to reinstall Dreamweaver, you can quickly find and add your collection of extensions.

Extension filenames end with .zxp, the special file format that works with Adobe's Extension Manager, the helper program that actually installs the extension. (Note that the Extension Manager no longer works with older Extension files, ones that end with .mxp.)

Extension Sources

Adobe prefers that you use add-ons rather than extensions with Dreamweaver, so you're on your own in the search for an extension. If you do a web search using the keywords "Dreamweaver" and "extension," you're sure to find some sources. Here's a sampling to get you started:

- **WebAssist** (*www.webassist.com*) is one of the largest and most professional extension-development companies for Dreamweaver. It offers a variety of high-quality extensions, including a few for free.

- **Project Seven** (*www.projectseven.com*) offers both free and excellent commercial extensions that let you create animated HTML and CSS menus, scrolling text, CSS-based page layouts, photo galleries, and more.

- **Trent Pastrana** (*www.fourlevel.com*) sells extensions that build photo galleries, display whiz-bang effects (like menus that slide onto a page), and move text up and down (or left and right) across a page. He also provides several free extensions.

- **Trio Solutions** (*http://tinyurl.com/6k8q2zg*) sells lots of inexpensive extensions that let you add CSS-style calendars, Flash music players, and much more.

- **Hot Dreamweaver** (*www.hotdreamweaver.com*) sells extensions for server-side needs, like sending form submissions as emails, adding CAPTCHAs (those little hard-to-read pictures of letters and numbers you have to type into a form to prove you're a human), and uploading files to a web server.

- **DMXzone** (*www.dmxzone.com/index?3*) offers a range of extensions, including those that let you build a Facebook fan page for your business, embed an MP3 player on a page so visitors can listen to audio, and add extensions for PHP and

ASP server-side programming. They even have a bunch of free extensions, like YouTubizer, which makes it easy to embed YouTube videos on a page.

NOTE When this book went to press, some of the sites mentioned above still offered extensions in the older–and no longer Dreamweaver-compatible–MXP format. Hopefully, these developers will update the best and most useful extensions for Dreamweaver CC.

The Extension Manager

To add or remove a Dreamweaver extension, use the Extension Manager, a standalone program that handles add-ons for many Adobe programs, including Dreamweaver. It lets you install extensions, turn them on and off, and remove them (see Figure 23-5). It's also handy if you use Adobe's Photoshop, Illustrator, Flash, or Premiere programs—you get a single place to manage all your extensions.

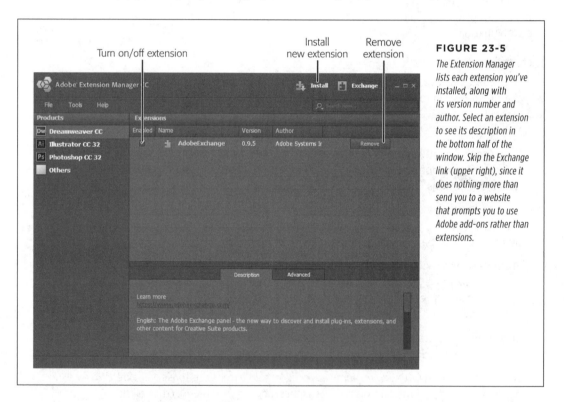

FIGURE 23-5

The Extension Manager lists each extension you've installed, along with its version number and author. Select an extension to see its description in the bottom half of the window. Skip the Exchange link (upper right), since it does nothing more than send you to a website that prompts you to use Adobe add-ons rather than extensions.

The first thing you need to do is install the extension manager through the Creative Cloud. Go to your Creative Cloud tool, which lives in your computer's taskbar. On Windows computers, you find the taskbar in the lower-right corner of your screen. For Mac systems, it's in the upper-right corner. Go to the Apps section, find Extension Manager CC, and then click Install. It may take a couple of minutes, but Creative Cloud installs the Extension Manager on your computer as a standalone application.

To install an extension:

1. **Find and download an extension (a .zxp file).**

   Extensions are distributed in a special compressed file format. Extension Manager knows how to unpack these files and install them for Adobe applications.

2. **Start up Extension Manager CC.**

   You start it as you would any other application on your Mac or PC. If you aren't exactly sure where to find it, try this: In Windows, press the Windows key on your keyboard and start typing *Extension Manager*. By the time you enter four or five letters, you'll see Adobe Extension Manager in the list of found files. Click it to fire up the program. On Macs, try the same process using Spotlight (⌘-space bar).

3. **Choose Dreamweaver CC 2014 from the left-hand list of Adobe products. If you don't see Dreamweaver listed, choose Others.**

   As you can tell from the program list, Extension Manager handles several products.

4. **Click Install in the upper-right corner of the Extension Manager.**

   Or choose File→Install Extension. The Extension Manager displays the "Select Extension to Install" window, listing all the folders on your hard drive.

5. **Navigate to and select the extension you want to add.**

   A disclaimer appears with a lot of legal text. In brief, it frees Adobe from liability if your computer melts down as a result of installing the extension.

6. **Click Accept in the Disclaimer window.**

   A message may appear that asks you to quit and restart Dreamweaver. If so, follow the directions.

TIP A faster way to install an extension is to simply double-click the .zxp file after you download it. This automatically launches the Extension Manager and installs the extension.

To remove an extension, select it from the list and then choose File→Remove Extension, or click Remove.

If you've installed a lot of extensions, Dreamweaver may take longer than usual to load; it needs to process every extension file as it starts up. If you want to temporarily turn off an extension (as opposed to deleting it), open the Extension Manager and turn off the Enable checkbox next to the extension's name. To turn it back on, simply turn on the checkbox once more. You may need to restart Dreamweaver to make the extension available again.

Working with Server-Side Programming

So far in this book, you've learned to build and maintain websites using Dreamweaver's powerful design, coding, and site-management tools. The pages you've created use straightforward HTML, and you can immediately preview them in a web browser. The web cognoscenti often call these kinds of pages *static*, because they don't change once you finish building them (unless you edit them, of course). For many websites, especially those where you carefully handcraft the design and content on a page-by-page basis, static web pages are the way to go.

But imagine landing a contract to build an online catalog of 10,000 products. After the initial excitement disappears (along with your plans for that trip to Hawaii), you realize that, even using Dreamweaver's Template tool (Chapter 22), building 10,000 pages is a lot of work!

For jobs like that, most developers use a database to store information about the many products the company sells, along with a kind of page template that's programmed to serve up just-in-time product-info pages. These dynamically created pages work their magic using a server-side programming language like PHP, ASP, ColdFusion, Java, or Ruby. When a visitor clicks a link to learn more about a product, he's actually requesting this template file, which talks to the database, retrieves the product information, and then returns a fully formed web page—one that looks just like a page you'd create by hand.

All major e-commerce sites work this way. Visit *www.amazon.com*, for example, and you'll find more books than you could read in a lifetime. In fact, you'll find more products—DVDs, CDs, even outdoor lawn furniture—than could fit inside a Walmart. In just an hour, you could browse through hundreds of products, each with its own web page. Do you think Amazon hired an army of web developers to create a web page for each product it sells? Not a chance.

Instead, when you search for a book on Amazon.com, you trigger a computer program running on what's called an *application server* that searches Amazon's gigantic database of products. When the program finds a product that matches your search criteria, it merges information about that product with HTML page elements (a banner, navigation buttons, a copyright notice, and so on) to stitch together a web page on the fly and send it to your browser. You see a page that's been created, perhaps for the first time ever (Figure 24-1).

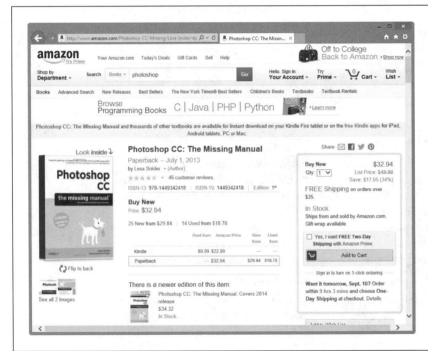

FIGURE 24-1

An infinite number of monkeys couldn't create a web page for each product Amazon.com sells. The solution? A dynamic website, which creates pages on the fly, made up of content chunks pulled from a database.

NOTE Luckily, you're not limited to *either* "static" *or* "dynamic" pages. Websites frequently use both—static pages for custom designs and handcrafted content, and dynamic pages for mass-produced catalog pages, for example.

Dynamic websites are generally the realm of professional programmers. If you're reading this chapter, you're either already programming these types of pages using PHP, ColdFusion, Ruby on Rails, C#, or some other programming language...or you're interested in learning how to do so.

NOTE   This chapter won't teach you how to program; its sole purpose is to show you how to set up Dreamweaver to work with dynamic websites. If you're interested in getting started with server-side programming, PHP is a very popular first step. Facebook and the popular blogging system WordPress use PHP, for example. A good place to start learning PHP is with *PHP Solutions: Dynamic Web Design Made Easy* (friends of ED) or *Head First PHP & MySQL* (O'Reilly).

FREQUENTLY ASKED QUESTION

What Happened to Dreamweaver's Server-Side Tools?

I own a previous version of this book, which included tutorials for building database-driven websites with Dreamweaver. Where did they go?

It's true that Dreamweaver used to provide tools for connecting to a database, adding and retrieving information from that database, password-protecting pages, and a lot more. Unfortunately, those tools, called "server behaviors," were left stagnant for several versions of Dreamweaver, and the code the program produced was just plain unprofessional. So, as of Dreamweaver CC, Adobe removed the server behaviors altogether.

Even if that weren't the case, it's been best to steer clear of Dreamweaver's antiquated server behaviors for quite some time now and either learn to program yourself or use a pre-programmed content management system like WordPress, Joomla, or Drupal to handle your database needs. Alternatively, you can jump to a third-party solution from companies like DMXzone (*http://www.dmxzone.com*) or WebAssist (*http://webassist.com*), which sells its own set of PHP server behaviors. You can find their server add-ons by choosing Window→Browse Add-ons. For more details, see the section on using add-ons on page 908.

■ Dynamic Website Basics

Dynamic websites are more complex than static sites. Static sites require only the computer you use to build your pages and a web server to dish them out. In fact, as you saw by previewing your site with a browser on your own computer (page 266), you don't even need a web server to effectively view a static website.

Dynamic web pages, by contrast, require more horsepower and a mix of technologies (see Figure 24-2). Not only do you need a web server to handle requests for web pages, you need two other types of servers, too, an *application server* and a *database server*.

You'll still use a lot of HTML (and CSS) in building a dynamic site—to provide, for example, the page layout, banner graphics, and display navigation bars. But you'll augment that mix with some form of programming code. The application server processes that code, often retrieving information from the database server, and then it sends a completed HTML page back to the web server, which, in turn, sends that page to your site's visitor.

Static HTML Page

Client → Request → Web Server

Web Server → Response → Client

Dynamic Page

Client → Request → Web Server

Web Server → Response → Client

Web Server → Unprocessed Page → Server Model (Application Server)

Server Model → Processed Page → Web Server

Server Model → Data Request → Database

Database → Data Results → Server Model

Database: MS Access, MySQL, SQL, Oracle, etc.

FIGURE 24-2

Top: The technology behind a website that uses plain old static HTML pages is straightforward: When you come to the site, a web server sends your computer (known as the client computer) the pages, graphics, and other elements of a page.

Bottom: When you visit a dynamic site, on the other hand, the web server must communicate with an application server, which in turn communicates with a database server. The final results come back to you through the web server.

NOTE When you talk about websites, a *server* refers to the software that dishes out particular types of information—web pages, database results, and so on. It doesn't necessarily mean a separate computer; web hosting firms can (and frequently do) have web, database, and application servers all running happily together on a single machine.

Because dynamic websites always coordinate the work of these servers, you can't just open dynamic site pages in your browser as you build them, as you can with a regular web page. You have to view dynamic pages through a web server that has an appropriate application server running. You may also have to set up a database and connect that database to your application server.

Although this arrangement can be quite complex, it's not difficult to set up on your own computer so you can build and test database-driven web pages. It's also easy to connect to remote computers that are already configured to serve up dynamic, database-driven pages.

NOTE The term *web application* refers to web pages that work together to complete a task. All the various pages that make up an online shopping site—pages that let you search a database of products, view individual product pages, and add products to a shopping cart, for example—are collectively considered a web application.

■ Setting Up a Dynamic Website

Now that your head is spinning and you're considering some noble career alternative like farmer, firefighter, or carpenter, it's time to set up Dreamweaver to work with an application server and database.

You can configure your setup in several ways. One involves using what Dreamweaver calls a *testing server*. Remember how you can create a website on your own computer (called a *local site*) before posting it online for all to see (the *remote site*)? Here the concept is similar. When you build web applications, it's a good idea to keep all your work-in-progress pages on your own computer, just as you did when you created static pages. After all, you don't want to fill up an online database with test data, or risk putting half-finished pages on the Internet to test them. But because dynamic websites require an application server and database to work, you need a testing server to store and preview your dynamic pages—a real web server, an application server, and a database, in other words, all running on the same machine. You create that server on your own computer, by following the instructions below.

Then, once you finish building your site, you transfer the pages to your remote site using Dreamweaver's built-in FTP feature (see Chapter 20). If you work in a group setting with other web developers, you can set up the testing server on a machine that's part of your group's local network. Each page author can then connect to the testing server and retrieve files to work on. (Dreamweaver's Check In/Check Out feature, described on page 821, is ideal for this type of environment.)

> **NOTE** You can test your dynamic pages on your remote site, but that doesn't mean it's a great idea. For one thing, pages on your remote server are visible to the public. Also, whenever you work on dynamic files directly on a remote server, be aware that mistakes you make along the way may affect a database that *other* dynamic pages use. For example, if, while hurriedly trying to complete your website, you accidentally create a page that deletes records from your database, important information may no longer be available on your site. So whenever possible, test dynamic pages on your local testing site.

Setting Up a Testing Server

If you want to set up your own local testing server and you're new to server-side programming, start with a set of technologies called AMP, which stands for Apache, MySQL, and PHP. Apache is the web server that sends finished pages to your visitor's browser. MySQL is the database that stores the detail info for things like the products you sell. PHP is the programming language that tells the server and database what to do. This is the most common trio of web server, database server, and application server components; you'll find AMP at almost all hosting companies, and it's a great foundation for server-side programming. Even better, it's easy to set up on both Windows and Mac PCs.

■ WINDOWS

For Windows, WAMP is a simple installer that puts Apache, MySQL, and PHP on your computer. It's free and works with Windows 7 and 8, Windows Vista, and Windows

XP. You can find it at *www.wampserver.com/en*. Because the software changes somewhat frequently, you'll find instructions that match the current version of the WAMP installer at *www.uptospeedguides.com/wamp*.

■ MACS

For the Mac, MAMP provides a simple way to get Apache, MySQL, and PHP up and running. MAMP is free and available from *www.mamp.info*. The MAMP software changes (as does its website) frequently, so make sure you get the most up-to-date directions at *www.uptospeedguides.com/mamp*.

If you plan to follow along with the tutorials in this section of the book (Part Six), download and install WAMP or MAMP now.

Localhost and the Local Site Root Folder

If you followed the previous instructions and installed a testing server on your computer, you've already visited a web page at either *http://localhost/* or *http://localhost/MAMP* (the home pages for WAMP and MAMP, respectively). You may be wondering, what's this *localhost* thing? For a computer, "localhost" is just another way of saying "me." When you instruct a browser to go to *http://localhost*, you're merely telling it to look for a web server that's running on the same computer as your browser is. Normally, when you visit a website, you type a web address like *http://www.google.com*. That sends your browser out over the Internet looking for a web page located on some computer identified as *www.google.com*. When you set up a web server on your own computer and you want to view the web pages you create there, your browser need look no further than your own system and *its* web server, a.k.a. that testing server you set up in the previous section.

> **TIP** On some Mac setups, the localhost address is *http://localhost:8888* rather than *http://localhost*. The colon and four numbers are known as a "socket." The important point here is that if you can't communicate with your Mac's localhost, try using the longer address.

But once the browser asks your local testing server for a web page, where does the server find that page on your computer? When you work with static web pages (like the ones you built earlier in this book), you can keep your website files pretty much anywhere you want: on your desktop, in your Documents folder, on an external hard drive, and so on.

Dynamic pages, on the other hand, work only with the help of a web server and its companions, the application and database servers. Because it has to coordinate the work of these machines, the web server expects files for a website to reside in a particular location on your computer. That folder is called the *site root* folder (you may also hear it referred to as the *document root* folder), just as it is for static pages. The exact name and location of the site root folder varies from web hosting company to web hosting company, which might name the folder *htdocs*, *webdocs*, or *public_html*. WAMP uses a folder named *www* as the site root (*C:*

WAMP\www, for example), while MAMP uses a folder called *htdocs*; head over to Applications→MAMP→htdocs to see it.

In the case of WAMP, if you type *http://localhost/my_page.html* into your browser, the browser requests a file named *my_page.html* from the web server running on your computer. The server then looks inside *C:\Program Files\WAMP\www* for a file named *my_page.html*; if it finds it, the server sends the file back to the browser. On a Mac running MAMP, the web server looks in *Applications→MAMP→htdocs* for the file *my_page.html*.

NOTE If you don't specify a particular file—for example, if you just surf to *http://localhost/*—the web server looks for a "default file," usually named *index.html* or *index.php*.

Remember, when you work on a dynamic, database-driven site, you need to keep your website files inside the site root folder of your testing server.

NOTE You can also put your site files in a folder *inside* the site root folder. If you placed a folder named *store* in the *www (WAMP)* or *htdocs (MAMP)* folder, you could visit a web page named *products.php* inside that folder by browsing to *http://localhost/store/products.php*.

In addition, as you build more and more dynamic sites, you might want to have separate folder names for each one. For example, you could put the site files for client X in a folder named *clientX* inside the *www* or *htdocs* folder. Then you could test that client's web pages by typing *http://localhost/clientX/* into a browser.

More elegantly, you could have separate local sites for each client. That way, you can type a URL as simple as *http://clientX/* into a web browser, and your local server would find the files for just that one client. If you use MAMP, you can do that with MAMP Pro ($59, and worth every penny), which easily lets you create and manage separate websites on the same server.

Setting Up a Dynamic Site in Dreamweaver

After you set up a testing server on your computer, the next step (as with any site you work on in Dreamweaver) is setting up a website on your machine. The process of setting up a dynamic site, however, differs slightly from that of a static site:

1. **Start Dreamweaver, and then choose Site→New Site.**

   Dreamweaver opens the Site Setup window (see Figure 24-3). You need to give this new site a name and tell Dreamweaver where to find the site files.

2. **Name the site in the Site Name box.**

   Use any name you like—it shows up only in Dreamweaver's Files panel. (This is the same step as described on page 23.)

3. **In the next box, click 🗀, and then navigate to and select the folder where you'll store your local files.**

   Again, this is the same step you used to set up a static website. However, if you've set up a local testing environment using a program like MAMP or WAMP (page 921), this folder should match the name of the local root folder for the testing server. In the case of WAMP, you'll find that root folder at *C:\WAMP\ www*; MAMP puts it in *Applications→MAMP→htdocs*. (If you installed Apache yourself, or used a program other than WAMP or MAMP, your local root folder will be elsewhere on your system; refer to the setup program's website to see where the program creates local root folders.)

You just told Dreamweaver the name you want for the new site and selected the local site's folder.

FIGURE 24-3

Setting up a dynamic site starts the same way as setting up a plain old HTML site: Name the site and tell Dreamweaver where to find its files.

4. **Click Servers in the left-hand list of categories (see Figure 24-4).**

   You use this screen to set up both the remote and testing servers for your dynamic site. In other words, you use this screen to add FTP information so you can upload your site files to your live web server (as described on page 812), *and* you use this screen to tell Dreamweaver where your local testing server resides.

5. **Click the Add New Server button (+ , circled in Figure 24-4).**

   Dreamweaver displays the Basic server settings window (see Figure 24-5). Here, you tell Dreamweaver how to connect to your testing server and where it can find the files for your site.

6. **In the Server Name box, type *local testing*.**

   It doesn't really matter what you type here—the name just helps you identify your server in the Servers window (Figure 24-4). In this case, use *local testing* since it denotes both a testing server and the fact that it's "local," on your own computer.

   The next step tells Dreamweaver how to connect to that server.

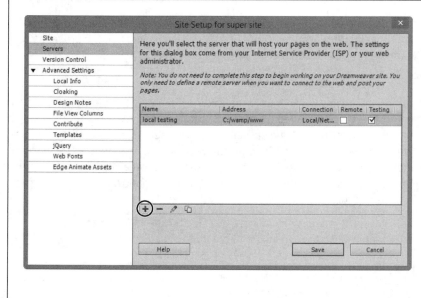

FIGURE 24-4

Dreamweaver lets you add more than one server to a site via the Add New Server button (circled), crucial if you're building a dynamic site. Dynamic sites, just like static websites, need a regular old web server on the Internet to serve up finished pages, and you have to tell Dreamweaver how to connect to it via FTP (discussed in Chapter 20). In addition, dynamic sites need a testing server, and you have to give Dreamweaver the connection details for that as well.

FIGURE 24-5

You want to test your dynamic site locally (on your own computer) before you upload your files to a live server on the Web. To do that, you need to tell Dreamweaver where to find the local testing server. Your setup window should look like this when you're done.

7. **Choose Local/Network from the "Connect using" drop-down menu.**

   This is the same window you use to set up connections to both local and remote servers, so even though you're setting up a local site, you'll see options like FTP,

SFTP, and so on here (see page 800 for more on these). Because you're setting up a local testing server, choose Local/Network.

8. **Click ▣ and select your local site folder (basically the same as step 2).**

If you're using WAMP, the *root* folder is at *C:\WAMP\www*. If you're using MAMP, select Applications→MAMP→htdocs. Next, you need to provide a web address so you can connect to your testing server.

9. **Type *http://localhost/* in the Web URL box.**

Although Dreamweaver asks for a "Web" URL, don't type in the address for your site out on the Web. Dynamic pages work only when you have a web server, and you just set one up, called a testing server, on your own computer. Therefore, you have to tell Dreamweaver to direct a web browser to your own local testing server. That way, when you use Dreamweaver's File→"Preview in Browser" command, Dreamweaver opens a browser and tells it to find the page on your machine's web server.

The Site Setup window should now look like the one in Figure 24-5. Lastly, you'll tell Dreamweaver that you want to create PHP pages.

> **NOTE** If you run MAMP and can't change the port Apache uses as described in the setup instructions at *www.uptospeedguides.com/mamp/*, you need to add port number 8888 to the web address, like this: *http://localhost:8888/*.

10. **Click the Advanced tab and choose PHP MySQL from the drop-down Server Model menu (see Figure 24-6).**

This lets Dreamweaver know the type of web pages you'll create. This step doesn't do much else, but it does ensure that Dreamweaver adds the proper file extension when you create a new file. For example, if you select PHP MySQL from this list, Dreamweaver appends ".php" to new-page filenames. If you're using a language that Dreamweaver doesn't list, like Ruby on Rails, you can still use Dreamweaver to edit those files. You need to name the files yourself, and Dreamweaver doesn't automatically append an extension, but Live view still displays the site, and you can still preview it by using a web browser to launch it from your local testing server.

11. **Click Save to close the advanced settings window. In the Site Setup window, turn off the Remote checkbox and then turn on the Testing checkbox (see Figure 24-4).**

This last step identifies your machine as your testing server. When Dreamweaver previews your pages in a browser, it loads the pages from this server. You're just about done.

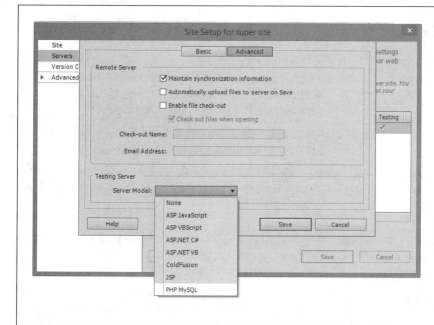

FIGURE 24-6

*The Advanced server
settings in the Site Setup
window let you choose
options related to your live
web server (they're listed
under "Remote Server"),
and pick the server model
you'll use when you build
web pages. These options
come into play only when
you build a new, blank
web page—Dreamweaver
creates a file with the correct file extension (.aspx
or .jsp, for example), but
that's about it.*

> **NOTE**   If you forget to turn on the Testing checkbox as described in step 11, Dreamweaver pops up an error
> message when you try to use the "Preview in Browser" command with a PHP page. It tells you that you need
> to set up a testing server first and gives you the option to go to the Site Setup window. If you see this message,
> click Yes, and then just turn on the Testing checkbox for the appropriate server.

12. **Click Save to save the new site.**

    Whew! That took a few steps, but you've successfully set up a local site so you can
    build and view dynamic pages. You're now ready to start *creating* those pages.

■ Creating a Dynamic Page

Once you set up an application server and a database server, you're ready to connect
to a database, retrieve information, and display it on a web page.

You already know how to handle the first step: Design an HTML page to display
database information (Chapter 10). Dynamic pages differ from regular HTML pages
in a couple of ways. For starters, the name of a dynamic file doesn't end with .html.
Depending on which server model you use, dynamic pages end in .php (for PHP
pages), .asp (ASP), .aspx (.NET), or .cfm or .cfml (ColdFusion). The file extension
you use is important because web servers use it to identify the type of page you're

requesting. If a server gets a request for an .html file, it simply finds the file and sends it to the web browser. But if it gets a request for a page that ends in, say, .php, it sends the page to the application server to sort out all the messy programming.

The good news is that the basic process of creating a new, blank, dynamic page is the same as creating your standard HTML page:

- Choose File→New to open the New Document window. Select the Blank Page category; from the Page Type list, choose a dynamic page type (PHP, for example). From the Layout list, choose a layout (or <none> if you wish to start with a fresh, blank page), and then click Create.

  When you save the file, Dreamweaver automatically adds the proper extension: .asp for ASP pages, .cfm for ColdFusion, or .php for PHP pages.

NOTE When you create a new page from the New Document window, Dreamweaver lets you select many different types of dynamic page, including JSP, ASP.NET, and ASP JavaScript.

- Or, more simply, right-click (Control-click) in the Site panel and choose New File from the shortcut menu. Dreamweaver creates a file in the correct server model format, with the proper extension.

NOTE For ASP pages, just renaming a file in the Site panel (from *about.html* to *about.asp*, for example) does *not* give the file the code necessary to apply the correct server model to the page. However, PHP and ColdFusion pages don't start life with any special code embedded in them, so you could start with an .html page, change the extension to .php, and then add PHP programming.

Once you create a blank page, you can use any of the page-building tools described in this book—Cascading Style Sheets, JavaScript, Library items, and so on—to design it. Even though the file is officially a PHP page (or an ASP or ColdFusion page), it still contains lots of HTML. Unlike a plain-vanilla HTML page, though, this one can also contain server-side programming that lets the page communicate with a database.

Finally, you can edit your newly created page in Design view, Split view, or Code view, but to add server-side programming, you need to switch to Code view.

■ Using Server-Side Includes

Even if you don't want to dive into the weird (but wonderful) world of server-side programming, you can take advantage of one timesaving feature that dynamic web pages offer: server-side includes (SSIs). SSIs are like the Dreamweaver Library items discussed in Chapter 21; they're individual files with code that you can reuse on pages throughout a site. They're great for banners, footers, copyright notices, sidebars, and other chunks of HTML. For example, you might use the same banner (logo, navigation bar, search box, and so on) at the top of each page. Instead of replicating that HTML over and over again, you can store it in a single file and "include" that file on your site's pages.

The advantage to this approach is that if you need to change anything on the banner, you open its file, make the change, save it, upload it to your web server, and voilà, your entire site is updated. Server-side includes actually make site updates easier than Library items do. As you can read on page 847, when you change a Library item, Dreamweaver has to update all the relevant pages on your site. Granted, that process is fast and automated, but it still requires that you upload all the changed files to your web server, and if the Library item appears on 10,000 pages, you have to update and upload 10,000 pages! That takes time.

Web servers incorporate server-side includes into a web page on the fly, when a visitor requests the page. That means that you can update your entire site just by changing and uploading the Include file. Now, that's fast and efficient!

With SSIs, a web server acts like an automated copy-and-paste machine. Say your home page includes an SSI that holds the HTML for the page's banner. When someone requests that page, the web server opens the file (*index.php*, for example), sees the SSI for the banner, opens the banner file (*banner.php*, for example), copies its code, pastes it into the home page, and then sends the just-constructed page to your visitor. If your guest goes to another page on the site, the server again copies the banner code and pastes it into the newly requested page. While all this repeated copying and pasting might sound inefficient, servers are fast—so fast that the use of server-side includes are extremely common on the Web.

Creating a Server-Side Include

SSIs are simply text files that contain programming code, HTML, or both. They can be as simple as a paragraph of text with a copyright notice, or as complex as the programming required to retrieve information from a database. Generally, SSI filenames end in the extension of the programming language you're using (.php, for example). In addition, since the SSI gets added to a web page, it shouldn't include the elements of a complete HTML file. In other words, just like a Dreamweaver Library item, the SSI should contain no doctype, <head> tag, or style sheet. It's just a text file that has only the content you wish to appear on a page.

Here's a simple way to create a server-side include:

1. **Choose File→New.**

   Dreamweaver opens the New Document window.

2. **Click Blank Page in the left-hand list of categories, choose a page type that matches your programming language (PHP, for example), and then click Create.**

   Dreamweaver creates a new blank page. However, it's full of the usual scaffolding that web pages require, including a doctype and <html>, <head>, and <body> tags. You don't need (or want) any of that for the small snippet of HTML you'll add to the include.

3. **Click the Code or Split view button in the Document toolbar, position your cursor in Code view, and then select and delete all the text.**

   For example, choose Edit→Select All and then Edit→Cut. Now that you have a truly empty page, you can save it.

4. **Choose File→Save, and use the extension that matches your programming language.**

   For example, save the file as *banner.php*.

TIP One common practice among web developers is to include both .inc *and* the programming-language extension in the filename—*banner.inc.php*, for example. The .inc in the middle makes it clear that the file is a server-side include.

---

5. **Add content to the server-side include.**

   You can switch to Design view for this task and use tools you're already familiar with, such as the Insert bar, to add HTML. Note, however, that you can't add styles to the Include file—the SSI is just *part* of a complete web page, so you add any styles you want to the page itself. But if you use Dreamweaver's Design-Time style sheet feature (page 425), you can overcome this limitation; it "tricks" Dreamweaver into thinking that the SSI actually does have a style sheet attached to it, and you can edit the styles.

NOTE When you add links or images to an SSI, always use root-relative paths (see page 179). An SSI is simply copied and pasted by the server into other files on your site. If the server pastes the SSI into a file that's within a folder or subfolder of your site, a document-relative path probably won't work when the SSI gets pasted into the page.

Adding a Server-Side Include to a Web Page

Once you create an SSI, you can add it to any dynamic page on your site; that is, to any page that ends in .php or another server-side programming extension.

1. **Open the page to which you wish to add the SSI.**

   This page must end in .php (or .asp or .cfm). They have to be dynamic pages, because you're about to add some "call-and-response" code to them.

2. **Click the spot in the page where you want to insert the SSI.**

   While you can do this in Design view, it's usually less error-prone to do it in Code view. For example, it's easy in Design view to add an SSI within a page's <p> tag, and if the SSI includes <div>s, headers, or other block-level HTML, you'll generate invalid code.

   Say you create an SSI banner for your site. To add it to a page, you'd go into Code view and place the cursor just after the opening <body> tag. Alternatively, if you want to insert a footer SSI (like a copyright notice or contact information), click just before the closing </body> tag.

3. **Choose Insert→PHP→Include (or ASP→Insert→Include Coldfusion or Insert→Coldfusion→CFINCLUDE).**

   If you aren't already in Code view, Dreamweaver changes to Split view. It writes the code for a server-side include, positioning your cursor between a pair of quotation marks—that's the spot where you identify the Include file. For example, the PHP code looks like this:

   ```
   <?php include(""); ?>
   ```

4. **Type in the name of the file you want to include.**

   Dreamweaver adds the necessary code to attach the SSI. For example, in PHP it will look something like this:

   ```
   <?php include("banner.php"); ?>
   ```

   If the SSI contains any HTML, Dreamweaver displays it in Design view so you can see your full-fledged page. (You won't, however, see the results that any server-side programming should produce, such as fulfilling a database request.)

You can continue to use the SSI on additional pages. You can even use it in Dreamweaver templates (Chapter 22), thereby combining two time-saving features.

NOTE When you add a server-side include to a page, make sure you use a document-relative path to the file that you're including in your page (see page 178).

■ Working with Related PHP Files

As discussed on page 343, Dreamweaver provides a special toolbar for identifying files associated with a web page, such as an external style sheet or a JavaScript file. This Related Files toolbar not only shows you which files you've added to a page, but, with just a click of the mouse, it also lets you jump directly to the code for that file. Dreamweaver considers server-side includes "related files" too, so you can easily edit an SSI file by clicking its name in the toolbar.

In fact, server-side programming often involves adding lots of files to a page: files for connecting to a database server, for running a database query, for sending email, and more. For example, the popular blogging system WordPress uses a single file, *index.php*, to control an entire blog. That one file manages every one of the blog's pages, from the home page to a category page to a single blog post. To do this, the *index.php* file includes tons (really, a *lot*) of other PHP files. If you're using a web page editor other than Dreamweaver, the only way to edit a WordPress site is to open each file individually. Dreamweaver, however, can "discover" related PHP files and display them in the Related Files toolbar for easy access. To take advantage of this important feature, you need to follow a few steps:

1. **Open a PHP file.**

   If you used the Insert Server-Side Include command discussed previously, Dreamweaver automatically sees these PHP files and displays them in the Related Files toolbar with no further effort on your part. But you might also include PHP files within *other* Include files. In cases like that, you need to tell Dreamweaver to "discover" them.

2. **Click the Discover link in the information toolbar in the document window (see Figure 24-7, top).**

   Dreamweaver finds all the PHP files the currently open dynamic page uses. That may be just a few files or, in the case of complex PHP applications like WordPress, quite a few. For example, you can see that the Related Files toolbar in the bottom image in Figure 24-7 is chock-full of filenames.

FIGURE 24-7

With PHP pages, you find all related PHP files by clicking the Discover link (top). You can then work on a related file by clicking its name in the Related Files toolbar or, if there are a lot of files, by clicking the "Show more related files" button (bottom).

3. **Select a related file you want to work on.**

Once Dreamweaver discovers all the related PHP files, you can use the Related Files toolbar as you normally would to open a file. If there are a lot of files, as is the case with WordPress, navigate through the list by clicking the left and right arrow buttons, or click the Show More button to see a drop-down menu of all the files. Select a name from that list to open the file in Code view.

4. **Filter the list if necessary.**

You may not want to see or work on some of the files Dreamweaver discovers. For example, in the case of WordPress, you won't want to touch most of the discovered files because they're part of the core WordPress program, and editing them might break your blog.

Fortunately, you can see just the files you want. The Filter button in the top-right corner of the Related Files toolbar lets you filter files in a couple of ways. First, you can filter by file type, meaning you can show or hide JavaScript, CSS, or PHP files, along with any other file type your web page taps. On its own, Dreamweaver selects all the file types, so to hide one, click the Filter button, and then click the relevant extension (.css, .php, .js, and so on). To show those file types later, select them again from the Filter menu.

You can also create a custom filter. Click the Filter button, choose Custom Filter, and Dreamweaver displays a dialog box. Type in the filenames and/or file types you want to see. For example, with WordPress, you're interested in editing the PHP theme files—the ones WordPress uses to create your blog's look. To see the relevant files, enter their names separated by a semicolon, like this: *index. php; footer.php; header.php*, and so on. You can also filter by file type. To show all JavaScript files plus *index.php, footer.php*, and *header.php*, type this in the Related Files toolbar: *index.php; footer.php; header.php; .js*.

When you're done, click OK to close the Custom Filter window. Now, in the Related Files toolbar, Dreamweaver displays only the files you specified.

NOTE Custom filters are useful but, unfortunately, Dreamweaver doesn't remember a custom filter, so once you close a file, that filter is lost and you have to recreate it the next time you want to use it. In addition, you can't filter by folder (you can filter all PHP files within a particular folder only), although that would be really helpful when you work with certain content management systems like WordPress, which keep files related to the design of a site in one particular folder. Maybe next time.

■ PHP Code Hints

Dreamweaver includes advanced code hints for the PHP language, but not for other server-side technologies, like .NET, ColdFusion, Java Server Pages, and Ruby on Rails. Not only does Dreamweaver support code-hinting for built-in PHP functions, but it also makes note of variables, functions, and classes you create (see Figure 24-8).

Since it's common for programmers to create multiple PHP files and then add them all to (or include them all in) a master file, Dreamweaver searches all the files identified in the current working file and analyzes them. Then, as you type more PHP code, Dreamweaver displays code hints based on the names of the variables, functions, and classes you defined in those files. In other words, Dreamweaver personalizes its code hints for your site and for the PHP programming you added to it. Pretty nice.

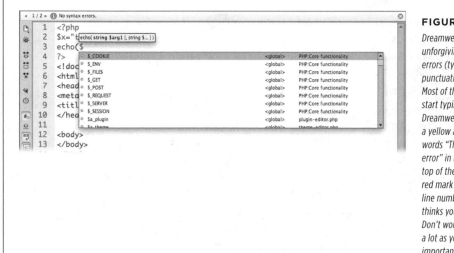

FIGURE 24-8

Dreamweaver is pretty unforgiving of syntax errors (typos or missing punctuation) in PHP code. Most of the time, you start typing PHP code and Dreamweaver displays a yellow alert with the words "There is a syntax error" in the info bar at the top of the code window. A red mark appears on the line number at the point it thinks you made an error. Don't worry, this happens a lot as you program; the important thing is that, once you finish, there are no syntax error messages left. If there are, you probably left off a closing), }, ', or ".

In addition, since many PHP frameworks, like CakePHP and Zend, and many PHP-based content management systems (CMSes), like WordPress, Joomla, and Drupal, rely on many separate PHP files, Dreamweaver includes something called site-specific code hints. They let you identify which folders Dreamweaver scans to create its code hints for your site, but, alas, they come with a hitch: they offer hints for PHP-based sites only.

Dreamweaver's site-specific code hints have a few benefits. First, if you often include PHP files outside the root folder (for example, the Zend framework keeps its Include files outside the web-accessible root folder), you can tell Dreamweaver to scan the folder above the current local root folder. Second, many CMSes and PHP frameworks use tons of files with tons of variables, functions, and class names. Sites like those use the files internally, in the programming that drives the systems. You, as a programmer, don't ever need to see most of them, and you certainly don't want their elements cluttering up your code-hint window. By specifying a folder that Dreamweaver should scan, you pare down that number of files.

You can turn site-specific code hints on by choosing Site→Site-Specific Code Hints. This opens a new window (see Figure 24-9). If you're using WordPress, Joomla, or Drupal, you can select your environment from the top Structure menu, and Dreamweaver automatically identifies the proper folders, files, and paths. Click OK and you're done.

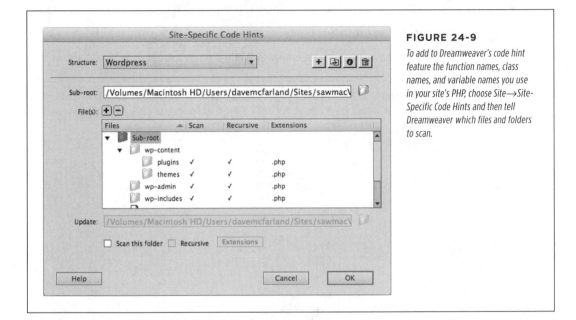

FIGURE 24-9

To add to Dreamweaver's code hint feature the function names, class names, and variable names you use in your site's PHP, choose Site→Site-Specific Code Hints and then tell Dreamweaver which files and folders to scan.

If, however, you're using a PHP framework or some other PHP CMS, you need to tell Dreamweaver which folders to analyze by following these steps:

1. **Identify the folder that has your site and all the PHP files you want Dreamweaver to scan by clicking 📁 and selecting a folder.**

   If you don't have any PHP files outside your local root folder, you can skip this step because Dreamweaver automatically selects the local root folder. However, you may have PHP files one level up from the local folder. In this case, click 📁 and select the folder one level up, which should contain both the PHP files you want to scan and your local site root.

2. **Click + .**

   Dreamweaver opens the Add File/Folder window. You can select either one particular PHP file or a folder's worth of PHP files. If you pick a folder, turn on the Recursive checkbox if you want Dreamweaver to scan the files in subfolders within this main folder. You can ensure that Dreamweaver searches only .php files by clicking + to the right of the Extensions label and then typing *.php*. Dreamweaver won't look through any other file types and, as a result, it displays code hints faster. However, if you do use other extensions for your PHP files, such as .inc, make sure you type in those extensions as well. To add another extension, click + again. Dreamweaver displays a new line in the extension pane where you can type in the extension.

You can prevent Dreamweaver from scanning a folder you added from the main Site-Specific Code Hints window, too. Select the folder from the Files list and then turn off the "Scan this folder" checkbox. You can also turn off recursive scanning and change file extensions from this window.

3. **Click OK to finish.**

Dreamweaver scans the selected files and creates a list of code hints for your site.

NOTE You may find that Dreamweaver doesn't always automatically pop up a box for site-specific code hints, as it does for regular PHP functions. You may need to coax Dreamweaver into displaying them by using the keyboard shortcut Ctrl+space bar.

Appendixes

Getting Help

Hard as it may be to believe, even a book as voluminous as this one may not answer all your questions about Dreamweaver. Fortunately, many other resources await you when a feature is giving you trouble.

▮ Getting Online Help

Adobe puts all its resources for help with Dreamweaver on its support site, so you need an Internet connection to use any of them. Articles, videos, tutorials, and discussions abound, so Adobe gives you several ways to navigate its support system, depending on what you're looking for. Some might say there are so many options that you may need help for the help section. If you're in that camp, read on.

Dreamweaver lists five choices at the top of the Help menu. (At the bottom of the menu, you'll find Creative Cloud tools that let you sign into and manage your account.) The help options are:

- **What's New In Dreamweaver**. Adobe shows off the features it added to the most recent update to the program. The features are displayed in brief animations with minimal text. You won't find a complete "how to" tutorial here, but you will get a first look at the new features. If something looks different since the last time you updated your copy of the program (page xviii), check here to see what's up. Adobe usually debuts significant updates to Dreamweaver in the spring and fall, so that's when you're likely to find new features.

- **New Feature Videos.** This page provides links to videos that explain how to use Dreamweaver's newest features. The videos are professionally produced and most run between 2 and 4 minutes.

- **Learn Dreamweaver**. Here you find tutorials grouped under the topics Get Started, Learn Essentials, and Key Techniques. The Get Started tutorials are pretty basic, but you'll find some real help in the Learn Essentials (50 topics) and Key Techniques (13 topics) sections.

- **Help and Support**. This is where you find the most thorough help options, divided among three submenus:

- **Dreamweaver Online Help** is a traditional text-based help system. For more details, see the next section.

- **Dreamweaver Support Center** links to the pages described above as well as to a page of common questions, a page of top issues, and the community forums page. You'll find more details on help and support in the next section.

- **Adobe Online Forums** is a direct link to the forums page mentioned in the previous bullet point. Adobe's forums are a valuable resource for web developers and designers. See page 943.

- **Submit Bug/Feature Request**. As the name suggests, this is the place to go when Dreamweaver behaves badly or if you have a great idea to improve the program.

> **TIP** You can find links to some of these same help pages on Dreamweaver's Welcome Screen. Dreamweaver displays the Welcome Screen when you don't have any pages open in the document window. For example, the Learn Dreamweaver link in the window takes you to the Learn Dreamweaver tutorials. The Help and Support link takes you to Dreamweaver Online Help.

Dreamweaver Online Help

This is the place to go if you're looking for articles on specific topics, like CSS, site management, linking, and navigation. This text-based resource is fairly well organized and covers topics you may not find in the video tutorials. You can get to this page several ways:

- On the Welcome Screen, click Help & Support in the lower-left corner.

- Choose Help→Help and Support→Dreamweaver Online Help.

- Go to *http://helpx.adobe.com/dreamweaver/topics.html*.

- In Windows, press F1; on a Mac, press fn-F1.

All these roads lead to the web page titled "Learn & Support/Dreamweaver Help," shown in Figure A-1. It looks like a rather boring page full of links, so the trick is to know what you're looking for.

Click a blue link at the top of the page, and the page scrolls to the relevant section below, where you find more links on that topic. For example, if you click "Site management," the page scrolls to a spot where you see several links to articles on site management. The contents in the first two sections, What's New and Get Started, have a promotional feel to them, but the rest of the articles feel more like traditional technical help.

FIGURE A-1

To search for help on a specific topic, type keywords into the gray Adobe Community Help box in the upper-left corner of Dreamweaver's support page. Don't let the name of the box fool you: It searches Adobe's entire support site for relevant articles and blog entries, not just the discussion forums.

TIP You can download a PDF that has all the articles found in Dreamweaver's Learn & Support site. Go to Help→Help and Support→Dreamweaver Online Help and then, on the left side of the page, look for Help PDFs. Choose Dreamweaver CC (October 2014). Once you have the PDFs, you can use them even if you're not connected to the Internet.

Dreamweaver Support Center

To get to Dreamweaver's support center, choose Help→Help and Support→ Dreamweaver Support Center. The page that appears serves as a table of contents for the other help and support pages (Figure A-2). In the Learn section, you find links to tutorials that have names like Learn Essentials and Key Techniques. Below those, in the Get Support area, you see links to categories like Common Questions and Top Issues. Here's a rundown of the topics:

- **Common Questions** provides answers to frequently asked questions. Many of the questions and answers are sales-oriented, like "What is Dreamweaver, and who is it for?" Some are technical, such as "What are the minimum system requirements to run Dreamweaver CC 2014?" However, there's not a lot of technical depth here when it comes to working with Dreamweaver.

- **Top Issues** deals with known problems with Dreamweaver. You find descriptions of the issues and possible workarounds.

- **Ask the Community** lists some of the hottest discussions going on in the Adobe community forums (page 942). To ask a new question, fill in the search box at the top of the page and then click "Ask now."

- **Contact Us** starts by asking *you* questions and boring down through a couple of possible solutions. If you don't find the answer you need, you get to a link where you can contact someone at Adobe. The options there include talking to someone in an online chat or by phone. Alternatively, you can select a link to Adobe's forums, where you can query the Dreamweaver community.

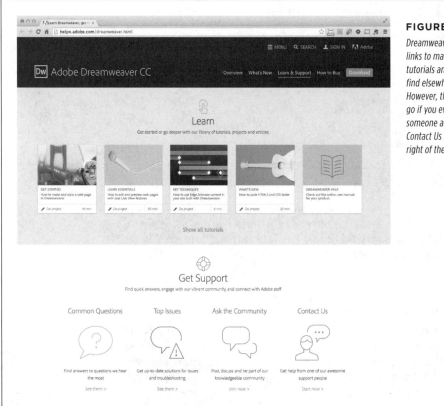

FIGURE A-2

Dreamweaver's support center links to many of the same tutorials and help pages you find elsewhere on the site. However, this is the place to go if you ever need to contact someone at Adobe. Click the Contact Us link at the bottom right of the page.

Adobe TV

Why read the book when you can wait for the movie? That's the sort of thinking behind Adobe TV. You may have encountered these videos before, in the Learning Dreamweaver tutorials. To see the full assortment of videos (Figure A-3), go to the Adobe TV page (*http://tv.adobe.com*), click the Products tab in the top bar, and then choose Dreamweaver.

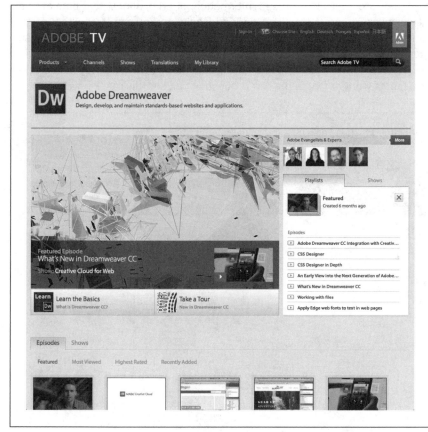

FIGURE A-3

Much of what's on Adobe TV (and it covers all the Creative Cloud programs, not just Dreamweaver) are tutorials in video form, presented by Adobe employees and other experts.

Some introductory videos are just a couple of minutes long, while in-depth lessons can run 10 minutes or so. And, hey, they were made using Adobe tools, so you can count on clear visuals and professional production quality.

■ Getting Help from Other Dreamweaver Fans

Adobe provides online community forums that offer the free exchange of advice among many helpful souls. Knowledgeable souls, too, including MVPs—Most Valuable Participants. These forum mavens have been recognized by Adobe for their expertise and skill in sorting out Dreamweaver difficulties. In addition, according to Adobe, about 1,000 company employees comb the forums and answer questions.

To get to the forums:

- Choose Help→Help and Support→Adobe Online Forums.

- Go to *http://forums.adobe.com/community/dreamweaver*.

The forums are a terrific source of information, offering almost real-time answers on Dreamweaver and related web-design techniques. You can start with the list of Frequently Asked Questions in the middle of the page (Figure A-4). It's an unusual Dreamweaver question that hasn't already been asked, answered, and debated on the support forum. If you don't find an answer among the Frequently Asked Questions, type a word or two in the Ask a Question box and click "Ask now."

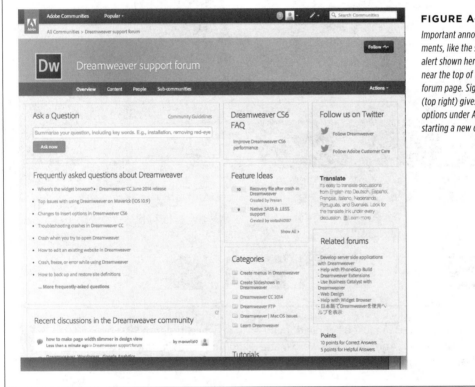

FIGURE A-4

Important announcements, like the security alert shown here, appear near the top of the support forum page. Signing in (top right) gives you more options under Actions, like starting a new discussion.

You can start a new discussion if you have a unique question, but Adobe makes it a bit difficult—it prefers you search existing discussions first. After that, look for the Action drop-down menu in the gray bar at the top of the page, and then click Discussion under the heading Create.

You need to be signed in to begin a new discussion. Click "Sign in" at the top right of the page and then enter your Adobe ID (page 4) and password. If this is your first time logging in, Adobe asks you to create a user name to represent your online identity.

TIP   In your travels through Adobe's labyrinth of online help, you may stumble on a page called Adobe Communities (*www.adobe.com/communities*). This catch-all page contains links to the forums and user groups mentioned in this appendix, along with other resources for contacting Dreamweaver experts—or becoming one.

Dreamweaver CC 2014, Menu by Menu

Dreamweaver CC: The Missing Manual is quite comprehensive; in its pages, you'll find descriptions of every major Dreamweaver function (and most minor ones). In the interest of completeness, however, here's a quick reference to every command in every Dreamweaver menu—and the answer to the occasional "What does that mean?" mystery. This menu-by-menu summary was written for the Dreamweaver 2014 CC October Release. These commands (except where noted) are available in Design view as you edit a page. Editing in Live view is more limited, so many commands are "grayed out" in that view. Then again, there are a few commands that are only available in Live view, and those are clearly noted in the list.

■ File Menu

The commands in Dreamweaver's File menu include basic functions like saving and closing files, and controlling an open Dreamweaver document:

- **New**. Opens the New Document window, which lets you create various types of new Dreamweaver files. On the left side, four document categories are listed:

  - **Blank Page.** Creates an empty Dreamweaver document using any of several types of web page, from basic HTML and CSS pages to dynamic pages built on JavaScript and PHP.

  - **Fluid Grid Layout**. This option provides a basic framework for creating a site that works in mobile, tablet, and desktop browsers. Using some pre-packaged CSS and JavaScript, as well as a fancy user interface, you can basically "draw" three layouts—one for smartphones, one for tablets, and one for desktop computers—that use the same content.

— **Starter Templates**. These templates help you set up web pages destined for mobile devices.

— **Site Templates**. If you've created your own templates, they show up here.

- **Open**. Launches the standard Open File dialog box so you can navigate to and open a Dreamweaver document. You can set the Enable drop-down menu to display only specific types of documents—just HTML pages or style sheets, for example.

- **Open Recent**. Displays a submenu that lists the 10 most recently opened documents. Selecting a document from the list opens it. The last option in this menu, "Reopen Documents on Startup," is kind of cool. If you quit Dreamweaver with documents still open and have this option turned on, Dreamweaver automatically reopens those documents the next time you launch the program.

- **Close**. Closes the currently open Dreamweaver document. If you have unsaved changes, Dreamweaver gives you the opportunity to save them. This action also closes the files in the Related Files toolbar (see page 343).

- **Close All**. Closes *all* the currently open documents. If you have unsaved changes in any of them, Dreamweaver gives you the opportunity to save them.

- **Save**. Saves any changes you made to your document. Dreamweaver dims the Save command if you haven't made any changes to the document since the last time you saved it.

- **Save As**. As with most other programs, this command saves a copy of the current document under a new name.

- **Save All**. Saves changes to all your open documents, including other web pages, external CSS and JavaScript files, and any files listed in the Related Files toolbar (see page 343). This handy command makes sure all your changes are saved to every document you edited since opening Dreamweaver.

- **Save All Related Files**. Saves changes to the document you're currently editing, as well as files that the current document uses, such as external CSS and JavaScript files, and server-side programs such as PHP Includes. This is a good way to make sure you save every edit that affects the current file, whether you made the change in a CSS file, the HTML source code, or an external JavaScript file.

- **Save as Template**. Saves the current document as a Dreamweaver template with the extension .dwt. The "Save as Template" dialog box appears so you can specify the template's filename, and indicate which site it belongs to. Dreamweaver automatically saves all template documents in a Templates subfolder in the selected site's folder. You'll find templates discussed in Chapter 22.

- **Revert**. Undoes any changes you made to a document since the last time you saved it. Edit→Undo is often a better choice; it takes a few more steps to undo all the changes you made, but it can actually undo changes *past* your last save.

So if you're one of those gotta-save-it-every-5-seconds types, the Undo command is for you.

- **Print Code**. Prints the underlying code for the currently selected document. You can be in any view to use this command—you don't need to be in Code or Split view.

- **Import**. Lets you import data from other sources into your Dreamweaver document. For example, you can import XML data into a template, or tabular data from a CSV (comma separated value) file into an HTML file. Windows users can also import text from a Microsoft Word document or tabular data from an Excel spreadsheet.

- **Export**. Extracts tabular data or template data in XML format from your Dreamweaver document, for use in other applications.

- **Preview in Browser**. Opens the current document in your web browser. By selecting Edit Browser List, you can add new browsers to, or delete browsers from, your browser list, or specify a preferred browser.

- **Validate**. Lets you check XML files to make sure they conform to XML standards and document type definitions. In other words, it checks to make sure your XML is correct. In addition, you can check an HTML file using the W3C's online validator—right from within Dreamweaver. Select the "Validate current document" option and Dreamweaver connects to the Web, contacts the W3C validator, and checks your page's HTML. If it finds errors, it lists them in the W3C validation pane below the Property Inspector. If you're working on a server-side page (like a WordPress page), choose the Validate Live Document option—it first processes a page through a web server and then contacts the W3C site. That way, you're actually checking the finished HTML (after the server has completed all its server-side antics and produced a real HTML file).

- **Compare with Remote/Compare with Testing**. Lets you use a third-party code-comparison tool to see how the local copy of a page differs from either the remote copy (the one on your web server) or the copy on your testing server. It identifies all code differences. You can learn more about this feature on page 358.

- **Design Notes**. Opens the Design Notes window (Chapter 20) to add information about an open document, set its status, and choose to have the Design Note appear whenever you open the document.

> **NOTE** To use Design Notes, make sure you select the Maintain Design Notes option in the Site Definition window's "Design notes" section; see page 831.

- **Exit (Windows only)**. Exits Dreamweaver. If any of your open Dreamweaver documents have unsaved changes, the program prompts you to save them before quitting. (Mac users will find a "Quit Dreamweaver" option under the Dreamweaver menu.)

■ Edit Menu

The Edit menu lets you make common changes to your documents, like copying and pasting text:

- **Undo**. Undoes the most recent change you made to your document. Choose this command repeatedly to step progressively backward through your changes, even *after* you save the document. You can take 50 steps back in time, unless you change Dreamweaver's default in Preferences→General.

- **Redo (Repeat)**. Restores whatever changes you just made using the Undo command. Selecting Redo multiple times moves you progressively forward through the changes you made. If you just used a command other than Undo, Repeat appears instead of Redo. This property lets you repeat the last action. For example, if you just pressed Delete, the Repeat command presses it again.

- **Cut**. Deletes the selected text or objects from a document and copies them to the invisible Windows or Macintosh Clipboard so you can paste them elsewhere. (The Clipboard holds only one selection at a time.)

- **Copy**. Copies the selected text or object to the Clipboard so you can paste it elsewhere, without disturbing the original.

- **Paste**. Places the most recent selection from the Clipboard into your document at the insertion point.

- **Paste Special**. Opens the Paste Special window, which lets you choose how to paste a Clipboard item into your document. Options range from Text Only for just plain text to increasingly more elaborate options, which force Dreamweaver to attempt to preserve various kinds of formatting, such as styles, bold text, italic text, bulleted lists, and so on. See page 71.

- **Clear**. Deletes the selected text or object from a document without placing it in the Clipboard.

- **Delete (Live view only).** Deletes elements on the page while editing in Live view. In Live view, you insert page elements, like paragraphs and images, using the Insert menu or Insert panel.

- **Duplicate (Live view only).** Makes a copy of the selected elements and pastes it back into the page. For example, if you want to create several paragraphs, you can first choose File→Insert→Structure→Paragraph. Then, to create a second paragraph, choose Duplicate.

- **Select All**. Selects all the content in the current <div>, <header>, <article>, <footer>, or whatever section the cursor is in. To expand the selection, choose this command to select the parent of the selected element. Keep selecting the command and, ultimately, you'll select the entire <body> of the page.

- **Select Parent Tag**. Broadens the current selection to include everything within its *parent tag*, including the content. For example, if you have a table cell selected, this command increases the selection to include the entire table *row*. Choose the command a second time and you increase the selection to include the entire table. In short, this command ensures that any changes you make apply to the entire tag.

- **Select Child**. Narrows the current selection to include everything within the *child tag*, including its contents. If you select a table row, choosing this command decreases that selection to include only the first table *cell* and its contents.

- **Find and Replace**. Lets you search a document—or an entire site—for a specific word, tag, or piece of source code, and replace it with something different (see Chapter 8). This command lets you make these changes either en masse or one instance at a time.

- **Find Selection**. This command lets you find another instance of the current selection. Say you select the word "mothball" on a page. This command searches the page for another instance of "mothball."

- **Find Again**. Uses the most recent search setting from the "Find and Replace" window to search the current document, highlighting the next instance of the search item.

- **Live Search (Mac only)**. Unlike "Find and Replace," this tool works both inside and outside of Design view. It uses OS X's Spotlight search tool to look for text throughout a site. Instead of the "Find and Replace" dialog box, you type your search terms into a box in the Files panel.

- **Go to Line**. Opens the "Go to Line" dialog box. Type in a number, and Dreamweaver positions the cursor at the beginning of the specified line of code (available only in Code view).

- **Show Code Hints**. Immediately displays any code hints (overriding the delay set in the Preferences window) available for the current tag. Code hints, described in Chapter 7, provide a drop-down menu of properties appropriate for the current tag (available only in Code view, and only when you use the Insert Tag command Ctrl+T [⌘-T]).

- **Refresh Code Hints**. Doesn't seem to do much of anything.

- **Code Hint Tools**. When you work in Code view, this command lets you access Dreamweaver's color picker, its "Browse for File" button, and its list of fonts so you don't have to type in things like *#FF6633*, *../../images/dog.gif*, or *Arial, Helvetica, sans-serif* every time you use a color, link to a file, or want to use a font. In addition, you can display a pop-up menu of all the ID, class, and element names on a page, which you'll find useful for JavaScript programming.

- **Indent Code**. Adds one indent before the selected line of code (available only in Code view).

- **Outdent Code**. Removes one indent from the selected line of code (available only in Code view).

- **Balance Braces**. When you edit a script in Code view, this command helps you check for unbalanced braces (that is, an introductory "{" without a closing "}") by highlighting the matching tags enclosing the selected code. It doesn't do anything for plain HTML, but if you're writing a JavaScript program or using a dynamic programming language like PHP or ASP, it helps identify missing braces—a common source of programming errors. Works with opening and closing parentheses and brackets ([and]) as well.

- **Repeating Entries**. Lets you cut, copy, paste, and delete repeating regions in templates. You can learn about repeating regions in Chapter 22.

- **Code Collapse**. Hides a selection of code in Code view so you see only the code you want to work on. You'll find this feature discussed on page 338, and since the same options are available more directly from the coding toolbar, you can skip this command.

- **Tag Libraries**. Lets you modify the way Dreamweaver writes code for various types of tags, such as those for HTML, PHP, ASP, and ColdFusion. You can create new tag libraries for other types of tag-based languages or modify the ones that ship with Dreamweaver.

- **Keyboard Shortcuts (Windows only).** Opens the Keyboard Shortcuts window and shows you all of Dreamweaver's current keyboard shortcuts. You can create a new set of shortcuts for specific sites or programs, or export the settings to HTML so you can share them with others. (You must duplicate the factory settings before you add or delete your own shortcuts, however.) You'll find details on page 904. (On the Mac, this option appears under the Dreamweaver menu.)

- **Preferences (Windows only).** Opens the Preferences window, which is full of options that customize the way Dreamweaver works. You can choose from 19 categories of options, including those that let you edit the color and format of HTML tags, create shorthand versions of CSS styles, and change the order in which Dreamweaver's info panels appear onscreen. (On the Mac, this option appears under the Dreamweaver menu.)

■ View Menu

The View menu controls the document window's appearance. A checkmark in the menu lets you know which view you're in:

- **Code**. Displays the file's source code.

- **Split Code**. Displays the file's source code in split view, side by side. You use this feature to edit both the HTML near the top of a page (on one side of the document window), and the HTML elsewhere on the page (on the other side of the Document window). But it's most useful when you use it in conjunction with Dreamweaver's Related Files feature (page 343). In Split Code view, you can view the HTML of the page in one pane and the CSS of an external style sheet in the other.

- **Design/Live**. When you have Design selected from the drop-down menu in the Document toolbar, this option displays the file's visual design. When you have Live selected in the Document toolbar, you see your page as it will appear in a web browser.

- **Code and Design/Code and Live**. Splits the document window into two panes: source code on the left (or top), and either visual design on the right (or bottom) or Live view on the right (or bottom), depending on the option you selected in the Design/Live view drop-down menu. You can adjust how much of each pane you see by dragging the center divider left or right or up or down.

- **Split Vertically**. When you're in Code and Design view, you see the page's code and its design side by side...great for really wide monitors. Unselecting this option displays the Code and Design views one on top of the other—unless you have an unusually tall monitor, this option doesn't let you see much of either.

- **Design View on Left/Top**. When you're in Code and Design view, this option dictates where Dreamweaver puts the Design view pane relative to the Code view pane. If you select Split Vertically, you can display the Design view either to the right or left of the Code view; when you stack Code and Design views on top of each other, you can place the Design view either above or below the Code view.

- **Switch Views**. Switches your cursor position between Code and Design views... of course, so does just clicking into the code in Code view, or clicking into the design in Design view!

- **Refresh Design View**. Updates the Design view to reflect changes you make directly to the source code in either Code view or Split view.

- **Refresh Styles**. Who knows what this does? You can select it only when viewing a page in Live view, and even then it doesn't seem to do anything.

- **Toggle Live View**. Displays a web page as it would appear in a web browser (actually, as it would appear in Apple's Safari or Google's Chrome browser). You can preview JavaScript, Flash movies, and other interactive page features in this view.

- **Live View Options**. Lets you control the display of Live view. You can pause JavaScript—a useful way to see the HTML that JavaScript creates on the fly—disable JavaScript, turn off plug-ins, and control settings that affect how Dreamweaver displays the page in Live view.

- **Live Code**. In Live view, choose this option to display the HTML as it appears to a web browser—useful for pages that include JavaScript that can dynamically change the HTML of a page by adding classes to tags and even inserting or removing entire chunks of HTML. This feature is a good way to make sure the JavaScript code you write does what you want it to do to the HTML of a page.

This feature is also good for server-side pages composed of multiple server-side includes (page 928) so you can see, for example, what the HTML looks like for a site using the WordPress content management system (see page 347).

- **Inspect**. This option lets you inspect the CSS of page elements in Live view. Discussed on page 348, this feature is a great way to inspect page styles in dynamically generated server-side pages (such as PHP pages), which you often can't see in Design view.

- **Element Quick View**. This new tool works hand in hand with Live view editing. It displays the HTML elements in your page in outline form. Using Element Quick View, you can drag elements to different positions in the outline, repositioning them on your web page.

- **Visual Aids**. Lets you summon onscreen symbols that represent typically invisible page elements, like image maps, anchors, and the borders of a <div> tag,.

- **Style Rendering**. Lets you hide or show the effects of all style sheets on a page.

- **Code View Options**. Lets you adjust the way your HTML appears in Code view. You can turn on (or off) options that wrap lines of text to fit in the document window, add line numbers, highlight invalid HTML, turn on syntax coloring, and indent lines of code.

- **Window Size**. Lets you change the size of the page that Dreamweaver displays in the document window. Best used in conjunction with media queries (Chapter 12) to see how a page looks on different-size screens, such as the 320 x 480-pixel screen of a smartphone.

- **Magnification**. Lets you zoom in, zoom out, and generally magnify your view of the document window. It has no effect on the HTML or how a page displays in a web browser; it merely zooms in to get a close-up view of the page or zooms out to get a bird's-eye view.

- **Rulers**. When you choose Show, Dreamweaver displays rulers along the top and left sides of the document window. Using the options you find here, you can choose your ruler units: pixels, inches, or centimeters. You can also reset the orientation of the two rulers so that both start from zero in the screen's upper-left corner.

- **Grid**. Places a grid of vertical and horizontal lines over the document window that you use as a guide to build your layouts. Choose Grid Settings to open a dialog box where you can adjust the grid's colors, spacing, behaviors, and line appearance.

- **Guides**. Shows, hides, locks, and erases guidelines you drag from a ruler onto the current page. Also controls options for guides and displays guidelines that mark the visible area of a browser window for monitors of different resolutions.

- **Tracing Image**. Adjusts the document's background tracing image. You can load a new tracing image, make a current one visible, or adjust its position.

- **Display External Files**. You can insert images and other files into a page from your own or other websites on the Internet. When you insert an image from another site, you can type in or paste an absolute URL. Dreamweaver even displays the image in Design view, but only if you check this option. Because this feature requires an Internet connection, pages with links to external files may take longer to display in Dreamweaver (since it has to get the images and files from the Web). If you have lots of external images and files and your pages open sluggishly in Dreamweaver, uncheck this option.

- **Hide Panels (Show Panels)**. Hides all open panels. If you've already hidden the panels, the command says Show Panels instead; it restores the panels to their original positions.

- **Toolbars**. Displays toolbars for use with Dreamweaver. Select Document from the submenu to display the Document toolbar at the top of the document window. It displays the current page's title and offers common commands, like display options, file-management options, code-navigation options, and browser previews. The Standard toolbar displays buttons for common commands for opening files, closing files, and cutting, copying, and pasting content. The Coding toolbar appears along the left edge of Code view and provides options for working with HTML, JavaScript, CSS, and PHP, such as wrapping the code in comments, indenting the code, and so on.

- **Related Files**. Lists all external CSS, JavaScript, and server-side programming files the current page uses. Select one and you'll see the code for that file. Better yet, use the Related Files toolbar that appears in the document window—it's much faster.

- **Related Files Options**. Lets you filter the files displayed in the Related Files toolbar (page 343). For example, you can hide all server-side includes, display just external CSS files, or create a custom filter to show files that match a certain pattern (like all PHP files that include *DB* in the filename). You'll find filters most useful for really complicated server-side programs (like WordPress, Joomla, or Drupal) that often overwhelm the Related Files toolbar with dozens of included PHP files.

- **Code Navigator**. Pops open the Code Navigator window so you can scan all CSS rules that apply to the current HTML element (see page 418).

Insert Menu

The Insert menu adds selected page elements to a document at the cursor's current position. The commands listed here correspond to the buttons on the Objects panel:

- **Div.** In Design view, opens the Insert Div dialog box, which lets you easily create a new <div> container, either around something you selected or anywhere on the page. This box helps you remember to give the <div> a class or ID, or to go ahead and create a new CSS rule. In Live view, this command adds a <div> element to the page, along with placeholder text.

- **HTML5 video.** Adds the <video></video> tags to your page's code so you can place a video at that point (see page 708).

- **Canvas.** Adds the tags for an empty canvas, with an ID of "canvas," to your page. The Canvas Properties panel opens, so you can size the new canvas.

- **Image**. Inserts an image file (such as a JPG, PNG, or GIF), a rollover image, or a Fireworks HTML file into the current document. The Select Image Source window appears so you can navigate to the file on your hard drive. You can choose to make the URL for the file relative to either the document or to the site root folder. For a rollover image, you need to choose two image files.

- **Table**. Inserts a new table into a document. The Table dialog box appears and lets you format the table by specifying the number of rows and columns; the table width; measurements for cell padding, cell spacing, and the table border; and whether (and where) to include table headers.

- **Head**. Lets you choose from four dialog boxes—Meta, Keywords, Description, and Viewport—that help you add the appropriate tags and content to the head section of your page. You type in the dialog box; Dreamweaver creates the code.

- **Script**. Lets you insert programming code.

- **Hyperlink**. Inserts a link. The Hyperlink dialog box lets you specify the label for the link, the link's address, as well as many other link options, such as the target window and tab index.

- **Email Link**. Creates a new email link at the insertion point. The Email Link dialog box appears; you specify both the email address and the link's label (such as "Click to email me").

- **Horizontal Rule**. Places an <hr> tag at the insertion point. This is a tricky one, especially in Code view, since there's no dialog box and no chance to click OK to confirm what you've just done. In Design view, a simple black line appears across the page, and the Properties panel opens so you can style the rule.

- **Date**. Inserts the current date into a document. The Insert Date dialog box lets you format the appearance of the day of the week, the date, and the time. You can also automatically update the date each time you save the document.

- **IFrame**. Creates an empty IFrame—an inline frame—at the insertion point. A frame is a self-contained HTML document inside your HTML document. You can use an IFrame to embed an ad, a Google map, or other content on your page.

- **Character**. This handy little submenu lets you insert common symbols, like ©, £, and even ". Also handles line breaks and nonbreaking spaces.

- **Structure.** HTML forms the structure of a web page, and so the Structure submenu gives you a quick way to place various HTML elements—divs, lists, paragraphs, and so on—on your page.

- **Media**. Inserts media files including Edge Animate compositions, HTML5 video, HTML5 audio, Flash, Flash video, and plug-ins. In most cases, the standard Select File window appears, which you can use to navigate to the desired file.

- **Form**. Inserts Form Objects—the <form> tag, text fields, buttons, checkboxes, or lists—into a document. (If you don't insert the <form> tag when you insert a form object, Dreamweaver prompts you to do so.)

- **jQuery Mobile**. Lets you insert code needed to build mobile applications using the jQuery Mobile JavaScript library. For example, you can embed specialized user interface elements, like a toggle switch. See page 581.

- **jQuery UI**. Offers a direct route to interactive objects from the jQuery user interface (UI) library, like buttons users can click or date pickers they can use to enter dates in a form.

- **Template**. When you work on template files, this menu lets you insert many of Dreamweaver's template features, such as Optional, Editable, and Repeating regions.

- **Favorites**. Opens the Customize Favorite Objects dialog box, where you can pick the items you use most often—divs, canvases, Flash videos, or most other items that appear on the Insert menus. From then on, these items are just a click away in the Favorites section of the Insert panel.

- **Recent Snippets**. Lists the snippets you most recently inserted. Select a snippet from the list and Dreamweaver inserts it into the document. You'll see snippets discussed in Chapter 21.

■ Modify Menu

Commands in the Modify menu adjust the properties of common document objects, like links, tables, and layers:

- **Page Properties**. Opens the Page Properties window, where you can specify document-wide attributes—such as a page's title, background and link colors, margins, and background.

- **Template Properties**. Opens the Template Properties window, where you can modify settings for template features, like the visibility of optional regions, the properties of editable attributes, and the values of any template expressions you create. Available only when you work on template-based pages, as described in Chapter 22.

- **Manage Fonts**. Opens a dialog box of the same name, where you can choose the fonts you want to use on your websites. You can choose from the new-in-Creative-Cloud Adobe Edge Web Fonts, fonts stored on your computer, or custom font stacks (sets of fonts that work in most browsers). Once you choose a font in Manage Fonts, it will appear on the Font menu in the CSS properties panel so you can add it to a style. See page 141 for more about working with fonts.

- **Quick Tag Editor**. Lets you edit an HTML tag without leaving Design view. If you don't have anything selected on a page, the Quick Tag editor prompts you to enter a new HTML tag at the insertion point (by choosing from an alphabetical list). If you have text or an object already selected, the window displays the selection's tags so you can edit them.

- **Make Link**. Turns a highlighted page element (graphic or text) into a link. The standard Select File dialog box appears; choose the document you want a browser to open when someone clicks the link.

- **Remove Link**. This command is available only when you select a link or have the cursor positioned inside a link. Remove Link deletes hyperlinks by removing the <a> tag from the selected text or image.

- **Open Linked Page**. Opens the linked page in a new document window. This command is available only when you have a link selected or have the cursor positioned inside a link. (You can, however, hold down the Ctrl key [⌘] and double-click a link to open the linked page.)

- **Table**. Opens a list of options to modify a selected table. You can adjust the number of rows and columns, add row or column spans, or completely clear cells' defined heights and widths (see Chapter 6).

- **Image**. Opens a list of options to modify a selected image, including optimizing it in Fireworks or editing it with one of Dreamweaver's built-in image-editing features, such as the Crop, Resample, and Sharpen tools. See page 255 for more.

- **Arrange**. Lets you change the Z-index (the front-to-back order) of overlapping page elements. You can send one element in front of another, send it to the back, and so on. You can also tell Dreamweaver to disallow overlapping elements altogether. If you select two or more elements, you can choose from one of this menu's alignment options to align the components, like the tops of the two elements. See Chapter 10 for more on positioning elements.

- **Library**. Lets you add selected document objects to a site's Library folder (Chapter 21). You can also update the current document, or multiple documents, to reflect any changes you make to a Library object.

- **Templates**. These commands work with Dreamweaver's—or your own—templates (see Chapter 22). Using them, you can apply a preexisting template to the current page, separate the page from its template, or update the page to reflect changes you made to its template. If you have a template file open, you can create or delete editable regions (remove the template markup, in other words) and update all site files based on that template. You can also add repeating template regions and editable tag attributes.

Format Menu

The commands in this menu let you format and modify a document's text:

- **Indent**. In the case of bulleted or numbered lists, this option indents the selected list items to create a nested (indented) list (see page 96). For other HTML tags, this option wraps the element in a <blockquote> tag (an HTML tag used to represent a quotation). In cases where it's against the rules of HTML to wrap the selected tag in a <blockquote> tag—an HTML table, for example—this option simply inserts an empty <blockquote> tag (really, though, a better approach to indenting text is to use the CSS Margin property, as described on page 465).

- **Outdent**. Turns selected bulleted or numbered list items into paragraph tags; for nested list items, it removes the indent. If your cursor is within a <blockquote> tag, this option removes the blockquote.

- **Paragraph Format**. Applies a paragraph format, such as Heading 1, Heading 2, or preformatted text, to all the text in the current block-level element. You can also go to this menu's submenu and choose "None" to remove the paragraph formatting.

- **Align**. Aligns text in the selected paragraph to the left margin, center, or right margin of a document. If the paragraph sits inside a table cell or layer, Dreamweaver aligns it with the left, center, or right of that cell or layer. (The CSS text-align property [page 153] is a better option.)

- **List**. Turns the selected paragraph into an ordered, unordered, or definition list. You can edit the list's format by selecting the submenu's Properties option.

- **HTML Style**. Applies predefined text styles—such as bold, italic, or strikethrough—to the selected text.

- **CSS Styles**. Lets you apply CSS styles to selected text (Chapter 3). You can also choose to attach an existing style sheet to the current document, or use a Design-Time style sheet (page 425).

Commands Menu

Use the Commands menu to apply advanced features to your Dreamweaver document. Some menu items, like the Record command, eliminate repetitive tasks; others, such as the Clean Up HTML command, fix common problems in a single sweep:

- **Edit Command List**. Opens a list of all custom commands. You can rename the commands or delete them permanently.

- **Check Spelling**. Checks the current document for spelling errors (see page 107).

- **Apply Source Formatting**. Lets you apply Dreamweaver's formatting preferences to existing HTML and CSS documents. (Normally, changes you make to Dreamweaver's HTML source formatting, defined in the Preferences window and the *SourceFormat.txt* file, apply only to newly created documents.)

- **Apply Source Formatting to Selection**. Same as the previous command, Apply Source Formatting, but applies only to selected content. This command lets you selectively apply source formatting so you can, for example, make sure that Dreamweaver nicely formats a <table> element but leaves the rest of your finely crafted HTML alone. Works with CSS as well.

- **Clean Up HTML**. Opens a list of options to correct common HTML problems, such as empty tags or redundant nested tags. Once you select what you want to fix, Dreamweaver applies those changes to the current document, and, if requested, provides a log of the number and type of changes it made (see Chapter 19).

- **Clean Up Word HTML**. If you import HTML generated by Microsoft Word, you often end up with unnecessary or cluttered HTML tags that can affect your site's performance. This command opens a list of options that corrects common formatting problems in Word's HTML. Dreamweaver applies the selected changes to the document and, if requested, displays a log of the number and type of changes it made.

- **Clean Up Web Fonts Script Tag (Current Page)**. When you use the new Adobe Edge Web Fonts, Dreamweaver adds a bit of JavaScript to your page code. That JavaScript grabs the font from the Adobe server and delivers it to the browser. If you find that the font isn't working, this command attempts to fix the link to the server.

- **Externalize JavaScript**. Lets you take all the JavaScript code in a web page and dump it into an external JavaScript file. External files can make web pages download more quickly and let you reuse common JavaScript programs throughout your site.

- **Remove FLV Detection**. If you used Dreamweaver CS3 to add a Flash Movie and you then delete that movie, this command removes the JavaScript code left behind. Again, this applies only if you have old Flash video pages you created way back when, with Dreamweaver CS3.

- **Optimize Image**. Opens the selected image in the Image Preview window so you can experiment with different compression settings to find the best balance between file size and image quality. See page 263.

- **Sort Table**. Sorts the information in a selected table alphabetically or numerically, in ascending or descending order. You can't apply this command to tables that include *rowspans* or *colspans*.

■ Site Menu

As its name suggests, the commands in this menu apply to your entire website rather than single documents. These commands help keep your site organized and promote collaboration between large workgroups:

- **New Site**. Opens the Site Setup window, where you can set up a site to start working in Dreamweaver.

- **Manage Sites**. Opens the Manage Sites panel where you can create, delete, or edit site definitions. See Chapter 18.

> **NOTE** The next five menu commands let you transfer files between your computer (the *local* site) and a web server (the *remote* site). These commands, in other words, don't work unless you first define a local and remote site in the Site Definition window. In addition, you have to download the files you want to work on by *selecting* them in the Site window (see below).

- **Get**. Copies files (those you select in the Site window) from the remote server to your local site folder so you can edit them. Note that if you have Dream-weaver's file Check In and Check Out feature active (see Check In and Check Out below), you can't edit the downloaded files if someone downloaded a copy before you did.

- **Check Out**. Copies files (those you select in the Site window) from the remote server to your local site, and marks them on the remote server as *checked out*. No one else can make changes to the document until you upload it back onto the remote server to check it back in.

- **Put**. Uploads files (those you select in the Site window) from your local site to the remote site. The uploaded files replace the previous version of the document.

- **Check In**. Uploads files you've checked out and copied to your local site back up to your remote site, and makes them available for others to edit. Once you check a file in, the version on your local site becomes read-only (you can open it, but you can't edit it).

- **Undo Check Out**. Removes the checked-out status of selected files. Dream-weaver doesn't upload the file back to the remote server, so any changes you made to the file locally aren't transmitted to the server. In addition, your local copy of the file becomes read-only.

- **Show Checked Out By**. Lets you see who's checked out a file.

- **Locate in Site**. When you select this option while working on a document, it opens the Site window and highlights that document's filename in the site's local folder.

> **NOTE** See Chapter 18 for the full scoop on local sites, remote sites, and checking files in and out.

- **Reports**. Opens the Reports window and lists options for generating new reports (see Chapter 20). Reports can monitor pages (such as their Design Notes and check-out status) and highlight common HTML problems (such as missing Alt text, empty tags, and untitled documents). You can generate a report on an open document, multiple documents, or your entire site.

- **Site-Specific Code Hints**. This option, available only for PHP websites, lets you specify how code hints (the tooltips that pop up as you type code) work. This advanced feature is for serious PHP programmers.

- **Synchronize Sitewide**. Opens the Synchronization window, which lets you compare all your local files with the files on your web server. Use it to make sure you transfer all the files you update locally to your web server, or that you transfer all the site files on the server to your local site.

- **Check Links Sitewide**. Analyzes the current site for broken links, external links, and orphaned pages, and then generates a report of the problems it found. You can fix problematic links directly in the Report window—or click the filename to open the errant file in a new document window, with the link highlighted and ready to repair.

- **Change Link Sitewide**. Replaces a broken link throughout your site in one step. In the Change Link dialog box, you specify the incorrect link; below it, you enter the correct link. Dreamweaver searches your site, replacing every instance of the old link.

- **Advanced**. Provides access to advanced site options, such as the FTP Log—a record of all FTP file transfers; Recreate Site Cache, which forces Dreamweaver to rescan the site's files and update its cache to reflect any changes to the files or links in the site; and Remove Connection Scripts to remove the script files Dreamweaver creates to work with dynamic, database-driven websites.

◾ Window Menu

This menu controls which panels and windows Dreamweaver displays or hides at the moment. A checkmark in the menu denotes open panels:

- **Insert**. Opens the Insert panel, from which you can insert various types of objects (such as images, layers, or forms) into your document. You get all the same options as in the Insert menu (page 11).

- **Properties**. Opens the Property Inspector, where you can edit the properties for a selected object. The options in the Property Inspector depend on the page element you select.

- **Extract.** Opens the Extract window, which you use to grab assets and image details from Photoshop files (.psd). You use the Extract workspace and its tools when you've created a prototype page in Photoshop—it speeds the process of converting that image file into a real web page in Dreamweaver. See the box on page 264 for more details.

- **CSS Designer**. Opens the CSS Designer panel, from which you can define and edit CSS styles and selectors, or apply existing styles to selected text.

- **CSS Transitions**. Opens the CSS Transitions panel, which lets you add, edit, and remove animated transitions between two different CSS styles. You can read about this window on page 425. Click the + sign in the panel to create a new transition.

- **Files**. Opens the Files panel. From this window, you can open any file, and transfer files between your computer and your remote server.

- **Assets**. Opens the Assets panel, which conveniently groups and lists all the assets (such as colors, links, scripts, graphics, library items, and templates) you use in your site.

- **Snippets**. Opens the Snippets panel, which contains reusable snippets of HTML, JavaScript, and other types of code. You can create your own snippets to save your fingers from retyping code you use often on a site.

- **jQuery Mobile Swatches**. Opens the jQuery Mobile Swatches window, which lets you apply different "themes" to jQuery Mobile page elements. This option works only with the jQuery mobile pages discussed on page 581.

- **Behaviors**. Opens the Behaviors panel, which lets you associate *behaviors* (such as swapping images on a mouse rollover or checking for necessary plug-ins) to selected page elements (see Chapter 15).

- **History**. Displays the History panel, a record of all the actions you took in working on the current document.

- **Code Inspector**. Opens a pop-up window that displays the HTML for the current document. It's different from plain Code view, since the code sits in a pop-up window. While you can edit the code directly in this window, it's often easier just to use Dreamweaver's Code view or Code and Design view (View→Code and Design).

- **Results**. Lets you open Dreamweaver's many site-wide tools, such as the "Find and Replace," Link Checker, and Reports commands. Pick the operation of choice from the submenu.

  Browse Add-ons. Opens the Adobe Add-ons web page, where you can find and install miniprograms that add bells and whistles to Dreamweaver, as described on page 908. The buttons along the left side of the web page help you find the Add-on you want.

- **Add-ons**. Lets you see the Add-ons you download from the Adobe Add-ons website.

Before Dreamweaver CC 2014, Adobe used "Extensions" to add mini programs and new features to the program. In current Creative Cloud applications, Add-ons have replaced extensions. However, you can still install some of the old extensions in Dreamweaver CC 2014. Once you install an extension, you'll find it listed in this menu.

- **Workspace Layout**. Lets you choose preset layouts of panels and windows. You can also use this menu to save the position and size of Dreamweaver's current panels and windows setup. This command is your ticket to customizing your Dreamweaver work environment.

- **Hide Panels**. Closes all currently open panels. Choosing Show Panels reopens only those panels displayed before you selected Hide Panels.

- **Application Frame (Macs only)**. The Application Frame treats all of Dreamweaver's panels and windows as one big window (or frame). Grabbing the bottom-right corner of the frame (usually the bottom-right corner of the Files panel) lets you resize the frame. Some people like this unified feel; others don't. If you don't like it, uncheck this option. When you do, all the windows and panels act as individual units you can resize independently of one another.

- **Application Bar (Macs only)**. Opens and closes the Application toolbar at the top of the screen. The Application bar includes the Workspace Switcher, which lets you change the layout of the Dreamweaver document window and its assorted panels. Out of the box, Dreamweaver provides workspaces for Design, Extract, and Code, but you can create and save your own custom workspaces. The Appilcation toolbar also includes a button to run the Creative Cloud synchronization tools. That way, you can synchronize files and preferences when you use Dreamweaver on more than one computer. The button with the "i" in a circle opens your browser and displays Adobe's web page of Dreamweaver tutorials. On Macs, you can turn off the Application bar only if you also turn off the Application Frame. For Windows computers, the application bar is always displayed and this command is absent from the Window menu.

- **Cascade**. This and the next two options let you "undock" the current documents so you have all open documents floating and resizable within the document area. (Normally, when you have multiple documents open, you switch from page to page by clicking tabs at the top of the document window.) The Cascade option resizes each open document and places them one on top of the other. Windows folks can re-dock pages by clicking the Maximize button on any currently open document. Mac people can select the Combine As Tabs option.

> **TIP** If the Cascade command is grayed out, choose Window→Application Frame to free up the open documents. You can also unlock a document by dragging its tab out of the document window. You can then use the Cascade command to organize the windows.

- **Tile**. Places all open documents one on top of the other. The documents don't float on top of one another; rather, they fill the available document area as a grid of windows. With more than a few documents open, you see so little of each page that it's difficult to work on any one.

- **Combine As Tabs (Mac only)**. Returns either tiled or cascaded documents to the single, unified tab interface in the document window.

- **Next Document, Previous Document (Mac only)**. These commands let you step through all your open documents, bringing each one front and center in turn so you can edit it.

■ Help Menu

The Help menu offers useful links and reference documents that give you more information about using, troubleshooting, and extending Dreamweaver. For a full tour of Help resources, see Appendix A.

NOTE On a Mac, the topmost command on the Help menu is a Search field. But beware: This field searches only Mac help, not Dreamweaver help. To search Adobe's online help system, choose one of the following commands and then type into the Search field on the right side of the web page.

- **What's New in Dreamweaver**. Launches the Dreamweaver Help and Tutorials page (page 939) in your desktop browser. You also arrive at this page when you click the "Dreamweaver CC manual (help and tutorials)" link in the "Help and tutorials" list at the upper right of the Dreamweaver Help page (described next).

- **New Feature Videos**. Opens the main Dreamweaver Help page (page 940), which provides access to tutorials, videos, and troubleshooting tips. You can also get to this page by clicking the Resources link at the bottom of the Welcome screen.

- **Learn Dreamweaver**. Launches your desktop browser and loads a page called Dreamweaver Exchange Classic on Adobe.com, where you can find extensions—add-on features—that add new capabilities to Dreamweaver. (See Chapter 23 for details on extensions).

- **Help and Support**. Choose from three submenus. Dreamweaver Online Help launches the Dreamweaver Help and Tutorials page (page 940) in your desktop browser. Dreamweaver Support Center opens the main Dreamweaver Help page (page 940), which provides access to tutorials, videos, and troubleshooting tips. You can also get to this page by clicking the Resources link at the bottom of the Welcome screen. Adobe Online Forums opens an index of forums on Adobe's website. You can interact with other Adobe customers, post questions, share techniques, or answer questions posted by others. Requires Internet access and a newsgroup reader.

- **Submit Bug/Feature Request**. Opens your browser and displays Adobe's Feature Request/Bug Report Form. Fill in the blanks to suggest improvements to the program or to provide information about Dreamweaver's bad behavior in specific circumstances.

- **Manage My Account**. Ever since Dreamweaver CS6, Adobe has required owners of the software to create an Adobe ID. This menu option lets you update your profile (if you want to change your email address or password, for example).

- **Sign Out**. Logs you out of your Adobe account under the email address shown. With some licenses, you can use Dreamweaver CC on only one computer at a time, and you must sign out of your current computer before you can launch the program on another one.

- **Updates**. Launches the Adobe updater. It finds updates for Dreamweaver (and every other Adobe product on your computer).

Index